THE

HISTORY

OF

THE UNITED STATES

OF

NORTH AMERICA

VOL. I.

J. Graham

THE

HISTORY

OF

THE UNITED STATES

OF

NORTH AMERICA,

FROM THE

PLANTATION OF THE BRITISH COLONIES

TILL

THEIR ASSUMPTION OF NATIONAL INDEPENDENCE.

———

By JAMES GRAHAME

———

IN TWO VOLUMES.

VOL. I.

SECOND EDITION, ENLARGED AND AMENDED.

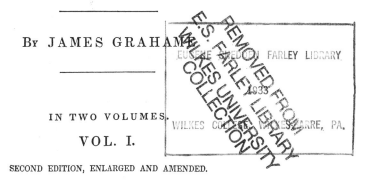

BOOKS FOR LIBRARIES PRESS
FREEPORT, NEW YORK

First Published 1845
Reprinted 1971

INTERNATIONAL STANDARD BOOK NUMBER:
0-8369-5737-7

LIBRARY OF CONGRESS CATALOG CARD NUMBER:
74-152985

PRINTED IN THE UNITED STATES OF AMERICA

PREFACE

TO THE

AMERICAN EDITION.

In December, 1842, the undersigned was appointed by the Massachusetts Historical Society " to prepare a Memoir of Mr. Grahame, the historian of the United States," who had been one of its corresponding members. In fulfilment of that duty, he entered into a correspondence with Mr. Grahame's family and European friends, in the course of which he learned that Mr. Grahame had left, at his death, a corrected and enlarged copy of his " History of the United States of North America," and had expressed, among his last wishes, an earnest hope that it might be published in the form which it had finally assumed under his hand.

This information having been communicated to Mr. Justice Story, Messrs. James Savage, Jared Sparks, and William H. Prescott, they concurred in the opinion, that it " scarcely comported with American feelings, interest, or self-respect to permit a work of so much laborious research and merit, written in a faithful and elevated spirit, and relating to our own history, to want an American edition, embracing the last additions and corrections of its deceased author." Influenced by considerations of this kind, those gentlemen, in connection with the undersigned, undertook the office of promoting and superintending the publication of the work in its enlarged and amended form. A copy, prepared from that left by the author, was accordingly placed at their disposal by his son, Robert Grahame, Esq.; who subsequently transmitted the original, also, to be deposited in the library of Harvard University. The supervision of the work, during its progress through the press, devolved on the undersigned, — a charge which he has executed with as thorough fidelity to Mr. Grahame and the public as its nature and his official engagements have permitted.

A wish having been intimated by the son of Mr. Grahame, that the Memoir, prepared at the request of the Massachusetts Historical Society, should be prefixed to the American edition of the History, it has been acceded to. The principal materials for this Memoir — consisting of extracts from Mr. Grahame's diary and correspondence, accompanied by interesting notices of his sentiments and character — were furnished by his highly accomplished widow, his son-in-law, John Stewart, Esq., and his friend, Sir John F. W. Herschel, Bart., who had maintained with him from early youth an uninterrupted intimacy. Robert Walsh, Esq., the present American consul at Paris, well known and appreciated in this country and in Europe for his moral worth and literary eminence, who had enjoyed the privilege of an intimate personal acquaintance with Mr. Grahame, also transmitted many of his letters. Like favors were received from William H. Prescott, Esq., and the Rev. George E. Ellis. In the use of these materials, the endeavour has been, as far as possible, to make Mr. Grahame's own language the expositor of his mind and motives.

The portrait prefixed to this work is from an excellent painting by Healy, engraved with great fidelity by Andrews, one of our most eminent artists ; the cost both of the painting and the engraving having been defrayed by several American citizens, who interested themselves in the suc cess of the present undertaking.

JOSIAH QUINCY.

CAMBRIDGE, September 9, 1845.

MEMOIR

OF

JAMES GRAHAME, LL. D.

JAMES GRAHAME, the subject of this Memoir, was born in Glasgow, Scotland, on the 21st of December, 1790, of a family distinguished, in its successive generations, by intellectual vigor and attainments, united with a zeal for civil liberty, chastened and directed by elevated religious sentiment.

His paternal grandfather, Thomas Grahame, was eminent for piety, generosity, and talent. Presiding in the Admiralty Court, at Glasgow, he is said to have been the first British judge who decreed the liberation of a negro slave brought into Great Britain, on the ground, that "a guiltless human being, in that country, *must* be free"; a judgment preceding by some years the celebrated decision of Lord Mansfield on the same point. In the war for the independence of the United States, he was an early and uniform opponent of the pretensions and policy of Great Britain; declaring, in the very commencement of the contest, that "it was like the controversy of Athens with Syracuse, and he was persuaded it would end in the same way."

He died in 1791, at the age of sixty, leaving two sons, Robert and James. Of these, the youngest, James, was esteemed for his moral worth, and admired for his genius; delighting his friends and companions by the readiness and playfulness of his wit, and commanding the reverence of all who knew him, by the purity of a life under the guidance of an ever active religious principle. He was the author of a poem entitled "The Sabbath," which, admired on its first publication, still retains its celebrity among the minor effusions of the poetic genius of Britain.

Robert, the elder of the sons of Thomas Grahame, and father of the subject of this Memoir, inheriting the virtues of his ancestors, and imbued with their spirit, has sustained, through a long life, not yet terminated, the character of a uniform friend of liberty. His zeal in its cause rendered him, at different periods, obnoxious to the suspicions of the British government. When the ministry attempted to control the expression of public opinion by the prosecution of Horne Tooke, a secretary of state's warrant was issued against him; from the consequences of which he was saved through the acquittal of Tooke by a London jury. When Castlereagh's ascendant policy had excited the people of Scotland to a state of revolt, and several persons were prosecuted for high treason, whose poverty prevented them from engaging the best counsel, he brought down, at his own charge, for their defence, distinguished English lawyers from London, they being deemed better acquainted than those of Scotland with the law of high treason; and the result was the acquittal of the persons indicted.   He sympathized with the Americans in their struggle for independence, and rejoiced in their success.   Regarding the French Revolution as a shoot from the American stock, he hailed its progress in its early stages with satisfaction and hope. So long as its leaders restricted themselves to argument and persuasion, he was their adherent and advocate ; but withdrew his countenance, when they resorted to terror and violence.

By his profession as writer to the signet[1] he acquired fortune and eminence.   Though distinguished for public and private worth and well directed talent, his political course excluded him from official power and distinction, until 1833, when, after the passage of the Reform Bill, he was unanimously chosen, at the age of seventy-four, without any canvass or solicitation on his part, at the first election under the reformed constituency, Lord Provost of Glasgow.   His character is not without interest to the American people ; for his son, whose respect for his talents and virtues fell little short of admiration, acknowledges that it was his father's suggestion and encouragement which first turned his thoughts to writing the history of the United States.

Under such paternal influences, James Grahame, our historian, was early imbued with the spirit of liberty.   His mind became familiarized with its principles and their limitations.   Even in boyhood, his thoughts were directed towards that Transatlantic people whose national existence was the work of that spirit, and whose institutions were framed with an express view to maintain and perpetuate it.   His early education was domestic.   A French emigrant priest taught him the first elements of learning.   He then passed through the regular course of instruction at the Grammar School of Glasgow, and afterwards attended the classes at the University in that city.   In both he was distinguished by his proficiency.   After pursuing a preparatory course in geometry and algebra, hearing the lectures of Professor Playfair, and reviewing his former studies under private tuition, he entered, about his twentieth year, St. John's College, Cambridge.   But his connection with the University was short.   In an excursion during one of the vacations, he formed an attachment to the lady whom he afterwards married ; becoming, in consequence, desirous of an early establishment in life, he terminated abruptly his academical connections, and commenced a course of professional study preparatory to his admission to the Scottish bar.

At Cambridge he had the happiness to form an acquaintance, which ripened into friendship, with Mr. Herschel, now known to the world as Sir John F. W. Herschel, Bart., and by the high rank he sustains among the astronomers of Europe.   Concerning this friendship Mr. Grahame thus writes in his diary : — " It has always been an ennobling tie.   We have been the friends of each other's souls and of each other's virtue, as well as of each other's person and success.   He was of St. John's College, as well as I. Many a day we passed in walking together, and many a night in studying together."   Their intimacy continued unbroken through Mr. Grahame's life.

In June, 1812, Mr. Grahame was admitted to the Scottish bar as an advocate, and immediately entered on the practice of his profession.   It seems, however, not to have been suited to his taste ; for about this time he writes, — " Until now, I have been my own master, and I now resign my independence for a service I dislike."   His assiduity was, nevertheless, unremitted, and was attended with satisfactory success ; indicative, in the opinion of his friends, of ultimate professional eminence.

---

[1] An attorney.

In October, 1813, he married Matilda Robley, of Stoke Newington, a pupil of Mrs. Barbauld ; who, in a letter to a friend, wrote concerning her, — "She is by far one of the most charming women I have ever known. Young, beautiful, amiable, and accomplished ; with a fine fortune. She is going to be married to a Mr. Grahame, a young Scotch barrister. I have the greatest reluctance to part with this precious treasure, and can only hope that Mr. Grahame is worthy of so much happiness."

All the anticipations justified by Mrs. Barbauld's exalted estimate of this lady were realized by Mr. Grahame. He found in this connection a stimulus and a reward for his professional exertions. "Love and ambition," he writes to his friend Herschel, soon after his marriage, "unite to incite my industry. My reputation and success rapidly increase, and I see clearly that only perseverance is wanting to possess me of all the bar can afford." And again, at a somewhat later period, — "You can hardly fancy the delight I felt the other day, on hearing the Lord President declare that one of my printed pleadings was most excellent. Yet, although you were more ambitious than I am, you could not taste the full enjoyment of professional success, without a wife to heighten your pleasure, by sympathizing in it."

Soon after Mr. Grahame's marriage, the religious principle took predominating possession of his mind. Its depth and influence were early indicated in his correspondence. As the impression had been sudden, his friends anticipated it would be temporary. But it proved otherwise. From the bent which his mind now received it never afterwards swerved. His general religious views coincided with those professed by the early Puritans and the Scotch Covenanters ; but they were sober, elevated, expansive, and free from narrowness and bigotry. Though his temperament was naturally ardent and excitable, he was exempt from all tendency to extravagance or intolerance. His religious sensibilities were probably quickened by an opinion, which the feebleness of his physical constitution led him early to entertain, that his life was destined to be of short duration. In a letter to Herschel, about this period, he writes, — "I have a horror of deferring labor ; and also such fancies or presentiments of a short life, that I often feel I cannot afford to trust fate for a day. I know of no other mode of *creating time*, if the expression be allowable, than to make the most of every moment."

Mr. Grahame's mind, naturally active and discursive, could not be circumscribed within the sphere of professional avocations. It was early engaged on topics of general literature. He began, in 1814, to write for the Reviews, and his labors in this field indicate a mind thoughtful, fixed, and comprehensive, uniting great assiduity in research with an invincible spirit of independence. In 1816, he sharply assailed Malthus, on the subject of "Population, Poverty, and the Poor-laws," in a pamphlet which was well received by the public, and passed through two editions. In this pamphlet he evinces his knowledge of American affairs by frequently alluding to them and by quoting from the works of Dr. Franklin. Mr. Grahame was one of the few to whom Malthus condescended to reply, and a controversy ensued between them in the periodical publications of the day. In the year 1817, his religious prepossessions were manifested in an animated "Defence of the Scottish Presbyterians and Covenanters against the Author of ' The Tales of my Landlord ' "; these productions being regarded by him "as an attempt to hold up to contempt and ridicule those Scotchmen, who, under a galling temporal tyranny and spiritual persecution, fled from their homes and

*

comforts, to worship, in the secrecy of deserts and wastes, their God, according to the dictates of their conscience ; the genius of the author being thus exerted to falsify history and confound moral distinctions." Mr. Grahame also published, anonymously, several pamphlets on topics of local interest ; "all," it is said, "distinguished for elegance and learning." In mature life, when time and the habit of composition had chastened his taste and improved his judgment, — his opinions, also, on some topics having changed, — he was accustomed to look back on his early writings with little complacency, and the severity with which he applied self-criticism led him to express a hope that all memory of these publications might be obliterated. Although some of them, perhaps, are not favorable specimens of his ripened powers, they are far from meriting the oblivion to which he would have consigned them.

In the course of this year (1817), Mr. Grahame's eldest daughter died, — an event so deeply afflictive to him, as to induce an illness which endangered his life. In the year ensuing, he was subjected to the severest of all bereavements in the death of his wife, who had been the object of his unlimited confidence and affection. The effect produced on Mr. Grahame's mind by this succession of afflictions is thus noticed by his son-in-law, John Stewart, Esq. : — "Hereafter the chief characteristic of his journal is deep religious feeling pervading it throughout. It is full of religious meditations, tempering the natural ardor of his disposition ; presenting curious and instructive records, at the same time showing that these convictions did not prevent him from mingling as heretofore in general society. It also evidences that all he there sees, the events passing around him, the most ordinary occurrences of his own life, are subjected to another test, — are constantly referred to a religious standard, and weighed by Scripture principles. The severe application of these to himself, — to self-examination, — is as remarkable as his charitable application of them in his estimate of others."

To alleviate the distress consequent on his domestic bereavements, Mr. Grahame extended the range of his intellectual pursuits. In 1819, he writes, — "I have been for several weeks engaged in the study of Hebrew ; and, having mastered the first difficulties, the language will be my own in a few months. I am satisfied with what I have done. No exercise of the mind is wholly lost, even when not prosecuted to the end originally contemplated."

For several years succeeding the death of his wife, his literary and professional labors were much obstructed by precarious health and depressed spirits. His diary during this period indicates an excited moral watchfulness, and is replete with solemn and impressive thoughts. Thus, in April, 1821, he remarks, — "In writing a law-pleading to-day, I was struck with what I have often before reflected on, the subtle and dangerous temptations that our profession presents to us of varnishing and disguising the conduct and views of our clients, — of mending the natural complexion of a case, filling up its gaps and rounding its sharp corners." And in October following, — "Why is it that the creatures so often disappoint us, and that the fruition of them is sometimes attended with satiety ? We try to make them more to us than God has fitted them to be. Such attempts must ever be in vain. We do not enjoy them as the gifts and refreshments afforded us by God, and in subordination to his will and purpose in giving. If we did so, our use would be humble, grateful, moderate, and happy. The good that God puts in them is bounded ; but when that is drawn off, their highest sweetness and best use may be found in the testimony they afford of his exhaustless love and goodness." And again, in February, 1822, — " We are all travelling to the grave, — but in very different attitudes ; — some feasting and jesting, some fasting and praying ; some eagerly and anxiously struggling for things temporal, some humbly seeking things eternal."

An excursion into the Low Countries, undertaken for the benefit of his health, in 1823, enabled Mr. Grahame to gratify his "strong desire to become acquainted with *extrema vestigia* of the ancient Dutch habits and manners." In this journey he enjoyed the hospitalities, at Lisle, of its governor, Marshal Cambronne, and formed an intimacy with that noble veteran, which, through the correspondence of their sympathies and principles, ripened into a friendship that terminated only with life itself.

About this period he was admitted a fellow of the Royal Society of Edinburgh, and soon after began seriously to contemplate writing the history of the United States of North America. Early education, religious principle, and a native earnestness in the cause of civil liberty concurred to incline his mind to this undertaking. He was reared, as we have seen, under the immediate eye of a father who had been an early and uniform advocate of the principles which led to American independence. In 1810, while yet but on the threshold of manhood, his admiration of the illustrious men who were distinguished in the American Revolution was evinced by the familiarity with which he spoke of their characters or quoted from their writings. The names of Washington and Franklin were ever on his lips, and his chief source of delight was in American history.[1] This interest was intensely increased by the fact, that religious views, in many respects coinciding with his own, had been the chief moving cause of one of the earliest and most successful of the emigrations to North America, and had exerted a material effect on the structure of the political institutions of the United States. These combined influences elevated his feelings to a state of enthusiasm on the subject of American history, and led him to regard it as "the noblest in dignity, the most comprehensive in utility, and the most interesting in progress and event, of all the subjects of thought and investigation." In June, 1824, he remarks in his journal, — "I have had some thoughts of writing the history of North America, from the period of its colonization from Europe till the Revolution and the establishment of the republic. The subject seems to me grand and noble. It was not a thirst of gold or of conquest, but piety and virtue, that laid the foundation of those settlements. The soil was not made by its planters a scene of vice and crime, but of manly enterprise, patient industry, good morals, and happiness deserving universal sympathy. The Revolution was not promoted by infidelity, nor stained by cruelty, as in France ; nor was the fair cause of Freedom betrayed and abandoned, as in both France and England. The share that religious men had in accomplishing the American Revolution is a matter well deserving inquiry, but leading, I fear, into very difficult discussion."

Although his predilections for the task were strong, it is apparent that he engaged in it with many doubts and after frequent misgivings. Nor did he conceal from himself the peculiar difficulties of the undertaking. The elements of the proposed history, he perceived, were scattered, broken, and confused ; differently affecting and affected by thirteen independent sovereignties ; and chiefly to be sought in local tracts and histories, hard to be ob-

---

[1] Sir John F. W. Herschel's letters.

tained, and often little known, even in America, beyond the scenes in which they had their origin, and on which their light was reflected. It was a work which must absorb many years of his life, and task all his faculties. Not only considerations like these, but also the extent of the outline, and the number and variety of details embraced in his design, oppressed and kept in suspense a mind naturally sensitive and self-distrustful. Having at length become fixed in his purpose, — chiefly, there is reason to believe, through the predominating influence of his religious feelings and views, — on the 4th of December, 1824, he writes in his journal, — " After long, profound, and anxious deliberation, and much preparatory research and inquiry, I began the continuous (for so I mean it) composition of the history of the United States of North America. This pursuit, whether I succeed in it or not, must ever attract my mind by the powerful consideration, that it was first suggested to me in conversation with my father, Mr. Clarkson, and Mr. Dillwyn." And, at a subsequent date, — " May God (whom I have invoked in the work) bless, direct, and prosper my undertaking! The surest way to execute it well is to regard it always as a service of body and spirit to God; that the end may shed its light on the means."[1] In the same spirit, he writes to Mr. Herschel, on the 31st of December, — " For a considerable time I have been meditating a great literary work, and, after much preparatory reading, reflection, and note-writing, have at length begun it. If I continue it, as I hope to do, it will absorb much of my time and mind for many years. It is a history of North America, — the most interesting historical subject, I think, a human pen ever undertook. I have always thought the labors of the historian the first in point of literary dignity and utility. History is every thing. Religion, science, literature, whatever men do or think, falls within the scope of history. I ardently desire to make it a religious work, and, in writing, to keep the chief end of man mainly in view. Thus, I hope, the nobleness of the end I propose may impart a dignity to the means."

The undertaking, once commenced, was prosecuted with characteristic ardor and untiring industry. All the time which professional avocations left to him was devoted to this his favorite field of exertion. His labors were continued always until midnight, and often until three or four o'clock in the morning, and he became impatient of every other occupation. But late hours, long sittings, and intense application soon seriously affected his health, and symptoms of an overstrained constitution gradually began to appear. Of this state of mind, and of these effects of his labors on his health, his letters give continual evidence. " I am becoming increasingly wedded to my historical work, and proportionally averse to the bar and forensic practice. At half past three this morning I desist, from motives of prudence (tardily operating, it must be confessed) rather than from weariness." — " Sick or well, my History is the most interesting and absorbing employment I have ever found. It is a noble subject."[2]

By application thus active and incessant, the first volume of his work, comprehending the history of the settlement of Virginia and New England, was so nearly completed early in the ensuing May, as to admit of his then

[1] A manuscript journal of the progress of this History, including the authorities consulted, was sent by Mr. Grahame, in the year 1835, to the President of Harvard College, and was deposited in the library of that institution, to which it now belongs. It is one of the documents used in the preparation of this Memoir.
[2] Letters to Herschel, January and February, 1825.

opening a negotiation for its publication. In a letter to Longman, his bookseller, Mr. Grahame expresses in the strongest terms his devotedness to the undertaking, and adds, — " Every day my purpose becomes stronger to abandon every other pursuit, in order to devote to this my whole time and attention."

He now immediately set about collecting materials for his second volume. Having ascertained that in England it was impossible to obtain books essential to the success of his historical researches, and that rich treasures in the department of American history were deposited at Göttingen, he undertook a journey to that city, and found in its library many very valuable materials for his work. To these resources his attention had been directed by Sir William Hamilton, whose " unwearied labors in supplying him with information on the subject of his historical work, and whose interest in its success," he gratefully acknowledges in his letters ; adding, — " To him nothing is indifferent that concerns literature, or the interests of his friends." During Mr. Grahame's short residence on the continent of Europe, his mother, to whom he was tenderly attached, died ; and he returned to England in the following September (1825) under a heavy depression of spirits. He resumed, however, his favorite labors, but, in consequence of the failure of his health, was soon obliged to desist.

" The latter part of 1825 and the beginning of 1826," his friend Herschel states, " was passed by Mr. Grahame in London, under pressure of severe and dangerous as well as painful illness, the exhausting and debilitating effects of which were probably never obliterated from his constitution, and which made it necessary for him to seek safety in a milder climate than that of Scotland. Thither, however, he for a while returned, but only to write in a strain like the following : — ' Whitehill, April 24, 1826. My bodily health is nearly reëstablished ; but my mind is in a wretched state of feebleness and languor, and indifference to almost every thing. My History is completely at a stand. The last month has been the most disagreeable of my life. If I am not to undergo some great change in the state of my faculties, I do sincerely hope my life may not be long. My discontent and uneasiness are, however, mitigated by the thought, that our condition is appointed by God, and that there must be duties attached to it, and some degree of happiness connected with the performance of those duties. Surely, the highest duty and happiness of a created being must arise from a willing subservience to the designs of the Creator.' "

Being apprized by his physicians that an abode in Scotland during another winter would probably prove fatal to him, he transferred his residence to the South of England, and thenceforth, abandoning his profession of advocate, devoted himself exclusively to the completion of his historical work, as appears by the following entry in his diary : — " March, 1826. Edinburgh. I am now preparing to strike my tent, that is, dissolve my household and depart for ever from this place ; my physicians requiring me not to pass another winter in the climate of Scotland. I quit my profession without regret, having little liked and greatly neglected it ever since I undertook the history of America, to which I shall be glad to devote uninterruptedly all my energies, as soon as I succeed in re-collecting them."

His journal bears continued testimony to the deep interest he took in every thing American, and the philosophic views which he applied to the condition and duties of the people of the United States. — " American writers are too apt to accept the challenge of Europeans to competitions quite unsuitable to their country. Themistocles neither envied nor emulated the boast of the flute-player, to whose challenge he answered : ' I cannot, indeed, play the flute like you ; but I can transform a small village into a great city.' From evils of which America is happily ignorant there arise some partially compensating advantages, which she may very well dispense with. Titular nobility and standing armies, for example, develope politeness and honor (not honor of the purest and noblest kind) among a few, at the expense of depraving and depressing vast multitudes. Great inequalities of wealth, the bondage of the lower classes, have adorned European realms with splendid castles and cathedrals, at the expense of lodging the mass of society in garrets and hovels. If American writers should succeed in persuading their countrymen to study and assert equality with Europeans, in dramatic entertainments, in smooth polish of manners, and in those arts which profess to enable men to live idly and uselessly, without wearying, they will form a taste inconsistent with just discernment and appreciation of their political institutions. Vespasian destroyed the palace of Nero, as a monument of luxury and pernicious to morals. The absence of such palaces as Trianon and Marly may well be compensated by exemption from such tyranny as the revocation of the edict of Nantes, which was coeval with their erection."

Of Mrs. Trollope's " Domestic Manners of the Americans," and her depreciating view of " the society which he regarded with love, admiration, and hope," he thus writes in a subsequent page of his journal : — " What is truth ? Is it not as much in the position of the observer as in the condition of the observed ? Mrs. Trollope seems to me full-fraught with the most pitiful vulgarities of aristocratical ignorance and pretension ; and these would naturally invite the shock of what she seems to have met with in the antipathy of democratic insolence and coarseness ; — she is Basil Hall in petticoats. Think of such a brace of pragmatical pretenders and adventurers as he and she, sitting in judgment on America ! "

It is impossible not to remark the delight his mind took in any associations connected with America. " At the printing office of Messrs. Strahan and Spottiswoode," he writes, " I corrected a proof-sheet of my History of North America, *sitting within the walls of that establishment where Franklin once was a workman.*" Again, at Kensington : — " I delight to stroll amid the sombre grandeur of these gardens. The lofty height and deep shade of these magnificent trees inspire a pleasing, solemn, half-melancholy gloom. Here *Penn* and Addison walked. Here Rousseau, when in England, was wont to sit and muse. Sometimes, in spirit, I meet their spirits here."

The first two volumes of his work, bringing the narrative down to the period of the English Revolution, being at length completed, were in February, 1827, published. But Mr. Grahame was now destined to sustain a severe disappointment. His History was received with little interest by the British public, and by all the greater Reviews with neglect. The Edinburgh, the Quarterly, and the Foreign Quarterly maintained towards it an ominous silence. Some of the minor Reviews, indeed, noticed it with qualified approbation. For Englishmen the colonial history of the United States had but few attractions ; and the spirit in which Mr. Grahame had treated the subject was not calculated to gratify their national pride. He was thought to have " drunk too deep of the spirit of the Puritans " ; it was said that his " hatred of tyranny had terminated in aversion to monarchy," — that to-

wards the church of England " his feelings were fanatical," towards the
church of Rome " illiberal and intolerant."

Conscious of the labor he had bestowed upon it, and of the fidelity with
which it was executed, Mr. Grahame was not disheartened by the chilling
reception his work met with from the British public, nor deterred from pursuing his original design ; the conviction predominating in his mind, that
sooner or later it would conciliate public esteem. Accordingly, in the autumn of the same year in which his first two volumes were published, he not
only commenced their revision, but began an extension of his History to the
period of the declaration of American independence. His interest in his
subject evidently increased. " American history," he writes, " is my favorite field." — " I am averse to all other occupation." — " I am pleased
to gather from any quarter wherewith to decorate my beloved North America." — " God bless the people and institutions of North America ! So
prays their warm friend, and obscure, but industrious, historian."

About this time, through the kindness of James Chalmers, nephew of the
late George Chalmers, he obtained admission to the library of that distinguished American annalist. The treasures there opened to him rekindled
his zeal, and he renewed his historical labors with an intense assiduity, ill
comporting with the critical state of his health. Apprehending a fatal termination of his disease, his medical advisers urged him to pass the ensuing winter at the island of Madeira ; and thither his friend Herschel, through anxiety for his life, offered to accompany him. But no consideration could induce him to leave England, where alone the researches which occupied his
mind could be pursued with advantage ; and for the purpose of availing himself of the books on American history which London afforded, he established
himself in the vicinity of that city.

In May, 1828, Mr. Grahame visited Paris, accompanied by his father,
who introduced him to La Fayette. " I was received," he writes, " by this
venerable and illustrious man with the greatest kindness. His face expresses
grave, mild, peaceful worth, the calm consciousness and serene satisfaction
of virtue. I was charmed with his dignified simplicity, his mild but generous
benevolence, and the easy, gentle, superior sense and virtue of his thinking."
From Paris, Mr. Grahame travelled with his father along the banks of the
Loire, visited Nantes, renewed his acquaintance with Marshal and Madame
Cambronne, and spent some days in their family. " The modest, simple,
chivalrous character of Marshal Cambronne," says Mr. Stewart, " attracted Mr. Grahame's esteem and admiration, and strengthened those ties of
mutual interest and attachment which their former intercourse had originated."

Returning to the neighbourhood of London in June following, his health
recruited by his excursion, he immediately resumed, with characteristic ardor, his favorite historical pursuits. At this time the Catholic emancipation
question strongly agitated the British nation, and Mr. Grahame's ardent love
of liberty and religious toleration excited in him a keen interest in the success of this measure. Having found the climate of Nantes adapted to his
constitution, and enabling him, as he expressed himself, " to labor night and
day at his historical work," he returned to that city in October of the same
year, and fixed his residence there during the ensuing winter and spring.

In May, 1829, on his homeward journey, he passed through Paris, again
visited La Fayette, and saw him in the midst of his family, " surrounded,"
he writes, " by a troop of friends, some of distinguished character and as-

pect, and all regarding him with respect and admiration. Thus serene is the evening of his troubled but glorious life." Mr. Grahame adds : — " I had the honor and happiness of long and most interesting conversations with him, respecting the origin and commencement of his connection with the American cause. Nothing could be more friendly, kind, or benevolent than his manners ; nothing more instructive, entertaining, or interesting than the conversation he bestowed upon me. How mild, wise, and good La Fayette is ! Mr. Clarkson described him to me *as a man who desires the happiness of the human race, in consistence with strict subservience to the cause of truth and the honor of God.* I deem this a very honorable diploma. In the company of La Fayette, I feel an elevation of spirit and expansion of heart. What a roll of great deeds, heroic virtues, and interesting scenes is engraven on the lines of the venerable face of *the prisoner of Olmütz !* "

From these and other conversations Mr. Grahame acknowledges that he derived the materials for various passages in the text and notes of the fourth volume of his History of the United States. This work he finished in December, 1829. The intense labor which he had applied to its completion brought on a severe nervous fever, which, for a short time, threatened a fatal result.

In April, 1830, Mr. Grahame was married, at Nantes, to Jane A. Wilson, daughter of the Rev. John Wilson, the Protestant pastor of that city. Concerning this connection, John Stewart, Esq., his son-in-law, thus writes : — " From this period till his death, Mr. Grahame's home was at Nantes ; and in the society of his pious, amiable, and accomplished wife, and under her tender and vigilant care, Mr. Grahame enjoyed a degree of tranquil happiness and renewed health to which he had been long a stranger ; — interrupted only, at times, by his tendency to excessive literary exertion ; but at a later period more seriously and permanently, by the dangerous, lingering, and almost hopeless illness of his daughter. Between Mr. and Mrs. Grahame existed the most devoted attachment, based upon a complete appreciation of and profound esteem for each other's qualities and principles. They were both interesting, even in appearance ; tall and well proportioned ; — their features bearing the impress of a happy seriousness, while their demeanour evinced that peculiarly attractive stamp of real gentility which Christian principles add to natural good-breeding."

After his marriage, Mr. Grahame resided for several years at L'Eperonnière, an ancient chateau in the environs of Nantes ; Mr. and Mrs. Wilson, the aged parents of his wife, being inmates of his family. " Through their long standing connections," continues Mr. Stewart, " Mr. Grahame found himself at once in the best French society of Nantes. There the worth of his character soon made itself respected. The interest he took in every thing affecting the welfare of the city (to which, if necessary, he was accustomed liberally to subscribe), the urbanity of his demeanour in his intercourse with individuals, united with the generosity of his disposition, soon caused him to be regarded more in the light of a fellow-citizen than as a stranger ; and in process of time all such local distinctions as his numerous friends could bestow upon him, or induce him to accept, were conferred on him. The influence he thus acquired was chiefly and successfully exerted in the support of the small but increasing church professing the Protestant faith at Nantes. To several Frenchmen residing at Nantes Mr. Grahame became warmly attached ; but though his spirit of general benevolence led him to take a warm interest in those among whom he lived, and notwithstanding he saw much among the French to admire and respect, yet the character of his mind and habits, staid, serious, and retired, did not permit his feelings towards that country to approach to any thing like the warmth of his affection and admiration for either America or England."

Although Mr. Grahame had finished writing his History in December, 1829, he was far from regarding it as ready for the press. He attributed the ill success of his first two volumes to the haste with which they had been published ; he therefore resolved to devote several years to the revision of the entire work, and often expressed a doubt of its publication in his lifetime.

Nearly four years had now elapsed since the appearance of Mr. Grahame's volumes, yet the general silence concerning them had not been broken by any voice from this side of the Atlantic. The high price of the English edition rendered any considerable circulation in this country hopeless ; and American editors were yet to learn that it was possible for a foreigner and a Briton to treat the early history of the United States with fairness and impartiality. The knowledge of the nature and true value of this composition was confined to a few individuals. At length, in January, 1831, a just and discriminating critical notice of the work appeared in the North American Review. After expressing regret at the neglect with which it had hitherto been treated in America, and pointing out the causes of the little interest it had excited in this country, the reviewer proceeds to do justice to the independent spirit of the author ; to his freedom from prejudice ; to " the happy discrimination he had manifested in the selection of the leading principles that led to the colonization of the several States, and the able exposition of the results that followed " ; and to his having " corrected, with a proper boldness, the mistakes, whether of ignorance or malignity, which his predecessors in the same labors had committed." The reviewer adds, — " Mr. Grahame, with a spirit able to appreciate the value of his subject, has published what we conceive to be the best book that has anywhere appeared, upon the early history of the United States." " He has not invariably avoided error, but he has coped very successfully with the disadvantages of his situation." This is believed to be the first time Mr. Grahame's History had been made, either in America or Europe, the special subject of notice in any leading Review.

This high commendation of the two volumes then published appears by his journal to have been " very gratifying " to Mr. Grahame, and to have encouraged him to proceed with the revision and preparation of his extended work. While, under this new incitement, he was assiduously employed in reëxamining the details of his History, and exerting himself to render it as accurate as possible, he was interrupted by events which filled his domestic circle with grief and anxiety. In May, 1833, the death of his wife's mother, Mrs. Wilson, for whom he entertained an affection truly filial, was immediately followed by the dangerous illness of his only daughter. Her physicians, both in France and England, having declared that her life depended upon a change of climate, Mr. and Mrs. Grahame immediately accompanied her to Madeira ; whence, after a residence of nine months, they returned, her restoration being now deemed hopeless. She eventually recovered, however, in a manner " incomprehensible and unparalleled in medical experience," and ultimately attained a state of fair and permanent health, to which the assiduous attention of her excellent mother-in-law greatly contributed.

On his return from Madeira, Mr. Grahame first heard of the death of La Fayette, to whose memory he pays the following tribute in his diary : — " La Fayette is dead ! This ' sun of glory ' is blotted from the political firmament, which he has so long adorned. Every honest and generous breast must ' feel the sigh sincere ' for the loss of this great man, — the extinction of an effulgence of honor, virtue, and wisdom so benignly bright. Fully and beautifully did he exemplify the words of Wolsey : ' Love thyself last,' and ' Corruption wins not more than honesty.' He drew his last breath, and ceased to be a part (how honored, how admirable a part !) of human nature, at an early hour on the twentieth of this month [May], at the age of nearly seventy-seven. Pity that his last days must have been embittered by the existing dissensions in his beloved America ! Of the human beings I have known, and knowing have regarded with unmingled veneration, there exist now only Mr. Clarkson and my father. It seems strange to me that La Fayette should be no more, — that such an illustrious ornament of human nature should disappear, and yet the world continue so like what it was before. Yet the words ' La Fayette is dead ' will cause a keen sensation to vibrate through every scene of moral and intellectual being on earth. A thousand deep thoughts and earnest remembrances will awaken at that name, over which ages of renown had gathered, while yet its owner lived and moved and had his being among us. France, in losing this man, seems to me to have lost the brightest jewel in her national diadem, and to have suffered an eclipse of interest and glory."

During his residence in Madeira, Mr. Grahame continued the revision of his History, and on his return, after devoting another year to the same object, he took up his residence in London for the purpose of superintending its publication. Here, again, his anxiety and unremitting industry induced a dangerous illness. His restoration to health he attributed to the assiduous care of two of his friends, Mrs. Reid and Dr. Boott. The former took him from his hotel to her own house, and thus secured for him retirement, quiet, and her undivided attention. " From her," he says, " I have received the most comfortable and elegant hospitality, the kindest and most assiduous care, and conversation seasoned with genius, piety, and benevolence, and the finest accomplishments of education." Concerning Dr. Boott, who is a native of Boston, Massachusetts, established as a physician in London, Mr. Grahame remarks in his diary, — " His knowledge is great ; his abilities excellent ; his flow of thought incessant ; his heart and dispositions admirable. He insists that his valuable attendance upon me be accepted as friendly, and not remunerated as professional, service. In this man, America has sent me one of her noblest sons, to save the life of her historian."

After an interruption of six weeks, Mr. Grahame resumed the revision of the proof-sheets of his work ; and in December, having finished this labor, returned to his family, at Nantes. In the ensuing January (1836), his History was published.

Eleven years had now elapsed since Mr. Grahame had commenced writing the History of the United States. More earnest and assiduous research had seldom been exerted by any historian. His interest in the subject was intense. His talents were unquestionable. There was no carelessness in the execution, no haste in the publication. A Briton, highly educated, universally respected, of a moral and religious character which gave the stamp of authority to his statements and opinions, had devoted the best years of his life to the task of introducing his countrymen and the world to an acquaintance with the early fortunes of a people who had risen with unparalleled rapidity to a high rank among the nations of the earth ; yet a second time his work was received with neglect by those literary Reviews in Great Britain which chiefly guide the public taste, and distribute the rewards and honors of literary industry.   Although highly wrought, elevated in sentiment, generous and noble in its design, all its views and influences made subservient to the cause of pure morals and practical piety, yet, as has been already observed, it was obviously not adapted to conciliate either the prejudices, the feelings, or the interests of the British people.   It could not well be expected, that, under an Episcopal hierarchy, whose Roman Catholic origin and tendencies are manifest, a history of successful Puritanism would be favorably received.   It could not be hoped, that, in a nation which had risen to the height of civilization and power under a monarchy based on an aristocracy, a work illustrative and laudatory of institutions strictly republican would be countenanced, — much more, generally patronized.   Mr. Grahame, moreover, had not only imbibed the political principles of the Puritans, but had caught much of their devotional spirit.   Hence his language, at times, is ill suited to the genius of an age which does not regard religion as the great business of life, nor the extension of its influences as one of the appropriate objects of history.   Owing to these causes, his work received little encouragement in Europe, and the knowledge of its claims to respect and attention was limited.   Nor were these consequences confined to Great Britain.   American readers commonly rely on the leading Reviews of that country for notices of meritorious productions of British authors, and are not apt to make research after those which they neglect or depreciate.   As Mr. Grahame belonged to no political or literary party or circle, he was without aid from that personal interest and zeal which often confer an adventitious popularity. He trusted the success of his work wholly to its own merits, and, when disappointed a second time, neither complained nor was discouraged, — supported, as before, by a consciousness of his faithful endeavours, and by a firm belief in their ultimate success.   He had assumed the whole pecuniary risk of his extended publication, in four volumes octavo, which resulted in a loss of one thousand pounds sterling, — and that, at a time, as he states, when it was not easy for him to sustain it.   Taking no counsel of despondency, however, he immediately began to prepare for a second edition of his entire work, and devoted to it, during the remaining years of his life, all the time and strength which a constitutional organic disease permitted.

Hitherto, Mr. Grahame's interest in America had been derived from the study of her history and institutions ; but in 1837 he formed an acquaintance with a few distinguished Americans, and received from them the respect due to his historical labors.   Among these was Robert Walsh, Esq., who, after a brilliant and effective literary career in this country, had transferred his residence to Paris ; by him Mr. Grahame was introduced to Washington Irving.   Both these eminent Americans united in urging him to write the history of the American Revolution ; Mr. Walsh offering to procure for him materials, and a sufficient guaranty against pecuniary loss.

Under this influence he now entered upon a course of reading embracing that period of American history ; but, as may be gathered from the general tenor of his subsequent remarks and the result, more from curiosity and interest in the subject than from any settled purpose of writing upon it ; for early in August of this year (1837), he observes in his diary, — " Mr. Walsh, in his letters to me, renews his urgency that I should write the history of the Revolutionary War. But I think I have done enough as a historian, and that a prudent regard to my own reputation bids me rather enforce my title than enlarge my claim to public attention." And about the same time he wrote to Mr. Walsh, — " I cannot agree with you in thinking that our beloved America will regard with equal complacency a historic garland attached to her brows by foreign hands, and one in which a son of her own blends his own renown with hers." Yet, from a letter to the same gentleman in September following, it is evident that Mr. Grahame entertained a strong predilection for the design ; for he thus writes : — " The more I pursue my present American studies, the more I am struck with a pleasing astonishment. The account of the formation of the federal constitution of North America inspires me with delight and admiration. I knew but the outline of the scene before. Now, I find that the more its details are examined, the more honorable and interesting it proves. Truly does it deserve to be termed the greatest scene of human glory that ever adorned the tide of human time. I wish, that, ere my health and spirit had been broken, I had ventured to be the historian of that scene. But surely the country, the *magna mater virûm*, that has produced such actors and such deeds, is herself destined to afford their fittest historian." In a similar strain he writes in his journal, under the same date, — " The account (by Pitkin and others), which I am reading, of the formation of the federal constitution of North America, after the achievement of her national independence, fills me with astonishment and admiration. It would make me glad to be convinced that the present people of America and their leaders are altogether such as were the Americans of those days. Far more was gained to America (and through her, I hope, eventually to the whole world) by the wisdom, virtue, and moderation exhibited by her children after the War of Independence, than by the valor that brought that war to its happy close. Such a scene the history of no other country ever exhibited. I wish I had been its historian. But a fit historian will surely arise one day."

Botta, who had written the history of the American Revolution, died about this time in Paris. Mr. Grahame's feelings were deeply moved by the event. " I hope," he wrote in his diary, " that the Americans at Paris attended his funeral. *Though only in heart an American*, I would have desired leave to attend, had I been there." And in a letter to Mr. Walsh, he remarks, — " I hope some memoir of Botta will appear. It should gratify Americans to learn, that, on his death-bed, he related (it was to myself), that his son, in some distant part of the world, received civilities from the officers and crew of an American vessel, who instantly recognized as a friend the son of the historian of their country, — adding, ' That was a rich reward of my labors.' When I told him that Jefferson had expressed admiration of his work, he squeezed my hand and testified much delight. And when I told him that both Jefferson and John Adams condemned his *speeches* as fictitious, he smiled, and answered with *naïveté*, ' They are not wholly invented.' "

Mr. Walsh having, in conversation, expressed to Mr. Grahame his surprise at the partiality he evinced for his country and countrymen, he replied, — " As Hannibal was taught by his father to hate the Romans, so was I trained by mine to love the Americans." And, in writing to that gentleman in October, 1837, he remarks, in the same spirit, — " I regret, when I see the defence of America conducted with recrimination against Great

Britain. But I must confess that my own indignation at the conduct and language of some of my countrymen towards America is at times uncontrollable. I wish that Americans could regard these follies with indulgence, or magnanimous (perhaps disdainful) indifference. For my part, I can truly say, that my daughter is hardly dearer to me than America and American renown."

His admiration of the character of Washington is thus expressed in his journal, under the date of September, 1837 : — " O, what a piece of work of divine handicraft was Washington ! What a grace to his nation, his age, and to human nature was he ! I know of no other military and political chief who has so well supported the character delineated in these lines of Horace : —

> ' Justum ac tenacem propositi virum
> Non civium ardor prava jubentium,
> Non vultus instantis tyranni,
> Mente quatit solidâ.'

With the same feeling that tempted the clergyman, who read the funeral service over the body of John Wesley, to substitute, for the formula, ' our dear *brother* here departed,' the words, ' our dear *father* here departed,' I am inclined to regard Washington rather as a father than a brother of his fellow-men. What a master, what a pupil, were Washington and La Fayette ! One day, when I was sitting with La Fayette, he said to me, ' I was always a republican, and Washington was always my model and my master.' " During the same month, he wrote to Mr. Walsh, — " Washington impresses me with so much veneration, that I have become more than ever anxious to know what really was the state and complexion of his religious opinions " ; and recurring, in a subsequent letter, to the same topic, he remarks, — " I find McGuire's ' Religious Opinions and Character of Washington ' heavy, tiresome, and, in general, unsatisfactory. But last night I reached a passage which gave me lively delight ; for now I can look on Washington as a Christian."

Until near the close of this year, Mr. Grahame continued to pursue his researches on the subject of the American Revolution, although laboring under a constant depression of health and spirits, and a prevailing apprehension that his life would be short, and that his constitutional disorders were symptomatic of sudden death. But in December, 1837, his physicians prohibited him from " writing or reading for some months, on any subject likely to provoke much thinking " ; and on the 19th of this month, he wrote to Mr. Walsh, that he had reason to attribute his recent illness to his " late historic studies, and to the anxiety of mind earnest meditation had induced." " For me to undertake such a work," he says, " or even contemplate it, or diligently prepare for it, until my health be totally renovated (which, in all human probability, it never will be), would, I clearly see, be to do to the subject and to myself unreasonable injustice. *I therefore renounce it altogether.* I hope you will not blame me, nor regret the trouble you have taken and the kindness you have shown me with the view of my prosecuting the career from which I have now retreated. For a long time before I had the pleasure of your acquaintance, I had resolved, from a sense of both moral and physical incompetency, as well as on account of the slenderness of my success, the heaviness of my pecuniary loss, and other considerations, to carry my historic narrative no farther. It was your flattering encouragement — the *laus laudati viri* — that tempted me to mistake an agreeable vision for a reasonable hope, and to embrace the purpose I must now painfully, but decidedly, forego.

> ' Hos successus alit : possunt quia posse videntur.'

Neither category was mine. I had no success to sustain me, and no internal confidence to impel me ; but the very reverse."

The charge of "invention," preferred against Mr. Grahame by Mr. Bancroft, in his History,[1] on account of the epithet "baseness" applied by him to the conduct of Clarke, the agent of Rhode Island, in negotiating for that colony the charter it obtained in 1663 from Charles the Second, first came to Mr. Grahame's knowledge early in the year 1838, and excited in him feelings of surprise and a deep sense of wrong. "There is here," he immediately wrote to Mr. Walsh, "a plentiful lack of the kindness I might have expected from an American, and of the courtesy which should characterize a gentleman and a man of letters. I had deserved even severer language, if the *invention* with which I am charged were justly laid to me. But the imputation is utterly false. — I have written under the guidance of authorities, on which I have, perhaps erringly, certainly honestly, relied. I would rather be convicted of the grossest stupidity, than of the slightest degree of wilful falsification ; for I greatly prefer moral to intellectual merit and repute." A defence against this attack upon Mr. Grahame's veracity as a historian was soon after published by Mr. Walsh in "The New York American " ; and was succeeded by another, from Mr. Grahame himself, in the same paper.

Mr. Bancroft, in a subsequent edition of his History,[2] silently withdrew the charge of "invention," and substituted in its stead that of "unwarranted misapprehension." It is not apparent how this charge is more tenable than was the other.

Mr. Grahame's strictures on Clarke's conduct in the negotiation referred to drew upon him the animadversions of "some of the *literati* of Rhode Island." Through them, he became acquainted with the intrinsic worth of Clarke's general character, and readily acknowledged him to be "a true patriot and excellent man, and well deserving the reverence of his natural and national posterity." Yet Mr. Grahame's mind was so deeply and unalterably impressed with the opinion, that Clarke had exceeded "the line of honor and integrity" in that negotiation, that he appears to have been unable to reconcile it to his sense of truth, as a historian, wholly to exonerate his conduct from censure. Accordingly, in the present edition of his History,[3] Mr. Grahame thus alters the sentence which had occasioned the animadversions alluded to : — "The envoy conducted his negotiation with a suppleness of adroit servility, that rendered the success of it dearly bought " ; implying that Clarke, in suing for favors under such pretences as he urged to obtain them, had exhibited a "servile" spirit, "supple" in respect of policy, and "adroit" in the color he gave to the facts on which he based his hopes of success ; and intimating that he could find no other apology for his conduct, than "the aptitude even of good men to be transported beyond the line of honor and integrity, in conducting such negotiations as that which was confided to Clarke."[4]

---

[1] Vol. II., p. 64, edit. 1837.   [2] Vol. II., p. 64, edit. 1841.   [3] See Vol. I., p. 224.

[4] It is due to the subject of this Memoir here to inquire into those general facts and circumstances which led Mr. Grahame (the tenor of whose mind towards the people of the United States was kind, candid, and laudatory) to express so strongly and adhere so perseveringly to the opinion he had formed concerning Clarke's conduct in the negotiation above adverted to.

At the time of Clarke's negotiation, Massachusetts and Rhode Island were both present by deputy at the court of Charles the Second, — *both moved alike by fear;* Massachusetts of the king, being apprehensive it was his intention to vacate her old charter; Rhode Island of Massachusetts, who had shown a disposition to extend her jurisdiction over territory which Rhode

From Mr. Grahame's position as a distant observer, his views of character and events may sometimes conflict with those entertained in this country ; yet his spirit is *wholly American*, and it is his desire and delight to do justice to the actors in the scenes he describes. The high moral tone, and the ever active, all-controlling religious principle and feeling, which pervade his work, inspire the strongest confidence in all that he writes ; and it seems impossible for any one, in the exercise of a sound and unprejudiced judgment, to believe that a mind impelled by motives so pure and elevated, having no personal ends to serve, no party purposes to answer, could, under any circumstances, knowingly warp the truth, invent or suppress facts, or give to them any false or delusive coloring. Mr. Grahame never visited the United States, and his opportunities for intercourse with its citizens were few ; but he spared neither time, labor, nor expense to acquaint himself with the authentic materials of its history ; he laid the public libraries of Scotland, England, France, and Germany under contribution to the completeness and accuracy of his work ; and if he has occasionally fallen into mistakes, they are either such as all historians, who rely for their facts on the authority of others, are subject to, or such as might naturally be expected under the peculiar circumstances of the case, — being chiefly on points of local history, in their nature of little interest or importance beyond the immediate sphere

---

Island claimed, as also to interfere with the local government and religious liberties of this colony. It was no motive of *loyalty* that induced the appearance of either of them at court ; nor was there any thing in their previous history which could entitle the deputies of either colony to vaunt any sentiment of this sort on the part of their constituents.

In this state of things, and notwithstanding " Rhode Island had solicited and accepted a patent from the Long Parliament, in the commencement of its struggles with Charles the First, while Massachusetts declined to make a similar recognition, even when the Parliament was at the utmost height of its power and success," (Grahame, I., 323,) — Chalmers represents Clarke as boasting of the loyalty of the inhabitants of Rhode Island, and, in order to depreciate Massachusetts in the opinion of King Charles the Second, and exalt Rhode Island, as challenging the deputies of the former colony " to display any one act of duty or loyalty shown by their constituents to Charles the First or to the present king, from their first establishment in New England." " The challenge thus confidently given," adds Chalmers, " was not accepted." — *Political Annals of the United Colonies*, p. 273. — The agents of Massachusetts would not condescend, for the sake even of saving their charter, to feign a sentiment which they were sensible had no existence. Their silence, under such circumstances, it is impossible for any fair mind not to honor and approve.

Furthermore, Chalmers states that the Rhode-Islanders " procured from the chiefs of the Narragansets a formal surrender of their country, which was afterwards called the King's Province, to Charles the First, in right of his crown," and that their " *deputies boasted to Charles the Second of the merits of this transaction.*" — *Ibid.* — Now, *in point of fact*, the name of King's Province was not given to the Narraganset country until 1666, three years after Clarke's negotiation ; — see *Collections of Rhode Island Historical Society*, Vol. IV., p. 69 ; — and in respect of the surrender of the Narraganset country, Gorton, who was the chief agent in receiving it, explicitly states, that it was *self-moved* on the part of the Indians ; that they sent to the colonists and voluntarily offered it ; and does not pretend that the Rhode-Islanders had any further agency in the affair than encouraging the disposition of the Indians to make the surrender, aiding them in doing it in legal form, and promising to transmit their deed and desire of protection to the English government. — See Gorton's *Simplicities Defence*, pp. 79 – 81.

In view of Clarke's hollow pretences of loyalty on the part of his constituents, and the supposititious proofs of it adduced by him, it is not wonderful that a mind like that of Mr. Grahame should have become immovably fixed in the opinion, that the conduct of the Rhode Island deputy was not reconcilable with truth and integrity, and that it was unbecoming a historian who meant to be just, and was conscious of being impartial, to refrain from expressing with fidelity the convictions forced upon him by a knowledge of the facts and circumstances.

Clarke was unquestionably faithful to his agency. He acted according to the views and wishes of his constituents, and in vaunting their loyalty probably followed their instructions ; he was therefore fully entitled to all the thanks they expressed, and all the honors they conferred upon him. A Christian moralist, like Grahame, who had drunk deep of " Siloa's brook," which flowed fast by the oracles of God," naturally can allow no compromise with truth for the sake of effect or success, and must unavoidably apply to the conduct of men, whether acting as private individuals or as public agents, one and the same pure and elevated moral standard ; a strictness of moral principle, which, it must be confessed, in respect of public agents, the customs and opinions of the world do not regard as either practicable or politic.

or the particular persons they affect ; and when traced to their sources, it will often be found that even into these he was led by authorities whose errors have been detected only by recent research, in some instances subsequent to the publication of his volumes.

In February, 1839, Mr. Grahame writes to Mr. Walsh, — " You propose (and deeply I feel the honor and kindness of the proposal) to have an American edition of my work published at Philadelphia. Now, pray, ponder wisely and kindly these suggestions. Much as I should otherwise like a republication of my work in America, I could not enjoy it, ' with unreproved pleasure free,' if I thought it would be at all disagreeable to Mr. Bancroft, or that it would be construed in America as a competitory challenge of an English to an American writer. Let there be, if it be necessary or profitable, a rivalry (a generous one) between England and America. But I am far too much Americanized to think, without chagrin and impatience, of *my* seeming the rival (the foreign rival) of a great American writer. Dear to me is the fame of every man whose fame is interwoven with the fame of America, and whose career tends to justify to myself and to the world the delightful feelings of admiration and hope with which she inspires me." And, in a subsequent letter on the same topic, he writes to the same correspondent, — " Most sincerely do I wish that an American may prove the great, the conclusive, and the lasting historian of America. I shall be content, if of my work some Englishmen and perhaps a few Americans say, ' *So* thought an Englishman who loved his country, but affected still more warmly the cause of truth, justice, and universal human welfare.' "

In his correspondence with this gentleman during this and the ensuing year, the American bias of his mind appears on almost every occasion and every subject. Intermingled with this, we continually meet with manifestations of that all-pervading religious sentiment, and of that tenderness of the domestic affections, which constituted the most striking and beautiful elements of his character. Thus, in congratulating Mr. Walsh on the restored health of his "*wife*," he remarks, — " They say that Americans, in general, say *lady* and *female*, when we say *wife* and *woman*. Now, I reckon *wife*, *woman*, and *mamma* to be the three loveliest words in the English language." And, writing concerning his having completed the forty-ninth year of his age, he adds, — " The period of life, at which, I believe, Aristotle fixes the decline of human abilities. I would give all the abilities I have, and ten times more, if I had them, for a deep, abiding sense of piety and the love of God. May that, my dear, kind friend, be yours and mine ! And can we wish a happier portion to those whom we love ? All else fades away."

In the course of this year (1839), a highly laudatory review of the "History of the United States" was read before the Royal Academy of Nantes, by M. Malherbe, in which its merits were analyzed and acknowledged ; and Mr. Grahame was, in consequence, unanimously elected a member of the Academy.

In August, of the same year, the degree of Doctor of Laws was conferred on Mr. Grahame by the Corporation and Overseers of Harvard University. It was the first public evidence of respect he had received from this side of the Atlantic ; and it drew from him unqualified expressions of satisfaction. In a letter to the Rev. George E. Ellis, of Massachusetts, in November following, he writes, — " Harvard College has long been a spot round which my heart hovered.

> ' Ille terrarum mihi præter omnes
> Angulus ridet.'

Now, indeed, it is doubly dear to me ; for I feel myself, in a manner, one of its sons. The view of the College buildings in Peirce's History awakened and detained my fondest regards. May truth, virtue, and happiness flourish within those walls, and beam forth from them to the divine glory and human welfare ! Though somewhat broken by years and infirmities, I yet cherish the hope to see Harvard University before I die." In a letter to Mr. Walsh, in October following, he thus refers to the same topic : — " I am now an American. Your dear country has adopted me. Never let me hear again of America or Americans owing any thing to me. I am the much indebted party. I feel with the keenest sensibility the honor that Harvard University has conferred upon me."

The writer of a critical notice of Bancroft's History of the United States, in the North American Review, for January, 1841, introduced some incidental remarks on that of Mr. Grahame. After bearing testimony to his capacity, though a foreigner, to appreciate the motives and institutions of the Puritans, and acknowledging the fidelity and candor, the extent and accuracy, of his researches, the critic adds, — " Mr. Grahame's work, with all its merit, is the work of a *foreigner*. And that word comprehends much that cannot be overcome by the best writer. He may produce a beautiful composition, faultless in style, accurate in the delineation of prominent events, full of sound logic and most wise conclusions. But he cannot enter into the sympathies, comprehend all the minute feelings, prejudices, and peculiar ways of thinking, which form the idiosyncrasy of the nation."

The author of this review was well understood to be William H. Prescott, Esq., and Mr. Grahame thus remarks upon it in his journal : — " Prescott's critical notice of Bancroft's third volume, in the North American Review, contains some handsome commendation of my work ; — qualified by that favorite canon of American literary jurisprudence, that no man not born and bred in America can perform, *as such a function ought to be performed*, the task of describing the people, or relating even their distant history. Now, I am inclined to suspect that this theorem is unsound in principle and false in fact. I think a man may better describe objects, from not having been inveterately habituated and familiarized to them ; and at once more calmly contemplate and more impartially estimate national character, of which he is not a full, necessitated, born partaker, — and national habits, prejudices, usages, and peculiarities, under the dominance of which his own spirit has not been moulded, from its earliest dawn of intelligent perception."

In a letter to Mr. Prescott, dated March 3d, 1841, he recurs to this topic. " On the general censure of your countrymen, that, ' personally unacquainted with America, I cannot correctly delineate even her distant history,' — Queen Elizabeth desired that her portrait should be painted without shade ; because, by a truly royal road to the principles of that art, she had discovered that shade is an accident. Are not some of your countrymen possessed of a similar feeling, and desirous that every historic portrait of America should represent it *as it ought to be*, and not *as it is ?* When I look into the works of some of your greatest American writers, and see how daintily they handle certain topics, — elusively playing or rather fencing with them, as if they were burning ploughshares, — I must respectfully doubt, if, as yet at least, an American is likely to be the best writer of American history. That the greatest and most useful historian that has ever instructed mankind will yet arise in America, I fondly hope, desire, and believe. It would be my pride to be regarded as the pioneer of such a writer, and to have, in

A *

any wise, contributed to the utility of his work and the extension of American fame. I trust it is with you, as it is with me, a sacred maxim, that to good historiography elevation and rectitude of soul are at least as requisite as literary resource and intellectual range and vigor."

In June of this year, he received, and in his journal thus comments on, Quincy's History of Harvard University : — " Read it with much interest. No other country, from the first syllable of recorded time, ever produced a seat of learning so honorable to its founders and early supporters as Harvard University. This work is the only recent American composition with which I am acquainted that justifies his countrymen's plea, that there is something in their history that none but an American born and bred can adequately conceive and render. His account of the transition of the social system of Massachusetts, from an entire and punctilious intertexture of church and state, to the restriction of municipal government to civil affairs and occupations, is very curious and interesting, and admirably fills up an important void in New England history. He wounds my prejudices by attacking the Mathers, and other persons of a primitive cast of Puritanism, with a severity the more painful to me that I see not well how I can demur to its justice. But though I disapprove and dissent from many of their views, and regret many of their proceedings, yet the depths of my heart are with the primitive Puritans and the Scottish Covenanters ; and even their errors I deem of nobler kind than the frigid merits of some of the emendators of their policy."

In the same strain he wrote to Mr. Quincy on the 4th of July following, — " I regard the primitive Puritans much as I do the Scottish Covenanters ; respectfully disapproving and completely dissenting from many of their views and opinions ; especially their favorite scheme of an intertexture of church and state, which appears to me not only unchristian, but antichristian. But I cordially embrace all that is purely doctrinal in their system, and regard their persons with a fond, jealous love, which makes me indulgent even to their errors. Carrying their heavenly treasures in earthly vessels, they could not fail to err. But theirs were the errors of noble minds. How different from those of knaves, fools, and lukewarm professors ! I forget what poet it is that says,

'Some failings are of nobler kind
Than virtues of a narrow mind.' "

The complete restoration to health of his only daughter, and her marriage to John Stewart, Esq., the brother-in-law of the friend of his youth and manhood, Sir John F. W. Herschel, shed bright rays of happiness over the last years of Mr. Grahame's life. These were passed at Nantes in his domestic circle, in the companionship of the exemplary and estimable lady who had united her fortunes with his, and cheered by the reflected happiness and welfare of his children. His only son, who was pursuing successfully the career of a solicitor in Glasgow, occasionally visited him as his professional avocations permitted. His daughter and son-in-law divided their time between Nantes and England. Always passionately fond of children, and having the power of rendering himself singularly attractive to them by his gentle, quiet, playful manner, he was devotedly attached to his little granddaughter, who became his frequent companion. Under the influence of these tranquil scenes of domestic happiness his health visibly improved ; nor was there the slightest suspicion of the organic disease which was destined soon to terminate his life. By direction of his medical attendant, Dr. Fouré, an eminent physician of Nantes, he abstained from all severe literary toil ; yet whatever study was permitted to him was directed to the improvement of his History of the United States, to which he made many additions and amendments, and which he declared, shortly before his death, he had finally completed to his own satisfaction, and thoroughly prepared for a second edition.

Circumstances in which Mr. Grahame had been accidentally placed had forcibly directed his mind to the subject of slavery, the enormity of the evil, and its effects on the morals and advancement of the people among whom it existed. He had acquired, in right of his first wife, an estate in the West Indies, which was cultivated by slaves. His feelings in respect of this slave-derived income are strongly expressed in a letter to Sir John F. W. Herschel, dated the 24th of February, 1827. " A subject has for some time been giving me uneasiness. My children are proprietors of a ninth share of a West India estate, and I have a life-rent in it. Were my children of age, I could not make one of the negroes free, and could do nothing but appropriate or forego the share of produce the estate yielded. Often have I wished it were in my power to make the slaves free, and thought this barren wish a sufficient tribute to duty. My conscience was quite laid asleep. Like many others, I did not do what I could, because I could not do what I wished. For years past, something more than a fifth part of my income has been derived from the labor of slaves. God forgive me for having so long tainted my store ! and God be thanked for that warning voice that has roused me from my lethargy, and taught me to feel that my hand offended me ! Never more shall the price of blood enter my pocket, or help to sustain the lives or augment the enjoyment of those dear children. They sympathize with me cordially. Till we can legally divest ourselves of our share, every shilling of the produce of it is to be devoted to the use of some part of the unhappy race from whose suffering it is derived." Subsequently, with the consent of his children, Mr. Grahame entirely gave up this slave-property, amounting to several thousand pounds.

His interest in the fate of the African race had been excited several years before by a circumstance which he thus relates in his diary, under date of October, 1821 : — " My father is most vigorously engaged in protecting three poor, forlorn Africans from being carried, against their wills, back to the West Indies. They were part of the crew of a vessel driven by stress of weather into the port of Dumbarton. While the vessel was undergoing some repairs, the people of the town remarked with surprise the precautions by which unnecessary communication with the shore was prevented ; and their surprise was converted into strong suspicion, when they perceived sometimes, in the evening, a few black heads on the deck, suffered to be there a short time, and then sent below. A number of the citizens applied to the magistrates, but the magistrates were afraid to interfere ; so the people had the sense and spirit to convey the intelligence by express to my father, whose zeal for the African race was well known. He instantly caused the vessel to be arrested, and has cheerfully undertaken the enormous damages, as well as the costs of suit, to which he will be subjected, if the case be decided against him." In a subsequent entry in his diary, Mr. Grahame writes, — " But it was decided in his favor."

By the same daily record it appears, that, in 1823, his feelings were still further excited on the subject of slavery by an incident which he thus notices : — " Zachary Macaulay showed me to-day some of the laws of Jamaica, and pointed out how completely every provision for restraining the

cruelty of the masters and alleviating the bondage of the slaves is defeated
by counter provisions that render the remedy unattainable. — What a stain
on the history of the church of England is it, that not one of her wealthy
ministers, not one of her bishops who sit as peers of the realm in the House
of Lords, has ever attempted to mitigate the evils of negro slavery, or ever
called the public attention to that duty ! No, they leave the field of Christian labor to Methodists and Moravians."

Actuated by such feelings and sentiments, he published, in 1823, a pamphlet, entitled " Thoughts on the Projected Abolition of Slavery," — a
production, which, in the latter years of his life, he declared that he looked
back upon with unalloyed pleasure and satisfaction. In 1828, Mr. Grahame
relates in his journal, that he had had a long conversation on this subject with
the celebrated Abbé Grégoire, to whom he had been introduced by La
Fayette. In the course of this conversation, the Abbé stated to him that
he " had written to Jefferson, combating the opinions expressed in Jefferson's ' Notes on Virginia,' of the inferiority of the intellectual capacity of
the negroes, and that Jefferson had answered, acknowledging his error."

The prevalent language on the subject of negro slavery in some parts of
the United States, and the apparently general acquiescence of the people in
the continuance of that institution, led him, in the latter years of his life, to
apprehend, that, in the first edition of his History, he had treated that subject with more indulgence than was consistent with truth and duty. Under
this impression, he remarks in his diary, in December, 1837, — " My admiration of America, my attachment to her people, and my interest in their
virtue, their happiness, their dignity, and renown, have increased, instead of
abating. But research and reflection have obliged me, in the edition of my
work which I have been preparing since the publication in 1835, to beat
down some American pretensions to virtue and apologies for wrong, which
I had formerly and too hastily admitted. Much as I value the friendship
and regard of the Americans, I would rather serve than gratify them, —
rather deserve their esteem than obtain their favor."

Early in the year 1842, a pamphlet, published in London in 1835, entitled
" A Letter to Lord Brougham on the Subject of American Slavery, by an
American," was put into Mr. Grahame's hands, as he states, " by another
American, most honorably distinguished in the walks of science and philanthropy," who bid him " read there the defence of his (the American's)
country." The positions maintained by this writer — that " slavery was
introduced into the American colonies, now the United States, by the British government," and that " the opposition to it there was so general, that,
with propriety, it may be said to have been universal " — roused Mr. Grahame's indignation ; which was excited to an extreme when he perceived
these statements repeated and urged in a memorial addressed to Daniel
O'Connell by certain Irish emigrants settled at Pottsville, in the United
States. Having devoted some time to a careful perusal of this pamphlet, he
felt himself called upon as a Briton, from a regard to the reputation of his
country and to truth, and from a belief that " no living man knew more of
the early history of the American people than himself," to contradict, in the
most direct and pointed manner, the statements referred to ; pledging himself " to prove that the abovementioned pamphlet was a production more
disgraceful to American literature and character (in so far as it was to be
esteemed the representative of either) than any other literary performance
with which he was acquainted."

He accordingly applied himself forthwith to an extended discussion of this subject in a pamphlet to which he affixed the title, — "Who is to blame? or Cursory Review of American Apology for American Accession to Negro Slavery." In this pamphlet Mr. Grahame admits that Great Britain "facilitated her colonial offspring to become slaveholders," — that " she encouraged her merchants in tempting them to acquire slaves," — that " her conduct during her long sanction of the slave-trade is indefensible," — that " she excelled all her competitors in slave-stealing, for the same reason that she excelled them in every other branch of what was then esteemed legitimate traffic " ; — but denies that she "*forced* the Americans to become slaveholders," — denies that " the slave-trade was comprehended within the scope and operation of the commercial policy of the British government until the reign of Queen Anne," — and asserts, that, " prior to that reign, negro slavery was established in every one of the American provinces that finally revolted from Great Britain, except Georgia, which was not planted until 1733." The argument in this pamphlet is pressed with great strength and spirit, and the whole is written under the influence of feelings in a state of indignant excitement. Without palliating the conduct of Great Britain, he regards the attempt to exculpate America, by criminating the mother country, as unworthy and unjust ; contending that neither was under any peculiar or irresistible temptation, but only such as is common to man, when, in the language of the Apostle, " he is drawn away of his own lust and enticed." His argument respecting the difference, in point of criminality, between America and Great Britain results as another identical question has long since resulted concerning the comparative guilt of the receiver and the thief.

In the month of June, 1842, at the urgent request of his and his father's friend, Thomas Clarkson, the early and successful asserter of the rights of Africans, he repaired to London, for the purpose of superintending the publication of this pamphlet. On arriving there, he placed his manuscript in the hands of a printer, and immediately proceeded to Playford Hall, Ipswich, the residence of Mr. Clarkson. Concerning this distinguished man, Mr. Grahame, under date of the 25th of June, thus writes in his diary : — " Mr. Clarkson's appearance is solemnly tender and beautiful. Exhausted with age and malady, he is yet warmly zealous, humane, and affectionate. Fifty-seven years of generous toil have not relaxed his zeal in the African cause. He watches over the interests of the colored race in every quarter of the world, desiring and promoting their moral and physical welfare, rejoicing in their improvement, afflicted in all their afflictions. The glory of God and the interests of the African race are the mastersprings of his spirit."

After two days passed in intercourse with this congenial mind, Mr. Grahame returned to London and occupied himself zealously in correcting the proof-sheets of his pamphlet. On the morning of the 30th of June, he was assailed by severe pain, which his medical attendant attributed at first to indigestion, and treated as such. But it soon assumed a more alarming character. Eminent physicians were called for consultation, and his brother, Thomas Grahame, was sent for. From the nature and intensity of his suffering, Mr. Grahame soon became sensible that his final hour was approaching, and addressed himself to meet it with calmness and resignation. He proceeded to communicate his last wishes to his son-in-law, directed where he should be buried, and dictated his epitaph : — " James Grahame, Advocate, Edinburgh, Author of the History of the United States of North America ; aged 51." He, at the same time, expressed the hope concerning his recently published pamphlet, that no efforts might be spared to secure its sale and distribution, " as he had written it conscientiously and with single-heartedness, and had invoked the blessing of God upon it."

Notwithstanding the distinguished skill of his physicians, every remedy failed of producing the desired effect. His disorder was organic, and beyond the power of their art. Such was the excruciating agony which preceded his death, that his friends could only hope that his release might not be long delayed. This wish was granted on Sunday morning, the 3d of July.

" His endurance of the pain and oppression of breathing which preceded his death," says Mr. Stewart, " was perfectly wonderful. His features were constantly calm, placid, and at last bore a bright, even a cheerful expression. His attendants, while bending close towards him, caught occasionally expressions of prayer ; his profound acquaintance with the Scriptures enabling him, in this hour of his need, to draw strength and support from that inexhaustible source, where he was accustomed to seek and to find it."

He was buried in Kensall Green Cemetery, in the neighbourhood of London. His son-in-law, John Stewart, and his brother, Thomas Grahame, attended his remains to the grave. His son, also, who had set out from Scotland on hearing of his illness, though arriving too late to see him before he expired, was not denied the melancholy satisfaction of being present at his interment. A plain marble monument has been erected over his tomb, bearing the exact inscription he himself dictated.

These scanty memorials are all that it has been possible, in this country, to collect in relation to James Grahame. Though few and disconnected, they are grateful and impressive.

The habits of his life were domestic, and in the family circle the harmony and loveliness of his character were eminently conspicuous. His mind was grave, pure, elevated, far-reaching ; its enlarged views ever on the search after the true, the useful, and the good. His religious sentiments, though exalted and tinctured with enthusiasm, were always candid, liberal, and tolerant. In politics a republican, his love of liberty was nevertheless qualified by a love of order, — his desire to elevate the destinies of the *many*, by a respect for the rights and interests of the *few*. As in his religion there was nothing of bigotry, so in his political principles there was nothing of radicalism.

As a historian, there were combined in Mr. Grahame all the qualities which inspire confidence and sustain it ; — a mind powerful and cultivated, patient of labor, indefatigable in research, independent, faithful, and fearless ; engaging in its subject with absorbing interest, and in the development of it superior to all influences except those of truth and duty.

To Americans, in all future times, it cannot fail to be an interesting and gratifying circumstance, that the foreigner, who first undertook to write a complete history of their republic from the earliest period of the colonial settlements, was a Briton, eminently qualified to appreciate the merits of its founders, and at once so able and so willing to do justice to them. The people of the United States, on whose national character and success Mr. Grahame bestowed his affections and hopes, owe to his memory a reciprocation of feeling and interest. As the chief labor of his life was devoted to illustrate the wisdom and virtues of their ancestors and to do honor to the institutions they established, it is incumbent on the descendants to hold and perpetuate in grateful remembrance his talents, virtues, and services.

PREFACE.

THIS historical work is the fruit of more than eleven years of eager research, intense meditation, industrious composition, and solicitous revisal. To the author, the scene of labor which he now concludes has been one of the most agreeable features of his life. And, should the perusal of his work afford to others even a slight share of the entertainment that its production has yielded to himself, he may claim the honor and gratification of a successful contributor to the stock of human happiness and intelligence.

In the year 1827, I published a work in two volumes, entitled *The History of the Rise and Progress of the United States of North America, till the British Revolution in* 1688. My plan, as I then announced, was, and it still is, restricted to the history of those provinces of North America (originating, all except New York and Delaware, from British colonization), which, at the era of the American Revolution, were included in the confederacy of *The United States ;* — the illustration of the parentage and birth of this great republic being the main object of my labors.

The first and second volumes of the present work may be considered as a republication of the former one. They embrace the rise of such of those States, comprehended within my general plan, as were founded prior to the British Revolution in 1688 ; and trace their progress till that epoch, and, in several instances, till a period somewhat later. Various additional researches which I have made since my first historical publication, and in which I have been assisted by suggestions communicated to me from America, have enabled me to correct some important errors by which that work was deformed, and now to reproduce it in an enlarged and greatly amended condition. Of some of these emendations the nature and effect are such as to render it impossible (without making one volume contradict the statements in another) to publish a continuation of the History, except in connection with the present republication of the first portion of it, — a circumstance which will perhaps expose me to blame, and which I most sincerely regret. The respect which I feel for the judgment of some intelligent and estimable friends (and in particular of my brother[1]) has induced me to cancel various passages in the original publication, which were censured as obtruding superfluous (perhaps irrelevant) reflections, or accumulating an excess of detail and illustration. A diligent and laborious revision, frequently repeated, has been productive

---

[1] Author of *A Treatise on Internal Intercourse and Communication in Civilized States,* and other scientific works.

of numerous alterations, and, I hope, proportional improvement, in the style of my performance.

The third and fourth volumes of the present work form the second composition which was prospectively announced in the preface to my first historical publication. They continue the history (commenced in the first two volumes) of the older American States, and also embrace the rise and progress of those younger colonial commonwealths which were subsequently founded, — till the revolt of the United Provinces from the dominion of Britain, and their assumption of national independence. Strictly speaking, they form a continuation, not of my original publication, but of my original work as it has been subsequently altered and amended.

In the preface to my first publication, I announced a third historic composition, which was intended to embrace the Revolutionary War, and the establishment and consolidation of the North American republic. But I have been induced, on farther reflection, to abandon the purpose I had entertained of this ulterior effort. Since my first publication, I have met with and read Botta's *History of the War of American Independence,* — a work of so much merit, and so well suited, I think, to the present era, that it seems to me to render any other composition (at least, any other *European* composition) on the same subject, *at present,* superfluous. Fifty or sixty years hence, a final and more compendious delineation of the scene may be required.

In the collection of materials for the production of this work, I have been obliged to incur a degree of toil and expense, which, in my original contemplation of the task, I was far from anticipating. Considering the connection that so long subsisted between Great Britain and the American States, the information concerning the early condition and progress of many of these communities, which the public libraries of Britain are capable of supplying, is, or at least till very lately was, amazingly scanty. Many valuable works, illustrative of the history and statistics both of particular States and of the whole North American commonwealth, I found had no place and were entirely unknown in the British libraries ; a defect the more discreditable, as the greater part of these works might have been obtained without much difficulty in London or from America.

After borrowing all the materials that I could so procure, and purchasing as many more as I could find in Britain or obtain from America, my collection proved still so defective in many respects, that, in the hope of enlarging it, and in compliance with the advice of my friend, Sir William Hamilton[1] (of whose counsel and assistance I can better feel the obligation than express the value), I undertook a journey, in the year 1825, from Edinburgh, where I then resided, to Göttingen ; and in the library of this place, as I had been taught to expect, I found a richer treasury of North American literature than any, or indeed all, of the libraries of Britain could at that time supply. From the resources of the Göttingen library, and the liberality with which its administrators have always been willing to render it subservient to the purposes of literary inquiry, I derived great advantage and assistance. I am indebted, also, to the private collections of various individuals in England and France for the perusal of some very rare and not less valuable and interesting works, illustrative of the subject of my labors. To particularize all the persons who have thus or otherwise assisted my exertions and enriched my stock of ma-

---

[1] Professor of Universal History, and afterwards of Logic and Metaphysics, in the University of Edinburgh.

terials would weary rather than interest the reader, — whom it less imports to know what opportunities I have had than what use I have made of them. Yet I must be indulged in one grateful, perhaps boastful, allusion to the advantage I have enjoyed in the communications which I had the honor of receiving from that illustrious friend of America and ornament of human nature, the late General La Fayette.

History addresses her lessons to all mankind ; but when she records the fortunes of an existing people, it is to them that her admonitions are especially directed. There has never been a people on whose character their own historical recollections were calculated to exercise a more animating or salutary influence than the nation whose early history I have undertaken to relate.

In national societies established as the United States of North America have been, history does not begin with obscure traditions or fabulous legends. The origin of the nation, and the rise and progress of all its institutions, may be distinctly ascertained ; and the people enabled to acquire a complete and accurate conception of the character of their earliest national ancestors, as well as of every succeeding generation through which the inheritance of the national name and fortunes has devolved on themselves. When the interesting knowledge thus unfolded to them reveals, among other disclosures, that their existence as a nation originated in the noblest efforts of wisdom, fortitude, and magnanimity, and that every successive acquisition by which their liberty and happiness have been extended or secured has proceeded from the exercise of the same qualities, and evinced their faithful preservation and unimpaired efficacy, — respect for antiquity becomes the motive and pledge of virtue ; the whole body of the people feels itself ennobled by the consciousness of ancestors whose renown will constitute, to the end of time, the honor or reproach of their successors ; and the love of virtue is so interwoven with patriotism and with national glory, as to prevent the one from becoming a selfish principle, and the other a splendid or mischievous illusion.[1] If an inspired apostle might with complacency proclaim himself *a citizen of no mean city*, a North American may feel grateful exultation in styling himself the native of no ignoble land, — but of a land that has yielded as rich a harvest of glory to God and of happiness to man, as any other portion of the world, from the earliest lapse of recorded time, has ever had the honor of affording. Were the dark and horrible blot of negro slavery obliterated from this scene, the brightness of its aspect would awaken universal admiration, and shed a cheering and ameliorating ray through the whole expanse of human nature and society. A more elevated model of human character could hardly be proposed to the imitation of the American people than that which their own early history, and the later scene of their achievement of national independence, bequeath to them. It is at once their interest and their honor to preserve with sacred care a bequest so richly fraught with the instructions of wisdom and the incitements of duty. Acquaintance with the past is essential to a wise estimate and use of the present, and to enlightened consideration of the future. The diffusion of knowledge, the progress of popular liberty and improvement, have deprived of

[1] " Certainly, we cannot wish to see perpetuated among us the old Asiatic and European notions of indelible hereditary excellence. But surely there is a point at which good feeling and sound philosophy can meet, and agree in ascribing the best parts of our character to the moral influence of a virtuous and intelligent ancestry." Verplanck's *Anniversary Discourse* (1818) *before the New York Historical Society.*

its exclusive and aristocratic import the oft-repeated maxim of other days, that *History is the lesson of kings.*   The American people will cherish a generous and profitable self-respect, while they comply with the canon of divine wisdom, to " remember the days of old, and consider the years of many generations " ; and the venerated ashes of their fathers will dispense a nobler influence than the relics of the prophet of Israel in reviving piety and invigorating virtue.[1]

The most important requisite of historical compositions, and that in which, I suspect, they are commonly most defective, is truth,[2] — a requisite, of which even the sincerity of the historian is insufficient to assure us.   In tracing ascertained and remarkable facts, either backward to their source, or forward in their operation, the historian frequently encounters, on either hand, a perplexing variety of separate causes and diverging effects ; among which it is no less difficult than important to discriminate the predominant or peculiar springs of action, and to preserve the main and moral stream of events.   Indiscriminate detail would produce intolerable fatigue and confusion ; while selection necessarily infers the risk of error.   The sacred historians often record events with little or no reference to their moral origin and lineage : and have thus given to some parts of the only history that is infallibly authentic an appearance of improbability, which the more reasoning narratives of uninspired writers have exchanged, at least as frequently, for substantial misrepresentation.   It may be thought an imprudent avowal, and yet I have no desire to conceal, that, in examining and comparing historical records, I have more than once been forcibly reminded of Sir Robert Walpole's assurance to his son, that " *History must be false.*" [3]   Happily, this apothegm applies, if not exclusively, at least most forcibly, to that which Walpole probably regarded as the main trunk of history, but which (especially in modern times, and in relation to free and civilized communities) is, indeed, the most insignificant branch of it, — the intrigues of cabinets, the secret schemes and machinations of ministers, and the conflicts of selfish and trading politicians.

In contemplating scenes of human dissension and strife, it is difficult, or rather it is impossible, for an observer, partaking the infirmities of human nature, to escape entirely the contagion of those passions which the controversies arose from or engendered.   Thus partialities are secretly insinuated into the mind ; and, in balancing opposite testimony, they find a subtle and so much the surer means of exerting their influence.   I am not desirous of concealing that I regard America with sentiments of ardent, perhaps partial,

---

[1] " No people can be bound to acknowledge and adore the invisible hand which conducts the affairs of men more than the people of the United States.   Every step by which they have advanced to the character of an independent nation seems to have been distinguished by some token of providential agency."   Washington's Speech to Congress, 30th April, 1789.

[2] " Truth is the eye of History."   Polybius.   No writer, ancient or modern, has so well explained and inculcated the main duties of a historian as Polybius ; and few, if any, have better exemplified them.   He is one of the rare exceptions to Dr. Johnson's maxim, that *Every historian discovers his country.*

[3] Horace Walpole's *Works.*   A curious illustration of historical inaccuracy was related by the late President Jefferson to an intelligent English traveller   The Abbé Raynal, in his *History of the British Settlements in America,* has recounted a remarkable story which implies the existence of a particular law in New England.   Some Americans, being in company with the Abbé at Paris, questioned the truth of the story, alleging that no such law had ever existed in New England.   The Abbé maintained the authenticity of his History, till he was interrupted by Dr. Franklin, who was present, and, after listening for some time in silence to the dispute, said, " I can account for all this: you took the anecdote from a newspaper, of which I was at that time editor ; and, happening to be very short of news, I composed and inserted the whole story."   Hall's *Travels in Canada and the United States.*

affection ; and, in surveying various scenes in her history, I derive a warm, unreproved pleasure from the conviction, that, in dignity, wisdom, and worth, they transcend the highest conception suggested by the annals of any other people in ancient or in modern times. If my consciousness of the existence of feelings somewhat partial should not exempt my judgment from their influence, I hope the avowal, at least, will prevent the error from extending to my readers.

I am far from thinking, or from purposing to assert or insinuate, that every part of the conduct of the American States, throughout the various controversies in which they have been involved, was pure and blameless. Guile, evil passion, violence, and injustice have in some instances dishonored the councils and transactions of the leaders and assemblies of America ; and it was the conduct of one of the States, the most renowned for piety and virtue, that suggested to her historian the melancholy observation, that, " in all ages and countries, communities of men have done that, of which most of the individuals of whom they consisted would, acting separately, have been ashamed." [1]   But mingled masses are justly denominated from the elements and qualities that preponderate in their composition ; and sages and patriots must be regarded as the mere creations of fancy, if we can never recognize the lineaments of worth and wisdom under the vesture of human imperfection. There exists in some romantic, speculative minds a *Platonic* love of liberty, as well as virtue, that consists with a fastidious disgust for every visible and actual incarnation of either of these principles ; and which, when not corrected by sense and experience, conducts to ingenious error or to *seemingly* generous misanthropy.

Whoever, with attention minute and impartial, examines the histories of individuals or communities, should prepare himself to be disappointed and perplexed by numberless imperfections and inconsistencies, which, wisely pondered, confirm the Scriptural testimony of the inherent frailty of human nature and the reflected lustre of human virtue. Much error is produced and prolonged in the world by unwillingness or inability to make candid concessions or to admit charitable interpretations, — to acknowledge in an adversary the excellence that condemns our undiscriminating hate, — in a friend or hero, the defects that sully the pleasing image of virtue, that diminish our exultation, and rebuke the excesses of inordinate confidence. There is not a more common nor more unhappy mistake than that which confounds the impulse of sincerity with the virtue of candor. With partial views, sincerely embraced, but not candidly appreciated, we encounter the opposite partialities of antagonists ; and, by mutual commission and perception of injustice, confirm, augment, and reciprocate each other's misapprehensions. It should be the principal object of every man, who undertakes the office of a historian, to correct, as far as he may, the errors by which experience is thus rendered useless ; and this object I have purposed and endeavoured to keep steadily in view.

L'EPERONNIERE, NEAR NANTES,
 September, 1835.

---

[1] Hutchinson's *History of Massachusetts*. This observation referred immediately to the dispute between Massachusetts and the confederated States of New England in 1649 ; but the general proposition which it involves is one which Hutchinson (himself an ambitious and disappointed antagonist of popular assemblies) snatches, throughout his work, every occasion to propound and illustrate.

P. S. The variations which distinguish the second from the first edition of this work consist of the retrenchment of superfluities in some quarters, the introduction of additional facts and remarks in others, and numerous emendations of the style, — the result of a severe revision, in which I have been aided by the taste and sagacity of some accomplished friends, and especially of my father-in-law, the Rev. John Wilson, President of the Protestant Consistory of Nantes and La Vendée. To the kindness of those distinguished American writers, Robert Walsh and Josiah Quincy (whose friendship has been one of the most agreeable fruits of my labors), I owe my recent access to some valuable literary materials and my acquaintance with some curious historic details.

It may be proper to observe (which I omitted to do in the preface to the former edition), that, in the course of this historical digest, I have frequently illustrated particular portions of my narrative by citation of various authorities not one of which accords entirely either with the statements of the others or with my own. To explain, in every such instance, how I have been led, from comparison of conflicting authorities, to the view that I have considerately embraced, would encumber every chapter of my work with a long series of subsidiary disquisitions. Much of the labor of an honest historian must either be painfully shared by his readers, or remain wholly unknown to them.

5 PLACE DE LAUNAY, NANTES,
June, 1842.

CONTENTS

OF

THE FIRST VOLUME.

BOOK I.

PLANTATION AND PROGRESS OF VIRGINIA, TILL THE BRITISH REVOLUTION, IN 1688.

CHAPTER I.

Cabot despatched by Henry the Seventh — visits the Coast of North America. — Neglect of Cabot's Discovery by Henry — and by his immediate Successors. — Reign of Elizabeth — favorable to maritime Adventure. — Rise of the Slave-trade. — Sir Walter Raleigh — projects a Colony in North America — first Expedition fails. — Elizabeth names the Country Virginia. — Grenville despatched by Raleigh — establishes a Colony at Roanoke. — Misfortunes of the Colonists — their Return. — Use of Tobacco introduced into England. — Farther Efforts of Raleigh — terminate unsuccessfully. — Accession of James to the English Crown. — Gosnold's Voyage — its Effects. — James divides North America between two Companies. — Tenor of their Charters. — Royal Code of Laws. — The first Body of Colonists embarked by the London Company — arrive in the Bay of Chesapeake — found Jamestown. — Dissensions of the Colonists. — Hostility of the Indians. — Distress and Disorder of the Colony. — Services of Captain Smith — he is taken Prisoner by the Indians — his Liberation — he preserves the Colony. — The Colonists deceived by Appearances of Gold. — Smith surveys the Bay of Chesapeake — elected President of the Colony. — New Charter. — Lord Delaware appointed Governor. — Newport, Gates, and Somers sent to preside till Lord Delaware's Arrival — are wrecked on the Coast of Bermudas. — Captain Smith returns to England. . . 25

CHAPTER II.

The Colony a Prey to Anarchy — and Famine. — Gates and Somers arrive from Bermudas. — Abandonment of the Colony determined upon — prevented by the Arrival of Lord Delaware. — His wise Administration — his Return to England. — Sir Thomas Dale's Administration. — Martial Law established. — Indian Chief's Daughter seized by Argal — married to Rolfe. — Right of private Property in Land introduced into the Colony. — Expedition of Argal against Port Royal and New York. — Tobacco cultivated by the Colonists. — First Assembly of Representatives convened in Virginia. — New Constitution of the Colony. — Introduction of Negro Slavery. — Migration of young Women from England to Virginia. — Dispute between the King and the Colony. — Conspiracy of the Indians. — Massacre of the Colonists. — Dissensions of the London Company. — The Company dissolved. — The King assumes the Government of the Colony — his Death. — Charles the First pursues his Father's arbitrary Policy. — Tyrannical Government of Sir John Harvey. — Sir William Berkeley appointed Governor. — The provincial Liberties restored. — Virginia espouses the royal Cause — subdued by the Long Parliament. — Restraints imposed on the Trade of the Colony. — Revolt of the Colony. — Sir William Berkeley resumes the Government. — Restoration of Charles the Second. 59

CONTENTS.

CHAPTER III.

The Navigation Act — its Impolicy. — Discontent and Distress of the Colonists. — Naturalization of Aliens. — Progress of the provincial Discontent. — Indian Hostilities. — Bacon's Rebellion. — Death o Bacon — and Restoration of Tranquillity. — Bill of Attainder passed by the colonial Assembly. — Sir William Berkeley superseded by Colo nel Jeffreys. — Partiality of the new Governor — Dispute with the Assembly. — Re newal of Discontents. — Lord Culpepper appointed Governor — Severity and Rapacity of his Administration. — An Insurrection — Punishment of the Insurgents. — Arbitrary Measures of the Crown. — James the Second — augments the Burdens of the Colonists. — Corrupt and oppressive Government of Lord Effingham. — Revolution in Britain. — Complaints of the Colonies against the former Governors discouraged by King William. — Effect of the English Revolution on the American Colonies. — State of Virginia at this Period — Population — Laws — Manners. 90

BOOK II.

FOUNDATION AND PROGRESS OF THE NEW ENGLAND STATES, TILL THE YEAR 1698.

CHAPTER I.

Attempts of the Plymouth Company to colonize the northern Coasts of America. — Popham establishes a Colony at Fort Saint George. — Sufferings and Return of the Colonists. — Captain Smith's Voyage and Survey of the Country — which is named New England. — His ineffectual Attempt to conduct a Colony thither. — The Company relinquish the Design of colonizing New England. — History and Character of the Puritans. — Rise of the Brownists or Independents. — A Congregation of Independents retire to Holland — they resolve to settle in America — their Negotiation with King James — they arrive in Massachusetts — and found New Plymouth. — Hardships — and Virtue of the Colonists. — Their civil Institutions. — Community of Property. — Increase of civil and ecclesiastical Tyranny in England. — Project of a new Colony in Massachusetts. — Salem built. — Charter of Massachusetts Bay obtained from Charles the First by an Association of Puritans. — Embarkation of the Emigrants — Arrival at Salem. — Their ecclesiastical Institutions. — Two Persons banished from the Colony for Schism. — Intolerance of some of the Puritans. 121

CHAPTER II.

The Charter Government transferred from England to Massachusetts. — Numerous Emigration. — Foundation of Boston. — Hardships endured by the new Settlers. — Disfranchisement of Dissenters in the Colony. — Influence of the provincial Clergy. — John Cotton and his Colleagues and Successors. — Williams's Schism — he founds Providence. — Representative Assembly established in Massachusetts. — Arrival of Hugh Peters — and Henry Vane, who is elected Governor. — Foundation of Connecticut — and New Haven. — War with the Pequod Indians. — Severities exercised by the victorious Colonists. — Disturbances created by Mrs. Hutchinson. — Colonization of Rhode Island — and of New Hampshire and Maine. — Jealousy and fluctuating Conduct of the King. — Measures adopted against the Liberties of Massachusetts — interrupted by the Civil Wars. — State of New England — Population — Laws — Manners. . . . 161

CHAPTER III.

New England embraces the Cause of the Parliament. — Federal Union between the New England States. — Provincial Coinage of Money. — Disputes occasioned by the Disfranchisement of Dissenters in Massachusetts. — Impeachment and Trial of Governor Winthrop. — Arbitrary Proceedings against the Dissenters. — Attempts to convert and civilize the Indians. — Character and Labors of Eliot and Mayhew. — Indian Bible printed in Massachusetts. — Effects of the missionary Labor. — A Synod of the New England Churches. — Dispute between Massachusetts and the Long Parliament. — The Colony foils the Parliament — and is favored by Cromwell. — The Protector's Administration beneficial to New England. — He conquers Acadia. — His Propositions to the

Inhabitants of Massachusetts — declined by them. — Persecution of the Anabaptists in
Massachusetts. — Conduct and Sufferings of the Quakers. — The Restoration. — Address of Massachusetts to Charles the Second. — Alarm of the Colonists — their Declaration of Rights. — The King's Message to Massachusetts — how far complied with. —
Royal Charter of Incorporation to Rhode Island and Providence — and to Connecticut
and New Haven.   191

CHAPTER IV.

Emigration of ejected Ministers to New England. — Royal Commissioners sent thither. —
Petition of the Assembly of Massachusetts to the King — rejected. — Policy pursued by
the Commissioners. — Their Disputes with the Government of Massachusetts — and
Return to England. — Policy of the Colonists to conciliate the King — Effects of it. —
Cession of Acadia to the French. — Prosperous State of New England. — Conspiracy of
the Indians. — Philip's War. — The King resumes his Designs against Massachusetts.
— Controversy respecting the Right to Maine and New Hampshire. — Progress of the
Dispute between the King and the Colony. — State of Parties in Massachusetts. — State
of Religion and Morals in New England. — Surrender of the Charter of Massachusetts
demanded by the King — refused by the Colonists. — Writ of Quo Warranto issued
against the Colony. — Firmness of the People. — Their Charter adjudged to be forfeited. 227

CHAPTER V.

Designs — and Death of Charles the Second. — Government of Massachusetts under a
temporary Commission from James the Second. — Andros appointed Governor of New
England. — Submission of Rhode Island. — Effort to preserve the Charter of Connecticut. — Oppressive Government of Andros. — Colonial Policy of the King. — Sir William Phips. — Indian Hostilities renewed by the Intrigues of the French. — Insurrection
at Boston. — Andros deposed — and the ancient Government restored. — Connecticut
and Rhode Island resume their Charters. — William and Mary proclaimed. — War with
the French and Indians. — Sir William Phips conquers Acadia. — Ineffectual Expedition
against Quebec. — Impeachment of Andros by the Colony discouraged by the English
Ministers — and dismissed. — The King refuses to restore the ancient Constitution of
Massachusetts. — Tenor of the new Charter. — Sir William Phips Governor. — The
New England Witchcraft. — Death of Phips. — War with the French and Indians. —
Loss of Acadia. — Peace of Ryswick. — Moral and Political State of New England.   . 255

BOOK III.

PLANTATION AND PROGRESS OF MARYLAND, TILL THE CLOSE OF THE SEVENTEENTH CENTURY.

Charter of Maryland obtained from Charles the First by Lord Baltimore. — Condition of
the Roman Catholics in England. — Emigration of Roman Catholics to the Province. —
Friendly Treaty with the Indians. — Generosity of Lord Baltimore. — Opposition and
Intrigues of Clayborne. — First Assembly of Maryland. — Representative Government
established. — Early Introduction of Negro Slavery. — An Indian War. — Clayborne's
Rebellion. — Religious Toleration established in the Colony. — Separate Establishment
of the House of Burgesses. — Clayborne declares for Cromwell — and usurps the Ad-
ministration. — Toleration abolished. — Distractions of the Colony — terminated by the
Restoration. — Establishment of a provincial Mint. — Happy State of the Colony. —
Naturalization Acts. — Death of the first Proprietary. — Wise Government of his Son
and Successor. — Law against importing Felons. — Establishment of the Church of
England suggested. — Dismemberment of the Delaware Territory from Maryland. —
Arbitrary Projects of James the Second. — Rumor of a Popish Plot. — A Protestant Association is formed — and usurps the Administration. — The Proprietary Government
suspended by King William. — Establishment of the Church of England, and Persecution of the Catholics. — State of the Province — Manners — Laws.   .   .   .   301

BOOK IV.

PLANTATION AND PROGRESS OF NORTH AND SOUTH CAROLINA, TILL THE BEGINNING OF THE EIGHTEENTH CENTURY.

CHAPTER I.

Early Attempts of the Spaniards and the French to colonize this Territory. — First Charter of Carolina granted by Charles the Second to Lord Clarendon and others. — Formation of Albemarle Settlement in North Carolina. — Settlement of Ashley River in South Carolina. — Second Charter of the whole united Province. — Proceedings at Albemarle. — The Proprietaries enact the Fundamental Constitutions of Carolina. — Expedition of Emigrants to South Carolina. — John Locke created a Landgrave. — Hostilities with the Spaniards in Florida — and with the Indians. — Disgusts between the Proprietaries and the Colonists. — Affairs of North Carolina. — Culpepper's Insurrection. — He is tried in England — and acquitted. — Discord among the Colonists. — Sothel's tyrannical Administration. — He is deposed. 340

CHAPTER II.

Affairs of South Carolina. — Indian War. — Practice of kidnapping Indians. — Emigrations from Ireland — Scotland — and England. — Pirates entertained in the Colony. — Emigration of French Protestants to Carolina. — Disputes created by the Navigation Laws. — Progress of Discontent in the Colony. — Sothel usurps the Government. — Endeavours of the Proprietaries to restore Order. — Naturalization of French Refugees resisted by the Colonists. — The Fundamental Constitutions abolished. — Wise Administration of Archdale. — Restoration of general Tranquillity. — Ecclesiastical Condition of the Province. — Intolerant Measures of the Proprietaries. — State of the People — Manners — Trade, &c. 369

BOOK V.

FOUNDATION AND PROGRESS OF NEW YORK, TILL THE BEGINNING OF THE EIGHTEENTH CENTURY.

CHAPTER I.

Hudson's Voyage of Discovery. — First Settlement of the Dutch at Albany. — The Province granted by the States General to the West India Company of Holland. — The Dutch Colonists extend their Settlements into Connecticut. — Disputes with the New England Colonies. — Delaware first colonized by the Swedes. — War between the Dutch and Indians. — Farther Disputes with New England. — Designs of Charles the Second. — Alarm and Exertions of the Dutch Governor. — The Province granted by Charter to the Duke of York — invaded by an English Fleet — surrenders. — Wise Government of Colonel Nichols. — Holland cedes New York to England — recaptures it — finally cedes it again. — New Charter granted to the Duke of York. — Arbitrary Government of Andros. — Discontent of the Colonists. — The Duke consents to give New York a free Constitution. 397

CHAPTER II.

Colonel Dongan's Administration. — Account of the Five Indian Nations of Canada. — Their Hostility to the French. — Missionary Labors of the French Jesuits. — James the Second abolishes the Liberties of New York — commands Dongan to abandon the Five Nations to the French. — Andros again appointed Governor. — War between the French and the Five Nations. — Discontents at New York. — Leisler declares for King William, and assumes the Government. — The French attack the Province, and burn Schenectady. — Arrival of Governor Sloughter. — Perplexity of Leisler — his Trial — and Execution. — Wars and mutual Cruelties of the French and Indians. — Governor Fletcher's Administration. — Peace of Ryswick. — Piracy at New York. — Captain Kidd. — Factions occasioned by the Fate of Leisler. — Trial of Bayard. — Corrupt and oppressive Administration of Lord Cornbury. — State of the Colony at the Close of the seventeenth Century. 427

BOOK VI.

PLANTATION AND PROGRESS OF NEW JERSEY, TILL THE BEGINNING OF THE EIGHTEENTH CENTURY.

Sale of the Territory by the Duke of York to Berkeley and Carteret. — Liberal Frame of Government enacted by the Proprietaries. — Emigration from Long Island to New Jersey. — Arrival of the first Governor and Settlers from England. — Discontent and Disturbance in the Colony. — Renovation of the Titles to New Jersey. — Equivocal Conduct of the Duke of York. — Situation of the Quakers in England. — Sale of Berkeley's Share of the Province to Quakers. — Partition of the Province between them and Carteret. — Emigration of Quakers from England to West Jersey. — Encroachments of the Duke of York. — Remonstrance of the Quakers — causes the Independence of New Jersey to be recognized. — First Assembly of West Jersey. — The Quakers purchase East Jersey. — Robert Barclay — appointed Governor. — Emigration from Scotland to East Jersey. — Designs of James the Second against the Proprietary Governments — defeated by the Revolution. — Inefficient State of the Proprietary Government. — Surrender of the provincial Patent to the Crown — and Reunion of East and West Jersey. — Constitution of the provincial Government. — Administration of Lord Cornbury. — State of the Colony. 461

BOOK VII.

PLANTATION AND PROGRESS OF PENNSYLVANIA AND DELAWARE, TILL THE BEGINNING OF THE EIGHTEENTH CENTURY.

CHAPTER I.

Birth and Character of William Penn. — He solicits a Grant of American Territory from Charles the Second. — Charter of Pennsylvania. — Object and Meaning of the Clauses peculiar to this Charter. — English and American Opinions thereon. — Penn's Policy to people his Territories. — Emigration of Quakers to the Province. — Letter from Penn to the Indians. — Penn's first Frame of Government for the Province. — Grant of Delaware by the Duke of York to Penn — who sails for America — his joyful Reception there. — Numerous Emigrations to the Province. — First legislative Assembly. — Pennsylvania and Delaware united. — Controversy with Lord Baltimore. — Treaty with the Indians. — Second Assembly — new Frame of Government adopted. — Philadelphia founded. — Penn's Return to England — and Farewell to his People. . . . 492

CHAPTER II.

Penn's Favor at the Court of James the Second. — Dissensions among the Colonists — their Disagreement with Penn about his Quitrents. — He appoints five Commissioners of State. — Rumor of an Indian Conspiracy. — Penn dissatisfied with his Commissioners — appoints Blackwell Deputy-Governor. — Arbitrary Conduct of Blackwell. — Displeasure of the Assembly. — Dissension between the People of Delaware and Pennsylvania. — Delaware obtains a separate executive Government. — George Keith's Schism in Pennsylvania. — Penn deprived of his Authority by King William. — Fletcher appointed Governor. — Penn's Authority restored. — Third Frame of Government. — Quaker Accession to War. — Penn's second Visit to his Colony. — Sentiments and Conduct of the Quakers relative to Negro Slavery. — Renewal of the Disputes between Delaware and Pennsylvania. — Fourth and last Frame of Government. — Penn returns to England. — Union of Pennsylvania and Delaware dissolved. — Complaints of the Assembly against Penn. — Misconduct of Governor Evans. — He is superseded by Gookin. — Penn's Remonstrance to his People. — State of Pennsylvania and Delaware at the Close of the seventeenth Century. 521

APPENDIX I.

State and Prospects of the North American Provinces at the Close of the seventeenth Century. — Sentiments and Opinions of the Colonists respecting the Sovereignty and the Policy of Great Britain, &c. 551

NOTES 567

THE

HISTORY

OF

NORTH AMERICA.

BOOK I.

VIRGINIA.

CHAPTER I.

Cabot despatched by Henry the Seventh — visits the Coast of North America. — Neglect of Cabot's Discovery by Henry — and by his immediate Successors. — Reign of Elizabeth — favorable to Maritime Adventure. — Rise of the Slave-trade. — Sir Walter Raleigh — projects a Colony in North America — first Expedition fails. — Elizabeth names the Country Virginia. — Grenville despatched by Raleigh — establishes a Colony at Roanoke. — Misfortunes of the Colonists — their Return. — Use of Tobacco introduced into England. — Farther Efforts of Raleigh — terminate unsuccessfully. — Accession of James to the English Crown. — Gosnold's Voyage — its Effects. — James divides North America between two Companies. — Tenor of their Charters. — Royal Code of Laws. — The first Body of Colonists embarked by the London Company — arrive in the Bay of Chesapeake — found Jamestown. — Dissensions of the Colonists. — Hostility of the Indians. — Distress and Disorder of the Colony. — Services of Captain Smith — he is taken Prisoner by the Indians — his Liberation — he preserves the Colony. — The Colonists deceived by Appearances of Gold. — Smith surveys the Bay of Chesapeake — elected President of the Colony. — New Charter. — Lord Delaware appointed Governor. — Newport, Gates, and Somers sent to preside till Lord Delaware's Arrival — are wrecked on the Coast of Bermudas. — Captain Smith returns to England.

It was on the third of August, 1492, a little before sunrise, that Christopher Columbus, undertaking the grandest enterprise that human genius has ever conceived, or human talent and fortitude have ever accomplished, set sail from Spain for the discovery of the western world. On the 13th of October, about two hours before midnight, a light in the island of San Salvador was descried by Columbus from the deck of his vessel, and America for the first time beheld by European eyes.[1] Of the wide train of impor-

---

[1] Dr. Robertson espoused the opinion, that the ancients had no notion of the existence of the western world, and has collected from ancient writers many proofs, not only of ignorance, but of most barbarous error, respecting the extent and dimensions of the earth. *Hist. of America*, Book I. Yet a Roman writer, to whose sentiments he has not adverted, is supposed by some to have prophesied the discovery of America, 1400 years before this event took place. The passage occurs in one of Seneca's tragedies.

" Venient annis
Secula seris, quibus oceanus
Vincula rerum laxet, et ingens
Pateat tellus, Tiphysque novos
Detegat orbes ; nec sit terris
Ultima Thule."   *Medea*, Act II. Chorus.

This passage attracted a good deal of comment from the early Spanish and Flemish writers on America. Acosta opposed the common notion of its being a prophecy, and maintained that it was (as most probably it was) a mere conjecture of the poet. *Natural and Moral History of the Indies*, B. I. Certain passages in Virgil's *Æneid*, in Lucan's *Pharsalia*, and even in the works of still older writers, have been equally cited, with more zeal and ingenuity than discretion and success, as containing allusions to America. See, on this subject, that

tant consequences that depended on this spectacle, perhaps not even the penetrating and comprehensive mind of Columbus was adequately sensible; but to the end of time, the heart of every human being who reads the story will confess the interest of that eventful moment, and partake the feelings of the illustrious man. On the following day, the Spanish adventurers, preceded by their commander, took possession of the soil; the external emblems of Christianity were planted on the shores of the western hemisphere; and a connection, pregnant with a vast and various progeny of good and evil, was established between Europe and America. By one of those accidents to which the solidest titles to human fame are exposed, the discoverer of the new world was defrauded of the honor of blending his own name with the great fruit of his noble adventure; which has derived its now unalterable denomination from the bold imposture by which an earlier writer, though much later visitor of the region, Amerigo Vespucci, of Florence, contrived for a while to persuade mankind that he was the first European to whom America had revealed her existence.[1]

The intelligence of the successful voyage of Columbus was received in Europe with the utmost surprise and admiration. In England, more especially, it was calculated to produce a strong impression, and to awaken at once emulation and regret. While Columbus was proposing his schemes with little prospect of success at the court of Spain, he had despatched his brother Bartholomew to the court of Henry the Seventh in England, there to solicit patronage and tender the fruits of discovery. Bartholomew was taken prisoner by pirates, and after a long detention was reduced to such poverty, that, on his arrival in London, he was compelled by the labor of his hands to procure the means of arraying himself in habiliments becoming his interview with a monarch. His propositions were favorably entertained by Henry; but before a definitive arrangement was concluded, Bartholomew was recalled by the intelligence, that his brother's plans had at length been sanctioned and espoused by Ferdinand and Isabella of Spain.

If the wareful and penurious disposition of Henry contributed to diminish his regrets for the abandonment of a hazardous and expensive undertaking, the astonishing success which attended its actual prosecution by others revived the former projects of his mind, and inspired a degree of enterprise that showed him both instructed and provoked by the better fortune of the Spanish crown.[2] In this temper he hearkened with satisfaction to the proposals of one Gabato or Cabot, a Venetian, residing in Bristol; who, from reflection on the discoveries of Columbus towards the southwest, had conceived the opinion, that lands might likewise be discovered towards the northwest, and now offered to the king to conduct an expedition in this direction. Henry, prompted by his avarice and stung with envy and disappointment, readily closed with this proposal, and not only bestowed on its author a commission of discovery, but, on two subsequent occasions, issued similar commissions to other individuals for exploring and appropriating the territorial resources of unknown portions of the globe.[3]

---

portion of Basnage's *Histoire des Juifs* which is appended to Stowe's translation of Jahn's *History of the Hebrew Commonwealth.*

[1] By a late and honorable reparation of this injustice, at the period when America achieved her highest glory in the establishment of the independence and the federal constitution of the United States, the central and federal District received the name of Columbia.

Joanna Baillie's *Legend of Christopher Columbus* is the grandest poetical tribute ever rendered to the discoverer of America.

[2] Bacon's *History of Henry the Seventh.*   [3] Bacon.

The commission to Cabot, the only one which was productive of interesting consequences, was granted on the 5th of March, 1495, (about two years after the return of Columbus from America,) and empowered that adventurer and his sons to sail under the flag of England in quest of countries yet unappropriated by Christian sovereigns ; to take possession of them in the name of Henry, and plant the English banner on the walls of their castles and cities, and to maintain with the inhabitants a traffic exclusive of all competitors and exempted from customs ; under the condition of paying a fifth part of the free profit of every voyage to the crown.[1]   About two years after the date of his commission, Cabot, with his second son, Sebastian, embarked at Bristol[2] in a ship provided by the king, and attended by four small vessels equipped by the merchants of that city.   Sebastian Cabot appears to have greatly excelled his father in genius and nautical science ; and it is to him alone that historians have ascribed all the discoveries with which the name of Cabot is associated.

The navigators of that age were as much influenced by the opinions as incited by the example of Columbus, who erroneously supposed that the islands he discovered in his first voyage were outskirts or dependencies of India, not far remote from the Indian continent.   Impressed with the same notion, Sebastian Cabot conceived the hope, that, by steering to the northwest, he might fulfil the design and improve the performance of Columbus, and reach India by a shorter course than the great navigator himself had attempted.   Accordingly pursuing that track, he discovered the islands of Newfoundland and St. John ; and, continuing to hold a westerly course, soon reached the continent of North America, and sailed along it from the confines of Labrador to the coast of Virginia.   Thus, conducted by Cabot, whose own lights were derived from the genius of Columbus, did the English achieve the honor of being the second European nation that visited the western world, and the first that discovered the vast continent that stretches from the Gulf of Mexico towards the North Pole : for it was not till the succeeding year [1498] that Columbus, in his second voyage, was enabled to complete his own discovery, and advance beyond the islands he had first visited to the continent of America.

Cabot, disappointed in his main object of finding a western passage to India, returned to England to relate the discoveries he had already accomplished, — without attempting, either by settlement or conquest, to gain a footing on the American continent.[3]   He would willingly have resumed his exploratory enterprise in the service of England, but he found that in his absence the king's ardor for territorial discovery had greatly abated.   Seated on a throne which he acquired by conquest, in a country exhausted by civil wars, — involved in hostilities with Scotland, — and harassed by the insurrections of his subjects and the machinations of pretenders to his crown, — Henry had little leisure for the execution of distant projects ; and his sordid disposition found small attraction in the prospect of a colonial settlement which was not likely to be productive of immediate pecuniary gain.   He was engaged, likewise, at this time, in negotiating the marriage of his son with the daughter of Ferdinand of Spain, — a transaction that supplied additional reasons for relinquishing designs which could not fail to give umbrage to this jealous prince, who claimed the whole continent of America in virtue

[1] Hakluyt.   Chalmers's *Annals of the United Colonies.*   Hazard's *Historical Collections.*
[2] Smith's *History of Virginia, New England, and the Somer Isles.*
[3] Churchill's *Collection of Voyages.*

of a donative from the pope. Nor were the subjects of Henry in a condition to avail themselves of the ample field thrown open by Cabot's discovery to their enterprise and activity. The civil wars had dissipated wealth, repressed commerce, and even excluded the English people from partaking the general improvement of the other nations of Europe ; and all the benefit, which for the present they derived from the voyage of Cabot, was that right of territorial property which is supposed to arise from priority of discovery, — an acquisition, which, from the extent of the region, the mildness of its climate, and the fertility of its soil, afforded an inviting prospect of advantageous colonization. But by the counteracting circumstances to which we have already adverted, was England prevented from occupying this important field, till the moral and religious advancement which her people were soon to attain should qualify her to become the parent of civility and population in North America. Cabot, finding that Henry had abandoned all colonial projects, soon after transferred his own services to the Spaniards ; and the English seemed contented to surrender their discoveries and the discoverer to the superior fortune of that successful people. The only immediate fruit of his enterprise is said to have been the importation from America of the first turkeys [1] that were ever seen in Europe.

It is remarkable, that, of these earliest expeditions to the western world by Spain and England, not one was either projected or conducted by a citizen of the state which supplied the subordinate adventurers, defrayed the expense of the equipment, and reaped the benefit of the enterprise. The honor of the achievement was thus more widely distributed. The Spanish adventurers were conducted by Columbus, a native of Genoa ; the English, by John Cabot, a citizen of Venice ; [2] and though Sebastian Cabot, whose superior genius assumed the direction of the enterprise, was born in England, it was by the experience and instructions of his father that his capacity was trained to naval affairs, and it was to the father that the projection of the voyage was due, and the chief command of it intrusted. Happily for the honor of the English people, the parallel extends no farther ; and the treatment which the two discoverers experienced from the nations that employed them differed as widely as the histories of the two empires which they respectively contributed to found. Columbus was loaded with chains in the region which he had the glory of discovering, and died, the victim of ingratitude and disappointment, among the people whom he had conducted to wealth and renown. Cabot, after spending some years in the service of Spain, also experienced her ingratitude ; and returning in his old age to England, obtained a kind and honorable reception from the nation which had as yet derived only barren hopes and a seemingly relinquished title from his expedition. He received the dignity of knighthood, the appointment of Grand Pilot of England, and a pension that enabled him to spend his declining years in circumstances of honor and comfort. [3]

From this period till the reign of Elizabeth, no fixed views were entertained nor any deliberate purpose evinced in England of occupying territory or establishing colonies in America. In the earlier part of the reign of Henry the Eighth, the attention and energy of the English government were

---

[1] Why this bird received the name it enjoys in England has never been satisfactorily explained. By the French it was called *coq d'Inde*, on account of its American original; America being then generally termed Western India.

[2] The first expedition of the French to America was conducted, in like manner, by an Italian, John Verazzan, a native of Florence.

[3] Smith.

absorbed by wars and intrigues on the continent of Europe ; and the innovations in religious doctrine and ecclesiastical constitution, that attended its
close, supplied ample employment at home for the minds of the king and of
the great bulk of the people. It was during this reign that (after many pre-
lusive gleams supplied during successive ages by that small Christian community which never admitted the sway nor adopted the errors of the church
of Rome [1]) the full light of the Reformation broke forth in Germany,
whence it was rapidly diffused on all sides over the rest of Europe.
Henry, at first, resolutely opposed himself to the adversaries of the church
of Rome, and even attempted by his pen to stem the progress of the innovations, — a service which the pope rewarded by conferring on him the
title of *Defender of the Faith*. But his subsequent controversy with the
papal see awakened and sanctioned a spirit of inquiry among his own subjects, which spread far beyond his expectations and desires, and eluded all
his attempts to control and restrain it. A discussion of the pretensions of
the church of Rome naturally begot inquiry into her doctrines ; for her
grand pretension to infallibility formed the only authority to which many of
these doctrines were indebted for their currency. This pretension, indeed,
was so closely interwoven with the whole fabric of her canons and institutions, that even a partial dissent from any one of them attacked a principle
that pervaded them all. In a system so overgrown with abuses, the spirit
of inquiry, wherever it gained admission, could not fail to detect error ; and
even a single instance of such detection, by shaking the fundamental tenet
of infallibility, arraigned the solidity of the whole structure. This danger,
which could not have been entirely evaded, was aggravated by the alarm
with which it inspired the Roman pontiffs, and the imprudence of the defensive policy which they adopted. Utterly proscribing the spirit of inquiry
which it was no longer possible to suppress, they only inflamed its vigor and
hostility, and compelled the Reformers to extend their views from an emen-
dation of the actual state of the church of Rome to an unqualified impugnation of her authority and revolt from her communion.

The progress of this growing spirit of inquiry operated with strong and
salutary influence on the character and fortune of the nations in which it
prevailed. A subject of rational investigation had at length been found,
that could interest the dullest and engross the most vigorous capacities ; the
contagion of fervent zeal and bold excursive thought was widely propagated ; and every people by which the reformed doctrines were embraced
was elevated in force and dignity of intellectual character. Introduced into
England by the power of a haughty, capricious, and barbarous tyrant, whose
object was, not the emancipation of his subjects, but the deliverance of himself from an authority which he wrested from the pope only to wield with
his own hands, — some time elapsed before these doctrines worked their
way into the minds of the people, and, expelling the corruptions and adul-
terations of the royal teacher, attained a full maturity of reasonable influence. Besides leavening the national *creed* with the spirit of the ancient
superstition, Henry encumbered the national worship with many of the
Romish institutions ; retaining whatever was calculated to prove a useful
auxiliary to royal prerogative, or to gratify the pomp and pride of his own
sensual imagination. In the composition of the ecclesiastical body, he preserved the splendid hierarchy ; and in the solemnities of worship, the gor-

---

[1] Bost's *History of the Moravian Church.*

c *

geous ceremonial of the church of Rome. But he found it easier to promulgate ecclesiastical ordinances, than to confine the stream of human opinion, or stay the heavenly shower by which it was gradually reinforced and enlarged ; and in an after age, the repugnance that manifested itself between the constitution of the English church and the religious sentiments of the English people produced consequences of very great importance in the history of England, and the origination of civilized society in North America.

The rupture between Henry the Eighth and the Roman see removed whatever obstacle the papal donative to Spain might have opposed to the appropriation of American territory by the English crown ; but of the two immediate successors of that monarch, the one neglected this advantage, and the other renounced it. During the reign of Edward the Sixth, the court of the royal minor was distracted by faction, or occupied with the conduct and the vicissitudes of a war with Scotland ; and the attention of the king, and of a great portion of his people, was engrossed by the care of extending and confirming the establishment of the Protestant doctrines. Introduced by Henry and patronized by Edward, these doctrines multiplied their converts with a facility that savored somewhat of the influence of human authority and the suggestions of secular interest ; till, under the direction of Providence, the same temporal power that had been employed to promote the introduction of truth was permitted to attempt its extinction. The royal authority, which Henry had blindly made subservient to the spread and recognition of the Protestant doctrines, was now employed by Mary, with equal blindness, as an instrument to sift and purify the collective mass of Protestant professors, to separate the genuine from the spurious portions of it, and to enable the sound and sincere believers, by a wonderful display of fortitude, faithfulness, and patience, to illustrate the perfection of Christian character in unison with the purity of Christian faith. This princess, restoring the connection between England and the church of Rome, and united in marriage to Philip of Spain, was bound by double ties to refrain from contesting the Spanish claims on America. It was not till the reign of Elizabeth, that the obstacles created by the pretensions of Spain were finally removed ; and then, indeed, the prospect of collision with the designs of this state, so far from appearing objectionable, presented the strongest attraction to the minds of the English.

But although, during this long period, the occupation of America was entirely neglected, the naval resources adapted to the formation and maintenance of colonies were diligently cultivated in England, and a vigorous impulse was communicated to the spirit of commercial enterprise. Under the directions of Cabot, in the reign of Henry the Eighth, the English merchants visited the coast of Brazil, and traded with the colonial settlements of the Portuguese. In the reign of Edward the Sixth, the fisheries on the Banks of Newfoundland, which had been previously established, were extended and encouraged ; and an association of adventurers for the discovery of new countries was incorporated by royal charter. Even Mary contributed to promote this direction of the national disposition and faculties : she founded the Corporation of Merchants trading to Russia, and studied to augment the security of their traffic by cultivating a friendly relation with the sovereign of that country. During her reign, an attempt highly creditable to English enterprise and energy, and not wholly unsuccessful, was made to reach India by land;[1] and a commercial intercourse was established with the coast of Africa. Many symptoms conspired to indicate with what adventurous vigor and persevering ardor the English might be expected to improve every opportunity of exerting and enlarging their resources, and how high a rank they were destined to hold in the scale of nations, when the force of their genius should be thoroughly developed by the progress of their recent improvement, and when the principles and policy of their government should more perfectly coincide with the temper and character of the people.

The Spaniards, meanwhile, had spread their settlements over the southern regions of the new world, and achieved an extent of conquest and accession of treasure that dazzled the eyes and awakened the emulation of all Europe. Men of active and enterprising disposition in Spain, curbed and restricted at home by the illiberal genius of their municipal government, eagerly rushed into the outlet of grand adventure presented to them on the vast theatre of Mexico and Peru. The paganism of the natives of these regions allured the invasion of bigots wedded to a faith that recognized compulsion as an instrument of conversion; and their wealth and effeminacy not less powerfully tempted the cupidity and ambition of men in whom pride inflamed the thirst of riches, while it inspired contempt of useful industry. Thus every prospect that could address itself prevailingly to human desires, or to the peculiarities of Spanish taste and character, contributed to promote that series of rapid and vigorous invasions by which the Spaniards overran so large a portion of the continent of South America. The real and lasting effect of their acquisitions has corresponded, in a manner very satisfactory to the moral eye, with the character and merit of the achievements by which they were earned. The history of the expeditions which terminated in the conquest of Mexico and Peru displays, perhaps, more strikingly than any other portion of the records of the human race, what amazing exertions the spirit of man can prompt him to attempt, and sustain him to endure, — how signally he is capable of misdirecting the energy with which his Creator has endowed him, and of disgracing the most admirable capacities of his nature, by rendering them instrumental to sordid, unjust, and barbarous ends. Religion, the grand corrective of human evil, error, and woe, shared this fatal perversion; and the crosses, which, as emblems of Christianity, successively announced the advent of this faith to each newly discovered region, proved far other than the harbingers of glory to God or good-will to men. The deliberate pride, and stern, unsparing cruelty of the Spanish adventurers, their arrogant disregard of the rights of human nature, and calm survey of the desolation of empires and destruction of happiness and life, are rendered the more striking and impressive by the humility of their own original circumstances, which seemed practically to level and unite them by habit and sympathy with the mass of mankind. Their conquests were accomplished with such rapidity, and followed with such barbarous oppression, that a very few years sufficed not only to subjugate but almost wholly to extirpate the slothful and effeminate idolaters who were fated to perish by their hands. Yet the fate of these victims of Spanish cruelty was not unavenged. To their conquerors, and through them to all Europe, they communicated the most loathsome and horrible disease that has ever afflicted and corrupted the human frame. The settlements that were founded in the conquered countries produced, from the nature of the soil, a vast influx of gold

---

[1] Hakluyt.

and silver into Spain, and finally exercised a pernicious influence on the liberty, industry, and prosperity of her people. But it was long before the bitter harvest of this golden shower was reaped ; and in an age so darkly blind to the liberal truths of political science, it could not be foreseen through the dazzling pomp and renown with which the acquisition of so much empire and the administration of so much treasure invested the Spanish monarchy. The exploits of the original adventurers, embellished by the romantic genius of Spain, and softened by national partiality, had now occupied the pens of Spanish historians, and excited a thirst for kindred enterprise and hopes of similar enrichment in every nation to which the tidings were conveyed. The study of the Spanish language, and the acquaintance with Spanish literature, which the marriage of Philip and Mary introduced into England, contributed to cherish this impulse in the minds of the English, and gave to the rising spirit of adventure among them a strong determination towards the continent of America.

The reign of Elizabeth was productive of the first attempts of the English people to establish a permanent settlement in America. But many causes conspired to enfeeble their exertions for this purpose, and to retard the accomplishment of so great a design. The civil government of Elizabeth, in the commencement of her reign, was acceptable to her subjects ; and her commercial policy, though frequently perverted by the interests of arbitrary power and the principles of a narrow and erroneous system, was in the main, perhaps, not less laudably designed than judiciously directed to the cultivation of their resources and the enlargement of their prosperity. By permitting a free exportation of corn, she promoted at once the agriculture and the commerce of England ; and by treaties with foreign powers, she endeavoured to establish commercial relations between their territories and her own.[1] Sensible how much the dignity and security of her crown and the welfare of her people depended on a naval force, she studiously encouraged navigation ; and so greatly increased the shipping of the kingdom, both by building large vessels herself, and by promoting ship-building among the merchants, that she was styled by her subjects the Restorer of Naval Glory and the Queen of the Northern Seas.[2] Rigidly just in discharging the ancient debts of the crown, as well as in fulfilling all her own particular engagements, — yet forbearing towards her people in the imposition of taxes ; frugal in the expenditure of her resources, and yet exerting a firm and deliberate perseverance in the prosecution of well directed projects ; the policy of her civil government at once conveyed good lessons to her subjects, and happily coincided with the general cast and bent of their genius and disposition.

During a reign thus favorable to commercial enterprise, the spirit that had been gradually pervading the steady minds of the English was called forth into active and vigorous exertion. Under the patronage of Dudley, Earl of Warwick, and conducted by Martin Frobisher, an expedition was de-

---

[1] She obtained from John Basilides, the czar of Muscovy, a patent which conferred the whole trade of his dominions on the English. With this grant, the tyrant, who lived in continual dread of a revolt of his subjects, purchased from Elizabeth the assurance of an asylum from their fury in England. But his son Theodore revoked it, and answered to the queen's remonstrances, that he was determined to rob neither his own subjects nor foreigners by subjecting to monopolies what should be free to all mankind. Camden. So superior was the commercial policy which natural justice taught this barbarian to the system which Elizabeth derived from her boasted learning and renowned ability, and which, in the progress of her reign, loaded the freedom and industry of her people with patents, monopolies, and exclusive companies.

[2] Camden. Strype.

spatched for the discovery of a northwest passage to India [1578] : but after exploring the coasts of Labrador and Greenland, Frobisher was compelled to return with the tidings of disappointment.   If the ardor of the English was damped by this failure, it was speedily reanimated by the successful effort of Sir Francis Drake, who, with a feeble squadron, undertook and accomplished the same enterprise that for sixty years had formed the peculiar glory of the Portuguese navigator Magellan, and obtained for England the honor of being the second nation that completely circumnavigated the globe.   A general enthusiasm was produced by this splendid achievement, and a passion for naval exploits laid hold of almost all the leading spirits of the age.

Yet still, no project of effecting a permanent settlement abroad had been entertained or attempted by the English.   The social happiness enjoyed by the subjects of Elizabeth enhanced those attractions that bind the hearts of men to their native land, and that are rarely surmounted but by the experience of intolerable hardships at home, or the prospect of sudden enrichment abroad.   Now the territory of North America presented none of the allurements that had incited and rewarded the Spanish adventurers ; it encouraged no hopes but of distant gain, and invited no exertions but of patient industry.   The prevalence of the Protestant doctrines in England, and the increasing influence of a sense of religion on the minds of the people, disinclined many persons to abandon the only country where the Reformation appeared to be securely established ; engrossed the minds of others with schemes for the improvement of the constitution and ritual of their national church ; and probably repressed in some ardent spirits the epidemical thirst of adventure, and reconciled them to that moderate competency which the state of society in England rendered easily attainable, and the simplicity of manners preserved from contempt.

But if the immediate influence of religious principle was unfavorable to projects of colonization, it was to the further development of that noble principle that England was soon to be indebted for the most remarkable and interesting colonial establishment that she has ever possessed.   The ecclesiastical policy of Elizabeth was far from giving the same general satisfaction that her civil government afforded to her subjects.   Inheriting the arrogant temper, the lofty pretensions, and the taste for pompous pageantry by which her father had been distinguished, without partaking his earnest zeal and sincere bigotry, she frequently blended religious considerations with her state policy, but suffered religious sentiments to exert little, if any, influence on her heart.   Like him, she wished to render the establishments of Christian worship subservient to the indulgence of human pomp and vanity, and, by a splendid hierarchy and gorgeous ceremonial, mediate an agreement between the loftiness of her heart and the humility of the gospel.   But the trials and afflictions which the English Protestants underwent from Mary had deepened and purified the religious sentiments of a great body of this people, and at the same time associated with many of the ceremonies retained in the national church the idea of popery and the recollection of persecution.   This repugnance between the sentiments of the men who now began to be termed *Puritans* and the ecclesiastical policy of the English government continued to increase during the whole of Elizabeth's reign : but as the influence which it exercised on the colonization of America was not manifested till the succeeding reign, the further account of it must be de-

ferred till we come to trace its effects in the rise and progress of the settlements in New England.

During the present reign, there was introduced into England a branch of
that inhuman traffic in negro slaves which afterwards engrossed so large a
share of her commercial wealth and activity, and converted a numerous body
of her merchants into a confederacy of robbers, and much of what she termed
her *trade* into a system of the basest fraud and the most atrocious rapine and
violence.   The first Englishman who exposed himself and his country to
this foul reproach was Sir John Hawkins, who subsequently attained a high
nautical celebrity, and was created an admiral and treasurer of the British
navy.   His father, an expert English seaman, having made several voyages
to the coast of Guinea and from thence to Brazil and the West Indies, had
acquired considerable knowledge of these countries, which he transmitted to
his son in the copious journals he preserved of his travels and observations.
In these compositions, he described the soil of America and the West Indies
as endowed by nature with extraordinary richness and fertility, yet languishing in total unproductiveness from the actual want of cultivators.   Europeans
were represented as unequal to the toil of agriculture in so sultry a climate ;
but the natives of Africa as peculiarly well adapted to this employment.
Forcibly struck with his father's remarks, Hawkins deduced from them the
project of transporting Africans into the western world ; and having composed a plan for the execution of this design, he produced it to some persons with whom he was acquainted, of opulent estate and enterprising disposition, and solicited their approbation and concurrence.   A subscription
was opened, and speedily completed, by Sir Lionel Ducket, Sir Thomas
Lodge, Sir William Winter, and other individuals, who plainly perceived
the large emolument that might be derived from the adventure proposed to
them.   By their assistance, Hawkins was enabled to set sail for Africa in
the year 1562 ; and having reached Sierra Leone, he began his commerce
with the negroes.   While he trafficked with them in the usual articles of
barter, he took occasion to give them an inviting description of the country
to which he was bound ; contrasting the fertility of its soil and the wealth of
its inhabitants with the barrenness of Africa and the poverty of the African
tribes.   Finding that the unsuspecting negroes listened to him with implicit
belief, and were greatly captivated with the European luxuries and ornaments which he displayed to their view, — he offered, if any of them were
willing to exchange their destitute circumstances for a happier condition, to
transport them to this more bountiful region, where he assured them of a
friendly reception, and an ample participation in the enjoyments with which
he had made them acquainted, as a certain recompense of easy labor.   The
negroes were ensnared by his flattering promises ; and three hundred of
them, accepting his offer, consented to embark along with him for Hispaniola.   On the night before their embarkation, they were attacked by a hostile tribe ; when Hawkins, hastening with his crew to their assistance, re
pulsed the assault, and carried a number of the assailants as prisoners on
board his vessels.   The next day he set sail with his mixed lading of human
ware, and during the passage treated the negroes who voluntarily accompanied him with more kindness and indulgence than he extended to his
prisoners of war.   On his arrival at Hispaniola, he disposed of the whole
cargo to great advantage, and endeavoured to inculcate on the Spaniards
who bought the negroes the same distinction in the treatment of them which

he himself had observed. But, having now put the fulfilment of his promises out of his own power, it was not permitted to him so to limit the evil consequences of his perfidy ; and the Spaniards, who had purchased all the Africans at the same rate, considered them as slaves of the same condition, and treated them all alike.

When Hawkins returned to England with a rich freight of pearls, sugar, and ginger, obtained in exchange for his slaves, the success of his voyage excited universal interest and curiosity respecting the sources from which so much wealth had been derived. At first the nation was shocked with the barbarous aspect of a traffic in the persons of men ; and the public feeling having penetrated into the court, the queen sent for Hawkins to inquire in what manner this novel and extraordinary description of commerce was conducted ; declaring to him, that, " if any of the Africans were carried away without their own consent, it would be detestable, and call down the vengeance of Heaven upon the undertakers." Hawkins, in vindication of himself, protested, that, in no expedition which he conducted should any of the people of Africa (except captives obtained in defensive and legitimate war) be compulsorily removed from their native soil ; and he declared, that, so far from entertaining any scruple respecting the righteous nature of his traffic, he deemed it an act of humanity to carry men from a worse condition to a better, from a state of heathen barbarism to an opportunity of sharing the blessings of Christianity and civilization.[1] It is believed, indeed, and seems consonant with probability, that Hawkins did not himself contemplate the perpetual slavery of the negroes whom he sold, but expected that they would be advanced to the condition of free servants whenever their labor had produced to their masters an equivalent for the expense of their purchase. The queen was satisfied with his explanation, and dismissed him with the assurance, that, while he and his associates acted with humanity, they might depend on her countenance and protection.

The very next voyage that Hawkins undertook demonstrated still more clearly than the former the deceitfulness of that unction which he had applied to his conscience, and the futility even of those intentions of which the fulfilment seemed to depend entirely on himself. In his passage he met with an English ship-of-war, which joined itself to the expedition and accompanied him to the coast of Africa. On his arrival, he began as formerly to traffic with the negroes, and endeavoured, by reiteration of his former topics of persuasion, to induce them to embark in his vessels. But they now treated his advances with a reserve that betrayed jealousy of his designs. As none of their countrymen had returned from the former voyage, they were apprehensive that the English had killed and devoured them ; a supposition which, however offensive to the English, did greatly and erroneously extenuate the inhumanity of which they were actually guilty. The crew of the ship-of-war, observing the Africans backward and suspicious, began to deride the gentle and dilatory procedure to which Hawkins confined himself, and proposed immediate recourse to the summary process of impressment. The sailors belonging to his own vessels joined with the crew of the man-of-war, and,

---

[1] This was the plea by which all the conductors and apologists of the slave-trade attempted to vindicate the practice in its infancy. The danger of hearkening to a policy that admits of " doing evil that good may come " was never more strikingly illustrated than by the descendants of those men, whom we have seen (both in America and the West Indies) enact laws prohibiting all education, moral, political, or religious, of their negro slaves, and even of emancipated negroes.

applauding their suggestion, made instant preparation for carrying it into effect. Hawkins protested against such lawless barbarity, and vainly endeavoured to prevail on them to desist from their purpose. But the instructions of the queen and the dictates of conscience were ineffectually cited to men whom he had initiated in piratical injustice, and who were not able to discover the moral superiority of courteous treachery over undisguised violence. They pursued their design, and, after various unsuccessful attacks, in which many of them lost their lives, another cargo of human beings was at last forcibly collected.[1] Such was the origin of the English branch of the slave-trade, which is here related the more minutely, not only on account of the remarkable and instructive circumstances that attended the commencement of the practice,[2] but on account of the influence which it subsequently exercised on the colonization and condition of some of the provinces of North America.

The spirit of adventure which had been awakened in the English nation found a more inviting scene of exertion in the southern than in the northern regions of America ; and when, after twenty years of peace, Elizabeth was engaged in war with her brother-in-law, Philip, the prospect of enrichment and renown to be gathered from the plunder of the Spanish colonies opened a new career, which was eagerly embraced and successfully prosecuted by numerous bands of enterprising men issuing from every rank of society in England. Accordingly, for many years the most popular and notable exploits of the English were performed in the predatory hostilities which they waged with the colonies and colonial commerce of Spain. Even in scenes so unfavorable to the production or display of the better qualities of human nature, the manly character and moral superiority of the English were frequently and strikingly disclosed. Drake and other adventurers in the same career were men equally superior to avarice and fear ; and though willing to encounter hardship and danger in quest of wealth, they did not esteem it valuable enough to be acquired at the expense of honor and humanity.

And yet it was to this spirit, so unfavorable to industrious colonization, and so strongly attracted to a more congenial sphere in the South, that North America was indebted for the first attempt to colonize her territory. Thus irregular and incalculable (to created wisdom) is the influence of human passions on the stream of human affairs.

The most illustrious adventurer in England was Sir Walter Raleigh, a man endowed with brilliant genius, unbounded ambition, and unconquerable activity ; whose capacious mind, stimulated by an ardent, elastic, and versatile spirit, and strongly impregnated with the enthusiasm, credulity, and sanguine expectation peculiar to the age, no single project, however vast or arduous, could wholly absorb. The extent of his capacity combined acquirements that are commonly esteemed remote and almost incompatible with each other. Framed in the prodigality of nature, he was at once the most industrious scholar and the most accomplished courtier of his age ; as a projector, profound, ingenious, and indefatigable ; as a soldier, prompt, daring, and heroic ; so contemplative (says an old writer) that he might have been judged unfit for action, so active that he seemed to have no leisure for contemplation.[3] The chief defect of his mental temperamant

---

[1] Hakluyt. Hill's *Naval History.* Hewit's *History of South Carolina and Georgia.*
[2] See Note I., at the end of the volume.
[3] Lloyd's *State Worthies.* Raleigh's friend, Edmund Spenser, the poet, with a strange, fantastic mixture of images, has termed him, in a sonnet, *The Shepherd of the Ocean.*

was the absence of moderation and regulation of thought and aim. Smitten with the love of glorious achievement, he had unfortunately embraced the maxim, that " whatever is not extraordinary is nothing"; and his mind (till the last scene of his life) was not sufficiently pervaded by religion to recognize that nobility of purpose, which ennobles the commonest actions, and elevates circumstances, instead of borrowing dignity from them. Uncontrolled by steady principle and sober calculation, the fancy and the passions of Raleigh transported him, in some instances, beyond the bounds of rectitude, honor, and propriety ; and, seconded by the malevolence of his fortune, entailed reproach on his character and discomfiture on his undertakings. But though adversity might cloud his path, it could never depress his spirit, or quench a single ray of his genius. He subscribed to his fortune with a noble grace, and by the universal consent of mankind his errors and infirmities have been deemed within the protection of his glory. The continual discomfiture of his efforts and projects served only to display the exhaustless opulence and indestructible vigor of that intellect, of which no accumulation of disaster nor variety of discouragement could either repress the ardor or narrow the range. Amidst disappointment and impoverishment, pursued by royal hatred, and forsaken by his popularity, he continued to project and attempt the foundation of empires ; and in old age and a prison he composed the History of the World. Perhaps there never was another instance of distinguished reputation as much indebted to genius and as little to success. So powerful, indeed, is the association that connects merit with success, and yet so strong the claim of Raleigh to elude the censure which this view implies, that we find it difficult to pronounce him, even amidst uninterrupted disaster, an unsuccessful man. Whatever judgment may be formed of his character, it must be acknowledged that in genius he was worthy of the honor which he may, perhaps, be considered to have attained, of originating the settlements that grew up into the North American commonwealth.

In conjunction with a kindred spirit, his half-brother, Sir Humphrey Gilbert, Raleigh projected the establishment of a colony in that quarter of America which Cabot had visited ; and a patent for this purpose was procured without difficulty, in favor of Gilbert, from Elizabeth. [1578.] This patent authorized him to explore and appropriate remote and barbarous lands, unoccupied by Christian powers, and to hold them as a fief of the crown of England, to which he was obliged to pay the fifth part of the produce of their gold or silver mines ; it permitted the subjects of Elizabeth to accompany the expedition,[1] and guarantied to them a continuance of the enjoyment of the rights of free denizens of England ; it invested Gilbert with the powers of civil and criminal legislation over the inhabitants of the territory which he might occupy ; but with this limitation, that his laws should be framed with as much conformity as possible to the statutes and policy of England, and should not derogate from the supreme allegiance due to the English crown. The endurance of the patent, in so far as related to the appropriation of territory, was limited to six years ; and all other persons

---

[1] This provision was necessary to evade the obstructions of the existing law of England. By the ancient law, as declared in the Great Charter of King John, all men might go freely out of the kingdom; retaining, indeed, their allegiance to the king. But no such clause appears in the charter of his successor ; and during the reign of Elizabeth it was enacted, that any subject, departing the realm without a license under the Great Seal, should forfeit his personal estate, and the rent of his landed property. 13 Eliz. cap. 3.

D

were prohibited from establishing themselves within two hundred leagues of any spot which the adventurers might occupy during that period.[1]

The arbitrary power thus committed to the leader of the expedition did not prevent the accession of a numerous body of subordinate adventurers. Gilbert had earned high and honorable distinction by his services, both in France and Ireland ; and the attractive influence of his reputation, combining with the spirit of the times, and aided by the zeal of Raleigh and the authority of Secretary Walsingham, enabled him speedily to collect a sufficient body of associates, and to accomplish the equipment of the first expedition of British emigrants to America. But in the composition of this body there were elements very ill fitted to establish an infant commonwealth on a solid or respectable basis ; the officers were disunited, the crew mutinous and licentious ; and, happily for the credit of England, it was not the will of Providence that the adventurers should gain a footing in any new region. Gilbert, approaching the American continent by too northerly a course, was dismayed by the inhospitable aspect of the coast of Cape Breton ; his largest vessel was shipwrecked ; and two voyages, in the last of which he himself perished, finally terminated in the defeat of the enterprise and dispersion of the adventurers.[2] [1583.]

But the ardor of Raleigh, neither daunted by difficulties nor damped by miscarriage, and continually refreshed by the suggestions of a fertile and uncurbed imagination, was incapable of abandoning a project that had gained his favor and exercised his energy. Applying to the queen, in whose esteem he then held a distinguished place, he easily prevailed with her to grant him a patent in all respects similar to that which had been previously bestowed upon Gilbert.[3] [1584.] Not less prompt in executing than intrepid in projecting his schemes, Raleigh soon despatched two small vessels, commanded by Amadas and Barlow, to visit the districts which he intended to occupy, and to examine the accommodations of their coasts, the productions of the soil, and the condition of the inhabitants. These officers, avoiding the error of Gilbert in steering too far north, shaped their course by the Canaries, and, approaching the North American continent by the Gulf of Florida, anchored in Roanoke Bay, off the coast of North Carolina. Worthy of the trust reposed in them, they behaved with much courtesy to the inhabitants of the region, whom they found living in all the rude independence, and laborless, but hardy, simplicity, of savage life, and of whose hospitality, as well as of the mildness of the climate and the fertility of the soil, they published a flattering encomium on their return to England. This intelligence diffused general satisfaction, and was so agreeable to Elizabeth, that, in exercise of the parentage she proposed to assume over the country, and as a memorial that the acquisition of it originated with a virgin queen, she thought proper to bestow on it the name of Virginia.[4]

A prospect so encouraging not only pricked forward the enthusiastic spirit of Raleigh; but, by its influence on the minds of his countrymen, enabled him the more speedily to complete his preparations for a permanent colonial settlement ; and he was soon in a condition to equip and despatch a

---

[1] Stith's *History of Virginia.* Hazard's *Historical Collections.*
[2] Hakluyt, III. 143.
[3] Stith. Hazard.
[4] Smith. The country was so called (says Oldmixon) either in honor of the virgin estate of the queen, " or, as the Virginians will have, because it still seemed to retain the virgin purity and plenty of the first creation." Oldmixon's *British Empire in America,* 2d edit.

squadron of seven ships under the command of Sir Richard Grenville, one of the most heroic spirits of the time, and eminent for valor in an age distinguished by the numbers of the brave. But this gallant leader, unfortunately, was more infected with the spirit of predatory enterprise, at that time so prevalent among the English, than endued with the qualities which his peculiar duty on the present occasion required ; and, commencing his expedition by cruising among the West India islands and capturing the vessels of Spain, he initiated his followers in pursuits and views very remote from peaceful industry, patient perseverance, and moderation. At length he landed a hundred and eight men[1] at Roanoke [August, 1585] ; and left them there to attempt, as they best might, the arduous task of founding and maintaining a social establishment. The command of this feeble band was committed to Captain Lane, assisted by some persons of note, of whom the most eminent were Amadas, who had conducted the former voyage, and Thomas Heriot, the improver of algebraical calculation, — a man whose generous worth and wisdom might have preserved the colony, if these qualities had been shared by his associates, and whose unremitted endeavours to instruct the savages, and diligent inquiries into their habits and character, by adding to the stock of human knowledge, and extending the example of virtue, rendered the expedition not wholly unproductive of benefit to mankind. The selection of such a man to accompany and partake the enterprise reflects additional honor on his friend and patron, Raleigh. On their first arrival, the adventurers were regarded with the utmost awe and veneration by the savages, who, seeing no women among them, were inclined to believe them not born of woman, and therefore immortal. Heriot endeavoured to avail himself of the admiration they expressed for the guns, the clock, the telescopes, and other implements that attested the superiority of their visitors, in order to lead their minds to the great Source of all sense and science. But while they hearkened to his instructions, they accommodated the import of them to their own depraved notions of Divine Nature ; they acknowledged that the God of the strangers was more powerful and more beneficent to his people than the deities whom they served, and expressed an eager desire to touch and embrace the Bible, and apply it to their breasts and heads.[2] In the hands of an artful or superstitious priest, such practices and dispositions would probably have produced a plentiful crop of pretended miracles and imaginary cures of diseases, and terminated in an exchange of superstition, instead of a renovation of moral nature. But Heriot was incapable of flattering or deceiving the savages, by encouraging their idolatry and merely changing its direction ; he labored to convince them that the benefits of religion were to be obtained by acquaintance with the contents of the Bible, and not by an ignorant veneration of the exterior of the book. By these labors, which were too soon interrupted, he succeeded in making such impression on the minds of the Indians, that Wingina, their king, finding himself attacked by a dangerous malady, rejected the assistance of his own priests, and solicited the attendance and prayers of the English ; and his example was followed by many of his subjects.[3]

But, unfortunately for the stability of the settlement, the majority of the colonists were much less distinguished by piety or prudence, than by eager and impetuous desire to obtain immediate wealth ; their first pursuit was gold ; and, smitten with the persuasion that every part of America was per-

---

[1] Smith, B. I.　　　　[2] Heriot, *apud* Smith.　　　　[3] Ibid.

vaded by ramifications of the mines which enriched the Spanish colonies, their chief efforts were directed to the acquisition of treasures that happily had no existence. The natives, discovering the object which the strangers sought with so much avidity, amused them with tales of a neighbouring region abounding with the precious metals, and possessing such quantities of pearl, that even the walls of the houses glittered with its lavish display.[1] Eagerly listening to these agreeable fictions, the adventurers consumed their time and endured extreme hardships in pursuit of a phantom, while they neglected entirely the means of providing for their future subsistence. The detection of the imposture produced mutual suspicion and disgust between them and the savages, and finally led to open enmity and acts of bloodshed. The stock of victuals brought with them from England was exhausted ; the additional supplies they had been taught to expect did not arrive ; and the hostility of the Indians left them no other dependence than on the precarious resources of the woods and rivers. Thus, struggling with increasing scarcity of food, and surrounded by enemies, the colonists were reduced to a state of the utmost distress and danger, when a prospect of deliverance was unexpectedly presented to them by the arrival of Sir Francis Drake with a fleet, which he was conducting home from a successful enterprise against the Spaniards in the West Indies. Drake consented to supply them with an addition to their numbers and a liberal contribution of provisions ; and if this had been done, it seems probable, that, with the ample reinforcement soon after transmitted by Raleigh, the colonists might have been able to maintain their establishment in America. But Drake's intentions were frustrated by a storm, that carried out to sea the very ship which he had freighted with the requisite supplies ; and as he could not afford to weaken his fleet by a further contribution for their defence or subsistence, the adventurers, now completely exhausted and discouraged, unanimously determined to abandon the settlement. In compliance with their desire, Drake accordingly received them on board his vessels, and reconducted them to England.[2] [1586.] Such was the abortive issue of the first colonial settlement planted by the English in America.

Of the political consequences that resulted from this expedition, the catalogue, though far from copious, is not devoid of interest. An important accession was made to the scanty stock of knowledge respecting North America ; the spirit of mining adventure received a salutary check ; and the use of tobacco, already introduced by the Spaniards and Portuguese into other parts of Europe, was now imported into England. This herb the Indians esteemed their principal medicine ;[3] and some tribes are said to have ascribed its virtues to the inhabitation of one of those spiritual beings which they supposed to reside in all the extraordinary productions of nature. Lane and his associates, contracting a relish for its properties, brought a quantity of tobacco with them to England, and taught the use of it to their countrymen. Raleigh, in particular, adopted, and, with the help of some young men of fashion, encouraged the practice, which soon established itself, and spread with a vigor that outran the help of courtiers, and defied the hinderance of kings ; and awakening a new and almost universal appetite in human nature, formed an important source of revenue to England, and multiplied the ties that united Europe with America.[4]

[1] Smith.   [2] Ibid.   [3] Heriot, ap. Smith.
[4] Queen Elizabeth herself, in the close of her life, became one of Raleigh's pupils, in the accomplishment of smoking. One day, as she was partaking this indulgence, Raleigh betted

But the disappointment that attended this enterprise did not terminate with the return of Lane and his followers to England. A few days after their departure from Roanoke, a vessel, despatched by Raleigh, reached the evacuated settlement with a plentiful contribution of all necessary stores; and only a fortnight after this bark set sail to return from its bootless voyage, a still larger reinforcement of men and provisions arrived in three ships, equipped by Raleigh, and commanded by Sir Richard Grenville. Disconcerted by the absence of the vessel that preceded him, and unable to obtain any tidings of the colonists, yet unwilling to abandon the possession of the country, Grenville landed fifty men at Roanoke, and, leaving them in possession of an ample supply of provisions, returned to England to communicate the state of affairs and obtain further directions.[1]

These successive defeats and mishaps excited much gloomy speculation and superstitious surmise in England,[2] but could neither vanquish the hopes nor exhaust the resources of Raleigh, whose dauntless and aspiring mind still rose superior to all mischance. In the following year [1587], he fitted out and despatched three ships under the command of Captain White, with directions to join the small body that Grenville had established at Roanoke, and thence to transfer the settlement to the Bay of Chesapeake, of which the superior advantages were remarked in the preceding year by Lane. A charter of incorporation was granted to White and twelve of his principal associates, as Governor and Assistants of the City of Raleigh in Virginia. In the hope of evading the unprosperous issue of the former expeditions, more efficacious means were adopted, in the equipment of this squadron, for preserving and continuing the colony. The stock of provisions was more abundant; the number of men greater, and the means of recruiting their numbers afforded by a competent intermixture of women. But the full extent of the precedent calamities had yet to be learned; and on landing at Roanoke, in quest of the detachment that Grenville had placed there, White and his companions could find no other trace of it than the significant memorial presented by a dismantled fort and a heap of human bones.[3] The apprehensions excited by this melancholy spectacle were confirmed by the intelligence of a friendly native, who informed them that their countrymen had fallen victims to the enmity of the Indians. Instructed rather than discouraged by this calamity, they endeavoured to cultivate the good-will of the savages; and determining to remain at Roanoke, they hastened to repair the houses and restore the colony. One of the natives was baptized into the Christian faith, and, retaining an unshaken attachment to the English, contributed his efforts to pacify and conciliate his countrymen.[4] But finding themselves destitute of many articles which they judged essential to their comfort and preservation, in a country thickly covered with forests and peopled only by a few scattered tribes of savages, the colonists deputed their governor to solicit for them the requisite supplies; and White repaired for this purpose to England. In his voyage thither he

with her that he could ascertain the weight of the smoke that should issue in a given time from her Majesty's mouth. For this purpose, he weighed first the tobacco, and afterwards the ashes left in the pipe, and assigned the difference as the weight of the smoke. The queen acknowledged that he had gained his bet; adding, that she believed he was the only alchemist who had ever succeeded in turning smoke into gold. Stith.
   [1] Smith. "The Virginians positively affirm that Sir Walter Raleigh made this voyage in person." Oldmixon's *British Empire in America*, 2d edit. But the generous wish alone seems to have been the parent of this notion.
   [2] Smith.   [3] Ibid.   [4] Ibid.

touched at a port in Ireland, where he is reported to have introduced the first specimens ever seen in Europe of the potato plant, which he had brought with him from America. But whether this memorable importation was due to him, or, as some writers have affirmed, to certain of the earlier associates of Raleigh's adventures, it must be acknowledged that to the enterprise of Raleigh, and the soil of America, Great Britain is indebted for her acquaintance with the potato and with tobacco, the staple article of diet, and the most cherished, as well as the most innocent, luxury of a great portion of her people.

White arrived at a juncture very unfavorable for the success of his mission. England was now engrossed with the more immediate concern of self-preservation : the formidable armada of Spain was preparing to invade her, and the whole naval and military resources of the empire were placed under requisition for the purposes of national defence. The hour of his country's danger could not fail to present the most interesting employment to the generous spirit of Raleigh ; yet he mingled, with his distinguished efforts to repel the enemy, some exertions for the preservation of the colony which he had planted. For this purpose he had, with his usual promptitude, equipped a small squadron, which he committed to the conduct of Sir Richard Grenville, when the queen interposed to detain the ships that were adapted for fight, and to prohibit Grenville from leaving England at such a crisis. White, however, was enabled to reëmbark for America with two small vessels [1588] ; but, yielding to the temptation of trying his fortune by the way in a cruise against the Spaniards, he was beaten by a superior force, and totally disabled from pursuing his voyage. The colony at Roanoke was, in consequence, left to depend on its own feeble resources, of which the diligent cultivation was not likely to be promoted by the hopes that were entertained of foreign succour. [1589.] What its fate was may be easily guessed, but never was certainly known. White, conducting an expedition to Roanoke in the following year, found the territory evacuated of the colonists, of whom no further tidings were ever obtained.[1]

This last expedition was not despatched by Raleigh, but by his successors in the American patent ; and our history is now to take leave of that illustrious man, with whose schemes and enterprises it ceases to have any farther connection. The ardor of his mind was not exhausted, but diverted by a multiplicity of new and not less important concerns. Intent on peopling and improving a large district in Ireland, which the queen had conferred on him ; engaged in the conduct of a scheme, and the expense of an armament, for establishing Don Antonio on the throne of Portugal ; and already revolving his last and wildest project of an expedition for the discovery of mines in Guiana ; he found it impossible to continue either the attention or the expenditure which he had devoted to his American colony. Yet desiring with earnest inclination that a design, which he had so gallantly and steadfastly pursued, should not be entirely abandoned, and, hoping that the spirit of commerce would preserve an intercourse with America that might terminate in a colonial settlement, he consented to assign his patent to Sir Thomas Smith and a company of merchants in London, who undertook to establish and maintain a traffic between England and Virginia. The patent which he thus transferred had already cost him forty thousand pounds, without affording him the slightest return of pecuniary profit ; yet the only

---

[1] Smith. Stith. Williamson's *History of North Carolina.*

personal consideration for which he stipulated with the assignees was a small share of whatever gold or silver ore they might eventually discover; and he now bestowed on them, in addition to his previous disbursements, a donation of one hundred pounds, in aid of the efforts to which they pledged themselves for the propagation of Christianity in America.[1]

It appeared, very soon, that Raleigh had transferred his patent to hands very different from his own. The last mentioned expedition, which was productive of nothing but tidings of the miscarriage of a prior adventure, was the most notable effort that the London company exerted. Satisfied with a paltry traffic conducted by a few small vessels, they made no attempt to take possession of the country; and at the period of Elizabeth's death, not a single Englishman was settled in America. The exertions of Raleigh, however, had united the views and hopes of his countrymen, by a strong association, with settlements in Virginia, and given a bias to the national spirit, which only the encouragement of more favorable circumstances was wanting to develope. But the war with Spain, that endured till the close of Elizabeth's reign, allured men of enterprise and activity into the career of predatory adventure, and obstructed the formation of peaceable and commercial settlements.

The accession of James to the English crown [1603] was, by a singular coincidence, an event no less favorable to the colonization of America than fatal to the illustrious projector of this design. Peace was immediately concluded with Spain; and England, in the enjoyment of uninterrupted tranquillity, was enabled to direct to more bloodless pursuits the energies matured in a war which had excited the spirit of the nation without impairing its strength. From the inability of government, in that age, to collect all the disposable force of the empire for combined operation, war was chiefly productive of a series of partial efforts and privateering expeditions, which widely diffused the allurements of ambition and multiplied the opportunities of advancement. This had been remarkably exemplified in the contest with Spain; and many ardent spirits, to which this contest had supplied opportunities of animating exertion and flattering ascendency, became impatient of the restraint and inactivity to which the peace consigned them, and began to look abroad for a new sphere of activity and distinction.

The prevalence of such dispositions naturally led to a revival of the project of colonizing North America, which gained an additional recommendation to public favor from the success of a voyage undertaken in the last year of Elizabeth's reign. Bartholomew Gosnold, who planned and performed this voyage in a small vessel containing only thirty men, was led, by his experience in navigation, to suspect that the proper track from Europe to America had not yet been discovered, and that, in steering by the Canary Islands and the Gulf of Florida, a circuit of at least a thousand leagues was unnecessarily made. In prosecution of his conjecture, he abandoned the southern track, and, steering more to the westward, was the first navigator who reached America by this directer course. He arrived at a more northerly quarter of the continent than any of Raleigh's colonists had visited, and, landing in the region which now forms the State of Massachusetts, he pursued an advantageous traffic with the natives, and freighted his vessel with abundance of rich peltry. He visited two adjacent islands, one of which he named Martha's Vineyard, the other Elizabeth's Island.

---

[1] Hazard. Campbell's *History of Virginia*.

The aspect of the country appeared so inviting, and the climate so salubrious, that twelve of the crew at first determined to remain there ; but reflecting on the melancholy fate of the colonists at Roanoke, they found their resolution unequal to their wishes ; and the whole party, reluctantly quitting the agreeable region, returned to England after an absence of less than four months.[1]

The report of this expedition produced a strong impression on the public mind, and led to important consequences. Gosnold had discovered a route that greatly shortened the voyage to North America, and found a healthy climate, a fertile soil, and a coast abounding with excellent harbours. He had seen many fruits, that were highly esteemed in Europe, growing plentifully in the American woods ; and having sown some European grain, beheld it germinate with rapidity and vigor. Encouraged by his success, and perhaps not insensible to the hope of finding gold and silver, or some new and lucrative article of commerce, in the unexplored interior of so fine a country, he endeavoured to procure associates in an enterprise to transport a colony to America. Similar projects were generated in various parts of the kingdom ; but the spirit of adventure was controlled by a salutary caution, awakened by the recollection of former disappointments.

These projects were zealously promoted by the counsel and encouragement of Richard Hakluyt, prebendary of Westminster, a man of eminent attainments in naval and commercial science, the patron and counsellor of many of the English expeditions of discovery, the correspondent of the leaders who conducted them, and the historian of the exploits they gave rise to. At his suggestion,[2] two vessels were fitted out by the merchants of Bristol, and despatched to examine the discoveries of Gosnold, and verify his statements. [1603.] They returned with an ample confirmation of the navigator's veracity. A similar expedition was equipped and despatched by the Earl of Southampton and Lord Arundel of Wardour[3] [1605], which not only produced farther testimony to the same effect, but reported so many additional particulars commendatory of the region, that all doubt and hesitation vanished from the minds of the projectors of American colonization ; and an association, sufficiently numerous, wealthy, and powerful to undertake this enterprise, being speedily formed, a petition was presented to the king for his sanction of the plan, and the interposition of his authority towards its execution.

The attention of James had been previously directed to the advantages attending the plantation of colonies, at the time when he attempted to civilize the more barbarous clans of his original subjects by introducing detachments of industrious traders from the low country into the Highlands of Scotland.[4] Well pleased to resume a favorite speculation, and willing to encourage a scheme that opened a safe and peaceful career to the active genius of his new subjects, he hearkened readily to the application ; and, highly commending the plan, acceded to the wishes of its projectors. Letters patent were issued [April, 1606] to Sir Thomas Gates, Sir George Somers, Richard Hakluyt, and their associates, granting to them those territories in America lying on the seacoast between the thirty-fourth and forty-fifth degrees of north latitude, together with all islands situated within a hundred miles of their shores. The design of the patentees was declared to be, " to make

1 Purchas. Smith. Stith.   2 Smith.
3 Smith. Oldmixon.   4 Robertson's *History of Scotland.*

habitation and plantation, and to deduce a colony of sundry of our people into that part of America commonly called Virginia " ; and, as the main recommendation of the design, it was proclaimed, that " so noble a work may, by the providence of Almighty God, hereafter tend to the glory of his Divine Majesty, in propagating of Christian religion to such people as yet live in darkness and miserable ignorance of the true knowledge and worship of God, and may, in time, bring the infidels and savages living in those parts to human civility, and to a settled and quiet government." The patentees were required to divide themselves into two distinct companies ; the one consisting of London adventurers, whose projected establishment was termed the first or southern colony ; the second or northern colony devolving on a company composed of merchants belonging to Plymouth and Bristol.

The territory appropriated to the first or southern colony was generally called Virginia, and preserved that appellation after the region assigned to the second or northern colony obtained, in 1614, the name of New England. The adventurers were authorized to transport to their respective territories as many English subjects as might be willing to accompany them, and to make shipments of arms and provisions for their use, with exemption from custom-house dues for the space of seven years. The colonists and their children were to enjoy the same liberties and privileges in the American settlements as if they had remained or been born in England.[1] The administration of each of the colonies was committed to two boards of council ; the supreme government being vested in a board resident in England, which was to be nominated by the king, and directed in its proceedings by such ordinances as he might enact ; and a subordinate jurisdiction, which included the functions of executive power, devolving on a colonial council, which, like the other, was to be created by royal appointment, and regulated by the application of royal wisdom and authority. Liberty to search for and open mines (which, under all the feudal governments, were supposed to have been originally reserved to the sovereign) was conferred on the colonists, — with an appropriation, however, of part of the mineral and metallic produce to the crown ; and the more valuable privilege of unrestrained freedom of trade with other nations was also extended to them. The president and council within the colonies were authorized to levy duties on foreign commodities, which, for twenty-one years, were to be applied to the use of the adventurers, and afterwards to be paid into the royal exchequer.[2]

The terms of this charter afford an illustration both of the character of the monarch who granted, and of the designs of the persons who procured it. By neither of these parties was the formation of a solid and liberal social establishment either aimed at or preconceived. The arbitrary spirit of the royal grantor is discernible in the subjection of the emigrant body to a corporation in which they were not represented, and over whose delibera-

---

[1] This provision (whether suggested by the caution of the prince or the apprehension of the colonists) occurs in almost all the colonial charters. It is, however, omitted in the most elaborate of them all, the charter of Pennsylvania, which was revised and finally adjusted by that eminent lawyer, the Lord Keeper Guildford. When King William was about to renew the charter of Massachusetts, after the British Revolution, he was advised by the ablest lawyers in England that such a provision was nugatory ; the law necessarily inferring (they declared) that the colonists were Englishmen, and both entitled to the rights, and obliged to the duties, attached to the character of subjects of the English crown. Chalmers's *Annals*.
[2] Stith. Hazard.

tions they possessed no control. There is likewise a manifest inconsistency between the assurance of participation in all the privileges of Englishmen to the colonists, and the reservation of legislative power exclusively to the king, the control of whose legislative functions constitutes the most valuable political privilege that Englishmen enjoy. But we have no reason to suppose that the charter was unacceptable to the patentees; on the contrary, its most objectionable provisions are not more congenial to the character of the king, than conformable to the views which the leading members of that body plainly appear to have entertained. Their object (notwithstanding the more liberal designs professed in the charter) was rather to explore the continent and appropriate its supposed treasures, by the agency of a body of adventurers over whom they retained an entire control, than to establish a permanent and extensive settlement. The instructions to the provincial governors, which accompanied the second shipment despatched by the London company, demonstrated, very disagreeably to the wiser emigrants and very injuriously to the rest, that the purposes with which their rulers were mainly engrossed were not patient industry and colonization, but territorial discovery and hasty gain.[1] In furtherance of these views, the leading patentees were careful, by mixing no women with the first emigrants, to retain the colony in dependence upon England for its supplies of people, and to give free scope to the cupidity and the roving spirit of minds, undivided by the cares, and unfixed by the habits and attachments, of domestic life.

The king appears to have entertained ideas somewhat more liberal, and a more genuine purpose of colonization, than the patentees. While their leaders were employed in making preparations to reap the benefits of their charter, James was assiduously engaged in the task, which his vanity rendered a rich enjoyment, and the well guarded liberties of England a rare one, of digesting a code of laws for the projected colonies. This code, issued under the sign manual and privy seal, enjoined the preaching of the gospel in America, and the performance of divine worship, in conformity with the doctrines and rites of the church of England. Legislative and executive functions within the colonies were conferred on the provincial councils; but with this controlling provision, that laws originating there should, in substance, be consonant to the English laws; that they should continue in force only till modified or repealed by the king or the supreme council in England; and that their penal inflictions should not extend to death or demembration. Persons attempting to withdraw the colonists from their allegiance to the English crown were to be imprisoned; or, in cases highly aggravated, to be remitted for trial to England. Tumults, mutiny, rebellion, murder, and incest were to be punished with death; and for these offences the culprit was to be tried by a jury. Summary trial was appointed for inferior misdemeanours, and their punishment intrusted to the discretion of the president and council. Lands were to be holden by the same tenures that prevailed in England; but, for five years after the plantation of each colony, a community of labor and gains was to have place among the colonists. Kindness to the heathen inhabitants of America, and the communication of religious instruction to them, were enjoined. And, finally, power was reserved to the king and his successors to enact further laws, in consistence always with the jurisprudence of England.[2]

These regulations, in the main, are creditable to the sovereign who com-

---

[1] Smith.   [2] Stith.

posed them. No attempt was made, nor right pretended, to legislate for the Indian tribes of America ; and if the large territories, which these savages rather claimed than occupied, were appropriated and disposed of without any regard to their pretensions, at least no jurisdiction was assumed over their actions, and, in point of personal liberty, they were regarded as an independent people. This was an advance in equity beyond the practice of the Spaniards and the ideas of Queen Elizabeth, whose patent asserted the jurisdiction of the English crown and laws over the old as well as the new inhabitants of her projected colonies. In the criminal legislation of this code, we may observe a distinction which trial by jury has enabled to prevail over that ingenious and perhaps expedient rule of ancient colonial policy, which intrusted proconsular governors with the power of inflicting death, but restrained them from awarding less formidable penalties, as more likely to invite the indulgence of interest or caprice. If the charter, in some of its provisions, betrayed a total disregard of political liberty, the code, in establishing trial by jury, interwove with the very origin of society a habit and practice well adapted to cherish the spirit and principles of freedom.

The London company, to which the plantation of the southern colony was committed, applied themselves promptly to the formation of a colonial settlement. But, though many persons of distinction were included among the proprietors, their funds at first were scanty, and their early efforts proportionally feeble. Three small vessels, of which the largest did not exceed a hundred tons burden,[1] under the command of Captain Newport, formed the first squadron that was to execute what had been so long and so vainly attempted, and sailed with a hundred and five men destined to remain in America. Several of these emigrants were members of distinguished families, — particularly George Percy, a brother of the Earl of Northumberland ; and several were officers of reputation, — of whom we may notice Bartholomew Gosnold, the navigator, and Captain John Smith, one of the most distinguished ornaments of an age that was prolific of memorable men.

Thus, at length, after a research fraught with perplexity and disappointment, but assuredly not devoid of interest, into the sources of the great transatlantic commonwealth, we have reached the first inconsiderable spring, whose progress, opposed by innumerable obstructions, and nearly diverted in its very outset, yet always continuous, expands under the eye of patient inquiry into the grand and grandly spreading stream of American population. After the lapse of a hundred and ten years from the discovery of the continent by Cabot, and twenty-two years after its first occupation by Raleigh, was the number of the English colonists limited to a hundred and five ; and this handful of men [2] undertook the arduous task of peopling a remote and uncultivated land, covered with woods and marshes, and inhabited only by tribes of savages and beasts of prey. Under the sanction of a charter, which bereaved Englishmen of their most valuable rights, and banished from the constitution of American society the first principles of liberty, were the foundations laid of the colonial greatness of England, and of the freedom and prosperity of America. From this period, or at least very shortly after, a regular and connected history ensues of the progress of Virginia and New England, the two eldest-born colonies, whose example promoted the rise,

---

[1] Smith.

[2] " Never was the prophetic declaration, that ' a little one shall become a thousand, and a small one a strong nation,' more wonderfully exemplified than in the planting and rearing of these colonies." General Cass. *Discourse.* (1836.)

as their shelter protected the weakness, of the others which were successively planted and reared.

Newport and his squadron, pursuing, for some unknown reason, the wider compass taken by the first navigators to America, instead of the less circuitous track that had been recently ascertained, did not accomplish their voyage in a shorter period than four months ; but its termination was rendered peculiarly fortunate by the effect of a storm, which defeated their purpose of landing and settling at Roanoke, and carried them into the Bay of Chesapeake. [April, 1607.] As they advanced through its waters, they easily perceived the advantage that would be gained by establishing their settlement on the shores of this spacious haven, replenished by the tributary floods of so many great rivers, which fertilize the soil of that extensive district of America, and, affording commodious inlets into the interior parts, facilitate their foreign commerce and mutual communication. Newport first landed on a promontory forming the southern boundary of the bay, which, in honor of the Prince of Wales, he named Cape Henry. Thence, coasting the southern shore, he entered a river which the natives called Powhatan, and explored its banks for the space of forty miles from its mouth. Impressed with the superior convenience of the coast and soil to which they had been thus happily conducted, the adventurers unanimously determined to make this the place of their abode. They gave to their infant settlement, as well as to the neighbouring river, the name of their king ; and Jamestown retains the distinction of being the oldest existing habitation of the English in America.[1]

But the dissensions that broke out among the colonists soon threatened to deprive them of all the advantages of their fortunate territorial position. Their animosities were inflamed by an arrangement, which, if it did not originate with the king, at least betrays a strong affinity to that ostentatious mystery and driftless artifice which he affected as the perfection of political dexterity. The names of the provincial council were not communicated to the adventurers when they departed from England ; but the commission which contained them was inclosed in a sealed packet, which was directed to be opened within twenty-four hours after their arrival on the coast of Virginia, when the counsellors were to be installed in their office, and to elect their own president. The disagreements, incident to a long voyage and a band of adventurers rather conjoined than united, had free scope among men unaware of the relations they were to occupy towards each other, and of the subordination which their relative and allotted functions might imply ; and when the names of the council were proclaimed, the disclosure was far from affording satisfaction. Captain Smith, whose superior talents and spirit excited the envy and jealousy of his colleagues, was excluded from a seat in the council which the commission authorized him to assume, and even accused of traitorous designs so unproved and improbable, that none less believed the charge than the persons who preferred it. The privation of his counsel and services in the difficulties of their outset was a serious loss to the colonists, and might have been attended with ruin to the settlement, if his merit and generosity had not been superior to their mean injustice. The jealous suspicions of the individual who was elected president restrained the use of arms, and discouraged the construction of fortifications ; and a misunderstanding having arisen with the Indians, the

---

[1] Stith.

colonists, unprepared for hostilities, suffered severely from one of the sudden attacks characteristic of the warfare of those savages.[1]

Newport had been ordered to return with the ships to England ; and as the time of his departure approached, the accusers of Smith, with affected clemency, proposed that he also should return with Newport, instead of abiding a criminal prosecution in Virginia. But, happily for the colony, he scorned so to compromise his integrity ; and, demanding a trial, was honorably acquitted, and took his seat in the council.[2]

The fleet was better victualled than the magazines of the colony ; and while it remained with them, the colonists were permitted to share the plenty enjoyed by the sailors. But when Newport set sail for England, they found themselves limited to scanty supplies of unwholesome provisions ; and the sultry heat of the climate, and moisture of a country overgrown with wood, coöperating with the defects of their diet, brought on diseases that raged with fatal violence. Before the month of September, one half of their number had miserably perished ; and among these victims was Bartholomew Gosnold, who planned the expedition, and materially contributed to its accomplishment. This scene of suffering was embittered by internal dissensions. The president was accused of embezzling the public stores, and finally detected in an attempt to seize a pinnace and escape from the colony and its calamities. At length, in the extremity of their distress, when ruin seemed to impend alike from famine and the fury of the savages, the colonists obtained a complete and unexpected deliverance, which the piety of Smith ascribed to the influence of God in suspending the passions and controlling the sentiments and purposes of men. The savages, actuated by a sudden and generous change of feeling, not only refrained from molesting them, but gratuitously brought to them a supply of provisions so liberal, as at once to dissipate their apprehensions of famine and hostility.[3]

Resuming their spirit, the colonists now proved themselves not wholly uninstructed by their misfortunes. In seasons of exigency merit is illustrated, and the envy that pursues it is absorbed by deeper interest and alarm. The sense of common and urgent danger promoted a willing and even eager submission to the man whose talents were most likely to extricate his companions from the difficulties with which they were encompassed. Every eye was now turned on Smith, and with universal acclaim his fellow-colonists devolved on him the authority which they had formerly shown so much jealousy of his acquiring. This individual, whose name will be for ever associated with the foundation of civilized society in America, was descended of a respectable family in Lincolnshire, and born to a competent fortune. At an early age, his lively mind was deeply smitten with the spirit of adventure that prevailed so strongly in England during the reign of Elizabeth ; and yielding to his inclination, he had passed through a great variety of military service, with little pecuniary gain, but high reputation, and with the acquisition of an experience the more valuable that it was obtained without exhausting his ardor or tainting his morals.[4] The vigor of his constitution had preserved his health unimpaired amidst the general sickness ; the undaunted mettle of his soul retained his spirits unbroken, and his judgment unclouded, amidst the general misery and dejection ; and his adventurous zeal, which once attracted the reproach of overweening ambition, was now felt to diffuse an animating glow of hope and courage among all around him.

---

[1] Smith.   [2] Ibid.   [3] Ibid.   [4] Stith.

A strong sense of religion predominated over the well proportioned qualities of his mind, refreshed his confidence, extended and yet regulated his
views, and gave dignity to his character and consistency to his conduct.
Assuming the direction of the affairs of the colonists, he promptly adopted
the only policy that could save them from destruction. Under his directions, Jamestown was fortified by such defences as were sufficient to repel
the attacks of the savages ; and by dint of great labor, which he was always
the foremost to partake, its inhabitants were provided with dwellings that
afforded shelter from the weather, and contributed to restore and preserve
their health. Finding the supplies of the savages discontinued, he put himself at the head of a detachment of his people, and penetrated into the interior of the country, where, by courtesy and liberality to the tribes whom
he found well disposed, and vigorous retribution of the hostility of such as
were otherwise minded, he succeeded in procuring a plentiful stock of
provisions.[1]

In the midst of his successes, he was surprised [1607] during an expedition by a band of hostile savages, who, having made him prisoner, after a
gallant and nearly successful defence, prepared to inflict on him the usual
fate of their captives. His genius and presence of mind did not desert him
in this trying emergency. He desired to speak with the sachem or chief
of the tribe to which he was a prisoner ; and presenting him with a mariner's
compass, expatiated on the wonderful discoveries to which this little instrument had contributed, — descanted on the shape of the earth, the extent of
its lands and oceans, the course of the sun, the varieties of nations, and the
singularity of their relative terrestrial positions, which made some of them
antipodes to the others. With equal prudence and magnanimity he refrained
from any expression of solicitude for his life, which would infallibly have
weakened or counteracted the effect which he studied to produce. The
savages listened to him with amazement and admiration. They had handled
the compass, and viewing with surprise the play of the needle, which they
plainly saw, but found it impossible to touch, from the intervention of the
glass, were prepared by this marvellous object for the reception of those
sublime and interesting communications by which their captive endeavoured
to gain ascendency over their minds. For an hour after he had finished his
discourse, they remained undecided ; till, their accustomed sentiments reviving, they resumed their suspended purpose, and, having bound him to a
tree, prepared to despatch him with their arrows. But a deeper impression
had been made on their chief ; and his soul, enlarged for a season by the
admission of knowledge, or subdued by the influence of wonder, revolted
from the dominion of habitual barbarity. This chief bore the harsh and
uncouth appellation of Opechancanough, — a name which the subsequent
history of the province was to invest with no small terror and celebrity.
Holding up the compass in his hand, he gave the signal of reprieve ; and
Smith, though still guarded as a prisoner, was conducted to a dwelling,
where he was kindly treated and plentifully entertained.[2] But the strongest
impressions pass away, while the influence of habit remains. After vainly
attempting to prevail on their captive to betray the English colony into their
hands, the Indians referred his fate to Powhatan, the emperor or principal
sachem of the country, to whose presence they conducted him in triumphal
procession. This prince received him with much ceremony, ordered a

---

[1] Smith. Stith.   [2] Ibid.

plentiful repast to be set before him, and then adjudged him to suffer death by having his head laid on a stone and beaten to pieces with clubs. At the place appointed for his execution, Smith was again rescued from impending destruction by the interposition of Pocahontas, the favorite daughter of the king, who, finding her first entreaties, in deprecation of the captive's intended fate, disregarded, threw her arms around him, and passionately declared her determination to save him or die with him. Her generous humanity prevailed over the cruelty of her tribe ; and the king not only gave Smith his life, but soon after sent him back to Jamestown, where the beneficence of Pocahontas continued to follow him with supplies of provisions, that delivered the colonists from famine.[1]

After an absence of seven weeks, Smith returned to Jamestown, barely in time to prevent the desertion of the colony. His associates, reduced to the number of thirty-eight, impatient of farther stay in a country where they had met with so many discouragements, and in which they seemed fated to reënact the disasters of Roanoke, were preparing to abandon the settlement ; and it was not without the utmost difficulty, and alternately employing persuasion, remonstrance, and even violent interference, that Smith prevailed on them to relinquish their design.[2] The provisions that Pocahontas sent to him relieved their present wants ; his account of the plenty he had witnessed among the Indians revived their hopes ; and he endeavoured, by a diligent improvement of the favorable impressions he had made on the savages, and by a judicious regulation of the intercourse between them and the colonists, to promote a coalition of interests and reciprocation of advantages between the two races of people. His generous efforts were successful ; he preserved a steady and sufficient supply of food to the English, and extended his influence and consideration with the Indians, who began to respect and consult their former captive as a superior being. If Smith had sought only to magnify his own repute and establish his supremacy, he might easily have passed with the savages for a demi-god ; for they were not more averse to yield the allegiance which he claimed for their Creator, than forward to tender an abject homage to himself, and to ratify the loftiest pretensions he might advance in his own behalf. But no alluring prospect of dominion over men could tempt him to forget that he was the servant of God, or aspire to be regarded in any other light by his fellow-creatures. With uncompromising sincerity he labored to divert the savages from their idolatrous superstition, and made them all aware, that the man, whose superiority they acknowledged, despised their false deities, adored the true God, and obtained from his gracious communication the wisdom which they so highly commended. His pious exertions were obstructed by imperfect acquaintance with their language, and very ill seconded by the conduct of his associates, which contributed to persuade the Indians that his religion was something peculiar to his own person. Partly from the difficulties of his situation, partly from the defectiveness of his tuition, and, doubtless, in no small degree, from the stubborn blindness and wilful ignorance of the persons whom he attempted to instruct, Smith succeeded no farther than Heriot had formerly done. The savages extended their respect for the man to a Being whom they termed " the God of Captain Smith " ; and some of them acknowledged that this Being excelled their own deities in the same proportion that artillery excelled bows and arrows, and sent deputies

---

[1] Smith.   [2] Ibid.

to Jamestown to entreat that Smith would pray for rain, when their idols
seemed indisposed or unable to afford them a supply.[1] They were willing
enough to believe in gods made after the image of themselves, and in the
partial control exercised by those *superior beings* over the affairs of men ;
but the announcement of an *Almighty Creator*, the great source and support of universal existence, presented a notion which their understandings
refused to admit, and required a homage which their hearts revolted from
yielding.

While the affairs of the colony were thus prospering under the direction
of Captain Smith, a reinforcement of a hundred and twenty men, with an
abundant stock of provisions, and a supply of vegetable seeds and instruments of husbandry, arrived in two vessels from England. [1608.] The
colonists were not a little gladdened by this accession to their comforts and
their force. But, unhappily, the jealousies, which danger had restrained
rather than extinguished, again budded forth in this gleam of prosperity ;
the ascendency which Smith exercised over the Indians excited the envy
of the very persons whose lives it had preserved ; and his authority now
began sensibly to decline. Nor was it long before the cessation of his influence, together with the defects in the composition of the new body of emigrants, gave rise to the most serious mischiefs in the colony. The restraints
of discipline were relaxed, and a free traffic was permitted with the natives,
who speedily began to complain of fraudulent and unequal dealing, and to
exhibit their former animosity. In an infant settlement, where the views
and pursuits of men are unfixed, and habitual submission to authority has
yet to be formed, the welfare, and indeed the existence, of society are
much more dependent on the manners and moral character of individuals,
than on the influence of laws. But in recruiting the population of this
colony, too little consideration was shown for those habits and occupations
which must everywhere form the basis of national prosperity. This arose
as well from the peculiar views of the proprietors, as from the circumstances
of the English people, whose working classes were by no means over-
crowded, and among whom, consequently, the persons, whose industry and
moderation best qualified them to form a new settlement, were the least disposed to abandon their native country. Of the recruits newly arrived in the
colony, a large proportion were *gentlemen*, a few were *laborers*, and several
were *jewellers* and *refiners of gold*.[2] Unfortunately, some of this latter
description of artists soon found an opportunity of exercising their peculiar departments of industry, and of demonstrating (though too late) their
complete deficiency even of the worthless qualifications which they professed.

A small stream of water, issuing from a bank of sand near Jamestown,
was found to deposit in its channel a glittering sediment which resembled
golden ore, and was fondly mistaken for this precious material by the colonists. Only this discovery was wanting to reawaken the passions which
America had so fatally kindled in the bosoms of her first European invaders.
The deposition of the ore was supposed to indicate the neighbourhood
of a mine ; every hand was eager to explore ; and considerable quantities
of the dust were amassed, and subjected to the scrutiny of ignorance prepossessed by the strongest and most deceptive of human passions, and misled by the blundering guidance of superficial pretenders to superior skill.

---

[1] Smith.   [2] Ibid.

Smith exerted himself to disabuse his countrymen, and vainly strove to stem the torrent that threatened to devastate all their prospects ; assuring them, with prophetic wisdom, that to addict themselves to mining in preference to agriculture would be to squander and misdirect, in pursuit of a phantom, the exertions on which their subsistence depended. The deceptive dust, having undergone an unskilful assay of the refiners who had recently been united to the colony, was pronounced to be ore of a very rich quality ; and from that moment the thirst of gold was inflamed into a rage that reproduced those extravagant excesses, but, happily, without conducting to the same profligate enormities, for which the followers of Cortés and Pizarro were distinguished. All productive industry was suspended, and the operations of mining occupied the whole conversation, engrossed every thought, and absorbed every effort of the colonists. The two vessels that had brought their late supplies, returning to England, the one laden with this valueless dross, and the other with cedar wood, carried the first remittance that an English colony ever made from America. [June, 1608.] They conveyed back with them, also, some persons who had been invested and despatched to the colony with the absurdly inappropriate appointments of Admirals, Recorders, Chronologers, and Justices of the Peace, — a supply as useless to America as the remittance of dust was to Europe.[1]

Foreseeing the disastrous issue to which the delusion of his associates inevitably tended, Captain Smith, with the hope of preventing some of its most fatal consequences, conceived the project of extending his researches far beyond the range they had hitherto attained, and of exploring the whole of the great Bay of Chesapeake, for the purpose of ascertaining the qualities and resources of its territories, and promoting a beneficial intercourse with the remoter tribes of its inhabitants. This arduous design he executed with determined resolution and proportional success ; and while his fellow-colonists were actively engaged in disappointing the hopes of England, and rivalling the sordid excesses that had characterized the adventurers of Spain, he singly sustained the honor of his country, and, warmed with a nobler emulation, achieved an enterprise that equals in dignity, and surpasses in value, the most celebrated exploits of the Spanish discoverers. When we compare the slenderness of the auxiliary means which he possessed, with the magnitude of the results which he accomplished, with the hardships he endured, and the difficulties he overcame, we recognize in this achievement a monument of human power no less eminent than honorable, and willingly transmit a model so well calculated to warm the genius, to animate the fortitude, and sustain the patience of mankind. With his friend, Dr. Russell, and a small company of followers, whose fortitude and perseverance he was frequently obliged to resuscitate, and over whom he possessed no other authority than the ascendant of a vigorous character and superior intelligence, he performed, in an open boat, two voyages of discovery, that occupied more than four months, and embraced a navigation of above three thousand miles. With prodigious labor and extreme peril, he visited every inlet and bay on both sides of the Chesapeake, from Cape Charles to the River Susquehannah ; he sailed up many of the great rivers to their falls, and diligently examined the successive territories into which he penetrated, and the various tribes that possessed them. He brought back with him an account so ample, and a plan so accurate, of that great portion of the Ameri-

---

[1] Smith. Stith.

E *

can continent now comprehended in the States of Virginia and Maryland, that all the subsequent researches which it has undergone have only expanded and illustrated his original view; and his map has been made the groundwork of all posterior delineations, with no other diversity than what has inevitably arisen from the varieties of appropriation and the progress of settlements. But to come and to see were not his only objects; to win was also the purpose of his enterprise, and the effect of his exertions. In his intercourse with the various tribes which he visited, he displayed the genius of a commander, in a happy exercise of all those talents that overcome the antipathies of a rude people, and gain at once the respect and good-will of mankind. By the wisdom and liberality with which he negotiated and traded with the friendly, and by the courage and vigor with which he repelled and overcame the hostile, he succeeded in inspiring the savages with the most exalted opinion of himself and his nation, and paved the way to an intercourse that promised important advantage to the Virginian colony.[1] This was, indeed, the heroic age of North America; and such were the men, and such the labors, by which the first foundations of her greatness and prosperity were laid.

While this expedition was in progress, the golden dreams of the colonists were finally dispelled; and they had awaked to all the miseries of sickness, scarcity, disappointment, and discontent, when Smith once more returned to reanimate their drooping spirits with his success, and relieve their wants by the resources he had created. Shortly after his return, he was chosen President by the council [10th Sept. 1608]; and accepting the office, he employed his influence so efficiently with the savages, that immediate scarcity was banished, and exerted his authority so vigorously and judiciously in the colony, that orderly dispositions and industrious habits began generally to prevail, and gave promise of lasting plenty and steady improvement.[2] If we compare the actions of Smith, during the period of his presidency, with the enterprise that immediately preceded his election, it may appear, at first view, that the sphere of his exertions was contracted and degraded by his official elevation; and we might almost be tempted to regret the returning reasonableness of the colonists, which, by confining this active spirit to the petty details of their government, withdrew it from a range more congenial to its excursive vigor, and more fraught with general advantage to mankind. Yet, deeper and wiser reflection suggests, that a truly great mind, especially when united with an ardent temper, will never be contracted by the seeming restriction of its sphere, but will always be nobly as well as usefully employed, and not the less nobly when it dignifies what is ordinary, and improves those models that invite the widest imitation and are most level with common opportunities.

Accordingly, when we examine the history of that year over which the official supremacy of Captain Smith was extended, and consider the results of the multifarious details which it embraces,[3] we discern a dignity as real, though not so glaring, as that which invests his celebrated voyage of discovery; and are sensible of consequences even more interesting to human nature than any which this expedition produced. In a small society, where no great actual inequality of accommodation could exist, where power derived no aid from pomp, circumstance, or mystery, and where he owed his office to the appointment of his associates, and held it by the tenure of their

[1] Russell, *apud* Smith. Bagnal, *eod. loc.*   [2] Stith.   [3] Smith.

good-will,[1] he preserved order and enforced morality among a crew of dissolute and disappointed men ; and so successfully opposed his authority to the allurements of indolence, strengthened by their previous habits and promoted by the community of gains that then prevailed, as to introduce and maintain a respectable degree of laborious and even contented industry. What one governor afterwards achieved, in this respect, by the influence of an imposing rank, and others by the strong engine of martial law, Smith, without such aid, and with greater success, accomplished by the continual application of his own superior sense and his preëminent vigor, fortitude, and activity. Some plots were formed against him ; but these he detected and defeated without either straining or compromising his authority. The caprice and suspicion of the Indians involved him in numberless trials of his temper and capacity. Even Powhatan, notwithstanding the friendly ties that united him to his ancient guest, was induced, by the treacherous artifices of certain Dutchmen who deserted to him from Jamestown, first to form a secret conspiracy, and then to excite and prepare open hostility against the colonists. [1609.] Some of the fraudful designs of the royal savage were revealed by the unabated kindness of Pocahontas ; others were detected by Captain Smith ; and from them all he contrived to extricate the colony with honor and success, and yet with little and only defensive bloodshed ; displaying to the Indians a vigor and sagacity they could neither overcome nor overreach, a courage that excited their admiration, and a generosity that carried his victory into their minds, and reconciled submission with their pride. He was ever superior to that political timidity, which, in circumstances of danger, suggests not the proportionate, but always the strongest and most violent, remedy and counteraction ; and admirably illustrated the chief political uses of talent and virtue, in accomplishing the objects of government by gentler efforts and milder means than stupidity and ferocity would have ventured to employ. In demonstrating (to use his own words) " what small cause there is that men should starve or be murdered by the savages, that have discretion to manage them with courage and industry," [2] he bequeathed a valuable lesson to his successors in the American colonies, and to all succeeding settlers in the vicinity of savage tribes ; and in exemplifying (though, it must be confessed, only for a brief period and on a small scale) the power of a civilized people to anticipate the cruel and vulgar issue of battle, and to prevail over an inferior race without either extirpating or enslaving them, he obtained a victory, which Cæsar, with all his boasted superiority to the rest of mankind, was too ungenerous to appreciate, or was incompetent to achieve.

There was one point, indeed, in which it must be confessed that his conduct to the Indians was chargeable with defect of justice and good policy ; though the blame of this error must be divided between himself and the royal patentees whom he served, and, in addition to other palliating circum-

---

[1] It was the testimony of his soldiers and fellow-adventurers, says Stith, "that he was ever fruitful in expedients to provide for the people under his command, whom he would never suffer to want any thing he either had or could procure ; that he rather chose to lead than send his soldiers into danger ; " that, in all their expeditions, he partook the common fare, and never gave a command that he was not ready to execute ; " that he would suffer want rather than borrow, and starve sooner than not pay ; that he had nothing in him counterfeit or shy, but was open, honest, and sincere." Stith adds, respecting this founder of civilized society in North America, what the son of Columbus has, with a noble elation, recorded of his father, that, though habituated to naval manners, and to the command of factious and licentious men, he never was guilty of profane swearing.

[2] Smith.

stances, was disguised by its conformity with the universal and unreproved practice of European settlers in barbarous lands. No part of the territory which the first colonists occupied was purchased from the rude tribes who considered themselves its owners, and who probably at first regarded with little apprehension the settlement of a handful of strangers in a valueless corner of their wide domains. The colonists, indifferent to the opinion of the Indians, seem not to have conceived that the important right of property in land could be derived from occasional visitations of savage hunters, and readily took, as from the hands of nature, the territory which appeared to them to have been never reclaimed from its natural wildness and vacancy by deliberate occupation or industrial use. If they had reasoned upon the matter, they would probably have denied the right of the Indians to defeat the chief end of so large a portion of the earth, and restrict to an ignoble ministration to the idle subsistence of a few barbarians the soil which industry and virtue might render subservient to the diffusion of civility and the extension of life. But if their views had been regulated by the same equity and moderation which distinguished the later colonists of North America, they might have ascertained that their interests would be at once more cheaply and more humanely promoted by recognizing than by disputing the pretensions of the Indians; who, if they claimed land by a title which Europeans accounted unworthy of respect, were generally willing to part with it for a price which Europeans found it very easy to pay. It was reserved for the Puritan fathers of New England to set the first example of more liberal justice, and more impartial consideration of the rights of mankind; and, by a transaction in which sound policy and refined morality were happily blended, to mediate an amicable agreement between their own wants and the claim which the Indians asserted on the territorial resources of the country.

Captain Smith was not permitted to complete the work which he so well began. His administration was unacceptable to the company in England, for the same reasons that rendered it beneficial to the settlers in America. The patentees, very little concerned about the establishment of a happy and respectable community, had fondly counted on the accumulation of sudden wealth by the discovery of a shorter passage than was yet ascertained to the South Sea, or the acquisition of territory replete with mines of the precious metals. In these hopes they were hitherto disappointed; and the state of affairs in the colony was far from betokening even the retribution of the expenditure which they had already incurred. The prospect of a settled and improving state of society at Jamestown, so far from meeting their wishes, threatened to promote the growth of habits and interests perfectly incompatible with them. Still hoping, therefore, to realize their avaricious dreams, they conceived it necessary for this purpose to resume all authority into their own hands, and to abolish every semblance or substance of jurisdiction originating in America.[1] In order to fortify their pretensions, as well as to increase their funds, they now courted the acquisition of additional associates; and, having strengthened their interests by the accession of some persons of the highest rank and influence in the realm, they applied for and obtained a new charter.

If the arbitrary introduction of a new charter [23d May, 1609] proclaimed an entire disregard of the rights of the colonists who had emigrated on the

---

[1] Smith.

faith of the original one, the provisions peculiar to the new charter demonstrated no less plainly the intention of restricting the civil liberty of those
emigrants, and increasing their dependence on the English patentees. The
new charter was granted to twenty-one peers, ninety-eight knights, and a
great multitude of doctors, esquires, gentlemen, merchants, and citizens, and
sundry of the corporations of London, in addition to the former adventurers ;
and the whole body was incorporated by the title of " The Treasurer and
Company of Adventurers of the City of London for the first Colony in
Virginia." The boundaries of the colonial territory and the power of the
corporation were enlarged ; the offices of president and council in Virginia
were abolished ; a new council was established in England, and the company empowered to fill all future vacancies in it by election ; and to this
council was committed the power of new-modelling the magistracy of the
colony, of enacting all the laws that were to have place in it, and nominating
all the officers by whom these laws were to be carried into execution.
Nevertheless, was it still formally stipulated that the colonists and their posterity should retain all the rights of Englishmen. To prevent the doctrines
of the church of Rome from gaining admission into the plantation, it was
announced that no persons would be allowed to settle in Virginia without
having previously taken the oath of supremacy.[1]

The new council appointed Lord Delaware governor and captain-general
of the colony ; and the hopes, inspired by the distinguished rank and respectable character of this nobleman, contributed to strengthen the company
by a considerable accession of funds and associates. Availing themselves
of the favorable disposition of the public, they equipped without loss of time
a squadron of nine ships, and despatched them with five hundred emigrants,
under the command of Captain Newport, who was authorized to supersede
the existing administration, and to govern the colony till the arrival of Lord
Delaware with the remainder of the recruits and supplies. But by an unlucky combination of caution and indiscretion, the same powers were severally intrusted to Sir Thomas Gates and Sir George Somers, without any
adjustment of precedence between the three functionaries ; and they, finding
themselves unable to settle this point among themselves, agreed to embark
on board the same vessel, and to be companions during the voyage, — thus
deliberately provoking and eventually producing the disappointment of the
main object which their association in authority was intended to secure.
The vessel that contained the triumvirate was separated from the fleet by a
storm, and stranded on the coast of Bermudas.[2] The residue of the squadron arrived safely at Jamestown ; but so little were they expected, that,
when they were first descried at sea, they were mistaken for enemies ; and
this rumor gave occasion to a very satisfactory proof of the friendly dispo-

---

[1] Stith. Hazard.

[2] It was probably this disaster which produced the only mention of the American regions
which we find in the works of Shakspeare. In *The Tempest*, which was composed about
three years after this period, Ariel celebrates the stormy coast of " the still vexed Bermudas."
An allusion to the British settlements in America is couched in the prophecy which Shakspeare, in the last scene of *King Henry the Eighth*, imputes to Cranmer respecting King James,
— that,

> " Wherever the bright sun of heaven shall shine,
> His honor and the greatness of his name
> Shall be, and *make new nations*."

Milton, I believe, has never mentioned America, except in his casual allusion (*Paradise
Lost*, B. IX.) to the condition of the Indians when they were first visited by Columbus.

sition of the Indians, who came forward with the utmost alacrity, and offered to fight in defence of the colony.[1]

These apprehensions, which were dissipated by the nearer approach of the fleet, gave place to more substantial and more formidable evils, arising from the composition of the reinforcement which it brought to the colonial community. A great proportion of the new emigrants consisted of profligate and licentious youths, sent from England by their friends with the hope of changing their destinies, or for the purpose of screening them from the justice or contempt of their country ; of indigent gentlemen, too proud to beg, and too lazy to work ; tradesmen of broken fortunes and broken spirit ; idle retainers, of whom the great were eager to rid themselves ; and dependents too infamous to be decently protected at home ; with others, like these, more likely to corrupt and prey upon an infant commonwealth than to improve or sustain it.[2] The leaders of this pernicious crew, though devoid of legal documents entitling them to supersede the existing authority, proclaimed the changes which the constitution of the colony had undergone, and hastened to execute that part of the innovation which consisted in the overthrow of the provincial presidency and council. Their conduct soon demonstrated that their title to assume authority was not more defective than their capacity to exercise it. Assuming supreme jurisdiction, they were unable to devise any frame of government, or establish even among themselves any fixed subordination ; sometimes the old commission was resorted to ; sometimes a new model attempted ; and the chief direction of affairs passed from hand to hand in one uninterrupted succession of folly and presumption. The whole colony was thrown into confusion by the revolutionary state of its government ; and the Indian tribes were alienated and exasperated by the turbulence, injustice, and insolence of the new settlers.

This emergency summoned the man, who had already more than once rescued the settlement from ruin, again to attempt its deliverance. The call was seconded by the wishes of the best and wisest of the colonists ; and, aided as much by the vigor of his own character as by the coöperation of these individuals, Smith reassumed his natural ascendant and official supremacy, and declared his intention of retaining the authority created by the old commission, till a legal revocation of it and legitimate successors to himself should arrive. With a determined vigor of purpose, to which instant acquiescence was yielded, he imprisoned the chief promoters of tumult ; and, having restored order and obedience, endeavoured to prevent a recurrence of the former mischiefs by detaching from Jamestown a portion of the new colonists to form a subordinate settlement at some distance from this place. This was an unfortunate step ; and it is remarkable that the only signal failing in the policy of this eminent commander was evinced in the only instance in which he seemed to distrust his own vigor and capacity. The detachments which he removed from Jamestown conducted themselves so imprudently as to convert all the neighbouring Indians into enemies, and to involve themselves in continual difficulty and danger. The Indians assailed him with complaints ; the detached settlers with requisitions of counsel and assistance ; and Smith, who never spent in lamenting misfortunes the time that might be employed in repairing them, was exerting himself with his usual activity and good sense in redressing these disorders, when he received a dangerous wound from the accidental explosion of a mass of gun-

---

[1] Smith. Stith.   [2] Stith.

powder.   Completely disabled by this misfortune, and destitute of surgical aid in the colony, he was compelled to resign his command, and take his departure for England.[1] [Oct. 1609.] He never returned to Virginia again. It was natural that he should abandon with regret the society which he had exerted so much admirable vigor to preserve, — the settlement which he had conducted through difficulties as formidable as those which obstructed the infant progress of Carthage or Rome, — and the scenes which he had dignified by so much wisdom and virtue.   But our sympathy with his regret is abated by the reflection, that a longer residence in the colony would speedily have consigned him to very subordinate office,[2] and might have deprived the world of that stock of valuable knowledge, and his own character of that accession of fame,[3] which the publication of his travels has secured and perpetuated.

CHAPTER II.

The Colony a Prey to Anarchy — and Famine. — Gates and Somers arrive from Bermudas. — Abandonment of the Colony determined upon — prevented by the Arrival of Lord Delaware. — His wise Administration — his Return to England. — Sir Thomas Dale's Administration. — Martial Law established. — Indian Chief's Daughter seized by Argal — married to Rolfe. — Right of private Property in Land introduced into the Colony. — Expedition of Argal against Port Royal and New York. — Tobacco cultivated by the Colonists. — First Assembly of Representatives convened in Virginia. — New Constitution of the Colony. — Introduction of Negro Slavery. — Migration of young Women from England to Virginia. — Dispute between the King and the Colony. — Conspiracy of the Indians. — Massacre of the Colonists. — Dissensions of the London Company. — The Company dissolved. — The King assumes the Government of the Colony — his Death. — Charles the First pursues his Father's arbitrary Policy. — Tyrannical Government of Sir John Harvey. — Sir William Berkeley appointed Governor. — The provincial Liberties restored. — Virginia espouses the royal Cause — subdued by the Long Parliament. — Restraints imposed on the Trade of the Colony. — Revolt of the Colony. — Sir William Berkeley resumes the Government. — Restoration of Charles the Second.

AT the period of Smith's departure, the infant commonwealth was composed of five hundred persons, and amply provided with all necessary stores of arms, provisions, cattle, and implements of agriculture ;[4] but the sense to improve its opportunities was wanting ; and fortune forsook it along with its preserver.   For a short time, the government was administered by George Percy, a man of sense and probity, but devoid of the vigor that gives efficacy to virtue ; and the direction of affairs soon relapsed into the same mischievous channel from which Smith had recalled it.   The colony was delivered up to the wantonness of a giddy and distracted rabble, and presented a scene of riot, folly, and profligacy, strongly invoking vindictive retribution, and speedily overtaken by it.   The magazines of food were exhausted with reckless improvidence ; and the Indians, incensed by repeated injuries, and aware that the man whom they so much respected had ceased to govern the colonists, not only refused them all assistance, but harassed them with continual hostilities.   Famine ensued, and completed their wretchedness and degradation by transforming them into cannibals, and compelling them to support their lives by feeding on the bodies of the In-

---

[1] Smith. Stith.
[2] See Note II., at the end of this volume.
[3] He became so famous in England before his death, that his adventures were dramatized and represented on the stage, to his own great annoyance. Stith.
[4] Stith.

dians whom they slew, and of their own companions who perished of hunger or disease. Six months after the departure of Smith, there remained no more than sixty persons alive at Jamestown, still prolonging their misery by a vile and precarious diet, but daily expecting its final and fatal close.[1]

In this wretched predicament was the colony found by Gates, Somers, and Newport, who at length arrived from Bermudas [May, 1610], where the shipwreck they encountered had detained them and their crew for ten months.[2] The bounty of nature in that happy region maintained them in comfort while they constructed the vessels that were to transport them to Jamestown, and might have supplied them with ample stores for the use of the colony ; but they neglected these resources, and arrived almost empty-handed, in the confident assurance of receiving from the magazines of a thriving settlement the relief that was now vainly implored from themselves by the famishing remnant of their countrymen. Their disappointment was equalled only by the difficulty of ascertaining, amidst the mutual and contradictory accusations of the surviving colonists, how or by whose fault a calamity so unexpected had actually come to pass. But there was no time for deliberate inquiry, or adjustment of complaints. It was determined to abandon the settlement ; and with this view all the people embarked in the vessels that had arrived from Bermudas, and set sail for England. Their stores were insufficient for so long a voyage ; but they hoped to obtain an additional supply at the English fishing station on the coast of Newfoundland. Such abhorrence of the scene of their misery was entertained by some of the colonists, that they importuned the commanders to burn the fort and houses at Jamestown. But Gates could not discern in their or his own distresses any reason for demolishing the buildings, that might afford shelter to future settlers ; and happily, by his interposition, the edifices were preserved from destruction, and the colonists prevented from wreaking additional vengeance on themselves.[3]

For it was not the will of Providence that this little commonwealth should perish ; the calamities with which it had been visited were appointed to punish merely, but not entirely to destroy ; and the most vicious members being now cut off, and a memorable lesson afforded both to the patrons who collect[4] and the persons who compose such communities, a deliverance no less signal was vouchsafed by the Disposer of all events, just when hope was over, and the colony advanced to the very brink of annihilation. Before the fugitives had reached the mouth of James River, they were met by Lord Delaware, who arrived with three ships, containing a large supply of provisions, a considerable number of new settlers, and an ample stock of every implement and commodity requisite for defence or cultivation.[5]

Lord Delaware, who now presented himself as captain-general of the colony, was singularly well fitted for the exigency of the predicament in which he was thus unexpectedly placed. To an ancient lineage and a title

---

[1] Stith.   [2] Smith.   [3] Smith. Stith.
[4] The fate of this settlement probably suggested to Lord Bacon the following passage in his *Essay on Plantations*. "It is a shameful and unblessed thing to take the scum of the people, and wicked, condemned men, to be the people with whom we plant ; and not only so, but it spoileth the plantation ; for they will ever live like rogues and not fall to work, but be lazy and do mischief and spend victuals." Britain boasts the honor of producing two such philosophers and teachers of colonial policy as Lord Bacon and Adam Smith, but cannot claim the higher honor of having appreciated and followed their counsels.
[5] Smith. Stith.

of nobility, in an age when such distinctions were regarded with much veneration, he joined a dignified demeanour, a disinterested character, respectable sense, and a firm and resolute temper. The hope of rendering an important service to his country, and the generous pleasure of coöperating in a great design, had induced him to exchange ease and splendor at home for a situation of the general difficulties of which he was perfectly aware ; and the same firmness and elevation of purpose preserved him undaunted and unperplexed by the astounding scene of calamity which he encountered on his arrival in Virginia. Stemming the torrent of evil fortune, he carried back the fugitives to Jamestown, and commenced his administration by attendance on divine worship. After some consultation respecting the affairs of the settlement, he summoned all the colonists together, and addressed them in a short, but judicious and impressive harangue. [1611.] He rebuked the folly, sloth, and immorality that had produced such disasters, and recommended a return to the virtues most likely to repair them ; he declared his determination not to hold the sword of justice in vain, but to punish the first recurrence of disorder by shedding the blood of the delinquents, — though he would infinitely rather (he protested) shed his own to protect the colony from injury. He nominated proper officers for every department of the public service, and allotted to every man his particular station and business. This address was received with general applause and satisfaction ; and the factious humors of the people seemed readily and entirely to subside beneath the dignity and the prudent and resolute policy of Lord Delaware's administration. The deference which had been reluctantly extorted by the superior talent and genius of Smith was more willingly yielded to claims of superior birth and hereditary elevation, more palpable to the apprehension, and less offensive to the self-complacency, of the mass of mankind. By an assiduous attention to his duty, and a happy union of qualities fitted equally to inspire esteem and command submission, Lord Delaware succeeded in maintaining peace and good order within the settlement, in awakening a spirit of industry and alacrity among the colonists, and in again impressing the dread and reverence of the English name on the minds of the Indians. This promising beginning was all that he was permitted to accomplish. Oppressed by disease occasioned by the climate, he was compelled to quit the country ; having first committed the administration of his authority to George Percy.[1]

The restoration of Percy [March, 1611] to the official dignity which he had once before enjoyed was attended with the same relaxation of discipline, and would probably have issued in a repetition of the same disorders that so fatally distinguished his former presidency. But, happily for the colony, a squadron that had been despatched from England, before Lord Delaware's return, with a supply of men and provisions, brought also with it Sir Thomas Dale, whose commission authorized him, in the absence of that nobleman, to assume the chief command. [May, 1611.] This new governor found the colonists fast relapsing into idleness and penury ; and though he exerted himself strenuously, and not unsuccessfully, to restore better habits, yet the loss of Lord Delaware's imposing rank and authoritative character was sensibly felt. What Dale could not accomplish by milder means, he was soon enabled to produce by a system of notable rigor and severity. A code of rules had been compiled by Sir Thomas Smith, the treasurer of the com-

---

[1] Stith. Lord Delaware's *Discourse, apud* Smith.

F

pany of patentees, from the martial law of the Low Countries, the most severe and arbitrary frame of discipline then subsisting in the world; and having been printed by the compiler for the use of the colony, but without the sanction or authority of the council, was transmitted by him to the governor.[1] This code did not long remain inoperative. Dale caused it to be proclaimed as the established law of the colony; and some conspiracies having broken out, he administered its provisions with great rigor, but not greater than was judged by all who witnessed it to have been requisite for the general safety. The wisdom and honor of the governor, who thus became the first depositary of those formidable powers, and the salutary consequences that resulted from the first exercise of them, prevented the alarm which the introduction of a system so arbitrary and despotic was calculated to provoke. Dale was succeeded in the supreme command by Sir Thomas Gates [August, 1611], who arrived with six vessels, containing a powerful reinforcement to the numbers and resources of the colonists. The late and the present governor were united by mutual friendship and similarity of character. Gates approved and pursued the system of strict discipline, and steady, but moderate, execution of the martial code introduced by Dale; and under the directions of Dale, who remained in the country and cheerfully occupied a subordinate station, various detached parties of the colonists began to form additional settlements on the banks of James River, and at some distance from Jamestown.[2]

An application was now made by the company of patentees to the king, for an enlargement of their territory and jurisdiction. The accounts they received from the persons who were shipwrecked on Bermudas, of the fertility and convenience of this region, impressed them with the desire of obtaining possession of its resources for the benefit of Virginia.[3] Their request was granted without difficulty; and a new charter was issued [March, 1612], investing them with all the islands situated within three hundred leagues of the Virginian coast. Some innovations were made, at the same time, in the structure and forms of the corporation; the term of exemption from customs was prolonged; the company was empowered to apprehend and remand persons deserting the settlement, in violation of their engagements; and in order to promote the advancement of the colony and the reimbursement of the large sums that had been expended on it, license was granted to open lotteries in any part of England. The lottery which was established in virtue of this license was the first institution of the kind that ever received public countenance in England; it brought twenty-nine thousand pounds into the treasury of the company, but loaded this body with the reproach of defrauding the English people and corrupting their manners. The House of Commons remonstrated against the permission of the lottery, as a measure equally unconstitutional and impolitic; and the license was shortly after recalled. Happy if their example had been sooner copied by after ages, and the rulers of mankind restrained from polluting their financial administration by a system of chicane, promoting in their subjects those gambling

---

[1] Stith. Nothing can be more fanciful or erroneous than Dr. Robertson's account of the introduction of this system, which, without the slightest authority, he ascribes to the advice of Lord Bacon, and, in opposition to all evidence, represents as the act of the company. See Note III., at the end of the volume.

[2] Smith. Stith.

[3] Stith. About this time, the patentees promoted a subscription among devout persons in London for building churches in the colony; but the money was diverted to other purposes; and it was not till some years after, that churches were built in Virginia. Oldmixon.

tastes and habits which dissolve industry and virtue and frequently beget even the most atrocious crimes ! Notwithstanding the eagerness of the company to acquire the Bermuda Islands, they did not long retain this territory, but sold it to a junto of their own associates, who were united by royal charter into a separate corporation, named the Somer Islands Company.[1]

The colony of Virginia had once been saved, in the person of its own deliverer, Captain Smith, by Pocahontas, the daughter of the Indian king, Powhatan. This princess maintained ever since a friendly intercourse with the English, and was destined now again to render them a service of the highest importance. A scarcity prevailing at Jamestown, and supplies being obtained but scantily and irregularly from the neighbouring Indians, with whom the colonists were often embroiled, Captain Argal was despatched to the shores of the river Potomac in quest of a cargo of corn. Here he learned that Pocahontas was living in retirement at no great distance from him ; and hoping, by possession of her person, to obtain such an ascendant over Powhatan as would insure an ample contribution of provisions, he prevailed on her, by some artifice, to come on board his vessel, and then set sail with her to Jamestown, where she was detained in captivity, though treated with ceremonious respect. But Powhatan, (who, like many Indian chiefs, though devoid of steady, generous wisdom, yet possessed a wild, uncultivated virtue,) more indignant at such treachery than subdued by his misfortune, rejected with scorn the demand of a ransom ; he even refused to hold any communication with the pirates who still kept his daughter a prisoner ;[2] declaring, nevertheless, that, if she were restored to him, he would forget the injury, and, feeling himself at liberty to regard the authors of it as friends, would gratify all their wishes. The colonists, however, were too conscious of not deserving the performance of such promises, to be able to give credit to them ; and the most injurious consequences seemed likely to arise from an unjust detention, which they could no longer continue with advantage, nor relinquish with safety, — when, behold ! all at once the aspect of affairs underwent a happy and surprising change. During her residence in the colony, Pocahontas, whose pleasing manners and other personal attractions have been celebrated with warm commendation, gained the affections of a young man named Rolfe, a person of rank and estimation among the planters, who offered her his hand, and, with her approbation and the cordial encouragement of the governor, solicited the consent of Powhatan to their marriage. This the old prince readily bestowed, and despatched certain of his relatives to attend the ceremonial, which was performed with extraordinary pomp [April, 1613], and laid the foundation of a firm and sincere friendship between his tribe and the English. This fortunate event also enabled the provincial government to conclude a treaty with the Chickahominies, a horde distinguished by their bravery and their military experience, who consented to acknowledge themselves subjects of the British monarch, and to style themselves henceforward Englishmen, — to assist the colonists with their arms in war, and to pay an annual tribute of Indian corn.

But a material change, which now took place in the social structure of

---

[1] Stith. Chalmer's *Annals.*
[2] He would not deem
" The soil of her fair rape
Wiped off in honorable keeping her."
Shakspeare.

the colony, contributed to fix its prosperity on foundations more solid and respectable than the alliance or dependence of the Indian tribes. The industry, which had been barely kept alive by the severe discipline of martial law, languished under the discouraging influence of that community of property and acquisition which was introduced, as we have seen, by the provisions of the original charter. As a temporary expedient, this system could not have been easily avoided; and the censure which historians have so readily bestowed on its introduction seems to be far from reasonable. The real impolicy consisted in prolonging its duration beyond the time when the colony acquired stability, when modes and habits of life were fixed, and when, the resources of the territory and the productive powers of labor being fully understood, the government might safely and beneficially have remitted every individual to the stimulus of his own interest and dependence on his own exertions. But in the outset, it was necessary, or at least highly expedient, that the government should charge itself with the support of its subjects and the regulation of their industry; and that their first experimental exertions should be referred and adapted to the principle and governance of a system of partnership. How long such a system may endure, when originated and maintained by a strong and general impulse of that Christian spirit which directs every man to regard his office on earth as a trust, his life as a stewardship, and the superiority of his faculties and advantages as designating, not the enlargement of his privileges, but the extent of his responsibility, is a problem to be solved by the future history of mankind. But as a permanent arrangement, supported only by municipal law, it attempts an impossibility, and commits its practical administration to an influence destructive of its own principles. As soon as the sense of individual interest and security begins to dissolve the bond of common hazard, danger, and difficulty, the law is felt to be an irksome and injurious restriction; but as in theory it retains a generous aspect, and the first symptoms of its practical inconvenience are the idleness and immorality promoted by its secret suggestions, it is not surprising that rulers should seek to remove the effect, while they preserve the cause, and even by additional severities of regulation extinguish every remains of the virtue which they vainly attempt to rekindle.

Sir Thomas Dale, by his descent from the supreme direction of affairs to a more active participation in the conduct of them, was enabled to discern with accurate and unprejudiced observation the influence of the provincial laws on the dispositions of the colonists; and soon discovered the violent repugnance between a system which enforced community of property, and all the ordinary motives by which human industry is sustained. He saw that every one was eager to evade or abridge his own share of labor; that the universal reliance on the common stock impaired, universally, the diligence and activity on which the accumulation of that stock depended; that the slothful trusted to the exertions of the industrious, while the industrious were deprived of alacrity by impatience of supporting and confirming the slothful in their idleness; and that the most conscientious citizen would hardly perform as much labor for the community in a week as he would for himself in a day. Under Dale's direction, the evil was redressed by a radical and effectual remedy: a sufficient portion of land was divided into lots, and one of them was appropriated to every settler. From that moment, industry, freed from the obstruction that had relaxed its incitements and intercepted its recompense, took vigorous root in Virginia, and the prosperity of the colony experienced a steady and rapid advancement.[1] Gates returning to England [1614], the supreme direction again devolved on Sir Thomas Dale, whose virtue seems never to have enlarged with the extension of his authority. He retained for two years longer the governance of the colony, and in his domestic administration continued to promote its real welfare ; but he launched into foreign operations little productive of advantage, and still less of honor. In Captain Argal, the author of the flagitious but fortunate abduction of Pocahontas, he found a fit instrument, and perhaps a counsellor, of designs of a similar character.

The French settlers in Acadia had, in the year 1605, built Port Royal, in the Bay of Fundy, and ever since retained quiet possession of the adjacent country, and successfully cultivated a friendly intercourse with the neighbouring Indians. Under the pretext, that the French, by settling in Acadia, invaded the rights which the English derived from prior discovery of the continent, was Argal despatched, in a season of profound peace, to make a hostile attack on Port Royal. Nothing could be more unjust or unwarranted than this enterprise. The Virginian charters, with the protection of which alone Sir Thomas Dale was intrusted, did not embrace the territory which he now presumed to invade, and which the French had peaceably possessed for nearly ten years in virtue of charters from their sovereign, Henry the Fourth. Argal easily succeeded in surprising and plundering a community totally unsuspicious of hostility and unprepared for defence ; but as he established no garrison in the place, the French soon resumed their station ;[2] and the expedition produced no other permanent effect than the indignant recollections it left in the minds of the French, and the unfavorable impression it produced on the Indians. Returning from this expedition, Argal undertook and achieved a similar enterprise against New York, which was then in possession of the Dutch, whose claim was derived from Captain Hudson's visit to the territory in 1609, when he commanded one of their vessels, and was employed in their service. Argal, however, maintained, that, as Hudson was an Englishman by birth, the benefit of his discovery accrued by indefeasible right to his native country ; and the Dutch governor, being unprepared for resistance, was compelled to submit, and declare the colony a dependency of England, and tributary to Virginia. But another governor arriving shortly after, with better means of asserting the title of his countrymen, the concession was retracted, and the English claim successfully defied.[3]

One of the first objects which engaged the increasing industry of the colonists was the cultivation of tobacco, a commodity now for the first time introduced into the commerce of Virginia. [1615.] King James had conceived a strong antipathy to the use of this herb, and in his celebrated treatise, entitled *Counterblast against Tobacco*, endeavoured to prevail over one of the strongest appetites of human nature by the force of pedantic fustian, and reasoning as ridiculous as the title of his performance. The issue of the contest corresponded better with his interests than with his wishes ; his testimony, though pressed with all the vehemence of exalted

---

[1] Smith. Stith.

[2] Stith. Escarbot's *History of New France.* Purchas. Argal's piratical attack on Port Royal was revenged by the French on Captain Smith in the following year. See Book II. Chap. I. *post.*

[3] Stith. See the *History of New York*, in Book V. *post.*

folly, could not prevail with his subjects over the solicitation and evidence of their own senses ; and though he summoned his prerogative to the aid of his logic, and guarded the soil of England from pollution by forbidding the domestic culture of tobacco, he found it impossible to withstand its importation from abroad ; the demand for it continually extended, and its value and consumption daily increased in England. Incited by the hopes of sharing a trade so profitable, the colonists of Virginia devoted their fields and labor almost exclusively to the production of this commodity. Sir Thomas Dale, observing their inconsiderate ardor, and sensible of the danger of neglecting the cultivation of the humbler but more necessary productions on which the subsistence of the colony depended, interposed his authority to check the excesses of the planters ; and adjusted by law the proportion between the corn crop and the tobacco crop of every proprietor of land. But after his departure [1616], his wise policy was forgotten, and his regulations disregarded ; and the culture of tobacco so exclusively occupied the attention of the settlers, that even the streets of Jamestown were planted with it, and a scarcity of provisions very soon resulted. The colonists, unable to devise any better remedy for this evil than the renewal of exactions from the Indians, involved themselves in disputes and hostilities which gradually alienated the regards of these savages, and paved the way to one of those schemes of vengeance which they are noted for forming with impenetrable secrecy, maturing with consummate artifice and executing with unrelenting ferocity.[1] This fatal effect was not experienced till after the lapse of one of those intervals which to careless eyes seem to disconnect the misconduct from the sufferings of nations, but impress reflective minds with an awful conception of that strong, unbroken chain, which, subsisting unimpaired by time or distance, preserves and extends the moral consequences of human actions.

But a nobler produce than any that her physical soil could supply was to grace the dawn of civilization in Virginia ; and we are now to contemplate the first indication of that active principle of liberty which was destined to obtain the most signal development from the progress of American society. When Sir Thomas Dale returned to England, he committed the government of the province to George Yeardley, whose lax administration, if it removed a useful restraint on the improvident cupidity of the planters, enabled them to taste, and prepared them to value, the dignity of independence and the advantages of freedom. He was succeeded [1617[2]] by Captain Argal, a man of considerable talent and activity, but sordid, haughty, and tyrannical. Argal provided with ability for the wants of the colony, and introduced some politic regulations of the traffic and intercourse with the Indians ; but he

[1] Smith. Stith. Purchas. In the year 1615, was published at London *A true Discourse of the present State of Virginia*, by Ralph Hamor, Secretary to the Colony ; a tract which has no other merit but its rarity.

[2] In the present year died Pocahontas. She had accompanied her husband on a visit to England, where her history excited much interest, and the grace and dignity of her manners no less respect and admiration. Captain Smith introduced her to the queen, and her society was courted by the most eminent of the nobility. But the mean soul of the king regarded her with jealousy ; and he expressed alternate murmurs at Rolfe's presumption in marrying a princess, and alarm at the title that this planter's posterity might acquire to the sovereignty of Virginia. Pocahontas died in the faith, and with the sentiments and demeanour, of a Christian. Smith. Stith. She left a son by Rolfe, whose posterity, says a modern historian of Virginia, " are not unworthy of their royal ancestry." Campbell. An American writer, in 1787, remarks, that the descendants of Rolfe and Pocahontas had then lost all the exterior characteristics of their Indian origin. Dr. Smith's *Essay on the Causes of the Variety of Complexion and Figure in the Human Species.*

cramped the liberty of the people by minute and vexatious restrictions, and enforced a practical conformity to them by harsh and constant exercise of martial law.   While he affected to promote piety in others by punishing absence from ecclesiastical ordinances with a temporary servitude, he postponed, in his own personal practice, every other consideration to the acquisition of wealth, which he greedily pursued by a profligate abuse of the opportunities of his office, and defended by the terrors of despotic authority. Universal discontent was excited by his administration ; and the complaints of the colonists at length reached the ears of the company in England. Lord Delaware, who had always been the zealous friend and advocate of the colonists, now consented, for their deliverance, to resume his former office, and again to undertake the direction of their affairs.   He embarked for Virginia [1618] with a splendid train, but died on the voyage.   His loss was deeply lamented by the colonists.   Yet it was, perhaps, an advantageous circumstance for them, that an administration invested with so much pomp and dignity was thus seasonably intercepted, and the improvement of their affairs committed to men whose rank and manners were nearer the level of their own condition ; and it was no less advantageous to the memory of Lord Delaware, that he died in the demonstration of a generous willingness to attempt what he would most probably have been unable to accomplish.   The tidings of his death were followed to England by increasing complaints of the odious and tyrannical proceedings of Argal ; and the company having conferred the office of Captain-General on Yeardley [April, 1619], this new governor received the honor of knighthood, and repaired to the scene of his administration.[1]

Sir George Yeardley, on his arrival in Virginia, perceived at a single glance that it was impossible to compose the prevalent jealousy of arbitrary power and impatience for liberty, or to conduct his own administration in a satisfactory manner, without reinstating the colonists in full possession of the rights of Englishmen ; and accordingly, to their inexpressible joy, he promptly signified his intention of convoking a provincial assembly, framed with all possible analogy to the parliament of the parent state.   This first representative legislature that America ever beheld consisted of the governor, the council, and a number of burgesses, elected by the seven existing boroughs, who, assembling at Jamestown, in one chamber, discussed all matters that concerned the general welfare, and conducted their deliberations with good sense, moderation, and harmony.   The laws which they enacted were transmitted to England for the approbation of the treasurer and company, and are no longer extant ; but it is asserted by competent judges, that they were, in the main, wisely and judiciously framed, though (as might reasonably be expected) somewhat intricate and unsystematical.[2]   The company soon after passed an ordinance by which they substantially approved and ratified the platform of the Virginian legislature.   They reserved, however, to themselves the nomination of a council of state, which should assist the governor with advice in the executive administration, and should also form a part of the legislative assembly ; and they provided, on the one hand,

[1] Smith. Stith.
[2] Rolfe, *apud* Smith. Stith. The assembly, when they transmitted their own ordinances to England, requested the general court to prepare a digest for Virginia of the laws of England, and to procure for it the sanction of the king's approbation, adding, " that it was not fit that his subjects should be governed by any other rules than such as received their influence from him."   Chalmers.

that the decrees of the assembly should not have the force of law till sanctioned by the court of proprietors in England ; and conceded, on the other hand, that the orders of this court should have no force in Virginia till ratified by the provincial assembly.[1]   Thus early was planted in America that representative system which forms the soundest political frame wherein the spirit of liberty was ever embodied, and at once the safest and most efficient organ by which its energies are exercised and developed.   So strongly imbued were the minds of Englishmen in this age with those generous principles which were rapidly advancing to a first manhood in their native country, that, wherever they settled themselves, the institutions of freedom took root and grew up along with them.

It had been happy for the morals and the welfare of Virginia, if her inhabitants, like their countrymen in Massachusetts, had oftener elevated their eye from subordinate agency to the great First Cause, and had referred, in particular, the signal blessing that was now bestowed on them to the will and bounty of God.   Liberty, so derived, acquires at once its firmest and noblest basis ; it becomes respected as well as beloved ; the dignity of the origin to which it is referred influences the ends to which it is rendered instrumental ; and all men are taught to feel that it can neither be violated nor abused without provoking the divine displeasure.   It is this preservative principle alone, which, recognizing in the abundance of divine goodness the extent of the divine claims, prevents the choicest blessings and most admirable talents from cherishing in human hearts an ungrateful and counteracting spirit of insolence and pride, — a spirit which led the Virginians too soon to plant the rankest weeds of tyrannic injustice in that field where the seeds of liberty had been so happily sown.

The company of patentees had received orders from the king to transport to Virginia a hundred idle, dissolute persons who were in prison for various misdemeanours in London.[2]   These men were dispersed through the province as servants to the planters ; and the degradation of the provincial character and manners, produced by such social intermixture, was overlooked, in consideration of the advantage that was expected from so many additional and unpaid laborers.   Having once associated felons with their pursuits, and committed the cultivation of their fields to servile and depraved hands, the colonists were prepared to yield to the temptation which speedily presented itself, and to blend, in barbarous combination, the character of oppressors with the claims and condition of freemen.   A Dutch ship, from the coast of Guinea, arriving in James River, sold to the planters a part of her cargo of negroes ;[3] and as this hardy race was found more capable of enduring fatigue in a sultry climate than Europeans, the number was increased by continual importation, till a large proportion of the inhabitants of Virginia was composed of men degraded to a state of slavery by the selfishness and ungrateful barbarity of others, who, embracing the gifts without imbibing the beneficence of their Creator, turned into a scene of bondage for their fellows the territory that had proved a seat of liberty and happiness to themselves.

---

[1] Stith.   Hazard.
[2] Stith.   Captain Smith relates, that, since his departure from the colony, the number of felons and vagabonds transported to Virginia brought such evil report on the place, " that some did choose to be hanged ere they would go thither, *and were.*"   " This custom," says Stith, " hath laid one of the finest countries in America under the unjust scandal of being another Siberia, fit only for the reception of malefactors and the vilest of the people."
[3] Beverly, *History of Virginia.*

Another addition, at this epoch [1620], more productive of virtue and felicity, was made to the number of the colonists. Few women had as yet ventured to cross the Atlantic ; and the English, restrained by the pride and rigidity of their character from that incorporation with the native Americans, which the French and Portuguese have found so conducive to their interests and so accordant with the pliancy of their manners, were generally destitute of the comforts and connections of married life. Men so situated could not regard Virginia as a permanent residence, and must have generally entertained the purpose of returning to their native country after amassing as expeditiously as possible a competency of wealth. Such views are inconsistent with patient industry, and with those extended interests that produce or support patriotism ; and in conformity with the more liberal policy which the company now began to pursue towards the colony, it was proposed to send out a hundred young women of agreeable persons and respectable characters, as wives for the settlers. Ninety were sent ; and the speculation proved so profitable to the company, that a repetition of it was suggested by the emptiness of their exchequer in the following year [1621], when sixty more were collected and transported. They were immediately disposed of to the young planters, and produced such an accession of happiness to the colony, that the second consignment fetched a larger profit than the first. The price of a wife was estimated first at a hundred and twenty, and afterwards at a hundred and fifty pounds of tobacco, which was then sold at three shillings per pound. The young women were not only bought with avidity, but received with such fondness, and so comfortably established, that others were invited to follow their example ; and virtuous sentiments and provident habits spreading consequently among the planters enlarged the happiness and prosperity of the colony.[1] To the blessings of marriage naturally succeeded some provision for the benefits of education. A sum of money was collected by the English bishops, by direction of the king, for the maintenance of an institution in Virginia for the Christian education of Indian children ; and in emulation of this good example, various steps were taken by the chartered company towards the foundation of a provincial college, which was afterwards completed in the reign of William and Mary.

It is remarkable that the rise of civil liberty in North America was nearly coeval with the first dispute between her inhabitants and the government of the mother country. With the increasing industry of the colony, the produce of its tobacco fields became more than sufficient for the supply of England, where, also, its disposal was vexatiously restricted by the wavering and arbitrary policy of the king, in granting monopolies for the sale of it, in limiting the quantities permitted to be imported, in appointing commissioners " for garbling the drug called tobacco," with arbitrary powers to confiscate whatever portions of it they might consider of base quality, in loading the importation with a heavy duty, and at the same time encouraging the import of tobacco from Spain. The company, harassed by these absurd and iniquitous restraints, opened a trade with Holland, and established warehouses in that country, to which they sent their tobacco directly from

---

[1] Stith. This interesting branch of traffic appears to have subsisted for many years, during which its seeming indelicacy was qualified as far as possible by the nice attention that was paid to the ascertainment of the moral character of every woman aspiring to become a Virginian matron. In the year 1632, by an order of the provincial council, two young women, who had been seduced during their passage from England, were ordered to be sent back, as " unworthy to propagate the race of Virginians." Burk's *History of Virginia*.

Virginia ; but the king interposed to prohibit such evasion of his revenue, and directed that all the Virginian tobacco should be brought in the first instance to England. A lengthened and acrimonious dispute arose between this feeble prince and the colonists and colonial corporation. Against the monopoly established in England, they petitioned the House of Commons ; and in support of their practice of trading directly with Holland, they contended for the general right of Englishmen to carry their commodities to the best market they could find, and pleaded the special concessions of their own charter, which expressly conferred on them unlimited liberty of commerce. At length, the dispute was adjusted by a compromise, by which the company obtained, on the one hand, the exclusive right of importing tobacco into the kingdom, and engaged, on the other, to pay an import duty of ninepence per pound, and to send all the tobacco produce of Virginia to England.[1]

But a cloud had been for some time gathering over the colony ; and even the circumstances that were supposed most forcibly to betoken the prosperity of its inhabitants were provoking the storm to burst with more destructive violence on their heads. [1622.] At peace with the Indians, unapprehensive of danger, and wholly engrossed with the profitable cultivation of a fertile territory, their increasing numbers had spread so extensively over the province, that no fewer than eighty settlements were already formed ; and every planter being guided only by his own peculiar taste or convenience in the choice of his dwelling, and more disposed to shun than to court the neighbourhood of his countrymen, the settlements were universally straggling and uncompact.[2] In the Scriptures, which the colonists received as their rule of faith, they might have found ample testimony to the cruelty and treachery of mankind in their natural state ; and from their own experience they might have derived the strongest assurance that the savages, by whom they were surrounded, could claim no exemption from this testimony of divine wisdom and truth. Yet the pious labors by which the evil dispositions of the Indians might have been corrected, and the military exercises and precautions by which their hostility might have been overawed or repelled, were equally neglected by the English settlers ; who, moreover, contributed to foster the martial habits of the Indians by employing them as hunters, and enlarged their resources of destruction by furnishing them with firearms, which they very soon learned to use with dexterity.

The marriage of the planter Rolfe to the Indian princess did not produce as lasting a friendship between the English and the Indians as at first it seemed to portend. The Indians eagerly courted a repetition of such intermarriages, and were painfully stung by the disdain with which the English receded from their advances and declined to become the husbands of Indian women.[3] The colonists forgot that they had inflicted this mortification ; but it was remembered by the Indians, who sacredly embalmed the memory of every affront in lasting, stern, silent, and implacable resentment. Earnest recommendations were repeatedly transmitted from England to attempt the conversion of the savages ; but these recommendations were not promoted by a sufficient attention to the means requisite for their accomplishment. Yet neither were they entirely neglected by the colonists. Some attempts at conversion were made by a few pious individuals, and the success of one of them undoubtedly mitigated the calamity that was impending ;

---

[1] Stith.   [2] Smith.   [3] Beverly.

but these efforts were feeble and partial, and the majority of the colonists had contented themselves with cultivating a friendly acquaintance with the Indians, who were admitted at all times into their habitations, and encouraged to consider themselves as welcome and familiar guests.[1]

It was in the midst of this free and unguarded intercourse, that the Indians formed, with deliberate and unrelenting ferocity, the project of a general massacre of the English, which devoted every man, woman, and child in the colony to indiscriminate destruction. On the death of Powhatan, in 1618, the power of executing a scheme so daring and sanguinary devolved on a man fully capable of contriving and conducting it. Opechancanough,[2] who succeeded to the supremacy over Powhatan's tribe, and possessed extensive influence over all the neighbouring tribes of Indians, was distinguished by his ferocious bravery, his profound dissimulation, and a rancorous hatred and jealousy of the European colonists of America. He renewed the pacific treaty which Powhatan had concluded with the English after the marriage of his daughter to Rolfe ; and he availed himself of the security into which it lulled the objects of his guile, to prepare, during the four ensuing years, his friends and followers for the several parts they were to act in the tragedy which he contemplated. The tribes in the neighbourhood of the English, except those on the eastern shore, whom, on account of their peculiar friendship for the colonists, he did not venture to intrust with the design, were successively gained over ; and all coöperated with that singlemindedness and intensity of purpose characteristic of Indian conspiracy and revenge.

In a tribe of savage idolaters, the passions of men are left unpurified by the influence of religion, and unrestrained by a sound or elevated morality ; and human character is not subjected to that variety of impulse and impression which it undergoes in civilized society. The sentiments inculcated and the dispositions contracted in the family and in the tribe, in domestic education and in public life, in all the scenes through which the savage passes from his cradle to his grave, are the same ; there is no contest of opposite principles or conflicting habits to dissipate his mind or weaken its determinations ; and the system of morals (if it may be so called) which he embraces being the offspring of wisdom and dispositions congenial to his own, a seeming dignity of character arises from the simple vigor and consistency of that conduct which his moral sentiments never disturb or reproach. The understanding, neither refined by variety of knowledge, nor elevated by the grandeur of its contemplations, instead of moderating the passions, becomes the abettor of their violence and the instrument of their gratification. Men in malice, but children in sense, it is in the direction of fraud and cunning that the intellectual faculties of savages are chiefly exercised ;

[1] Stith. To the remonstrances of certain of the colonists against their worship of demons, some of the Indians of Virginia answered that they believed in two great spirits, a good and an evil one ; that the first was a being sunk in the enjoyment of everlasting indolence and ease, who showered down blessings indiscriminately from the skies, leaving men to scramble for them as they chose, and totally indifferent to their concerns ; but that the second was an active, jealous spirit, whom they were obliged to propitiate, that he might not destroy them. Oldmixon.

[2] Stith. Opechancanough, in imitation of the English, had built himself a house, and was so delighted with the contrivance of a lock and key, that he used to spend whole hours in repetition of the experiment of locking and unlocking his door. Oldmixon. No European invention struck the Indians with greater surprise than a windmill ; they came from vast distances and continued for many days to gaze at a phenomenon which they ascribed to the agency of demons shut up within the edifice.

and so perfect is the harmony between their passions and their reflective powers, that the same delay which would mitigate the ferocity of more cultivated men serves but to harden their cruelty and mature the devices for its indulgence. Notwithstanding the long interval that elapsed between the formation and the execution of their present enterprise, and the continual intercourse that subsisted between them and the white people, the most impenetrable secrecy was preserved by the Indians; and so fearless, consummate, and inscrutable was their dissimulation, that they were accustomed to borrow boats from the English to cross the river, in order to concert and communicate the progress of their design.[1]

An incident, which, though minute, is too curious to be omitted, contributed to stimulate the malignity of the Indians by the sense of recent provocation. There was a man, belonging to one of the neighbouring tribes, called Nemattanow, who, by his courage, craft, and good fortune, had attained the highest repute among his countrymen. In the skirmishes and engagements which their former wars with the English produced, he had exposed his person with a bravery that commanded the esteem of his fellow-savages, and an impunity that excited their astonishment. They judged him invulnerable, whom so many dangers had vainly menaced; and the object of their admiration partook, or at least encouraged, the delusion which seemed to invest him with a character of sanctity. Opechancanough, the king, whether jealous of this man's reputation, or desirous of embroiling the English with the Indians, sent a message to the governor of the colony, to acquaint him that he was welcome to cut Nemattanow's throat. Such an indication of Indian character as this message afforded ought to have produced alarm and distrust in the minds of the English.

Though the offer of the king was disregarded, his wishes were not disappointed. Nemattanow, having murdered a planter, was shot by one of the servants of his victim, who attempted to arrest him. In the pangs of death, the pride, but not the vanity, of the savage was subdued, and he entreated his captors that they would never reveal that he had been slain by a bullet, and that they would bury him among the English, in order that the secret of his mortality might remain unknown to his countrymen. The request seems to infer the possibility of complying with it; and the colonists, by whom it was neglected, had cause to regret their imprudent disclosure of the fatal event. The Indians were filled with grief and indignation; and Opechancanough inflamed their anger by pretending to share it. Having counterfeited displeasure for the satisfaction of his subjects, he affected placability for the delusion of his enemies, and assured the English that the sky should sooner fall than the peace be broken by him. But the plot meanwhile advanced to maturity, and, at last, the day was fixed on which all the English settlements were at the same instant to be attacked. The respective stations of the various troops of assassins were assigned to them; and that they might be enabled to occupy their posts without awakening suspicion, some carried presents of fish and game into the interior of the colony, and others presented themselves as guests soliciting the hospitality of their English friends, on the evening before the massacre. As the fatal hour drew nigh, the rest, under various pretences, and with every demonstration of kind and peaceful intent, assembled around the detached and unfortified settlements of the colonists; and not a sentiment of compunction,

---

[1] Stith.

not a rash expression of hate, nor an unguarded look of exultation, had occurred to disconcert or disclose the purpose of their well disciplined ferocity.

The universal destruction of the colonists seemed unavoidable, and was prevented only by the consequences of an event, which, perhaps, at the time when it came to pass, appeared but of little importance in the colony, — the conversion of an Indian to the Christian faith. On the night before the massacre, this man was made privy to it by his own brother, who communicated to him the command of his king and his countrymen to share in the exploit that would enrich their race with spoil, revenge, and glory. A summons of such tenor was well calculated to prevail with a savage mind ; but a new mind had been given to this convert, and, as soon as his brother left him, he revealed the secret to an English gentleman in whose house he was residing. This planter immediately carried the tidings to Jamestown, from whence the alarm was communicated to the inhabitants of the nearest settlements barely in time to prevent the last hour of the perfidious truce from being the last hour of their lives.

But the intelligence came too late to be more generally available. At mid-day [March 22, 1622], the moment they had previously fixed for this execrable deed, the Indians, raising a hideous yell, rushed at once on the English in all their scattered settlements, and butchered men, women, and children with undistinguishing fury, and every aggravation of brutal outrage and enormous cruelty. In one hour, three hundred and forty-seven persons were cut off, almost without knowing by whose hands they fell. The slaughter would have been still greater, if the English, even in some of those districts where no prior intimation of the danger was received, had not flown to their arms with the energy of despair, and defended themselves so bravely as to repulse the assailants, who almost universally displayed a cowardice proportioned to their malignity, and fled at the sight of weapons in the hands even of the women and boys, whom, unarmed, they were willing to attack and destroy.[1]

The colony received a wound no less deep and dangerous than painful and alarming. Six of the members of council, and several of the wealthiest and most respectable inhabitants, were among the slain ; at some of the settlements, the whole of their population had been exterminated ; at others, a remnant escaped the general destruction by the efforts of despair ; and the survivors were impoverished, terrified, and confounded by a stroke that at once bereaved them of friends and fortune, and showed that they were surrounded by legions of foes, whose enmity was equally furious and unaccountable, and whose treachery and ferocity seemed to proclaim them a race of fiends rather than men.[2] To the massacre succeeded a vindictive and exterminating war between the English and the Indians ; and the colonists were at last provoked to retaliate, in some degree, the fraudful guile and indiscriminate butchery to which they found themselves exposed from their savage adversaries. But though a dire necessity was thought to justify or palliate such proceedings, yet the warfare of the colonists was never wholly divested of honor and magnanimity. During this disastrous period, the

---

[1] Smith. Stith.

[2] It was long before the British colonists were properly on their guard against the ferocity of a race of men capable of such consummate treachery, and who " in anger were not, like the English, talkative and boisterous, but sullen and revengeful." Trumbull's *History of Connecticut.*

design that had been entertained of erecting a provincial college, and various other public institutions, was abandoned ; the number of the settlements was reduced from eighty to six ; and an afflicting dearth of food was added to the horrors of war.[1]

When the tidings of this calamity arrived in England, they excited, along with much disapprobation of the defective policy and inefficient precautions of the company of patentees, a lively sympathy with the danger and distress of the colonists. By order of the king, a supply of arms from the Tower was delivered to the treasurer of the company ; and vessels were despatched to Virginia with cargoes of such articles as were supposed to be most urgently needed by the planters. Captain Smith submitted to the company the project of an enterprise, which he offered to conduct, for the deliverance of the colony by the expulsion or subjugation of all the Indian tribes within the limits of its territory ; but, though generally approved, this proposition was not embraced. By dint of the exertions which they made in their own behalf, and with the assistance of the supplies that were actually sent to them from England, the colonists were barely saved from perishing with hunger ; and it was not till after a severe and protracted struggle that they were enabled again to resume their prosperous attitude and extend their settlements.

More ample supplies and more active assistance would have been afforded to the colonists from England, but for the dissensions among the associated patentees, which had been spreading for a considerable period, and at this juncture attained a height that portended the dissolution of the corporation. The company was now a numerous body ; and being composed of able and enterprising men, drawn from every class in society, it presented a faithful abstract of the state of political feeling in the nation ; while its frequent courts or convocations afforded a convenient arena in which the parties tried their strength, and a conspicuous organ by which the prevailing sentiments were publicly expressed. At every meeting, the transaction of business was impeded by the intrigues of rival factions, and the debates were inflamed and protracted by their mutual altercations. At every election, the offices of the company were courted and contested by the most eminent persons in the state. [1623.] The controversy between the court party and the country party, that was spreading through the nation, was the more readily insinuated into those assemblies from the infrequency and irregularity of its more legitimate theatre, the parliament ; and various circumstances in the history of the company tended to nourish and extend this source of disagreement. Many of the proprietors, dissatisfied with the slender pecuniary returns that the colony afforded, were disposed to blame the existing officers and administration for the disappointment of their hopes ; not a few resented the procurement of the third charter, the exclusion of Captain Smith from the direction which he had shown himself so well qualified to exercise, and the insignificance to which they were themselves condemned by the arbitrary multiplication of their associates ; and a small but

---

[1] Stith. As far as I am able to discover, the retaliatory deceit practised by the colonists in their hostilities with the Indians has been greatly overrated. Stith seems to have mistaken expressions of indignation for deliberate designs; and Dr. Robertson has extended the error by mistaking purposes for the execution they never attained. The contemplation, and especially the endurance, of cruelty tends to make men cruel; yet, to the honor of the colonists, be it remembered, that, even during the prevalence of these hostilities, a deliberate attempt to cozen and subjugate a body of Indians was punished by the provincial magistrates, as an offence against the law of God and against national faith and honor. Stith.

active and intriguing party, who had labored with earnest though unsuccessful rapacity to engross the offices of the company, to usurp the direction of
its affairs, and to convert the colonial trade into their own private patrimony
by monopolies which they bought from needy courtiers, naturally ranged
themselves on the side of the court, and by their complaints and misrepresentations to the king and privy council, sought to interest them in the
quarrels, and infect them with suspicions of the corporation.[1]

At the head of this least numerous, but most dangerous, faction was the
notorious Captain Argal, who continued to display a rancorous enmity to
the liberty of Virginia, and hoped to compass by intrigue and servility at
home the same objects which he had pursued by tyranny and violence
abroad.   Sir Thomas Smith, too, the treasurer, whose predilection for arbitrary government we have already had occasion to remark, encouraged
every complaint and proposition that tended to abridge the privileges of
the colonial company, and give to its administration a less popular form.
The arbitrary changes which the charter had already undergone taught all
the malcontents to look up to the crown for such farther alterations as
might remove the existing obstructions to their wishes ; and the complete
ascendency which the country party acquired in the company strongly disposed the king to suppress or modify an institution that served to cherish
public spirit and disseminate liberal opinions.   " These Virginia courts,"
said Gondemar, the Spanish envoy, to him, " are but a seminary to a
seditious parliament." [2]   The hardihood which the company had displayed
in their late dispute with him concerning the restrictions of their tobacco
trade, the freedom with which his policy was canvassed in their deliberations, the firmness with which his measures were resisted, and the contempt
they had shown for the supremacy alike of his wisdom and his prerogative
in complaining to the House of Commons, eradicated from the mind of
James all that partiality to an institution of his own creation, that might
have sheltered it from the habitual dislike and suspicion with which he regarded the authority of a popular assembly.   But the same qualities that
rendered them odious caused them also to appear somewhat formidable,
and enforced some attention to equitable appearances, and deference to
public opinion, in wreaking his displeasure upon them.   The murmurs and
discontents, that were excited in England by the intelligence of the Indian
massacre, furnished him with an opportunity which he did not fail to
improve.

Having signalized his own concern for the misfortunes of the colony by
sending thither a quantity of military stores for defence against the Indians,
and by issuing his mandate to the company to despatch an ample supply of
provisions, he proceeded to institute an inquiry into the cause of the disaster.   A commission was addressed to certain of the English judges and
other persons of distinction [May, 1623], requiring them to examine the
transactions of the corporation since its first establishment ; to report to
the privy council the causes of the late disasters ; and to suggest the expedients most likely to prevent their recurrence.[3]   In order to obstruct the
efforts of the company for their own vindication, and to discover, if pos-

---

[1] Stith.

[2] So powerful were the leaders of the Virginia Company, that they could influence the election of members of parliament.   Under their auspices, the pious and accomplished Nicholas
Ferrar obtained about this time a seat in the House of Commons, where he distinguished himself by an active opposition to the court.   Bishop Turner's *Life of Ferrar.*

[3] Stith.

sible, additional matter of accusation against them, measures the most arbitrary and tyrannical were employed. All their charters, books, and papers were seized ; two of their principal officers were arrested ; and all letters from the colony intercepted and carried to the privy council. Among the witnesses whom the commissioners examined was Captain Smith, who might reasonably be supposed to entertain little favor for the existing constitution of the corporate body by which his career of honor and usefulness had been abridged, and who had recently sustained the mortification of seeing his offer to undertake the defence of the colony and subjugation of the Indians treated with thankless disregard, notwithstanding the approbation of a numerous party of the proprietors. Smith ascribed the misfortunes of the colony, and the slenderness of the income derived from it, to the neglect of military precautions ; the rapid succession of governors, which stimulated the rapacity of their dependents ; the multiplicity of public offices, by which industry was loaded and revenue absorbed ; and, in general, to the inability of a numerous body of men to conduct an undertaking so complex and arduous. He recommended the annexation of the colony and of all the jurisdiction over it to the crown, the introduction of greater simplicity and economy into the frame of its government, and an abandonment of the practice of transporting criminals to its shores.[1]

The commissioners did not communicate any of their transactions to the company, who first learned the tenor of the report in which they were so deeply interested from an order of the king and privy council [Oct. 1623], signifying to them that the misfortunes of Virginia had arisen from their misgovernment, and that, for the purpose of repairing them, his Majesty had determined to revoke the old charter and issue a new one, which should commit the powers of government to fewer hands. In order to quiet the minds of the colonists, it was declared, that private property would be respected, and that all past grants of land should remain inviolate. An instant surrender of their privileges was required from the company ; and, in default of their voluntary submission, they were assured that the king was prepared to carry his purpose into effect by process of law.[2]

This arbitrary mandate produced so much astonishment and consternation in the assembled court of proprietors, that a long and deep silence ensued on its communication. But, resuming their spirit, they prepared to defend their rights with a resolution, which, if it could not avert their fate, at least redeemed their character. They indignantly refused to sanction the stigma affixed to their conduct by the order of council, — to surrender the franchises which they had legally obtained, and on the faith of which they had expended large sums of money, — or to consent to the abolition of a popular frame of government, and deliver up their countrymen in Virginia to the dominion of a narrow junto wholly dependent on the pleasure of the king. In these sentiments they persisted, in spite of all the threats and promises by which their firmness was assailed ; and by a vote, which only the dissent of Captain Argal and seven of his adherents rendered not quite unanimous,

---

[1] Smith.

[2] Stith. It was in the midst of those distractions, says Stith, that the Muses for the first time opened their lips in North America. One of the earliest literary productions of the English colonists was a translation of Ovid's *Metamorphoses*, made in 1623 by George Sandys, treasurer of the Virginia Company. It was afterwards published in England, and dedicated to Charles the First. Stith terms it "a laudable performance for the times" ; and Dryden mentions the author with respect, in the preface to his own translations from Ovid.

they finally rejected the king's proposal, and declared their resolution to defend themselves against any process he might institute.

Incensed at their audacity in disputing his will, James directed a writ of *quo warranto* to be issued against the company, in order to try the validity of their charter in the Court of King's Bench. With the hope of collecting additional proofs of their maladministration, he despatched envoys to Virginia to inspect the condition of the colony, and attempt to form a party there opposed to the pretensions of the court of proprietors. The royal envoys, finding the provincial assembly embodied [Feb. 1624], endeavoured, with great artifice and magnificent promises of military aid, and of other marks of royal favor, to detach the members from their adherence to the company, and to procure an address to the king, expressive of " their willingness to submit to his princely pleasure in revoking the ancient patents." But their exertions were unsuccessful. The assembly transmitted a petition to the king, professing satisfaction to find themselves the objects of his especial care, beseeching him to continue the existing form of government, and soliciting, that, if the promised military force should be granted to them, it might be placed under the control of their own governor and house of representatives. The domestic legislation of this assembly was marked by the same good sense and patriotism that appeared in the reception which it gave to the propositions of the royal envoys. The governor was deprived of an arbitrary authority which he had hitherto exercised. It was ordained that he should no longer have power to withdraw the inhabitants from their private labors to his own service, and should levy no taxes but such as the provincial assembly should impose and appropriate. White women still were objects of great scarcity and value in the colony ; and to obviate an inconvenience that resulted from the ardor and frequency of amorous competition, a fine was now imposed on any woman who should encourage the matrimonial addresses of more than one man at a time. Various wise and judicious laws were enacted for the improvement of manners and the reformation of abuses, the support of divine worship, the security of civil and political freedom, and the regulation of traffic with the Indians.

Whether the suit between the king and the company was prosecuted to a judicial consummation or not is a point involved in some uncertainty, and truly of very little importance ; for the issue of a suit between the king and any of his subjects at that period could never be doubtful for a moment. Well aware of this, the company looked to protection more efficient than the ordinary administration of law could afford them, and presented a petition to the House of Commons, detailing a part of their grievances, and soliciting redress. Their application was entertained by the House so cordially, that, had it been sooner presented, it might have saved the corporation ; but they had deferred this last resource till so late a period of the session of parliament, that there was not time to enter on the wide inquiry which their complaints demanded ; and fearing to exasperate the king by preferring odious charges which they could not hope to substantiate, they confined their pleading before the House to the discouragement of their tobacco trade, which the Commons without hesitation pronounced a national grievance. They gained no other advantage from their complaint, nor from their limitation of it. The king, enraged at their presumption, and encouraged by their timidity, launched forth a proclamation [July, 1624], suppressing the courts of the company, and committing the temporary administration of the colonial affairs to certain of his privy counsellors, in conjunction with Sir Thomas Smith and a few other persons.[1] The Virginia Company was thus dissolved, and its rights and privileges reabsorbed by the crown.

James did not suffer the powers he had resumed to remain long unexercised. He issued a special commission [August, 1624], appointing a governor and twelve counsellors, to whom the direction of the affairs of the colony was intrusted. No mention was made in this instrument of a house of representatives ; a circumstance, which, coupled with the subsequent imposition of royal proclamations as legislative edicts, has led almost all the historians of Virginia into the mistaken belief, that the provincial assembly was abolished along with the mercantile corporation. The commission ascribes the disasters of the settlement to the popular shape of its late government, which intercepted and weakened the beneficial influence of the king's superior understanding ; and, in strains of the most vulgar and luscious self-complacency, prospectively celebrates the prosperity which the colony must infallibly attain, when blessed with the directer rays of royal wisdom. With this demonstration of hostility to the political liberties of the colonists, there was mingled some favorable attention to their commercial interests ; for, in consequence of the remonstrance of the English parliament [Sept. 1624], James renewed by proclamation his former prohibition of the culture of tobacco in England, and restricted the importation of this commodity to Virginia and the Somer Isles, and to vessels belonging to British subjects.[2]

This was James's last public act in relation to the colony ; for his intention of composing a code of laws for its domestic administration was frustrated by his death. [1625.] He died the first British sovereign of an established empire in America ; and thus closed a reign, of which the only illustrious feature was the colonization which he impelled or promoted. To this favorite object both the virtues and the vices of his character proved subservient. If the merit he might claim from his original patronage of the Virginian colonists be cancelled by his subsequent efforts to bereave them of their liberties ; and if his persecution of the Puritans in their native country be but feebly counterbalanced by his willingness to grant them an asylum in New England ; — his attempts to civilize Ireland by colonization connect him more honorably with the great events of his reign. Harassed by the turbulent and distracted state of Ireland, and averse to the sanguinary remedy of military operation, he endeavoured to impart a new character to its inhabitants by planting colonies of the English in the six northern counties of that island. He prosecuted this plan with so much wisdom and steadiness, as to cause, in the space of nine years, greater advances towards the reformation of Ireland than were made in the four hundred and forty years which had elapsed since the conquest of the country was first attempted, and laid the foundation of whatever affluence and security it has since been enabled to attain.[3] It is difficult to recognize the dogmatical oppressor of the Puritans, and the weak and arrogant tyrant of Virginia, in the wise and humane legislator of Ireland.

The fall of the Virginia Company excited the less concern, and the arbi-

[1] Rymer. Hazard.   [2] Ibid.
[3] Leland's *History of Ireland.* Hume's *History of England.*

trary measures of the king the less odium, in England, from the disappoint-ments and calamities with which the colonial plantation had been attended. More than a hundred and fifty thousand pounds [1] were already expended on this settlement, and upwards of nine thousand inhabitants had been sent to it from the mother country. Yet, at the dissolution of the company, the gross value of the annual imports from Virginia did not exceed twenty thousand pounds, and the population of the province was reduced to about eighteen hundred persons.[2] The effect of this unprosperous issue, in facili-tating the overthrow of the corporation, may be regarded as a fortunate cir-cumstance for Virginia ; for, however unjust and tyrannical were the views and conduct of the king, they were overruled to the production of a most important benefit to the colony, in the suppression of an institution which would have dangerously loaded and cramped its infant prosperity and free-dom. It is an observation of the most eminent teacher of political science, that, of all the expedients that could possibly be contrived to stunt the natural growth of a new colony, the institution of an exclusive company is the most effectual ; [3] and the observation is confirmed by the experience of history. In surveying the constitutions and tracing the progress of the various colo-nial establishments which the nations of Europe have successfully formed, we find a close and invariable connection between the decline and the revival of their prosperity and the ascendency and overthrow of sovereign mercantile corporations.

A sovereign company of merchants must ever consider their political power as an instrument of commercial gain, and as deriving its chief value from the means it gives them to repress competition, to buy cheaply the commodities they obtain from their subject customers, and to sell as dearly as possible the articles with which they supply them ; that is, to diminish the incitement and the reward of industry to the colonists, by restricting their powers and opportunities of acquiring what they need and disposing of what they have. The mercantile habits of the rulers prevail over their political interest, and lead them not only to prefer immediate profit to permanent revenue, but to adapt their administration to this policy, and render govern-ment subservient to the purposes of monopoly. They are almost necessa-rily led to devolve a large discretionary power on their provincial officers, over whom they retain at the same time but a feeble control. Whether we regard the introduction of martial law into Virginia as the act of the com-pany, or (as it really seems to have been) the unauthorized act of the treasurer and the provincial governors, the prevalence it obtained displays, in either case, the unjust and arbitrary policy of an exclusive company, or the inability of such a sovereign body to protect its subjects against the op-pression of its officers. How incapable an organ of this description must be to conduct a plan of civil policy on fixed and stable principles, and how strongly its system of government must tend to perpetual fluctuation, is at-tested by the fact, that, in the course of eighteen years, no fewer than ten successive governors had been appointed to preside over the province. Even after the vigorous spirit of liberty, which was so rapidly gaining ground in that age, had enabled the colonists to extort from the company the right of composing laws for the regulation of their own community, still, as the company's sanction was requisite to give legal prevalence to the enactments of the provincial legislature, the paramount authority resided with men who

---

[1] Smith.   [2] Chalmers's *Annals*.   [3] Smith's *Wealth of Nations*.

had but a temporary interest in the fate of their subjects and the resources of their territories. While, therefore, we sympathize with the generous indignation which the historians of America have expressed at the tyrannical measures by which the company was dissolved, we must regard with satisfaction an event, which, by its concomitant circumstances, inculcated an abhorrence of arbitrary power, and by its operation overthrew a system under which no colony has ever grown up to a vigorous maturity.

Charles the First inherited [March, 1625], with his father's throne, all the maxims that had latterly regulated his colonial policy. Of this he hastened to give assurance to his subjects by a series of proclamations, which he issued soon after his accession to the crown, and which distinctly unfolded the arbitrary principles which he entertained, and the tyrannical administration he intended to pursue. He declared, that, after mature deliberation, he had adopted his father's opinion, that the misfortunes of the colony were occasioned by the democratical frame of its civil constitution, and the incapacity of a mercantile company to conduct even the most insignificant affairs of state; that he held himself in honor engaged to accomplish the work that James had begun; that he considered the American colonies to be a part of the royal empire devolved to him with the other dominions of the crown; that he was fully resolved to establish a uniform course of government through the whole British monarchy; and that henceforward the entire administration of the Virginian government should be vested in a council nominated and directed by himself, and responsible to him alone. This unlimited arrogation of power has given rise to the common belief, that Charles deemed the provincial assembly already abolished; and the arbitrary manner in which the functions of this body were repeatedly superseded by exertions of royal prerogative in the earlier part of the present reign has induced the greater number of the historians of Virginia erroneously to suppose and relate, that no assembly was actually convoked in the province during that period. But in truth neither the king nor his father seems to have entertained the design of extirpating the popular branch of the constitution. Their object appears to have been to reduce it to what they conceived a due subordination to the supremacy of their own prerogative; and to vindicate and develope the efficacy of royal proclamations, both in suspending laws already made, and in legislating for cases not yet regulated by statutory provision.

While Charles expressed the utmost scorn of the capacity of a mercantile corporation, he did not disdain to embrace its illiberal spirit, and copy its interested policy. As a specimen of the extent of legislative authority which he intended to exert, and of the purposes to which he meant to render it subservient, he prohibited the Virginians, under the most absurd and frivolous pretences, from selling their tobacco to any persons but certain commissioners appointed by himself to purchase it on his own account.[1] Thus the colonists found themselves subjected to a municipal administration that combined the vices of both its predecessors, — the unlimited prerogative of an arbitrary prince, with the narrowest maxims of a mercantile corporation; and saw their legislatorial rights invaded, their laws and usages rendered uncertain, all the profits of their industry engrossed, and their only valuable commodity monopolized by the sovereign, who pretended to have resumed the government of the colony only in order to blend it more perfectly with the general frame of the British empire.

[1] Rymer. Hazard. Burk.

Charles conferred the office of governor of Virginia on Sir George Yeardley, and empowered him, in conjunction with a council of twelve persons, to exercise the authority of an indefinite prerogative ; to make and execute laws ; to impose and levy taxes ; to seize the property of the late company, and apply it to public uses ; and to transport the colonists to England, to be tried there for offences committed in Virginia. The governor and council were specially directed to exact the oaths of allegiance and supremacy from every inhabitant of the colony, and in all points to conform their own conduct to the instructions which from time to time the king might transmit to them.[1] [1627.] Yeardley's early death prevented the full weight of his authority from being experienced by the colonists during his short administration. He died in the beginning of the year 1627, and, two years after, was succeeded by Sir John Harvey. Meanwhile, and during a long subsequent course of time, the king, who seems to have inherited his father's prejudices respecting tobacco,[2] continued to restrict and encumber the importation and sale of this commodity by a series of regulations so vexatious, oppressive, multifarious, and unsteady, that it is impossible to undergo the fatigue of perusing them without a mixture of contempt for the fluctuations and caprice of his counsels, and of indignant pity for the wasted prosperity and abused patience of his people. Notwithstanding these disadvantages, however, the colonial population increased with rapidity ; and in the year 1628 more than a thousand persons emigrated from Europe to Virginia.[3]

Sir John Harvey, the new governor, proved a fit instrument to carry the king's system of arbitrary rule into complete execution. Haughty, rapacious, and cruel, he exercised an odious authority with the most offensive insolence, and by the rigor of his executive energy increased the provocation inspired by his legislatorial usurpation and injustice. His disposition was perfectly congenial with the system which he conducted ; and so thoroughly did he personify as well as administer tyranny, as not only to attract, but to engross in his own person, the odium of which a large share was properly due to the prince who employed him. He added every decree of the Court of High Commission in England to the ecclesiastical constitutions of Virginia ; and selected for especial enforcement every regulation of English law which was unsuitable to the circumstances of the colonists, and therefore likely to entail and multiply legal penalties, all of which were commuted into fines and forfeitures appropriated to the governor.[4] Of the length to which he carried his arbitrary exactions and tyrannical confiscations some notion may be formed from a letter of instructions by which the royal committee of council for the colonies in England at length thought proper [July, 1634] to inculcate on him a more moderate demeanour. It signified, that the king, in the plenitude of his bounty, and for the encouragement of the planters, desired that the interests which had been acquired under the late corporation should be respected, and that the colonists, "*for the present*, shall enjoy their estates with the same freedom and privilege as they did before the recalling of the patent."[5]

---

[1] Chalmers.

[2] That he inherited also his father's style of writing against the use of this commodity appears from a letter which he addressed to the governor and council of Virginia in 1627, in which he declares, that " it may well be said that the plantation is wholly built on *smoke*, which will easily turn into *air*, if either English tobacco be permitted to be planted, or Spanish imported." Burk.

[3] Rymer. Chalmers. Hazard. Campbell.   [4] Beverly. Burk.

[5] State Papers, *ap.* Chalmers.

We might suppose this to be the mandate of an Eastern sultan to one of his satraps ; and, indeed, the rapacious tyranny of the governor seems hardly more odious than the cruel mercy of the prince, who interposed to mitigate oppression only when it had reached an extreme which is proverbially liable to inflame the wise with madness and drive the patient to despair.   The most significant comment on the letter is, that Harvey was neither censured nor displaced for the injustice which it commanded him to restrain.   The effect, moreover, which it was calculated to produce, in ascertaining the rights and quieting the apprehensions of the colonists, was counterbalanced by large and vague grants of territory within the province, which Charles inconsiderately bestowed on his courtiers, and which gave rise to numerous encroachments on established possession, and excited general distrust of the validity of titles and the stability of property.   The consequence of one of these grants was the formation of the State of Maryland, by dismembering a large portion of territory that was previously annexed to Virginia. For many years, this event proved a source of much discontent and serious incon-venience to the Virginian colonists, who had endeavoured to improve their trade by restricting themselves to the exportation only of tobacco of superior quality, and now found themselves deprived of all the advantage of this sac-rifice by the transference of a portion of their own territory to neighbours who refused assent to their regulations.[1]

The instructions communicated by the letter of the royal committee left Harvey still in possession of ample scope to his tyranny [1635] ; and the colonial assembly, respecting or overawed by the authority with which he was invested, endured it for some time longer without resistance, and prac-tically restricted their own functions to the degrading ceremonial of register-ing the edicts and decrees of their tyrant.   At length, after a spirited, but ineffectual, attempt to curb his excesses by enactments which he disregarded, the assembly, yielding to the general desire of their constituents, suspended him from his office, and sent him a prisoner to England, along with two deputies from their own body, who were charged with the duty of repre-senting the grievances of the colony and the misconduct of the governor. But their reliance on the justice of the king proved to be very ill founded. Charles was fated to teach his subjects, that, if they meant to retain their liberties, they must prepare to defend them ; that neither submissive pa-tience nor respectful remonstrance could avail to relax or divert his arbitrary purposes ; and that, in order to obtain justice to themselves, they must de-prive him of the power of withholding it.   The inhabitants of Virginia en-dured oppression (of which he had already avowed his consciousness) with long resignation, and, even when their yoke became intolerable, showed that they neither imputed their wrongs to him nor doubted his disposition to re-dress them.   Against the hardships and ill treatment to which they were exposed, they appealed to him as their protector, and implored a relief to which their claim was supported by every consideration that could impress a just or move a generous mind.   Yet, instead of commiserating their suf-ferings, or redressing their wrongs, Charles resented their conduct on this occasion as an act of presumptuous audacity little short of rebellion ; and all the applications of their deputies were rejected with calm injustice and inflexible disdain.   Harvey, released from his bonds, became in his turn the accuser ; and the calumnies of the disgraced and banished tyrant were

---

[1] Beverly.

listened to with complacency and attention, while the representatives of the brave and loyal people whom he had oppressed were regarded as traitors, and forbidden to appear in the presence of their sovereign.   The king refused to hear a single word from the provincial deputies, either in defence of their countrymen or in crimination of Harvey ; and, having reinstated this obnoxious governor in his office, sent him back to Virginia [April, 1637] with a renovation of the powers which he had so grossly abused.   There, elated with his triumph, and inflamed with rage, Harvey resumed and aggravated a tyrannical sway that has entailed infamy on himself and disgrace on his sovereign, and provoked complaints so loud and vehement, that they began to penetrate into England, where they produced an impression, which, mingling with the general irritation in the parent state, could not be safely disregarded.[1]

If the administration of Sir John Harvey had been protracted much longer, it must have ended in the revolt or the ruin of the colony.   So great was the distress it occasioned, as to excite the earnest attention of the Indians, and awaken their slumbering hostility by suggesting the hope of exerting it with success.   Opechancanough, the ancient enemy of the colonists, was now far advanced in years [1638] ; but age, though it had bent his body and dimmed his eyes, had neither impaired his discernment nor extinguished his animosity.   Proud, subtle, sly, fierce, and cruel, he watched, with enduring and considerate hate, the opportunity of redeeming his glory and satiating his revenge.   Seizing the favorable occasion presented by the distracted state of the province, he again led his warriors to a sudden and furious attack, which the colonists did not repel without the loss of five hundred men.   A general war ensued between them and all the Indian tribes under the influence of Opechancanough.[2]

But a great change was now [1639] to reward the patience of the Virginians with a bloodless redress of their grievances.   The public discontents, which had for many years been gathering force and virulence in England, were advancing with rapid strides to a full maturity, and threatened to issue in some violent eruption.   After a long intermission, Charles was forced to contemplate the reassembling of a parliament ; and perfectly aware of the ill-humor already engendered by his government at home, he had reason to apprehend that the displeasure of the Commons would be inflamed, and their worst suspicions confirmed, by representations of the despotism exercised in Virginia.   There was yet time to soothe the irritation, and even secure the adherence of a people, who, in spite of every wrong, retained a generous attachment to the prince whose sovereignty was regarded as the bond of political union between them and the parent state ; and from the propagation of the complaints of colonial grievances in England, it was easy to foresee that the redress of them, if longer withheld by the king, would be granted, to the great detriment of his credit and influence, by the parliament.   To this assembly the Virginians had applied on a former occasion, and the encouragement they had met with increased the probability both of a repetition of their application and of a successful issue to it.   These considerations alone seem to account for the entire and sudden alteration which the colonial policy of the king underwent at this period.   Harvey was recalled, and the government of Virginia was committed [1641], first, to Sir Francis Wyatt, and afterwards to Sir William Berkeley, — a person

---

[1] Chalmers. Oldmixon. Burk.   [2] Beverly.

not only of superior rank and abilities to any of his immediate predecessors, but distinguished by every popular virtue of which Harvey was deficient, — of upright and honorable character, mild and prudent temper, and manners at once dignified and engaging. A change not less gratifying was introduced into the system of government. The new governor was instructed to recognize in the amplest manner the legislative privileges of the provincial assembly, and to invite this body to compose a code of laws for the province, and improve the administration of justice by introduction of the forms of English judicial procedure.

Thus, all at once, and when they least expected it, was restored to the colonists the full enjoyment of those liberties which they had originally procured from the Virginian Company, and which had been exposed to continual peril and violation from the same authority by which the company itself was subverted. Universal joy and gratitude were excited throughout the colony ; and the king, who, amidst the hostility that lowered upon him from every other quarter of his dominions, was addressed in the language of grateful loyalty by this people, seems to have been a little touched by the generous sentiments which he had so ill deserved, and which forcibly proved to him how cheap and easy were the means by which princes may render their subjects attached and happy. And yet so strong were the illusions of his self-love, or so deliberate his artifice, that, in his answer to an address of the colonists, he eagerly appropriated the praise for which he was indebted to their generosity alone, and endeavoured to extend the application of their expressions of gratitude even to the policy from which he had desisted in order to awaken this sentiment.[1]

While Charles thus again introduced the principles of the British constitution into the domestic government of Virginia, he was not inattentive to the policy of preserving its dependence on the mother country, and securing to England the exclusive possession of the colonial trade. [1641.] For this purpose Sir William Berkeley was directed to prohibit all commerce with other nations, and to require a bond from the master of every vessel sailing from Virginia, obliging him to land his cargo in some part of the king's dominions in Europe. Yet the pressure of this restraint was more than counterbalanced by the gracious strain of the other contemporary measures of the crown ; and with a mild and liberal domestic government, which offered a peaceful asylum and distributed ample tracts of land to all emigrants who sought its protection, the colony advanced so rapidly in prosperity and population, that, at the beginning of the civil war in the parent state, it contained upwards of twenty thousand inhabitants. By the vigor and conduct of Sir William Berkeley, the Indian war, after a few campaigns, was brought to a successful close ; Opechancanough was taken prisoner ;[2] and a peace concluded with the savages, which endured for many years.

It was happy for Virginia that the restitution of her domestic liberties was accomplished in this manner, and not deferred till a later period, when the

---

[1] Beverly. Chalmers. Campbell.
[2] Beverly. It was the intention of Sir William Berkeley to send this remarkable personage to England ; but he was shot, after being taken prisoner, by a soldier, in resentment of the calamities he had inflicted on the province. He lingered under the mortal wound for several days, and continued proud and stout-hearted to the last. Indignant at the crowds who came to gaze at him on his death-bed, he exclaimed, "If I had taken Sir William Berkeley prisoner, I would not have exposed him as a show to the people." He would probably have made him expire under Indian torture.

boon would probably have been attended with the reëstablishment of the company of patentees. To this consummation some of the members of the suppressed company had been eagerly looking forward; and notwithstanding the disappointment inflicted on their hopes by the redress of those grievances whose existence would have aided their pretensions, they endeavoured to turn to their own advantage the jealous avidity with which every complaint against the royal government was received in the Long Parliament, by presenting a petition in the name of the assembly of Virginia, praying for a restoration of the ancient patents. This petition, though supported by some of the colonists, who were justly dissatisfied with the discouragement which the Puritan doctrines, and certain preachers of them whom they had invited from Massachusetts,[1] experienced from the domestic government of Virginia, was, undoubtedly, not the act of the assembly, nor the expression of the prevailing sentiment in the colony. The assembly had tasted the sweets of unrestricted freedom, and were not disposed to hazard or encumber their system of liberty by reattaching it to the mercantile corporation under which it was originally established. No sooner were they apprized of the petition to the House of Commons than they transmitted an explicit disavowal of it; and at the same time presented an address to the king, acknowledging his bounty and favor to them, and desiring to continue under his immediate protection. In the fervor of their loyalty, they framed and published a declaration [1642], " that they were born under monarchy, and would never degenerate from the condition of their births by being subject to any other government." [2]

The only misfortune attending the manner in which the Virginians had regained their liberties was, that it allied their partial regards to an authority which was destined to be overthrown in the approaching civil war, and which could no more reward than it deserved their allegiance. During the whole period of the struggle between the king and parliament in England, they remained unalterably attached to the royal cause; and after Charles the First was beheaded, and his son driven out of the kingdom, they acknowledged the fugitive prince as their sovereign, and conducted the provincial government under a commission which he despatched to Sir William Berkeley from Breda.[3] The royal family, though they had little opportunity during their exile of cultivating their interest in the colony, were not entirely regardless of it. [June, 1650.] Henrietta Maria, the queen-mother, obtained the assistance of the French government to the execution of a scheme projected by Sir William Davenant, the poet, of emigrating in company with a large body of artificers whom he collected in France, and founding with them a new plantation in Virginia. The expedition was intercepted by the English fleet; and Davenant, who was taken prisoner, owed the safety of his life to the friendship of Milton.[4]

---

[1] This transaction forms a part of the history of New England.

[2] Chalmers. Gordon's *History of America*. Burk.

[3] Hume's *England*. Chalmers. This year a tract was published at London, by one Edward Williams, recommending the culture of silk in Virginia.

[4] Johnson's *Life of Milton*. *Encyclopædia Britannica*, V. 688. Cowley, in a poem addressed to Davenant, exclaims,
"Sure 't was the noble boldness of the Muse
Did thy desire to seek new worlds infuse."
But the motive of Davenant is, perhaps, better illustrated by the example than by the genius of Cowley. Impatient of the tumultuous distractions of Europe, these votaries of the peaceful pursuits of literature sighed for a sojourn in the " safer world " of America. In the preface to a volume of his poems, published in 1656, Cowley declares, that " his desire had been for

But the parliament, having subdued all opposition in England, was not disposed to suffer its authority to be questioned in Virginia. Incensed at the open defiance of its power in this quarter, it issued an ordinance [Oct. 1650], declaring that the settlement of Virginia, having originated from the wealth and population of England and the authority of the state, ought to be subordinate to and dependent upon the English commonwealth, and subject to the legislation of parliament ; that the colonists, instead of rendering this dutiful submission, had audaciously disclaimed the supremacy of their parent state, and rebelled against it ; and that, consequently, they now deserved to be regarded as notorious robbers and traitors. Not only was all connection prohibited with these refractory colonists, and the council of state empowered to send out a fleet and army to reduce them to obedience, but all foreign nations were expressly interdicted from trading with any of the English settlements in America.[1] It might reasonably be supposed that this latter restriction would have created a common feeling, throughout all the English colonies, of opposition to the government of the parent state. But the colonists of Massachusetts were much more cordially united by similarity of political sentiments and religious opinions with the leaders of the English commonwealth, than by identity of commercial interest with the inhabitants of Virginia. The religious views that had founded their colonial society long regulated all its municipal policy, and prevailed over every other consideration. And no sooner were the people of Massachusetts apprized of the parliamentary ordinance, than they hastened to corroborate its prohibition of intercourse with Virginia, by a corresponding enactment of their own domestic legislature.[2]

The measures of the republican rulers of England were as prompt and decisive as their language. They quickly despatched Sir George Ayscue with an armament sufficient to overpower the provincial royalists, and extinguish the last traces of living monarchical authority that still lingered in the extremities of the empire. The commissioners who were appointed to accompany this expedition received instructions more creditable to the vigor than to the moderation and humanity of the parliamentary councils. They were empowered to try, in the first instance, the efficacy of pardons and other conciliatory propositions in reducing the colonists to obedience ; but if their pacific overtures should prove ineffectual, they were directed then to employ every species of hostile operation, to set free the servants and slaves of all the planters who continued refractory, and furnish them with arms to assist in the subjugation of their masters.[3] This barbarous plan of hostility resembles less a war than a massacre, and suggests the painful reflection, that an assembly possessed of absolute power, and continually protesting that the glory of God and the liberty of mankind were the chief ends for which they assumed it, never once projected the liberation of the negro slaves in their own dominions, except for the purpose of converting them into instruments of bloodshed, ravage, and conquest.

The English squadron, after reducing the colonies in Barbadoes and other islands to the sway of the commonwealth, entered the Bay of Chesapeake. [1651.] Berkeley, apprized of the invasion, hastened to engage the assistance of a few Dutch ships which were then trading to Virginia, contrary

some time past, and did still very vehemently continue, to retire himself to some of the American plantations, and to forsake this world for ever."

[1] Scobell's *Acts*, 1650, cap. 28.   [2] Hazard.
[3] Thurloe's *State Papers*. Hazard.

both to the royal and the parliamentary injunctions, and with more courage than prudence prepared to oppose the invading armament ; but though he was cordially supported by the royalists, who formed the great majority of the inhabitants, it was evident that he had undertaken an unequal contest. Yet his gallant demonstration of resistance, though unavailing to repel the invaders, enabled him to procure to his people favorable terms of submission. By the articles of surrender, a complete indemnity was stipulated for all past offences ; and the colonists, recognizing the authority, were admitted into the bosom of the English commonwealth, and expressly assured of an equal participation in all the civil rights of the people of England. In particular, it was conditioned that the provincial assembly should retain its wonted functions ; and that "the people of Virginia shall have as free trade as the people of England to all places and with all nations," and "shall be free from all taxes, customs, and impositions whatsoever, without the consent of their own assembly." Berkeley disdained to make any stipulation for himself with those whom his principles of loyalty taught him to regard as usurpers. Without leaving Virginia, he withdrew to a retired situation, where he continued to reside as a private individual, universally beloved and respected, till a new revolution was to summon him once more to defy the republican forces of England, and restore the ascendency of royalty in the province.[1]

But it was the dependence, and not the mere adherence of the colonies, that the rulers of the English commonwealth were desirous to obtain ; and their shameless disregard of the treaty concluded by their own commissioners demonstrated in a striking manner with how little equity absolute power is exercised, even by those who have shown themselves most prompt to resent the infliction of its rigor upon themselves. Having now obtained from the colonies a recognition of the authority which they administered, they hastened to adopt measures for promoting their dependence on England, and securing the exclusive possession of their increasing commerce. With this view, as well as for the purpose of provoking a quarrel with the Dutch, by aiming a blow at their carrying trade,[2] the parliament not only forbore to repeal the ordinance of the preceding year, which prohibited commercial intercourse between the English colonies and foreign states, but framed another law [1652] which was to introduce a new era of commercial jurisprudence, and to found the celebrated navigation system of England. By this remarkable law, (of which the general policy was warmly commended in the parliamentary speeches and political writings of the learned Selden,) it was enacted that no production of Asia, Africa, or America should be imported into the dominions of the commonwealth, except in vessels belonging to English owners or inhabitants of the English colonies, and navigated by crews of which the captain and the majority of the sailors should be Englishmen.[3] Willing, at the same time, to encourage the cultivation of the staple commodity of Virginia, the parliament soon after passed an act confirming all the royal proclamations against planting tobacco in England.[4]

---

[1] Beverly.   Oldmixon.   Chalmers.   Burk.   [2] Hume's *England.*
[3] Scobell's *Acts*, 1651, cap. 22. The germ of this famous system of policy occurs in English legislation so early as the year 1381, when it was enacted by the statute of 5 Rich. II. cap. 3, " that, to increase the navy of England, no goods or merchandises shall be either exported or imported but only in ships belonging to the king's subjects." This enactment was premature, and soon fell into disuse. A bill proclaiming its revival to a limited extent, in 1460, was rejected by Henry the Sixth. These measures were probably suggested by the commercial policy of Aragon. See Prescott's *History of Ferdinand and Isabella*, Introduct. § 2.
[4] Scobell's *Acts*, 1652, cap. 2.

This unjust restriction of the colonial traffic, though by no means rigorously enforced, tended to keep alive in Virginia the attachment to the royal cause, which was farther maintained by emigrations of the distressed cavaliers, who resorted thither in such numbers, that the population of the colony amounted to thirty thousand persons at the epoch of the Restoration. But Cromwell had now prevailed over the parliament [1653], and held the reins of the commonwealth in his vigorous hands ; and though the flame of discontent was secretly nourished in Virginia by the passions and intrigues of so many cavalier exiles, yet the eruption of it was repressed by the terror of his name, and the energy which he infused into every department of his administration. Other causes, too, which have been long obscured by the misrepresentations of partial or ignorant historians, contributed to the tranquillity and security of Cromwell's dominion in Virginia. For a century and a half it had been repeatedly asserted, without contradiction, by successive generations of writers,[1] that the government of the Protector in this province was illiberal and severe ; that he appointed governors whose dispositions rendered them fit instruments of a harsh policy, and yet frequently displaced them from distrust of their exclusive devotion to his interest ; and that, while he indulged his favorite colonists of Massachusetts with a dispensation from the commercial laws of the Long Parliament, he exacted the strictest compliance with them from the Virginians. But the reputation of Cromwell's colonial policy has been triumphantly vindicated by the intelligent industry and research of a modern historian[2] of this province, who has proved, beyond the possibility of further doubt or denial, that the treatment which the Virginians experienced under the protectorate was mild and humane ; that their privileges were rather enlarged than circumscribed ; and that Cromwell dignified his usurped dominion over them by the most liberal justice and fearless magnanimity.

So far from having regulated the appointment and dismission of governors by the principles which have been imputed to him, he never appointed or displaced a single governor of the province ; but, from the first, surrendered this branch of the sovereign's prerogative to the legislative assembly of a state which he knew to be the resort of his own most implacable enemies ; and though he appears not to have granted to the Virginians an express exemption from the commercial ordinances of the Long Parliament, he suffered them practically to indulge a total disregard of these oppressive restrictions. Though his government was not fitted to inspire attachment, it seems to have gained the esteem and approbation of impartial and considerate men in Virginia, and to have trained their minds to freer reflection and inquiry than they had ever before entertained with respect to the reasonable objects and purposes for which municipal governments are instituted. But from a numerous and increasing party of the inhabitants of Virginia neither dispassionate reflection nor impartial judgment could reasonably be expected. To many of them the name of Cromwell was associated with recollections of personal disappointment and humiliation ; and to all of them it recalled the ruin of their friends and the death and exile of their kings. Hatred and hope combined to unite their hearts to the downfall

[1] Among whom we find the respectable names of Beverly. Oldmixon, Chalmers, Robertson, and Gordon.
[2] Burk. The history of Virginia has derived the most valuable and important illustration from the industry and genius of this writer. His style is defaced by florid, meretricious ornament.

of the protectorate and commonwealth ; and as passionate are much more contagious than merely reasonable sentiments, the public mind in Virginia, notwithstanding the liberality of Cromwell's administration, was strongly leavened with the wish and expectation of change.

The Puritan colonists of New England had always been the objects of suspicion and dislike to a great majority of the inhabitants of Virginia ; and the manifest partiality which Cromwell entertained for them now increased the aversion with which they were heretofore regarded. New England was generally considered by the cavaliers as the centre and focus of Puritan sentiment and republican principle ; and, actuated partly by religious and partly by political feelings, the Virginian cavaliers conceived a violent antipathy against all the doctrines, sentiments, and practices that were reckoned peculiar to the Puritans ; and rejected all communication of the knowledge that flourished in New England, from hatred of the authority under whose shelter it grew and of the principles to which it administered support.[1] At length the disgust and impatience of the royalist party in Virginia spurned further restraint. Matthews, the last governor appointed during the supremacy of Cromwell [1658], died nearly at the same period with the Protector ; and before an assembly could be convened to nominate his successor, a numerous body of the inhabitants, though yet unacquainted with Cromwell's death, assembled in a tumultuous manner, and, having forced Sir William Berkeley from his retirement, declared him the only governor whom they would acknowledge in Virginia.[2] Berkeley declining to act under usurped authority, the insurgents venturously erected the royal standard, and proclaimed Charles the Second to be their lawful sovereign ; a measure which entailed apparently a contest with the arms of Cromwell and all the force of the parent state. Happily for the colonists, the distractions that ensued in England deferred the vengeance which her rulers had equal ability and inclination to inflict, till the sudden and unexpected restoration of Charles to the throne of his ancestors [1660] converted imprudent temerity into meritorious service, and enabled the Virginians safely to exult in the singularity which they long and proudly commemorated, that they were the last of the British subjects who renounced, and the first who resumed, their allegiance to the crown.[3]

---

[1] The prejudices of an old cavalier against popular education are strikingly displayed by Sir William Berkeley, in a letter descriptive of the state of Virginia, some years after the Restoration. "I thank God," he says, "there are no free schools nor printing ; and I hope we shall not have them these hundred years. For learning has brought heresy and disobedience and sects into the world, and printing has divulged them, and libels against the best government: God keep us from both !" Chalmers.

[2] That Cromwell meditated some important changes in Virginia, which death prevented him from attempting to accomplish, may be inferred from the publication of a small treatise at London in the year 1657, entitled "Public Good without Private Interest," written by Dr. Gatford, and dedicated to the Protector. In this little work, the Protector is urged to reform the numerous abuses extant in Virginia,—the disregard of religion,—the neglect of education,—and the fraudulent dealings of the planters with the Indians; on all which topics the author descants very forcibly. Of this treatise, as well as of the tracts by Hamor and Williams and some others, which I have had occasion to notice elsewhere, I found copies in the library of the late George Chalmers.

[3] Oldmixon. Beverly. Chalmers. Burk. Campbell.

CHAPTER III.

The Navigation Act — its Impolicy. — Discontent and Distress of the Colonists. — Naturalization of Aliens. — Progress of the provincial Discontent. — Indian Hostilities. — Bacon's
Rebellion. — Death of Bacon — and Restoration of Tranquillity. — Bill of Attainder passed
by the colonial Assembly. — Sir William Berkeley superseded by Colonel Jeffreys. — Partiality of the new Governor — Dispute with the Assembly. — Renewal of Discontents. —
Lord Culpepper appointed Governor — Severity and Rapacity of his Administration. — An
Insurrection — Punishment of the Insurgents. — Arbitrary Measures of the Crown. — James
the Second — augments the Burdens of the Colonists. — Corrupt and oppressive Government of Lord Effingham. — Revolution in Britain. — Complaints of the Colonies against
the former Governors discouraged by King William. — Effect of the English Revolution
on the American Colonies. — State of Virginia at this Period — Population — Laws —
Manners.

THE intelligence of the restoration of the House of Stuart to the throne
of Britain excited very different emotions in the various British colonies
which were now established in America. We shall have occasion hereafter
to notice the gloomy impressions it produced in the States of New England.
In Virginia, whose separate history we still exclusively pursue, it was received by a great majority of the people like the surprising fulfilment of an
agreeable dream, and hailed with acclamations of unfeigned and unbounded
joy. Even that class of the inhabitants, which had recently expressed
esteem and approbation of the protectoral government, manifested a new-
born zeal for royalty hardly inferior to the more consistent ardor of the
genuine cavaliers. These sentiments, confirmed by the gracious expressions
of regard and good-will[1] which the king very readily vouchsafed, begot
hopes of substantial favor and recompense which it was not easy to gratify,
and which were fated to undergo a speedy and severe disappointment.
Sir William Berkeley, having received a new commission from the crown
to exercise the office of governor [1660], convoked the provincial assembly, which, after zealous declarations of loyalty and satisfaction, undertook
a general revision of the laws and institutions of Virginia. Trial by jury,
which had been discontinued for some years, was now again restored ;
judicial procedure was disencumbered of various abuses ; and a provision
of essential importance to the interests of liberty was made for enlarging the
number of representatives in the assembly in proportion to the increase of
the province in peopled and cultivated territory. The supremacy of the
church of England was recognized and established by law ; stipends were
allotted to its ministers ; and no preachers but those who had received their
ordination from a bishop in England, and who should subscribe an engagement of conformity to the forms and constitutions of this established church,
were permitted to exercise their functions either publicly or privately within
the colony.[2] A law was shortly after enacted against the importation of
Quakers into Virginia, under the penalty of five thousand pounds of tobacco
inflicted on the importers ; but with a special exception of such Quakers as

---

[1] Sir William Berkeley, who made a journey to England to congratulate the king on his
restoration, was received at court with distinguished regard ; and Charles, in honor of his loyal
Virginians, wore at his coronation a robe manufactured of Virginian silk.   Oldmixon.
    This was not the first royal robe that America supplied.   Queen Elizabeth wore a gown
made of the silk grass, of which Raleigh's colonists sent a quantity to England.   Coxe's
Description of Carolana.   There is a copy of this curious work in the library of the Royal
Institution of Great Britain.
[2] Chalmers.   Burk.

might be judicially transported from England for breach of her legislative ordinances.[1]

The same principles of government which prevailed in England after the Restoration uniformly extended their influence, whether salutary or baneful, across the Atlantic ; and the colonies, no longer deemed the mere property of the prince, were considered as adjunctions of the British territory, and subject to parliamentary legislation.   The explicit declaration by the Long Parliament of the dependence of the colonies on the parent state introduced maxims which received the sanction of the courts of Westminster Hall, and were thus interwoven with the fabric of English law.   In a variety of cases which involved this great constitutional point, the judges pronounced, that, by virtue of those principles of the common law which bind the territories to the state, the American plantations were included within the pale of British dominion and legislation, and affected by acts of parliament, either when specially named or when reasonably supposable within the contemplation of the legislature.[2]   In conformity with the adjudications of the courts of law was the uniform tenor of the parliamentary proceedings ; and the colonists soon perceived, that, although the Long Parliament was no more, it had bequeathed to its successors the spirit which influenced its commercial councils.   The new House of Commons determined not only to retain the system of colonial policy which the Long Parliament had introduced, but to mature and extend it, — to render the trade of the colonies completely subject to parliamentary governance, and exclusively subservient to the interests of English commerce and navigation.

No sooner was Charles seated on the throne, than a duty of five *per cent.* was imposed by the parliament on all merchandise exported from, or imported into, any of the dominions belonging to the crown ;[3] and the same session, in producing the celebrated *Navigation Act* [1660], originated the most memorable and important branch of the commercial code of England. By this statute, (in addition to many other important provisions, which are foreign to our present consideration,) it was ordained, that no commodities should be imported into any British settlement in Asia, Africa, or America, or exported from thence, but in vessels built in England or her colonial plantations, and navigated by crews of which the masters and three fourths of the mariners should be English subjects, under the penalty of forfeiture of ship and cargo ; that none but natural-born subjects of the English crown, or persons legally naturalized, should exercise the occupation of merchant or factor in any English colonial settlement, under the penalty of forfeiture of goods and chattels ; that no sugar, tobacco, cotton, wool, indigo, ginger, or woods used in dyeing, produced or manufactured in the colonies, should be shipped from them to any other country than England ; and to secure the observance of this regulation, ship-owners were required, at the port of lading, to give bonds with surety for sums proportioned to the tonnage of their vessels.[4]   The commercial wares thus restricted were termed *enumerated commodities ;* and when new articles of colonial produce, as the rice of Carolina and the copper ore of the northern provinces, were raised into importance, and brought into commerce by the increasing industry of the

---

[1] Chalmers. In 1663, the assembly entertained a complaint against one of its own members, of " being loving to the Quakers."   Burk.

[2] Freeman's *Reports*, 175. *Modern Reports,* III. 159, 160, IV. 225. Vaughan's *Reports*, 170, 400.   Salkeld's *Reports*, II. 6.

[3] 12 Car. II. cap. 4.   [4] Ibid. cap. 18.

colonists, they were successively added to the original list which we have noted, and subjected to the same regulations.

As some compensation to the colonies for these commercial restraints, the parliament at the same time conferred on them the exclusive supply of tobacco, by prohibiting its cultivation in England, Ireland, Guernsey, and Jersey.[1] The Navigation Act was soon after enlarged, and additional restrictions imposed by a new law [1663], which prohibited the importation of European commodities into the colonies, except in vessels laden in England and navigated and manned in conformity with the requisitions of the original statute. More rigorous and effectual provisions were likewise devised for securing the infliction of the penalties attached to the transgression of the Navigation Act ; and the principles of commercial policy on which the whole system was founded were openly avowed in a declaration, that, as it was the practice of other nations to keep the trade of their plantations to themselves, so the colonies that were founded and peopled by English subjects ought to be retained in firm dependence upon England, and obliged to contribute to her advantage in the employment of English shipping, the vent of English commodities and manufactures, and the conversion of England into a settled mart or emporium, not only of the productions of her own colonies, but also of such commodities of other countries as the colonies themselves might require to be supplied with.[2] Advancing a step farther in the prosecution of its domineering policy, the parliament assumed the prerogative of regulating the trade of the several colonies with each other ; and as the Act of Navigation had left all the colonists at liberty to export the enumerated commodities from one settlement to another without paying any duty, this exemption was subsequently withdrawn, and they were subjected, in trading with each other, to a tax equivalent to what was levied on the consumption of their peculiar commodities in England.[3]

The system pursued by these regulations, of securing to England a monopoly of the trade of her colonies, by shutting up every other channel which competition might have formed for it, and into which the interest of the colonists might have caused it preferably to flow, excited in their minds the utmost disgust and indignation. In England, it was long applauded as a masterpiece of political sagacity ; retained and cherished as a main source of national opulence and power ; and defended on the plea of expediency, deduced from its supposed advantages. The philosophy of political science, however, has amply refuted these illiberal principles, and would long ago have corrected the views and amended the institutions which they sanctioned or introduced, but that, from the general prevalence of narrow jealousies, and of those obstinate and violent prepossessions that constitute wilful ignorance, the cultivation of political science has much more frequently terminated in knowledge merely speculative, than visibly operated to improve human conduct, or increase human happiness.

Nations, biased by virulent enmities, as well as mean partialities, have suffered an illiberal jealousy of other states to contract the views they have formed of their own interests, and to induce a line of policy, of which the operation is to procure a smaller amount of exclusive gain, in preference to a larger contingent in the participation of general advantage. Too passionate or gross-sighted to discern the bonds that connect the interests

---

[1] 12 Car. II. cap. 34.   [2] 15 Car. II. cap. 7.   [3] 25 Car. II. cap. 7, Anno 1672.

of all the members of the great family of mankind, they have accounted the detriment and exclusion of their rivals equivalent to an extension of benefit to themselves. The prevalence of this mistaken policy has commonly been aided by the interested representations of the few who contrive to extract a temporary and partial advantage from every abuse, however generally pernicious ; and when, in spite of a faulty commercial system, the prosperity of a state has been augmented by the force of its natural advantages, this effect has been eagerly ascribed to the very causes which really impeded and abridged, without being able entirely to intercept it. But the discoveries obtained by the cultivation of political science have, in this respect, coincided with the dictates of Christian morality, and demonstrated, that, in every transaction between nations and individuals, the intercourse most solidly and lastingly beneficial to both and each of the parties is that which is founded on the principles of fair reciprocity and mutual accommodation ; that all policy suggested by jealous or malevolent regard of the advantage of others implies a narrow and perverted view of our own ; that that which is morally wrong can never be politically right ; and that to do as we would be done by is not less the maxim of prudence than the precept of piety. So coherent must true philosophy ever be with the prescriptions of divine wisdom. But, unfortunately, this coherence has not always been recognized even by those philosophers whose researches have tended to its illustration ; and confining themselves to reasonings sufficiently clear and convincing, no doubt, to persons contemplating human affairs in the simplicity and disinterested abstraction of theoretical survey, they have neglected to promote the acceptance of important truths by reference to those principles that derive them from infallible wisdom, and connect them with the strongest sanctions of human duty.

They have demonstrated[1] that a parent state, by restraining the commerce of her colonies with other nations, impairs the industry and productiveness both of the colonies and of foreign nations ; and hence, by enfeebling the demand of foreign purchasers, which must be proportioned to their ability, and lessening the quantity of colonial commodities actually produced, which must be proportioned to the actual demand for them, enhances the price of the colonial produce to herself as well as to the rest of the world, and so far diminishes its power to increase the enjoyments and animate the industry of her own citizens as well as of other states. . Besides, the monopoly of the colonial trade produces so high a rate of profit to the merchants who carry it on, as to attract into this channel a great deal of the capital that would, in the natural course of things, be directed to other branches of trade ; and in these branches the profits must consequently be augmented in proportion to the diminished competition of the capitals employed in them. But whenever the ordinary rate of profit in any country is raised by artificial means to a higher pitch than it would naturally attain, that country is necessarily subjected to great disadvantage in every branch of trade of which she does not command a monopoly. Her merchants cannot obtain such higher profit without selling dearer than they otherwise would do both the commodities of foreign countries which they import into their own, and the goods of their own country which they carry abroad. The country thus finds herself undersold at foreign markets in many branches of commerce ; a disadvantage to which she is the more exposed,

---

[1] Smith's *Wealth of Nations.*

that in foreign states much capital has been forced into those branches by her exclusion of foreigners from partaking her colonial trade, which would have absorbed a part of it.   Thus, by the operation of a monopoly of the colonial trade, the parent state obtains an overgrowth of one branch of distant traffic, at the expense of diminishing the advantages which her own citizens might derive from the unrestricted produce of the colonies, and of impairing all those branches of nearer trade, which, by the greater frequency of their returns, afford the most constant and beneficial excitement to national industry.   Her commerce, instead of flowing in a variety of moderate channels, is trained to seek principally one great conduit ; and hence the whole system of her trade and industry is rendered dangerously liable to obstruction and derangement.

But the injurious consequences of this exclusive policy are not confined to its immediate operation upon trade.   The progress of our history will demonstrate, that the connection, which a parent state seeks, by the aid of such a system, to maintain with colonies in which the spirit and institutions of liberty obtain any prevalence, carries within itself the principles of its own dissolution.   During the infancy of the colonies, a perpetual and vexatious exertion is required from the parent state to execute and develope her restraining laws ; while a corresponding activity is awakened in the colonies to obstruct or elude their operation.   Every rising branch of trade, which is left, for a time or for ever, free to the colonists, serves, by the effect of contrast, to render more striking and sensible the disadvantages of their situation in the regulated branches ; and every extension of the restrictions provokes additional discontent.   As the colonies increase their internal strength, and make advances in the possession and appreciation of social importance, the disposition of their inhabitants to emancipate themselves from such restraints is combined with ability to accomplish their deliverance, by the very circumstances and at the very period which will expose the trade of the parent state to the greatest injury and disorder. And the advantages which the commerce of other nations must expect from the destruction of the monopoly unites the wishes of the whole world with the revolt of the colonies, and gives assurance of the most powerful assistance to promote their emancipation.

A better apology for the system which England adopted towards her colonies, than the boasted expediency of her measures would thus appear to supply, may be derived from the admitted fact, that her colonial policy, on the whole, was much less illiberal and oppressive than that which any other nation of Europe had ever been known to pursue.   While the foreign trade of the colonies was restrained for the supposed advantage of England, whose prosperity they partook, and by whose power they were or were supposed to be defended, their internal liberty was in the main suffered to flourish and mature itself under the shelter of wise and liberal domestic institutions ; and even the commercial restrictions imposed on them were much less rigorous and injurious than those which the colonies of France, Spain, Portugal, and Denmark endured from their respective parent states.   The trade of the British settlements was not committed, according to the practice of some of those states, to exclusive companies, nor restricted, according to the practice of others, to a particular port ; but, being left free to all the people, and admitted to all the harbours of England, employed a body of British traders too numerous and dispersed to admit of their renouncing mutual competition and uniting in a general confederacy to oppress the colonists and extort exorbitant profits to themselves.   This apology is obviously very unsatisfactory, as every attempt to palliate injustice must necessarily be.   It was urged with a very bad grace by the people of England, and totally disregarded by the inhabitants of America.

In none of the American colonies did this tyrannical system excite greater resentment than in Virginia, where the larger commerce of the people, their preëminent loyalty, and the recent experience of the lenient and liberal policy of Cromwell, rendered the pressure of the burden more severe, and the infliction of it more exasperating.[1]   No sooner was the Navigation Act promulgated in Virginia, and its effects perceived, than the colonists warmly remonstrated against it as a grievance, and petitioned earnestly for relief. But, although the English monarchs were accustomed at this period to exercise a dispensing power over the laws, — insomuch, that, when the court at a later period ventured openly to pursue a system of arbitrary government, even the Act of Navigation itself, so great a favorite with the nation, was suspended for a while by an exertion of this stretch of prerogative, — yet, during the early period of his reign, Charles, unassured of the stability of his throne, and surrounded by ministers of constitutional principles, was compelled to observe the limits of a legal administration, and to aid with his authority the execution even of those laws that were most repugnant to his principles and wishes.[2]   So far from lending a favorable ear to the petition of Virginia, Charles and his ministers adopted measures for carrying the act into strict execution.   Intelligence having been received that its provisions were violated almost as generally as they were detested, and that the provincial authorities were reluctant to promote the efficacy of a system which they perceived was so hateful to the persons over whom they presided, — a royal mandate was issued to the governors of the settlements, reprimanding them for the " neglects, or rather contempts," which the law had sustained, and enjoining their future attention to its rigid enforcement ; [3] and in Virginia, more especially, demonstration was made of the determined purpose of the English government to overcome all provincial resistance, by the erection of forts on the banks of the principal rivers, and the appointment of vessels to cruise on the coasts.   But, notwithstanding the threatening measures employed to overawe them, and the vigilance of the British cruisers, the Virginians contrived to evade the law, and to obtain some vent to the accumulating stores of their depreciated produce, by a clandestine traffic with the settlement of the Dutch on Hudson's River.   This relief, however, was inconsiderable ; and the discontent of

[1] It was to Virginia alone that Montesquieu's justificatory principle of the system of restricted trade could be considered as in any degree applicable.   " It has been established," says this writer, " that the mother country alone shall trade in the colonies, and that from very good reason, — because the design of the settlement was the extension of commerce, and not the foundation of a city or of a new empire."   *Spirit of Laws.*   This was in some measure true in regard to Virginia, though her first charter professes more enlarged designs; but it was not applicable to New England, Maryland, or the other posterior settlements of the English.

[2] When the parliament, in 1666, proposed the unjust and violent law, which they finally established, against the importation of Irish cattle into England, the king was so much struck with the remonstrances of the Irish people against this measure, that he not only exerted all his interest to oppose the bill, but openly declared that he could not conscientiously assent to it ; but the Commons were inflexible in their purpose, and the king was compelled to submit. " The spirit of tyranny," says Hume, " of which nations are as susceptible as individuals, had extremely animated the English to exert their authority over their dependent state."

[3] Chalmers. *State Papers*, ibid.

the planters, inflamed by the hostilities which the frontier Indians now resumed, began to spread so widely as to inspire some veteran soldiers of Cromwell, who had been banished to Virginia, with the hope of rendering themselves masters of the colony, and delivering it entirely from the yoke of England. A conspiracy, which has received the name of *Birkinhead's Plot*, was formed for this purpose ; but the design, having been seasonably disclosed by the fear or remorse of one of the persons engaged in it, was easily defeated by the prudence and vigor of Sir William Berkeley, and with no farther bloodshed than the execution of four of the conspirators.[1]

The distress of the colony continuing to increase with the increasing depreciation of tobacco, now confined almost entirely to one market, and with the augmentation of the price of all foreign commodities, now derivable only from the supplies which one country could furnish, — various efforts were made from time to time by the provincial assembly for the relief of their constituents. Retaliating, in some degree, the injustice with which they were treated, they framed a law ordaining, that, in the payment of debts, foreign creditors should be postponed to Virginian claimants, and that the provincial tribunals should give precedence in judgments to engagements contracted within the colony. Statutes were enacted for restraining the culture of tobacco ; and attempts were made to introduce a new staple, by encouraging the plantation of mulberry-trees and the manufacture of silk ; but neither of these projects was successful. Numerous French Protestant refugees being attracted to Maryland by a statute of naturalization in their favor, which was enacted in this province in the year 1666, the Virginian assembly endeavoured to recruit the wealth and population of its territories from the same source, by framing, in like manner, a series of laws which empowered the governor to confer on aliens taking the oath of allegiance all the privileges of naturalization [1671] ;[2] but it was provisionally subjoined, that this concession should not be construed to vest aliens with the power of exercising any function which they were disabled from performing by the statutes of the English parliament relative to the colonies. This prudent reference to a restriction which the provincial patents of naturalization must inevitably have received from the common law was intended to guard against the disputes and confiscations which might ensue from the attempts of naturalized aliens to infringe the Navigation Act. But the precaution was unavailing ; and at an after period many forfeitures of property were occasioned, and much judicial controversy produced, by the traffic which aliens in the colonies carried on under the

[1] Oldmixon. Beverly. Burk.

[2] It was not till after the Revolution of 1688 that the population of Virginia received any accession from the influx of these or other foreigners. In 1671, Sir William Berkeley thus describes the state of its population : — " There are in Virginia above 40,000 persons, men, women, and children ; of which there are 2,000 black slaves, 6,000 Christian servants for a short time, and the rest have been born in the country, or have come in to settle or serve in hope of bettering their condition in a growing country. Yearly, we suppose, there come in of servants about 1,500, of which most are English, few Scotch, and fewer Irish ; and not above two or three ships of negroes in seven years." *Answers to the Lords of the Committee of Colonies, apud* Chalmers. The numerous importations of servants mentioned by Sir William Berkeley were probably checked by the troubles that preceded and attended *Bacon's Rebellion.* The later importations were more available than the earlier ones ; the diseases of the country having diminished in frequency and violence as the woods were progressively cut down; diseases occasioned by the repugnance of the human constitution to novelty of climate were diminished by the lapse of time and the consequent gradual compliance of the bodily frame with the properties of the region. The mortality among the new comers, we learn from Sir William Berkeley, was at first enormous, but had become very trifling prior to 1671.

authority of general patents of denization granted to them by the ignorance or inattention of the royal governors. Their pretensions, though quite repugnant to the navigation laws, were supported by the American courts of justice, but uniformly disallowed by the English privy council, which, after repeated decisions in conformity with the principle, that the ordinances of a provincial legislature cannot derogate from the general jurisprudence of the empire, finally prohibited all farther denizations by the provincial governors or assemblies.[1]

Far from being mitigated by the lapse of time, the discontents in Virginia were exasperated by the increasing pressure of the commercial restrictions, corresponding with the successive exertions of the English government to promote their more effectual operation. Various additional causes contributed to inflame the displeasure of the colonists ; and a considerable native population having now grown up in Virginia, the resentment of these persons was no way abated by the habitual regard and fond remembrance which emigrants retain for the parent state which is also the land of their individual nativity. The defectiveness of their education excluded the influence of literature from acting in this respect as a substitute to experience ; and they knew little of England beyond the wrongs which they heard daily imputed to her injustice. It was natural that all the political leaders and reasoners, who either sincerely undertook to demonstrate or factiously endeavoured to magnify these wrongs, should contrast the oppression that followed restored royalty in England with the liberality which the colony had experienced from Oliver Cromwell ; and the effect of this suggestion was to associate national prosperity with democratical ideas in the minds of a numerous and increasing party of the Virginian planters.[2]

The Indian hostilities, after infesting the frontiers, began now to penetrate into the interior of the province ; and while the colonists were reduced to defend their property at the hazard of their lives, they found it additionally endangered [1673] by the large and improvident grants of land which the king, after the example of his father, yielded with lavish profusion and facility to the solicitations of his favorites. The fate of that parent had warned him to avoid, in general, rather the arrogance that provoked than the injustice that deserved it ; and in granting those applications, without fatiguing himself by any inquiry into their merits, he at once indulged the indolence of his disposition, and exerted a liberality that cost him nothing that he cared for. Many of the royal grants not only were of such exorbitant extent as to be unfavorable to the progress of cultivation, but, from ignorance or inaccuracy in the definition of their boundaries, were so conceived as to include tracts of land that had already been planted and appropriated. Such a complication of exasperating circumstances brought the discontents of the colony to a crisis.

In the beginning of the year 1675, two slight insurrections, which were rather the hasty explosions of popular irritation than the fruits of matured design, were easily suppressed by the governor, but gave significant intimation of the state and the tendency of public feeling in Virginia. In the hope of averting the crisis, and obtaining redress of the more recent grievances

---

[1] Chalmers.

[2] The partial and contradictory accounts that have been transmitted of the subsequent events bear unhappy testimony to the influence of the distinction that now began to prevail in Virginia between a royalist and a democratical party. The misrepresentations of faction continue to hide and disguise truth, after its passions have ceased to disturb happiness.

which were provoking it, the assembly despatched deputies to England, who, after a tedious negotiation with the king and his ministers, had brought matters to the point of a happy adjustment, and obtained the promise of a royal charter, defining both the constitution and the territory of Virginia, when their expectations were frustrated and the proceedings suspended by intelligence of a formidable rebellion in the colony. A tax, imposed by the assembly to defray the expense of the deputation [1676], increased the discontent which the deputation was intended to remove ; and when the dilatory proceedings of the English ministers, who disdained to allow the intelligence of past or the apprehensions of future insurrection to quicken their diligence, seemed to confirm the assurances of the factious leaders of the colonists that even their last sacrifice was thrown away, the tide of rage and disaffection began again to swell to the point of rebellion. It did not long wait for additional provocation to excite, or an able leader to impel, its fury. For, to crown the provincial distress, the Indian warfare, which continued to prevail notwithstanding all the governor's attempts to suppress it, now spread out with redoubled extent and fury, and threatened a formidable addition of danger, hardship, and expense.

The Indians were alarmed and irritated by a series of enterprises which the governor promoted for exploring the large and yet unvisited districts adjoining the colonial occupation, and which the savages regarded as a preparatory step to farther encroachments on their domains. Even the popularity of the long tried and magnanimous friend of Virginia, Sir William Berkeley, was overcast by the blackness of this cloud of calamities. The spirit and fidelity with which he had adhered to the colony through every variety of fortune, his earnest remonstrances with the English government against the commercial restraints, his generosity in devoting a considerable part of his own private fortune to the improvement and embellishment of the province, and the disinterestedness he had shown in declining, during the unprosperous state of the provincial finances, to accept an addition, proposed by the assembly, to his official emoluments, were disregarded, denied, or forgotten. [1676.] To his age and incapacity were now attributed the burdens of the people and the distractions of the time ; and he was loudly accused of wanting alike honesty to resist the tyrannical policy of the mother country, and courage to repel the hostility of the savages.[1] Such ungrateful injustice is rarely, if ever, committed by any people advanced beyond a state of national barbarism, except when the insidious suggestions of factious leaders have imposed on their credulity and fanned their passions into fury. The populace of Holland, when, a few years before this period, they tore in pieces their benefactor, John De Witt, were not only terrified by the progress of their national calamities, but deluded by the profligate artifices of the retainers of the House of Orange. To similar influence (exerted in similar circumstances) were the enraged and misguided Virginians now exposed from the artifice and ambition of Nathaniel Bacon.

This man was educated to the profession of a lawyer in England ; and only three years had elapsed, since, for some unexplained reason, he emigrated to Virginia. Short as this interval was, it sufficed to advance him to a conspicuous station in the colony, and to illustrate the disposition and talents of a popular leader. The consideration he derived from his legal attainments, and the esteem he acquired by an insinuating address, had pro-

---

[1] Beverly.   Chalmers.   Oldmixon (2d edit.).   Campbell.   Burk.

cured him already a seat in the council, and the rank of colonel in the provincial militia. But his temper was not accommodated to subordinate office ; and, unfortunately, the distractions of the colony presented to him a sphere of action more congenial to his character and capacity. Young, sanguine, eloquent, and daring, yet artful and ambitious, he presented himself in the assemblies of the discontented planters, and, by his spirited harangues on the grievances under which they labored, he promoted their exasperation and attracted their favor. He was implicated in the abortive insurrection of the preceding year, and had been imprisoned and subsequently pardoned by the governor ; but less affected by the clemency than encouraged by the impunity which he experienced, and sensible that the avenue to legitimate promotion was now for ever closed against him, he determined to unite his lot with the fortune of the malcontent party ; and taking advantage of their present excitation, he once again came forward, and addressed them with artifice which their uncultivated understandings were unable to detect, and with eloquence which their untamed passions rendered quite irresistible. Finding that the sentiments most prevalent with his auditory were the alarm and indignation excited by the Indian ravages, he hastened to strike in with the impressions of which he proposed to lay hold, and loudly charged the governor with neglect or incapacity to exert the vigor that was requisite for the general safety ; and having expatiated on the facility with which the whole Indian race might be exterminated, he exhorted his fellow-colonists to take arms in their own defence, and achieve the deliverance they must no longer expect from any other quarter. So acceptable was this address and the speaker to the temper of the popular mind, that his exhortation was instantly obeyed, and his main object no less successfully accomplished.

A great multitude hastened to embody themselves for an expedition against the Indians ; and electing Bacon to be their general, committed themselves to his direction. He assured them, in return, that he would never lay down his arms, till he had avenged their sufferings and redressed their wrongs. To give some color of legitimacy to the preëminence he had obtained, and, perhaps, expecting to precipitate matters to the extremity which his interest required that they should speedily reach, he applied to the governor for an official confirmation of the popular election, and offered to march immediately against the common enemy. Berkeley, suspecting his real designs, thought it prudent to temporize, and try the effect of negotiation ; but he had to deal with a much more practised adept in dissimulation than himself ; and encountered in Bacon a man precautioned by his own guile and insincerity against the craft of others, and fully conscious that promptitude and resolute perseverance alone could extricate him with safety or credit from the dangers of his situation. Pressed for an answer, and finding that the applicants were not to be soothed by his conciliating demeanour, Berkeley issued a proclamation, commanding the multitude to disperse under pain of incurring the guilt of rebellion.

Bacon, no more disconcerted by this assumption of vigor than he had been duped by the previous negotiation, instantly marched to Jamestown at the head of six hundred of his followers, and, surrounding the house where the governor and assembly were engaged in deliberation, he demanded the commission which his proceedings and retinue showed how little he either needed or regarded. Berkeley, undismayed by the dangers that environed him, was sensible of his inability to repel the force of the insurgents, and yet disdained to bend his authority before their menacing attitude, or yield to their imperious demands. Confronting, with invincible courage, the men who reproached him with defect of this virtue, he peremptorily commanded them to depart; and when they refused, he presented his breast to their weapons, and calmly defied their rage. But the council, more considerate of their own safety, and fearful of driving the multitude to some fatal act of fury, hastily prepared a commission, by which Bacon was appointed captain-general of all the forces of Virginia, and, by dint of earnest entreaty, prevailed with the governor to unite with them in subscribing it. The insurgents, thus far successful, retired in triumph; and the council no sooner felt themselves delivered from the immediate presence of danger, than, passing from the depth of timidity to the height of presumption, they enacted and published an ordinance annulling the commission they had granted, as having been extorted by force, proclaiming Bacon a rebel, commanding his followers to deliver him up, and summoning the militia to arm in defence of the constitution. They found too little difficulty in persuading the governor to confirm, by his sanction, this indiscreet affectation of an authority which they were totally incapable of supporting. The consequences might have been easily foreseen. Bacon and his associates, flushed with their recent triumph, and incensed at the impotent menace, which they denounced as a base and treacherous breach of compact, returned directly to James-town; and the governor, destitute of any force sufficient to cope with the insurgents, retired across the bay to Accomac on the eastern shore. Some of the counsellors accompanied him thither; the rest retired to their estates; the frame of the provincial administration seemed to be dissolved, and Bacon took unresisted possession of the vacant government.

The preëminence which he attained by this vigorous conduct Bacon employed with much address to add strength and reputation to his party. To invest his usurped jurisdiction with the semblance of a legal establishment, he summoned a convention of the principal planters of the province, and prevailed with a numerous body of them to pledge themselves by oath to support his authority and resist his enemies. A declaration or manifesto was published, in the name of this body, setting forth that Sir William Berkeley had wickedly fomented a civil war among the people, and that, after thus violating his trust, he had abdicated the government, to the surprise and confusion of the country; that General Bacon had raised an army for the public service and with the public approbation; that the late governor having, as was reported, abused the ear of the king by falsely representing that the general and his followers were rebels, and pressing his Majesty to send forces to subdue them, the welfare of the colony and their true allegiance to his most sacred Majesty alike required that they should oppose and suppress all forces whatsoever, except those commanded by the general, till the king should be fully informed of the real merits and nature of the case by persons despatched to him by Bacon, to whom, in the interim, all the inhabitants were required to take an oath of allegiance. It was remarked by the wise, that this manifesto, which might have been expected to display the genuine source of the revolt, mentioned none of the original causes of quarrel; and hence they justly suspected that the leader of the insurgents entertained personal and ambitious designs, to which he purposed to render the discontents of his followers subservient, which extended beyond the immediate measures in relation to the Indians, and which had already suggested to him a specious pretence for exposing the colony to a war with the forces of the mother country. Yet such was the spirit of the times, and so prompt the sympathy with resistance to every branch of an administration which Charles was daily rendering more odious and suspected, that, when the rebel manifesto was promulgated in England, it found admirers among the people, and even within the walls of that parliament whose injustice formed the only real grievance that Virginia had at present to complain of. Though Bacon designedly omitted to remind his adherents that the conduct of the Indian war was the object for which they had originally intrusted him with military command, it was to this object that his first exertions were actually directed. To redeem his promise and to exercise his troops, he marched at the head of an expedition against the hostile savages, who, rashly awaiting a general engagement, were defeated with a loss which they never were able to repair.

Berkeley, meanwhile, having collected a force from levies among the planters who remained well affected to him, and from the crews of the English shipping on the coasts, prepared to give battle to the army of the usurper; and several sharp encounters ensued between the parties with various success. All the horrors of civil war descended on the colony. Jamestown, which already contained several elegant buildings, erected at considerable expense by the governor and the more opulent planters, was reduced to ashes by the insurgents, at the command of Bacon, who judged it a station which he could not safely retain; the estates of the loyalists were pillaged, their friends and relatives seized as hostages, and the richest plantations in the province laid waste. The governor was prompted by his indignation, as well as by the rage of his partisans, to retaliate these extremities, and even to execute some of the insurgents by martial law; and the animosity of both parties was rapidly mounting to a pitch that threatened a war of mutual extermination. The superiority of the insurgent force had hitherto confined the efforts of the loyalists in the field to mere skirmishing engagements; but the tidings of an approaching armament, which the king despatched from England under Sir John Berry to the assistance of the governor, gave promise of a wider range of carnage and desolation. Charles had issued a proclamation [Oct. 1676], declaring Bacon a traitor and the sole promoter of the insurrection; tendering pardon to all his followers who should forsake him, and freedom to all slaves who would assist in suppressing the revolt. However elated the loyalists might be with the intelligence of the approaching succour, the leader of the insurgents was no way dismayed by it; and his influence over his followers was unbounded. Conscious now that his power and his life were indissolubly connected, he determined to encounter whatever force might be sent against him. He was aware, at the same time, of the importance of striking a decisive blow while the advantage of numbers remained with him; and with this view, having enlarged his resources by proclaiming a general forfeiture of the property of all who either opposed his pretensions or even affected neutrality, he was preparing to take the field, when his career was arrested by that Power which can wither in an instant the sinews of abused strength, and arrest the uplifted arm of the most formidable destroyer. Happily for his country, and to the manifest advantage not less of his followers than his adversaries, Bacon unexpectedly sickened and died. [Jan. 1677.]

I*

The ascendency with which this remarkable person had predominated, as the master-spirit of his party, was illustrated by the effect of his death on their sentiments and conduct.   The bands of their confederacy seemed to be cut asunder by the loss of their general, nor did any successor even attempt to reunite them ; and their sanguine hopes and resolute adherence to Bacon were succeeded by mutual distrust and universal despondency. Ingram, who had been lieutenant-general, and Walklate, who had been major-general of the insurgent forces, showed some disposition to prolong the struggle by maintaining possession of a stronghold which was occupied by their party ; but after a short treaty with Sir William Berkeley, they consented to surrender it, on condition of receiving a pardon for their offences.   The other detachments of the rebel army, finding themselves broken and disunited, afraid to protract a desperate enterprise, and hoping, perhaps, to be included in the indemnity granted to Walklate and Ingram, or at least to experience equal lenity, laid down their arms [1677], and submitted to the governor.

Thus suddenly and providentially was dissipated a tempest that seemed to portend the entire ruin of Virginia.   From the man whose evil genius excited and directed its fury, this insurrection has been distinguished by the name of *Bacon's Rebellion.*   It placed the colony for seven months in the power of that daring adventurer, involved the inhabitants during all that period in bloodshed and confusion, and was productive of a devastation of property to the extent of at least a hundred thousand pounds.[1]   To the mother country it conveyed a lesson which she appears never to have understood, till the loss of her colonies illustrated its meaning, and the consequence of disregarding it.   For, after every allowance for the ability and artifice of Bacon, it was manifest that the general discontent and irritation, occasioned by the commercial restrictions, had formed the groundwork of his influence ; and it required little sagacity to foresee that those sentiments would be rendered more inveterate and more formidable by the growth of the province, and by the increased connection and sympathy with the other colonial settlements, which the lapse of time and the habitual consciousness of common interests and grievances would infallibly promote.   Had Bacon been a more honest and disinterested leader, this lesson would perhaps have been more distinctly unfolded, and the rebellion, it is probable, would not have ended with his life.   But, instead of sincerely embracing the cause of his associates, he contrived to render their passions instrumental to the gratification of his own sinister ambition.   The assertors of the interests of Virginia were thus converted into the partisans of an individual ; and when his presence and influence were withdrawn, they perceived at once that they were embarked in a contest which to themselves had neither interest nor object.

No sooner were the insurgents disbanded, and the legitimate government restored, than Sir William Berkeley developed the vindictive powers of the law with a rigor more proportioned to the guilt of the rebels and the provocation he had received from them, than akin to the general humanity

---

[1] Beverly.   Oldmixon. *Modern Universal History*, XLI. Sir William Keith's *History of Virginia.* Chalmers. Burk. Campbell. Mrs. Aphra Behn celebrated this rebellion in a tragi-comedy, entitled *The Widow Ranter, or the History of Bacon in Virginia,* to which Dryden wrote a prologue. The play was acted unsuccessfully, and afterwards published in 1690. There is a copy of it in the British Museum. It sets historical truth entirely and avowedly at defiance, and is replete with coarse humor and indelicate wit.

of his character and the lenity which he had extended to the promoters of former insurrections. But the recent rebellion had produced a scene of outrage and bloodshed to which nothing similar had occurred in the preceding commotions, and which he probably regarded as the reproach and requital of his lenity on those occasions. Refusing to publish the royal proclamation which he now received from England, offering pardon to all who would lay down their arms, he caused several of the rebels who were not included in his treaty with Walklate and Ingram to be brought to trial for treason. All who confessed their guilt and implored mercy seem to have been exempted from the extremity of legal rigor ; but of others who abided the issue of a trial, ten were convicted and executed. The number of the guilty, which at first had seemed to betoken their security, served now to aggravate and diffuse the terror of these proceedings, which were at last interrupted by an address from the provincial assembly, beseeching the governor to forbear from the farther infliction of capital punishment. By this assembly a few of the surviving ringleaders of the insurrection were subjected to fines and disabilities, and Bacon, together with certain of his officers who had perished in the contest, was attainted.

An attainder of the dead seems an arrogant attempt of human power to extend its arm beyond the scene of human life, to invade with its vengeance the inviolable sanctuary of the grave, and to reclaim to the jurisdiction of transient authority and fallible judgment the defenceless being and supposed offender, who has already been removed by the act of divine power to abide the decree of eternal and unerring justice. In England the measure was regarded as an act of sovereignty beyond the competence of a subordinate legislature, and held to be void from defect of power ; but this objection was obviated, and the attainder subsequently reënacted, by a bill to the same effect, which was framed in England, and transmitted under the great seal to the colonial assembly.[1]

The tardy aid despatched from England to the defence of the provincial government did not reach Virginia till after the rebellion was suppressed. With the fleet arrived Colonel Jeffreys [April, 1677], appointed by the king to signify the recall and succeed to the office of Sir William Berkeley, who now closed in peace an administration of nearly forty years ; and shortly after, closing his life, may be said to have died in the service of Virginia. This gallant and honorable man was thus spared the mortification of beholding the injustice and impolicy with which the royal authority was soon after employed to blacken his fame, and to weaken all those sentiments of loyalty in the colony, which it had been the great object of his

---

[1] *Abridgment of the Laws of Virginia.* Oldmixon. Keith. Chalmers. Burk. Campbell. The account which I have given of the penal proceedings which followed the suppression of the rebellion is derived from a strict examination and comparison of the statements of these and other writers, and coincides entirely with none of them. Except Burk and Campbell (who merely repeats, without vouching for, the statements of Burk), every other writer has declared that Sir William Berkeley punished none of the rebels capitally, and ascribed this forbearance to his having procured their surrender by a promise of general pardon. Burk expressly asserts that Berkeley gave such assurance to the rebels, and charges him with having violated it both by the executions which I have related and by others inflicted by the more summary process of martial law. But an attentive examination of the documents to which he refers has satisfied me that there is no credible evidence of any person having been put to death by martial law, except during the subsistence of the rebellion, or of any promise of pardon having been made to those who were tried and convicted after its suppression. Neither the colonial assembly, in their address against further capital punishments, nor the royal commissioners, in their subsequent charges against the governor, have given any countenance to the suppositions adopted by Burk.

wishes to cultivate and cherish. Entertaining all the principles of an old cavalier, endowed with a character well formed to recommend his principles, and presiding in a colony where the prevailing sentiments of the people were for a long time entirely congenial with his own, he had hoped to render Virginia a scene where the loyalty that was languishing in Europe might be renovated by transmigration into a young and growing body politic, and expand to a new and more vigorous maturity. But this was not the destination of the provinces of America. The naked republican principle, that substitutes the respect and approbation of citizens toward their magistrate, in place of the reverence and attachment of subjects to their sovereign, was held by all the cavaliers in utter abhorrence ; and a more favorable specimen of the opposite principle which they embraced, and of that mixed system of opinion and sentiment which it tended to produce, will not easily be found than in the character and conduct of Sir William Berkeley. The courageous regard he demonstrated for his people not only excited their grateful admiration, but recommended to their esteem the generous devotion to his king with which it was in his language and demeanour inseparably blended. When the hopes of the royalists were extinguished in every other quarter of the empire, this governor of an infant province boldly arrayed his scanty forces on the banks of James River, in defence of his people and his principles, against the victorious arms of the most formidable power in Europe ; and afterwards, emerging from retirement, and seconding the popular impulse, he again braved the same unequal contest, and, disowning the authority, defied the forces, of the protectoral government. For many years, his influence in Virginia was unbounded, and his virtues expanded with the growth and the enjoyment of his popularity. But in the close of his administration, — when he saw the efficacy of these virtues impaired, his long labors defeated, and the scene of all his loyal and disinterested service gradually pervaded by discontent and democratical sentiment, and finally defaced and convulsed by rebellion, — his disposition seemed to derive a tincture from the bitterness of disappointment, and his conduct, both during the continuance and after the suppression of Bacon's rebellion, has been reproached with splenetic impatience and vindictive severity. In happier times, he approved himself a wise legislator, as well as a benevolent and upright magistrate ; and we are informed by the editor of the *Laws of Virginia*, that the most judicious and most popular of them were suggested by Sir William Berkeley. When his death was known, and he was no longer an object of flattery or of fear, the provincial assembly recorded the sentiments which the colony entertained of his conduct in the grateful declaration, "that he had been an excellent and well deserving governor" ; and earnestly recommended his widow to the justice and generosity of the king.[1] The bosom of the king, however, was little accessible to such sentiments ; and his reign was calculated to dispel, instead of confirming, the impressions of cavalier loyalty.

The most remarkable event that distinguished the government of Colonel Jeffreys was the conclusion of the Indian war, which had raged so long, and contributed, with other causes, to the production of the late rebellion, by a treaty which gave universal satisfaction. This, too, was the only act of his administration that was attended with consequences so agreeable.

---

[1] Chalmers. Preface to Moryson's edition of the *Laws of Virginia*. *Life of Sir William Berkeley.*

Jeffreys, Sir John Berry, and Colonel Moryson were appointed commissioners to investigate and report the causes of Bacon's rebellion. They commenced their inquiries with an avowed prepossession in favor of the insurgents, and conducted them with the most indecent partiality. The temptation which their office presented to magnify the importance of their labors by new and unexpected discoveries, and to prove, by arraignment of the late administration, that they had not been appointed its censors in vain, contributed, no doubt, to inspire the malevolence and injustice which they displayed in a degree that would otherwise seem quite unaccountable. Instead of indemnifying, or even applauding, they discountenanced the loyalists who had rallied in the time of danger around the provincial government ; and having invited all persons who were engaged in the insurrection to come forward and state their grievances without fear, and unequivocally demonstrated the favorable acceptance which such representations might expect, they succeeded in collecting a mass of confused and passionate complaints, which they digested into a report fraught with crimination of Sir William Berkeley and his council, and with insinuations against the honesty and the courage of all the planters who had united with the governor in withstanding the rebels.[1] While their folly or malignity thus tended to rekindle the dissensions of the colonists, their intemperance involved them in a dispute that united all parties against themselves. Finding that the assembly hesitated to comply with a requisition they addressed to it, that all its books and journals should be submitted to their inspection, they seized these records by force, and withdrew them from the clerk who was intrusted with their custody. Incensed at this insult, the assembly demanded satisfaction from Jeffreys ; and when he appealed to the authority of the great seal of England, under which the commissioners acted, they replied to him, in language worthy of the descendants of Englishmen and the parents of Americans, " that such a breach of privilege could not be commanded under the great seal, because they could not find that any king of England had ever done so in former times." The spirit thus displayed by the assembly appears the more deserving of applause, when we consider that a body of regular troops, the first ever sent to Virginia, were now stationed in the colony, under the command of Sir John Berry. Informed of this proceeding, the king, in strains that rival the arrogance of his father and grandfather, commanded the governor " to signify his Majesty's indignation at language so seditious, and to give the leaders marks of the royal displeasure." Berry and Moryson soon after returned to England, leaving the colony in a state of ferment, and all parties disgusted and disappointed.

---

[1] The memory of Sir William Berkeley was defended against the misrepresentations of the commissioners by his brother, Lord Berkeley, (Chalmers,) and his fame suffered no diminution from their report. Burk, who has evidently conceived a strong prejudice against Berkeley, expresses a different opinion. He asserts, that Berkeley, on his return to England, found that his conduct was disapproved by the king. But Oldmixon, whose authority on a point like this is entitled to the highest respect, declares that Berkeley before his death received an assurance of the esteem and approbation of his sovereign.

During the disputes that preceded the war of independence, it was common for the writers who espoused the cause of America to aggravate the blame of the British government by exaggerating the previous loyalty of the Americans. But this representation has ceased to please in America ; and some of her late writers have preferably devoted their labor and ingenuity to the illustration of the antiquity of her republican spirit. Burk, in particular, has magnified beyond their due importance the first manifestations of discontent and democratical feeling in Virginia ; and, for the credit both of his representations and of his countrymen, has eagerly adopted every factious charge and injurious supposition with respect to Sir William Berkeley.

To the other causes of discontent was added the burden of supporting the soldiery, who, receiving no remittances of pay from England, indemnified themselves by their exactions from the planters. The impatience created by this treatment, however, was mitigated by the mild and prudent conduct of an aged officer and venerable man, Sir Henry Chicheley, to whom, as lieutenant-governor, the administration devolved, on the death of Jeffreys [1678] ; and as, during his presidency, some of the large and improvident donations of land by the crown, that had been so much complained of, were revoked, and certain other grievances corrected, a short gleam of prosperity was shed on the colony, and an interval of comparative repose gave the people time to breathe, before the resumption of tyranny with a violence which was to endure till the British Revolution.[1]

It was not to royal generosity or benevolence that the colonists were indebted for the lenient administration of Sir Henry Chicheley. Charles had some time before conferred the government of the province on Lord Culpepper, who, though very willing to accept this important office, showed so little readiness to perform the duties of it, that it was not till he had been reprimanded by the king for his neglect that he made his voyage to Virginia. [May, 1680.] His administration was conducted with the same arbitrary spirit that the royal government had now begun to indulge without control in the mother country. Having wrested from the assembly the nomination of its own most confidential officer, the secretary who composed its journals ; having abolished the power it had hitherto exercised of entertaining appeals from the decisions of the provincial judicatories ; having accumulated a considerable sum of money by official pillage ; and having guarded his tyranny from complaint by a proclamation, that interdicted, under the severest penalties, all disrespectful speeches against the governor or his administration, — he returned [Aug. 1680], after a very short stay in Virginia, to dissipate the spoils of the province in the luxury of England. Yet on this ignoble lord did the king confer the commission of governor for life, and a salary twice as large as the emoluments of Sir William Berkeley.

The irritation created by these proceedings sharpened the sense of the hardships which the colonists were now enduring from the depressed price of tobacco ; and the public impatience exploded in a tumultuary attempt to destroy all the new tobacco plantations that threatened to increase the depression of price by multiplying still farther the quantities of produce. [May, 1682.] The insurrection might have proceeded to very serious extremities, if the prudence and activity of Sir Henry Chicheley had not again been exerted to compose the public discontent, and restore the peace of the colony. To any mind influenced by liberal justice, or susceptible of humane impressions, this slight and short-lived insurrection was strongly recommended to indulgent consideration. It was but a momentary expression of popular impatience created by extreme suffering ; and the earnest, though ineffectual, addresses by which the assembly had recently solicited from the king a prohibition of the increase of tobacco plantations both suggested and seemed to sanction the object to which the violence of the rioters was directed. But to the king it appeared in the light of an outrage to his dignity, which imperiously demanded a severe, vindictive retribution ; and Lord Culpepper, again obeying the royal mandate to repair to Virginia, caused a number of the insurgents to be tried for high treason ; and by a

---

[1] Chalmers.

series of bloody executions impressed that mute terror which tyrants denominate tranquillity.   Having thus enforced a submission not more propitious to the colony than the ferment which attended his former departure,
Lord Culpepper again set sail for England, where he was immediately put
in confinement for returning without leave ; and, on a charge of misappro-
priating the provincial revenues, was shortly after arraigned before a jury,
and in consequence of their verdict deprived of his commission.[1]

In displacing this nobleman, it was the injury done to himself, and not
the wrongs of the colony, that Charles intended to redress.   The last exertion of his royal authority, which Virginia experienced, was the appointment of a successor to Culpepper, in Lord Effingham [Aug. 1683], whose
character was very little if at all superior, and whom, among other instructions, the king expressly commanded to suffer no person within the colony
to employ a printing-press on any occasion or pretence whatsoever.   Along
with the new governor was sent a frigate, which was appointed to be stationed on the coast with the view of compelling a stricter execution of the
Navigation Act than this obnoxious measure had yet been able to obtain.[2]

On the death of Charles the Second, his successor, James, was proclaimed [Feb. 1685] in Virginia with demonstrations of joy, indicating less
the attachment of the colonists to the person of their new sovereign, than
that impatient desire with which men, under the pressure of hardship and
annoyance, are ready to hail any change in their prospects or situation.
Acclamation far more warmly expressive of gladness and hope had attended
the commencement of the preceding reign ; and if the hopes that were now
awakened were more moderate, they were not on that account the less
fallacious.   The colonists soon learned with regret, that, in his first parliament, James had procured the imposition of a tax on the consumption of
tobacco in England ; and in imploring the suspension of this tax, which
threatened still farther to obstruct the sale of the only vendible production
of their soil, they descended to an abjectness of entreaty which produced
no other effect than to embitter their disappointment with the consciousness
of humiliating and yet fruitless prostration.   Though the assembly judged it
expedient to present an address of felicitation to the king on the defeat of
Monmouth's invasion of England, the colonists found an opportunity of indulging very different sentiments on that occasion, in the kindness with which
they treated some of the insurgents, whom James, from a satiety of bloodshed, which he termed the plenitude of royal mercy, appointed to be transported to the American plantations ; and even the assembly paid no regard
to the signification of the royal desire that they should frame a law to prevent these unfortunate persons from redeeming themselves from the servitude to which they were consigned.   This conduct, however, of the colonists and their assembly, in so far as it was not prompted by simple humanity, expressed merely their dissatisfaction with the king's treatment of
themselves, and denoted no participation of their wishes or views in the
designs of Monmouth.   The general discontent was increased by the personal character of the governor, through whom the rays of royal influence
were transmitted.   Lord Effingham, like his predecessor, ingrafted the baseness of a sordid disposition on the severity of an arbitrary and despotic
administration.   He refused to convoke the provincial assembly.   He instituted a court of chancery, in which he himself presided as judge ; and,

----

[1] Beverly.   Chalmers.   [2] Chalmers.

besides multiplying and enhancing the fees attached to his own peculiar
functions, he condescended to share with clerks the meaner perquisites of
subordinate office. For some time he contrived to stifle the remonstrances
which his extortions produced, by the infliction of arbitrary imprisonment
and other tyrannical severities ; but at length the public displeasure became
so general and uncontrollable, that he found it impossible to prevent the
complaints of the colony from being carried to England, — for which country
he in consequence resolved himself to embark, in order to be present at his
own arraignment. [1688.] He was accompanied by Colonel Ludwell,
whom the assembly appointed their agent to advocate the complaints of his
conduct and urge his removal from office.[1]

But before the governor and his accuser arrived in England, the Revolution, which the tyranny of James provoked in that country, had transferred
the allegiance of all parties to new sovereigns. The Virginians, though
they readily acquiesced in the change, appear to have surveyed with very
little emotion an event which coincided with none of their anticipations, and
to the production of which their concurrence had not been demanded.
Whatever might be its remoter consequences, its immediate effect was forcibly to remind them of their own insignificance, as the appendage of a distant empire, whose political changes they were fated to follow, but unable
to control. The most deep-seated and lasting grievances under which they
labored, having proceeded from the English nation and parliament, were
such as the present event gave no promise of alleviating. Their immediate
complaints were to be submitted to sovereigns of whom they knew absolutely nothing ; and their late experience had diminished their trust in
princes, and discouraged hopes of advantage from changes of royalty. The
coolness, then, with which the Virginians are said to have regarded the
great event of the British Revolution [1688], so far from implying that their
minds were not touched with a concern for freedom, may, with much greater
probability, be referred to the ardor with which they cherished this generous
principle, and the deliberate reflection which they combined with it.[2] In
some respects, too, the policy of the new government that arose in the
parent state was but ill formed to convey to them more satisfactory impressions of the change that had taken place, or to invite their sympathy with
the feelings of that portion of their fellow-subjects by whose exertions it
was accomplished.

Notwithstanding the representations of Colonel Ludwell (who himself was
gratified with the appointment of governor of Carolina), King William, disinclined and perhaps unable to dismiss those officers of his predecessor who
were willing to transfer their personal adherence and official service to himself, retained Lord Effingham in the government of Virginia. This nobleman, however, did not again return to the province ; and as long as his
commission was suffered to endure, the administration was conducted by a
deputy governor. He was removed in the year 1692, and replaced by
a successor still more obnoxious to the colonists, Sir Edmund Andros,
whose tyrannical conduct, prior to the Revolution, in the government of
other American provinces, more justly merited the brand of legal punishment and disgrace than continuance of official trust and dignity. If such

[1] Beverly.   Oldmixon.   Chalmers.
[2] Colonel Quarry's *Memorial to the Lords of Trade*, in the year 1703, on the state of the
American provinces, represents the Virginian planters as a numerous and wealthy race, deeply
infected with " republican notions and principles."

appointments remind us that the English ministry was still composed of many of the persons who had dispensed patronage in the preceding reigns, they may also in part be accounted for by other considerations. Of the officers who were thus undeservedly retained, some pretended to great local experience and official ability. This was particularly the case of Sir Edmund Andros, whose administration eventually proved highly beneficial to Virginia. And they excused the arbitrary proceedings which they had conducted in the former reigns, by pleading the authority of the sovereign whose commands they had obeyed, — a plea which always finds favor with a king, when not opposed to wrongs which he deems personal to himself. Moreover, the complaints of the colonists were not always accurate ; for anger is a more copious than discriminating accuser. Justice suffered, as usual, from the defect of temper and moderation with which it was invoked ; and the guilty artfully availed themselves of the inconsiderate passion by which their accusers were transported, in order to defeat or discredit the charges which they preferred. The insolence and severity, for example, that pervaded the whole of Lord Effingham's government, had elicited many complaints, in which the accusers either neglected or were unable to discriminate between the legality of official acts and the tyrannical demeanour or malignant motives of the party by whom they were performed. Accordingly, while some of the remonstrances which the Virginians transmitted to England by Colonel Ludwell were favorably received and approved by the British government, there were others that produced only explanations, by which the assembly was given to understand that it had mistaken certain points of English constitutional law.[1] In the infancy of a free state, collisions and disputes not unfrequently arise from conflicting pretensions of different, but coördinate, branches of its municipal constitution, before time has given consistence to the whole structure, and those relative limits, which abstract reason finds it difficult to prescribe to the respective parts, have been determined by the convenience of practice and the authority of precedent.

The revolution of the British government, both in its immediate and its remote operation, was attended with consequences highly beneficial to Virginia, in common with all the existing provinces of America. Under the patronage and by the pecuniary aid of William and Mary, the college which had been projected in the reign of James the First was established.[2] The political institutions, under which the manly character of Englishmen is formed, were already planted in the soil to which so large a portion of their race had migrated ; the literary and religious institutions, by which that character is refined and elevated, were now, in like manner, transported to Virginia ; and a fountain opened within her own territory, which promised

[1] Beverly. Chalmers. One of the grievances complained of by the assembly of Virginia was, that Lord Effingham, having by a proclamation declared the royal dissent to an act of assembly which repealed a former law, gave notice that this law was now in force. This was erroneously deemed by the assembly an act of legislation.

[2] Beverly. Seymour, the English attorney-general, having received the royal commands to prepare the charter of the college, which was to be accompanied with a grant of two thousand pounds, remonstrated against this liberality, protesting that the nation was engaged in an expensive war, that the money was wanted for more important purposes, and that he did not see the slightest occasion for a college in Virginia. Blair, the commissary for the Bishop of London in Virginia, represented to him that the object of the institution was to educate and qualify young men to be ministers of the gospel, and begged Mr. Attorney would consider that the people of Virginia had souls to be saved, as well as the people of England. " *Souls!* " said he ; " *damn your souls ! make tobacco.* " Franklin's *Correspondence.*

J

to dispense to her children the streams of science, physical, moral, and religious.

But the most important and decisive influence which the British Revolution exercised on the condition of the colonies, consisted in the abridgment and almost entire abolition of their dependence on the personal character of the king. A conservative principle was infused by that great event into the main trunk of the British constitution in England, and into all the filial shoots that had issued from the parent stem, and germinated in the settlements abroad. The continuity of existence and supremacy of power, which the parliament acquired in Britain, extended the constitutional superintendence of this national assembly to every subordinate organ of popular rights ; and if it oppressed the trade, it protected the chartered liberties, of the provinces of America. The king still continued to appoint the governors of Virginia and of some of the other settlements ; and men of sordid dispositions and of feeble or profligate character were frequently the objects of this branch of the royal patronage. But the powers of these officers were in general circumscribed and distinctly defined ; and the authority of the provincial assemblies was able to restrain, and even overawe, the most vigorous administration of the executive functionaries. Whatever evil influence a wicked or artful governor might exert on the domestic harmony of the people, or on their opinions of the royal prerogative which he administered, he could commit no serious inroad on the constitution of the province over which he presided. From this period a tolerably equal and impartial policy distinguished the British dominion over the American provinces ; the diminution of the personal influence of the sovereign effaced in a great degree the inequalities of treatment previously occasioned by the different degrees of favor with which he might happen to regard the religious or political sentiments of the inhabitants of the respective states ; and consequently extinguished, or at least greatly abated, the jealousies which the several colonial communities had hitherto entertained of each other. A farther abatement of these mutual jealousies was produced by the religious toleration which the provincial governments were henceforward compelled to observe. Even when intolerant statutes were permitted to subsist, their execution was generally disallowed ; and the principles cherished in one province were no longer exposed to persecution in another.

We must now transfer our inquiry to the rise of the other colonies in North America which were founded antecedently to the British Revolution, and trace their separate progress till that era. But before our undivided attention be withdrawn from this, the earliest of the settlements, it seems proper to subjoin a few particulars of its civil and domestic condition at the period at which we have now arrived.

Notwithstanding the unfavorable circumstances to which the colony was exposed in a greater or less degree ever since the Restoration, the number of its inhabitants had continued to increase. The deputies to Charles the Second, in 1675, represented the population as amounting, at that time, to 50,000 persons.[1] If their statement were not exaggerated (as it probably was), we must suppose that Bacon's Rebellion and the subsequent tyranny gave a very severe check to this rapid increase ; for there is no reason to suppose that the colony contained a much greater number than 50,000 at the Revolution of 1688. From a table appended to the first

---

[1] Chalmers.

edition of Beverly's *History*, it appears, that, in 1703, the population of Virginia (exclusive of 800 French refugees conveyed thither by King William) amounted to 60,606 souls. Of this number, 20,023 were *tithables* (a denomination implying liability to a poll tax, and embracing all white men above the age of sixteen, and all negro slaves, male and female, above that age), and 35,583 were children of both races, and white women. The most intelligent and accomplished of the modern historians of Virginia has conjectured, that, at the period of the British Revolution, one half of the population of the province consisted of slaves.[1] Many circumstances contributed to give free scope to the increase of the provincial population, and to counterbalance the influence of commercial restraint and despotic government. The healthfulness of the country had greatly improved ; and the diminution of disease not only closed a drain from which the population had severely suffered, but rendered the general strength more available to the general support. The use of tobacco now prevailed extensively in Europe ; and the diminution of its price was compensated by the increased demand for the commodity. In 1671, it was computed, that, on an average, eighty vessels came annually from England and Ireland to Virginia for tobacco. In 1675, there were exported from Virginia above 23,000 hogsheads of tobacco, and in the following year upwards of 25,000. In this latter year, the customs on tobacco from Virginia and Maryland, collected in England, amounted to £135,000.[2] Sir William Berkeley rates the number of the militia, in the year 1671, at nearly 8,000, and adds, that the people were too poor to afford the equipment of cavalry. In the year 1680, the militia amounted to 8568, of whom 1300 served as cavalry.[3] Our estimate, however, of the increased wealth which the cavalry establishment seems to indicate, must be abated by the consideration of the increased exertions which the Indian war and Bacon's Rebellion had rendered necessary. In the year 1703, we learn from Beverly that the militia amounted to 9522, of whom 2363 were light horse, and the remainder foot and dragoons ; and that, as few of the planters were then destitute of horses, it was judged that the greater part of them might, if necessary, be converted into dragoons.[4] Every freeman (a denomination embracing all the inhabitants, except the slaves and the indented servants), from sixteen to sixty years of age, was enrolled in the militia ; and as the people were much accustomed to shoot in the woods, they were universally expert in the use of firearms.[5] The militia was commanded by the governor, whose salary was £1000 a year, till the appointment of Lord Culpepper, who, on the plea of peerage, procured it to be doubled.[6]

The twelve provincial counsellors, as well as the governor, were appointed by the king ; and a salary of £350, assigned to the council, was divided in proportion to the official services which the members respectively performed. In all matters of importance, the concurrence of the council with the governor was indispensably requisite. The provincial assembly was composed of the counsellors, who termed themselves the Upper House, and claimed privileges correspondent with those exercised by the English House of Lords ; and the burgesses, who were elected by the freemen of the respective counties, and performed the functions of the House of Commons,

---

[1] Beverly.   Burk.
[2] Chalmers. In the year 1604, the whole customs of England amounted only to £127,000, of which £110,000 was collected in the port of London.   Hume.
[3] Chalmers.   [4] Beverly.   [5] Beverly (edit. 1722).   [6] Beverly.

receiving wages proportioned to their services, and derived, like all the other provincial salaries, from provincial taxation. A poll tax long continued to be the only domestic tribute imposed on the Virginians ; and subjection to this tax inferred the qualification of a freeman. The poorer classes were reconciled to the poll tax by this identification of its burden with the enjoyment of the political franchise, and by the specious application of a maxim which became current in the colony, that *the lives and industry of the citizens were objects of greater value than lands and houses.* Until the year 1680, the several branches of the assembly had collectively formed one deliberative body ; but in that year the counsellors separated themselves from the burgesses, and assumed a distinct political existence. In conjunction with the governor, the counsellors formed the supreme tribunal of the province ; from whose judgments, however, in all cases involving more than £ 300, an appeal was permitted to the king and privy council of England. In 1681, the province contained twenty counties ; in 1703, it contained twenty-five. A quitrent of two shillings for every hundred acres of land was paid by the planters to the crown.[1]

In the year 1688, the province contained forty-eight parishes, embracing upwards of 200,000 acres of appropriated land. A church was built in every parish, and a house and glebe assigned to the clergyman, along with a stipend, which was fixed by law at 16,000 pounds of tobacco. This mode of remuneration obviously tends to give a secular cast to the life and character of the ministers, and to entangle them with concerns remote from their spiritual duties. The equalization which it proposes is deceptive ; the different degrees of fertility of different parishes rendering the burden unequal to the people, and the varying quality of the tobacco produced in various soils making the remuneration unequal to the clergymen. The privilege of collating to ecclesiastical benefices, prior to the British Revolution, belonged to the governor, but was generally usurped or controlled by the parishioners. After the British Revolution, it was grasped by the hands of parochial vestries, which, though originally elected by the people, came, in process of time, to exercise the power of supplying vacancies in their numbers by their own appointment. The bishop of London was accounted the diocesan of the province ; and a resident commissary (generally a member of the council), appointed by that prelate, presided over the clergy, with the power of convoking, censuring, and even suspending them from the exercise of their ministry. The doctrines and rites of the church of England were established by law ; attendance at divine worship in the parochial churches, and participation in the sacraments of the church, were enjoined under heavy penalties ; the preaching of dissenters, and participation in the rites and worship of dissenting congregations, were prohibited, and subjected to various degrees of punishment. There was one bloody statute, which menaced Quakers returning from banishment with the punishment of death ; but no execution ever took place in consequence of this law, and it was repealed soon after the Revolution of 1688. The other intolerant laws were not then abolished, but they were no longer strictly or generally executed ; and though the statute-book continued to forbid the promulgation of tenets and performance of worship dissenting from the established model, the prohibition was little regarded, and a practical liberty of conscience was considerably realized. In 1688, a great majority of the people belonged to

---

[1] Chalmers. Burk.

the established church. Other opinions and practices, however, began to arise, and were doubtless promoted by the influence of the free schools, of which a great many were founded and endowed soon after that period ; and the provincial government, being restrained from executing the intolerant laws against dissenters, endeavoured to cherish the ecclesiastical establishment by heaping temporal advantages upon its ministers.   This policy produced its usual fruits, and generated in the state clergy a spirit and character so odiously contrasted, and so inadequate to cope, with the zeal and diligence of dissenting teachers stimulated by the most powerful motives both temporal and spiritual, that at the era of the American Revolution two thirds of the inhabitants of Virginia had become dissenters from the episcopal church, and were obnoxious, on that account, to the ban of their own municipal law.[1]

Of every just and humane system of laws one main object should be to protect the weak against the strong, and to temper and correct, instead of promoting and perpetuating, the inequalities of social condition created from time to time by inequalities of human strength, skill, success, or industry. This wise and benevolent principle must be sacrificed, to a considerable extent, in the code of every country where slavery is admitted.   By the laws of Virginia, all persons arriving voluntarily or involuntarily in the colony by sea or land, not having been Christians in their native country, were subjected to slavery, even though they might be converted to Christianity after their arrival.   A slave accused of a capital crime was remitted to the judgment of commissioners named by the governor, without the intervention of a jury ; and if the punishment of death were inflicted, indemnification to the extent of the pecuniary value of the slave was awarded from the provincial treasury to the master.   This last regulation has prevailed in every State into which negro slavery has gained admission ; notwithstanding its manifest tendency to injure the public by relaxing the domestic vigilance of masters, and its injustice to the slaves in weakening the slight but sole security of humane treatment which they derive from the pecuniary interest of their owners in the preservation of their lives.   In the year 1669, it was enacted that the death of a slave occasioned by the correction of a master should not be accounted felony ; " since it cannot be presumed," says the act, " that prepensed malice, which alone makes murder felony, should induce any man to destroy his own estate."   But reason and experience alike refute this pernicious sophistry, which ascribes to absolute power a tendency to repress human irascibility, and accounts avarice and selfishness sufficient motives and pledges of justice, humanity, and moderation.   Neither infidels nor negroes, mulattoes nor Indians, were allowed to purchase Christian white servants ; and if any person, having Christian white servants, should marry an infidel, or a negro, mulatto, or Indian, all such servants were made free.   Any free white person intermarrying with a negro or mulatto, and any minister celebrating such marriage, were punished with fine and imprisonment.

---

[1] *Abridgment of the Laws of Virginia.* Beverly.   Burnaby's *Travels through the Middle Settlements of America.* Chalmers. Jefferson's *Notes on Virginia.* From the *Journal* of Thomas Chalkley, the Quaker, it appears that many of his fellow-sectaries were peaceably and happily established in Virginia before the end of the seventeenth century.   Among these, he mentions one Porter, who (in the year 1698), at the age of ninety-two, had a daughter two years old.   Porter died at the age of a hundred and seven, full of days, wisdom, and piety, leaving seventy descendants in the province.

It will excite the merriment of a satirist, the disgust of a philosopher, and the indignant concern of a Christian, to see, combined with such inhuman and tyrannical laws, the strictest injunctions of the worship of that great Teacher of charity and humility who commanded his worshippers to *honor all men ;* together with many solemn denunciations and penal enactments against *travelling on Sunday, profane cursing, and profanely getting drunk.* 'Justices of the peace were commanded to hear and determine the complaints of all servants, *except slaves,* against their masters. Various regulations were established for securing mild and equitable treatment to indented servants ; at the close of their indentures, they received from their masters each a musket, a small sum of money, and a quantity of corn ; but if, during the currency of their term of service, they presumed to marry without consent of their master or mistress, they were punished with an additional year of servitude. To divert the planters from employing female indented servants in agricultural labor, it was decreed that all white women exempted from such labor should be also exempted from poll tax, but that any of them who might be employed in rustic toil should forthwith be enrolled in the list of tithables. All persons riotously assembling, to the number of eight or more, for the purpose of destroying tobacco, incurred the guilt of treason. Every person, not being a servant or slave, committing adultery or fornication, was for the greater offence fined one thousand, and for the lesser, five hundred, pounds of tobacco. Women convicted of slander were adjudged to be ducked, in default of their husbands' consenting to redeem them from the penal immersion at the cost of a pecuniary mulct. There being no inns in the country, strangers were entertained at the houses of the inhabitants, and were frequently involved in lawsuits by the exorbitant claims of their hosts for indemnification of the expenses of their mercenary hospitality ; for remedy whereof, it was ordained, that an inhabitant, neglecting in such circumstances to forewarn his guest and to make an express compact with him, should be reputed to have entertained him from mere courtesy and benevolence.[1] All the foregoing laws continued in force long after the British Revolution.

It appears from the first of these statutes, that Indians visiting the territories of the State were liable to be enslaved by the colonists ; and in Jefferson's statistical account of Virginia, it is admitted that the practice of subjecting those savages to slavery did at one time actually prevail.[2] But with the Indian tribes situated in their immediate vicinity, and comprehended in the pacification negotiated by Colonel Jeffreys, the colonists maintained relations more approaching to friendship and equality. The Indians paid, indeed, in conformity with the treaty of peace, an annual tribute of beaver-skins to the provincial government.[3] But their territories were ascertained by the treaty, and secured to them by the guaranty of the provincial laws ; and every wrong they might sustain at the hands of any of the colonists was punished in the same manner as if it had been done to an Englishman.[4] By the aid of a donation from that distinguished religious philosopher,

---

[1] *Abridgment of the Laws of Virginia.* Beverly. Burk.
[2] *Notes on Virginia.*   [3] Beverly.
[4] *Abridgment of the Laws of Virginia.* "That the lands of this country were taken from the Indians by conquest is not so general a truth as is supposed. I find, in our historians and records, repeated proofs of purchases which cover a considerable part of the lower country ; and many more would doubtless be found on farther search. The upper country, we know, has been acquired altogether by purchases made in the most unexceptionable form." *Notes on Virginia.*

Robert Boyle, an attempt was made to render the institution, which, from its founders, has been called William and Mary College, subservient to the instruction of the Indians.   Some young persons, belonging to the friendly tribes, received at this seminary the rudiments of civil and religious education ; and the colonists, sensible of the advantages they derived from possessing in the persons of such pupils the most valuable hostages of the pacific demeanour of their parents, prevailed with some of the more remote nations of the Indians to send a few of their children to drink of the same fountain of knowledge.   But as the pupils were restored to their parent tribes, when they attained the age that fitted them for hunting and warlike exercises, it is not likely that the course of collegiate instruction which they pursued produced any wide or permanent impression on the character of the Indians, or made any adequate compensation for the destructive vices and diseases which the Europeans were unhappily much more successful in imparting.[1]

Attempts to convert barbarians very frequently disappoint their promoters ; and not those persons only who have assisted the undertaking from merely secular ends, but those also, who, truly regarding the divine glory in the end, disregard, at least in some measure, the divine agency in the means.   As an instrument of temporal improvement merely, and civilization, the preaching of the gospel will ever be found to disappoint all those who have no higher or ulterior views.   In a civilized and Christian land, the great bulk of the people are Christians merely in name ; reputation, convenience, and habit are the sources of their religious denomination ; an early and habitual familiarity with mysterious doctrine evades the difficulty of reasonable assent to it ; vices are so disguised, that the testimonies of Christian preachers against them often miss their aim ; and a professed devotedness to the service of piety and the pursuit of spiritual good is easily reconciled with, and esteemed a decent livery of, more real and substantial devotion to all that is worldly, selfish, and sensual.   But among heathens and savages, a convert to Christianity must change his style of life, overcome his habits, renounce his opinions, and forfeit his reputation ; and none, or at least very few, become professors, except from the influence of real conviction, more or less lasting and profound.   Those who remain unconverted, if they be honestly addressed by the missionary preachers, are incensed at the testimony against their evil deeds and sullied nature ; and the conduct of many professing Christians among their civilized neighbours too often contributes to mislead and confirm them in error.   But this topic will derive an ampler illustration from occurrences that relate to others of the North American States, than the early history of Virginia is fitted to supply.

Literature was but very slightly cultivated in Virginia.   There was not at this period, nor for many years after, a single bookseller's shop in the colony.[2] Yet a history of Virginia was written some years after by Beverly,   a native of the province, who had taken an active part in public affairs prior to the Revolution of 1688.   The first edition of this work in 1705, and a later edition in 1722, were published in England.   Beverly   is a brief and some-

[1] Beverly (edit. 1722). In citing this author, it is the edition of 1705 that I refer to, when the other is not expressly named.

[2] The literature of North America was at this time monopolized almost entirely by New England.   In the beginning of the eighteenth century, when Boston contained five printing-offices and many booksellers' shops, there was but one bookseller's shop in New York, and not one in Virginia, Maryland, or Carolina.   Neal's *History of New England.*   Even in the provincial towns of the parent state booksellers' shops were very rare at this period.   Boswell's *Life of Johnson.*

what agreeable annalist, and has appended to his narrative of events an account of the institutions of the province, and of the manners of the colonial and aboriginal inhabitants.   He is chargeable with great ignorance and incorrectness in those parts of his story that embrace events occurring in England, or elsewhere beyond the immediate precincts of Virginia.   Only the initial letters of his name appear on the title-page of his book, — whence Oldmixon was led into the mistake of supposing his name to have been *Bullock;* and in some of the critical catalogues of Germany he has received the erroneous appellation of *Bird.*[1]   A much more enlarged and elaborate history of Virginia (but, unfortunately, carried no further down than the year 1624) was written at a later period by Stith, also a native of the province, and one of the governors of William and Mary College.   Stith is a candid, accurate historian, and accomplished scholar ; tediously minute in relating the debates in the Court of Proprietors of the Virginia Company, and their disputes with the king ; but generally impressive and interesting. A manly and liberal spirit pervades every page of his work, which was first published at Williamsburg in 1747.

Beverly warmly extols the hospitality of his countrymen ; a commendation which the peculiarity of their condition renders sufficiently credible, though the preamble of one of their laws, which we have already noticed, demonstrates that its application was by no means universal. He reproaches them with indolence, which he ascribes to their residence in scattered dwellings, and their destitution of that collected life which promotes mutual cooperation and competition, invigorates industry, and nourishes the spirit of adventurous enterprise.   It may be ascribed, also, to the influence of slavery in fostering pride and discrediting labor.   A life like that of the first Virginian colonists, remote from crowded haunt, unoccupied by a multitude and variety of objects and purposes, sequestered from the intelligence of passing events, and yet connected, by origin, remembrance, and interest, with a distant and distinguished realm, is the life of those to whom the company of strangers is peculiarly acceptable.   All the other circumstances of such a lot contribute to the promotion of hospitable habits.   As for many of their hours the inhabitants can find no more interesting occupation, so of much of their superfluous produce they can find no more profitable use, than the entertainment of visitors.[2]

It was the remarkable and fortunate peculiarity of their local situation, that prevented a people so early devoted to commerce as the Virginians from congregating in large towns and forming marts of trade.   The same peculiarity characterized that portion of their original territory which was subsequently formed into the separate province of Maryland ; and there, too, it was attended with similar effects.   The whole of that vast region is pervaded by numerous streams, that impart fertility to the land, and carry the produce they have promoted to the great highway of nations. From the Bay of Chesapeake, where all those streams unite, the greater number of

[1] Warden, a late American writer, has repeated this error, and described as the production of Bird what in reality was the first edition of Beverly's work.   There really was a history of Virginia written and published by a Colonel Bird, in the beginning of the eighteenth century ; but 1 have never been able to meet with it.   Oldmixon, in his Preface, gives some account of the author, and refers to his work among the other materials which he himself had made use of.

[2] "Mr. Jefferson told me, that in his father's time it was no uncommon thing for gentlemen to post their servants on the main road for the purpose of amicably waylaying and bringing to their houses any travellers who might chance to pass."   Hall's *Travels in Canada and the United States.*

them afford an extensive navigation into the interior of the country ; and the colonists, perceiving that in order to embark the produce of their land they needed not to quit their plantations, but might load the merchant ships at the doors of their country warehouses, dispersed themselves[1] along the banks of the rivers, and united the healthful felicity of rural life with the advantages of commerce.   Except the small towns of Williamsburg, which succeeded Jamestown as the capital of Virginia, and Annapolis, the capital of Maryland, no cities grew up for a very long period in either of these provinces. This social condition proved highly favorable to those two great sources of national happiness, — good morals, and the facility of gaining by industry a moderate competence and a respectable station in society.   The convicts who were transported to the colony, finding none of the opportunities of confederacy, pillage, and concealment, that large towns afford, either returned to Europe at the expiration of their periods of service, or, impressed with the advantages which the country so liberally tendered to honest toil and sobriety of manners, they melted into the mass of humble and respectable free laborers.   To this important class of society the virtues of industry and economy were recommended by prizes both greater and nearer than any other social community ever before presented.   Labor was so valuable, and land so cheap, that a very few years of diligent exertion could promote the laborer to the condition of a land-owner ;[2] no one needed to despair of a competence ; and none found it practicable to amass enormous wealth. Manual work, no longer the badge of hopeless poverty, was respected as the certain passport to independence ; nor was there among the free population any distinction of rank which industry and virtue were unable to surmount.   A constant and general progression, accomplished without scramble or peril, gave a quiet alacrity to life ; and fellow-feeling was not obstructed, nor insolence and servility engendered, by numerous instances of a wide inequality of condition.   They were, and are, undoubtedly, a happy people.

Two causes, however, have contributed, in this and others of the American provinces, to impede the operation and abridge the influence of circumstances so favorable to happiness and virtue.   Of these, by far the most important is the institution of domestic slavery ; a practice fraught with incalculable evil to the morals, manners, and felicity of every country into which it has gained admission.   The slaves are reduced to a state of misery and degradation ; to a state which experience has pronounced so destructive to virtue, that, in many languages, the condition of a slave and the character of a thief are expressed by the same word.   The experience of every age has confirmed the maxim of Homer, that *the day which makes man a slave takes half his worth away.*   The masters are justly loaded with the guilt of all the wretchedness and worthlessness which the condition of slavery inevitably infers ; every mind is tainted with the evil which it engenders and displays, and sustains an abatement either of happiness or virtue.   Every master of a slave, whether he term himself citizen or subject, is a monarch endowed with more uncontrolled authority than any sovereign in Europe enjoys ; and every country where slavery is admitted, whether it call itself

---

[1] " But, as the bees which have no hive collect no honey, the commerce which was thus dispersed accumulated no wealth."   Tucker's *Life of Jefferson.*

[2] " I remember the time when five pounds were left by a charitable testator to the poor of the parish he lived in ; and it lay nine years before the executors could find one poor enough to be entitled to any part of this legacy ; and at last it was all given to one old woman. So that this may in truth be termed the best poor man's country in the world."   Beverly.

kingdom or republic, is a country subject to the dominion of tyrants. Nay, the more liberal its political constitution, the more severe in general is its system of domestic tyranny ; and the experience of every age has verified the Grecian proverb, that *none are so completely enslaved as the slaves of the free.* Human character is as much corrupted and depraved by the arrogance of domination as by the depression of servitude ; and slavery is a state wherein *one man ruleth over another to his own hurt.* The same wisdom which assigned to man his duties adapted them to the development of his understanding and the refinement of his sensibility. This adaptation is particularly visible in the duties that regulate the mutual intercourse of men. To violate therein the law of kindness and the principles of equity is to warp the understanding,[1] as well as to corrupt the heart ; to lower the dignity of rational, and the happiness of sensible beings. There is a perpetual reciprocation of evil between a master and his slaves. His injustice consigns them to their servile state ; and the evil qualities that this condition engenders in them tend continually to provoke his irascibility. His power inflicts their degradation ; and their degradation at once provokes and facilitates the excesses of his power. In proportion to the rigor of their treatment is the hatred which he inspires in them, and which, reacting on its own dire cause, imparts a wider scope and keener edge to his cruelty. Hence the commerce between master and slave tends to stimulate and exhibit all that is odious and revolting in human passion and conduct. The delicate susceptibility of women is exposed to the impression of this spectacle, and the imitative disposition of children exercised amidst its continual display. In the picture that Juvenal has drawn of the toilet of a Roman lady we behold a striking illustration of the influence of domestic slavery in corrupting even the gentler sex with the direst cruelty ; and that the picture was far from being overcharged may unhappily be deduced from the delineations, still more odious, that present themselves in the pages of modern travellers in North America and the West Indies. Female slaves, regarding the freemen as a superior race of beings, lose alike the virtues and the rights of women in their intercourse with them, and introduce into rural life modes of vice even more disgraceful and corruptive than those which are generated by the temptations of profligate cities. The freemen, habituated to consider the great majority of the females with whom they associate as an inferior race, are consequently exposed to an influence hostile to those sentiments and manners which constitute the moral grace and symbol of civilized life ; and proportionally descend to the level of that barbarous state in which women are regarded merely as instruments of drudgery or ministers of voluptuousness. Every description of work that is committed to slaves is performed with as much neglect and indolence as they dare to indulge, and is so degraded in common estimation, that the poorest freeman disdains to undertake it except when he is working for himself. White servants in America have been always distinguished for a jealous impatience of their position, and a reluctant and imperfect regard to the will of their masters. As the numbers of the slaves are multiplied, the industry of the free is thus repressed by the extension of slave labor ; and the safety of the state is endangered by the strength of a body of internal enemies ready to conspire against its tranquillity or to join its first invader.[2] The number of the slaves

---

[1] See Note IV., at the end of the volume.

[2] "I tremble for my country," says Jefferson, in his observations on the slave population

and gladiators contributed to the downfall of Rome ; and, indeed, every body politic, compounded of parts so heterogeneous as freemen and slaves, plainly contains within itself a principle of progressive disease and corruption. Such a mixture tends also to pervert and confound the moral sentiments of all mankind, and to degrade the value of those free institutions which are seen to form a canopy for the shelter of domestic tyranny,[1] to mock one portion of the people with such liberty and dignity as jailers enjoy, and to load all the rest with such fetters as only felons should wear.

Of all the forms under which slavery has ever appeared in the world, negro slavery is the most odious and mischievous. The difference of color aggravates the distinction of condition between the master and the slave ; and the mutual hatred and fear generated between individuals by this accidental relation are extended to natural distinctions of bodily feature, and perpetuated between whole races of men. Long as well as grievous are the consequences of guilt and injustice. The first introduction of slavery into a country plants a canker, of which the entire malignity is not perceived till in an after age, when it has attained an extent, which, concurring with the attendant train of prejudices and antipathies, renders its extirpation exceedingly difficult. This consideration, without tending to diminish our abhorrence of a system so fraught with mischief and danger, mitigates the severity of our censure on those to whom the system, already matured by long continuance and fortified by inveterate prejudice, has unhappily descended. And even with regard to the race who first introduced it we shall not fulfil the duty of fellow-men, if we omit to consider the apologies which may reasonably be supposed to have deluded their conscience and understanding, and veiled from their view the wickedness they committed and the misery they prepared. The negroes first brought to Virginia were enslaved before they came there, and by the purchase of the colonists were delivered from the hold of a slave-ship and the peculiar and notorious cruelty of the Dutch. Some little good might thus at first seem to result from the commission of evil. When the slaves were few in number, and consequently incapable of awakening public jealousy and alarm, they appear to have been kindly treated ;[2] and their masters perhaps intended to emancipate them at that *convenient season* for adjusting the accounts of interest and conscience, which every added year and every addition to their numbers tended still farther to postpone. Even at a later pe-

of this province, " when I reflect that God is just ; that his justice cannot sleep for ever ; that, considering numbers, nature, and natural means only, a revolution of the wheel of fortune, an exchange of situation, is among possible events ; that it may become probable by supernatural interference ! The Almighty has no attribute which can take side with us in such a contest." *Notes on Virginia.* So early as the year 1687, we are told that " a plan of insurrection of the blacks was at this time discovered in the Northern Neck, just in time to prevent its explosion." Seneca relates that it was once proposed at Rome to discriminate the slaves by a peculiar dress ; but it was justly apprehended that there might be some danger in acquainting them with their own numbers. This information is conveyed to the negroes by their color ; and this color being always a mark of contempt, even those negroes, who become free in countries where their race is generally enslaved, continue allied, both by the most irritating feelings, and by the sympathy they must entertain for men of the same complexion, with all those who remain in a state of bondage.

[1] *To dream of freedom in his slave's embrace* — is represented with bitter satire and melancholy truth by the Irish bard, Moore, as the felicity of many an American planter.

[2] The treatment of slaves at Rome, latterly distinguished by the most enormous cruelty, was originally kind and humane. Plutarch, *Life of Coriolanus.* In the reign of the Emperor Claudius, it was found necessary to pass a law forbidding masters to kill their slaves on account of age or infirmity. The original admission of the Hebrews into Egypt was an act of benevolence ; and it was only when they had waxed numerically strong that they experienced the rigors of bondage.

riod and in altered circumstances, numerous instances have been known of what is most inappropriately termed the *humane* treatment of negro slaves by masters, who, freely dispensing physical comforts and indulgences to them, and carefully barring them from the knowledge that would waken aspiration for a higher moral condition, appeal to their unmanly contentment with degradation as a proof that slavery may be a happy state.[1]

Negro slavery lingered long in the settlements of the Puritans in New England, and of the Quakers in New Jersey and Pennsylvania; although in none of these States did the climate, or the soil and its appropriate culture, suggest the same temptations to this inhumanity which presented themselves in the southern quarters of America. Las Casas, so distinguished by the warmth of his philanthropy, first suggested its introduction into Mexico and Peru; George Fox, the most intrepid and enthusiastic of reformers, demanded no more of his followers than a mitigation of its rigor in Barbadoes; and the illustrious philosopher, John Locke, renowned also as the champion of religious and political freedom, introduced an express sanction of it into the fundamental constitutions of Carolina. Georgia is the only one of the North American States in which slavery was expressly disallowed by the fundamental laws; but these laws were soon repealed; and in none of the other States has slavery proved a more rigorous and oppressive yoke than in Georgia. Considerations such as these are calculated to increase at once our indulgence for mankind, and our abhorrence of that insidious and formidable mischief which has so signally baffled the penetration of the wise, and triumphed over the benevolence of the humane.

The other cause which has been alluded to, as operating unfavorably on the prosperity of Virginia, is the inordinate cultivation of tobacco. As long as Virginia and Maryland were the only provinces of North America where this commodity was produced, their inhabitants devoted themselves almost exclusively to a culture which is attended with much inconvenience to the persons engaged in it, and no small disadvantage to their country even when moderately pursued. It requires extremely fatiguing labor from the cultivators, and exhausts the fertility of the ground; and, as little food of any kind is raised on the tobacco plantations, the men and cattle employed on them are badly fed, and the soil is progressively impoverished.[2] This disadvantage was long experienced in Virginia; but has been diminished by the introduction into the markets of Europe of the tobacco produce of territories more recently subjected to cultivation.[3]

---

[1] One of the best pictures I have ever met with of the actual operation of negro slavery occurs in Pinckard's *Notes on the West Indies.*

[2] Jefferson's *Notes on Virginia.*   [3] Priest's *Travels in America.* Warden.

BOOK II.

THE NEW ENGLAND STATES.

CHAPTER I.

Attempts of the Plymouth Company to colonize the northern Coasts of America. — Popham establishes a Colony at Fort Saint George. — Sufferings and Return of the Colonists. — Captain Smith's Voyage and Survey of the Country — which is named New England. — His ineffectual Attempt to conduct a Colony thither. — The Company relinquish the Design of colonizing New England. — History and Character of the Puritans. — Rise of the Brownists or Independents. — A Congregation of Independents retire to Holland — they resolve to settle in America — their Negotiation with King James — they arrive in Massachusetts — and found New Plymouth. — Hardships — and Virtue of the Colonists. — Their civil Institutions. — Community of Property. — Increase of civil and ecclesiastical Tyranny in England. — Project of a new Colony in Massachusetts. — Salem built. — Charter of Massachusetts Bay obtained from Charles the First by an Association of Puritans. — Embarkation of the Emigrants — Arrival at Salem. — Their ecclesiastical Institutions. — Two Persons banished from the Colony for Schism. — Intolerance of some of the Puritans.

WHEN James the First of England gave his sanction to the project of colonizing the vast district of North America which was comprehended at that time [1606] under the name of Virginia, he made a partition, which we have already remarked, of the territory between two trading companies, and established the residence of the one at London, and of the other at Plymouth. If the object of this partition was to diminish the inconvenience of monopoly, and diffuse the benefit of colonial relations more extensively in England, the means were ill adapted to the end ; and eventually the operation of this act of policy was far from corresponding with its design. The resources of the adventurers, who had already prepared to undertake the enterprise of colonization, were divided so unequally, and yet so much to the disadvantage of all parties, that even the more powerful company was barely enabled to maintain a feeble and precarious settlement in Virginia ; while the weaker, without ability to accomplish the purpose of its institution, obtained little more than the privilege of debarring the rest of the world from attempting it. We have seen that the southern colony, — though promoted by a corporation which reckoned among its members some of the richest and most considerable persons in the realm, and enjoyed the advantage of being situated in a town then engrossing almost all the commercial wealth of England, — even with the aid of these favorable circumstances, made but slow and laborious advances to a secure establishment. The Plymouth Company possessing much narrower resources and a less advantageous situation, its efforts were proportionally more feeble and inadequate.

The most conspicuous members of the Plymouth Company were Sir John Popham, lord chief justice of England, Sir Ferdinando Gorges, governor of Plymouth Fort, and Sir John Gilbert, nephew of that distinguished adventurer who has already engaged our notice as the first obtainer of a patent of colonization from Queen Elizabeth, and the earliest conductor of emigrants to America. Animated by the zeal of these men, and especially of Popham, who assumed the principal direction of their measures, the Plymouth Company, shortly after their association, despatched a small vessel to inspect their territories ; but soon received the mortifying intelligence of its capture by the Spaniards, who still pretended right to exclude every other people from the navigation of the American seas. The chief justice and his friends, however, were too much bent on the prosecution of their purpose to be deterred by this disaster. At his own expense, Popham equipped and despatched another vessel to resume the survey ; and having received a favorable report of the appearance of the country, he availed himself of the impression produced by the tidings to raise a sufficient supply of men and money for the formation of a colony. [May, 1607.] Under the command of his brother, Henry Popham, and of Raleigh Gilbert, brother of Sir John, a hundred emigrants, embarking in two vessels, repaired to the territory of what was still called Northern Virginia ; and took possession of a piece of ground near the River Sagadahoc, where they built a stronghold and named it Fort Saint George. The district where they established themselves was rocky and barren ; and their provisions were so scanty, that they were obliged, soon after their arrival, to send back to England all but forty-five of their number. The winter proved extremely severe, and confined this small remnant to their miserable dwelling, and a helpless contemplation of the dreary waste that surrounded it. Disease, the offspring of scarcity and hardship, augmented the general gloom ; and before the return of spring, several of the adventurers, and among others their president, Henry Popham, had sunk into the grave. With the spring [1608], arrived a vessel laden with supplies from England ; but the intelligence that accompanied these supplies more than counterbalanced the satisfaction they afforded ; for the colonists were now informed of the deaths of Chief Justice Popham and Sir John Gilbert, the most powerful of their patrons and most active of their benefactors. Their resolution was completely subdued by so many misfortunes ; and, unanimously exclaiming against longer continuance in those dismal scenes, they forsook the settlement and returned to their native land, which they filled with the most disheartening accounts of the soil and climate of Northern Virginia.[1] The American historians have been careful to note that this disastrous expedition originated with the judge, who (odious and despicable in every part of his professional career) had, three years before, presided with the most scandalous injustice at the trial of Raleigh, and condemned to the death of a traitor the man to whom both England and America were so greatly beholden.

The miscarriage of this colonial experiment, and the evil report raised against the scene where it had been attempted, deterred the Plymouth Company for some time from any farther exertion to plant a settlement in Northern Virginia, and produced an impression on the minds of the people of England very unfavorable to emigration to that territory. For several years, the operations of the company were confined to a few fishing voyages to Cape Cod, and a traffic in peltry and oil with the natives. At length their prospects were cheered by a gleam of better fortune ; and the introduction of Captain Smith — already known to us by his guardianship of the

[1] Smith's *History of Virginia, New England*, &c. Stith's *History of Virginia.* Neal's *History of New England.* Hutchinson's *History of Massachusetts.*

infant province of Virginia — into their service, seemed to betoken more vigorous and successful enterprise. Sir Ferdinando Gorges and some other leading members of the Plymouth Company, justly appreciating the genius and merit of this man, were fain to engage his valuable services, which the London Company had unworthily neglected. [1614.] Six years after the abandonment of the settlement at Sagadahoc, two vessels were despatched, under the command of Captain Smith and Captain Hunt, on a voyage of trade and discovery to the Plymouth Company's territories. Smith, having concluded his traffic with the natives, left his crew engaged in fishing, and, accompanied by only eight men, travelled into the interior of the country, surveyed its condition, explored with care and diligence the whole coast from Cape Cod to Penobscot, and composed a map in which its features were accurately delineated. On his return to England, he presented his map, with an account of his travels and observations, to Prince Charles, who was so much pleased with the description of the country, that he bestowed on it the name of New England, which it has ever since retained.

The successful voyage of Captain Smith, and the favorable account that he gave of the territory, though they contributed not a little to animate the spirit of commercial adventure, could not overcome the general reluctance to a permanent settlement in this region, which the misfortunes of the first colonists had created in England. The impediments to a colonial establishment in this quarter of America, besides, were greatly increased by the conduct of Hunt, who had been associated with Smith in the late voyage. That sordid and profligate man, unwilling that the benefit of the existing narrow traffic with the company's territories, which was exclusively shared by himself and a few others who were aware of its advantages, should be more generally diffused by the formation of a colony, resolved to defeat the design by embroiling his countrymen with the natives ; and for this purpose, having enticed a number of these people on board his ship, he set sail with them for Malaga, where he had been ordered to touch on his homeward voyage, and sold them for slaves to the Spaniards. The company, indignant at his wickedness, instantly dismissed him from their service ; but his mischievous purpose was accomplished ; and the next vessel that returned from New England brought intelligence of the vindictive hostilities of the savages. Undismayed by all these difficulties and dangers, Smith determined to make an effort for the colonization of the northern territory ; and having communicated a portion of his own resolute hope and spirit to some of the leading patentees, he was enabled, by their assistance, to equip a small squadron, and set sail at the head of a band of emigrants for New England. [1615.] Thus far could energy prevail ; but in a struggle with fate, farther advancement was impracticable ; and Smith, who had now accomplished all that man could do, was destined to experience that all was unavailing. The voyage was one uninterrupted scene of disaster. After encountering a violent tempest by which the vessels had nearly perished, and escaping more than once from the attacks of pirates, Smith was made prisoner by the commander of a French fleet, who mistook or pretended to mistake him for Captain Argal, and charged him with the guilt of the piratical enterprise which Argal had conducted in the preceding year against Port Royal.[1] On this unjust charge, Smith was separated from his crew, and detained

---

[1] Book I., Chap. II., ante.

long in captivity. It was happy for himself and for mankind that he lived to return to his country and write the history of his travels, instead of reaching New England, where his blood would probably have stained the land which his genius and virtue have contributed to illustrate. Several years afterwards [1619], the Plymouth Company, having discovered that an Indian, named *Squanto*, one of the persons kidnapped by Hunt, had escaped from the Spaniards, and found his way to Britain, acquitted themselves to his satisfaction of the injury he had suffered, enriched him with valuable gifts, and sent him back to New England along with a small expedition commanded by one Dormer, who was directed to avail himself of Squanto's assistance in regaining the friendship of the Indians. But although Squanto earnestly labored to pacify his abused countrymen, and assured them that Hunt's treachery had been condemned and punished in England, they would hearken to no suggestion that forbade the gratification of their burning revenge, and, watching a favorable opportunity, attacked and dangerously wounded Dormer and several of his party, who, escaping with difficulty from the hostile region, left Squanto behind to urge at more leisure and with better success his topics of apology and conciliation. Disgusted by so many disappointments, the company laid aside all thoughts of establishing colonies in New England. An insignificant traffic bounded their own adventures ; and they exercised no farther dominion over the territory than the distribution of small portions of the northern quarter of it to private adventurers, who occupied them in summer as mercantile factories or victualling stations for the use of vessels resorting thither for trade.[1]

We have sufficient assurance that the course of this world is not governed by chance ; and that the series of events which it exhibits is regulated by divine ordinance, and adapted to purposes, which, from their transcendent wisdom and infinite range, often elude the conceptive grasp of created capacity. As it could not, then, be without high design, so it seems to have been for no common object, that discomfiture was thus entailed on the counsels of princes, the schemes of the wise, and the efforts of the brave. It was for no ordinary people that the land was reserved, and of no common qualities or vulgar superiority that it was appointed the prize. New England was the destined asylum of oppressed piety and virtue ;[2] and its colonization, denied to the pretensions of greatness and the efforts of might, was reserved for persons whom the great and mighty despised for their insignificance, and persecuted for their integrity. The recent growth of the Virginian colony, and the repeated attempts to form a settlement in New England, naturally attracted to this quarter the eyes of men who felt little reluctance to abandon a country, where, for conscience's sake, they had already incurred the loss of temporal ease and enjoyment ; whom persecution had fortified to the endurance of hardship, and piety had taught to despise it. It was at this juncture accordingly, that the project of colonizing New England was undertaken by the Puritans ; a class of men of whose origin, sentiments, and previous history it is proper that we here subjoin some account.

Of all the national churches of Europe, which, at the era of the Reformation, renounced the doctrine and revolted from the dominion of the see of Rome, there was none in which the origin of the separation was so discreditable, or the proceedings to which it immediately gave rise so unrea-

---

[1] Smith. Neal.   [2] " Jupiter illa piæ secrevit littora genti." Horace.

sonable and inequitable, as the church of England.[1] This arose partly from the circumstance of the alteration in this church having mainly originated with the temporal magistrate, and partly from the character of the individuals by whom the interposition of magisterial authority was exerted. In the Palatinate, in Brandenburg, Holland, Geneva, and Scotland, where the reform proceeded from the general conviction, the doctrine and constitution of the national church corresponded with the religious sentiments of the people. The Biblical Christianity taught by Calvin and Luther (with circumstantial varieties, occasioned by variety of human capacity, sensibility, and attainment) superseded the traditional dogmas of the church of Rome ; and the primitive simplicity of the Presbyterian administration (with proportionate varieties, of similar origin) superseded the pageantry of her ceremonial and the pomp of her constitution. In England, the Reformation originating from a different source, its institutions received a tincture from qualities proportionally different. The same haughty and imperious disposition, that prompted Henry the Eighth to abolish the authority of the church of Rome in his dominions, regulated all his views and conduct in constructing a substitute for the abrogated system. Abetted by a crew of servile dependents and sordid nobles, whom he enriched with the spoils of the plundered monasteries, and by a compliant House of Commons, whose profession of faith veered about with every variation of the royal creed, he neither felt nor affected the slightest respect for the sentiments of the mass of the people, a portion of his subjects to whose petitions he once answered, by a public proclamation, that they were " but brutes and inexpert folk," and as unfit to advise him as blind men were to judge of colors.[2] His object was to substitute himself and his successors as heads of the church, in place of the pope ; and for the maintenance of this usurped dominion, he retained, both in the ceremonies of worship and in the constitution of the clerical order, a great deal of the machinery which his predecessor in the supremacy had found useful. The unbridled vehemence of his temper detracted somewhat from the policy of his devices, and greatly disguised their aspect as a politic system by that show of good faith and sincerity which accompanied all his actions, and which was but the natural result of sincere and impetuous selfishness, and of a presumptuous and undoubting conviction of the superiority of his own understanding and the infallibility of its dictates.[3] While he rigidly denied the right of private judgment to his subjects, his own incessant and imperious exercise of this right continually tempted them to partake the satisfaction it seemed to afford him ; and the frequent variations of the creeds he promulgated at once excited a spirit of speculation akin to his own, and practically refuted the only pretence that could recommend or entitle his judgment to the implicit assent of fallible men. The pope, expressly maintaining, that, in virtue of his sacred office, he could never be in the

[1] " The work, which had been begun by Henry, the murderer of his wives, was continued by Somerset, the murderer of his brother, and completed by Elizabeth, the murderer of her guest. Sprung from brutal passion, nurtured by selfish policy, the Reformation in England displayed little of what had in other countries distinguished it, unflinching and unsparing devotion, boldness of speech, and singleness of eye." *Edinburgh Review.*

[2] Lord Herbert's *Life of Henry the Eighth.*

[3] The public disputation which he held with one of his subjects, the noble-minded and unfortunate Lambert, who denied the doctrine of the real presence, was, perhaps, regarded at the time as an act of admirable zeal and most generous condescension. It might have merited this praise, if the horrid death by which he revenged the impotence of his logic did not prove it to have been an overflowing of arrogance and vain-glory.

wrong, was disabled from correcting either his own errors or those bequeathed to him by his predecessors. Henry, merely pretending to the privilege of being always in the right, defeated this pretension by the variety and inconsistency of the systems to which he applied it. While he insisted on retaining much of the peculiar doctrine of the church of Rome, he attacked, in its infallibility, a tenet not only important in itself, but the sole sanction and foundation of a great many others. Notwithstanding his desire to restrain it, — nay, promoted, indeed, by some part of his own conduct, — a spirit of religious inquiry began to arise among the multitude of professors who blindly or interestedly had followed the fortunes and the fluctuations of the royal creed ; and the knowledge of divine truth, combined with a growing regard for simplicity of divine worship, arising first in the higher classes, spread downwards through the successive grades of society in this and the following reigns. The administration of inquisitorial oaths, and the infliction, in various instances, of decapitation, torture, and burning, for the crime of heresy, during Henry's reign, demonstrate how fully he embraced the character as well as the pretensions of the haughtiest pontiffs that ever filled the Romish see,[1] and how ineffectually he labored to impose his own heterogeneous system of opinions on the understandings of his subjects. Even in his lifetime, the Protestant doctrines had spread far beyond the limits of any of the peculiar creeds which he adopted and promulgated ; and in their illegitimate extent made numerous proselytes in his court and kingdom. The propagation of them was aided by the translation and diffusion of the Scriptures, which he vainly endeavoured to prevent, and which enabled his people to imbibe religious knowledge, unstinted and unadulterated, from its everlasting fountains. The open profession of those illicit opinions was in many instances repressed by the terror of his inflexible cruelty, and by the influence over his measures which his lay and clerical courtiers found it easy to obtain by feigning implicit submission to his capricious and impetuous temper.[2] The temptations which these men were exposed to proved fatal, in some instances, to their integrity ; and several of them (even the vaunted Cranmer) concurred, though reluctantly, in punishing by a cruel death the public avowal of sentiments which they secretly cherished in their own breasts.

By the death of Henry the Eighth his Protestant subjects were released from the necessity of farther dissimulation. In the reign of his son, Edward the Sixth, the Catholic doctrines were wholly expunged from the national creed, and the fundamental articles of the Protestant faith recognized and established by law. As, among other practices of the preceding reign, the absurd and tyrannical device of promoting uniformity of faith and worship by persecution was still pursued,[3] the influence of temporal fear and favor contributed, no doubt, to encumber the Protestant church with many reluctant and hypocritical professors. In the hope of reconciling the English nation as extensively as possible to the system which they established, the ministers of Edward preserved not only the ecclesiastical constitution which Henry had retained, but as much of the ancient ceremonial of worship as they judged likely to gratify the taste and predilections of minds that still hankered after Catholic pageantry. They rather complied in this respect

---

[1] One of his laws (31 Henry VIII. Cap. 14) bears the presumptuous title of " An act for *abolishing diversity of opinions* in certain articles concerning the Christian religion."
[2] Lord Herbert.
[3] 2 & 3 Edward VI. Cap. I. Burnet's *History of the Reformation.* Rymer.

with the prevalent temper and disposition of the people, than indulged their own sentiments or followed out their principles ; and plainly insinuated their opinion, that, whenever the public mind was sufficiently prepared for it, a farther reformation should be introduced into the establishment, by inserting a prayer to this purpose in the liturgy.[1] But, in the exercise of their temporizing policy, the rulers of the English reformed church encountered a spirit of resistance, originating in the Protestant body itself. During the late reign, the disaffection that had been cherished in secret towards the national church was not confined to the doctrines savoring of Popery, which she retained, and which many Protestants connected in their opinion and esteem with the ceremonial rites and clerical habits that had for ages been their inveterate associate and distinctive livery. With their enmity to the doctrines of the Romish church, they combined an aversion to those ceremonies which her ministers had too often rendered subservient to imposture ; which seemed to owe their survivance in the national system to the same cloud of error and superstition that had long sheltered so much doctrinal heresy ; and which diverted the mind from that spiritual worship expressly claimed for the Most High in the Scriptures of truth.

These sentiments, which were subsequently developed and ripened into the doctrines of the Puritans, had already taken possession of the minds of some of the English Protestants ; but their operation was yet comparatively feeble and partial. One of the most remarkable manifestations of their influence that has been transmitted to us was afforded by Bishop Hooper, who, in the reign of Edward, refused to be consecrated to his office in the superstitious habits (as he deemed them) appropriated by the church to the episcopal order. The Protestant opinions of this prelate had rendered him an exile from England during the latter part of the preceding reign, and his Puritan sentiments were confirmed by the conversation of the Presbyterian teachers with whom he associated during his residence abroad. Cranmer and Ridley, who were afterwards his fellow-sufferers under the persecution of Mary, resorted to arguments, threats, entreaties, and imprisonment, in order to overcome Hooper's objections ; and it was not without great difficulty and reluctance that his rigid spirit condescended to terminate the dispute by a compromise.[2] The sentiments which had thus received the sanction of a man distinguished no less by the purity and elevation of his character than by the eminence of his station in the church, continued to manifest themselves throughout the short reign of Edward ; and there was scarcely a rite of the established worship, or an article of ecclesiastical apparel, that escaped impugnation and contentious discussion.[3] The defenders of the controverted practices (or at least the more enlightened of this party) did not pretend that they were of divine appointment, or in themselves of essential importance. They maintained that they were in themselves inoffensive, and that by long establishment and inveterate association they had taken possession of the reverence of the people, and contributed to attach their affections to the national worship. They admitted, that, as useless and exotical appendages, it was desirable that time and reason should gradually obliterate such practices ; but insisted that it would be both unwise and illiberal to abolish them abruptly, and at the risk of unhinging the important sentiments with which they had accidentally connected themselves. This reasoning was very unsatisfactory to the Puritans, who rejected such

[1] Neal.   [2] Burnet. Heylin's *History of the Reformation.*   [3] Strype.

temporizing policy as the counsel of lukewarm piety and worldly wisdom, and regarded with abhorrence the mixture of superstitious attractions with the motives to that which should be entirely a reasonable service ; [1] and whatever weight the arguments of the prevailing party may be considered to possess, they certainly cannot justify the violent imposition of observances, which their own patrons regarded as indifferent, on persons who deemed them sinful and pernicious. The sentiments of the Puritans, whether supported or not by superior force of reason, were overborne by the force of superior numbers, and might perhaps have gradually died away, if the reign of Edward had been farther prolonged, or his sceptre been transmitted to a Protestant successor. But the reign of Mary was destined at once to purify the Protestant body by separating the true and sound members from the false or formal professors, and to radicate every Protestant sentiment by exposing it to the fiery test of tyrannical rage and persecution.

The administration of this queen was productive of events that tended to enliven and extend the Puritan sentiments, and at the same time to animate the opposition of some of their adversaries. During the heat of her bloody persecution, many of the English Protestants forsook their country, and sought refuge in the Protestant states of Germany and Switzerland. There, in regulating for themselves the forms and ordinances of divine worship, their ancient disputes naturally recurred, and were exasperated by the approach of the two parties to an equality of numbers that never before subsisted between them, and protracted by the utter want of a spirit of mutual compliance, and the absence of any tribunal from which an authoritative decision could be obtained. The Puritans beheld with pleasure in the continental churches the establishment of a constitution and ritual which had been the object of their own warm approbation and earnest desire ; and they either composed for themselves a formula of religious association on a similar model, or entered into communion with the churches established in the places where they resided. Their opponents, on the other hand, clung more firmly than ever to their ancient practices ; refused to surrender any one of the institutions of the faith, for the sake of which they had forsaken their country ; and plumed themselves on reproducing, amidst the desolation of their church at home, an entire and accurate model of her ordinances in the scene of their exile. Both parties were willing to have united in church-fellowship with each other, if either could have yielded in the dispute concerning forms of office, habits, and ceremonies. But though each considered itself strongest in faith, neither felt disposed on that account to succumb to what it deemed the infirmities of the other ; and though united in the great fundamental points of Christian belief, and associated by the common calamity that rendered them fellow-exiles in a foreign land, their fruitless controversies separated them more widely than they had ever been before, and inflamed them with mutual dislike and animosity.[2] On the death of Mary, both parties returned to England ; the one joyfully expecting to see their ancient style of worship restored ; the other more firmly wedded to their Puritan sentiments by the opportunity they had obtained of freely indulging them, and entertaining (in common with many who had remained at home) an increased antipathy to the habits and ceremonies which the recent ascendency and measures of Catholic bigots forcibly associated with the odious features of superstitious delusion and tyrannic cruelty.

---

[1] Strype.   [2] Neal.

The views, of which the Puritans expected the accomplishment from the accession of Elizabeth to the throne, were seconded by the disposition of not a few even of their opponents among the leading Protestant churchmen who had weathered the storm at home. Several of the most distinguished persons of this class expressed the strongest reluctance, in restoring the Protestant constitution, to interweave with its fundamental canons any subordinate or merely ceremonial regulations that might be offensive to men endeared to them by their common calamity, and so recently associated with them as confessors not merely for the forms but for the very substance of the Christian religion. Some of the Puritans, no doubt, were stiffly bent on reducing the model of the church to a strict conformity with their own peculiar sentiments and standard of propriety ; and some of their opponents were as stoutly resolved to prohibit and suppress every trace of Puritan practice.[1] The majority, however, as well as the leading members of both parties, were sincerely desirous to promote an accommodation on the principle of mutual forbearance ; and willingly agreed that the disputed habits and ceremonies should be retained in the church as observances merely of a discretionary and indifferent nature, not to be controverted by the one party nor enforced by the other, but left to be confirmed or abolished, extended or qualified, by the silent progress of sentiment and opinion.[2] But these wise and candid concessions were frustrated by the views and temper of the queen; whose authority soon defaced the fair prospect that had arisen of concord and happiness, and involved the people committed to her care in a long and widening scene of strife, malevolence, and misery.

Elizabeth inherited the headstrong and arrogant disposition of her father, and his taste for splendid pageantry. And though she was educated with her brother Edward, and her understanding had received a strong tincture of Protestant opinion, her sentiments inclined her, with manifest bias, in favor of the rites, discipline, and even doctrine of the Catholics ; of every thing, in short, that could lend an imposing aspect to the ecclesiastical establishment of which she was the supreme head, and extend the dominion which she was resolved to maintain over the clergy. She publicly thanked one of her chaplains for preaching in defence of the Real Presence, and rebuked another for mentioning with little reverence the Catholic notion of an inherent virtue in the symbol of the cross.[3] She desired to make the clergy priests, and not preachers ; discouraged their sermons ; and would have interdicted them from marriage, had she not been restrained by the remonstrances of her minister, Lord Burleigh.[4] Disregarding the wishes and entreaties both of Churchmen and Puritans, she restored King Edward's constitutions, with no other alteration than the omission of a few passages in the liturgy which were offensive to the Catholics ; and caused a law to be framed, commanding, under the penalties of fine, imprisonment, and deprivation of ministerial office, a strict uniformity of religious worship.[5] This was the first step in a line of policy which the church of England has had deep and lasting cause to deplore, and which, by compelling thousands of her best and ablest ministers reluctantly to forsake her communion, afflicted her with a decay of internal piety, of which the traces continued to be visible after the lapse of many generations.

But this law was for some time neither strictly nor generally executed. The queen could not at once find a sufficient number of persons fitted to

[1] Neal.   [2] Strype's *Life of Parker.* Neal.   [3] Heylin.   [4] Strype.   [5] Neal.

sustain the dignity of episcopal elevation, and yet willing to become the instruments of her arbitrary designs ; nor could all her efforts for a while excite general strife and ill-will among men, of whom so many, though differing from each other on subordinate points, had but lately been united by community of sentiment and suffering in the noblest cause that can interest human hearts.   Her first bench of bishops were not only eager to clear themselves of the reproach of having composed or approved the existing laws,[1] but, by a general forbearance to exact compliance with them, enabled the Puritan ministers and the practices of Puritanism to obtain a considerable footing in the church.   And though she reprimanded the primate, Parker, for his negligence, and at length stimulated him to the exertion of some rigor in the execution of the Act of Uniformity, it was far from obtaining general prevalence ; and by various acts of connivance on the one side, and prudent reserve or simulated compliance on the other, the Puritans were enabled to enjoy the semblance of toleration.   Their tranquillity was promoted by the accession of Grindall to the primacy.   The liberal principles and humane disposition of this man revolted against the tyrannical injustice which he was required to administer ; and at the expense of his own temporal liberty and dignity (for the queen disgraced and imprisoned him), he prolonged the duration of lenient policy and the peace of the church.[2]

At length, on the death of Grindall, the primacy was bestowed on Whitgift, a man of severe temper, a rigid votary of the established system of ecclesiastical discipline and policy, and an implacable adversary of the Puritans, against whom he had repeatedly directed the hostility of his pen, and now gladly wielded a more formidable weapon.   From this period, all the force of the law was spent in uninterrupted efforts to harass the persons or violate the consciences of the Puritans.   A great number of Puritan ministers were deprived of their benefices ; and many of their parishioners were punished by fine and imprisonment for attending their ministry in the fields and woods, where they continued to exercise it.   Vainly were the exertions of wise and good men employed to move the queen, ere yet it was too late, to recede from her fatal policy, and stifle the flame of discord which she was essaying to kindle among her people.   Burleigh and Walsingham earnestly interceded for the suspended ministers ; urging the indulgence due to their conscientious scruples, the humane concern to which their families were entitled, and the respect which sound policy demanded for the sentiments of that numerous portion of the people by whom they were revered and beloved.   The House of Commons, too, showed a desire to procure some relief for the oppressed Puritans.   But Whitgift flung himself on his knees before the queen, and implored her to uphold the sinking church, and to admit no alteration of its ritual that would authorize men to say *that she had maintained an error*.[3]   His humiliation, most probably, was prompted rather by flattery than fear ; for Elizabeth had shown no inclination whatever to mitigate an imperious policy so congenial to her own character.

[1] In their letters to their friends at home and abroad, they not only reprobate the obnoxious institutions, but promise to withstand them "till they be sent back to hell, from whence they came to sow discord, confusion, and vain formality in the church." Burnet. Neal.

[2] Strype's *Life of Grindall*. Neal.

[3] Walton, a great admirer of this prelate, thus characterizes his policy with the queen. " By justifiable sacred insinuations, such as St. Paul to Agrippa, ' Agrippa, believest thou ? I know that thou believest,' he wrought himself into so great a degree of favor with her, as, by his pious use of it, hath got both of them a great degree of fame in this world and of glory in that into which they are now both entered." *Life of Hooker.*

The exaction of implicit deference to her judgment, and of rigid conformity to the ecclesiastical model she had preferred, was the result of her
early and stubborn choice, and pursued with her usual firmness and vigor
of determination. She overbore all opposition ; and the primate and his
associates being encouraged to proceed in the course which they had commenced, their zeal, enlarging as it flowed, soon transported them beyond
all bounds of decency and humanity. They were empowered to establish a
court of commissioners for the detection of non-conformity, which even the
privy council complained of as a copy of the detested tribunal of the Inquisition. By the assistance of this tyrannical engine, they gave freer course
to the severities of the law ; and having rendered integrity hazardous, they
made prudence unavailing to the Puritans. In vain were they reminded of
the maxim of the earliest Christian council, which recommended the imposition of no greater burden on the people than the observation of duties
undeniably necessary and of primary importance. For the purpose of imposing a load of ceremonies, which they could not pretend to characterize
as essential requisites to salvation, they committed such oppression as rendered the ceremonies themselves tenfold more obnoxious to those persons
to whom even indulgent treatment would have failed to recommend them ;
and roused the opposition of others, who would willingly have complied with
the ceremonial ordinances, if they had been proposed to them merely as
matters of convenient observance, but revolted from them, as fraught with
danger and mischief, when it was attempted to bind them on the conscience,
and place them on a level with the most sacred obligations.

The chief fruits of this increased severity were the enkindling of much
additional zeal and fervor in the minds of the Puritans ; the multiplication of
their numbers, by the powerful influence of sympathy with their courage and
compassion for their sufferings ; and a growing abhorrence among them of
the order of bishops and the whole frame of a church which to them was an
organ of injustice and tyranny. It is certain that all or almost all the
Puritans of those times were at first averse to separate from the church of
England ; and their ministers were still more reluctant to abet a schism and
renounce their preferments. They willingly recognized in her the character
of a true Christian church, and merely claimed for themselves indulgence
with regard to a few ceremonies which did not affect the substance of her
constitution. But the injurious treatment which they received held forth a
premium to very different considerations, and at once aroused their passions, stimulated their inquiries, and extended their arguments and objections. Expelled from fellowship with the national church, they were forcibly invited to inquire if they could not dispense with that which they found
they could not obtain ; and were easily led to question if the genuine features of a Christian church could be recognized in that society which not
only rejected but persecuted them for conscientious adherence, in a matter
of ceremonial observance, to what they believed to be the manifest will of
God. As the Puritan principles spread through the mass of society, and
encountered in their progress a greater variety of character in their votaries
and of treatment from their adversaries, considerable varieties and inequalities of sentiment and conduct appeared in different portions of the Puritan
body. Some of them caught the spirit of their oppressors, and, in words
at least, retaliated the unchristian usage they underwent. They combined
the doctrines of the New with the practices of the Old Testament, in a man-

ner which will not excite the wonder of those who recollect that some of the very earliest votaries of Christianity in the world committed the same error, and so far forgot the meekness they had been commanded to evince, as even in the presence of their Divine Master to propose the invocation of fire from heaven on the men who rejected their society. But the instances of this spirit were at first exceedingly rare ; and it was not till the following reigns that it prevailed either strongly or widely. In general, the oppressed Puritans conducted themselves with the fortitude of heroes and the patience of saints ; and, what is surprising, they made more zealous and successful efforts to preserve their loyalty than the queen and the bishops did to extinguish it. Many, in defiance of every danger, followed the preaching of their favorite ministers into the highways and fields, or assembled privately in conventicles, which the general sympathy, or the connivance of their secret partisans among the adherents of the ecclesiastical establishment, sometimes preserved from detection. Others reluctantly tarried within the pale of the national church, unweariedly pursuing their ineffectual attempts to promote parliamentary interference in behalf of the Puritan cause, and casting a wistful eye on the presumptive succession of a prince who was educated in a Presbyterian society. Some, at length, openly disclaimed the national system, and were led by the cruel excesses of magisterial power to the conviction, that magisterial power ought to be banished entirely from the administration of the kingdom of Christ.[1]

The designs of the queen were cordially abetted by the angry zeal of those Churchmen who had fled from England in the preceding reign, and taken part in the controversy that arose with the Puritans during their common exile. But the whole civil and ecclesiastical policy of the present reign was mainly and essentially the offspring of Elizabeth's own character and disposition. The Puritan writers, bestowing an undue proportion of their resentment on those persons whose functions rendered them the instruments as well as the apologists of the queen's ecclesiastical system, have been disposed to impute the tyrannical features of this system exclusively to the bishops, and particularly to Whitgift, whose influence with Elizabeth they ascribe to his constant habit of addressing her on his knees.[2] But Whitgift, in seconding her enmity to the Puritans, did no more than subminister to her favorite and declared purpose ; with zeal half courtly, half clerical, he flattered a temper which she had already unequivocally manifested, and swam with the stream of that resolute determination, which, he saw, would have its way. The abject homage which he paid her was nothing more than she was accustomed generally to receive ; and the observation which it has attracted from the Puritans denotes rather a peculiarity in their own sentiments and manners, than any thing remarkable in the conduct of their ecclesiastical adversary. Not one of her subjects was permitted to address the queen without kneeling ; wherever she turned her eye, every one was expected to fall on his knees ; and even in her absence, the nobles, who were alone deemed worthy to cover her table, made three genuflections every time they approached or retired from it in the performance of their menial duty.[3] This was an exact counterpart of the homage rendered by the Catholics to the Real Presence, which they believed to reside in the

---

[1] Strype's *Life of Whitgift.* Fuller's *Church History.* Neal.   [2] Neal.
[3] Hentzner's *Journey into England* in 1598. Much of this abject ceremonial was abolished by King James, who, though highly relishing adulation, found himself embarrassed by a mode of displaying it so ill suited to his awkward manners and ungainly appearance.

Host ; and the sentiments which it tended to implant, both in the prince who received and the subjects who proffered it, were confirmed by the language of parliament, in which the queen was continually flattered with attributes and praise befitting the homage of creatures to their Creator. Nor was this servile system of manners peculiar to the reign of Elizabeth. On the contrary, it was carried even to a greater extent under the government of her predecessors ; and her ministers frequently noted and deplored the decay of that *fearfulness and reverence of their superiors* which had formerly characterized the inferior estates of the realm.[1] Sense and reason shared the ignominy and degradation of manners ; arrogance disordered the understanding of the prince, while servility deformed the sentiments of the people ; and if Henry the Eighth, by a royal proclamation, assured the populace that they were *brutes*, — the same populace, in their petitions against his measures, represented the promotion of *low-born persons* to public trust and honor as one of the most serious and intolerable grievances of which they had reason to complain.[2]

The sentiments which such practices and manners tended to create or nourish in the mind of the queen enhanced the displeasure with which she regarded the Puritans, who were fated to offend her by their political conduct, as well as their religious opinions. Many persons of note among them obtained seats in parliament, where they studied to cherish and invigorate a spirit of liberty, and direct its energy to the protection of their persecuted brethren. Impelled, by the severity of the restraints they experienced, to investigate the boundaries of that authority by which such restraints were imposed, — and regulating their sentiments rather by the consequences they foresaw than by the precedents they remembered, — they questioned the rational legitimacy of the most inveterate practices, and obtained the confidence of the people by showing themselves the indefatigable and fearless defenders of all who were oppressed. In the annals of those times, we find them continually supporting petitions in parliament against monopolies, and advocating propositions for reformation of ecclesiastical abuses and corruptions. Attracting popular favor, and willing to undergo the labor of parliamentary service, they gradually multiplied their numbers in the House of Commons, and acquired an ascendant over its deliberations. The queen, observing that the Puritans were the sole abettors of measures calculated to restrict her prerogative, was easily led to ascribe the peculiarity of their religious and political opinions to the same source, — a malignant aversion to exalted rank, and mutinous impatience of subordination. Their reluctance to render to the Deity that ceremonious homage which she herself received from the most illustrious persons in the land, and their inclination to curtail the royal authority, which from no other quarter experienced resistance, seemed to her the manifest proofs of an insolent disregard no less of the Supreme Being than of her, his acknowledged vicegerent and representative, — a presumptuous insurrection of spirit against the reverence due to God and the loyalty due to the prince.[3]

---

[1] Hayne's *Collection of State Papers.*   [2] Lord Herbert.

[3] In a speech from the throne, she informed the Commons (after a candid confession that she knew nobody who had read or reflected as much as herself), that whoever attacked the constitutions of the church slandered her as its supreme head, divinely appointed ; and that, if the Papists were inveterate enemies to her person, the modern sectaries were no less formidable to all regal government. She added, that she was determined to suppress their overboldness in presumptuously scanning the will of God Almighty. D'Ewes's *Account of Queen Elizabeth's Parliaments.* The cruel law that was passed in the thirty-fifth year of the queen's

Nothing could be more unjust and fallacious than this royal reasoning. The religion as well as the loyalty of the Puritans was the less ceremonious, only because it was the more reflective, profound, and substantial. To preserve an unstained conscience, they encountered the extremities of ecclesiastical rigor. Notwithstanding the most oppressive and tyrannical treatment, they exhibited a resolute constancy of regard to their sovereign. And neither intimidated by danger nor dispirited by defeat, they maintained a continual effort to check the excesses of despotic authority, and to rear and sustain the infant liberties of their country. They have incurred the reproach of gloomy and unseasonable melancholy from those who rendered their lives at once bitter and precarious ; of a neglect of general literature, and an exclusive study of the Bible, from those who destroyed their writings, subjected the press to episcopal licensers, and deprived them of every source of comfort and direction but what the Bible could supply ; of an exaggerated estimate of little matters, from those who rendered such matters the occasion of cruel suffering and enormous wrong to them ; of a stern jealousy of civil power, from those who made it continually their interest to question and abridge the authority by which they were oppressed. A great philosopher and historian, who will not be suspected of any undue partiality for Puritan tenets, whether religious or political, has been constrained to acknowledge that the Puritans were the preservers of civil and religious liberty in England.[1] It was a scion of the same stock that was destined to propagate these blessings in America.

The minds of a numerous party among the Puritans had been gradually prepared to disclaim the authority of the national church, and to deny the lawfulness of holding communion with it ; insomuch, that, when these sentiments were first publicly proclaimed by Robert Brown, in 1586, they readily gained the assent and open profession of multitudes. Brown, who obtained the distinction of bestowing his name on a sect which derived very little credit from the appellation, was a young clergyman of good family, endowed with a restless, intrepid disposition, a fiery temper, and an insatiable thirst for controversy. Encountering the wrath of ecclesiastics with still fiercer wrath, and trampling on their arrogance with more than clerical pride, he roamed about the country, inveighing against bishops, ecclesiastical courts, religious ceremonies, and episcopal ordination of ministers, and exulting, above all, in the boast that he had been committed to thirty-two prisons, in some of which he could not discern his hand at noonday. His impetuous and illiberal spirit accelerated the publication of opinions which were not yet matured in the Puritan body, and which, but for his unseasonable

reign, against all ecclesiastical recusants, is entitled " An Act to retain her Majesty's Subjects in their due Obedience," and was intended, as the preamble declares, to repress the evil practices of " sectaries and disloyal persons," — synonymous descriptions of guilt, in the estimation of Elizabeth.

[1] " So absolute, indeed, was the authority of the crown, that the precious spark of liberty had been kindled and was preserved by the Puritans alone ; and it was to this sect, whose principles appear so frivolous and habits so ridiculous, that the English owe the whole freedom of their constitution." Hume's *England*. Again, " It was only during the next generation that the noble principles of liberty took root, and, spreading themselves under the shelter of Puritanical absurdities, became fashionable among the people." Ibid.

In a well known passage, Hume has represented the domestic leisure and social converse of the Puritan leaders as polluted by a barbarous sullenness, vulgarity, and fanaticism ; most unjustly, as every one must have felt, who, in reading the *Memoirs of Colonel Hutchinson*, has paused over the delightful picture they present of ease and leisure devoted to elegant studies, virtuous pursuits, useful occupations, polite amusements, rational converse, and cheerful hospitality.

interposition and perverting influence, might sooner have been ripened into the system of the Independents. The queen and the bishops applied the usual remedy of persecution to this innovation, with even more than the usual evidence of the unfitness of such instrumentality to accomplish their purpose. Supported by strong argument, maintained with striking zeal and courage, and opposed by cruelties that disgraced the name of religion, the principles of the Brownists spread widely through the land. Brown himself, and a congregation more immediately attached to him, expatriated to Middelburg, in Zeeland, where they were permitted to express and cultivate their opinions without molestation. But Brown had collected around him spirits too congenial to his own to preserve their union when the iron band of oppression was withdrawn. The congregation crumbled into parties, and was soon dissolved ; and Brown, returning to England, rejoined the national church, and, contracting dissolute habits, ended his days in indolence and contempt. But the doctrines which he had been the means of introducing to public notice had firmly rooted themselves in the Puritan body, and received daily accessions to the numbers and respectability of their votaries.[1]

The Brownists did not dissent from the church of England in any of her articles of faith, but they accounted her ritual and discipline unscriptural and superstitious, and all her sacraments and ordinances invalid ; and they renounced communion not only with her, but with every other Protestant church that was not constructed on the same model as their own. Their ecclesiastical model was derived from the closest imitation of the apostolical institutions as delineated in Scripture. When a church or congregation was to be formed, all the persons who desired to be members of it professed the particulars of their religious faith in each other's presence, and signed a covenant by which they obliged themselves to make the Bible and its ordinances the sole guide of their conduct. Each congregation formed an independent church, and the admission or exclusion of members resided with the brethren composing it. Their ecclesiastical officers were elected from among themselves, and invested with their several charges of preaching the gospel, administering the sacramental ordinances, and relieving the poor, — after fasting and prayer, by the imposition of the hands of certain of the brethren. They did not account the priesthood a distinct order, nor the ministerial character indelible ; but deemed, that, as the appointment of the church conferred on a minister his function (which in its exercise, too, was limited to the special body to which he was attached), so the same authority was sufficient to deprive him of it. It was permitted to any one of the brethren to exercise *the liberty of prophesying*, which meant the addressing of occasional exhortation to the people ; and it was usual for some of them, after the customary religious service, to promulgate questions and considerations relative to the doctrines that had been preached.[2] The condition to which the Puritans were reduced by their oppressors favored the prevalence of all that was separative and unsocial in the principles of the Brownist teachers ; for, as they could assemble only by stealth, it was impossible to preserve a regular intercourse between their churches, or to ascertain how far they mutually agreed in doctrine and discipline.

Against these men, in whose characters were united more piety, virtue, courage, and loyalty than any other portion of her people displayed, did

---

[1] Fuller. Neal.   [2] Neal.

Elizabeth and her ecclesiastical counsellors direct the whole fury of the law. John Udall, one of their ministers, was tried in the year 1591, for having published a defence of their tenets, which he entitled, *A Demonstration of the Discipline which Christ hath prescribed in his Word for the Government of the Church in all Times and Places until the World's End.* This performance, consistently with Elizabeth's maxim, that whoever attacked the established church slandered the queen, was regarded as a political libel, and Udall was arraigned on a charge of capital felony. In conformity with the barbarous jurisprudence which then prevailed in England, the witnesses against the prisoner were not confronted with him; his proposition to adduce exculpatory evidence was disallowed, as an affront to the majesty of the crown; and because he refused at the bar to swear that he was not the author of the book, his refusal was urged against him as the strongest proof of his guilt. When he was told by one of the judges that a book replete with sentiments so inconsistent with the established institutions tended to the overthrow of the state by the provocation of rebellion, he replied, " My Lords, that be far from me; for we teach, that, reforming things amiss, if the prince will not consent, the weapons that subjects are to fight withal, are repentance and prayers, patience and tears." The judge offered him his life, if he would recant; and added, that he was now ready to pronounce sentence of death. " And I am ready to receive it," exclaimed this magnanimous man; " for I protest before God (not knowing that I have to live an hour) that the cause is good; and I am contented to receive sentence, so that I may leave it to posterity how I have suffered for the cause." [1] He was condemned to die; and being still urged to submit to the queen, he readily expressed his regret that any of his writings had given her offence, and disclaimed any such wish or intention, but firmly refused to disown what he believed to be truth, or to renounce liberty of conscience. By the interest of some powerful friends, a conditional pardon was obtained for him; but before the terms of it could be adjusted, or the queen prevailed on to sign it, he died in prison.

Penry, Greenwood, Barrow, and Dennis, of whom the first two were clergymen, and the others laymen, were soon after tried on similar charges, and perished by the hands of the executioner. A pardon was offered to them, if they would retract their profession; but, inspired by a courage which no earthly motive could overcome, they clung to their principles, and left the care of their lives to Heaven. Some more were hanged for dispersing the writings, and several for attending the discourses, of the Brownists. Many others endured the torture of severe imprisonment, and numerous families were reduced to indigence by heavy fines.[2] Who could doubt the final triumph of a cause that already produced so noble an army of heroes and martyrs? As the most virtuous and honorable are ever, on such occasions, most exposed to danger, every stroke of the oppressor's arm is aimed at those very qualities in his adversaries that constitute his own defence and security; and hence, severities, so odious to mankind, and so calculated to unite by a strong sympathy the minds of the spectators and the sufferers,

---

[1] Howell's *State Trials.* It is remarkable, that, although one devoted victim of royal vengeance and persecution (Sir Nicholas Throgmorton) was enabled to escape during the reign of Mary, not one of the objects of Elizabeth's hostility was equally fortunate. A great addition to the power, as well as the pretensions, of the first Protestant sovereigns of England was derived from their assumption of the ecclesiastical supremacy previously ascribed to the Roman pontiff.

[2] Strype's *Life of Whitgift.* Fuller. Neal.

are more likely to diminish the virtue than the numbers of a party.   By dint of long continuance and of the exertion of their influence on a greater variety of human character, they finally divested a great many of the Puritans of the spirit of meekness and non-resistance for which the fathers of the party had been so highly distinguished.   But this fruit was not gathered till a subsequent reign ; and the first effect of the system of rigor was not only to multiply the numbers, but to confirm the virtue of the Puritans.   When persecution had as yet but invigorated their fortitude without inspiring fero- city, a portion of this people was happily conducted to the retreat of Ameri- ca, there to plant and extend the principles of their cause, — while their brethren in England remained behind to revenge its accumulated wrongs.

When the queen was informed, by Dr. Reynolds, of the firm and ele- vated, yet mild and gentle, piety which the martyrs of her cruelty had dis- played, — how they blessed their persecuting sovereign, and turned the scaffolds to which she consigned them into scenes of holy charity, whence they prayed for her long and happy reign, — her heart was touched with a sentiment of remorse, and she expressed regret for having taken their lives away.   But repentance with all mankind is too often but a fruitless anguish ; and princes have been known to bewail, even with tears, the mortal con- dition of multitudes whom they were conducting to slaughter, and the brevity of that life which their own selfish and sanguinary ambition was contributing still farther to abridge.   Elizabeth, so far from alleviating, increased, the legislative severities whose effects she had deplored ; and was fated never to see her errors, till it was too late to repair them.   In the year 1593, a few months after the executions which we have remarked, a new and se- verer law was enacted against the Puritans.   These sectaries were not only increasing their numbers every day, but furnishing so many votaries of the Brownist or Independent doctrines, that, in the debate which took place in the House of Commons on the introduction of this measure, Sir Walter Raleigh stated that the number of professed Brownists alone then amounted to twenty thousand.   The humane argument, however, which he derived from this consideration, was unavailing to prevent the enactment of a law,[1] which ordained, that any person above sixteen years of age, who obstinately refused, during the space of a month, to attend public worship in a legiti- mate parochial church, should be committed to prison ; that, if he persisted three months in his refusal, he must abjure the realm ; and that, if he either refused this condition, or returned after banishment, he should suffer death as a felon.   If this act was not more fortunate than its predecessors in ac- complishing the main object of checking the growth of Puritan principles, it promoted at least the subordinate purpose of driving a great many of the professors of ecclesiastical independency out of England.

A numerous society of these fugitives was collected, about the close of the sixteenth century, at Amsterdam, where they flourished in peace and piety for upwards of a hundred years.   Others retired to various Protestant states on the continent, whence, with fond, delusive hope, they looked to be recalled to their native land on the accession of Elizabeth's successor. The remainder continued in England, to fluctuate between the evasion and the violation of the law, — cherishing along with their principles a stern im-

---

[1] 35 Eliz. Cap. 1.   Raleigh was not the only favorite of Elizabeth who was opposed to her ecclesiastical policy.   One of the causes of her displeasure at Lord Essex was the counte- nance he gave to the Puritans, who had previously received still more active patronage from her haughty minion, Lord Leicester.   Walton's *Life of Hooker.*

patience, generated by the galling restraint that impeded the free expression of them ; and yet retained in submission by the hope, which, in common with the exiles, they indulged, of a mitigation of their sufferings on the demise of the queen.[1]   Some historians have expressed surprise at the close concurrence of that general and impatient desire of a new reign, which was manifested in the conclusion of Elizabeth's life,[2] with the strong and sudden disgust which the government of her successor experienced ; and hence have taken occasion, with censorious but inapplicable wisdom, to deplore the ingratitude and fickleness of mankind.   But the seeming inconsistency admits of an explanation more honorable to human nature, though less creditable to royal wisdom and virtue.   Elizabeth had exhausted the patience and loyalty of a great portion of her subjects ; and the adherence to her policy, which her successor unexpectedly manifested, disappointed all the hopes by which those virtues had been sustained.

The hopes of the Puritans were derived from the education of the Scottish king, and supported by many of his declarations, which were eagerly cited and circulated in England.   James (pupil of the great George Buchanan, who succeeded no farther than in rendering the object of his tuition, what Sully termed him, the wisest fool in Europe) was bred a Presbyterian ; he had publicly declared that the church of Scotland was the best ecclesiastical constitution in the world, and that the English liturgy resembled, to his apprehension, an ill-chanted mass.   On his accession to the English crown, he was solicited by numerous petitions to interpose his authority for the protection and relief of the Puritans ; and at first he showed himself so far disposed to comply with their wishes as to appoint a solemn conference between their leaders and the heads of the Church party at Hampton Court. But the hopes inspired by the proposition of this conference were disappointed by its result.   [Jan. 1604.]   If James ever sincerely preferred a Presbyterian to an Episcopal establishment, his opinion was entirely reversed by the opportunity he now enjoyed of comparing them with each other, and by the very different treatment he experienced from their respective ministers.

In Scotland he had been engaged in perpetual contentions with the clergy, who did not recognize in his kingly office any supremacy over their church, and who differed from him exceedingly in their estimate of his piety, capacity, and attainments.   Precluded by his poverty from a display of regal pomp, that might have dazzled their eyes, and hid the weakness of the man behind the grandeur of the monarch, he stood plainly revealed to their keen glance, an awkward personification of conceit and pedantry, obstinate but unsteady, filled with the rubbish and subtilty of scholastic learning, void of manly sense and useful knowledge.   They have been accused, and not without reason, of disturbing his government by exercising a censorial power over it ; but it was he himself that first taught, or at least encouraged, them thus to overstep their functions.   Extending his administration into their peculiar province, where it had no right to penetrate, he seemed to sanction as well as provoke their retributive strictures on his intrusion.   Mingling religious notions with his political views, he attempted to remodel the church ; and the clergy, mingling political doctrines with their theological sentiments, complained of his interference, and censured the whole strain of his government.   In an appeal to the public opinion and will, they easily triumphed

---

[1] Strype's *Life of Whitgift.* D'Ewes. Neal.
[2] " Four days after her death, she was forgotten."   Carte's *England.*

over the unpopular pretensions of their feeble sovereign, and gained a victory which they used with little moderation, and which he resented not less as a theological than as a political affront.   One of the ministers of the church of Scotland had so far transgressed the limits of decency and propriety as to declare publicly that " all kings are the Devil's children " ;[1] and James retorted the discourtesy, when he found himself safe from their spleen and turbulence in England, by warmly protesting that " a Scottish presbytery agrees as well with monarchy as God and the Devil."[2]   The sentiments that naturally resulted from offended arrogance and mortified presumption were expanded to their amplest plenitude by the blaze of flattery and adulation with which the dignitaries of the English church greeted their new sovereign.   By them he was readily hailed the supreme head of their establishment, the protector of its privileges, the centre of its splendor, the fountain of its dignities ; and Whitgift did not scruple to declare, in the conference at Hampton Court, that *undoubtedly his Majesty spake by the special assistance of God's spirit.*[3]

This was the last impulse that the deluded ecclesiastic was destined to impart to royal pride and folly.   Confounded at the wide and spreading explosion of Puritan sentiment, which he had flattered himself with the hope of having almost entirely extinguished, his grief and concern so violently affected his aged frame as to cause his death very shortly after. [Feb. 1604.]   But he had already contributed to instil the ecclesiastical spirit of Elizabeth into the mind of her successor ; and James, inflamed with admiration of a church, which, like a faithful mirror (he thought), so justly reflected and illustrated his royal perfections, became henceforward the determined patron of the church of England, and the persecutor of all who opposed her institutions.   He was the first prince who assumed the title of *Sacred Majesty*, which the loyalty of bishops transferred from their God to their king.   His natural conceit, fortified by the testimony of the English prelates, soared to a height of surpassing arrogance and presumption ; and he, who, in Scotland, had found himself curbed in every attempt to interfere with the religious institutions of his own narrow realm, now reckoned himself qualified and entitled to dictate the ecclesiastical policy of foreign nations.

Engaging in a dispute with Vorstius, professor of theology in a Dutch university, and finding his adversary insensible to the weight of his arguments, he resolved to make him feel at least the weight and the stretch of his power ; and, roused on this occasion to a degree of energy and haughtiness to which no other foreign concernment was ever able to excite him, he remonstrated so strenuously with the States of Holland, that, to silence his clamor, they stooped to the mean injustice of deposing and banishing the professor.   With this sacrifice to his insulted logic James was forced to be contented, though he had endeavoured to inspire his allies with the purpose of more sanguinary vindication, by acquainting them, " that, as to the *burning* of Vorstius for his blasphemies and atheism, he left them to their own Christian wisdom, — though, surely, never heretic better deserved the flames."   He did not fail to reinforce this charitable counsel by his own example ; and in the course of his reign burned at the stake two persons who entertained the Arian system of doctrine,[4] and an unfortunate lunatic

---

[1] Spottiswoode.   [2] Fuller.   [3] Kennet.
[4] One of these victims is termed by Fuller, in his *Church History*, " our English Vorstius."

who mistook himself for the Deity, and whose frenzy was thus cruelly treated by a much more dangerous and deliberate invader of divine attributes.

If James had not been restrained by the growing political ascendency of the Puritans, there would probably have been more of such executions in England. He did, however, as much as he dared; and finding in Bancroft a fit successor to Whitgift, he made, with his assistance, so vigorous a commencement, that in the second year of his reign three hundred Puritan ministers were deprived of their benefices, and either imprisoned or banished. To preclude the communication of light from abroad, the importation of any books hostile to the restraints imposed by the laws of the realm or the king's proclamations was forbidden under the severest penalties; to prevent its rise and repress its spread at home, no books were suffered to be printed in England without the license of a committee of bishops or their deputies; and arbitrary jurisdictions for the trial of ecclesiastical offences were multiplied and extended. Persons suspected of entertaining Puritan sentiments, even though they adhered to the established ecclesiastical system, were subjected to fine and imprisonment for barely repeating to their families, in the evening, the substance of the discourses they had heard at church during the day, — under the pretence, that this constituted the crime of irregular preaching. One Peacham, a Puritan minister, in whose study there was seized, by a tyrannical stretch of power, a manuscript discourse never preached, nor intended to be preached, containing censures on the royal government, was, by the king's desire, first tortured on the rack, and then condemned to the death of a traitor.

Some of the Puritans having conceived the design of withdrawing to Virginia, where they hoped that distance would at least mitigate the violence of oppression, a small party of them did actually repair thither; and a larger number were preparing to follow, when Bancroft, apprized of their intention, obtained a proclamation from the king, commanding that none of his subjects should settle in Virginia without the authority of an express license under the great seal. [1620.] Thus harassed and oppressed in England, and denied a refuge in Virginia, the Puritans began to retire in considerable numbers to the Protestant states of the continent of Europe; and the hopes of the still greater and increasing portion that remained at home were fixed on the House of Commons. In this assembly the Puritan ascendency at length became so manifest, that, in spite of the king's proclamations for encouraging mirthful games on Sunday, a bill was introduced for compelling a more strict and solemn observance of the day, to which it gave the denomination of the Sabbath; and when one member objected to this as a Puritan appellation, and ventured to justify dancing on Sunday by a jocose misapplication of some passages of Scripture, he was, on the suggestion of Pym, expelled from the House for his profanity.[1] But we have now reached the period at which we forsake the main stream of the history of the Puritans, to follow the fortunes of that illustrious branch which was destined to visit and ennoble the deserts of America. In reviewing the strange succession of events which we have beheld, and the various impressions they have produced on our minds, it may perhaps occur to some, as a

The king, in imitation of Henry the Eighth's generosity to Lambert, held a personal dispute with him, and concluded it by delivering him into the hands of the executioner.

[1] K. James's *Works. Journals of the House of Commons.* Rymer. Neal. Stith's *Virginia. State Trials.*

humiliating consideration, that the crimes and follies, the cruelties and weaknesses, which would excite no other sentiments but horror, grief, or pity in an angelic beholder, are capable of presenting themselves in such an aspect to less purified eyes, as to excite the splenetic mirth even of beings whose nature is reproached by the odious or absurd display.

In the year 1610, a congregation of Brownists, expelled by royal and ecclesiastical tyranny from their native land, removed to Leyden, where they were permitted to establish themselves in peace under the ministry of their pastor, John Robinson.[1] This excellent person may be justly regarded as the founder of the society of Independents, having been the first teacher who steered a middle course between the narrow path of Brownism and the broader Presbyterian system ; to one or other of which the views and inclinations of the Puritans were now generally tending. The sentiments which he entertained, when he first quitted his country, bore the impress of the persecution under which they had been formed, and when he commenced his ministry at Leyden he was a rigid Brownist ; but after he had seen more of the world, and enjoyed opportunities of familiar converse with learned and good men of different ecclesiastical denominations, he began to entertain a more charitable opinion of those minor differences, which he plainly perceived might subsist without injury to the essentials of religion, and without violating charity or generating discord. Though he always maintained the legitimacy and expediency of separating from the established Protestant churches in the country where he lived, he willingly allowed them the character of churches substantially Christian ; esteemed it lawful to unite with them in preaching and prayer ; and freely admitted their members to partake the sacrament of the Lord's Supper with his own congregation. He considered that each particular church or society of Christians possessed the power of electing its officers, administering the gospel ordinances, and exercising over its own members every necessary act of discipline and authority ; and, consequently, that it was independent of all ecclesiastical synods, convocations, and councils. He admitted the expediency of synods and councils for composition of emergent differences between particular churches by the communication of friendly advice to them ; but denied their competence to exercise any act of jurisdiction, or authoritatively to impose any articles or canons of doctrine. These sentiments Robinson recommended to esteem, by exemplifying in his life and demeanour the best fruits of that divine spirit by whose tuition they were imparted, — by a character and behaviour, in which the most eminent faculties and the highest attainments were leavened and controlled by the predominating influence of a solemn, affectionate piety.[2] [1620.]

Enjoying the counsel and direction of such a pastor, and entertaining a just sense of his value, the English exiles composing this congregation remained for ten years at Leyden, in harmony with each other and in peace with their neighbours. But at the end of that period, the same pious views that had prompted their original departure from England incited them to undertake a more distant migration. They beheld with strong concern the prevalence around them of manners which they esteemed loose and profane; more particularly, the general neglect among the Dutch of a reverential

[1] Cardinal Bentivoglio, in his *Account of the United Provinces*, describes these exiles as *a body of English heretics, called Puritans, who had resorted to Holland for purposes of commerce.*
[2] Mather's *Ecclesiastical History of New England.* Neal. Robinson's *Apology for the Brownists.*

observance of Sunday; and they reflected with apprehension on the danger to which their children were exposed from the natural contagion of habits so inimical to serious piety. Their country, too, still retained a hold on their affections; and they were loath to behold their posterity commingled and identified with the Dutch population. The smallness of their numbers, together with the difficulties occasioned by difference of language, discouraged them from attempting to propagate in Holland the principles, which, with so much peril and suffering, they had hitherto maintained; and the conduct of the English government extinguished every hope of toleration in their native land. The famous *Arminian Controversy*, moreover, which was now raging in Holland with a fury that produced the barbarous execution of the Grand Pensionary Barneveldt and the imprisonment of the illustrious Grotius, probably contributed to alienate the desires of the English exiles from farther residence in a land where the Calvinistic tenets which they cherished were thus disgraced by practical cruelty and intolerance. In these circumstances, it occurred to them that they might combine the indulgence of their patriotic attachment with the propagation of their religious principles, by establishing themselves in some remote, sequestered part of the British dominions; and after many days of earnest supplication for the counsel and direction of Heaven, they unanimously determined to transport themselves and their families to the territory of America. It was resolved that a select portion of the congregation should proceed thither before the rest, to prepare a settlement for the whole; and that the main body meanwhile should continue at Leyden with their pastor. In choosing the particular scene of their establishment, they hesitated for some time between the territory of Guiana, of which Sir Walter Raleigh had published a most dazzling and attractive description (mainly the offspring of his own lively and fertile imagination), and the province of Virginia, to which they finally gave the preference; but Providence had ordained that their residence should be established in New England.

By the intervention of agents, whom they deputed to solicit the sanction of the English government to their enterprise, they represented to the king, "that they were well weaned from the delicate milk of their mother country, and inured to the difficulties of a strange land; that they were knit together in a strict and sacred bond, by virtue of which they held themselves bound to take care of the good of each other and of the whole; and that it was not with them as with other men, whom small things could discourage, or small discontent cause to wish themselves at home again." The king, wavering between his desire to promote the colonization of America, and his reluctance to suffer the consciences of any portion of his subjects to be emancipated from his control, refused to grant them a charter assuring the full enjoyment of ecclesiastical liberty, but promised to connive at their practices, and to refrain from molesting them. They were forced to accept this precarious security, and would hardly have obtained it but for the friendly interposition of Sir Robert Nanton, one of the secretaries of state, and a favorer of the Puritans; but they relied with more reason on their distance from the ecclesiastical tribunals of England, and from the eye and arm of their persecuting sovereign. Having procured from the Plymouth Company a grant of a tract of land, situated, as was supposed, within the limits of its patent, some members of the congregation sold their estates, and expended the purchase-money in the equipment of two vessels, in which a hundred and twenty of their number were appointed to embark from an English port for North America.[1] [1620.]

All things being prepared for the departure of this detachment of the congregation from Delft Haven, where they took leave of their associates, for the English port of ultimate embarkation, Robinson and his people devoted their last meeting in Europe to an act of solemn and social worship, intended to implore a blessing from Heaven upon the hazardous enterprise. He preached a sermon to them from Ezra viii. 21 : — *I proclaimed a fast there, at the river of Ahava, that we might afflict ourselves before our God, to seek of him a right way for us, and for our little ones, and for all our substance ;* — and concluded his discourse with the following exhortation, to which, with the fullest perception of its intrinsic merits, our sentiments will fail to do justice, unless we remember that such a spirit of Christian candor and liberality as it breathes was then hardly known in the world.

" Brethren," said he, " we are now quickly to part from one another, and whether I may ever live to see your faces on earth any more the God of heaven only knows ; but whether the Lord has appointed that or no, I charge you, before God and his blessed angels, that you follow me no farther than you have seen me follow the Lord Jesus Christ.

" If God reveal any thing to you by any other instrument of his, be as ready to receive it as ever you were to receive any truth by my ministry ; for I am verily persuaded, I am very confident, the Lord has more truth yet to break forth out of his holy word. For my part, I cannot sufficiently bewail the condition of the reformed churches, who are come to a period in religion, and will go at present no farther than the instruments of their reformation. The Lutherans cannot be drawn to go beyond what Luther saw ; whatever part of his will our good God has revealed to Calvin, they will rather die than embrace it ; and the Calvinists, you see, stick fast where they were left by that great man of God, who yet saw not all things.

" This is a misery much to be lamented ; for though they were burning and shining lights in their times, yet they penetrated not into the whole counsel of God ; but, were they now living, would be as willing to embrace farther light, as that which they first received. I beseech you, remember it, 't is an article of your church covenant, *that you be ready to receive whatever truth shall be made known to you from the written word of God.* Remember *that,* and every other article of your sacred covenant. But I must herewithal exhort you to take heed *what* you receive as truth. Examine it, consider it, and compare it with other scriptures of truth, before you receive it ; for 't is not possible the Christian world should come so lately out of antichristian darkness, and that perfection of knowledge should break forth at once.

" I must also advise you to abandon, avoid, and shake off the name of Brownist ; 't is a mere nickname, and a brand for the making religion, and the professors of it, odious to the Christian world."

Having said thus much, he exchanged with them embraces and affectionate farewells ; and kneeling down with them all on the seashore, commended them, in a fervent prayer, to the blessing and protection of Heaven.[2] Such

---

[1] Mather. Neal. Hutchinson. Hazard. Oldmixon. If the Puritans would have stooped to intrigue and duplicity, they might have had more powerful partisans at court than Sir Robert Nanton. The Duke of Buckingham, in imitation of the policy of Lord Leicester and Lord Essex, in the preceding reign, vainly attempted to obtain an ascendency over the Puritans by caressing their leaders.

[2] Mather. Hazard.

were the men whom the English monarch cast out of his dominions ; and such the scenes of wisdom and piety, which the control of Divine Providence elicited from the folly, arrogance, and bigotry of a tyrant.   The emigrants were at first driven back by a storm which destroyed one of their vessels ; but finally reëmbarking in the other at Plymouth, on the 6th of September, they succeeded, after a long and dangerous voyage, in reaching the coast of America. [9th Nov., 1620.] Hudson's River was the place where they had proposed to disembark, and its banks were the scene of their intended settlement ; but the Dutch, who conceived that a preferable right to this territory accrued to them from its discovery by Captain Hudson, had maintained there, for some years, a small commercial establishment, and were actually projecting a scheme of more extensive occupation, which they were neither disposed to forego, nor yet prepared to defend.   In order to defeat the design of the English, they bribed the captain of the vessel in which the emigrants sailed, who was a Dutchman, to carry his passengers so far towards the north, that the first land which they reached was Cape Cod, a region not only beyond the precincts of their grant, but beyond the territories of the company from which the grant was derived.   The advanced period of the year, and the sickliness occasioned by the hardships of a long voyage, compelled the adventurers to settle on the soil to which they were thus conducted, and which seemed to have been expressly prepared and evacuated for their reception by a pestilential disease, which, during several preceding years, had swept away nine tenths of its savage and idolatrous population.   After exploring the coast, they chose for their station a place afterwards included within the province of Massachusetts, to which they gave the name of New Plymouth, in commemoration of the city with which their last recollections of England were associated.   To supply, in some measure, the absence of a more formal title, they composed and subscribed an instrument declaratory of the purpose with which they had come to America, recognizing the sovereign authority of the English crown, and expressing their own combination into a body politic, and their determination to enact just and righteous laws, and to evince and enforce a strict obedience to them.[1]   Here, then, remote from scenes and circumstances of temporal grandeur, these men embarked on a career, which, if the true dignity of human actions be derived from the motives that prompt them, the principles they express, and the ends they contemplate, must be allowed to claim no common measure of honor and elevation.   To live for eternity, and in the prospect of it, they deemed the great business of their lives ; this was a just and noble calculation of the value of existence.

   The speedy approach and intense severity of their first winter in America painfully convinced the settlers that a more unfavorable season of the year could not have been selected for the plantation of their colony ; and that the slender stores with which they were provided were greatly short of what was requisite to comfortable subsistence, and formed a very inadequate preparation to meet the rigor of the climate.   Their exertions to procure for themselves suitable dwellings were obstructed, for a time, by the hostile attacks of some of the neighbouring Indians, who had not forgotten the injurious conduct of Captain Hunt ; and the colonists had scarcely succeeded in repulsing them, when sickness, occasioned by scarcity of provisions and

---

[1] Mather. Neal. Oldmixon. Hutchinson. The fraud by which the Dutch contrived to divert these emigrants from Hudson's River was discovered and stated in a memorial, which was published in England before the close of this year. Prince's *New England Chronology.*

the increasing horrors of the season, afflicted them with a calamity, perhaps less dangerous to their virtue, but more fatal to their strength and security, than the perils of war. More than one half of their number, including John Carver, their first governor, perished by hunger or disease before the return of spring ; and during the whole of the winter, only a few were capable of providing for themselves, or rendering assistance to the rest. But hope and virtue survived ; and, rising in vigor beneath the pressure of accumulated suffering, surmounted and ennobled every circumstance of distress. [1621.] Those who retained their strength became the servants of the weak, the afflicted, and the dying ; and none distinguished himself more in this humane employment than Carver, the governor. He was a man of large estate, but more enlarged benevolence ; he had spent his whole fortune on the colonial project ; and now, willingly contributing his life to its accomplishment, he exhausted a feeble body in laboriously discharging the humblest offices of kindness and service to the sick.   He was succeeded by William Bradford, who, inheriting the merit and the popularity of his predecessor, was reëlected to the same office for many successive years, — notwithstanding his own earnest desire to be released from the charge, and his oft repeated remonstrance, that, *if this office were an honor, it should be shared by his fellow-citizens, and if it were a burden, the weight of it should not always be imposed upon him.*

When the distress of the colonists was at its height, the approach of a powerful Indian chief with a band of his followers seemed to portend their utter destruction ; but, happily, in the train of this personage was the ancient guest and friend of the English, Squanto, who eagerly and successfully labored to mediate a good understanding between them and his countrymen. He afterwards cancelled the merit of this useful service, and endeavoured to magnify his own importance by fabricating charges of plots and conspiracies against some of the neighbouring tribes, while at the same time he maintained an empire of terror over these tribes by secretly assuring them that the English were in possession of a cask filled with the plague, which only his influence prevented them from setting abroach for the destruction of the Indians.   But, before he resorted to this mischievous policy, the colonists had become independent of his services.   His friendship with the English was never entirely dissolved ; and on his death-bed, soon after, he desired Governor Bradford to pray for him, *that he might go to the Englishman's God in heaven.* Some of the neighbouring tribes, from time to time, made alarming demonstrations of hostility ; but they were at length completely overawed by the conduct and valor of Captain Miles Standish, a gallant and skilful officer, who, with a handful of men, was always ready to encounter their strongest force, and foil their most dexterous stratagems and rapidest movements.[1]

On the arrival of summer, the health of the colonists was restored ; and their numbers continued to be recruited occasionally, by successive emigrations of oppressed Puritans from Europe.   But these additions fell far short of their expectations ; and of the reinforcement which they had mainly looked for from the accession of the remanent congregation at Leyden, they

---

[1] Mather. Neal. Oldmixon. Belknap's *American Biography.* Peter Martyr declares, that the hardships endured by the Spaniards in South America were such as none but Spaniards could have supported. But the hardships sustained by the first colonists of New Plymouth appear to have exceeded them both in duration and intensity. See Hutchinson, II., Appendix.

were unhappily disappointed. The unexpected death of Robinson, their pastor, deprived his people of the only leader whose animating counsels could have overcome the timidity inspired by the accounts of the manifold hardships and distresses sustained by their friends in New England ; and upon that event, the greater part of those who had remained behind at Leyden now retired to join the other English exiles at Amsterdam, and very few had the courage to proceed to New Plymouth. This small colony, however, had displayed a hardy virtue that showed it was formed for endurance ; and, having surmounted its first misfortunes, continued to flourish in the cultivation of piety, and the enjoyment of religious and political freedom. A generous attachment was formed to the soil which had been so worthily earned, and to the society whose continuance attested so manly and glorious a struggle with every variety of ill. While the colonists demonstrated a proper respect for the claims of the original inhabitants of the country, by purchasing from them the territory over which their settlement extended, they neglected no preparation to defend by force what they had acquired with justice ; and, alarmed by the tidings of the massacre of their countrymen in Virginia, they erected a timber fort [1622], and adopted other prudent precautions for their security. This purchase from savages, who rather occasionally traversed than permanently occupied the territory, is perhaps the first instance on record of the entire prevalence of the principles of justice in a treaty between a civilized and a barbarous people.

The ecclesiastical constitution which the emigrants established was the same with that which had prevailed among them at Leyden ; and their system of civil government was founded on those ideas of the natural equality of men, to which their religious policy, so long the main object of their concern, had habituated their minds. The supreme legislative body was composed at first of all the freemen who were members of the church ; and it was not until the year 1639 that they established a house of representatives. The executive power was committed to a governor and council, annually elected by the members of the legislative assembly. Their jurisprudence was founded on the laws of England, with some diversity in the appreciation and punishment of crimes, wherein they approximated more nearly to the Mosaic institutions. Deeming the protection of morals more important than the preservation of wealth, they punished fornication with flogging, and adultery with death, — while on forgery they inflicted only a moderate fine. The clearing and cultivation of the ground, fishing, and the curing of fish for exportation, formed the temporal occupations of the colonists. The peculiarity of their situation naturally led them, like the Virginians, for some time to throw all their property into a common stock, and, like members of one family, to carry on every work of industry by their joint labor for the public behoof. But the religious zeal which promoted this self-denying policy was unable to overcome the difficulties which must always attend it, and which are peculiarly aggravated in a society deriving its principle of increment not so much from internal growth as from the confluence of strangers. About three years after the foundation of New Plymouth, it was judged proper to introduce separation of possessions, though the full right of separate property was not admitted till a much later period ; and even that first change is represented as having produced a great and manifest improvement of the industry of the people.[1]

[1] Mather. Neal. Chalmers.

The slow increase, which, for a considerable period of time, the population of the colony exhibited, has been ascribed to the prolonged operation of this system of equality ; but it seems more likely that the slowness of the increase (occasioned by the poverty of the soil and the report of the hardships attending a settlement in New England) was itself the reason why the complete ascertainment of the rights of separate property was so long retarded. In the first society of men collected by the bond of Christianity, and additionally united by persecution, we find an attempt made to abolish individual property ; and from the apostolic direction, that *he who would not work should not eat*, we may conclude that the disadvantage, which the operation of this principle is exposed to in a society mainly deriving its increase from the accession of strangers of dissimilar characters, was pretty early experienced. In Paraguay, the Jesuits formed a settlement where this peculiar disadvantage was not experienced, and which affords the only authenticated instance of the introduction and protracted endurance of a state of equality in a numerous society. But there the great fundamental difficulty was rather evaded than encountered, by a system of tuition, adapted, with exquisite skill, to confound all diversities of talent and disposition among the savage or barbarous natives in an unbounded and degrading dependence on their Jesuit instructors.

After remaining for some years without a patent legalizing their territorial occupation, the colonists, whose numbers now amounted to a hundred and eighty, employed one Pierce as their agent in England, to solicit a grant of this nature from the English government, and the Grand Council of Plymouth, — a new corporation, by which James, in the year 1620, had superseded the original Plymouth Company, and on which he conferred all the American territory lying between the fortieth and forty-eighth degrees of north latitude. This corporate body continued to subsist for a considerable time, notwithstanding a vote of the House of Commons, in the year after its creation, declaring its privileges a public grievance, and its patent void. Pierce procured a charter from the council, and caused it to be framed in his own name, with the appropriation of large territories and privileges to himself and his family [1623] ; but, having embarked with a numerous body of associates, whom he collected in England, and induced to accompany him, and assist in the prosecution of his ambitious designs, his vessel was shipwrecked, and Pierce himself so dismayed with the disastrous issue of his enterprise, that he made a public declaration of remorse, and resigned his unjust acquisition. The colonists, informed of their agent's treachery, despatched Winslow, one of their own number, to resume the solicitation for a charter. Winslow did not succeed in procuring a patent from the crown, but he obtained, after a long delay, a grant of land and a charter of privileges from the council. It was directed [Jan. 1630] to William Bradford, the existing governor ; and the immunities it bestowed were appropriated to him, his heirs, associates, and assignees ; but Bradford instantly surrendered all that was personal in the charter and grant, and associated the general court of the freemen to the privileges it conferred.[1]

By this charter of the Grand Council of Plymouth, the colonists were authorized to choose a governor, council, and general court, for the enactment and execution of laws instrumental to the public good. Some American historians have mistaken this charter for a patent from the crown. But

---

[1] Hazard. Chalmers. Trumbull's *History of Connecticut.*

no such patent was ever issued; and the social community of New Plymouth was never incorporated with due legal formality into a body politic, but remained a subordinate and voluntary municipal association, until it was united to its more powerful neighbour, the colony of Massachusetts. Both before and after the reception of their charter, the colonists were aware of the doubts that might be entertained of the validity of the acts of government which their magistrates exercised. This circumstance, perhaps, was not altogether unfavorable to the interests of the people, and may have contributed to the liberal principles and conciliatory strain by which the administration of their domestic government was honorably distinguished from that which afterwards unhappily prevailed among their neighbours in New England. But the soil around New Plymouth was so meagre, and the supplies received by the planters from Europe were so scanty and infrequent, that in the tenth year of their colonial existence their numbers did not exceed three hundred.[1] Their exertions, nevertheless, were productive of consequences most happy and interesting. They held up to the view of the oppressed Puritans in the parent state a retreat to which persecuted virtue might retire, and where only the enduring virtue which persecution had failed to conquer seemed capable of obtaining a permanent establishment. At the expense of the noblest sacrifices and most undaunted efforts, this handful of men laid the foundation of civilized and Christian society in New England. A few years after their arrival at New Plymouth, a messenger was despatched to this colony by the governor of the Dutch plantation on Hudson's River, with letters congratulating the English on their prosperous and commendable enterprise, tendering the good-will and friendly services of the Dutch, and proposing a commercial intercourse between the two settlements. The governor and council of Plymouth returned a courteous answer, expressing their grateful remembrance of the hospitality which they had received in the native country of the Dutch, and a willing acceptance of the proffered friendship.[2] Nothing farther ensued from this overture than a series of small commercial dealings, and an occasional interchange of similar civilities, which, but a few years after, gave place to the most inveterate jealousy, and a continual reciprocation of complaint and menace between the Dutch and English colonists.

Various attempts had latterly been made to emulate the successful establishment of New Plymouth; but they had all failed, in consequence of the neglect or inability of their promoters to emulate the virtues from which the success of this colonial enterprise was derived. In the year 1622, a rival colony was planted in New England by one Weston, and a troop of disorderly adventurers, who, in spite of the friendly assistance of the settlers at New Plymouth, speedily sunk into a state of such misery and degradation, that several of them were reduced to become servants to the Indians; some perished by hunger; others betook themselves to robbery, and by their depredations involved both themselves and the colonists of New Plymouth in hostilities with the natives; and the rest were glad to find their way back to Europe. In the following year, an attempt was made on a larger scale, under the patronage of the Grand Council of Plymouth, which bestowed on Captain Gorges, the leader of the expedition, the title of governor-general of New England, with an ample endowment of arbitrary power, and on a

---

[1] Neal. Chalmers. See Note V., at the end of the volume.
[2] *Collections of the Massachusetts Historical Society.* Neal.

clergyman who accompanied him the office of bishop and superintendent of all churches in this quarter of America. But the condition of New England was very ill suited to the entertainment of such functionaries, and the intro-duction of such institutions ; and the governor and bishop, deserting their charge, made haste to return to a region more adapted to the culture of civil and ecclesiastical dignity. Of their followers, some retired to Virginia, and others returned to England.[1] At a later period [1626], a similar undertaking, conducted by Captain Wollaston, was attended with a repetition of the same disastrous issue. The followers of Wollaston first taught the savage inhabitants of this part of America the use of firearms, — a lesson which ere long the colonists of New England had abundant reason to de-plore.[2] All these unsuccessful plantations were attempted on land more fertile, and in situations more commodious, than the settlers at New Ply-mouth enjoyed. The scene of their brief and unprosperous existence was the coast of Massachusetts Bay, where, a few years later, a colony, which was formed after the model and principles of the society at New Plymouth, and whose origin now claims our attention, afforded the second example of a successful establishment in New England.

The reign of Charles the First was destined to produce the consummation and the retribution of royal and ecclesiastical tyranny. Charles committed the government of the English church to men who openly professed the most arbitrary principles, and whose sentiments far more inclined them to promote an approximation to the rites and practices of the church of Rome than to mediate an agreement among the professors of the Protestant faith. Abbot, the archbishop of Canterbury, being restrained by the liberality of his principles and the mildness of his temper from lending his instrumen-tality to the views of the court, was treated with harshness, and, at length, finally suspended from his office [1627], of which the functions were com-mitted to a board of prelates, of whom the most eminent was Laud, who afterwards succeeded to the primacy. From this period, both in the civil and ecclesiastical administration of the realm, a system of deliberate and in-solent invasion of every right most valued by freemen and most revered by Protestants was pursued with a stubborn pride, folly, and cruelty, that at length exhausted the patience of the English people. To the historian of England the political abuses that distinguished this period will probably ap-pear the most interesting features in its history ; and, doubtless, they con-

---

[1] The most important act of Captain Gorges's administration, that has been transmitted to us, is one which affords an explanation of a passage in *Hudibras*, where the New Englanders are accused of hanging an innocent, but bedrid, weaver, instead of a guilty, but useful, cobbler : —
"That sinners may supply the place
Of suffering saints is a plain case.
Our brethren of New England use
Choice malefactors to excuse,
And hang the guiltless in their stead,
Of whom the churches have less need, —
As lately happened. In a town
There lived a cobbler," &c.   *Hudibras.*
Some of Gorges's people had committed depredations on the Indians, who insisted that the ringleader should be put to death. Gorges satisfied and deceived them by hanging up either a dying man or a dead body. Hutchinson. Butler's witty malice, studious to defame the Puri-tans, has rescued from oblivion an act, of which the whole merit or demerit is exclusively due to his own party. Morrell, the clergyman who accompanied Gorges, notwithstanding his dis-appointment, conceived a very favorable opinion of New England, which he expressed in an elegant Latin poem descriptive of the country. *Collections of the Massachusetts Historical Society.*
[2] Neal. Oldmixon (2d edit.).

M *

tributed at least as powerfully as any other cause to the production of the
ensuing scene of civil rage and warfare.   But, as it was the ecclesiastical
administration that mainly conduced to the peopling of America, it is this
branch of the English history that chiefly merits our attention, in investigating
the sources of the colonization of New England.

Not only were the ancient ceremonial observances, which long oppression
had rendered so obnoxious, exacted with additional rigor from the increasing
numbers of the Puritans, but new and more offensive rites were added to
the ecclesiastical canons.   A design seems to have been formed of enabling
the church of England to vie with the Romish see in splendid pageantry,
elaborate ceremonial, and temporal power.   Laud, indeed, boasted that he
had refused the offer of a cardinal's hat from Rome; but the offer was
justly considered a more significant circumstance than the refusal; and,
having already assumed to himself the papal title of *His Holiness*, which he
substituted in place of *His Grace*, his titular style would have been lowered
instead of elevated by the Romish promotion which he rejected.   The communion table was converted into an altar, and all persons were commanded
to bow to it on entering the church.   [1627.]   All the week-day lectures,
and all afternoon sermons on Sunday, were abolished; and, instead of them,
games and sports were permitted to all the people, "*excepting known recusants*," who were thus, with matchless absurdity, penally debarred from
practices which they regarded with the utmost detestation.   Every minister
was commanded, under pain of deprivation of his benefice, to read from
the pulpit a royal proclamation recommendatory of games and sports on
Sunday.   This ordinance, like all the other novelties, was productive of the
greater dissatisfaction, from the extent to which Puritan sentiments had
penetrated into the church, and the number of Puritan ministers within the
establishment whom habit had taught to fluctuate between the fulfilment and
the evasion of the ancient obnoxious canons, and trained partially to submit,
without at all reconciling to the burden.   Nothing could be more ill-timed
than an aggravation of the load under which these men were laboring; it
reduced many to despair, inflamed others with vindictive resentment, and
deprived the church of a numerous body of her most zealous and most
popular ministers.   Nor were these the only measures of the day that were
calculated to excite discontents within as well as without the pale of the
ecclesiastical establishment.   Three fourths of the English clergy were
Calvinists; yet Laud and the ruling prelates, who were Arminians, caused
a royal edict to be issued against the promulgation of the Calvinistic tenets;
and while the Arminian pulpits resounded with the sharpest invectives
against these tenets, a single sentence that could be construed into their
defence exposed the preacher to the undefined and arbitrary penalty attached to contempt of the king's authority.

In the reign of Elizabeth, the Churchmen were eager to shift from themselves upon the courts of common law as great a portion as they could of
the odium of administering the ecclesiastical statutes.   But Laud and his
associates, inaccessible to fear, remorse, or shame, courted a monopoly of
the function and repute of persecution; and in the Court of High Commission exercised such arbitrary power, and committed such enormous cruelty,
as procured to this odious tribunal the name of *the Protestant Inquisition*.
Fines, imprisonment, banishment, the pillory, were the most lenient of the
punishments inflicted by the judges who presided in it.   Its victims were

frequently condemned to have their flesh torn from their bodies by the lash of the executioner, their nostrils slit, and their ears cut off; and in this condition were exhibited to the people as monuments of what was termed the righteous justice of their sovereign and the holy zeal of the prelates. Of the extent to which this tyrannical policy was carried some notion may be formed from the accounts that have been transmitted to us of the proceedings within the diocese of Norwich alone. In the articles of impeachment subsequently exhibited against Bishop Wren, it is affirmed, that, during his possession of that diocese, which lasted only for two years and a half, fifty ministers were ejected from their pulpits for not complying with the prescribed innovations, and three thousand of the laity were compelled to abandon the kingdom.[1]

Consonant with the ecclesiastical was the civil policy of Charles's government. Parliamentary taxation was superseded by royal imposts ; the tenure of judicial office was altered from the good behaviour of the judges to the arbitrary pleasure of the king ; every organ of liberty was suspended or perverted ; and the kingdom at length subjected to the exclusive dominion of a stern and uncontrolled prerogative. Insult was employed, as if purposely to stimulate the sensibility which injuries might not have sufficiently awakened. A clergyman having alleged, in a sermon which he preached before the court, that his Majesty's simple requisition of money from his subjects obliged them to comply with it " under pain of eternal damnation," Charles at first coldly remarked that he owed the man no thanks for giving the king his due ; but when the discourse attracted a censure of the House of Commons, its author was forthwith accounted a proper object of royal favor, and promoted, first to a valuable benefice, and afterwards to a bishopric.[2] A system of such diffusive and exasperating insolence and violence, employed by the government against a numerous and increasing body of the people, needed only sufficient duration to provoke from general rage a vindictive retribution, the more to be dreaded from the patience with which the heavy arrear of injury had been endured and permitted to accumulate. But before this tyrannical system had time to mature the growing discontents, and to produce extremities so perilous to the moderation and humanity of all who were to abide them, it was destined to inspire efforts of nobler energy and purer virtue ; much good was to be educed from the scene of evil and disorder ; and great and happy consequences were yet to be engendered by the steady and beneficent dominion of Providence over the malevolent and irregular passions of men.

The severities exercised on the Puritans in England, and the gradual extinction of their fondly cherished hopes of a mitigation of ecclesiastical rigor, had for some time directed their thoughts to that distant territory in which their brethren at New Plymouth had achieved a secure establishment and attained the enjoyment of civil and religious liberty. In the last year of James's reign [1625], a few Non-conformist families removed to New England and took possession of a corner of Massachusetts Bay ; but being disappointed in the hope they had entertained of the accession of a sufficient number of associates to secure the formation of a permanent settlement, they were on the point of returning to Britain, when they received the agreeable intelligence of the approach of a numerous reinforcement. White, a Non-conformist minister at Dorchester, conceived the project of a new

---

[1] Neal.   [2] Sanderson's *Life of Charles the First*. Rushworth's *Hist. Collect.*

settlement on the shore of Massachusetts Bay; and by his zeal and activity he succeeded in forming an association of a number of the gentry in his neighbourhood who cherished Puritan opinions, for the purpose of conducting a colony to that region. The views and sentiments that actuated the leaders of this enterprise were committed to writing, and circulated among their friends under the title of *General Considerations for the Plantation of New England.*

The authors of this remarkable proclamation began by alluding to the progress of the Jesuit establishments in South America; and expatiated on the duty and advantage of counteracting the influence of these institutions by the introduction of a purer system of Christianity into that quarter of the world. They observed that all the other churches of Europe had been brought under desolation; that the same fate seemed to impend over the church of England; and that it might reasonably be supposed that the Deity had provided the unoccupied territory of America as a land of refuge for those of his people yet inhabiting the scene of approaching convulsion, whom he purposed to snatch from its dangerous vortex. England, they remarked, grew weary of her inhabitants; insomuch that man, the most precious of all creatures, was there reckoned more vile and base than the earth he trod on; and children and friends (if unwealthy) were accounted a burdensome incumbrance, instead of being prized and relished as the choicest of earthly blessings. A taste for expensive living, they added, prevailed so strongly among their countrymen, and the means of indulging it had become so exclusively the object of men's desires, that all arts and trades were tainted by sordid maxims and dishonest practices; and the English seminaries of learning abounded with so many spectacles and temptations of dissolute irregularity, that vice was there more effectually communicated by example than knowledge and virtue were imparted by precept. " The whole earth," they declared, " is the Lord's garden, and he hath given it to the sons of Adam to be tilled and improved by them. Why, then, should any stand starving here for places of habitation, and in the mean time suffer whole countries, as profitable for the use of man, to lie waste without any improvement ? " They concluded by adverting to the situation of the colony of New Plymouth, and strongly urged the duty of supporting the infant church which had there been so happily planted.

Actuated by such views, these magnanimous projectors purchased from the Council of Plymouth all the territory extending in length from three miles north of the River Merrimac to three miles south of Charles River, and in breadth from the Atlantic to the Southern Ocean. [1628.] Their measures were as vigorous as their designs were elevated. As the precursors of the main body of emigrants whom it was intended to transport, a small troop of planters and servants were despatched under John Endicott, one of the leading projectors, who, arriving safely in Massachusetts, were cordially greeted and kindly assisted by the colonists of New Plymouth, and laid the foundations of a town, which they denominated Salem, from a Hebrew word that signifies *peace.*[1] [1628.]

---

[1] Mather. Neal. An earlier writer than these has described Endicott as " a fit instrument to begin this wilderness work; of courage bold, undaunted, yet sociable, and of a cheerful spirit, loving, or austere, as occasion served " Johnson's *Wonder-working Providence in New England.* (London, 1654.) This contemporary historian of the first emigrations from Britain to New England represents their leaders as " gentlemen of good estate and reputation, descendants or connections of noble families; having large means, and great yearly revenue, sufficient in all reason to content; wanting nothing of a worldly nature which could contribute to the pleasures, the prospects, or the splendor of life."

But all the ardor and enthusiasm of these adventurers could not blind them to the perception of their inability to maintain effectual possession of the extensive territory that was ceded to them, without the participation of more opulent coadjutors in the enterprise ; of whom, chiefly by the influence and activity of White, they were enabled to procure a sufficient number in London, among the commercial men who openly professed, or secretly favored, the tenets of the Puritans. These auxiliaries brought an accession of prudent forecast, as well as of pecuniary resources, to the conduct of the design ; and justly doubting the expediency of founding a colony on the basis of a grant from a company of patentees, who might, indeed, convey a right of property in the soil, but could not confer municipal jurisdiction, or the privilege of governing the society which it was proposed to establish, they persuaded their associates to unite with them in an application to the crown for a royal charter.

The readiness with which this application was granted [4th March, 1629], and the liberal tenor of the charter which was obtained, are perfectly unaccountable, except on the supposition that the king and his counsellors were willing, at this season, even at the expense of some concessions to the Puritans, to disencumber the realm, in which they were preparing to introduce the ecclesiastical innovations to which we have already adverted, of a body of men from whom the most unbending opposition to the new measures might be expected ; a politic design which appears sufficiently credible ; although, at a subsequent period, Charles and his ministers resorted to an opposite line of policy, when they were sensible of the reflective influence exercised on the Puritan body in England by the spread and predominance of their tenets in America. It seems impossible, on any other supposition, to account for the remarkable facts, that, at the very time when this monarch was sanctioning the exercise of despotic authority in Virginia, he extended to a colony of Puritans a constitution containing all the immunities of which the Virginians were divested ; and that, well aware of the purpose of the applicants to escape from the constitutions of the church of England, he granted them a charter containing ample commendation of the religious ends they had in view, without the imposition of a single ordinance respecting the system of their church government, or the forms and ceremonies of their worship. Nay, so completely did he surrender the maxims of his colonial policy to the demands of the projectors of a Puritan settlement, that, although he had recently declared, in a public proclamation, that a mercantile company was utterly unfit to administer the affairs of a remote colony ; yet, on the present occasion, he scrupled not, in compliance with the wishes of the mercantile portion of the adventurers, to commit the supreme direction of the colony, which was to be planted in the province of Massachusetts Bay, to a corporation consisting chiefly of merchants resident in London.

The new adventurers were incorporated as a body politic ; and their right to the territory which they had purchased from the Council of Plymouth being confirmed by the king, they were empowered to dispose of the soil, and to govern the people who should settle upon it. Among other patentees specially named in this charter were Sir Henry Rosewell, one of the earliest promoters of the design ; Sir Richard Saltonstall, the descendant of an ancient family in Northamptonshire ; Isaac Johnson, son-in-law of the Earl of Lincoln ; John Ven, a distinguished citizen of London, and commemorated by Clarendon, as *leading the city after him in seditious remonstrances ;* and Samuel Vassal,[1] who was afterwards member of parliament for London, and had already signalized himself by a strenuous opposition to the arbitrary collection of tonnage and poundage. The first governor of the company and the first members of a council of assistants were named by the king ; the right of electing their successors was vested in the freemen of the corporation. The executive power was committed to the governor and council ; the legislative, to the body of freemen, who were empowered to enact statutes and ordinances for the good of the community, not inconsistent with the laws of England. The adventurers obtained the same temporary exemption that had been granted to the Virginian company from duties on goods exported or imported ; and it was declared, that, notwithstanding their migration to America, they and their descendants should be entitled to all the rights of home-born subjects of England.[2]

The meaning of this charter, with respect to the ecclesiastical rights of the colonists of Massachusetts, has been made the subject of much controversial discussion. By the Puritans and the Puritan writers of that age, it was sincerely believed, and confidently maintained, that the intendment of the charter was to bestow on the colonists unrestricted liberty to regulate their ecclesiastical estate by the dictates of their own judgments and consciences.[3] The grantors were fully aware, and the grantees had neither the wish nor the power to conceal, that the object of the intending emigrants was to make a peaceable secession from a church which they could no longer conscientiously adhere to, and to establish for themselves, at Massachusetts Bay, an ecclesiastical constitution similar to that which was already created and supported without objection at New Plymouth. A silent acquiescence in such designs was all that could reasonably be expected from the king and his ministers ; and when this emphatic silence, on a point which could not but be intimately present to the thoughts of both parties, is coupled with the king's ready departure, on the same occasion, from all the arbitrary principles which he was preparing to enforce in every other branch of his domestic and colonial administration, it seems to follow, by inevitable inference, that Charles was at this time not unwilling to make a partial sacrifice of authority, in order to rid himself of those Puritan petitioners ; and that the interpretation which they gave to their charter was perfectly correct. And yet writers have not been wanting, whom enmity to the Puritans has induced to explain this charter in a manner totally repugnant to every rule of legal or equitable construction. It is a maxim of English law, and the dictate of common sense and universal equity, that, in all cases where the import of a compact is doubtful, the bias of presumptive construction ought to incline against the pretensions of that party whose office

---

[1] From the monument erected to the memory of this man by his great-grandson at Boston, it appears that he was the son of the gallant John Vassal, who, in 1588, at his own expense, equipped and commanded two ships of war against the Spanish Armada. The son, exerting himself as strenuously against domestic tyranny as the father had done against foreign invasion, was deprived of his liberty and of the greater part of his fortune by the Court of Star Chamber. The Long Parliament voted him upwards of £10,000, as a compensation for his losses, and resolved that his personal sufferings should be further considered. "But the rage of the times," says his epitaph, " and the neglect of proper application since, have left to his family only the honor of that vote and resolution." Dodsley's *Annual Register,* 1766.

[2] Mather. Neal. Hutchinson's *Collection of Massachusetts Papers.* Hazard. Oldmixon (2d edit.).

[3] Mather. Neal. Neal's *History of the Puritans.*

it was to speak, and who had the power to clear every ambiguity away. In defiance of this rule, those writers have insisted that the silence of the charter respecting the ecclesiastical state of the colony implied the imposition on the colonists of every particular ordinance and institution of the church of England. The most eminent writer of this party has taken occasion from hence to reproach the colonists of Massachusetts Bay with having laid the foundations of their church establishment in fraud. " *Without regard*," says this distinguished author, " *to the sentiments of that monarch*, under the sanction of whose authority they settled in America, and from whom they derived right to act as a body politic, and in contempt of the laws of England, with which the charter required that none of their acts or ordinances should be inconsistent, they adopted in their infant church that form of policy which has since been distinguished by the name of Independent." He accounts for the pretermission in the charter of a particular which was unquestionably uppermost in the minds of both parties, by remarking, that " the king seems not to have foreseen, nor to have suspected, the secret intentions of those who projected the measure"; and he explains the conduct of the colonists, by pronouncing that they were " animated with a spirit of innovation in civil policy as well as in religion." [1] But surely no impartial inquirer will ever esteem it a reproach to the Puritans, driven by persecution from their native land, that they did not cross the Atlantic Ocean and settle in a desert for the purpose, or with the intention, of cultivating a more perfect conformity with the principles and policy of their oppressor. The provision in their charter, that the laws to be enacted by them should not be repugnant to the jurisprudence of England, could never be understood to enjoin any thing farther than a general conformity with the legislation of the parent state, suitable to the acknowledged dependence of the colony on the main trunk of the British dominions. The unsuspecting ignorance, too, that is imputed to the king and his counsellors, appears quite incredible, when we consider that the example of New Plymouth, where a bare exemption from express restrictions had been followed by the establishment of an Independent church, was fresh in their recollection ; that they were avowed and notorious Puritans who now applied for permission to repair to the land where that constitution was established ; and above all, that, in their application to the king, they expressly desired leave to withdraw in peace from the bosom of a church to whose ordinances they confessed that they could not conscientiously conform.[2] Whether the king and Laud were or were not aware of the intentions of the Puritans, they must surely be regarded as the best judges of the extent of concession which they themselves intended to convey ; and by their acquiescence in the constitution which the planters of Massachusetts Bay forthwith established, they ratified a practical interpretation of the charter in conformity with the views of the Puritans, and confessed that this proceeding imported no violation either of general law or particular paction. When they afterwards became sensible that the progress of Puritan establishments in New England increased the ferment which their own measures were creating in the parent state, they interposed to check the intercourse between the two countries ; but yet tacitly acknowledged that the intolerant system which they pursued in England was excluded by understood compact from the colonial territory.

Soon after the power of the adventurers to establish a colony was rendered

---

[1] Robertson's *History of America*, B. x.   [2] Mather.

complete by the royal charter [1st May, 1629], they equipped and despatched five ships for New England, containing three hundred and fifty
emigrants, chiefly zealous Puritans, accompanied by some eminent Non-
conformist ministers.   The regrets which an eternal farewell to their native
land was calculated to inspire, the distressing inconvenience of a long
voyage to persons unaccustomed to the sea, and the formidable scene of
toil and danger that confronted them in the barbarous land where so many
preceding emigrants had found an untimely grave, seem to have vanished
entirely from the minds of these men, supported by the worth and dignity
of the design which they were combined to accomplish.   Their hearts were
knit to each other by community of generous purpose ; and they experienced none of those jealousies which invariably spring up in confederacies
for ends merely selfish, among persons unequally qualified to promote the
object of their association.   Behind them, indeed, was the land of their
fathers ;[1] but it had long ceased to wear towards them a benign or paternal
countenance ; and in forsaking it they fled from the prisons and scaffolds to
which Christians and patriots were daily consigned.   Before them lay a vast
and dreary wilderness ; but they hoped to irradiate its gloom by kindling
and preserving there the sacred fire of religion and liberty, which regal and
pontifical tyranny was striving to extinguish in the shrines of England,
whence they carried its embers.[2]   They confidently believed that the religious and political tenets which had languished under a protracted persecution in Europe would now, at length, shine forth in their full lustre in
America.   Establishing an asylum where the professors of these doctrines
might at all times find shelter, they justly expected to derive continual accessions to the vigor of their own principles from the fresh arrival of succeeding emigrants, willing, like them, to transplant their uprooted patriotic
affection to a soil where it might flourish in alliance with the cultivation and
enjoyment of truth and liberty.   They did not postpone the practice of piety
till the conclusion of their voyage ; but, occupied continually with the exercises of devotion, they caused the ocean which they traversed to resound
with unwonted acclaim of praise and thanksgiving to its Creator.   The sea-
men, catching their spirit, readily joined in all their religious exercises and
ordinances, and expressed their belief that they had practised the first voluntary *sea-fasts* that had ever been performed in the world.   After a prosperous voyage, the emigrants had the satisfaction of reuniting themselves to
their friends already established at Salem under John Endicott, who had
been appointed deputy-governor of the colony.[3]   [June 24, 1629.]

    To the assemblage of men thus collected the formation of a church ap-
peared the most interesting of all their concerns, and it occupied, accordingly, their earliest and earnest deliberation.   They had been advised to

---

[1] Francis Higginson, one of the most able, devout, and popular ministers in England, was
a passenger in this fleet.   When he perceived that he was taking his last look of the English
coast, he summoned his children and the other passengers to the deck of the vessel, and said
to them, " We will not say, as the separatists were wont to say at their leaving of England,
' Farewell, Babylon ! Farewell, Rome ! ' But we will say, Farewell, dear England ! Farewell,
the church of God in England, and all Christian friends there ! We separate not from the church
of England, but from its corruptions.   We go to practise the positive part of church reforma
tion, and propagate the gospel in America."
[2] Even the pious George Herbert, though devotedly attached to royalty and the church of
England, thus expressed himself at this period in his *Temple of Sacred Poems : —*
                   " Religion stands a-tiptoe in our land,
                   Ready to pass to the American strand."
[3] Mather.   Neal.   Eliot's *New England Biography.*   Walton's *Life of Herbert.*

discuss and settle, before their departure from England, the form of church government which was to be established in the colony ; but, neglecting this advice, they had proceeded no farther than to express their general assent to the principle, that *the reformation of the church was to be attempted according to the written word of God.* They now applied to their brethren at New Plymouth, and desired to be acquainted with the grounds of the constitution which was there adopted ; and, having heard these fully explained, and devoted some time to a diligent comparison of the model with the warrants of Scripture which were cited in its vindication, and earnestly besought the enlightening aid of that Being who alone can teach his creatures how to worship him in an acceptable manner, they declared their entire approbation of the sister church, and closely copied her structure in the composition of their own. [Aug. 6, 1629.] They united together in religious society by a covenant, in which, after a solemn dedication of themselves to live in the fear of God, and practise a strict conformity to his will, so far as he should be pleased to reveal it to them, they engaged to each other to cultivate watchfulness and tenderness in their mutual intercourse ; to repress jealousies, suspicions, and secret emotions of spleen ; and, in all cases of offence, to suffer, forbear, and forgive, after the example of their divine pattern. They promised in the congregation to restrain the indulgence of a vain-glorious forwardness to display their gifts ; and in their intercourse, whether with sister churches or with the mass of mankind, to study a conversation remote from offence and from every appearance of evil. They engaged, by a dutiful obedience to all who should be set over them in church or commonwealth, to encourage them to a faithful discharge of their functions ; and they expressed their resolution to approve themselves, in their particular callings, the stewards and servants of God ; shunning idleness as the bane of every community, and dealing hardly or oppressively with none of the human race. The system of ecclesiastical policy and discipline which they adopted was that which distinguished the churches of the Independents, and which we have already had occasion to consider. The form of public worship which they instituted rejected a liturgy and every superfluous ceremony, and was adapted to the strictest standard of Calvinistic simplicity. They elected a pastor, a teacher, and an elder, whom they consecrated to their respective offices by imposition of the hands of the brethren. All who were on that occasion admitted members of the church signified their assent to a confession of faith digested by their teachers, and gave an account of the foundation of their own hopes as Christians ; and it was established as an ordinance, that no person should thereafter be permitted to subscribe the covenant, or be received into communion with the church, until he had satisfied the elders with respect to the soundness of his faith and the purity of his conduct.[1]

The constitution, of which we have now beheld an abstract, and especially the covenant or social engagement so fraught with sentiments of exalted piety and genuine benevolence, has excited the derision of some writers, who refuse to regard the speculative liberality which it indicates in any other point of view than as contrasted with the practical intolerance which the framers of it soon after displayed. But however agreeable this aspect may be to eyes that watch for the follies and frailties of the wise and good, it is not the only light in which the transaction we have now considered will

---

[1] Mather. Neal.

present itself to humane and liberal minds. Philosophy admits that the human soul is enlarged and ennobled by the mere purpose of excellence ; and religion has pronounced that even those designs which men are not able or worthy to accomplish may beneficially affect the minds that have sincerely entertained them. The error of the inhabitants of Salem was a universal trait and feature of the era to which they belonged ; the virtues they demonstrated were peculiar to themselves and their Puritan brethren.

In the ecclesiastical constitution which they established, and the sentiments and purposes which they declaratively interwove with it, they rendered a sincere and laudable homage to the rights of conscience and the requirements of piety ; and these principles, no doubt, exercised a beneficial influence on the practice, which, unhappily, they did not entirely control. The influence of principles that tend to the restraint of human ferocity and intolerance is frequently invisible to mortal eyes, because it is productive chiefly of negative consequences ; and when great provocation or alarm has prompted the professors of those principles to violate the relative restraint, they will be judged with little candor, if charity neglect to supply the imperfection of that knowledge to which we are limited by the narrow and partial range of our view, and to suggest the secret and difficult forbearance which may have preceded the visible action which we condemn or deplore. In the very first instance of intolerant proceeding with which the adversaries of the Puritans have reproached this American community, the influence of genuine piety in mitigating human impatience was strikingly apparent. It is a notable fact, that, although these emigrants were collected from a body of men embracing such diversity of opinion respecting church government and the rites of worship as then prevailed among the Puritans of England, and though they had landed in America without having previously ascertained how far they were likely to agree on this very point, for the sake of which they incurred banishment from their native country, the constitution which was copied from the church of New Plymouth gave satisfaction to almost every individual among them.

Two brothers, however, of the name of Brown, one a lawyer, and the other a merchant, both of them men of note and among the number of the original patentees, dissented from this constitution, and arguing, with great absurdity, that all who adhered to it would infallibly become Anabaptists, endeavoured to procure converts to their opinion, and to establish a separate congregation, on a model more approximated to the forms of the church of England. The defectiveness of their argument was supplied by the vehemence of their clamor ; and they obtained a favorable audience from a few persons who regarded with unfriendly eye the discipline which the provincial church was disposed to exercise upon offenders against the rules of morality. Endicott, the governor, called those men, together with the ministers, before a general assembly of the people, who, after hearing both parties, repeated their approbation of the system that had been established ; and, as the two brothers still persisted in their attempts to create a schism in the church, and even endeavoured to excite a mutiny against the government, they were declared unfit to remain in the colony, and compelled to reëmbark and depart in the vessels in which they had accompanied the other emigrants in the voyage from England.[1] Their departure restored

---

[1] Mather. Neal. On their return to England, they preferred a complaint against the colonists of oppressive demeanour to themselves and enmity to the church of England. The total

harmony to the colonists, who were endeavouring to complete their settlement and extend their occupation of the country, when they were interrupted by the approach of winter, and the ravages of disease, which quickly
deprived them of nearly one half of their number, but produced no other
change on their minds than to cause the sentiments of hope and fear to con-
verge more steadily to the Author of their existence.

Notwithstanding the censure with which some writers have commented
on the banishment of the two individuals whose case we have remarked,
the justice of the proceeding must commend itself to the sentiments of all
impartial men ; nor would it have been necessary to advert to the charge
of intolerance to which the colonists have been exposed, if their conduct
had never given juster occasion to it. But, unfortunately, a great proportion
of the Puritans at this period were deeply infected with the prevalent error
of their age,[1] and regarded as impossible the peaceable coëxistence of dif-
erent sects in the same community, — a notion strongly confirmed, if not
originally suggested to them, by the treatment which they received from their
adversaries. If it was reasonably incumbent on men, who were themselves
the victims of persecution, to abstain from what their own experience had
feelingly shown them to be hateful and odious, it was natural that these
men, flying to deserts for the sake of particular practices and opinions,
should desire and expect to see the objects of their painful sacrifice flourish
unmolested and undisputed in the scene of their retirement. The sufferings
they had endured from their adversaries they considered as the legitimate
consequence of the pernicious errors that these adversaries had imbibed ;
and they customarily regarded their opponents as the enemies of their persons, as well as persecutors of their tenets. The activity of government in
support of a system of religious doctrines they were far from condemning
in the abstract. They admitted the propriety of such interposition, and
condemned it only when it seemed to them erroneously directed. Even
when oppressed themselves, they exclaimed against indiscriminate toleration. They contradicted so far their own principles ; and maintained that
human beings might and ought to punish what God alone could correct and
alter. Some of them, it is true, had already anticipated the sentiments by
which at a later period the Independents were generally characterized, and
which induced them to reject all connection between church and state, and
disallow the competence of interposing magisterial authority to sustain one
church or to suppress or discourage another.

But very opposite sentiments prevailed among the bulk of the colonists
of Massachusetts, who came to America fresh from the influence of perse-

disregard which their complaint experienced (Chalmers) strongly confirms the opinion I have
expressed of the understanding of all parties with regard to the real import of the charter.
[1] The richest endowment of reason could not exempt the most distinguished of modern philosophers from intolerance ; nor could the experience of persecution always demonstrate its
injustice even to its own victims. Lord Bacon considered that uniformity in religious sentiment and worship was essential to the support of government, and that no toleration could
with safety be granted to sectaries. Bacon, *De Unitate Ecclesiæ*. During the administration
of Cromwell, a Presbyterian minister, who had himself felt the rod of persecution, published
a treatise against what he was pleased to term "*this cursed intolerable toleration.*" Orme's
Life of Owen.
To the objection, that persecution tends to make men hypocrites, an eminent minister in
New England answered, " Better tolerate hypocrites and tares, than briers and thorns."
Another, in a work published in 1645, thus expresses himself: " It is said that men ought to
have liberty of conscience, and that it is persecution to debar them of it. I can rather stand
amazed than reply to this. It is an astonishment that the brains of men should be parboiled
in such impious ignorance." Belknap's *History of New Hampshire.*

cution, and had not, like their brethren at New Plymouth, the advantage of an intermediate residence in a land where (to a certain extent, at least[1]) a peaceful coëxistence of different sects was demonstrated to be not merely practicable, but signally promotive of the most excellent graces of Christian character. Much might be urged, and will doubtless suggest itself to every liberal mind, in extenuation of their error, of which the bitter leaven continued long to disturb their peace and felicity. But indulgence must not be confounded with approval ; and the considerations which may be allowed to mitigate our censure of the intolerant spirit which these people displayed can never entitle this spirit to the commendation of virtue. It was sharpened by the copious infusions which the colony received of the feelings excited in England by the increased severity of persecution, from which the victims began to fly in increasing numbers to America.

The British empire in America underwent, about this period, some vicissitudes, which in after years affected materially the prosperity both of New England and of the other colonial establishments in the same quarter of the world. The war which the king so wantonly declared against France in 1627, and which produced only disgrace and disaster to his arms in Europe, was attended with events of a very different complexion in America. Sir David Kirk, having obtained a commission to attack the American dominions of France, invaded Canada in the summer of 1628 ; and so successful was the enterprise, that in July, 1629, Quebec was reduced to surrender to the arms of England. Thus was the capital of New France subdued by the English, about one hundred and thirty years before they achieved its final conquest by the sword of Wolfe. But the important tidings had not been received in Europe when peace was reëstablished between France and England ; and Charles, by the subsequent treaty of St. Germain, not only restored this valuable acquisition to France, but expressed the cession in terms of such extensive application, as undeniably inferred a recognition of the French, and a surrender of the British claims to the province of Nova Scotia.[2] This arrangement portended vexation and injury to the settlements of the English ; and the sequel of our narrative will demonstrate how fully the sinister portent was accomplished.

---

[1] It was not till the year 1619 (the year preceding the departure of the Plymouth settlers from Leyden), that the sanguinary persecution of the Arminians, to which I have already alluded, occurred in Holland.

[2] Champlain's *Voyage*. Oldmixon. Chalmers. "It is remarkable," says Professor Kalm, "that the French were doubtful whether they should reclaim Canada from the English, or leave it to them. Many were of opinion that it was better to keep the people in France, and employ them in all sorts of manufactures, which would oblige the other European powers who had colonies in America to bring their raw goods to French ports, and take French manufactures in return." But the prevalent opinion was, that the reclamation and retention of Canada would promote the naval power of France, and was necessary to counterbalance the rising colonial empire of England. Kalm's *Travels in North America.*

CHAPTER II.

The Charter Government transferred from England to Massachusetts. — Numerous Emigration. — Foundation of Boston. — Hardships endured by the new Settlers. — Disfranchisement of Dissenters in the Colony. — Influence of the provincial Clergy. — John Cotton and
his Colleagues and Successors. — Williams's Schism — he founds Providence. — Representative Assembly established in Massachusetts. — Arrival of Hugh Peters — and Henry Vane,
who is elected Governor. — Foundation of Connecticut — and New Haven. — War with
the Pequod Indians. — Severities exercised by the victorious Colonists. — Disturbances
created by Mrs. Hutchinson. — Colonization of Rhode Island — and of New Hampshire and
Maine. — Jealousy and fluctuating Conduct of the King. — Measures adopted against the
Liberties of Massachusetts — interrupted by the Civil Wars. — State of New England —
Population — Laws — Manners.

THE directors of the New England Company in Britain now exerted the
utmost diligence to reinforce the colony they had founded with a numerous
body of additional settlers. [1629.] Their designs were promoted by the
rigor and intolerance of Laud's administration, which progressively multiplying the hardships imposed on all Englishmen who scrupled entire conformity
to his ecclesiastical ordinances, proportionably diminished, in their estimation, the danger and hardships attending a removal to America. Many
people began to treat with the company for a settlement in New England ;
and several of those new adventurers were persons of distinguished family
and opulent estate.   But foreseeing the misrule inseparable from the residence of the legislative authority in Britain, they demanded, as a previous
condition of their emigration, that the chartered rights and all the powers
of government should be transferred to New England, and exercised within
the territory of the colony.   The directors of the company, who had incurred a considerable expense, with little prospect of speedy remuneration,
were willing to secure the settlement of so many wealthy and respectable
colonists in their domains, even at the expense of the surrender that was
demanded from them ; but, doubting its legality, they thought proper to consult lawyers of eminence on the subject.   Unaccountable as it must appear
to every person in the slightest degree conversant with legal considerations,
the lawyers who were consulted delivered an opinion favorable to the wishes
of the emigrants ; and accordingly it was determined, by general consent,
" that the charter should be transferred, and the government be settled in
New England." [29th Aug., 1629.]   To the existing members of the
corporation who should still remain in Britain was reserved a share in the
trade, stock, and profits of the company, for the term of seven years.[1]   By
this transaction, — one of the most singular that is recorded in the history
of a civilized people, — were the municipal rights and liberties of the inhabitants of New England established on a firm and respectable basis.
   When we consider the means by which this was accomplished, we find
ourselves beset with doubts and difficulties, of which the only rational solution that presents itself is the supposition we have already adopted, that the
king was at this time exceedingly desirous to rid the realm of the Puritans,
and had unequivocally signified to them, that, if they would withdraw to
some other part of his dominions, and employ their energies in subduing
the deserts of America, instead of disturbing his operations in England, they

---

[1] Mather. Hutchinson.

should have permission to arrange the structure, civil and ecclesiastical, of their provincial commonwealth, according to their own discretion. An English corporation, appointed by its charter to reside in London, resolved itself, by its own act, into an American corporation, and transferred its residence to Massachusetts ; and this was openly transacted by men whose principles rendered them peculiarly obnoxious to their rulers, and under the eyes of a prince no less vigilant to mark, than prompt to repress, every encroachment on the limits of his prerogative. So far was Charles from entertaining the slightest dissatisfaction at this proceeding, or from desiring, at the present period of his reign, to obstruct the removal of the Puritans to New England, that about two years after this signal change was carried into effect, when a complaint of arbitrary and illegal measures was preferred against the colony by a Roman Catholic who had been banished from it, and who was supported by Sir Ferdinando Gorges, — the king, after a deliberate examination of the case in the privy council, issued a proclamation not only justifying but commending the whole conduct of the provincial government, reprobating the prevalent reports that he " had no good opinion of that plantation," and engaging not only to maintain the privileges of its inhabitants, but to supply whatever else might contribute to their farther comfort and prosperity.[1]

From the terms of this document (of which no notice is taken by the writers inimical to the Puritans), and from the whole complexion of the king's conduct towards the founders of this settlement, it would appear, that, whatever designs he might secretly cherish of adding the subjugation of New England, at a future period, to that of his British and Virginian dominions, his policy at the present time was, to persuade the leaders of the Puritans, that, if they would peaceably abandon the contest for their principles in England, they were at liberty to embody and enjoy them in whatever institutions they might think fit to establish in America. And yet some writers [2] — whom it is impossible to tax with ignorance, as they had access to all the existing materials of information, — whom it might justly be reckoned presumptuous to charge with defect of discernment, — and whom it may, perhaps, appear uncharitable to reproach with malignity towards the Puritans — have not scrupled to accuse the founders of this colony of pursuing their purposes by a policy not less impudent than fraudful, and by acts of disobedience little short of rebellion. The colonists themselves, notwithstanding all the facilities which the king presented to them, and the unwonted liberality and consideration with which he showed himself willing to grace their departure from Britain, were so fully persuaded of his rooted enmity to their principles, and so little able to reconcile his present demeanour with his favorite policy, that they openly declared they had been conducted by Providence to a land of rest, through ways which they were contented to admire without comprehending ; and that they could ascribe the blessings they obtained to nothing else than the special interposition of that Being who orders all the steps of his people, and holds the hearts of kings, as of all men, in his hands. It is, indeed, a strange coincidence, that this arbitrary prince, at the very time when he was oppressing the royalists in Virginia, should have been cherishing the principles of liberty among the Puritans in New England.

Having achieved this important innovation in the structure of their politi-

---

[1] Neal.   [2] Chalmers. Robertson.

cal system, the adventurers proceeded with equal prudence and vigor to execute the ulterior designs which they had undertaken. By a general court of assembly, John Winthrop was appointed governor, and Thomas Dudley deputy-governor ; eighteen counsellors, or assistants, were also chosen ; and in these functionaries, together with the whole body of freemen residing in New England, were vested all the corporate rights of the company.   So active was the spirit of emigration, that, in the course of the ensuing year [1630], above fifteen hundred settlers, among whom were several wealthy and high-born persons, both men and women, who expressed their determination to follow truth and liberty into a desert, rather than to enjoy all the pleasures of the world under the dominion of superstition and slavery, set sail from Britain aboard a fleet of seventeen ships for New England. [July 6.] Among them there came Nathaniel Rogers (and his family), a clergyman of Ipswich, in Suffolk ; the lineal descendant of that excellent Rogers, who, burned at Smithfield under Mary's reign, attained the highest fame in English martyrology. On their arrival at Salem, many of them were so displeased with its local circumstances, that they explored the country in quest of more agreeable stations ; and, settling in various places around the adjacent bay, according to their particular predilections, laid the foundation of Boston, Charlestown, Dorchester, Roxbury, and other societies, which have since expanded into considerable towns.   In each of these settlements, a church was established on the same model with that of Salem. This concernment, together with the care of providing for their subsistence during winter, afforded ample occupation to the emigrants for several months after their arrival.   The approach of winter was attended with a repetition of those trials and distresses, through the ordeal of which every band of European settlers in New England was long fated to pass.   Afflicted with severe scarcity, which all the generous contributions of the other settlements in the province could but slightly alleviate, — attacked with various distempers, the consequence of hunger, cold, and the peculiarities of a soil and climate uncongenial to constitutions formed in Europe, — and lodged for the most part in booths and tents that afforded but imperfect protection from the weather, — great numbers of the new colonists were speedily carried to the grave. " Many," says Cotton Mather, " merely took New England in their way to heaven."   But the noble determination of spirit which had impelled them to emigrate preserved all its force ; the survivors endured their calamities with unshaken fortitude ; and the dying expressed a grateful exultation in the consciousness of having promoted and beheld the foundation of a Christian church in this desolate and benighted quarter of the earth.   The continuance of deadly disease enforced the devout supplications of the colonists ; and its cessation, which they recognized as the answer to their prayers, excited their pious gratitude.   This calamity was hardly removed, when they were alarmed by the tidings of a conspiracy of the neighbouring Indians for their destruction.   The colonists, instead of relying on their patent from the British crown, had, on their first arrival, fairly purchased from the Indians all the tracts of land which they proposed to occupy ; and in the hour of their peril, both they and the faithless vendors who menaced them reaped the fruit of their compliance or collision with the designs of Eternal Justice.   The hostility of the savages was interrupted by a pestilential distemper, that broke out among them, and with rapid desolation swept whole tribes away.   This distemper was the small-pox, which has always proved a much more formidable malady to Indian than to European constitutions. In spite of the most charitable exertions on the part of the colonists to arrest the progress of the malady by their superior medical skill, nine tenths of the neighbouring Indians were cut off; and many of the survivors, flying from the infection, removed their habitations to more distant regions.[1]

When the departure of winter and the arrival of supplies from England [1631] permitted the colonists to resume their assemblies for the transaction of public business, their very first proceedings demonstrated that a great majority of them were strongly imbued with a spirit of intolerance, and were determined that their commonwealth should exemplify a thorough intertexture and mutual dependence of church and state. A law was framed, enacting that no persons should hereafter be admitted freemen, or entitled to any share in the government, or capable of being chosen magistrates, or even of serving as jurymen, but such as had been or should hereafter be received members of one or other of the congregations of the established church of the province. This law at once divested every person who did not hold the prevailing opinions, not only on the fundamental points of Christian doctrine, but with respect to ecclesiastical discipline and the ceremonies of worship, of all the privileges of a citizen. An uncontrolled power of approving or rejecting the claims of those who applied for admission into communion with the church being vested in the ministers and elders of each congregation, the most valuable civil rights were made to depend on their decision with respect to qualifications purely ecclesiastical. Even at a later period, when the colonists were compelled by the remonstrances and menaces of Charles the Second to make some alteration of this law, they altered it at first rather in appearance than in reality, and still required that every candidate for the rank of a freeman should produce a certificate from some minister of the established church, that he was a person of orthodox principles and of honest life and conversation, — a certificate which dissenters from the established church solicited with great disadvantage. The consequence of such laws was to elevate the clergy to a very high degree of influence and authority;[2] and, happily, the colony was long blessed with a succession of ministers whose disinterested virtue and superior sense served not merely to counteract the mischief of this inordinate influence, but even to convert it in some measure into an instrument of good. Though dissenters from the provincial church were thus deprived of political privileges, it does not appear that they were exposed to any positive molestation,

---

[1] Mather. Neal. Hutchinson. Peirce's *History of Harvard University.* "The first planters, far from using the barbarous methods practised by the Spaniards on the southern continent, which have made them detestable to the whole Christian world, sought to gain the natives by strict justice in their dealings with them, as well as by all the endearments of kindness and humanity. To lay an early foundation for a firm and lasting friendship, they assured the Americans that they did not come among them as invaders, but purchasers, and therefore called an assembly of them together to inquire who had the right to dispose of their lands; and being told it was their sachems or princes, they thereupon agreed with them for what districts they bought, publicly, and in open market." Dummer's *Defence of the New England Charters.*

[2] Some instances of their influence in matters of importance will occur in the further progress of our narrative. An instance of their control over public opinion on a point, which, being quite beyond the province of reason, was the more likely to interest the most obstinate and unassailable prejudices, is mentioned by Hutchinson. Tobacco was at first prohibited under a penalty; and in some writings that were popular in the colony, the smoke of it was with profane absurdity compared to the fumes of the bottomless pit. But some of the clergy having fallen into the practice of smoking, tobacco was instantly, by an act of government, "set at liberty."

except when their tenets were considered as blasphemous, or when they endeavoured by the propagation of them to detach other persons from the established system, or to disturb the public peace. The exclusion from political franchises to which they were subjected seems not at first to have given them any annoyance, but to have been recognized as the necessary operation of that system of policy in conformity with which the preservation of the church estate was accounted the main object of political institutions; and the chief value of political rights was supposed to consist in their subservience to that object.   Various persons resided in peace within the colony, though excluded from political franchises ; and one minister in particular, of the episcopal persuasion, provoked more mirth than displeasure, when, signifying his refusal to join any of the provincial congregations, he declared, that, *as he had left England because he did not like the lords bishops, so they might rest assured that he had not come to America to live under the lords brethren.*[1]

The diminution of their original numbers [1632[2]], which the colonists underwent from hardship and disease, was much more than compensated by the ample reinforcements which they continually received from their persecuted brethren in England.   Among the new settlers who arrived not long after the transference of the seat of government to Massachusetts, were some eminent Puritan ministers, of whom the most remarkable were Eliot and Mayhew, the first Protestant missionaries to the Indians, and John Cotton, a man whose singular worth procured, and long preserved, to him a patriarchal repute and authority in the colony.   After ministering for twenty years in England to a congregation by whom he was highly respected and beloved, Cotton was summoned before the Court of High Commission, on a charge of neglecting to kneel at the sacrament.   Lord Dorset and other persons of distinction, by whom he was known and esteemed, employed the strongest intercession in his behalf with Laud ; but their exertions were unavailing ; and Dorset was constrained to inform his friend, " that, *if it had been only drunkenness or adultery* that he had committed, he might have found favor ; but the sin of Puritanism was unpardonable." Cotton, in consequence, retired to New England, where he soon found an ample solace of exile in an enlarged sphere of usefulness and virtue.   To an earnest concern for the propagation of religion he united a deep and constant personal sense of its influence ; and habitually seeking to illustrate and adorn by his life the doctrine which he taught, he promoted its acceptance by the weight of his character and the animation of his example.

The loftiness of the standard to which his constant regard was directed, and the assimilating influence of that strong admiration which he entertained for it, communicated to his character an elevation that commanded respect; while the continual sense of his dependence on divine aid, and of his inferiority to the great object of his imitation, graced his manners with a humility that attracted love, and disarmed the contentious opposition of petulance and envy.   It is recorded of him, that, having been once followed from the

---

[1] Neal. Hutchinson. Chalmers.

[2] "One pleasant thing happened this year, acted by the Indians. Mr. Winslow, coming in his bark from Connecticut to Narraganset, went to Ousamequin, the sagamore, his old ally, who offered to conduct him to Plymouth. Ousamequin sent a man to Plymouth to say that Winslow was dead. Being afterwards asked the reason, he said it was their custom, in order to make their friends more joyful on seeing them." *Collections of the Rhode Island Historical Society.* Even the wise Ulysses is described by Homer as employing a similar device with his father, and *moving the old man's sorrow to enhance his joy.*

church where he preached by a sour, peevish fanatic, who announced to him, with a frown, that his ministry had become dark and flat, he replied, " *Both, brother, — it may be both ; let me have your prayers that it may be otherwise.*" On another occasion, being accosted in the street by a pragmatical disputer, who insolently called him an old fool, Cotton, with forgiving mildness blended with a solemnity that showed him incapable of contemning the opinion of his neighbour, answered, "*I confess I am so ; the Lord make thee and me wiser than we are ; even wise unto salvation.*"[1] The character, at once so venerable and so amiable, of this excellent clergyman, and of many of his colleagues, seems to have been formed by Providence for the express purpose of moderating, by a happy influence, the violent, divisive, and controversial spirit that long continued to ferment in a community of men whom persecution had rendered rigid and inflexible in opinion, — whose sentiments had not been harmonized by previous habits of union and accommodation, — who were daily receiving into their body a fresh infusion of dissimilar characters and exasperated spirits, — and among whom each naturally considered the notions and practices for which he had individually suffered as the most important feature of the common cause.

When we recollect the presence of such elements of discord, and the severe and protracted operation that had been given to that influence which tends to drive even the wise to frenzy, we shall be less disposed to marvel at the vehement heats and acrimonious contentions which in some instances broke forth to disturb the peace of the colony, than that in the midst of those alarming symptoms so much coherence and stability was preserved, and so much virtue, happiness, and prosperity attained. Nor should it ever be forgotten, that the polemical strife that arose among the fathers of New England was not the selfish strife of ambition. It arose from their common attachment to the truths of Christianity ; but, unfortunately, to these truths partially conceived, and beheld in different points of view by different men. Among the instruments happily qualified and providentially employed to compose and unite the spirits of the people, were this eminent individual, John Cotton ; Thomas Hooker, a man very little inferior to him in worth and influence ; and, at a later period, Dr. Increase Mather, who succeeded to the estimation which Cotton had enjoyed, and whose family supplied no fewer than ten of the most popular ministers of the age which they adorned to the churches of Massachusetts, and produced the celebrated author of the ecclesiastical history of New England. If all the provincial churches had been guided by such spirits as these, the agitated minds of the inhabitants would doubtless have sooner attained a settled composure ; but, unfortunately, the intolerant and contentious disposition which many of the people had contracted did not long wait for ministerial leaders to excite and develope its activity.

The first theological dissension that arose in the colony was promoted by Roger Williams [1634], who emigrated to New England in 1630, and officiated for some time as pastor of New Plymouth. Not finding there an audience of congenial spirits, he obtained leave to resign that charge, and had recently been appointed minister of Salem. This man was a stubborn Brownist, keen, unpliant, illiberal, unforbearing, and passionate ; seasoning evil with good, and error with truth, he began to vent from the pulpit, which he had gained by his substantial piety and fervid zeal, a singular medley of

---

[1] Neal.

notions, some wildly speculative, some boldly opposed to the constitutions of civil society, and some, which, if unexceptionable in the abstract, were unsuitable to the scene of their promulgation, and to the exercises and sentiments with which he endeavoured to blend them. He insisted that it was not lawful for an unregenerate man to pray, nor for Christians to join in family prayer with those whom they judged unregenerate ; that it was not lawful to take an oath to the civil magistrate, — not even the oath of allegiance, which he had declined himself to take, and advised his congregation equally to repudiate ; that King Charles had unjustly usurped the power of disposing of the territory of the Indians, and hence the colonial patent was utterly invalid ; that the civil magistrate had no right to restrain or direct the consciences of men ; and that any thing short of unlimited toleration for all religious systems was detestable persecution.

These liberal principles of toleration he combined with a spirit so rigid and separative, that he not only refused all communion with persons who did not profess every one of the foregoing opinions, but forbade the members of the church at Salem to communicate with any of the other churches in the colony ; and when they refused to obey this prohibition, he forsook his ministerial office among them, and established a separate meeting in a private house. He even withdrew from the society of his wife, because she continued to attend the church of Salem, and from that of his children, because he accounted them unregenerate. In his retirement he was attended by a select assembly of zealous admirers, consisting of men in whose minds an impetuous temper, inflamed by persecution, had greatly impaired the sense of moral perspective ; who entertained disproportioned ideas of those branches of the trunk of godliness, for the sake of which they had endured severe affliction, and had seen worth and piety foully wronged ; and who abhorred every symbol, badge, and practice, that was associated with the remembrance, and stained, as they conceived, with the iniquity, of their idolatrous oppressors. One of these individuals, Endicott, a magistrate of the place, and formerly deputy-governor of the colony, in a transport of devouring zeal against superstition, was instigated by Williams to cut the red cross out of the royal standard ; and many of the trained bands, who had hitherto followed this standard without objection, caught the contagion of Endicott's fervor, and protested that they would no longer follow a flag on which the *popish* emblem of a crucifix was painted. The intemperate and disorderly conduct of Endicott was generally disapproved, and the provincial authorities punished his misdemeanour by reprimand and disability of holding office for a year ; but they were obliged to compromise the dispute with the protesters among the trained bands, and to comply with their remonstrances. It is a notable fact, and illustrative perhaps of the extent of their compliance, that, only two years after, when they were pressed with (apparently) friendly counsel to dissipate English jealousy by hoisting the British flag on the walls of their little fort, not a single royal ensign could be found in Massachusetts. They were preparing to call Williams to a judicial reckoning, when Cotton and some other clergymen interposed, and desired to be allowed to reason with him ; alleging that his vehemence and breach of order betokened rather a misguided conscience, than seditious principles ; and that there was hope that they might gain, instead of losing, their brother. *You are deceived in that man, if you think he will condescend to learn of any of you,* was the prediction of the governor ; and the result of the conference proving the justice of it,[1] sentence of banishment from the colony was forthwith pronounced against Williams.

This sentence excited a great uproar in Salem, and was so successfully denounced as persecution by the adherents of Williams, that the bulk of the inhabitants of the place were preparing to follow him into exile, when an earnest and pious admonition, addressed to them by Cotton and the other ministers of Boston, induced them to relinquish their purpose, to acknowledge the justice of the proceeding, and abandon Williams to his fate. Still, was he not abandoned by his more select admirers, whose esteem and affection he had gained to such a degree, that they resolved to brave every hardship, in order to live and die with him. Accompanying him in his exile, they directed their march towards the south ; and settling at a place beyond the jurisdiction of Massachusetts, they purchased a considerable tract of land from the Indians, and bestowed on their plantation the name of Providence. Had Williams encountered the severities to which the publication of his peculiar opinions would have exposed him in England, he would probably have lost his senses ; the wiser and kinder treatment he experienced from the Massachusetts authorities was productive of happier effects ; and Cotton and his colleagues were not wholly mistaken in supposing that they would gain their brother. They gained him, indeed, in a manner less flattering to themselves than a controversial victory would have been, but much more beneficial to the interests of America. He contributed, as we shall see, to found the colony of Rhode Island, and was one of its most eminent benefactors. He lived to an advanced age ; and gradually emancipating himself from the impetuous and yet punctilious spirit with which his doctrinal sentiments had originally been leavened, he regained the friendship and esteem of his ancient fellow-colonists, and preserved a friendly correspondence with Cotton and others of them till his death. The principles of toleration, which he had formerly discredited by the rigidness with which he disallowed the slightest difference of opinion between the members of his own communion, he now recommended by the exercise of meekness, charity, and forbearance. The great fundamental principles of Christianity progressively acquiring a more exclusive and absorbing influence on his mind, he began to labor for the conversion of the Indians ; and in addition to the benefits of which his ministry among them was productive to this race of people, he acquired over them an influence which he rendered highly advantageous to his old associates in Massachusetts, whom he was enabled frequently to apprize of conspiracies formed against them by the savages in their vicinity, and revealed to him by the tribes with whom he maintained relations of friendship.[2] Endicott's vehemence was not less mellowed by time and the ascendency of sound wisdom and piety. He remained in Massachusetts ; and, at a later period, held for many years the chief office in its government with great public advantage and general esteem.[3]

---

[1] Though he would not retract his dogmas, it seems that some of the arguments that were employed with him sank into his mind, and at least reduced him to silence. Hooker, one of the ministers who were sent to deal with him, urged, among other reasonings, — "If it be unlawful for an unregenerate person to pray, it is unlawful for your unregenerate child to ask a blessing on his meat ; and if so, it is unlawful for him to eat, since food is sanctified by prayer, and without prayer unsanctified (1 Tim. iv. 4, 5) ; and it must be equally unlawful for you to invite him to eat, since you ought not to tempt him to sin." To this he declined making any answer. Mather.
[2] Mather. Neal. Hutchinson.   [3] Mather.

The colony of Massachusetts continued meanwhile to advance in stability and prosperity, and to extend its settlements ; and this year [1634] an important and beneficial change took place in its municipal constitution. The mortality that had prevailed among the Indians vacated a great many stations formerly occupied by their tribes ; and as most of these were advantageously situated, the colonists took possession of them with an eagerness and latitude of appropriation that dispersed their settlements widely over the face of the country. This necessarily led to the introduction of representative government ; and, accordingly, at the period of convoking the General Court, the freemen, instead of personally attending it, which was the literal prescription of the provincial charter, elected deputies from their several districts, whom they authorized to appear in their name and act in their behalf. Without demur or objection from any quarter, the pretensions of the persons thus elected were recognized ; and the popular representatives thenceforward considered themselves, in conjunction with the governor and council of assistants, as the supreme legislative assembly of the province. The abstract wisdom of this innovation is undeniable ; and, in defence of its legitimacy, it was forcibly urged that the colonists did no more than construct an improved and necessary access to the enjoyment of an advantage already belonging to them, and prevent their assemblies from becoming either too numerous to transact business, or inadequate to represent the general interest and administer the general will. The number of freemen was greatly augmented since the date of the charter ; many resided at a distance from the places where the general courts or assemblies of the freemen were held ; personal attendance had become inconvenient ; and, in such circumstances, little if any blame can attach to the colonists for effecting with their own hands the improvement that was necessary to preserve their existing rights, instead of applying to the government of England, which was steadily pursuing the plan of subverting the organs of liberty in the mother country, and had already begun to exhibit an altered countenance towards the colonial community. In consequence of this important measure, the colony advanced beyond the state of a mercantile society or corporation, and acquired by its own act the condition of a commonwealth endowed with political liberty. The representatives of the people, having established themselves in their office, asserted its appropriate privileges by decreeing that no legal ordinance should be framed within the province, no tax imposed, and no public officer appointed, in future, except by the provincial legislature.[1]

The increasing violence and injustice of the royal government in Britain coöperated so forcibly with the tidings that were circulated of the prosperity of Massachusetts, — and the simple frame of ecclesiastical policy that was established in the colony presented a prospect so desirable, and (by the comparison which it invited) exposed the gorgeous hierarchy and recent superstitious innovations in the ceremonies of the English church to so much additional odium, — that the flow of emigration rather enlarged than subsided, and crowds of new settlers continued to flock to New England. Among the passengers in a fleet of twenty vessels that arrived in the ensuing year [1635] were two persons who afterwards made a distinguished figure in a more conspicuous scene. One of these was Hugh Peters, the celebrated chaplain and counsellor of Oliver Cromwell ; and the other was Vane, whose father, Sir Henry Vane the elder, enjoyed the dignity of a

---

[1] Hutchinson. Chalmers.

privy counsellor at the English court, and afterwards filled the office of principal secretary of state. Peters, who united an active and enterprising genius with the warmest devotion to the interests of religion and liberty, became minister of Salem, where he not only discharged his sacred functions with zeal and advantage, but suggested new hints of profitable industry to the planters, and recommended his wise counsels by his own successful example. His labors were blessed with a produce not less honorable than enduring. The spirit which he fostered has continued to prevail with unabated vigor; and nearly two centuries after his death, the piety, good morals, and industry, by which Salem has always been characterized, were ascribed with just and grateful commemoration to the effects of Peters's residence there. He remained in New England till the year 1641, when, at the request of the colonists, he went to transact some business for them in the mother country, from which he was fated never to return. But his race remained in the land thus highly indebted to his virtue ; and the name of Winthrop, one of the most honored in New England, was acquired and transmitted by his daughter.

Vane, afterwards Sir Henry Vane the younger, had been for some time restrained from indulging his wish to reside in New England by the prohibition of his father, who was at length induced to waive his objections by the interference of the king. The Puritan principles which Vane had imbibed, and to which he had already sacrificed his collegiate rank in the university of Oxford, were distasteful alike to his father and his king ; and while the one dreaded the effect of his intercourse with the Puritans of Massachusetts, the other feared the influence of his example in England. A young man of patrician family, animated with such ardent devotion to the cause of pure religion and liberty, that, relinquishing the most brilliant prospects in Britain, he chose to inhabit an infant colony which as yet afforded little more than a bare subsistence to its inhabitants, was received in New England with the fondest regard and admiration. He was then little more than twenty-four years of age. His youth, which seemed to magnify the sacrifice he made, increased no less the impression which his manners and appearance were calculated to produce. The fixed, thoughtful composure of his aspect and demeanour stamped a serious grace and somewhat (according to our conceptions) of angelic grandeur on the bloom of manhood ; his countenance disclosed the surface of a character not less resolute than profound, and of which the energy was not extinguished, but concentrated into a sublime and solemn calm. He possessed a prompt and clear discernment of the characters and purposes of other men, and a wonderful mastery of his own spirit. Clarendon ascribes to him "a quick conception and ready, sharp, and weighty expression, an unusual aspect, a *vultum clausum*, which, though no man could guess what he intended, yet made men think there was something in him extraordinary ; and his whole life made good that imagination." He has been charged with a wild enthusiasm [1] by some who have remarked the intensity with which he pursued purposes which to them appeared worthless and ignoble ; and with hypocrisy by others, who have contrasted the vigor of his resolution with the calmness of his manners.

---

[1] One ingenious writer speaks more respectfully of Vane's enthusiasm ; declaring that "it seems never to have precipitated him into injudicious measures, but to have added new powers to his natural sagacity." "He mistook," continues the writer, "his deep penetration for a prophetic spirit, and the light of his genius for divine irradiation." I see no proof that he entertained the first of these notions, and no mistake in the second.

But a juster consideration, perhaps, may suggest that it was the habitual energy of his determination that repressed every sympton of vehement impetuosity, and induced an equality of manner that scarcely appeared to exceed the pitch of a grave, deliberate constancy. So much did his mind predominate over his senses, that, although constitutionally timid,[1] and keenly susceptible of impressions of pain, yet his whole life was one continued course of great and daring enterprise ; and when, amidst the wreck of his fortunes and the treachery of his associates, death was presented to him in the appalling form of a bloody execution, he prepared for it with a heroic and smiling intrepidity, and encountered it with tranquil and dignified resignation. The man who could so command himself was formed to acquire ascendency over the minds of others. He was instantly admitted a freeman of Massachusetts ; and extending his claims to respect by the address and ability which he displayed in conducting business, was elected governor in the year subsequent to his arrival [1636], by unanimous choice, and with the highest expectations of a happy and advantageous administration. These expectations were disappointed. Vane, not finding in the political affairs of the colonists a wide enough field for the excursion of his active spirit, embarked its energy in their theological discussions ; and, unfortunately, connecting himself with a party who had conceived singularly clear and profound views of Christian doctrine, but associated them with some dangerous errors, and discredited them by a wild extravagance of behaviour, he very soon witnessed the abridgment of his usefulness and the decline of his popularity.[2]

The incessant flow of emigration to Massachusetts, causing the inhabitants of some of the towns to feel themselves straitened for room, suggested the formation of additional settlements. A project of founding a new colony on the banks of the River Connecticut was now embraced by Hooker, one of the ministers of Boston, and a hundred of the members of his congregation. After enduring extreme hardship, and encountering the usual difficulties that attended the foundation of civilized society in this quarter of America, with the usual display of Puritan fortitude and resolution, they succeeded in establishing a plantation, which gradually enlarged into the flourishing State of Connecticut. Some Dutch settlers from New York, who took prior possession of a post in this country, were compelled to surrender it to the British colonists, who, moreover, obtained shortly after from Lord Brooke and Lord Say and Seal an assignation to a district which these noblemen had acquired in the same quarter, with the intention of flying from royal tyranny to America.[3] Hooker and his comrades relied for a

---

[1] See Note VI., at the end of the volume.

[2] *America Painted to the Life*, by Ferdinando Gorges. There is a copy of this work in the Redcross-street Library of London. Neal. Hutchinson. Dwight's *Travels in New England and New York*. Upham's *Life of Sir Henry Vane*, in Sparks's *American Biography*. New England has now repaid Vane's noble devotion by the best (Mr. Upham's) memoir of that great man that has ever been given to the world. Vane was accompanied to America by Lord Leigh, son of the Earl of Marlborough, who had conceived a curiosity to behold the New England settlements.

[3] Lord Brooke and Lord Say and Seal so far pursued their design as to send an agent to take possession of their territory, and build a fort. Happily for America, the sentiments and habits that rendered them unfit members of a society where complete civil liberty and perfect simplicity of manners were esteemed requisite to the general happiness, prevented these noblemen from carrying their project into execution. They proposed to establish an order of nobility and hereditary magistracy in America ; and consumed so much time in arguing this important point with the other settlers who were to be associated with them, that at length their ardor for emigration subsided, and nearer and more interesting prospects opened to their activity in England. Chalmers.

while on a commission which they procured from the government of Massachusetts for the administration of justice in their new settlement; but subsequently ascertaining that their territory was beyond the jurisdiction of the
magistrates from whom the commission was derived, they combined themselves by a voluntary association into a body politic, constructed on the
model of the colonial society from which they had separated. They continued in this condition till the Restoration, when they obtained a charter
for themselves from King Charles the Second. That this secession from
the colony of Massachusetts was occasioned by lack of room in a province
yet imperfectly peopled has appeared so improbable to some writers, that
they have thought it necessary to assign another cause, and have found none
so credible or satisfactory as the jealousy which they conclude that Hooker
must inevitably have entertained towards Cotton, whose patriarchal authority
had attained such a height in Massachusetts, that even a formidable civil
broil was quelled by one of his pacific discourses. But envy was not a
passion congenial to the breast of Hooker, or likely to be generated by the
character or influence of Cotton. The notion of a redundant population
was the more readily conceived at this period from the unwillingness of the
settlers to penetrate far into the interior of the country, and thus deprive
themselves of an easy communication with the coast. Another reason, indeed, appears to have suggested the formation of the new settlement; but
it was a reason that argued not dissension, but community of feeling and
design between the planters who remained in Massachusetts and those who
removed to Connecticut. By the establishment of this advanced station,
a barrier, it was hoped, would be erected against the vexatious incursions
of the Pequod Indians.[1] Nor is it unlikely that some of the seceders to the
new settlement were actuated by a restless spirit, which had expected too
much from external change, and which vainly urged a farther pursuit of that
spring of contentment which must arise in the minds of those who would
enjoy it.

In the immediate neighbourhood of this new settlement another plantation
was formed, about two years after [1638], by a numerous band of emigrants who arrived from England under the guidance of Theophilus Eaton,
a man of large fortune, and John Davenport, an eminent Puritan minister.
Averse to erect the social institutions which they projected upon foundations previously laid by other hands, these adventurers declined to settle in
Massachusetts, which already presented the scene of a thriving and well
compacted community; and smit with the attractions of a vacant territory
skirting the large and commodious sound to the southwest of Connecticut
River, they purchased from its Indian owners all the land that lies between
that stream and the line which now separates New England from New York.
Repairing to the shores of this sound, they built, first the town of New
Haven, which gave its name to the whole colony, and then the towns of
Guilford, Milford, Stamford, and Branford. After some time they crossed
the sound, and planted various settlements in Long Island; in all places
where they came, erecting churches on the model of the Independents.

---

[1] Mather. Hutchinson. Trumbull. It appears from Mather's *Lives*, that Cotton and Hooker
were knit together in the firmest bonds of Christian friendship and cordial esteem. Yet these
men, who forsook houses, lands, and country for the sake of the gospel, are described by Dr.
Robertson as " rival competitors in the contest for fame and power "! This is the only light
in which many eminent and even reverend writers are capable of regarding the labors of the
patriot, the saint, and the sage. It is not uncommon for men, in attempting to paint the character of others, unconsciously to transcribe their own.

When we observe the injustice and cruelty exercised by the government of Britain, thus contributing to cover the earth with cities and to plant religion and liberty in the savage deserts of America, we recognize the overruling providence of that Being who can render even the insolence of tyrants who usurp his attributes conducive to his honor. Having no royal patent, nor any other title to their lands than the vendition of the natives, and not being included within the boundaries of any provincial jurisdiction established by British authority, the planters of New Haven united in a compact of voluntary association of the same nature and for the same ends with that which the founders of Connecticut had embraced; and in this condition they remained till the Restoration, when New Haven and Connecticut were united together by a charter of King Charles the Second.[1]

When the plantation of Connecticut was first projected, hopes were entertained that it might conduce to overawe the hostility of the Indians; but it produced a perfectly opposite effect. The tribes of Indians in the immediate vicinity of Massachusetts Bay were comparatively feeble and unwarlike; but the colonies of Providence and Connecticut were planted in the midst of powerful and martial hordes. Among these, the most considerable were the Narragansets, who inhabited the shores of the bay which bears their name; and the Pequods, who occupied the territory which stretches from the River Pequod[2] to the banks of the Connecticut. The Pequods were a numerous tribe, and renowned for their prowess and ferocity. They entertained, from the first, a jealous hatred of the European colonists, and for some time past had harassed them with unprovoked attacks, and excited their abhorrence and indignation by the monstrous outrages to which they subjected their captives. Unoffending men, women, and children, who fell into their hands, were scalped and sent back to their friends, or put to death with every circumstance of torture and indignity, — while the assassins, with diabolical glee and derision, challenged them to invoke the God of the Christians, and put to the proof his power to save them. The extension of the English settlements excited anew the fury of the savages, and produced a repetition of injuries, which Vane, the governor of Massachusetts, determined at length to retaliate and punish by offensive operations. Receiving intelligence of a serious attack by the Pequods on the Connecticut settlers [1637], he summoned all the New England communities to assemble and despatch the strongest force they could contribute to the defence of their countrymen and of the common cause of European colonization. The Pequods, aware of the impending danger, were not negligent of prudent precautions, as well as active endeavours to repel it. To this end, they sought a reconciliation with the Narragansets, their hereditary enemies and

---

[1] Neal. The colonists of Massachusetts were very desirous that Davenport and his associates should settle among them. But "it had been an observation of Mr. Davenport's, that, whenever a reformation had been effected in any part of the world, it had rested where it had been left by the reformers. It could not be advanced another step. He was now embarked in a design of forming a civil and religious constitution as near as possible to Scripture precept and example. The principal gentlemen who had followed him to America had the same views. In laying the foundation of a new colony, there was a fair probability that they might accommodate all matters of church and commonwealth to their own feelings and sentiments. But in Massachusetts the principal men were fixed in the chief seats of government, which they were likely to keep, and their civil and religious polity was already formed." Trumbull. In the history of every great public reform, religious or political, we may remark the operation, among the leading reformers, of a narrow, selfish, arrogant spirit, timidly or ambitiously contending for *finality* and opposed to ulterior progress.

[2] The Thames.

rivals in power ; proposing that on both sides the remembrance of ancient quarrels and animosities should be buried, or at least suspended ; and urging the Narragansets for once to coöperate cordially with them against a common foe, whose progressive encroachments threatened to confound them both in one common destruction.   But the Narragansets had long cherished a fierce and deep-rooted hatred against the Pequods ; and, less moved by a distant prospect of danger to themselves, than by the hope of an instant gratification of their implacable revenge, they rejected the proposals of accommodation, and determined to assist the English in the prosecution of the war.[1]

Enraged, but not dismayed, by this disappointment, the Pequods hastened, by the vigor of their operations, to anticipate the junction of the allied provincial forces ; and the Connecticut troops, while as yet they had received but a small part of the succour which their friends had engaged to afford them, found it necessary to advance against the enemy.   The Pequod warriors, amounting in number to more than fifteen hundred, commanded by Sassacus, their principal sachem, occupied two fortified stations, against one of which Captain Mason and the Connecticut militia, consisting only of ninety men, attended by a troop of Indian allies, directed their attack. The approach of Mason was quickened by the information he obtained, that the enemy, deceived by a seemingly retrograde movement of the provincial force, had abandoned themselves to the conviction that the English dared not encounter them, and were celebrating with festive revel and premature triumph the supposed evacuation of their country.   About daybreak, while wrapped in deep slumber and supine security, they were approached by the colonists ; and the surprise would have been complete, if an alarm had not been communicated by the barking of a dog.   The war-whoop was instantly sounded, and they flew to their arms.   The English troops rushed on to the attack ; and while some of them fired on the Indians through the palisades, others forced their way by the entrances into the fort, and, setting fire to the huts, which were covered with reeds, involved their enemies in the confusion and horror of a general conflagration.   The Pequods, notwithstanding the disadvantage of their predicament, behaved with great intrepidity ; but, after a stout and obstinate resistance, they were defeated, with the slaughter of at least five hundred of their tribe.   Many of the women and children perished in the flames ; and the warriors, endeavouring to escape, were slain by the colonists, or, falling into the hands of the Indian allies of the English, who surrounded the fort at a distance, were reserved for a more cruel fate. Soon after this action, Captain Stoughton having arrived with the auxiliary troops from Massachusetts, it was resolved to pursue the victory.   Several engagements took place, which terminated unfavorably for the Pequods ; and in a short time they sustained another general defeat, which put an end to the war.   A few only of this once powerful nation survived, who, abandoning their country to the victorious Europeans, dispersed themselves among the neighbouring tribes, and lost their existence as a separate people.   Sassacus had been an object of superstitious terror to the Narragansets, who at first endeavoured to dissuade the colonists from risking a personal encounter with him, by the assurance that his life was charmed and his person invulnerable.   After the destruction of his people, and when he fled for refuge to a distant tribe, the Narragansets passing, by natural progress, from terror

[1] Mather. Neal. Trumbull.

to cruelty, solicited and prevailed with his hosts to cut off his head.[1] Thus terminated a struggle, more important from its consequences than from the numbers of the combatants or the celebrity of their names. On its issue there had been staked no less than the question, whether Christianity and civilization, or paganism and barbarity, should prevail in New England.

This first military enterprise of the colonists was conducted with vigor and ability, and impressed the Indian race with a high opinion of their steadfast courage and superior skill. Their victory, it must be confessed, was sullied by cruelties, which it is easy to account for and extenuate, but painful to recollect. The Massachusetts militia, previously to their march, exerted no small diligence in purging their ranks of all persons whose religious senti- ments did not fully correspond with the general standard of faith and ortho- doxy.[2] It had been happy, if they could have purged their own bosoms of the vindictive feelings which the outrages of their savage foes were but too well fitted to inspire. Some of the prisoners were tortured by the Indian allies, whose cruelties we can hardly doubt that the English might have pre- vented ; a considerable number were sold as slaves in Bermudas,[3] and the rest were reduced to servitude in the New England settlements. In aggra- vation of the reproach which these proceedings undoubtedly merit, it has been urged, but with very little reason, that the Pequods were entitled to the treatment of an independent people gallantly striving to defend their property, their rights, and their freedom. But, in truth, the Pequods were the aggressors in an unjust quarrel, and were fighting all along in support of unprovoked and ferocious purposes of extermination. The colonists had conducted themselves with undeviating justice, civility, and Christian benev- olence towards the Indians. They treated fairly with them for the ceded territories ; assisted them by counsel and help in their diseases and their agriculture ; and labored to communicate to them the blessings of religion. They disallowed all acquisitions of territory from the Indians, but such as underwent the scrutiny and received the sanction of the colonial magistracy ; and they offered a participation of all the rights and privileges of their com- monwealth to every Indian who would embrace the faith of a Christian and the manners of a civilized human being. In return for these demonstrations of good-will, they experienced the most exasperating outrage and barbarity, directed against all that they reverenced or loved ; and were forcibly im- pressed with the conviction, that they must either extirpate those sanguinary idolaters, or leave themselves and their wives, children, and Christian kin- dred exposed to a far more horrid extermination.[4] Even in the course of

---

[1] Mather. Neal. Hutchinson. Trumbull. The destruction of the brave Pequods, though provoked by their own aggressive hostility, was lamented about one hundred and fifty years after by an American divine and poet : —

> "Indulge, my native land ! indulge the tear
> That steals impassioned o'er a nation's doom ;
> To me each twig from Adam's stock is near,
> And sorrows fall upon an Indian's tomb." — Dwight.

[2] Regimental chaplains accompanied the New England forces in their campaigns ; and in circumstances of doubt or danger, the chaplain was invited to pray for divine direction and assistance. When a commander-in-chief was appointed, his truncheon was delivered to him by one of the clergy. Trumbull.

[3] A similar punishment was inflicted, some years after, in England, on a number of the royalists who were implicated in Penruddock's insurrection. Hume.

[4] The colonists considered themselves in some degree accessory to the crimes which they failed to prevent by neglect of any of the means warranted by strict justice. Belknap cites the following entry in a MS. *Journal of Events in New England*, some years posterior to this period. "The house of John Keniston was burned, and he killed, at Greenland. The In-

the war, they made propositions of lenity to the savages, on the condition of their delivering up the murderers of the English ; but their offers were uniformly rejected ; and the people who thus avouched the murders as national acts invited the avengers of blood to visit them with national punishments.

The mutual hostilities of civilized nations, waged by dispassionate mercenaries, and directed by leaders more eager for fame than prompted by animosity or personal apprehension, may be conducted on the principles of a splendid game. But such hostilities as those which the New England colonists were compelled to wage with the hordes of savage assassins who attacked them will always display human passions in their naked horror and ferocity. The permission (for we must suppose that they could have prevented it) of the barbarity of their savage allies appears the least excusable feature in their conduct. And yet, in considering it, we must add to our allowance for passion inflamed by enormous provocation a reasonable regard to the danger and inexpediency of checking that mutual enmity of the savages, which prevented a combination that might have proved fatal to all the European settlements. The reduction of their captives to servitude was unquestionably an illaudable measure ; but one for which it would not be easy to suggest a substitute. The captive Pequods were treated with all possible kindness, and regarded rather as indented servants than slaves. It must be acknowledged, at least, that the colonists observed a magnanimous consistency in their international policy, and gave the Indians the protection of the same stern principles of justice of which they had taught them to feel the vindictive energy. They not only tendered a participation of their own privileges and territory to all civilized and converted Indians ; but, having ascertained the stations which the savages most highly valued, and the range of territory that seemed necessary to their comfort and happiness, they prohibited and annulled every transaction by which these domains might be added to the European acquisitions. A short time after the termination of the Pequod war, an Indian having been wantonly killed by some vagabond Englishmen, the murderers were solemnly tried and executed for the crime ; and the Indians beheld with astonishment the blood of three men deliberately shed by their own countrymen for the slaughter of one stranger. The sense of justice, coöperating with the repute of valor, secured to the English settlements a long rest from war.[1]

While the military force of Massachusetts was thus externally employed, the provincial commonwealth was shaken by intestine dissension, generated by theological controversy, and inflamed by the gall of bitterness of unruly tongues. [1637.] It was the custom at that time in Boston, that the members of every congregation should assemble in weekly meetings to reconsider the sermons of the preceding Sunday ; to discuss the doctrinal instructions they had heard ; to revive the impressions that had been produced by their Sabbatical exercises ; and extend the sacred influence of the Sabbath throughout the week. Anne Hutchinson, the wife of one of the most respectable inhabitants of the colony, a lady of masculine spirit, subtle, ambitious, and enthusiastic, submitted with impatience to the restriction by which women at these meetings were debarred from the privilege of joining in the debates ; and conceiving that she was authorized to exercise her di-

---

dians are Simon, Andrew, and Peter. Those three we had in prison, and should have killed. *The good Lord pardon us!*" *History of New Hampshire.*
[1] Mather. Neal. Hutchinson.

dactic powers by the precept of Scripture which enjoins *the elder women to teach the younger*, she established separate female assemblages, in which her zeal and talent soon procured her a numerous and admiring audience. These women, who had partaken the struggles and perils of the male colonists, had also caught no small portion of the various hues of their spirit ; and as many of them had been accustomed to a life more replete with external elegance and variety of interest and employment than the state of the colony could supply, they experienced a restless craving for something to animate and engage their faculties, and judged nothing fitter for this purpose than an imitation of those exercises for the promotion of the great common cause, which seemed to minister so much comfort and support to the spirits of the men. Mrs. Hutchinson, their leader, gained by her devout behaviour the cordial esteem of John Cotton, whose charity never failed to recognize in every human being the slightest trace of those graces which he continually and ardently longed to behold ; and towards him she entertained and professed for some time a very high veneration. The friendship of Vane and some others had a less favorable influence on her mind ; and their admiring praise of the depth and vigor of her genius seems to have elevated, in her estimation, the gifts of intellect above the graces of character. She acquired the title of *The Nonsuch*, which the ingenuity of her admirers derived from an anagrammatical transposition of the letters of her name ; and gave to her female assemblies the title of *gossipings*,—a term, at that time, of respectable import, but which the scandalous repute of female congregation and debate has since consigned to contempt and ridicule. Doing amiss what the Scriptures plainly forbade her to do at all, she constituted herself not only a dictator of orthodoxy, but a censor of the spiritual condition and value of all the ministers and inhabitants of the province. Her canons of doctrine were received by her associates as the unerring standard of truth ; and a defamatory persecution was industriously waged against all who accounted them unsound, uncertain, or unintelligible. A scrutiny was instituted into the characters of all the provincial clergy and laity ; and of those who refused to receive the doctrinal testimony of the conclave, few found it easy to encounter the test of a censorious inquisition stimulated by female petulance and controversial rancor. In the assemblies which were held by the followers of Mrs. Hutchinson, there was nourished and trained a keen, contentious spirit, and unbridled license of tongue, of which the influence was speedily felt in the serious disturbance, first of domestic happiness, and then of the public peace. The matrons of Boston were transformed into a synod of slanderous praters, whose inquisitorial deliberations and audacious decrees instilled their venom into the innermost recesses of society ; and the spirits of a great majority of the citizens being in that combustible state in which a feeble spark will suffice to kindle a formidable conflagration, the whole colony was inflamed and distracted by the incontinence of female spleen and presumption.[1]

The tenets embraced and inculcated by the faction of which Mrs. Hutchinson was the leader were denounced by their adversaries as constituting the heresy of Antinomianism, — a charge, which, when preferred by the world at large, indicates no more than the reproach which the gospel, from

[1] " When the minds of men are full of reforming spirit, and predisposed to the distempers which are engendered by such fulness, a little matter sometimes occasions rather than causes dangerous symptoms to appear." Sir James Mackintosh.

its first promulgation, has been fated to sustain, and when advanced by Christians against each other generally implies nothing else than the conclusion which the accusers logically deduce from certain articles of doctrine, but which the holders of these articles reject and disallow. Nothing can be more perfectly free and gratuitous than the tender of heavenly grace in the gospel ; nor any thing more powerfully operative than the influence which the faithful acceptance of this grace is calculated to exercise. Mrs. Hutchinson and her adherents contended more earnestly for the freedom than for the constraining influence of divine grace ; and, with female eagerness and polemical impetuosity, were prompt and swift to brand with terms of heretical and contemptuous designation every inhabitant of the colony, and especially every minister, whose views did not entirely coincide with their own. The doctrines which they taught, and the censures which they pronounced, were received with avidity and delight by a considerable party ; and, proportionally provoking the displeasure of others, excited the most violent dissensions throughout the whole colony. Cotton endeavoured to moderate the heats that arose, by representing to the parties that their strife was prejudicial to the great purpose in which he firmly believed the minds of both were united, — the exalting and honoring of divine grace ; *the one* (said he) *seeking to advance the grace of God within us in the work of sanctification, the other seeking to advance the grace of God without us in the work of justification.* But the strife was not to be stayed ; his endeavours to pacify and reconcile only attracted upon himself the fulmination of a censure of timorous and purblind incapacity from the assembly of the women ; and, as even this insult was not able to provoke him to declare himself entirely opposed to them, he incurred a temporary abatement of his popularity with the majority of the colonists. Some of the tenets promulgated by the sectaries he reverenced as the legitimate fruit of profound and perspicuous meditation of the Scriptures ; but he viewed with grief and amazement the fierce and arrogant spirit with which they were maintained, and the wild and dangerous errors with which they were associated.

The controversy raged with a violence very unfavorable to the discernment and recognition of truth. Mrs. Hutchinson and her adherents, both male and female, firmly persuaded of the superior soundness and purity of their system of doctrine, forgot to consider how far the opposition which it encountered might be traced to the obscurity and imperfection with which they themselves received and proclaimed it ; — a consideration which no human being is entitled to disregard, and which is peculiarly fitted to embellish superior attainments, and promote their efficacy by uniting them with the amiable graces of candor and humility. The principles they discarded from their creed laid hold of their spirits ; and while they contended for the sovereignty of divine grace in communicating truth, they assailed their adversaries with an acrimony and invective that might well seem to imply that truth was easily and exclusively attainable by the mere will and endeavour of men. The most enlightened and consistent Christian will ever be the most ready to acknowledge that *he knows nothing yet as he ought to know*, and may have more cause than in this life he can ever discover to blush for the defectiveness of a testimony, which, exhibited with more clearness and consistency, might have found a readier and more entire acceptance with mankind. But no such considerations suggested themselves to mitigate the vehemence, or soften the asperity, of those busy, bold, and presumptuous spirits ; nor did it ever occur to them that the doctrines they proclaimed would be discredited by association with the venom of untamed, audacious tongues. It is asserted that the heat of their tempers gradually communicated itself to the understandings of Mrs. Hutchinson and her party ; and that — in addition to their original tenets, that believers are personally united with the spirit of God, that commands to *work out salvation with fear and trembling* apply only to those who are under a covenant of works, and that sanctification is not the proper evidence of Christian condition — they adopted that dangerous and erroneous notion of the Quakers, that the spirit of God communicates with the minds of believers independently of the written word ; and, in consistency with this, received many revelations of future events announced to them by Mrs. Hutchinson, as equally infallible with the prophecies of Scripture. But the accounts transmitted of such theological dissensions are always obscured by the cloud of contemporary passion, prejudice, and error ; hasty effusions of irritated zeal are mistaken for deliberate sentiments ; and the excesses of the zealots of a party held up as the standard by which the whole body may fairly be measured.[1]

Some ministers, who espoused Mrs. Hutchinson's opinions, began to proclaim them from the pulpit with such opprobrious invectives against all by whom they were rejected, as at length brought the dissensions to a crisis ; and Vane being accounted the confederate and protector of Mrs. Hutchinson, his continuance in office, or privation of it at the approaching annual election, was the first test by which the parties were to try with which of them resided the power of imposing silence on the other. So much ill-humor and mutual jealousy had now been instilled into the minds of the people, that the utmost efforts of the sober and humane barely sufficed to prevent the election from being disgracefully signalized by a general riot. All the exertions of Vane's partisans failed to obtain his reappointment ; and, by a great majority of votes, Winthrop was chosen governor. [May, 1637.] Vane, nevertheless, still remained in Massachusetts, professing his willingness to undertake even the humblest function in the service of a commonwealth composed of the undoubted people of God ; and the followers of Mrs. Hutchinson, regarding his deprivation of office as a dangerous blow to themselves, ceased not to labor for his reinstatement with as much warmth as they had exerted for the propagation of their religious tenets. The government was loudly and insultingly vilified, and Winthrop openly slighted and affronted. At length the prevailing party resolved to cut up this source of contention by the roots ; and a general synod of the churches of the colony having been assembled, the doctrines recently broached were condemned as erroneous and heretical. As this proceeding served only to provoke the professors of these doctrines to assert them with increased warmth and per-

---

[1] That to a certain extent, however, the heresy which I have particularized had crept in among them seems undeniably manifest ; and it is remarkable that the notion which united them with the fundamental tenet of the Quakers should have issued from a society, which, with farther resemblance to the Quakers, admitted the antiscriptural irregularity of female preaching. Captain Underhill, one of Mrs. Hutchinson's followers, carried that error to a monstrous length, and combined with it the grossest immorality of conduct. Much scandal was occasioned by his publicly affirming that he had received a special communication of his everlasting safety while he was smoking a pipe. He was banished along with his patroness ; and, a few years after, returned to Boston, where he made a public confession of hypocrisy, adultery, and delusion. Belknap's *History of New Hampshire.* Another of Mrs. Hutchinson's followers was a woman named Mary Dyer, who retired to Rhode Island, where she subsequently became a Quaker. Winthrop's *Journal* (Savage's edition).

tinacity, the leaders of the party were summoned before the General Court. Mrs. Hutchinson rebuked her judges for their wicked persecution of truth, compared herself to the prophet Daniel cast into the den of lions, and attempted to complete the similitude by exercising what she believed to be the gift of prophecy, and predicting that her exile would be attended with the ruin of her adversaries and all their posterity.[1] To this punishment, nevertheless, she was condemned, together with her brother, Wheelwright, who was a clergyman, and had been the chief pulpit-champion of her doctrines ; and some of the inferior members of the faction, partly on account of the violence with which they still proclaimed their theological tenets, and partly for the seditious insolence with which they had treated the new governor, were fined and disfranchised. In consequence of these proceedings, Vane quitted the colony and returned to England, " leaving a caveat," says Cotton Mather, " that all good men are not fit for government." [2]

From the unpleasing contemplation of these religious dissensions, we turn to the more agreeable survey of some of the consequences which attended their issue. A considerable number of persons, dissatisfied with the policy and conduct of the synod and the General Court of Massachusetts, voluntarily forsook the colony ; some of these united themselves with Roger Williams and his friends at Providence ; and being soon after abandoned by Mrs. Hutchinson, they fell under the guidance of that meliorated spirit which Williams now began to display. By a transaction with the Indians, these associated exiles acquired the property of a fertile island in Narraganset Bay, which obtained the name of Rhode Island.[3] Williams remained among them upwards of forty years, respected as the father and director of the colony, of which he was several times elected governor. In the year 1643, he made a journey to England, and, aided by the interest of Sir Henry Vane, obtained and conveyed to his fellow-colonists a parliamentary charter, by which Providence and Rhode Island were politically united till the Restoration. Others of the exiles, under the guidance of Wheelwright, betook themselves to the

---

[1] Her presumption was signally punished. The ruin she predicted as the consequence of her exile fell on herself and her family. She went to Rhode Island ; but not liking that situation, removed to one of the Dutch settlements, where she and all her family were murdered by the Indians. Before she quitted Massachusetts, she published a disclamation of some of the erroneous tenets which were imputed to her ; but maintained (in the face of the clearest evidence to the contrary) that she had never entertained them. This was considered a proof of dissimulation. Perhaps it might rather have warranted the inference, that the visionary and violent spirit which had laid hold of her had departed or subsided, and that she no longer recognized the opinions, which, through its medium, formerly presented themselves to her imagination.

[2] Mather. Neal. Hutchinson. Milton differed from Mather in his estimate of Vane's capacity. His fine sonnet to him begins thus : —

" Vane, young in years, but in sage counsels old,
- Than whom a better senator ne'er held
The helm of Rome."

And ends thus : —

" Therefore on thy right hand Religion leans,
And reckons thee in chief her eldest son."

[3] The price paid to the Indians was fifty fathoms of white beads, ten coats, and twenty shoes. Chalmers. " When a fourth part of a township of the common size was sold by one Englishman to another for a wheelbarrow, it will be easily believed that it was of still less value to the aborigines. To the Indians, without an English purchaser, the land was often worth nothing ; and to the colonist, its value was created by his labor." Dwight's *Travels*. " At Rhode Island, the settlers, in March, 1638, subscribed the following civil compact : — ' We, whose names are underwritten, do hereby solemnly, in the presence of Jehovah, incorporate ourselves into a body politic ; and, as he shall help, will submit our persons, lives, and estates, to our Lord Jesus Christ, the King of Kings and Lord of Lords, and to all the perfect and absolute laws given in his holy word.' " Pitkin's *History of America*.

northeast parts of New England, and, being joined by associates who were allured by the prospects of rich fisheries and an advantageous beaver trade, they gradually formed and peopled the provinces of New Hampshire and Maine. These provinces had been respectively purchased from the Council of Plymouth by Mason and Gorges, who made sundry ineffectual attempts to colonize their acquisitions with advantage to themselves. Mason and Gorges were actuated by views widely different from those which prevailed in general among the colonists of New England; they wished to become the proprietaries or hereditary chiefs of vast manors and seigniories, and to establish in America the very institutions from which emigrants to America were generally seeking to escape. They found it impracticable to obtain a revenue from the settlers in New Hampshire and Maine, or to establish among them a form of government suited to their own views. These settlers, composed partly of adventurers from England, and partly of exiles and voluntary emigrants from Massachusetts, framed for themselves separate governments, to which for a few years they yielded a precarious obedience; till, wearied with internal disputes and divisions, they besought the protection of the General Court of Massachusetts, and obtained leave to be included within the pale of its jurisdiction.[1]

A schism, akin to that which Mrs. Hutchinson created in Massachusetts, was fomented at Plymouth by one Samuel Gorton; but his career in this place was cut short by a conviction for swindling. He removed from Plymouth to Rhode Island, where he excited such disturbance, that, even in this community, where unlimited toleration was professed, he was sentenced to be flogged and banished. Repairing to the plantation of Providence, he nearly involved the people of this settlement in a war with the Indians; but at length, in compliance with the entreaty of Roger Williams, the government of Massachusetts laid hold of him and some of his adherents, and, after subjecting them to a temporary imprisonment, obliged them to depart the country.[2] [1638.]

The population of Massachusetts, impaired by the various drains from this territory which we have noticed, was recruited in the following year by the arrival of a fleet of twenty ships conveying three thousand emigrants from England. Of these the most eminent and memorable person was Charles Chauncy, an English clergyman, and one of the greatest scholars and theologians of his age. Flying from the persecution which his own generous but passionate temper provoked from the bigotry of Laud, he devoted himself, with the most admirable zeal, patience, industry, and success, to the ministry of the gospel, and the tuition of youth, in his adopted country. So animating and impressive was the Christian example he sustained, that the church with which he connected himself celebrated, on a day of thanksgiving to God, the privilege by which they were distinguished in obtaining the society and converse of such a man. Resigning wealth, ease, and distinction, he cheerfully entertained a lot of penury, toil, and obscurity; and at the age of fourscore, resisted all solicitations to repose, and expressed an earnest desire to die in his pulpit. The same year witnessed the founda-

---

[1] Neal. Hutchinson. Sullivan's *History of Maine.* Belknap. The province of Maine was thus denominated in honor of the British queen, with whom Charles the First received as a dowry the revenues of a French province of the same name. Sullivan. Sullivan has been represented to me as an intelligent man; but he is certainly not a perspicuous historian.
[2] Gorges's *America painted to the Life.* Neal. Gorton went to England, and, during the civil wars, occasioned some trouble to the colony by his complaints of the treatment which he had undergone.

P

tion of an establishment calculated to improve and preserve the moral condition of the people. This was Harvard College (which has subsequently expanded into Harvard University), at Cambridge, in Massachusetts, the first seminary of learning erected in North America. So highly prized were the advantages of knowledge and the influence of education by these generous parents of American society, that in the year 1636, while the colony, in addition to the feebleness and suffering of its infant condition, was struggling with the calamity of the Pequod War, the General Court at Boston appropriated four hundred pounds to the erection of a college or academy. "For a like spirit, under like circumstances," says the president and historian of this institution, "history will be searched in vain." The bequest of an emigrant clergyman, who appointed his whole fortune to be applied to the same design, enabled them in the present year to enrich their country with an establishment whose operation has proved as beneficial to their posterity, as its institution, at this early period of their history, is honorable to themselves. In the year 1642, the degree of Bachelor of Arts was conferred by Harvard College on nine young men, the first persons who ever received collegiate honors, the growth of North America.[1]

The national growth of the New England societies was now to be left to depend on their own resources; and the impulse which had been communicated to it by the stream of emigration from the parent state was for a while to cease. For some time past, the policy of the English government in relation to these settlements had savored of fear, aversion, and undecided purpose; various demonstrations were made of arbitrary design and tyrannical encroachment; but, not being steadily prosecuted, they served merely to keep the colonists united by a sense of common danger, and to endear the institutions of liberty by the destruction with which they were ineffectually menaced. The king, in reviewing his first proceedings towards the emigrants, seems to have doubted pretty early the soundness of that policy which had prompted so wide a departure from the general principles of his administration; the experience of every year tended to enhance his doubts; and he wavered some time in irresolute perplexity between his original wish to evacuate England of the Puritans, and his apprehensions of the dangerous and increasing influence which their triumphant establishment in America was visibly exerting. The success of his politic devices appeared for a short time to answer all his expectations; and he seemed likely to prevail over the Puritans by the demonstration of a hollow good-will or lenity, suspended on the condition of their abandoning the realm. A considerable portion of the embers of Puritan and patriotic feeling had been removed from England, and consigned to deserts, where as yet no colony had been able to survive; but they had neither languished nor perished; and, on the

[1] Mather. Neal. Hutchinson. Winthrop's *Journal* (Savage's edition). Quincy's *History of Harvard University.* For some time the college possessed but a scanty collection of books. The efforts of the managers to accumulate a library were aided by considerable donations of books made to them by that great and pious ecclesiastic, Archbishop Usher; by the celebrated Non-conformist minister, Richard Baxter; the great Whig lawyer and partisan, Sergeant Maynard; and that distinguished warrior and philosopher, Sir Kenelm Digby. This last mentioned benefactor to a Puritan library was himself a Roman Catholic. It is an interesting fact, and serves to dignify and embellish the relationship between the two countries, that many of the most illustrious men whom England has ever produced contributed to lay the foundation of civilized society in America. The enumeration of the patentees in the Virginian charters includes almost every distinguished individual in England at the time. The people of New England have always retained that generous zeal for the cultivation of knowledge which their fathers thus early displayed. In the year 1780, and in the midst of the Revolutionary War, an Academy of Arts and Sciences was established at Boston.

contrary, had kindled in America a flame so powerful and diffusive that even distant England was warmed and enlightened by the blaze.   The jealous attention of Laud was soon awakened to the disastrous issue of that experiment ; and while he revolved the means by which its farther effects might be counteracted, he maintained spies in New England, whose reports increased his misgivings, and who courted his favor by traducing the objects of his dislike.   The detection of this correspondence served to animate the resentment and promote the caution and the union of the colonists.

So early as the year 1633, the English government, inspired with alarm, made a hasty and ill-considered attempt to repair its error, by issuing a proclamation reprobating the designs that prompted emigration to New England, and ordering all ships that were ready to proceed thither with passengers to be detained.   It was soon perceived that this measure was premature, and that the only, or at least the most certain, consequence of it would be to inflame the impatience of the Puritans to obtain, either at home or abroad, the institutions which they had made preparation to establish and enjoy.   Not only was the proclamation suffered to remain unexecuted, but even, at a later period, Charles reverted so far to his previous policy as to promote, by his own interposition, the expatriation of young Vane, of whose political and religious sentiments he was perfectly well informed.   After an interval of hesitation, measures more deliberate were adopted for subverting the system of liberty that had been established in the provincial territory. In the year 1635, a commission was granted to the great officers of state and some of the nobility, for the regulation and government of the American plantations.   By this commission the Archbishop of Canterbury (Laud) and a few other distinguished associates were authorized to make laws and constitutions for the colonists of New England ; to establish an order of clergy, and assign them a maintenance ; and to punish capitally, or otherwise, all who should violate their ordinances.   The same persons, in conjunction with a more numerous body of commissioners, were directed to examine all existing colonial patents and charters, *and if they found that any had been unduly obtained, or that the liberties they conferred were hurtful to the prerogative royal, to cause them to be revoked and quashed.*   The English Grand Council of New Plymouth were easily persuaded to give the first example of submission to this arbitrary authority ; and accordingly surrendered their useless patent to the king, under reservation of their claims as private individuals to the property of the soil.   These reserved claims gave occasion at an after period to much dispute, perplexity, and inconvenience.   The only proceeding, however, which immediately ensued against the New England colonists, was the institution of a process of *quo warranto* against their charter in the Court of King's Bench, of which no intimation was given to the parties interested, and which was never prosecuted to a judicial issue.

It is vain to speculate on all the fluctuating motives and purposes that from time to time guided and varied the policy of the king.   He was formed to hate and dread alike the growth of religious and political freedom ; but fated to render the highest service to the objects of his aversion by an ill-directed and unavailing hostility.   In the year 1637, he granted a commission to Sir Ferdinando Gorges, appointing him governor-general of New England, and issued a proclamation prohibiting all persons from transporting themselves, or others, to that country, without a special permission under the great seal, — which, it was added, would be granted to none who could not produce credible certificates of their having taken the oaths of supremacy and allegiance, and of their having fully conformed to the ritual and ordinances of the church of England. But the critical state of affairs in Britain prevented the adoption of measures requisite to give effect to Gorges's commission ; and the irresistible impatience of the oppressed Puritans and votaries of liberty to escape from the increasing heat of persecution, or the approach of civil war, completely defeated the restrictions imposed on their emigration. We have seen, that, in the year 1638, a numerous transportation of additional emigrants took place. But before the close of that year, the king gave way to a singleness and obstinate directness of purpose which now alone was wanting to assure and accelerate his ruin ; and after a long course of wavering policy and unsuccessful experiment, he adopted a measure, which, unfortunately for himself, was effectual.

Learning that another fleet was preparing to sail for New England with a band of emigrants, among whom were some of the most eminent leaders of the patriots and Puritans, he caused an order of council to be issued for its detention ; and the injunction being promptly enforced, the intended voyage was prevented. On board this fleet there appear to have been, among other distinguished individuals, Hazlerig, Hampden, Pym, and Oliver Cromwell;[1] — men to whom, but a few years after, Charles was fain to tender the highest offices in his realm, and whom his blind injustice now detained to avenge the tyranny by which so many of their friends had been driven away. Various proclamations were issued the same year for the prevention of emigration to New England, which, accordingly, from this time was for many years discontinued.[2] These measures inflamed to the highest pitch the discontent that had long rankled in the minds of a great body of the people. Even the hospitality of rude deserts, it was declared, was denied to the oppressed inhabitants of England ; and men were constrained to inquire if the evils which could not be evaded might not be repelled, and, since retreat was impracticable, if resistance might not be availing. By promoting emigration at first, the king opened a vein which it was impossible to close, without incurring considerable danger ; and the increased severity of his administration augmented the flow of evil humors at the very time when he thus imprudently

---

[1] That Hampden and Cromwell were on board this fleet, or that they even intended to repair to America, has been doubted, but I think without good reason. Hume (contrary to his own intention) has rather confirmed than removed the doubt, by the manner in which he has referred to a passage in Hutchinson, the meaning of which he has evidently misunderstood. But Dr. Mather, who preceded Hutchinson, expressly names all the individuals mentioned in the text as having prepared for their voyage, and been arrested by the order of council. Oldmixon recites the grant of land in America in favor of *Hampden* and others, which the emigrants were proceeding to occupy. Mather's statement is confirmed by Neal, Clarendon, Bates, and Dugdale. The strong mind of Cromwell appears long to have retained the bias it had once received towards emigration, and the favorable opinion of the colonists of New England, from which that bias was partly derived. After the *Remonstrance* was voted in the Long Parliament, he told Lord Falkland, that, if the debate had been attended with a different result, he was prepared next day to have converted his effects into ready money and to quit the kingdom. When he was invested with the Protectorate, he treated Massachusetts with distinguished partiality. Hume considered himself as levelling a most sarcastic reflection against Hampden and Cromwell, when he described them as willing to cross the Atlantic Ocean for the sake of saying their prayers. Other writers, who partake the political, but not the religious, sentiments of these eminent persons, have been very willing to defend them from this imputation.

Some historians have asserted that Hampden did actually, at one time, visit North America; and, doubtless, in the year 1623, there was at New Plymouth an Englishman named John Hampden, whom Winslow describes as "a gentleman of London, who then wintered with us, and desired much to see the country." Belknap's *American Biography.*

[2] Mather. Neal. Hutchinson. Oldmixon. Chalmers. Hazard.

deprived them of their accustomed vent. The previous emigration had already drained the Puritan body of a great number of those of its members whose milder tempers and meeker strain of piety rendered them more desirous than the generality of their brethren to decline a contest with their sovereign ; the present restrictions forcibly retained in the realm men of more daring spirit and trained in experience of enmity to his person and opposition to his measures.[1] He now at last succeeded in stripping his subjects of every protection that the law could extend to their rights ; and was destined soon to experience how completely he had divested them of every restraint that the law could impose on the vindictive retribution of their wrongs. From this period till the assembling of the Long Parliament, he pursued a short and headlong career of disgrace and disaster ; while a gross infatuation veiled from his eyes the gulf of destruction to which his steps were advancing.

In pursuance of the policy which the king at length determined openly and vigorously to employ, a requisition was transmitted by the privy council to the governor and General Court of Massachusetts, commanding them to deliver up their patent, to be conveyed by the first ship that should sail for England, in order that it might abide the issue of the process of *quo warranto* that was depending against the colony. To this requisition the General Court [September, 1638] returned for answer a humble and earnest petition that the colonists might be suffered to plead in their own behalf before they were condemned. They declared that they had transported their families to America, and embarked their fortunes in the colonial project, in reliance on his Majesty's license and encouragement ; that they had never willingly or knowingly offended him, and now humbly deprecated his wrath, and solicited to be heard with their patent in their hands. If it were forcibly withdrawn from them, they protested that they must either return to England or seek the hospitality of more distant regions. But they prayed that they might " be suffered to live in the wilderness," where they had till now found a resting-place ; and might experience in their exile some of that favor from the ruler of their native land which they had largely experienced from the Lord and Judge of all the Earth. They retained possession of their patent while they waited an answer to this petition, which, happily for their liberties, they were destined never to receive. The insurrections which soon after broke out in Scotland directed the whole attention of the king to matters which more nearly concerned him ; and the long gathering storm, which was now visibly preparing to burst upon him from every corner of his dominions, engaged him to contract as far as possible the sphere of hostility in which he found himself involved.[2] The benefit of his altered views was experienced by the Virginians, in the abolition of the despotism to which he had previously subjected them ; and by the inhabitants of New England, in the cessation of his attempts to supersede by a similar despotism the liberal institutions which they had hitherto enjoyed. He would doubtless now

---

[1] The commencement of resistance in Scotland originated with some individuals of that country who had purchased a tract of territory in New England, and made preparation to transport themselves thither, but were prevented (it does not appear how) from carrying their design into execution. They had obtained from the assembly of Massachusetts an assurance of the free exercise of their Presbyterian form of church government. Mather.

[2] Hutchinson. Chalmers. This year (1638) was distinguished by an earthquake in New England, which extended through all the settlements, and shook the ships in Boston harbour and the neighbouring islands. The sound of it reminded some of the colonists of the rattling of coaches in the streets of London. Winthrop's *Journal*. Trumbull.

have readily consented to disencumber himself of some of his domestic adversaries by promoting the emigration which of late he so imprudently obstructed ; but such a revolution of sentiment had taken place in England, and such interesting prospects began to open to the patriots and Puritans at home, that the motives which formerly induced them to migrate to the New World ceased any longer to prevail.

When the intercourse which for twenty years had subsisted between New England and the parent state was thus interrupted, the number of the colonists amounted to about twenty thousand persons,[1] or four thousand families, including a hundred ministers. The expenditure already incurred in equipping vessels and transporting emigrants amounted to nearly two hundred thousand pounds, — a prodigious sum in that age, and which nothing but the grand and unconquerable principle which animated the Puritans could have persuaded men to expend on the prospect of forming an establishment in a remote, uncultivated desert, offering to its inhabitants merely a plain, unadorned freedom and difficult subsistence. When the civil war broke out in the parent state, the colonists had already founded fifty towns and villages ; they had erected upwards of thirty churches and ministers' houses ; and combining with their preponderating regard to the concerns of religion a diligent and judicious conduct of their temporal affairs, they had improved their estates to a high degree of cultivation. During the first seven years of the infancy of the settlement that was founded in 1630, even subsistence was procured with difficulty, and trade was not generally attempted ;[2] but soon after that period, the people began to extend their fishery, and to open a trade in lumber, which subsequently proved the staple article of New England commerce. In the year 1637, there were but thirty ploughs in the whole province of Massachusetts, and less than the third of that number in Connecticut. The culture of the earth was generally performed with hoes, and was consequently slow and laborious. Every commodity bore a high price. Though money was extremely scarce, the price of a good cow was thirty pounds ; Indian corn cost five shillings a bushel ; labor and every other useful commodity was proportionably dear.

Necessity at first introduced what the jurisprudence of the colonists afterwards confirmed ; and desiring to perpetuate the habits that had proved so conducive to piety and virtue, they endeavoured by legislative enactments to exclude luxury and promote industry. When the assembling of the Long Parliament opened a prospect of safety, and even of triumph and supremacy, to the Puritans in England, many persons who had taken refuge in America returned to their native country ; but a great majority of the emigrants had experienced so much of the substance and happiness of religious life in the societies already formed within the colony, that they felt themselves united to New England by stronger and nobler ties than any that patriotic recollections could supply; and resolved to abide in the region which their virtue had converted from a wilderness into a garden. In these infant societies of men, devoted to godliness and liberty, all hearts were strongly united by community of feeling on subjects the most interesting and important ; the inhabitants were in general very nearly on a level in point of temporal con-

---

[1] Josselyn's *Voyage to New England*. Hutchinson. Josselyn, who visited New England more than once, was intrusted by Quarles, the poet, with some of his metrical versions of Scripture, to be submitted to the perusal and judgment of John Cotton.
[2] Yet in the year 1636, a ship of one hundred and twenty tons was built at Marblehead by the people of Salem. *Collections of the Massachusetts Historical Society.*

dition ; the connections of neighbourhood operated as extended family ties ; and the minds of all were warmed and invigorated by a primitive friendliness, freedom, and simplicity of mutual communication.[1] And yet some indications of an aristocratical disposition, arising, not unnaturally, from peculiar circumstances that occurred in the formation of the colonial settlements, did occasionally manifest themselves. Several of the first planters, particularly Dudley, Winthrop,[2] Bradford, Bellingham, and Bradstreet, were persons of ample fortune ; and besides the transportation of their own families, they had borne the charge of transporting many poor families who must otherwise have remained in England. Others were members of the original body of patentees, and had incurred expenses in the procurement of the charter, the formation of the company, the equipment of the first body of adventurers, and the purchase of the soil from the natives, of which they had now no prospect of obtaining reimbursement. On this class of planters the chief offices of government naturally devolved during the infancy of the settlements, and long continued to be discharged by them without other pecuniary recompense than presents, which were occasionally voted to them by the gratitude of their fellow-citizens. It was probably owing to the prevalence of the peculiar sentiments inspired by the services of these persons, that, in the first General Court which was assembled in Massachusetts, the election of the governor, the appointment of all the other officers, and even the power of legislation, were withdrawn from the freemen, and vested in the Council of Assistants ; and although the freemen reclaimed and resumed their rights in the following year, yet the practical exercise of legislation was confined almost entirely to the Council of Assistants, till the introduction of the representative system in the year 1634. From this time the council and the freemen, assembled together, formed the *General Court*, till the year 1644, when it was arranged that the governor and assistants should sit apart ; and thence commenced the separate existence of the democratic branch of the legislature, or House of Representatives. Elections were conducted by *ballot*, in which the balls or tickets tendered by the electors consisted of Indian beans.[3]

Some notice of the peculiarities of jurisprudence that already prevailed

---

[1] The following passage in a sermon of Robert Cushman, one of the earliest ministers of New Plymouth, is characteristic of this state of society : — " Remember, brethren, that ye have given your names and promises to one another, here to cleave together. You must, then, seek the wealth of one another, and inquire, as David, How liveth such a man ? how is he clad ? how is he fed ? He is my brother, my associate, and we ventured our lives together. Is his labor harder than mine ? surely, I will ease him. Hath he no bed to lie on ? I have two ; I 'll lend him one. He is as good a man as I, and we are bound each to other ; so that his wants must be my wants, and his welfare my welfare." Belknap's *American Biography.*

[2] Winthrop " had not so high an opinion of a democratical government as some other gentlemen of equal wisdom and goodness." He remarked that " the best part of a community is always the least, and of that best part the wiser is still less. Therefore it is written, Choose ye judges, and bring the cause before the judge." Belknap's *American Biography.* Not accounting superiority of wealth or of bodily accomplishments (the only distinctions universally palpable to mankind) infallible indications of superiority in moral and intellectual worth, Winthrop suggests no better success for the ascertainment and promotion of the good and wise minority, than the elective judgment of the less wise and worthy majority. Nor has a more honest or rational suggestion been ever propounded. The greatest happiness of all might and should be the motive principle of political institutions in communities of men all wise and good. But with the actual imperfection of human intelligence and virtue, we are content to accept the term (continually enlarged by human advancement) of the *greatest happiness of the greatest number.*

[3] Winthrop's *Journal.* Neal. Hutchinson. Chalmers. Trumbull. Holmes's *American Annals.* (This is, perhaps, the most excellent chronological digest of its history that any nation has ever possessed.) Belknap's *American Biography.*

in the various communities of New England will serve to illustrate the state of society and manners that sprung up at first among this singular people. By a fundamental law of Massachusetts it was enacted, " that all strangers professing the Christian religion, who shall flee to this country from the tyranny of their persecutors, shall be succoured at the public charge till some provision can be made for them." Jesuits and other Romish priests, however, were doomed to banishment, and, in case of their return, to death. This cruel ordinance was afterwards extended to Quakers ; and all persons were forbidden, under the severest penalties, to import any of " that cursed sect," or of their writings, into the colony. By what behaviour the Quakers of that age provoked so much aversion and such rigorous treatment we shall have an opportunity of considering hereafter. An ordinance of the General Court of Massachusetts in the year 1637 (prompted apparently by Mrs. Hutchinson's schism) forbade the residence within that colony of any stranger unprovided with the license of a provincial magistrate ; but this illiberal ordinance (which was warmly combated by Henry Vane) seems never to have obtained any practical efficiency. These persecuting edicts had no place in Rhode Island, where nobody was exposed to active molestation for religious opinions, and all professors of Christianity, except Roman Catholics, were admitted to the full rights of citizenship. All persons were forbidden to run, or even walk, " except reverently to and from church," on Sunday, or to profane the day by sweeping their houses, cooking their victuals, or shaving their beards. Mothers were even commanded not to kiss their children on that sacred day. The usual punishments of great crimes were disfranchisement, banishment, and temporary servitude ; but perpetual slavery was not permitted to be inflicted upon any persons except captives lawfully taken in war ; and these were to be treated with the gentleness of Christian manners, and to be entitled to all the mitigations of their lot enjoined by the law of Moses. Disclaiming all but defensive war, the colonists considered themselves entitled and constrained in self-defence to deprive their assailants of a liberty which they had abused and rendered inconsistent with the safety of their neighbours. The practice, nevertheless, was impolitic, to say no worse, and served to pave the way, at a later period, for the introduction of negro slavery into New England.

Adultery was punished by death ; and fornication by compelling the offending parties to marry (an absurd device, which discredits the state of marriage), or by fine and imprisonment. Burglary and robbery were punished, for the first offence, by branding ; for the second, by branding and flogging ; for the third, by death : but if either of these crimes, while yet not inferring a capital punishment, were committed on Sunday, an ear was to be cut off in addition to the other inflictions. We must beware of supposing that such penal enactments indicate the frequency or even the actual occurrence of the crimes to which they refer. In those communities where civilization has been a gradual attainment, penal laws denote the prevalence of the actions they condemn. But in communities at once infant and civilized, many of the laws must be regarded merely as the expression of the opinion of the legislators, and by no means as indicating the actual condition of society. Blasphemy and idolatry were punishable by death ; and though it was acknowledged in the preamble to one of the laws, " that no human power is lord over the faith and consciences of men," yet heresy, by this very law, was declared to infer banishment from the province. Pecuniary

mulcts were imposed on every person "observing any such day as Christ-
mas." Witchcraft and perjury, directed against human life, were capitally
punished. No capital charge was deemed capable of being proved by evidence less weighty than the oaths of two witnesses, — a principle that deserves to be universally established, as well on account of its own intrinsic
rectitude as of the sanction it received from divine legislation. By a singular
law, which, both from its peculiar terms and from its never having been
carried into effect, is more discreditable to the wisdom of its framers than
to the humanity of the people at large, it was enacted, that, although torture
should not be ordinarily inflicted, yet a convicted criminal, known to have
had accomplices, and refusing to disclose them, might be subjected to torture, — " yet not to such tortures as are barbarous and inhuman."

All gaming was prohibited ; cards and dice were forbidden to be imported ;
and assemblies for dancing were proscribed. Public registers were instituted,
in which all the marriages, births, and deaths of the colonists were recorded.
By a law enacted in 1646, kissing a woman in the street, even in the way
of honest salute, was punished by flogging, which was not considered an infamous punishment by the people of Massachusetts. Even so late as the
middle of the eighteenth century, there were instances of persons, who,
after undergoing public flagellation, associated with the most respectable
circles of society in Boston. This doubtless arose from the peculiar character of the government, which, seeming to hold a patriarchal relation to
the people, could never be supposed, in correcting an offender, to divest
itself entirely of respect and good-will for him. The economy of inns was
regulated with a strictness which deserves to be noted, as explanatory of a
circumstance that has frequently excited the surprise of European travellers
in America. The intemperance and immorality to which these places are
so often made subservient was punished with the utmost rigor ; and all inn-
keepers were required, under the severest penalties, to restrain the excesses
of their guests, or to acquaint the magistrate with their perpetration. To
secure a stricter execution of this law, it was judged expedient that inn-
keepers should be divested of the temptation that poverty presents to its
infraction, and should enjoy such personal consideration as would facilitate
the exercise of their difficult duty ; and, accordingly, none were permitted
to follow this calling but persons of approved character and competent estate.
One of the consequences of this policy has been, that an employment, very
little respected in other countries, has ever been creditable in New England,
and not unfrequently pursued by men who have retired from honorable stations in the civil or military service of the state.

Persons wearing apparel, which the grand jury should account disproportioned to their fortune, were to be admonished in the first instance, and,
if contumacious, fined. A fine was imposed on every woman cutting her
hair like a man's, or suffering it to hang loosely upon her face. Idleness,
lying, swearing, and drunkenness were visited with various penalties and
marks of disgrace.[1] The *selectmen* assessed, in every family, the quantity

[1] That these laws were not permitted to be a dead letter appears from the following extracts
from the earliest records of the court of Massachusetts. " John Wedgewood, *for being in the
company of drunkards*, to be set in the stocks. Catharine, the wife of Richard Cornish, was
found *suspicious of incontinency*, and seriously admonished to take heed. Thomas Petit, for
suspicion of slander, idleness, and stubbornness, is sentenced to be severely whipped. Captain
Lovel admonished to take heed of *light carriage*. Josias Plaistowe, for stealing four baskets
of corn from the Indians, is ordered to return them eight baskets, to be fined five pounds, and
hereafter to be called by the name of Josias, and not Mr., as formerly he used to be." Hutch-

of spinning which the young women were reckoned capable of producing, and enforced by fines the production of the requisite quantities. Usury was forbidden ; and the prohibition was not confined to the interest of money, but extended to the hire of laboring cattle and implements of husbandry. Persons deserting the English settlements, and living in heathen license and profanity, were punished by fine and imprisonment. A male child above sixteen years of age, accused by his parents of rebellion against them and general misconduct, incurred (conformably with the Mosaic code) the doom of capital punishment ; and any person courting a maid, without the sanction of her parents, was fined and imprisoned. Yet the parental authority was not left unregulated. All parents were commanded to instruct and cate-chize their children and servants, whom the selectmen or overseers were directed to remove from their authority and commit to fitter hands, if the parents or masters were found deficient in this duty ; and children were al-lowed to seek redress from the magistrate, if they were arbitrarily restrained from marriage. The celebration of the nuptial ceremony was confined to the magistrate, or such other persons as the General Court might authorize to perform it. The provincial law of tenures was exceedingly simple and concise. The charter had conveyed the territory to the company and its assigns ; and by an early law of the province, it was provided, " that five years' quiet possession shall be deemed a sufficient title." Instead of pro-claiming or intending that the deficiencies of the provincial code should be supplied by the common or statute law of England, it was announced, that, in cases where redress of wrongs or remedy of inconvenience was not pro-vided by the ordinances or customary practice of the province, recourse should be had to the pages of holy writ.[1]

Like the tribes of Israel, the colonists of New England had forsaken their native land after a long and severe persecution, and journeyed into a wilder-ness for the sake of religion. Like the Israelites, they compared themselves to a vine brought out of Egypt, and planted by the Lord in a land from

inson. Few obtained the title of Mr. in the colony; still fewer that of Esquire. Goodman and Goodwife were the common appellations. It was by merit and public services, rather than wealth, that the distinctive appellations were gained. Ibid. The strictness and scrupulosity of manners, affected by many of the inhabitants, exceeded the standard of the laws ; and asso-ciations were formed for suppressing the practices of drinking healths, and of wearing long hair and periwigs. Ibid. In some instances, the purposes of these associations were after-wards sanctioned and enforced by the laws. " They thought the magistrates, being God's ministers, were bound to punish all offences in their courts in the same proportion as the Su-preme Judge would punish them in the court of heaven." Ibid. This notion frequently in-volved the magistrates in most absurd and indecent inquisitions ; some of which, to the dis-grace of Puritan jurisprudence, have been preserved in Winthrop's *Journal.* It is related of some of the earlier settlers, that, with an outrageous exaggeration of rigidity, they refrained from brewing on Saturday, because the beer would *work* upon Sunday. Douglas, *Summary of the British Settlements in America.* A farmer in New Hampshire found great difficulty in escaping excommunication for having shot, on Sunday, a bear that was wasting his fields. Graham's *Sketch of Vermont.*
[1] *Abridgment of the Ordinances of New England, apud* Neal. Hutchinson. Trumbull. Josselyn. Burnaby's *Travels in America.* Chalmers. Winthrop's *Journal.* Holmes's *Account of the Blue Laws of Connecticut,* in the *Rhode Island Farmers' and Manufacturers' Journal.* The primitive rigidity discernible in some of these laws was tempered by a patriarchal mild-ness of administration. Many instances of this occur in Mather's *Lives of the Governors of New England.* One I may be permitted to notice as a specimen. Governor Winthrop, being urged to prosecute and punish a man who pillaged his magazine of firewood in winter, de-clared he would soon cure him of that malpractice ; and, accordingly, sending for the delin-quent, he told him, " You have a large family, and I have a large magazine of wood ; come as often to it as you please, and take as much of it as you need to make your dwelling comfortable." — " And now," he added, turning to his friends, " I defy him to steal my fire-wood again."

which the heathen were cast forth.   They endeavoured to cherish a resemblance of condition, so honorable and so fraught with incitements to piety, by cultivating a conformity between their laws and customs and those which distinguished the ancient people of God.   Hence arose some of the peculiarities which we have observed in their legislative code ; and hence arose also the practice of commencing their sabbatical observances on Saturday evening.   The same predilection for Jewish customs begot, or at least promoted, among them the habit of bestowing significant names on children, of whom the first three that were baptized in Boston church received the names of Joy, Recompense, and Pity.   This custom seems to have obtained the greatest prevalence in the town of Dorchester, which long continued to be remarkable for such names as Faith, Hope, Charity, Deliverance, Dependence, Preserved, Content, Prudence, Patience, Thankful, Hate-evil, Holdfast, and others of a similar character.[1]

CHAPTER III.

New England embraces the Cause of the Parliament. — Federal Union between the New England States. — Provincial Coinage of Money. — Disputes occasioned by the Disfranchisement of Dissenters in Massachusetts. — Impeachment and Trial of Governor Winthrop. — Arbitrary Proceedings against the Dissenters. — Attempts to convert and civilize the Indians. — Character and Labors of Eliot and Mayhew. — Indian Bible printed in Massachusetts. — Effects of the Missionary Labor. — A Synod of the New England Churches. — Dispute between Massachusetts and the Long Parliament. — The Colony foils the Parliament — and is favored by Cromwell. — The Protector's Administration beneficial to New England. — He conquers Acadia. — His Propositions to the Inhabitants of Massachusetts — declined by them. — Persecution of the Anabaptists in Massachusetts. — Conduct and Sufferings of the Quakers. — The Restoration. — Address of Massachusetts to Charles the Second. — Alarm of the Colonists — their Declaration of Rights. — The King's Message to Massachusetts — how far complied with. — Royal Charter of Incorporation to Rhode Island and Providence — and to Connecticut and New Haven.

THE coincidence between the principles of the New England colonists and those of the prevailing party in the Long Parliament [1641] was cemented by the consciousness, that with the success of this party was identified the security of the provincial institutions from the dangers that had so recently menaced them.   As soon as the colonists were informed of the convocation of that famous assembly, they despatched Hugh Peters and two other persons to promote their interests in the parent state.   The mission proved more fortunate for New England than for her ambassadors.   By an ordinance of the House of Commons[2] in the following year, the inhabitants of all the various plantations of New England were exempted from payment of any duties, either upon goods carried thither, or upon goods imported by them into the mother country, " until the House shall make further order therein to the contrary."   The colonists, in return, cordially embraced the cause of their benefactors ; and when the civil wars broke out in England [1642], they published a decree expressive of their approbation of the measures of parliament, and denouncing capital punishment against all per-

---

[1] *History of the British Dominions in America.*

[2] The reasons assigned by the House for this ordinance are, that the plantations of New England are likely to conduce to the propagation of the gospel, and already " have, by the blessing of the Almighty, had good and prosperous success, *without any public charge to the state.*"

sons who should disturb the peace of the commonwealth by endeavouring to
raise a party for the king of England, or by discriminating between the king
and the parliament, which pursued (it was declared) the true interests of the
king as well as its own.   Happily for themselves, the colonists were unable
to signalize their predilection by more active interference in the contest ;
and, with a prudent regard to their commercial interests, they gave free
ingress into their harbours to trading vessels from the ports in possession of
the royalists.   They had likewise the good sense to decline an invitation they
received to depute John Cotton, and others of their ministers, to attend,
as provincial delegates, the celebrated Assembly of Divines convoked at
Westminster.

Encouraged by the privileges that were conferred on them, they pursued
the cultivation of their soil with unremitting ardor ; and their wealth and
population rapidly increased.   From the continent they began to extend
their occupation to the adjacent islands ; and one planter, in particular, having obtained a grant of Martha's Vineyard, Nantucket, and the Elizabeth
Islands, laid the foundation there of settlements that afterwards proved
highly serviceable to the conversion and civilization of the Indians.   But a
contemporaneous attempt which they made to extend, if not their settlements, at least their principles, in another quarter of the continent, was attended with unfortunate results.   The colonists of Virginia were in general
stanch royalists ; and, with little concern for the substance of religion, professed a strong attachment to the forms and institutions of the church of
England.   Yet, as we have seen, they received, even as early as the reign
of James, an accession to their numbers, composed of persons who had
imbibed Puritan sentiments, and were fugitives from ecclesiastical persecution in Britain.   A deputation from this class of the Virginian planters
had been lately sent to Boston to represent their destitution of proper ministers, and solicit a supply of pastors from the New England churches.   In
compliance with this request, three clergymen were selected to repair as
missionaries to Virginia, and furnished with recommendatory letters from the
governor of Massachusetts to Sir William Berkeley.   [1642.]   On their
arrival in Virginia, they began to preach in various parts of the country, and
the people flocked to hear them with an eagerness that might have been
productive of important consequences.   But the Puritan principles, as well
as the political sentiments, of the colonists of New England were too much
the objects of aversion to Sir William Berkeley, to admit of his patronage
being afforded to an enterprise intended and adapted to propagate their influence among his own people.   So far from complying with the desire of
his brother governor, he issued a proclamation, by which all persons who
would not conform to the ceremonial of the church of England were commanded straightway to depart from Virginia.   The preachers accordingly
returned to New England ; and thus was laid the foundation of a jealousy
which long subsisted between the two oldest provinces of North America.[1]

The disappointment occasioned by this fruitless attempt to establish a
friendly connection with the sister colony of Virginia was counterbalanced
in the following year [1643] by an important event in the history of the
New England settlements ; — the formation of a league by which they were
knit together in a federal union that greatly augmented their security and
power.   The Narraganset Indians had by this time reflected at leisure on

[1] Hutchinson. Neal. Hazard.

the policy of their conduct towards the Pequods; and the hatred which they formerly cherished against this tribe, being extinguished in the destruction of its objects, was succeeded by an angry jealousy of those strangers who obviously derived the chief and only lasting advantage which the conflict had yielded. They saw the territories of their ancient rivals occupied by a much more formidable neighbour; and mistaking their own inability to improve their condition for the effect of fraud and injustice on the part of the colonists, who were rapidly surpassing them in number, wealth, and power, they began to complain that the plunder of the Pequods had not been fairly divided, and concerted measures with some of the neighbouring tribes for a general insurrection of the Indians against the English. Their designs had advanced but a little way towards maturity, when they were detected, in consequence of an emergent quarrel with another tribe, which they pursued with an imprudent indulgence of that inordinate appetite for present revenge which seemed fated to disconcert and defeat their political views. The colonists, from the groundless murmurs they found themselves exposed to, and which proved only the rooted dislike of the savages, were sensible of their own danger, without yet being aware of its extent, or feeling themselves authorized to anticipate by defensive hostility some more certain indication of it; when, fortunately, they were invited to act as mediators between two contending tribes. The Narragansets, having conceived some disgust against a neighbouring chief, employed an assassin to kill him; and, failing in this attempt, plunged into a war, with the declared intention of exterminating the whole of his tribe. This tribe, who were at peace with the English, implored the protection of the Massachusetts government, which agreed to interpose in their behalf. The Narragansets, apprized of this transaction, recollecting the terrible punishment inflicted on the Pequods, and conscious that they themselves justly merited a similar visitation, were struck with dismay, and, throwing down their arms, acceded to a treaty of peace dictated to them by the English. When their immediate apprehensions subsided, they showed so little regard to the performance of their paction, that it was not till the colonists made a demonstration of readiness to employ force that they sullenly fulfilled it.

Alarmed by such indications of fickleness, dislike, and furious passion, and ascertaining by dint of inquiry the design that had been recently proposed and entertained of a general conspiracy of the Indians, — the authorities of Massachusetts conceived the defensive project of providing, by a mutual concert of the colonies, for the common danger which they might expect to encounter at no distant day, when the savages, instructed by experience, would sacrifice their private feuds to combined hostility against a race of strangers whose progressive advancement seemed to minister occasion of increasing and incurable jealousy to the whole Indian race. Having composed, for this purpose, a plan which was framed in imitation of the bond of union between the Dutch provinces, and which readily suggested itself to some leading personages among the colonists who had resided with the Brownist congregation in Holland, they communicated it to the neighbouring settlements of New Plymouth, Connecticut, and New Haven, by which it was cordially embraced. These four colonies, accordingly, entered into a league of perpetual confederacy, offensive and defensive. [May 19, 1643.] The instrument of confederation between them announced that their respective inhabitants *had all come into these parts of America with the same errand and aim, to advance the Christian religion, and enjoy the liberty of their consciences with purity and peace.* It was stipulated, that the confederates should thenceforth be distinguished by the title of The United Colonies of New England ; that each province should remain a separate and distinct municipal association, and retain independent jurisdiction within its own territory ; that in every war, offensive or defensive, each of the confederates should furnish its quota of men, money, and provisions, at a rate to be fixed from time to time in proportion to the population of the respective communities ; that a council, composed of two commissioners from each province, should be annually convoked and empowered to deliberate and decide on all points of common concern to the confederacy ; and that every resolve, sanctioned by the approbation of six of the commissioners, should be binding on all the associated provinces. Every province renounced the right of protecting fugitive debtors or criminals from the legal process of the particular community which they might have wronged and deserted. The State of Rhode Island, which was not included in this confederacy, petitioned a few years after to be admitted into it ; but her request was refused, except on the condition, which she declined, of merging her separate existence in an incorporation with the colony of New Plymouth. Thus excluded from the benefit of the federal union, and in a manner dissociated from the other States, the inhabitants of Rhode Island and Providence endeavoured to promote their separate security by conciliating the friendship of the Indians ; and the humane and courteous policy which this purpose taught them to pursue proved remarkably successful.[1]

The colonists have been reproached with arrogating the prerogative of sovereignty in this transaction, — which, doubtless, wears all the features of a direct approach to political independence. Yet it was a measure that could hardly be avoided by a people surrounded with enemies, and abandoned to their own guidance and resources, in a territory many thousand miles distant from the seat of the government that claimed supreme dominion over them. Of a community so situated every progressive step in social advancement, whether consisting in the enlargement of its numbers or the concentration of its resources, or otherwise tending to increase its power and promote its security, was a step towards national independence. Nothing but some curiously politic system, or such a series of events as might have kept the various settlements continually disunited in mutual jealousy and consequent weakness, could have secured their protracted existence as a dependent progeny of England. But whatever effects the transaction which we have remarked may have silently produced on the course of American sentiment and opinion, and however likely it may now appear to have planted the seminal idea of independence in the minds of the colonists, it was regarded neither by themselves nor by their English rulers as indicating pretensions unsuitable to their condition. Even after the Restoration, the commissioners of the federal union were repeatedly noticed and recognized in the letters and official instruments of Charles the Second ; and the league itself, with some alterations, subsisted till very near the era of the British Revolution. A few years after its establishment, the principal object which engaged its deliberations and exertions was the religious instruction of the Indians, — an object which was pursued in coöperation with the society instituted by parliament in Britain for propagating the gospel in New England.[2]

---

[1] Increase Mather's *New England Troubles.* Neal. Hutchinson. Pitkin's *History.*
[2] Hutchinson.

While the colonists were thus employed in devising measures calculated to guard, confirm, and mature their institutions, the parliament enacted an ordinance of which the principle menaced those institutions with an entire overthrow. [1643.] It appointed the Earl of Warwick governor-in-chief, and lord high admiral of all the British colonies, with a council of five peers and twelve commoners to assist him ; it empowered him, in conjunction with his associates, to investigate the actual condition of the colonies ; to require the production of their patents and records, and the personal attendance and testimony of any of their inhabitants ; to remove governors and other provincial magistrates ; to replace them by proper successors ; and to delegate to these new functionaries as much of the power conferred on himself as he should think proper. This ordinance, which created an authority that might have new-modelled all the provincial governments, and abrogated all their charters, was not suffered to remain wholly inoperative. To some of the colonial commonwealths the parliamentary council extended protection, and even granted new patents.[1]   Happily for Massachusetts, either the peculiar favor and indulgence of which she was deemed worthy, or the absorbing interest of the great struggle with which England was shaken, prevented any interference with her institutions, until a period when her provincial assembly was able, as we shall see, to employ defensive measures that eluded the undesirable interposition without disputing the formidable authority of the parliamentary council.

Various disputes had arisen of late years between the inhabitants of New England and the French settlers in Acadia or Nova Scotia. These differences were now [1644] adjusted by a treaty between a commissioner for the king of France on the one part, and *John Endicott, governor of New England, and the rest of the magistrates there,* on the other.[2] The colonists had already debarred themselves from recognizing the king as a distinct authority from the parliament ; and they probably found it difficult to explain to the other contracting parties to what denomination of sovereign power they owned allegiance. This state of things, as it engendered practices, so it may have secretly fostered sentiments, that savored of independence. A practice strongly denoting pretension to sovereign authority was adopted a few years after,[3] when the increasing trade of the colonists with the West Indies, and the quantity of Spanish bullion that was conveyed through this channel into New England, induced the provincial authorities to erect a mint for the coinage of silver money at Boston. The coin was stamped with the name of New England on the one side ; of Massachusetts, as the principal settlement, on the other ; and with a tree, as the symbol of national vigor and increase. Maryland was the only other colony that ever presumed to coin money ; and, indeed, this prerogative has been always regarded as the peculiar attribute of sovereignty. " But it must be considered," says one of the New England historians, " that at this time there was no king in Israel." In the distracted state of the mother country, it might well be judged unsafe to send bullion there to be coined ; and from the uncertainty respecting the form of government which would finally arise out of the civil wars, it might reasonably be apprehended that an impress received during their continuance would not long retain its currency. The practice gave no umbrage whatever to the English government. It received the tacit allowance of the par-

---

[1] *Journals of the House of Lords.* Chalmers. The people of Maine solicited the protection of the council in 1651.   Hazard.
[2] Hutchinson.   [3] In 1652.

liament, of Cromwell, and even of Charles the Second, during twenty years of his reign.[1]

The separation of the two branches of the legislature of Massachusetts naturally gave rise to some disputes respecting the boundaries of jurisdiction in a constitution not yet matured by practice. But what precedent could not supply, the influence of the provincial clergy was able to accomplish. [1644.] By common consent, all the ministers were summoned to attend the session of the assembly, and the points at issue being submitted to them, their decision was honored with immediate and universal acquiescence.[2] But in the following year [1645], a dispute more violent in its nature, and less creditable and satisfactory in its result, was occasioned in this commonwealth by the intolerance which we have already noted in its original institutions. With the growing prosperity and importance of the provincial society, the value of its political franchises was felt to be proportionably augmented; and the increasing opulence and respectability of the dissenters seemed to aggravate the hardship of the disfranchisement to which they were subjected. Some of these persons, having proceeded with violence to assume the privileges from which they were excluded by law, and disturbed an election by their interference, were punished by Winthrop, the deputy-governor, who vigorously resisted and defeated their pretensions. They complained of this treatment to the General Court by a petition couched in very strong language, demanding leave to impeach the deputy-governor before the whole body of his fellow-citizens, and to submit to the same tribunal the consideration of their general sufferings, as well as of the particular severities they had experienced from Winthrop. The grievances under which they labored were enumerated in the petition, which contained a forcible remonstrance against the injustice of depriving them of the rights of freemen, because they could not conscientiously unite with the congregational churches, or when they solicited admission into them were arbitrarily rejected by the ministers. They contended that either the full rights of citizenship should be communicated to them, or that they should no longer be required to obey laws to which they had not given assent, to contribute to the maintenance of ministers from whose labors they derived no advantage, or to pay taxes imposed by an assembly in which they were not represented. The court was so far moved by the petition, or by the respectability of its promoters, that Winthrop was commanded to defend himself publicly, before the magistrates, from the charges which it advanced against him.

On the day appointed for his trial, he descended from his official seat on the bench, he being one of the magistrates, and, placing himself at the bar in presence of a numerous assemblage of the inhabitants, he addressed himself to explain and vindicate his conduct. Having clearly proved that the proceedings for which he was impeached were sanctioned by law, and that the sole object of them was to maintain the existing institutions, by the exercise of the authority confided to him for this purpose, he concluded an excellent harangue in the following terms :—" Though I be justified before men, yet it may be, the Lord hath seen so much amiss in my administration as calls me to be humbled; and, indeed, for me to have been thus charged by men is a matter of humiliation, whereof I desire to make a right use before the Lord. If Miriam's father spit in her face, she is to be ashamed."

---

[1] Hutchinson. [2] Ibid.

Then desiring leave to propose some considerations by which he hoped to rectify the opinions of the people on the nature of government : " The questions," he observed, " that have troubled the country have been about the authority of the magistracy and the liberty of the people. It is you who have called us unto this office ; but being thus called, we have our authority from God.   Magistracy is the ordinance of God, and it hath the image of God stamped upon it ; and the contempt of it has been vindicated by God with terrible examples of his vengeance.   I entreat you to consider, that, when you choose magistrates, you take them from among yourselves, men subject unto like passions with yourselves.   If you see our infirmities, re-flect on your own, and you will not be so severe censurers of ours.   The covenant between us and you is the oath you have exacted of us, which is to this purpose, *that we shall govern you and judge your causes according to God's laws and the particular statutes of the land, according to our best skill.*   As for our skill, you must run the hazard of it ; and if there be an error only therein, and not in the will, it becomes you to bear it.   Nor would I have you to mistake in the point of your own liberty.   There is a liberty of corrupt nature, which is affected both by men and beasts, to do what they list.   This liberty is inconsistent with authority ; impatient of all re-straint (by this liberty *sumus omnes deteriores*), 't is the grand enemy of truth and peace, and all the ordinances of God are bent against it.   But there is civil, a moral, a federal liberty, which is the proper end and object of authority ; it is a liberty for that only which is just and good.   For this liberty you are to stand with the hazard of your very lives ; and whatsoever crosses it is not authority, but a distemper thereof.   This liberty is main-tained in a way of subjection to authority ; and the authority set over you will, in all administrations for your good, be quietly submitted unto by all but such as have a disposition to shake off the yoke, and lose their true lib-erty by their murmuring at the honor and power of authority."

The circumstances in which this address was delivered recall the most interesting scenes of Greek and Roman story, while in the wisdom, piety, and dignity that it breathes, it resembles the magnanimous vindication of a judge of Israel.   Winthrop was not only acquitted by the judicial sentence of the court and the approving voice of the public, but recommended so strongly to the esteem of his fellow-citizens by this and all the other indi-cations of his character, that he was chosen governor of Massachusetts every year after as long as he lived.[1]   [1646.]   His accusers incurred a pro-portional degree of public displeasure ; their petition was rejected, and several of the chief promoters of it were severely reprimanded, and adjudged to make open acknowledgment of their fault in seeking to subvert the funda-mental laws of the colony.   Refusing to acknowledge that they had acted amiss, and still persisting in their clamor for an alteration of the law, with very indiscreet threats of complaining to the parliament, they were punished

---

[1] This excellent magistrate (says Cotton Mather) continually exemplified the maxim of Theodosius, that, *If any man speak evil of the ruler, if it be through lightness, 't is to be con-temned ; if it be through madness, 't is to be pitied ; if through malice, 't is to be forgiven.*   One of the colonists, who had long manifested much ill-will towards his person, at length wrote to him, " Sir, your overcoming of yourself hath overcome me."   At his third election to the office of governor, he declared, in a speech to his fellow-citizens, that he had hitherto accepted *with a trembling hand* the presents by which they had acknowledged his services, and could no longer consent to a repetition of them.   In the close of his life, he is said to have expressed regret for the sanction he had given to intolerance.   His death, in 1649, was deeply and uni-versally bewailed ; and all declared that he had been the father of the colony, and the first alike in virtue and in place.

with fine or imprisonment. Most of them were known or believed to incline to the ecclesiastical form of presbytery ; and as this peculiar constitution was also affected by the prevailing party in the English House of Commons, the menace of a complaint to parliament excited general anger and
alarm. A deputation of the malcontents having made preparation to sail for
England, and given significant hints of the changes they hoped to procure
by their machinations in the parent state, some of them were placed under
arrest, and their papers were seized and examined. Among these papers
were found petitions to Lord Warwick, urging a forfeiture of the provincial
charter, the introduction of a Presbyterian establishment, and of the whole
code of English jurisprudence, into the provincial institutions, together with
various other innovations, which were represented as at once accordant with
legislatorial wisdom and justice, and conducive to the important object of
securing and enlarging the sovereign authority of the parliament over the
colony. The discovery of the intolerance contemplated by these persons
served to exasperate the intolerance which they themselves were experiencing from the society of which they formed but an insignificant fraction.
The contents of their papers excited so much resentment, that not a voice
was raised against the iniquity of the process by which the documents had
been intercepted ; and the alarm was increased by the manifest impossibility
of preventing designs so dangerous from being still pursued. The ardor of
the public sentiment, as well as the peculiar nature of the subject that excited it, introduced this all-prevalent topic into the pulpit ; and even John
Cotton was so far heated and transported by the contagion of passionate
zeal, as to declare, in a sermon, "that, if any one should carry writings or
complaints against the people of God in this country to England, he would,
doubtless, find himself in the predicament of Jonah in the vessel." This
was a prediction to which a long voyage was not unlikely to give at least a
seeming fulfilment. In effect, a short time after, certain deputies from the
petitioners, having embarked for England, were overtaken by a violent storm;
whereupon, the sailors, recollecting the prediction that had gone abroad, and,
happily, considering the papers, and not the bearers of them, as the offending part of the shipment, insisted so vehemently on casting all obnoxious
writings overboard, that the deputies were obliged to commit their credentials to the waves. Yet, when they arrived in England, they did not fail to
prosecute their mission ; but the attention of the parliamentary leaders at
that time being deeply engaged with more important matters, and Winslow
and Hugh Peters, on behalf of the colony, actively laboring to traverse the
designs of the applicants, they obtained little attention and no redress.[1]
   From the painful survey of intolerance and contentious zeal for the forms
of religion, it is pleasing to turn to the substantial fruits of Christian sentiment
displayed in those memorable exertions for the conversion of the Indians,
that originated in the same year that witnessed so much dispute and animosity. [1646.] The circumstances that promoted the emigrations to New
England had operated with especial force on the ministers of the Puritans ;
and so many of these spiritual directors had accompanied the other settlers,
that, among a people who derived less enjoyment from the exercises of piety,
the numbers of the clergy would have been reckoned exceedingly burdensome, and very much disproportioned to the wants of the laity. This circumstance was highly favorable to the promotion of religious habits among

----

[1] Mather. Neal. Hutchinson. Chalmers.

the colonists, as well as to the extension of their settlements, in the plantation of which the coöperation of a minister was accounted indispensable. It contributed also to suggest and facilitate missionary labor among the neighbouring heathens, to whom the colonists had associated themselves by superadding the ties of a common country to those of a common nature. While the people at large were progressively extending their industry, and subduing by culture the rudeness of desert nature, the ministers of religion with earnest zeal aspired to an extension of *their* peculiar sphere of usefulness ; and at a very early period entertained designs of redeeming to the dominion of piety and civility the neglected wastes of human life and character that lay stretched in savage ignorance and idolatry around them. John Eliot, one of the ministers of Roxbury, a man whose large soul glowed with the intensest flame of holy charity, was deeply penetrated with a sense of this duty, and for some time had been laboriously qualifying himself to overcome the preliminary difficulty by which its performance was obstructed. He had now by diligent study attained such acquaintance with the Indian language as enabled him not only to speak it with fluency, but to facilitate the acquisition of it to others, by the construction and publication of a system of *Indian Grammar*. Having completed his preparatory inquiries, he began, in the close of this year [October, 1646], a scene of pious labor which has been traced with great interest and accuracy by the ecclesiastical historians of New England, and still more minutely, we may believe, in that eternal record where alone the actions of men obtain their just, their final, and everlasting proportions. It is a remarkable feature in his long and arduous career, that the spirit and energy by which he was supported never incurred the slightest abatement, but, on the contrary, manifested a steady and continual increase. He confidently relied on its unfailing endurance ; and always referring it to divine infusion, felt assured of its derivation from a fountain incapable of being wasted by the most liberal communication. Every thing he saw or knew occurred to him in a religious aspect ; every faculty, and every acquisition that he derived from the employment of his faculties, was received by him as a ray imparted to his soul from that supreme source of sentiment and intelligence which was the object of his earnest contemplation and continual desire. As he was one of the holiest, so was he also one of the happiest and most beloved of men. When he felt himself disabled from preaching by the infirmities of old age, he proposed to his parishioners of Roxbury to resign his ministerial salary ; but these good people unanimously declared that they would willingly pay the stipend, for the advantage and honor of having him reside among them. His example, indeed, was the most valuable part of his ministry among Christians ; his life, during many years, being a continual and manifest effusion of soul in devotion to God and charity to mankind.

The mild, persuasive address of Eliot soon gained him a favorable audience from many of the Indians ;[1] and having successfully represented to them the expediency of an entire departure from their savage habits of life, he obtained from the General Court a suitable tract of land adjoining to the settlement of Concord, in Massachusetts, where a number of Indian families began, under his counsel, to erect fixed habitations for themselves, and where they eagerly received his instructions, both spiritual and secular. It was not long before a violent opposition to these innovations was excited by the

---

[1] See Note VII., at the end of the volume.

powwows, or Indian priests, who threatened death, and other inflictions of the vengeance of their idols, on all who should embrace Christianity. The menaces and artifices of these persons caused several of the seeming proselytes to draw back, but induced others to separate themselves entirely from the society and converse of the main body of their countrymen, and court the advantage of a closer association with that superior race of men who showed themselves so generously willing to diffuse and communicate the capacity and benefits of their own improved condition. A considerable number of Indians resorted to the land allotted to them by the provincial government, and exchanged their wild and barbarous habits for the modes of civilized life and industry. Eliot was continually among them, instructing, animating, and directing them. They felt his superior wisdom, and saw him continually and serenely happy ; and there was nothing in his exterior condition that indicated sources of enjoyment from which they were necessarily debarred. On the contrary, it was obvious, that of every article of merely selfish comfort he was willing to divest himself, in order to communicate to them a share of what he esteemed the only true riches of an immortal being. The women in the new settlement learned to spin ; the men to dig and till the ground ; and the children were instructed in the English language, and taught to read and write, or, as the Indians expressed themselves, to get *news from paper, and mark their thoughts on it.*

As the numbers of domesticated Indians increased, they built a town by the side of Charles River, which they called *Natick ;* and they desired Eliot to frame a system of municipal government for them. He directed their attention to the counsel that Jethro gave to Moses ; and, in conformity with it, they elected for themselves rulers of hundreds, of fifties, and of tens. The provincial government also established a tribunal, which, without assuming jurisdiction over them, tendered the assistance of its judicial mediation to all who might be willing to refer to it the adjustment of their more difficult or important controversies. In endeavouring to extend their missionary influence among the surrounding tribes, Eliot and the associates of his labors (men like-minded with himself) encountered a variety of success, corresponding to the visible varieties of human character, and the invisible predeterminations of the divine will. Many persons expressed the utmost abhorrence and contempt of Christianity ; some made a hollow profession of willingness to learn, and even of conviction, — with the view, as it afterwards proved, of obtaining the tools and other articles of value that were furnished to every Indian who proposed to embrace the habits of civilized life. In spite of great discouragement, the missionaries persisted ; and the difficulties that at first mocked their efforts seeming at length to vanish under an influence at once mysterious and irresistible, their labors were crowned with astonishing success. The character and habits of the lay colonists promoted the efficacy of these pious exertions, in a manner which will be forcibly appreciated by all who have examined the history and progress of missions. Simple in their manners, devout, moral, and industrious in their conduct and demeanour, they enforced the lessons of the missionaries by demonstrating their practicability and beneficial effects, and exhibited a model of life, which, in point of refinement, was not too elevated for Indian imitation.

While Eliot and an increasing company of associates were thus employed in the province of Massachusetts, Thomas Mayhew, a man who combined the gentlest manners with the most ardent and enthusiastic spirit, together with a few coadjutors, diligently prosecuted the same design in Martha's Vineyard, Nantucket, and the Elizabeth Islands, and the territory comprehended in the Plymouth patent. Abasing themselves that they might elevate their species and promote the divine glory, and counting their work their wages, they labored with their own hands among those Indians whom they persuaded to forsake savage habits ; and zealously employing all the influence they acquired to the communication of moral and spiritual improvement, they beheld their exertions rewarded by the happiest results. The character and manners of Mayhew were singularly calculated to excite the tenderness, no less than the veneration, of the objects of his benevolence. His address derived a penetrating interest from that earnest concern and high and holy value which he manifestly entertained for every member of the family of mankind. Many years after his death, the Indians could not hear his name mentioned without shedding tears and betraying transports of grateful emotion. Both Eliot and Mayhew found great advantage in the practice of selecting the most docile and ingenious of their Indian pupils, and by especial attention to their instruction, qualifying them to act as schoolmasters among their countrymen. To a zeal that seemed to increase by exercise they added insurmountable patience and admirable prudence ; and steadily fixing their view on the glory of the Most High, and declaring, that, whether outwardly successful or not in promoting it, they felt themselves blessed and happy in pursuing it, — they found its influence sufficient to light them through the darkness of every perplexity and peril, and finally conduct them to a degree of success and victory unparalleled, perhaps, since that era when the miraculous endowments of the apostolic ministry caused multitudes to be converted in a day. They were not hasty in urging the Indians to embrace improved institutions ; they desired rather to lead them insensibly forward, — more especially in the establishment of religious ordinances. Those practices, indeed, which they accounted likely to commend themselves by their obviously beneficial effects to the natural understanding of men, they were not restrained from recommending to their early adoption ; and trial by jury very soon superseded the savage modes of determining right or ascertaining guilt, and contributed to improve and refine the sense of equity. In the dress and mode of cohabitation of the savages they also introduced, at an early period, alterations calculated to form and develope a sentiment of modesty, of which the Indians were found to be grossly and universally deficient. But all those practices which are, or ought to be, exclusively the fruits of renewed nature and divine light, they desired to teach entirely by example, and by diligently radicating and cultivating in the minds of their flocks the principles out of which alone such visible fruits of piety can lastingly and beneficially grow. It was not till the year 1660, that the first Indian church was founded by Eliot and his fellow-laborers in Massachusetts. There were at that time no fewer than ten settlements within the province, occupied by Indians comparatively civilized.

Eliot had occasionally translated and printed various approved theological dissertations for the use of the Indians ; and at length, in the year 1664, the Bible was printed, for the first time, in one of the native languages of the New World, at Cambridge, in Massachusetts.[1] This, indeed, was not ac-

---

[1] I have seen a copy of this edition of the Bible in the library of the late George Chalmers. It is a beautiful piece of typography. Many earlier publications had already issued from the

complished without the assistance of pecuniary contributions from the mother country. The colonists had zealously and cheerfully coöperated with their ministers, and assisted to defray the cost of their charitable enterprises ; but the increasing expenses threatened at last to exceed what their narrow means were competent to afford. Happily, the tidings of this great work excited a kindred spirit in the parent state, where, in the year 1649, there was formed, by act of parliament, a *Society for propagating the Gospel in New England,* whose coöperation proved of essential service to the missionary cause. This society, dissolved at the Restoration, was afterwards reëstablished by a charter from Charles the Second, obtained by the exertions of the pious Richard Baxter and the influence of the illustrious Robert Boyle, who thus approved himself the benefactor of New England as well as of Virginia. Supported by its ample endowments, and the liberal contributions of their own fellow-colonists, the American missionaries exerted themselves with such energy and success in the work of converting and civilizing the savages, that, before the close of the seventeenth century, there were collected in the province of Massachusetts more than thirty congregations of Indians, comprising upwards of three thousand persons, reclaimed from a gross barbarism and degrading superstition, and advanced to the comfort and respectability of civilized life, and the dignity and happiness of worshippers of the true God. There were nearly as many converts to religion and civility in the islands of Massachusetts Bay ; there were several Indian congregations in the Plymouth territories ; and among some of the tribes that still pursued their wonted style of roving life there was introduced a considerable improvement in civil and moral habits. Several Indians received education at Harvard College ; from which, in the year 1665, one of their number obtained the degree of Bachelor of Arts.

Among the various difficulties that obstructed the improvements which the missionaries attempted to introduce into the temporal condition of the Indians, it was found that the human constitution had been greatly deteriorated by ages of savage life. Unacquainted with moderation, and accustomed to vibrate between intense toil and sluggish supineness, the Indians at once relished indolence and loathed the even tenor of tranquil exertion. Habits of alternate sloth and activity, indulged from generation to generation, seemed to have gradually imparted a character or bias to their animal faculties, scarcely less fixed and inveterate than the depraved hue of the negro body, and to have deeply impaired the capacity of continuous application. In every employment that demanded steady labor, the Indians were found unequal to the Europeans. The first missionaries and their immediate successors sustained this discouragement without shrinking, and animated their converts to resist or endure it. But at a later period, when it appeared that the taint which the Indian constitution had received continued to be propagated among descendants educated in habits widely different from those of their forefathers, many persons began too hastily to apprehend that the imperfection was incurable ; and missionary ardor was abated by the very circumstance that most strongly solicited its revival and enlargement. In concurrence with this cause of decline, the ardent gratitude awakened in the first converts was chilled in its transmission to succeeding generations ; and the consequence unhappily was, that a considerable abatement ensued of the

fertile press of New England. One of the first was a new metrical translation of the Psalms, — very literal and very inelegant. To this last imputation the New Englanders answered, " that God's altars need not our polishings." Oldmixon.

piety, morality, and industry of the Indian communities that had been reclaimed from savage life. The members of these communities were depressed by many mortifying circumstances incident to their condition, being exposed to the aversion and contempt of the mass of their race, from which they were socially cut off, though still visibly allied to it by their color ; while from the same color and other qualities, even when kindly treated, they were regarded with little respect by the generality of the white colonists, who considered them rather as children and inferiors than as men and equals. Yet the missionary work was never entirely abandoned, nor its visible fruits suffered wholly to disappear. Amidst occasional decline and revival, the New England missions have been always pursued ; and converts to piety and civility have continued to attest their beneficial efficacy upon the Indian race.[1]

Having already transgressed considerably the march of time, in order to exhibit a brief but unbroken view of the foregoing scene of missionary labor, we now return to follow more leisurely the general stream of affairs in New England.

Shortly after the dissensions which we have remarked in the year 1646, the General Court of Massachusetts recommended the convocation of a synod of the churches of New England, in order to frame a uniform scheme of church discipline for all the provincial congregations. The proposal was resisted by several of the churches, which expressed apprehension of the arbitrary purposes and superstitious devices which might be promoted by the dangerous practice of convocating synods. But at length, the persuasion generally prevailing that an assembly of this description possessed no positive authority, and that its functions were confined to the tendering of counsel, the second synod of New England was convoked at Cambridge. [1648.] The confession of faith that had recently been published by the Assembly of Divines at Westminster was thoroughly examined and unanimously approved. Three of the most eminent of the provincial ministers, Cotton, Partridge, and Mather, were then appointed to prepare a model of discipline for the New England churches. The *Platform of Church Discipline*, which they composed accordingly, and presented to the synod, after many long debates, received general approbation and almost universal acquiescence.[2]

A dispute had for some time prevailed between Massachusetts and Connecticut respecting a commercial tax imposed by the legislature of Connecticut, and which operated with very questionable equity and most unquestionable disadvantage on the inhabitants of Massachusetts. [1649.] Having complained to the commissioners of the confederated provinces, and not obtaining redress as speedily as they deemed themselves entitled to expect, the legislative authorities of Massachusetts issued an ordinance imposing a retaliatory duty not only on goods imported from Connecticut, but on importations from all the other States of the confederation. This unjust proceeding could be defended only by superior strength ; an advantage which

---

[1] *Day-breaking of the Gospel in New England.* Shepherd's *Clear Sunshine of the Gospel upon the Indians.* Eliot's and Mayhew's *Letters.* Mayhew's *Indian Converts.* Whitfield's *Discovery of the present State of the Indians.* Of these, and of various other works on the same subject, copies exist, partly in the Redcross-street Library of London, and partly in the Advocate's Library of Edinburgh. *Baxter's Life.* Mather. Neal. Hutchinson. Peirce's *History of Harvard University.* The Indian tribes within the Connecticut territory proved remarkably indocile. Some individuals were converted ; but no Indian church was ever gathered in this State. Trumbull.
[2] Neal.

so manifestly resided with Massachusetts, that the other confederates had
nothing to oppose to it but an appeal to those principles of equity which
one of their own number had already set the example of disregarding.
Happily for them, and for herself, their ally, though liable to be betrayed
into error by resentment and partiality, was not intoxicated with conscious
power.   They presented a remonstrance to the General Court of Massachusetts, desiring it " seriously to consider whether such proceedings agree
with the law of love, and the tenor of the articles of confederation."   On
receiving this remonstrance, the government of Massachusetts, superior to
the mean shame of acknowledging a fault, consented to suspend the obnoxious ordinance.[1]   [1650.]

   But Massachusetts, in the following year [1651], was engaged in controversy with a power more formidable to her than she was to her confederates, and much less accessible to sentiments of moderation and forbearance.
The Long Parliament, having now established its authority in England, was
determined to exact an explicit recognition of it from all the foreign dependencies of the state, and even to introduce such recognition into the charters
and official style and procedure of subordinate communities.   A mandate
was accordingly transmitted to the governor and assembly of Massachusetts,
requiring them to send their charter to London ; to accept a new patent
from the keepers of the liberties of England ; and to express in all public
writs and judicial proceedings the dependence of the provincial authorities
on those existing depositaries of supreme power in the parent state.   This
command excited the utmost alarm in the colony ; nor could all the attachment of the people to the cause of the parliament[2] reconcile them to a surrender of the title under which their settlements and institutions had been
formed, and which had never obstructed their obedience to the authorities
that now proposed to revoke it.   The parliament, indeed, had no more
right to supersede the original patent of the colony, than to require the city
of London, or any of the other corporations of England, to submit their

   [1] Hutchinson. Chalmers. Another dispute, which occurred about three years after, between
Massachusetts and the other confederated States, is related with great minuteness, and I think
with no small injustice and partiality, by the respectable historian of Connecticut.   In 1653, a
discovery was supposed to have been made of a conspiracy between Stuyvesant, the governor
of the Dutch colony afterwards called New York, and the Indians, for the extermination of the
English.   The evidence of this sanguinary project (which Stuyvesant indignantly disclaimed)
was judged sufficient, and the resolution of a general war embraced by all the commissioners
of the union except those of Massachusetts.   The General Court of this province reckoned the
proof inconclusive, and were fortified in this opinion by the judgment of their clergy, which
they consented to abide by.   To all the remonstrances of their allies they answered, that no
articles of confederation should induce them to undertake an offensive war which they considered unjust, and in which they could not expect the advantage of divine favor.   The historian of Connecticut, not content with reprobating this infringement of the articles of union,
indignantly censures the scruples of Massachusetts as insincere.   Trumbull.   But, in truth, the
evidence of the Dutch plot labored under very serious defects, which were much more coolly
weighed by the people of Massachusetts than by the inhabitants of Connecticut and New
Haven, exasperated by frequent disputes with the Dutch, and exposed by their local situation
to the greatest danger from Dutch hostilities.   In the beginning of the following century, the
situation of the provinces was so far reversed, that Massachusetts was compelled to solicit the
aid of Connecticut in a war with the Indians ; and, on this occasion, Connecticut, remote from
the scene of action, at first refused her aid, upon scruples (which she afterwards ascertained
to be groundless) respecting the justice of the cause to which her support was desired.—
Trumbull.
   [2] Though attached to the cause of the parliament, the people of New England had so far
forgotten their own wrongs, and escaped the contagion of the passions engendered in the civil
war, that the tragical fate of the king appears to have excited general grief and concern.   The
public expression of such sentiments would have been equally inexpedient and unavailing ;
but that they were entertained is certain.   See Hutchinson.

charters to similar dissolution and renovation. But the colonists were aware that the authorities which issued this arbitrary mandate had the *power* to give it practical effect; and, accordingly, declining a direct collision with superior force, they reverted to the same policy which they had once before successfully employed to counteract the tyrannical designs of the late king; and now succeeded in completely foiling the leaders of that parliamentary assembly, so renowned for its success, resolution, and capacity. The General Court, instead of surrendering the provincial patent, transmitted a petition to the parliament against the obnoxious mandate, setting forth, that "these things not being done in the late king's time or since, it was not able to discern the need of such an injunction." It represented the authority and understanding on which the colonists originally repaired to New England, their steadfast adherence to the cause of the parliament throughout the civil wars, and their present explicit recognition of its supremacy; and prayed that the people might not now be worse dealt with than in the time of the king, and, instead of a governor and magistrates annually chosen by themselves, be required to submit to others imposed on them against their will.

The General Court at the same time addressed a letter to " the Lord General Cromwell," for the purpose of interesting his powerful mediation in their behalf, as well as of dissuading him from the prosecution of certain measures which he himself had projected for their advantage. The peculiar character which the New England colonists displayed, the institutions they established, and their predilection for the independent model of church government which he himself approved, recommended them warmly to the esteem of this extraordinary man; and his favorable regards were enhanced by the recollection of the project which he had conceived, and so nearly accomplished, of uniting his destiny with theirs in America. Nor were they at all abated by the compassion and benevolence with which the colonists received a considerable body of unfortunate Scots whom Cromwell banished to Massachusetts after the battle of Dunbar, and of which he was apprized by a letter from John Cotton. He seemed to consider that he had been detained in England for their interests as well as his own; and never ceased to desire that they should be more nearly associated with his fortunes, and more warmly cheered with the rays of his grandeur. He was touched with a generous ambition to be the author of an enterprise so illustrious as the revocation of these men to their native country; and as an act of honorable justice to them, as well as for the advantage of Ireland, he had recently broached the proposal of transporting them from America, and establishing them in a district of that island, which was to be evacuated for their reception. In their letter to him, the General Court, alluding to this scheme, acknowledged, with grateful expressions, the kind consideration which it indicated; but declined to comply with it, or abandon a land where they had experienced so much of the favor of God, and were blessed with a fair prospect of converting the neighbouring heathens. They recommended, at the same time, their petition against the parliamentary measures to his friendly countenance, and besought " his Excellence to be pleased to show whatsoever God shall direct him unto, on the behalf of the colony, to the most honorable parliament." It is probable that Cromwell's mediation was successfully employed, as the requisition that had been addressed to the General Court was not urged any farther.[1]

---

[1] Hutchinson. Hutchinson's *Collection of Papers*. Chalmers. The commissioners who

R

The successes of the Long Parliament produced or promoted in its leading members a domineering spirit, to the exercise of which the colonies were peculiarly exposed. [1652.[1]] In the history of Virginia, we have remarked the laws by which the traffic of all the colonies with foreign states was prohibited, and the martial counsel and conduct by which the subjugation of that refractory settlement was decreed and accomplished. The province of Massachusetts, which was desirous, as far as possible, to act in harmonious concurrence with the parliament, and was perfectly sincere in recognizing its supremacy, coöperated with the ordinance against Virginia, by prohibiting all intercourse with this colony till it was reduced by the parliamentary forces. But it was not over those settlements alone which opposed its supremacy that the parliament was disposed to indulge the spirit of domination; and though Massachusetts was protected from its undesirable handling by the interference of Cromwell, Maryland, which had received its establishment from Charles the First, was compelled to admit the alterations of its official style which Massachusetts evaded; and Rhode Island beheld the very form of government which it derived from the parliament itself, in 1643, suspended by a warrant of the council of state. What might have ensued upon this warrant, and what similar or ulterior proceedings might have been adopted by the parliament relative to the other colonies, were intercepted by its own dissolution, and the convergence of the whole authority of the English commonwealth in the powerful hands of Oliver Cromwell.[2] [1653.]

The ascendency of this great usurper (the perfidious servant, yet magnanimous master, of his country) proved highly beneficial to all the American colonies, except Maryland, where, unfortunately, it was rendered instrumental to much injustice, discord, and confusion. Rhode Island, immediately after his elevation to the protectorate, resumed the form of government which the parliament had recently suspended; and, by the decisive vigor of his interference, the people of Connecticut and New Haven were relieved from the apprehensions they had long entertained of the hostile designs of the Dutch colonists of New York. All the New England States were thenceforward exempted from the operation of the parliamentary ordinance against trade with foreign nations; and both their commerce and their security were promoted by the conquest, which the protector's arms achieved, of the province of Acadia from the French. But it was Massachusetts that occupied the highest place in his esteem; and to the inhabit-

were sent to New England by Charles the Second asserted, in their narrative, that the colonists of Massachusetts solicited Cromwell to declare it an independent state. Hutchinson's *Collection of Papers.* This is a very improbable statement, and was suggested, perhaps, by misrepresentation or misapprehension of the circumstances related in the text. The publication of Governor Winthrop's *Journal* has now clearly proved that the leading men in Massachusetts entertained from the beginning a considerable jealousy of parliamentary jurisdiction. " In 1641," says Winthrop, " some of our friends in England wrote to us advice to send over some to solicit for us in the parliament,— giving us hopes that we might obtain much; but, consulting about it, we declined the motion for this consideration,— that, if we should put ourselves under the protection of the parliament, we must then be subject to all such laws as they should make, or, at least, such as they might impose upon us; in which course, though they should intend our good, yet it might prove very prejudicial to us." Hence it is obvious, that the people of New England, in acknowledging the supremacy of parliament, had respect to it, not as a legislative body, but as administering the functions of supreme executive power. They never willingly admitted that the mother country possessed a legislative control over them; or that, in forsaking her shores, they left behind them an authority capable of obstructing or defeating the objects of their migration.

[1] This year, Massachusetts lost its eminent preacher and patriarch, John Cotton. Finding himself dying, he sent for the magistrates and ministers of the colony, and, with much solemnity and tenderness, bade them farewell for a while.

[2] Chalmers.

ants of this settlement he earnestly longed to impart a dignity of civil condition corresponding to the elevation which he believed them to enjoy in the favor of the great Sovereign of the universe. The reasons for which they had declined his offer of a settlement in Ireland, however likely to obtain his acquiescence, were still more calculated to enlarge his regard for a people who were actuated by such generous considerations. When his arms had achieved the conquest of Jamaica, he conceived the project of transplanting the colonists of Massachusetts to that island [1655] ; and, with this view, he represented to them, that, by establishing themselves and their principles in the West Indies, they would carry the sword of the gospel into the very heart of the territories of popery, and that consequently they ought to deem themselves as strongly invited to this ulterior removal, as they had been to their original migration. He endeavoured to incite them to embrace this project by assurances of the countenance and support which he would extend to them, and of the amplest delegation of the powers of government in their new settlement, as well as by descanting on the rich productions of the torrid zone, with which their industry would be rewarded ; and with these considerations he blended an appeal to their conscience, in pressing them to fulfil, in their own favor, the promise of the Almighty *to make his people the head, and not the tail*.[1] He not only urged these views upon the agents and correspondents of the colonists in England, but despatched one of his own confidential officers to Massachusetts to solicit their compliance with his proposal. But the colonists were exceedingly averse to abandon a country where they found themselves happy and in possession of a sphere of increasing usefulness and virtue ; and the proposal was the more unacceptable to them from the unfavorable reports they received of the climate of Jamaica. The General Court, accordingly, returned an address, declining, in the name of their fellow-citizens, to embrace the protector's offer [1656], and withal beseeching his Highness not to impute their refusal to indifference to his service, or an ungrateful disregard of his concern for their welfare.[2] Thus, happily for themselves, were the colonists, on two several occasions, deterred from acceding to the proposals of Cromwell for the advancement of their welfare and dignity. Had they removed to Ireland, they would have incurred in the sequel a diminution both of happiness and liberty ; had they proceeded to Jamaica, they would have been exposed, amidst the prevalence of negro slavery, to circumstances highly unfavorable to piety and virtue. In the mind of Cromwell, a vehement ardor was singularly combined with the most profound and deliberate sagacity ; and enthusiastic sentiments were not unfrequently blended with politic considerations, in proportions which it is little likely that he himself was aware of, or that any remote spectator of his actions can accurately adjust. It is obvious, on the one hand, that his propositions to the colonists were connected with the securer establishment of his own dominion in Ireland and the preservation of his conquest in the West Indies. But it is equally certain, on the other hand, that the colonists incurred neither his displeasure, nor even abatement of

---

[1] He alluded, I suppose, to Deuteronomy xxviii., 13.

[2] Hutchinson. Chalmers. Hazard. A similar answer was returned by New Haven to a similar application from the protector. Trumbull. There were not wanting some wild spirits among the colonists, who relished Cromwell's proposals. The notorious Venner, who headed the insurrection of the *Fifth Monarchy Men* in England after the Restoration, was for some time an inhabitant of Salem, and prevailed with a party of zealots there to unite in a scheme of emigration to the West Indies. But the design was discouraged by the clergy, and intercepted by the magistrates. Oldmixon.

his cordial regard, by thus refusing to promote schemes on which he was strongly bent. Nay, so powerfully had they captivated his steady heart, that they retained his favor, even while their intolerance discredited the independent principles which he and they united in professing ; and none of the complaints against them, with which he was long assailed by the Anabaptists and Quakers, whose conduct and treatment in the colony we are now to consider, could ever deprive the people of the place they had gained in the protector's esteem.

The colonists had been of late years involved occasionally in hostilities with some of the Indian tribes, and in disputes with the Dutch; by whose machinations they suspected that the Indians were prompted to attack them. But these events were productive of greater alarm than injury ; and by far the most serious troubles with which the colonists were infested arose from religious dissensions. Of all the instances of persecution that deform the history of New England, the most censurable in its principle, though happily also the least inhuman in the severity to which it mounted, was the treatment inflicted on the Anabaptists by the government of Massachusetts. The first apparition of these sectaries in the province occurred in the year 1651, when, to the great astonishment and concern of the community, seven or eight persons, of whom the leader was one Obadiah Holmes, professed the Baptist tenets, and separated from the congregation to which they had previously belonged, protesting that they could no longer take counsel, or partake divine ordinances, with unbaptized men, as they pronounced all the other inhabitants of the province to be. The peculiar doctrine which thus unexpectedly sprung up was at that time regarded with extreme aversion and jealousy, on account of the horrible enormities wherewith the first professors of it in Germany had associated its repute ;[1] and no sooner did Holmes and his friends establish a Baptist conventicle in Massachusetts, than complaints of their conduct, as a scandalous and intolerable nuisance, came pouring into the General Court from all quarters of the colony.

From the tenor of these complaints, it is manifest that the minds of the colonists were strongly impressed with the recollection of the licentious sentiments and infamous practices by which the wretched Boccold and his insane followers at Munster had sullied and discredited the Baptist tenets ; and that the bare profession of these tenets was calculated to awaken suspicions of the grossest immorality of conduct. Holmes was accused of having dishonored the Almighty, not only by dividing his people and resisting his ordinance, but by the commission of profligate impurities, and the gross indecency with which, it was alleged, the rite distinctive of his sect was administered. It is admitted by the provincial historians, that no sufficient evidence was adduced in support of these latter charges. The Court refused to hearken to the plea of liberty of conscience in behalf of Holmes and his followers, but, in the first instance, exerted its authority no farther against their persons, than to adjudge that they should desist from their unchristian separation ; and they were permitted to retire, having first, however, publicly declared that they were determined to pursue the dictates of their conscience, and to obey God rather than man. Some time after, they were apprehended on a Sunday, while attending the ministry of one Clarke,

---

[1] See Robertson's *History of Charles the Fifth.* The primitive Anabaptists have been not unhappily termed the Jacobins of the Reformation. Violence and exaggeration, prejudicial alike to the interests of religion and liberty, are incident to all great awakenings and revolutions of human sentiment and opinion.

a Baptist, from Rhode Island, who had come to propagate his tenets in Massachusetts. The constables who took them into custody carried them to one of the Congregational churches, where Clarke put on his hat as soon as the clergyman began to pray. Clarke, Holmes, and another were sentenced to pay small fines, or to be flogged ; and thirty lashes were actually inflicted on Holmes, who resolutely persisted in choosing a punishment that would enable him to evince the constancy with which he could suffer for the rights of conscience and the defence of what he conceived to be truth. A law was at the same time passed, subjecting to banishment from the colony every person who should openly condemn or oppose the baptism of infants, — who should attempt to seduce others from the practice or approbation of infant baptism, — or ostentatiously depart from a church when that rite was administered, — " *or deny the ordinance of the magistracy, or their lawful right or authority to make war.*" [1]

From these last words, it seems that the Baptists (naturally, or at least naturally accounted, inimical to the authority of their oppressors) either held, or were reputed to hold, along with the proper tenets from whence they derived their denomination, principles opposed to the acknowledgment of magisterial power and authority. In addition to this, we are assured by Cotton Mather, that it was the practice of the Baptists, in order to multiply their partisans, and manifest their contempt for the ecclesiastical institutions of the colonists, to admit the fellowship of all persons whom the established churches in New England had excommunicated for licentiousness of conduct, and even to appoint such persons administrators of the sacramental rites. Yet, even with these and other extenuating considerations, it is impossible to acquit the government of Massachusetts of having violated in this instance the rights of conscience, and molested men for the fidelity with which they adhered to what they firmly believed to be the will of God, in relation to a matter purely ecclesiastical.[2] The greediness with which every collateral charge against the Baptists was received in the colony, and the passionate impatience with which their claim of toleration was rejected, forcibly indicate the illiberality and delusion by which their persecutors were governed ; and may suggest to the Christian philosopher a train of reflections, no less instructive than interesting, on the self-deceit by which men commonly infer the honesty of their convictions, and the rectitude of their proceedings, from that resentful perturbation which far more truly indicates a latent consciousness of injustice and inconsistency.

It is mortifying to behold such tares spring up in a field already so richly productive of missionary exertion and other fruits of genuine and exalted piety. The severities that were employed proved in the sequel incompetent to restrain the spread of the Baptist tenets ; though for the present the professors of these doctrines appear to have either desisted from holding separate assemblies, or to have retired from Massachusetts. Some of them repaired to England, and complained to Cromwell of the persecution they

---

[1] Mather. Neal.

[2] The Baptists who were exiled from Massachusetts were allowed to settle in the colony of Plymouth (Hutchinson), — whence it may be inferred that they did not in reality profess (as they were supposed by the people of Massachusetts to do) principles adverse to civil subordination. This charge against them probably originated in the extravagance of a few of their own number, and the impatience and injustice of their adversaries.

The government of Massachusetts was by no means inquisitorial in its intolerance. Dunster, the first president of Harvard College, was deprived of this office, not for entertaining, but for refusing to desist from teaching, the Baptist tenets which he had embraced. Peirce.

had undergone ; but, instead of espousing their sentiment, he rejected their supplication, and applauded the conduct of the provincial authorities.[1]

The treatment which the Quakers experienced in Massachusetts was much more severe, but certainly much more justly provoked. It is difficult for us, in the calm and rational deportment of the Quakers of the present age, to recognize the successors of those wild enthusiasts who first appeared in the North of England, about the year 1644, and received from the derision of the world the title which they afterwards adopted as their sectarian denomination. In the mind of George Fox, the collector of this sect, and the founder of its system of faith, there existed a singular mixture of Christian sentiment and doctrinal truth with a deep shade of error and delusion. Profoundly pious and contemplative, but constitutionally visionary and hypochondriacal, he at first suspected that the peculiarities of his mental impressions might be derived from some malady which human science or friendly suggestion could remove ; and an old clergyman, to whom he applied for counsel, advised him to attempt a cure of what was spiritual in his disorder by singing psalms, and of what was bodily by smoking tobacco.[2] Fox rejected both parts of the prescription, as unsuitable to his condition, because disagreeable to his taste ; and being now convinced that others were incapable of understanding his case, he took it entirely into his own hands, and resolved to study, cherish, and cultivate the vague, mysterious motions of his spirit, — in short, to follow the impulse of his restless humor as far as it would lead him. Unsuspicious of morbid influence, or of the deceitfulness of his own imagination, he yielded implicit credence to every suggestion of his mind, mistook every impulse for inspiration, and was given up in an amazing degree to delusions, which, by prayer to the Almighty, he might have been enabled to overcome and dispel. Yet the powerful hold which the Scriptures had already taken of his mind, and the strong determination towards solid and genuine piety which his spirit thence derived, prevented him from personally wandering into the same monstrous extravagance which the conduct of many of his associates and disciples too soon disclosed. In his *Journal* (one of the most curious and interesting productions of the human mind), he has faithfully related the influence which his tenets produced on the sentiments and conduct both of himself and his followers. This singular record displays, in many parts, a wonderful depth of thought and keenness of penetration, together with numberless examples of that delusion, by which its author mistook a strong perception of wrong and disorder in human nature and civil society for a supernatural vocation and power to rectify whatever he deemed amiss. He relates with deliberate approbation various instances of contempt of decency and order in his own conduct, and of insane and disgusting outrage in that of his followers ; and though he reprobates the frenzy of some whom he denominates *Ranters*, it is not easy to discriminate between the extravagance which he sanctions and that which he condemns. Amidst much darkness, there glimmers a bright and beautiful ray of religious truth ; many passages of Scripture are illustrated with happy sagacity ; and labors of zeal and piety, of courage and integrity, are recorded, that would do honor to the ministry of an inspired apostle. That his personal character was elevated and excellent in an unusual degree appears from the impression it produced on the minds of all who approached him. Penn and Barclay, in particular, who to the most eminent virtue

---

[1] Hutchinson.   [2] Fox's *Journal*.

added talents and accomplishments of the first order, regarded Fox with the warmest love and veneration.[1] He was, perhaps, the only founder of any religious sect or order, in whom no lust of power, no lurking sentiment of selfish or ambitious aspiration, was ever discovered.

It was this man who first embraced and promulgated those tenets which have subsisted ever since as the distinctive principles of Quaker doctrine, — that the Holy Spirit, instead of operating (as the generality of Christians believe it in all ordinary cases to do) by insensible control of the bent and exercise of our faculties, acts by direct and cognizable impulse on the spirit of man ; that its influence, instead of being obtained in requital or accompaniment of believing prayer to God, is procured by an introversion of the intellectual eye upon the mind, where it already resides, and in the stillness and watchful attention of which the hidden spark will blaze into a clear inward light and sensible flame ; and that the Holy Spirit, instead of simply opening the minds of men to understand the Scriptures and receive their testimony, can and does convey instruction independently of the written word, — and communicate knowledge which is not to be found in the pages of holy writ. The Quaker regulations with respect to plainness of speech and apparel, abstinence from music and other amusements, and general simplicity of manners, are too well known and too little pertinent to our purpose, to require that they should here be particularly described. We may, however, with propriety remark, that the precepts injunctive of plainness of apparel received very early a practical interpretation in some respects contradictory of their own intendment. Forbidden to court an arrogant distinction by fineness of apparel, the Quakers soon procured to themselves a distinction, ridiculous indeed, yet of great and mixed importance, by adopting and retaining the plainest garb exemplified by the tasteless fashion of one particular age ; and, instead of the modesty of simple attire, challenged the general gaze by ostentatious adherence to a sectarian *uniform* or *livery*. The doctrinal errors to which we have alluded have never been renounced by the Quakers, though their practical influence has long since abated, and, indeed, had considerably declined before the end of that century in the middle of which they arose. In proportion as they have been cultivated and practically regarded, has been the progress of the sect into pestilent heresy of opinion, wild delusion of fancy, and outrageous extravagance of conduct; in proportion as they have subsided into mere theoretical speculation, has been the ascendency which real piety or rational and philosophical principle has obtained over the minds of the Quakers.

Even in the present day, we behold the evil influence of those erroneous doctrines, in the frequently silent meetings of the Quakers, in the license which they give to women to assume the office of teachers in their church, and in the rejection of the sacraments so distinctly instituted and enjoined in Scripture. But when the doctrines of Quakerism were first promulgated, the effects which they produced on many of their votaries far exceeded the influence to which modern history restricts them, or which the experience of a rational and calculating age finds it easy to conceive. In England, at that time, the minds of men were in a state of feverish agitation and excitement, inflamed with the rage of innovation, strongly imbued with religious sentiment, and yet strongly averse to restraint. The bands that so long repressed liberty of speech being suddenly broken, many crude thoughts were

---

[1] See Note VIII., at the end of the volume.

eagerly broached, and many fantastic notions that had been vegetating in the unwholesome shade of locked bosoms were abruptly brought to light ; and all these were presented to the souls of men roused and whetted by civil war, kindled by great alarms or by vast and indeterminate designs, and latterly so accustomed to partake or contemplate the most surprising changes, that with them the distinction between speculation and certainty was considerably effaced. The Presbyterians alone, or nearly alone, were generally willing to submit to, as well as to impose, restraint on the lawless license of speculation ; and to them the doctrines of Quakerism, from their earliest announcement, were the objects of unmixed disapprobation and even abhorrence. But to many other persons, this new scheme, opening a wide field of enthusiastic conjecture, and presenting itself without the restrictive accompaniment of a creed, exhibited irresistible attractions, and it rapidly absorbed a great variety of human character and feeling.

Before many years had elapsed, the numbers of the Quakers were enlarged, and their tenets, without being substantially altered, were moulded into a more systematic shape, by such an accession of philosophical votaries, as, in the early ages of the church, Christianity itself derived from the pretended adoption and real adulteration of its doctrines by the disciples of the Alexandrian school of Platonic philosophy. But it was the wildest and most enthusiastic visionaries of the age, whom Quakerism counted among its earliest votaries, and to whom it afforded a sanction and stimulus to the boldest excursions of unregulated thought, and a principle that was adduced to consecrate the rankest absurdity of conduct. And, accordingly, these sectarians, who have always professed and inculcated the maxims of inviolable peace, — who, not many years after, were accounted a society of philosophical deists, seeking to pave the way to a scheme of *natural religion*, by allegorizing the distinguishing articles of the Christian faith, — and who are now in general remarkable for a guarded composure of language, an elaborate stillness and precision of demeanour, and a peculiar remoteness from every active effort to make proselytes to their distinctive tenets, — were, in the commencement of their sectarian history, the most impetuous zealots and inveterate disputers ; and in their eagerness to proselytize the world, and to launch testimony from the fountain of oracular truth, which they supposed to reside within their own bosoms, against a regular ministry which they called a priesthood of Baal, and against the sacraments which they termed carnal and idolatrous observances, many of them committed the most revolting blasphemy, indecency, and disorderly outrage.[1] The unfavorable impression which these actions created long survived the extinction of the frenzy and folly that produced them.

While, in pursuance of their determination to proselytize the whole world, some of the Quakers travelled to Rome, in order to illuminate the pope, and others to Constantinople, for the purpose of converting the Grand Turk, — a party of them embarked for America and established themselves in Rhode Island, where persons of every religious (Protestant) denomination

---

[1] The frenzy that possessed many of the Quakers had reached its height in the year 1656, the very year in which the Quakers first presented themselves in Massachusetts. See the proceedings in the House of Commons against James Naylor, a Quaker, for blasphemy. Howell's *State Trials.* This unhappy person represented himself as the redeemer of the human race. Some particulars of his frenzy are related in Note VIII., at the end of the volume. He lived to recant his errors, and even write sensibly in defence of the Quakers, who were by this time increasing in respectability, and were yet magnanimous enough to acknowledge as a friend and associate the man who had done such disservice to their cause.

were permitted to settle in peace, and no one gave heed to the sentiments or practices of his neighbours. From hence they soon made their way into the Plymouth territory, where they succeeded in persuading some of its inhabitants to embrace the doctrine that a sensible experience of inward light and spiritual impression was the meaning and end of Christianity, and the essential characteristic of its votaries, — and to oppose all regulated order, forms, and discipline, whether civil or ecclesiastical, as a vain and judaizing substitution of the *kingdom of the flesh* for the *kingdom of the spirit.* On their first appearance in Massachusetts [July, 1656], where two male and six female Quakers arrived from Rhode Island and Barbadoes, they found that the reproach entailed on their sect by the insane extravagance of some of its members in England had preceded their arrival, and that they were regarded with the utmost terror and dislike by the great bulk of the people. They were instantly arrested by the magistrates, and diligently examined for what were considered bodily marks of witchcraft. No such indications having been found, they were sent back to the places whence they came, by the same vessels that had brought them, and prohibited with threats of severe punishment from ever again returning to the colony. A law was passed at the same time, subjecting every ship-master importing Quakers or Quaker writings to a heavy fine ; adjudging all Quakers who should intrude into the colony to stripes and labor in the house of correction, and all defenders of their tenets to fine, imprisonment, or exile.

The four associated States adopted this law, and urged the authorities of Rhode Island to coöperate with them in stemming the progress of Quaker opinions ; but the assembly of this settlement wisely replied, that they could not punish any man for declaring his mind with regard to religion ; that they were much incommoded by the presence of the Quakers, and the tendency of their doctrines to unsettle the relations of mankind and dissolve the bonds of society ; but that they found that the Quakers delighted to encounter persecution, speedily sickened of a patient, uncontradicting audience, and had already begun to loathe Rhode Island as a scene in which their talent of heroic endurance was ingloriously buried.[1] It is much to be lamented that the counsel insinuated in this good-humored reply was not embraced. The penal enactments resorted to by the other settlements served only to inflame the impatience of the Quaker zealots to carry their ministry into places that seemed to them to stand so greatly in need of it ; and the persons [2] who had been disappointed in their first attempt returned almost im-

<hr>

[1] Gordon and other writers have represented the letter from Rhode Island to Massachusetts as conveying a dignified rebuke of intolerance, and have quoted a passage to this effect, which they have found somewhere else than in the letter itself. We shall find, in the sequel, that the forbearance exerted by the government of that province towards the Quakers did not last many years.

Roger Williams, who contributed to found the State of Rhode Island, endeavoured, some years after this period, by challenging certain of the leaders of the sect, who had come from England on a mission to their brethren, to hold a public disputation with him on their tenets. They eagerly accepted his challenge ; and their historians assure us, that the disputation, which lasted for several days, ended " in a clear conviction of the envy and prejudice of the old man." Gough and Sewell's *History of the Quakers*. It is more probable, that, like other public disputations, it ended as it began. Williams never doubted that it had issued in his own favor, and signalized his triumph by publishing a book bearing the incourteous title of *George Fox digged out of his Burrow ;* to which Fox promptly replied by a publication entitled, *A New England Firebrand quenched, being an Answer to a lying, slanderous Book by one Roger Williams, confuting his blasphemous Assertions.* Eliot's *New England Biography.*

[2] Except one of the women, Mary Fisher, who travelled to Adrianople, and had an interview with the Grand Vizier, by whom she was received with courteous respect. Bishop, the

mediately to Massachusetts, and, dispersing themselves through the colony, began to proclaim their mystical notions, and succeeded in communicating them to some of the inhabitants of Salem. They were soon joined by Mary Clarke, the wife of a tailor in London, who announced tha she had forsaken her husband and six children in order to convey a message from heaven, which she was commissioned to deliver to New England. Instead of joining with the provincial missionaries in attempts to reclaim the neighbouring savages from their barbarous superstition and profligate immoralities, or themselves prosecuting separate missions with a like intent, the apostles of Quakerism raised their voices in vilification of every thing that was most highly approved and revered in the doctrine and practice of the provincial churches. Seized, imprisoned, and flogged, — they were again dismissed with severer threats from the colony, and again they returned by the first vessels they could procure. The government and a great majority of the colonists were incensed at their stubborn pertinacity, and shocked at the impression which it had already produced on some minds, and which threatened to corrupt and subvert a system of piety, whose establishment, fruition, and perpetuation supplied their fondest recollections their noblest enjoyment, and most energetic desire. New punishments were introduced into the legislative enactments against the intrusion of Quakers and the profession of Quakerism [1657] ; and, in particular, the abscission of an ear was added to the former ineffectual severities. Three male Quaker preachers endured the rigor of this cruel law.

But all the exertions of the provincial authorities proved unavailing, and seemed rather to stimulate the zeal of the obnoxious sectaries to brave the danger and court the glory of persecution. Swarms of Quakers descended upon the colony ; and, violent and impetuous in provoking persecution, — calm, resolute, and inflexible in sustaining it, — they opposed their power of enduring cruelty to their adversaries' power of inflicting it ; and not only multiplied their converts, but excited a considerable degree of favor and pity in the minds of men, who, detesting the Quaker tenets, yet derived from their own experience a peculiar sympathy with the virtues of heroic patience, constancy, and contempt of danger. When the Quakers were committed to the house of correction, they refused to work ; when they incurred pecuniary fines, they refused to pay them. In the hope of enforcing compliance with its milder requisitions, the court adjudged two of those contumacious persons to be sold as slaves in the West Indies ; but as even this dismal prospect could not move their stubborn resolution, the court, instead of executing its inhuman threat, reverted to the unavailing device of banishing them beyond its jurisdiction. [1658.] It was by no slight provocations that the Quakers attracted these and additional severities upon themselves. Men trembled for the faith and morals of their families and their friends, when they heard the blasphemous denunciations that were uttered against the worship of " a carnal Christ," and when they beheld the frantic and indecent outrages that were prompted by the mystical impressions which the Quakers

---

Quaker, in his *New England Judged*, observes, that she fared better among heathens than her associates did among professing Christians. He was perhaps not aware that the Turks regard insane persons as inspired. But whether insane or not, she was not altogether divested of a prudential regard to her own safety ; for " when they asked her what she thought of their prophet Mahomet, she made a cautious reply, that she knew him not." Kelsey, another Quaker, displayed less prudence, and experienced less courtesy from the Turks. He preached in the streets of Constantinople to crowds who understood not one word of his language ; and by the advice of Lord Winchelsea, the English ambassador at the Porte, was punished by the Turkish authorities with the bastinado.

inculcated and professed to be guided by. In public assemblies and in crowded streets, it was the practice of some of the Quakers to denounce the most tremendous manifestations of divine wrath on the people, unless they forsook their carnal system. One of them, named Faubord, conceiving that he experienced a celestial encouragement to rival the faith and imitate the sacrifice of Abraham, was proceeding with his own hands to shed the blood of his son, when his neighbours, alarmed by the cries of the lad, broke into the house and prevented the consummation of this blasphemous atrocity. Others interrupted divine service in the churches by loudly protesting that *these* were not the sacrifices that God would accept ; and one of them illustrated this assurance by breaking two bottles in the face of the congregation, exclaiming, " Thus will the Lord break you in pieces ! " They declared that the Scriptures were replete with allegory, that the inward light was the only infallible guide to religious truth, and that all were *blind beasts and liars* who denied it.

The female preachers far exceeded their male associates in folly, frenzy, and indecency. One of them presented herself to a congregation with her face begrimed with coal-dust, announcing it as a pictorial illustration of *the black pox*, which Heaven had commissioned her to predict as an approaching judgment on all carnal worshippers. Some of them in rueful attire perambulated the streets, proclaiming the speedy arrival of an angel with a drawn sword to plead with the people ; and some attempted feats that may seem to verify the legend of Godiva of Coventry. One woman, in particular, entered stark naked into a church in the middle of divine service, and desired the people to take heed to her as a sign of the times, and an emblem of the unclothed state of their own souls ; and her associates highly extolled her submission to the inward light, that had revealed to her the duty of illustrating the spiritual nakedness of her neighbours by the indecent exhibition of her own person. Another Quakeress was arrested as she was making a similar display in the streets of Salem. The horror, justly inspired by these insane enormities, was inflamed into the most vehement indignation by the deliberate manner in which they were defended, and the disgusting profanity with which Scripture was linked in impure association with notions and behaviour at once ridiculous and contemptible. Among other singularities, the Quakers exemplified and inculcated the forbearance of even the slightest demonstration of respect to courts and magistrates ; they declared that governors, judges, lawyers, and constables were trees that cumbered the ground, and presently must be cut down, in order that the true light might have leave to shine and space to rule alone ; and they freely indulged every sally of distempered fancy which they could connect, however absurdly, with the language of the Bible. A Quaker woman, who was summoned by the provincial court to answer for some extravagance, being desired to tell where she lived, refused to give any other answer than that she lived in God, " for in him we live, and move, and have our being." Letters replete with coarse and virulent railing were addressed by other members of the sect to the magistrates of Boston and Plymouth. Such was the inauspicious outset of the Quakers in America, — a country, where, a few years after, under the guidance of sounder judgment and wiser sentiment and purpose, they were destined to extend the empire of piety and benevolence, and to found establishments that have been largely productive of happiness and virtue.

It has been asserted by some of the modern apologists of the Quakers, that these frantic excesses, which excited so much indignation and produced such tragical consequences, were committed, not by genuine Quakers, but by the *Ranters*, or wild separatists from the Quaker body. Of these Ranters, indeed, a very large proportion certainly betook themselves to America ; attracted chiefly by the glory of enduring persecution, — but in some instances, perhaps, by the hope of attaining among their brethren in that country a distinction from which they were excluded in England by the established preëminence of George Fox.[1] It is certain, however, that the persons whose conduct we have particularized assumed the name of Quakers, and traced all their absurdities to the peculiar Quaker principle of searching their own bosoms for sensible admonitions of the Holy Spirit, independent of the Scriptural revelation of divine will. And many scandalous outrages were committed by persons whose profession of Quaker principles was recognized by the Quaker body, and whose sufferings are related, and their frenzy applauded, by the pens of Quaker writers.[2]

Exasperated by the repetition of these enormities, and the extent to which the contagion of their radical principle was spreading in the colony, the magistrates of Massachusetts, in the close of this year [1658], introduced into the assembly a law, denouncing the punishment of death upon all Quakers returning from banishment. This legislative proposition was opposed by a considerable party of the colonists ; and various individuals, who would have hazarded their own lives to extirpate the heresy of the Quakers, solemnly protested against the cruelty and iniquity of shedding their blood. It was at first rejected by the assembly ; but finally adopted by the narrow majority of a single voice. In the course of the two following years [1659, 1660], this barbarous law was carried into execution on three separate occasions, — when four Quakers, three men and a woman, were put to death at Boston. It does not appear that any of these unfortunate persons were guilty of the outrages which the conduct of their brethren in general had associated with the profession of Quakerism. Oppressed by the prejudice created by the frantic conduct of others, they were adjudged to die for returning from banishment and continuing to preach the Quaker doctrines. In vain the court entreated them to accept a pardon on condition of abandoning for ever the colony from which they had been repeatedly banished. They answered by reciting the heavenly call to continue there, which, on various occasions, they affirmed, had sounded in their ears, in the fields and in their dwellings, distinctly syllabling their names, and whispering their prophetic office and the scene of its exercise.[3] When they were conducted to the scaffold, their

---

[1] One of the most noted of these separatists was John Perrot, who, in order to convert the pope, had made a journey to Italy, where he was confined for some time as a lunatic. This *persecution* greatly endeared him to the Quakers, and exalted him so much in his own esteem, that he began to consider himself more enlightened than George Fox. He prevailed with a considerable party among the Quakers to refrain from shaving their beards, and to reject the practice of uncovering their heads in the act of prayer, as a vain formality. Fox having succeeded, by dint of great exertions, in stemming these innovations, Perrot repaired to America, where he appears to have multiplied his absurdities, and propagated them among the Quakers to an amazing extent. Various missions were undertaken by George Fox and other English Quakers to reclaim their brethren in America from the errors of Perrot, who finally abandoned every pretence to Quakerism, and became a strenuous asserter of all the doctrines and observances against which he had formerly borne testimony. Gough and Sewell.

[2] See Note IX., at the end of the volume.

[3] The first Quakers, instead of following the injunction of our Saviour to his apostles, that when persecuted in one city they should flee to another, seem to have found strong attractions in the prospect of persecution. One of those who were put to death in Massachusetts

demeanour expressed unquenchable zeal and courage, and their dying declarations breathed in general a warm and affecting piety.[1]

These executions excited much clamor against the government; many
persons were offended by the exhibition of severities against which the establishment of the colony itself seemed intended to bear a perpetual testimony;
and many were touched with an indignant compassion for the sufferings of
the Quakers, that effaced all recollection of the indignant disgust which the
principles of these sectaries had previously inspired. The people began
to flock in crowds to the prisons, and load the unfortunate Quakers with
demonstrations of kindness and pity. The magistrates at first attempted to
combat the censure they had provoked, and published a vindication of their
proceedings, for the satisfaction of their fellow-citizens and of their friends
in other countries, who united in blaming them; but at length the rising sentiments of humanity and justice attained such general and forcible prevalence, as to overpower all opposition. On the trial of Leddra, the last of
the sufferers, another Quaker, named Wenlock Christison, who had been
banished with the assurance of capital punishment in case of his return, came
boldly into court with his hat on, and reproached the magistrates for shedding innocent blood. He was taken into custody, and soon after brought
to trial. Summoned to plead to his indictment, he desired to know by what
law the court was authorized to put him on the defence of his life. When
the last enactment against the Quakers was cited to him, he asked, who empowered the provincial authorities to make that law, and whether it were not
repugnant to the jurisprudence of England. The governor answered, with
little regard to sense or propriety, that an existing law in England appointed
Jesuits to be hanged. But Christison replied, that they did not even accuse
him of being a Jesuit, but acknowledged him to be a Quaker, and that there
was no law in England that made Quakerism a capital offence. The court,
nevertheless, overruled his plea, and the jury found him guilty. When sentence of death was pronounced upon him, he desired his judges to consider
what they had gained by their cruel proceedings against the Quakers. "For
the last man that was put to death," said he, "here are five come in his
room; and if you have power to take my life from me, God can raise up
the same principle of life in ten of his servants, and send them among you
in my room, that you may have torment upon torment." The magnanimous
demeanour of this man, who seems to have been greatly superior in understanding to the bulk of his sectarian associates, produced an impression
which could not be withstood. The law now plainly appeared to be unsupported by public consent, and the magistrates hastened to interpose between
the sentence and its execution. Christison and all the other Quakers who
were in custody were forthwith released and sent beyond the precincts of
the colony; and as it was impossible to prevent them from returning, only
the minor punishments of flogging and reiterated exile were employed. Even

declared, that, as he was holding the plough in Yorkshire, he was directed by a heavenly voice
to leave his wife and children, and repair to Barbadoes; but hearing of the banishment of the
Quakers from New England, and of the severe punishments inflicted on persons returning
there after banishment, he began to ponder on the probability of his receiving a spiritual direction to proceed thither, and very soon after received it accordingly. Tomkins's and Ken-
dall's *Lives, Services, and Dying Sayings of the Quakers.*

The woman who was executed was Mary Dyer, who, twenty years before, had been a fol
lower of Mrs. Hutchinson and a disturber of New England.

[1] There is a striking resemblance between the dying behaviour of these Quaker martyrs
and the sublime scene delineated in 2 Maccabees, vi. and vii.

these penal rigors were relaxed in proportion as the demeanour of the Quakers became more quiet and orderly ; and in the first year after the restoration of Charles the Second, the infliction of flogging was suspended by a
letter from the king to Governor Endicott[1] and the other magistrates of the
New England settlements, requiring that no Quakers should thenceforward
undergo any corporal punishment in America, but, if charged with offences
that were reckoned deserving of such severity, they should be remitted for
trial to England.   Happily the moderation of the provincial government was
more steady and durable than the policy of the king, who retracted his interposition in behalf of the Quakers in the course of the following year.

The persecution thus happily closed was not equally severe in all the New
England States ; the Quakers suffered most in Massachusetts and Plymouth,
and comparatively little in Connecticut and New Haven.   It was only in
Massachusetts that the inhuman law inflicting capital punishment upon them
was ever carried into effect.[2]   At a subsequent period, the laws relating to
vagabond Quakers were so far revived, that Quakers disturbing religious
assemblies, or violating public decency, were subjected to corporal chastisement.   But little occasion ever again occurred of executing these severities ;
the wild excursions of the Quaker spirit having generally ceased, and the
Quakers gradually subsiding into a decent and orderly submission to all the
laws except such as related to the militia and the support of the clergy, —
in their scruples as to which, the provincial legislature, with reciprocal
moderation, consented to indulge them.[3]

During the long period that had now elapsed since the commencement of
the civil war in Britain, the New England provinces experienced a steady
and vigorous growth, in respect both of the numbers of their inhabitants and
the extent of their territorial occupation.   The colonists were surrounded
with abundance of cheap and fertile land, and secured in the enjoyment of
that ecclesiastical estate which was the object of their supreme desire, and
of civil and political freedom.   They were exempted from the payment of
all taxes except for the support of their internal government, which was conducted with great economy ; and they enjoyed the extraordinary privilege
of importing commodities into England free from the duties which all other
importers were constrained to pay.   By the favor of Cromwell, too, the

---

[1] Endicott was in an especial degree the object of dislike to Charles the Second. Hutchinson relates that he had seen a letter from the secretary of state, some time after this period,
containing an intimation that " the king would take it well, if the people would leave out Mr.
Endicott from the place of governor."   But the people continued to elect him to this office as
long as he lived.   He died at the age of seventy-seven, in the year 1665, leaving behind him
the character of " a sincere Puritan."   Holmes.

[2] This law, though never executed in Connecticut, was embraced by the assembly of this
province, which also adjudged that " No food or lodging shall be afforded to a Quaker, Adam-
ite, or other heretic."   *Blue Laws of Connecticut*, Art. 13 and 14.

[3] Mather. Neal. Hutchinson. Chalmers. Hazard. Oldmixon. Oldmixon, who entertained
no predilection for either of the parties, has pronounced this impartial censure on the treatment which the Quakers experienced from the Puritan magistrates of New England.   " If the
Quakers ran about the streets, crying out against the sins of the people, there might have been
a mad-house set apart for them. If Deborah Wilson marched through Salem stark naked, the
hangman might have flogged her with the more advantage. I meet with some signs of frenzy
and folly in the rants and riots of the Quakers, but nothing for which they should have been
hanged ; and these New England magistrates acted like the ignorant surgeon, that knew no
way of curing a bad limb but by cutting it off."

My venerated friend, that illustrious Quaker philanthropist, William Allen, of London, in
the doctrinal and historical *Summary* prefixed to his edition of Woolman's *Journal*, has related
all the sufferings, without making any allusion to the offences, of either the Quakers or the
Ranters. He has also erroneously ascribed the first tolerating law in favor of the Quakers
to Massachusetts, instead of Connecticut.

ordinances by which the Long Parliament had restricted their commerce were not enforced ; and they continued to trade wherever they pleased. Almost all the peculiar circumstances, which thus combined to promote the prosperity of New England during the suspension of monarchy, contributed proportionally to overcast the prospects awakened by the Restoration. There was the strongest reason to expect an abridgment of commercial advantages, and to tremble for the security of religious and political freedom. Various other circumstances conspired to retard the recognition of the royal authority in New England.   On the death of Cromwell, the colonists were successively urged to recognize, first, his son Richard as protector, afterwards, the Long Parliament, which for a short time resumed its ascendency, and subsequently, the Committee of Safety, as the legitimate organs of sovereign power in England. But, doubtful of the stability of any of these forms of government, they prudently declined to commit themselves by positive declaration.   In the month of July [1660], a vessel, on board of which were Generals Whalley and Goffe, two of the late king's judges, arrived with intelligence of the restoration of Charles the Second ; but no authoritative or official communication of this event was received ; and England was represented as being in a very unsettled and distracted condition.   Massachusetts had no inducement to imitate Virginia in a premature declaration for the king ; and while farther intelligence was anxiously expected, Whalley and Goffe were permitted to travel through the province, and accept the friendly civilities which many persons tendered to them, and with which Charles afterwards bitterly reproached the colonists.[1]

At length, authentic tidings were obtained that the royal authority was firmly established in England [December, 1660], and that complaints against the colony of Massachusetts had been presented, by various royalists, Quakers, and other enemies of its policy or institutions, to the privy council and the houses of parliament.   The General Court was straightway convened, and an address voted to the king, in which, with considerable ability, and with that conformity which they studied to the language of Scripture, the colonists justified their whole conduct, tendered assurances of a dutiful attachment to their sovereign, and entreated his protection and favor, which they professed to expect the more confidently from one, who, having been himself a fugitive, was no stranger to the lot and the feelings of exiles. Having vindicated their proceedings against the Quakers, by an exposition of the heretical doctrines that were introduced, and of the seditious and indecent excesses that were committed by these sectaries, they expressed their entire readiness and earnest desire to defend themselves against every other charge that already had been, or in future might be, preferred against them.   " Let not the king hear men's words," they said ; " your servants are true men, fearers of God and the king, and not given to change, zealous of government and order, orthodox and peaceable in Israel.   We are not seditious as to the interest of Cæsar, nor schismatics as to matters of religion.   We distinguish between churches and their impurities ; between a living man, though not without sickness and infirmity, and no man.   Irregularities either in ourselves or others we desire may be amended.   We could not live without the worship of God ; we were not permitted the use of public worship, without such a yoke of subscription and conformity as we could not consent unto without sin.   That we might, therefore, enjoy divine wor-

---

[1] Hutchinson.   Chalmers.

ship without human mixtures, without offence either to God, or man, or our consciences, we, with leave, but not without tears, departed from our country, kindred, and fathers' houses, into this Patmos." They assimilated their secession from England to that of "the good old non-conformist Jacob" from Syria; but declared that "the providential exception of us thereby from the late wars and temptations of either party we account as a favor from God." They solicited the king to protect their ecclesiastical and civil institutions, protesting that they considered the chief value of the latter to consist in their subservience to the cultivation and enjoyment of religion.

A similar address was made to parliament; and letters were written to Lord Manchester, Lord Say and Seal, and other persons of distinction, who were known to be friends of the colony, soliciting their interposition in its behalf. Leverett, the agent for the colony at London, was instructed, at the same time, to use every effort in order to procure a continuance of the exemption from customs which the colonists had hitherto enjoyed. But before he had time to make any such vain attempt, the parliament had already established the duties of tonnage and poundage over every portion of the empire. This disappointment was softened by a gracious answer which was returned by the king to the provincial address, and was accompanied by an order for the apprehension of Whalley and Goffe. [1661.] So prompt a display of good-will and confidence excited general satisfaction; and a day of thanksgiving was appointed, to acknowledge the favor of Heaven in moving the heart of the king to incline to the desires of the people. With regard to Whalley and Goffe, the provincial authorities were greatly perplexed between the obligation of a duty which it was impossible to decline, and their reluctance to betray to a horrible fate two men who had lately been members of a government acknowledged and obeyed by the whole British empire, who had fled to New England as an inviolable sanctuary from royal vengeance, and were recommended to the kindness of the colonists by letters from the most eminent ministers of the Independent persuasion in the parent state. It is generally supposed, and is sufficiently probable, that intimation was privately conveyed to the fugitive regicides of the orders that had been received; and, although warrants for their apprehension were issued, and by the industry of the royalists a diligent search for their persons was instituted, they were enabled, by the assistance of their friends, by dexterous evasion from place to place, and by strict seclusion, to end their days in New England.[1]

But the apprehensions which the colonists had originally entertained of danger to their civil and ecclesiastical institutions were speedily reawakened by intelligence that reached them from England of the industrious malignity which was exerted in circulating the most unfavorable representations of their conduct, of the countenance that these representations received from the king, and of the vindictive and tyrannical designs against them which gen-

---

[1] Mather. Neal. Hutchinson. Chalmers. Small as was the number of royalists in Massachusetts, it was too great to enable the people to afford permanent shelter to Goffe and Whalley. But in New Haven there were no royalists at all; and even those who disapproved of the great action of the regicides regarded it (with more of admiration than abhorrence) as the error of noble and generous minds. Leet, the governor of New Haven, and his council, when summoned by the pursuers of Goffe and Whalley to assist in the apprehension of them, first consumed abundance of time in deliberating on the extent of their powers, and then protested, that, in a matter of such importance, they could not act without the orders of an assembly. The royalist pursuers, incensed at this answer, desired the governor to declare at once whether he owned and honored the king; to which he replied, "We do honor his Majesty; but we have tender consciences, and wish first to know whether he will own us." Trumbull.

eral opinion ascribed to the court.   It was reported that their commercial
intercourse with Virginia and the West India Islands was to be cut off;
that three frigates were preparing to sail from England, in order to facilitate
the introduction of arbitrary power ; and that this armament was to be accompanied by a governor-general, whose jurisdiction was to extend over all
the North American plantations. Apprehensions of these and other changes
at length prevailed so strongly in Massachusetts, as to produce a public
measure of very remarkable character.   The General Court, having proclaimed the necessity of promoting unity of spirit and purpose among the
colonists for the vindication of their provincial liberties, in consistence with
a dutiful recognition of the paramount authority of England, appointed a
committee of eight of the most eminent persons in the State to prepare a
report, ascertaining the extent of their rights and the limits of their obedience ; and shortly after [May, 1661], the Court, in conformity with the report of the committee, framed and published a series of declaratory resolutions expressive of their solemn and deliberate judgment on those important
subjects.   It was declared that the patent (under God) is the original compact and main foundation of the provincial commonwealth, and of its institutions and policy ; that the governor and company are, by the patent, a
body politic empowered to confer the rights of freemen ; and that the freemen so constituted have authority to elect annually their governor, assistants,
representatives, and all other officers ; that the magistracy, thus composed,
hath all requisite power, both legislative and executive, for the government
of all the people, whether inhabitants or strangers, without appeal, except
against laws repugnant to those of England ; that the provincial government
is entitled by every means, even by force of arms, to defend itself both by
land and sea against all persons attempting injury to the province or its inhabitants ; and that any imposition injurious to the provincial community,
and contrary to its just laws, would be an infringement of the fundamental
rights of the people of New England.   This firm and distinct assertion of
provincial rights was accompanied with a recognition of the duties to which
the people were engaged by their allegiance, and which, it was declaratorily
announced, consisted in preserving the colony as a dependency of the English crown, and preventing its subjection to any foreign prince ; in defending, to the utmost of their power, the king's person and dominions ; and in
maintaining the dignity and prosperity of the king and people, by punishing
crimes, and by propagating the gospel.[1]

These proceedings disclose without disguise or ambiguity the alarming
suspicions which the colonists entertained of the character and policy of
their new sovereign, and the firm determination with which they clung to the
dear-bought rights of which they anticipated an attempt to bereave them.
How far they are to be considered as indicating a settled purpose to resist
tyrannical aggression by force is a matter of uncertain conjecture.   It is not
improbable that the authors of them hoped, by strongly proclaiming their
rights, and suggesting the extremities which an attempt to violate them would
legally warrant and might eventually provoke, to deter the king from awakening, in the commencement of his reign, the recollection of a contest which

[1] Hutchinson. Chalmers. During the subsistence of the Commonwealth in England, John
Eliot, the missionary, on one occasion, so far overstepped his proper functions as to publish a
little treatise against monarchical government. The General Court of Massachusetts now
deemed it expedient to cite him before them to answer for this impugnation of regal authority.
Eliot acknowledged that he had acted rashly and culpably; and, desiring forgiveness, obtained it.
s *

had proved fatal to his father, — and which, if once rekindled, even to an extent so little formidable as a controversy with an infant colony implied, might soon become less unequal, by presenting an occasion of revival and exercise to passions hardly yet extinguished in England. If such were the views of the provincial leaders, the soundness of them was approved by the event. But, in the mean time, the provincial authorities, in order to manifest a dutiful subordination to the parent state, issued injunctions for the pursuit and apprehension of Goffe and Whalley, and publicly announced that no persons obnoxious to the laws of England, and flying from her tribunals, would receive shelter in a colony that acknowledged her supreme authority.

Having now declared the terms on which they recognized the dominion of the English crown, the General Court caused the king to be solemnly proclaimed as their undoubted prince and sovereign lord. They published, at the same time, an ordinance prohibiting all disorderly behaviour on the occasion, and commanding in particular that none should presume to drink his Majesty's health, "which," it was added, "he hath, in an especial manner, forbidden," — an injunction the most alien to the sentiments and habits of the king, and imputed to him on no better grounds than that drinking of healths was prohibited by the statutes of his colony of Massachusetts. This senseless practice had been offensive, on account of its heathen origin, to the more scrupulous of the Puritan planters, who were desirous in all things to study a literal and exclusive conformity to the revealed will of God, — and, accounting nothing unworthy of human regard that afforded occasion to exercise such conformity, finally prevailed to have the ceremonial of drinking healths interdicted by law. Though many of the colonists entertained little favor or respect for this regulation, yet almost all of them were desirous that the restoration of royal authority should not be signalized by a triumph over any, even the least important, of the provincial constitutions. Intelligence having arrived soon after of the progress of the complaints that were continually exhibited to the privy council against the colony, and an order at the same time being received from the king that deputies should be sent forthwith to England to make answer to those complaints, the Court committed this important duty to Simon Bradstreet, one of the magistrates, and John Norton, one of the ministers of Boston. [December, 1661.] These agents were instructed to vindicate the loyalty and justify the conduct of the colony ; to discover, if possible, what were the designs which the king meditated, or the apprehensions that he entertained ; and neither to do nor submit to any thing prejudicial to the provincial charter. They undertook their thankless office with great reluctance, and obtained before their departure a public assurance of being indemnified by the General Court for whatever damage they might sustain by detention of their persons or other maltreatment in England.[1]

Whether from the vigor and resolution which the recent conduct of the provincial government displayed, or from the moderation of the wise counsellors by whom Charles was then surrounded, promoted by the influence which Lord Say and some other eminent persons employed in behalf of the colony, the agents were received with unexpected favor, and were soon enabled to return to Boston [1662] with a letter from the king, confirming the provincial charter, and promising to renew it under the great seal, whenever this formality should be desired. The royal letter likewise announced an

---

[1] Hutchinson. Chalmers.

amnesty for whatever treasons had been committed during the late troubles, to all persons but those who were attainted by act of parliament, and who had fled, or might hereafter fly, to New England. But it contained other matters by no means acceptable to the colonists. It required that the General Court should pronounce all the ordinances that had been enacted during the abeyance of royalty invalid, and forthwith revise them and repeal every one that might seem repugnant to the royal authority; that the oath of allegiance should be duly administered to every person; that justice should be distributed in the king's name; that all who desired it should be permitted to use the *Book of Common Prayer*, and to perform their devotions according to the ceremonial of the church of England; that, in the choice of the governor and assistants, or counsellors, of the colony, the only qualifications to be regarded should be wisdom and integrity, without any reference to peculiarities of religious faith; and that all freeholders of competent estates, and not immoral in their lives, should be admitted to vote in the election of officers, civil and military, whatever might be their opinions with respect to forms of church-government. "We cannot be understood," it was added, "hereby to direct or wish that any indulgence should be granted to Quakers, whose principles being inconsistent with any kind of government, we have found it necessary, with the advice of our parliament here, to make a sharp law against them, and are well content you do the like there."[1]

However reasonable some of the foregoing requisitions may now appear, the greater number of them were highly disagreeable to the persons to whom they were addressed. The colonists considered themselves entitled to maintain the form of polity in church and state, which they had fled to a desert in order to cultivate, without the intrusion and commixture of different principles; and they regarded with the utmost jealousy the precedent of an interference with their fundamental constitutions by a prince, who, they were firmly persuaded, was aiming at present to enfeeble the system which he waited only a more convenient season to destroy. To comply with the royal injunctions, they apprehended, would be to introduce among their children the spectacles and corruptions which they had incurred the mightiest sacrifices in order to withdraw from their eyes; and to throw open every office in the state to Roman Catholics, Socinians, and every heretic and unbeliever who might think power worth the purchase of a general declaration that he was (according to his own unexamined interpretation of the term) a Christian. The king, never deserving, was never able to obtain, credit with his subjects for good faith or moderation; he was from the beginning of his reign suspected of a predilection for the church of Rome; and the various efforts which he made to procure a relaxation of the penal laws against the Protestant dissenters in England were jealously and censoriously regarded by all these dissenters themselves, — with the solitary exception of the Quakers, who considered the other Protestants and the Catholics as nearly on a level with each other, and were made completely the dupes of the artifices by which Charles and his successor endeavoured to introduce the ascendency of the Catholic church under the preliminary guise of universal toleration.

Of all the requisitions in the royal letter, the only one that was complied

---

[1] Hutchinson. Belknap. The royal invitation to persecute the Quakers was disregarded by the government of Massachusetts. Whether from greater deference to the king's pleasure or from some other cause, the government of Rhode Island, in the year 1665, passed an act of outlawry against the Quakers for refusing to bear arms. *Collections of the Massachusetts Historical Society.*

with was that which directed that judicial proceedings should be conducted in the king's name. The letter commanded that its contents should be published in the colony; which was accordingly done, — with an intimation, however, that the directions relative to political and ecclesiastical matters were reserved for the deliberate consideration which would be requisite to adjust them to the existing constitutions. The treatment which the provincial agents experienced from their countrymen, it is painful, but necessary, to relate. The ill-humor which some of the requisitions provoked was unjustly extended to these men ; and their merits, though at first gratefully acknowledged, were speedily forgotten. Impressed with the danger from which the colony had obtained a present deliverance, but which still impended over it from the designs of a prince who visibly abetted every complaint of its enemies, the agents increased their unpopularity by warmly urging that all the requisitions should be instantly and literally obeyed. Norton, who, on the first inofficial intelligence that was received of the king's restoration, had ineffectually counselled his fellow-citizens to proclaim the royal authority, — in now again pressing upon them a measure to which they were still more averse, went the length of declaring to the General Court, that, if they complied not with the terms of the king's letter, they must blame themselves for the bloodshed that would ensue. Such language was ill calculated to soothe the popular disquiet, or recommend an ungracious counsel ; and the deputies, who were actuated by the most disinterested zeal to serve, rather than flatter, their fellow-citizens, now found themselves opprobriously identified with the grievances of the colony, and heard the evils, which it was not in their power to prevent, ascribed to their neglect or unguarded concession. Bradstreet, endowed with a robust, philosophical temper, was the less moved by this ingratitude, and entertained his evil fortune without surprise or repining ; but Norton, who was a man of keen and delicate sensibility, could not behold the altered eyes of his countrymen without the most stinging sensations of grief and mortification. When he heard many say of him, that " *he had laid the foundation for the ruin of his country's liberty*," he expressed no resentment, but sunk into a profound and consuming melancholy. Vainly struggling with his anguish, and endeavouring to embrace his lot with patience and do his duty to the last, he died soon after of a broken heart. His death was regarded by the people as a public misfortune, and felt as a poignant reproach, and the universal mourning that overspread the province expressed a late but lasting remembrance of his virtue, and bewailed an ungrateful error, which only repentance was now permitted to repair.[1]

The colony of Rhode Island received the tidings of the restoration of royalty with much real or apparent satisfaction. It was hoped by the inhabitants that the suspension of their charter by the Long Parliament would more than compensate the demerit of having accepted a charter from such authority ; and that their exclusion from the confederacy, of which Massachusetts was the head, would operate as an additional recommendation to royal favor. The restored monarchical government was proclaimed with eager haste in this colony ; and Dr. John Clarke was employed as deputy from the colonists to carry their dutiful respects to the foot of the throne, and to solicit a new charter in their favor. The envoy conducted his negotiation with a suppleness of adroit servility that rendered the success of it

---

[1] Mather. Hutchinson. See Note X., at the end of the volume.

dearly bought. He not only vaunted in courtly strains the loyalty of the inhabitants of Rhode Island, of which not the slightest proof could be adduced, but meeting this year the deputies of Massachusetts at court, he publicly challenged them to cite any one demonstration of duty or loyalty by their constituents to the present king or his father, from the period of their first establishment in New England.[1] Yet the inhabitants of Rhode Island had solicited and accepted a patent from the Long Parliament in the commencement of its struggle with Charles the First ; while Massachusetts declined to make a similar recognition, even when the Parliament was at the utmost height of its power and success.[2] Clarke succeeded in obtaining, this year[3] [1662], a charter which assured to the inhabitants of Rhode Island and Providence the amplest enjoyment of religious liberty, and most unlimited concession of municipal jurisdiction. Certain of the leading colonists, together with all other persons who should in future be admitted freemen of the society, were incorporated by the title of the Governor and Company of the English Colony of Rhode Island and Providence. The supreme or legislative power was vested in an assembly, consisting of the governor, assistants, and representatives elected from their own number by the freemen. This assembly was empowered to enact legal ordinances, and establish forms of government and magistracy, with as much conformity to the laws and institutions of England as the state of the country and condition of the people would admit ; to erect courts of justice ; to regulate the manner of appointment to places of trust ; to inflict all lawful punishments ; and to exercise the prerogative of pardon. A governor, deputy-governor, and ten assistants were to be annually chosen by the assembly ; and the first board of these officers, nominated by the charter, on the suggestion of the provincial agent, were authorized to commence the work of carrying its provisions into execution. The governor and company were empowered to transport all merchandise not prohibited by the statutes of the kingdom, on payment of the usual duties ; to exercise martial law, when necessary ; and, upon just causes, to invade and destroy the native Indians or other enemies. The territory, granted to the governor and company and their successors, was described as that part of the dominions of the British crown in New England, which embraced the islands in Narraganset Bay and the countries and districts adjacent, — which were appointed to be holden of the manor of East Greenwich in common soccage. The inhabitants and their children were declared to be entitled to the same immunities which would have accrued to them, if they had resided or been born within the realm. This is

[1] Mr. Bancroft has, with strange lack of courtesy and correctness, reproached me with having *invented* the charge I have preferred against Clarke. I am incapable of such dishonesty; and sincerely hope that Mr. Bancroft's reproach is, and will continue, on his part, a solitary instance of deviation from candor and rectitude.

With a mixture of pain and admiration, I have witnessed the displeasure with which some of the *literati* of Rhode Island have received my strictures on Clarke. The authorities they have cited prove undeniably that he was a true patriot and excellent man and well deserving the reverence of his natural and national posterity. But every person acquainted with history and human nature ought to know how apt even good men are to be transported beyond the line of honor and integrity, in conducting such negotiations as that which was confided to Clarke.

[2] The Rhode Islanders had also presented an address to the rulers of England in 1659, beseeching favor to themselves as "a poor colony, an outcast people, formerly from our mother nation in the bishops' days, and since from the New-English over-zealous colonies." Douglass's *Summary.*

[3] Although the charter was framed in 1662, yet, in consequence of a dispute between Connecticut and Rhode Island, it was not completed till July, 1663.

the first instance of the creation, by a British patent, of an authority of that peculiar description which was then established in Rhode Island. Corporations had been formerly constituted within the realm, for the government of colonial plantations ; but now a body politic was created with specific powers for administering all the affairs of a colony within the colonial territory itself. The charter was received with great satisfaction by the colonists, who entered immediately into possession of the democratical constitution which it appointed for them, and continued to pursue the same system of civil and ecclesiastical policy that they had heretofore observed.[1]

Though the inhabitants of Connecticut neither felt nor affected the same joy that Rhode Island expressed at the restoration of the king, they did not fail to send a deputy to England to express their recognition of the royal authority and to solicit a new charter.[2] They were fortunate in the choice of the man to whom they committed this important duty, — John Winthrop, the son of the eminent person of the same name who had presided with so much honor and virtue over the province of Massachusetts. Winthrop, deriving an hereditary claim on the kindness of the king from a friendship that had subsisted between his own grandfather and Charles the First,[3] employed it so successfully, as to obtain for his constituents a charter in almost every respect the same with that which was granted to Rhode Island. The most considerable differences were, that by the Connecticut charter the governor was directed to administer the oaths of allegiance and supremacy to the inhabitants, — a formality which was not required by the charter of Rhode Island, where many of the people scrupled to take an oath ; and that, by the last-mentioned charter, liberty of conscience was expressly conceded in its fullest extent, while the other made no express mention of the concerns of religion, and no other allusion to them than what might seem to be implied in the requisition of the oath of supremacy. [1662.] By this charter New Haven was united with Connecticut ; an arrangement which for some time did not obtain the unanimous approbation of the people of New Haven, although they afterwards heartily acquiesced in it ; and the description of the provincial territory was indefinite and incorrect. But on the whole it gave so much satisfaction, that Winthrop, on his return, was received with grateful approbation by his fellow-citizens, and annually chosen governor of the united colony as long as he lived.[4]

There was thus established by royal charter, both in Connecticut and

---

[1] Chalmers. Hazard.

[2] At New Haven the republican spirit was so strong, that several of the principal inhabitants declined to act as magistrates under the king. Trumbull. It was here that Goffe and Whalley found the securest asylum, and ended their days. When a party of royal officers were coming in pursuit of them to New Haven, Davenport, the minister of the place, preached publicly in favor of the regicides, from the text (Isaiah xvi. 3, 4), " Take counsel, execute judgment ; make thy shadow as the night in the midst of the noonday ; hide the outcasts ; bewray not him that wandereth. Let mine outcasts dwell with thee, Moab ; be thou a covert to them from the face of the spoiler." Holmes. It is remarkable that Salem and New Haven, so highly distinguished among the towns of New England by the Puritan and republican zeal of their founders, have so long continued to be graced by the superior piety, morality, industry, and prosperity of their inhabitants. Dwight's description of New Haven, in the commencement of the nineteenth century, is one of the most animating and agreeable pictures that were ever delineated of a social congregation of mankind. Dwight's *Travels*.

[3] Mather relates, that, when Winthrop presented the king with a ring which Charles the First had given to his grandfather, " the king not only accepted his present, but also declared that he accounted it one of his richest jewels ; which, indeed, was the opinion that New England had of the hand that carried it." Yet Charles had, little more than a year before, consigned to a horrid death Hugh Peters, the father-in-law of Winthrop. See Note XI., at the end of the volume.

[4] Mather. Chalmers. Hazard.

Rhode Island, a model of government the most perfectly democratic, together with the additional singularity of subordinate political corporations almost wholly disconnected by any efficient tie or relation with the organ of sovereign authority.   All power, as well deliberative as active, was vested in the freemen of the corporation or their delegates ; and the supreme executive magistrate of the empire was excluded from every constitutional means of interposition or control.   A conformity to the laws of England, no doubt, was enjoined on the provincial legislatures ; and this conformity was conditioned as the tenure by which their privileges were enjoyed ; but no method of ascertaining or enforcing its observance was provided.   At a later period, the crown lawyers of England were sensible of the oversight which their predecessors had committed ; and proposed that an act of parliament should be obtained, requiring those colonies to transmit the records of their domestic ordinances to Britain for the inspection and consideration of the king.   But this suggestion was never carried into effect.[1]

CHAPTER IV.

Emigration of ejected Ministers to New England. — Royal Commissioners sent thither. — Petition of the Assembly of Massachusetts to the King — rejected. — Policy pursued by the Commissioners. — Their Disputes with the Government of Massachusetts — and Return to England. — Policy of the Colonists to conciliate the King — Effects of it. — Cession of Acadia to the French. — Prosperous State of New England. — Conspiracy of the Indians. — Philip's War. — The King resumes his Designs against Massachusetts. — Controversy respecting the Right to Maine and New Hampshire. — Progress of the Dispute between the King and the Colony. — State of Parties in Massachusetts. — State of Religion and Morals in New England. — Surrender of the Charter of Massachusetts demanded by the King — refused by the Colonists. — Writ of Quo Warranto issued against the Colony. — Firmness of the People. — Their Charter adjudged to be forfeited.

ALTHOUGH New England now [1663] consisted of a variety of distinct social communities independent of each other, yet a common and harmonious policy was naturally engendered in societies founded by men acknowledging the same national origin, conducted to America by the same motives, and assimilated by religious tenets, manners, laws, and municipal institutions. The commercial system which the English parliament thought fit to pursue tended still farther to unite these colonies by identity of views, interests, and purposes.   The Navigation Acts which it framed, and which we have considered at much length in the history of Virginia, created for a time more discontent than inconvenience, and served rather to proclaim than to enforce the restrictions designed to be imposed on the colonial commerce.   These restrictions were a copious and continual source of displeasure and controversy between the two countries.   The colonies had been accustomed in their infancy to a free trade ; and its surrender was required with the more injustice, and yielded with the greater reluctance, because England was not then a mart in which all the produce of the colonies could be vended, or from which all the wants of their inhabitants could be supplied.   Even in the southern colonies, where the governors were appointed either by the

---

[1] Chalmers.   " The charters of Rhode Island and Connecticut were carelessly given by a very careless monarch."   Macpherson's *Annals of Commerce.*

crown or by proprietaries closely connected with the parent state, the Act
of Navigation was very imperfectly executed ; and in New England, where
the governors were elected by the people, it appears, for a considerable
time, to have been entirely disobeyed.[1]

While the commercial system of the English parliament thus tended to
unite the colonies by community of interest and opposition to the parent
state, the ecclesiastical policy which now prevailed in England was calculated to promote among the colonists the remembrance of the original causes
of secession from her territory, and at once to revive their influence, and
recommend the exercise of toleration by sympathy with the victims of an
opposite principle. Charles the Second had obtained the assistance of the
English Presbyterians to his restoration by express and solemn promise of
an ecclesiastical constitution framed on a compromise between Episcopalian
and Presbyterian principles ; but by the advice, or at least with the cordial
approbation, of Lord Clarendon, he scrupled not to violate this engagement
as soon as he found himself securely established on the throne. In consequence of the rigorous execution of that shameless act of perfidy, the statute
of uniformity, in the close of the preceding year, about two thousand of the
English clergy, the most eminent of their order for learning, virtue, and
piety, were ejected from the established church ; and, to the astonishment
of the prevailing party, sacrificed temporal interest to the dictates of conscience. They were afterwards banished to the distance of five miles from
every corporation in England ; and many of them died in prison for privately
exercising their ministry in contravention of the law. While the majority
of them remained in Britain, to preserve by their instructions the decaying
piety of their native land, a considerable number were conducted to New
England, there to invigorate American virtue by a fresh example of conscientious sacrifice, and to form a living and touching memorial of the cruelty
and injustice of religious intolerance. The merits and the sufferings of
these men strongly excited the admiration and sympathy of the people of
New England ; and this year an invitation was despatched to Dr. John Owen,
one of the most eminent scholars and theologians that the world has ever
produced, to accept an ecclesiastical appointment in Massachusetts. Owen
declined to avail himself of this invitation, on account of the cloud of royal
displeasure which he perceived to be gathering against Massachusetts, and
the measures which he had reason to believe would ere long be adopted for
the subjugation of its civil and religious liberties. Other countries besides
America contended for the honor of sheltering this illustrious man from the
persecution of the church of England, and for the happiness and advantage
expected from his presence, example, and counsels ; for his character was
equal to his genius and learning. But he preferred suffering in a land of which
he fully understood the language, to enjoyment and honor among a people
with whom his communication must necessarily have been more restricted.
At a later period, when the presidency of Harvard College was offered to
him, he consented to embrace this sphere of useful and important duty ;
and having shipped his effects for New England, was preparing to accompany them, when his steps were arrested by an order from Charles, expressly
commanding him not to depart from the kingdom.[2]

The apprehension which the inhabitants of Massachusetts had entertained,
ever since the Restoration, of hostile designs of the English government,

[1] Chalmers.	[2] Neal. Hutchinson.

and which had been confirmed by the reasons assigned by Dr. Owen for refusing the first invitation they tendered to him, was strengthened by all the other intelligence they obtained from England. A great number of the ejected Non-conformist ministers who had made preparation for emigrating to Massachusetts now declined to settle in a country on which the extreme of royal vengeance was expected to descend ; and at length the most positive information was received, that Charles had openly avowed, that, although he was willing to preserve the provincial charter, he was nevertheless determined to institute an inquiry for the purpose of ascertaining how far the provisions of this charter had been practically observed. It was reported soon after, that the king had associated this object with the design which he cherished of provoking a quarrel with Holland ; and that for this double purpose he was preparing to despatch an expedition for the reduction of the Dutch settlement of New York, and meant to send along with it a board of commissioners empowered to investigate and judge (according to their own discretion) all complaints and disputes that might exist within New England, and to take every step they might judge necessary for settling the peace and security of the country on a solid foundation. In effect, a commission for these purposes, as well as for the reduction of New York, had already been issued by the king to Sir Robert Carr, Colonel Nichols, George Cartwright, and Samuel Maverick. This measure, conspiring with the reports that had long prevailed of the projects harboured by the court of England against the liberties of the colonists, was calculated to strike them with dismay. They knew that plausible pretexts were not wanting to justify a censorious view of certain parts of their conduct ; and they were firmly persuaded that the dislike and suspicion with which the king regarded them would never be satisfied by any measure short of the entire abrogation of their institutions.

Various controversies had arisen between the different settlements, concerning the boundaries of their respective territories ; and loud complaints were preferred by the representatives of Mason, and by Gorges, and other members of the old Council of Plymouth, of the occupation of districts and the exercise of jurisdiction to which these complainers pretended a preferable right. The claim of Mason to New Hampshire, derived from the assignment of the Plymouth Council, had never been expressly surrendered ; and Gorges's title to Maine was confirmed and enlarged by a grant from the late king, in the year 1639. As Gorges adhered to the royal cause in the civil wars, the death of the king produced the temporary demise of his patent ; both he and Mason's heirs had long abandoned their projects, in despair of ever prosecuting them to a successful issue. But now the restoration of royalty in England presented them with an opportunity of vindicating their claims ; and the congregation of inhabitants in the territories promised advantage from such vindication. They had as yet reaped no benefit from the money expended on their acquisitions ; but they now embraced the prospect, and claimed the right of the labors of others, who, in ignorance of their pretensions, had occupied and colonized a vacant soil, and held it by the right of purchase from its native proprietors. In addition to this formidable controversy, many complaints were preferred by royalists, Quakers, and Episcopalians, of abuses in the civil and ecclesiastical administration of Massachusetts. The investigation and adjustment of these complaints and controversies were the principal reasons assigned for the royal commission. But, doubtless, the main object of concern to the English

T

court was the suppression or essential modification of institutions founded and administered on principles that had so long warred with monarchy, and so recently prevailed over it. The colonists readily believed the accounts they received from their friends in England of this hostile disposition of their sovereign ; and the proclamation by which they cautioned the enemies of his government not to expect shelter in Massachusetts was intended to remove or appease it. When intelligence was received of the expected visitation from England, the General Court of Massachusetts appointed a day of solemn fast and prayer throughout its jurisdiction, in order to implore the mercy of God under their many distractions and troubles ; and deeming it a point of the highest importance that the patent or charter should be kept " safe and secret," they ordered their secretary to bring it into court, and deliver it to four of the members, who were directed to dispose of it in such manner as they should judge most conducive to its secure preservation. Aware of the profane, licentious manners of European sailors and soldiers, and reflecting on the peculiar strictness of the provincial laws, the Court adopted at the same time the most prudent precautions for preventing the necessity of either a hazardous enforcement or a pusillanimous suspension of its municipal ordinances.[1]

On the arrival of the royal armament at Boston in the following year [1664], the commissioners exhibited their credentials to the governor and council, and demanded, in the first instance, that a troop of provincial militia should be embodied to accompany the English forces in the invasion of New York. Endicott, the governor, neither relishing the enterprise, nor empowered by the forms of the provincial constitution to levy forces without express permission from the General Court, judged it necessary to convoke this body ; but the commissioners, who had not leisure to await its deliberations, proceeded with the fleet against New York, desiring that the provincial auxiliaries should follow as quickly as possible, and signifying to the governor and council that they had much important business to transact with them on their return from New York, and that in the mean time the General Court would do well to bestow a fuller consideration than they seemed yet to have done on the letter which the king addressed to them two years before. The vague, mysterious terms of this communication were certainly calculated, and would seem to have been deliberately intended, to increase the disquiet and apprehensions of the colonists. That they produced this impression is manifest from the transactions that ensued in the General Court.

On the assembling of this body, it was declared by an immediate and unanimous vote, that they were " resolved to bear true allegiance to his Majesty, and to adhere to a patent so dearly obtained and so long enjoyed by undoubted right." In compliance with the requisition of the commissioners, they equipped a regiment of two hundred men, who were preparing to embark for New York, when intelligence arrived that the place had already surrendered, and that the junction of the English and provincial forces was no longer necessary. The assembly then resumed consideration of the king's letter, which was so emphatically commended to their attention ; and passed a law extending the elective franchise to all the inhabitants of English or provincial birth, paying public rates to a certain amount, and attested by a minister as orthodox in their religious principles and not im-

---

[1] Hutchinson. Belknap. Sullivan. Hazard.

moral in their lives, whether within or without the pale of the established church.   They next proceeded to frame and transmit to the king a petition strongly expressive of their present apprehensions and their habitual sentiments.   They represented at considerable length the dangers and difficulties they had encountered in founding and rearing their settlement ; the explicit confirmation which their privileges had received, both from the reigning monarch and his predecessor ; and their own recognition of royal authority, and willingness to testify their allegiance in every righteous way.   They expressed their concern at the appointment of four commissioners, one of whom (Maverick) was their known and professed enemy, who were vested with an indefinite authority, in the exercise of which they were to be guided, not by the known rules of law, but by their own discretion ; and they declared, that even the little experience which already they had obtained of the dispositions of these persons was sufficient to assure them that the powers conferred by the commission would be employed to the complete subversion of the provincial constitution.   If any advantage was expected from the imposition of new rules and the infringement of their liberties, the design, they protested, would produce only disappointment to its authors ; for the country was so poor, that it afforded little more than a bare subsistence to its inhabitants, and the people were so much attached to their institutions, that, if deprived of them in America, they would seek them in new and more distant habitations ; and if they were driven out of their present territory, it would not be easy to find another race of inhabitants who would be willing to sojourn in it.[1] They averred, in a solemn appeal to God, that they came not into this wilderness in quest of temporal grandeur or advantage, but for the sake of a quiet life ; and concluded in the following strains of earnest anxiety :—" Let our government live, our patent live, our magistrates live, our laws and liberties live, our religious enjoyments live ; so shall we all yet have farther cause to say from our hearts, Let the king live for ever ! "

Letters suing for favor and friendly mediation were addressed at the same time to several of the English nobility, and particularly to the chancellor, Lord Clarendon.   But these applications were unsuccessful.   Clarendon was no friend to Puritan establishments ; he had instigated, or at least cordially abetted, the existing persecution against sectaries of every denomination in England ; and he was at present too painfully sensible of his declining credit with the king, to risk the farther provocation of his displeasure by moving the suit of a people whom the monarch disliked, and opposing a favorite scheme of royal policy.   In a letter to the provincial governor, he defended the commission as a constitutional exercise of royal power and wisdom, and a manifest indication of his Majesty's grace and goodness ; and advised the colonists, by a prompt submission, to deprecate the consequences of that indignation which their ungrateful clamor must already have excited in the breast of the king.   The answer of Charles, which was transmitted by Secretary Morrice, to the petition of the General Court, excited less surprise.   It reproached this assembly with making unreasonable and groundless complaints ; represented the commission as the only proper means

---

[1] It is curious to observe the expression of a similar sentiment by the inhabitants of the province of Aragon.   The preamble to one of the laws of Aragon declares that such was the barrenness of the country, that, but for the sake of the liberties by which they were distinguished from other nations, the people would abandon it, and repair in quest of a settlement to some more fruitful region.   Robertson's *History of Charles the Fifth.* Thucydides (B. I.) ascribes to the poverty of its soil the peculiar adherence of the Athenians to their country.

of rectifying the provincial disorders ; and affected to consider the petition as " the contrivance of a few persons who infuse jealousies into their fellow-subjects as if their charter were in danger."[1]

No sooner was the conquest of New York completed,[2] than the commissioners addressed themselves to the discharge of their civil functions in New England. One of the first official acts that they had occasion to perform was the adjustment of a dispute respecting boundaries, that arose out of the occupation of New York. [1665.] A patent had been granted to the Duke of York, of all the territory occupied or claimed by the Dutch, including large districts already comprehended in the charter of Connecticut. A controversy concerning limits was thus created by the act of the crown, between the State of Connecticut and the new province designated by the patent of the Duke of York. Their boundaries were now adjusted by the commissioners in a manner which appears to have been highly satisfactory to the people of Connecticut, but which entailed a great deal of subsequent dispute. Another controversy, in which Connecticut was involved, arose out of a claim to part of its territory preferred by the Duke of Hamilton, and other persons, in virtue of rights that had accrued to themselves or their ancestors as members of the Grand Council of Plymouth. The commissioners, desirous of giving satisfaction to both parties, adjudged the property of the disputed soil to these individual claimants, but declared that the municipal government of the territory appertained to Connecticut. It appears manifestly to have been their policy to detach the other New England States from the obnoxious province of Massachusetts, and to procure their cooperation (by the example of implicit submission on their own part, and the accumulation of complaints against that province) in the design of curtailing her liberties and altering her institutions. In the prosecution of this policy they were but partially successful. The people of Connecticut received the commissioners with frigid respect, and plainly showed that they disliked their mission, and regarded the cause of Massachusetts as their own. Nay, so strongly were they impressed with the danger to their liberties from the interposition of such arbitrary power, that some disagreements, which had arisen between Connecticut and New Haven, and hitherto prevented their union in conformity with the recent charter, were entirely composed by the mere tidings of the approach of the commissioners. At Plymouth the commissioners met with little opposition ; the inhabitants being deterred from expression of their sentiments by a consciousness of their weakness, and being exempted from the apprehensions that prevailed in the provinces of greater consideration by a sense of their insignificance.

In Rhode Island alone was their insidious policy attended with success. There, the people received them with studious deference and submission ; their inquiries were answered, and their mandates obeyed, without a syllable of objection to the authority from which they emanated ; and during their stay in this settlement they were enabled to amplify their reports with numberless complaints of injustice and misgovernment alleged to have been committed in Massachusetts. The inhabitants of Rhode Island, as we have seen, gained their late charter by a display of subservience and devotion to the crown ; and the liberal institutions which it introduced had not yet had time to form a spirit that disdained to hold the enjoyment of liberty by so ignoble a tenure. The freedom thus spuriously begotten was tainted in its

---

[1] Hutchinson. Chalmers.   [2] See Book V., chap. I., *post.*

birth by principles that long rendered its existence precarious; and we shall find these colonists, a few years after, abjectly proposing to strip themselves of the rights which they gained so ill, and of which they now showed themselves unworthy, by their willingness to coöperate in attacking the liberties of Massachusetts. We must not, however, discard from our recollection that Rhode Island was yet but a feeble community, and that the unfavorable sentiments with which many of its inhabitants regarded Massachusetts arose from the persecution which their religious tenets had experienced in this province. Their conduct to the commissioners received the warmest approbation from Charles, who assured them that he would never be unmindful of the claims they had acquired on his goodness by a demeanour so replete with loyalty and humility.[1] In justice to the king, whose word was proverbially the object of very little reliance, we may observe that he never actually contradicted these professions of favor for Rhode Island ; and in justice to a moral lesson that would be otherwise incomplete, we may here so far transgress the pace of time, as to remark, that, when Charles's successor extended to Rhode Island the same tyrannical system which he introduced into the other New England provinces, and when the people endeavoured to avert the blow by a repetition of the abject pliancy that had formerly availed them, their prostration was disregarded, and their complete subjugation pursued and accomplished with an insolence that forcibly taught them to detest oppression and despise servility.

It was in Massachusetts that the commission was expected to produce its most important effects ; and from the difference between the views and opinions entertained by the English government and by the provincial authorities, it was easily foreseen that the proceedings of the commissioners would provoke a keen and resolute opposition. Among other communications, which the commissioners were charged to convey to the colonists, was, that the king considered them to stand in precisely the same relation to him as the inhabitants of Kent or Yorkshire in England. Very different was the opinion which the colonists themselves entertained. They considered, that, having been forced by persecution to depart from the realm of England, and having established themselves by their own unassisted efforts in territories which they purchased from the natural proprietors, they retained no other political connection with their sovereign than what was created by their charter, which they regarded as the sole existing compact between the English crown and themselves, and as defining all the particulars and limits of their obedience. The acknowledged difference of sentiment in religion and politics between them and their ancient rulers, from which their colonial settlement originated, and the habits of self-government that they had long been enabled to indulge, confirmed these prepossessions, and tended generally and deeply to impress the conviction, that their primitive allegiance, as natives of England and subjects of the British crown, was entirely dissolved and superseded by the stipulations which they had voluntarily contracted by accepting their charter. Such opinions, though strongly cherished, it was not prudent distinctly to profess ; but their prevalence is attested by a respectable provincial historian, on the authority of certain manuscript compositions of the leading persons in Massachusetts at this period, which he had an opportunity of perusing. The colonists were not the less attached to these notions, from the apprehension that they would find as little favor in the eyes of the English government as the tenets which had led to the persecution and emigration of their ancestors ; they were, indeed, quite repugnant to the principles of the English law, which regards the allegiance of subjects to their sovereign, not as a local or provincial, but as a perpetual and indissoluble tie, which distance of place does not sunder, nor lapse of time relax. Forcibly aware of these differences of opinion, of the dangerous collisions which might result from them, and of the disadvantage with which they must conduct a discussion with persons who sought nothing so much as to find or make them offenders, the colonists awaited, with much anxiety, the return of the commissioners to Boston.[1]

The character and disposition of these commissioners increased the probability of an unfriendly issue to their debates with the provincial authorities. If conciliation was, as the king professed, the object which he had in view in instituting the commission, he was singularly unfortunate in the selection of the instruments to whom the discharge of its important duties was confided. Nichols, indeed, was a man of honor, good sense, and ability ; but it was mainly for the reduction and subsequent governance of New York that he had been appointed to accompany the expedition ; he remained at that place after its capitulation ; and when he afterwards rejoined his colleagues, he found himself unable to control their conduct, or repair the breach which they had already occasioned. The other commissioners were utterly destitute of the temper,[2] sense, and address which their office demanded ; and Maverick added to these defects an inveterate hostility to the colony, which had induced him for years to solicit the functions which he now hastened to execute with malignant satisfaction. On their return to Boston [April, 1665], the very first communication which they addressed to the governor demonstrated the slight respect they entertained for the provincial authorities ; for they required that all the inhabitants of the province should be assembled to receive and reply to their communication ; and when the governor desired to know the cause of this requisition, they answered, " that the motion was so reasonable, that he who would not attend to it was a traitor." Perceiving, however, that this violent language served rather to confirm the suspicions than to shake the resolution of the provincial magistrates, they condescended for a while to adopt a more conciliating tone, and informed the General Court that they had favorably represented to the king the promptness with which his commands had been obeyed in the equipment of a provincial regiment ; but it was soon ascertained that they had actually transmitted a representation of perfectly opposite import.

The suspicions which the commissioners and the General Court reciprocally entertained of each other prevented, from the outset, any cordial cooperation between them. The communications of the commissioners display the most lofty ideas of their own authority as representatives of the

---

[1] Hutchinson.

[2] The senselessness of their conduct is strongly illustrated by a case related at considerable length by the provincial historians. They had been drinking, one Saturday night, in a tavern, after the hour when, by the provincial laws, all taverns were ordered to be shut. A constable, who warned them not to infringe the law, was beaten by them. Hearing that Mason, another constable, had declared that *he* would not have been deterred by their violence from doing his duty, they sent for him, and extorted from him an admission that he would have arrested the king himself, if he had found him drinking in a public house after lawful hours. They insisted that he should be tried for high treason, and actually prevailed to have this injustice committed. The jury returned a special verdict ; and the court, considering the words offensive and insolent, but not treasonable, inflicted only a slight punishment. Hutchinson.

crown, with a preconceived opinion that there was an indisposition on the part of the General Court to pay due respect to their authority, as well as to the source from which it was derived. The answers of the General Court manifest an anxious desire to avoid a quarrel with the king, and to gratify his Majesty by professions of loyalty and submission, and by every municipal change that seemed likely to meet his wishes, without compromising the fundamental principles of their peculiar polity. They expressed, at the same time, a deliberate conviction of having done nothing that merited displeasure or required apology, and a steady determination to abide by the charter. The correspondence gradually degenerated into altercation. At length, the commissioners demanded from the Court an explicit answer to the question, if they acknowledged the authority of his Majesty's commission. But the Court desired to be excused from giving any other answer than that they acknowledged the authority of his Majesty's charter, with which they were much better acquainted. Finding that their object was not to be gained by threats or expostulations, the commissioners attempted a practical assertion of their pretensions ; they granted letters of protection to persons who were prosecuted before the provincial tribunals ; and in a civil suit, which was already determined by the provincial judges, they promoted an appeal to themselves from the unsuccessful party, and summoned him and his adversary to plead before them. The General Court perceived that they must now or never make a stand in defence of their authority ; and with a decision which showed the high value they entertained for their privileges, and the vigor with which they were prepared to guard them, they publicly proclaimed their disapprobation of this measure, and declared, that, in discharge of their duty to God and the king, and in faithfulness to the trust reposed in them by the king's good subjects in the colony, they must protest against the proceedings of the commissioners, and disclaim friendship with all who would countenance or abet them. They accompanied this vigorous demonstration with an offer to compromise the dispute by rejudging the cause themselves in presence of the commissioners ; but this proposition was scornfully rejected, and every effort to establish harmony between these conflicting authorities proved unavailing.

Suspending for a time their operations at Boston, the commissioners repaired to New Hampshire and Maine, and instantly pronouncing sentence in favor of the claims of Mason and Gorges against the jurisdiction of Massachusetts, they suppressed the existing authorities, and erected a new system of government in each of those provinces. On their return to Boston, the General Court declared that these measures tended to the disturbance of the public peace, and demanded a conference with the commissioners, which was refused with an asperity of reproach that excluded all farther correspondence. Sir Robert Carr even went the length of assuring the General Court that the king's pardon for their manifold treasons during the civil war had been merely conditional and was now forfeited by their evil behaviour, and that the contrivers of their late measures would speedily endure the same punishment which their associates in rebellion had recently experienced in England.

The king, having been apprized of these transactions, and assured by the commissioners that it was fruitless for them to prolong a discussion with persons who were determined to misconstrue all their words and actions, issued letters, recalling these functionaries to England [1666], expressing his satis-

faction with the conduct of all the colonies except Massachusetts, and commanding the General Court of this province to send deputies to answer in
his presence the charges preferred against their countrymen.   But the inhabitants of Massachusetts were aware that in such a controversy they had
not the remotest chance of success, and that it was not by reasonable pleas,
or the cogency of argument, that they could hope to pacify the displeasure
of their sovereign.   Instead of complying with his injunction, the General
Court addressed a letter to the secretary of state, in which they hinted real
or pretended doubts of the authenticity of the royal mandate, and declared
that their cause had already been so plainly and minutely unfolded, that the
ablest among them would be utterly incapable of rendering it any clearer.
At the same time they endeavoured to appease his Majesty by humble addresses expressive of their loyalty ; and in order to demonstrate the sense
they attached to these professions, they purchased a ship-load of masts which
they presented to the king ; and learning that his fleet in the West Indies
was distressed by want of provisions, they promoted a contribution among
themselves, and victualled it at their own expense.   Charles accepted their
presents very graciously ; and a letter under the sign manual having been
transmitted to the General Court, declaring that their zeal for the royal service was " taken well by his Majesty," the cloud that had gathered over the
colony in this quarter seemed for the present to be dispersed.[1]   Nevertheless,
the design that had been so far disclosed of remodelling the institutions of
New England was by no means abandoned.   The report of the commissioners furnished Charles with the very pretexts that were wanting to the
accomplishment of his plans ; and the measures which he embraced, at a
later period, demonstrated that it was not the dutiful professions or laberali-
ties of the colonists that would deter him from availing himself of the advantages which he had made such efforts to obtain.   But the dreadful affliction
of the *plague*, — which broke out with such violence, as in one year to
destroy ninety thousand of the inhabitants of London, and to transfer for a
time the seat of government to Oxford, — the great fire of London,[2] the
wars and intrigues on the continent of Europe, and the rising discontents
of the people of Britain, so forcibly engaged the attention of the king, as to
suspend for a while the execution of his designs against the institutions of
New England.

   After the departure of the royal commissioners, the provinces of New
England enjoyed for some years a quiet and prosperous condition.   The
only disturbance which their internal tranquillity sustained arose from the
persecutions, which, in all the States except Rhode Island, continued to be

[1] Hutchinson. Chalmers.

[2] A liberal contribution was made by the people of Massachusetts, and transmitted to London, for relief of the sufferers by the fire. Hutchinson. We have seen their kindness honorably repaid [1836], by a subscription among the citizens of London for relief of the sufferers by a vast conflagration at New York. The people of New England have always been
honorably distinguished by their charitable participation of the misfortunes of other communities. In the year 1703, they contributed £2,000 for the relief of the inhabitants of Nevis and
St. Christophers, which had been ravaged by the French. Holmes. In the same year, they
had an opportunity of showing that their hands were as ready to repel the danger as to relieve
the calamities of their friends. The planters of Jamaica having besought the assistance of
New England to repel an invasion that was apprehended from the French, two regiments
were promptly embodied and despatched for this purpose to Jamaica, where they remained
two years. Oldmixon (2d edit.). Military aid was not the only benefit which the West India
planters derived from New England, which appears frequently to have supplied them, at
their request, with ministers of religion. Holmes. Of the generous exertions of the New-
Englanders, both for the instruction and the defence of the colonists of Carolina, some notice
will be found in Book IV., Chap. II., and Book VIII., Chap. II., *post*.

waged against the Anabaptists, as these sectaries, from time to time, attracted notice by attempting to propagate their tenets. Letters were written in their behalf to the provincial magistrates by the most eminent dissenting ministers in England ; but though it was strongly urged by the writers of these letters, that the severe persecution which the Anabaptists were then enduring in the parent state should recommend them to the sympathy of the colonists, and that their conversion was more likely to be accomplished by exemplifying to them the peaceable fruits of righteousness than by attacking their doctrines with penal inflictions, which could have no other effect than to render them martyrs or hypocrites, the intercession, though respectfully received, was completely unavailing. The provincial authorities persisted in believing that they were doing God service by employing the civil power with which they were invested to guard their territories from the intrusion of what they deemed heresy, and to maintain the purity of those religious principles for the culture and preservation of which their settlements were originally founded. A considerable number of Anabaptists were fined, imprisoned, and banished ; and persecution produced its usual effect of confirming the sentiments and propagating the tenets which it sought to extirpate, by causing their professors to connect them in their own minds, and to exhibit them to others in connection, with suffering for conscience's sake. These proceedings, however, contributed more to stain the character of the colonists than to disturb their tranquillity. Much greater disquiet was created by the intelligence of the cession of Acadia, or, as it was now generally termed, *Nova Scotia*, to the French by the treaty of Breda. [1667.] Nothing had contributed more to promote the commerce and security of New England than the conquest of that province by Cromwell ; and the inhabitants of Massachusetts, apprized of the extreme solicitude of the French to regain it, and justly regarding such an issue as pregnant with mischief and danger to themselves, sent agents to England to remonstrate against it. But the influence of France prevailed with the British monarch over the interest of his people ; and the conduct of Charles on this occasion betrayed as much indifference for the external security of the colonies, as his previous measures had disclosed for their domestic liberties. The French regained possession of their ancient settlement ; and both New England and the mother country had afterwards abundant cause to regret the admission of a restless and ambitious neighbour, who for a long course of time exerted her peculiar arts of intrigue to interrupt the pursuits and disturb the repose of the British colonists.[1]

The system of government that prevailed in Massachusetts coincided with the sentiments of a great majority of the people ; and even those acts of municipal administration that imposed restraints on civil liberty were reverenced on account of their manifest design and their supposed efficiency to promote an object which the people held dearer than civil liberty itself. A printing-press had been established at Cambridge for upwards of twenty years ; and the General Court had recently appointed two persons to be licensers of the press, and prohibited the publication of any book or other composition that was not sanctioned by their censorial approbation. The licensers having authorized the publication of Thomas à Kempis's admirable treatise *De Imitatione Christi*, the Court interposed [1668], and, declaring that "the book was written by a popish minister, and contained some things

[1] Neal. Chalmers.

less safe to be infused among the people," recommended a more diligent revisal to the licensers, and in the meantime suspended the publication. In a constitution less popular, a measure of this nature would have been regarded as an outrage upon liberty. But the government of Massachusetts expressed and was supported by the feelings and opinions of the people; and so generally respected was its administration, that the inhabitants of New Hampshire and Maine, rejecting the form of municipal authority which they received from the royal commissioners, again solicited and were received into the rank of dependencies on its jurisdiction. All traces of the visitation of these commissioners being thus effaced, and the apprehensions excited by their measures forgotten, the affairs of the New England colonies continued for several years to glide on in a course of silent but cheerful prosperity.[1] The Navigation Act, not being aided by the establishment of an efficient custom-house, and depending for its execution upon officers annually elected by their own fellow-citizens, was completely disregarded. [1668–1672.] The people enjoyed a commerce practically unrestricted; a consequent increase of wealth was visible among the merchants and farmers; and habits of industry and economy continuing to prevail with unabated force, the plantations underwent a progressive improvement, and many new settlements arose.

From a document preserved in the archives of the colonial office of London, and published by Chalmers, it appears, that, in the year 1673, New England was estimated to contain one hundred and twenty thousand souls, of whom about sixteen thousand were able to bear arms; and of the merchants and planters there were no fewer than five thousand persons, each of whom was worth £ 3,000.[2] Three fourths of the wealth and population of the country centred in the territory of Massachusetts and its dependencies. The town of Boston alone contained fifteen hundred families. Theft was rare, and beggary unknown in New England. Josselyn, who returned about two years before this period from his second visit to America, commends highly the beauty and agreeableness of the towns and villages of Massachusetts and Connecticut, and the substantial structure and interior comfort of all the private dwellings.[3] During this interval of tranquil pros-

---

[1] In the year 1669, the inhabitants of Portsmouth, in New Hampshire, presented an address to the General Court of Massachusetts, signifying, "that, although they had articled with them for exemption from taxes, yet they had never articled with God and their own consciences for exemption from gratitude," and that they now pledged themselves for seven years to an annual contribution of sixty pounds sterling to the funds of Harvard College. Quincy's *History of Harvard University.*

In the year 1672, the laws of Connecticut (till then preserved in manuscript, and promulgated by oral proclamation) were collected into a code, printed, and published. The Preface, written with great solemnity, commences in this manner : — " To our beloved brethren and neighbours, the inhabitants of Connecticut, the General Court of that colony wish grace and peace in our Lord Jesus." It was ordered that every householder should have a copy of the code, and should read it weekly to his family. Trumbull. The legislators of Connecticut seem to have thought, like Agesilaus, that the duties of a citizen should form part of the earliest education of a child.

In Connecticut, by a law of 1667, three years' voluntary separation of married persons is held to dissolve their matrimonial engagement. It is strange that a law departing so widely from the injunctions of Scripture should have gained admission into the codes of Scotland and of New England, — two countries long distinguished above all others by the general and zealous desire of their people to harmonize their municipal ordinances with the canons of Scripture.

[2] John Dunton, who visited New England about twelve years after this period, mentions a merchant in Salem worth £ 30,000. Dunton's *Life and Errors.*

[3] Josselyn's *Second Voyage.* Even at this early period, Josselyn has remarked the prevalence of that inveterate but unexplained peculiarity, of the premature decay of the teeth of white persons, and especially women, in North America.

perity, many of the more aged inhabitants of New England closed the career of a long and eventful life ; and the original race of settlers was now almost entirely extinguished.   The annals of this period are filled with accounts of their deaths, — of the virtues by which they contributed to the foundation of the new commonwealth, and of the fondness with which their closing eyes lingered upon its flourishing estate.   To our retrospective view, enlarged by the knowledge which history supplies of the impending calamities from which these persons were thus seasonably removed, not the least enviable circumstance of their lot appears to have been, that they died in scenes so fraught with serene enjoyment and cheering promise, and bequeathed to their descendants at once the bright example of their virtue, and the substantial fruits of it, in a singularly happy and prosperous condition.   Yet, so shortsighted and fallacious are the prospective regards of men, — so strongly are they led by an instinctive and unquenchable propensity to figure and desire something better than they behold, — and so apt to restrict to the present fleeting and disordered scene the suggestions of this secret longing after original and immortal perfection, — that many of the fathers of the colony, even when, full of days and honor, they beheld their latter end crowned with peace, could not refrain from lamenting that they had been born too soon to see more than the first faint dawn of New England's glory. Others, with greater enlargement of wisdom and piety, remembered the Scriptural declaration, that *the eye is not satisfied with seeing ;* acknowledged that the conceptions of an immortal spirit are incapable of being adequately filled by any thing short of the vision of its Divine Author, for whose contemplation it was created ; and were contented to drop like leaves into the bosom of their adopted country, and resign to a succeeding race the enjoyment and promotion of her glory, in the confidence of their own renovated existence in scenes of more elevated and durable felicity.[1]

The state of prosperous repose which New England enjoyed for several years was interrupted by a general conspiracy of the Indian tribes [1674], that produced a war so bloody and formidable as to threaten for some time the utter destruction of all the settlements.   This hostile combination was promoted by a young chief whose history reminds us of the exploits of Opechancanough in Virginia.   He was the second son of Massasoit, a prince who ruled a powerful tribe inhabiting territories adjacent to the settlement of Plymouth at the time when the English first gained a footing in the country.   The father had entered into an alliance with the colonists, and, after his death, his two sons expressed an earnest desire to retain and cultivate their friendship.   They even requested of the magistrates of Plymouth, as a mark of identification with their allies, that English names might be given them ; and, in compliance with their desire, the elder received the name of Alexander, and the younger of Philip.   But these expressions of good-will were prompted entirely by the artifice that regulated their schemes of hostility ; and they were both shortly after detected and disappointed in a treacherous attempt to involve the Narragansets in hostilities with the colonists.   The haughty spirit of the elder brother was overwhelmed by this disgrace.   Unable to brook the detection and discomfiture of his perfidy, and perhaps additionally stung by the generous clemency of the colonists, which lent aggravation to his infamy, he abandoned himself to despair, and died of the corrosion of rage and mortification.   Philip, after the death of

---

[1] Hutchinson.   Chalmers.   Neal.

his brother, renewed the alliance between his tribe and the English ; but nothing was farther from his thoughts than the fulfilment of his engagements. Subtle, fierce, artful, and dissembling, yet stern in adventurous purpose and relentless cruelty, he meditated a universal conspiracy of the Indians for the extirpation of the colonists, and for several years pursued this design as secretly and successfully as the numerous difficulties that encompassed him would permit. Next to the growing power of the European settlers, nothing more keenly provoked his indignation than the progress of their missionary labors ; and, in reality, it was to these labors, and some of the consequences they produced, that the colonists were indebted for their preservation from the ruin that would have attended the success of Philip's machinations. Some of the tribes to whom he applied revealed his propositions to the missionaries ; and several Indians who had embraced his schemes were persuaded by their converted brethren to renounce them. The magistrates of Plymouth frequently remonstrated with him on the dishonor he incurred and the danger he provoked by the perfidious machinations of which from time to time they obtained information ; and by renewed and more solemn engagements than before, he endeavoured to disarm their vigilance and allay their apprehension. For two or three years before the present period, he pursued his hostile projects with such successful duplicity as to elude discovery and even suspicion ; and had now succeeded in uniting some of the fiercest and most powerful of the Indian tribes in a confederacy to make war on the colonists to the point of extermination.

A converted Indian, who was laboring as a missionary among the tribes of his countrymen, having discovered the plot, revealed it to the governor of Plymouth, and was soon after found dead in a field, under circumstances that left no doubt of assassination. Some neighbouring Indians, suspected of being the perpetrators of this crime, were apprehended, and solemnly tried before a jury consisting half of English and half of Indians, who returned a verdict of guilty. At their execution, one of the convicts confessed the murder, — declaring, withal, that its commission had been planned and instigated by Philip ; and this crafty chief, alarmed at the perilous disclosure, now threw off the mask, and summoned his confederates to his aid. The States of Massachusetts, Plymouth, and Connecticut took arms for their common defence, — having first employed every means to induce Philip to accommodate the quarrel by a friendly treaty. But a bloodless issue was not what Philip desired ; and perceiving that the season of secret conspiracy was over, he rejected all negotiation, and commenced a general war [1675] which was carried on with great vigor and various success. Though Philip's own tribe supplied no more than five hundred warriors, he had so increased his force by alliances that he was able to bring three thousand men into the field. This formidable host, conducted by a chief who was persuaded that the war must terminate in the total ruin of one or other of the conflicting parties, made exertions of which the Indians were hitherto supposed incapable. Several battles were fought, and all the fury, havoc, and cruelty which distinguish Indian warfare were experienced in their fullest extent by the English. Wherever the enemy marched, their route was marked with slaughter and desolation. Massachusetts and Plymouth were the States that suffered principally from the contest. There, especially, the Indians were so mingled with the European colonists, that there was scarcely a part of the country which was not exposed to danger, or a family which had not to bewail the loss of a relative or friend. In a woodland scene near the village of Deerfield, in Massachusetts, Captain Lothrop and a party of the provincial troops were suddenly attacked by an Indian force commanded by Philip himself; and, unaware that to encounter such an enemy with effect he ought to place his men in phalanx, Lothrop posted them separately behind trees, where he and every one of them, to the number of ninety-three, were presently shot down; other provincial troops now pressing up with unavailing succour, defeated the Indians and put them to flight. But, more elated with their first success than daunted by their final check, these savages speedily reappeared before the village and shook the scalps and bloody garments of the slaughtered captain and his troop before the eyes of the inhabitants. Deerfield was shortly after deserted by its harassed settlers, and destroyed by the triumphant Indians. It is a truth not yet sufficiently illustrated, that, in all the Indian wars of this period, the savages, from the condition of the country, their own superior acquaintance with it, and their peculiar habits of life and qualities of body and mind, enjoyed advantages which well nigh counterbalanced the superiority of European science. They seemed to unite the instinct and ferocity of the brutal creation with the art and sagacity of rational beings, and were, in single combat and in the conflict of very small numbers, as superior, as in more numerous encounter they were inferior, to civilized men. Changing their own encampments with facility, and advancing upon those of the colonists with the wary, dexterous secrecy of beasts of prey, with them there was almost always the spirit and audacity of attack, and with their adversaries the disadvantages of defence and the consternation produced by surprise; nor could the colonists obtain the means of attacking, in their turn, without following the savages into forests and swamps, where the benefit of their higher martial qualities was lost, and the system of European warfare rendered impracticable. The savages had long been acquainted with firearms, and were remarkably expert in the use of them.

For some time the incursions of the Indians could not be restrained; and every enterprise or skirmish in which they reaped the slightest credit or advantage increased the number of their allies. But the savage artifice which Philip employed, on one occasion, for the purpose of recruiting his forces, recoiled with merited injury on himself. Repairing with a band of his adherents to the territory of a neutral tribe, he caused certain of the people who belonged to it to be surprised and assassinated; and then, proceeding to the head-quarters of the tribe, he affirmed that he had seen the murder committed by a party of the Plymouth soldiers. The tribe, in a flame of rage, declared war on the colonists; but their vindictive sentiments soon took another direction; for one of the wounded men, having recovered his senses, made a shift to crawl to the habitations of his countrymen, and, though mortally injured, was able, before he expired, to disclose the real author of the tragedy. Revoking their former purpose, the tribe thereupon declared war on Philip, and espoused the cause of his enemies. Hostilities were protracted till near the close of the following year, when the steady efforts and determined courage of the colonists prevailed; and, after a series of defeats, and the loss of all his family and chief counsellors, Philip himself was killed by one of his own tribe whom he had offended. [Aug., 1676.] Deprived of its chief abettor, the war was soon terminated by the submission of the Indians. Yet to certain of the tribes the colonists sternly denied all terms of capitulation, and warned them, before their surrender, that their treachery had been so gross and unprovoked, and their outrages so atrocious and unpardonable, that they must abide the issue of judicial arbitrament. In conformity with this declaration, some of the chiefs were tried and executed for murder ; and a number of their followers were transported to the West Indies, and sold as slaves.   Never before had the people of New England been engaged in hostilities so fierce, so bloody, or so desolating. Many houses and flourishing villages were reduced to ashes ; and in the course of the warfare six hundred persons of European birth or descent, composing the flower and strength of several of the districts, either fell in battle, were massacred in their dwellings, or expired beneath the tortures inflicted by the savages on their captives.   The military operations of the colonists in these campaigns were thought, and perhaps justly, to disclose less skill and conduct than had been displayed in the Pequod War. They were, indeed, no longer commanded by the experienced officers who accompanied their ancestors from Europe ; and they were opposed to an enemy much more formidable than the Pequods.   But the firm, enduring valor they manifested was worthy of men whose characters were formed under institutions no less favorable to freedom than virtue, and who fought in defence of all they held dear and valuable.   Among other officers, Captain Church, of Massachusetts, and Captain Denison, of Connecticut, have been particularly celebrated by the provincial historians for their heroic ardor and fortitude.   In the commencement of the war, the surprising treachery practised by the hostile Indians naturally excited apprehensions of the defection of the Indian congregations which the missionaries had collected and partly civilized.   But not one of these people proved unfaithful to their benefactors.[1]

The Indian warfare by which New England was desolated during this period was not bounded by the hostilities of Philip and his confederates. An attack was made at the same time on New Hampshire and Maine, by the tribes that were situated in the vicinity of these settlements.   The Indians complained that they had been defrauded and insulted by some of the English traders in that quarter ;[2] but strong suspicions were entertained that their hostilities were promoted by the French government, now reëstablished in Acadia.   The invasion of those territories was distinguished by the usual guile, ferocity, and cruelty of the savages.   Many of the inhabitants were massacred, and others carried into captivity.   Prompt assistance was rendered to her allies by Massachusetts ; and after a variety of sharp engagements, the Indians sustained a considerable defeat.   They were, notwithstanding, still able and willing to continue the war ; and both their numbers and their animosity were increased by a measure which the provincial government adopted against them.   It was proposed to the General Court of

---

[1] Mather. Neal. Hutchinson. See Note XII., at the end of the volume.

[2] One of these complaints was occasioned by the brutal act of some English sailors in overturning an Indian canoe in which they observed an infant child, in order to ascertain the truth of a story they had heard, that swimming was as natural to a young Indian as to a young duck. The child died in consequence of the immersion ; and its father, who was highly respected as a necromancer by the Indians, became the inveterate enemy of the English. Belknap. An action that excited still greater resentment was committed by Major Waldron, of New Hampshire, during the war. He had made a treaty of friendship with a band of four hundred Indians ; but on discovering that some of them had served in Philip's army, he laid hold of these by a stratagem and sent them as prisoners to Boston. Their associates never forgave this breach of compact ; and thirteen years after, a party of them, having surprised the major in his house by a stratagem still more artful than his own, put him to death by the most horrible inflictions of cruelty. Ibid.

Massachusetts to invite the Mohawk tribe, who, from time immemorial, had been the enemies of the Eastern Indians, to make a descent on their territories at this juncture. The lawfulness of using such auxiliaries was questioned by some ; but it was deemed a satisfactory answer to the objection, that Abraham confederated with the Amorites for the rescue of his kinsman, Lot, from the hands of a common enemy ; [1] and messengers were accordingly despatched to solicit the coöperation of the Mohawks. Little entreaty was necessary to induce them to comply with the invitation ; and a band of Mohawk warriors quickly marched against their hereditary foes. The expedition, however, so far from producing the slightest benefit, was attended with serious disadvantage to the cause of the colonists. The Indians who were their proper enemies suffered very little from the Mohawk invasion ; while some powerful tribes, who had been hitherto at peace with the colonists, exasperated by injuries or affronts which they received from those invaders, now declared war both against them and their English allies. At last, the intelligence of Philip's overthrow, and the probability of stronger forces being thus enabled to march against them, inclined the Eastern Indians to hearken to proposals of peace. The war in this quarter was terminated by a treaty favorable to the Indians, to whom the colonists engaged to pay a certain quantity of corn yearly as a quitrent for their lands. [2]

Although the neighbouring province of New York was now a British settlement, no assistance was obtained from it by the New England States in their long and obstinate conflict with the Indians. On the contrary, a hostile demonstration from that quarter augmented the distress and inquietude of the Indian war. Andros, who was then governor of the newly acquired province, having claimed for the Duke of York a considerable tract of land which in reality formed part of the Connecticut territory, asserted the denied pretension of his master by advancing with an armament against the town and fort of Saybrook, which he summoned to surrender. The inhabitants, though at first alarmed to behold the English flag unfurled against them, speedily recovered from their surprise ; and hoisting the same flag on their walls, prepared to defend themselves against the assailants. Andros, who had not anticipated such resolute opposition, hesitated to fire upon the English flag ; and learning that Captain Bull, an officer of distinguished bravery and determination, had marched with a party of the Connecticut militia for the defence of the place, judged it expedient to abandon his enterprise and return to New York. [3]

The cessation of the Indian hostilities was not attended with a restoration of the happiness and tranquillity which they interrupted. The king had now matured the scheme of arbitrary government which he steadily pursued during the remainder of his inglorious reign ; and the colonists, while yet afflicted with the smart of their recent calamities, were forced to resume their ancient controversies with the crown, which they had vainly hoped were forgotten or abandoned by the English government. [4] Instead of approbation for the bravery and the manly reliance on their own resources with which they had conducted their military operations, and repelled hostilities partly occasioned by the disregard of their interests exemplified by the mother country in restoring Acadia to the French, — they found themselves overwhelmed with

---

[1] Francis the Second, of France, had previously employed the same defensive argument in the proclamation by which he apologized for his alliance with the Turks.   Millot.
[2] Neal. Hutchinson. Belknap.   [3] Trumbull.
[4] See Note XIII., at the end of the volume.

reproaches for a haughty, factious obstinacy in refusing to solicit assistance from the king, and a sordid parsimony in the equipment of their levies, which (the British court declared) had caused the war to be so greatly protracted, and showed them utterly unfit to be longer intrusted with the government of a country in which their sovereign possessed so large a stake.[1] Indications of the revival of royal dislike, and of the resumption of the king's former designs, had occurred before the conclusion of the war with Philip. While hostilities were still raging in the province, the government of Massachusetts found it necessary to direct a part of its attention to the claims of Mason and Gorges with respect to New Hampshire and Maine. In the summer of 1676, Randolph, a messenger despatched by the king, announced to the General Court that a judgment would be pronounced by his Majesty in council against their pretensions, unless, within six months, deputies were sent to plead in their behalf ; and as letters were received at the same time from the friends of the colonists in England, giving assurance that the king was determined to fulfil his threat, and that any apparent contumacy or procrastination on the part of the provincial government would but accelerate the execution of more formidable designs on which the English court was deliberating, the royal message received immediate attention, and Stoughton and Bulkeley were despatched as deputies to represent and support the interests of Massachusetts.[2]

The respective titles and claims of the parties having been submitted to the consideration of the two chief justices of England, the legal merits of the question were speedily extricated by their practised intelligence from the confused mass of inconsistent grants in which they had been enveloped. [1677.] It was adjudged that municipal jurisdiction in New Hampshire was incapable of being validly conveyed by the Council of Plymouth, and therefore reverted to the crown in consequence of the dissolution of the Council, with reservation, however, of Mason's claims on the property of the soil, — a reservation which for many years rendered all property in New Hampshire insecure, and involved the inhabitants in continual inquietude, dispute, and litigation. As Gorges, in addition to his original grant from the Plymouth Council, had procured a royal patent for the province of Maine, the entire property, both seigniorial and territorial, of this province was adjudged to be vested in him. In consequence of this decision, the jurisdiction of Massachusetts over New Hampshire ceased ; but it was preserved in the province of Maine by an arrangement with the successful claimant. The king had been for some time in treaty for the purchase of Maine, which he designed to unite with New Hampshire, and to bestow on his natural son, the Duke of Monmouth ; but, straitened for money, and expecting no competitor in the purchase, he deferred the completion of the contract. The government of Massachusetts, aware of this, and urgently solicited by the inhabitants of Maine to prevent their territories from being severed from its jurisdiction, proposed to Gorges an immediate purchase of his rights, which he readily consented to sell for twelve hundred pounds. This transaction gave much offence to the king, who peremptorily insisted that the authorities of Massachusetts should waive their title and relinquish the acquisition to him ; but they firmly declined to gratify him by such compliance, and main-

[1] " You are poor, and yet proud," said Lord Anglesey, one of the king's ministers, in a letter to the domestic authorities of Massachusetts, " and you wish to be independent of the king's protection."
[2] Hutchinson.

tained that their conduct needed no other justification than its conformity to the wishes of the people of Maine.

The inhabitants of New Hampshire were no less reluctant to be separated from Massachusetts ; but they were compelled to submit, and to receive a royal governor.[1] [1677.] One of the first acts of their legislature was to vote a grateful address to Massachusetts, acknowledging the former kindness of this colony, and protesting that only the commands of the king now interrupted a connection which it had been their anxious desire to preserve. The government thus forced upon them proved incapable of preserving tranquillity or commanding respect.   The attempts that were made to enforce Mason's title to the property of the soil, and to render the inhabitants tributary to him for the possessions which they had purchased from others and improved by their own labor, excited violent ferments, and resulted in a train of vexatious, but indecisive, legal warfare.[2] Cranfield, the governor, after involving himself in controversies and altercations with the planters and their legislative assembly, in which he was continually foiled, transmitted an assurance to the British government, " that, while the clergy were allowed to preach, no true allegiance could be found in those parts."   He wreaked his vengeance upon some Non-conformist ministers, to whose eloquence he imputed the stiff, unbending spirit of the people, and whose general denunciations against vice he construed into personal reflections on himself and his favorites, by arbitrarily commanding them to administer the sacrament to him according to the liturgy of the church of England, and committing them to prison on receiving the refusal which he expected.   His misgovernment at length provoked a few rash individuals, hastily and without concert, to revolt against his authority.   The insurrection was suppressed without the slightest difficulty ; and the insurgents, having been arraigned of high treason, were convicted and condemned to die.   But Cranfield, conscious of the unpopularity of his government, had exercised an unfair and illegal control in the selection of the jury, which excited universal indignation ; and afraid to carry his sentence into effect within the colony, he adopted the strange and unwarrantable proceeding of sending the prisoners to be executed in England.   The English government actually sanctioned this irregularity, and were preparing to obey the sentence of a provincial magistrate, and to exhibit to the people of England the tragical issue of a trial, with the merits of which they were totally unacquainted, when a pardon was obtained for the unfortunate persons, by the solicitation of Cranfield himself, who, finding it impracticable to maintain order in the province, or to withstand the numerous complaints of his injustice and oppression, had solicited his own recall.   Shortly after his departure, New Hampshire spontaneously reverted to the jurisdiction of Massachusetts, and shared her fortunes till the period of the British Revolution.[3]

[1] In the first commission that was issued for the government of this province, the king engaged to continue to the people their ancient privilege of an assembly, " unless, by inconvenience arising therefrom," he or his heirs should see cause to alter the same."   Belknap.

[2] The people were sometimes provoked to oppose what they termed *swamp law* to parchment law. An irregular judgment having been pronounced in favor of Mason, against some persons who refused to submit to it, the governor sent a party of sheriff's officers to serve a writ on them while they were in church. The congregation was incensed at this proceeding ; a young woman knocked down a sheriff's officer with her Bible ; and the conflict becoming general, the whole legal army was routed. It was found necessary to abandon the judgment. Belknap.

[3] Hutchinson. Chalmers. Belknap. These events, and the particular history of New Hampshire at this period, are related in considerable detail, with every appearance of accu-

Although the troubles of the *Popish Plot* began now to engage and per-
plex the mind of the king [1678], he was no longer to be diverted from
his purpose of attempting the subjugation of Massachusetts ; and though the
concern of the Duke of Monmouth with that celebrated imposture, and the
connections he formed with the profligate Shaftesbury and its other promoters or patrons, might diminish the king's regret for the privation of the
appanage which he had meant to bestow on him, yet the presumptuous interference of Massachusetts to defeat this design inflamed his displeasure and
fortified his tyrannical resolution.   That additional pretexts might not be
wanting to justify his measures, every complaint that could be collected
against the colony was promoted and encouraged.   The Quakers, who refused, during the Indian war, either to perform military service or to pay
the fines imposed on defaulters, complained bitterly of the *persecution* they
had incurred by the exaction of those fines, as well as of the law which
obliged them to contribute to the maintenance of the provincial clergy.
When the dangers of the Indian war were at their height, some of the colonists, interpreting the calamity as a judgment of Heaven upon the land for
harbouring such heretics as the Quakers within its bosom, procured the re-
enactment of an old law prohibiting assemblies for Quaker worship ; and
though it does not appear that this law was executed, its promulgation was
justly regarded as persecution, and alienated the regards of many persons
who had hitherto been friends of the colony.   The agents, deputed to defend the interests of Massachusetts in the controversies respecting New
Hampshire and Maine, were detained to answer the complaints of the Quakers, — gravely preferred by these sectaries to a government which was itself administering with far greater rigor upon them the very policy which it
now encouraged them to impute to one of its own provincial dependencies
as the most scandalous cruelty and injustice.

Other and more serious imputations contributed to detain the agents and
increase their perplexity.   Randolph, who was distinguished by a stanch and
sagacious activity in support of the views and interests of arbitrary power,
and whom the people of New England described as " going up and down
seeking whom he might devour," had ably and diligently fulfilled his instructions to collect as much matter of complaint as he could obtain within the
colony ; and loaded with the hatred of the people, which he cordially recip-
rocated, he now returned to England and opened his budget of arraignment
and vituperation.   The most just and most formidable of his charges was,
that the Navigation Act was entirely disregarded, and a free trade pursued
by the colonists with all parts of the world.   This was a charge which the
provincial agents could neither deny nor extenuate ; and they anxiously
pressed their constituents to put an end to the occasion of it.   Any measures
which the king might adopt, either for promoting the future efficacy of the
Navigation Acts, or for punishing the past neglect which they had experienced, were the more likely to coincide with the sentiments of the English
people, from the interest which a considerable portion of the mercantile
class of their countrymen enjoyed in the monopoly which it was the object
of those laws to secure.   A petition was presented to the king and privy
council by a number of English merchants and manufacturers, complaining
of the disregard of the Navigation Acts in New England, and praying that

racy, and with much spirit, good sense, and liberality, by Dr. Belknap.   It is to this author's
History of New Hampshire that I refer, wherever his *American Biography* (the very inappropriate title of a valuable work) is not expressly mentioned.

they might hereafter be vigorously executed, for the sake of promoting the commerce of the parent state, as well as of preserving her dominion over her colonies. That a stronger impression might be made on the public mind, the petitioners were solemnly heard in presence of the privy council, and indulged with the amplest latitude of pleading in support of their commercial complaints and political views.

The General Court of Massachusetts [1679], alarmed by these measures, intimated, by letter to their agents, that "they apprehended the Navigation Acts to be an invasion of the rights, liberties, and properties of the subjects of his Majesty in the colony ; — *they not being represented in parliament ;* and, according to the usual sayings of the learned in the law, the laws of England being bounded within the four seas, and not reaching to America." They added, however, that, " as his Majesty had signified his pleasure that those acts should be observed in Massachusetts, they had made provision, by a law of the colony, that they should be strictly attended to from time to time, although it greatly discouraged trade, and was a great damage to his Majesty's plantation." These expressions, and the recent provincial law to which they refer, demonstrate the peculiar views which were entertained by the people of Massachusetts of the connection that subsisted between themselves and the parent state. Their pretensions were the same with those which a few years after were advanced by the people of Ireland ; — that, although dependent on the crown, and obliged to conform their jurisprudence, as far as possible, to the law of England, the statutes of the English parliament did not operate within their territory, till reënacted, or otherwise recognized, by their own domestic legislature. So fully did this notion possess the minds of the people of New England, and so obstinately did their interests resist the execution of the commercial regulations, that even the submissive province of Rhode Island, although, about this time, in imitation of Massachusetts, it took some steps towards a conformity with these regulations, never expressly recognized them till the year 1700, when its legislature *empowered* the governor " to put the Acts of Navigation in execution." [1]

The provincial agents, aware of the strong interests that prompted their countrymen still to overstep the boundaries of their regulated trade, furnished them with correct information of the threatening aspect of their affairs in England, and assured them that only an entire compliance with the Navigation Acts could shelter them from the impending storm of royal vengeance and tyranny. These honest representations produced the too frequent effect of unwelcome truths ; they diminished the popularity of the agents, and excited suspicions in Boston that they had not advocated the interests of the colony with sufficient zeal. The people were always too apt to suspect that their deputies in England were overawed by the pomp and infected with the subservience that prevailed at the royal court ; and they neglected to make due allowance for the different aspect which a dispute with England presented to men who beheld face to face her vast establishments and superior power, and to others who speculated on the probability of such dispute at the opposite extremity of the Atlantic Ocean. At last the agents obtained leave to return ; and though some impatience and ill-humor had been excited by their fidelity in the discharge of a disagreeable duty, the deliberate sentiments of their countrymen were so little perverted,

---

[1] Neal. Hutchinson. Chalmers.

that, when the king again intimated his desire of the reappointment of agents in England, the colonists twice again elected the same individuals to their former office, — which, however, these persons could never again be persuaded to undertake.   They carried back with them to America a letter containing the requisitions of the king, of which the most material were, that the formula of the oath of allegiance should be rendered more explicit, and should be subscribed by every person holding an office of public trust in New England ; that all civil and military commissions should be issued in the king's name ; and all laws repugnant to the English commercial statutes abolished. The General Court, eagerly indulging the hope, that, by a compliance with these moderate demands, they could appease their sovereign and avert his displeasure, made haste to enact laws in conformity with his requisitions.   They trusted that he had now abandoned the designs which they had been taught to apprehend ; and which, in reality, were merely suspended by the influence of the proceedings connected with the *Popish Plot*, and with the parliamentary bill that was in agitation for excluding the Duke of York from the throne.

Although the requisitions which the king transmitted by the hands of Stoughton and Bulkeley were obeyed, he continued to intimate, from time to time, his desire that new agents might be appointed to represent the colony in London ; but partly from the apprehensive jealousy with which the colonists regarded such a measure, and partly from the reluctance that prevailed among their political leaders to undertake so arduous and delicate an employment, the king's desires on this point were not complied with.   The short interval of independence which the colonists were yet permitted to enjoy was very remote from a state of tranquillity.   Randolph, who had commended himself to the king and his ministers by the adroit and active prosecution of their views, was appointed collector of the customs at Boston ; and a custom-house establishment, which some years before had been erected without opposition in Virginia and Maryland, was now extended to New England.[1] But it was in Massachusetts that this measure was intended to produce the effects which it was easily foreseen would result from its own nature, as well as from the temper and unpopularity of the person who was appointed to conduct it.   The Navigation Acts were evaded in Rhode Island, and openly contemned and violated in Connecticut ; yet these States were permitted to practise such irregularities without reprehension.   It was less the execution of the commercial statutes themselves that the king desired, than the advantage which would accrue from an attempt to enforce them after such long neglect in the obnoxious province of Massachusetts. To this province he confined his attention ; and justly considered that the issue of a contest with it would necessarily involve the fate of all the other settlements in New England.   Randolph exercised his functions with the most offensive rigor, and very soon complained that the stubbornness of the people defeated all his efforts, and presented insuperable obstacles to the execution of the laws. Almost every suit that he instituted for the recovery of penalties or forfeitures issued in a judicial sentence against himself.   He repaired to England in order to lay his complaints before his employers

[1] As a measure, partly of terror, and partly of punishment, it was determined by the English privy council, about this time, "that no Mediterranean passes shall be granted to New England, to protect its vessels against the Turks, till it is seen what dependence it will acknowledge on his Majesty, or whether his custom-house officers are received as in other colonies." Chalmers.

[1680], and returned invested with more extensive powers, — in the exercise of which he was not more successful. He reproached the provincial authorities with injustice and partiality ; while they denied the charge, and taxed him with superfluous, unnecessary, and vexatious litigation.

The requisitions and remonstrances which the king continued to address to the General Court, from time to time, were answered by professions of loyalty, and by partial compliances ; but on one point the colonists were determined, either entirely or as long as possible, to evade the royal will ; and though repeatedly directed, they still delayed, to send deputies to England. The General Court was at this time divided between two parties, who cordially agreed in the esteem and attachment by which they were wedded to their chartered privileges, but differed in opinion as to the extent to which it was expedient to contend for them. Bradstreet, the governor, at the head of the moderate party, promoted every compliance with the will of the parent state short of a total surrender of the civil and ecclesiastical constitution of Massachusetts. Danforth, the deputy-governor, at the head of another party, obstructed the appointment of deputies, and opposed all submission to the acts of trade ; maintaining that the colonists should adhere to the strict construction of their charter, resist every abridgment of it as a dangerous precedent, no less than an injurious aggression, and, standing firm in defence of their utmost right, commit the event to Divine Providence. These parties conducted their debates with warmth, but without acrimony ; and as the sentiments of one or other alternately prevailed, a greater or lesser degree of compliance with the demands of the king was infused into the undecided policy of the General Court.[1]

The scene of trouble and misfortune in which the inhabitants of this quarter of America had for a series of years been involved could not fail to produce a grave and earnest impression on the minds of men habituated to regard all the events of life in a religious aspect, and contributed to revive among the descendants of the original planters the piety for which New England was at first so highly distinguished. A short time before the commencement of their late distresses, a natural phenomenon[2] that excited much awe and tribulation at the time, and was long pondered with earnest and solemn remembrance, was visible for several nights successively in the heavens. It was a bright meteor in the form of a spear, of which the point was directed towards the setting sun, — and which, with slow, majestic motion, descended through the upper regions of the air, and gradually disappeared beneath the horizon. This splendid phenomenon produced a deep and general impression on the minds of the people ; and the magistrates, without expressly alluding to it, acknowledged and endeavoured to improve its influence by seizing the opportunity to promote a general reformation of manners. Circular letters were transmitted to all the clergy, urging them to increased diligence in exemplifying and inculcating the precepts of religion, especially on the young, and instructing their parishioners from house to house. The dupes of science, falsely so called, may deride these impressions, and ascribe to ignorant wonder the piety which they enkindled ; but enlightened philosophy will confess the worth and dignity of that prin-

---

[1] Hutchinson. Chalmers. From a report presented this year (1680) to the Lords of Trade, it appears that Connecticut then contained twenty-one churches, each of which had its minister ; a militia of 2,500 men ; a very few indented servants, and thirty slaves. Holmes.

[2] In the *Journal* of John Evelyn there are descriptions of the occurrence of similar phenomena in England, in the years 1643 and 1680.

ciple which recognizes in every display of the great phenomena of nature an additional call to worship and glorify its Almighty Creator, and which elevates and refines human faculties by placing every object that forcibly strikes them in a noble and graceful light derived from connection with the interests of morality and the honor of God. The events of the Indian war, the agricultural losses that were occasioned by the peculiar inclemency of the ensuing season, and, latterly, the disquiet excited by the contentions with the English government, served, in like manner, to humble the people beneath the hand of that Sovereign Power which controls the passions of men as well as the elements of nature; and were equally productive of increased diligence in the cultivation of piety and the reformation of manners.

Deeply lamenting the moral imperfections and deficiencies which they experienced in themselves and remarked in those around them, many of the ministers, magistrates, and principal inhabitants of Massachusetts and Connecticut urgently besought their countrymen to consider if the interruption of divine favor did not betoken disregard of the divine will ; and by precept and example labored to eradicate every evil habit or licentious practice that a state of war and an influx of commercial wealth were supposed to have produced or promoted. Men were strongly exhorted to carry a continual respect to the divine will into the minutest ramifications of their affairs, and to refine and sanctify whatever they did by *doing it to the Lord*. The General Court published a catalogue of the epidemical vices of the times, in which we find enumerated, neglect of the education of children, pride displayed in the manner of cutting and curling hair, excess of finery, immodesty of apparel, negligent carriage at church, failure in due respect to parents, a sordid eagerness of shopkeepers to obtain high prices, profane swearing, idleness, and frequenting of taverns. Grand juries were directed to *present* (that is to signalize for trial and punishment) all offenders in these respects ; but either the happier influence of example and remonstrance was sufficient to control the obnoxious practices, or they never attained such extent of prevalence as to justify the infliction of legal severities.[1] In many instances, the scrupulous piety of the provincial magistrates has reprobated existing vices, and the extent to which they prevailed, in language which is apt to beget misapprehension, if it be interpreted in conformity with the general notions and tone of the world ; and, hence, a writer no less acute than Chalmers has fallen into the gross mistake of deriving a charge of extraordinary immorality against the inhabitants of Massachusetts from the very circumstances that prove the strength of their piety, the purity of their moral habits, and the still higher purity of their moral aspirations. The strong sense that religious impressions awaken of the depraved propensities inherent in human nature causes the expression of the moral sentiments of truly religious men to appear to the world at large as the ravings of hypocritical cant or fanatical delusion.[2]

[1] Neal. Hutchinson. Trumbull.
[2] After this manner the New England ministers were accustomed to address their hearers. "It concerneth New England always to remember that they are originally a plantation religious, not a plantation of trade. Let merchants, and such as are increasing *cent. per cent.*, remember this, that worldly gain was not the end and design of the people of New England, but religion. And if any man among us make religion as twelve, and the world as thirteen, such an one hath not the spirit of a true New-Englandman." Higginson's *Election Sermon*, 1663, *apud* Belknap. Robert Keayne, a colonist of great wealth, piety, talent, and consideration in Massachusetts, and a liberal benefactor of the colony, having on one occasion become obnoxious on account of the "corrupt practice" of selling dearer than most traders, "was, for this offence, after solemn trial, fined two hundred pounds by the General Court, publicly ad-

The king had never lost sight of his purpose of remodelling the constitution of Massachusetts ; although some appearance of moderation had been latterly enforced upon him by the more personal and pressing concern of resisting the attempts of Shaftesbury to reëxemplify the deep and daring policy of the Duke of Guise, and control his sovereign by the formation and supremacy of a Protestant league in England.   While Shaftesbury and his party were able to retain their influence on the public mind by the artifice of the *Popish Plot*, and to attack the monarchy by the device of the exclusion bill, it was probably deemed unsafe to signalize the royal administration by any public act of extraordinary tyranny in a province so distinguished for zeal in the Protestant cause as Massachusetts.   But Charles had now obtained a complete victory over his domestic adversaries [1681] ; and, among other excesses of retaliatory violence and arbitrary power by which he hastened to improve his success, he instituted writs of *quo warranto* against the principal corporations in England, and easily obtained judgments from the courts of law that declared all their liberties and franchises forfeited to the crown.   About two years before this period, he deliberated on the possibility of superseding entirely the constitution of Massachusetts without the intermediate recourse of any legal solemnity ; but, on consulting Jones and Winnington, the attorney and solicitor general, he learned that his object could not be securely or effectually attained except by the instrumentality of a writ of *quo warranto*, which at that time it was not deemed expedient to employ.   But now every impediment to the gratification of his wishes was removed ; and the colonists received such intelligence from their friends in England as permitted them no longer to doubt that the abrogation of their charter was finally resolved on and was to be instantly attempted.   Randolph, who made numerous voyages between England and America, and had lately affixed a protest on the exchange of Boston against the legitimacy of the provincial government and its official acts, now brought from London a letter from the king, dated the 26th of October, 1681, recapitulating all the complaints against the colony, and commanding that deputies should instantly be sent to him, not only to answer these complaints, but " with powers to submit to such regulations of government as his Majesty should think fit " ; which if the colonists failed to do, it was intimated that a writ of *quo warranto* would be directed against their charter.

A new criminatory charge, suggested by the inquisitive hostility of Randolph, was at the same time preferred against them, — that they coined money within the province, in contempt of the king's prerogative.   The General Court, in answer to this sudden arraignment of a practice which had been permitted so long to prevail without objection, explained in what manner and at what time it originated, and appealed to these circumstances as decisively proving that no contempt of royal authority had been designed ; but withal declared, that, if it were regarded as a trespass on his Majesty's prerogative, they humbly entreated pardon for the offence, and indulgence for the ignorance under which it was committed.   Among the other complaints that were urged by the king, were the presumptuous purchase of the province of Maine, which the colonists were again commanded to surrender, and the disallowance of religious worship except on the model of the Congregational churches within the colony.   To the first of these they answered by repeating their former apology, and still declining what was re-

monished by the church, and hardly escaped excommunication." Quincy's *History of Harvard University*.

quired of them ; and to the second, that liberty of worship was now granted
to all denominations of Christians in Massachusetts.   The royal letter contained many other charges ; but they were all answered by solemn protestations that either the commands they imported were already fulfilled, or the
disobedience they imputed had not been committed.   An assembly of the
General Court having been held for the purpose of electing deputies to
represent the province in England, and Stoughton again declining to accept
this office, it was conferred on Dudley and Richards, two of the wealthiest
and most respectable citizens of Massachusetts.   But as the plenary powers
which the royal letter required that they should be invested with, of acceding to whatever regulations of government the king might think fit to propose,
were nothing else than powers to surrender all the rights of their countrymen, the Court was careful to grant no such authority, and, on the contrary,
plainly expressed in their instructions that the deputies were not to do or
consent to any thing that should infringe the liberties bestowed by the charter, or infer the slightest alteration of the existing form of government.

The deputies set sail for England, whither they were soon followed by
Randolph, eager to confront them and counteract their exertions.[1]   A public
fast was appointed to be observed throughout the province ; and prayers
were addressed to Heaven for the preservation of the charter and the success of the deputation.   Means less pure, though certainly not unjustifiable,
were adopted, or at least sanctioned, by the provincial council or board of
assistants, for promoting at the English court the wishes and interests of
their countrymen.   Cranfield, the late royal governor of New Hampshire,
happening to visit Boston at this juncture, suggested to those authorities
that the provincial deputies should be directed to wait on Lord Hyde, and
tender the sum of two thousand guineas for the private service of the king,
which he assured them, from the notorious poverty and venality of the court,
would infallibly procure a suspension of all hostile proceedings.   Novices in
craft, they fell headlong into the snare, and addressed letters to this effect
to the deputies, while Cranfield despatched letters at the same time to the
king, which he represented to them as containing the strongest recommendations of their cause to royal favor.   But though these men were willing,
in a cause where no interests except their own were involved, to sacrifice
their money for their liberty, and to buy their country out of the hands of a
sordid and dissolute tyrant, — it was not the will of Providence that the
liberties of Massachusetts should be bartered for gold, or that devotional
prayers associated with such unholy exertions should prevail.   Letters soon
arrived from the deputies, informing their constituents that Cranfield had
written a ludicrous account of the affair to the king, and vaunted his dexterity in outwitting the people of Boston, whom he described as a crew of
seditious miscreants and rebels ; and that the publication of the story had
exposed them to the derision of the royal court.[2]

The American deputies found their sovereign intoxicated with the triumph of his victorious prerogative, impatient of all farther vacation of his

[1] To such a degree had Randolph excited the jealousy and abhorrence of the colonists, that
a great fire happening on one occasion to break out in Boston, soon after his arrival in the city,
he was generally believed by the populace to have been the author of it (Hutchinson) ; and
so conscious was he of the provocation he had given to popular vengeance, that he expressed
his apprehensions to the British ministers, that the people of Massachusetts would account him
guilty of treason, and punish him with death, for attempting to subvert their political constitution. Holmes.
[2] Hutchinson. Chalmers.

revenge, and incensed to the highest degree against a province that had so long presumed to withstand his will. Their credentials, which were exhibited to Sir Lionel Jenkins, the secretary of state, were at once declared to be insufficient ; and they were informed, that, unless a commission more ample and satisfactory were immediately produced, it was his Majesty's pleasure that a writ of *quo warranto* against their country's charter should issue without delay. The deputies communicated this peremptory injunction to their constituents ; assuring them, at the same time, that the predicament of the colony was desperate ; and leaving them to determine whether it was most advisable to submit themselves unreservedly to his Majesty's pleasure, or to abide the issue of a process which would certainly be fatal. This important question, the determination of which was to be the last exercise of their highly prized liberty, was solemnly debated, both in the General Court, and, as was meet, by the inhabitants of the province at large ; and the prevailing sentiment was declared to be, " that it was better to die by other hands than by their own." [1683.[1]] An earnest address to the king was framed by the General Court ; a corresponding one was signed by the inhabitants at large ; and the agents were directed to present or suppress these addresses according to their own discretion. They were likewise authorized to resign the title-deeds of the province of Maine, if, by so doing, they could preserve the charter of Massachusetts, — and they were, finally, assured of the irrevocable determination of their constituents to adhere to the charter, and never to show themselves unworthy of liberty by making a voluntary surrender of it. The communication of this magnanimous answer put an end to the functions of the deputies ; and a writ of *quo warranto* having been issued forthwith against the colony, they desired leave to retire from the scene of this procedure, and were permitted to return to Boston.

They were instantly followed by Randolph, who had presented to the Committee of Plantations a catalogue of crimes and misdemeanours which he imputed to the provincial government, and was now selected to carry the fatal writ across the Atlantic. The communication was highly agreeable to the messenger who conveyed it ; and Randolph performed [October, 1683] his part with an ostent of triumphant satisfaction that added insult to injury, and increased the detestation with which he was universally regarded. The king, at the same time, made a last endeavour to induce the colonists to spare him the tedious formalities of legal process. He declared, that, if before judgment they would unreservedly submit and resign themselves to his pleasure, he would study their interest as well as his own in composing the new charter, and make no farther innovation on the original constitution of the province than should be necessary for the due support of his authority. To add weight to this suggestion, the colonists were apprized, that all the corporations in England, except the city of London, had surrendered their privileges to the king ; and abstracts of the legal proceedings which had proved fatal to the charter of London were circulated through the province, — that all might learn the hopelessness of a contest with royal authority. But the people of Massachusetts were not to be moved from

---

[1] This year, died Roger Williams, founder of the settlement of Providence, and one of the founders of the State of Rhode Island ; his admirable piety and philanthropy and singularly virtuous and useful life have been strikingly illustrated in the third volume of the *Collections of the Rhode Island Historical Society*, — a composition of very great merit, but defaced by a strain of hostile prejudice against the early colonists of Massachusetts and Connecticut.

their purpose by the threats of despotic power or the example of general servility. They had acted well, and had now to suffer well; and disdainfully refused to diminish the infamy of their oppressor by sharing it with him. A majority of the council, dejected and overwhelmed by their calamities, voted an address of submission to the king; but, with more erect spirit, the house of delegates, imbued with the general feeling of the people, and supported by the approbation of the clergy, rejected the address, and adhered to their former resolutions: [1683.] The process of *quo warranto* was in consequence urged forward with all the expedition that was compatible with forensic formality. Among other instances of tyrannical contempt of justice, the summons which required the colony to defend itself was transmitted so tardily, that, before compliance with it was possible, the space assigned for such compliance had elapsed. In Trinity Term of the following year [1684], judgment was pronounced by the English Court of King's Bench against the Governor and Company of Massachusetts, " that their letters patent and the enrolment thereof be cancelled "; and in the year after, an official copy of this judgment was received by the secretary of the General Court. [2d July, 1685.][1]

Thus was the system of liberty that flourished for sixty years in Massachusetts overthrown by the descendant of the princes whose tyranny had led to its establishment, after being defended by the children of the original settlers with the same hardy and generous virtue that their fathers had exerted in founding and rearing it. The venerable Bradstreet, who accompanied the first emigrants to Massachusetts in 1630, was still alive, and was governor of the colony at the period of the subversion of those institutions which he had contributed to plant in the desert, and had so long continued to adorn and enjoy. Perhaps he now discerned the vanity of those sentiments that had prompted so many of the coevals whom he survived to lament their deaths as premature. But the aged eyes that beheld this eclipse of New England's prosperity were not yet to close till they had seen the return of better days.

That the measures of the king were in the highest degree unjust and tyrannical appears manifest beyond all decent denial; and that the legal adjudication by which he masked his tyranny was never annulled by the English parliament is a circumstance very little creditable to English justice. The House of Commons, indeed, shortly after the Revolution, inflamed with indignation at the first recital of the transactions which we have now witnessed, voted a resolve declaring " that those *quo warrantos* against the charters of New England were illegal and void"; and followed up this resolve by a bill for restoring the charter of Massachusetts. But the progress of the bill was arrested in the House of Lords by a sudden prorogation of parliament; and the Commons were afterwards prevailed with to depart from their purpose by the arguments of Treby, Somers, and Holt,[2] whose eminent faculties and liberal principles could not exempt them from the influence of a superstitious prejudice, generated by their professional habits, in favor of the sacredness of legal formalities.

---

[1] Hutchinson. Chalmers.   [2] Ibid.

CHAPTER V.

Designs — and Death of Charles the Second. — Government of Massachusetts under a temporary Commission from James the Second. — Andros appointed Governor of New England.
— Submission of Rhode Island. — Effort to preserve the Charter of Connecticut. — Oppressive Government of Andros. — Colonial Policy of the King. — Sir William Phips. — Indian
Hostilities renewed by the Intrigues of the French. — Insurrection at Boston. — Andros
deposed — and the ancient Government restored. — Connecticut and Rhode Island resume
their Charters. — William and Mary proclaimed. — War with the French and Indians. —
Sir William Phips conquers Acadia. — Ineffectual Expedition against Quebec. — Impeach-
ment of Andros by the Colony discouraged by the English Ministers — and dismissed. —
The King refuses to restore the ancient Constitution of Massachusetts. — Tenor of the new
Charter. — Sir William Phips Governor. — The New England Witchcraft. — Death of
Phips. — War with the French and Indians. — Loss of Acadia. — Peace of Ryswick. —
Moral and Political State of New England.

So eager was Charles to complete the execution of his long cherished
designs on Massachusetts, that, in November, 1684, immediately after the
judgment of the Court of King's Bench against its charter was pronounced,
he began to make arrangements for the new government of the colony.
Though not even a complaint was pretended against New Plymouth, he
scrupled not to involve this settlement in the same fate ; and as if he purposed to consummate his tyranny and vengeance by a measure that should
surpass the darkest anticipations entertained in New England, he selected as
the delegate of his prerogative a man, than whom it would be difficult, in
all the records of human wickedness and oppression, to find one who has
excited to a greater degree the abhorrence and indignation of his fellow-
creatures. The notorious Colonel Kirke, whose ferocious and detestable
cruelty has secured him an immortality of infamy in the history of England,
was appointed governor of Massachusetts, New Hampshire, Maine, and New
Plymouth ; and it was determined that no representative assembly of the
colonists should be permitted to exist, but that all the functions of municipal
authority should be vested in the governor and a council appointed during
the royal pleasure. This arbitrary policy was approved by all the ministers
of Charles, except the Marquis of Halifax, who espoused the cause of the
colonists with generous zeal, and warmly, but vainly, urged that they were
entitled to enjoy the same laws and institutions that prevailed in the parent
state.[1] Though Kirke had not yet committed the enormities by which he
was destined to illustrate his name in the West of England, he had already
given such indications of his disposition, in the government of Tangier, that
the tidings of his appointment filled the inhabitants of the colony with horror
and dismay. But before the royal commission and instructions to this ruffian
were completed, the career of the monarch himself was interrupted by death ;
and Kirke was reserved to contribute by his sanguinary violence in England
to bring hatred and exile on Charles's successor. This successor, James
the Second, from whose stern, inflexible temper and lofty ideas of royal prerogative the most gloomy presages of tyranny were derived, was proclaimed
in Boston with melancholy solemnity. [April, 1685.] [2]

---

[1] The French court and the Duke of York remonstrated with Charles on the impolicy of
retaining in office a man who professed such sentiments. Barillon's *Correspondence* in the
Appendix to Fox's *History of James the Second.* " Even at this early period," says Mr. Fox,
" a question relative to North American liberty, and even to North American taxation, was
considered as the test of principles friendly or adverse to arbitrary power at home."

[2] Hutchinson. Chalmers.

These presages were verified by the conduct of the new sovereign. Soon after his accession to the throne, he appointed, by special commission, a provisional government of Massachusetts, New Hampshire, Maine, and New Plymouth, to be administered by a president and council selected from the inhabitants of Massachusetts, whose functions were merely executive, and were to endure till the establishment of a fixed and permanent system. The functionaries thus appointed were directed to concede liberty of conscience to all persons, but to bestow peculiar encouragement on the votaries of the church of England ; to determine all suits originating within the colony, but to admit appeals from their sentences to the king ; and to defray the expenses of their government by levying the taxes previously imposed. This commission was appointed to be produced before the General Court at Boston, not as still considered a body administering legal authority, but as a convocation of individuals of the greatest influence and consideration in the province.   In answer to the communication of its contents, the Court voted [May, 1686] a unanimous resolution, in which they protested that the inhabitants of Massachusetts were deprived of the rights of freemen by the system of government which had been announced to them, and that it deeply concerned both those who introduced and those who were subjected to the operation of this system to reflect how far it was safe to pursue it.   For themselves, they declared, that, if the newly appointed officers should think proper to exercise their functions, though they could never regard them as invested with constitutional power, they would demean themselves, notwithstanding, as loyal subjects, and humbly make their addresses to God, and in due time to their prince, for relief.

The president named in the commission was Dudley, who had previously been one of the deputies of the province to England, and whose conduct justified, in some degree, the jealousy with which the colonists ever regarded the persons to whom they were constrained to intrust that important office. The patriotic virtue of this man, without being utterly dissolved, was relaxed by the beams of regal splendor ; and he had not been able to look on the pomp and show of aristocratical institutions with philosophic composure or undesiring eyes.   Despairing of his ability at once to serve and gratify his country, he applied himself with more success to cultivate his own interest at the English court ; and in pursuing this crooked policy, he seems to have flattered himself with the hope that the interest of his fellow-citizens might be more effectually promoted by his own advancement to official preëminence among them, than by the exclusion which he would incur, in common with themselves, by a stricter adherence to the line of integrity.   Though he accepted the commission, and persuaded the other persons who were associated with him to imitate his example, he continued to demonstrate a friendly regard to the rights of the people, and to the municipal institutions which they so highly valued.   Not only was immediate change in the provincial magistracy avoided, but the commissioners, in deference to the public feeling, transmitted a memorial to the English court, affirming that a well regulated assembly of the representatives of the people was urgently necessary, and ought in their opinion to be established without delay.   This moderate conduct, however, gave little satisfaction to any of the parties whom they desired to please.   The people were indignant to behold a system which was erected on the ruins of their liberty administered by their own fellow-citizens, and above all by the man whom they had lately ap-

pointed to resist its introduction among them ; and nothing but the apprehension of seeing him replaced by Kirke, whose massacres in England
seemed gloomily to foretell the treatment of America, prevented an open
expression of their displeasure. The conduct of the commissioners was no
less unsatisfactory both to the abettors of arbitrary government in England,
and to the creatures and associates of Randolph within the province, who
were eager to pay court to the king by prostrating beneath his power every
obstacle to the execution of his will. Complaints were soon transmitted by
these persons to the English ministers, charging the commissioners with
conniving at wonted practices by which the trade laws were evaded, countenancing ancient principles of civil and ecclesiastical policy, and evincing,
in general, but a lukewarm affection to the king's service.[1]

In addition to these causes of dissatisfaction with the commissioners, the
king was incited to proceed to the completion of his plans by the imperfection of the temporary arrangement to which he had resorted. It was
found that the provincial acts of taxation were ready to expire ; and the
commissioners, being devoid of legislative authority, had no power to renew
them. They employed this consideration to support their suggestion of a
representative assembly ; but it determined the king to enlarge the arbitrary
authority of his provincial officers, and at the same time to establish a permanent administration for New England. He consulted the crown lawyers,
and in particular Sir William Jones, the attorney-general, respecting the
extent of his powers ; and they pronounced, as their official opinion, "that,
notwithstanding the forfeiture of the charter of Massachusetts, its inhabitants
continued English subjects, invested with English liberties, and consequently
that the king could no more grant a commission to levy money on them,
without their consent in an assembly, than they could discharge themselves
from their allegiance " ; a truth, of which the discovery implies no extraordinary legal knowledge or acuteness, but of which this open declaration
bespeaks more honesty than we might have expected from persons selected
by the monarch from a society of lawyers, which, in that age, could supply
such instruments as Jeffries and Scroggs. We must recollect, however,
that lawyers, though professionally partial to the authority which nominally
and theoretically constitutes the source and mainspring of the system which
they administer, cherish also, in their strong predilection for those forms and
precedents that practically constitute their own influence and the peculiar
mystery of their science, a principle that frequently protects liberty and befriends substantial justice.

But James was too much enamoured of arbitrary power to be deterred
from the indulgence of it by any obstacle inferior to invincible necessity ;
and accordingly, without paying the slightest regard to an opinion supported
only by the pens of lawyers, he determined to establish a complete tyranny
in New England, by combining the whole legislative and executive authority
in the persons of a governor and council to be named by himself. Kirke
had been found too useful, as an instrument of terror in England, to be spared
to America. But Sir Edmund Andros, who had signalized his devotion to
arbitrary power in the government of New York, was now appointed captain-
general and vice-admiral of Massachusetts, New Hampshire, Maine, New
Plymouth, and certain dependent territories, during the pleasure of the king.
He was empowered, with consent of a board of counsellors, to make ordi-

---

[1] Neal. Hutchinson. Chalmers.

258 HISTORY OF NORTH AMERICA. [BOOK II.

nances for the colonies, not inconsistent with the laws of England, and which were to be submitted to the king for his approbation or dissent, and to impose taxes for the support of government. He was directed to govern the people in conformity with the tenor of his commission, of a separate letter of instructions with which he was at the same time furnished, and of the laws which were then in force or might be afterwards enacted. The governor and council were also constituted a court of record ; and from their decisions an appeal was competent to the king. The greater part of the instructions that were communicated to Andros are of a nature that would do honor to the patriotism of the king, if the praise of this virtue were due to a barren desire to promote the welfare of his people, accompanied with the most effectual exertions to strip them of every security by which their welfare might be guarded.

Andros was directed to promote no persons to offices of trust, but colonists of fair character and competent estate, and to displace none without *sufficient cause* ; to respect and administer the existing laws of the country, in so far as they were not inconsistent with his commission or instructions ; to dispose of the crown lands at moderate quitrents ; " to take away or to harm no man's life, member, freehold, or goods, but by established laws of the country, not repugnant to those of the realm " ; to discipline and arm the inhabitants for the defence of the country, but not to obstruct their attention to their own private business and necessary affairs ; to encourage freedom of commerce by restraining engrossers ; to check the excessive severity of masters to their servants, and to punish with death the slayers of Indians or negroes ; *to allow no printing-press to exist ;* and to grant universal toleration in religion, but special encouragement to the church of England. Except the restraint of printing (which, though enjoined, appears not to have been carried into effect), there is not one of these instructions that expresses a spirit of despotism ; and yet the whole system was silently pervaded by that spirit ; for as there were no securities provided for the accomplishment of the king's benevolent directions, so there were no checks established to restrain the abuse of the powers with which the governor was intrusted. The king was willing that his subjects should be happy, but not that they should be free, or entitled to pursue a scheme of happiness independent of his instruction and control ; and this conjunction of a desire to promote human welfare, with an aversion to the means most likely to secure it, suggests the explanation, perhaps the apology, of an error to which despotic sovereigns are inveterately liable. Trained in habits of indulgence of their own will, and in sentiments of respect for its force and efficacy, they learn to consider it as what not only ought to be, but must be, irresistible ; and feel no less secure of ability to make men happy without their own cooperation, than of the right to balk the natural desire of mankind to be the providers and guardians of their proper welfare. The possession of absolute power renders self-denial the highest effort of virtue ; and the absolute monarch, who should demonstrate a just regard to the rights of his fellow-creatures, would deserve to be honored as one of the most magnanimous of human beings. Furnished with the instructions which we have seen for the mitigation of his arbitrary power, and attended by a few companies of soldiers for its support, Andros arrived in Boston [December, 1686] ; and presenting himself as the substitute for the dreaded and detested Kirke, and commencing his administration with many gracious expressions of good-will, he was received more favorably than might have been expected. But his popularity was shortlived. Instead of conforming to his *instructions*, he copied and even exceeded the arbitrary behaviour of his master in England, and committed the most tyrannical violence and oppressive exactions.[1] Dudley, the late president, and several of his colleagues, were associated as counsellors of the new administration, — which was thus loaded, in the beginning of its career, with the weight of their unpopularity, and in the end involved them in deeper odium and disgrace.

It was the purpose of James to consolidate the force of all the British colonies in one general government ; and Rhode Island and Connecticut were now to experience that their destiny was involved in that of Massachusetts. The inhabitants of Rhode Island, on learning the accession of the king, instantly transmitted an address congratulating him on his elevation, acknowledging themselves his loyal subjects, and begging his protection of their chartered rights. Yet the humility of their supplications could not protect them from the consequences of the plans he had embraced for the general government of New England. Articles of high misdemeanour were exhibited against them before the Lords of the Committee of Colonies, charging them with breaches of their charter, and with opposition to the Acts of Navigation ; and before the close of the year 1685, they received notice of the institution of a process of *quo warranto* against their patent. Without hesitation, they protested that they would not contend with their sovereign, and passed an act, in full assembly, formally surrendering their provincial charter and all the powers it conferred. By a fresh address they " humbly prostrated themselves, their privileges, their all, at the gracious feet of his Majesty, with an entire resolution to serve him with faithful hearts." This abject language emboldened, without conciliating, the king ; who, accounting legal solemnities a superfluous ceremony with persons so obsequious to his will, proceeded, without farther delay, to impose the yoke which the people sought to evade by deserving it. But his eagerness to accomplish his object with rapidity, though it probably inflicted a salutary disappointment on this people at the time, proved ultimately beneficial to their political interests by preserving their charter from a legal extinction ; and this benefit, which a similar improvidence afforded to the people of Connecticut, was ascertained at the era of the British Revolution. In consequence of the last address from Rhode Island, Andros was charged to extend his administration to this province ; and in the same month that witnessed his arrival at Boston he visited Rhode Island, where he dissolved the provincial corporation, broke its seal, and, admitting five of the inhabitants into his legislative council, assumed the exercise of all the functions of government.[2]

Connecticut had also transmitted an address to the king on his accession, and vainly solicited the preservation of her privileges. When the articles of misdemeanour were exhibited against Rhode Island, a measure of similar import was employed against the governor and assembly of Connecticut, who were reproached with framing laws contrary in tenor to those of England ; of extorting unreasonable fines ; of administering an oath of fidelity to their own corporation, in contradistinction to the oath of allegiance ; of intolerance in ecclesiastical polity ; and of denial of justice. These charges, which were supposed to infer a forfeiture of the charter, were remitted to Sawyer, the attorney-general, with directions to expedite a writ of *quo warranto*

---

[1] Hutchinson. Chalmers.	[2] Ibid.

against the colony. The writ was issued, and Randolph, the general enemy of American liberty and officious partisan of arbitrary power, offered his services in conveying it across the Atlantic. The governor and the assembly of Connecticut had for some time remarked the storm approaching, and, knowing that direct resistance was vain, they endeavoured, by address, to elude what they were unable to repel. After delaying, as long as possible, to make any signification of their intentions, they were convinced, by the arrival of Sir Edmund Andros at Boston, and his conduct in Rhode Island, that the designs of the king were to be vigorously pursued, and that they could not hope to be indulged with farther space for deliberation. They wrote, accordingly, to the secretary of state, expressing a strong desire to retain their present constitution ; but requesting, if it were the irrevocable purpose of their sovereign to dispose otherwise of them, that they might be incorporated with Massachusetts, and share the fortunes of a people with whom they had always maintained a friendly correspondence, and whose principles and manners they understood and approved. This was hastily construed by the British government into a surrender of the provincial constitution ; and Andros was commanded to annex this province, also, to his jurisdiction.

Randolph, who seems to have been qualified not less by genius than inclination to promote the success of tyrannical designs, advised the English ministers to prosecute the *quo warranto* to a judicial issue ; assuring them that the government of Connecticut would never consent to do, nor acknowledge that they had actually done, what was equivalent to an express surrender of the rights of the people. It was matter of regret to the ministers and crown lawyers of a later age, that this politic suggestion was not adopted. But the king was too eager to snatch the boon that seemed within his reach, to wait the tedious formalities of the law ; and no farther judicial proceedings ensued on the *quo warranto*. In conformity with his orders, Andros marched at the head of a body of troops to Hartford [October, 1687], the seat of the provincial government, where he demanded that the charter should be delivered into his hands. The people were extremely desirous to preserve at least the document of rights, which the return of better times might enable them to assert with advantage. The charter was laid on the table of the assembly, and some of the principal inhabitants of the colony addressed Andros at considerable length, recounting the exertions that had been made, and the hardships that had been incurred, in order to found the institutions which he was come to destroy ; entreating him yet to spare them, or at least to leave the people in possession of the patent, as a testimonial of the favor and happiness they had hitherto enjoyed. The debate was earnest, but orderly, and protracted to a late hour in the evening. As the day declined, lights were introduced into the hall, which was gradually surrounded by a numerous concourse of the bravest and most determined men in the province, prepared to defend their representatives against the apprehended violence of Andros and his armed followers. At length, their arguments proving quite ineffectual, a measure, supposed to have been previously concerted by the inhabitants, was coolly, resolutely, and successfully conducted. The lights were extinguished, as if by accident ; and Captain Wadsworth, laying hold of the charter, disappeared with it before they could be rekindled. He conveyed it securely through the crowd, — who opened to let him pass, and closed their ranks as he proceeded, — and deposited it in the hollow of an ancient oak, which retained the precious deposit till the era of the British Revolution, and was long regarded with veneration by the people, as the memorial and associate of a transaction so interesting to their liberties. Andros, disappointed in all his efforts to recover the charter, or ascertain the person by whom it was secreted, contented himself with declaring that its institutions were dissolved; and assuming to himself the exercise of supreme authority, he created two of the principal inhabitants members of his legislative council.[1]

Having thus united all the New England States under one comprehensive system of arbitrary government, Andros, with the assistance of his grand legislative council, selected from the inhabitants of the several provinces, addressed himself to the task of composing laws and regulations calculated to fortify his authority. An act restoring the former taxes obtained the assent of the council; and yet even this indispensable provision was obstructed by the reluctance with which the counsellors, though selected by Andros himself, consented to become the instruments of riveting the shackles of their country. The only farther opposition which he experienced proceeded from the inhabitants of the county of Essex, in Massachusetts, who, insisting that they were freemen, refused to pay the contingent assessed upon them of a taxation which they deemed unconstitutional. But their resistance was easily overpowered, and their leaders were severely punished. Andros soon discovered that the revenues of the ancient government were inadequate to the support of his more costly administration; and while he signified this defalcation to the king, he declared, at the same time, with real or affected humanity, that the country was so much impoverished by the effects of the Indian war, by recent losses at sea, and by scanty harvests, that an increase of taxation could hardly be endured. But James, who had exhausted his lenity in the letter of instructions, answered this communication by a peremptory mandate to raise the taxes to a level with the charges of administration; and Andros, thereupon, either stifling his tenderness for the people, or discarding his superfluous respect to the moderation of the king, proceeded to exercise his power with a tyrannical rigor that rendered his government universally odious.

The weight of taxation was oppressively augmented, and the fees of all public functionaries screwed up to an enormous height. The ceremonial of marriage was altered, and the celebration of that rite, which had been hitherto committed to the civil magistrates, was confined to the ministers of the church of England, of whom there was only one in the province of Massachusetts. The fasts and thanksgivings appointed by the Congregational churches were arbitrarily suppressed by the governor, who maintained that the regulation of such matters belonged entirely to the civil power. He took occasion repeatedly, and with the most offensive insolence, to remark, in presence of the council, that the colonists would find themselves mistaken, if they supposed that the privileges of Englishmen followed them to the extremity of the earth; and that the only difference between their condition and that of slaves was, that they were neither bought nor sold. It was declared unlawful for the colonists to assemble in public meetings, or for any one to quit the province without a passport from the governor; and Randolph, now at the summit of his wishes, was not ashamed to boast in letters to his friends that the rulers of New England were "as arbitrary as the Great

---

[1] Hutchinson. Chalmers. Dwight's *Travels.* Trumbull.

Turk." While Andros mocked the people with the semblance of trial by jury, he contrived, by intrigue and partiality in the selection of jurymen, to wreak his vengeance on every person who offended him, as well as to screen the misdeeds of his own dependents from the punishment they deserved. And, as if to heighten the discontent excited by such tyrannical insolence, he took occasion to question the validity of the existing titles to landed property, pretending that the rights acquired under the sanction of the ancient government were tainted with its vices and obnoxious to its fate.[1] New grants or patents from the governor, it was announced, were requisite to mend the defective titles to land ; and writs of intrusion were issued against all who refused to apply for such patents, and to pay the large fees that were charged for them. Most of the landed proprietors were compelled to submit to this extortion in order to save their estates from confiscation, — an extremity, which, however, was braved by one individual, Colonel Shrimpton, who preferred the loss of his property to the recognition of a principle which he deemed both injurious and dishonorable to his country. The king had now encouraged Andros to consider the people whom he governed as a society of felons or rebels ; for he transmitted to him express directions to grant his Majesty's most gracious *pardon* to as many of the colonists as should apply for it. But none had the meanness to solicit a grace that exclusively befitted the guilty. The only act of the king that was favorably regarded by the inhabitants of the colony was his *Declaration of Indulgence,* which excited so much discontent in Britain, even among the Protestant dissenters who shared its benefit. Notwithstanding the intolerance that has been imputed to New England, this declaration produced general satisfaction there ; though some of the inhabitants had discernment enough to perceive that the sole object of the king was the gradual introduction of the Catholic church into Britain.[2]

After many ineffectual remonstrances against his violence and injustice had been addressed by the colonists to Andros himself, two deputies, one of whom was Increase Mather, the most eminent theologian and most popular minister in Massachusetts, were sent to England, to submit the grievances of the colony to the humane consideration of the king. [April, 1688.] Randolph, whose subservience to the royal policy was rewarded with the offices of postmaster-general and licenser of the press in New England, exerted himself to defeat the success of the deputation, by writing to the English court that Mather was a seditious and profligate incendiary, and that his object was to pave the way to the overthrow of regal government. Yet the petitions which the colonists transmitted by Mather were remarkably moderate. Whatever they might desire, all that they demanded was, that their freeholds should be respected, and that a representative assembly should be established for the purpose, at least, of adjusting their taxation. The first of these points was conceded by the king ; but with respect to the other, he was inexorable. When Sir William Phips, whose spirit and gallantry had gained this monarch's esteem, pressed him to grant the colonists an assembly, he replied, "Any thing but that, Sir William" ; and even the opinion of Powis, the attorney-general, to whom the application of the deputies was

[1] The titles of many of the proprietors of estates in New England depended upon conveyances executed by the Indians ; but Andros declared that Indian deeds were no better than " the scratch of a bear's paw." Belknap.
[2] *Life of Phips, apud* Mather. Neal. Dummer's *Defence of the New England Charters.* Hutchinson. Chalmers. Trumbull.

remitted, and who reported that it was just and reasonable, produced no change in his determination.

James, who had now enlarged and completed his views of colonial policy, determined to reduce all the American communities and constitutions, as well those which were denominated *proprietary* as the others, to an immediate dependence on the crown ; for the double purpose of effacing examples that might diminish the resignation of the people of New England, and of combining the force of all the colonies, from the banks of the Delaware to the shores of Nova Scotia, in a compact system capable of presenting a barrier to the formidable encroachments of France. A general dislike of liberal establishments conspired with these views ; and the declamations that resounded from his oppressed subjects in Britain, on the happiness and liberty which America was reputed to enjoy, contributed, at this period, to increase his aversion to American institutions.[1] In prosecution of his politic design, he had recently commanded writs of *quo warranto* to be issued for the purpose of cancelling all the colonial patents that still remained in force ; and shortly before the arrival of the deputation from Massachusetts, a new commission had extended the jurisdiction of Andros to New York and New Jersey, and conferred the appointment of lieutenant-governor on Colonel Francis Nicholson. Andros, with his usual promptitude, accomplished this enlargement of his authority ; and having appointed his deputy to reside at New York, he conducted his wide dominion with a vigor that rendered him formidable to the French, but, unhappily, still more formidable and odious to the people whom he governed.[2]

Sir William Phips, whose fruitless interposition we have remarked in behalf of the deputation from Massachusetts, was himself a native of this province, and, notwithstanding a mean education and the depression of the humblest social position, had ascended by the mere force of superior genius to a conspicuous rank, and gained a high reputation for spirit, capacity, and success. He followed the employment of a shepherd at his native place till he was eighteen years of age, and was afterwards apprenticed to a ship-carpenter. When he was freed from his indentures, he pursued a seafaring life, and attained the station of captain of a merchant-vessel. An account which he happened to peruse of the wreck of a Spanish ship, loaded with bullion, near the Bahama Islands, about fifty years before, inspired him with the bold design of extricating the buried treasure from the bowels of the deep ; whereupon, transporting himself to England, he stated his scheme so plausibly, that the king was struck with it, and, in 1683, sent him with a vessel to undertake the experiment. It proved unsuccessful ; and all his urgency could not induce James to engage in a repetition of it. But the Duke of Albemarle, resuming the project, equipped a vessel for the pur-

---

[1] Dryden, whose servile Muse faithfully reëchoed the sentiments of the court, thus expresses himself in a dramatic prologue written in the year 1686 : —

"Since faction ebbs, and rogues grow out of fashion,
    Their penny scribes take care to inform the nation
    How well men thrive in this or that plantation :

"How Pennsylvania's air agrees with Quakers,
    And Carolina's with associators;
    Both e'en too good for madmen and for traitors.

"Truth is, our land with saints is so run o'er,
    And every age produces such a store,
    That now there 's need of two New Englands more."

[2] Neal   Hutchinson.   Chalmers.

pose, and gave the command of it to Phips, who now succeeded in accomplishing his expectations, and achieved the recovery of specie, to the value of at least £ 300,000, from the bottom of the ocean. Of this treasure he obtained a portion sufficient for his own enrichment, with a still larger meed of general consideration and applause.. The king was advised by some of his courtiers to confiscate the whole of the specie thus recovered, on pretence that he had not received a fair representation of the project ; but he declared that the representation had been perfectly fair, and that nothing but his own misgivings, and the timorous counsels and mean suspicions of those courtiers themselves, had deprived him of the riches which this honest man had sought to procure for him. He conceived a high regard for Phips, and conferred on him the rank of knighthood. Sir William employed his influence at court for the benefit of his country ; and his patriotism seems never to have harmed him in the opinion of the king. Finding that he could not prevail to obtain the restoration of the chartered privileges, he solicited and received the appointment of high sheriff of New England ; in the hope, that, by remedying the abuses that were committed in the empanelling of juries, he might create a barrier against the tyranny of Andros. But the governor and his creatures, incensed at this interference, hired ruffians to attack his person, and soon compelled him to quit the province and take shelter in Britain. James, shortly before his own abdication, among the other attempts he made to conciliate his subjects, offered Phips the government of New England ; but Phips refused to accept this appointment from a falling tyrant, and under a system, which, instead of seeking any longer to mitigate, he hoped speedily to behold entirely overthrown.[1]

The discontent of the people of New England continued meanwhile to increase, insomuch that every act of the government, however innocent or even laudable, was viewed through the perverting gloom of a settled jealousy, and ascribed with undoubting confidence to the most sinister designs. In order to discredit the former provincial authorities, Andros and Randolph sedulously inculcated the notion that the Indians had hitherto been treated with a cruelty and injustice, to which all the hostilities of these savages ought reasonably to be imputed ; and vaunted their own ability to pacify and propitiate them by gentleness and equity.[2] But this year their theory and their policy were alike disgraced by the furious hostilities of the Indians on the eastern frontiers of New England. The movements of these savages were excited on this, as on former occasions, by the insidious artifices of the French, whose suppleness of character and demeanour, contrasted with the grave, unbending spirit of the English, gave them in general a great advantage in the competition for the favor of the Indians ; and who found it easier to direct and employ than to check or eradicate the treachery and ferocity of their savage neighbours. The English colonists offered to the Indians terms of accommodation, which at first they seemed willing to accept ; but the encouragement of their French allies soon prevailed with them to reject all friendly overtures, and their native ferocity prompted them to signalize this declaration by a series of unprovoked and unexpected massacres. Andros published a proclamation requiring that the murderers should be delivered up to him ; but the Indians treated him and his proclamation with

[1] *Life of Phips, apud* Mather. Neal. Hutchinson.
[2] It appears that Randolph cultivated the good opinion of William Penn, by writing to him in this strain, as well as by condemning the former persecution of the Quakers in Massachusetts. Hutchinson. Chalmers.

contempt. In the depth of winter, he found himself obliged to march with a considerable force against these enemies ; and though he succeeded in occupying and fortifying positions which enabled him somewhat to restrain their future incursions, he inflicted but little injury upon them, and lost a great many of his own men, who perished in vain attempts to follow the Indians into their fastnesses, in the most rigorous season of the year. So strong and so undiscriminating was the dislike he excited among the people of New England, that this expedition was unjustly ascribed to a deliberate purpose to destroy the troops whom he conducted, by cold and famine.[1] Every reproach, however groundless, stuck fast to the hated characters of Andros and Randolph.

At length [1689] the smothered rage of the people broke forth. In the spring, some vague intelligence was received, by letters from Virginia, of the transactions of the Prince of Orange in England. The ancient magistrates and principal inhabitants of the province, though they ardently wished and secretly prayed that success might attend the Prince's enterprise, yet determined in so great a cause to incur no unnecessary hazard, and quietly to await a revolution which they believed that no movement of theirs could either promote or retard. But New England was destined to accomplish by her own efforts her own liberation ; and the inhabitants of Massachusetts were now to exercise the gallant privilege, which, nearly a century after, and in a conflict still more arduous, their children again were ready to assert, of being the foremost in resisting oppression and vindicating the rights and honor of their country. The cautious policy and prudential dissuasions from violence that were employed by the wealthier and more aged colonists were contemned by the great body of the people, whose spirit and courage prompted them to achieve the deliverance which they were less qualified by foresight and patience to await. Stung with the recollection of past injuries, their patriotic ardor, on the first prospect of relief, could not be restrained. In seasons of revolution, the wealthy and eminent mingle with their public spirit a less generous concern for their valuable private stakes, and their prospect of sharing in official dignities. The poor have no rich private stakes in their possession ; no dazzling preferments within their reach ; and consequently less restraint on the full flow of their social affections. All at once, and apparently without any preconcerted plan, an insurrection burst out in the town of Boston ; the drums beat to arms, the people flocked together, and in a few hours the revolt became universal, and the energy of the people so overpowering, that every purpose of resisting their will was abandoned by the government. The scruples of the more wealthy and cautious inhabitants were completely overcome by the obvious necessity of interfering to calm and regulate the fervor of the populace. Andros, Dudley, and others, to the number of fifty of the most obnoxious characters, were seized and imprisoned. On the first intelligence of the tumult, Andros sent a party of soldiers to apprehend Simon Bradstreet ; a measure that served only to suggest to the people who their chief ought to be, and to anticipate the unanimous choice by which this venerable man was reinstated in the office he had held when his country was deprived of her liberties. Though now bending under the weight of ninety years, his intellectual powers had undergone but little decay ; he retained (says Cotton Mather) a vigor and wisdom that would have recommended a younger man

---

[1] Neal. Hutchinson.

to the government of a greater colony. As the tidings of the revolt spread through the province, the people eagerly flew to arms, and hurried to Boston to coöperate with their insurgent countrymen. To the assembled crowds a proclamation was read from the balcony of the court-house, detailing the grievances of the colony, and imputing the whole to the tyrannical abrogation of the charter. A committee of safety was appointed by general consent ; and an assembly of representatives being convened soon after, this body, by a unanimous vote, and with the hearty concurrence of the whole province, declared their ancient charter and its constitutions to be resumed ; reappointed Bradstreet and all the other magistrates who were in office in the year 1686 ; and directed these persons in all things to conform to the provisions of the charter, " that this method of government may be found among us when order shall come from the higher powers in England." They announced that Andros and his fellow-prisoners were detained in custody to abide the directions that might be received concerning them from his Highness the Prince of Orange and the English parliament.[1] What would be the extent and final issue of the revolution that was in progress in the parent state was yet unknown in the colonies.

The example of Massachusetts was followed by the other provinces of New England. When the tidings of the revolution at Boston reached Connecticut, the inhabitants determined no longer to acknowledge a governor, who, from the command of one half of the English colonies, was now reduced to the situation of an imprisoned delinquent. Their charter reappeared from its concealment ; and their democratical constitution, which had not been either expressly surrendered or legally dissolved, was instantly restored with universal satisfaction. The people of Rhode Island had never been required to give up the charter whose privileges they so formally and unequivocally resigned ; and now, without a moment's scruple or hesitation, they protested that it was still in force, and removed as well as they could the only obstruction to this plea, by retracting every prior declaration of a contrary tenor. New Plymouth, in like manner, resumed instantaneously its ancient form of government. In New Hampshire, there assembled a general convention of the inhabitants, who promptly and unanimously determined to reannex their territory to Massachusetts. In pursuance of this purpose, they elected deputies to represent them in the General Court at Boston ; but King William refused to comply with their wishes, and in the sequel appointed a separate governor for New Hampshire.[2]

Although the people of Massachusetts at first distinctly intimated their intention to reëstablish by their own act their ancient charter, the calm reflection that succeeded the ferment during which this purpose had been broached convinced them that its accomplishment was impracticable, and that the renovation of a charter, vacated by legal process before the tribunals of the parent state, could proceed only from the crown or legislature of England. Informed of the convention of estates convoked by the Prince of Orange in England, the revolutionary government of Massachusetts assembled a similar convention of the counties and towns of the province ; and it was the opinion of the majority of this assembly, that, although the charter

---

[1] Lives of Bradstreet and Phips, *apud* Mather. Neal. Hutchinson. The provisional government at Boston would willingly have released Andros, after they had deprived him of power ; but the people vehemently insisted that he should be detained in prison. " I am deeply sensible that we have a wolf by the ears," says Danforth, in a letter written on this occasion to Mather, the provincial agent in England. Hutchinson's *Massachusetts Papers.*

[2] Hutchinson. Chalmers.

might be restored, it could not be resumed.   Intelligence having arrived of the settlement of England, and of the investiture of William and Mary with the crown, these sovereigns were proclaimed in the colony with sincere gratulation and extraordinary solemnity. [May 29, 1689.]   A letter was soon after addressed by the king and queen *to the Colony of Massachusetts*, expressing the royal sanction and ratification of the late transactions of the people, and authorizing the present magistrates to retain provisionally the administration of the provincial government, till their Majesties, with the assistance of the privy council, should establish it on a basis more permanent and satisfactory.   An order was communicated, at the same time, to send Andros and the other prisoners to England, that they might answer the charges preferred against them.   Additional agents were deputed by the colony to join Mather, who still continued in England, and, in concurrence with him, to prosecute the charges against Andros, and, above all, to solicit the restoration of the charter.[1]

But before the colonists were able to ascertain if their favorite desire was to be promoted by the English Revolution, they felt the evil effects of this great event, in the consequences of the war that ensued between England and France.   The rupture between the two parent states quickly extended itself to their possessions in America; and the colonies of New England and New York were now involved in bloody and desolating warfare with the forces of the French in Canada and their Indian auxiliaries and allies.   The hostilities that were directed against New York belong to another branch of this history.   In concert with them, various attacks were made by numerous bands of the Indians, in the conclusion of the present year, on the settlements and forts in New Hampshire and Maine; and proving successful in some instances, they were productive of the most horrid extremities of savage cruelty.   Aware that these depredations originated in Canada and Acadia, the General Court of Massachusetts prepared, during the winter, an expedition against both Port Royal and Quebec.   The conduct of it was intrusted to Sir William Phips, who, on the dissolution of the late arbitrary government, returned to New England, in the hope of being able to render some service to his countrymen.   Eight small vessels, with seven or eight hundred men, sailed under his command, in the following spring [April, 1690], and, with little opposition, took possession of Port Royal and of the whole province of Acadia; and, within a month after its departure, the fleet returned loaded with plunder enough to defray the whole expense of the expedition.   But Count Frontignac, the governor of Canada, retorted by sharp and harassing attacks on the remote settlements of New England; and, stimulating the activity of his Indian allies, kept the frontiers in a state of incessant alarm by their predatory incursions.

In letters to King William the General Court of Massachusetts had forcibly represented the importance of the conquest of Canada, and urgently solicited his aid in an expedition for that purpose; but he was too much occupied in Europe to extend his exertions to America; and the provincial government determined to prosecute the enterprise without his assistance. New York and Connecticut engaged to furnish a body of men who were to march overland to attack Montreal, while the troops of Massachusetts should repair by sea to Quebec.   The fleet destined for this expedition consisted of nearly forty vessels, the largest of which carried forty-four guns; and the

----

[1] Neal. Hutchinson.

number of troops on board amounted to two thousand. [Aug. 9, 1690.] The command of this armament was intrusted to Sir William Phips, who, in the conduct of the enterprise, demonstrated his usual courage, and every other military qualification except that which experience alone can confer, and without which, in warfare with a civilized enemy, all the rest commonly prove unavailing. The troops of Connecticut and New York, retarded by defective arrangements, and disappointed of the assistance of the friendly Indians who had engaged to furnish them with canoes for crossing the rivers they had to pass, were compelled to retire without attacking Montreal; and, in consequence, the whole force of Canada was concentrated to resist the attack of Phips. His armament arrived before Quebec so late in the season [October], that only an immediate assault could have enabled him to carry the place; but by unskilful delay the opportunity of making such an attempt with advantage was irretrievably lost. The English were worsted in various sharp encounters, and finally compelled to make a precipitate retreat; and the fleet, after sustaining great damage in its homeward voyage, returned to Boston. [November 13.]   Such was the unfortunate issue of an enterprise which involved Massachusetts in an enormous expense, and cost the lives of at least a thousand of her people. The French had so strongly foreboded its success, that they ascribed its discomfiture to the immediate interposition of Heaven, in confounding the devices of the enemy, and depriving them of common sense; and under this impression, the citizens of Quebec established an annual procession in commemoration of their deliverance. That the conduct of Phips, however, was no way obnoxious to censure may be safely inferred from the fact that a result so disastrous brought no reproach upon him, and deprived him in no degree of the favor of his countrymen.   And yet the disappointment, in addition to the mortification which it inflicted, was attended with very injurious consequences.

The General Court of Massachusetts had not even anticipated the possibility of miscarriage, and confidently expected to derive, from the success of the expedition, the same reimbursement of expenses which their former enterprise had afforded.   "During the absence of the forces," says Cotton Mather, with an expression too whimsical for a matter of so much solemnity, "the wheel of prayer for them in New England had been kept continually going round"; and this attempt to reinforce the expedition by spiritual co-operation was pursued in conjunction with an entire neglect of provisions applicable to an unsuccessful result. The returning army, finding the government unprepared to satisfy their claims, were on the point of mutinying for their pay; and it was found necessary to issue bills of credit, which the troops consented to accept in place of money. The colony was now in a very depressed and suffering state. Hoping to *improve* (as they expressed themselves) the calamities which they were unable to evade, the provincial magistrates endeavoured to promote the increase of piety and the reformation of manners; and pressed upon the ministers and the people the duty of strongly resisting that worldliness of mind which the necessity of contending violently for temporal interests is apt to engender. The attacks of the Indians on the eastern frontiers were attended with a degree of success and barbarity that diffused general terror; and the colonists in this quarter were yielding to anticipations of a speedy expulsion from their settlements, when, all at once, the savages, of their own accord, proposed a peace of six months, which was accepted by the provincial government with great willingness and devout gratitude. As it was clearly ascertained that the hostilities of the Indians were continually fostered by the intrigues, and rendered the more formidable by the counsel and assistance, of the French authorities in Canada, the people of New England began to regard the conquest of that province as indispensable to their safety and tranquillity. With the hope of prevailing on the king to sanction and embrace this enterprise, as well as for the purpose of aiding the other deputies in the no less interesting application for the restoration of the provincial charter, Sir William Phips, soon after his return from Quebec, by desire of his countrymen, repaired to England.[1]

In the discharge of the duties of their mission [1691], the deputies employed every effort that patriotic zeal could prompt, and honorable policy admit, to obtain satisfaction to their constituents, by the punishment of their oppressors, and the restitution of their charter. But in both these objects their endeavours were unsuccessful ; and the failure was generally (whether justly or not) ascribed to the unbending integrity with which Mather and Phips rejected every art and intrigue that seemed inconsistent with the honor of their country. It was soon discovered that the king and his ministers were averse to an inquiry into the conduct of Andros and Randolph, and not less so to the restoration of the ancient charter of the colony. The conduct of the British court on this occasion presents a confused and disgusting picture of intrigue and duplicity. The deputies were beset by a multitude of importunate counsellors, and real or pretended partisans ; — some doubtless indiscreet, and some perhaps insincere. They were persuaded by certain of their advisers to present to the privy council the charges against Andros *unsigned*, and assured by others that in so doing they had *cut the throat of their country*. When they attended to present their charges, they were anticipated by Andros and Randolph, who came prepared with a charge against the colonists of resistance to the authority of the parent state, and rebellious deposition of their legitimate governor. Sir John Somers, the lawyer employed by the deputies, consented that they should abandon the situation of accusers and stand on the defensive ; and he tendered the unsigned charges as an answer to the accusations of Andros and Randolph. The council hesitated to receive a plea presented in the name of a whole people, and required that some individuals should appear and personally avouch it. " Who was it," said the Lord President, " that imprisoned Sir Edmund and the rest ? You say it was the country, and that they rose as one man. But that is nobody. Let us see the persons who will make it their own case." The deputies thereupon offered to sign the charges, and to undertake the amplest personal responsibility for the acts of their countrymen. But they were deterred from this proceeding by the remonstrances of Sir John Somers, who insisted (for reasons that have never been satisfactorily explained) on persisting in the course in which they had begun. Some of the counsellors protested against the injustice and chicanery of encountering the complaint of a whole nation with objections so narrow and technical. " Is not it plain," they urged, " that the revolution in Massachusetts was carried on exactly in the same manner as the revolution in England ? Who seized and imprisoned Chancellor Jeffries ? Who secured the garrison of Hull ? These were the acts of the people, and not of private individuals." This difference of opinion on a point of form seems to have been the object which the ministry studied to promote. Without determining the point, the

---

[1] Neal. Hutchinson. Colden's *History of the Five Indian Nations of Canada.*

w *

council interrupted the discussion by a resolution that the whole matter should be referred to the king; and his Majesty soon after signified his pleasure that the complaints of both parties should be dismissed.[1] [1691.] Thus terminated the impeachment of Andros, in a manner very ill calculated to impress the people of Massachusetts with respect for the justice of the British government. They soon after had the mortification of seeing him add reward to impunity, and honored with the appointment of governor of Virginia and Maryland. They had previously seen Dudley, whom they arrested and sent to England with Andros, appointed chief justice of New York, where he condemned to death the unfortunate Leisler, who excited the first revolutionary movement in that colony in favor of King William.[2]

The deputies, finding that the House of Commons, though at first disposed to annul the judicial decree against the charter of Massachusetts, had been persuaded, by the arguments of Somers and other lawyers who possessed seats in the house, to depart from this purpose, and that the king was resolved not to restore the old charter, employed every effort to obtain at least a restitution of the privileges it conferred. But William and his ministers, though restrained from imitating the tyrannical measures of the former reign, were eager and determined to avail themselves of whatever acquisitions these measures might have gained to the royal prerogative; and finding that the crown had acquired a specious legal pretext to exercise much greater authority over the colony than was reserved in its original constitution, they scrupled not to take advantage of this pretext, without regard to the tyrannical cast of the policy by which it had been obtained. The restoration of their ancient privilege of electing their own municipal officers was ardently desired by the colonists, and demanded by the deputies with a warmth which the king would probably have resented as disrespectful to himself, if he had not felt himself bound to excuse the irritation provoked by his own injustice. In vain did Archbishop Tillotson urge him not to withhold from the people of Massachusetts the full measure of those privileges, which, even under the arbitrary sway of Charles the First, had been conceded to them. He adhered inflexibly to his determination of retaining, as far as possible, every advantage, however surreptitiously acquired, that fortune had put into his hands; and at length a new charter was framed on principles that widely departed from the primeval constitution of the colony, and transferred to the crown many valuable privileges that originally belonged to the people. [October 7, 1691.]

By this charter the territories of Massachusetts, Plymouth, and Maine, together with the conquered province of Acadia, or Nova Scotia, were united together under one jurisdiction,—an arrangement that was by no means satisfactory to the parties included in it; for Plymouth, which earnestly solicited a separate establishment, was forcibly annexed to Massachusetts; and New Hampshire, which as earnestly petitioned to be included in this annexation, was made a separate province.[3] The appointment of the

---

[1] Neal. Hutchinson.

[2] Randolph was not sent back to America. He received, however, an appointment in the West Indies, where he died, retaining, it is said, his dislike of the people of New England to the last. Eliot's *Biographical Dictionary of New England.* Cranfield, the tyrant of New Hampshire, was appointed collector of customs at Barbadoes. He repented of his conduct in New England, and endeavoured to atone for it by showing all the kindness in his power to the New England traders who resorted to Barbadoes. Belknap.

[3] The union, so much desired by the people of Massachusetts and New Hampshire, was overruled by the interest, and for the convenience, of Samuel Allen, a merchant in London,

governor, deputy-governor, secretary, and all the officers of the admiralty, was reserved to the crown.   Twenty-eight counsellors were directed to be chosen by the house of assembly, and presented to the governor for his approbation.   The governor was empowered to convoke, adjourn, prorogue, and dissolve the assembly at pleasure ; to nominate, exclusively, all military officers, and (with consent of the council) all the judges and other officers of the law.   To the governor, was reserved a negative on the laws and acts of the general assembly and council ; and all laws enacted by these bodies and approved by the governor were to be transmitted to England for the royal approbation ; and if disallowed within the space of three years, they were to become absolutely void.   Liberty of conscience and of divine worship, which had not been mentioned in the old charter, was, by the present one, expressly assured to all persons except Roman Catholics.[1]

The innovations thus introduced into their ancient municipal constitution [1691] excited much discontent in the minds of the people of Massachusetts ; the more especially because the enlargement of royal authority was not attended with a proportional communication of the royal protection.   At the very time when the king thus extended the limits of his prerogative at the expense of popular liberty, he found himself constrained, by the urgency of his affairs in Europe, to refuse the assistance which the people besought from him to repel the hostilities of the Indians and of the French forces in Canada.   The situation of the provinces of Connecticut and Rhode Island, which were permitted to reassume all their ancient privileges, rendered the injustice with which Massachusetts was treated more flagrant and irritating. Though legal technicalities might be thought by lawyers and special pleaders to warrant the advantageous distinction which those States enjoyed, a conclusion so illiberal was utterly repugnant to the enlarged views of justice and equity which ought to regulate the policy of a legislator.   Only mistake on the one side, or artifice on the other, could be supposed to have procured to Connecticut and Rhode Island an advantage that made the treatment of Massachusetts more invidious ; and a dangerous lesson was taught to the colonial communities, when they were thus given to understand that it was their own vigilant dexterity and successful intrigue, or the blunders of the parent state, that they were to rely on as the safeguards of their rights. The injustice of the policy now applied to Massachusetts was rendered still more glaringly apparent by the very different treatment obtained by the powerful corporation of the city of London, whose charter, though annulled with the same legal formality, and on grounds as plausible, as the ancient charter of Massachusetts, was restored by a legislative act immediately after the Revolution.   Nor was any real political advantage obtained by the English government from its violation of just and equitable principles.   The

to whom Mason's heirs had sold their claim to the soil of New Hampshire.   He was appointed the first governor of the province ; and employing his authority in vexatious, but unsuccessful, attempts to extract pecuniary profit from his purchased claim, rendered himself extremely odious to the people.   Belknap.   He was superseded in the office of governor by Lord Bellamont, in 1698.

[1] Mather, *Life of Sir William Phips.* Neal. Hutchinson. Belknap. Bancroft. " That charter effected in Massachusetts as perfect and thorough a revolution as ever was produced by a similar act in any state or nation.   It changed not only the form of the government and the relations of power among the people, but also the entire foundation and objects of the government.   By making freehold and property, instead of church-membership, the qualification of the right of electing and being elected to office, religion became no longer the end and object of the civil government."   Quincy's *History of Harvard University.*   This change was for a while disguised by the coincidence between the sentiments of the first boards of new magistrates and the ancient system of municipal polity.

power that was wrested from the colonists, and appropriated by the crown, was quite inadequate to the formation of an efficient royal party in the province. The usurped prerogative of nominating the governor and other officers was regarded as a badge of dependence, instead of forming a bond of union. The popular assemblies retained sufficient influence over the governors to curb them in the administration of an illiberal policy, and sufficient power to restrain them from making any serious inroad on the constitution. It is a remarkable fact, that the dissensions between the two countries, which eventually terminated in the dissolution of the British empire in America, were not a little promoted by the pernicious counsels and erroneous information conveyed to the English ministry by the governors of those provinces in which the appointment to that office was exercised by the king.

Aware of the dissatisfaction with which the new charter was regarded, the ministers of William judged it prudent to waive in the outset the full exercise of the invidious prerogative, and desired the provincial deputies to name the person whom they considered most likely to be acceptable to their countrymen as governor of Massachusetts ; and the deputies having united in recommending Sir William Phips, the appointment to this office was bestowed on him accordingly. This act of courtesy was attended with a degree of success in mollifying the ill-humor of the people, that attests the high estimation in which Phips was held by his countrymen ; for on his arrival at Boston [May, 1692], though some discontent was betrayed, and several of the members of the General Court warmly insisted that the new charter should be absolutely rejected,[1] yet the great body of the people received him with acclamations ; and a majority of the General Court resolved that the charter should be heartily accepted, and appointed a day of thanksgiving for the safe arrival of their worthy governor and of Increase Mather, whose services they acknowledged with grateful commemoration. The new governor hastened to approve himself worthy of the favorable regard thus expressed for him. Having convoked the General Court of the province, he addressed the members in a short, characteristic speech, recommending to them the composition of a code of good laws with all the expedition they could exert. " Gentlemen," said he, " you may make yourselves as easy as you will for ever. Consider what may have a tendency to your welfare ; and you may be sure that whatever bills you offer to me, consistent with the honor and interest of the crown, I 'll pass them readily. I do but seek opportunities to serve you. Had it not been for the sake of this thing, I had never accepted of this office. And whenever you have settled such a body of good laws, that no person coming after me may make you uneasy, I shall desire not one day longer to continue in the government." His conduct seems in general to have corresponded with these professions.[2]

And yet, the administration of Sir William Phips was neither long nor prosperous. Though he might give his sanction as governor to popular laws, it was not in his power to prevent them from being rescinded by the crown ;

---

[1] Mather and the other deputies, when they found it impossible to obtain an alteration of the new charter, proposed at first to reject it altogether, and to institute a process for trying the validity of the judgment pronounced on the *quo warranto*. They were deterred from this proceeding by the solemn assurance of Treby, Somers, and the two chief justices of England (Holt and Pollexfen), that, if the judgment were reversed, a new *quo warranto* would be issued, and inevitably followed by a sentence exempt from all ground of challenge. These learned persons assured the deputies, that the colonists, by erecting judicatories, constituting a house of representatives, and incorporating colleges, had forfeited their charter, which gave no sanction to such acts of authority. Hutchinson.

[2] Mather, *Life of Phips*. Neal. Hutchinson.

and this fate soon befell a law that was passed by the provincial assembly, declaring the colonists exempt from all taxes but such as should be imposed by their own representatives, and asserting their right to share all the privileges of Magna Charta. He found the province involved in a distressing war with the French and Indians, and in the still more formidable calamity of that delusion which has been termed *the New England witchcraft*. When the Indians were informed of the elevation of Sir William Phips to the office of governor of Massachusetts, they were struck with amazement at the fortunes of the man whose humble origin they perfectly well knew, and with whom they had familiarly associated but a few years before in the obscurity of his primitive condition. Impressed with a high opinion of his courage and resolution, and a superstitious dread of that fortune that seemed destined to surmount every obstacle and prevail over every disadvantage, they would willingly have made peace with him and his countrymen, but were induced to continue the war by the artifices and intrigues of the French. A few months after his arrival, the governor, at the head of a small army, marched to Pemmaquid, on the Merrimack River, and there caused to be erected a fort of considerable strength, and calculated by its situation to form a powerful barrier to the province, and to overawe the neighbouring tribes of Indians, and interrupt their mutual communication.

The beneficial effect of this operation was experienced in the following year [1693], when the Indians sent ambassadors to the fort at Pemmaquid, and there concluded with English commissioners a treaty of peace, by which they renounced for ever the interests of the French, and pledged themselves to perpetual amity with the inhabitants of New England.[1] The colonists, who had suffered severely from the recent depredations of these savages,[2] and were still laboring under the burdens entailed on them by former wars, were not slow to embrace the first overtures of peace ; and yet they murmured with great discontent and ill-humor at the measure to which they were principally indebted for the deliverance they had so ardently desired. The expense of building the fort, and of maintaining its garrison and stores, occasioned an addition to the existing taxes, which provoked their impatience. The party who had opposed submission to the new charter eagerly promoted every complaint against the conduct of a system which they regarded with rooted aversion ; and labored so successfully on this occasion to vilify the person and government of Sir William Phips in the eyes of his countrymen, that his popularity sustained a shock from which it never afterwards entirely recovered. The people were easily persuaded to regard the increase of taxation as the effect of the recent abridgment of their political

---

[1] Neal. Hutchinson.

[2] The situation of the people of New Hampshire, in particular, had become so irksome and dangerous, that at one time they entertained the purpose of abandoning the province. Belknap. When Adam Smith declared that " nothing can be more contemptible than an Indian war in North America," he alluded to a period much later than this, and in which the proportion between the numbers of the savage and civilized races had undergone a great alteration. Even then, the observation was just only in so far as respected apprehensions of conquest ; for no hostilities were ever more fraught with cruelty, misery, and horror, than those of the North American Indians. When Chalmers pronounced the Indians " a foe that has never proved dangerous, except to the effeminate, the factious, and the cowardly," he was transported into this injustice by the desire of lowering the reputation of the people of New Hampshire, — a portion of the American population who seem to have provoked in a peculiar degree his spleen and malevolence. New Hampshire has been more justly characterized by an American historian as " a nursery of stern heroism ; producing men of firmness and valor, who can traverse mountains and deserts, encounter hardships, and face an enemy without terror." Belknap.

privileges, and to believe, that, if they had retained their ancient control over the officers of government, the administration of their affairs would have been more economically conducted. But another cause, which we have already cursorily remarked, and must now more attentively consider, rendered the minds of the colonists at this time unusually susceptible of gloomy impressions, and of suspicions equally irritating and unreasonable. [1693.]

The belief of witchcraft was at this period almost universal in Christian countries; and the existence and criminality of the practice were recognized in the penal code of every civilized state. Persons suspected of being witches and wizards were frequently tried, condemned, and put to death by the authority of the most enlightened tribunals in Europe; and, in particular, but a few years before the present epoch, Sir Matthew Hale, a man highly and justly renowned for the strength of his understanding, the variety of his knowledge, and the eminent Christian graces that adorned his character, after a long and anxious investigation, adjudged a number of men and women to die for this offence at an assize in Suffolk.[1] The reality of witchcraft had never yet been questioned; nor were there any individuals to whom that reality appeared unimportant or incredible, except those who regarded the spiritual world altogether as a mere speculation of visionary fancy, and delusive. Among other believers in the practice, were some of the unfortunate beings themselves who were put to death as witches. Instigated by fraud, folly, or malignity, or possessed by demoniacal frenzy, some of these unhappy persons professed, more or less openly, to hold communication with the powers of darkness; and by the administration of subtle poisons, by disturbing the imagination of their victims, or by an actual appropriation of that unhallowed agency which Scripture assures us did once operate in the world, and of which no equal authority has ever proclaimed the extinction, they committed crimes and inflicted injuries which were punished, doubtless sometimes, perhaps frequently, under an erroneous name.

The colonists of New England, participating in the general belief of this practice, regarded it with a degree of abhorrence and indignation corresponding to the piety for which they were so remarkably distinguished. Their experience in America had tended to strengthen the sentiments on this subject which they brought with them from Europe; for they found the belief of witchcraft firmly rooted among the Indian tribes, and the practice (or what was so termed and esteemed) prevailing extensively, and with perfect impunity, among those people, whom, as heathens, they regarded as the worshippers of demons.[2] Their conviction of the reality of witchcraft was, not unreasonably, confirmed by such evidence of the universal assent of mankind; and their resentment of its enormity was proportionally increased by the honor and acceptance which they saw it enjoy under the shelter of superstitions that denied and dishonored the true God. The first trials for

---

[1] Howell's *State Trials*. Even so late as the middle of the eighteenth century, the conviction of the witches of Warbois, in the reign of Queen Elizabeth, was still commemorated in an annual sermon at Huntingdon. Johnson's *Works, Observations on the Tragedy of Macbeth.* The seceders from the established church in Scotland published an act of their associate presbytery at Edinburgh, in 1743 (reprinted at Glasgow in 1766), denouncing the repeal of the penal laws against witchcraft as a national sin. Arnot's *Criminal Trials in Scotland.*
The last executions for witchcraft in the British dominions were at Huntingdon in 1716, and in Sutherlandshire in 1722. Arnot.

[2] Hubbard, a Puritan minister, and one of the earliest historians of New England, cites with approbation the opinion of a Mr. Mede, that America was originally peopled by a crew of witches, transported thither by the devil. *Collections of the Rhode Island Historical Society,* Vol. III.

witchcraft in New England occurred in the year 1645, when four persons charged with this crime were put to death in Massachusetts. Goffe, the regicide, in his *Diary*, records the conviction of three others at Hartford, in Connecticut, in 1662, and remarks, that, after one of them was hanged, a young woman, who had been bewitched, was restored to health. For more than twenty years after, few instances occurred, and little notice has been preserved of similar prosecutions. But in the year 1688, a woman was executed for witchcraft at Boston, after an investigation conducted with a degree of solemnity that made a deep impression on the minds of the people. An account of the whole transaction was published ; and so generally were the wise and good persuaded of the justice of the proceeding, that Richard Baxter, the celebrated Non-conformist divine, wrote a preface to the narrative, in which he scrupled not to declare every one who refused to believe it an obdurate Sadducee. The attention of the people being thus strongly excited, and their suspicions awakened and attracted in this dangerous direction, the charges of witchcraft became gradually more frequent, till, at length, there commenced at Salem that dreadful tragedy which rendered New England for many months a scene of bloodshed, terror, and madness.

In the beginning of the year 1692, Massachusetts was visited with an epidemical complaint resembling epilepsy, which the physicians, unable to explain or cure, readily imputed to supernatural operation. Some young women, and among others the daughter and niece of Paris, the minister of Salem village, were first attacked by this distemper, and induced by the suggestions of their medical attendants to ascribe it to withcraft. The delusion was encouraged by a perverted application of the means best fitted to strengthen and enlighten the understanding. Solemn fasts were observed, and assemblies convoked for extraordinary prayer ; and the supposition of witchcraft, which in reality had been previously assumed, was thus confirmed and consecrated in the apprehension of the public. The imaginations of the patients, disturbed by morbid sensation, and inflamed by the contagious terror which their supposed malady excited, readily prompted accusations against particular individuals as the authors of the calamity. The flame was now kindled, and finding ample nourishment in all the strongest passions and most inveterate weaknesses of human nature, carried havoc and destruction through the community. The bodily symptoms of the prevailing epidemic, frequently pondered by timorous and susceptible persons, were propagated with amazing rapidity ; and having been once regarded as symptoms of witchcraft, were ever after referred to the same diabolical origin. The usual and well known contagion of nervous disorders was quickened by dread of the horrid and mysterious agency from which they were now supposed to arise ; and this appalling dread, enfeebling the reason of its victims, led them to confound the visions of their disturbed apprehension with the realities of sound experience. To think earnestly upon any thing implies its influence and engraves its presence on the mind ; and to dread it is partly to realize and still farther to invite its dominion. Symptoms before unheard of, and unusually terrific,[1] attended the cases of the sufferers, and were supposed

---

[1] Swelling of the throat, in particular, now well known to be a symptom of hysterical affection, was considered at that time a horrible prodigy. Medical science was still depraved by an admixture of gross superstition. The touch of a king was believed to be capable of curing some diseases ; and astrology formed a part of the course of medical study, because the efficacy of drugs was believed to be promoted or impeded by planetary influence. " In consequence of the greater nervous irritability of women," says Dugald Stewart, " their muscular system seems to possess a greater degree of that mobility by which the principle of sympathetic imi-

to prove beyond a doubt that the disorder was no natural ailment; while, in truth, they denoted nothing else than the extraordinary terror of the unhappy patients, who augmented the malignity of their disease by the darkness and horror, of the source to which they traced it.   Every case of nervous derangement was now referred to this source, and every morbid affection of the spirits and fancy diverted into the most dangerous channel.   Accusations of particular individuals easily suggested themselves to the disordered minds of the sufferers, and were eagerly preferred by themselves and their relatives, in the hope of obtaining deliverance from the calamity by the punishment of its guilty authors.

These charges, however unsupported by proof, and however remote from probability, alighted with fatal influence wherever they fell.   The supernatural intimation, by which they were supposed to be dictated, supplied and excluded all ordinary proof; and when a patient, under the dominion of nervous affections, or in the intervals of epileptic paroxysms, declared that he had seen the apparition of a particular individual occasioning his sufferings, no consideration of previously unblemished character could screen the accused from a trial, which, if the patient persisted in the charge, invariably terminated in a conviction.   The charges were frequently admitted without any other proof, for the very reason for which they should have been absolutely rejected by human tribunals, — that their truth was judged incapable of ordinary proof, or of being known to any but the accuser and the accused. So general and inveterate was the belief in the reality of the supposed witchcraft, that no one dared openly to gainsay it, whatever might really be his opinion on the subject; and the innocent victims of the charges were constrained to argue on the assumption, that the apparitions of themselves, described by their accusers, had actually been seen, — and reduced to plead that their semblance was assumed by an evil spirit that sought to screen his proper instruments, and divert the public indignation upon unoffending persons.   It was maintained, however, by Stoughton, the deputy-governor of Massachusetts, most gratuitously, but, unhappily, to the conviction of the public, that an evil spirit could sustain only the appearance of such persons as had given up their bodies to him and devoted themselves to his service. The semblance of legal proof, besides, was very soon added to the force of those charges; and seeming to put their truth past doubt in some cases, was thought to confirm it in all.   Some of the accused, terrified by their danger, sought safety in avowing their guilt, recanting their supposed impiety, and denouncing others as their tempters and associates.   In order to beget favor and verify their recantation, they now declared themselves the victims of the witchcraft they had formerly practised, counterfeited the nervous affections of their own accusers, and imputed their sufferings to the vengeance of their ancient accomplices.

These artifices and the general delusion were promoted by the conduct of the magistrates, who, with a monstrous inversion of equity and sound sense, offered impunity to all who would confess the imputed crime and betray their associates, while they inflexibly doomed to death every accused person who maintained his innocence.   Thus one accusation produced a multitude of others, — the accused becoming accusers and witnesses, and hastening to escape from danger by fastening the guilt on other persons.

tation operates." The first and the most numerous of the supposed victims of witchcraft in New England were young women. It is not improbable, that, in some cases, the other morbid symptoms were complicated with the mysterious phenomena of somnambulism.

From Salem, where its main fury was exerted, the evil spread over the whole province of Massachusetts ; and wherever it was able to penetrate, it effectually subverted the happiness and security of life.   The sword of the law was wrested from the hand of dispassionate justice, and committed to the grasp of the wildest fear and fury, while the shield of the law was denied to the unfortunate objects of these headlong and dangerous passions. Alarm and terror pervaded all ranks of society.   The first and the favorite objects of arraignment were ill-favored old women, whose dismal aspect, exciting horror and aversion instead of tenderness and compassion, was reckoned a proof of their guilt, and seemed to designate the appropriate agents of mysterious and unearthly wickedness.   But the sphere of accusation was progressively enlarged to such a degree, that at length neither age nor sex, neither ignorance nor innocence, neither learning nor piety, neither reputation nor office, could afford the slightest safeguard against a charge of witchcraft.   Even irrational creatures were not exempted from this fatal charge ; and a dog, belonging to a person accused of witchcraft, was hanged as the accomplice of a crime which the poor brute was alike incapable of confessing, denying, or comprehending.   Under the dominion of terror, all mutual confidence was destroyed, and the kindest feelings of human nature were trampled under foot.   The nearest relations became each other's accusers ; and one unhappy man, in particular, was condemned and executed on the testimony of his wife and daughter, who impeached him merely with the view of preserving themselves.   Many respectable persons fled from the colony ; others, maintaining their innocence, were capitally convicted, and died with a serene courage and piety, that affected, but could not disabuse, the spectators.

The accounts that have been preserved of the trials of these unfortunate persons present a most revolting and humiliating picture of frenzy, folly, and injustice.   In support of the charge of witchcraft against some of the prisoners, the court permitted testimony to be given of losses and mishaps that had befallen the accusers or their cattle (even as long as twenty years before the trial), after some meeting or some disagreement between them and the prisoners.   Against others it was deposed, that they had performed greater feats of strength, and walked from one place to another in a shorter space of time, than the accusers judged possible without diabolical assistance.   But the main article of proof was the spectral apparitions of the persons of the pretended witches to the eyes of their supposed victims during the paroxysms of their malady.   The accusers sometimes declared that they could not see the prisoners at the bar of the court ; which was construed into a proof of the immediate exertion of Satanic influence in rendering the persons of the culprits invisible to those who were to testify against them.   The bodies of the prisoners were commonly examined for the discovery of what were termed witch-marks ; and as the examiners did not know what they were seeking for, and yet earnestly desired to find it, every little puncture or discoloration of the skin was easily believed to be the impress of infernal touch. In general, the accusers fell into fits, or complained of violent uneasiness, at the sight of the prisoners.   On the trial of Burroughs, a clergyman of the highest respectability, some of the witnesses being affected in this manner, the judges replied to his protestations of innocence, by asking if he would venture to deny that these persons were then laboring under the malignant influence of the powers of hell.   He answered that he did not deny it, but

x

that he denied having any concern with it.   " If you were not a friend of the devil," replied the presiding judge, " he would not exert himself in this manner to prevent these persons from speaking against you."   When a prisoner in his defence uttered any thing that seemed to move the audience in his favor, some of the accusers were ready to exclaim that they saw the devil standing by and putting the words in his mouth ; and every feeling of humanity was chased away by such absurd and frantic exclamations.   While one of the convicts, at the foot of the scaffold, was addressing a last assurance of his innocence to the spectators, the executioner sat by him smoking tobacco ; and some of the smoke having been wafted by the wind into the eyes of the dying man, the accusers thereupon set up a shout of brutal triumph, and exclaimed, " See how the devil wraps him in smoke ! " It cannot be doubted that fraud and malignity had a share in inciting these prosecutions.

The principle that was practically avowed in the courts of justice, that, in cases of witchcraft, accusation was equivalent to conviction, presented the most subtle and powerful allurements to the indulgence of natural ferocity and the gratification of fantastic terror and suspicion ; and there is but too much reason to believe, that rapacity, malice, and revenge were not vainly invited to seize this opportunity of satiating their appetites in confiscation and bloodshed.   So strong meanwhile was the popular delusion, that even the detection of manifest perjury, on one of the trials, proved insufficient to weaken the credit of the most unsupported accusation.   Sir William Phips, the governor, Stoughton, the lieutenant-governor, and the most learned and eminent persons, both among the clergy and laity of the province, partook and promoted the general infatuation.   Nothing but an outrageous zeal against witchcraft seemed capable of assuring any individual of the safety of his life ; and temptations, that but too frequently overpowered human courage and virtue, arose from the conviction impressed on every person that there remained no other alternative than that of becoming the oppressor or the oppressed.   The *afflicted* (as the accusers were termed) and their witnesses and partisans began to form a numerous and united party in every community, which none dared to oppose, and which none who once joined or supported it could forsake with impunity.   A magistrate, who for a while took an active part in examining and committing the supposed delinquents, beginning to suspect that the charges originated in some fatal mistake, showed an inclination to discourage them, and straightway found that he had drawn the dangerous imputation on himself.   A constable, who had apprehended many of the accused, was smitten with a similar suspicion, and hastily declared that he would meddle in this matter no farther.   Reflecting with alarm on the danger he had provoked, he attempted to fly the country, but was overtaken in his flight by the vengeance of the accusers ; and, having been brought back to Salem, was tried for witchcraft, convicted, and executed.   Some persons, whom the instinct of self-preservation had induced to accuse their friends or kinsfolk, touched with remorse, confessed the crime they had been guilty of, and retracted their testimony.   They were convicted of relapse into witchcraft, and died the victims of their returning virtue.

At last, the very excess of the evil brought about its cure.   About fifteen months had elapsed since it first broke forth ; and so far from being extinguished or abated, it was growing every day more formidable.   Of twenty-eight persons capitally convicted, nineteen had been hanged ; and one, for refusing to plead, was *pressed to death* ; — the only instance in which this engine of legal barbarity was ever employed in North America. The number of the accusers and pardoned witnesses multiplied with alarming rapidity. The sons of Governor Bradsteet, and other individuals of eminent station and character, had fled from a charge belied by the whole tenor of their lives. A hundred and fifty persons were in prison on the same charge, and impeachments of no less than two hundred others had been presented to the magistrates. Men began to ask where this would end. The constancy and piety with which the unfortunate victims encountered their fate produced an impression on the minds of the people, which, though counterbalanced at the time by the testimony of the pardoned witnesses, gained strength from the reflection that these witnesses purchased their lives by their testimony, while the persons against whom they had borne evidence sealed their own testimony with their blood.

It was happy, perhaps, for the country, that, while the minds of the people were awakening to reflections thus reasonable and humane, some of the accusers carried the audacity of their arraignment to such a pitch, as to prefer charges of witchcraft against Lady Phips, the governor's wife, and against certain of the nearest relatives of Dr. Increase Mather, the most pious minister and popular citizen of Massachusetts. This circumstance at once opened the eyes of Sir William Phips and Dr. Mather ; so far, at least, as to induce a strong suspicion that many of the late proceedings which they had countenanced were rash and indefensible. They felt that they had dealt with others in a manner very different from that in which they were now reduced to desire that others should deal with them. A kindred sentiment beginning also to prevail in the public mind encouraged the resolute exertion by which a citizen of Boston succeeded in stemming the fury of these terrible proscriptions. Having been charged with witchcraft by some persons at Andover, he anticipated an arrest, by promptly arresting his accusers for defamation, and preferring on oath against them a claim of damages to the amount of a thousand pounds. The effect of this vigorous conduct surpassed his most sanguine expectations. It seemed as if a spell that had been cast over the people of Andover was dissolved by one bold touch ; the frenzy subsided in a moment, and witchcraft was heard of in that town no more. The impression was quickly diffused throughout the province ; and the influence of it appeared at the very next assize that was held for the trial of witchcraft, when, of fifty prisoners who were tried on such evidence as was formerly deemed sufficient, the accusers could obtain the conviction of no more than three, who were instantly reprieved by the governor. These acquittals were doubtless in part produced by a change which the public opinion underwent as to the sufficiency of what was denominated *spectral evidence* of witchcraft.

An assembly of the most eminent divines of the province, convoked for the purpose by the governor [June 15th, 1693], after solemn consideration, pronounced and promulgated as their deliberate judgment, " That the apparitions of persons afflicting others was no proof of their being witches," and that it was by no means inconsistent with Scripture or reason that the devil should assume the shape of a good man, or even cause the real aspect of that man to produce impressions of pain on the bodies of persons bewitched. The ministers, nevertheless, united in strongly recommending to the government the rigorous prosecution of all persons still accused of witchcraft. . But the judgment they pronounced respecting the validity of the customary evidence rendered it almost impossible to procure a judicial conviction ; and produced, at the same time, so complete a revolution in the public mind respecting the late executions, that charges of witchcraft were found to excite no other sentiments than deep disgust, and angry suspicion of the parties who preferred them. The dark cloud that had overcast the peace and happiness of the colony vanished entirely away,—and universal shame and remorse succeeded to the frenzy that previously prevailed. Even those who continued to believe in the reality of the diabolical influence of which the accusers had complained, were satisfied that most, if not all, of the unfortunate convicts were unjustly condemned, and that their accusers, in charging them, were deluded by the same infernal agency by which their sufferings were occasioned. Many of the witnesses now came forward and published the most solemn recantations of the testimony they formerly gave, both against themselves and others ; apologizing for their perjury, by a protestation, of which all were constrained to admit the force, that no other means of saving their lives had been left to them. These testimonies were not able to shake the opinion which was still retained by a considerable party both among the late accusers and the public at large, that the recent malady was caused in part by real witchcraft, whether the real culprits had yet been detected or not. This opinion was supported in learned[1] treatises by Dr. Mather and other eminent divines. But it was found impossible ever after to reiterate prosecutions that excited such painful remembrances, and had been rendered instrumental to so much barbarity and injustice. Sir William Phips, soon after he reprieved the three persons last convicted, gave order that all who were in custody on charges of witchcraft should be released ; and, with prevenient dread of the dissensions that might arise from retributory proceedings against the accusers and their witnesses, he proclaimed a general pardon to all persons for any participation imputable to them in the recent prosecutions. The surviving sufferers from those persecutions, however, and the relatives of those who had perished, were enabled to enjoy whatever consolation they could derive from the sympathy of their countrymen and the earnest regret of their persecutors.

The House of Assembly appointed a general fast and solemn supplication, "that God would pardon all the errors of his servants and people in a late tragedy raised among us by Satan and his instruments." Sewell, one of the judges who had presided on the trials at Salem, stood up in his place in church on this occasion,[2] and implored the prayers of the people that the errors which he had committed might not be visited by the judgments of an avenging God on his country, his family, or himself. Many of the jurymen subscribed and published a declaration lamenting and condemning the delusion to which they had yielded, and acknowledging that they had brought the reproach of wrongful bloodshed on their native land. Paris, the clergyman who instituted the first prosecutions and promoted all the rest, found himself exposed to a resentment not loud or violent, but fixed and deep ; and was at length generally shunned by his fellow-citizens, and entirely for-

---

[1] "Here learning, blinded first, and then beguiled,
        Looks dark as ignorance, as frenzy wild." — Savage.
[2] When Stoughton, the deputy-governor and chief justice, was informed of this, he " observed for himself, that when he sat in judgment he had the fear of God before his eyes, and gave his opinion according to the best of his understanding ; and although it might appear afterwards that he had been in error, yet he saw no necessity of a public acknowledgment of it." Hutchinson.

saken by his congregation. He appears, throughout the whole proceedings, to have acted with perfect sincerity, but to have been transported by a violent temper, and a strong conviction of the rightfulness of the ends he pursued, into the adoption of means for their attainment, inconsistent with honor, justice, or humanity. While the delusion lasted, his violence was applauded as zeal in a righteous cause, and little heed was given to accusations of artifice and partiality in conducting what was believed to be a controversy with the devil. But when it appeared that all these efforts had in reality been directed to the shedding of innocent blood, his popularity gave place to incurable odium and disgust. [1694.] Perceiving, too late, how dreadfully he had erred, he hastened to make a public profession of repentance, and solemnly begged forgiveness of God and man. But as the people declared their fixed resolution never more to attend the ministry of an individual who had been the instrument of misery and ruin to so many of their countrymen, he was obliged to resign his charge and depart from Salem.[1]

Thus terminated a scene of fury and delusion that justly excited the astonishment of the civilized world, and exhibited a fearful picture of the weakness of human nature in the sudden transformation of a people renowned over all the earth for piety and virtue into the slaves or associates, the terrified dupes or helpless prey, of a band of ferocious lunatics and assassins. Among the various evil consequences that resulted from the preceding events, not the least important was the effect they produced on the minds of the Indian tribes, who began to conceive a very unfavorable opinion of a people that could inflict such barbarities on their own countrymen, and of a religion that seemed to instigate its professors to their mutual destruction. This impression was the more disadvantageous to the colonists, as there had existed for some time a competition between their missionaries and the priests of the French settlements, for the conversion of the Indians,[2] who invariably embraced the political interests of that nation whose religious instructors were most popular among them. The French did not fail to improve to their own advantage the odious spectacle that the late frenzy of the people of New England had exhibited ; and to this end they labored with such diligence and success, that in the following year, when Sir William Phips paid a visit to the tribes with whom he had concluded the treaty of Pemmaquid, and endeavoured to unite them in a solid and lasting friendship with his own people, he found them more firmly wedded than ever to the interests of the French, and prepossessed with sentiments unfavorable in the

[1] Mather, *Life of Sir William Phips.* Increase Mather's *Cases of Conscience concerning Evil Spirits.* Neal. Hutchinson. Calef's *Wonders of the Invisible World.* Oldmixon. "I find these entries in the MS. *Diary* of Judge Sewell : ' Went to Salem, where, in the meeting-house, the persons accused of witchcraft were examined ; a very great assembly. 'T was awful to see how the afflicted persons were agitated.' But in the margin is written, in a tremulous hand, probably on a subsequent review, the lamenting Latin interjection, *Væ, væ, væ!*" Holmes. "It is likely," says Wynne, "that this frenzy contributed to work off the ill-humors of the New England people, — to dissipate their bigotry, — and to bring them to a more free use of their reason."

[2] It was a very corrupted edition of Christianity that the French priests unfolded to the Indians, — a system that harmonized too well with the passions and sentiments which genuine Christianity most strongly condemns. By rites and devices, material and yet mysterious, it brought some portion of the spiritual doctrine of Christianity within the range of the coarse capacity of the Indians, and facilitated the transition from their ancient and peculiar mode of superstition and idolatry ; while, by stigmatizing their enemies as heretics, it afforded additional sanction and incitement to hatred, fury, and cruelty. The French priests who ministered amongst the Indians were Jesuits; and their maxim, that it was unnecessary to keep faith with heretics, proved but too congenial to the savage ethics of their pupils.

highest degree to the formation of friendly relations with the English.   To
his proposition of renewing the treaty of peace they readily agreed ; but all
the urgency which he exerted to induce them to desist from their correspondence with the French proved unavailing.   They refused to listen to
the missionaries who accompanied him ; having learned from the French
priests to believe that the English were heretics, and enemies to the true
religion of Christ.   Some of them, with blunt sincerity, acquainted Phips,
that, since they had received the instructions of the French, witchcraft had
lost all perceptible existence among their tribes, and that they desired not
to recall its presence by familiar intercourse with a people among whom it
was reputed to prevail still more extensively than it had ever yet done with
themselves.[1]

There were not wanting signs foreboding the renewal of war between the
colonists and the Indians, which accordingly broke out very soon after, —
and was perhaps accelerated by the departure of Sir William Phips from
New England.   The administration of this officer, though in the main highly
and justly popular, had not escaped some share of reproach.   The discontents excited by the taxation imposed for the support of the fortification at
Pemmaquid, combining with the resentments and enmities which the prosecutions for witchcraft gave rise to, produced a party in the province who
labored on every occasion to thwart the measures and vilify the character
of the governor.   Finding their exertions in Massachusetts insufficient to
deprive him of the esteem which a great majority of the people entertained
for him, his political enemies transmitted articles of impeachment against
him to England, and petitioned the king and council for his recall and punishment.   King William having declared that he would hear and judge the
controversy himself, an order was communicated to the governor to meet his
accusers in the royal presence at Whitehall ; in compliance with which,
Phips set sail for England [November, 1694], carrying with him an address
of the assembly expressive of the strongest attachment to his person, and
beseeching that the province might not be deprived of the services of so
able and meritorious an officer.   On his appearance at court, his accusers
vanished, and their charges were dismissed ; and having rendered a satisfactory account of his administration, he was preparing to return to his government, when a malignant fever put an end to his life.   [February, 1695.]
As a soldier, Phips, if not preëminently skilful, was active and brave ; as a
civil ruler, he was upright, magnanimous, and disinterested.   It was remarked of him, as of Aristides, that, with a constant and generous under-
bearing of his fortune, *he was never visibly elated by any mark of honor or
confidence that he received from his countrymen ;* nor could all his success
and advancement ever make him ashamed to recall the humbleness of his
original condition.   In the midst of a fleet that was conveying an armament
which he commanded on a military expedition, he addressed himself to some
young soldiers and sailors who were standing on the deck of his vessel, and,
pointing to a particular spot on the shore, said, "Young men, it was upon
that hill that I kept sheep a few years ago ; — you see to what advancement
Almighty God has brought me ; do you, then, learn to fear God and act uprightly ; and you also may rise as I have done."   His natural temper was
somewhat hasty and impetuous ; and the occasional ebullitions of this infirmity, which his elevated station rendered more conspicuous, contributed,

[1] Neal.

with the other causes which we have remarked, to attaint the lustre of his reputation.[1]

On the departure of Sir William Phips, the supreme authority in Massachusetts devolved on Stoughton, the lieutenant-governor [1695], who continued to exercise it during the three following years; the king being so much engrossed with his wars and negotiations on the continent of Europe, that it was not till after the peace of Ryswick that he found leisure even to nominate a successor to Phips. During this period, the colony was much disturbed by internal dissension, and harassed by the dangers and calamities of war. The passions bequeathed by the prosecutions for witchcraft (which Stoughton had zealously promoted) continued long to divide and agitate the people; and the political factions which sprung up during the administration of Phips prevailed with increased virulence after his departure. The mutual animosities of the colonists attained such a height, that they seemed to be on the point of kindling a civil war; and the operations of the provincial government were cramped and obstructed at the very time when the utmost exertions of vigor and unanimity were requisite to encounter the hostile enterprises of the French and the Indians. [June, 1695.] Incited by their French allies, the Indians recommenced the war with all the suddenness and fury of their military operations. Wherever surprise or superior numbers enabled them to prevail over parties of the colonists, or detached plantations, their victory was signalized by the extremities of barbarous cruelty.[2] The colony of Acadia, or Nova Scotia, once more reverted to the dominion of France. It had been annexed, as we have seen, to the jurisdiction of Massachusetts, and governed hitherto by officers deputed from the seat of the superior authority at Boston. But Port Royal (or Annapolis, as it was afterwards termed) having been now recaptured by a French armament, the whole settlement revolted, and reannexed itself to the French empire, — a change that was ratified by the subsequent treaty of Ryswick.

A much more serious loss was sustained by Massachusetts in the following year, when, in consequence of a combined assault by the French and Indians, the fort erected by Sir William Phips at Pemmaquid was compelled to surrender to their arms, and was levelled with the ground. [1696.]

---

[1] Mather, *Life of Sir William Phips.* Neal. Constantine, son of Sir William Phips, became Lord Chancellor of Ireland; and his descendants have since enjoyed the titles of Earl of Mulgrave and Marquis of Normanby in Britain.

[2] Numerous cases are related by the provincial historians of the torture and slavery inflicted by the Indians on their captives, and of the desperate efforts of many of the colonists to defend themselves and their families, or to escape from the hands of their savage enemies. Wherever the Indians could penetrate, war was carried into the bosom of every family. The case of a Mrs. Dunstan, of Haverhill, in Massachusetts, is remarkable. She was made prisoner by a party of twelve Indians, and, with the infant of which she had been delivered but a week before, and the nurse who attended her, forced to accompany them on foot into the woods. Her infant's head was dashed to pieces on a tree before her eyes; and she and the nurse, after fatiguing marches in the depth of winter, were lodged in an Indian hut, a hundred and fifty miles from their home. Here they were informed that they were to be made slaves for life, but were first to be conducted to a distant settlement, where they would be stripped, scourged, and forced to run the gantlet, naked, between two files of the whole tribe to which their captors belonged. This intelligence determined Mrs. Dunstan to make an attempt that would issue either in her liberation or her death. Early in the morning, having awaked her nurse, and a young man who was their fellow-prisoner, she got possession of an axe, and, with the assistance of her two companions, despatched no fewer than ten Indians in their sleep. The other two awoke and escaped. Mrs. Dunstan returned in safety with her companions to Haverhill, and was rewarded for her intrepidity by the legislature of Massachusetts. — Dwight's *Travels.*

Whatever other cruelties the Indians might exercise on the bodies of their captives, it is observable that they never attempted to violate the chastity of women. They showed a strong aversion to negroes, and generally killed them whenever they fell into their hands. Belknap.

Chubb, the commander of this fort, at first replied to the summons of the invaders, that *he would not surrender it, even though the sea were covered with French vessels, and the land with Indian allies of France*; and the capitulation to which he finally acceded was extorted from him by the terror of his garrison, to whom the French commander announced, that, in case of a successful assault, they would be abandoned to the rage of his Indian auxiliaries. This severe and unexpected blow spread equal surprise and consternation; and the alarming consciousness of the danger, imparted by the loss of a barrier of such consequence, rebuked in the strongest manner the factious discontent that had murmured at the expense of maintaining it. These apprehensions were but too well justified by the increased ravages of Indian warfare, and the increased insolence and fury with which a triumph so signal inspired the Indian tribes. Stoughton and his council exerted the utmost promptitude and vigor to repair or retaliate the disaster, and despatched forces to attack the enemy both by land and sea; but miscarriage attended both these expeditions; and, at the close of the year, the provincial troops had been unable, by the slightest advantage, to check the assaults of the enemy, or to cheer the drooping spirits of their countrymen.

In the following year [1697[1]], the province, after being severely harassed by the inroads of the Indians, was alarmed by the intelligence of a formidable invasion which the French were preparing, with a view to its entire subjugation. The commander of a French squadron which was cruising on the northern coasts of America had concerted with Count Frontignac, the governor of Canada, a joint attack by sea and land, with the whole united force of the French and Indians, on the colony of Massachusetts; and little doubt was entertained of the conquest of this people, and the complete destruction of their settlements. On the first intelligence of this design, all the dauntless and determined spirit of New England seemed again to awake; and, factious animosities being swallowed up by more generous passion, the people vied with each other in zealous coöperation with the energetic measures by which Stoughton prepared to repel the threatened assault. He caused the forts around Boston to be repaired, the whole militia of the province to be embodied and trained with the strictest discipline, and every other precaution conducive to an effectual defence to be promptly employed. In order to ascertain, and, if possible, anticipate, the operations of the enemy by land, he despatched a considerable force to scour the eastern frontiers of the province; and these troops, encountering a detachment of the Indians, proceeding to join the French invaders, overthrew and dispersed it, after a short engagement. This check, though in itself of little importance, so deranged the plans of the governor of Canada as to induce him to defer the invasion of Massachusetts by land till the following year; and the French admiral, finding his fleet weakened by a storm, and apprized of the vigorous preparations for his reception, judged it prudent, in like manner, to abandon the projected naval attack. During the whole of this protracted contest, Connecticut and Rhode Island, though exempted from territorial ravage, shared in the burdens of war. Connecticut, in particular, was distinguished by the promptitude and liberality of the succours which she extended to the warfare

---

[1] In the midst of these troubles, died, this year, full of days and honor, the venerable Simon Bradstreet, the last survivor of the original planters, — for many years governor of Massachusetts, — and termed by his countrymen the Nestor of New England. He died in his ninety-fifth year, earnestly desiring to be at rest, — insomuch (says Cotton Mather) that it seemed as if death were conferred upon him, instead of life being taken from him.

of her friends, both in the eastern parts of New England and on the frontiers of New York.[1]

In the commencement of the following year [1698], intelligence reached America of the treaty of Ryswick, by which peace was reëstablished between Britain and France. By this treaty it was agreed that the two contracting powers should mutually restore to each other all conquests that had been made during the war, and that commissioners should be appointed to investigate and determine the extent and limits of the adjacent territories of both monarchs in America. The evil consequences of thus leaving the boundaries of growing settlements unascertained were sensibly experienced at no distant date.

Count Frontignac, on receiving notice of this treaty, acquainted the chiefs of the Indian tribes, whose martial coöperation he had obtained, that he could no longer assist or countenance their hostilities against the English, and advised them to deliver up their captives, and make peace on the best terms they could obtain. The government of Massachusetts, to which their pacific overtures were addressed, sent two commissioners to Penobscot to meet their principal sachems, who endeavoured to apologize for their unprovoked hostilities by ascribing them to the artifice and instigation of the French Jesuits. They expressed, at the same time, the highest esteem, and even a filial regard, for Count Frontignac, and an earnest desire, that, in case of any future war between the French and English, the Indians might be permitted to observe a neutrality between the belligerent parties. After some conferences, a new treaty was concluded with them, in which they consented to acknowledge a more unqualified dependence on the crown of England than they had ever before admitted.

On the settlement of his affairs in Europe, the British king found leisure to direct some portion of his attention to America, and nominate a successor to the office that had been vacant since the death of Sir William Phips. The Earl of Bellamont was appointed governor of New York, Massachusetts, and New Hampshire. [May, 1698.] The office of deputy-governor of the two latter States was bestowed by this nobleman on Stoughton, whose recent services and disinterested patriotism effaced the jealousy with which at one time he was regarded by his countrymen, for having accepted a seat in the legislative council of New England during the arbitrary sway of Sir Edmund Andros.[2]

Having pursued the separate history of the New England States up to this period, we shall now leave these interesting settlements in the enjoyment (unhappily, too short-lived) of a peace, whereof a long train of previous warfare and distresses had taught the inhabitants fully to appreciate the value. They were now more united than ever among themselves, and enriched with an ample stock of experience of both good and evil. When Lord Bellamont visited Massachusetts in the following year [1699], the recent heats and animosities had entirely subsided ; he found the inhabitants generally dis-

---

[1] Mather. Neal. *History of the British Dominions in North America.* Trumbull. Holmes.
[2] Mather. Neal. Hutchinson. Belknap. Stoughton died in the year 1702. As the colonial agent in England, he had tendered advice that proved unacceptable to his countrymen ; as a member of the grand council of Andros, he had occupied a post which they regarded with aversion ; and as lieutenant-governor, he had promoted the odious prosecutions for witchcraft. Yet his repute for honest and disinterested patriotism finally prevailed over all the obstructions of these untoward circumstances ; and a bright reversion of honor attended the close of his life. "Instead of children," says Hutchinson, "he saw before his death a college reared at his expense, which took the name of Stoughton Hall, and will transmit a grateful remembrance of his name to succeeding ages."

posed to harmony and tranquillity, and he contributed to cherish this disposition by a policy replete with wisdom, integrity, and moderation. The
virtue that so signally distinguished the original settlers of New England was
now seen to shine forth among their descendants with a lustre less dazzling,
but with an influence in some respects more amiable, refined, and humane,
than attended its original display.

One of the causes, perhaps, that conduced to the restoration of harmony
and the revival of piety among this people, was the publication of various
histories [1] of the New England settlements, written with a spirit and fidelity
well calculated to commend to the minds of the colonists the just results of
their national experience. The subject was deeply interesting ; and, happily,
the treatment of it was undertaken by writers whose principal object was to
render this interest subservient to the promotion of piety and virtue.

Though New England might be considered as yet in a state of political
infancy, it had passed through a great variety of fortune. It was the adopted
country of many of the most excellent men of the age in which its colonization began, and the native land of others who inherited the character of
their ancestors, and transmitted it in unimpaired vigor and with added renown. The history of man never exhibited an effort of more resolute and
enterprising virtue than the original migration of the Puritans to this distant
and desolate region ; nor have the annals of colonization ever supplied
another instance of the foundation of a commonwealth, and its advancement
through a period of weakness and danger to strength and security, in which
the principal actors have left behind them a reputation more illustrious and
unsullied, together with fewer memorials calculated to pervert the moral
sense or awaken the regret of mankind. The relation of their achievements
had a powerful tendency to animate hope and perseverance in brave and
virtuous enterprise. They could not, indeed, boast, as the founders of the
settlement of Pennsylvania have done, that, openly professing non-resistance
of injuries, and faithfully adhering to that profession, they had so fully
merited and obtained the divine protection by an exclusive dependence on
it, as to disarm the ferocity of barbarians, and conduct the establishment
of their commonwealth without violence and bloodshed. But if they were
involved in numerous wars, it was the singular and honorable characteristic
of them all, that they were invariably the offspring of self-defence against the
unprovoked malevolence of their adversaries, and that not one of them was
undertaken from motives of conquest or plunder. Though they considered
these wars as necessary and justifiable, they sincerely deplored them ; and,
more than once, the most distressing doubts were expressed, at the close
of their hostilities, if it were lawful for Christians to press even the natural
right of self-defence to such fatal extremity. They behaved to the Indian

---

[1] Of these productions two of the earliest in point of composition were Governor Bradford's
History of the Colony of Plymouth, and Governor Winthrop's *Journal of Events in New England*. But neither of these was published till more than a century after. The conclusion of
Winthrop's *Journal* was not published till the year 1826.
    A voluminous history of New England was composed by William Hubbard, a Puritan cler-
gyman ; but never having been published, it is known only to scholars. It is frequently
referred to as an authority by other New England historians. The author was rewarded for
his labors by the following order of the General Court of Massachusetts, in the year 1682 : —
" Whereas it has been thought necessary, and a duty incumbent upon us, to take due notice
of all occurrences and passages of God's providence towards the people of this jurisdiction
which may remain to posterity, and that the Rev. Mr. William Hubbard hath taken pains
to compile a history of this nature, the Court doth with thankfulness acknowledge his labor,
and hereby orders the treasurer to pay him fifty pounds ; he transcribing the work fairly into
a book, that it may be the more easily perused." Eliot's *New England Biography*.

tribes with as much good faith and justice as they could have shown to a powerful and civilized people,[1] and were incited by the manifest inferiority of those savage neighbours to no other acts than a series of the most magnanimous and laudable endeavours to instruct their ignorance and improve their condition. If they fell short of the colonists of Pennsylvania in the exhibition of Christian meekness, they unquestionably excelled them in extent and activity of Christian exertion. The Quakers succeeded in conciliating the Indians ; the Puritans endeavoured to civilize them.

The chief, if not the, only fault, with which impartial history must ever reproach the conduct of these people, is the religious intolerance that they cherished, and the persecution, which, on too many occasions, it prompted them to inflict. Happily for their own character, the provocation which in some instances they received from the objects of their severity tended greatly to extenuate the blame ; and happily, no less, for the legitimate influence of their character on the minds of their posterity, the fault itself, notwithstanding every extenuation, stood so manifestly opposed to the very principles with which their own fame was for ever associated, that it was impossible for a writer of common integrity, not involved in the immediate heat of controversy, to render a just tribute to their excellence, without finding himself obliged to remark and condemn this signal departure from it. The histories that were now published were the compositions of the friends, associates, and successors of the original colonists. Written with an energy of just encomium that elevated every man's ideas of his ancestors and his country, and of the duties which arose from these natural or patriotic relations, these works excited universally a generous sympathy with the characters and sentiments of the fathers of New England. The writers, nevertheless, were too conscientious and too enlightened to confound the virtues with the defects of the character they described ; and while they dwelt apologetically on the causes by which persecution had been provoked, they lamented the infirmity that (under any degree of provocation) had betrayed good men into conduct so oppressive and unchristian. Even Cotton Mather, the most encomiastic of the historians of New England, and who cherished very strong prejudices against the Quakers and other persecuted sectaries, has expressed still stronger disapprobation of the severities they encountered from the objects of his encomium. These representations could not fail to produce a beneficial effect on the people of New England. They saw that the glory of their native land was associated with principles that could never coalesce

---

[1] Not only was all the territory occupied by the colonists fairly purchased from its Indian owners, but, in some parts of the country, the lands were subject to quitrents to the Indians, "which." says Belknap, in 1784, "are annually paid to their posterity." A great English writer has represented an Indian chief as moralizing on the policy and pretensions of the European colonists in the following strains : — "Others pretend to have purchased a right of residence and tyranny; but surely the insolence of such bargains is more offensive than the avowed and open dominion of force." Dr. Johnson's *Idler*. The Indians, indeed, were no strangers to such sentiments. Beholding with ignorant wonder and helpless envy the augmented value which the lands they had sold derived from the industry and skill of the purchasers, they very readily admitted the belief that they had been defrauded in the original vendition. But abundant evidence has been preserved by the New England historians, that the prices paid by the colonists, so far from being lower, were in general much higher than the just value of the land.

I am sorry to observe some modern (even American) writers indulge a spirit of perverse paradox in palliating and even defending the conduct of the Indians at the expense of the first race of British colonists, who in reality treated the Indians with an equity which succeeding generations would do better liberally to imitate than captiously to depreciate. The new historian of already recorded times ought diligently to guard at once against the force of prejudice and the effects of novelty.

with or sanction intolerance ; and that every instance of persecution with which their annals were stained was a dereliction of those principles, and an impeachment of their country's claim to the admiration of mankind. Inspired with the warmest attachment to the memory, and the highest respect for the virtue, of their ancestors, they were forcibly admonished, by the errors into which they had fallen, to suspect and repress in themselves those erring sentiments from which even virtue of so high an order had not afforded exemption. From this time the religious zeal of the people of New England was no longer perverted by intolerance or disgraced by persecution; and the influence of Christianity, in mitigating enmity and promoting kindness and indulgence, derived a freer scope from the growing conviction that the principles of the gospel were utterly irreconcilable with violence and severity ; and that, revealing to every man his own infirmity much more clearly than that of any other human being, they were equally adverse to confidence in himself and to condemnation of others. Cotton Mather, who recorded and reproved the errors of the first colonists, lived to witness the success of his monitory representations in the charity and liberality of their descendants.[1]

New England, having been colonized by men not less eminent for learning than piety, was distinguished at an early period by the labors of her scholars and the dedication of her literature to the nurture of religious sentiment and principle. The theological works of John Cotton, Hooker, the two Mathers, and other New England divines, have always enjoyed a high degree of esteem and popularity, not only in New England, but in every Protestant country of Europe. The annals of the various States, and the biography of their founders, were written by contemporary historians with a minuteness which was very agreeable and interesting to the first generation of their readers, and to which the writers were prompted, in some measure at least, by the conviction they entertained that their countrymen had been honored with the signal favor and especial guidance and direction of Divine Providence. This conviction, while it naturally betrayed these writers into the fault of prolixity, enforced by the strongest sanctions the accuracy and fidelity of their narrations. Recording what they considered the peculiar dealings of God with a people peculiarly his own, they presumed not to disguise the infirmities of their countrymen ; nor did they desire to magnify the divine grace in the infusion of human virtue beyond the divine patience in enduring human frailty and imperfection. Nay, the errors and failings of the illustrious men whose lives they related gave additional weight to the impression which above all they desired to convey, that the colonization of

---

[1] A discourse, which he published some years after this period, contains the following passage : — " In this capital city of Boston there are ten assemblies of Christians of different persuasions, who live so lovingly and peaceably together, doing all the offices of neighbourhood for one another in such a manner, as may give a sensible rebuke to all the bigots of uniformity, and show them how consistent a variety of rites in religion may be with the tranquillity of human society ; and may demonstrate to the world that persecution for conscientious dissents in religion is an *abomination of desolation*, a thing whereof all wise and just men will say, ' Cursed be its anger, for it is fierce, and its wrath, for it is cruel.' " Neal's *Present State of New England.* The first Episcopal society was formed in Massachusetts in 1686 (before the arrival of Andros) ; and the first Episcopal chapel was erected at Boston in 1688. *Collections of the Massachusetts Historical Society.* A Quaker meeting-house was built at Boston in 1710. Ibid. Mass was performed for the first time in Boston, by a Roman Catholic priest, in 1788. Holmes. " It is remarkable," says this writer, " that the same church, which was originally built [at Boston] for French Protestants who had fled from the persecution of the Roman Catholics, was the first to receive the Roman Catholics who fled from the persecution of the Jacobins of France."

New England was an extraordinary work of Heaven ; that the counsel and the virtue by which it was conducted and achieved were not of human origin ; and that the glory of God was displayed no less in imparting the strength and wisdom than in controlling the weakness and perversity of the instruments which he condescended to employ.[1]

The most considerable of these historical works, and one of the most interesting performances that the literature of New England has ever produced, is the *Magnalia Christi Americana*, or History of New England, by Cotton Mather. Of this work, the arrangement is exceedingly faulty ; and its vast bulk must continue to render its exterior increasingly repulsive to modern readers. The continuity of the narrative is frequently broken by the introduction of long discourses, epistles, and theological reflections and dissertations ; biography is intermixed with history ; and events of local or temporary interest are related with tedious superfluity of detail. It is not so properly a single or continuous historical narration, as a collection of separate works illustrative of the various scenes of New England history, under the heads of *Remarkable Providences*, *Remarkable Trials*, and numberless other subdivisions. A plentiful intermixture of puns, anagrams, and other barbarous conceits, exemplifies a peculiarity (the offspring partly of bad taste and partly of superstition) which was very prevalent among the prose-writers, and especially the theologians, of that age. Notwithstanding these defects, the work will amply repay the labor of every reader. The biographical portions, in particular, possess the highest excellence, and are superior in dignity and interest to the compositions of Plutarch. Cotton Mather was the author of a great many other works,[2] some of which have been highly popular and eminently useful. One of them bears the title of *Essays to do Good*, and contains a lively and forcible representation (conveyed with more brevity than the author usually exemplifies) of the opportunities which every rank and every relation of human life may present to a devout mind, of promoting the glory of God and the good of mankind. Dr. Franklin, in the latter years of his active and useful life, declared that all the good he had ever done to his country or his fellow-creatures must be ascribed to the impression produced on his mind by perusing that little work in his youth.[3] It is curious to find an infidel philosopher thus ascribe his

---

[1] " If we look on the dark side, the human side, of this work, there is much of human weakness and imperfection hath appeared in all that hath been done by man, as was acknowledged by our fathers before us. Neither was New England ever without some fatherly chastisements from God ; showing that he is not fond of the formalities of any people upon earth, but expects the realities of practical godliness according to our profession and engagement unto him." Higginson's *Attestation*, prefixed to Cotton Mather's *History*. " To vindicate the errors of our ancestors," says Jefferson, " is to make them our own."

[2] His biographers have given us a catalogue of his works, amounting to no fewer than *three hundred and eighty-two*, — many, no doubt, of small dimensions, but others of considerable bulk. He was a singular economist of time, and at once the most voluminous and popular writer and the most zealous and active minister of his age. Among his manuscripts was a theological work which he had prepared for publication, and which is reported to have been " enough constantly to employ a man, unless he be a miracle of diligence, the half of the threescore years and ten allowed us." Holmes. In conversation he is said to have particularly excelled : — " Here it was seen how his wit and fancy, his invention, his quickness of thought, and ready apprehension were all consecrated to God, as well as his will and affections." Ibid. Above his study door was inscribed this impressive admonition to his visitors, " *Be short.*" He was the son of Dr. Increase Mather. Born in 1663, he died in 1727. From President Quincy's *History of Harvard University*, it appears to me, much more clearly than agreeably, that, in the instance of Cotton Mather as well as of his father, a strong and acute understanding, though united with real piety, was sometimes corrupted by a deep vein of passionate vanity and absurdity.

[3] Franklin's *Works*.

own practical wisdom to the lessons of a Christian divine, and trace the stream of his beneficence to the fountain of the gospel.

History and divinity were the chief, but not the only subjects which exercised the labors of the scholars of New England. John Sherman, an eminent Puritan divine, who was one of the first emigrants from Britain to Massachusetts, where he died in 1685, obtained a high and just renown as a mathematician and astronomer. He left at his death a large manuscript collection of astronomical calculations ; and for several years published an almanac which was interspersed with pious reflections and admonitions.[1]

A traveller, who visited Boston in the year 1686, mentions several booksellers there who had already made fortunes by their trade. The learned and ingenious author of the *History of Printing in America* has given a catalogue of the works published by the first New England printers in the seventeenth century. Considering the circumstances and numbers of the people, the catalogue is amazingly copious. One of the printers of that age was an Indian, the son of one of the first Indian converts.[2]

The education and habits of the people of New England prepared them to receive the full force of those impressions which their national literature was fitted to produce. In no country have the benefits of knowledge been ever more highly prized or more generally diffused. Institutions for the education of youth were coeval with the foundation of the first provincial community, and were propagated with every accession to the population and every extension of the settlements. Education was facilitated in New England by the peculiar manner in which its colonization was conducted. In many other parts of America, the planters dispersed themselves over the face of the country ; each residing on his own farm, and, in choosing the spot where his house was to be placed, guided merely by considerations of agricultural convenience. The advantages resulting from this mode of inhabitation were gained at the expense of such dispersion of dwellings as rendered it difficult to fix upon proper spots for the erection of churches and schools, and obstructed the enjoyment of social intercourse. But the colonization of New England was conducted in a manner much more favorable to the improvement of human character and manners. All the original townships were formed in what is termed in America *the village manner ;*[3] the inhabitants having originally planted themselves in societies, from regard to the ordinances of religion and the convenience of education. Every town containing fifty householders was obliged by law to provide a schoolmaster qualified to teach reading and writing ; and every town containing a hundred householders, to maintain a grammar school.[4] But the generous ardor of the people continually outstripped the provisions of this law. We have seen Harvard College arise in Massachusetts within a few years after the foundation of the colony was laid.[5] With allusion to the flourishing and efficient condition of this seminary, Lord Bellamont, the provincial governor, in an address to the General Court, in 1699, remarked, " It is a very great advantage you have above other provinces, that your youth are not put to travel for learning, but have the Muses at their doors." The other States, for some time after, were destitute of the wealth and population necessary to

[1] Eliot's *New England Biography.*
[2] Dunton's *Life and Errors.* Thomas's *History of Printing in America.*
[3] Dwight's *Travels.*
[4] *Abridgment of the Laws of New England.* Neal.
[5] See Note XIV., at the end of the volume.

support similar establishments within their own territories ; but they frequently assessed themselves in the most liberal contributions for the maintenance and enlargement of Harvard College.   The contributions, even at a very early period, of Connecticut, New Haven, and New Hampshire, have been particularly and deservedly noted for their liberality.[1] The close of the same century was illustrated by the establishment of Yale College in Connecticut.   So high was the repute which this quarter of North America long continued to enjoy for the moral excellence and intellectual efficiency of its seminaries of education, that many respectable persons, both in the other American States and in Europe, and even some of patrician rank and lineage in Britain, sent their children to be educated in New England.[2]

A general appetite for knowledge, and a universal familiarity with letters, were thus maintained from the beginning of their national existence among the New England colonists.   The rigid discouragement of frivolous amusements, and of every recreation that bordered upon vice, tended to devote their leisure hours to reading ; and the sentiments and opinions derived through this avenue of knowledge sunk deeply into vigorous and undissipated minds.   The historical retrospections of this people were peculiarly calculated to exercise a favorable influence on their character and turn of thinking, by awakening a generous emulation, and connecting them with a uniform and progressive course of manly, patient, and successful virtue.

Notwithstanding the general diffusion of knowledge among the early colonists of New England, the lower classes of the people were not entirely exempt from the prevalent delusions of the age.   In particular, the notion then generally received in the parent state, and consecrated by a special office long retained in her church liturgy, of the efficacy of the royal touch for the cure of the disorder called the king's evil, was imported into New England, to the great inconvenience of those victims of the malady who were so unhappy as to entertain it.   Belknap has transcribed from the records of the town of Portsmouth, in New Hampshire, the petition of an inhabitant to the assembly of this province, in the year 1687, for assistance to undertake a journey to England, that he might be cured of his disease by coming in contact with a king ;[3] a circumstance which Heaven (it may be hoped) has decreed a perpetual impossibility within the confines of North America.

The amount of the population of New England at the present era has been very differently estimated by different writers. According to Sir William Petty, the number of inhabitants amounted, in the year 1691, to one hundred and fifty thousand.[4] A much lower computation is adopted by Neal ; and a much higher by a later historian.[5] The population, it is certain, had been considerably augmented, both by the emigration of Dissenters from various of the European states, and by domestic propagation in circumstances so favorable to increase.   Yet no quarter of North America has had its own population so extensively drained by emigration as New England, which, from a very early period of its history, has continually furnished swarms of

[1] Trumbull. Belknap.
[2] *History of the British Dominions in America.* Peirce's and Quincy's *Histories of Harvard University.* In aid of the library of Yale College, copies of their works were contributed by the most illustrious writers in England ; and among others by Sir Isaac Newton, Sir Richard Blackmore, Sir Richard Steele, Bishop Burnet, Dr. Woodward, Dr. Halley, Dr. Bentley, Calamy, Henry, and Whiston. — Holmes.
[3] Belknap. Smollett's *History of England.*   [4] *Political Arithmetic.*
[5] *History of the British Dominions in North America.*

hardy, sober, intelligent, enterprising, and educated men to recruit and improve every successive settlement that has offered its resources to industry
and virtue. The severe restraint of licentious intercourse, the facility of
acquiring property and maintaining a family, and the prevalence of industrious and frugal habits among all classes of people combined with happy efficacy to render marriages both frequent and prolific in New England. Boston,
the capital of Massachusetts, and during many years the largest city in North
America, appears to have contained a population of more than 10,000 persons at the close of this century. In the year 1720, its inhabitants amounted
to 20,000.   Every inhabitant of the province was required by law to keep
a stock of arms and ammunition in his house ; and all males above sixteen
years of age were enrolled in the militia, which was assembled for exercise
four times a year.[1]

The whole territory of New England was comprehended at this period
in four jurisdictions, — Massachusetts, New Hampshire, Connecticut, and
Rhode Island.   To Massachusetts there were annexed the settlements of
New Plymouth and Maine, and to Connecticut that of New Haven.   The
territories of these governments were divided into constituted districts called
townships, each of which was represented by one or two deputies (according
to the number of freeholders) in the assembly of the State to which it belonged.   Besides this elective franchise, the freeholders of each township
enjoyed the right of appointing the municipal officers denominated selectmen, by whom the domestic government of the township was exercised.
The qualification of a freeholder in Massachusetts was declared by its charter to be an estate of the value of forty shillings *per annum*, or the possession
of personal property to the amount of fifty pounds ; communion with the
Congregational churches having ceased to be requisite to the enjoyment of
political privileges.   In the other States of New England, the qualification
was nearly the same as in Massachusetts.   The expenses of government
were defrayed originally by temporary assessments, to which every man was
rated according to the value of his whole property ; but since the year 1645,
excises, imposts, and poll taxes were in use. The judicial procedure in the
provincial courts was conducted with great expedition, cheapness, and simplicity.   In all trials by jury in New England, whether of civil or criminal
causes, the juries were not, as in Britain, nominated by the sheriffs, but
elected by the inhabitants ; and these elections were conducted with the
strictest precautions for preventing the intrusion of partiality or corruption.[2]

Massachusetts and New Hampshire — the one enjoying a chartered, the
other an unchartered municipal constitution — were the only two provinces
of New England in which the superior officers of the domestic government
were appointed by the crown, and from the tribunals of which an appeal
was admitted to the king in council.   As New Hampshire was too inconsiderable to support the substance as well as the title of a separate government, it was the practice at this period, and for some time after, to appoint
the same person to be governor of Massachusetts and New Hampshire. In
Connecticut and Rhode Island, all the officers of government (excepting
the members of the Court of Admiralty) were elected by the inhabitants ;
and so resolutely was this highly valued privilege defended, that, when King
William appointed Fletcher, the governor of New York, to command the

---

[1] Neal.
[2] *History of the British Dominions in North America.* Wynne's *History of British America.*

Connecticut militia, the province refused to acknowledge his authority.[1]   It was not provided by the charters of these States that their laws should be subject to the negative, or the judgments of their tribunals to the review, of the king.   But the validity of their laws was declared to depend on a very uncertain criterion, — a conformity, as close as circumstances would admit, to the jurisprudence of England.[2]   So perfectly democratic were the constitutions of Connecticut and Rhode Island, that in neither of them was the governor suffered to withhold his formal sanction from the resolutions of the assembly.   The spirit of liberty was not suppressed in Massachusetts by the encroachments of royal prerogative on the ancient privileges of the people, but was vigorously exerted through the remaining and important organ of the provincial assembly.   All the patronage that was vested in the royal governor was never able to create more than a very inconsiderable royalist party in this State.   The functionaries whom he or whom the crown appointed depended on the popular assembly for the emoluments of their offices ; and although the most strenuous efforts and the most formidable threats were employed by the British ministers to free the governor himself from the same dependence, they were never able to prevail with the assembly to annex a fixed salary to his office.   The people and the popular authorities of Massachusetts were always ready to set an example to the other colonies of a determined resistance to the encroachments of royal prerogative.

   In all the provinces of North America, and especially in those of New England, there existed at this period, and for a long time afterwards, a mixture of very opposite sentiments towards Great Britain.   As the posterity of Englishmen, the colonists cherished a warm attachment to a land which they habitually termed the *Mother Country* or *Home*,[3] and to a people whom, though contemporaries with themselves, they regarded as holding an ancestral relation to them.   As Americans, their liberty and happiness, and even their national existence, were associated with the idea of escape from royal persecution in Britain ; and the jealous and unfriendly sentiments engendered by this consideration were preserved, more particularly in Massachusetts, by the unjust abridgment of the privileges which she had originally enjoyed, and which still subsisted unimpaired in Connecticut and Rhode Island ; and were maintained in every one of the provinces by the oppressive commercial policy which Great Britain pursued towards them, and of which their increasing resources rendered them increasingly sensible and proportionally impa-

[1] Wynne. Trumbull. Book V., Chap. II., *post.*

[2] There were no prescribed or customary means of ascertaining this conformity ; these States not being obliged, like Massachusetts, to transmit their laws to England. On a complaint from an inhabitant of Connecticut, aggrieved by the operation of a particular law, it was declared by the king in council, " that their law, concerning dividing land-inheritance of an intestate, was contrary to the law of England, and void " ; but the colony paid no regard to this declaration.   *History of the British Dominions in North America.*

[3] They have left one indestructible mark of their origin, and their kindly remembrance of it, in the British names which they extended to American places.   When New London, in Connecticut, was founded in the year 1648, the assembly of the province assigned its name by an act commencing with the following preamble : — " Whereas it hath been the commendable practice of the inhabitants of all the colonies of these parts, that, as this country hath its denomination from our dear native country of England, and thence is called New England, so the planters, in their first settling of most new plantations, have given names to these plantations of some cities and towns in England, thereby intending to keep up and leave to posterity the memorial of several places of note there," &c., " this court, considering that there hath yet no place in any of the colonies been named in memory of the city of London," &c. Trumbull.

" Certus enim promisit Apollo
     Ambiguam tellure nova Salamina futuram." — Horace.

tient.   The loyalty of Connecticut and Rhode Island was in no degree
promoted by the preservation of their ancient charters, — an advantage
which they well knew had been yielded to them with the utmost reluctance
by the British government, and of which numerous attempts to divest them
by act of parliament were made by King William and his immediate successors.   Even the new charter of Massachusetts was not exempted from
such attacks; and the defensive spirit that was thus excited and kept alive
by the aggressive policy of Britain contributed, no doubt, to influence, in a
material degree, the subsequent destinies of America.

In return for the articles which they required from Europe, and of which
the English merchants monopolized the supply, the inhabitants of New England could offer no staple commodity which might not be obtained more
cheaply in Europe by their customers.   They possessed, indeed, good
mines of iron and copper, which might have been wrought with advantage ;
but the manufacture of these metals in the colonies was obstructed by the
dearness of labor ; and till the year 1750, the export of American iron, even
to the mother country, was restrained by heavy duties.   The principal commodities exported from New England were the produce and refuse of her
forests, or, as it was commonly termed, lumber, and the produce of her cod-
fishery.   In the beginning of the eighteenth century, the annual imports into
these provinces from Britain were estimated by Neal at £100,000.   The
exports by the English merchants consisted of a hundred thousand quintals
(the quintal weighing one hundred and twelve pounds) of dried codfish, which
were sold in Europe for £80,000, and of three thousand tons of naval
stores.   To the other American plantations, and to the West Indies, New
England sent lumber, fish, and other provisions, valued at £50,000 annually.
An extensive manufacture of linen cloth was established about this time in
New England ; — an advantage for which this country was indebted to the
migration of many thousands of Irish Presbyterians to her shores about the
beginning of the eighteenth century.   Ship-building was from an early period
carried on to a considerable extent at Boston and other seaport towns.   It
was the practice of some merchants to freight their vessels, as soon as they
were built, with cargoes of colonial produce, and to sell the vessels in the
ports where the cargoes were disposed of.   The manufacture of tar was promoted for some time in New Hampshire by an ordinance of the assembly of
this province in the beginning of the eighteenth century, which allowed the
inhabitants to pay their taxes in tar rated at twenty shillings per barrel.   A
great part of the trade of the other American colonies was conducted by
the shipping of New England.   For many years both before and after the
present era, specie was so scarce in this quarter of America, that paper
money formed almost exclusively the circulating medium in use among the
inhabitants.   Bills, or notes, were circulated for sums as low as half-a-
crown.[1]

The progress of population in the district of Maine was remarkably slow.
For many years after its first colonization, the greater number of the emigrants to this region were not husbandmen, but traders and fishermen, — a
description of persons qualified neither by their views nor their habits to promote the culture and population of a desert.   The soil of a great part of
Maine was erroneously supposed, by the first European colonists, to be ungrateful to tillage, and incapable of yielding a sufficient supply of bread to

[1] Neal. Belknap. Wynne. Raynal. Douglass. Winterbotham.

its inhabitants. This notion produced the deficiency which it presupposed; and, injurious as it was to the increase and prosperity of the inhabitants, it prevailed even till the period of the American Revolution. Prior to this event, the greater part of the bread consumed in the district of Maine was imported from the middle colonies.[1] New England was long infested with wolves; and at the close of the seventeenth century, laws were still enacted by the provincial assemblies, offering bounties for the destruction of those animals.[2]

Except in Rhode Island, the system of religious doctrine and ecclesiastical order embraced by the Congregational church established by the first colonists prevailed generally in New England. Every township was required by law to choose a minister, and to fix his salary by mutual agreement of the parties; in default of which, a salary proportioned to the ability of the township was decreed to him by the justices of the peace. In case of the neglect of any township to appoint a minister within a certain period of time prescribed by law, the right of appointment for the occasion devolved on the Court of Quarter Sessions. By a special custom of the town of Boston, the salaries of its ministers were derived from the voluntary contributions of their respective congregations, collected every Sunday on their assembling for divine service; and it was remarked that none of the ministers of New England were so liberally provided for as those whose emoluments, undetermined by legal provision, thus represented the diligence of their labors, and the conscientious regard of their people.[3] In Rhode Island there was no legal provision for the celebration of divine worship, or the maintenance of religious institutions. This colony was peopled by a mixed multitude of sectarians, who, having separated from Christian societies in other places, had continued, ever since in a broken and disunited state. In their political capacity, the inhabitants of Rhode Island admitted unbounded liberty of conscience, and disavowed all connection between church and state. In their Christian relations, they made no account of the virtue of mutual forbearance, and absolutely disowned the duty of submitting to one another on any point, whether essential or circumstantial. Few of them held regular assemblies for public worship; still fewer had stated places for such assemblage; and an aversion to every thing that savored of *restraint* or *formality* prevailed among them all. Notwithstanding the unlimited toleration that was professedly established in this settlement, its rulers, in 1665, passed an ordinance to outlaw Quakers and confiscate their estates, because they refused to bear arms. But the people, in general, resisted this regulation, and would not suffer it to be executed.[4] Cotton Mather declares, that, in 1655, " Rhode Island colony was a colluvies of Antinomians, Famalists, Anabaptists, Anti-sabbatarians, Arminians, Socinians, Quakers, Ranters, and every thing but Roman Catholics and true Christians; *bona terra, mala gens.*" In the town of Providence, which was included in this colony, and was inhabited by the descendants of those schismatics who accompanied Roger Williams and Mrs. Hutchinson in their exile from Massachusetts, the aversion to legal establishments and every species of subordination was car-

---

[1] Sullivan's *History of Maine.* Dwight's *Travels.*
[2] Trumbull. *Ordinances of New England to the Year* 1700. Chalmers.
[3] Neal.
[4] *Collections of the Massachusetts Historical Society.* In the year 1688, an inhabitant of Rhode Island was " fined by the Quarter Sessions for planting a peach-tree on Sunday." This occurred during the administration of Andros. *Collections of the Rhode Island Historical Society.*

ried to such an extreme, that, at the present period, the inhabitants had neither magistrates nor ministers among them. They entertained an invincible antipathy to all rates and taxes, as devices invented for the benefit of *hirelings,* — by which opprobrious term they designated all civil and ecclesiastical functionaries who refused to serve them for nothing. Yet they lived in great amity with their neighbours, and, though every man did whatever seemed right in his own eyes, it was seldom that any crime was committed among them ; " which may be attributed," says the historian from whom this testimony is derived, " to their great veneration for the Holy Scriptures, which they all read, from the least to the greatest." [1] Massachusetts and Connecticut, as they were the most considerable of the New England States in respect of wealth and population, so were they the most distinguished for piety, morality, and the cultivation and diffusion of knowledge. At the close of the seventeenth century, there were a hundred religious assemblies in Massachusetts, exclusive of numerous congregations of Christian Indians.[2] The censorial discipline exercised by these societies over their members was highly conducive to the preservation of sound morality, guarded by exact and sober manners ; and the efficacy of this and of every other incitement to virtue was enhanced by the thinly peopled state of the country, where no person could screen his character or pursuits from the observation of the public eye.

Perhaps no country in the world was ever more distinguished than New England was at this time for the general prevalence of those sentiments and habits that render communities respectable and happy. Sobriety and industry reigned among all classes of the inhabitants. The laws against immoralities of every description were extremely strict, and not less strictly enforced ; [3] and, being cordially supported by the executive principle of pub-

---

[1] Neal. We have an account of the religious condition of Rhode Island, about thirty years after the period to which we have conducted the separate history of New England, from the pen of the great and good Bishop Berkeley, who resided some years in this colony. A general indifference to religion, and a great relaxation of morality, had then become the characteristics of the majority of the people. Several churches, however, some on the Congregational, and others on the Episcopal model, had been established ; and through their instrumentality, the blessings of religion were yet preserved in the colony. Berkeley's *Works.*

" So little," says a writer much esteemed in America, " has the civil authority to do with religion in Rhode Island, that no contract between a minister and a society (unless incorporated for that purpose) is of any force. It is probably for these reasons that so many sects have ever been found here ; and that the Sabbath and all religious institutions, as well as good morals, have been less regarded in this than in any other of the New England States." Jedediah Morse.

So late as the beginning of the nineteenth century, the legislature of Rhode Island discouraged the project of a turnpike road, alleging that turnpike duties and ecclesiastical establishments were *English practices,* and badges of slavery, — from which their people were distinguished above all the other Americans by a happy exemption. It was not till the year 1805 that the advantages of turnpike roads prevailed over the imaginary dignity of this exemption. Dwight.

It would be well for the Americans, if, in the system of management which they adopt with regard to roads and canals they would ponder and avoid the monstrous vices inherent in *the style* of those *English practices* to which the people of Rhode Island were opposed. No municipal government in the world has greater reason than the American to dread the evil effects of those vices ; and from its popular structure, none is so well fitted to adopt the only means of effectually preventing or eradicating them. This important subject is strikingly elucidated in Sir Henry Parnell's *Treatise on Roads,* but especially in *A Treatise on Internal Intercourse and Communication in Civilized States,* by Thomas Grahame, brother of the author of this *History.*

[2] Neal.

[3] Josselyn, who visited New England, for the first time, in 1638, relates, that in the *village* of Boston there were then two licensed inns. " An officer visits them," he adds, " whenever a stranger goes into them ; and if he calls for more drink than the officer thinks in his judg-

lic opinion, they rendered every vicious and profligate excess alike dangerous and discreditable to the perpetrator. We are assured by a well informed
writer, that at this period there was not a single beggar in the whole province ; and a person of unquestioned veracity, who resided in it for seven
years, relates, that during all that period he never heard a profane oath, nor
witnessed an instance of inebriety.[1] Labor was so valuable, land so cheap,
and the elective franchise so widely extended, that every industrious man
might acquire a stake in the soil, and a voice in the civil administration of
his country. The general diffusion of education caused the national advantages, which were vigorously improved, to be justly appreciated ; and a
steady and ardent patriotism knit the hearts of the people to each other and
to their country.

The condition of society in New England, the circumstances and habits
of the people, tended to form among their leading men a character more
solid than brilliant : — not (as some have imagined) to discourage the cultivation or exercise of talent, but to repress its idle display, and train it to
its legitimate and respectable end, of giving efficacy to wisdom, prudence,
and virtue. Yet this state of society was by no means incompatible either
with politeness of manners or with innocent hilarity. Lord Bellamont was
agreeably surprised with the graceful and courteous behaviour of the gentlemen and clergy of Connecticut, and confessed that he found the manners and
address which he had thought peculiar to feudal *nobility* in a land where
this aristocratical distinction was unknown.[2] From Dunton's account of his
residence in Boston in 1686, it appears that the inhabitants of Massachusetts were at that time distinguished in a very high degree by their cheerful
vivacity, their hospitality, and a courtesy the more estimable that it was indicative of genuine benevolence.[3] From the circumstances of the country,
it is impossible to suppose that the manners of its inhabitants could exhibit
that perfection of exterior polish and factitious elegance generated in old
societies by leisure, wealth, and the necessity of refining the means of procuring social distinction. But if (as has been finely suggested by an ingenious American, in reference to a later period in his country), "in the equal
intercourse of all classes, the higher had some degree of polish rubbed off,
the humbler were gainers by what the others lost"; and while the absence
of unsuitable pretensions and mean competitions banished the most copious
source of vulgarity, the diffusion of literary taste and of liberal piety supplied an influence amply sufficient to soften and ennoble human manners.
Elegance may consist with great plainness of external circumstances ; nay,
in proportion as it is unaided by exterior trapping and decoration, its origin
seems the more pure and exalted, and its excellence the more genuine and
durable. It was a remark of the great Prince of Condé, that the New Testament displayed the most perfect model of a kind and graceful politeness
that he had ever met with. Good manners consist in conducting ourselves

ment he can soberly bear away, he countermands it, and appoints the proportion, beyond
which he cannot get one drop." Josselyn's *Voyage.* In 1694, the selectmen of the several
towns in Massachusetts were ordered to hang up in every alehouse lists of all *reputed* tipplers
and drunkards within their districts; and alehouse-keepers were forbidden to supply liquor to
any person whose name was thus posted. Holmes. The magistrates of some of the towns
of Scotland exercised similar acts of authority. An instance occurred in the town of Rutherglen in 1668. Ure's *History of Rutherglen.*
    [1] Neal. Trumbull.   [2] Trumbull. Dwight's *Travels.*
    [3] Dunton's *Life and Errors.* Dunton, who was familiar with the tables of the rich in Lon-
don, was yet struck with the plenty and elegance of the entertainments he witnessed in
Boston.

towards every person with a demeanour graciously expressive of the relation which he holds to ourselves and others.   Christianity at once affords
the justest, the most endearing, and most enlarged view of the relations of
human beings to each other, and enforces by the strongest sanctions the duties and courtesies which these relations infer.   Men devoted to the service
of God, like the first generations of the inhabitants of New England, carried
throughout their lives an elevated strain of sentiment and purpose, which
must have communicated some portion of its own grace and dignity to their
manners.

   In the historical and statistical accounts of the various provinces[1] we continually meet with instances of the beneficial influence exercised by superior
minds on the virtue, industry, and happiness of particular districts and infant
settlements.   In no country has the ascendency of talent been greater, or
been more advantageously exerted.   The dangers of Indian invasion were
encountered and repelled ; the dejection and timidity produced by them,
surmounted ; the feuds and contentions peculiarly incident to newly formed
societies of men, collected from different countries, and varying in race,
habits, and opinions, were composed ; the temptations to slothful and degenerate modes of living, resisted ; the self-denial requisite to the endowment
of institutions for preaching the gospel and the education of youth, resolutely practised.   In founding and conducting to maturity the new settlements that progressively arose, men of talent and virtue enjoyed a sphere
of noble employment.   They taught both by action and example.   They
distinguished themselves from the rest of mankind by excelling them in their
common pursuits, and exercising a manifest superiority of understanding on
the ordinary subjects of human reflection and consideration.   They exemplified a species of dignity at once the most substantial and the most generally attainable ; which depends not on opportunities of performing remarkable deeds, but consists in discharging the ordinary duties of life with a
generous elevation of sentiment and view.   They read their history in the
approving eyes, and improving manners and condition, of a free and happy
people.   Mankind have a greater aptitude to copy characters than to yield
obedience to precepts ; and virtue is much more effectually recommended
to their imitation and esteem by the exhibition of zeal than by the force of
argument.   Let the votaries of glory remember, that, if a life thus spent cir-
cumscribe the diffusion of the patriot's name, it extends the influence of his
character and sentiments to distant generations ; and that, if posthumous
fame be any thing more than a brilliant illusion, it is such distinction as this
from which the surest and most lasting satisfaction will be derived.

   The esteem of the community was considered so valuable a part of the
emoluments of public office, that the salaries of all municipal officers, except
those who were appointed by the crown, were, if not scanty, yet exceedingly moderate.   In Connecticut, where the public expenditure, without
being sordidly or unjustly abridged, was contracted to the greatest exact-
ness of thrift, it was remarked, that the whole annual expense of its public
institutions (about £ 800) did not amount to the salary of a royal governor.[2]
The slender emoluments of public offices, and the tenure of popular pleasure by which they were held, tended very much to exempt them from the
pretensions of unworthy candidates, and those who were invested with them

---

[1] See, in particular, the *Histories* of Trumbull and Belknap, and the *Travels* of Dwight,
passim.
[2] Trumbull.

from calumny and envy. Virtue and ability were fairly appreciated ; and we frequently, find the same individuals reëlected for a long series of years to the same offices,[1] and in some instances succeeded by their sons, when inheritance of merit recommended inheritance of dignity. In more than one of the settlements, the first codes of law were the composition of single, persons ; the people desiring an eminent citizen to compose for them a body of laws, and then legislating unanimously in conformity with his suggestions. The estimation and the disinterestedness of public services were not unfrequently attested by legislative appropriations of public money to defray the funeral charges of men who for many years had enjoyed the highest official dignities. The public respect for distinguished patriots, though not perpetuated by titles of nobility, was preserved in the recollection of their actions, and stimulated, instead of relaxing, the ardor of their descendants. The virtue of remarkable benefactors of their country was more diffusively beneficial from their never being disjoined from the main trunk of the community by titular distinctions. Remaining incorporated with the general order of citizens, their merit more visibly reflected honor upon it, than if they had been advanced to an imaginary eminence, tending to engender in themselves or their descendants contempt for the mass of their countrymen.

The most lasting, if not the most effectually pernicious, evil with which New England has been afflicted, was the institution of slavery, which continued till a late period to pollute all its provinces, and lingered the latest, though to a very slight extent, in the province of New Hampshire.[2] The practice, as we have seen, originated in the supposed necessity created by Indian hostilities ; but, once introduced, it was banefully calculated to perpetuate itself, and to derive accessions from various other sources. For some time, indeed, this was successfully resisted ; and instances have been recorded of judicial interposition to confine the mischief within its original limits. In the year 1645, a negro, fraudfully brought from Africa, and enslaved within the New England territory, was liberated by the magistrates and sent back to his native country.[3] No law expressly authorizing slavery was ever enacted by any of the New England States ; and such was the

---

[1] In the year 1634, the people of Massachusetts having elected a particular individual to the office of governor, in place of Winthrop, who had previously enjoyed this dignity, their conduct was censured by John Cotton, who, in a sermon preached before the General Court, maintained that a magistrate ought not to be reduced to the condition of a private individual, without some cause of complaint publicly established against him. This curious proposition was discussed by the Court, and " referred for farther consideration." Winthrop's *Journal.*

Strikingly applicable to the early magistrates of New England is the following description, by a great German writer, of the regents or judges of Israel. " They were not only simple in their manners, moderate in their desires, and free from avarice and ambition, but noble and magnanimous men, who felt that whatever they did for their country was above all reward, and could not be recompensed; who desired merely to promote the public good, and who chose rather to deserve well of their country than to be enriched by its wealth. This exalted patriotism was partly of a religious character; and these regents always conducted themselves as the officers of God." Jahn's *History of the Hebrew Commonwealth.*

[2] The assembly of this province, as early as the reign of George the First, passed a law, enacting, that, " if any man smite out the eye or tooth of his man or maid servant, or otherwise maim or disfigure them, he shall let him or her go free from his service, and shall allow such farther recompense as the Court of Quarter Sessions shall adjudge "; and that, " if any person kill his Indian or negro servant, he shall be punished with death." The slaves in this province are said to have been treated in all respects like white servants. Warden's *United States.* By an act of the legislature of Rhode Island, in the year 1704, all *negroes and Indians* were prohibited from being abroad after nine o'clock of the evening. *Collections of the Rhode Island Historical Society.* Yet Rhode Island writers eagerly vaunt the superior equity of the treatment experienced by the Indians from their countrymen.

[3] Belknap.

influence of religious and moral feeling in all these States, that, even while there was no law prohibiting the continuance of slavery, it never succeeded in gaining any considerable prevalence.   To this end the qualities and produce of the soil coöperated with the moral sentiments of the people, who were not exposed to the same temptations to the employment of slave labor that presented themselves in the Southern provinces of America. By the early laws of Connecticut, man-stealing was declared a capital crime. In the year 1703, the assembly of Massachusetts imposed a duty of four pounds on every negro imported into the province ; and nine years after, passed an act prohibiting the importation of any more Indian servants or slaves.[1]   In Massachusetts, the slaves never exceeded the fiftieth part of the whole population ; in Connecticut and Rhode Island, when slaves were most numerous (about the middle of the eighteenth century), the proportion was nearly the same ; and in the territory that afterwards received the name of Vermont, when the number of inhabitants amounted to nine thousand, there were only sixteen persons in a state of slavery.[2]   The cruelties and vices that slavery tends to produce were repressed at once by so great a preponderance of the sound over the unhealthy part of the body politic, and by the moral circumstances to which this preponderance was owing. The majority of the inhabitants were decidedly hostile to slavery ; and numerous remonstrances were addressed to the British government against the encouragement she afforded to it by supporting the slave-trade.   When North America attained independence, the New England States adopted measures, which, in the course of a few years, effected the abolition of this vile institution.[3]

[1] *Blue Laws of Connecticut.* Holmes. "In the early part of the eighteenth century, Judge Sewell, of New England, came forward as a zealous advocate for the negroes. He addressed a memorial to the legislature, which he entitled *The Selling of Joseph*, and in which he pleaded their cause both as a lawyer and a Christian. This memorial produced an effect upon many, but particularly upon those of his own religious persuasion." Clarkson's *History of the Abolition of the Slave Trade.*

[2] Warden. Winterbotham's *America.* Dwight.

[3] There is a strange, I hope not a disingenuous, indistinctness in the statements of some writers respecting the negro slavery of New England. Winterbotham, writing in 1795, asserts that there are no slaves in Massachusetts. If he meant that a law had been passed which denounced and was gradually extinguishing slavery, he was right ; but the literal sense of his words is contradicted by Warden's *Tables*, which demonstrate that fifteen years after (the law not yet having produced its full effect) there were several thousand slaves in Massachusetts. Dwight relates his travels, in the end of the eighteenth and beginning of the nineteenth century, through every part of New England, without giving us the slightest reason to suppose that such beings as slaves existed in any one of its provinces, except when he stops to defend the legislature of Connecticut from an imputation on the manner in which her share of the abolition of slavery had been conducted. It was actually conducted in a style the most tenderly regardful of the iniquitous interests of the whites, and disdainfully negligent of the just rights of the negroes. Warden himself says, in one page, that "slavery no longer exists in New England," even while, in another, he admits and seeks to palliate the occurrence of its lingering traces in New Hampshire.

It is easier to commit than to repair injustice. Obstinate and protracted are its consequential evils. Hatred, contempt, and ill-usage of the negro race have long continued, in New England and other of the North American communities, to survive the abolition of negro slavery within their limits. See Note XXXVIII., at the end of Vol. II.

BOOK III.

MARYLAND.

Charter of Maryland obtained from Charles the First by Lord Baltimore. — Condition of the Roman Catholics in England. — Emigration of Roman Catholics to the Province. — Friendly Treaty with the Indians. — Generosity of Lord Baltimore. — Opposition and Intrigues of Clayborne. — First Assembly of Maryland. — Representative Government established. — Early Introduction of Negro Slavery. — An Indian War. — Clayborne's Rebellion. — Religious Toleration established in the Colony. — Separate Establishment of the House of Burgesses. — Clayborne declares for Cromwell — and usurps the Administration. — Toleration abolished. — Distractions of the Colony — terminated by the Restoration. — Establishment of a provincial Mint. — Happy State of the Colony. — Naturalization Acts. — Death of the first Proprietary. — Wise Government of his Son and Successor. — Law against importing Felons. — Establishment of the Church of England suggested. — Dismemberment of the Delaware Territory from Maryland. — Arbitrary Projects of James the Second. — Rumor of a Popish Plot. — A Protestant Association is formed — and usurps the Administration. — The Proprietary Government suspended by King William. — Establishment of the Church of England, and Persecution of the Catholics. — State of the Province. — Manners. — Laws.

FROM the history of Massachusetts, and of the other New England States, which were the offspring of its colonization, our inquiry is now transferred to the origin and early progress of a colony which arose from the plantation of Virginia. In relating the history of this province, we had occasion to notice, among other circumstances that disquieted its inhabitants during the administration of Sir John Harvey, the arbitrary grants, obtained by certain courtiers from the crown, of large tracts of territory situated within its chartered limits. The most remarkable of these was the grant of Maryland to Lord Baltimore.

Sir George Calvert, afterwards Lord Baltimore, was secretary of state to King James the First, and one of the original members of the Virginian Company. Conceiving a high opinion of the value of landed property in America, and foreseeing the improvement it must derive from the progress of colonization, he employed his political influence to secure an endowment of it to himself and his family. He was a strenuous asserter of the supremacy of that authority from the exercise of which he expected his own enrichment; and when a bill was introduced into the House of Commons for rendering the Newfoundland fishery free to all British subjects [1620], he opposed it, on the plea that the American territory, having been acquired by conquest, was subject exclusively to the control of the royal prerogative. The first grant that he succeeded in obtaining was of a district in Newfoundland which he named Avalon [1622], and where, at a considerable expense, he formed the settlement of Ferryland;[1] but finding his expectations disap-

---

[1] His colonial policy is thus contrasted by an old writer with that of Chief Justice Popham, the promoter of the first attempts to colonize New England: "Judge Popham and Sir George Calvert agreed not more unanimously in the public design of planting, than they differed in the private way of it; the first was for extirpating heathens, the second for converting them. He sent away the lewdest, this the soberest people; the one was for present profit, the other for a reasonable expectation; ..... the first set up a common stock, out of which the people should be provided by proportions; the second left every one to provide for himself." Lloyd's *State Worthies*.

pointed by the soil and climate of this inhospitable region, he paid a visit to
Virginia, for the purpose of ascertaining if some part of its territorial resources might not be rendered more subservient to his advantage. [1628.]
But he had now embraced and professed the tenets of the Church of Rome ;
and the officers of the Virginian government, whether from jealousy of his
territorial views, or from a conscientious regard to their own duty, compelled him after a short stay to abandon the province, by insisting on their
right to administer to him *the oath of supremacy*.[1] This proceeding, however, had no other effect than to prompt him to consummate his purpose,
and pursue the very encroachment which it is probable that the Virginians
apprehended. His visit to the province inspired him with a predilection
for its soil and climate ; and the treatment he received from the provincial
authorities, if it did not originally suggest, at least confirmed, his design of
procuring a grant that would render him independent of their jurisdiction.
Observing that the Virginians had not yet formed any settlements to the
northward of the river Potomac, he resolved to apply for a royal donative
of territory in that quarter ; and easily prevailed with Charles the First to
bestow on him the investiture he solicited. With the intention of promoting
the aggrandizement of his own family he combined the more generous project of founding a new commonwealth, and colonizing it with the persecuted
votaries of the church of Rome. But the design to which he had paved the
way by an act of injustice he was not permitted himself to accomplish. His
project, which was interrupted by his death, just when every preparation
was made for carrying it into effect, was resumed by his son and successor,
Cecilius, Lord Baltimore [June, 1632], in whose favor the king completed
the charter that had been destined for his father.[2]

If the charter which shortly before was obtained from Charles by the
Puritan colonists of Massachusetts may be regarded as the exercise of policy, the investiture which he now bestowed on Lord Baltimore was not less
manifestly the expression of favor. This nobleman, like his father, was a
Roman Catholic ; and his avowed purpose was to people his territory with
colonists of the same persuasion, and erect an asylum in North America
for the Catholic faith. By the charter which he received, it was declared
that the grantee was actuated by a laudable zeal for extending the Christian
religion and the territory of the British Empire ; and the district assigned
to him and his heirs and successors was described as " that region bounded
by a line drawn from Watkins's Point of Chesapeake Bay ; thence to that
part of the estuary of Delaware on the north which lies under the fortieth
degree, where New England is terminated ; thence in a right line, by the
degree aforesaid, to the meridian of the fountain of Potomac ; thence following its course by the farther bank to its confluence." In compliment to the
queen, the province thus bestowed on a nobleman of the same faith with her
Majesty was denominated Maryland ; and in compliment, perhaps, to her
Majesty's creed, the endowment was accompanied with immunities more

---

[1] The formula of the oath of supremacy then in use (prescribed by Stat. 1 Eliz., cap. 1, § 19)
declared the king governor of all his dominions and countries, " as well in all spiritual or ecclesiastical things or causes as temporal." Lord Baltimore, though an Englishman by birth,
was a peer of Ireland, and doubtless knew that Pope Urban the Eighth had but a few years
before addressed a bull to the Irish Catholics, charging them " rather to lose their lives, than
to take that wicked and pestilent oath of supremacy, whereby the sceptre of the Catholic
church was wrested from the hand of the vicar of God Almighty." Leland's *History of
Ireland*.
[2] Chalmers. Bozman's *History of Maryland*.

ample than any of the other colonial establishments possessed.   The new
province was declared to be separated from Virginia, and no longer subordinate to any other colony, but immediately subject to the crown of England,
and dependent thereon for ever.   Lord Baltimore was created the absolute
proprietary of it ; saving the allegiance and sovereign dominion due to the
crown.   He was empowered, with the assent of the freemen or their delegates, whom he was required to assemble for this purpose, to make laws for
the province, not repugnant to the jurisprudence of England ; and the acts
of the assembly he was authorized to execute.   For the population of the
new colony, license was given to all his Majesty's subjects to transport themselves thither ; and the emigrants and their posterity were declared to be
liegemen of the king and his successors, and entitled to the same liberties as
native-born Englishmen.   The proprietary was authorized, with the consent
of the people, to impose all just and proper subsidies, which were declared
to pertain to himself for ever ; and it was covenanted on the part of the king,
that neither he nor his successors should at any time impose, or cause to be
imposed, any tallages on the colonists, or on their goods, tenements, or
commodities.   Thus was conferred on Maryland, in perpetuity, the same
fiscal benefit which had been granted to other colonies for a term of years.
The territory was erected into a palatinate ; and the proprietary was invested
with the same royal rights which were enjoyed by the palatine Bishop of
Durham ; and authorized to appoint provincial officers, to repel invasions,
and to suppress rebellions.   The advowsons of all churches, which should
be established in conformity with the ecclesiastical constitutions of England,
were granted to him.   The charter finally provided, that, if any doubt should
ever arise concerning its true meaning, the interpretation most favorable to
the proprietary should always be adopted ; excluding, however, any construction derogatory to the Christian religion, or to the allegiance due to the
crown.[1]

Though the sovereignty of the crown was thus reserved over the province, and a conformity enjoined between its legislation and the jurisprudence
of England, no means were provided for the exercise of the royal dominion
or the ascertainment of the stipulated conformity.   The charter contained
no definition of the method or occasions of royal interference in the municipal administration, and no obligation on the proprietary to transmit the acts
of assembly for confirmation or annulment by the king.   In erecting the
province into a palatinate, and vesting the hereditary government of it in the
family of Lord Baltimore, the king exercised the highest attributes of the
prerogative of a feudal sovereign.   A similar trait of feudal prerogative appears in the perpetual exemption from royal taxation which was assured to
the colonists by the charter, and which, at a later period, gave rise to much
intricate and elaborate controversy.   It was maintained, when this provision
became the subject of critical comment, that it ought not to be construed to
import an exemption from parliamentary taxation, since the king could not
be supposed to intend to abridge the jurisdiction of the parliament, or to renounce a privilege that was not his own ;[2] and that, even if such construction had been intended, the immunity was illegal, and incapable of restrain-

---

[1] *Laws of Maryland.*   Hazard.
[2] Yet, at an after period, it was considered by English lawyers that an exclusion of parliamentary taxation, whether effectually constituted, would be at least imported by such a clause ;
and, in the Pennsylvania charter, when an exemption from customs was conceded, it was
qualified by an express reservation of the authority of the English parliament.

ing the functions of the British legislature. In addition to the general reasoning that was employed to demonstrate this illegality, reference was made to the authority of a parliamentary transaction related by Sir Edward Coke, who, in a debate on the royal prerogative in the year 1620, assured the Commons that a dispensation from subsidies, granted to certain individuals within the realm in the reign of Henry the Seventh, had been subsequently repealed by act of parliament. But even if this authority could be reinforced by supposing that every act of parliament which introduced a particular ordinance was also declaratory of the general law in all similar cases, the application of it to the charter of Maryland might, nevertheless, very fairly be questioned. Colonies, at the time of which we treat, were regarded entirely as dependencies on the monarchical branch of the government ; the rule of their governance was the royal prerogative, except where this authority was specially limited or excluded by the terms of a royal charter ; and the same power that gave a political being to the colony was considered adequate to determine the political privileges of its inhabitants. The colonists of Maryland undoubtedly conceived that their charter bestowed on them an exemption from all taxes but such as should be imposed by their own provincial assembly ; for it discharged them for ever from the taxation of the only other organ of power that was deemed competent to exercise this authority over them. Not the least remarkable peculiarity of this charter is, that it affords the first example of the dismemberment of an established colony, and the creation of a new one within its original limits, by the mere act of the crown.

Lord Baltimore having thus obtained the charter of Maryland, hastened to execute the design of colonizing the new province, of which he appointed his brother, Leonard Calvert, to be governor. Of a ready resort of inhabitants to his domain, and especially of persons, who, like himself, professed the faith of the Church of Rome, the state of England at that period encouraged a reasonable expectation. The Roman Catholic inhabitants of this kingdom had been for many years the objects of increasing dread and antipathy to all other classes of their fellow-subjects, and had experienced from the English government a progressive severity of persecution. All the indulgence which the first proceedings of Queen Elizabeth seemed to betoken to them was defeated by the sentence of excommunication and deposition fulminated against herself by the head of the Catholic church, and by the repeated attempts of some of her own subjects, who were votaries of this church, to effectuate the Papal sentence by revolt and assassination ; and, notwithstanding the generous ardor displayed by the more respectable portion of the English Catholics, in defending her against the Armada of Spain, which was expected to restore the preëminence of their church, the progress of her reign was distinguished by the enactment of a series of vindictive and rigorous laws against a faith which was believed by her Protestant subjects to menace her with unappeasable hatred and continual danger. The accession of the House of Stuart to the English throne produced no less disappointment to the Catholics than to the Puritans of England. The favor which the Catholics expected from the birth and the character of James the First was intercepted by the necessity of his situation ; while the hopes that the Puritans derived from his early education and habits were frustrated by the flattery of their Protestant adversaries, and his unexpected display of rancor and aversion toward themselves. In the particular history of New

England, we have had occasion to consider the treatment which the Puritans experienced from this prince. To the application which he received from the Catholics on his accession to the crown, his answer was, that he reckoned himself obliged to support the system which he found established in the kingdom; and, though he was compelled to maintain and even enlarge the code of legal severity to which they were subjected, he frequently interposed to mitigate the actual infliction of its rigor, by the exercise of his royal prerogative.

The tenets of the Puritans and the Catholics could hardly differ more widely than the conduct which ensued on the disappointment of their respective expectations. The Catholics, whose hopes had been the most chimerical, and who plainly perceived the indulgence which the king entertained, and would willingly have demonstrated more unreservedly to them, were at first transported with indignation, and stimulated to revenge; while the Puritans, whose hopes had been more reasonable, and whose experience of the actual regards of their sovereign was more fraught with substantial disappointment, expressed much less resentment than regret. It was long before the Puritans were provoked to resistance and civil war; and emigration was the earliest remedial measure to which the more zealous of their number had recourse. The sentiments that were at first excited in the zealots of the Catholic persuasion were of a very different complexion; and one of the earliest measures which they embraced was the atrocious contrivance of the *Gunpowder Plot.* The detection of that horrid enterprise, though it was unable to extinguish the king's partiality to the Catholics, rendered this sentiment much less available than it might otherwise have proved for the relief of their sufferings. New statutes of persecution were enacted by the parliament against the Catholics; and new disabilities, restraints, penalties, and forfeitures were inflicted on the whole Catholic body, for an action which truly indicated only the extravagant zeal and criminal rage of a few of its most intemperate members. The assassination of Henry the Fourth, of France, which occurred not long afterwards, increased the antipathy of all classes of English Protestants against the Catholics, and, leading James to believe that nothing short of an entire devotion to the church of Rome could enable him securely to associate with its votaries, prompted him, from an increased apprehension of personal danger, to employ more than once his royal proclamations to quicken, instead of restraining, the execution of the penal laws. And although the deliberate sentiments both of this monarch and his successor were averse to the infliction of the extreme of legal rigor on the Catholics, yet to discerning eyes the advantage of this circumstance was more than counterbalanced by the increasing influence of the Puritans in the English House of Commons, and the increasing propagation of Puritan sentiments in the minds of the English people.

Thus exposed to molestation from the existing authorities in England, and apprehending still greater severity from the predominance of a party gradually advancing in strength and hardening in sternness of spirit, many of the Catholics were led to meditate a retreat from the scene of persecution to some vacant corner in the British dominions. The most liberal and moderate of the members of the Romish church were the most forward to embrace this purpose, and of such consisted the first emigrants to Lord Baltimore's territory. Sensible of the inveterate odium that their persuasion had incurred in England, both from the criminal enterprises of unworthy votaries, and from the bigotry of intolerant adversaries, they purposed, perhaps, to redeem its reputation, and to teach a lesson of wisdom and charity both to Catholics and Protestants, by conducting their colonial settlement on principles diametrically opposite to the illiberal maxims and practices with which the church of Rome was reproached, and by rendering Maryland a scene of greater liberty of conscience than was enjoyed in any other quarter of the world. Whether in the commencement of their enterprise they distinctly conceived this generous design or not, they are entitled to the higher praise of having practically realized it.

The first band of emigrants, consisting of about two hundred gentlemen of considerable rank and fortune, professing the Roman Catholic faith, with a number of inferior adherents, in a vessel called *The Ark and the Dove,* sailed from England, under the command of Leonard Calvert, in November, 1632; and, after a prosperous voyage, reached the coast of Maryland, near the mouth of the river Potomac, in the beginning of the following year. [1633.] The governor, as soon as he landed, erected a cross on the shore, and took possession of the country *for our Saviour and for our sovereign lord the king of England.* Aware that the first settlers of Virginia had given umbrage to the Indians by occupying their territory without demanding their permission, he determined to imitate the wiser and juster policy that was pursued by the colonists of New England, and to unite the new with the ancient race of inhabitants by the ties of equity, good-will, and mutual advantage. The Indian chief, to whom he addressed his proposition of occupying a portion of the country, answered at first with a sullen affectation of indifference, — the result, most probably, of aversion to the measure and of conscious inability to resist it, — that he would not bid the English go, neither would he bid them stay, but that he left them to their own discretion. The liberality and courtesy, however, of the governor's demeanour succeeded at length in conciliating the Indian's regard so powerfully, that he not only established a friendly league between the colonists and his own people, but persuaded the other neighbouring tribes to accede to the treaty, and warmly declared, *I love the English so well, that, if they should go about to kill me, if I had so much breath as to speak, I would command my people not to revenge my death ; for I know they would not do such a thing, except it were through my own fault.* Having purchased the rights of the aborigines at a price which gave them perfect satisfaction, the colonists obtained possession of a large district, including an Indian town, which they forthwith occupied, and distinguished by the name of St. Mary's. It was not till their numbers had undergone a considerable increase, that they judged it necessary to frame a code of laws and establish their political constitution. They lived for some time in a social union, resembling the domestic regimen of a patriarchal family ; and confined their attention to the providing of food and habitations for themselves and the associates by whom they expected to be reinforced. The lands which were ceded to them yielded a ready increase, because they had already undergone the discipline of Indian tillage ;[1] and this circumstance, as well as the proximity of Virginia, which now afforded an abundant supply of the necessaries of life, enabled the colonists of Maryland to escape the ravages of that calamity which had afflicted the infancy, and nearly proved fatal to the existence, of every one of the other settlements of the English in America. So luxuriant were

[1] " They found fat pasture and good, and the land was wide, and quiet, and peaceable ; for they of Ham had dwelt there of old." 1 Chron. iv. 40.

their crops, that, within two years after their arrival in the province, they exported ten thousand bushels of Indian corn to New England, for the purchase of salted fish and other provisions. The tidings of their safe and comfortable establishment, conspiring with the uneasiness experienced by the Roman Catholics in England, induced considerable numbers of the professors of this faith to follow the original emigrants to Maryland ; and no efforts of wisdom or generosity were spared by Lord Baltimore to promote the population and the happiness of the colony. The transportation of people and of necessary stores and provisions, during the first two years, cost him upwards of forty thousand pounds. To every emigrant he assigned fifty acres of land in absolute fee ; and with a liberality unparalleled in that age, he united a general recognition of Christianity as the established faith of the land, with an exclusion of the political predominance or superiority of any one particular sect or denomination of Christians. This wise administration soon converted a desolate wilderness into a flourishing commonwealth, enlivened by industry and adorned by civilization. It is a proof at once of the success of his policy, and of the prosperity and happiness of the colonists, that, a very few years after the first occupation of the province, they granted to their proprietary a large subsidy of tobacco, in grateful acknowledgment of his liberality and beneficence.[1] Similar tributes continued, from time to time, to attest the merit of the proprietary and the attachment of the people.

The wisdom and virtue by which the colonization of the new province was signalized could not atone for the arbitrary encroachment by which its territory had been wrested from the jurisdiction of Virginia ; and while it is impossible not to regret the troubles which this circumstance engendered, there is something not altogether dissatisfactory to the moral eye in beholding the evil fruits of usurpation. Such lessons are most agreeable, when the requital which they exhibit is confined to the immediate perpetrators of wrong ; but they are not the less salutary, when the admonition they convey is derived from punishment extended to the remote accessories, who have consented to avail themselves of the injustice of the actual or principal delinquents. The king had commanded Sir John Harvey, the governor of Virginia, to render assistance and encouragement to Lord Baltimore in establishing himself and his associates in Maryland. But though the governor and his council declared their readiness, in humble submission to his Majesty's will, to maintain a good correspondence with their unwelcome neighbours, they determined at the same time to defend the rights of the prior settlement. The planters of Virginia presented a petition against the charter of Lord Baltimore ; and both parties were admitted to discuss their contradictory pretensions before the privy council. [July, 1633.] After vainly endeavouring to promote an amicable adjustment, the council decreed that Lord Baltimore should retain his charter, and the petitioners their remedy at law, — a remedy which probably had no existence, and for which the Virginians never thought it worth while to inquire. For the prevention of farther differences, it was enjoined by the council that free and mutual commerce should be permitted between the two colonies ; that neither should harbour fugitives from the other, nor commit any act that might provoke a war with the natives ; and that each should on all occasions assist and befriend the other in a manner becoming fellow-subjects of the same empire.

[1] Oldmixon. Chalmers. Bozman.

But although the Virginian planters were thus compelled to withdraw their opposition, and the Virginian government to recognize the independence of Maryland, the establishment of this colony encountered an obstinate resistance from interests far less entitled to respect ; and the validity of Lord Baltimore's grant was disputed with much violence and pertinacity by a prior, but less legitimate, intruder. This competitor was William Clayborne, a member of Sir John Harvey's council, and secretary of the province of Virginia ; and the friendship between Harvey and this individual may perhaps account for a singularity in the conduct of that tyrannical governor, and explain why, on one occasion at least, he was disposed to defend the interests of the Virginian planters in opposition to the arbitrary policy of the king. About a year before the date of Lord Baltimore's charter, the king granted to Clayborne a license under the sign manual to traffic in those parts of America not comprehended in any preceding patent of exclusive trade ; and in corroboration of this license, Harvey superadded to it a commission in similar terms under the seal of his own authority. The object of Clayborne and his associates was, to monopolize the trade of the Chesapeake ; to which end they had established a small trading settlement in the isle of Kent, which is situated in the very centre of Maryland, and which Clayborne now persisted in claiming as his own, and refused to subject to the newly erected jurisdiction. The unreasonableness of a plea, which engrafted a territorial grant upon a mere commercial license, did not prevent the government of Virginia from countenancing Clayborne, who, encouraged by the approbation thus afforded to his pretensions, scrupled not to support them by acts of profligate intrigue and even sanguinary violence. He infused a spirit of insubordination into the inhabitants of the isle of Kent, and scattered jealousies among the Indian tribes, some of whom he was able to persuade that the new settlers were Spaniards and enemies to the Virginians. Lord Baltimore, now perceiving the necessity of a vigorous effort in defence of his rights, commanded the governor to vindicate the provincial jurisdiction, and maintain an entire subordination within its limits. [Sept., 1634.] Till this emergency, the colony had subsisted without the formal establishment of municipal institutions ; but the same occasion that now called forth the powers of government tended also to develope its organization. Accordingly, in the commencement of the following year [Feb., 1635], was convened the first popular assembly of Maryland, consisting of the whole body of the freemen, by which various regulations were framed for the maintenance of good order in the province. One of the statutes of this assembly ordained that all perpetrators of murder and other felonies should incur the same punishments that were appointed for such offences by the laws of England ; an enactment, which, besides its general utility, was necessary to pave the way to the judicial proceedings that were contemplated against Clayborne. This individual, still persisting in his outrages, was indicted soon after for murder, piracy, and sedition. Finding that those who had encouraged his pretensions left him unaided to defend his crimes, he fled from penal inquisition, and his estate was confiscated. Against this adjudication he appealed to the king, and petitioned at the same time for the renewal of his license and the grant of an independent territory adjoining to the isle of Kent. By the assistance of powerful friends and the dexterity of his representations, he very nearly obtained a complete triumph over his antagonists, and eventually prevailed so far as to involve Lord Baltimore and the colonists of Maryland in a controversy that was not terminated for several years. At length the Lords Commissioners of the Colonies, to whom the matter was referred, pronounced a final sentence, dismissing Clayborne's appeal, and adjudging that the whole territory belonged to Lord Baltimore, and that no plantation or trade with the Indians, unsanctioned by his permission, could be lawfully established within the limits of his patent. Thus divested of every semblance of legal title, Clayborne exchanged his hopes of victory for schemes of revenge ; and watching with considerate hate every opportunity of hostile intrigue that the situation of the colony might present to him, he was unfortunately enabled, at an after period, to wreak the vengeance of disappointed rapacity upon his successful competitor.[1]

The colony meanwhile continued to thrive, and the numbers of its inhabitants to be augmented by copious emigration from England. With the increase of the people and the extension of the settlements to a greater distance from St. Mary's, the necessity of a legislative code became apparent ; and Lord Baltimore, having composed a body of laws for the province, transmitted them to his brother, with directions to propose them to the assembly of the freemen. The second assembly of Maryland was in consequence convoked by the governor, with the expectation, doubtless, of an immediate ratification of the suggestions of the proprietary. [Jan., 1637.] But the colonists, along with a sincere attachment to Lord Baltimore, entertained a just and liberal conception of their own political rights ; and while they made an ample provision for the support of his government, they refused to accept his legislative propositions. It was in vain that the governor urged upon them that the provisions of this code were confessedly salutary and judicious, and that it was the wish of the proprietary that the proposition of all laws should originate with himself, and that they should restrict their legislative functions to the acceptance or rejection of his suggestions. This was an arrangement which they were determined not to admit. In place of Lord Baltimore's code, they prepared a collection of ordinances for themselves. The province was divided into baronies and manors. Various regulations were enacted for securing popular liberty, for ascertaining the titles to landed property, and for regulating the course of intestate succession. A law was passed for the support of the proprietary government ; and an act of attainder against Clayborne. In almost all the laws, where prices were stated or payments prescribed, tobacco, and not money, was assumed as the measure of value. The first colonists of Maryland devoted themselves as eagerly as the Virginians did at first to the cultivation of this valuable commodity. With indiscriminate desire to enlarge their contributions to the market, and obtain a price for the whole produce of their fields, they refused to accede to the regulations by which the planters of Virginia improved the quality by diminishing the quantity of their supply ; and this dissension was productive of much ill-humor and jealousy between the two colonies, and tended to keep alive the original disgust which the establishment of Maryland had inspired in Virginia.

The third assembly of Maryland, convoked two years afterwards [Feb., 1639], was rendered memorable by the introduction of a representative body into the provincial constitution. The population of the province had derived so large an increase from recent emigrations, that it was impossible for all the freeholders to continue longer to exercise the right of legislation by per-

---

[1] Oldmixon. Chalmers. Hazard. Bozman.

sonal attendance. An ordinance was consequently established for the election of representatives, and the modification of the house of assembly. It was now ordained, that the persons, elected in pursuance of writs issued, should be termed burgesses, and should supply the place of the freemen who chose them in the same manner as the representatives of the people in the parliament of England ; and in conjunction with a smaller body, convoked by the special nomination of the proprietary, together with the governor and secretary, should constitute the General Assembly. But though the election of representatives was thus introduced for the convenience of the people, they were not restricted to this mode of exercising their legislatorial rights ; for, by a very singular provision, it was ordained that all freemen declining to vote at the election of burgesses should be entitled to assume a personal share in the deliberations of the assembly. The several branches of the legislature were appointed to meet in the same chamber ; and all acts assented to by the united body were to be deemed of the same force as if the proprietary and every one of the freemen had been personally present. It was not long before the people were sensible of the advantage that the democratic part of the constitution would derive from the separate establishment of its appropriate organ ; but, although this innovation was suggested by the burgesses very shortly afterwards, the form of convocation that was now adopted continued to be retained by the legislature of Maryland till the year 1650. Various acts were passed in this assembly for the security of liberty, and the administration of justice, according to the laws and customs of England. All the inhabitants were required to take the oath of allegiance to the king ; the prerogatives of the proprietary were distinctly recognized ; and the great charter of England was declared to be the measure of the liberties of the colonists. To obviate the inconveniences that were apprehended from the almost exclusive attention of the people to the cultivation of tobacco, it was judged expedient to enjoin the planting of corn by law. A tax was imposed for the supply of a revenue to the proprietary. But notwithstanding this indication of prosperity, and the introduction of representative government, that the colonists were not yet either numerous or wealthy may be inferred from the imposition of a general assessment to erect a water-mill for the use of the province. Slavery seems to have been established in Maryland from its earliest colonization ; for an act of this assembly describes *the people* to consist of all Christian inhabitants, *slaves only excepted*.[1] That slavery should gain a footing in any community of professed Christians will excite the regret of every one who knows what slavery and Christianity mean. Some surprise may mingle with our regret, when we behold this baneful institution adopted in a community of Roman Catholics, and of men who not only were themselves fugitives from persecution, but so much in earnest in the profession of their distinctive faith, as for its sake to incur exile from their native country. The unlawfulness of slavery had been solemnly proclaimed by the pontiff, whom the Catholics regarded as the infallible head of their church ; for when the controversy on this subject was submitted to Leo the Tenth, he declared that " *not only the Christian religion, but nature herself, cried out against a state of slavery.*" But the good which an earthly potentate can accomplish or promote is far from being commensurate with his power of doing evil. When one pope divided the undiscovered

---

[1] Bacon's *Laws*. Oldmixon. Chalmers. Bozman. This author, unfortunately, has not continued his history of Maryland beyond the year 1638.

parts of the world between Castile and Portugal, his arrogant distributive decree was held sacred ; when another uttered his humane and equitable canon against the lawfulness of slavery, his authority was contemned, and proved quite inefficient.

The discontent with which the Virginians regarded the establishment of the new colony was heightened by the contrast between the liberty and happiness which the planters of Maryland were permitted to enjoy, and the tyranny which they themselves endured from the government of Sir John Harvey. The arguments by which the Maryland charter had been successfully defended against them tended to associate the invasion of their liberties with the existence of this colony ; for the complaint of dismemberment of their original territory was encountered by the plea, that the designation of the territory perished with the charter which contained it, and that, by the dissolution of the company to which the charter had belonged, all the dominion it could claim over unoccupied regions reverted by legal necessity to the crown. From the company, or at least during its existence, the Virginians had obtained a degree of liberty, which, since the dissolution of that corporate body, was greatly circumscribed by the encroachments of the royal governor ; and hence their ardent wishes for the restoration of their privileges were naturally connected with the reëstablishment of a corporation, whose patent, if revived, would annul the charter of Maryland. It was fortunate for both the colonies, that the king, in consenting to abandon the illiberal system of government which he had been pursuing in Virginia, granted to the inhabitants rather what they wanted than what they asked, and restored to them the enjoyment of liberty, without the appendage of the ancient corporation under which it had been acquired ; and that the Virginians, justly appreciating the advantage thus accruing to them, now regarded with aversion the proposed revival of the patent, and were sensible that their interests would be rather impaired than promoted by the event that would enable them to reannex Maryland to their territory. Had this change of circumstances and interests been deferred but a short time, the most injurious consequences might have resulted to both the colonies ; for the assembling of the Long Parliament [1640], and the encouragement which it bestowed on every complaint of royal misgovernment, inspired the partners of the suppressed Virginia Company with the hope of obtaining a restitution of their patent. Fortified by the opinion of eminent lawyers whom they consulted, and who confidently assured them that the ancient patents of Virginia still remained in force, and that the grant of Maryland, as derogatory to them, was legally void, they presented an application to the parliament, complaining of the unjust invasion that their privileges had suffered, and demanding that the government of Virginia (embracing all the territory formerly denoted by this name) should be restored to them. This application would undoubtedly have prevailed, if it had been seconded by the Virginian colonists. Its failure was mainly occasioned by the vigorous opposition of the assembly of Virginia.[1] [1641.]

Under the constitution which was thus preserved to them by the exertions of their formal rivals, the colonists of Maryland continued to flourish in the enjoyment of a happy and prosperous estate, and to demonstrate, by their unabated gratitude to the proprietary, that the spirit of liberty rather enhances than impairs the attachment of a free people to its ruler, and that a

---

[1] Chalmers. *Ante*, Book I., Chap. II.

strong sense of the rights of men is no way incompatible with a just impression of their duties. The wise and friendly policy which the governor pursued towards the Indians had hitherto preserved a peace which proved highly beneficial to the colony in its infant state. But, unfortunately, the intrigues of Clayborne had infected the minds of these savages with a jealous suspicion, which was nourished by the visibly increasing strength of the colony, and which the immoderate avidity of some of the planters tended to extend and inflame. The rapid multiplication of the stranger race seemed to threaten the extinction of the aboriginal inhabitants ; and the augmented value, which the territory they sold to the colonists had subsequently derived from the industry and skill of its new proprietors, easily suggested to their envy and ignorance the angry surmise that they had been defrauded in the original vendition. This injurious suspicion was confirmed by the conduct of various individuals among the planters, who, without the authority of government, procured additional grants of land from the Indians, for considerations which were grossly inadequate, and which, upon reflection, inspired the defrauded vendors with anger and discontent.[1] These causes at length produced the calamity which the governor had earnestly labored to avert. An Indian war broke out in the beginning of the year 1642, and continued for two years after to administer its accustomed evils, without the occurrence of any decisive issue, or the attainment of any considerable advantage by either party. Peace having been with some difficulty reëstablished [1644], the provincial assembly enacted laws for the prevention of the more obvious causes of complaint and animosity. All acquisitions of land from the aborigines, without the consent of the proprietary, were pronounced derogatory no less to his dignity and rights than to the safety of the community, and therefore void and illegal. It was declared a capital felony to kidnap or sell any friendly Indians ; and a high misdemeanour to supply them with spirituous liquors, or with arms or ammunition. Partly by these regulations, but chiefly by the humane and prudent demeanour of the officers who conducted the proprietary government, the peace that was now concluded between the colonists and the Indians subsisted, without interruption, for a considerable space of time.[2]

But the province was not long permitted to enjoy the restoration of its tranquillity. Scarcely was the Indian war concluded, when the intrigues of Clayborne exploded in mischiefs of far greater magnitude and more lasting

---

[1] Similar causes of offence undoubtedly begot or promoted many of the wars between the Indians and the other colonies. "Such things," says the historian of New Hampshire, "were indeed disallowed by the government, and would always have been punished, if the Indians had made complaint ; but they knew only the law of retaliation, and when an injury was inflicted, it was never forgotten till revenged." The fraud, or supposed fraud, of an individual might, at the distance of many years from its perpetration, involve the whole colony to which he belonged in an Indian war. Belknap.

"The Indians," says a pious, accurate, and impartial writer, "need not much provocation to begin a war with the white people : a trifling occurrence is readily laid hold of as a sufficient pretence. They frequently first determine upon war, and then wait a convenient opportunity to find reasons for it. Sometimes they have sold districts of land for the purpose of disputing the transaction and finding in the dispute a desired occasion of war." Loskiel's *History of the Moravian Missions.*

"Unprincipled and avaricious traders sometimes resided among the Indians ; and, that they might the more easily cheat them, first filled the savages drunk, and then took all manner of advantage of them in the course of traffic. When the Indian recovers from his fit of drunkenness, and finds himself robbed of his treasures, for procuring which he had, perhaps, hunted a whole year, he is filled with fury, and spurns every check upon his vengeance." Hewit's *History of South Carolina and Georgia.*

[2] Chalmers.

malignity. The activity of this enterprising and vindictive spirit had been curbed hitherto by the deference which he affected to the pleasure of the British court, at which he cultivated his interest so successfully, that, in the year 1642, he received from the king the appointment of treasurer of Virginia for life.[1] But the civil wars which now broke out in England, leaving him no longer any thing to hope from royal patronage, he made no scruple to declare himself a partisan of the popular cause, and to espouse the fortunes of a party from whose predominance he expected the gratification at once of his ambition and his revenge. In conjunction with his former associates in the isle of Kent, and aided by the contagious ferment of the times, he kindled a rebellion in Maryland in the beginning of the year 1645. Calvert, destitute of forces suitable to this emergency, was constrained to take shelter in Virginia ; and the vacant government was instantly appropriated by the insurgents, and exercised with a violence characteristic of the ascendency of an unpopular and unprincipled faction. Notwithstanding the most vigorous exertions of the governor, seconded by the well-affected part of the community, the revolt was not suppressed till the autumn of the following year. [August, 1646.] The afflictions of that calamitous period are indicated by a statute of the assembly, which recites "that the province has been wasted by a miserable dissension and unhappy war, which has been closed by the joyful restitution of a blessed peace." To promote the general tranquillity and confidence, an act of pardon and oblivion was passed, from the benefits of which only a few leading agitators were excepted ; and all suits were disallowed for wrongs perpetrated during the revolt. But the additional tributes which it was found necessary to exact from the people were consequences of the insurrection that did not so soon pass away ; and three years afterwards [1649], a temporary impost of ten shillings on every hundred-weight of tobacco exported in Dutch vessels was granted to the proprietary, — the one half of which was expressly appropriated to the liquidation of expenses incurred for the recovery and defence of the province, — while the other was declared to be conferred on him for the purpose of enabling him the better to provide for the public safety in time to come.[2]

In the assembly by which the imposition of this tribute was decreed, a magnanimous attempt was made to preserve the peace of the colony, by extinguishing within its limits one of the most fertile sources of human strife and animosity. It had been proclaimed from the very beginning by the proprietary, that religious toleration should constitute one of the fundamental principles of the social union over which he presided ; and the assembly of the province, composed chiefly of Roman Catholics, now proceeded, by a memorable *Act concerning Religion*, to interweave this noble principle into its legislative constitutions. The statute commenced with a preamble, declaring that *the enforcement of the conscience had been of dangerous consequence in those countries wherein it had been practised* ; and ordained, that, thereafter, no persons professing to believe in Jesus Christ should be molested on account of their faith, or denied the free exercise of their particular modes of worship ; that persons molesting any individual, on account of his religious tenets or ecclesiastical practices, should pay treble damages to the party aggrieved, and twenty shillings to the proprietary ; that those who should reproach their neighbours with opprobrious names or epithets, inferring religious distinctions, should forfeit ten shillings to the persons so in-

---

[1] Hazard.   [2] Preface to Bacon's *Laws*. Chalmers.

sulted ; that any one speaking reproachfully against the blessed Virgin or the apostles should forfeit five pounds ; and that blasphemy against God should be punished with death.[1] By the enactment of this statute, the Catholic planters of Maryland procured to their adopted country the distinguished praise of being the first of the American States in which toleration was established by law ;[2] and graced their peculiar faith with the signal and unwonted merit of protecting those rights of conscience which no other Christian association in the world was yet sufficiently humane and enlightened to recognize. It is a striking and instructive spectacle, to behold at this period the Puritans persecuting their Protestant brethren in New England ; the Protestant Episcopalians inflicting similar rigor and injustice on the Puritans in Virginia ; and the Catholics, against whom all the others were combined, forming in Maryland a sanctuary where Christians of every denomination might worship, yet none might oppress, and where even Protestants sought refuge from Protestant intolerance. If the dangers to which the Maryland Catholics must have felt themselves exposed, from the disfavor with which they were regarded by the other colonial communities in their vicinity, and from the ascendency which their most zealous adversaries, the Presbyterians, were acquiring in the councils of the parent state, may be supposed to account in some degree for their cultivation of a principle of which they manifestly needed the protection, the surmise will detract very little from the merit of the authors of this excellent law. The disposition of mankind towards moderation has ever needed adventitious support ; and Christian sentiment is not depreciated by the supposition that deems it capable of deriving an accession to its purity from the experience of persecution. It is by divine grace alone that the fire of persecution thus sometimes tends to refine virtue and consume the dross incident even to this celestial principle in its coexistence with human frailty ; and the progress of our history will abundantly demonstrate, that, without such overruling agency, the commission of injustice naturally tends to its own reproduction, and that the experience of it engenders a much stronger disposition to retaliate its severities than to sympathize with its victims. It had been happy for the credit of the Protestants, whose hostility perhaps promoted the moderation of the Catholics of Maryland, if they had imitated the virtue thus elicited by apprehension of their own violence and injustice. But, unfortunately, a great proportion even of those fugitives who were constrained to seek shelter among the Catholics from the persecutions of their own Protestant brethren carried with them into exile the same intolerance of which they had themselves already been the victims ; and the Presbyterians and other dissenters, who now began to flock in considerable numbers from Vir-

[1] Bacon's *Laws.*
[2] Rhode Island was at this time the only one of the Protestant settlements in which the principle of toleration was recognized ; and even there Roman Catholics were excluded from participating in the political rights that were enjoyed by the rest of the community.
The toleration thus early established in Maryland is one of the most remarkable events in the modern history of the Catholic church. If this church (which obtained temporal power long before any other, and had been accustomed to exercise it during a period when it was universally associated with a fierce, vindictive spirit) supplied the first Christian persecutors, — it also supplied the first professors and practitioners of toleration. "One is astonished," says Dr. Robertson (*History of America,* Book V.), "to find a Spanish monk of the sixteenth century among the first advocates against persecution and in behalf of religious liberty." No Christian church, which enjoyed temporal power or an alliance with temporal power, prior to the eighteenth century, is entitled to reproach another with intolerance. This interesting subject has received the most admirable illustration from Mr. Hallam in his *Constitutional History of England.*

ginia to Maryland,[1] gradually formed a Protestant confederacy against the
interests of the original settlers ; and, with ingratitude still more odious than
their injustice, projected the abrogation not only of the Catholic worship, but
of every part of that system of toleration under whose sheltering hospitality
they were enabled to conspire its downfall.   But though the Catholics were
thus ill requited by their Protestant guests, it would be a mistake to suppose
that the calamities that subsequently desolated the province were produced
by the toleration which her assembly now established, or that the Catholics
were really losers by this act of justice and liberality.   From the disposition
of the prevailing party in England, and the state of the other colonial settlements, the catastrophe that befell the liberties of the Maryland Catholics
could not possibly have been evaded ; and if the virtue they now displayed
was unable to avert their fate, it exempted them at least from the reproach
of deserving it ; it redoubled the guilt and scandal incurred by their adversaries, and achieved for themselves a reputation more lasting and honorable
than political triumph or temporal elevation.

From the establishment of religious liberty [1650], the assembly of Maryland extended its attention to the security of political freedom : and in the
following year the constitution of this province received that structure, which,
with some short interruptions, it continued to retain for more than a century
after.   So early as the year 1642, the burgesses who were then elected
members of the existing assembly expressed a desire " that they might be
separated, and sit by themselves, and have a negative."   Their proposition
was disallowed at that time ; but now, in conformity with it, a statute was
enacted, ordaining that members called to the assembly by special writ of
the proprietary should form the upper house, while those who were chosen
by their fellow-colonists should form the lower house ; and that all bills
approved by the two branches of the legislature and ratified by the governor
should be acknowledged and obeyed as the laws of the province.   An act
of recognition of the rights of Lord Baltimore was passed in the same session.   The assembly declared itself bound by the laws both of God and
man to acknowledge his just title by virtue of the grant of the late King
Charles of England ; it accepted his authority, and obliged its constituents
and their posterity for ever to defend him and his heirs in his seigniorial
privileges and preëminences, so far as they should not infringe the just liberties of the free-born subjects of England ; and it besought him to accept
this act, as a testimony to himself and his posterity of its fidelity and thankfulness for the manifold benefits which the colony had derived from him.
Blending a due regard to the rights of the people with a just gratitude to the
proprietary, the assembly at the same time enacted a law prohibiting the
imposition of taxes without the consent of the freemen, and declaring in its
preamble, " that, as the proprietary's strength doth consist in the affections
of his people, so on them he doth rely for his supplies, not doubting of their
duty and assistance on all just occasions." [2]   In prosecution of its patriotic
labors, the assembly framed laws for the relief of the poor, and the encouragement of agriculture and commerce ;[3] and a short gleam of tranquil prosperity preceded the calamities which the province was fated again to experience from the evil genius of Clayborne and the mischievous interference of
the parent state.

The parliament, having now established its supremacy in England, had

_____
[1] Oldmixon. Wynne. Pitkin.   [2] *Laws.*   [3] Ibid.

leisure to extend its views beyond the Atlantic ; and if the people of Virginia were exposed by their political sentiments to a collision with this formidable power, the inhabitants of Maryland were not less obnoxious to its bigotry from their religious tenets. This latter province was not denounced by the parliamentary ordinance of 1650 as in a state of rebellion, like Virginia ; but it was comprehended in that part of the ordinance which declared that the plantations were, and of right ought to be, dependent on England, and subject to her laws. In prosecution of the object and purpose of this ordinance, certain commissioners, of whom Clayborne was one, were appointed to reduce and govern the colonies within the Bay of Chesapeake. [September, 1651]. In Virginia, where resistance was attempted, the existing administration was instantly suppressed : but as the proprietary of Maryland professed his willingness to acknowledge the parliamentary jurisdiction, the commissioners were compelled (in conformity with their instructions) to respect his rights [1652] ; and he was suffered to rule the province, though as a dependent functionary of the keepers of the liberties of England.[1] But Clayborne was not to be thus deterred from availing himself of an opportunity so favorable to the gratification of his malignity ; and, unfortunately, his designs were favored by the distractions in England that preceded the elevation of Cromwell to the protectorate, and by the disunion which began to prevail in the province from the pretensions of the Protestant exiles who had recently united themselves to its population. Ever the ally of the strongest party, Clayborne hastened to espouse the fortunes of Cromwell [1653], whose triumph he easily foresaw ; and inflamed the dissensions of the province, by encouraging the Protestants to combine the pursuit of their own ascendency with the recognition of the protectoral government. The contentions of the two parties were at length exasperated to the extremity of civil war ; and after various skirmishes, which were fought with alternate success, the Catholics and the other partisans of the proprietary were defeated in a decisive engagement [1654], the governor deposed, and the administration usurped by Clayborne and his associates.[2]

Although the victorious party did not consider themselves warranted expressly to deny the title of the proprietary, they made haste to signalize their triumph by abolishing his institutions. Fuller and Preston, whom Clayborne appointed [July] commissioners for directing the affairs of Maryland under his Highness the Lord Protector, convoked a provincial assembly [October] ; and some of the persons who were elected burgesses having refused to serve in a capacity which they deemed inconsistent with their obligations to Lord Baltimore,[3] the legislative power was the more exclusively appropriated by the partisans of innovation. The assembly having, as a preliminary measure, passed an act of recognition of Cromwell's just title and authority, proceeded to frame an ordinance concerning religion, which derogated not less signally from the credit of the Protestant cause than from the justice and liberality of the Protector's administration.[4] By this ordinance

---

[1] Bacon's *Preface.* Thurlow's *State Papers.*   [2] Bacon's *Preface.*   [3] Chalmers.

[4] Cromwell is at least obnoxious to the charge of having suffered the triumph of his own and of the Protestant cause to be signalized by the extinction of a toleration established by Roman Catholics. That he incited, or even approved, this proceeding is by no means apparent. In the records of the province, there is a letter from him to his commissioners, desiring them not to busy themselves about religion, but to settle the civil government. Chalmers. Yet in writing to the governor and council of Virginia, he reproached them with impiety in having given countenance and support to the Catholic interest in Maryland. Burk. The Protector was much more distinguished by the vigor of his conduct than the perspicuity of his

it was declared that no persons professing the doctrines of the Romish church could be protected in the province by the laws of England formerly established and yet unrepealed, or by the protectoral government ; and that such as professed faith in God by Jesus Christ, though dissenting from the doctrine and discipline generally established in the British dominions, should not be restrained from the exercise of their religion ; " provided such liberty be not extended to popery or prelacy ; or to such as, under the profession of Christianity, practise licentiousness." [1] Thus the Roman Catholics were deprived of the protection of law in the commonwealth which their own industry and virtue had reared, and by those Protestants to whom their charity had given a country and a home. This unworthy triumph was hailed by the zealots against popery in London, where a book was published soon after under the title of *Babylon's Fall in Maryland*. But the Catholics were not the only parties who experienced the severity of the new government. All the Protestant Dissenters were exposed more or less to persecution ; and a number of Quakers, having resorted some time after to the province, and begun to preach against judicial oaths and military pursuits, were denounced by the government as heretical vagabonds, and underwent the punishment of flogging and imprisonment.[2]

As Lord Baltimore's right to the proprietariship of the province was still outwardly recognized, the commissioners, either deeming it requisite to the formality of their proceedings, or more probably studying to embroil him with the Protector, demanded his assent to the changes which were thus introduced. But he firmly refused to sanction either the deposition of his governor, or any one of the recent measures of the commissioners and their adherents ; and declared in particular, with respect to the free exercise of religious worship, that he never would assent to the repeal of a law which protected the most sacred rights of mankind. The commissioners, with expressions of surprise either hypocritical or ridiculous, complained of his contumacy to Cromwell, to whom they continued from time to time to transmit the most elaborate representations of the *tyranny*, *bigotry*, and royalist predilections of Lord Baltimore, and the expediency of depriving him of the proprietariship of the province.[3] [1655.] But all their representations were ineffectual. Lord Baltimore was allowed by Cromwell to retain, at least nominally, the rights which he was practically debarred from enjoying ; and the commissioners remained in the province to exercise the tyranny and bigotry of which they falsely accused him. Their conduct, as intemperate as their counsels, disturbed the peace of the colony, and rendered their own power insecure. The people, lately so tranquil and happy, were now a prey to all those disorders which never fail to result from religious persecution embittered by the triumph of party in civil contention. In this situation an insurrection was easily raised by Josias Fendal, a restless and profligate adventurer, destined by his intrigues to become the Clayborne of the next generation, and who now sought occasion to indulge his natural turbulence

---

diction ; and his correspondents were sometimes unable to discover the meaning of his letters. In one of his communications to the Maryland commissioners, we find him reprimanding them for having misunderstood his former directions. Chalmers. Hazard. He seems, on many occasions, to have studied an ambiguity of language, that left him free to approve or disapprove the measures of his officers, according to the success that might attend them.
[1] *Laws.*   [2] Chalmers.
[3] Langford's *Refutation of a Scandalous Pamphlet, named " Babylon's Fall in Maryland."* Chalmers. Hazard. The only copy of Langford's tract that I have ever met with was in the library of Mr. Chalmers.

under pretence of supporting the rights of the proprietary and the original constitution of the province. [1656.] This insurrection was productive of very unhappy consequences to the colony. It induced Lord Baltimore to repose an ill-grounded confidence in Fendal ; and its suppression was attended with increased severities on the part of the commissioners, and additional exactions from the people.[1]

The affairs of the colony remained for two years longer in this distracted condition ; when at length the commissioners, disgusted with the disorders which they had produced, but were unable to compose, and finding all their efforts unavailing to procure the abrogation of Lord Baltimore's title, to which they ascribed the unappeasable discontent of a great part of the population, surrendered the municipal administration into the hands of Fendal, who had been appointed governor by the proprietary. [1658.] But this measure, so far from restoring the public quiet, contributed to aggravate the mischiefs which infested the province, by giving scope to the machinations of that unprincipled agitator, whose habitual restlessness and impetuosity had been mistaken for attachment to the proprietary system. No sooner had he convoked an assembly [February, 1659], than with unblushing treachery he surrendered into the hands of the burgesses the trust which Lord Baltimore had committed to him, and accepted from *them* a new commission as governor : and the burgesses, at his instigation, dissolved the upper house and assumed to themselves the whole legislative power of the state. Fendal and his associates were probably encouraged to pursue this lawless course by the distractions of the English commonwealth that followed the death of the Protector. Their administration, which was chiefly distinguished by the imposition of heavy taxes, and a bitter persecution of the Quakers, was happily soon terminated by the restoration of Charles the Second [1660] ; when Philip Calvert, producing a commission to himself from the proprietary, and a letter from the king commanding all his officers and other subjects in Maryland to assist in the reëstablishment of Lord Baltimore's jurisdiction, found his authority universally recognized and peaceably obeyed. Fendal was now tried for high treason, and found guilty ; but the clemency of the proprietary prevailed over his resentment; and he granted the convict a pardon, qualified by the imposition of a moderate fine, and a declaration of his perpetual incapacity of public trust. This lenity was very ill-requited by its worthless object, who was reserved by farther intrigues and treachery to disturb at an after period the repose of the province. [1661.] His accomplices, upon a timely submission, were pardoned without even undergoing a trial. The recent usurpations were passed over in prudent silence, and buried in a generous oblivion ; toleration was forthwith restored ; and the inhabitants of Maryland once more experienced the blessings of a mild government and internal tranquillity.[2]

Happily for mankind, amidst the contentions of political factions and the revolutions of government, there generally subsists, in every community, an under-current of peaceful and industrious life, which pursues its course undisturbed by the tempests that agitate and deform the upper region of society. Notwithstanding the disorders to which Maryland was so long a prey, the province had continued to increase in population, industry, and wealth ; and at the epoch of the Restoration it contained about twelve thousand inhabitants.[3] The reëstablishment of a humane government and

---

[1] *Laws.* Chalmers.   [2] Ibid.   [3] Chalmers.

general subordination, however, had manifestly the effect of quickening the march of prosperity ; for, about five years after the present epoch, we find the population increased to sixteen thousand persons. At this latter period, the number of ships trading from England and other parts of the British dominions to Maryland was computed at one hundred.[1] So great was the demand for labor in the colony, and so liberal its reward, that even the introduction of negro slavery had not been able to degrade it in public esteem. Industry, amply recompensed, was animated and cheerful ; and, closely connected with independence and improvement of condition, was the object of general respect. Every young person was trained to useful labor ; and though a legal provision was made for the support of the poor, pauperism and beggary were practically unknown ; and the public bounty, though sometimes delicately conveyed to the necessities of proud poverty or modest misfortune, was never openly solicited.[2] An account of the condition of Maryland was published at London, in the year 1666, by George Alsop, who resided in the province both prior and subsequent to the Restoration. From his representation it appears that a great deal of the agricultural work of the colonists was performed by indented servants ; and that the treatment of these persons was so humane, and the allotment of land and stock which they received from their masters at the end of their quadrennial servitude so ample, that the author, who himself had served in this capacity, declares he was much happier as an indented servant in Maryland than as an apprentice in London. It was common for ruined tradesmen and indigent laborers in England to embrace this resource for retrieving or improving their worldly circumstances ; though many were deterred by the misrepresentations circulated by shallow politicians who dreaded the depopulation of the realm, or by interested employers who apprehended an augmentation of the wages of labor at home. No emigrants (says Alsop) were more successful in bettering their condition than female servants ; they invariably obtained an immediate and respectable establishment in marriage. Money was very scarce in the colony, and was never employed in its domestic transactions ; tobacco being the universal medium of exchange, the remuneration of all services, civil, military, and ecclesiastical, and the measure of all penal amercements. This author, when he has occasion to mention the troubles that preceded the Restoration, alludes to them simply as affairs of state and events of merely partial interest and importance. Of some of the personages who were culpably implicated in them, it was his opinion " that their thoughts were not so bad at first, as their actions would have led them into in process of time." [3]

A great proportion of the inhabitants of Maryland, and in particular all the Catholic part of the population, were sincerely attached to the royal government ; [4] and the gratification they derived from the restoration of the king enhanced the satisfaction with which they returned to the patriarchal sway of their benevolent proprietary. [May, 1661.] During the general festivity that ensued in the province, the house of assembly was convoked by the governor. One of the first measures undertaken by this body aimed

---

[1] Oldmixon. Blome's *Present State of his Majesty's Isles and Territories in America.*

[2] Alsop's *Maryland.* The English civil wars produced a considerable improvement in the condition of laborers in North America, by interrupting the emigration of additional competitors for employment. Winthrop's *Journal.*

[3] Alsop. The Advocates' Library of Edinburgh contains a copy of this little work.

[4] It was one of the charges preferred against the proprietary by Cromwell's commissioners, that Charles the Second had been proclaimed by the people of Maryland, without any signification of displeasure from Lord Baltimore. Hazard.

at providing a remedy for the scarcity of money, which, it was declared, formed a serious obstruction to the advancement of trade. For this purpose, they besought the proprietary to establish a mint in the province ; and enacted that the money to be coined should be of as good silver as English sterling, and that the proprietary should accept it in payment of his rents. This is the second instance that we have witnessed, and the last that ever occurred, of a pretension to the right of coining money in the British provinces of North America. A coinage accordingly took place in Maryland ; and the measure seems neither to have offended the British government, nor to have disappointed the colonists ; for the law was confirmed and declared perpetual by the assembly in the year 1676. Yet, in consequence, perhaps, of the blame that Massachusetts incurred for a similar proceeding, the practice of coining soon after fell into disuse, and the ordinances that sanctioned it were repealed. In the same session there was passed an act for the imposition of port duties, which conferred on the proprietary half a pound of powder and three pounds of shot for every ton of the burden of vessels not belonging to the province.[1] This act, as we shall afterwards find, gave rise to some controversy at the period of the British Revolution.

The happiness and prosperity of the colonists were promoted by the arrival, in the following year [1662], of Charles Calvert, eldest son of the proprietary, whom his father appointed the resident governor of Maryland, for the purpose of enabling him to form acquaintance with the people over whom he was destined to maintain the hereditary jurisdiction. From the various *acts of gratitude* (as they were termed) that emanated from the assembly during his presidency, Charles Calvert appears to have followed, with successful virtue, the wise and generous policy of his father ; and his administration, first as governor, and afterwards as proprietary, proved for a considerable period alike honorable to himself, beneficial to the public weal, and acceptable to the people. The provincial records, during this period, are occupied exclusively with details of jurisprudence and the progress of legislation. Various laws were enacted by the assembly for the ascertainment of public and private right, the promotion of commerce, and the encouragement of agricultural and manufacturing industry. Acts were passed for engrafting more perfectly the English statute law on the jurisprudence of the colony ; for securing the stability of possessions, and the fulfilment of contracts ; and for the encouragement of the culture of English grain, and the rearing and manufacturing of hemp and flax. As the agitations of the parent state had ever been found to diffuse their influence through the colonial territories, and the perturbing spirit of political rumor to gain force and malignity proportioned to the distance from which it was wafted, an attempt was made to protect the quiet of the province by a law imposing penalties on divulgers of false news [1662–1666] ; but this desirable object was much more respectably as well as effectually promoted by the merit and popularity of the governor's administration. The public tranquillity sustained some disturbance from the encroachments of the Dutch on the western banks of the Delaware, and from the hostile incursions of a distant tribe of Indians. But the remonstrances of Calvert obliged the Dutch intruders to evacuate the whole country around Cape Henlopen, of which he instantly took possession ;[2] and his prudence, sec-

---

[1] *Laws.* Chalmers.
[2] A more particular account of the disputes and various transactions between the English and the Dutch in this quarter occurs in Book V., Chap. I., *post.*

onded by the friendly demonstrations of the Indian allies of the province, restored peace with the hostile tribe by a treaty, which was confirmed by act of assembly. [May, 1666.] The fidelity of the Indian allies was rewarded by settling on them and their descendants an extensive and valuable territory, which, being assured to them on various occasions by successive acts of the legislature, continued in their possession for near a century after. All the Indian tribes within the limits of the province now declared themselves subject to the proprietary government; and in testimony of their subjection, the inferior chiefs or princes, on the death of their principal sachem, refused to acknowledge the sway of his successor, till this pretender's claim to the dignity was sanctioned by Governor Calvert. The removal of the Dutch from Cape Henlopen induced many of those planters to unite themselves to the colony of Maryland, into which they were readily admitted; and, in the year 1666, the Maryland assembly enacted, in favor of them and of certain French Protestant refugees, the first law ever framed by any provincial legislature for the naturalization of aliens. Many similar laws were enacted in every subsequent session, till the British Revolution; and, during the intervening period, great numbers of foreigners transported themselves to this province, and became completely incorporated with its other inhabitants.[1]

The principal, if not the only, inconvenience, of which the people of Maryland were sensible at this time, was that which they shared with all the other colonies, and which was inflicted by the parliamentary Acts of Navigation. In Virginia, where the pressure of these restrictions was sooner and more severely experienced, an attempt was made to enhance the price of the staple commodity, by a temporary restraint of the cultivation of tobacco; but as Maryland refused to embrace this measure, its efficacy was defeated, and the former animosity of the Virginians against the inhabitants of the neighbouring province unhappily revived. To this animosity we must ascribe the various complaints against the colonists of Maryland which Virginia from time to time addressed to the king; all of which, on examination, proved entirely groundless.[2] As the inconvenience arising from the Navigation Laws began to be more sensibly experienced in Maryland, the policy that had been ineffectually suggested by Virginia was more favorably regarded; and at length a prohibitory act, suspending the growth of tobacco, was passed in the present year by the assembly; but the dissent of the proprietary and governor, who apprehended that it might prove injurious to the poorer class of planters, as well as detrimental to the royal customs, prevented this regulation from being carried into effect.[3] The popularity of Lord Baltimore and his son incurred no abatement from their opposition to this project of the assembly. Though averse to impose any direct restraint on the cultivation of tobacco, they willingly promoted every plan that was suggested by the provincial legislature for the encouragement of other branches of industry; and their efforts to alleviate the public inconvenience were justly appreciated, as well as actively seconded, by a

---

[1] Bacon's *Laws*. Oldmixon. Chalmers.

[2] One of these complaints, which the proprietary was summoned to answer, was for making partial treaties with the Indians, and contenting himself with exempting the Maryland territory from their hostilities, without stipulating the same advantage for the province of Virginia. The Committee of Plantations, to which the complaint was referred, on examining the treaties of both parties, reported to the king that Maryland had included Virginia in all her treaties, but that Virginia had demonstrated no such concern for Maryland. Chalmers.

[3] Bacon's *Laws*. Chalmers.

people more ready to improve the remaining advantages of their situation, than to resent the injustice of the parent state, by which these advantages were circumscribed.   While Virginia was a prey to discontent and insurrection, Maryland continued to enjoy the blessings of peace and prosperity, and to acknowledge the patriotic superintendence of its generous proprietary.   By an act passed in the year 1671,[1] the assembly imposed a duty of two shillings sterling on every hogshead of tobacco exported ; the one half of which was to be applied in maintaining a magazine of arms, and defraying the necessary expenses of government ; and the other half was settled on the proprietary, in consideration of his accepting merchantable tobacco for his rents and alienation fines, at the rate of two pence a pound. This provision was soon after continued during the life of the heir of the proprietary, by " An act of gratitude," as the assembly termed their ordinance, " to Charles Calvert, the governor."[2] [1674.]

Cecilius, Lord Baltimore, the father of the province, having lived to reap these happy and honorable fruits of the plantation which he had reared with so much wisdom and virtue, died, in the forty-fourth year of his supremacy, crowned with venerable age and illustrious reputation. [1676.]   It was his constant maxim, which he studiously inculcated on the provincial assembly, " that by concord a small colony may grow into a great and renowned nation ; but that by dissension mighty and glorious kingdoms have declined and fallen into nothing."   Some observations on the state of the province at the period of his death occur in a letter written in the same year by a clergyman of the church of England, resident there, to the Archbishop of Canterbury.   Maryland, it thence appears, was already divided into ten counties, and contained upwards of twenty thousand inhabitants. The Catholics, says this writer, provided for their priests ; and the Quakers supported their ministers ; but no care was taken to establish by law a Protestant Episcopal church.   There were but three or four ministers of the church of England in Maryland ; and from the want of a legal establishment for them, the colony, he declares, had fallen into a most deplorable condition, — having become a *pest-house of iniquity*, in which the Lord's day was openly profaned.   As a remedy for this evil, he suggests an endowment of the church of England at the public expense.[3]   The remedy discredits the representation, which, besides, is totally unconfirmed by any other account; and it seems neither uncharitable nor unreasonable to suppose, that this writer contemplated the existing condition of society through the inverted medium of the same systematic view that represented to him the future advancement of the spiritual interests of the laity, originating from the promotion of the temporal interests of the clergy.   The brightness of distant hope tends to darken the realities of present experience ; and the associations that serve

---

[1] Bacon's *Laws*. " Reflecting with gratitude," says the preamble of this enactment, " on the unwearied care of the proprietary, and the vast expense that he has been put to in preserving the inhabitants in the enjoyment of their lives and liberties, and the increase and improvement of their estates," &c.   History should delight to record the expressions of popular gratitude for conspicuous service, — the public honors rendered to wisdom and virtue.

The same year, there was passed an act "for encouraging the importation of negroes and slaves."

[2] Bacon's *Laws*.

[3] Chalmers. Yeo, *apud* Chalmers. This representation is as incredible as the statement that was published about twelve years after, by the Protestant Association of Maryland, of the daily murders and persecutions incited by the proprietary and committed by the Catholics. No reliance can be placed on the accounts that men give of the character and conduct of those whom they are preparing or longing to plunder.

to embellish and illustrate the one are able to deform and obscure the other. The Protestant part of the population of Maryland was less distinguished by that Christian zeal which leads men to impose sacrifices on themselves, than by that ecclesiastical zeal which prompts them to impose burdens on others ; they were probably less wealthy, from having been more recently established in the province, than the Catholics ; and the erection of their churches was farther retarded by the state of dispersion in which the inhabitants generally lived.   The Protestant Episcopal pastors, like the clergy of every other order, depended on the professors of their own particular tenets for support ; and it is not easy to discern the soundness of the argument that assigns the liberality of other sectarians to clergymen of their own persuasion, as a reason for loading them with the additional burden of supporting the ministers of the church of England, — or the existing incompetency of these ministers to control the immoralities of their people, as a reason for endowing them with a provision that would render them independent of the discharge of their duty.   This logic, however, was quite satisfactory to the primate of England, who eagerly undertook to reform the morals of the people of Maryland, by obtaining a legal establishment and wealthy endowment to a Protestant Episcopal church in the province.

The deceased proprietary was succeeded by his son Charles, Lord Baltimore, who had governed the province for fourteen years with a high reputation for virtue and ability.   With the religious tenets, he inherited the tolerant principles of his father ; and one of the first acts of his administration was to confirm the remarkable law of 1649, which established an absolute political equality among all denominations of Christians.   Having convoked an assembly, where he presided in person, he performed, with their assistance, what has often been recommended to other legislatures, but rarely executed by any, — a diligent revision of all the existing laws ; repealing those that were judged superfluous or inexpedient, confirming the salutary, and explaining the obscure.[1]   In this assembly, an attempt was made to stem the progress of an evil with which the colony was afflicted, by a regulation more wisely, perhaps, than competently opposed to the policy of the mother country.   The morals of the colonists were endangered in a much greater degree by the transportation of felons to Maryland, than by the want of a legislative endowment to the clergy of the Protestant Episcopal church.   To the common law of England this punishment of transportation was quite unknown ; though in some cases it permitted a felon who preferred exile to death to abjure the realm.   It was a statute of Elizabeth which first inflicted banishment on dangerous rogues ; and it was James the First, who, without any regard to this law, but in the plenitude of his royal prerogative, introduced the practice of transporting felons to Virginia.   He was indebted for the suggestion to Chief Justice Popham, who, being a proprietor of colonial territory, as well as a judge, conceived the

[1] *Laws.* No human society is stationary in its condition ; but the changes to which all are inevitably subject are less rapid and obvious in old than in young communities. The peculiarly progressive state of society in America was calculated to suggest to the Americans that wise principle which their revolt from Britain afforded them an opportunity of interweaving into their municipal constitutions, and in conformity with which provision is made for periodical revisions and corrections of their systems of law and government, in order to adapt them more perfectly to the altered and actual condition of the community. The Americans, in this as in many other respects, have taught by example a grand and useful lesson to mankind. They have placed the science of politics on the same footing with other sciences, by opening it to improvements derived from experience and the discoveries of successive ages.

project of rendering the administration of justice subservient to his private interests as a planter, and had destined New England in particular to anticipate the uses of Botany Bay,[1] The practice of transporting felons to the colonies was resumed soon after the Restoration, and received so far the countenance of the legislature, that an act of parliament authorized the king to inflict this punishment on persons convicted of the crime of Quakerism.[2] The effects of it proved so disagreeable to the people of Maryland, that a law was now framed by their assembly against the importation of convicts into this province,[3] and afterwards reënacted at various subsequent periods till the commencement of the reign of Queen Anne. Whether any notice was taken of this demonstration of resistance to a measure of the British government, or what were the effects of it, I am unable to discover. It is certain, that, at a later period, the practice was continued and extended, in spite of the remonstrances of the more wealthy and intelligent planters, who regarded it as at once disgraceful to the province, and subversive of those notions of the superiority of white men which they studied to impress on their negro slaves ; and shortly prior to the American Revolution, no fewer than three hundred and fifty felons were annually imported into Maryland from the parent state.[4]

At the conclusion of the legislative session, the proprietary having announced his intention of visiting England, the assembly, in acknowledgment of the many signal benefits which he had rendered to the people, and as a token of their love and respect, unanimously desired his acceptance of all the tobacco which remained unappropriated in the public stores of the province.[5] Lord Baltimore was undoubtedly worthy of these demonstrations of regard ; and the experience of his own, together with the remembrance of his father's merits, might have been expected to recommend the system of proprietary government to the lasting approbation of the colonists. This species of magistracy, however, was destined to enjoy but a transient popularity in America. Allied by congruity to no similar institution, and surrounded by no kindred order of persons in the provincial communities, it stood wholly unsheltered from envy, a solitary specimen of hereditary grandeur ; and its objectionable features were exhibited in the most offensive light, when, in the progress of succession, exclusive dignity became the portion of despicable, or the instrument of unjust and odious men. These considerations, it must be acknowledged, afford no explanation of the sudden decline which Lord Baltimore's popularity was doomed to undergo ; and we must seek elsewhere for the causes of that revolution of public opinion in which his merits were ungratefully depreciated or forgotten. If he had lived in an age less subject to jealousy and alarm, or presided in a colony composed entirely of Catholics, he would probably have enjoyed a larger and more enduring harvest of popular gratitude. But the toleration which his father established, and the naturalization of foreigners which he himself introduced, had attracted to the provincial territory a multitude of Protestants,

---

[1] Lloyd's *State Worthies*. Many persons have been transported as felons to America whom no community of wise and honorable men would be ashamed to recognize as fellow-citizens. The crews of the first squadron conducted by Columbus to America were partly composed of convicts, pardoned on condition of undertaking the voyage. In the reign of Charles the Second, before the voluntary emigration of the Quakers, a considerable number of these sectaries, and, in the reign of James the Second, a great many of the gallant and unfortunate partisans of the Duke of Monmouth, were transported as felons to America.
[2] 13, 14 Charles II., Cap. 1.   [3] 1676, Cap. 16.
[4] *History of the British Dominions in America.*   [5] 1676, Cap. 18.

both French and English. The liberal principles of the proprietary were not able to disarm the French Protestants of their enmity against a faith associated in their previous experience with perfidy and persecution; and the English Protestants, impressed with the opinion which their friends in the mother country deduced from the policy of the king, regarded toleration but as a cloak under which Catholic bigotry disguised the most dangerous designs. These unhappy impressions were confirmed by the alarms and intrigues of which the ensuing period of English history was abundantly prolific, and which invariably extended their influence to the minds of the people of Maryland, where a mixture of opinions unknown in any other of the provinces gave a peculiar interest to the conflict of the same opinions that was carried on in the parent state.

On his arrival in England [1677], Lord Baltimore was assailed with complaints, preferred against him to the Committee of Plantations by the colony of Virginia and the prelates of England. The accusations of Virginia, which related to provincial boundaries and Indian treaties, were easily repelled ; but the controversy with the prelates was not so satisfactorily adjusted. Compton, Bishop of London, to whom the primate had imparted his ecclesiastical project for the colony, represented to the committee that true religion was deplorably neglected in Maryland; that, while Roman Catholic priests were enriched there with valuable possessions, the Protestant ministers of the church of England were utterly destitute of support ; and that heresy and immorality had consequently overspread the province. Lord Baltimore, in justification of himself and of the provincial legislature, exhibited the act of 1649, together with the recent confirmation of it, which assured freedom and protection to every society of Christians, but allowed special privileges to none. He stated that four ministers of the church of England were in possession of plantations which afforded them a decent subsistence ; but that, from the variety of religious opinions prevalent in the assembly, it would be extremely difficult, if not impossible, to induce this body to consent to a law that should oblige any religious society to maintain other ministers than its own. Satisfactory as this answer ought to have been, the impartial policy which it disclosed obtained little or rather no approbation. The committee declared that they thought fit there should be a public maintenance assigned to the church of England, and that the proprietary ought to propose some means of supporting a competent number of her clergy. The king's ministers at the same time signified to him the royal pleasure that immorality should be discouraged, and laws for the repression of vice enacted and punctually executed in Maryland.[1]

This last injunction, to which its authors probably attached very little meaning or importance, was the only one that received any attention from the provincial government. A law was framed by the assembly [1678], enjoining a reverential observance of Sunday ;[2] and after the return of the proprietary [1681], new regulations were adopted for the speedier prosecution of offences, and the stricter definition of punishments. As the more rigorous enforcement of the Navigation Act began now to occasion an increased depreciation of the staple produce of the colony, numerous attempts

[1] Chalmers.
[2] " Yes, far beyond the high-heaved western wave,
    Amid Columbia's wildernesses vast,
    The words which God in thunder from the Mount
    Of Sinai spake are heard, and are obeyed." — Grahame's *Sabbath*.

were made by the proprietary and assembly, during the two following years, to counteract or diminish this inconvenience, by giving additional encouragement and a new direction to the provincial industry and commerce. Laws were framed for promoting tillage and raising provisions for exportation ; for restraining the export of leather and hides, and otherwise encouraging the labor of tanners and shoemakers ; and for rearing manufactures of linen and woollen cloth. Thus early did the legislature endeavour to introduce manufactures into the province ; but the attempt was premature ; and though domestic industry was able to supply some articles for domestic uses, it was found impracticable even at a much later period to render Maryland a manufacturing country. For the encouragement of trade, various ports were established, where merchants were enjoined to reside, and commercial dealings to be carried on, and where all trading vessels were required to unlade the commodities of Europe, and take on board the productions of the province. But from the situation of the country, abounding with navigable rivers, and from the great variety of ports that were erected in conformity with the wishes of the planters, every one of whom desired to have a port on his own plantation, this regulation was attended with very little effect. It was now that there occurred the last instance of the expression of that reciprocal regard which had reflected so much honor on the proprietary and the people. By a vote of the assembly, in the year 1682, this body, " to demonstrate its gratitude, duty, and affection to the proprietary," desired his acceptance of a liberal subsidy,— a testimony of esteem to which he returned a courteous acknowledgment, though he declined to appropriate the contribution, on account of the straitened circumstances of the colony.[1]

But amidst all this seeming cordiality, and the mutual endeavours of the proprietary and the assembly to promote the public welfare, there lurked in the province a secret heartburning and discontent pregnant with future quarrel and convulsion. The fiction of the Popish Plot extended its baneful influence to Maryland, and was employed there by some profligate politicians as the instrument of designs similar to those which it engendered or from which it originated in England. The insurrections that had been provoked by the oppression of the Covenanters in Scotland ; the discontents in England ; the disputes with regard to the proposed exclusion of the Duke of York from the throne ; the continued disagreement between the king and parliament, — all, transmitted through the magnifying and uncertain medium of rumor to a country so remote from the means of accurate information, seemed to forebode a renewal of the distractions of the preceding reign. A general ferment was excited in men's minds ; and in the strong expectation that prevailed of some great change, parties and individuals prepared with anxiety to defend their interests, or intrigued with eagerness for the enlargement of their advantages. The absence of the proprietary from the province, during his visit to England, probably served to promote the machinations of the factious, which, however, received a seasonable check from his return. Fendal, who had raised insurrection against the administration of Cromwell, and afterwards betrayed and resisted the government of the proprietary, now availed himself of the lenity he had experienced to reëxcite commotions in Maryland. He seems to have had no other purpose than to scramble for property and power amidst the confusion which he expected to ensue ; and he encouraged his partisans with the assurance, that, during

[1] *Laws.*

the approaching civil wars of England, they might easily possess themselves of whatever plantations they pleased to appropriate. But Lord Baltimore, partly by a steady application of the laws, and partly by the influence of the tidings which were received of the king's triumph over his opponents at the dissolution of the Oxford Parliament, was able as yet to preserve, even without a struggle, the tranquillity of the province. Fendal was tried for his seditious practices in the year 1681 ; and though the provincial laws annexed the penalty of death to the offence of which he was convicted, he was now only fined, and banished from Maryland for ever. But unfortunately his influence was not banished with his person ; and one of his associates, John Coode, who was tried along with him, but acquitted, remained behind to renovate at a fitter season those dark intrigues which were dissipated for the present by the last ray of good fortune that attended the proprietary's administration. A few others of the less guilty associates of Fendal and Coode were convicted of sedition, and punished by fine.[1]

The last years of Lord Baltimore's administration were embittered by the retribution of that injustice in which the establishment of his hereditary jurisdiction began ; and the wrong inflicted half a century before on Virginia was now avenged by the disruption of a considerable portion of the territory that had been allotted to Maryland. If the historian of this transaction were permitted to adapt the particulars of it to his own conceptions of moral consistency, he would ascribe the requital of the Maryland usurpation to other instrumentality than that of the venerable patriarch of Pennsylvania. Such, nevertheless, was the mode of this occurrence ; and as the founder of American toleration committed the encroachment on Virginia, so another illustrious friend of truth, justice, and liberty promoted the retributory partition of Maryland. On the arrival of William Penn in America, a conference took place between him and Lord Baltimore (two of the most prudent and virtuous persons that have ever ruled over mankind) with the purpose of effecting an amicable adjustment of the boundaries of their respective territorial grants. Penn was received by Lord Baltimore with dignified respect and courtesy ; and perhaps that eminent person entertained some degree of corresponding regard for a legislator whose institutions had long afforded a peaceful asylum to persecuted Quakers. The pretensions of the parties, however, were so completely inconsistent with each other, that it proved impossible to adjust them in a manner satisfactory to both. Penn was authorized to appropriate, among other districts, the whole of the peninsula lying between the Bays of Chesapeake and Delaware, which formed a considerable portion of the territory included within the charter of Maryland, and part of which had been colonized by Dutch and Swedish settlers before the commonwealth of Maryland existed. Lord Baltimore's was certainly the juster and more legitimate claim ; but Penn was encouraged to persist in his counter pretension by the declaration of the Committee of Plantations, that it had never been intended to grant to Lord Baltimore any territory except such as at the time was inhabited by savages alone, and that the tract which he now claimed, having been planted by Christians anterior to his grant, was therefore excluded from its intendment, though it might be embraced by its literal construction. The controversy between these two distinguished men was conducted with a greater conformity to the general principles of human nature than it is pleasing to record. While

---

[1] Chalmers.

the conflicting claims were yet unsettled, Penn attempted to appropriate the disputed district ; and as Lord Baltimore insisted that the inhabitants should either acknowledge the jurisdiction of Maryland or abandon their dwellings, proclamations were issued by each of the contending parties, asserting his own exclusive title, and condemnation of the proceedings of his opponent. But the pretensions of Penn, whether sanctioned by the principles of equity or not, were supported by an influence of much greater practical efficacy in regulating extent of dominion and territorial limits.   Aware of his superior interest at the English court, he complained of his antagonist to the king and the Duke of York, and prevailed in obtaining a decree of the privy council, adjudging that the litigated region should be divided into two equal parts, one of which was appropriated to himself and the other to Lord Baltimore. This adjudication was carried into effect [1682–1685] ; and the territory which now composes the State of Delaware was thus dismembered from the provincial limits of Maryland.[1]

Meanwhile, the late proceedings against Fendal and his associates ministered occasion of fresh complaints in England against Lord Baltimore for partiality to Roman Catholics.   It was in vain for him to represent that the laws of his province gave equal encouragement to persons of every Christian denomination, without dispensing peculiar favor to any ; that in order to conform his administration to the principles of the constitution, he had always endeavoured to distribute the offices of government as equally as possible among Protestants and Catholics ; and that, to allay the jealousy by which the Protestants were disquieted, he had latterly suffered them to engross nearly the whole command of the militia, and to assume the custody of the arms and military stores of the province.   From the record of Fendal's trial, he showed that the proceedings against this individual had been perfectly fair, — nay, so indulgent, that the culprit, impudently protesting against being tried by Catholics, obtained a jury composed entirely of Protestants.   Notwithstanding the satisfactoriness of this explanation, the ministers of the king, less desirous of doing justice to others than of shifting the dangerous imputation of *Popery* from themselves, commanded that all the offices of government should in future be committed exclusively to the hands of Protestants, and thus meanly sanctioned the unjust suspicions under which the proprietary government was already laboring.   It was less easy for Lord Baltimore to defend himself against another charge which was now preferred against him, and which, having some foundation in truth, involved him in considerable perplexity.   He was accused of obstructing the custom-house officers in the collection of the duties imposed by the Navigation Acts ; and it did certainly appear, that, biased perhaps by the desire of alleviating as far as possible the pressure of the commercial restrictions, he had construed them in some points in a manner too favorable to the freedom and wishes of the colonists.   While he endeavoured unsuccessfully to maintain the legitimacy of his conduct, he charged the collectors of the customs with wilfully disturbing the commerce and peace of the colony by wanton interference and groundless complaint.   It seems probable that this recrimination was well founded, and that the revenue officers, provoked to find that the unpopularity of their duties prevailed over the respect they conceived

[1] Chalmers. Clarkson's *Life of Penn.* Mr. Clarkson's account of this dispute is very defective, and tends to create an impression of the conduct of Lord Baltimore not less unfavorable than erroneous. The controversy between Lord Baltimore and Penn is resumed and farther illustrated in the history of Pennsylvania, *post*, Book VII., Chap. I.

due to their station, had labored to convert their own private disagreements with individuals into the occasion of national dispute ; for when, shortly after, a new surveyor-general of the customs in Maryland was appointed, he had the honesty to report that the colonists had been greatly misrepresented with regard to their opposition to the Trade Laws. [1685.] The proprietary, however, incurred a severe rebuke from the king for his erroneous construction of the law. Charles expressed indignant surprise that his service should be obstructed and his officers discouraged by Lord Baltimore, whom he upbraided with the many royal favors conferred on his family, and even threatened with the visitation of a writ of *quo warranto*.[1] It seems never to have occurred to the English government, nor did Lord Baltimore presume to urge, that the king, in pretending right to exact imposts in Maryland, violated the most express provisions of the royal charter, and claimed to himself what truly belonged to the proprietary.

On the accession of James the Second to the throne of his brother [1685], he transmitted to the colonies a proclamation of this event, which was published in Maryland with partial, but lively and unaffected, demonstrations of joy. The Committee of Plantations had taken so much pains, during the preceding reign, to obtain accurate information of the affairs of the colonies and the temper of their inhabitants, that it was perfectly well known how deeply they were affected by reports from England, and how much provincial disturbance the prospect of confusion in the mother country was apt to engender. When the invasions of Monmouth and Argyle were defeated [June], the king conveyed accounts of these occurrences to the proprietary of Maryland ; assigning, as the object of this communication, the prevention of any false rumors which might be propagated among his people in that distant province of the empire, by the malicious insinuations of ill-disposed men. He informed Lord Baltimore, at the same time, in strains of exultation, that the parliament had cheerfully granted to the crown an aid, to be levied by a new tax on the importation of sugars and tobacco, — which, however, he remarked, inferred no new burden on the inhabitants of Maryland, who possessed a high place in his interest and regard, since the imposition was not laid on the planters, but on the retailers and consumers.[2] But the impost could not be disarmed of its injurious efficiency by such royal logic and barren good-will ; and both in Virginia and in Maryland it operated to straiten the circumstances and cool the loyalty of the people. As the other impediments of commerce were aggravated in Maryland by the continued prevalence of a scarcity of money, an attempt was now made to remedy this evil by a law " for the *advancement* of coins." [1686.] French crowns, pieces of eight, and rix dollars were appointed to be received in all payments at six shillings each ; all other coins, at an advance of threepence in the shilling ; and the sixpences and shillings of New England, according to their denominations, as sterling.[3] This law first gave rise in Maryland to the peculiarity of provincial currency, in contradistinction to sterling money.

At the same time that the king undertook to subvert the political constitution of England, he determined to overthrow the proprietary governments of the colonies. The existence of such independent jurisdictions, he declared, embarrassed him, in conducting both his domestic and colonial government ; and it was requisite no less to his interest than his dignity, to

---

[1] Chalmers. *State Papers*, ib.   [2] Ibid.   [3] *Laws.*

reduce them to more immediate subjection to the crown.   Alarmed by the communication of this arbitrary purpose, the proprietary of Maryland again repaired to England, and vainly represented to the inflexible despot that the administration of his province had been at all times conducted in conformity with the terms of his charter ; that he had never consciously violated his duty to his sovereign ; and that neither he nor his father had committed a single act which could infer the forfeiture of a patent which they had dearly purchased, in adding, at their own risk and expense, a large and flourishing province to the British empire.   These remonstrances were disregarded by the king ; and the attorney-general received orders to issue a writ of *quo warranto* against Lord Baltimore's charter. [1687.]   The writ was issued accordingly ; but from the dilatory pace of the requisite legal procedure, and the important events that soon after diverted the monarch's attention to nearer concerns, no judgment upon it was ever pronounced.[1]   Thus, with relentless and impartial tyranny, which even the predilections of the bigot were unable to control, James, contemning alike the wishes of the Puritans of Massachusetts and of the Catholics of Maryland, involved both in the same undistinguishing system of oppression and degradation.   Whether the singular friendship, which, in this monarch and William Penn, seemed to unite the two extremes of human nature, might have suspended for a while the destruction of the institutions of Pennsylvania, — this cousummation would have infallibly followed in due time ; and the royal regards that Penn shared with Judge Jeffries and Colonel Kirke would have secured him no other advantage than that of being, perhaps, the last of the American proprietaries that was sacrificed.   Fortunately for the interests of mankind, bigotry, infatuated by the exercise of tyranny, at length obtained ascendency over the king's mind ; and, depriving the bigot of the adherents of the tyrant, involved even Jeffries in disgrace, and constrained even the prelates of England to seek protection in the principles of liberty.

The birth of a son to James the Second [1688], which was regarded with mingled skepticism and disappointment by his English subjects, and contributed to hasten the British Revolution, was no sooner communicated by the proprietary (who was still in England) to his officers in Maryland, than it produced a general expression of satisfaction throughout the province.   In the assembly, which was convoked on this occasion, a law was passed appointing an annual commemoration of the happy event.[2]   If this proceeding seem to indicate the prevalence of a feeling that may be supposed peculiar to the Catholics, other parts of the conduct of the same assembly betrayed with more authentic semblance the existence of those jealousies with which the Protestants were infected, which the mean injustice of the late king's ministers had sanctioned, and which the unfortunate absence of Lord Baltimore now contributed to promote.   The burgesses at first demurred to take the oath of fidelity to the proprietary ; and afterwards exhibited to the deputy-governors a remonstrance against certain pretended grievances, which in truth disclosed nothing else than the ill-humor and alarm of the parties complaining ; for the articles were all so vague and so frivolous, and, if true, imported only such petty and easily remediable violations of law and usage, that it is impossible to peruse them without perceiving that the promoters of complaint either industriously sought a cause of quarrel, or had already found one which they were backward to avow.   The re-

---

[1] Chalmers.   [2] *Laws.*

monstrance, however, received a courteous and obliging answer from the deputy-governors ; and, as its authors were not yet transported by passion beyond the control of reason and common sense, they returned thanks for this issue,[1] and the flame of jealousy and discontent, from the want of any thing which it could presently lay hold of, subsided as abruptly as it had arisen.   But the embers remained, and waited only a more suitable juncture to show what a conflagration they were capable of producing.   The spirit of party in the province, excited and preserved by religious differences, in an age in which to differ was to dislike and suspect, had been hitherto moderated by the liberal spirit of the laws and the prudent administration of the proprietary.   But no sooner were the tidings of the revolution in England conveyed to the province, than those latent heats, aroused by fresh aliment, burst forth in a blaze of insurrectionary violence ; and the agitators who had long been sowing discontent in the minds of their fellow-citizens, now prepared to reap a plentiful harvest in the season of public disorder.

When the deputy-governors of Maryland were first informed of the invasion of England by the Prince of Orange [January, 1689], they judged it expedient to take measures for preserving the tranquillity of the province, where as yet none could foresee, and none had been informed, of the extraordinary issue to which that memorable enterprise was to be conducted. They collected the public arms that were dispersed in the different counties, and imprisoned several persons who were accused of attempts to excite disturbance.   But their purposes were completely frustrated by the rumor of a *popish plot*, which suddenly and rapidly disseminated the alarming intelligence, that the deputy-governors and the Catholics had formed a league with the Indians for the massacre of all the Protestants in the province.   Confusion, rage, and terror instantly laid hold of the minds of almost all the Protestant colonists ; and every exertion that was made to demonstrate the folly and absurdity of the report proved ineffectual.   Like the kindred fiction in England, the tale was corroborated by various unhappily contingent circumstances, that tended wonderfully to support the general delusion. Though Lord Baltimore received orders to proclaim William and Mary, which he readily promised and prepared to obey, yet some cross accident or treacherous machination intercepted the relative commands which he punctually transmitted to his deputies ; and they still awaited official orders respecting this important transaction, long after the corresponding proclamation was published in Virginia.   It happened unfortunately, too, that the time had now arrived when it was usual to repeat the annual confirmation of the existing treaty of peace with the Indians.   These occurrences, distorted by the arts of the factious and the credulity of the timid, increased the prevailing panic, and accelerated the explosion it had threatened to produce. A *Protestant Association* was formed [April, 1689] by John Coode, who had already illustrated his genius for sedition as the accomplice of Fendal ; and soon gaining strength from the accession of numerous votaries, took arms under this worthless leader for the defence of the Protestant faith and the vindication of the royal title of William and Mary.   A declaration or manifesto was published by the associators, replete with charges against the proprietary, that reflect the utmost dishonor on their own cause.   The reproaches of tyranny and wickedness, of murder, torture, and pillage,[2] with

---

[1] See Note XV., at the end of the volume.

[2] "If the Papists," says Hume, " have sometimes maintained that no faith was to be kept

which Lord Baltimore is loaded in this production, are refuted not only by the gross inconsistency between such heinous enormities and the recent limitation of the public grievances to the frivolous complaints exhibited to the deputy-governors, but by the utter inability of the associators to establish by evidence any one of their charges, even when the whole power and authority of the provincial government were in their own hands. With matchless impudence and absurdity, the affronts formerly complained of by the custom-house officers were now recited as injuries inflicted on the province by Lord Baltimore, — who, if he ever participated in them at all, must have been induced to do so by resentment of the real grievance inflicted on his people by the policy of the parent state. A charge of this description, however artfully calculated to recommend the cause of the associators to the favor of the British government, would never have suggested itself to a passionate multitude ; and it is probable that the whole composition was the work of Coode, whose subsequent conduct showed how little he participated in the popular feelings, which he was able notwithstanding to excite and direct with such energy and success. The deputies of Lord Baltimore endeavoured at first to oppose by force the designs of the associators ; but as the Catholics were afraid to justify the prevalent rumors against themselves by taking arms, and as the well-affected Protestants showed no eagerness to support a falling authority, they were compelled to deliver up the provincial fortress, and surrender the powers of government, by capitulation. The king, apprized of these transactions, hastened to express his approbation of them, and authorized the leaders of the insurgents to exercise in his name the power they had acquired, until he should have leisure to settle the administration of affairs on a permanent basis. Armed with this commission, Coode and a junto of his confederates continued for three years after to conduct the government of Maryland, with a predatory tyranny, that exemplified the demerits they had falsely imputed to the proprietary, and produced loud and numerous complaints from persons of every religious denomination in the province.[1] Thus, even in the midst of their own insolent triumph, the Maryland Protestants were unable to escape entirely the visitation of retributive justice.

King William, meanwhile, endeavoured to gain the same advantage to the royal authority in Maryland, which the tyranny of his predecessor bequeathed to him in Massachusetts. But to persist in the iniquitous process of *quo warranto* was no longer feasible ; and all that could be done was to summon Lord Baltimore to answer before the privy council the complaints expressed in the manifesto of the associators. After a tedious investigation, which loaded this nobleman with a heavy expense, it was found impossible to convict him of any other charge than that of differing in religious opinion from the men by whom he was so ungratefully persecuted and so calumniously traduced. He was accordingly suffered to retain the patrimonial interest attached by his charter to the office of proprietary, but deprived by an act of council of the political administration of the province, of which Sir Edmund Andros was at the same time appointed governor by the king.[2] [1692.] The unmerited advancement of this man was not less

with heretics, their adversaries seem also to have thought that no truth ought to be told of idolaters ! ''

[1] Chalmers.

[2] Oldmixon. " I know not how it happened, but so it was, that in King William's reign, Queen Anne's, &c., there were periods when the friends or tools of the abdicated king were more hearkened to than the instruments of the Revolution." Ibid. (2d edition). It is to the first edition of Oldmixon's work that I refer, when the second is not expressly designated.

discreditable to the British court than the unjust deposition of the proprietary. Lord Baltimore, having exercised his power with a liberal respect for the freedom of other men's consciences, now parted with it from a noble regard to the sanctity of his own. Andros, who had previously gained elevation by his active subserviency to a Catholic despot, now purchased its continuance by rendering himself instrumental to Protestant intolerance.

In this manner fell the proprietary government of Maryland, after a duration of fifty-six years, during which it was conducted with unexampled mildness, and with a regard to the liberty and welfare of the people, deserving a very different requital from that which we have had the pain of reviewing. The slight notice which the policy of Lord Baltimore has received from the philosophic encomiasts of liberal institutions attests the capricious distribution of fame, and has probably been occasioned by dislike of his religious tenets, which, it was feared, would share the commendation bestowed on their votary. It was apprehended, perhaps, that the charge of intolerance, so strongly preferred by Protestants and philosophers against Catholic potentates and the Romish Church, would be weakened by the praise of a toleration which Catholics established and Protestants overthrew. But, in truth, every deduction that is made by the most uncharitable of their adversaries from the liberality of Catholics in general, and every imputation that is more or less justly thrown on the ordinary influence of their tenets in contracting the mind, ought to magnify the merit of Lord Baltimore's institutions, and enhance the praise by illustrating the rarity of his virtue. One of the most respectable features of the proprietary administration was the constant regard that was shown to justice, and to the exercise and cultivation of benevolence, in all transactions and intercourse with the Indians. But though this colony was more successful than the New England States (who conducted themselves no less unexceptionably towards the Indians) in avoiding war with its savage neighbours, yet we have seen that it was not always able to avert this extremity. In Maryland as well as in New England, doubtless, the pacific endeavours of the colonists were counteracted, not only by the natural ferocity of the Indians, but by the hostilities of other Europeans, by which that ferocity was, from time to time, enkindled and developed. Yet the Quakers of Pennsylvania, who were exposed to the same disadvantage, escaped its evil consequences, and were never attacked by the Indians. Relying implicitly and exclusively on the protection of Heaven, they renounced every act or indication of self-defence that could awaken the contentiousness of human nature, or excite apprehensive jealousy, by ostentation of the power to injure. But the Puritan and Catholic colonists of New England and Maryland, while they professed and exercised good-will to the Indians, adopted the hostile precaution of demonstrating their readiness and ability to repel violence. They displayed arms and erected forts, and thus provoked the suspicion they expressed, and invited the injury they anticipated.

Before toleration was defended by Locke, it was practically established by Lord Baltimore; and in the attempts which both of these eminent persons made to construct the frame of a wise and liberal government in America, it must be acknowledged that the Protestant philosopher was greatly excelled by the Catholic nobleman.[1] The constitutions of William Penn

[1] At a social entertainment, where Sir Isaac Newton, John Locke, and William Penn happened to meet together, the conversation turned on the comparative excellence of the governments of Carolina and Pennsylvania. Locke ingenuously yielded the palm to Penn (Clark-

have been the theme of general panegyric ; but of those who have commended them, how few have been found to celebrate or even acknowledge
the prior establishment of similar institutions by Lord Baltimore ! [1]   Assimilated in their maxims of government, thése two proprietaries were assimilated in their political fortunes ; both having witnessed an eclipse of their
popularity in America, and both being dispossessed of their governments by
King William.   Penn, indeed, was restored a few years after : but Lord
Baltimore's deprivation continued during his life.   On his death, in 1716,
his successor, being a Protestant, was restored to the enjoyment of proprietary powers.   These powers, however, had in the interim sustained some
abatement from an act of the English parliament,[2] which applied not only
to this but to all the other feudatory principalities in North America, and
rendered the royal sanction necessary to confirm the nomination of the proprietary governors.

Immediately after his appointment to the office of governor, Sir Edmund
Andros repaired to Maryland, where he convoked an assembly, in which the
title of William and Mary was recognized by a legislative enactment, and
in which an attempt was made to divest the proprietary of the port-duties
that were settled on his family in the year 1661.   The assembly now made
a tender of the produce of this tax to the king, alleging, that, although the
provision was granted in general terms to the proprietary, the real intention
of the legislature had been to confer it merely as a trust for the uses of
the public.   The king, however, declined to accept the offer, or sanction
the assembly's construction of the grant ; Sir John Somers, to whom the
legitimacy of the proposition was referred, having pronounced as his opinion
that the duty truly belonged to Lord Baltimore, and was intended for his own
use, and that it would be of dangerous consequence to admit parol proof
of legislative intention, contradictory of the plain meaning of the words of
enacted law.   The ingratitude which was thus manifested towards the proprietary met with a just retribution from the administration of Andros, who,
though he subsequently approved himself a good governor in Virginia, exercised much severity and rapacity in Maryland.   Not the least offensive part
of his conduct was, that he protected Coode against the complaints he had

son's *Life of Penn*), and would doubtless have yielded it to Lord Baltimore. But Penn's reputation (from the interest which the Quakers have felt in promoting it, and the willingness of
philosophers to acknowledge him as an ally) has been much better protected than that of Lord
Baltimore: and to this, perhaps, may be ascribed the very different treatment which the descendants of these proprietaries experienced from the communities of which they were the
chiefs at the period of the American Revolution. The proprietary of Maryland was then a
minor ; yet his estates were confiscated, and no indemnification could ever be obtained.
Winterbotham. The descendants of Penn, after a long series of quarrels with the people,
embraced the cause of Britain ; yet the legislature of Pennsylvania indemnified them in the
most liberal manner for the loss of their property.   Brissot's *Travels.*
    [1] From one English poet the two proprietaries have received an equal tribute of praise :—
            " Laws formed to harmonize contrarious creeds,
            And heal the wounds through which a nation bleeds ;
            Laws mild, impartial, tolerant, and fixed,
            A bond of union for a people mixed :
            Such as good Calvert framed for Baltimore,
            And Penn, the Numa of the Atlantic shore." — Burroughs.
    [2] 7 and 8 Will. III., Cap. 22, § 16. This was the first instance in which the English parlia-
ment assumed the right of modifying the charter and altering the constitution of an American
province. — By another clause in the same statute, it was enacted, "that on no pretence whatever any kind of goods from the English American plantations shall hereafter be put on shore
either in the kingdoms of Ireland or Scotland, without being first landed in England, and having also paid the duties there, under the penalty of a forfeiture of the ship and cargo." The
Union in 1707 rendered this restriction void, in so far as related to Scotland.

provoked, and enabled this profligate hypocrite a little longer to protract the period of his impunity. But Coode's fortunes soon became more appropriate to his deserts. Finding himself neglected by Colonel Nicholson, the lieutenant and successor of Andros, he began to practise against the royal government the same treacherous intrigues that he had employed with success against the proprietary administration. Inferior in talent to Bacon, the disturber of Virginia, and far inferior in sincerity to Leisler, the contemporary agitator of New York, Coode was chiefly indebted for his success to the implicit reliance which he placed on the influence of panic and the extent of popular credulity. He had an unbounded confidence in the power of copious and persevering calumny, and endeavoured to impress it as a maxim on his disciples in sedition, that, " if plenty of mud be thrown, some of it must infallibly stick." In 1695, this president of the Protestant Association of Maryland was indicted for treason and blasphemy ; and, justly apprehending that he would be treated with less lenity under the Protestant, than he formerly experienced under the Catholic administration, he declined to stand a trial, and fled from the province which he had contributed so signally to dishonor.[1]

The suspension of the proprietary government was accompanied with a notable departure from the principles on which its administration was previously conducted. The political equality of religious sects was disallowed, and the toleration that had been extended to every form of Christian worship was abolished. The Church of England was declared to be the established ecclesiastical constitution of the state ; and an act passed in the year 1692 having divided the several counties into parishes, a legal maintenance was assigned to a minister of this communion in every one of these parishes, — consisting of a glebe, and an annual tribute of forty pounds of tobacco from every Christian male, and every male or female negro above sixteen years of age. The appointment of the ministers was vested in the governor, and the management of parochial affairs in vestries elected by the Protestant inhabitants. For the instruction of the people, free schools and public libraries were established by law in all the parishes ; and an ample collection of books was presented to the libraries, as a commencement of their literary stock, by the Bishop of London. This design was originally suggested by Dr. Thomas Bray, an English clergyman, who distinguished himself by the zeal and activity with which he labored to extend the doctrine and authority of the church of England, both in this, and the other North American colonies. But notwithstanding all these encouragements to the cultivation of knowledge, and the rapid increase of her wealth and population, it was not till after her separation from the parent state, that any considerable academy or college was formed in Maryland. All Protestant Dissenters were admitted to partake the full benefit of the act of toleration passed in the commencement of William and Mary's reign by the English parliament. But this grace was strictly withheld from the Roman Catholics ; and the Protestants, who thus enacted toleration to themselves, with the most impudent injustice and unchristian cruelty denied it to the men by whose toleration they had been permitted to gain an establishment in the province. Sanc-

---

[1] Oldmixon. Chalmers. Among other expressions that Coode's indictment laid to his charge, as constituting the offence of blasphemy, he was accused of having said " that there was no religion but what was in Tully's *Offices*." To make these words the more intelligible, the indictment illustrated them by this innuendo, " that they were spoken of *one Tully*, a Roman orator meaning."

tioned by the authority, and instructed by the example of the British government, the legislature of Maryland proceeded, by the most tyrannical persecution of the Catholics, to confirm and disgrace the Protestant ascendency.
Not only were these unfortunate victims of a conscientious belief, which
the actions of their opponents contributed additionally to fortify, excluded
from all participation in political privileges, but they were debarred from the
exercise of their peculiar form of worship, and from the advantages of education.   By an act of the provincial assembly, passed in the year 1704, and
renewed in the year 1714, it was ordained that any Catholic priest, attempting to convert a Protestant, should be punished with fine and imprisonment ;
and that the celebration of mass, or the education of youth by a Papist,
should be punished by transmission of the offending priest or teacher to
England, that he might there undergo the penalties which the English statutes attached to such conduct.   Transported by their eagerness to deprive
the Catholics of liberty, the Protestants of Maryland seem not to have perceived that this last measure tended to subvert their own pretension to
independent legislation.   They maintained that the statutes of the English
parliament did not extend, by the mere operation of their own intrinsic authority, to Maryland ; and in conformity with this notion, we find an act of
assembly, in the year 1706, giving to certain English acts of parliament the
force of law within the province.   But it was manifestly inconsistent with
such pretended independence to declare any of the colonists amenable to
the peculiar jurisprudence of England, for actions committed in the province
and not punishable by the provincial laws.   Though laws thus unjust and
oppressive were framed, it was found impossible to carry them into complete execution.   Shortly after the act of 1704 was passed, the assembly
judged it expedient to suspend its enforcement so far as to admit of Catholic
priests performing their functions in private houses ; and the act of 1714
was suspended in a similar manner, in consequence of an express mandate
to the assembly from Queen Anne.[1]

Thus were the Catholics of Maryland, under the pretence of vices which
none exemplified more forcibly than their persecutors, deprived of those
privileges, which, for more than half a century, they had exercised with
unparalleled justice and moderation.   In addition to the other odious features
of the treatment they experienced, there was a shameful violation of national
faith in suffering Protestant persecution to follow them into the asylum from
its severity, which they had been encouraged to seek, and with laborious
virtue had established.   Sensible of this injustice, or rather, perhaps, willing
to induce the Catholics, whom they had determined not to tolerate at home,
to expatriate to Maryland, the British government continued from time to
time to set bounds to the exercise of that provincial bigotry which its own
example had prompted and its own authority still maintained. From the
still more unjust and perfidious treatment which the Catholics of Maryland
beheld their brethren in Ireland undergo from Great Britain they might derive at least the consolation of perceiving that they themselves were not
delivered up to the utmost extremity of Protestant tyranny and intolerance.

Before the overthrow of the Catholic church in Maryland, its clergy had
signalized themselves by some attempts to convert the Indians to the Christian faith ; but their endeavours have been represented as being neither judicious nor successful.   Eager to prevail on the savages to receive the for-

---

[1] Smollett's *History of England.   Acts of the Assembly of Maryland, from* 1692 *to* 1715.

malities, before they were impressed with the substance of Christian faith, they are said to have administered the rite of baptism to persons who understood it so little, that they considered their acceptance of it as a favor they conferred on the missionaries in return for the presents they received from them, and used to threaten to renounce their baptism unless these presents were repeated.[1] But if the Catholics of Maryland were chargeable with a superstitious forwardness to administer this rite, some of their Protestant fellow-colonists betrayed sentiments far more inexcusable, in their determination to withhold it. An act of assembly, passed in the year 1715, recounts that many people refused to permit their slaves to be baptized, in consequence of an apprehension that baptism would entitle them to their freedom ; and accordingly, to overcome their reluctance, ordains that no negro receiving the holy sacrament of baptism should derive therefrom any right or claim to be made free.[2] It was the peculiar unhappiness of the lot of the Maryland Protestants, that they were surrounded at the same time by Catholics, whom they were incited to persecute, and by slaves, whom they were enabled to oppress ; and it was not till some time after the Revolution of 1688, that they began to show more genuine fruits of the tenets they professed, than the persecution of those who differed from them in religious opinion.[3]

At the close of the seventeenth century, the population of Maryland amounted to thirty thousand persons ; and whether from superiority of soil, or industry, or from the absence of laws restrictive of cultivation, this province is said to have exported at least as much tobacco as the older and more populous province of Virginia. At a later period, a law was passed, prohibiting the cultivation on any estate of a greater quantity than six thousand plants of tobacco for every taxable individual upon the estate. Maryland was the first of the provinces in which the right of private property was from the beginning recognized in its fullest extent ; and community of possessions had never even a temporary establishment. This peculiarity, it is probable, contributed to promote the peculiar industry by which the people of Maryland have been distinguished. In the year 1699, Annapolis was substituted for St. Mary's, as the capital of the province ; and all roads leading thither were ordered to be marked by notches cut on the trees growing on either hand : but the same causes that prevented the growth of towns in Virginia also repressed their rise in Maryland. There were few merchants or shopkeepers who were not also planters ; and it was the custom for every man to maintain on his plantation a store for supplying the usual accommodations of shops to his family, servants, and slaves.[4] Living dispersed over the province, and remote from each other, the effects of their comparative solitude are said to have been generally visible in the physiognomy, manners, and apparel of the planters ; their aspect expressing less cheerful frankness, their demeanour less vivacity, their dress less attention to neatness, and their whole exterior less *urbanity*, than were found in those colonies where cities engendered and diffused the graceful quality to which they have given a name. But even those who have reproached them with this defect have not failed to recognize a more respectable characteristic of their situation, in that hospitality by which they were universally distinguish-

---

[1] Neal's *New England.*
[2] *Acts of the Maryland Assembly, from* 1692 *to* 1715.   [3] Oldmixon.
[4] Oldmixon. *History of the British Dominions in America.*

ed.[1] At a later period, the towns of Maryland seemed to acquire a sudden principle of increase ; and Baltimore, in particular, has grown with a rapidity unrivalled even in the United States.   In none of the provinces have the effects of a wise or illiberal system of government been more plainly apparent than in Maryland. For nearly a century after the British Revolution, difference in religious opinion proved a source of animosity, and was made the apology for injustice ; and during all that period, not one considerable seminary of learning arose in the province.   Within a few years after the return of equal laws and universal toleration, in the train of American independence, the varieties of doctrinal opinion among the people served but to illustrate religious charity ; numerous colleges and academies were founded ; and the same people among whom persecution had lingered longest became distinguished for a remarkable degree of courteous kindness, liberal indulgence, and generous humanity.[2]

During the suspension of the proprietary government, the legislature of the province consisted of three branches ; after its revival, of four: the proprietary, the governor, the council, and the burgesses. The proprietary, besides a large domain cultivated by himself, enjoyed a quitrent of two shillings sterling yearly for every hundred acres of appropriated land.   This was increased at an after period to four shillings in some districts ; and an unsuccessful attempt was made to raise it as high as ten shillings.   The proprietaries, it must be confessed, had received little encouragement to rely on the recompense of popular gratitude, and persist in their original moderation and liberality.   The salaries of the governor and deputy-governor consisted of official fees, and a tax on exported tobacco, decreed to them successively on their appointment to office, and proportioned to their popularity.   The council consisted of twelve persons, appointed by the proprietary, and, during the abeyance of his political rights, by the royal governor ; each of whom received, during the session of the assembly, an allowance of one hundred and eighty pounds of tobacco daily from the province. The house of representatives or burgesses consisted of four members from each of the counties, and two from the capital ; the daily allowance of each of them being one hundred and sixty pounds of tobacco.   From the decisions of the provincial courts, in all cases involving property to the amount of three hundred pounds, an appeal was admitted to the king in council. The office of the selectmen in New England was performed in Maryland by the parochial vestries, which engrossed the management of all the public affairs of their districts, and which soon betrayed an entire departure from the popular principle of their original constitution ; for, though at first elected by the inhabitants, the vestrymen held their office for life, and very early assumed the privilege of renovating their own body, and supplying its vacancies by their own appointment.[3] In the year 1704, it was provided by " An act for the advancement of the natives and residents of this province," that no office of trust, except those that were conferred by immediate commission from the crown, could be held by any person who had not previously resided three years in the colony.[4]

---

[1] Winterbotham. " That pride which grows on slavery, and is habitual to those who from their infancy are taught to believe and feel their superiority, is a visible characteristic of the inhabitants of Maryland." Ibid.

[2] Warden's *Account of the United States.*

[3] *History of the British Dominions in America.*

[4] *Acts of Assembly, from* 1692 *to* 1715.

The situation of slaves and of indented servants appears to have been very much the same in Maryland as in Virginia. Any white woman, whether a servant or free, becoming pregnant from the embrace of a negro, whether a slave or free, was punished with a servitude of seven years ; and the children of " those unnatural and inordinate connexions " (as they were termed by law) were doomed to servitude till they should attain the age of thirty-one.   A white man begetting a child by a negress was subjected to the same penalty as a white woman committing the corresponding offence.[1] Thus pride produced in Maryland regulations, less extensive, indeed, in their range, but not less rigid in their operation, than those which piety had established in New England.   An indented servant, at the expiration of his dependence, was entitled to demand an ample allowance of various useful commodities from his master, some of which he was prohibited, under a penalty, from selling for twelve months after his emancipation.[2]   A tax was imposed on the importation of servants from Ireland, " to prevent the importing too great a number of Irish Papists into this province."[3]

To obstruct the evasion of provincial debts or other obligations, by flight to England, or to the other American States, all persons preparing to leave the colony were required to give public intimation of their departure, and obtain a formal passport from the municipal authorities.[4]   An act was passed in the year 1698, bestowing a large tract of land in Dorchester county on two Indian kings, who, with their subjects, were to hold it as a fief from the proprietary, and to pay for it a yearly rent of one bear-skin. In common with the other colonies, Maryland was much infested by wolves ; and so late as the year 1715, a previous act was renewed, offering " *the sum* of three hundred pounds of tobacco " as a reward for every wolf's head that should be brought by any colonist or Indian to a justice of the peace.[5]   An act proposing a similar recompense had been passed in Virginia, but was repealed in the year 1666.

---

[1] *Acts of the Assembly, from* 1692 *to* 1715.   [2] Ibid.
[3] Ibid.   [4] Ibid.   [5] Ibid.

BOOK IV.

NORTH AND SOUTH CAROLINA.

CHAPTER I.

Early Attempts of the Spaniards and the French to colonize this Territory. — First Charter of Carolina granted by Charles the Second to Lord Clarendon and others. — Formation of Albemarle Settlement in North Carolina. — Settlement of Ashley River in South Carolina. — Second Charter of the whole United Province. — Proceedings at Albemarle. — The Proprietaries enact the Fundamental Constitutions of Carolina. — Expedition of Emigrants to South Carolina. — John Locke created a Landgrave. — Hostilities with the Spaniards in Florida — and with the Indians. — Disgusts between the Proprietaries and the Colonists. — Affairs of North Carolina. — Culpepper's Insurrection. — He is tried in England — and acquitted. — Discord among the Colonists. — Sothel's tyrannical Administration. — He is deposed.

WE have beheld New England colonized by Puritans exiled by royal and episcopal tyranny ; Virginia replenished by cavalier and episcopal fugitives from republican triumph and Puritan ascendency ; and Maryland founded by Catholics retiring from Protestant intolerance. By a singular coincidence, the settlement whose history we are now to investigate originally seemed to have been destined to complete this series of reciprocal persecution ; and if the first colonists who were planted in it had been able to maintain their establishment, Carolina would have been peopled by Huguenots flying from Catholic bigotry.[1]

This territory has been contested by a variety of pretensions and distinguished at successive periods by a variety of names. The claim of England to the first discovery of it was disputed by the Spaniards, who maintained that Cabot never advanced so far to the south, and that it had been yet unvisited by any European, when Ponce de Leon, the Spanish governor of Porto Rico, arrived on its shores [1512], in the course of a voyage he was making in quest of a land which was reported to contain a brook or fountain endowed with the miraculous power of restoring the bloom and vigor of youth to age and decrepitude.[2] Believing that he had here attained the favored region, he hastened to take possession, in his sovereign's name, of so rare and valuable an acquisition. He bestowed on it the name of Florida, either on account of the vernal beauty that adorned its surface, or because he discovered it on the Sunday before Easter, which the Spaniards call *Pascua de Flores* ; but, though he chilled his aged frame by bathing in every stream that he could find, he had the mortification of returning an older instead of a younger man to Porto Rico. A few years afterwards, another Spanish officer, who was sent to inspect more minutely the territory supposed to have been thus newly discovered, performed an exploit too congenial with the

---

[1] At a subsequent period, the descendants of one of the most illustrious people of antiquity were induced to seek a refuge in America from Turkish oppression. In the latter part of the eighteenth century, Sir William Duncan, an eminent English physician, conceived the project of founding a Grecian colony in North America, and actually transported, for this purpose, several hundred Greeks to East Florida. Galt's *Letters from the Levant.*

[2] An account of a fountain in Ethiopia endowed with similar efficacy (manifestly little credited by the relater) occurs in Book III. of the *History* of Herodotus.

contemporary achievements of his countrymen, in kidnapping a number of the natives, whom he carried away into bondage. Some researches for gold and silver, undertaken shortly after by succeeding adventurers of the same nation, having terminated unsuccessfully, the Spaniards seemed to have renounced the intention of any immediate settlement in this region, and left it to repose under the shadow of the name they had bestowed, and to remember its titular owners by their cupidity and injustice.

The whole of its coast was subsequently [1523 – 1525] explored with considerable accuracy by Verazzan, an Italian navigator, employed in the service of the French, and whom Francis the First [1] had commissioned to attempt the discovery of new territories in America for the benefit of his crown. But the colonial projects of the French were suspended during the remainder of this reign, by the wars and intrigues which were conducted with such eager and obstinate rivalry between Francis and the Emperor Charles the Fifth.[2] During succeeding reigns, they were impeded by still more fatal obstructions ; and all the benefit that France might have derived from the territory explored by Verazzan and neglected by the Spaniards was postponed to the indulgence of royal and papal bigotry in a war of extermination against the Huguenots. The advantages, however, thus disregarded by the French court, were not overlooked by the objects of its persecution ; and in process of time, the project of appropriating a part of that territory as a retreat for French Protestants was embraced by one of their leaders, the renowned Admiral Coligni. [1562.] Two vessels which he equipped for this purpose were accordingly despatched with a band of Protestant emigrants to America, who landed at the mouth of Albemarle River, and in honor of their sovereign (Charles the Ninth), gave the country the name of Carolina, — a name which the English first obliterated and finally restored. Though the French colonists had only to announce themselves as strangers to the faith and the race of the Spaniards, in order to obtain a friendly reception from the Indians, they suffered so many privations in their new settlement, from the inability of the admiral to furnish them with adequate supplies, that, after a short residence in America, they were compelled to return to France.

A treacherous pacification having been negotiated, meanwhile, between the French court and the Protestants, Coligni employed the interval of repose, and the unwonted favor which the king affected to entertain for him, in providing a refuge for his party from that tempest, which, though unhappily for himself he did not clearly foresee, yet his sagacity and experience enabled him partially to anticipate. Three ships, furnished by the king, and freighted with another detachment of Huguenots, were again despatched to Carolina [1564], and followed soon after by a more numerous fleet with additional settlers and a copious supply of arms and provisions. The as-

---

[1] The kings of Spain and Portugal remonstrated against the projects of Francis as a direct impugnation of ecclesiastical authority. To this remonstrance the French monarch is said to have pleasantly replied, "I should be glad to see the clause in Adam's will, which makes that continent their exclusive inheritance." Raynal.

[2] A slight demonstration was made by Francis, in the year 1540, of an intention to colonize a different quarter of America, by the letters patent which he then granted to Jacques Quartier for the establishment of a colony in Canada. But the French made no permanent settlement even there till the reign of Henry the Fourth. Escarbot's *History of New France.* Champlain's *Voyage.* In the commission to Quartier, the territory is described as " possessed by savages living without the knowledge of God or the use of reason." Yet Pope Paul the Third had previously by a solemn decree pronounced the American Indians to be rational creatures, possessing the nature and entitled to the rights of men.

sistance which the king of France thus vouchsafed to the Huguenots reminds us of the similar policy by which Charles the First promoted, in the following century, the departure of the Puritans from England. The French monarch was a little more liberal than the English, in the aid which he granted ; but he was infinitely more perfidious and cruel in the design which he secretly entertained. Befriended by the Indians, and vigorously applying themselves to the cultivation of their territory, the colonists had begun to enjoy the prospect of a permanent and happy establishment in Carolina, when they were suddenly attacked by a force despatched against them by the king of Spain. The commander of the Spanish troops, having first induced them to surrender as Frenchmen, put them all to the sword as heretics ; announcing, by a placard erected at the place of execution, that this butchery *was inflicted on them not as subjects of France, but as followers of Luther.* Nearly a thousand French Protestants were the victims of this massacre ; and only one soldier escaped to carry tidings to France, which charity does not oblige us to believe communicated any surprise to the projectors of the league of Bayonne and the massacre of St. Bartholomew.[1] Though the colony had been planted with the approbation of the French court, and peace subsisted at the time between France and Spain, the assault and extirpation of the colonists produced no demonstration of resentment from the French government, and would have been totally unavenged in this world, if De Gorgues, a French nobleman, incensed at such heinous insolence and barbarity, had not determined to vindicate the claims of justice and the honor of his country. Having fitted out three ships at his own expense [1567], he set sail for Carolina, where the Spaniards, in careless security, possessed the fort and settlement which they had acquired by the murder of his countrymen. He easily obtained the coöperation of the neighbouring Indians, and with their assistance overpowered and put to the sword all the Spaniards who resisted his enterprise, and hanged all whom he made prisoners on the nearest trees ; erecting, in his turn, a placard which announced that this execution *was inflicted on them not as Spaniards, but as murderers and robbers.* Having thus accomplished his purposed vengeance, he returned to France ; first razing the fort to the ground and destroying every trace of the settlement, which neither Frenchmen nor Spaniards were destined ever again to occupy.[2] Religious dissensions excited a much greater degree of mutual hatred and of public confusion in France than in England, and were proportionally unfavorable to French colonization. Canada, which was the first permanent occupation of the French in America, was not colonized till six years after Henry the Fourth had issued the memorable edict of Nantes.

About eighteen years after the destruction of the French colony founded by Coligni, there was planted, within the same territorial limits, in the isle of

---

[1] Coligni, in conjunction with John Calvin, made attempts on a larger scale to colonize South America with French Huguenots. But the settlement that he planted in this quarter, also, was subverted by treachery and violence. Southey's *History of Brazil.*

[2] L'Escarbot. Millot's *History of France.* Oldmixon. Hewit. Williamson. The French, however, retained their pretensions to the country. D'Aubigny, the father of Madame Maintenon, having formed the purpose of establishing himself in Carolina, found he had incurred the serious displeasure of the French court for having solicited the permission of the English government. Voltaire's *Age of Louis the Fourteenth.* Voltaire is mistaken in supposing that the daughter of this adventurer, who afterwards became queen of the country where she had been born in a prison, received her early education in Carolina, where as yet there were none but savage inhabitants. It was to Martinique that her father actually removed himself and his family. *Mémoires et Lettres de Maintenon.* *Vie de M. Maintenon.*

Roanoke, the first settlement established by Raleigh, of whose enterprises we have remarked the progress and the fate in the early history of Virginia. There was an analogy between the fortunes of their colonial enterprises, as well as between the personal destinies of the two illustrious adventurers ; and, transient as it proved, it was still the most lasting trace of his exertions witnessed by Raleigh, that the name of the country was changed by the English from Carolina to Virginia, — a name of which we have already traced the final application and peculiar history.[1] Even the subsequent and more durable colonial appropriations of the English did not extend to this territory, till the year 1622, when a few planters and their families, flying from the hostilities of the Indians in Virginia and New England, sought refuge within its limits, and are said to have acted the part of Christian missionaries in their new settlement with some promising appearance of success. They suffered extreme hardship from scarcity of provisions, and were preserved from perishing by the generous contributions of the people of Massachusetts, whose assistance they implored. An attempt was made to assume a jurisdiction over them by Sir Robert Heath, attorney-general to Charles the First, who obtained from his master a patent of the whole of this region by the name of *Carolana*. But as he neglected to execute the powers conferred on him, the patent was afterwards declared to be vacated by his failure to perform the conditions on which it was granted.[2] Much collision and contestation between claimants and occupiers of colonial territory would have been prevented, if the principle of this adjudication had been more generally extended and more steadily enforced.

The country which so many unsuccessful attempts had been made to colonize was finally indebted for its cultivation to a project formed by certain courtiers of Charles the Second for their own aggrandizement, but which they were pleased to ascribe to a generous desire of propagating the blessings of religion and civility in a barbarous land. An application, couched in these terms [1663], having been presented to the king by eight of the most eminent persons whose fidelity he had experienced in his exile, or whose treachery had contributed to his restoration, easily procured for them a grant of that extensive region, situated on the Atlantic Ocean, between the thirty-sixth degree of north latitude and the river Saint Matheo. This territory was accordingly declared an English province, by the name of Carolina, and conferred on the Lord Chancellor Clarendon, Monk, Duke of Albemarle, Lord Craven, Lord Berkeley, Lord Ashley (afterwards Earl of Shaftesbury), Sir George Carteret, Sir John Colleton, and Sir William Berkeley, the brother of Lord Berkeley, and already introduced to our acquaintance as governor of Virginia ; *who* (as the charter set forth), *being*

---

[1] The denomination, which, in honor of himself, he conferred on a projected town (see *ante*, Book I., Chap. I.), was revived and bestowed upon an actual city, more than two hundred years after ; when, by an ordinance of the legislature of North Carolina, the name of Raleigh was given to the seat of government of this province.

[2] Coxe's *Description of Carolana*. Hutchinson. Oldmixon. Chalmers. Heath had previously sold his patent to the Earl of Arundel and Surrey, who made expensive preparations for founding a colony, but was diverted from his design by a domestic calamity. Daniel Coxe, a physician in London, who, at the close of the seventeenth century, became an extensive purchaser of proprietary rights in North America, contrived, among other acquisitions, to obtain an assignation to Sir Robert Heath's patent ; and maintained, with the approbation of King William's ministers, that this patent was still a valid and subsisting title, in so far as it embraced territory occupied by the Spaniards, and not included in any posterior English patent. His son (author of the *Description*) resumed his father's claims, and made various unsuccessful attempts to colonize the territory which he persisted in denominating *Carolana*. Coxe.

excited with a laudable and pious zeal for the propagation of the gospel, have begged a certain country in the parts of America not yet cultivated and planted, and only inhabited by some barbarous people who have no knowledge of God. The territory was bestowed on these personages, and their heirs and assigns, as absolute lords proprietaries for ever, saving the sovereign allegiance due to the crown ; and they were invested with as ample privileges and jurisdiction within their American palatinate, as the Bishop of Durham enjoyed within his diocese. This charter, composed by the parties themselves who received it, seems to have been copied from the prior charter of Maryland, — the most liberal in the communication of privileges and authority that had ever been granted by an English monarch.

A meeting of all the proprietaries who were in England was held soon after, for the purpose of concerting the best means of carrying the purposes of their charter into effect ; when a joint stock was formed by general contribution for transporting emigrants and defraying other preliminary expenses. At the desire of the New England settlers, who already inhabited the province, and had stationed themselves in the vicinity of Cape Fear, the proprietaries published, at the same time, a document entitled *Proposals to all that will plant in Carolina.* They proclaimed that all persons inhabiting the vicinity of Charles River to the southward of Cape Fear, and consenting to take the oath of allegiance to the king, and to recognize the proprietary government, should be entitled to continue the possession they had assumed and to fortify their settlements ; that the planters should present to the proprietaries a list of thirteen persons, in order that they might select from them a governor and council of six, to exercise authority for three years ; that an assembly, composed of the governor, council, and delegates of the freemen, should be convoked as soon as the circumstances of the colony would admit, with power to make laws, of which the validity was to depend on their congruity with the jurisprudence of England and the approbation of the proprietaries ; that all the colonists should enjoy the most perfect religious freedom ; that every freeman arriving in the province during the next five years should obtain a hundred acres of land for himself and fifty for a servant, — paying only a halfpenny of rent for every acre ; and that the same exemption from customs, which was conferred on the proprietaries by the royal charter, should be extended to all classes of the inhabitants.[1] Such was the original compact between the rulers and the inhabitants of Carolina ; and assuredly it must strike every reflecting mind with surprise, to behold a regular system of civil and religious freedom thus established as the basis of the provincial institutions by the same statesmen, who, in the parent country, had framed the intolerant *act of uniformity,* and were executing its provisions with the most relentless rigor. While they silenced such teachers as John Owen, and filled the prisons of England with such victims as Baxter, Bunyan, and Alleine, they tendered freedom and encouragement to every variety of opinion in Carolina ; thus forcibly impeaching the wisdom and good faith of their domestic administration by the avowal which their colonial policy manifestly implies, that diversities of opinion and worship may peaceably coexist in the same society, and that implicit toleration is the surest political means of making a commonwealth flourish and endearing a country to its inhabitants. It is humiliating to observe a man like Lord Clarendon adopt, in conformity with his private inter-

[1] Oldmixon. Chalmers.

est as a proprietor of colonial territory, the principles which his eminent faculties and enlarged experience were insufficient to induce him, as an English statesman, to embrace.

Besides the emigrants from New England who were seated at Cape Fear, there was another small body of inhabitants already established in a different quarter of the proprietary domains. In the history of Virginia, we have seen, that, as early as the year 1609, Captain Smith judged it expedient, for political reasons, to remove a portion of the Virginian colonists to a distance from the main body at Jamestown. With this view he despatched a small party to form a plantation at Nansemond, on the southern frontier of Virginia, where, notwithstanding the formidable obstructions that they encountered from the hostility of the natives, they succeeded in maintaining and extending their settlement. As the Indians receded from the vicinity of these intruders, the planters naturally followed their tracks, — extending their plantations into the bosom of the wilderness ; and as their numbers increased and the most eligible situations were occupied, they traversed the forests in quest of others, till they reached the streams which, instead of discharging their waters into the Chesapeake, pursued a southeastern course to the ocean. Their numbers are said to have been augmented, and their progress impelled, by the intolerant laws that were enacted in Virginia against sectarians of every denomination. At the epoch of the Carolina charter of 1663, a small plantation, formed in this manner, had existed for some years within its specified territorial boundaries on the northeastern shores of a river formerly called the Chowan, but which now received the name of Albemarle, in compliment to the title by which General Monk's services were rewarded.

Notwithstanding the assertion of an intelligent historian of North Carolina, there is no reason to believe that the planters of Albemarle were composed entirely or even generally of exiles for conscience's sake ; yet that a number of conscientious men had mingled with them may be inferred from the fact that they purchased their lands at an equitable price from the aboriginal inhabitants. Remote from the seat of the Virginian government, they paid little regard to its authority, and for some time had lived without any ascertainable rule ; when at length the governor of Virginia assumed, in a new capacity, a stricter and more legitimate superintendence of their affairs. In September, 1663, Sir William Berkeley was empowered by the other proprietaries to nominate a president and a council of six persons, with authority to govern this little community according to the prescriptions of the royal charter ; to confirm existing possessions ; to grant lands to new planters ; and, with the consent of the delegates of the freemen, to frame laws which were to be transmitted for the consideration of the proprietaries. Berkeley was desired to visit the colony, and to employ skilful persons to explore its bays, rivers, and shores ; a duty which he performed in the following year. Having confirmed existing possessions, and made sundry new grants of land, in conformity with his instructions, he appointed Drummond, a man of prudence and ability, the first governor of his fellow-colonists, and then returned to Virginia, leaving the people to follow their various pursuits in peace. [1664.] The colonists for some time continued perfectly satisfied with an arrangement that seemed rather to secure than impair the advantages of their former condition ; but as the day approached when the payment of quitrents was to commence, they began to manifest impatience of the

tenure by which they held their lands.   In the year 1666, they constituted
an assembly, probably the first that was ever held in Carolina, and from this
body a petition was transmitted to the proprietaries, desiring that the people
of Albemarle might hold their possessions on the same terms that were enjoyed by the inhabitants of Virginia.   The proprietaries, who were exceedingly solicitous to promote the population of the province, and to avoid
every measure that might discourage the resort of settlers, readily acceded
to this request, and commanded the governor in future to confer grants of
land on the terms prescribed by the colonists themselves.   Notwithstanding
the apostolical views which the proprietaries had professed, they made not
the slightest attempt to provide for the spiritual instruction of the colonists
or the conversion of the Indians ; and the little commonwealth for a series
of years was conducted without even a semblance of religious worship.[1]

    The proprietaries, after this endeavour to rear and organize the settlement
of Albemarle, directed their chief regard to the finer region that extends
along the more southerly coast.   Having caused a survey to be made of
these shores, by a vessel which they despatched from Virginia, for the
purpose of ascertaining what spots and districts were the most proper for
habitation, they resolved, among other projected settlements, to establish a
new colony to the southward of Cape Fear, along the banks of the river
Charles, in the district which was now denominated the county of Clarendon.   Several of the planters of Barbadoes, dissatisfied with their existing
condition, and desiring to become the chiefs of a less numerous community,
had for some time projected to remove to that region, and now submitted a
proposition to this effect to the proprietaries [1664] ; and though their first
demands, of being invested with a district thirty-two miles square and all
the powers of a distinct and independent corporation, were deemed inadmis-
sible, their application, on the whole, received so much encouragement as
determined them to undertake the migration.   In furtherance of a project
so agreeable to their wishes, the proprietaries bestowed on John Yeamans,
a respectable planter of Barbadoes, and the son of a man who had lost his
life in the king's service during the civil wars, the appointment of commander-
in-chief of Clarendon county, stretching from Cape Fear to the river Saint
Matheo ; and obtained for him, at the same time, the title of a baronet,
partly in recompense of the loyalty of his family, and partly in order to give
weight to his official authority, and some appearance of splendor to the provincial establishment. [Jan., 1665.]   The same powers were now conferred,
and the same constitution was appointed, as those which had contented the
inhabitants of Albemarle ; and Yeamans was particularly directed to " make
every thing easy to the people of New England," whence the proprietaries
announced that they expected very copious emigrations to Carolina.   This
expectation, more creditable to their discernment than to their integrity,
was obviously derived from the intolerance which yet prevailed to some
extent in New England, and the effects of which were thus distinctly recognized and deliberately anticipated by men who themselves unreservedly
pursued the same illiberal principle in the parent state.   A resolution was
signified at the same time by the proprietaries that the commission of
Yeamans should not prevent the appointment of another governor for a new
settlement which was projected in a district to the southward of Cape Ro-
main, and which acquired soon after the name of Carteret.   The policy

----

[1] Chalmers.   Williamson.

which the proprietaries were thus pursuing, in the establishment of a variety of separate and independent communities in Carolina, each of which had its own distinct assembly, customs, and laws, supplied them in the sequel with abundance of trouble and embarrassment, and contributed to the prolonged feebleness and disunion by which the English settlements in this province were unhappily distinguished. Meanwhile, however, their proceedings obtained the approbation of the king, who presented them with twelve pieces of ordnance, which were conveyed to Charles River along with a collection of military stores.[1]

Having now obtained a minute acquaintance with the whole coast of Carolina, and discovered, at both extremities of their territory, large tracts of land of which the acquisition seemed to them highly desirable, the proprietaries easily procured from their sovereign a gift of these additional domains. A second charter, which was consequently issued in their favor [June, 1665], recited and confirmed the former grant, and gave renewed assurance and commendation of " *the pious and noble purpose* " under which these insatiable courtiers judged it decent to cloak their ambition or rapacity. It granted to the same patentees " that province situated within the king's dominions in America, extending northeastward to Carahtuke Inlet, and thence in a straight line to Wyonoke, which lies under the thirty-sixth degree and thirtieth minute of north latitude, southwestward to the twenty-ninth degree ; and from the ocean to the South Seas." The patentees or proprietaries were endowed with all the rights, jurisdictions, and royalties which the Bishop of Durham ever possessed, and were to hold the territory as a feudal dependence of the manor of East Greenwich, paying a rent of twenty marks, and one fourth of all the gold and silver that might be found within it. All persons, except those who should be specially forbidden, were allowed to transport themselves to Carolina ; and the colonists and their posterity were declared to be denizens of England, and entitled to be considered as the same people, and to enjoy the same privileges, as those dwelling within the realm. They were empowered to trade in all commodities which were not prohibited by the statutes of England ; and to convey the productions of the province into England, Scotland, or Ireland, on payment of the same duties as other subjects. And they were exempted, for seven years, from the payment of customs, on the importation, into any of the dominions of the crown, of wines and other enumerated articles of colonial produce. The proprietaries were authorized to make laws for the province, with the consent of the freemen or their delegates, under the general condition that their legislation should be reasonable, and assimilated with as much conformity as possible to the jurisprudence of England. They were permitted to erect ports for the convenience of commerce, and to appropriate all imposts decreed by the assembly. They were authorized to create an order of nobility, by conferring titles of honor, differing, however, in style, from the titles bestowed by the British monarch. Carolina was declared independent of every other province, and subject immediately to the crown ; and the inhabitants were exempted from all liability to judicial suit or process in any other part of his Majesty's dominions, except the realm of England. The proprietaries were empowered to grant indulgences to such colonists as might be prevented by conscientious scruples from conforming to the church of England ; to the end that all persons might have liberty to follow

[1] Hewit. Chalmers.

their own judgments and consciences in religious concerns, provided they disturbed not the civil order and peace of the province.[1]

Such is the tenor of the last of the Carolina charters, which conferred on the grantees a territory of vast extent, and rights which it is not easy to discriminate from royalty. By a strange anomaly, the king, in divesting himself, as it were, of a part of his dominions, in behalf of a junto of his ministers, ostentatiously recommended to them a system of ecclesiastical policy diametrically opposite to the intolerance, which, at this very time, and by the counsels of this very junto, characterized his own domestic administration.[2] As Clarendon still held the office of Lord Chancellor, this charter, as well as the former, in favor of himself and his colleagues, was sealed by his own hands ; and when we consider how liberally it endowed the proprietaries with privileges, at the expense of the prerogative of the crown, it seems the less surprising that he should not have suggested a similar objection to the charters which Connecticut and Rhode Island obtained while the great seal was in his keeping. The arbitrary commission for Massachusetts, which we have seen him defend, shows that he entertained no general design of abridging the royal prerogative in the British colonies.

Animated by this fresh acquisition, the proprietaries exerted themselves, for several years, to promote the resort of inhabitants to their domains from Scotland, Ireland, the West Indies, and the northern colonies of America ; but, notwithstanding all their endeavours, the province, partly from the unhealthiness of its climate, but chiefly from the state of dispersion in which the planters chose to live, advanced but slowly in population and strength. In the autumn of the present year, the emigrants from Barbadoes, conducted by Sir John Yeamans, arrived at their place of destination, on the southern bank of the river of Cape Fear, where they corroborated their formal title from the proprietaries by an equitable purchase of the territory from the neighbouring Indians. While they were employed in the first rude toils requisite to their establishment in the wilderness which they had undertaken to subdue, their leader ruled them with the mildness of a parent, and cultivated the good-will of the aborigines so successfully, that for some years they were enabled to prosecute their labors without danger or distraction. As the planters opened the forest to obtain space for the operations of tillage, they necessarily prepared timber for the uses of the cooper and builder, which they transmitted to the insular colony whence they had emigrated ; a commencement of commerce, which, however feeble, served to cherish their hopes and encourage their industry.[3]

The inhabitants of Albemarle continued, meanwhile, to pursue their original employments in peace, and from the cultivation of tobacco and Indian corn obtained the materials of an inconsiderable traffic with the merchant-vessels of New England. About two years after the acquisition of their second charter [Oct., 1667], the proprietaries appointed Samuel Stevens, a man whose parts and virtue were judged equal to the trust, to succeed Drummond as governor of Albemarle ; and at the same time bestowed on this settlement a constitution, which, had it been faithfully maintained,

---

[1] Lawson's *History of Carolina.* Williamson.

[2] A remarkable counterpart of this inconsistency was exhibited in 1766, when George the Third, at the very time when he was inflicting privations and disabilities on his Catholic subjects in Ireland and his Socinian subjects in England, addressed a pious remonstrance to the Polish diet against similar treatment of the Socinian dissidents of Poland.

[3] Chalmers. Williamson.

would doubtless have promoted the content and prosperity of the people. Stevens was directed to conduct his administration in conformity with the advice of a council of twelve, of which he himself was to appoint one half, and the other six were to be elected by the assembly. This was an approach to a principle disallowed entirely in Virginia and Maryland, but exemplified still more perfectly in the New England States, and by which the democratical branch of the government was admitted to a share in composing and controlling that body which in the colonial constitutions formed equally the senatorial or aristocratical branch of the legislature, the privy council of the supreme magistrate, and the judicial court of appeals. The assembly was to be composed of the governor, the council, and a number of delegates, annually chosen by the freeholders. The legislature, in which democratic interests were admitted thus strongly to preponderate, was invested not only with the power of making laws, but with a considerable share of the executive authority ; with the right of convoking and adjourning itself, of appointing municipal officers, and of nominating and inducting ministers to ecclesiastical benefices. Various regulations provided for the security of property ; in particular, it was proclaimed that no taxes should be imposed without the consent of the assembly ; and the lands possessed by the colonists were anew confirmed to them, and declared to be now holden by the free tenure of soccage. Perfect freedom in respect of religion was offered to a people who were very willing to accept freedom without concerning themselves at all about religion ; and an entire equality of political rights was assured to all classes of persons taking the oath of allegiance to the king and of fidelity to the proprietaries. As we have but too much reason to suppose that the proprietaries did not sincerely intend to preserve the constitution which they now affected to establish, it is due to the character of Lord Clarendon to remark that he had no share whatever in this transaction ; his impeachment and exile from England having previously sequestrated him from all farther concern with the government of Carolina.

The system, however, which was tendered to their acceptance, was received by the inhabitants of Albemarle with perfect satisfaction ; gratitude, perhaps, it would have been unreasonable to expect from them towards proprietaries who had in no way contributed to their occupation of the province, but had followed them into a desert with the obvious intent of reaping where they had not sown, and congregating a scattered flock for the purpose of enriching themselves with its tributary fleeces. It was not till two years after [1669], that an assembly constituted on the new model was convened to enact laws for men, who, being yet few in number, seem to have been governed till then chiefly by the usages they had brought with them from their former settlement. Their first efforts in legislation were characteristic of persons accustomed to live remote from the discipline of strict law and an active government, and to shift their local position whenever it ceased to be perfectly agreeable to them, instead of seeking to alter and improve its circumstances. From the number of persons of broken fortunes who resorted to the American colonies, and from the conviction that was early and most justly entertained by all the colonists, that their industry was fettered and their advantages impaired by the legislature of England, for the benefit of her own domestic population, a defensive, or perhaps retributory, spirit was too readily admitted by the provincial legislatures ; and, if not a universal, it was at least a general, principle of their policy to obstruct the recovery

DD

of debts, especially of such as were due to European creditors. Of this disposition we have already noted some traces, about the same period of time, in the legislation of Virginia.

By the assembly now convened at Albemarle, it was declared that sufficient encouragement had not yet been afforded to the resort of settlers and the peopling of the province ; and to supply this defect, it was enacted that no settler could be sued, during five years after his arrival in the country, for any cause of action arising beyond its limits ; and that none of the inhabitants should be at liberty to accept a power of attorney to sue their neighbours for debts contracted abroad.[1] These complaints of thinness of population continued long to be reiterated by the inhabitants of Carolina ; though it was afterwards, justly enough, recriminated upon them by the proprietaries, that the inconvenience they complained of was promoted by their own aversion to settle in towns, and by the lazy rapacity with which every planter endeavoured to surround himself with a large expanse of property, over the greater part of which he could exercise no farther act of ownership than that of excluding other occupants by whom it might be profitably cultivated. The remedy, likewise, which was applied by the provincial assembly, seems to be defective in policy, no less than in justice. If industry might be expected to derive some encouragement from the assurance that its gains were not to be carried off by former creditors in a distant country, the nature of this encouragement, as well as its temporary duration, tended to attract neither a respectable nor a stationary race of inhabitants ; and accordingly this colony was long considered as the peculiar asylum of fugitive debtors and criminals. But a more suitable and reasonable encouragement to population was afforded by an act concerning marriage ; which provided, that, as people might desire to marry, while as yet there were no ministers of religion in the colony, — in order that none might be restrained from a step so necessary for the preservation of mankind, any man and woman presenting themselves to the governor and council, along with a few of their neighbours, and declaring their mutual purpose to unite in matrimony, should be legally deemed husband and wife.

The circumstances indicated by this law forcibly suggest the wide distinction between the sentiments and habits of the northern and the southern colonists of America. While all the colonial establishments of New England were conducted by clergymen, who long directed with almost equal authority in temporal and in spiritual concerns ; not a trace of the existence of such an order of men is to be found in the laws of Carolina, during the first twenty years of its history ; and it was not till after a considerable body of dissenters from the church of England had emigrated thither, that we hear of religious worship or inquiry, or indeed of any thing akin to religion, in the province. Other regulations, besides those which we have already noticed, were adopted by this assembly. New settlers were exempted from taxes for a year ; and every proprietor of land was restrained from transferring it for two years after its acquisition. The first of these laws was intended to invite settlers ; the second appears to have been a politic device to retain them. A duty of thirty pounds of tobacco was

[1] The same policy was pursued to a much greater extent by the ancient Romans, of whom Plutarch informs us, that, " not long after the first foundation of the city, they opened a sanctuary of refuge for all fugitives, which they called the temple of the god *Asylæus*, where they received and protected all, delivering back neither the servant to his master, the debtor to his creditors, nor the murderer into the hands of the magistrates." *Life of Romulus.*

imposed on every lawsuit,[1] in order to provide funds requisite for the expenses of the governor and council during the session of assemblies. These laws, which proclaim the weakness and illustrate the early policy of this commonwealth, were ratified in the following year by the proprietaries. As the colonists received little increase from abroad, their numbers advanced but slowly ; nor was it till some time after this period, that they extended their plantations to the southern bank of the river Albemarle.[2]

But although the proprietaries were willing to tender every concession and encourage every hope that seemed likely to retain or augment the population of Carolina, it was not for the purpose of founding and superintending institutions so homely and popular that they had solicited the extraordinary privileges which their charters conferred. Their ambition aimed at producing in Carolina a social scene adapted to the exhibition of all that grandeur, and the maintenance of all those distinctions, that have ever been known to coexist with the theory of liberty ; and the plumage which they had stripped from the royal prerogative, it was their intention to employ for the illustration of their own dignity, and the decoration of their provincial organs and institutions. With this view, about a year before they ratified the enactments of the assembly of Albemarle [March 1, 1669], they had subscribed that memorable instrument which bears the name of *The Fundamental Constitutions of Carolina*, the preamble of which assigns as the reason for its adoption, " that the government of this province may be made most agreeable to the monarchy under which we live ; and that we may avoid erecting a numerous democracy." The task of composing this political frame was devolved upon Shaftesbury, by the unanimous consent of his colleagues, all of whom were deeply impressed with the vigor and resources of his capacity, and some of whom had experienced, in the intrigues that preceded the Restoration, with what consummate dexterity he could accomplish his own purpose, and appropriate to this end the subordinate agency even of persons who were strongly interested to obstruct it. The instrument, indeed, was at first believed to have been actually the production of Shaftesbury,[3] but is now recognized as the composition of the illustrious John Locke, whom he had the sagacity to appreciate and the honor to patronize, and who was united to him by a friendship more creditable than beneficial to the statesman, and no way advantageous either to the character or the fortunes of the philosopher.[4]

The Constitutions of Carolina exhibit a mixture as discordant as the characters of these men ; though in what proportions they represent the peculiar sentiments of either, it is not easy to guess, or possible to determine.

---

[1] It is remarkable that the Carolinians, who thus obstructed by a tax the legal adjustment of disputes, have always been more addicted to duelling than the inhabitants of any of the other North American States. In Connecticut, according to the representation of Dr. Morse, there is more litigation than in any other quarter of North America; but a duel was never known to occur in Connecticut. Warden. In most of the provinces, legal controversy was promoted by the uncertainty of the law ; for although it had been authoritatively prescribed, and was universally recognized as a general principle, that there should be a substantial conformity of the colonial jurisprudence to the common and statute law of England, yet the ascertainment of the precise extent of this conformity in every case was committed to the discretion of the judges. Smith's *New York*.

[2] Chalmers. Williamson.

[3] It is so represented in the first edition of Oldmixon's work, which was published in 1708. But it was afterwards inserted in the collection, published in 1719, by Des Maiseaux, of the anonymous compositions of Locke, from a copy corrected by the philosopher's own hand, and which he had presented to a friend expressly as one of his own works.

[4] See Note XVI., at the end of the volume.

It has been said (whether conjecturally or authoritatively), that Shaftesbury, smitten alike with reverence for antiquity and admiration of Locke, desired to revive in his person the alliance that once subsisted between philosophy and legislation ; to restore the practice of that age when societies accepted their municipal constitutions more willingly from the disciples of Pythagoras than from the cabinets of kings. It is certain, however, that Shaftesbury, along with a very high value for the genius and talents of Locke, reposed implicit confidence in his own ability to employ the full vigor of Locke's understanding, and yet inject into it regulating views that would enable him securely to anticipate and define the general results of its application. What instructions were communicated to Locke by his patron cannot now be known ; but it must be admitted that the philosopher was indulged with so much liberty, that he afterwards represented the *Fundamental Constitutions* as his own performance, and himself as a competitor with William Penn for the praise of enlightened legislation ; and hence, this instrument, whatever may be thought of its intrinsic merits, must ever be regarded with interest, as the link that connects the genius of Locke with the history of America.

By the *Fundamental Constitutions*, it was appointed that the eldest of the eight proprietaries should be palatine of the province during his life ; and that this dignity, on every vacancy, should devolve to the eldest of the surviving proprietaries. Seven other of the chief offices of state, namely, the offices of admiral, chamberlain,[1] chancellor, constable,[2] chief justice, high steward, and treasurer, were appropriated exclusively to the other seven proprietaries ; and the duties of those functionaries, as well as of the palatine, might be executed by deputies residing within the province. Corresponding to these offices, there were to be (besides the ordinary courts of every county) *eight supreme courts*, to each of which was annexed a college of twelve assistants. The palatine was to preside in the palatine's court, wherein he and three others of the proprietaries formed a quorum of functionaries ; and this court represented the king, ratified or negatived the enactments of the legislature, and, in general, was vested with the administration of all the powers conferred by the royal charter, except in so far as limited by collateral provisions of the Fundamental Constitutions. By a complicated frame of *counties, seigniories, baronies, precincts,* and *colonies,* the whole land of the province was divided into five equal portions, one of which was assigned to the proprietaries, another to the nobles, and the remaining three were left to the people. Two classes of hereditary nobility, with possessions proportioned to their respective dignities, and for ever unalienable and indivisible, were to be created by the proprietaries, under the titles of landgraves and caciques ; and these, together with the deputies of the proprietaries, and representatives chosen by the freemen, constituted the parliament of the province, which was appointed to be biennially convoked, and, when assembled, to form one deliberative body, and occupy the same chamber. No matter or measure could be proposed or discussed in the parliament that had not been previously considered and

---

[1] The chamberlain's court had the care of "all *ceremonies,* precedency, heraldry, and pedigrees," and also "power to regulate all *fashions, habits,* badges, games, and *sports.*" Art. 45. If the functions of this body resemble the ceremonial academy of China, the title at least of another body of functionaries recalls the institutions of old Rome. The assistants of the admiral bore the title of *proconsuls.*

[2] This was a military office, and the members of its relative college of assistants were termed lieutenant-generals.

approved by the grand council of the province, — a body resembling the *lords of the articles* in the ancient constitution of Scotland, and composed almost exclusively of the proprietaries' officers and the nobility.   No man was eligible to any office, unless he possessed a certain definite extent of land, larger or smaller in proportion to the dignity or meanness of the office. Trial by jury was established in each of the courts throughout the whole of the lengthened ramification of jurisdiction ; but the office of hired or professional pleaders was disallowed, as a base and sordid occupation ; and no man was admitted to plead the cause of another without previously deposing on oath that he neither had received nor would accept the slightest remuneration for his service.   To avoid the confusion arising from a multiplicity of laws, all acts of the provincial parliament were appointed to endure only one hundred years, after which they were to cease and expire of themselves, without the formality of an express repeal ; and to avoid the perplexity created by a multiplicity of commentators, all written comments whatever on the Fundamental Constitutions, or on any part of the common or statute law of Carolina, were strictly prohibited.   Every freeholder was required to pay a yearly rent of a penny for each acre of his land to the proprietaries ; and all the inhabitants above seventeen and under sixty years of age were obliged to bear arms, and serve as soldiers, whenever they should receive a summons to this duty from the grand council.   Every freeman of Carolina was declared to possess *absolute power and authority over his negro slaves, of what opinion or religion soever*.[1]   The apology that most readily suggests itself for such a regulation is excluded by the fact, that at this time [1669], and long after, there were no negroes in the province, except a very small number whom Sir John Yeamans and his followers brought with them from Barbadoes.[2]

A series of regulations that not only import the most ample toleration in religion, but manifestly infer the political equality of all religious sects and systems whatever, was ushered by this remarkable provision : — " Since the natives of the place who will be concerned in our plantation are utterly strangers to Christianity, whose idolatry, ignorance, or mistake, gives us no right to expel or use them ill ; and those who remove from other parts to plant there will unavoidably be of different opinions concerning matters of religion, the liberty whereof they will expect to have allowed them, and it will not be reasonable for us on this account to keep them out ; that civil peace may be maintained amidst the diversity of opinions, and our agreement and compact with all men may be duly and faithfully observed ; the violation whereof, upon what pretence soever, cannot be without great offence to Almighty God, and great scandal to the true religion which we profess ; and also that Jews, heathens, and other dissenters from the purity of Christian religion, may not be scared and kept at a distance from it, but, by having an opportunity of acquainting themselves with the truth and

---

[1] It is humiliating to reflect that this regulation was composed by the hand that wrote the *Essay on the Human Understanding*.   At a later period of his life, when the English Revolution and the controversies it engendered had enlightened Locke's ideas of the rights of men, we find him thus pronouncing his own condemnation, while he exposes and confutes the servile sophistry of Sir Robert Filmer.   " Slavery is so vile and miserable an estate of man, and so directly opposite to the generous temper and courage of our nation, that it is hardly to be conceived that an Englishman, much less a gentleman, should plead for it."   " The perfect condition of slavery " he afterwards defines to be " *the state of war* continued between a *lawful conqueror* and a captive."

[2] Hewit.

reasonableness of its doctrines, and the peaceableness and inoffensiveness of its professors, may by good usage and persuasion, and all those convincing methods of gentleness and meekness suitable to the rules and design of the gospel, be won over to embrace and unfeignedly receive the truth ; therefore any seven or more persons agreeing in *any religion* shall constitute a church or profession, to which they shall give some name to distinguish it from others." In the terms of communion of every such *church or profession*, it was required that the three following articles should expressly appear : that there is a God ; that public worship is due from all men to this Supreme Being ; and that it is incumbent on every citizen, at the command of the civil magistrate, to deliver judicial testimony with some ceremonial or form of words, indicating a recognition of divine justice and human responsibility. Only the acknowledged members of some *church or profession* of this description were to be capable of becoming freemen of Carolina, or of possessing any estate or habitation within the province ; and all persons were forbidden to revile, disturb, or in any way persecute the members of any of the religious associations thus recognized by law. What was *enjoined* to freemen was *permitted* to slaves, by an article which declared, that, " since charity obliges us to wish well to the souls of all men, and religion ought to alter nothing in any man's civil estate or right, *it shall be lawful* for slaves, as well as others, to enter themselves, and be of what church or profession any of them shall think best, and thereof be as fully members as any freeman." But the hope of political equality that dissenters from the church of England might derive from these provisions was completely defeated, and even the security of a naked tolerance of their tenets and practices was menaced, by an article, which, though introduced into the Fundamental Constitutions, was neither composed nor approved by Locke,[1] and by which it was provided, that, whenever the country should be sufficiently peopled and planted, the provincial parliament should enact regulations for the building of churches and the public maintenance of divines, to be employed in the exercise of religion, according to the canons of the church of England ; " which, being *the only true and orthodox*, and the national religion of all the king's dominions, is so also of Carolina ; and therefore it alone shall be allowed to receive public maintenance by grant of parliament." Finally, it was declared that these Fundamental Constitutions, consisting of one hundred and twenty articles, and forming a vast labyrinth of perplexing regulations (intended rather than calculated to secure an apt intertexture of all the parts in the general frame), should be the sacred and unalterable form and rule of government of Carolina for ever.[2] Thus, by the labor and genius of European philosophers and politicians, the most cumbrous, operose, and illiberal system of government ever engendered by theory or practice was composed for a country, which, under the guidance of sounder sense and manlier spirit in her own native population, has since been renowned over all the earth for the simplicity, efficacy, and generosity of her municipal institutions and policy.

The faults and absurdities of the foregoing system are at once so numerous and so palpably manifest, that to particularize them would be tedious and superfluous toil. It may be remarked, in general, that the authors

---

[1] " This article was not drawn up by Mr. Locke, but inserted by some of the chief of the proprietors, against his judgment ; as Mr. Locke himself informed one of his friends to whom he presented a copy of these Constitutions." Locke's *Works* (folio edit.), Vol. III., p. 676.
[2] Locke.

of it, in collecting materials for their composition, seem to have entirely disregarded or misconceived the actual situation and habits of the people for whom the legislative experiment was intended. Lawgivers, who derive their function from any other source than popular election, are so little accustomed, in the exercise of it, to consider themselves obliged to treat others as they would have others treat them, that the partiality and illiberality of these institutions would scarcely merit notice, if Locke had not been their principal author. It was a reproach more exclusively due to the proprietaries, that good faith was violated and existing rights disregarded. For a number of inhabitants had already settled in the province, on conditions which their rulers were no longer entitled to abrogate or qualify ; and forms of government having been actually established, the people had acquired an interest in them, which, without their consent, ought not to have been sacrificed to those innovating regulations. The proprietaries might perhaps have been led to doubt the reasonableness of their expectations, if not the equity of their purposes, had they fairly considered the motives which retained themselves in England, and anticipated the probable operation of similar sentiments on the minds of the inhabitants of Carolina. It is reported of some ancient legislators, that they sacrificed their own lives in order to secure the reception or the perpetuity of their constitutions. But while the proprietaries of Carolina could not prevail on themselves to resign the comforts and luxuries of England, and even deliberately anticipated their non-residence, by providing for the vicarious discharge of their functions, they expected that an infant colony of independent woodsmen and laborious tobacco-planters should at once renounce their manners and their habits of life, enchain their liberties, abridge their gains, and nearly metamorphose themselves into a new order of beings, for the sake of accumulating dignity on persons whom even the enjoyment of such dignity could not induce to live in the country. It is hard to say whether there was greater folly or injustice in projecting a social system where such overweening concern was admitted in the rulers, and such gross indifference supposed in the people, for their respective interests ; where the multitude were expected to sacrifice their liberty and prosperity, in order to enhance the advantages of certain conspicuous stations, which those for whom they were reserved judged unworthy of their personal occupation. Shaftesbury was the head of the anti-Catholic party in England ; and Locke assisted with his pen to propagate the suspicions which his patron professed to entertain of the designs of the Catholics against religious and political freedom. Yet if we compare the constitutions of Maryland and Carolina, we cannot hesitate to prefer the labors of the Catholic legislator to those of the Protestant philosopher and politician ; and to acknowledge that the best interests of mankind were far more wisely and effectually promoted by the plain, unvaunted capacity of Lord Baltimore, than by the united labors of Locke's elevated and comprehensive mind, and of Shaftesbury's vigorous, sagacious, and experienced genius.

The proprietaries, however, were so highly satisfied with the Fundamental Constitutions, that they determined to carry them into effect without delay ; and, as a preliminary step, exerted themselves to the utmost of their ability to promote the transportation of additional inhabitants to the province. The Duke of Albemarle was installed in the office of palatine [Jan., 1670], and the sum of twelve thousand pounds expended on the

* ห

equipment of a fleet, which set sail in the beginning of the following year with a considerable troop of emigrants. This expedition, which was destined to found a colony at Port Royal, was conducted by Colonel William Sayle, an officer of considerable experience in military service and command, who received the appointment of governor of that part of the coast lying southwestward of Cape Carteret. As these emigrants consisted chiefly of Dissenters, it is probable that religious freedom was the object they had principally in view ; and that they were not acquainted with the special article of the Constitutions by which the security of this important blessing was endangered. Indeed, at a subsequent period, the colonists indignantly complained that the Fundamental Constitutions had been interpolated, and some of their original provisions disingenuously warped to the prejudice of civil and religious liberty.[1] Sayle was accompanied by Joseph West, a man who for upwards of twenty years bore the chief sway in Carolina, and was now intrusted with the management of the commercial affairs of the proprietaries, on whom the colonists continued for some time to depend exclusively for their foreign supplies.

When the new settlers arrived at their place of destination, they prepared with more good faith than good sense to erect the structure of the political system to which they were required to conform ; but, to their great surprise, the first glance at their actual situation convinced them that this design was impracticable ; and that the offices which were appointed to be established were no less unsuitable to the numbers than to the occupations of the people. A wide scene of rough toil lay before them, and it was obvious that for many years a pressing demand for laborers must be experienced ; a state of things totally incompatible with the avocations of official dignitaries and the pompous idleness of an order of nobility. Neither landgraves nor caciques had yet been appointed by the proprietaries ; and to have peopled even the subordinate institutions would have been to employ all the inhabitants of the colony in performing a dramatic pageant, instead of providing the means of subsistence. Yet, although the colonists found themselves constrained at once to declare that it was *impossible to execute the grand model*, they steadily persisted in their adherence to it, and expressed their determination to *come as nigh to it as possible*. Writs were therefore issued, requiring the freeholders to elect five persons, who, with five others chosen by the proprietaries, were to form the grand council associated with the governor in the administration of the executive power. A parliament, composed of these functionaries, and of twenty delegates, chosen by the same electors, was invested with legislative authority. So great were the difficulties attending the commencement of their new scene of life, that, only a few months after their arrival in Carolina [1670], the colonists were relieved from the extremity of distress by a supply of provisions seasonably transmitted to them by the proprietaries. Along with this supply, there were forwarded to the governor twenty-three articles of instruction, called *temporary agrarian laws*, relative to the distribution of land, together with the plan of a magnificent town, which he was desired to build with all convenient speed, and to denominate Charles-Town, in honor of the king. To encourage the resort of settlers to Port Royal, one hundred and fifty acres of land were allotted to every emigrant, at a small quitrent, and clothes and provisions were distributed from the stores of the proprie-

[1] Chalmers.

taries to those who were unable to provide for themselves.   The friendly
assistance of the neighbouring Indians was purchased by liberal presents
to the native caciques, who thus performed the only service which dignitaries of this denomination were destined ever to render to the colony.

While the colonists were toiling to lay the foundation of civil society
in the province, the proprietaries were busied very unseasonably with the
superstructure of those aristocratical institutions which they designed to
establish.   The Duke of Albemarle, having died in the course of this year,
was succeeded in the dignity of palatine by Lord Craven ; and shortly afterwards John Locke was created a landgrave in recompense of his services ;
and the same dignity was bestowed on Sir John Yeamans, and on James
Carteret, a relative of one of the proprietaries.[1]   Perhaps it may excite
some elation in the mind of an American citizen to reflect, that, while the
fanciful distinction of an order of nobility, thus imported into his country,
continued to enjoy even a nominal subsistence, John Locke was one of its
members ; and that when he was expelled from the learned halls of Oxford, and a fugitive from England, he was denominated by a title of honor,
and regarded as a chief of the people in Carolina.   But it is disagreeable
to behold this eminent philosopher and truly estimable man accept a titular
distinction to himself in the society where he had contributed to sanction
and introduce the degrading institution of negro slavery.   Happily for the
country with which he was thus connected, and for his own credit with mankind, the order of Carolinian nobles enjoyed but a brief duration ; and the
attempt to incorporate feudal dignity with the institutions of North America
proved completely abortive.

Sayle had scarcely witnessed the establishment of his fellow-colonists
in the new territory to which they removed, when he fell a victim to the un-
wholesomeness of the climate.   On his death, Sir John Yeamans claimed
the administration of the vacant authority, as due to his rank of landgrave,
which no other inhabitant of the province enjoyed.   But the council, who
were empowered in such circumstances to elect a temporary governor, preferred to appoint Joseph West, a man of popular manners, and much esteemed by the other planters for his activity, vigor, and prudence.   West's
appointment, however, did not long endure ; for, notwithstanding this indication of his influence with the colonists, the proprietaries, desirous of promoting the consideration of their nobles, and satisfied with the conduct of
Yeamans in the government of the plantation around Cape Fear [1671],
judged it expedient to extend his command to the new settlement.   The
shores, the streams, and the interior of the country being now perfectly
well known, through the accurate surveys which they had undergone, the
planters from Clarendon on the north, and from Port Royal on the south,
began about this period to resort to the convenient banks of Ashley River ;
and here was laid, during the same year, the foundation of *Old Charlestown*,
which became, for some time, the capital of the southern settlements.   The
proprietaries, meanwhile, with the policy that characterized their previous
proceedings, promulgated *temporary laws*, which they appointed to be observed, till, by a sufficient increase of inhabitants, the government could be
administered in conformity with the Fundamental Constitutions.   One of
these laws, equally prudent and humane, enjoined the colonists to practise
equity and courtesy in their intercourse with the Indians ; to afford them

---

[1] Oldmixon. *History of the British Dominions in America.* Hewit. Chalmers. Williamson.

prompt and ample redress of any wrongs they might happen to sustain ; and
on no pretence whatever to enslave or send any of them out of the country.
Unfortunately, the object of this regulation was very soon defeated by the
intrigues of the Spaniards ; and the other temporary laws received little
attention or respect from the colonists, who were by no means disposed
to acquiesce in such arbitrary and irregular government ; and who very justly
thought, that, if the establishment of permanent laws was obstructed by the
circumstances of their present condition, the temporary arrangements by
which such laws were to be supplied ought to originate with themselves, to
whom alone the exact nature of the controlling circumstances was practically known.[1]

The proprietaries were more successful in their efforts to attract additional emigrants to the settlement on Ashley River than in their experi-
ments in the science of legislation.   To the Puritans, persecuted in England by the existing laws, and ridiculed and insulted by the Cavaliers, they
offered a secure asylum and ample grants of land in Carolina, on condition
of their transporting themselves and their families to this province.   Even
the most bigoted churchmen in the king's council are said to have cooperated
with much eagerness to promote this scheme ; considering severe labor a
wholesome remedy for enthusiasm, and enthusiasm a fit stimulus and auxiliary to novel and hazardous undertakings ; and judging it expedient to diminish, by every means, the farther extension of Puritan sentiments and
practices in Massachusetts.   And although it was to this favorite scene that
the major and the most zealous portion of the Puritan emigrants still resorted, yet a considerable number were tempted, by the flattering offers of the
proprietaries, to try their fortunes in Carolina.   Unfortunately for the repose
and prosperity of the province, the invitations and encouragements to emigrate thither were tendered indiscriminately to men of the most discordant
characters and principles.   Rakes and gamblers, who had wasted their substance in riot and debauchery, and Cavaliers who had been ruined by the
civil wars, were sent to associate with moody, discontented Puritans, and to
enter on a scene of life in which only severe labor and the strictest temperance and frugality could save them from perishing with hunger.   To the impoverished officers and other unfortunate adherents of the royalist party,
for whom no recompense was provided in England, the proprietaries and
the other ministers of the king offered estates in Carolina [1671], which
many of them were fain to embrace as a refuge from beggary.   A society,
composed of these Cavaliers, who ascribed their ruin to the Puritans, and
of Puritan emigrants, who imputed their exile to the Cavaliers, could not
reasonably be expected to exist long in harmony or tranquillity ; and the
feuds and distractions, that afterwards sprung up from the seeds of division
thus unseasonably imported into the infant commonwealth, inflicted a merited
retribution on the proprietaries for the reckless ambition they indulged, and
the absurdity of the policy they pursued.   The dangers and hardships, indeed, with which the emigrants found themselves encompassed on their arrival in the province, contributed for a time to repress the growth of civil and
religious dissension ; but, on the other hand, the same circumstances tended
to develope the mischievous consequences of sending men, whose habits
were already inveterately depraved, to a scene where only vigorous virtue
could maintain a secure and prosperous establishment.   Accordingly, it

----

[1] Hewit.   Chalmers.

was the effect of this part of their policy that afforded to the proprietaries the earliest occasion of repentance.   Of the extent to which impatience and disappointment prevailed among the settlers we may judge from this circumstance, that one of the earliest provincial laws was an ordinance that no person should be permitted to abandon the colony.[1]

The distress which thus attended the infancy of the colonial settlement was aggravated by the hostile intrigues and assaults of the Spaniards [1672], who had established a garrison at Augustine, in the territory to which the appellation of Florida was now restricted from its original comprehensiveness.   The hostile operations of the Spaniards, which even their original pretensions would hardly have warranted, were pursued in manifest violation of a treaty by which those pretensions had been expressly renounced. Prior to the year 1667, no mention was made of America in any treaty between Spain and England ; the former being contented to retain her ancient claims to the whole country, and the other bent on peaceably securing and improving the footing she had already acquired in it.   But at that epoch [1672], which was only a few years posterior to the English occupation of Carolina, Sir William Godolphin concluded a treaty with Spain, in which, among other articles, it was agreed, " that the king of Great Britain should always possess, in full right of sovereignty and property, all the countries, islands, and colonies, lying and situated in the West Indies, or any part of America, which he and his subjects then held and possessed, insomuch that they neither can nor ought to be contested on any account whatsoever." It was stipulated at the same time, that the British government should withdraw its protection from the buccaneers, who had for many years infested the Spanish dominions in America ; and, accordingly, all the commissions previously granted to these pirates were recalled and annulled.   By the same treaty, the right of both nations to navigate the American seas was formally recognized ; and it was declared that all ships, endangered either by storms or the pursuit of enemies or pirates, and taking refuge in places belonging either to Britain or Spain, should receive protection and assistance, and be suffered to depart without molestation.   But notwithstanding this treaty, a certain religious society in Spain continued to assert a claim to the whole region to which the name of Florida had been originally applied, not only on the footing of prior discovery, but by virtue of a special grant from the pope ; and in conformity with this pretension, the garrison that was maintained at Augustine, regarding the British settlement as an encroachment on their countrymen's domains, endeavoured, by every act of insidious and even violent annoyance, to compel the colonists to abandon their possessions.   They sent emissaries among the settlers at Ashley River, in the hope of moving them to revolt ; they encouraged indented servants to desert their masters and fly to the Spanish territory ; and they labored so successfully to awaken hatred and jealousy of the British in the minds of the adjacent tribes of savages, that these deluded Indians, at the instigation of a people whose treachery and injustice they had themselves severely experienced, took arms to extirpate a race who had never injured them, and whose whole demeanour, as well as the express instructions of their rulers, announced a desire to cultivate friendly relations with them.

The colonists were now involved in a scene of labor, danger, and misery, which it is impossible to contemplate without admiring the energy

---

[1] Hewit. Hewit's work was published without his name, which some writers have spelt *Hewit*, and others *Howat*.

and endurance which human nature with all its wants and weaknesses is still capable of exemplifying. Except a very few negroes, imported by Yeamans and his followers from Barbadoes, there were no other laborers but Europeans in the colony ; the brute creation could not replace or even partake human labor, till the ground was disencumbered of wood ; and the unassisted arm of man alone had to encounter the hardship of clearing a forest, whose stubborn strength and thickness seemed to bid defiance to his most strenuous efforts. The toil of felling the large and lofty trees, by which they were surrounded, was performed by the colonists under the dissolving heat of a climate to which their bodies were unaccustomed, and amidst the dread of barbarous enemies, whose stealthy approaches and abrupt assaults they could not otherwise repel, than by keeping a part of their own number under arms, to protect the remainder who were struggling with the forest, or cultivating the spaces that had been cleared. The provisions obtained by dint of such hardships were frequently devoured or destroyed by their enemies ; and the recompense of a whole year's toil was defeated in one night by the dexterous celerity of Indian depredation. The burden of these distresses was augmented by the feebleness, helplessness, and ill-humor of a great part of the recently arrived emigrants, and by the mistakes and disappointments arising from ignorance of the peculiar culture and produce appropriate to the soil of Carolina, to which European grain and tillage proved unsuitable. So much discontent and insubordination was produced by this scene of varied annoyance and calamity, that it was with the utmost difficulty that the governor could prevent the people from abandoning the settlement. An insurrection was even excited by Culpepper, one of the provincial officers ; but it was easily suppressed by the governor ; and the guilty were either mildly punished or humanely forgiven, in consideration of the misery to which their violence was imputed. While Yeamans was exerting himself to compose these disorders, the Spanish garrison at Augustine, learning their occurrence from some fugitive servants of the colonists, judged this a proper opportunity to strike a decisive blow ; and accordingly despatched an invading party, who advanced as far as the island of St. Helena, with the purpose of dislodging or destroying the inhabitants of Ashley River. But either the courage of the invaders was disproportioned to their animosity, or they had overrated the divisions among the English colonists ; for, being joined by only one traitor named Fitzpatrick, and finding that Yeamans was not only prepared to receive them, but had sent Colonel Godfrey with a party of fifty volunteers to attack them in St. Helena, they did not wait the encounter, but, evacuating the island, retreated to their quarters at Augustine. The more formidable hostilities of the Indians were quelled for a time, partly by the conciliatory address of Yeamans, but chiefly by a war which broke out between two of their own principal tribes, the Westoes and the Seranas, and was carried on with such destructive fury, that in the end it proved the ruin of them both.[1]

During the administration of Sir John Yeamans [1673], the colony received an addition to its strength from the Dutch settlement of Nova Belgia, or New Netherlands, which had been conquered by Colonel Nichols and annexed to the English empire. Charles the Second bestowed it on his brother James, who changed its name to New York ; and by the prudence and mildness of the first governor whom he appointed, the inhabitants were

---

[1] Hewit.

reconciled for a time to the change of dominion. But subsequently various circumstances occurred to render the Dutch discontented with their altered situation, and many of them had formed the intention of removing to some other region ; when the proprietaries of Carolina, understanding or anticipating their design, and ever on the watch to promote emigration to their own provincial territory, prevailed with them, by encouraging offers, to direct their course thither, and despatched two vessels, which conveyed a number of Dutch families to Charlestown. Stephen Bull, the surveyor-general of the colony, was directed to assign lands on the southwest side of Ashley River for their accommodation ; and here the Dutch emigrants, having drawn lots for their possessions, formed a village, or villatic settlement, which was called Jamestown. This first resort of Dutch settlers to Carolina produced an abundant flow of emigration to the province ; for, having surmounted amazing hardships by their patience and industry, the successful establishment which they attained induced many of their countrymen in ancient Belgia, at a later period, to follow them to the western world. The inhabitants of Jamestown, at length finding its precincts too narrow for their growing numbers, began to spread themselves over the province, till the original settlement, by degrees, was entirely deserted.[1]

The proprietaries had hitherto supplied the wants of the colonists with an unsparing hand ; insomuch that it was to their ample and seasonable consignments of provisions and other stores that the settlement owed more than once its deliverance from the brink of dissolution. But their patience was not proportioned to the liberality of their commencement ; in the expectations they formed of speedy reimbursement and grateful regard, they omitted to consider some of the most important circumstances in the condition of the persons for whom they had so freely provided ; and quite regardless of the injustice and imprudence with which they had hurried off great numbers of helpless, shiftless men to a scene where they could only encumber, disturb, and discourage the more useful members of the community, they were exclusively and deeply impressed with the largeness of their own pecuniary sacrifices, which seemed fully to warrant the conviction that the colonists had no cause whatever of complaint. Before the end of the year 1673, a debt of many thousand pounds was contracted, in this manner, by the colonists to the proprietaries ; while yet the colonists solicited fresh supplies, without being able to show how the past or the future disbursements were likely ever to be refunded ; and in alluding to the severity of the hardships they underwent, they complained of neglect, and insinuated reproach. The proprietaries were exceedingly provoked and disgusted with this result ; and their disappointment, in concurrence with the Dutch war, rendered their communication with the colony much less frequent than before. Willing, however, to encourage the settlers who had lately emigrated from New York, they despatched another supply, and promised an annual one [1674] ; but, withal, warned the planters to consider how the debt was to be liquidated, since they were now determined, they declared, to make no more advances without assurance of repayment. " It must be a bad soil," they observed, " that will not maintain industrious men, or we must be very silly that would maintain the idle." They transmitted at the same time a large assortment of vines and other useful plants, accompanied by a number of persons who were acquainted with the cul-

---

[1] Hewit.

ture of them ; but they refused an application for a stock of cattle, observing that they wished to encourage planters rather than graziers ; and
they strongly recommended the cultivation of tobacco, till more beneficial
staples could be introduced.   Mutual jealousy and dissatisfaction began
now to arise between the proprietaries and the colonists, and embittered
the whole of their future intercourse.   But a useful lesson was conveyed
to the colonists by the circumstances which thus diminished their reliance
on foreign support and enforced their dependence on their own unassisted
exertions.   The proprietaries ascribed the unproductiveness of the colony
and the poverty of its inhabitants to the misrule of Sir John Yeamans,
who, in the commencement of this year, was forced by ill health to resign
his command, and try to repair his constitution in Barbadoes, where he
soon found a grave.   The factions and confusion in which the colony was
shortly after involved have rendered the annals of this period extremely
perplexing and inconsistent, — obscuring, with an almost impenetrable cloud,
the real characters of men and the connection of events.   Yet, amidst conflicting testimonies, it seems reasonable to believe that the charges of the
proprietaries against Sir John Yeamans were unjust, and either the effusions
of spleen and disappointment, or (more probably) the artful suggestion of an
apology for the main body of the colonists, with whom it was not convenient
for them to quarrel irreconcilably.   The only offence of Yeamans appears to
have been his eagerness to procure ample supplies from the proprietaries to
the colonists ; a policy, which, while the proprietaries were determined to
discourage, they were naturally disposed to ascribe to his own misconduct.
When he abdicated his office, the council again appointed Joseph West his
successor ; and on this occasion the palatine thought proper to confirm the
popular choice, with many compliments to the object of it, which, however
gratuitous at the time, were eventually justified by the prudence and success
of his administration.[1]   The early annals of Carolina are chiefly interesting as
illustrative of a state of society not likely ever again to occur in the world.

From the affairs of the southern plantation, we must now transfer our
attention for a while to the northern settlement of Albemarle. Instructions,
similar to those which had been communicated to Sayle, in the year 1670,
were addressed to Stevens, the governor of Albemarle, at the same period ;
but a system, replete with innovations so unfavorable to the interests of freedom, was received with disgust and even derision by the people, who were
no more disposed to execute the plan of the *Fundamental Constitutions*
than the proprietaries had been to invite their assistance in its composition.
The promulgation of this instrument produced no other effect than to awak-
en the most inveterate jealousy of the designs of the proprietaries ; till, in
process of time, it was reported and believed, that they entertained the
project of partitioning the province, and bestowing Albemarle on Sir William Berkeley as his share of the whole.   This apprehension, though perfectly groundless, prevailed so strongly, that at length the assembly of
Albemarle [1675] presented a remonstrance to the proprietaries against
a measure which they declared to be at once injurious to individuals and
degrading to the country.   Although the remonstrance was answered in
a conciliatory strain by the proprietaries, who graciously confessed that they
had been deficient in attention to the people of Albemarle, and solemnly
promised to preserve the integrity of the province, the displeasure of the
colonists was too deeply rooted to be thus easily removed.   Little satisfac-

---

[1] Chalmers. Hewit.

tion was created by the expectation of more frequent attention from those whose policy had become the object of incurable suspicion ; and a jealous and refractory spirit, taking possession of the minds of the people, promoted sentiments and practices as hostile to subordination, as the policy of the proprietaries was repugnant to liberty. From this period, the history of the northern province, for a series of years, is involved in such confusion and contradiction, that it is impossible to render it interesting, and difficult to unravel its intricacy or make it even intelligible. Chalmers, the most accurate of its historians, has been enabled, by his access to the best sources of information, to rectify the mistakes of other writers respecting the nature and order of the principal events ; but has found it utterly impracticable to account for them. Unhappily, they have been involved in the deeper confusion, from being connected, in some degree, with the violent, but unsteady and mysterious, politics of Lord Shaftesbury.

Shortly after the remonstrance by the assembly of Albemarle, Miller, a person of some consideration in the province, was accused of sedition ; and having been acquitted, notwithstanding the grossest irregularity and injustice in the conduct of his trial, he repaired to England in order to complain to the proprietaries of the treatment he had undergone. Stevens, the governor, died soon after ; and the assembly made choice of Cartwright to replace him, until orders should be received from England ; but this man, after a short attempt to conduct the administration, was so disgusted with the scene of foolish, furious faction in which he found himself involved, that he abandoned the colony altogether and returned to England [1676], whither he was accompanied by Eastchurch, a person whose address and abilities had raised him to the dignity of speaker of the assembly, and who was deputed to represent to the proprietaries the actual situation of their people. The proprietaries, conceiving a favorable opinion of Eastchurch, appointed him governor of Albemarle ; and disapproving the treatment that Miller had received, bestowed on him as a compensation the office of provincial secretary, to which Lord Shaftesbury added a deputation of his proprietary functions. The commissioners of the customs appointed Miller, at the same time, the first collector of these duties in the province. The proprietaries observed with dissatisfaction how little their designs had been promoted or their directions regarded by the provincial functionaries. They had signified their desire to have settlements formed to the southward of Albemarle Sound, and a communication by land established with the southern colony. But this scheme was obstructed by the governor and council of Albemarle, who engrossed to themselves nearly the whole of the trade with the neighbouring Indians, and justly apprehended that the extension of the settlements would divert this profitable traffic into other hands. The proprietaries had endeavoured with no better success to alter the channel of the foreign trade of their dominions, and to promote a direct intercourse with Britain, in place of the narrow system of commercial dealing to which the colonists restricted themselves with the New England settlements. The traders from New England, penetrating into the interior of the province, and bringing their goods to every man's door, obtained a monopoly of the produce of Albemarle, and habituated the planters to a traffic which they preferred, on account of its safety and simplicity, to the superior emolument of more extended commercial transactions. It was hoped by the proprietaries that an important alteration in these particulars would result from the instructions which they now communicated to Eastchurch and Miller.   These officers departed to take possession of their respective appointments ; but Eastchurch, enticed by the prospect of a wealthy marriage in the West Indies, deemed it prudent to remain there till his object was accomplished, and despatched his companion with directions to administer the government of Albemarle till he himself should arrive.[1]

As chief magistrate and collector of the royal customs, Miller [July, 1677] was received with a hollow civility and affected consideration, of which he became the dupe and the victim.   Unaware or regardless of the aversion to his authority that prevailed with a considerable party among the planters, he at once proclaimed designs and commenced innovations that gave offence and alarm to them all.   The settlement, of which he now assumed the governance, consisted merely of a few insignificant plantations dispersed along the northeastern bank of the river Albemarle, and divided into four districts.   The planters were yet but an inconsiderable body ; the *tithables*, under which description were comprehended all persons from sixteen to sixty years of age, amounting only to fourteen hundred ; of whom one third was composed of Indians, negroes, and women.   Exclusive of the cattle and Indian corn, eight hundred thousand pounds of tobacco was the annual produce of their labor, and formed the basis of an inconsiderable commerce, which was monopolized by the traders from New England, who enjoyed unbounded influence in the province.   Remote from society, and destitute of the means of education, the planters were remarkable for ignorance and credulity, and were implicitly directed by the counsels of those traders, who regarded with the utmost jealousy the commercial designs which Miller was instructed by the proprietaries to pursue.   Unsupported by any effectual force, and possessing neither the reputation of eminent ability nor the advantage of popularity, this man commenced his work of reformation with a headlong and impetuous zeal that provoked universal disgust.   He was reproached, and perhaps justly, with some arbitrary exertions of power ; but the rock on which his authority finally split was an attempt to promote a more direct trade with Britain and with the other colonies,[2] in order to destroy the monopoly enjoyed by the traders of New England, whom the proprietaries regarded as insidious rivals, and pernicious associates of the people of Carolina.   On the arrest of a New England trader who was accused of smuggling, an insurrection[3] broke forth among the settlers of Pasquetanke [December, 1677], one of the districts of Albemarle ; and the flame spread through the whole colony.   The insurgents were conducted by Culpepper, who had formerly excited commotions in the settlement of Ashley River, and whose experience in such enterprises seems to have formed his sole recommendation to the regards of his present associates. As the government possessed no force capable of withstanding them, they

---

[1] Chalmers.   Williamson.

[2] Virginia, from her situation, might have absorbed the whole of this traffic, of which she then enjoyed only a very inconsiderable portion.   But so narrow were the commercial views by which she was governed, that two years after this period she passed an act prohibiting "the importation of tobacco from Carolina ; as it had been found very prejudicial." *Laws of Virginia*.   In the year 1681, the governor of Virginia, writing to the English Committee of Colonies, declares that " Carolina (I mean the north part of it) always was, and is, the sink of America, the refuge of our renegadoes, and, till in better order, dangerous to us." *State Papers, apud* Chalmers.

[3] This insurrection, it will be remarked, broke out but a few months after the suppression of Bacon's rebellion in Virginia.   But no connection has been traced between these two events.

overpowered it without difficulty or resistance ; and having deposed the president, who was the chief object of their indignation, they committed him and seven of the proprietary deputies to prison. They seized the provincial treasure, amounting to three thousand pounds, which they appropriated to the support of the revolt ; they established courts of justice, appointed officers, convoked a parliament, inflicted punishments on all who presumed to oppose them, and, for some time, exercised the authority of an independent government. As there had been no example of a revolt unaccompanied by a manifesto, the insurgents of Pasquetanke, in conformity with this usage, commenced their revolutionary movement, by publishing a feeble, frivolous composition, entitled *A Remonstrance to the People of Albemarle*, in which they complained of various wrongs, which they imputed to Miller, and declared the object they had in view to be the convocation of a free parliament, by whose instrumentality the grievances of the country might be ascertained and represented to the proprietaries. But the subsequent conduct of the insurgents demonstrated how little of real deference the proprietaries enjoyed with them ; for, on the arrival of Eastchurch [1678], to whose commission and conduct no objection could be made, they derided his authority, and denied him obedience. He applied for assistance to the governor of Virginia ; but died of vexation before a force sufficient for his purpose could be assembled.[1]

After two years of successful revolt, the insurgents, apprehensive of an invasion from Virginia [1679], despatched Culpepper and Holden to England, to offer submission to the proprietaries, on condition of their past proceedings being ratified, and Miller proclaimed and punished as a delinquent. This unfortunate president, and the other officers, who had languished meanwhile in imprisonment, having found means to escape, appeared in England at the same time [1680], and filled the court and the nation with complaints of their own sufferings, and accusations of their persecutors. If the proprietaries could have ventured to act with vigor, and in conformity with their own notions of right, it was the representation of this latter party that would doubtless have prevailed with them. But while they hesitated to embroil themselves irreconcilably with the colonists, their perplexity was increased by the encouragement which Shaftesbury thought proper to extend, in the most open manner, to Culpepper. That enterprising politician, who was now pursuing the last revolutionary projects that distinguished the career of his profligate ambition, and whose recent espousal of the popular cause in England placed him at variance with some of his brother proprietaries, plainly saw, that Culpepper, possessing the confidence of the people of Albemarle, was capable of becoming a useful instrument in the province, and that Miller, his ancient deputy, was unfit to lend him any assistance. Culpepper, thus powerfully countenanced, seemed to have prevailed over his opponents, and was preparing to return to Carolina, when he was accused by the commissioners of the customs (at the private instigation, most probably, of the palatine, and others of the proprietaries) of the offences of acting as collector without their authority, and of embezzling the king's revenue. He was arrested on board a vessel in the Downs, by a warrant from the privy council ; and his case being referred to the Committee of Plantations, the proprietaries no longer scrupled, nor indeed could in decency refuse, to come forward as his accusers ; in conse-

---

[1] Chalmers. Williamson.

E E *

quence of which, the report of the committee impeached him not only of embezzlement of the customs, but of having promoted a rebellion in the province. It was in vain for him to acknowledge the facts laid to his charge, and beg for mercy, or at least that his trial might take place in Carolina, where the offences had been committed ; his powerful accusers were determined to wreak the uttermost vengeance on so daring an opponent of legitimate authority ; and, in conformity with a statute of Henry the Eighth, which enacted that foreign treasons might be judged and punished in England, he was brought to trial in the Court of King's Bench, on an indictment of high treason committed without the realm. There is no departure from justice in requiring a colonial governor, or other public officer delegated by the parent state, to answer before her domestic tribunals for betraying the trust or perverting the power which he derived from her appointment. But Culpepper had not been an officer of the British government ; and, however consonant with the statute law of Henry the Eighth, it was plainly repugnant to the spirit of the English common law, as well as to the principles of equity, to compel him to take his trial at such a distance from all to whom his conduct and character were known, and in a community to which the witnesses on both sides must be strangers, and where conflicting testimony could not be properly balanced. It must be confessed, however, that, from the actual state of the province, the British government was reduced to the alternative of either trying him in England, or not trying him at all. His destruction at first appeared inevitable ; for the judges pronounced, that to take up arms against the proprietary government was treason against the king ; and the amplest evidence was produced of every circumstance requisite to substantiate the charge. But Shaftesbury, who was then at the zenith of his popularity, appearing in behalf of the prisoner, and representing, contrary to the most undoubted facts, that there had never been any regular government in Albemarle, and that its disorders were mere feuds between the planters, which at worst could amount to no higher offence than a riot, easily prevailed with the jury to return a verdict of acquittal.[1] [1680.] This was the last transaction by which Shaftesbury signalized his participation in the government or affairs of Carolina. His attention, thenceforward, was absorbed by the deep and daring cabals that preceded his exile ; and, about three years afterwards, having ruined or dishonored every party with which he had been connected, he was obliged to fly from England, and implore the hospitality and protection of the Dutch, whom he had formerly exhorted the English parliament to extirpate from the face of the earth. The ruin of this ablest of the proprietaries extended its influence to the fortunes of the most distinguished of the landgraves. Locke had been so intimately connected with Shaftesbury, that he deemed it prudent to retire from England at the same time ; but so remote was he from any accession to the guilt of his patron, that, when William Penn afterwards prevailed on James the Second to consent to the pardon and recall of Locke, the philosopher refused to accept a pardon, declaring that he had done nothing that required it.[2]

Meanwhile, the palatine, and the majority of the proprietaries, reduced to their former perplexity by the acquittal of Culpepper, pursued a temporizing policy, that degraded their own authority, and cherished the factions and ferments of the colony. Fluctuating between their resentments and

[1] *British Empire in America.* Ventris's *Reports.* Chalmers. Williamson.
[2] *Life of Locke.* Clarkson's *Life of Penn.*

their apprehensions, they alternately threatened the insurgents and reproached their own partisans. The inevitable consequence of this policy was to exasperate still farther all parties in the colony against each other, without attaching any to the proprietaries, who very soon discovered that it was no longer in their power either to overawe their mutinous subjects by vigor, or to conciliate them by lenity. [1681.] Abandoning, then, the hopeless attempt to vindicate their insulted authority, they are said to have adopted the humbler purpose of accommodating their pretensions and the strain of their government in future to whatever degree of obedience the colonists might be disposed to yield them. Having established a temporary administration, at the head of which they placed one Harvey as president, they announced, immediately after, their intention to send out as permanent governor Seth Sothel, who had purchased Lord Clarendon's share of the province, and whose interest and authority they hoped would effectually conduce to the restoration of order and tranquillity. But these measures were productive only of additional disappointment. Little regard was paid to the rule of Harvey by men who were already apprized that his government would have but a short duration ; and the proprietaries, along with the tidings of his inefficiency, received intelligence of the capture of Sothel on his voyage by the Algerines. Undismayed by so many disappointments, the proprietaries, now resolutely embracing a mild and accommodating policy, pursued it with commendable perseverance ; and Henry Wilkinson, a man from whose prudence more happy results were expected, was appointed governor of the whole of that portion of Carolina stretching from Virginia to the river Pamlico, and five miles beyond it. The most earnest endeavours were forthwith employed by the proprietaries to heal the existing disorders. To the governor and council they recommended in persuasive language the promotion and exemplification of forbearance and indulgence ; and, in compliance with their desire, an act of oblivion was passed by the assembly of Albemarle in favor of the late insurgents, on condition of their restoring the money of which they had plundered the provincial treasury. But it was found easier to inculcate the virtue of moderation on the parties who had suffered wrong, than on those who had inflicted it ; and the late insurgents, who were still the stronger, or at least the more vigorous, of the two factions, not only contemned the conditions of an act which they felt to be quite unnecessary to their security, but, acquiring the command of the assembly, proceeded, with triumphant insolence and injustice, to denounce and punish the party which had so far mistaken its situation as to proffer terms of pardon and indulgence to them. They inflicted fines and imprisonment on their opponents, who were forced to seek shelter in Virginia, and with whom every trace of justice and freedom took a long leave of the unhappy settlement.

The miserable scene of violence and anarchy that ensued was not abridged, nor was the condition of Albemarle in any degree meliorated, by the arrival of Sothel as governor, in the year 1683. The character, at once odious and despicable, of this unprincipled man disclosed itself in the very outset of his administration. Though required by the proprietaries to expel from office all those who had been concerned in the late disorders ; to establish a court, composed of the most respectable and impartial of the inhabitants, for the redress of wrongs committed during the distractions of the times ; and to assist the officers of the customs in collecting the royal revenue and executing

the Acts of Navigation, — he declined to comply with any of these mandates ; and, seeking only his own immediate enrichment, disregarded equally the happiness of the people, the interest of his colleagues, and the deep
stake which he himself possessed in the lasting welfare of the colony.
Newly escaped from captivity on the coast of Barbary, he was so far from
acquiring an increase of humanity or a stronger sense of equity from the
experience of hardship and injustice, that he seemed to have adopted the
policy of his late captors as the model of his own government ; nor have
the annals of colonial oppression recorded a name that deserves to be
transmitted to posterity with greater infamy than his.   Rapacity, cruelty,
and fraud, formed the prominent traits of his official conduct, which, after
afflicting the colony for a period of five years, finally exhausted the patience
of all parties, and produced at least one good effect, in uniting the divided
people by a sense of common suffering and danger.   Driven to despair,
the inhabitants universally took arms against his government in 1688, and,
having deposed and imprisoned him, were preparing to send him to England for trial, when, descending to the most abject supplications, he entreated to be judged rather by the provincial assembly, whose sentence he
declared himself willing to abide.   If the colonists, in granting this request,
arrogated a power that did not constitutionally belong to them, they exercised
it with a moderation that reflects honor on themselves, and aggravates the
guilt of their tyrannical governor.   The assembly declared him guilty of all
the crimes laid to his charge, and sentenced him to a year's banishment and
perpetual exclusion from office.   When the proprietaries received intelligence of these transactions, they deemed it proper to signify some disapprobation of the irregular justice of the colonists ; but they expressed a lively concern for their sufferings, and great astonishment and indignation at the
conduct of Sothel.   They summoned him still to answer for his crimes before the palatine's court in England ; and they protested, that, if their people
would render a dutiful obedience to legal authority, no governor should in
future be suffered to enrich himself with their spoils.[1]   Such was the condition to which North Carolina was reduced at the epoch of the British
Revolution.

---

[1] Williamson. Chalmers. Hewit. Hewit has related these proceedings against Sothel
as having occurred in South Carolina. Nor is this the only error with which he is chargeable. He perpetually combines events that are totally unconnected. His notation of dates
is extremely scanty, and sometimes very inaccurate. While he abstains from the difficult
task of relating the history of North Carolina, he selects the most interesting features of its
annals, and transfers them to the history of the southern province. His errors, though hardly
honest, were probably not the fruit of deliberate misrepresentation. Almost all the prior historians of America have been betrayed into similar inaccuracies with respect to the provinces
of Carolina. Even that laborious and generally accurate writer, Jedediah Morse, has been so
far misled by defective materials as to assert (*American Gazetteer*) that the first permanent
settlement in North Carolina was formed by certain German refugees in 1710.

CHAPTER II.

Affairs of South Carolina. — Indian War. — Practice of kidnapping Indians. — Emigrations from Ireland — Scotland — and England. — Pirates entertained in the Colony. — Emigration of French Protestants to Carolina. — Disputes created by the Navigation Laws. — Progress of Discontent in the Colony. — Sothel usurps the Government. — Endeavours of the Proprietaries to restore Order. — Naturalization of French Refugees resisted by the Colonists. — The Fundamental Constitutions abolished. — Wise Administration of Archdale. — Restoration of general Tranquillity. — Ecclesiastical Condition of the Province. — Intolerant Measures of the Proprietaries. — State of the People. — Manners — Trade, &c.

WE now resume the progress of the southern province of Carolina, which, under the governance of Joseph West, whose elevation to its presidency in 1674 we have already remarked, enjoyed a much greater share of prosperity than fell to the lot of the settlement of Albemarle. This governor has been celebrated for his courage, wisdom, and moderation ; and the state of the province over which he presided gave ample scope to the exercise of these qualities: Strong symptoms of mutual jealousy and dislike began to manifest themselves between the Dissenters and Puritans, on the one hand, who were the most numerous party in the colony, and the Cavaliers and Episcopalians, on the other, who were favored by the proprietaries in the distribution of land and of official power and emolument ; and although the firmness and prudence of West prevented the discord of those parties from ripening into strife and confusion, it was beyond his power to eradicate the evil, or to restrain his own council, which was composed of the leading Cavaliers, from treating the Puritans with insolence and contempt. The Cavalier party was reinforced by all those persons whom debauched habits and broken character and fortune had conducted to the province, not for a cure but a shelter of their vices, and who regarded the austere manners of the Puritans with as much dislike as the Cavaliers entertained for their political principles. The adversaries of the Puritans, finding that it was in their power to shock and offend them by a social behaviour opposed to their own, affected an extreme of gay and jovial license. Each party, considering its manners as the test of its principles, emulously exaggerated the distinctive features of its appropriate demeanour ; and an ostentatious competition ensued, in which the ruling party gave countenance and encouragement to practices and habits very unfavorable to the prevalence of industry and the acquisition of wealth. The proprietaries, whose imprudence had occasioned these divisions, were the first sufferers from them, and found all their efforts unavailing to obtain repayment of the large advances which they had made for the settlement. The colonists, who had undertaken to pay the small salary of one hundred pounds a year, allotted to West, the governor, proved unable or unwilling to discharge even this obligation ; and the proprietaries found it necessary, in April, 1677, to assign to him the whole stock of their merchandises and debts in Carolina, in recompense of his service and reimbursement of his expenditure. Meanwhile the population of the province received considerable accessions from the continued resort of English Dissenters, and of Protestant emigrants from the Catholic states of Europe. In the year 1679, the king, willing to gratify the proprietaries, and hoping, perhaps, to

divert the tide of emigration from Massachusetts, ordered two small vessels to be provided, at his own expense, for the conveyance of a band of
foreign Protestants to Carolina, who proposed to add wine, oil, and silk
to the other produce of the territory ; and he granted to the colonists an
exemption for a limited time from the payment of taxes on these commodities, in spite of a remonstrance from the commissioners òf customs, who
insisted that England would be ruined and depopulated if the colonies were
rendered a more desirable residence.   Although the new colonists were not
able to enrich the province with the valuable commodities which they had
hoped to introduce, they preserved their settlement in it, and formed a
useful and respectable addition to its population.   The proprietaries having
learned that the agreeable district called Oyster Point, formed by the confluence of the rivers Ashley and Cooper, enjoyed greater conveniences
than the station which the first settlers had chosen, encouraged the inclination of the people, who began to remove thither about this time ; and
there, in 1680, was laid the foundation of the modern Charleston, a city,
which, in the next century, was noted for the elegance of its streets, the
extent of its commerce, and the refinement of its society.   It was forthwith
declared the seaport and the metropolis of South Carolina.   For some
time it proved extremely unhealthful ; insomuch that from the month of
June till October the courts of justice were annually shut ; and during that
interval no public business was transacted, and the principal inhabitants retired to a distance from the pestilential vapors with which the atmosphere
was tainted.   The inconvenience at length was found to be so great, that
measures were taken for exploring and appropriating another metropolitan
situation more friendly to health.   But happily (in consequence, it has been
supposed, of the purification of the noxious vapor by the smoke of numerous culinary fires) the climate underwent a gradual change, which has
progressively diminished the insalubrity of Charleston.[1]   The lapse of time,
moreover, contributed to render the place less unhealthy to its inhabitants,
by attempering their constitutions to the peculiar qualities of its climate.

Notwithstanding the earnest desire of the proprietaries that the colonists
should cultivate the good-will of the Indians, a war that proved very detrimental to the settlement broke out, in the year 1680, with a powerful tribe
that inhabited the southern frontier.   The war seems to have originated
partly from the insolence with which some idle and licentious planters behaved to the Indians, and partly from the depredations of straggling parties
of Indians, who, being accustomed to the practice of killing whatever animals they found at large, accounted the planters' hogs, turkeys, and geese
lawful game, and freely preyed upon them.   The planters as freely made
use of their arms in defence of their property ; and several Indians having
been killed, the vengeance of their kindred tribe burst forth abruptly in
general hostilities, which for some time threatened the most serious consequences to the colony.   So divided were the colonists among themselves,
that the governor found it difficult to unite them in measures requisite even
for their common safety, or to persuade any one to undertake an effort that
did not promise to be attended with advantage immediately and exclusively
his own.   Conforming his policy to the selfish strain of their character, he
offered a price for every Indian who should be taken prisoner and brought
to Charleston ; and obtained the requisite funds by disposing of the captives

---

[1] Oldmixon. Hewit. Chalmers.

to the traders who frequented the colony, and who sold them for slaves in the West Indies. This system was productive of so much profit, and of enterprises so agreeable to the temper and habits of a number of the planters, that the war was carried on with a vigor that soon enabled the government to dictate a treaty of peace with the Indians. The proprietaries, desiring that this pacification should repose on a lasting and equitable basis [1681], appointed commissioners who were empowered to decide all future controversies between the contending parties ; and declared that all the tribes within four hundred miles of Charleston were under their special protection. But the practices that had been introduced during the war were too firmly established to be thus readily extirpated. Many of the colonists found it a more profitable as well as more interesting occupation to traffic in the persons of the Indians, than to clear the forests or till the ground ; and not only the principal inhabitants, but the officers of government, fomented the spirit of discord that prevailed among the savage tribes, and promoted their mutual wars, for the purpose of enlarging their own marketable stock of slaves, by purchasing the prisoners from their captors. It was in vain that the governor and council asserted, in justification of this system of intrigue and perfidy, that, by diverting the attention of the tribes, and prompting them to expend their force in mutual hostilities, it afforded the most effectual security to the colony against their attacks ; and that humanity sanctioned the purchase of prisoners who would otherwise have been put to death. The proprietaries were by no means satisfied with these reasons ; and, firmly persuaded that it was a sordid thirst for private gain, and not a generous concern for the public safety, that engendered a policy so unhallowed and ignoble, they ceased not to issue the strongest injunctions for its entire abandonment. But their humane interference was long unavailing ; and it was not till after the sharpest remonstrances and menaces that they were able to procure the enactment of a law to regulate, and at length utterly prohibit, this profligate and disgraceful practice. Its continuance was attended with consequences both immediately and lastingly injurious. The traders who carried the captives to the West Indies imported rum in exchange for them ; and a destructive habit of indulging to excess in this beverage depraved the manners and relaxed the industry of many of the colonists. A deep and mutual dislike was formed between them and the victims of their injustice, which the lapse of many years was unable to allay ; and at a subsequent period the Indians inflicted a severe retribution on the posterity of those who had been the authors of their wrongs and the insidious abettors of their ferocity.[1]

Governor West convoked a parliament at Charleston, in the close of the following year [1682] ; when laws were enacted for establishing a militia, which the late war had shown to be necessary ; for making ways through the vast forest that surrounded the capital on every side ; for repressing drunkenness and profanity, and otherwise promoting the morality of the people, who were generally destitute of the means of religious instruction. Shortly after this legislative session, West, who had incurred the displeasure of the proprietaries by supporting the practice of selling Indian captives, and by curbing the excesses of the Cavaliers, who were accounted the proprietary party, was removed from his command [1683] ; and the government of the colony was committed by Lord Craven to Joseph Moreton,

---

[1] Archdale's *Description of Carolina.* Oldmixon. Hewit. Chalmers.

who had been recently created a landgrave of Carolina. This was the commencement of a course of rapid succession of governors and of all the other public officers in the colony ; a system arising partly from unexpected casualties, and partly from unstable policy, and which produced its never-failing consequences, in the enfeeblement and degradation of the government, and the promotion of party spirit and cabals.   But however much the policy of the proprietaries might fluctuate in other respects, it continued long to be steadily and strenuously directed to the increase of population. At the desire of several wealthy persons, who proposed to emigrate to the province, they once more revised their Fundamental Constitutions, which, at the time of their first publication, were declared unalterable ; now again promulgating a similar declaration of their future inviolability.   The object of the present alterations was to relax somewhat in favor of popular liberty the rigor of the original constitutions ; but it is the less necessary to particularize them, as they were never acknowledged or accepted by the people of Carolina, who were more jealous of the power assumed to introduce such changes, than gratified with the particular advantages immediately tendered to their acceptance.

The alterations, notwithstanding, proving satisfactory to the parties who had solicited them, one Ferguson shortly after conducted to the province an emigration from Ireland, which soon mingled with the mass of the provincial inhabitants.   Lord Cardross (afterwards Earl of Buchan), a Scottish nobleman, also led out a colony from his native country [1] (then groaning under the barbarous administration of the Duke of Lauderdale), which settled on Port Royal Island, and, in pursuance of some agreement or understanding with the proprietaries, claimed for itself coördinate authority with the governor and grand council of Charleston.   This claim, however, was disallowed by the provincial government ; and the new occupants of Port Royal having been compelled to acknowledge submission, Lord Cardross, whether disappointed with this result, or satisfied with what he had already accomplished, forsook the colony and returned to Britain.   The settlers whom he left behind were some time after dislodged from their advantageous situation by a force despatched against them by the Spaniards at Augustine, whom they had wantonly provoked by inciting the Indians to make an irruption into the Spanish territory.   But the most valuable addition to its population, which the colony now received, was supplied by the emigration of a considerable number of pious and respectable Dissenters from Somersetshire in England.   This band of emigrants was conducted by Humphrey Blake, the brother and heir of the renowned Admiral Blake, under whom he had served for some time in the English navy, and by whom he was cashiered for deficiency of talent and spirit as a naval officer. Though constitutionally disqualified to excel as a warrior, Humphrey Blake was a worthy, conscientious, and liberal man ; and willingly devoted the moderate fortune bequeathed to him by his disinterested brother to facilitate the retirement of a number of Dissenters, with whom he was connected, from the persecutions they endured in England, and the greater calamities

---

[1] This was, probably, the issue of a transaction which occurred in the preceding year, and which is thus related by Hume : — " The Presbyterians (of Scotland) alarmed with such tyranny, from which no man could deem himself safe, began to think of leaving the country ; and some of their agents were sent to England in order to treat with the proprietaries of Carolina for a settlement in that colony.   Any condition seemed preferable to their living in their native country, which, by the prevalence of persecution and violence, was become as insecure to them as a den of robbers."

they apprehended from the probable accession of the Duke of York to the throne. Several other persons of similar principles and ample substance joined the expedition ; and the arrival of these new settlers contributed to strengthen the hands of the Puritan or sober party in the colony, and to counteract the influence of circumstances unfavorable to the character and manners of the planters. From the exertions of the proprietaries, and the condition of England at the present period, there is little doubt that Carolina would have received a much larger accession to its inhabitants, if the recent colonization of Pennsylvania had not presented an asylum more generally attractive to mankind. The liberality of William Penn's institutions, the friendly sentiments with which the Indians returned his courteous and pacific demeanour, the greater salubrity of the climate of Pennsylvania, and superior adaptation of its soil to the cultivation of British grain, strongly recommended this province to the preference of emigrants ; and such multitudes resorted to it, both from England and the other states of Europe, as soon enabled it to outstrip the older settlement of Carolina both in wealth and in population.[1]

A few months after his elevation to the office of governor, Moreton assembled a parliament [Sept., 1683], which promulgated a variety of regulations for the remedy of sundry inconveniences to which all colonial settlements are liable in their infancy. From a law that was now enacted for raising the value of foreign coins we may date the origin of the domestic currency of Carolina, which subsequently incurred an extreme depreciation. In imitation of the early policy of the community of Albemarle, all prosecutions for foreign debts were suspended. But the proprietaries, now disapproving a policy which had formerly obtained their own express acquiescence, interposed to annul this ordinance, declaring that it was repugnant to the king's honor, since it obstructed the course of justice ; and that the provincial parliament had no power to frame a law so inconsistent with the jurisprudence of England ; and the more sensibly to manifest their displeasure, they commanded that every public officer who had supported the obnoxious proposition should be cashiered. Another cause of dispute between the proprietaries and their people arose from the manner in which this parliament was constituted. The province, at the present time, was divided into the three counties of Berkeley, Craven (including the district formerly called Clarendon), and Colleton. The proprietaries directed, that, of the twenty members of whom the lower house of parliament was composed, ten should be elected by each of the two counties of Berkeley and Colleton ; the third being reckoned not yet sufficiently populous to merit a share of parliamentary representation. Berkeley, which contained the metropolis, was the only one of the counties which as yet possessed the machinery and accommodation of a county court; and the provincial government having appointed the election to take place at Charleston, the inhabitants of Berkeley combined to prevent the people of Colleton from voting at all, and themselves returned the whole twenty members. They insisted that this advantage was due to their own superiority in number of people, — a circumstance which at least enabled them to indulge the pretension it suggested.

When the proprietaries were informed of this disregard of their instruc-

---

[1] Archdale. Oldmixon. Hewit. Chalmers. Warden's *Population Tables of Pennsylvania and the Carolinas. Lives, English and Foreign*, Vol. II.

tions, they expressed the strongest displeasure, and commanded that the parliament should be immediately dissolved, and never again assembled in so irregular a manner.   But their commands were unavailing ; and the unjust encroachment of the Berkeley planters, after maintaining its ground for some time, obtained the countenance and assent of the proprietaries themselves, and continued to prevail, till, at a later period, its abettors were compelled to yield to the indignant and unanimous complaint of the people whom they had presumed to disfranchise.   The proprietaries, meanwhile, were exceedingly offended at the reiterated disobedience of their deputies, and, in a remonstrance which they addressed to the governor and council, reminded them, in language which at least expresses good intention, " that the power of magistracy is put into your hands for the good of the people, who ought not to be turned into prey, as we doubt hath been too much practised."   It was remarked that the dealers in Indian slaves were the keenest opponents of the claim of Colleton county to share in the exercise of the elective franchise ;—a coincidence forcibly demonstrating that the indulgence of selfishness and tyranny in any one relation or department of conduct tends entirely to pervert or extinguish in men's minds the sense of what is due to their fellows.   Although the proprietaries at times express-ed themselves, as on this last occasion, with vigor and wisdom, they seem to have been quite incapacitated, by ignorance or irresolution, from con-ceiving or pursuing a consistent scheme of policy.   It was found that some of the counsellors, and even the commissioners that were appointed to watch over the interests of the Indians, encouraged the traffic in Indian slaves ; and though Moreton was able to remove these delinquents from office, they succeeded in rendering his own situation so disagreeable to him, that he was constrained to resign his command, which was immediately con-ferred by the council on West, who suffered the people to continue the practice of inveigling and kidnapping the Indians without restraint.   The proprietaries then intrusted the government to Sir Richard Kyrle, an Irish-man, who died soon after his arrival in the province.   West, thereupon [1684], was again chosen interim governor by the council, whose ap-pointment, on this occasion, received the acquiescence of the proprietaries. But he was shortly after superseded by Colonel Quarry, who himself re-tained the office only till the following year, when, in consequence of the countenance he was found to have given to piracy, he, in his turn, was dismissed [1685], and Joseph Moreton reinstated in the government.[1]

The American seas had been long infested by a race of daring ad-venturers, privateers in time of war, pirates in time of peace, whose martial exploits, and successful depredations on the rich colonies and commerce of Spain, enabled them to conciliate the regard or purchase the connivance of many of the inhabitants of the British colonies, and even of the authori-

[1] Oldmixon. Hewit. Chalmers. From Oldmixon's *Lists*, it appears that Colonel Quarry held official situations under the crown in several of the provinces at the same time. In the year 1703, he presented to the Lords of Trade a memorial on the state of the American colonies, which is preserved among the *Harleian Collection*, in the British Museum. The main object of this memorial is to recommend an alteration of the colonial constitutions, for the promotion of the power of the crown in the several States, and facilitating the general de-fence of the territorial claims and possessions of England in America. Quarry expresses dislike and disapprobation of every colony in proportion to the freedom of its municipal con-stitution, and dwells with emphatic malignity on "the robbery and villany of the rulers of Connecticut." He undertakes to prove that the charter of Pennsylvania conferred no powers of government. He eulogizes Lord Cornbury, the tyrannical governor of New York, and strongly recommends his appointment to the command of Pennsylvania.

ties, supreme as well as subordinate, of the British empire.   The king himself, for several years after his restoration, extended to them his patronage ; and he even granted the honor of knighthood to one of their number, Henry Morgan, a Welshman, who plundered Portobello and Panama, and acquired a prodigious booty by his achievements.   Thus recommended by the king to the favorable regards of his subjects, those freebooters found it no less easy than advantageous to cultivate a friendly connection with the people of Carolina, who willingly opened their ports and furnished supplies of provisions to guests who lavishly spent their golden spoils in the colony.   The treaty between England and Spain in 1667, together with the increasingly lawless character of the adventurers, had caused the king to withdraw his protection from them ; but they continued, nevertheless, to maintain, and even extend, their intercourse with the planters and authorities of Carolina.   The governor, the proprietary deputies, and the principal inhabitants, degraded themselves to a level with the vilest of mankind, by abetting the crimes of pirates, and willingly purchasing their nefarious acquisitions.   The proprietaries warmly remonstrated against practices so disgraceful to the province, and corruptive of the manners of all who participated in them ; and their orders, backed by a proclamation from the king, prevailed so far as to restrain the colonists from indulging an inclination they had entertained of sharing in the enterprises as well as the gains of their piratical associates.   But they obstinately persisted in their wonted intercourse with these adventurers, — which, diffusing among them the infectious desire of sudden wealth and the relish of luxurious and expensive pleasure, contributed to the formation of habits pernicious to every community, but more particularly injurious to the prosperity of an infant settlement.   Traces of these habits continued long to be discernible in the manners of the inhabitants of Carolina.   The king, at length aroused by the complaints of his allies, and sensible how much the trade of his own subjects was injured by piratical ravages, transmitted to the colony, in April, 1684, " a law against pirates," which the proprietaries required their parliament to adopt and publish, and their executive officers strictly to execute.   The first part of this injunction was readily complied with ; but the evil had become so inveterate, that the law, instead of being carried into effect, was openly violated even by its promulgators.   It was not till three years after, that the evil received an effectual check, from an expedition which James the Second despatched under Sir Robert Holmes, for the suppression of piracy in the West Indies.   Of this expedition the proprietaries sent intimation to the governor and council of Charleston, and recommended to them a prompt submission to the authority, and cooperation with the enterprise, of Holmes ; and their mandates being now supported by a force sufficient to overcome all opposition, those disgraceful proceedings sustained a complete, though, unfortunately, only a temporary interruption.[1]

Meanwhile, the obloquy and disrepute which the province of South Carolina thus deservedly incurred was not the only inconvenience that resulted from its connection with the pirates.   The Spaniards at St. Augustine had always regarded the southern settlements of the English with jealousy and dislike ; they suspected, and not without reason, that the Scotch planters at Port Royal inflamed the Indians against them ; and they beheld with indignation the plunderers of their commerce openly encouraged at Charleston.

[1] Hewit.   Chalmers.

After threatening for some time to avenge themselves by hostilities, they
invaded the southern frontiers of the province, and laid waste the settlements of Port Royal.   The Carolinians, finding themselves unable to defend a widely extended frontier, resolved to carry their arms into the heart
of their enemy's territory ; and deeming themselves authorized by the tenor
of the provincial charter to levy war on their neighbours, they made preparations for an expedition against St. Augustine. [1686.]   But the proprietaries, informed of this project, hastened to withstand it by their remonstrance and prohibition.   Every rational being, they remarked, must have
foreseen that the Spaniards, provoked by such injuries as the colonists had
wantonly inflicted on them, would assuredly retaliate.   The clause of the
charter which was relied on by the colonists to justify their projected invasion
meant no more (they maintained) than a pursuit in heat of victory, and
never could authorize a deliberate prosecution of war against the king of
Spain's subjects within his own territories. " We ourselves," they protested, " claim no such power ; nor can any man believe that the dependencies
of England can have liberty to make war upon the king's allies, without his
knowledge or consent."   They signified, at the same time, their dissent
from a law which had been passed for raising men and money for the projected expedition against the Spaniards ; and the colonists, either convinced
by their reasonings, or disabled from collecting the necessary supplies,
abandoned the enterprise.   Learning this result, the proprietaries congratulated the governor and council on their timely retraction of a purpose,
which, had it been carried into effect, they declared, would have exposed
its authors to capital punishment.   They instructed them to address *a civil
letter* to the governor of St. Augustine, desiring to know by what authority
he had acted in committing the late hostilities ; and in the mean time to
put the province in a posture of defence.[1]   From this period, mutual suspicion and animosity rarely ceased to prevail between the Spanish and
English colonists in Florida and Carolina.

When the governor and council received intelligence of the death of
Charles the Second, they proclaimed his successor with expressions of
loyalty and joy, probably the effusions of mere levity and love of change,
but which gave so much satisfaction to James, that he communicated to
them, in return, the assurance of his favor and protection.   His sincerity
herein was on a par with their own ; for he already meditated the revocation of the colonial charter, and the annihilation of all their privileges.   He
was prevented, indeed, from completing these intentions, and his reign was
productive of events that proved highly advantageous to the colony.   Many
of his English subjects, apprehending danger from his arbitrary principles
and his adherence to the church of Rome, sought beyond the Atlantic
Ocean a retreat from his more direct and immediate sway ; being determined rather to endure the severest hardships abroad, than to witness the
establishment of popery and tyranny in England.   The population of
America, recruited by these emigrations, derived even a larger accession
from the persecution of the Protestants in France, that followed the revocation, in 1685, of the edict of Nantes.   Above half a million of her most
useful and industrious citizens, expelled from France, carried with them
into England, Holland, and other European states the arts and manufactures
to which their own native land chiefly owed her enrichment.   James, af-

[1] Chalmers.

fecting to participate the indignation that was expressed by his subjects at the persecution exercised by the French monarch, hastened to tender the most friendly assistance to the distressed Huguenots who sought shelter in his dominions ; and besides those who established themselves in England, considerable numbers were enabled to transport themselves to the British settlements in America.   Many, also, who needed not his bounty, and who dreaded his designs, purchased estates in America with their own money, and retreated to the same distant region.   Among the other colonies which thus reaped advantage from the oppression inflicted in France and the apprehensions entertained in England, Carolina obtained an acquisition of people.   A number of the French refugees, in particular, having purchased lands from the proprietaries, who were ever on the watch to encourage emigration to their territories, embarked with their families for this colony, and made a valuable addition to its industry, prosperity, and population.[1]

Although the colonists had as yet made but small progress in cultivating their territory, and still found their efforts impeded and their numbers abridged by the obstructions of the forest and the ravages of disease, they were now beginning to surmount the first difficulties and disadvantages of their situation.   Their cattle, requiring neither edifices nor attendance, found sufficient shelter and abundant nourishment in the woods, and increased to an amazing degree.   The planters traded to the West Indies for rum and sugar, in return for their lumber and provisions ; and England supplied them with clothes, arms, ammunition, and utensils for building and cultivation, in exchange for their deer-skins, furs, and naval stores.   This commerce, inconsiderable as it was, already began to attract attention ; and a collector of the customs was established at Charleston, soon after the accession of James to the throne.   The proprietaries enjoined their provincial officers to show a becoming forwardness in assisting the collection of the duty on tobacco transported to other colonies, and in seizing ships that presumed to trade without regard to the Acts of Navigation.   But, although the proprietaries enjoyed in theory the most absolute authority within the province, and seemed, indeed, to engross the whole powers of government, they had long been sensible of the practical inefficiency of every one of their mandates that were opposed to the sentiments or manners of the people.

The injunction which we have last remarked was not only violated, but openly and argumentatively disputed by the colonists and the provincial judges and magistrates, who insisted that they were exempted from the operation of the Navigation Acts by the terms of the provincial charter, — *against which*, they plainly informed the collector of the customs, that *they held an act of parliament to be of no force whatever*.   As the charter was posterior in date to the Navigation Act, this was in effect to contend for the dispensing power of the crown, and to urge against the king himself the very doctrine which he forfeited his throne by attempting to establish. Illegal and dangerous as a plea involving such doctrine may at first sight appear, it will be found, in proportion as we examine it, that it is very far from being destitute of support, whether from natural reason or legal principle.   It was the charter alone that had practically annexed the provincial territory to the British empire ; and it was to the execution and validity of this

---

[1] Hume's *England.* Hewit. Chalmers. Hallam. " Happy America ! " exclaimed the British statesman, Fox, about a century afterwards, — " you profit by the folly and madness of the governments of Europe ; and afford in your more congenial clime an asylum to those virtues and blessings they wantonly contemn."

charter alone that Great Britain could refer for legal evidence of the connection between herself and the provincial population.   The planters, possessing the power of transferring their residence and labor to any region where
they might please to settle, and the benefit of their allegiance to any sovereign whose stipulations in their favor might appear satisfactory to them,
had, on the faith of this charter, and of its due fulfilment in all points,
formed and reared, at a great expense, their present settlement ; and in all
the courts of Great Britain the charter was undoubtedly held a valid paction
in so far as it imposed obligations on them.   There appears, then, nothing
unjust or inequitable in the claim of these persons, that a charter which
formed their original paction and bond of union with the mother country,
on the faith of which their allegiance was pledged and their settlement created, and which was, on all hands, acknowledged to be strictly valid in so
far as it imposed obligations upon them, should be held no less sacred in
respect of the privileges which it conceded to them.   While it enjoyed a
legal subsistence, it was entitled to claim an entire and equal operation ;
and if it were to be set aside, the grantees should have been left at liberty to attach themselves to some other dominion, if they could not arrange
with Britain new terms of a prorogated connection with her.   Yet must
it be acknowledged, that the legal competence, if not the natural equity, of
this plea is not a little abated by the consideration, that it was disclaimed by
the proprietaries, and preferred exclusively by the resident provincial population.   The proprietaries vainly disputed the reasonableness of the provincial plea, and as vainly prohibited the continuance of the relative practices.
Neither awed by their authority, nor convinced by their reasonings, nor yet
deterred by the frequent seizures of their own vessels and merchandise,
the colonists continued to defend the legitimacy and persist in the practice
of trading wheresoever and in whatsoever commodities they pleased.
While the proprietaries were struggling with the difficulties of this controversy, they received a new and more painful addition to their embarrass-
ments, from the alarming intelligence, that the king, having adopted the resolution of annihilating all proprietary governments, had directed a writ of
quo warranto to be issued against the patent of Carolina.   Thus, neither
their submission to every royal mandate, nor their readiness to assist, with
their feeble power, the collection of the royal revenue and the execution of
the Acts of Navigation, could protect the chartered rights of the proprietaries
from the injustice of the king.   Yet prudentially bending beneath the violence which they were unable to resist, they eluded the force of an attack
which proved fatal to the charter of Massachusetts ; and by proposing a
treaty for the surrender of their patent, they gained such delay as left them
in possession of it at the period of the British Revolution.[1]

Governor Moreton, after his second appointment [1686] to the presidency of the colony, was permitted to retain it little more than a year.
Though endowed with a considerable share of sense and ability, and connected with some respectable provincial families, he found his instructions
from England so inconsistent with the prevailing views and general interests
of the people, that it was difficult to perform the duties of his office at all,
and impossible to discharge them satisfactorily.   He was a man of sober
and religious disposition ; and being married to the sister of Blake, it was
hoped by the friends of piety and good morals that his authority would

---

[1] Hewit. Chalmers. *State Papers*, ibid.

be strengthened by this alliance, and an effectual check imposed on the more licentious and disorderly portion of the colonists.   But a majority of the council entertained very different views and sentiments from those of the governor with respect to the conduct of the provincial administration, and incessantly claimed much greater indulgences for the people than he felt himself warranted to bestow.   Hence there arose in the colony two political parties ; the one attached to the prerogative and authority of the proprietaries, the other devoted to the interests of popular liberty.   By the one it was contended that the laws and regulations transmitted from England should be strictly and implicitly obeyed ; the other professed and exemplified more regard to the local circumstances of the colony, and maintained that the freemen were required to observe the injunctions of the proprietaries only in so far as they coincided with the interest of the resident population and the prosperity of the settlement.   In such circumstances, no governor could long maintain his authority over a community of bold and restless adventurers, averse to all restraint, and active in improving every occasion of advancing their own interests ; for, whenever he attempted to control their inclinations by the exercise of his official power, they insulted his person, and aspersed his conduct, till they succeeded in having him deprived of his functions.   The proprietaries finding that Moreton was become obnoxious to a considerable party among the people, now resolved, with their usual feeble policy, to sacrifice him to the enmity which his integrity had provoked ; and having accordingly displaced him [August, 1686], they appointed as his successor James Colleton, a brother of one of their own number, and on whose attachment to the proprietary interest they thought themselves entitled to rely.   Colleton's fortune and connections, it was expected, would add to the consideration of his official dignity ; and to lend him the greater weight, he was created a landgrave of the colony, with the appropriate endowment of forty-eight thousand acres of land.   A high opinion was entertained by his constituents of his good sense and address ; but either it was very ill-founded, or he was deprived of discretion and self-possession by the confusions and cabals in which he found himself involved.   To his great mortification, he was quickly made sensible that the proprietary government had acquired very little stability, and was continually declining in the respect of its subjects.   His own imprudence contributed materially to increase the weakness and discredit into which it had fallen.[1]

The commencement of Colleton's administration gave universal satisfaction.   But his instructions, requiring him to undertake what his authority was insufficient to accomplish, — the punishment of almost all the other provincial officers for various instances of disobedience to the proprietaries, and the rigorous execution of the unpopular law against pirates, — very soon embroiled him with a numerous party of the planters.   The form of the municipal constitution, composed of a variety of jurisdictions and investing the parliament with the choice of members for the grand council, afforded perpetual scope and temptation to political intrigue ; and a diversity of factions sprung up, *as rampant*, says Oldmixon, *as if the people had been made wanton by many ages of prosperity.*   A parliament having been summoned by Colleton [November, 1686], the majority of the members openly expressed their disapprobation of the Fundamental Constitutions ; and a committee of their number, whom they appointed to revise and amend that

---

[1] Hewit.

political compact, deliberately composed the frame of a new and very different scheme of government, which they denominated *the standing laws of Carolina*, and transmitted to England for the consideration of the proprietaries. The reception of such a communication might have been easily foreseen. The proprietaries hesitated not a moment to reject those audacious innovations, and to command an instant and unreserved submission to the Fundamental Constitutions thus irreverently handled. But men who had espoused such resolute policy were not to be deterred from the prosecution of their purpose by a consequence so obvious as the displeasure of the proprietaries ; and a majority of the assembly still positively refused to acknowledge the authority of the Fundamental Constitutions. The refractory members were then expelled from the house by the governor ; whereupon, after an open protest against the validity of any laws that might be enacted in their absence by a minority of the commons, they retired into the country, and diligently endeavoured to instil their own principles and discontents into the minds of their fellow-colonists. So successful were their exertions for this purpose, that, when a new parliament was convoked, the undisguised and unanimous purpose of the members was to thwart and contradict the governor in whatsoever proceedings he might embrace, recommend, or be supposed to approve. To this line of policy they adhered with the most inflexible pertinacity ; they even refused to frame a militia act, though the safety of the province, endangered by the Spaniards and their Indian allies, seemed urgently to demand this measure ; and, in fine, to make sure of giving sanction to nothing that could possibly be agreeable to the governor, they flatly declined to pass any laws at all. A dispute in which they engaged with him about the payment of quitrents afforded them an additional opportunity of indulging their spleen and increasing their popularity. Colleton urgently pressed for payment of the arrears of the quitrents due to the proprietaries by the colonists, which, though inconsiderable in amount, were reckoned extremely burdensome, inasmuch as not one acre among a thousand for which quitrents were demanded yielded as yet any profit to the possessors. [1687]. Finding it impossible to accomplish an object so unpopular, without the active coöperation of the other provincial officers, he wrote to the proprietaries, requesting them to appoint as deputies certain persons whom he knew to be favorably disposed towards their authority, and from whom he expected to receive a cordial support in the execution of his official duty. Apprized of this measure, the adverse party scrupled no violence or injustice to defeat or counteract it. Letters from England, suspected to contain deputations to persons obnoxious to the people, they seized and suppressed ; and themselves presumed to nominate other individuals better affected to the popular cause. Advancing in this lawless course, the leaders of the popular party ventured to issue writs in their own names [1688], and convoked assemblies in opposition to the governor, and in utter disregard of the sovereignty of the proprietaries. They imprisoned the secretary of the province, and took forcible possession of the public records ; and without appearing to have any fixed or definite object in view, effected a complete practical subversion of legitimate authority. Only a bold and determined usurper was wanting to possess himself of the power, which they seemed more eager to suspend or overthrow, than resolutely or permanently to appropriate ; and a personage altogether fitted to take advantage of the opportunity did not fail shortly after to present himself. Amidst this scene of confusion, the tidings of the birth of a Prince of Wales were received in the colony, and celebrated by all parties with appearances of sympathy and congratulation ; and yet so unmeaning were these expressions, or so absorbed were the colonists with their own domestic cabals, and so regardless of all changes beyond their own immediate sphere, that the intelligence of the revolution in England, though closely following the other event, excited no emotion whatever, and William and Mary were proclaimed [1689] with the most mechanical regularity and indifference.[1]

Colleton, mortified by the insignificance to which he was reduced, and alarmed by the bold and seditious spirit of the people, vainly perplexed himself with a variety of schemes for recalling them to the recognition of legal authority. His own conduct had been far from blameless, and even attracted censure from the quarter on which he principally relied for countenance and protection. Among other irregularities into which he was betrayed, he had imposed an arbitrary fine of one hundred pounds on a minister, *for preaching* what he accounted *a seditious sermon ;* and the proprietaries remitted the fine, not on account of the illegality of its infliction, but of the exorbitance of its amount. It was finally suggested to him, whether by imprudent partisans or insidious counsellors, that to proclaim martial law, and thereby appropriate to himself an exclusive and unlimited power to punish mutiny and sedition, was the only means that remained of reducing the people to subordination. Actuated by this purpose, though professing to apprehend an invasion of the Spaniards and Indians, he published a proclamation announcing the prevalence of martial law, and requiring every one of the inhabitants to appear in arms for the defence of the province. However legitimate, however consistent with the provisions of the charter, this measure was imprudent in the extreme ; because the colonists, thus summoned to arms, were far more inclined to turn their weapons against the governor himself than against the supposed public enemy. Colleton's policy was easily penetrated, and as easily defeated. The members of the provincial legislature, having spontaneously assembled, resolved, after a short deliberation, that the governor by his recent conduct had made a daring encroachment on their liberties, and an unwarrantable exertion of power at a time when the colony was in no danger from foreign hostility. Colleton, however, driven to extremity, persisted in his proclamation of martial law, and vainly attempted to enforce the articles of war. But he very soon discovered that the disaffection was too general to admit of such a remedy, and that all his efforts served but to unite the mass of the people more firmly in opposition to his authority. It was suggested by some of his opponents, that the sole object of his present operations was to acquire to himself a monopoly of the Indian trade ; and this surmise, with every other imputation, however groundless or improbable, was readily credited by a people to whom for years he had been an object of suspicion and dislike.[2]

During the ferment that ensued on these transactions, Seth Sothel, whom we have seen banished from Albemarle, and recalled by the other proprietaries to justify his conduct, suddenly presented himself at Charleston, and, in the double capacity of a proprietary of the province and a champion of popular rights against proprietary pretensions, laid claim to the possession of supreme authority. [1690.] Hailed at once with the rash and

¹ Archdale. Oldmixon. Hewit. Chalmers.   ² Hewit. Chalmers.

eager acclaim of a numerous party, he succeeded without difficulty in prevailing over the opposition of the governor and the more respectable inhabitants, and in possessing himself of the reins of government, which had long waited and invited the grasp of some vigorous hand. With a specious show of respect to petitions which had been suggested by himself, he consented to convene a parliament ; and, amidst the confusion and distraction to which the province was a prey, found it easy to procure the election of members who were ready to sanction by their votes whatever measures he might propose to them. Colleton was, in this assembly, impeached of high crimes and misdemeanours, and by their sentence not only adjudged incapable of ever again holding office in the government, but banished from the province. Other persons, who were accused of having abetted his misconduct, were subjected to fine, imprisonment, or exile. Having now gained firm possession of the supreme authority, and, under pretence of gratifying the resentments of the people, enriched himself by forfeitures, and disencumbered himself of rival candidates for office, Sothel exercised his power with a despotic energy and indiscriminate insolence, that effectually rebuked and punished the folly of those who permitted him to obtain it, and soon united the southern colony against him in the same unanimous hatred which he had provoked in the sister settlement of North Carolina. He is said to have trampled under foot every restraint of justice and equity, and to have ruled the colonists with a violence of undisguised tyranny, of which the endurance, even for the short period of two years, appears altogether surprising. The replenishment of his coffers was the sole object of his government ; and his financial operations were varied only by varieties of fraud and rapine. The fair traders from Barbadoes and Bermuda were seized by his orders, upon false accusations of piracy, and compelled to purchase their ransom from imprisonment by enormous fines ; bribes were accepted from real felons to favor their escape from justice ; and the property of unoffending individuals was seized and confiscated on the most groundless and tyrannical pretences. The proprietaries, hearing with astonishment of these outrageous proceedings, transmitted letters of recall to Sothel [1692], and threatened, in case of his disobedience, to procure a *mandamus* from the king to compel his appearance in England ; and their orders being now cordially seconded by the desire of the people, the usurper was constrained to vacate his functions and abandon the province. He retired, however, no farther than to North Carolina, where he died in the year 1694.[1]

The revolution of the British government excited very little attention in either of the provincial communities of Carolina, which were too remotely connected with the higher institutions of the empire to be sensibly affected by the changes they underwent. It was from the proprietaries alone that they could expect the interposition of a superior power to arrest or repair the misrule, contention, and other afflictions, that had so long composed the chief part of the history both of the northern and the southern settlements. In the hope of accomplishing this desirable object, the proprietaries, on the deposition of Sothel, intrusted the government of the whole of their domains to Colonel Philip Ludwell, a person totally unconnected with the province and the factions that prevailed in it, and who had been deputed by his countrymen in Virginia to present to the English government their complaints against Lord Effingham.[2] The proprietaries directed their new

---

[1] Hewit. Chalmers. Williamson.   [2] Book I., Chap. III., *ante.*

governor to publish to the inhabitants a general pardon for all crimes formerly committed, to inquire into all real or pretended grievances, and to propose
to themselves the measures he should judge best calculated to preserve order and restore happiness. He was accompanied by Sir Nathaniel Johnson,
who had been governor of the Leeward Islands in the preceding reign, and
who, having now embraced the design of retiring to Carolina, was appointed
a cacique of the province and a member of the council. Ludwell, who
was a man of sense and humanity, and possessed considerable experience
of colonial affairs, commenced his administration in a manner that gave
general satisfaction, and seemed to have completely allayed the ferments
and distractions of the provincial community. But this promising appearance
was of short duration ; the minds of men had been too long and too violently agitated to relapse at once into a settled composure ; and a circumstance which truly betokened the improvement and prosperity of the province proved the immediate occasion of the revival of public discontents.

In the year 1690, a great number of French Protestant exiles took refuge
in England, whence a large portion of them were conveyed, at the expense of the British government, to the colony of Virginia. Others, who
were less indigent, purchased lands in South Carolina (to which we have
already remarked a previous migration of some of their countrymen), and,
having transported themselves and their families to this province, brought
a valuable accession to the numerical strength as well as to the industry
and respectability of its people. The French settlers had taken the oath
of allegiance to the king, and promised fidelity to the proprietaries, and
were disposed to regard the colonists whom they joined in the friendly aspect of brethren and fellow-citizens. But, unhappily, these older colonists
were very far from regarding their new associates with reciprocal confidence and good-will. The numbers of the strangers, and the superior
wealth which some of them were reputed to possess, awakened envy, jealousy, and national antipathy in the minds of the English ; and when Ludwell, in compliance with the instructions of the proprietaries, proposed to
admit the refugees to a participation in all the franchises and immunities
of the other planters, the English and native inhabitants refused to acquiesce
in this measure, and resolutely opposed its execution. They insisted that
it was contrary to the laws of England, and therefore beyond the competence of the proprietaries, who were subject to these laws ; and that no
power but that of the English parliament could dispense with the legal inability of aliens to purchase lands within the empire, or could incorporate
them into the national community, and make them partakers of the rights
and privileges of natural-born Englishmen. They even maintained that
the marriages of the refugees, performed by the clergymen who accompanied
them, were unlawful, as being celebrated by ministers not consecrated by
episcopal ordination ; and for themselves they declared that they could not
brook the thought of sitting in the same assembly with the rivals of the
English nation, or of receiving laws from Frenchmen, the pupils of a system
of slavery and arbitrary government.

Alarmed by these menacing declarations, the unfortunate refugees implored the protection of the proprietaries ; and Ludwell found it necessary
to suspend the measure he had announced, and to apply to the same
quarter for farther directions. The proprietaries returned a conciliatory but
indecisive answer to the application of the refugees, who continued in a

state of anxious solicitude and entire privation of civil rights for several years after ;[1] when, at length, their mild and patient demeanour overcame the antipathy of their former adversaries, who then cordially sanctioned the pretensions they had so stoutly resisted, and passed a law of naturalization in favor of the aliens, without being disturbed by any scruples about invading the functions of the British parliament.   Meanwhile the dispute that had arisen on this subject spread a great deal of irritation through the province, which was increased by the arrival of a crew of pirates, whom Ludwell caused to be apprehended and brought to trial for their crimes.   The people exclaimed against the severity of this proceeding, and interested themselves so effectually in behalf of the pirates, who, previous to their apprehension, had spent a great deal of money very freely in the province, that on their trials they were all acquitted, and the government was even compelled to indemnify them for the expenses and molestation they had incurred.   It was not till more than twenty years after this period that Carolina was finally delivered from the resort of pirates.   Farther disputes now arose between the government and the people about the arrears of the quitrents that were due to the proprietaries, who at length becoming impatient of this untoward issue of Ludwell's administration, and suspecting him of bending too readily to the popular will, deprived him of his office, and conferred it, together with the dignity of landgrave, upon Thomas Smith, a wealthy planter, and a prudent, upright, and popular man.[2]

It was in the midst of these disputes, and with the hope of appeasing them, that the proprietaries surrendered to the general dislike of the people the *Fundamental Constitutions*, which had been originally declared sacred and changeless, but which an experience of twenty-three years had proved to be utterly absurd and impracticable. [1693.]   Apprized of the incurable aversion with which this instrument was now regarded by all classes of the colonists, and despairing of ever establishing a solid or respected frame of government among them without making some considerable sacrifice to their inclinations, the proprietaries with this view embraced and published the following resolution : " That, as the people have declared they would rather be governed by the powers granted by the charter, without regard to the *Fundamental Constitutions*, it will be for their quiet, and the protection of the well-disposed, to grant their request." [3]   Thus expired the political system devised by John Locke. Its fate was unregretted by any party ; for it had neither procured respect to the government, nor afforded happiness to the people. What is still more singular, it seems to have perished unheeded ; its abolition exciting no emotion whatever, and not being even noticed in any public act or order within the province. The convocations that were formerly termed parliaments were now called assemblies ;[4] and this was all the visible change that took place. So perfectly inappropriate and inapplicable had these celebrated Constitutions been found. All that remained of them was the order of provincial nobility, which continued to drag on a sickly existence for a few years longer.[5]

---

[1] This scene was reproduced on a larger scale in England in the following year, when a bill, entertained by the House of Commons, for the purpose of naturalizing the Protestant foreigners settled in the parent state, was withdrawn in consequence of the general indignation which it provoked. Smollett.

[2] Archdale. Oldmixon. Chalmers. Hewit. Williamson.

[3] Chalmers. Williamson.   [4] Williamson.

[5] The operation and fate of Locke's system strikingly exemplify the observation of an eminent American statesman, that " a man may defend the principles of liberty and the rights

This important measure, which had been deferred till the Constitutions which it repealed were practically abrogated by their own inefficiency, failed to produce any sensible effect in tranquillizing or conciliating the inhabitants of Carolina. Governor Smith, though he exerted himself with a zeal and prudence that have not been impeached by any party, to promote the peace and prosperity of the settlements intrusted to his care, found his endeavours so fruitless, and his situation so irksome, that he was constrained to solicit his own dismission from the proprietaries [1694], whom he strongly urged, as the only means of restoring order and tranquillity, to depute as governor one of their own number, invested with plenary power to hear and finally determine on the spot the complaints and controversies by which the province was distracted. The short administration of Smith, nevertheless, was signalized by an occurrence that produced lasting and extensive effects on the prosperity of Carolina. A vessel from Madagascar, on her homeward voyage to Britain, happening to touch at Charleston, the captain, in acknowledgment of the hospitable civilities which he received from Smith, presented him with a bag of seed-rice, which (he said) he had seen growing in Eastern countries, where it was deemed excellent food, and yielded a prodigious increase. The governor divided it between several of his friends, who agreed to attempt the experiment of its culture ; and planting their parcels in different soils, found the result to exceed their most sanguine expectations. From this casual occurrence Carolina derived her staple commodity, the chief support of her people, and the main source of her opulence.[1]

The proprietaries, disappointed in so many attempts to obtain a satisfactory administration of their authority in the province, determined the more readily to adopt the suggestion of Smith. Their first choice for this purpose fell upon Lord Ashley, grandson of the notorious Shaftesbury, and afterwards author of *The Characteristics*. It was supposed that his talents (of which the repute far exceeded the reality), his agreeable manners, and elevated rank, would promote the efficacy of his endeavours for the pacification of the colony. Happily, however, for all parties, his Lordship, either having little inclination for the voyage, or being detained, as he alleged, by the state of his private affairs in England, declined the appointment, which was then conferred on a far more estimable person, John Archdale, another of the proprietaries, a Quaker, and a man of great prudence and sagacity, united with admirable patience and command of temper. Accepting the office, he was invested with authority so absolute and extensive, that the proprietaries thought fit to record in his commission [August, 1695], that such powers were not to be claimed, in virtue of this precedent, by future governors. Archdale proved himself worthy of the distinguished trust that was reposed in him. He arrived first in South Carolina, where he formed a new council of sensible and moderate men ; and in a short time, by remitting some arrears of rent, and by other conciliatory measures, aided by a firmness and mild composure that were neither to be disturbed nor overcome, he prevailed so far in appeasing the public discontents, as to feel encouraged to call a meeting of the representative assembly.

An address of grateful thanks voted by this body to the proprietaries

of mankind with great abilities and success, and yet, after all, when called upon to produce a plan of legislation, he may astonish the world with a signal absurdity." Adams's *Defence of the American Constitutions.*

[1] Archdale. Oldmixon. Hewit.

(the first expression of such sentiments ever uttered in Carolina) attests the wisdom and benignity of Archdale's administration, and justifies the opinion, that, notwithstanding the inflammable materials of which the provincial society was composed, only a good domestic government had been hitherto wanting to render the colony flourishing and happy. Moreton, Ludwell, and Smith were, unquestionably, meritorious governors ; but they had been denied the power that was requisite to give efficacy to their wisdom, and could never grant the slightest indulgence to the people without assuming the dangerous liberty of transgressing their own commissions, or abiding the tedious intervention of correspondence with England. Though Archdale was a Quaker, and therefore opposed to military operations and the shedding of blood, yet he adapted his public policy to the sentiments of the people whom he had undertaken to govern ; and considering that a small colony, surrounded by savage enemies, and exposed to the attacks of the Spaniards, should maintain a constant state of defensive preparation, he promoted a militia law [1695], which, however, exempted all persons holding the same religious principles with himself from bearing arms.[1] While he thus adopted measures for insuring safety, he was far from neglecting the humaner means of preserving peace ; and for this purpose exerted himself so successfully, by the exercise of courtesy and liberality, to cultivate the good-will both of the civilized and savage neighbours of the province, that the Spaniards at St. Augustine expressed for the first time a desire to maintain friendly relations with the English ; and various tribes of Indians courted their alliance, and placed themselves under the protection of the government of Carolina. The Indians around Cape Fear, in particular, who had long pursued the practice of plundering shipwrecked vessels[2] and murdering their crews, renounced this inhumanity, and demonstrated the favorable change of their disposition by mitigating, with charitable relief, the numerous disasters by which the navigation of that coast was then unhappily signalized. Yet how inferior the worldly renown of Archdale, the instrument of so much good, to the more cherished fame of his less efficient and far less disinterested contemporary and fellow-sectary, William Penn !

In North Carolina, the administration of Archdale was attended with equal success, and conducted with greater facility from the coöperation of a number of Quakers who inhabited the settlements in this quarter, and with

---

[1] The following clause, by which this exemption was expressed, illustrates the confidence that Archdale enjoyed with the colonists. "And whereas there be several inhabitants called Quakers, who, upon a conscientious principle of religion, cannot bear arms, and because in all other civil matters they have been persons obedient to government, and ever ready to disburse their moneys in other necessary and public duties : Be it therefore enacted, that all such, whom the present governor, John Archdale, Esq., shall judge that they refuse to bear arms on a conscientious principle of religion only, shall, by a certificate from him, be excused." Archdale's *Preface.* Williamson.

Archdale manifested his own strict adherence to Quaker principles, when (after his return to England) he was elected, in the year 1698, member of parliament for the borough of Chipping Wycombe. He entered the House of Commons ; but, declining the usual oaths, and tendering a simple affirmation instead of them, was not permitted to take his seat in this assembly.

[2] It is remarked by a statistical writer (Warden), that, notwithstanding the temptations presented by the frequency of shipwrecks on the coast of Carolina, no instance ever occurred of the plunder of a wreck by the colonists. In this respect they have been distinguished, not, indeed, from the other colonists of North America, but from the inhabitants of the parent state, in which this inhumanity obtained so long and unreproved a prevalence, that, in the middle of the eighteenth century, Pope represents the enrichment of "a citizen of sober fame " as originating in two rich shipwrecks on his lands in Cornwall.

whom he enjoyed a large share of personal or sectarian influence. The esteem in which he was held by all ranks of men may be inferred from the elation with which the historian of North Carolina has recorded, as a circumstance redounding to the honor of this province, that Archdale purchased an estate at Albemarle, and gave one of his daughters in marriage to a planter at Pasquetanke. But it was not his design to remain longer in Carolina than was necessary for the adjustment of the existing controversies ; and having accomplished this object to an extent that surpassed the expectations of all parties, he returned to England in the close of the year 1696, loaded with the grateful benedictions of a people to whose peace and prosperity he had been so highly instrumental. The only portion of the inhabitants to whom he was unable to give complete satisfaction were the French refugees, against whom the jealous antipathy of the English settlers had not yet subsided. But while he soothed the public jealousy by declining to advocate the political enfranchisement of the refugees, he awakened public generosity by an impressive recommendation of these unfortunate strangers to the hospitality and compassion of his countrymen ; and to the refugees themselves he recommended a patient perseverance in those virtues that tend to disarm human enmity, and by the actual exercise of which they were enabled shortly after to overcome the aversion, and even conciliate the friendly regards, of their fellow-colonists.[1]

It was in this year that a regular administration of the ordinances of religion was first introduced into South Carolina, by the assistance of the colonists of New England. Intelligence of the destitute state of the province in this respect, seconded by the earnest applications of some pious individuals among the planters, had induced the New Englanders, in the preceding year, to form an association at Dorchester, in Massachusetts, which was designed to be removed to Carolina, "to encourage the settlement of churches and the promotion of religion in the southern plantations." The persons thus associated, having placed at their head a distinguished minister of the New England churches, arrived in the beginning of this year in South Carolina, which now for the first time was honored by the celebration of the rite of the Lord's supper. Proceeding to a spot on the northeast bank of Ashley River, about eighteen miles from Charleston, the pious emigrants founded there a settlement, to which, in commemoration of the place they had left, they gave the name of Dorchester.

Among other extraordinary privileges, there was granted to Archdale the power of nominating his successor ; and in the exercise of this power he propagated the benefit of his own administration, by delegating the office of governor to Joseph Blake (nephew of the English admiral), a man of probity, prudence, and moderation, acceptable to the people, and a proprietary of the province. Blake governed the colony wisely and happily for a period of four years. Shortly after his elevation to office, there was transmitted to Carolina a new code of fundamental constitutions, subscribed by the Earl of Bath, the actual palatine, and by the other proprietaries in England ; but it was never accepted or recognized by the provincial assembly. Blake exerted the most laudable endeavours to promote the religious

---

[1] Archdale. Oldmixon. Hewit. Williamson. Some years after his return to England, Archdale published his *Statistical and Historical Description of Carolina ;* a work replete with good sense, benevolence, and piety. He there relates, that, while he was governor, he caused an Indian to be hanged for having, in a fit of drunkenness, murdered another Indian of a different tribe. Here again the politician prevailed over the Quaker.

instruction of the people, and to facilitate the exercise of divine worship to all denominations of Christian professors.   In the year 1698, he had the satisfaction to see John Cotton, a son of the celebrated minister of Boston, remove from Plymouth, in New England, to Charleston, in South Carolina, where he gathered a church, and enjoyed a short, but happy and successful, ministry.   Though Blake was himself a Dissenter, yet, from regard to the wishes and the spiritual interests of the Episcopalian portion of the inhabitants of Charleston, he caused a bill to be introduced into the assembly for settling a perpetual provision of one hundred and fifty pounds a year, with a house and other advantages, on the Episcopal minister of that city. Marshall, the person who then enjoyed this pastoral function, had gained universal esteem by his piety and prudence ; and the Dissenters in the house of assembly acquiescing in the measure, from regard to this individual, the bill was passed into a law.[1] [1698.]   Those who may be disposed to think that the Dissenters acted amiss, and stretched their liberality beyond the proper limits of this virtue, in promoting the national establishment of a church from which they had themselves conscientiously withdrawn, may regard the persecution they soon after sustained from the Episcopal party as a merited retribution for their practical negation of dissenting principles.   Those who judge more leniently an error which there is little reason to suppose will be ever frequent in the world, must regret and condemn the ungrateful return which the Dissenters experienced from a party for whose advantage they had incurred so considerable a sacrifice.

With the administration of Blake, who died in the year 1700, ended the short interval of tranquillity which originated with the government of Archdale.   Under the rule of his immediate successors, James Moore and Sir Nathaniel Johnson, the colony was harassed with Indian wars, involved in a heavy debt by an ill-conducted and fruitless expedition against the Spaniards at St. Augustine, and agitated by religious disputes engendered by a series of persecuting laws against the Dissenters.   Henceforward the proprietary government continued (with the exception of one returning gleam of success and popularity, which it derived from the administration of Charles Craven, in 1712) to afflict the province with a vile and pernicious misrule, and to fluctuate between the aversion and contempt of its subjects, till they were relieved by its dissolution in the year 1729, when the chartered interests were sold to the crown.

The first Indian war by which this period was signalized broke out in the year 1703, and was occasioned by the influence of the Spaniards over the tribes that inhabited the region of Apalachia.   Resenting with cruel and disproportioned rage the affronts which these savages were instigated by the Spaniards to commit, Governor Moore determined by one vigorous effort to break their power, and by a sanguinary example to impress on all the Indian race a dread of the English name.   At the head of a strong detachment of the provincial militia, reinforced by a troop of Indian allies, he marched into the hostile settlements ; defeated the enemy with a loss of eight hundred of their number, who were either killed or taken prisoners ; laid waste all the Indian towns between the rivers Alatamaha and Savannah ; and reduced the whole district of Apalachia to submission.   To improve his conquest, he transported fourteen hundred of the Apalachian Indians to the territory which was afterwards denominated Georgia, where they were

---

[1] Oldmixon. Wynne. Hewit. *Collections of the Massachusetts Historical Society.* Holmes.

compelled to dwell in a state of dependence on the government of South Carolina.[1]

When the proprietaries of Carolina first embraced the project of a colonial plantation, they solemnly declared, and caused it to be recorded in their charters, that they were moved to embrace this great design by zeal for the diffusion of the Christian faith, and especially for its propagation among the Indian tribes of America. Yet a general provision in favor of toleration, which they permitted Locke to insert as an article of the Fundamental Constitutions, and which they fraudfully or insolently nullified by another article adjected to the same instrument by themselves, constituted the whole amount of their ecclesiastical operations during the first forty years of the proprietary government. They never made the slightest attempt to execute their pretended purpose of communicating instruction to the Indians ; and this important field of Christian labor was quite unoccupied till the beginning of the eighteenth century, when a few missionaries were sent to Carolina by the society incorporated in England for the propagation of the gospel in foreign countries. No cognizable fruits or vestiges of the labors of these missionaries have ever been mentioned. Prior to this enterprise, the only European instructions that the Indians received, under the auspices of the proprietary government, were communicated by a French dancing-master, who settled in Craven county, and acquired a large estate by teaching the savages to dance and play on the flute.[2]

At the close of the seventeenth century, there were only three edifices for divine worship erected within the southern province ; pertaining respectively to an Episcopal, a Presbyterian, and a Quaker congregation ; and all of them situated within the walls of Charleston. In no other quarter of the province were there either temples of public worship or schools for education. The first attempts that were made to supply these defects proceeded not from the proprietaries, but from Tennison, Archbishop of Canterbury, Compton, Bishop of London, Thomas Bray, an active minister of the church of England, and the society established in England for the propagation of the gospel ; but as, in most of these attempts, the paramount object was plainly to multiply adherents to the established church of the parent state, they were the less successful among a people, of whom many had personally experienced the persecution of this church, and more entertained a hereditary dislike to it. In the year 1707, the society for propagation of the gospel maintained six Episcopal ministers in South Carolina, and had sent two thousand volumes of books to be distributed gratuitously among the people. In the northern province, which was thinly peopled by colonists professing a great diversity of religious opinions, no visible institution of divine government was yet established, no religious worship recognized the providence of the Deity or besought his grace, and human life commenced and concluded without any solemnity expressive of its celestial origin and immortal renovation. An act was passed by the assembly of this province, in the year 1702, imposing an assessment of thirty pounds *per annum* on every *precinct*, for the maintenance of a minister ; and in 1705 and 1706, the first two religious edifices of North Carolina were erected. In the year 1715, the province was divided by an act of its domestic legisla-

---

[1] *Modern Universal History.* Hewit. In the year 1700, Charleston was attacked at once by fire, inundation, and pestilence. " Discouragement and despair sat on every countenance ; and many of the survivors thought of abandoning the country." Holmes.
[2] Hewit. Oldmixon.

ture into nine parishes ; in each of which a parochial vestry was established, and a ministerial stipend provided.   This northern province had for many years received from the proprietaries the appellation of *the county of Albemarle in Carolina*, and was sometimes, but not always, included in the commission of the governor of the southern settlement.   It now came to be termed North Carolina ; and at the dissolution of the proprietary government, was made a separate province with a distinct jurisdiction.[1]

After having for a long period disregarded entirely the ecclesiastical concerns of Carolina, the proprietaries, in the beginning of the eighteenth century, turned their attention to this subject with a spirit that caused the cessation of their previous indifference to be greatly lamented ; and made a first and last attempt to signalize their boasted zeal for Christianity, by the demonstration of a temper and the adoption of measures the most insolent, unchristian, and tyrannical.   The office of palatine had now devolved on Lord Granville, who entertained the utmost aversion and contempt for Dissenters of all descriptions, and who had already signalized his bigotry to the church of England by the vehement zeal with which he supported in parliament the bill against *occasional conformity*.[2]   His accession to the dignity of palatine presented him with an opportunity of indulging his favorite sentiments in the regulation of the ecclesiastical polity of Carolina. Contemning the remonstrances and overruling the opposition of Archdale, he eagerly laid hold of so fair an occasion of exerting his bigotry ; and in Moore and Johnson, on whom he successively bestowed the government of the province, he found able and willing instruments of the execution of his arbitrary designs.   These men, notwithstanding the great numerical superiority of the Dissenters, by a series of illegal and violent proceedings, acquired for themselves and a party of the Episcopalian persuasion a complete ascendency over the provincial assemblies, which they exercised in the formation of laws for the advancement of the church of England, and the depression of every other model of Christianity.   After various preparatory measures, which, under the impudent pretence of promoting the glory of God, effectually banished every trace of peace and good-will from a numerous society of his rational creatures, the Episcopal faction at length, in the year 1704, enacted two laws, by one of which Dissenters were deprived of all civil rights, and by the other an arbitrary *court of high commission* (a name of evil import to Englishmen) was erected for the trial of ecclesiastical causes and the preservation of religious uniformity in Carolina.   At the time when these laws were framed, not only the most wealthy and respectable inhabitants, but at least two thirds of the whole population of the province, were Dissenters.

The English Society for the Propagation of the Gospel, on receiving intelligence of the latter of those ordinances, declared their resolution to send no more missionaries to Carolina till it should be repealed.   Both the edicts, however, having been ratified by the proprietaries, and the complaints of the Dissenters treated with derision, these oppressed and insulted men were advised by the merchants of London, who traded to the province, to seek redress of their grievances from the supreme power of the realm.   A petition for this purpose was accordingly presented to the House of Lords, who

---

[1] Oldmixon. Hewit. Williamson. Holmes.

[2] This was a bill imposing severe penalties on any person, who, having conformed so far to the church of England as to entitle him to hold a municipal office, should ever after attend a dissenting place of worship.

were struck with surprise and indignation at the tyrannical insolence of those despotic proprietaries and their provincial officers; and forthwith voted an address to Queen Anne, praying her royal repeal of the obnoxious laws, and recommending that the authors of them should be brought to condign punishment. The Commissioners of Trade, to whom the matter was referred by the queen, reported, " that the making such laws was an abuse of the powers granted by the charter, and inferred a forfeiture of the same"; subjoining their advice that judicial steps should be adopted for having the forfeiture legally ascertained, and the government of the province resumed by the crown.[1] The queen, thereupon, issued an order, declaring the laws complained of null and void, and promised to institute a process of *quo warranto* against the provincial charter; but this promise was never fulfilled.[2] It was alleged that the forfeiture of the charter was obstructed by legal difficulties arising from the nonage of some of the proprietaries, who could not justly be held responsible for the acts of the rest;—as if the inability of these hereditary rulers of mankind to afford protection to their subjects had not itself furnished the strongest reason why they should be dispossessed of the power of exacting obedience from them. While incessant attempts were made by the British government to bereave the New England States of the charters by which popular liberty was guarded, this fair and legitimate occasion was neglected, of emancipating the people of Carolina from a patent which had confessedly been made subservient to the most odious oppression and intolerance; and even after the proprietaries had publicly declared (as they were soon after constrained to do) that it was not in their power to defend the province against the Indians, by whose attacks it was menaced, the proprietary government was suffered to endure until it sunk under its own weakness and incapacity. It was in the year 1706, that the intolerant policy of Lord Granville received this signal check; and from that period, the Dissenters were permitted to enjoy, not indeed the equality which they had originally been encouraged to expect, but a simple toleration. In the following year, an act of assembly was passed in South Carolina for the establishment of religious worship according to the forms of the church of England. By this act the province was divided into ten parishes; and provision was made for building a church in each parish, and for the endowment of its minister. The churches were soon after built, and supplied with ministers by the English Society for the Propagation of the Gospel.[3]

The progress of population, if not the most certain, is one of the most interesting tests of the prosperity of a commonwealth; but it is a test not easily applicable to societies subject, like all the American States, to a continual, but irregular, influx and efflux of people. The population of North Carolina appears to have sustained a considerable check from the troubles and confusions that attended Culpepper's insurrection and Sothel's tyranny; insomuch that, in the year 1694, the list of taxable inhabitants was found to contain only seven hundred and eighty-seven names,—about half the number that the colony had possessed at the commencement of Miller's admin-

---

[1] This report, among other signatures, has that of Prior, the poet, who was one of the Commissioners of Trade at the time.

[2] Oldmixon. Hewit. Preparatory to their address to the queen, the House of Lords passed a resolution containing these remarkable expressions:—that the law for enforcing conformity to the church of England in Carolina " is an encouragement to atheism and irreligion, destructive to trade, and tends to the ruin and depopulation of the province."

[3] Humphrey's *Historical Account of the Society for propagating the Gospel.*

istration.[1] Frequent emigrations were made from the northern to the southern province ;[2] and we may conclude that the diminution of inhabitants, ascertained in 1694, was occasioned, partly at least, in this manner, — since, prior to the year 1708, only two persons (a Turk for murder, and an old woman for witchcraft) perished on the scaffold in North Carolina,[3] — a fact, which, considering the violent convulsions that the province had undergone, appears highly creditable to the humanity of the people.   In the beginning of the eighteenth century, North Carolina received an accession to its inhabitants, first from a number of French refugees, who removed to it from Virginia ; and afterwards from a troop of Germans, who, many years before, were expelled from their homes by the desolation of the palatinate, and had since experienced a great variety of wretchedness and exile.[4]   In the year 1710, its whole population amounted to six thousand persons ;[5] but of these not two thousand were taxables.   There was no court-house in North Carolina before the year 1722 ; the assemblies and general courts till then being convened in private dwelling-houses.   Debts and rents were generally paid in hides, tallow, furs, or other productions of the country.   In the year 1705, it was appointed by law that marriages should be celebrated by the ministers of religion ; but magistrates were permitted to perform this function in parishes unprovided with ministers.   The executive power within the province was feeble and inefficient ; partly in consequence of the state of dispersion in which the bulk of the inhabitants lived, and partly from the corrupt dispositions or despicable characters of many of the executive officers.[6]   In the year 1709, Cary, the collector of the proprietary quitrents, resolving to appropriate, or at least refusing to account for, the produce of his collections, found it easy, with the aid of a few idle and dissolute partisans, to maintain himself in a state of resistance to the proprietary government, and suspend the operations of justice.   The people, though they neither approved nor abetted his fraudulent and rebellious conduct, made no opposition to it ; and the governor, unable to reduce him to obedience, applied for assistance to Virginia, where some regular troops were quartered at the time.   On the approach of a small party of these forces, Cary fled the colony, and his partisans dispersed.[7]

The population of South Carolina, in the year 1700, is said to have amounted to no more than five thousand five hundred persons,[8] — a computation probably short of the truth.   For several years after the first colonization of the territory, there were very few negro slaves in Carolina ; but the demand for them was increased by the increasing cultivation of rice, which was reckoned too unhealthy and laborious for European constitutions ;[9] and the slave-ships of Great Britain promoted the demand by the readiness with which they anticipated and supplied it.   At the close of the seventeenth century, Charleston was already a flourishing city, containing

---

[1] Williamson.   [2] Lawson's *History of Carolina.*   [3] Williamson.   [4] Ibid.

[5] Warden.   In the year 1717, the taxables amounted to two thousand.   Williamson.

[6] In 1701, Porter indicted a man for calling him " a cheating rogue."   The defendant justified the words, and, proving that they were properly applied, was acquitted, and allowed his costs from the prosecutor.   Yet a few years after, Porter was appointed a proprietary deputy and member of council.   Williamson.   In 1726, Burrington, who had previously held the office of governor, and afterwards held it again, was indicted for defamation, in saying of the existing governor, Sir Richard Everard, that " he was no more fit for a governor than Sancho Panza," and for riotously threatening to scalp " his d—d thick skull."   Ib.   Two years after, the grand jury *present Sir Richard, the governor*, for having with his cane twice or thrice struck George Allen.   Ib.

[7] Williamson.   [8] Warden.   [9] Hewit.

several handsome edifices, a public library, and a population of three thousand souls.[1] No printing press was established in Carolina till thirty years after ; and till then the provincial laws were promulgated by oral proclamation.

There prevailed in this province, from the period when the Fundamental Constitutions were enacted, a method of empanelling juries, which might have been copied with advantage both by the other colonies and the parent state. The names of all persons qualified to serve as jurymen were put into a ballot-box, from which a child drew out as many as were requisite to form four several juries ; and these having been put into a second ballot-box, another child drew forth the names that were to compose each respective petty jury. In the beginning of the eighteenth century, this valuable regulation was abolished by the palatine ; but the remonstrances of the people, aided by the zealous interposition of the agent at the court of London for the New England States, compelled him soon after to restore it.[2]

When the difficulties attending the establishment of the first settlers in Carolina were in some degree overcome, the fertility of the soil, the cheapness of food, and the agreeableness and general salubrity of the climate afforded a powerful encouragement to national increase. Families of ten and twelve children were frequently seen in the houses of the colonists at the close of the seventeenth century ;[3] and though some parts of both the provinces were for a time infected with severe epidemical diseases, and others still continue to be unfavorable to health at particular seasons, yet the statistical accounts and the registers of mortality sufficiently demonstrate that the climate of the whole region is in the main conducive to the preservation as well as to the production of life. The salubrity of these, as well as of the other provinces of North America, has been greatly promoted by the progress of industry in opening the woods, draining the marshes, and confining the streams within definite channels. Yet the influence of cultivation has not been uniformly favorable to health in the Carolinas ; and much of the disease with which these regions are afflicted at certain seasons is ascribed to the periodical inundations which the culture of the rice lands requires.[4]

During the infant state of the colony, the proprietaries sold the land at twenty shillings for every hundred acres, and sixpence of quitrent. They raised the price in the year 1694 to thirty shillings ; and in 1711, to forty shillings for every hundred acres, and one shilling of quitrent.[5] Lawson, who travelled through Carolina in the year 1700, celebrates the courtesy and hospitality of the planters ; but represents an aversion to labor, and a negligent contentment with immediate gratification, as qualities very prevalent among them. Fruit, he says, was so plentiful that the hogs were fed with peaches.[6] The Carolinians have always been characterized by a strong predilection for the sports of the field. The disposition that was evinced, at an early period of the history of these provinces, to treat insolvent debtors with extreme indulgence, has continued ever since to be a

---

[1] Oldmixon.   [2] Oldmixon (2d edit.).   [3] Oldmixon.
[4] Warden. Dr. Williamson has demonstrated that the *immediate* effects of the extirpation of wood in Carolina have always been unfriendly to health, from the exposure to the sun of a surface of fresh land covered with vegetable produce in a state of decay.
[5] Williamson.
[6] Lawson. Archdale speaks in nearly the same terms of the fertility of Carolina. Blome states that the province, in 1686, contained many wealthy persons who had repaired to it in a state of indigence.

prominent feature in their legislation, and has doubtless encouraged a loose and improvident readiness to contract debts.[1] The most serious evils with which the two provinces have been afflicted have arisen from the abuse of spirituous liquors, the neglect of education, and the subsistence of negro slavery. It was long before institutions for the education of youth were generally established in Carolina ; the benefits of knowledge were confined entirely to the children of wealthy planters, who were sent to the colleges of Europe or to the seminaries in the Northern States ; and the consequent ignorance of the great bulk of the people, together with the influence of a warm climate and the prevalent aversion to industry (increased by the pride which the possession of slaves inspires, and the discredit which slavery brings on labor), promoted an intemperate use of ardent spirits, which contributed additionally to deprave their sentiments, habits, and manners. It was an unfortunate supposition (whether well or ill founded) that was at one time entertained, that the water found in this part of America possessed deleterious qualities, which an infusion of rum was necessary to counteract. The various evils which we have enumerated (except those arising from negro slavery, which are more pernicious, perhaps, than all the rest) prevailed longest and most extensively in North Carolina. The improvement that after times have witnessed in all these respects has been considerable in both the provinces ; and the inhabitants of South Carolina, in particular, have long been distinguished for the cultivation of literature, the elegance of their manners, and their polite hospitality.[2]

In every community where slavery exists, the treatment experienced by the slaves depends very much on the proportion which they bear to the number of free men, and the consequent apprehensions which they are capable of inspiring.[3] No passion has a more insatiable appetite, or prompts to more unrelenting hatred and cruelty, than fear ; and no terror can be more selfish or more provocative of inhumanity than that which is inspired in men's bosoms by the danger of retaliation of the injustice which they have inflicted and are still continuing to inflict. In South Carolina, for a very considerable period, the number of slaves bore a greater proportion to that of the whole population than in any other of the North American colonies. The consequence of this state of things was, that the slaves of the South Carolina planters were treated with extreme severity ; and conspiracies were repeatedly formed by them for a general massacre of their masters. Their discontent was inflamed by the intrigues, and rendered the more dangerous from the vicinity, of the Spaniards.[4] Neither in this nor any other country, of which the history has yet been written, have the Protestant clergy of the Episcopal persuasion distinguished themselves by exertions to mitigate the evils of slavery. Wherever a Protestant Episcopal church has been established by law, the only ministers of the gospel, whose precepts have asserted and whose example has recognized the entire participation of negroes in the rights of human nature, have been Methodists, Moravians, or Dissenters of some other denomination. More practical Christianity and more humane enterprise, in this respect, have been evinced by the state

[1] Warden.   [2] Ibid
[3] Thucydides (Book VIII.) ascribes the peculiar cruelty with which slaves were treated by the Spartans and the Chians to the peculiarly large proportion, which, in these states, the number of the slaves bore to the total population of the commonwealth. In proportion to the increase of the number of slaves in North America has been the hatred awakened in the breasts of the white Americans against the whole negro race.
[4] Wynne. Hewit. Warden.

clergy in countries where the Catholic church has prevailed. The priests of this persuasion have generally constituted themselves the defenders and patrons of Indian savages and negro slaves.[1] Perhaps this has arisen in part from the strong peculiarities of moral and social position by which the Catholic priests are separated from the rest of mankind, and which may lessen in their estimation the differences of temporal condition by which the several classes of the laity are distinguished. The Catholic church, it must likewise be considered, exercises more temporal power than any Protestant church over its votaries ; and it has been very generally associated with despotic government, under which the rights enjoyed by individuals, whether in their slaves or in any other description of property, are more subjected to magisterial superintendence and control, than in states where the government is of a more popular description.

The early annals of Carolina have not transmitted to us any account of the manner in which the provincial assemblies were constituted, or of the extent of property to which political franchises were attached. All the executive officers were nominated by the proprietaries, who specified the amount of the official salaries in the warrants of appointment. So great was the difficulty of collecting money, or even agricultural produce, especially in the northern colony, that the proprietaries were frequently obliged to grant assignations of lands or quitrents to their officers in order to secure the performance of their duties. Sir Nathaniel Johnson, who was appointed governor of Carolina in the year 1702, received a warrant for a salary of two hundred pounds a year. The other contemporary officers had salaries, of which the highest was sixty pounds and the lowest forty pounds a year. The governor's salary was doubled in the year 1717.[2]

Carolina, by its amazing fertility in animal and vegetable produce, was enabled, from an early period, to carry on a considerable trade with Jamaica, Barbadoes, and the Leeward Islands, which, at the close of the seventeenth century, are said to have depended in a great measure on that colony for the means of subsistence.[3] Its staple commodities were rice, tar, and, afterwards, indigo. Oldmixon, whose history was published in the year 1708, observes that the trade of the colony with England had recently gained a considerable increase ; " for notwithstanding all the discouragements the people lie under," he adds, " seventeen ships came last year laden from Carolina with rice, skins, pitch, and tar, in the Virginia fleet, besides straggling ships." [4]

By an act of assembly, passed in the year 1715,[5] every planter of Carolina was required to purchase and inclose a burial-ground for all persons dying on his estate ; and, before interment of any corpse, to call in at least three

---

[1] The church of Rome, it has been asserted, is the only established church in which negroes have ever obtained the rank of priesthood. Several Catholic bishops have been negroes ; and one negro, at least, has been canonized as a saint at Rome. See Gregoire's Treatise *De la Noblesse de la Peau.* One instance may, however, be cited of the ordination of a negro as a priest of the church of England, by Keppel, Bishop, of Exeter, in 1765. *Annual Register for* 1765. It might move our surprise (if any inconsistency in an American slave-owner were justly surprising) to find Roman Catholics in America deny the entire rational capacity of men whom the supposed infallible church of Rome has consecrated as bishops and canonized as saints.

[2] Oldmixon. Hewit. Williamson.   [3] Archdale.

[4] Oldmixon. The materials of this statement seem to have been obtained from Archdale.

[5] *Laws of Carolina.*

I have not been able to learn either the precise date or any other particulars of the administration of Major Tynte, who, in the beginning of the eighteenth century, was for a short time governor of South Carolina. King, the English poet (who died in 1712), celebrated

or four of his neighbours to view it, for the purpose of insuring further inquiry in case of any suspicious appearance.

Tynte in some Latin stanzas, which he afterwards rendered into the following English version : —

> " Tynte was the man who first from Britain's shore
> Palladian arts to Carolina bore ;
> His tuneful harp attending Muses strung,
> And Phœbus' skill inspired the lays he sung.
> Strong towers and palaces their rise began,
> And listening stones to sacred fabrics ran ;
> Just laws were taught, and curious arts of peace,
> And trade's brisk current flowed with wealth's increase.
> On such foundations learned Athens rose ;
> So Dido's thong did Carthage first inclose ;
> So Rome was taught *old* empires to subdue,
> As Tynte creates and governs now the *new.*"

BOOK V.

NEW YORK.

CHAPTER I.

Hudson's Voyage of Discovery. — First Settlement of the Dutch at Albany. — The Province granted by the States General to the West India Company of Holland. — The Dutch Colonists extend their Settlements into Connecticut. — Disputes with the New England Colonies. — Delaware first colonized by the Swedes. — War between the Dutch and Indians. — Farther Disputes with New England. — Designs of Charles the Second. — Alarm and Exertions of the Dutch Governor. — The Province granted by Charter to the Duke of York — invaded by an English Fleet — surrenders. — Wise Government of Colonel Nichols. — Holland cedes New York to England — recaptures it — finally cedes it again. — New Charter granted to the Duke of York. — Arbitrary Government of Andros. — Discontent of the Colonists. — The Duke consents to give New York a Free Constitution.

NEW YORK is distinguished from the other American commonwealths whose history we have already considered, both by the race of the European settlers who first resorted to it, and by the mode of its annexation to the dominion of Britain. In all the other provinces, the first colonists were Englishmen ; and the several occupations of American territory, and corresponding extensions of the British empire, were the enterprises of English subjects, impelled by the spirit of commercial adventure, inflamed with religious zeal, or allured by ambitious expectation. The people of England derived, in all these instances, an increase of their commercial resources, and the crown an enlargement of its dominion, from the acts of private individuals, sanctioned no doubt by the approbation of public authority, but unaided by the treasure or troops of the nation. But the territory of New York was originally colonized, not from England, but from Holland ; and the incorporation of it with the rest of the British dominions was accomplished, not by settlement, but by conquest, — not by the enterprise of individuals, but by the forces of the state. It is a singularity still more worthy of remark, and illustrative of the slender influence of human views and purposes in the preadjustment and connection of events, that this military conquest proved the means of establishing a colony of Quakers in America ; and the sword of Charles the Second, in conquering an appanage for his bigot brother, prepared a tranquil establishment, in New Jersey and Pennsylvania, for the votaries of peace, toleration, and philanthropy.

The pretensions of the Dutch to this territory were certainly, from the first, more consistent with natural justice than with the commonly received law of nations, and the privilege which this law attaches to priority of discovery. For if, on the one hand, the voyage of Cabot, and his general and cursory survey of the North American continent, preceded by more than a century the occurrence from which the Dutch occupation originated, there seems, on the other hand, a monstrous disregard of the general rights of mankind, in maintaining that a privilege, so precariously constituted, could subsist so long unexercised, and that a navigator, by casually approaching North America, in a vain and erroneous search of a passage to the Indies, should acquire for his countrymen a right to prevent the whole continent from being inhabited for more than a hundred years. It is the dictate of reason, that the title accruing from discovery may be waived by dereliction, and extinguished by the sounder right created by occupation.

The prior right of England (yet unrecognized by the rest of the world) had produced no other permanent occupation than a feeble settlement on the distant shore of James River, in Virginia, which had now subsisted for two years, when Henry Hudson, an Englishman, employed by the East India Company of Holland, set sail from the Texel for the discovery of a northwest passage to India. Having attempted in vain to accomplish the object of his voyage [March, 1609], he steered for Cape Cod, and entered the Bay of Chesapeake, where he remarked the infant settlement of the English. He afterwards anchored his vessel off the Delaware, and proceeding thence to Long Island, sailed up the river Manhattan, on whose banks the chief fruits of his enterprise were destined to grow. Some authors have asserted that he sold his right as discoverer of this territory to the Dutch; but the assertion is equally unproved and improbable; as he could convey to the people in whose service he was engaged no right which the voyage itself did not vest in them by a much better title. Several voyages were afterwards made from Holland to the river Manhattan, which, at first, was called the North River, but, in process of time, received the name of the able and enterprising navigator, by whom, if not originally discovered, it was introduced for the first time to the acquaintance of the Dutch. This people now conceived that they had acquired a sufficient title to the adjacent territory, which they distinguished by the name of Nova Belgia, or New Netherlands.[1] The depending or recent conflicts of rival provinces, and even rival nations, lent at one time to all the circumstances attending the first occupation of this territory an interest which they have long ceased to possess, except in the estimation of antiquarians.

The favorable report that Hudson gave of the country having been confirmed by subsequent voyagers, an association of Dutch merchants embraced the resolution of establishing a trading settlement within its confines [1614]; and the States General promoted the enterprise by granting to its projectors a monopoly of the trade of Hudson's River. Encouraged by this act of favor, the adventurers, in the course of the same year, appropriated a small portion of land on the western bank of the river, near Albany, where they erected a fort, and intrusted the government of the place to one Henry Christiaens. This feeble settlement had scarcely been established, when it was invaded by a Virginian squadron, commanded by Captain Argal, and returning from the unjust and useless conquest of the French possessions in the Bay of Fundy. Argal claimed the territory occupied by the Dutch, as appertaining by the law of nations to the British dominion in America; and the provincial governor was compelled to obey a summons of surrender, and to stipulate allegiance to England, and tribute and subordination to the government of Virginia.[2] The States of Holland had too recently established an independence, promoted by the aid and recognized by the mediation of Great Britain, to suffer them to make this outrage the cause of quarrel with a powerful ally, whose friendship they did not yet deem themselves strong enough to dispense with. They forbore, therefore, to

---

[1] Purchas. Charlevoix, *History of New France.* Oldmixon. Stith's *Virginia.* Douglass's *Summary.* Smith's *History of New York.*
[2] See Book I., Chap. II., *ante.*

take any notice of Argal's hostile encroachment ; and it is even asserted by some writers, that, in answer to a complaint by the British court of their intrusion into America, they denied that the settlement was established by their authority, and represented it as the private enterprise of a few obscure individuals.   The same writers have alleged, that the Dutch, while they disavowed every pretension that could infringe on the claims of England, besought the English monarch to permit a few trading-houses to be erected within *his* territories on Hudson's River ; and that a permission to this extent was actually obtained.   Whatever truth or falsehood there may be in these statements, it is certain, that, in the year after Argal's invasion [1615], a new governor, Jacob Elkin, having arrived at the fort with an additional complement of settlers, the claim of the English to the stipulated dependence was forthwith defied, and the payment of tribute successfully resisted. For the better security of their resumed independence of English domination, the Dutch colonists now erected a second fort on the southwest point of Long Island ; and afterwards built two others at Good Hope, on Connecticut River, and at Nassau, on the east side of Delaware Bay. They continued for a series of years, in unmolested tranquillity, to mature their settlement, increase their numbers, and, by the exercise of their peculiar national virtues of patience and industry, to subdue the first difficulties and hardships incident to an infant colony.[1]

The States of Holland, finding their commerce enlarge with the duration of political freedom and the enjoyment of peace, and observing that their people were successful in preserving the footing they had gained on Hudson's River, began to entertain the design of improving this settlement, and rendering it the basis of more extended colonization in America.   With this purpose was combined the scheme of their celebrated West India Company, which was established in the year 1620, and to which, in pursuance of their favorite policy of colonizing by means of exclusive companies, it was determined to commit the administration of New Netherlands. They watched with a jealous eye the proceedings of the English Puritan exiles at Leyden,[2] and viewed with alarm their projected migration to the banks of Hudson's River.   Unable or unwilling to obstruct the design by an opposition which would have involved an immediate collision with the pretensions of Britain, they defeated it by bribing the Dutch captain, with whom the emigrants sailed,[3] to convey them so far to the northward, that their plantation was eventually formed in the territory of Massachusetts. This fraudful proceeding of the Dutch, though it prevented a rival settlement from being established on Hudson's River, discredited their own title to this territory, and proportionally ratified the claim of Great Britain, which, in the same year, was again distinctly asserted and exercised by the publication of King James's patent in favor of the Grand Council of Plymouth.   The Plymouth patent, however, which was declared void in the following year [November, 1621] by the English House of Commons, and surrendered a few years after by the patentees, seemed as little entitled to respect abroad as to favor at home ; for, even if its disregard of the Dutch occupation should not be supposed to infringe the law of nations, it unquestionably merited this reproach by appropriating territories where the French, in virtue

---

[1] Oldmixon. Stith. Wynne. Smith. In the year 1624, the exports from New Netherlands were " four thousand beavers' and seven hundred otters' skins, estimated at 27,150 guilders." Hazard.
[2] See Book II., Chap. I., *ante.*   [3] Mather. Neal. Hutchinson. Oldmixon.

of previous charters from their sovereign, had already established the settlements of Acadia and Canada.   The nullity of the Plymouth patent, in this last particular, was tacitly acknowledged by Charles the First, in 1630, when, by the treaty of St. Germain, he restored the French provinces which his arms had conquered in the preceding year.   Whether the States of Holland considered the patent equally unavailing against their pretensions, or not, they made a grant of the country which was now called New Netherlands to their West India Company, in the very year in which the English House of Commons protested against a similar patent of the same territory by their own monarch [1621], as inconsistent with the general rights of their countrymen and the true interests of trade.   If the States General, or their subjects on the banks of Hudson's River, were acquainted with this parliamentary transaction, they made more account of the benefit that might accrue from it to their territorial claim, than of the rebuke it conveyed to their commercial policy.   Under the management of the West India Company, the new settlement was soon both consolidated and extended.   The city of New Amsterdam, afterwards called New York, was built on York Island, then known by the name of Manhattan ; and at the distance of a hundred and fifty miles higher up the Hudson, were laid the foundations of the city of Albany.[1]

The precise extent of territory claimed by the Dutch, as comprehended within their colony of New Netherlands, has been differently represented even by their own writers, of whom some have explicitly declared that it embraced all the country lying between Virginia and Canada.   Whatever was its titular extent, which was probably unknown to the planters themselves, they hastened to enlarge their appropriation far beyond their immediate use ; and, by intrusion into the Connecticut and Delaware territories, laid the foundation of their subsequent disputes with the colonists of New England.   While these powerful neighbours as yet possessed no other establishment but the small settlement of Plymouth, to which the artifice of the Dutch had consigned the English emigrants from Leyden, the provincial authorities at New Amsterdam attempted to cultivate a friendly, or at least a commercial, correspondence with the English colony ; and for this purpose despatched their secretary, Razier, with a congratulatory communication to the governor of Plymouth. [1627.]   The English, from whose memory the fraud that deprived them of a settlement on the river Hudson had not banished the recollection of Dutch hospitality at Leyden, received with much courtesy the felicitations of their successful rivals on the courageous struggle they had maintained with the difficulties of their situation ;[2] and as some years had yet to elapse before Massachusetts became populous, and before the English establishments in Connecticut were formed, the Dutch colonists were enabled to flatter themselves with the hope that their stratagem would not be resented, nor their settlement disturbed.   They were aware of the reluctance of their government to exhibit publicly a title derogatory to the pretensions of Britain, and endeavoured to counteract the restraint which this policy might impose on their future acquisitions by the stretch of their immediate occupation.   Their first settlement was effected, apparently, without any equitable remuneration to the Indian proprietors of the land ; and hence, perhaps, arose those dissensions with the Indians which afterwards produced a great deal of bloodshed.   But when they

---

[1] Oldmixon. Smith. Chalmers.
[2] Smith. Neal's *New England*. *Collections of the Massachusetts Historical Society.*

extended their appropriations to Connecticut and Delaware, they were careful to facilitate their admission by purchasing the territory from its savage owners.[1] If their policy really was (as we may reasonably suppose, though we cannot positively affirm) to supply a defective, or at least non-apparent title, by largeness and priority of appropriation, it was completely disappointed by the result ; and when New England and Maryland began to be filled with inhabitants, the Dutch had the mortification of discovering that the early and immoderate extent of their occupation only served to bring their claims the sooner into collision with the pretensions of neighbours more powerful than they ; and to direct a severer scrutiny into a title which they were unable to produce, which their detected stratagem had contributed to discredit, and which the length of their possession was yet unable to supply.   These disagreeable results were not experienced till after the lapse of several years of uninterrupted peace ; and during the administration of Wouter Van Twiller [1629], who arrived at Fort Amsterdam as the first governor appointed by the West India Company, the Dutch colonists enjoyed a state of calm and monotonous ease, undisturbed by the commercial delirium that prevailed for several years in their parent state, and dissipated so many fortunes in the ruinous and ridiculous speculations of the *tulip trade*. This period affords no materials for history, and it served but indifferently to prepare the colonists for their impending contentions with men whose frames and spirits had been braced by the discipline of those severe trials that befell the first planters of New England.[2]

It was near the close of Van Twiller's administration, that the English colonists extended their settlements beyond the boundaries of Massachusetts into the territory of Connecticut [1636] ; an intrusion which the Dutch governor resented no farther than by causing his commissary, Van Curlet, to intimate a harmless protest against it.   He was succeeded in the following year by William Kieft [1637], a man of enterprise and ability, but choleric and imperious in temper, unfortunate in conduct, and more fitted to encounter with spirit than to stem with prudence the sea of troubles that began on all sides to invade the possessions of the Dutch.   These colonists now experienced a total change in the complexion of their fortune ; and their history for many subsequent years is little else than a chronicle of their struggles and contentions with the English, the Swedes, and the Indians.   Kieft's administration commenced [1638], as his predecessor's had concluded, with a protest against the advancing settlements of Connecticut and New Haven, accompanied by a prohibition of the trade which the English conducted in the neighbourhood of the fort of Good Hope.   His reputation for ability, and the sharpness of his remonstrance, excited at first some alarm among the English inhabitants of Connecticut, who had originally made their advances into this territory in equal ignorance of the proximity and the pretensions of the Dutch ; but soon suspecting that their imperious rival had no title to the country from which he proposed to exclude them, and encouraged by promises of assistance from the other New England States, they disregarded his remonstrance, and not only retained their settlements, but, two years after [1640], compelled the Dutch garrison to evacuate the fort at Good Hope, and appropriated the adjacent plantation to themselves.   This aggression, though passively endured, was loudly

---

[1] Smith.   [2] See Note XVII., at the end of the volume.

lamented by the Dutch,[1] who, notwithstanding the increase of their numbers, and the spirit of their governor, displayed a helplessness in their contentions with the English, which, if partly occasioned by the enervating influence of a long space of tranquillity, seems also to have been promoted by secret distrust of the validity of their claim to the territories they had most recently occupied. It is certain, at least, that the Dutch were not always so forbearing ; and an encroachment which their title enabled them more conscientiously to resist, was soon after repelled by Kieft, with a practical vigor and success very remote from the general strain of his conduct and fortune. Lord Stirling, who had obtained a grant of Long Island from the Plymouth Company, transferred a portion of it to certain of the inhabitants of New England, who removed to their new acquisition in the year 1639, and, unmolested by the Dutch, whose settlements were confined to the opposite quarter, these New Englanders peaceably inhabited the eastern part of the island. Receiving a considerable accession to their numbers, they ventured to take possession of the western quarter ; but from this station they were promptly dislodged by Kieft, who drove them back to the other end of the island, where they built the town of Southampton [1642], and subsisted as a dependency of Connecticut, till they were united to the State of New York, on the fall of the Dutch dominion in North America.[2]

Kieft, in the same year, equipped two sloops, which he despatched on an expedition against a body of English, who, advancing beyond the first settlements of their countrymen in Maryland, had penetrated into Delaware, — a territory which was claimed by the Dutch, but had, nevertheless, been included in the charter obtained by Lord Baltimore from Charles the First. As the number of these emigrants from Maryland was inconsiderable, and they were quite unprepared to defend their possession against this unexpected attack, they were easily dislodged by the forces of Kieft. But there still remained in another quarter of Delaware a different race of settlers, who, without any legal claim to the soil which they occupied, possessed a force that proved of more avail to them than the formal title of the English. This was a colony of Swedes, of whose transplantation to North America very few particulars have been recorded. Their migratory enterprise was suggested in the year 1626, when Gustavus Adolphus, king of Sweden, having received a flattering description of the country adjacent to the Dutch settlement of New Netherlands, issued a proclamation exhorting his subjects to associate for the establishment of an American colony. In conformity with the royal counsel, a large sum of money was collected by voluntary contribution ; and a number of Swedes and Fins emigrated, in the year 1627, to America. They first landed at Cape Henlopen, at the entrance of Delaware Bay, and were so much charmed with its aspect that they gave it the name of Paradise Point. Some time after, they pur-

---

[1] The Dutch preserved, for a series of years, a minute and formal record of the grievances which they laid to the charge of the English colonists. The insignificance of many of these complaints, and the homeliness of the subject matter of others, contrast somewhat ludicrously with the pompousness of the titles and the bitter gravity of the style. This singular chronicle, forming the earliest and very undignified annals of New York, is preserved in Hazard's *Collections.*

[2] Oldmixon. Smith. Chalmers. Trumbull's *Connecticut.* The histories of these events, by Oldmixon, Smith, and Chalmers, are exceedingly confused, and in some points erroneous. Their chronology, in particular, is remarkably careless. Trumbull is always distinguished by the accuracy of his statements, but not less distinguished by his partiality. Here, for example, he relates with great fidelity all the offences of the Dutch, but passes over in total silence every charge of this people against the English.

chased from the native inhabitants all the land between that cape and the Falls of Delaware ; and maintaining little intercourse with the parent state from which they were dissevered, but addicting themselves exclusively to agricultural pursuits, they possessed their colonial acquisition without challenge or interruption, till Kieft assumed the government of New Netherlands.[1] [1642.] Several of the Swedish colonists were scalped and killed, and in some instances their children were stolen from them, by the Indians. Yet commonly the two races lived on friendly terms together, and no general war ever arose between them.   The Indians sometimes attended the religious assemblies of the Swedes ; but with so little edification, that they expressed their amazement at the ill-breeding of the orator who could exercise the auditory patience of his tribe with such lengthened harangues without repaying their civility by a distribution of brandy.   One of the earliest of Kieft's political measures was the intimation of a formal protest against the intrusion of the Swedes, to whom he earnestly recommended the propriety of their instant departure from a territory which he assured them that his countrymen had purchased with their blood.   But as the Dutch discovered no inclination to purchase it over again at the same expense, the Swedes, unawed by this governor's power, paid no regard to his remonstrances.   A war, as it has been called, subsisted between the two communities for several years ; but, though attended with a cordial reciprocation of rancor and much flourish of verbal valor, it was unproductive of bloodshed.   Longing to destroy, but afraid to attack each other, they cherished their quarrel with an inveterate malice which might have been dissipated by a prompt appeal to the decision of more manly hostilities.   It seemed to be the object of both parties rather to forewarn their enemy of danger by menace, than to overcome him by active force.   At the treaty of Stockholm, in 1640, Sweden and Holland forbore to make any allusion to colonial disputes or American territory ;[2] and the two colonies being left to adjust their pretensions between themselves, their animosities subsided into an unfriendly peace.[3]   Even this faint color of good neighbourhood did not subsist for many years.

Meanwhile, numberless causes of dispute were continually arising between New Netherlands and the colonies of Connecticut and New Haven ; and the English, who had formerly been the objects of complaint, now became the complainers.   They charged the Dutch with disturbing, kidnapping, and plundering the English traders ; with enticing servants to rob and desert their masters ; and with selling arms and ammunition to the Indians. The unfriendly relations that subsisted between the Dutch themselves and

---

[1] The Swedish government appears to have made some attempt to obtain a recognition of its right to the territory.   An application to this effect was addressed by Oxenstiern, the Swedish ambassador, to the court of England; but though the Swedes alleged that the application was successful, and the legitimacy of their occupation admitted, no proof of this averment was ever produced.   Not less improbable was a pretence they seem to have urged, of having purchased the claim of the Dutch.   Samuel Smith's *History of New Jersey.*   This is a work of extreme rarity, and has been confounded by some writers with Smith's *History of New York.*   It contains much curious matter; but, as a composition, is tasteless, confused, and uninteresting.

[2] Smith.   Holmes.   Professor Kalm's *Travels in North America.*   Douglass.   Chalmers. Chalmers unfortunately seems to relax his usual attention to accuracy, when he considers his topics insignificant; and from this defect, as well as the peculiarities of his style, it is sometimes difficult to discover his meaning, or reconcile his apparent inconsistency in different passages.   Douglass's *Summary,* which is replete with prejudice and partiality when it treats of the New England States, is very frequently inaccurate when it travels beyond them.

[3] Trumbull represents the Dutch and Swedish governors, in 1642, as "uniting in a crafty design" to exclude an inhabitant of New Haven from trading at Delaware.

the Indians would render this last charge against them extremely improbable, if it were not notorious that their countrymen in Europe have, on various occasions, manufactured and sold to their enemies the cannon-balls which they perfectly well knew were to be fired back into their own towns.   To all those complaints the English could obtain no other answer from Kieft but haughty reproaches and angry recriminations ; and it was partly from apprehension of his designs, though chiefly, no doubt, for their own security against Indian hostility, that the New England colonies were induced to form the scheme of the federal union, which they carried into effect in the year 1643.[1]   That the complaints of the English against Kieft were by no means unfounded may be inferred from the fact, that the succeeding governor of New Netherlands, though warmly attached to the cause of his countrymen, declined to make any answer to those charges, and desired that he might not be held responsible for them.   And yet, notwithstanding their mutual disagreements, the Dutch and English colonists never suffered themselves to neglect entirely either the forms of courtesy, or the more substantial offices of humanity.   Kieft, perhaps with more politeness than sincerity, congratulated the United Colonies on the league they had formed ; and when, in the course of the same year [1643], he applied to New Haven for assistance against the Indians, with whom he was engaged in a bloody and dangerous war, the government of that colony, though precluded by the federal union, as well as by doubts of the justice of the Dutch cause, from embarking separately in hostilities, tendered the amplest contribution they could afford of provisions for men and cattle to supply the scarcity created by the Indian devastations.   So unwarlike were the Dutch colonists in general, that they found it necessary to hire the services of Captain Underhill, who had been banished from Boston as one of the associates of Mrs. Hutchinson,[2] and who, at the head of a mixed troop of English and Dutch followers, opposed the Indians with a skill and bravery that proved fatal to great numbers of them, both in Long Island and on the main land, and was regarded as the deliverer of New Netherlands from entire destruction.   Notwithstanding the need he had thus experienced of English assistance, and the benefit he derived from it, Kieft persisted, during the rest of his life, in exchanging with the colonies of Connecticut and New Haven, not only the sharpest remonstrances and vituperations, but menaces of vengeance and war, which, happily for himself, he had as little ability as they had inclination to execute.   He continued all this time to be involved in hostilities with the Indians, between whom and the Dutch there was fought [1646], towards the conclusion of his administration, a great and general battle on Strickland's Plain, where, after an obstinate conflict, and great slaughter on both sides, the Dutch with much difficulty kept the field, while the Indians withdrew unpursued.[3]

Kieft was succeeded, in the following year [1647], by the last of the Dutch governors of New Netherlands.   This was Peter Stuyvesant, a brave old officer, and one of those magnanimous spirits by which the re-

[1] See Book II., Chap. III., *ante.*   [2] See Book II., Chap. II., *ante.*
[3] Trumbull. Belknap. Yet the greater number of the writers of American history (copying each other's statements without examination) have asserted that the Dutch were never once involved in a quarrel with the Indians. One old writer, indeed, whose work is very scarce, has stated that the Dutch were continually harassed and endangered by the Indians. *Brief Description of New York, formerly called New Netherlands,* by Daniel Denton. In Samuel Smith's *History of New Jersey,* reference is made to some bloody contests between the Dutch and Indians.

publican service of Holland was in that age remarkably adorned. By his justice, prudence, and vigor, he succeeded in restoring peace with the Indians, and preserving it uninterrupted during the whole of his administration. His arrival was honored by an address of congratulation from the commissioners of the United Colonies of New England, accompanied with an earnest entreaty for reparation of the injuries they had sustained from his predecessor. One of the most serious of these injuries was the frequent seizure and confiscation of English trading-vessels on the pretence of infraction of the custom-house regulations of New Netherlands, which the Dutch, with insolent injustice, refused to promulgate, and yet rigidly enforced. Stuyvesant, though he declined to justify some of the acts of his predecessor, returned, as might have been expected, a counter claim of redress for the wrongs of New Netherlands, and in particular demanded a restoration of the territories of Connecticut and New Haven. This was a hopeless demand ; and Stuyvesant, soon perceiving that the state of his title and of his force would barely suffice to prevent farther invasion of the Dutch pretensions, was too prudent to insist on it. After various negotiations, a treaty was at length concluded [1650] between the commissioners of the United English Colonies and the governor of New Netherlands, by which the settlements of the respective nations in Long Island were mutually secured to them, and a boundary ascertained between the Dutch settlements and the Connecticut and New Haven occupations on the main land. This treaty was not productive of the good consequences that were expected from it. The English had enacted a law prohibiting the Dutch from trading within their territories, — a restriction that was highly resented by the Dutch ; and the disputes that arose concerning the execution of this law, together with the competition of the two nations to engross the profits of the Indian trade, engendered a degree of mutual jealousy and ill-humor that caused them to regard each other's proceedings and policy through a very unfavorable medium. The treaty seems not to have embraced any arrangement with regard to the Delaware territory, and Stuyvesant was determined to preserve entire all that yet remained uninvaded of his country's pretensions in this quarter. In support of these pretensions, he was soon constrained to make such efforts to resist a trading settlement which the colony of New Haven attempted to establish on the borders of Delaware, as completely effaced every semblance of good understanding between the Dutch and the English provincial governments. The breach between them was widened by a panic excited in the settlements of Connecticut and New Haven [1651], where a number of Indians volunteered a confession of a projected massacre of the English, to which they affirmed that they had been instigated by the governor of New Netherlands. [1652.] The only evidence in support of their story that they could produce was the ammunition which the Dutch had been always in the practice of selling to them, and which the English now the more readily believed to have been furnished for their destruction, as the Indians had frequently employed it for this purpose. Notwithstanding the confident assertions of a respectable historian of Connecticut, this confession manifestly appears to have derived the credit it received chiefly from the fears and prepossessions of the English, who suffered themselves to be made the dupes of perfidious savages, whose enmity was gratified by the dissensions of their powerful neighbours. What may be thought, indeed, to place this beyond a doubt is, that no future confirmation of the charge was ever obtained, even after the fall of the Dutch dominion had placed every facility for the procurement of evidence in the hands of their enemies.   The governments of Connecticut, New Haven, and Plymouth, however, blinded by rage and fear, gave implicit faith to a statement discredited no less by the habitual fraud and treachery of the Indians, than by the manly and honorable character of Stuyvesant.   To his indignant denial of the charge, they answered by reminding him of the massacre of their countrymen by the Dutch in Amboyna, about thirty years before ; and to his just exceptions to the value of Indian testimony, they replied that the Dutch governor of Amboyna had sought a pretext for his cruelty in the charges against the English which he extorted by torture from the Japanese.   The absurdity of their reasoning demonstrates the intensity of passion by which they were transported ; and the repeated introduction of the topic of Amboyna shows as clearly the strong though unconscious dominion of national prejudice and antipathy on their minds.   To the government of Massachusetts the evidence of the conspiracy did not appear satisfactory [1653] ; nor could all the instances of her confederates prevail with this State to join with them in a war against the Dutch.[1]   Judging their own forces alone inadequate to such an enterprise, the other colonies applied for assistance to Oliver Cromwell [1654], who was then engaged in the two years' war with Holland which the Long Parliament had begun, and who promptly complied with their request by despatching a squadron to undertake, in conjunction with the colonial troops, an invasion of New Netherlands.   But the expedition was intercepted by intelligence of the peace negotiated between the Protector and the States General ; and his squadron, having fortified the spirits of the English colonists by demonstrating to them and their adversary the readiness and determination of a powerful government to assist them, proceeded still farther to augment their security by the conquest of the French province of Acadia.[2]   It is remarkable that the treaty of peace, which was executed at this time between England and Holland, contained no express allusion to the claims or possessions of either in North America ; but as it was stipulated that war should cease and peace and friendship prevail between all the dominions and possessions of the two commonwealths in all parts of the world, and as the English expedition against New Netherlands was thereupon countermanded, the validity of the Dutch claim to this territory was manifestly implied and practically acknowledged.

It was in the Delaware territory that Stuyvesant exerted his most vigorous and successful efforts to defend the claims of his countrymen against the encroachments of the New England colonists and the Swedes.   As the war between the Dutch and the Swedes during Kieft's administration had in some respects resembled a peace, so the peace that ensued bore no little resemblance to a war.   To check the encroachments which the Swedish settlers were continually attempting, Stuyvesant erected a fort at a place then called New Amstel, and afterwards Newcastle.   This proceeding gave umbrage to the Swedes, who expressed their displeasure in a protest, which, with the usual fate of such instrumentality in these provincial

---

[1] *Ante*, Book II., Chap. III.

[2] Oldmixon. Chalmers. Trumbull. Smith. The whole voluminous correspondence that took place, both on this occasion and afterwards, between the governors of the Dutch and English colonies, is preserved in Hazard's *Collections*.

controversies, was totally disregarded. About a year afterwards [1654], Risingh, the Swedish governor, repaired with an armed vessel to the Dutch fort, and, obtaining admission into it by a stratagem somewhat discreditable to his own honor, as well as to the vigilance of its defenders,[1] easily over-powered the garrison, and expelled them with violence, but without blood-shed, not only from their strong-hold, but from the confines of Delaware. During the short time that the fortress remained in his possession, it re-ceived the name of Christina, in compliment to the queen of Sweden. Stuyvesant was not of a disposition to submit tamely to such an outrage, or to content himself with a simple recapture of the fort. He determined to invade and subdue the whole Swedish colony. Destitute of a force sufficient for this enterprise, and fully occupied at the time with a contro-versy more dangerous to his government, as well as more interesting to his honor, he was constrained to apply for reinforcement to the West India Company. This corporation, however, was then laboring under great em-barrassments; in so much that it was only by a friendly contribution of the city of Amsterdam, that its administrators were enabled to supply Stuyve-sant with a small body of troops. Thus reinforced, he marched into Dela-ware [1655], where the Swedes had employed their leisure in erecting another fort, as if they intended to defend their pretensions to the last extremity. But their resolution in facing danger was not equal to their au-dacity in provoking it; and no sooner did they perceive that these military demonstrations failed to answer their true object of deterring the enemy from approaching, and that they were now attacked in earnest by a warrior whose hostilities were not confined to stratagems and protests, than they peaceably surrendered the forts, together with the whole of their settle-ments, to the forces of Stuyvesant.

The conquest of Delaware was thus accomplished without bloodshed; — a circumstance the more extraordinary, as it certainly did not arise from ab-sence of the passions from which this fatal extremity might be expected to ensue; for many of the Swedes regarded the Dutch with such sincerity of detestation, that they determined to return to Europe, and to abandon a country which they had styled a paradise, rather than to submit to a union with the colony of New Netherlands. To this humiliation, however, the rest were reduced, and the settlement for some years continued to be ruled in peace by a lieutenant-governor appointed by Stuyvesant.[2] Thus, unas-sisted by the parent state, fell the only colony that Sweden ever founded. The historian would have little pretension to humanity, who would deride a bloodless adjustment of national disputes. But in timorous hostilities, a new feature of opprobrium is added to the deplorable aspect of war. When we recollect that these Swedes either had been the subjects of the heroic Gustavus Adolphus, or were the immediate descendants of his subjects, and when we see them provoke a war by fraud and outrage, and then decline the conflict by tamely submitting to the object of their insult and hatred, it must be acknowledged that they have enlarged the catalogue of those nations

---

[1] " Risingh, under the disguise of friendship, came before the works, fired two salutes and landed thirty men, who were entertained by the commandant as friends; but he had no sooner discovered the weakness of the garrison, than he made himself master of it, seizing also upon all the ammunition, houses, and other effects of the West Indian Company, and compel-ling several of the people to swear allegiance to Christina, queen of Sweden." Smith.

[2] Chalmers. Smith. A visit to Delaware and New Jersey, about a hundred years after, drew from a learned Swede a sigh of patriotic regret for the indifference of his countrymen to the preservation of " the finest and best province in all North America." Kalm's *Travels*.

whose spirit has degenerated in their colonial settlements.   The Dutch themselves have been generally obnoxious to this reproach ; and their conduct in New Netherlands will never be cited as an exception to its application.   All their colonies were the offspring of mere thirst for commercial gain ; no liberal institutions arose there to nourish generous sentiment or exercise manly virtue ; and the exclusive pursuit of the same objects which engaged them to extend their dominions engendered habits and tastes corruptive of the energy that was requisite to their defence and preservation. The valor of Stuyvesant[1] rebuked, without animating, the sluggish spirit of his fellow-colonists, whom his example could never teach either to repel injustice with spirit or to endure it with dignity.   Yet Holland was now in the meridian of her fame ; and this was the age of Tromp and De Ruyter.

The attention which had been awakened in the mother country to the state of the colony of New Netherlands was sustained by the prosperous result of her recent interposition, and farther manifested itself in the following year [1656], by an ordinance which was enacted by the West India Company and the burgomasters of Amsterdam, and approved by the States General of Holland.   It was decreed by this ordinance, that the colonists of New Netherlands should be ruled in future by a governor nominated by the municipal authorities of Amsterdam, and by burgomasters and a town council elected by the provincial people ; the council thereafter enjoying the power of filling up all vacancies in its own body.[2]   This constitution differed very little from the actual frame of government already established in New Netherlands ; and the attention of the mother country beginning soon to relax, with the decline of the colony's prosperity, no farther attempt was made to accomplish the projected alteration.   The West India Company transmitted about this time to Stuyvesant a ratification, which they had procured from the States General, of his treaty, in 1650, with the commissioners of the United English Colonies ; and the Dutch governor gave notice of this circumstance to the commissioners, in a letter replete with Christian benevolence and piety, and proposing to them that a friendly league and sincere good-will might thenceforward unite the colonies of England and Holland.   But the English were averse to believe the sincerity of a man whom they had recently accused of plotting their destruction with the Indians ; and, beginning to regard the Dutch occupation as altogether lawless and intrusive, they were determined not to sanction it by any new recognition.   The commissioners answered the governor's communication with austere civility ; recommending the continuance of peace, but declining either to ratify the former treaty or to execute a new one.[3]   They had for some time past indulged the hope that the English government would unite with them in regarding the Dutch settlers in America as mere intruders, who could derive no claim of forbearance from the peace with Holland, and whom it would be no less just than expedient to expel or subdue.   [1659.]   Their friends in England succeeded in im-

---

[1] This gallant veteran did not fail to attract a portion of that idle rumor and absurd exaggeration to which solitary superiority is exposed.   To the English he was an object of continual marvel and apprehension. He had lost a leg in fighting for the independence of Holland ; and the English believed that his artificial limb was made of silver (Josselyn) ; and with still greater credulity, that he *restrained the Dutch colonists* from immediate hostilities with them, in order to destroy them more cruelly by the hands of the Indians (Trumbull) ; so well did he cover the deficiency of his countrymen's military ardor.   The fable of the silver leg is also related by Blome.

[2] *Collections of the New York Historical Society.*

[3] Trumbull.

pressing these views upon Richard Cromwell, who, during his short enjoyment of the protectorate, addressed instructions to his commanders for an invasion of New Netherlands, and wrote letters to the provincial assemblies in America, desiring the coöperation of their forces in the enterprise.[1] But his speedy deposition spared him the actual guilt of attacking an unoffending people, whom his father had plainly regarded as comprehended in his treaty of peace with Holland.

Stuyvesant had already made attempts to improve his conquest of the Swedes by extending the Dutch settlements in Delaware [1660] ; and equitable as well as brave, he caused the lands which he appropriated to be fairly purchased from the Indians. But his success in this quarter was now drawing to a close. Fendal, the governor of Maryland, claimed the territory occupied by the Dutch and Swedes, as included within Lord Baltimore's patent ; and finding that Stuyvesant was determined to retain possession of the land and defend the supposed title of his country, he procured a remonstrance to be transmitted in the name of Lord Baltimore to the States General and the West India Company of Holland, who, with an inversion of their usual policy, publicly denied the pretensions of the English, but at the same time transmitted private orders to Stuyvesant to avoid hostilities, if they should seem likely to ensue, by retiring beyond Lord Baltimore's alleged frontier. This injunction was obeyed, though not to the extent of an entire evacuation of Delaware, when Charles Calvert a few years after assumed the government of Maryland.[2] Stuyvesant deplored the feeble policy of those whose mandates it was his duty to obey; and sensible of the total discredit to which the Dutch title would be exposed by thus practically avowing that its efficacy depended on the forbearance of the English, he earnestly solicited that a formal copy of the grant by the States General to the West India Company might be transmitted to New Netherlands, for the purpose of enabling him to assert, with proper form and dignity, the interests he was intrusted to defend. But his solicitations proved ineffectual. The States General were now more anxious than ever to avoid a rupture with England ; and the West India Company, either espousing their policy, or controlled by their orders, refused to exhibit a title which they feared that Stuyvesant might so employ as inevitably to provoke that extremity. Perhaps they expected that his prudence would be enforced by the consciousness of a defective title ; and such was at least the effect that their policy actually produced. Stuyvesant, willing by any honorable means to propitiate the English, and hoping to obtain a recognition of the title which he was unable to produce, sent an embassy to Sir William Berkeley, the governor of Virginia, to propose a treaty of mutual trade between this colony and New Netherlands, and an alliance against the Indian enemies of both. Berkeley received the ambassadors with much courtesy, and despatched Sir Henry Moody to New Netherlands, with the articles of a commercial treaty ; but he cautiously forbore every expression that might seem either to acknowledge, or even imply, assent to the territorial pretensions of the Dutch.[3]

The revolutionary rulers whose dominion in England was terminated by the Restoration had been regarded with continual uneasiness and apprehension by the inhabitants of New Netherlands. The Long Parliament had attacked their countrymen in Europe ; Cromwell had once been on the

---

[1] Thurloe's *Collection.*   [2] See *ante*, Book III   [3] Chalmers. Smith.

point of subduing their own colonial settlement in America ; and only the deposition of his successor again snatched them from a repetition of the same danger.   Of the government of Charles. the Second they were disposed to entertain more favorable hopes, which might, perhaps, derive some support from the well known fact, that their especial rivals, the inhabitants of New England, were as much disliked by the king as they had been favorably regarded by the Protector.   Accordingly, when the pursuers of Goffe and Whalley, baffled in their attempts to discover the retreat of these fugitive regicides in New England, besought Stuyvesant to deny them his protection in New Netherlands [1661], he readily seized the opportunity of ingratiating himself and his people with the English court, by undertaking to give instant notice of the arrival of any of the regicides within his jurisdiction, and to prohibit all vessels from transporting them beyond the reach of their pursuers.[1]   But this policy, which, it must be acknowledged, was no honorable feature of his administration, proved quite unavailing ; and every hope that the Dutch might have entertained, of an amelioration of their prospects, was speedily dissipated by intelligence of the designs entertained by the king of England.   Charles, though he had received, during his exile, more friendship and civility from the Dutch than from any other foreign power, ever regarded this people with enmity and aversion ; and he was the more disposed, at present, to embrace any measure that might humble the ruling party in Holland, by the interest he felt in a weaker faction, at the head of which was his nephew, the young Prince of Orange, whom he desired to see reinstated in the office of Stadtholder, which his ancestors had possessed ; — an office which the ruling party had pledged themselves to Cromwell never again to bestow on the Orange family.   These sentiments were promoted by the interest and urgency of the Duke of York [1663], who had placed himself at the head of a new African Company,[2] of which the expected commerce was circumscribed by the more successful traffic of the Dutch.   In imitation of the other courtiers, the duke, moreover, had cast his eyes on the American territory, which his brother was now distributing with a liberal hand ; and, accordingly, in addition to the other means which he employed to produce a quarrel with the Dutch, he solicited a grant of their North American plantations, on the specious pretence that they were usurped from the territory properly belonging to Britain.[3]   The influence of these motives on the mind of the king was doubtless aided by the desire to strike a blow that would lend weight to the arbitrary commission which he was preparing to despatch to New England, and teach the Puritan colonists there that it was in the power of their sovereign to punish and subdue his enemies in America.

The rumor of the king's intentions reached America before it was generally prevalent in Europe, owing to the vigilance and activity of the nu-

[1] Trumbull. It was notorious, at the time, that Goffe and Whalley were sheltered within the territory of New Haven, where the local authorities and the inhabitants, so far from assisting, had, with very little disguise, obstructed and defeated the attempts to apprehend them. This conduct of a people peculiarly distinguished by their enmity to the Dutch had probably some weight in inducing Stuyvesant to pledge himself to a line of conduct which would have compromised the honor and independence of his country.

[2] This company was formed with a view of extending and engrossing the *slave trade.* Under the patronage of the Duke of York, it treated every commercial rival with a violence and injustice worthy of the purpose of its institution. In return for the special favor it received from the English government, it lent its aid to harass the colonies by promoting a rigid execution of the Acts of Navigation. Oldmixon.

[3] Sir John Dalrymple's *Memoirs.* Hume's *England.* Chalmers.

merous friends of the English colonists, who collected and conveyed intelligence of the designs of the court. When the conjunction of the royal commission of inquiry with the expedition against New Netherlands was communicated to the inhabitants of New England, the first article of intelligence appeared to them much more unwelcome than the other was satisfactory. In Massachusetts, particularly, the language and measures of the *General Court* plainly indicated a strong apprehension that the military, no less than the civil, department of the expedition was intended against the liberties of the English colonists.[1] Stuyvesant, whose anxious eye explored the darkening horizon of his country's fortune, descried these symptoms of dissatisfaction in the New England settlements, and in the dimness of anguish and perplexity conceived from them the desperate and chimerical project of gaining the alliance, or at least securing the neutrality, of his ancient enemies. With this view he undertook a voyage to Massachusetts, where he was entertained by the governor and magistrates with much state and solemnity.[2] Former rivalship was forgotten in the season of common danger, or remembered only to enhance the respect with which Endicott and Stuyvesant recognized, each in the other, an aged, brave, and honorable champion of his country's cause. Perhaps some traces of the effect of this conference may be discerned in the slowness with which Massachusetts obeyed the requisition of the royal commanders to raise a body of men in aid of the invasion of New Netherlands. But it was impossible that Stuyvesant's negotiation could succeed, or his proposals, even to the extent of neutrality, be admitted. Notwithstanding this disappointment, he repaired subsequently to Connecticut, where he was engaged in vainly attempting to bring a similar negotiation to a more successful issue, when the tidings of the approach of the British fleet recalled him to the immediate defence of his province.[3]

The British monarch, who was unable to assign a just cause of war with Holland, after trying in vain to provoke the resentment of the States General by insulting memorials and groundless complaints,[4] determined to embrace the pretext that had been suggested to him of his right to the province of New Netherlands ; expecting, with good reason, that the assertion of this pretended right would supply the cause of quarrel which he was industriously seeking. In pursuance of this policy, a charter from the British crown was issued in favor of the Duke of York [March, 1664], containing a grant of the whole region extending from the western banks of the Connecticut to the eastern shore of the Delaware, together with the adjacency of Long Island ; and conferring upon the duke all the powers of government, civil and military, within these ample boundaries. This grant disregarded alike the existing possession of the Dutch, and the recent charter of Connecticut, which, whether from ignorance, or from carelessness in the definition of boundaries, it tacitly but entirely superseded. No sooner did the Duke of York obtain the object of his solicitation, than, without waiting to gain actual possession of the soil, he ventured to exercise his proprietary powers in their fullest extent, by assigning to Lord Berkeley and Sir George Carteret all that portion of the territory which afterwards received the name of New Jersey. But, as it was manifest that the title of the duke himself, equally with that of his assignees, would require to be supported by a military force, an armament was prepared for this purpose, with some attention

---

[1] See *ante*, Book II., Chap. IV.   [2] Josselyn.   [3] Trumbull.   [4] Hume.

to secrecy, — a precaution, which, if it proved ineffectual, was likewise unnecessary ; as the States of Holland reckoned it impossible that the British king would attack their possessions without the formality of a previous declaration of war, and were unwilling to provoke his injustice by seeming to expect it.   So little, indeed, was the hostile expedition against New Netherlands credited in Europe, that, but a few months before it sailed, a vessel arrived at the colony from Holland, bringing an addition to its population and a large supply of implements of husbandry.   Stuyvesant earnestly pressed upon the West India Company the alarming intelligence which he had received ; but the only defensive step to which they were moved by his urgency was, to send him now, when it was too late, the original grant from the States General, which, at the period when it might have availed him, he had solicited in vain.

. The command of the English troops that were embarked for this expedition, and the government of the province against which it was directed, were intrusted to Colonel Nichols, who had studied the art of war under Marshal Turenne, and who, with Carr, Cartwright, and Maverick, also held a commission to visit the colonies of New England, and investigate and determine, according to their discretion, all disputes and controversies within the various provincial jurisdictions.   After touching at Boston, where an armed force was ordered to be raised and sent to join the royal army, the fleet advanced to Hudson's River, and took its station before the capital of New Netherlands.   The requisition of a subsidiary force from Boston was so tardily obeyed, that the enterprise was concluded before the Massachusetts troops were ready to march ; but [August, 1664], on the communication of a similar mandate to Connecticut, Governor Winthrop, with several of the principal inhabitants of this province, repaired immediately to the English armament, and joined the standard of their king.[1]

The veteran governor of New Netherlands, and the pupil of Turenne, were, according to military notions, enemies worthy of each other ; though doubtless not even military morality can regard Nichols as worthily employed in executing the lawless rapacity and insolent ambition of a tyrant on a peaceful, industrious, and blameless community.   But the two commanders were very unequally supported.   Stuyvesant had vigorously exerted himself to put the city in the best posture of defence ; but he found it impracticable to awaken martial spirit in the unwarlike bosoms of its people.   It must, indeed, be confessed, in favor of these unfortunate Dutchmen, that the superior artillery and disciplined forces of the enemy forbade every hope of successful resistance.   Their inhabitance of the country had been too short to attach them to it by patriotic sentiments ; and their sluggish dispositions and ignoble habits rendered them totally unsusceptible of the impressions which their governor derived from the prospect of a contest, where the harvest of glory seemed to him to be proportioned to the hopelessness of victory. They felt themselves unjustly attacked ; and their resentment of this injury was so strong, that many of them were determined not to become the subjects of a tyrannical usurper : but it was not strong enough to overcome the rational conviction, that safety and independence were the only worthy objects of battle, and that, where independence could not be gained by fighting, safety should not be risked by it.   To add unnecessary combat to unavoidable subjugation appeared to them a driftless and fool-hardy waste

---

[1] Smith.   Chalmers.   Trumbull.

of life : and if they must surrender the image they had created of their native Holland in the wilderness, they would rather resign it entire to the pollution of hostile occupation than defaced and mutilated by the cannon of the enemy. They were willing to become exiles with their wives and children, or laborers for them ; to encounter, in short, every evil that hope could alleviate or virtue subdue. But to expose their kindred, their city, and themselves to the certainty of capture by storm, and the extremity of military fury, seemed to them an inversion of all the dictates of prudence and virtue.

Widely different were the sentiments, the views, and even the determinations of Stuyvesant ; and for several days his undaunted spirit upheld the honor and prolonged the dominion of his country, notwithstanding the desertion of her unwarlike children, and the impending violence of a stronger foe. On the arrival of the English armament, he sent a deputation to its commander, consisting of one of the ministers of New Amsterdam, one of the city counsellors, and two other inhabitants, with a courteous letter, desiring to know the reason and purpose of this hostile demonstration. Nichols answered, with equal politeness, that he was commanded by his royal master to take possession of the British territory which had been usurped by the Dutch, whom, though nearly allied to him, the king could not, consistently with his honor, allow to invade and occupy the dominions of his crown : that he must therefore now demand the instant surrender of the place ; that the king, being tender of the effusion of Christian blood, had authorized him to offer security of life, liberty, and estate to all who would readily submit to this requisition ; but that such as should oppose his Majesty's gracious intentions must prepare to abide the severest extremities of war. Governor Winthrop, who was connected by acquaintance and mutual esteem with Stuyvesant and the principal citizens of the Dutch colony, seconded the communication of Nichols by a letter, in which he strongly urged the prudence of doing soon what must unavoidably be done at last. Stuyvesant, on receiving the summons of the English commander, was sensible of no other consideration than the insolent injustice with which his country was treated ; and still earnestly hoping that her honor would be preserved unblemished, even though her dominion should be overthrown, he invited the burgomasters and council of the city to attend him, and vainly labored to instil a portion of his own spirit into the phlegmatic members of this municipal body. They coolly desired to see the letters he had received from the enemy ; but, as he judged, with good reason, that the easy terms of surrender that were proffered would not contribute to animate their ardor or further his own martial designs, he declined to gratify them in this particular ; and simply assured them that the English had declared their purpose of depriving Holland of her dominion, and themselves of their independence. Suspecting the truth, they became more importunate in their first request ; whereupon the governor, in a transport of indignation, tore the letters in pieces, and scattered them on the ground ; while the burghers, in amazement and dismay, protested against his conduct, and all the consequences that might attend it.

But Stuyvesant's courage needed not the aid of sympathetic bravery; and more incensed to see his country's honor disregarded than appalled to find himself its only defender, he determined to try the effect of an appeal to the justice and generosity of a gallant enemy ; and to express in his reply to the summons of the English commander, not what he painfully saw, but what he magnanimously wished, to be the sentiments of his fellow-citizens. He exhibited to a deputation sent to him by Nichols the original grant of the States General and his own commission from the West India Company; and in a firm and manly letter maintained that a province thus formally incorporated with the Dutch dominion could not, consistently with the law of nations, be attacked while peace subsisted between England and the republic. He represented the long possession of the territory which his countrymen had enjoyed, and the ratification which the Dutch claim received from his treaty with the English provincial authorities in the year 1650; and he protested that it was impossible that the king of England could have despatched this hostile armament, in the knowledge of these facts, or would hesitate to countermand it, if they were submitted to his consideration. To spare the effusion of blood, he proposed a treaty for a provisional arrangement, suspended on the issue of a reference to the two parent states; and to the denunciations of military havoc, in the event of a refusal to surrender, he returned this calm and undaunted reply : — " As touching the threats in your conclusion, we have nothing to answer, only that we fear nothing, but what God (who is as just as merciful) shall lay upon us ; all things being in his gracious disposal : and we may as well be preserved by him with small forces as by a great army ; which makes us to wish you all happiness and prosperity, and recommend you to his protection." But this simulation of force and confidence was unavailing ; and Stuyvesant found it far more easy to refute the pretensions than to resist the arms of his opponent. Even after the English had begun to invest the place, and occupied a position which announced immediate attack and inevitable capture, he still clung to the hope that his fellow-citizens would not surrender the rights of their country till they had defended them with valor and shed the blood of the invaders. But Nichols, who was informed how little the Dutch troops and colonists partook the martial ardor of their governor, caused a proclamation,[1] repeating his original offers, to be circulated through the country and introduced into the town ; a measure which so completely disarmed the spirit of the besieged, and extinguished the authority of Stuyvesant, that this brave and somewhat headstrong old man, after one more fruitless attempt to obtain a provisional treaty, was at length obliged to capitulate for surrender, in order to prevent the people from giving up the place without the formality of capitulation. [August 27, 1664.]

By the treaty which ensued, it was provided that the Dutch garrison should march out with all the accustomed honors of war, and that the States General and West India Company should preserve their ammunition and public stores, and be allowed the space of six months for transporting them to Holland ; that the inhabitants should have liberty either to sell their estates, and return to Holland, or to retain them and reside in the settlement ; that all who chose to remain should enjoy their ancient customs with respect to inheritance of property, liberty of conscience in ecclesiastical matters, and perpetual exemption from military service. All Dutchmen, either continuing in the province, or afterwards resorting to it, were to be allowed a free trade with Holland ; a privilege, which, as it was quite inconsistent with the

---

[1] The proclamation announced, that all who would " submit to this his Majesty's government, as his good subjects, shall be protected in his Majesty's laws and justice, and peaceably enjoy whatsoever God's blessing and their own honest industry have furnished them with." Smith. To the Swedish settlers in Delaware it was especially represented that it would be an honorable change for them to return from a republican to a monarchical government. S. Smith's *New Jersey.*

Navigation Act, neither Nichols nor even the king could legally confer, and which accordingly was withdrawn very soon after. As a concession to the inflexible obstinacy of the old governor, it was most superfluously provided, that, if at any time thereafter the king of England and the States General should unite in desiring that the province be redelivered to its former owners,[1] their commands should be promptly obeyed. These, and various other articles, of additional advantage to the Dutch, forming perhaps the most favorable terms that a capitulating city ever obtained, were satisfactory to every one except the fearless, stubborn veteran to whose solitary valor and pertinacity they were in no small degree a tribute ; and it was not till two days after they had been signed by the commissioners on both sides, that Stuyvesant, still erect amidst his forlorn circumstances, could be persuaded to ratify them. Yet the Dutch West India Company, whose blunders and imbecility promoted the fall of a dominion which they were unworthy to administer, had the mean ingratitude to express dissatisfaction with the conduct of this magnanimous man. The conquest of the capital, which now received the name of New York (a name also extended to the whole provincial territory), was followed by the surrender of Albany, and the general submission of the province, with its subordinate settlement of Dutch and Swedes in Delaware. The government of Britain was acknowledged over the whole region in the beginning of October, 1664.[2]

Thus, by an act of the most flagrant injustice and insolent usurpation, was overthrown the Dutch dominion in North America, after it had subsisted for more than half a century, and had absorbed the feebler colonial settlements of Sweden. It is impossible for a moment to suppose that the king of England was prompted to undertake this enterprise by an honest conviction of his right to the territory ; and that he was actuated by no concern for the interest of his other colonies was proved (if such proof were wanting) by his subsequent conduct with regard to Acadia. This region, to which the English had as fair a claim as to New York,[3] was conquered from its French occupiers by the fair and legitimate hostilities of Cromwell ; and yet the earnest entreaties of the New England colonies could not prevent the king from restoring it to France, a neighbour much more dangerous than Holland to his subjects. But Acadia was not, like New Netherlands, a settlement of Protestant republicans, but of the subjects of a brother despot, to whom Charles became a pensioner, and to whom he scrupled not to sell as much of the honor of England as was capable of being bartered by his hands. His object, in so far as it embraced the English colonies, was rather to intimidate them than to promote their advantage. Yet eventually it was they who derived the chief benefit from the acquisition of New York ; and this, as well as every other conquest of American territory achieved by Great Britain, only tended to undo the bands by which she retained her

---

[1] According to Hume, it would appear that this improbable condition did actually occur ; for he states, that, on the complaint of Holland, the King disavowed the expedition, and imprisoned the admiral. But he has confounded the invasion of New York with the expedition against Goree, which took place two years before, and which Charles, after despatching, affected to disavow.

[2] Oldmixon. Smith. Chalmers. Trumbull. Hutchinson.

[3] It was included in the claim derived from Cabot's voyage, and had been made the subject of various grants by James the First and Charles the First, to the Plymouth Council in the first instance, and afterwards to Lord Stirling. This nobleman was the king's secretary of state in Scotland ; and seeing the English courtiers obtaining grants of American territory, he applied for a share of this advantage ; and Acadia, under the name of Nova Scotia, was granted to him (very irregularly) by a patent under the great seal of *Scotland*.

colonies in a state of dependence. As they ceased to receive molestation or alarm from the neighbourhood of rival settlements, their strength and their jealousy converged against the power and pretensions of the parent state.

Colonel Nichols, who was appointed the first British governor of New York, — perhaps with the humane view of persuading his master to refrain from burdening or irritating the people by fiscal impositions, — studiously depreciated the actual condition of the settlement in his letters to the Duke of York. But all the early writers and travellers unite in describing the Dutch colonial metropolis as a handsome, well-built town ; and Josselyn declares that the meanest house in it was worth a hundred pounds.[1] Indeed, the various provisions that were introduced into the articles of surrender, for preserving the comforts of the inhabitants undiminished, attest the orderly and plentiful estate which these colonists had attained, as well as explain the causes of their unwarlike spirit. If the manners of the Dutch colonists corresponded with those of their countrymen in the parent state, they were probably superior in refinement to the manners which the English colonists could derive from similar imitation. Sir William Temple was surprised to find in Holland that he was expected not to spit upon the floors of gentlemen's houses.[2] Of the colonists who had latterly resorted to the province, some were persons who had enjoyed considerable affluence and respectability in their native country, and who imported with them, and displayed in their houses, costly services of family plate, and well-selected productions of the Dutch school of painting.[3] No account has been preserved of the total population of the province and its dependencies ; but the metropolis, at this time, contained about three thousand persons.[4] More than half of this number chose to continue in the place, after its annexation to the British empire ; the rest abandoned a settlement which was no longer to retain its Dutch aspect or name ; and their habitations were soon occupied by a supply of emigrants, partly from Britain, but chiefly from New England. The Duke of York, in order to allure the New England planters to settle in his province, published what he termed *conditions for plantations*, by which (among other provisions) it was declared that the inhabitants of every township should elect their own minister of religion, and determine his emoluments by private agreement between themselves and him.[5] Among the Dutch who remained at New York was the venerable Stuyvesant, who still adhered to the wreck of the institutions and community over which he had presided, and to the scenes that reminded him of the exploits of his old age. Here, for a few years more, he prolonged the empire of Dutch manners and the respect of the Dutch name, till, full of days and honor, he breathed his last amidst the tears of his countrymen. His descendants inherited his worth and popularity, and in the following century were frequently elected into the magistracy of New York.[6]

---

[1] Josselyn's *Second Voyage.* Oldmixon.   [2] Sir W. Temple's *Works.*
[3] Grant's *Memoirs of an American Lady.* An ingenious and observant traveller, in his contrasted sketch of Dutch and English colonial manners, remarks that Dutchmen are always more prone to improve the appearance than to enlarge the extent of their plantations; that the Dutch begin soonest to enjoy, and the English continue longest to pursue, their acquisitions ; and that the same funds which an English planter employs to increase the sphere of his industry and the sources of his revenue are preferably devoted by a Dutchman to the embellishment of his house and the refinement of his domestic accommodations. Bolingbroke's *Account of Demerara.*
[4] I found this calculation on a *Report to the Board of Trade* a few years after, published by Chalmers, together with a consideration of the intervening events.
[5] Oldmixon. Smith.   [6] Chalmers. Smith.

One of the earliest transactions in which Nichols was engaged [December, 1664] bore reference not to his authority as provincial governor, but to the functions which he shared with the other commissioners of the English monarch ; in conjunction with whom he had now to ascertain and determine the boundaries of New York and Connecticut. The claims of the latter of these provinces in Long Island were disallowed, and the whole of this insular region was annexed to the new British jurisdiction ; but in the arrangement of the boundaries on the main land, so little disposition was entertained to take advantage of the erroneous designation in the Duke of York's charter, — so ignorant also of the localities of the country were the commissioners, — and so much inclined, at the same time, to gratify the people of Connecticut, in order to detach them from the interest of Massachusetts, — that Connecticut undoubtedly received an allotment of territory far more liberal than equitable. At a subsequent period it was found necessary to make a more equitable adjustment of the limits of Connecticut and New York; which, however, was not accomplished without violent dispute and altercation between the two provincial governments.[1]

Leaving the other commissioners to proceed to the execution of their functions in New England, Nichols betook himself to the discharge [1665] of his own peculiar duty in the province which he was deputed to govern. The Duke of York had made an ample delegation of authority to his lieutenant, and the prudence and humanity of Nichols rendered his administration creditable to the proprietary and acceptable to the people. To confirm the acquisition that his arms had gained, and to assimilate, as far as possible, the different races of inhabitants of the province, Nichols judged it expedient to establish among them all a uniform frame of civil polity ; and with a prudent conformity to the institutions already established by the Dutch, he formed a court of assizes, composed of the governor, the council, and the justices of the peace, which was invested with every branch of authority, legislative and executive, within the colony. The only liberal institution that he was permitted to introduce was trial by jury ; and to this admirable check on judicial iniquity all suits and controversies were subjected. He encouraged the colonists to make purchases of land from the natives ; and these purchases he confirmed by charters from himself, in which he reserved to the proprietary a quitrent of a penny an acre. A dispute which occurred among the inhabitants of Long Island suggested to him a salutary regulation which continued long to obtain in the province. The dispute arose out of some conflicting Indian grants ; and to prevent a recurrence of such disagreements, as well as of the more fatal dissensions which were apt to spring from these transactions with the natives, it was ordained that henceforward no purchase from the Indians should be valid, unless the vendition were authorized by a license from the governor, and executed in his presence. The formidable number and martial spirit of the natives rendered it necessary to treat them with unimpeachable justice ; and to prevent their frequent sales of the same land to different persons (a practice in which they had been encouraged by the conflicting pretensions and occupations of the Dutch, Swedes, and English), it was judged expedient that the bargains should be signalized by some memorable solemnity. The friendly relations now established between the European colonists of this province and the powerful confederacy of Indian tribes distinguished by the title of *The Five*

[1] Smith. Chalmers.

Nations, and which will afterwards demand a considerable share of our attention, were promoted by the harmony which subsisted between the Dutch and Indians during the government of Stuyvesant, whose prudence thus bequeathed a wise lesson and a valuable opportunity to his successor.[1]

The Court of Assizes proceeded, without delay, to collect into one code the ancient customs of the province, with additional ordinances, rendered necessary by the recent change of empire [June, 1665], and which served to introduce a practical application of the supremacy ascribed to the jurisprudence of England. In this code, which was afterwards ratified by the Duke of York, there occur some laws that denote the influence which the New England settlers in Long Island[2] doubtless exercised in its composition. Any person above sixteen years of age, striking his father or mother (except in defence of his own life), "at the complaint of the said father and mother, and not otherwise, they being sufficient witnesses thereof," was adjudged to suffer death. Travelling on Sunday was forbidden; and fornication was *punished by marriage*, fine, flogging, or imprisonment, according to the discretion of the judges. The barbarous state of medical science and practice was indicated by an ordinance prohibiting all surgeons, physicians, and midwives from "presuming to exercise or put forth any act contrary to the known approved rules of art"; and the unsubdued state of nature appears from the proposition of rewards for the destruction of wolves in Long Island.[3] The city of New York, which had enjoyed extensive privileges under the old government, was now incorporated and placed under the administration of a mayor, aldermen, and sheriff; the English official nomenclature serving additionally to link the provincial institutions with English jurisprudence. One of the highest acts of power that was reserved to the Court of Assizes was the imposition of taxes; and this it was soon called to exercise in order to meet the exigencies of the war which Charles the Second had finally succeeded in kindling with Holland. But even the most ungracious acts of Nichols were disarmed of their offence by a conciliating demeanour that caused the Dutch to forget he had been their conqueror, and by the moderation and integrity which he uniformly displayed, and the personal sacrifices that he readily incurred for the public advantage. An assembly of deputies from the Dutch and English plantations in Long Island, which he summoned to adjust the relative boundaries of these settlements, took the opportunity of their congregation to transmit an address to the Duke of York, acknowledging their dependence on his sovereignty according to his patent; engaging to defend his rights, and to submit cheerfully to whatever laws might be enacted by his authority; and desiring that their declaration might be preserved and exhibited as a memorial against them and their posterity, if they should ever happen to fail in the performance of their duty.[4] Yet one portion of these people had but recently submitted to Nichols as the conquering leader of the troops of a foreign usurper; and the others had as recently been severed from the liberal institutions of New England.

The intelligence of the declaration of war with Holland [1666], which was communicated by the Lord Chancellor (Clarendon) to Colonel Nichols, was accompanied with the assurance that the Dutch were preparing an ex-

[1] Smith. Chalmers. Colden's *History of the Five Nations.*
[2] It was probably to them that Nichols alluded, when, in a letter to the Duke of York, he expressed his hope that "now even the most factious republicans must acknowledge themselves satisfied with the way they are in." Chalmers.
[3] *Collections of the New York Historical Society.*   [4] Smith. Chalmers.

pedition for the recovery of their American colony, and that De Ruyter had received orders to sail immediately for New York.[1] Nichols exerted himself, with his usual firmness and activity, to resist the assault of so formidable an invader ; and though it proved eventually, that either the chancellor's information was erroneous, or that the expedition was suspended by De Ruyter's more important avocations in Europe, the expense that attended the preparations for his reception, together with the other consequences of the war, inflicted much inconvenience and distress on the province.   As the people were destitute of shipping, their trade, which had been carried on by Dutch vessels, was completely suspended ; no supplies were obtained from England to alleviate this calamity ; and in addition to other concomitant burdens of war, a general rate or tax was imposed on the estates of the inhabitants by the Court of Assizes.   There was reason to apprehend that the product of this tax would be insufficient, and the preparations consequently inadequate to repel the expected invasion.   In this extremity, the governor, without pressing the people for farther contributions to defeat an enterprise which many of them must have contemplated with secret good-will, generously advanced his own money and interposed his private credit to supply the public exigencies.   Happily for the province, which Nichols, with the aid of the neighbouring English colonies, would have defended to the last extremity, neither the States General, nor the Dutch West India Company, made any attempt to repossess themselves of New York during this war ; and at the peace of Breda it was ceded to England [July, 1667] in exchange for her colony of Surinam, which had been conquered by the Dutch.   This exchange was no otherwise expressed, than by a general stipulation in the treaty that each of the two nations should retain what its arms had acquired since hostilities began.[2]   The Dutch had no reason to regret the transaction ; for it was impossible that they could long have preserved New York against the increasing strength and rivalry of the colonies of New England, Maryland, and Virginia.   It was by this treaty that Acadia was ceded to France, which had acted as the ally of Holland during the war, and was the only party that reaped advantage from it.   England saw her character sullied by the injustice of her hostilities ; the glory of her arms obscured by a signal disgrace at Chatham ; the conquest formerly achieved for her by Cromwell surrendered [1667] ; and every one of the purposes that induced her monarch to provoke the quarrel disappointed.

The security which the British dominion in New York derived from the treaty of Breda tended with seasonable occurrence to supply the loss of the services of Colonel Nichols, who, finding the pecuniary burdens of the war pressing too heavily on his own private fortune, was forced, in the beginning of this year, to resign a command which had proved not less honorable to himself than satisfactory and advantageous to the people over whom it was exercised.   The king expressed his sense of the meritorious conduct of Nichols, by a present of *two hundred pounds ;* and this brave and modest loyalist was more gratified with the expression of royal favor and remembrance, than disappointed by the meanness and inadequacy of the remuneration.   He was long remembered with respect and kindness by a people whom

---

[1] Hume says that De Ruyter actually committed hostilities on Long Island before the declaration of war, in revenge of the capture of New York. But De Ruyter was not accustomed so inadequately to avenge the wrongs of his country ; and Hume has been misled by an erroneous account, or by inaccurate recollection, of a more serious and successful attack on New York by the Dutch about seven years after this period, and in the course of a subsequent war.

[2] Smith. Chalmers. Douglass.

he had found hostile and divided ; and whom, notwithstanding that he was constrained to deprive them of liberty and independence, he left friendly, united, and contented.[1] The benefit of his successful exertions, together with the advantage of peace, and of the recognition by Holland of the British dominion, devolved on his successor, Colonel Lovelace, a man of quiet temper and moderate disposition, which in tranquil times so well supplied the absence of vigor and capacity, that the colony, during the greater part of six years that composed the period of his presidency, enjoyed a noiseless tenor of content and prosperity ;[2] and the most memorable occurrence that signalized his administration was the unfortunate event that brought it to a close.

The second war with Holland [1672], which the king undertook in subservience to the ambition of Louis the Fourteenth, was calculated no less to injure the trade of New York, than to disturb the harmony of its mixed inhabitants, and alienate the regards of the original colonists from their existing rulers. The false and frivolous reasons assigned by the English court for this profligate war rendered it more offensive to every Dutchman by adding insult to injury ; and the gallant achievements of De Ruyter, that extorted the admiration and applause even of his enemies, must have awakened in the most phlegmatic bosoms of the Dutch colonists some sympathy with the glory and danger of their country, and a reluctance to the destiny that associated them with her enemies. The intelligence of the Duke of York's recent profession of the Catholic faith contributed to increase their discontent, which at length prevailed so far with a considerable number of them, that they determined to abandon New York, and either return to Holland, or seek another colonial establishment in the new world. Happily for British America, they were retained within her territory by the address of the proprietaries of Carolina, who engaged them to direct their course towards this province, where, remote from foreign war, and surmounting hardships by patient industry, they formed a settlement that recompensed them for the habitations they had forsaken.[3] If more of their countrymen projected a similar retreat from New York, their purpose was suspended by an event which occurred the same year, and invited them to embrace a more gratifying deliverance from the irksomeness of their situation. A small squadron had been despatched from Holland, under the command of Binkes and Evertzen, to attack the shipping and harass the commerce of the English colonies ; and having performed this service with some effect on the Virginian coast, they were induced to attempt a more important enterprise, by intelligence of the negligent security of the governor of New York. Repairing with secrecy and expedition to this ancient possession of their country [July, 1673], they had the good fortune to arrive at the metropolis while Lovelace was at a distance, and the command was administered by Colonel Manning, whose own subsequent confession, added to the more credible testimony of his conduct, has branded him with the attributes of a traitor and poltroon. Now was reversed the scene that had been presented when

---

[1] From his monument in Ampthill church, Bedfordshire, it appears that Nichols was killed on board the Duke of York's ship, in a sea-fight with the Dutch in 1672. Within the pediment is fixed the cannon-ball that killed him, surmounted by this inscription : — *Instrumentum mortis et immortalitatis.*

[2] A feeble attempt was made in the year 1669, by one Coningsmark, a Swede, to excite an insurrection of his countrymen in the Delaware territory against the English. The attempt was defeated without bloodshed, and Coningsmark was condemned to be sold as a slave in Barbadoes. Samuel Smith's *History of New Jersey.*

[3] See *ante*, Book IV., Chap. I.

New York was invaded by Nichols. The English inhabitants prepared to defend themselves, and offered their services to Manning ; but he obstructed their efforts, rejected their aid, and, on the first intelligence of the enemy's approach, struck his flag before their vessels were even in sight. As the Dutch fleet advanced, his garrison could not forbear to demonstrate their readiness to fight ; but, in a transport of fear, he forbade a gun to be fired on pain of death, and surrendered the place unconditionally to the invaders.[1] The moderation of the conquerors, however, showed them worthy of their success ; and, hastening to assure all the citizens of the security of private rights and possessions, they inspired the Dutch colonists with triumph, and left the English no cause of resentment but against their pusillanimous commander. The same moderation being proffered to the other districts of the province, on condition of their sending deputies to swear allegiance to the States General, the inclinations of one party and the fears of the other induced the whole to submit ; the Dutch dominion was restored with a suddenness that exceeded the circumstances of its overthrow ; and the name of New Netherlands once more was applied to the province.[2] But neither the triumph of the one party, nor the mortification of the other, was destined to have a long endurance.

Great was the perturbation that these events excited in the adjoining colonies of the English. The government of Connecticut, with amazing absurdity, sent a message to the Dutch admirals, remonstrating against their usurpation of dominion over the territory of England and the property of her subjects ; desiring them to explain the meaning of their conduct and their further intentions ; and warning them that the United Colonies of New England were intrusted with the defence of their sovereign's empire in America, and would be faithful to their trust. To this ridiculous application the Dutch commanders returned a soldier-like answer, expressing their just surprise at the terms of it, and declaring that they were commissioned by their country to endamage the power and possessions of her enemies by sea and land ; and that, while they applauded the fidelity of the English colonies to their sovereign, they would emulously conform to an example so deserving of imitation, and endeavour to approve themselves not less zealous and faithful in the service of the States General. Active preparations for war ensued forthwith in Connecticut and the other confederated colonies ; but as each party stood on the defensive, awaiting the onset of the other, only a few insignificant skirmishes had taken place, when the arrival of winter suspended military operations. Early in the following spring [1674], the controversy was terminated, without farther blood-shed, by the intelligence of the treaty of peace concluded at London, and of the restoration of New York to the English by virtue of a general stipulation, that

---

[1] Manning, after all this extraordinary and unaccountable conduct, had the impudence to repair to England ; whence he returned, or was sent back, when the province was again given up by the Dutch in the following year. He was then tried by court-martial on a charge of treachery and cowardice, expressed in the strongest and most revolting terms. Confessing this charge to be well founded, he received a sentence almost as extraordinary as his conduct : — "That, though he deserved death, yet because he had since the surrender been in England, and *seen the king and the duke*, it was adjudged that his sword should be broke over his head in public, before the city hall, and himself rendered incapable of wearing a sword, and of serving his Majesty for the future in any public trust." Smith. The benefit of the old maxim, respected on this occasion, that grace is dispensed by the mere look of a king, was denied a few years after to the unfortunate Duke of Monmouth.

[2] When the intelligence of this disaster arrived in England, preparations were made for " sending succours to recover New York." Evelyn's *Diary*, 27th October, 1673.

all countries, conquered during the war, should be restored to the power that possessed them at its commencement.[1]

The events of this war, both in Europe and America, were attended with important consequences to that portion of the North American population which derived its origin from Holland. The elevation to the dignity of Stadtholder, which the Prince of Orange now obtained from the fear and danger of his countrymen, and from their desire to propitiate the king of England,[2] paved the way to his advancement to the English throne, and consequently to a reign under which the Dutch colonists, though disunited from Holland, ceased to regard the British sovereignty as a foreign domination. The reconquest of the province by the Dutch arms, and the final cession of it to England by a pacific and conventional arrangement, cured the wound that was inflicted by the insolent injustice of England's original acquisition. Many of the Dutch colonists, besides, apprehensive of molestation, or at least despairing of favor from a government whose temporary overthrow had provoked their undisguised triumph, were the more readily induced to follow their former companions who had emigrated to Carolina ;[3] and this dispersion of the Dutch tended at once to promote their friendly commixture with the English, and to divest New York of a distinctive character which might have obstructed harmony between her and the other provinces, with which she was henceforward to be indissolubly connected.

The Duke of York, understanding that some doubts existed concerning the validity of his original patent, which he had received at a time when the Dutch government was in peaceable possession of the country, and which, even though originally valid, yet seemed to have been vacated by the intervening conquest, thought it prudent to remedy this defect, and signalize the resumption of his proprietary functions by obtaining a new charter. This instrument, which he found no difficulty in obtaining [June 29, 1674], recited and confirmed the former grant of the province. It empowered the duke to govern the inhabitants " by such ordinances as he or his assigns should establish " ; and to administer justice according to the laws of England, with the admission of an appeal to the king in council. It prohibited all persons from trading to New York without his permission ; and though it allowed the colonists to import merchandises from England, it subjected them to payment of the same customs that were elsewhere prescribed by the laws of the realm. Under the authority of this charter, the duke continued to rule the province (diminished in extent by its partition from the New Jersey territory, which he had previously assigned to Berkeley and Carteret) till his proprietary right was merged in his regal title. It seems, at first sight, not a little surprising that neither in this nor in the former charter of the territory did the brother of the king obtain a grant of the same extraordinary powers and privileges that had been conferred on the proprietaries of Maryland and Carolina. But, relying on the greatness of his connection and his prospects, the duke probably was little solicitous to share the dignities and immunities which were coveted by those other proprietaries ; and while as counts palatine they assumed a style of independence in the administration of their governments, he contented himself with ruling his territory in the name of the king. The misfortunes and evident incapacity of Lovelace precluded his reappointment to the office of governor,

---

[1] Smith. Chalmers. Trumbull.   [2] Temple's *Works*.   [3] See *ante*, Book IV., Chap. I.

which was conferred on Edmund Andros [July 1, 1674], a man who disgraced superior talents by the unprincipled zeal and activity with which he rendered them subservient to the arbitrary designs of a tyrant.[1] This officer, whose subsequent conduct in New England has already introduced him to our acquaintance, now commenced that career in America which has gained him so conspicuous a place in her annals for twenty years after the present period. He was commanded to respect private rights and possessions, while he received the surrender of the province and its public property from the Dutch, and to distribute justice in the king's name according to the forms observed by his predecessors. But in order to raise a revenue and defray the expenses of government, a great variety of *rates* were at the same time imposed by the sole authority of the duke ; and an Englishman, named Dyer, was appointed the collector of these odious and unconstitutional impositions.[2]

The duke, in his instructions to Andros, recommended to him the exercise of gentleness and humanity ; but his selection of this officer to administer the arbitrary policy which he now began to pursue towards the colonists gave more reason to suppose that the admonition was necessary than that it would prove effectual ; and, accordingly, the new governor had not been long in the province [1675], when, besides embroiling himself with the neighbouring government of Connecticut, he excited the murmurs and remonstrances of the magistrates, the clergy, and a great majority of the people who were subjected to his command. The pressure of the arbitrary rates suggesting especially to the inhabitants of Long Island the benefit of a representative assembly, they began at length to broach this proposition as a matter of constitutional right ; but these first aspirations of liberty were checked by Andros with a vigor and decision for which he received the thanks of his master. A Dutch clergyman, named Renslaer, who was recommended by the duke to the patronage of Andros, proved unacceptable to the people, and was punished by the magistrates of Albany for some illegal and offensive language. The governor interfered, with his usual energy, in the dispute, and, having first loaded with insult a popular clergyman, whom Renslaer considered his rival, adjudged all the magistrates to find bail to answer Renslaer's complaints, to the extent of five thousand pounds each ; and threw Leisler, one of their number, into prison for refusing to comply. But finding that in this proceeding he had stretched his authority farther than he could support it, he was compelled to recede, barely in time to prevent a tumult that might have dissolved the government. Apparently somewhat daunted with his defeat, he conducted himself with greater regard to prudence, and was enabled for a while to enjoy a quiet administration ; but the seeds of popular discontent had been sown, and a strong desire for more liberal institutions took silent yet vigorous root in the colony. This disposition, which the contagious vicinity of liberty in New England doubtless tended to keep alive, was fomented by a measure to which the governor resorted, in order to supply the inadequate returns from the provincial rates, —the practice of soliciting pecuniary *benevolences* from the various communities and townships within his jurisdiction. [1676.] This policy, *the badge of bad times*, as a colonial historian has termed it, sometimes ef-

---

[1] See Note XVIII., at the end of the volume.
[2] Scott's *Model of the Government of East New Jersey.* The charter is here recited at length. Of this curious work (which will demand farther notice in Book VI.) I have seen copies in the library of Göttingen, and in the Advocates' Library of Edinburgh. Smith. Chalmers.

fectually befriends those rights which it attacks indirectly, and yet affects to recognize. In the close of the following year [1677], Andros was compelled to pay a visit to England in order to obtain farther instructions adapted to the new scene that was about to open.[1]

The rates imposed by the Duke of York, and which constituted the revenue he derived from the province, had been limited to the duration of three years ; and as the allotted period was on the point of expiring, the interest both of the government and the people was fixed on the issue to which this emergency would lead. The people anxiously hoped that the financial difficulties by which the government was embarrassed would induce their proprietary to consent to the desires they had expressed [1677], and to seek the improvement of his revenue from the establishment of a representative assembly. But the duke regarded this measure with aversion ; and thought that he made a sufficient sacrifice to the advantage of the colonists by simply proclaiming that the former rates should continue for three years longer. [1678.] When Andros returned to his government with this unwelcome edict, the province resounded with murmurs of disappointment ; and when a new edict, in the following year [1679], announced an increase of the tax on the importation of liquors, the public indignation was expressed so warmly, and so many complaints were transmitted to England, that the duke, in much surprise, recalled his governor to give account of an administration that plainly appeared to be universally odious. [1680.] This prince was determined that his subjects should be enslaved, and at the same time quite willing that they should be happy ; and seeing no incompatibility between those circumstances, he supposed the more readily that Andros might have perpetrated some enormities for which the exigence of his official position would not furnish an apology, and therefore called him home to ascertain if he had really so discredited legitimate tyranny. The inquiry, as might be expected, terminated in the acquittal of the governor, who easily demonstrated that he had committed no breach of trust ; that he had merely exerted a spirit suitable to the arbitrary system confided to his conduct, and enforced his master's commands with the rigor that was necessary to carry such obnoxious mandates into execution. But certain circumstances which occurred in the colony, during the absence of Andros, determined the duke to forbear for the present to reëmploy so unpopular an officer, or to risk his own authority in a farther struggle with the current of popular will, till his hand should be strengthened by the hold of a sceptre.

Dyer, the collector of the revenue, continued for some time after his appointment to execute his official functions with great odium, but little opposition. Latterly, however, the people had begun to question the legitimacy no less than the liberality of a system of taxation originating with the duke alone ; and when they learned that their doubts were sanctioned by the opinions of the most eminent lawyers in England, their indignation broke forth with a violence that nearly hurried them into the commission of injustice still more reprehensible than the wrongs they complained of. They accused Dyer of high treason, for having collected taxes without the authority of law ; and the local magistrates, seconding the popular rage, appointed a special court to try him on this absurd and unwarrantable charge. It was pretended, that, although he had not committed any one of the offences specified in the English statute of treasons, yet it was lawful to subject him

---

[1] Smith. Chalmers.

to the penalties of this statute, on the ancient and exploded charge of *en-croaching power* ; — one of those vague and unintelligible accusations which it was the express purpose of the statute to abolish. But reason and humanity regained their sway in the short interval between the impeachment and the trial ; and when the prisoner demanded to know whence his judges derived their functions, and if they did not act as servants and delegates of the same prince whose commission he had himself obeyed, — the court interposed to suspend farther prosecution of the affair within the colony, and ordered the prisoner to be sent with an accuser to England. [1681.] He was of course liberated immediately after his arrival ; and no accuser ventured to appear against him. But if the arraignment was any thing more than a bold, inconsiderate expression of popular displeasure and impatience, it accomplished the farthest purposes of its promoters ; and to their spirited, though irregular measures, New York was indebted for the overthrow of an odious despotism and her first experience of systematic liberty. While the duke regarded with astonishment the violent proceedings by which his officer had nearly perished as a traitor, and was banished from the colony without a voice being raised in his favor, he was assailed with expressions of the same sentiments that had produced this violence, in a more constitutional, and therefore, perhaps, more unwelcome shape. The governor's council, the Court of Assizes, and the corporation of the city of New York united with the whole body of the inhabitants in soliciting the duke to extend to the people a share of the legislative authority ; and while their conduct enabled him to interpret these addresses into a virtual declaration that they would no longer continue to pay taxes without possessing a representative assembly, he was informed by his confidential advisers that the laws of England would support them in this pretension. Overcome by the combined force of all these circumstances, and not yet advanced to the height whence he was afterwards enabled to regard the suggestions of legal obstructions with contempt, the duke first paused in his arbitrary career, and then gave a reluctant and ungracious assent to the demands of the colonists. Directions were sent to the deputy-governor, on whom the administration devolved in the absence of Andros, " to keep things quiet at New York in the mean time " ; and shortly after [February, 1682], it was intimated to him that the duke would condescend to grant the boon which the people desired, on condition of their raising enough of money for the support of government, and of the principal inhabitants assuring him by a written engagement that this should be done. In fine, after wavering a little longer between fear and aversion, the duke gave notice of his fixed determination to establish in New York the same frame of government that the other English colonies enjoyed, and particularly a representative assembly. The governor whom he nominated to conduct the new administration was Colonel Dongan, afterwards Earl of Limerick, a man of probity, moderation, and conciliating manners, and, though a professed Roman Catholic, which perhaps was his chief passport to the duke's favor, yet in the main acceptable, and justly so, to a people who regarded the Catholic faith with suspicion and dislike. The instructions that were given to Dongan required him to convoke an assembly, which was to consist of a council of ten nominated by the proprietary, and of a house of representatives, not exceeding eighteen, elected by the freeholders. Like the other provincial legislatures, this body was empowered to make laws for the colonists, under the condition of conformity to the general jurisprudence of the empire, and of dependence on the assent or dissent of the proprietary. Thus the inhabitants of New York, after having been treated as a conquered people for nearly twenty years, and governed by the arbitrary will of the Duke of York and his deputies, were elevated in the scale of political existence by their own spirit and vigor ; and, by a singular coincidence, obtained a free constitution at the very time when their old rivals, the colonists of New England, were deprived of it. Nothing could be more acceptable to them than this interesting change ; and the ardent gratitude of their acknowledgments expressed much more justly their relish of the benefit than the merit of their nominal benefactor.[1]

The most interesting monument of the tyrannical administration which was thus suspended is a report prepared by Andros, in reply to certain inquiries of the English Committee of Colonies in the year 1678 ; from which, and from a similar communication by the municipality of New York to the Board of Trade a few years after, some insight may be obtained into the condition of the province about this period. The city of New York, in 1678, appears to have contained three thousand four hundred and thirty inhabitants, and to have owned no larger navy than three ships, eight sloops, and seven boats. No account has been preserved of the population of the whole province, which contained twenty-four towns, villages, or parishes. About fifteen vessels, on an average, traded yearly to the port of New York, importing English manufactures to the value of fifty thousand pounds, and exporting the productions of the colony, which consisted of land produce of all sorts, among which are particularized beef, pease, lumber, tobacco,[2] peltry procured from the Indians, and sixty thousand bushels of wheat. Of servants the number was small ; and the demand for them was great. Some unfrequent and inconsiderable importations of slaves were made from Barbadoes ; and there were yet but very few of these unfortunate beings in the colony. Agriculture was more generally pursued than commerce. A trader worth five hundred pounds was considered a substantial citizen ; and a planter worth half that sum in movables was accounted rich. The united value of all the estates in the province was estimated at one hundred and fifty thousand pounds. "Ministers," says Andros, "are scarce, and religions many." The duke maintained a chaplain at New York, which was the only assured endowment of the church of England. There were about twenty churches or meeting-places, of which half were destitute of ministers. All districts were liable by law to the obligation of building churches and providing for ministers, whose emoluments varied from forty to seventy pounds a year, with the addition of a house and garden. But the Presbyterians and Independents, who formed the most numerous and thriving portion of the inhabitants, were the only classes of people who showed much willingness to procure and support ministers. Marriages were allowed to be solemnized either by ministers or by justices of the peace. There were no beggars in the province ; and the poor, of which the number was inconsiderable, were carefully tended and plentifully relieved. The number of the militia amounted to two thousand, comprehending one hundred and forty horsemen ; and a standing company of soldiers was maintained, as well as gunners and other officers, for the forts of Albany and New York. Such was the condition of the province about four years preceding the period at which we have now

---

[1] Smith. *History of the British Dominions in America.* Chalmers.

[2] Denton states that the New York tobacco was considered equal in quality to the finest produce of Maryland.

arrived. Four years after (in 1686) it was found to have improved so considerably, that the shipping of New York amounted to ten three-masted vessels, twenty sloops, and a few ketches of intermediate bulk. The militia had also increased to four thousand foot, three hundred horse, and a company of dragoons.[1] The augmentation of inhabitants, indicated by this increase of military force, appears the more remarkable, when we consider, that, some time prior to this last mentioned period, the province was diminished by the dismemberment of the Delaware territory, which had been partly surrendered to Lord Baltimore, and partly assigned to William Penn.

CHAPTER II.

Colonel Dongan's Administration. — Account of the Five Indian Nations of Canada. — Their Hostility to the French. — Missionary Labors of the French Jesuits. — James the Second abolishes the Liberties of New York — commands Dongan to abandon the Five Nations to the French. — Andros again appointed Governor. — War between the French and the Five Nations. — Discontents at New York. — Leisler declares for King William, and assumes the Government. — The French attack the Province, and burn Schenectady. — Arrival of Governor Sloughter. — Perplexity of Leisler — his Trial — and Execution. — Wars and mutual Cruelties of the French and Indians. — Governor Fletcher's Administration. — Peace of Ryswick — Piracy at New York. — Captain Kidd. — Factions occasioned by the Fate of Leisler. — Trial of Bayard. — Corrupt and oppressive Administration of Lord Cornbury. — State of the Colony at the Close of the Seventeenth Century.

COLONEL DONGAN did not arrive at the seat of his government till a year after the date of his appointment [August, 1683] ; a delay which appears to have created some uneasiness, and was probably beneficial to the people, in affording time for the first ardor of an ill-merited loyalty to cool, and suggesting precautions for preserving liberty that should signalize the first opportunity of exercising it. To appease the public inquietude, the governor, immediately after his arrival, issued writs to the sheriffs, directing them to convene the freeholders, for the purpose of electing their representatives in the assembly ; and this legislative body soon afterwards held its first meeting at New York, to the great satisfaction of the whole province. One of the earliest ordinances which it framed naturally arose from the mixture of nations of which the population was composed, and was an act of general naturalization, extending equal privileges to all. From this period the Dutch and English at New York were firmly compacted into one national body. They saw the daughter of their common proprietary married to the Stadtholder of Holland ; and willingly cemented their own union by frequent intermarriage and the ties of consanguinity. There was passed, at the same time, an act *declaring the liberties of the people*, and one for defraying the requisite charges of government for a limited time. These, with a few other laws regulating the internal economy of the province, and, in particular, appointing its division into counties, were transmitted to the Duke of York, and received his confirmation, as proprietary, in the following year. [1684.] An amicable treaty, which the governor concluded with the provincial authorities of Connecticut, extinguished the long-subsisting dispute with regard to the boundaries of Connecticut and New York.[2]

But the administration of Colonel Dongan was chiefly distinguished by the attention which he bestowed upon Indian affairs, and by the increasing

---

[1] *State Papers, apud* Chalmers.   [2] Chalmers.   Trumbull.

influence which now began to be exerted on the fortunes of the province by its connection with the tribes composing the celebrated confederacy of *The Five Nations of Canada.*   This federal association claimed an origin derived from the most remote antiquity ; and, as its title imports, comprehended five Indian nations, of which the Mohawks and Oneidas have obtained the most lasting name, and which were united, on terms of the strictest equality, in a perpetual alliance, for combined warfare and mutual defence and security.   The members of the united body reckoned themselves superior to all the rest of mankind, and the distinctive appellation which they adopted [1] was expressive of this opinion.   But the principles of their confederacy display far more policy and refinement than we might expect from the arrogance of their barbarous name.   They embraced the Roman principle, of increasing their strength by incorporating the people of other nations with themselves.   After every conquest of an enemy, when they had indulged their revenge by some bloody executions, they exercised their policy in the adoption of the remaining captives ; and frequently with so much advantage, that several of their most distinguished sachems and commanders were derived from vanquished foes.   Each nation had its own separate republican constitution, in which official power and dignity were claimed only by age, procured only by merit, and retained by the duration of public esteem ; and each was subdivided into three tribes, bearing respectively for their ensigns, and distinguished by the names of, the Tortoise, the Bear, and the Wolf.   In no community, savage or civilized, that has ever existed, was age regarded with more respect, or youth endowed with greater beauty.   Such was the efficacy of their mode of life in developing the grace and symmetry of the human frame, that, when the statue of the Apollo Belvidere was beheld, for the first time, by the American Apelles, Benjamin West, he started at the unexpected recognition, and exclaimed, "How like it is to a young Mohawk warrior ! "   The people of the several nations, and especially the Mohawks, were distinguished by the usual Indian qualities of attachment to liberty, stubborn fortitude in the endurance of pain, with equal sternness of ferocity in the infliction of it, and preference of craft and stratagem to undisguised operation in war ;[2] and by a more than usual degree of perseverance, resolution, and active intrepidity. It was universally reported of them, says Charlevoix, that *they advance like foxes, attack like lions, and retreat like birds.*   Almost all the tribes adjacent to this people, and even many at a great distance, though not included in the confederacy, yielding to the force or the reputation of its arms, acknowledged a subjection to it, paid a tribute, which two aged sachems were annually deputed to collect,[3] and were restrained from making war or peace without the consent of the Five Nations.   It was the habitual policy of the chiefs to affect peculiar poverty, and, in the distribution of plunder and tribute, to resign their own private shares to the people.   All matters of common concernment were transacted in general meetings of the sachems of each nation ; and the influence of time, seconded by a

---

[1] *Ongue-honwe,* — that is, " Men surpassing all others." Colden.

[2] In this peculiarity most of the Indian tribes resembled the ancient Spartans ; as they did also in their studious cultivation of conciseness of speech.   Plutarch's *Life of Lycurgus* resembles the anticipated biography of an early chief or patriarch of the Five Nations.

[3] " I have often had opportunity to observe what anxiety the poor Indians were under, while those two old men remained in that part of the country where I was.   An old Mohawk sachem, in a poor blanket and dirty shirt, may be seen issuing his orders with as arbitrary an authority as a Roman dictator." Colden.

course of judicious policy and victorious enterprise, had completely succeeded in causing the federal character and sentiments to prevail over the
peculiarities of their separate national subdivisions. In the year 1677, the
confederacy possessed two thousand one hundred and fifty fighting men.
Both the French and the English writers, who have treated of the character
or affairs of this people, agree in describing them as at once the most judicious and politic of the native powers, and the most fierce and formidable
of the native inhabitants of America.[1] There was only wanting to their
fame that literary celebration which they obtained too soon from the neighbourhood of a race of civilized men, who were destined to eclipse, and
finally extinguish, their greatness. They have received, in particular, from
the pen of an accomplished writer, Cadwallader Colden, one of the governors of New York, the same historic illustration which his own barbarian
ancestors derived from the writings of Cæsar and Tacitus.

When the French settled in Canada, in the beginning of this century,
they found the Five Nations engaged in a bloody war with the powerful tribe
of *Adirondacks*; in which, after having been themselves so severely pressed,
that they were driven from their possessions round Montreal, and forced
to seek an asylum on the southeast coast of Lake Ontario, the Five Nations
had succeeded in gaining a decided advantage, and in turn constrained
their enemies to abandon their lands situated above the *Three Rivers*, and
fly for safety behind the strait where Quebec was built. The tide of success, however, was suddenly turned by the arrival of Champlain, who conducted the French colony, and who naturally joined the Adirondacks, because he settled on their lands. The conduct, the bravery, and especially
the firearms, of these new allies of the enemy proved an overmatch for the
skill and intrepidity of the Five Nations, who were defeated in several
battles, and reduced to great distress. It was at this critical juncture that
the first Dutch ship arrived in Hudson's River with the colonists who established themselves at Albany. The Five Nations, procuring from these
neighbours a supply of that species of arms which had occasioned the superiority of their enemies, revived the war with such impetuosity and success,
that the nation of the Adirondacks was almost entirely destroyed [1684],
and the French too late discovered that they had espoused the fortunes
of the weaker people.[2] Hence originated the mutual dread and enmity that

---

[1] La Potherie's *History of North America*. Colden. Smith. Wentworth Greenhalph's
Journal, apud Chalmers. Galt's *Life of West*. Charlevoix's *Travels in North America*.
Though I have dwelt at some length on the character of the Five Nations, I should account
it a mere waste of words to particularize the names or discriminate the policy of all the various Indian tribes with whom the North American colonists were from time to time connected
by friendly or hostile relations. In general, the distinctions between them were few and
inconsiderable; and the revolutions of their condition and policy (as Milton remarked of the
annals of barbarians) not more interesting than the kindred vicissitudes of a commonwealth of
crows.

[2] To amuse the French, the Five Nations, at one time, made a proposal of peace, to which
the French heartily inclining, requested them to receive a deputation of Jesuits, whose exertions, they expected, would sincerely conciliate the friendship of the savages. The Five
Nations readily agreed, and desired to see the priests immediately; but the instant they got
hold of them, they marched to attack the Indian allies of the French, and taking the priests
with them as hostages, to enforce the neutrality of their countrymen, gave the Adirondacks a
signal defeat. Colden. The tribes opposed to the Five Nations in this war are called the
Hurons and *Algonquins* by Charlevoix, who acknowledges that the war was provoked by
the treachery and injustice of the allies of his countrymen. The Five Nations are often
termed by French writers the *Iroquois*, and by the English writers the *Mohawks*; though
this last was merely the distinctive name of one of the confederated tribes. Loskiel remarks
very justly, that "the numbers of the Indians have been often overrated, owing to the different names given to one nation." *History of the Moravian Missions in North America*.

long subsisted between the French and the confederated Indians and entailed so many calamities upon both.   The French, less accustomed to the
climate and less acquainted with the country than their savage enemies,
attempted vainly to imitate their rapid and secret expeditions.   A party
despatched in the winter of 1665, by Courcelles, the governor of Canada,
to attack the Five Nations, lost their way among wastes of snow, and, after
enduring extreme misery, arrived, without knowing where they were, at the
village of Schenectady, near Albany, which a Dutchman of consideration,
named Corlear,[1] had recently founded.   The French, exhausted, famished,
and stupefied with cold and hunger, resembled rather a crew of helpless
suppliants than an invading army, and would have fallen an easy prey to a
band of Indians who were reposing themselves in the village, if Corlear,
moved with compassion at their miserable appearance, had not employed
both influence and artifice with the Indians, to persuade them to spare their
unfortunate enemies, and depart to defend their own people against a more
formidable attack in a different quarter, of which he pretended to have received intelligence.   When the Indians were gone, Corlear and his towns-
men brought refreshments to the wretched Frenchmen, and supplied them
with provisions and other comforts, by which they were enabled to return in
safety to Canada, having received a touching lesson, that it is the mutual duty
of men to mitigate by kindness and charity, instead of aggravating by contention and ferocity, the evils arising from the rigor of nature and the frailty
of humanity.   The French governor expressed much gratitude for Corlear's
kindness, and the Indians never resented his benevolent stratagem ; but their
mutual hatred and warfare continued unabated.   After a long prevalence of
severe but indecisive hostilities, both parties, wearied of the struggle,
though not exhausted of animosity, acquiesced in a treaty of peace, which
was concluded in the year 1667, and had endured ever since without any
considerable interruption, at the period when Colonel Dongan was appointed
governor of New York.
     Of the relation that subsisted between the Dutch and the Five Nations
only confused and uncertain accounts have been preserved.   Those writers,
who assert that the Dutch were continually in close alliance and friendship with the Indians, seem to have derived their statements entirely from
their own conjectures of what was likely, and to have mistaken for an indication of particular good-will the indiscriminate readiness of the Dutch to
traffic with friend or foe.   It is certain, that, at one time, this people were
engaged in a bloody war with the Indians, — though with what particular
tribes there are no means of ascertaining ; and that during Stuyvesant's
administration they enjoyed a peace with their savage neighbours of which
the benefit descended to the English.   When Colonel Nichols assumed the
government of New York, he entered into a friendly treaty with the Five
Nations ; which, however, till the arrival of Dongan, was productive of no
farther connection than an extensive commercial intercourse, in which the
Indians supplied the English with peltry in return for arms and ammunition, of the use of which, as long as they were not employed against themselves, the colonists were entirely, and, as it is proved, unfortunately, regardless.   The Indians adhered to the treaty with strict fidelity, but always
evinced a jealous pride in punctiliously exacting the demonstrations of cere-

---

[1] This man enjoyed great influence with the Indians, who, after his death, always addressed
the governor of New York with the title *Corlear*, as the name most expressive of respect
with which they were acquainted. Colden.

monious respect due to an independent people ; and, in particular, when any of their forces had occasion to pass near the English forts, they expected to be saluted with military honors.   In the mean time the French Canadians were not remiss in availing themselves of their deliverance from the hostilities of these formidable Indians.   They extended their settlements along the river St. Lawrence, and, in the year 1672, built Fort Frontignac on its northwest bank, where, devolving from the parent lake of Ontario, it commences its rapid and majestic course.   With a policy proportioned to the vigor of their advances, they filled the Indian settlements with missionaries, whose active and successful exertions multiplied converts to the faith and allies to the interest of their countrymen.

The praying Indians, as the French termed their converts, were either neutral, or, more frequently, their auxiliaries in war.   The Jesuits preached not to their Indian auditors the doctrines that most deeply wound the pride of human nature, nor a system of pure, austere morality, which the conduct of the great mass of its nominal votaries practically disowns and disgraces. They required of their converts but a superficial change, — the adoption of one form of superstition in place of another ;[1] and they captivated their senses and impressed their imaginations by a ceremonial at once picturesque and mysterious.   Yet as, from the weakness and imperfection of man, an admixture of error is inseparable from the purest system of Christian doctrine, so, from the overruling goodness of God, a ray of truth is found to pervade even the most corrupted.   And the instructions of the Jesuits, from which the lineaments of Christianity, though disfigured by meretricious additament, were by no means obliterated, may have contributed, in some instances, to form the divine image in the minds of the Indians ; and the seed of heavenly truth, unchoked by the tares of human error, may in some places have yielded a holy and happy increase.[2]   The moral and domestic precepts contained in the Scriptures were frequently communicated with success and advantage ; and various congregations of Indian converts were persuaded by the Jesuits to build villages in Canada in the style exemplified by the French colonists ; to adopt European husbandry, and to renounce spirituous liquors.[3]   The visible separation of the Catholic priests from the general family of mankind, by renunciation of conjugal and parental ties, gave an awful sacredness to their character, and a strong prevailing power to their addresses.   In the discharge of what they conceived their duty, their courage and perseverance were equalled only by their address and activity.   They had already compassed sea and land to make proselytes ;

[1] There is preserved in Neal's *New England* a specimen of the French *Missionary Catechism*, containing a tissue of most absurd and childish fictions gravely propounded as the articles of Christian doctrine.   The following anecdote is related by Colden.   " About the time of the conclusion of the peace of Ryswick, Therouet, a noted Indian sachem, died at Montreal. The French gave him Christian burial in a pompous manner ; the priest that attended him at his death having declared that he died a true Christian.   For (said the priest) while I explained to him the passion of our Saviour, whom the Jews crucified, he cried out, ' O, had I been there, I would have revenged his death, and brought away their scalps ! ' "   " Some of the Iroquois," says Loskiel, about fifty years afterwards, " having been baptized by Romish priests, wore beads and crucifixes, which they considered merely as additions to their Indian finery."

[2] A number of the Indian converts of the Jesuits became themselves missionaries to their countrymen ; and several of them fell martyrs to their zeal, which had prompted them to attempt the conversion of tribes the enemies of their own.   These martyrs died with the usual fortitude of their race ; but they superadded to it a mildness and charity of demeanour and sentiment, which their murderers regarded with surprise, and ascribed to some magical influence exercised upon them by the rite of baptism.   Charlevoix's *Travels.*

[3] Their strict adherence to this difficult renunciation was remarked by a philosophic traveller in the year 1749.   Kalm's *Travels.*

and the threats of death and torture could not deter them from persisting to discharge what they regarded as a divine commission. Many of them, though commanded to depart, persisted in remaining among tribes that were at war with their countrymen; and some of them, from regard to the apostolical example of becoming *all things to all men*, embraced Indian habits of living. One of these last established himself so firmly in the affections of a tribe of the Five Nations, that, although they continued faithful to the national enmity against the French, they adopted him as a brother, and elected him a sachem. With such industry, resolution, and insinuation did the French Jesuits exert themselves to recommend their faith and the interests of their country to the favor of the Indians. The French laity, also, and especially their civil and military officers and soldiery, succeeded better than the generality of the English in conciliating the good graces of the savages. French vanity was productive of more politeness and accommodation[1] than English pride; and even the displeasure which the French sometimes excited by commission of injuries was less galling than the affronts which the English too frequently inflicted by a display of insolence. The firm, unyielding character of the English was best fitted to contend with the obstructions of physical nature; the pliancy and vivacity of the French, to prevail over the jealousy of the natives. There were as yet no Protestant missions in this quarter of America, which, in the following century, some New England clergymen, aided by a religious society in Scotland, and certain members of the Moravian brotherhood who emigrated from Germany, were destined to illustrate by memorable exertions of missionary labor.

Colonel Dongan, who was not encumbered, like his official predecessors, with a monopoly of all the functions of government, nor involved in collisions with popular discontent, had leisure for a considerate survey of the state of his countrymen's relations with the Indians, and very soon discovered that the peace which was so advantageous to the French Canadian colonists, by enabling them to extend their forts and their commerce over a wide extent of country, was attended with injurious consequences to some of the colonies of Britain, and threatened danger to them all. The Five Nations, inflamed with martial ardor, and finding a pretext for its gratification in the recollection of insults they had received from various quarters in the season of their adverse fortune, turned their arms southward, and conquered the whole country from the Mississippi to the borders of Carolina; exterminating numerous tribes and nations in their destructive progress. Many of the Indian allies of Virginia and Maryland sustained their attacks; and these colonies themselves were frequently compelled to take arms, both in defence of their allies and in defence of their own people, against allies incensed and alienated by discovering that their invaders derived the means of annoying them from the English at New York. But this year

[1] A curious instance of the complaisance of this people is related by Oldmixon, in his account of a tribe of savages who were greatly charmed with the good breeding of the French, in always appearing stark naked at their mutual conferences. Charlevoix boasts that the French are the only European people who have ever succeeded in rendering themselves agreeable to the Indians; and yet he himself has preserved a letter from Senonville, the governor of Canada in 1685, to Louis the Fourteenth, declaring that every attempt to approximate the two races, by intermarriage or otherwise, had issued in degrading the civilized, instead of elevating the savage people.

The excellent historian of the *Moravian Missions in America* observes, that "the French seem to possess the greatest share of the good-will of the Indians, by easily entering into the Indian manner of living, and appearing always good-humored." Loskiel.

[July, 1684], Colonel Dongan, in conjunction with Lord Effingham, the governor of Virginia, concluded with the Five Nations a definitive treaty of peace, embracing all the English settlements and all tribes in alliance with them.   Hatchets, corresponding to the numbers of the English colonies, were solemnly buried in the ground ; and the arms of the Duke of York, as the acknowledged supreme head of the English and Indian confederacy, were suspended along the frontiers of the territories of the Five Nations.[1] For this treaty the Five Nations long continued to demonstrate an inviolable respect ; and their fidelity to its engagements was speedily promoted by a renewal of hostilities between them and their ancient enemies, the French. It was at this time that the merchants of New York first adventured on the great lakes to the westward, hoping to participate in the fur trade, which the French were pursuing with much profit in this direction, and which they endeavoured to guard from invasion by prepossessing the Indians against the English, and by every artifice that seemed likely to obstruct the advances of their rivals.   Dongan, perceiving the disadvantages to which his countrymen were exposed, solicited the English ministry to take measures for preventing the French colonists from navigating the lakes which belonged to the Five Nations, and, consequently, as he apprehended, to England.   But, in answer to his application, he was admonished that it was preposterous to expect that France would command her subjects to desist from a lucrative commerce, for the benefit of their rivals ; and he was directed rather by acts of liberality and courtesy to encourage the Indians to retain their adherence to England, and to induce all the tribes, from regard to their own interest, to trade with the English in preference to the French ; observing withal such prudence as might prevent offence to European neighbours.[2]   So far were these views from being accomplished, that from this time there commenced a series of disputes between the two nations, which for the greater part of a century engaged them in continual wars and hostile intrigues, that threatened the destruction of their colonial settlements, cost the lives of many of the European colonists, and wasted the blood and promoted the barbarism of those unfortunate Indians who were involved in the vortex of their hostility.

On the death of Charles the Second [1685], the Duke of York ascended his brother's throne ; and the province of which he had been the proprietary devolved, with all its dependencies, on the British crown.   The people of New York received with improvident exultation the account of their proprietary's advancement to royalty, and proclaimed him as their monarch with the liveliest demonstrations of attachment and respect.   They had been for some time past soliciting with much eagerness a formal grant of the constitution that was now practically established among them ; and the duke had promised to gratify them in this particular, and actually proceeded so far as to sign a patent in conformity with their wishes, which, at his accession to the throne, required only some trivial solemnity to render it complete and irrevocable.   But James, though he could not pretend to forget, was not ashamed to violate, as king of England, the promise which he

[1] When this treaty was renewed, some years after, the sachem who acted as orator for the Indians thus addressed the provincial envoys : — "We make fast the roots of the tree of peace and tranquillity, which is planted in this place. Its roots extend as far as the utmost of your colonies : if the French should come to shake this tree, we would feel it by the motion of its roots, which extend into our country." Colden.
[2] Charlevoix. Colden. Smith. Kalm's *Travels*. Chalmers.

had made when Duke of York ; and a cool and unblushing refusal was
returned to the renewed solicitations of the inhabitants of the province.
Determined to establish the same arbitrary system in New York which he
designed for New England, — so far from conferring new immunities, he
withdrew what had been formerly conceded. In the second year of his
reign he invested Dongan with a new commission, empowering him, with
consent of a council, to enact laws and impose taxes ; and commanding
him to suffer *no printing-press to exist*.[1] Though he now appointed Andros
to administer the government of New England [June, 1686], he paused
awhile before he ventured to restore the authority of this obnoxious governor
in New York. But the people beheld in the appointment of Andros to govern the provinces in their neighbourhood an additional token of their
prince's character and of their own danger, and with impatient discontent[2]
endured a yoke which they were unable to break, and which they were prevented from exhibiting to public odium and English sympathy through the
medium of the press.

Dongan, having been a soldier all his life, was fitted rather by habit to
regard with indifference, than by disposition to conduct with rigor, a system
of arbitrary government ; and, accordingly, the remainder of his administration, though less favorable to his popularity, was not discreditable to his
character, and continued to disclose the same moderation and the same regard
to the public weal which its outset had demonstrated. Though himself a
Roman Catholic, he beheld with alarm, and resisted with energy, the intrusion
of the French priests into the settlements of the Five Nations ; and even when
his bigoted master was persuaded by the court of France to command him
to desist from thus obstructing the progress of the Catholic church, he continued nevertheless to warn the Indians that the admission of the Jesuits
among them would prove fatal to their own interests and to their friendship
with the English. He still insisted that the French should not treat with
the Indian allies of New York without his privity and intervention ; but
the French court again employed its influence with his master ; and Dongan
consequently received orders to depart from this pretension. The Five
Nations, however, seemed more likely to need the assistance of his forces
than the suggestions of his policy. Their untutored sagacity had long perceived, what the ministers of the court of England were not skilful enough
to discern, that the extensive projects of France both threatened themselves
with subjugation, and portended a serious injury to the English colonies, in
the diminution of their trade and the removal of the barrier that still separated them from the rival settlement of Canada. The treaty, that excluded
the Five Nations from hostile expeditions against the more distant tribes
allied to the other English colonies, gave them leisure to attend with less distraction to their nearer interests ; and finding themselves inconvenienced by
the supplies which their numerous enemies derived from the French, they
had of late pretended a right to consider this as a hostile act which they
were entitled to chastise and resist ; and, in conformity with this view,
attacked all the Canadian traders whom they encountered in the act of transporting military stores to any tribe with whom they were at war. The
French, under the conduct of two successive governors, De la Barre and

---

[1] Holmes. Chalmers.

[2] So great was the change produced in the sentiments of the colonists by this change of
treatment, that we find Dongan this year, in his letters to the English court, complaining of
their increasing numbers and turbulent disposition. *State Papers, apud* Chalmers

Senonville, vainly endeavoured, partly by negotiation and partly by force, to divert the Indians from operations so injurious to their commerce, their reputation, and their political designs ; when Dongan, perceiving that a war would probably ensue between the rivals and the allies of his countrymen, prevailed by the most urgent entreaties on the English court to authorize him to assist the Five Nations in the contest that menaced them. But the French ministers, gaining information of this proceeding, hastened to counteract it by a repetition of artifices which again proved successful. They had already more than once, by their hypocrisy and cunning, successfully practised on the sincere bigotry of the English king ; and they had now the address to conclude with him *a treaty of neutrality for America* [Nov., 1686], by which it was stipulated that neither party should give assistance to Indian tribes at war with the other. Armed with so many advantages, the French authorities in Canada resumed with increased vigor their endeavours to chastise by force, or debauch by intrigue, the Indian tribes who preferred the English alliance to theirs ; while Dongan was compelled to sacrifice the honor of his country to the erring policy of his master, and to abandon her allies to the hostility, and her barrier to the violation, of an insidious and enterprising rival. He could not, indeed, divest himself of the interest he had conceived in the fortunes of the Five Nations, and seized every opportunity of imparting to them advice no less prudent than humane, respecting the conduct of their enterprises and the treatment of their prisoners. But his inability to fulfil former engagements and afford additional aid greatly detracted from the efficacy of his counsel. Though the remonstrances of Dongan enabled the ministers of James to discover, in the following year [1687], that the treaty of neutrality for America was prejudicial to the interests of England, it was impossible to prevent the king from renewing, in the close of the same year, that impolitic arrangement with France.

But the king had no intention of relinquishing his empire in America ; and his mind, though strongly tinctured with bigotry, was not totally irrespective of political views ; though he seems rarely to have mingled these considerations together. As his bigotry had prompted him to deliver up the Indians to the French, his policy now suggested the measure of compacting all his northern colonies under one frame of government for their more effectual defence. To this design, assuredly, he was at least as strongly prompted by the desire of facilitating the exercise of his own prerogative in the colonies, as by concern for the safety of their inhabitants. As the scheme he had formed included New York, and as he thought the people of this province now sufficiently prepared to abide the extremity of his will, he indulged the more readily the sentiments of displeasure that Dongan had excited by obstructing the French Jesuits, which was a theme of continual complaint from the court of France. The commission of this meritorious officer was accordingly superseded by a royal command to deliver up his charge to Sir Edmund Andros [April, 1688] ; and New York not only reverted to the dominion of its ancient tyrant, but beheld its existence as a separate province practically merged in its annexation to the government of New England. Andros remained at Boston as the metropolis of his jurisdiction, committing the domestic administration of New York to Nicholson, his lieutenant-governor ; and though, by the vigor of his remonstrances, and his reputation for ability, he compelled the French to suspend some

encroachments which they were making or threatening to make on the English territories, he could lend no assistance to the Five Nations in the hostilities that were now carried on between them and that people with a mutual
fury and ferocity that seemed to obliterate the distinction between civilized
and savage men.   The people of New York, deprived of their liberties, and
mortified by their annexation to New England, felt themselves additionally
aggrieved by the policy which compelled them to stand aloof and behold
the fate of allies whom they had engaged to assist, together with their own
most important interests, suspended on the issue of a contest in which they
were not suffered to take a share ; while, at the same time, their countrymen in the eastern part of New England were harassed by a dangerous
Indian war ascribed on strong reasons to the intrigues of the French.[1] But,
though deserted by the English, the Five Nations maintained the struggle
with an energy that promised the preservation of their independence, and,
finally, with a success that excited hopes even of the subjugation of their
civilized adversaries. Undertaking an expedition against Montreal, they conducted their march with such rapidity and secrecy as to surprise the French
in almost unguarded security. [July, 1688.]   The suddenness and fury of
their attack proved irresistible.   They sacked the town, wasted the neighbouring plantations, put a thousand of the French to the sword, and carried
away a number of prisoners whom they burned alive ; returning to their
friends with the loss of only three of their own number.   It was now that
the disadvantage arising from the neutrality of the English was most sensibly
felt, in the cruelties with which the Indians stained the triumphs they obtained, and which the influence of a humane ally might have contributed
to moderate,[2] and also in the inability of the savages to improve their vic-
tories into lasting conquest.   They strained every nerve, indeed, to follow
up their advantage, and, shortly after the sack of Montreal, were enabled to
occupy the fort at Lake Ontario, which the garrison in a panic abandoned
to them ; and being now reinforced by the desertion of numerous Indian
allies of the French, they reduced the remaining possessions of this people
in Canada to a state of the utmost terror and distress.   Nothing could have
saved the French from total destruction, but the ignorance which disabled
the Indians from laying siege effectually to fortified places ; and it was
manifest to every intelligent observer that a single vigorous act of interposition by the English colonists would have sufficed to terminate for ever
the rivalry of France and England in this quarter of the world.[3]

  In the midst of a contest which the French and the Indians thus prolonged by indecisive hostilities, a scene of civil war and revolution was
gradually evolved at New York. [1689.]   A deep and increasing disaffection to the government prevailed there among all ranks of men ; and as the
general discontents of late had been plainly gathering to a head, some violent
crisis was fearfully anticipated ; and perhaps was suspended by divisions in
sentiment, arising from the different aspects in which the state of public
affairs presented itself to different minds.   To the wealthy and the dis-

---

[1] See *ante*, Book II., Chap. V.
[2] The conduct which we have already witnessed in some of the Indian allies of the New
England States, in the wars which they jointly carried on, may seem to render this a vain
speculation. But the Five Nations were a far more reasonable and intelligent race of men
than the Pequods and Narragansets. Colonel Dongan, whom they greatly loved and respected
(Colden), might have mollified their hostilities by his example, as he frequently, and not altogether ineffectually, attempted to do by his counsels.
[3] Oldmixon. Colden. Coxe's *Carolana*. Smith. Chalmers.

cerning the privation of liberty and the political degradation of the province appeared with justice the only public grievances which they had occasion to deplore, or were interested to remove. But an outrageous dread of *popery* had invaded the minds of the lower classes of people, and not only diminished real and substantial evils in their esteem, but nearly extinguished common sense in their understandings and common justice in their sentiments. The king's well known bigotry, his attempts to introduce the Romish faith and church into England, and the protection which he extended to the operations of the French Jesuits among the Indians, had inculcated this additional apprehension on their irritated minds ; and the servile apostasy of some of the officers of government at New York, who endeavoured to court royal favor by professing to adopt the king's religious faith, appeared strongly to confirm it. Some angry feelings that had been excited in the commencement of Colonel Dongan's administration were now suddenly reawakened from slumber, to augment and diversify the prevailing ferments. At that period, notwithstanding the exertions of a former governor to adjust the boundaries of property in Long Island, a variety of disputes on this subject prevailed in the same quarter between different individuals and different townships ; and on Dongan had devolved the thankless office of adjusting these controversies by judgments, which could hardly fail to engender some enmity against himself. In such cases it too commonly happens that the arbitrator, seeking to gratify both parties, disappoints them both, and is taxed on all sides with partiality ; or that, studying only to administer strict justice, he excites extreme discontent in those whom his award both deprives of the property they had hoped to keep or gain, and stigmatizes as unjust or unreasonable in their pretensions. Most men possess sufficient ingenuity to supply them with plausible reasons for imputing the disappointment of their expectations to the dishonesty of those who obstruct or withhold them ; and defeated litigants have in all ages been noted for the vehemence and acrimony of their spleen. A great many persons who accounted themselves wronged by Dongan's decrees made no scruple to impute their disappointments to the darkness and obliquity of his *popish* understanding. They conceived a violent jealousy of popish designs, which the recollection of their fancied wrongs preserved unimpaired either by the lapse of time or by the moderate and equitable strain of Dongan's administration. The rancorous sentiments harboured by these persons were revived and inflamed by recent events and appearances ; the apostasy of some of the public officers confirmed their apprehensions of popery ; and the painful stroke inflicted by the establishment of civil tyranny was chiefly felt by them as aggravating the smart of a former and totally different injury. This class of persons esteemed *popery* the most terrible feature in the aspect of the times, and their own disappointments the most signal exemplifications of popish wickedness ; and considered these as by far the fittest considerations to unite the general resentment and justify its vindictive reaction.

While the minds of men were thus agitated by common discontent, but restrained from cordial union by difference of opinion and variety of apprehension, the public expectation was still farther aroused by intelligence from Europe of the invasion of England by the Prince of Orange, and by sympathy with the swelling scene which was in progress in the parent state. Yet no commotion had arisen, when the important tidings arrived of the accession of William and Mary to the throne of England [May, 1689], and of the successful insurrection at Boston which terminated the government of Andros. Even the contagious ferment excited by this last intelligence might have subsided without producing an explosion of popular violence, if the conduct of the local authorities of New York had not indicated an intention to resist, or at least a hesitation to comply with, the general revolution of the empire. Nicholson, the lieutenant-governor, and his council, not only refrained from proclaiming William and Mary, but despatched a letter to Governor Bradstreet, at Boston, commanding, with haughty menace, the immediate release of Andros, and the chastisement of *the insurrectionary rabble* who had presumed to put him in confinement. Notwithstanding this demonstration of opposition to the Revolution, the more prudent and considerate citizens of New York clearly perceived that their local government must follow the fate of the rest of the empire, and were disposed calmly to await the spontaneous submission of Nicholson and his council to William and Mary, or the arrival of orders or help from Britain to reduce them. But the impatience of a numerous body of the people, and especially of those who were panic-struck with the terrors of *popery*, could not abide this tedious issue, and was inflamed by the apprehension of some notable stroke of craft from Nicholson and his associates in office.[1]

This party found a chief in Jacob Leisler, a man of eager, headlong temper, endowed with much plebeian prate, inordinate vanity, and a very shallow capacity ; whose blazing zeal against popery, and former ill-treatment by Andros, seemed to designate him the proper leader of the opposition to the political and religious enemies of the province. He had already committed the first act of resistance, by refusing to pay customs for some imported goods, alleging that the collector was a Papist, and that there was no legitimate government in the colony. Nicholson having begun to make preparations for defending the city against a foreign invasion, and summoned the trained bands to garrison the fort, — a report was circulated that the Papists were preparing to massacre the Protestants [June, 1689] ; and Leisler, who commanded a company of the trained bands, instantly marched at the head of a detachment of this body, and, gaining possession of the fort, assumed the command of it in defence of *the Protestant cause*, and in attendance on the orders of the king and queen of England. The precautions of the late monarch had withdrawn from the popular leaders the means of publishing and propagating their sentiments by the agency of the press ; but a written declaration was subscribed by Leisler and his followers, signifying, that, although they had endured much ill usage from " a *wicked popish* governor, Dongan," they would have patiently awaited redress from England, if the violence and oppression of Nicholson and the schemes of the Papists had not forced them to take arms and secure the fort, which they were ready to deliver up to any Protestant officer whom the king and queen might depute to command it. Leisler, finding that he was not joined by any persons of consideration in the province, despatched a messenger to King William, and, by dint of negotiations with Massachusetts and Connecti-

---

[1] Thucydides thus characterizes the conduct of the populace in one of the revolutions of Corcyra : — " Such as had the least wit had the best success ; for both their own defect and the subtlety of their adversaries putting them into a great fear to be overcome in words, or at least in pre-insidiation, by their enemies' great craft, they therefore went roundly to work with them with deeds." Book III., Hobbes's translation. Hobbes's own summary of this passage and the context is, — " In seditions and confusion, they that distrust their wits suddenly use their hands and defeat the stratagems of the more subtle sort."

cut, persuaded the revolutionary leaders in these colonies to countenance his enterprise. But a report arising that an English fleet was approaching to assist the insurgents, their cause was forthwith embraced by all classes of people in New York ; and Nicholson, apprehensive of sharing the treatment of Andros, fled to England. Unfortunately for Leisler, the command, which priority of resistance and the favor of the lower classes enabled him to acquire, his natural temper equally prompted him to retain, though surrounded by men who dreaded his precipitancy and reluctantly submitted to his elevation. These new associates had influence enough to cause a second proclamation to be issued, in which the unworthy censure on Dongan was omitted, and no stipulation whatever inserted as to the creed of the royal officer to whom the fort would be surrendered.

It had been happy for all parties, if the jealousy of Leisler's rivals had been satisfied with this wise and moderate control over his measures. But Courtlandt, the mayor of the city, Colonel Bayard, Major Schuyler, and several other persons of consideration, unable to brook the ascendency of a man whose birth and parts were inferior to their own, retired to Albany, and, seizing the fort there, declared that they held it for King William, and disclaimed all connection with Leisler. Each party now professed adherence to the same sovereign, and denounced the other as rebels to his authority. Leisler, though intrusted by the militia with the sole command of the province, judged it prudent to associate some respectable citizens with himself in the administration of his perilous functions. Having fortified his own power by the appointment of a committee of safety at New York, he despatched his son-in-law, Milbourn, against the adverse faction at Albany. Courtlandt and his associates, burning with resentment, yet averse to shed blood in such a quarrel, were relieved from their perplexity by a hostile irruption of French and Indians [1690], which, by the desolation it inflicted on the surrounding country, either rendered their post untenable, or induced them to sacrifice their pretensions, for the purpose of enabling their countrymen to unite all the force of the province against the common enemy. Abandoning the fort to their rival, they took refuge in the neighbouring colonies ; while Leisler, with rashly triumphant revenge, confiscated their estates. To add strength and reputation to his party, he summoned a convention of deputies from all the towns and districts to which his influence extended ; and this assembly, in which two deputies from Connecticut were admitted to assist as advisers, published various regulations for the temporary government of the province. But these legislative ordinances, and especially the financial impositions, were disputed by a powerful party among the colonists, whose indignation against Leisler was confined with difficulty to insults and menaces ; and many of the English inhabitants of Long Island, while they expressed a reluctant submission to his authority, privately applied to Connecticut, and solicited this province to annex their insular settlements to its jurisdiction.[1]

In this unhappy state of division and animosity the colonists of New York remained nearly two years, notwithstanding a revolution, which, by elevating the Stadtholder of Holland to the English throne, had promised to unite them together more firmly than ever. Happily, the quarrel exhibited no symptoms of national antipathy between the Dutch and English, who, without discrimination of races, embraced respectively the party to

[1] Smith. Hutchinson. Trumbull. Chalmers.

which their particular sentiments attached them ; and though a great deal
of rage and malignity was engendered between the two factions, no blood
was shed by either while their controversy lasted.   But, unfortunately, the
miseries of foreign war and hostile invasion were soon added to the calamity of internal discord.   The condition of the French in Canada was suddenly raised from the depth of adversity by the arrival of a strong reinforcement from the parent state, under the command of a skilful and enterprising officer, the old Count de Frontignac, who now assumed the government of the French settlements, and quickly gave an altered complexion
to the affairs of his countrymen.   He set on foot a treaty with the Five
Nations, and succeeded, meanwhile, in obtaining a suspension of their hostilities.   War had already been declared between France and England ;
and the dissensions among the inhabitants of New York seeming to invite an
attack upon this province, he undertook to revive the drooping spirits of
his people by improving the tempting opportunity of success.   A numerous
troop of French and Indians was accordingly collected, and despatched in
the depth of winter against New York.   By a strange coincidence, which
seemed to have been decreed for the purpose of branding the French name
in America with the blackest ingratitude and inhumanity, this party, like
their predecessors in 1665, after wandering for twenty-two days through
deserts rendered trackless by snow, approached the village of Schenectady, so travel-tainted, hunger-bitten, and benumbed with cold, that they proposed to surrender themselves to the inhabitants as prisoners of war. [Feb-
ruary, 1690.]   But, arriving at a late hour on an inclement night, and learning from the messengers whom they had sent forward to tender their submission, that the inhabitants were all in bed, without even the precaution of
a public watch, they exchanged the design of imploring mercy to themselves
for a plan of nocturnal attack and massacre of the defenceless people to
whose charity their own countrymen had once been so highly indebted.
This ungrateful and sanguinary purpose was executed with barbarous alacrity ; and the scene which ensued must be acknowledged to afford one of
the most loathsome and detestable pictures that have ever been exhibited
of human cruelty and ferocity, inflamed by the dire and maddening contagion of frantic example.   Dividing themselves into a number of parties,
they set fire to the village in various places, and attacked the inhabitants
with fatal advantage, when, alarmed by the conflagration, they endeavoured
to escape from their burning houses.   The exhausted strength of the French
seemed to revive with the blaze of destruction, and their spirits to catch a
fiery energy, and wild, ferocious glee, from the animated horror of the scene.
Not only were all the male inhabitants they could reach put to death, but
pregnant women were ripped up, and their unborn infants dashed against the
walls of the houses.   But either the delay occasioned by this elaborate
barbarity, or the more merciful haste of the flames to announce the calamity
to those who might still fly from the assassins, enabled many of the inhabitants to escape.   The bloodthirsty efforts of the assailants were also somewhat impeded by a careful discrimination which they judged it expedient to
exercise.   Though unmindful of benefits, they were not regardless of policy;
and of a number of Mohawk Indians who were residing in the village, not
one sustained an injury. Sixty persons perished in the massacre, and twenty-
seven were taken prisoners. Of the fugitives who escaped half naked,
and made their way through a storm of snow to Albany, twenty-five lost the

use of their limbs from the intensity of the frost. The French, having totally destroyed Schenectady, retired loaded with plunder from a place where it will probably be thought that even the celebrated contemporary atrocities of their countrymen in the Palatinate had been equalled, if not exceeded.

The destruction of Schenectady excited general consternation in the province of New York. Forces were quickly raised to repel or retort the hostility of the French ; and on the application of Leisler, the province of Connecticut sent a troop of auxiliaries to his aid. It was found difficult to persuade the Five Nations to join actively with allies who had once deserted them ; but they declared that no artifices of the French should ever prevail with them to adopt the quarrel or espouse the interest of an ancient enemy against an ancient friend. As the province of Massachusetts was severely harassed at the same time by Indian hostilities instigated and aided by Count Frontignac, a scheme was projected between the New England States and New York for a general invasion of Canada.[1] An expedition, commanded by Sir William Phipps, sailed from Boston against Quebec ; and the united forces of Connecticut and New York, under the command of General Winthrop, were to march against Montreal. But Leisler's son-in-law, Milbourn, who acted as commissary-general, had made such imperfect provision for the expedition, that, partly from this defect, and partly from the inability of the Indians to supply as many canoes as they were expected to furnish for crossing the rivers and lakes, the general was obliged to convoke a council of war, and, in conformity with the unanimous opinion of his officers, to order a retreat. [Sept., 1690.] The expedition against Quebec was equally unsuccessful. Leisler, transported with rage when he was informed of the retreat, caused Winthrop to be arrested ; but was instantly·compelled by universal indignation to release him. Infatuated and rendered giddy by his dangerous elevation, this man began to display the unbuckled spirit that precedes and portends a fall. The government of Connecticut, incensed at the affront by which he revenged the fruit of his kinsman's incapacity on the ablest officer and most respected inhabitant of their province, signified in very sharp terms their astonishment and displeasure at his presumption, and warned him that his own predicament demanded more than ordinary prudence and circumspection, and that he stood in urgent need of friends.[2]

Leisler, indeed, had reason to tremble. King William at first received his messenger with the most flattering encouragement, and admitted him to the honor of kissing his hand, in testimony of his satisfaction with the conduct of affairs at New York. But Nicholson, on his arrival in England, found means to gain the ear of the king, and instil into his mind a prejudice, of which the attainment of royalty rendered it extremely susceptible, against the insurgents both of Boston and New York. William returned thanks, indeed, to *the people* of New York, by Leisler's messenger, for their fidelity ; but in none of his communications with either Boston or New York did he recognize the governors whom the people had appointed ; and he demonstrated to the inhabitants of both those places how very lightly he regarded their complaints against Andros and Nicholson, by subsequently promoting these men to the government of others of the American provinces. He would, doubtless, have continued to keep New York and Massachusetts

---

[1] *Ante*, Book II., Chap. V.
[2] Smith. Trumbull. Sewell, *MS. Diary, apud* Holmes.

united under one political frame ; but plainly foreseeing that he must grant
a charter to Massachusetts, and that he might hope to evade a similar concession to New York, which had never yet possessed this advantage, he
consented to the separation which both desired, and in August, 1689, committed the separate government of this province to Colonel Sloughter.   In
consequence, however, of the embarrassed situation of his master's affairs
in England, Sloughter did not arrive at New York till the second year after
his appointment [March 19, 1691], and till Leisler and his partisans had
enjoyed power so long that they were naturally unwilling, and exercised it
with so much odium that they were exceedingly afraid, to resign it.   Leisler
seems to have hoped to the last that the king would either prolong his
authority, or expressly sanction and reward his services ; and when he found
himself no otherwise noticed than by a summons from Colonel Sloughter to
deliver up the fort, he answered, in the language of folly and fury, that he
would not surrender it, unless an order to this effect, under the king's own
hand, were exhibited.   Such a resolution it was, unfortunately, possible to
express, though quite impracticable to maintain ; and he only sealed his fate
by this sally of despair, and furnished his enemies with a legal pretext to
destroy him, which otherwise they would have found it no easy matter to
adduce.   The new governor's ears were now readily opened to all the
charges that Leisler's enemies hastened to prefer against him ; and although this ill-fated adventurer quickly abandoned the desperate purpose
of retaining the fort, he was proclaimed a rebel, and committed to prison,
with his kinsman Milbourn and various others of his adherents, on a charge
of high treason.

Colonel Sloughter, having thus established his authority in the province,
convoked an assembly [April, 1691], which voted addresses condemning
the rebellious conduct of Leisler in holding out the fort against the govern-
or.   A general act of abrogation was decreed, rescinding not only all the
regulations established by former royal governors and their councils, but
even the laws enacted by the popular assembly in 1683, on the strange
pretext, that, having been violated by the late king, they had ceased to be
binding on the people.   As some doubt was entertained, whether, in the absence of a provincial charter, the convocation of a representative assembly
proceeded from the inherent right of the people or the mere grace of the
king, a remarkable law declaratively adjudged that this and all the other liberties of Englishmen formed a part of the political birthright of the colonists ; but this law was afterwards annulled by King William.   Leisler and
Milbourn were now brought to trial, for high treason, before Dudley, whom
the king had recently appointed chief justice of New York, and who had
previously been expelled from office at Boston by the same revolution to
which the prisoners owed their recent elevation.   From a tribunal thus occupied by an exasperated antagonist a favorable or even a candid appreciation of the conduct of the accused was not to be expected.   Denying the
competency of the tribunal and refusing to plead, they were convicted,
and received sentence of death.   The governor, notwithstanding, shrunk
from inflicting the doom of traitors on the two persons, who, of all the inhabitants, had first declared themselves in favor of his sovereign ; and,
shortly after the trial [May, 1691], wrote to the English ministers, desiring them to direct him in what manner the convicts should be disposed
of ; but he had hardly taken this step, when the renewed instances of their

enemies induced him to alter his purpose, and issue the warrant of death, which was instantly carried into execution.[1] The adherents of Leisler and Milbourn, who had been much enraged at the sentence, were confounded with terror and astonishment when they beheld its fatal result, and began to fly in such numbers from the province, that it was judged expedient to pass in haste an act of general amnesty. Leisler's son complained to the king of the execution of his father and the confiscation of his property ; and the privy council, pronouncing, that, although the trial and execution were legal, it was advisable, under the peculiar circumstances of the case, to restore the forfeited estate, this was all the grace that could for some time be obtained. But a compensation more honorable and satisfactory was awarded soon after ; and, during the reign of the same king, the English parliament decreed a reversal of the provincial attainder. The passions, which Leisler's administration excited in one party, and which his execution communicated to the other, continued long to distract the public councils, and embitter the social intercourse of the inhabitants of New York.[2]

The most respectable circumstance of Sloughter's short administration was a conference which he held with the chiefs of the Five Nations, who admitted that they had hearkened to the enticing overtures of the French, and so far relaxed their hostile purposes against this people, as to entertain propositions for a lasting peace with them ; but now they willingly consented to *brighten*, as they termed it, *their ancient belt of friendship*, and to renew a league, offensive and defensive, with the English " We remember," they declared, " the deceit and treachery of the French ; the belt they have sent us is poison ; we spew it out of our mouths ; and are resolved to make war with them as long as we live." On his return from this conference, a sudden death put a period to Sloughter's administration.[3] [July, 1691.]

To confirm the Indians in the purposes they now professed, and to animate by exercising their hostility against the French, Major Schuyler, who had acquired extraordinary influence with the Five Nations by his courage, good sense, and friendly attention to their interests, undertook, in the close of this year, an expedition against Montreal at the head of a considerable body of provincial and Indian forces. Though the invaders were finally compelled to retreat, the French sustained great loss in several encounters, and the spirit and animosity of the Five Nations were whetted to such a pitch, that, even when their allies retired, they continued during the winter to harass the enemy with incessant attacks. Count Frontignac, whose sprightly manners and energetic character supported the spirits of his countrymen under every reverse, was so provoked with what he deemed the ingratitude of the Five Nations for the forbearance shown to them at Sche-

---

[1] " When no other measures could prevail with the governor, tradition informs us that a sumptuous feast was prepared, to which Colonel Sloughter was invited. When his Excellency's reason was drowned in his cups, the entreaties of the company prevailed on him to sign the death-warrant, and before he recovered his senses the prisoners were executed." Smith. At their execution, Leisler and Milbourn confessed their errors, ascribing them to ignorance, jealous fear, rashness, and passion, and evinced great courage, composure, and piety. " I hope these eyes shall see our Lord Jesus in heaven," were the words of Leisler when the executioner bound a handkerchief round his face. Bancroft.

[2] Smith. Chalmers.

[3] Colden. Smith. Of the language in which the Indians, when pressed by the French, applied for help to the governors of New York, the following, among other specimens, has been preserved by these writers. " We speak to you now in the name of the Five Nations, and come to you howling. This is the reason why we howl, — that the governor of Canada encroaches on our lands," &c.

nectady, that, besides encouraging his own Indian allies to burn their prisoners alive, he himself condemned to a death still more dreadful two Mohawk warriors who fell into his hands. [1692.]   In vain the French priests
remonstrated against this sentence, and urged him not to bring so foul a
stain on the Christian name ; the count declared that every other consideration must be postponed to the safety and defence of his people, and that he
could not suffer the Indians to entertain the belief that they might practise the
extreme of cruelty on the French without risk of requital.   If he had been
merely actuated by politic considerations, without being stimulated by revenge, he might have plainly perceived, from the conduct of all the Indian
tribes in their wars with each other, that the fear of retaliation had no efficacy whatever as a restraint upon their barbarous practices, which he now
undertook to sanction as far as his example was capable of doing.   The
priests, finding that their humane intercession was unavailing, repaired to the
prisoners, and labored to persuade them to embrace the Christian faith, as
a preparation for the dreadful fate which men calling themselves Christians
were prepared to inflict on them ; but their instructions were rejected with
scorn and derision, and they found the prisoners resolved to dignify by Indian sentiments and demeanour the Indian death they were doomed to undergo.   Shortly before the execution, some Frenchman, less inhuman than
his governor, threw a knife into the prison, — and one of the Mohawks despatched himself with it.   The survivor, collecting his soul, and expressing
contempt at his comrade's mean retreat from glory, walked to the scene
of blood, vaunting, in his death-song, that he was a Mohawk warrior, —
that all the power of man could not subdue his constancy, or extort an indecent expression of suffering from his lips, — and that it was ample consolation to him to reflect that he had caused many Frenchmen to undergo the
same pangs which he was now himself prepared to endure.   When attached to the stake, he looked round on his executioners, their instruments
of torture, and the assembled multitude of spectators, with all the calmness
and complacency of heroic fortitude ; and after sustaining for some hours
with composed mien, and retorting with proud language, a series of barbarities too horrible and disgusting to be recited, his sufferings were terminated
by the intercession of a French lady, whose urgency prevailed with the
governor to order the infliction of that mortal blow which human cruelty has
entitled to the name of *coup de grace*, or stroke of *favor*.[1]

It was with great reluctance that King William surrendered to the American colonies any of the acquisitions which regal authority derived from the
tyrannical usurpations of his predecessors ; and his reign was signalized by
various attempts to invade the popular rights which at first he had been compelled to respect or restore.   He was informed by the English lawyers that
he could not refuse to recognize the charter of Connecticut with all its ample privileges ; and he was baffled in his attempt to procure an act of parliament to annul it.   But as New York, never having had a charter, was
judged to be not legally entitled to demand one, he determined not only to
withhold from it this advantage, but, through the medium of its undefined
constitution, and the consequent absence of restriction on the authority
with which he might invest its governor, to attempt an encroachment on
the envied privileges of Connecticut.

Colonel Fletcher, a sordid, unprincipled man, of irascible disposition

[1] Colden. Smith.

and narrow understanding, yet endowed with a considerable share of activity, was the governor who next arrived to represent the king at New York ; [1] and to him was intrusted the execution of the design that William entertained against the neighbouring colony. [August, 1692.] Happily for the liberties which he undertook to invade, this officer was more fitted by his temper to disclose, than by his capacity to conduct, a system of arbitrary and encroaching policy.   By the commission which he now received from the crown, he was invested with plenary powers of commanding not merely the militia of New York, but all his Majesty's militia in the same quarter of America.   His first step towards achieving this encroachment was to tender a commission from himself to Governor Trent, who already commanded the militia of Connecticut in conformity with the directions of the provincial charter ; and the reception of this, even in the light of a mere supererogatory confirmation, it was doubtless expected, would pave the way to a more distinct and complete establishment of the king's pretensions.   But in the popular constitution of Connecticut, the offices of government were then filled by men, who, thoroughly appreciating the privileges they enjoyed, had sense to discern, and spirit to resist, every attempt to violate them ; and the proffer of Fletcher's commission was not only flatly rejected, but made the subject of a vigorous remonstrance.   Incensed at such contumacy, as he was pleased to regard it, Fletcher, with his usual impetuosity, repaired abruptly to Hartford [1693], and commanded the assembly of the State, who were convoked at the time, to place their militia forthwith under his orders.   He even carried his insolence to the length of declaring that he would issue a proclamation inviting all persons who were for the king to join him, and denouncing all others as guilty of disloyalty and sedition.   Finding his menacing injunctions received with calm but inflexible disregard, he presented himself with one of his council, Colonel Bayard, to the militia at their parade ; and, expecting that a royal warrant would find greater favor with the men than it had done with their civil rulers, he commanded Bayard to read his commission aloud, as an act of declaratory possession of the authority to which he pretended.   But Captain Wadsworth, who was always ready to confront any danger that menaced the liberties of his country, and who had once before saved the charter of Connecticut from invasion,[2] now stood forward to prevent the privileges it conveyed from being abridged or insulted, and, commanding the drums to beat, effectually drowned the obnoxious accents.   When Fletcher ventured to interpose, Wadsworth supported his orders with such an energy of determination, that the meaner spirit of his antagonist was completely outbraved and overmastered ; and seeing the countenances of all around kindling in sympathy with the patriot's fervor, he judged it prudent to consult his safety by a hasty return to New York.   The king, with the view of covering this defeat, or of trying whether legal chicane could repair it, caused the matter to be submitted to the deliberation of the attorney and solicitor general of England ; and on their reporting without hesitation in favor of the plea of Connecticut, an order of council was passed in conformity with their opinion ; — as if the question had involved a mere local dispute between two provincial jurisdictions, in which the king, without any precognition of its

---

[1] He was appointed also governor of Pennsylvania by the king, who had deprived William Penn of his proprietary functions.
[2] *Ante*, Book II., Chap. V.

LL

merits, was to exercise the dignified functions of supreme and impartial arbitrator.[1]

Fortunately for New York, the indiscretion of her governor was prevented from being so detrimental as it might otherwise have proved to her Indian interests, by the confidence he reposed in Major Schuyler, whose weighty influence was employed to preserve the affections and sustain the spirit of the Five Nations. Little or no assistance, indeed, was rendered by the provincial government to these allies ; and Frontignac, even while occupied with other hostilities in New England, was able by his vigor and activity to inflict on them a severe defeat. Stirred by this intelligence, Fletcher assembled the militia of New York, and abruptly demanded if any of them were willing to march to the aid of their allies against the French. The men threw up their hats in the air and answered warmly, " One and all." Their march was performed with a rapidity that highly gratified the Indians ; and though it produced no substantial advantage to them, it was so favorably regarded as a demonstration of promptitude to lend them assistance, that they were prevented from embracing Frontignac's offers of peace. They remarked, nevertheless, that it was too frequent with the English to defer their succour till it had become unavailing ; and that, while the whole power of France in America was concentrated in simultaneous efforts to maintain the French dominion, the English colonies acted with partial and divided operation, and Maryland and Delaware in particular (though the quarrel was said to be a national one) took no share in the hostilities at all.[2]

But the busy, yet contracted, spirit of Governor Fletcher was more frequently and strenuously exerted in contentions with the provincial legislature, than in succouring the Indians ; though it was to his services in this last particular that he owed what little popularity he enjoyed in the province. A bigot to the church of England, he labored incessantly to introduce a model of her establishment in New York, and naturally encountered much resistance to this project from the opposite predilections of the Dutch and other Presbyterian inhabitants. At length his efforts succeeded in procuring a bill to be carried through the lower house [September, 1693], or assembly of representatives, for placing and endowing ministers of religion in the several parishes : but when the council adjected to the clause which gave the people the privilege of electing their own ministers a proviso that the governor should exercise the episcopal power of approving and collating the incumbents, this amendment was directly negatived by the assembly. The governor, exasperated at their opposition, called the members before him, and prorogued their session with a passionate harangue. " You take upon you," said he, " as if you were dictators. I sent down to you an amendment of but three or four words in that bill, which, though very immaterial, yet was positively denied. I must tell you, it seems very unmannerly. It is the sign of a stubborn ill-temper. You ought to consider that you have but a third share in the legislative power of the government ; and ought not to take all upon you, nor be so peremptory. You ought to let the council have a share. They are in the nature of the House of Lords or upper house ; but you seem to take the whole power in your hands, and set up for every thing. You have sat a long time to little purpose, and have been a

off

[1] Smith. Trumbull. In the commission from George the Second to Sir Danvers Osborn (recited at length by Smith), the command of the Connecticut militia was again conferred on the governor of New York.
[2] Colden. Smith.

great charge to the country.   Ten shillings a day is a large allowance, and you punctually exact it.   You have been always forward enough to pull down the fees of other ministers in the government.   Why did not you think it expedient to correct your own to a more moderate allowance ? "   The members of assembly endured the ebullitions of his violence and spleen with invincible patience ; but not the less firmly did they withstand his pretensions. In the following year [1694], their disputes were so frequent that all public business was interrupted ; and the governor, with policy more splenetic than deliberate, announced his intention of convoking the assembly no more.   But though his own emoluments were secured by an act that established the public revenue for a series of years, the necessity of raising farther supplies to make presents to the Indians, and the arrival of a body of troops from Britain, obliged him to depart from his purpose.   He was directed also by the king to lay before the assembly an assignment which his Majesty had framed of the quotas [1] to be respectively contributed by the colonies for the maintenance of a force against the French.   The assembly could not be persuaded to pay the slightest attention to this royal proposition.   But they made a liberal grant of money for the support of the troops that had arrived, and added a present to the governor ; who now perceiving that the people of New York, though endowed with a spirit over which his insolence and passion could obtain no triumph, might yet be rendered subservient to his avarice, ceased to harass himself and them by farther pressing obnoxious schemes, and cultivated a good understanding with the assembly during the remainder of his administration.   In the prosecution of this altered policy he was more successful than some other royal governors of the American provinces, whose remarkable unpopularity during many years of honest and praiseworthy exertion has excited surprise in those who have not examined with sufficient minuteness the whole of their official career.   Like Fletcher, those officers were at first disposed to regard the provincial inhabitants as an inferior people, and commenced their administration with insolent, domineering carriage, and arbitrary pretensions ; like him, they learned wisdom from experience ; but before the lesson was taught, the opportunity of profitably applying it had been lost ; the people had ceased to be as tractable as in former days ; and the spirit of liberty, thoroughly exercised, had become prone to suspect encroachment, and prompt to repel as well as firm in resisting it.   Their administration was embarrassed by the total want of public confidence, which, having once deservedly forfeited it, they found that even a complete change of measures was insufficient to regain.   From ignorance or disregard of such considerations as these, it has been supposed, and plausibly maintained by many writers, that the executive government of the American provinces was obstructed by the factious obstinacy of a perverse and unreasonable people ; when, in truth, the governors were but reaping what themselves and their predecessors had sown, and struggling with the just suspicions that their original misconduct had created.   In all the provinces where either regal power was not circumscribed by charters, or where (as in Massachusetts) the nomination of the chief executive officer was by charter reserved to the crown, such were, not unfrequently, the pro-

---

[1] The list of the respective quotas was as follows : —

Pennsylvania	£ 80	Rhode Island and Providence	£ 48
Massachusetts	350	Connecticut	120
Maryland	160	New York	200
Virginia	240		

This assignment was disregarded by every one of the colonies.

ceedings of the British governors, and the complexion of their administrations ; and Britain, it must be confessed, by delegating authority to such
men, and abetting such policy, took infinite pains to nourish and educate the
spirit of liberty in those of her colonial dependencies, where it seemed least
likely to attain a flourishing growth.

The remainder of Fletcher's administration was not distinguished by any
domestic occurrrence that deserves to be particularly commemorated.   The
war between the French and the Five Nations sometimes languished by the
address of Frontignac's negotiations, and was oftener kindled into additional
fury and havoc by his enterprise and activity. Neither age nor sickness could
chill the ardor of this commander's spirit, or impair the resources of his
capacity.   On the threshold of his own fate,[1] and supported in a litter, he
flew to every point of attack or defence, to animate the courage of his soldiers, and contemplate the execution of his plans.   His own bodily infirmity
had as little effect in mitigating his rigor as in diminishing his activity ; and,
as their hostilities were prolonged, the French and the Indians seemed to be
inspired with a mutual emulation of cruelty[2] in victory, no less than of
prowess in battle. The prisoners on both sides expired in tortures ; and the
French, less prepared by education and physical habits for such extremities
of suffering, endured a great deal more pain than they inflicted. [1696.]
On one occasion, when Frontignac succeeded in capturing a Mohawk fort,
he found it deserted of all its garrison except a sachem in extreme old age,
who betrayed no symptom of trepidation ; but, seated with all the firmness
and gravity of an ancient Roman in his capitol, saluted his civilized com-
peer in age and decrepitude with calm, unbending dignity.   Every hand
was instantly raised to wound his time-stricken frame ; and while French and
Indian knives were plunged into his body, he contemptuously advised his
Indian enemies rather to burn him with fire, in order that their French allies
might learn, from his example, how to suffer like men. " Never, perhaps,"
says Charlevoix, " was a man treated with more cruelty ; nor ever did any
endure it with superior magnanimity and resolution."[3]

---

[1] He died very soon after the restoration of peace by the treaty of Ryswick. Smith. "He
was then," says Charlevoix, "seventy-eight years of age, and yet in full possession of the
firmness and vivacity of his prime. He was esteemed by all, and beloved by almost all who
approached him."

[2] In truth, this emulation was more than a mere semblance. On one occasion, a deliberate
competition took place between the French and an Indian tribe in alliance with them, to ascertain which people could inflict the most ingenious cruelty on a Mohawk prisoner. Of the
horrid tragedy that ensued I shall give no farther account than that the Indians greatly excelled
their competitors, and threw the French into transports of laughter by the fantastic variety of
the tortures they inflicted. The French soldiers appear to have been prompted to this brutal-
ity by mere revenge and ferocity. Their commander's object was to create irreconcilable enmity between a tribe newly allied to him and the Five Nations. Colden. But it was afterwards remarked, that Europeans, seduced by example into the imitation of savage practices, far
transcended their teachers, and indulged Indian cruelty without any regard to the limits within
which Indian principle confined it.

[3] Neither the French nor the Indians, however, slew all their prisoners. A great many remained to be exchanged at the end of the war ; and on this occasion it was remarked, that
all the Indians returned with alacrity to their friends, but that in many cases it proved very
difficult, and in some utterly impossible, to induce Frenchmen, who had lived a few years with
the Indians and embraced their habits, to return to civilized life. This seems to increase the
probability that the Indians are the degenerate descendants of civilized men. Civilization
implies a virtuous conflict, barbarism a natural compliance, with temptation. The English
found it no less difficult to prevail with their friends who had been taken prisoners by the
French Indians, and lived for any considerable time with them, to return to New York ;
" though no people enjoy more liberty, and live in greater plenty, than the common inhabitants of New York do." Colden. The exercise of mercy by the Indians was no less rare in
its occurrence than singular in its effects. For the captives whom they preserved they in-

The governor of New York from time to time encouraged the Five Nations to persevere in the contest, by endeavouring to negotiate alliances between them and other tribes, and by sending them valuable presents of ammunition, and of the European commodities which they principally esteemed; and their communications to him fluctuated between grateful acknowledgments of these occasional supplies, and angry complaints that he fought all his battles by the hands of the Indians.   Indeed, except repelling some insignificant attacks of the French on the frontiers of the province, the English governor took no actual share in the war, and left the most important interests of his countrymen to be defended against the efforts of a skilful and inveterate foe, by the unaided valor of their Indian allies.   The peace of Ryswick [September, 1697], which interrupted the hostilities of the French and English, threatened at first to be attended with fatal consequences to those allies to whose exertions the English were so highly indebted; and if Fletcher had been permitted to continue longer in the government of New York, this result, no less dangerous than dishonorable to his countrymen, would most probably have ensued.   A considerable part of the forces of Count Frontignac had been employed hitherto in warlike operations against Massachusetts and New Hampshire, in conjunction with the numerous Indian confederates of the French in that quarter.   But the peace of Ryswick, of which he now received intelligence, enabled him to concentrate his whole disposable force against the only foe that remained to him; and refusing to consider the Five Nations as identified with the English, he prepared to invade them with such an army as they never before had to cope with, and overwhelm them with a vengeance which they seemed incapable of resisting.

But Fletcher was now very seasonably succeeded by the Earl of Bellamont [April, 1698] in the government of New York and Massachusetts; and this new governor, who was well endowed with both resolution and capacity, perceiving the danger and injustice of suffering the French to execute their design, promptly interposed to counteract it.   He not only furnished the Five Nations with an ample supply of ammunition and military stores, but notified to Count Frontignac, that, if the French should presume to attack them, he would march with the whole forces of his province to their aid.   The count thereupon abandoned his enterprise, and complained to his sovereign (Louis the Fourteenth) of the interruption it had received; while Lord Bellamont, in like manner, apprized King William of the step he had taken.   The two monarchs commanded their respective delegates to lend assistance to each other, and exert a spirit of accommodation in making the peace effectual to both nations, and to leave all disputes concerning the dependency of the Indian tribes to the determination of commissioners who were to be named in pursuance of the treaty of Ryswick.   Shortly

dulged a degree of tenderness very remote from the stoicism which they commonly affected; and when obliged to surrender them, confessed the pain of the sacrifice by unwonted effusions of tears. See a description of the restoration of some of these prisoners in Dodsley's *Annual Register for* 1765. The celebrated Mrs. Grant of Laggan, even while enjoying and adorning, in mature age, the refined happiness of civilized society and literary distinction, confessed, that, from her accidental intercourse in early youth with the Mohawk Indians, she had imbibed an attachment for these savages, and even for their mode of life, which no after circumstances had been able to counteract.

So many English prisoners have remained and married in the Indian settlements (says Professor Kalm), and so many French traders have spontaneously united themselves to the Indians, that the "Indian blood in Canada is very much mixed with European blood, and a great part of the Indians now living (1749) owe their origin to Europe."

after the reception of these mandates, a peace was concluded between the French and the Five Nations ; but not till English insolence and French address had nearly detached these tribes entirely from the alliance they had so steadily maintained, by leading them to believe that the English interposed in their concerns for no other reason than that they accounted them their vassals.   The French endeavoured to take advantage of their ill-humor by pressing them to admit an establishment of Jesuits into their settlements.   But although the Indians at first entertained the proposition, and listened with their usual gravity and politeness to the enticing harangue of a Jesuit who was deputed to support it,[1] their habitual sentiments soon prevailed over a transient discontent, and they declared their determination to adhere to the English, and to receive, instead of the French priests, a mission of Protestant pastors which Lord Bellamont engaged to introduce among them.[2]

Some abuses that prevailed, and some disorders that were apprehended at New York, had prompted King William to bestow the government of this province on Lord Bellamont, whom he justly deemed peculiarly well qualified, by the influence of his elevated rank, added to the firmness and integrity of his character, to correct the one and compose the other.   Fletcher, the preceding governor, had proved a very unfaithful steward of the public revenue, and gratified his avarice and his partialities by unjust and exorbitant appropriations and grants of land.   Lord Bellamont, after investigating the particulars of Fletcher's administration, openly denounced him as a corrupt and profligate magistrate ; and not only caused judicial proceedings to be instituted against him and the favorites whom he had enriched with a share of the public spoils, but at one time proposed to send him as a prisoner to undergo a criminal trial in England.   The expense and difficulty of procuring what would be deemed requisite evidence by a judicial tribunal, together with other obstructions which commonly impede the success of schemes for accomplishing the exposure or compelling the restitution of official pillage rendered those purposes and proceedings abortive.

An attempt to correct another abuse proved at first extremely unfortunate, and was attended with remarkable circumstances in its progress, and important consequences in England.   The late war gave rise to a great deal of privateering, which in many instances degenerated into piracy ; and the evil was increased by the readiness with which James the Second, in his exile, granted commissions for naval service to adventurers adhering, or professing adherence, to his cause, and who preposterously hoped that these commissions would entitle their maritime robberies to be regarded as acts of legitimate warfare.   From New York, in particular, many piratical cruisers were known to have sailed ; and, indeed, there was strong reason to suspect that Fletcher's hunger for gold had been too voracious to scruple the acceptance of it from the hands of those robbers as the price of his connivance at their depredations.   Lord Bellamont, whom the king with especial urgency directed to adopt the most vigorous measures for the extirpation of this system (which he dreaded the more from its subservience to the intrigues of the

---

[1] See Note XIX., at the end of the volume.

[2] Smith.   Colden.   The fulfilment of the promise of sending Protestant pastors to the Five Nations seems to have been deferred till the year 1712, when one Andrews was sent among them by the English Society for propagating the Gospel.   The Indians at first received him with joy, but peremptorily refused to suffer him to teach the English language to their children.   After preaching and teaching among them, in the Indian tongue, for several years, he was universally forsaken by his auditors and scholars, and closed a fruitless mission in 1718. Humphrey's *Historical Account of the Society for propagating the Gospel.*

exiled monarch), was advised by some imprudent or disingenuous counsellor to invite the assistance of one Kidd, who was represented to him as a man of honor and intrepidity, and acquainted with the persons and the haunts of the pirates. Kidd, being in England at the time, was introduced to Lord Bellamont by the person who so characterized him, and readily offered to undertake the suppression and apprehension of the pirates, if the king would grant him a commission for the purpose, and place at his disposal a fast-sailing frigate of thirty guns. The earl laid the proposal before the king, who was fully disposed to embrace any feasible plan for extirpating piracy : but some difficulties having been started by the admiralty, the scheme was dropped ; and, unfortunately for the reputation of all parties, a private adventure to be conducted by Kidd against the pirates was suggested in its stead, and finally embraced. The king himself was concerned in the enterprise, and had a tenth share of its eventual profits reserved to him ; and the Lord Chancellor (Somers), the Duke of Shrewsbury, the Earls of Romney and Oxford, Sir Edmund Harrison, and various other persons of distinction, were associated in the adventure as partners with their sovereign. Kidd received an ordinary commission from the crown as a privateer, with special directions from the royal and noble owners of his vessel to attack the pirates, and to hold himself directly responsible to Lord Bellamont. Embarking on this important enterprise, with so much illustrious character intrusted to his keeping, Kidd reached New York long before the arrival of Lord Bellamont, whose assumption of his government did not take place till more than two years after his nomination. No sooner had this nobleman landed at New York, than he learned, with the deepest confusion and resentment, that by his patronage of Kidd he had been accessory to an enormous aggravation of the evil which he designed to suppress, as well as to the dishonor of his king and of all the distinguished persons associated in the privateering adventure ; and that Kidd had already rendered himself more infamous and formidable than any other pirate that infested the seas, by the extent of his depredations and his reckless disregard of human life. Lord Bellamont exerted the utmost vigor to repair this unhappy error ; and having fortunately succeeded in apprehending Kidd at Boston [1699], where the pirate rashly supposed himself unknown, he wrote to the secretary of state, desiring that a warrant might be sent for transmitting this daring offender to England, where already considerable interest was excited in the public mind by the tidings of the freebooter's desperate enterprises, and by vague rumors of the assistance he had derived from the first personages in the realm. A ship of war was instantly despatched to convey the prisoner to London, and repel any attempt that might be made for his rescue ; but, unfortunately, the vessel was disabled on her passage, and obliged to return to port.

A strong suspicion now arose of collusion between Kidd and the royal ministers, who, it was supposed, were determined at all hazards to screen him, lest in his own defence he should discover their infamous confederacy. This suspicion was inflamed by the artifices of the Tory party, opposed to King William's government, who vehemently pressed a motion in the House of Commons, that all persons concerned in Kidd's adventure might be dismissed from public employment. Though their motion was rejected, they prevailed with the house to have Kidd examined at the bar, — when at length the exertions of the ministers and of Lord Bellamont to vindicate their characters had succeeded in bringing him to England ; and though dis-

appointed at first in their hope of obtaining any valuable disclosures from
him, yet, either honestly suspecting what they professed to believe, or hoping
that he would be induced to become an instrument of their purposes (which
he discovered more inclination than ability to do), they endeavoured to have
his trial deferred, and prevailed with the house to call him again to its bar,
even after an address had been voted to the crown demanding that he should
be remitted forthwith to an English jury.　Kidd was brought to trial at the
Old Bailey in the year 1701, and, totally failing either to criminate the ministers or to defend himself, was convicted, with several of his accomplices,
of piracy and murder, and soon after underwent the just punishment of his
crimes.　The passionate violence of the Tory faction in England prevented
this matter from proving as injurious as, more moderately handled, it would,
and perhaps ought to, have been to Lord Bellamont and the Whig ministers
of the king.　Kidd's conduct previous to his employment as a privateer had
been in reality such that a proper investigation of it should have exposed him
to punishment, instead of recommending him to an important command.　A
charge derived from this gross and culpable neglect, and directed against all
who had been concerned in procuring Kidd's commission, was introduced
into the articles of impeachment preferred soon after by the Commons
against Lord Somers.　The character and conduct of the Earl of Bellamont
were severely arraigned in this charge ; though his recent death at New York
prevented him from being included in the impeachment.　But the managers
of the prosecution associating the charge of culpable neglect with other
weightier imputations which they were unable to prove, and involving themselves (purposely perhaps) in a dispute with the House of Lords, the impeachment ended in an acquittal, without producing a trial.[1]

The most formidable disorders that threatened the government and community of New York were portended by the increasing animosity of two
powerful factions, consisting of the friends and the enemies of the unfortunate Leisler.　The son of this man, incapable of forgetting or forgiving
the tragical fate of his parent, had labored incessantly for the reëstablishment of his character ; having obtained, by the assistance of the province
of Massachusetts (where the enemies of Leisler, and especially Dudley,
who had condemned him, were the objects of general aversion), an act of
parliament to reverse the attainder of his father, and now proceeding, with
every likelihood of success, to urge a claim for retribution of his family's
sufferings and losses, he elevated the spirits of his partisans in New York
by the hope of a triumph so humiliating to their adversaries.　The mutual
animosity of the two factions was excited to such a degree by the occurrence and the prospect of fresh opportunities of its indulgence, that the
conduct of public business began to be seriously obstructed by their intrigues
and collisions ; and in the very first assembly that Lord Bellamont convoked
at New York, — except a unanimous address of thanks to him for his speech
on the state of the province, — there was scarcely a single measure proposed, in which the members of assembly found it possible to agree.　The
character and manners of Lord Bellamont were happily adapted to compose
these dissensions ; a task, which, perhaps, if his administration had proved
more durable, he would have wisely attempted and successfully accomplished ; but, unfortunately, the circumstances in which he found himself placed,
on his first arrival at New York, and the line of conduct which he was

---

[1] Smith.　Smollett's *History of England.*　Howell's *State Trials.*

thereby prompted to pursue, tended rather to inflame than to mitigate the evil. His just displeasure against Fletcher, aggravated by the discovery of that profligate governor's encouragement of the pirates, at first extended itself to every person who had held office along with him, or been distinguished by any share of his intimacy or regard ; and as in this class were comprehended the principal adversaries of Leisler and his party, the spirits of this party were additionally revived, and their numbers augmented by the prospect of victorious supremacy. Young Leisler's solicitations in England eventually prevailed so far that a letter was addressed by the secretary of state to Lord Bellamont [February, 1700], announcing, that his Majesty, from " a gracious sense of the father's services and sufferings," desired that the son's claims of indemnification might be entertained by the general assembly of New York. No sooner was the royal letter laid before the assembly, of which a great majority now consisted of the friends of young Leisler, than a resolution was passed, appointing the sum of one thousand pounds to be levied on the province for his behoof.[1]

Lord Bellamont had now obtained a complete acquaintance with the circumstances and condition of New York ; and the resentment and disturbance he had suffered from the piratical transactions in which his own and his sovereign's honor were so deeply involved might reasonably be supposed to have subsided. But the influence which his good sense and moderation were expected to produce in assuaging the angry factions existing within his presidency was intercepted by his unexpected death, in the beginning of the year 1701. This event was attended with the most unhappy consequences. The faction that had appeared likely to be defeated received intelligence, that Lord Cornbury, who was expected soon to arrive as the successor of Bellamont, was prepossessed in their favor, because they were accounted partisans of the church of England, and began already to anticipate a favorable change in their relations with the adverse party ; while this party, at the head of which was Nanfan, the lieutenant-governor, made haste to exert their power with an energy enhanced by the probable shortness of its duration. Strenuous efforts were made by both to increase their strength in the assembly ; and furious disputes were engendered by the theoretical respect which both professed for the same constitutional principles, by the practical respect which each accordingly required for these principles from their adversaries, and by the practical disregard of them into which both were hurried by the violence of their passions. The party opposed to Leisler's friends, being generally defeated in these contests, vented their indignation in complaints of their adversaries to the king, the parliament, and, above all, to Lord Cornbury, on whose favor their hopes of victory and vengeance now mainly depended. Colonel Bayard, in particular, having promoted certain addresses [1702] in which the most scandalous charges of bribery, public plunder, and oppression were preferred against the lieutenant-governor, the chief-justice (for Dudley had ceased to hold this office), and the assembly, was committed to prison as a traitor, by Nanfan, in conformity with a law which Bayard and his friends had procured to be enacted in 1691,

---

[1] This year, no fewer than a thousand Scottish fugitives from the unfortunate and ill-used Scottish colony of Darien arrived at New York in various ships, during the absence of Lord Bellamont at Boston. Nanfan, the lieutenant-governor, in conformity with instructions from England, refused even the slightest relief or assistance to these unhappy adventurers. Oldmixon (2d edit.). Two years before, the royal governors of New York and New England had issued proclamations, forbidding all correspondence with, or assistance to, the Scottish colony. Holmes.

to curb their own adversaries, and which subjected to the pains of treason every person endeavouring, *by force of arms, or otherwise,* to disturb the peace, welfare, and quiet of the king's government.   Though the attorney-general of New York delivered in writing his solemn opinion that the addresses contained nothing criminal or illegal, Nanfan, finding the solicitor-general differently minded, urged on the prosecution ; and, after a trial more fair, perhaps, than in such a state of public feeling could have been reasonably expected, Bayard was dragged to the brink of the pit which he himself had dug for others, by a verdict of guilty and sentence of death.[1]   [March, 1702.]   Alderman Hutchins was shortly after tried, and convicted on a similar charge.   But here the adversaries of the prisoners were induced to pause.   Though the law on which the charges were founded was illiberal and unjust, it had been framed by the prisoners themselves and their party, and never yet repealed ; and though the convictions proceeded on a somewhat strained application of it, they were procured by no signal or undoubted departure from the ordinary principles of judicial procedure in the administration of penal law.   The prosecutors, therefore, had not incurred such guilt as to confound altogether their sense and humanity, or imperiously drive them to complete what they had begun, and destroy their victims while they were yet in their power.   Happily for themselves and for the province, they consented to reprieve the prisoners till the king's pleasure should be ascertained.   But long before this reference to the crown could be accomplished, Lord Cornbury arrived at New York [May 3, 1702] ; and not only caused the attainders of Bayard and Hutchins to be reversed, but, openly declaring himself the head of their party, conducted his administration with such violence and partiality, that the chief justice (who was dismissed from his office), and several other considerable persons of the opposite faction, deemed it prudent to depart from the province.[2]

Edward, Lord Cornbury, grandson of Lord Chancellor Clarendon, possessed not one of the qualities by which his distinguished ancestor was characterized, except an exaggeration of his zeal for the church of England, and his intolerance of all other ecclesiastical associations.   The rest of Lord Cornbury's character would have disgraced more estimable qualities ; and seems to have formed a composition, no less odious than despicable, of rapacity and prodigality, voluptuousness and inhumanity, the loftiest arrogance and the meanest chicane.   Whether from real difference in sentiment, or from a policy which in those days was not uncommon, — while his father adhered to the cause of James the Second, the son supported the pretensions of King William, and was one of the first officers who deserted with his troop to join the enterprise which produced the British Revolution ; and having now dissipated his substance in riot and debauchery, and being obliged to fly from his creditors in England, he obtained, by one of the last acts of his royal patron's administration, the government of New York as a reward of his services.   This appointment was confirmed by his kinswoman, Queen Anne, who added to it the government of New Jersey, which had

---

[1] The proceedings on this trial, which are reported at some length in Howell's *Collection,* are creditable to the legal knowledge, ability, and spirit of the lawyers employed to conduct them, and especially of the counsel for the prisoner.   Emot, one of the latter, maintained a plea which was not admitted till a much later period in England, — that " the jury are judges both of law and fact."   Even under the liberal sway of Oliver Cromwell, it was declared from the bench (on the first trial of Lilburne) that it was " a damnable doctrine " to hold that the jury were judges of law as well as fact.   Howell.

[2] Oldmixon.   Smith.   Howell's *State Trials.*

been recently surrendered by its proprietaries to the crown. The administration of Lord Cornbury is chiefly remarkable for the production of an effect not less remote from his own intentions than from the expectations which his character might reasonably suggest ; for it was during his pernicious and illiberal sway that the dissensions which we have seen carried to such a height in New York came to be, if not entirely suppressed, yet greatly mitigated and reduced. This desirable end, which was rather obstructed than advanced by the only respectable governor sent to New York since the Revolution, was now promoted by the administration of a successor who surpassed even Andros in his bad preëminence, and rendered himself more universally detested than any other officer to whom the government of this province was ever intrusted. For some time after his arrival in the colony, the majority of the assembly, composed, by his influence, of the faction which had recently smarted under the insolence and ascendency of a triumphant rival, adhered with unscrupulous zeal to him as its leader and protector ; and even after the intolerance he began to exert against the Presbyterians, and every other religious society, except the Protestant Episcopalians, had alienated many of his first political adherents, he found their loss nearly compensated by the increased attachment of those who now regarded him as their ecclesiastical ally.

Though the great mass of the inhabitants, including the principal families in the province, were Presbyterians, he refused to permit the ministers of this persuasion to preach without special license from himself, — which implied that they officiated, not by legal or natural right, but by precarious grace and indulgence. On one occasion, finding that in a township in Long Island there were a few Episcopalians intermixed with the Presbyterians, who formed the majority of the inhabitants, and had built a parsonage for their minister, he fraudulently contrived to get possession of the house, and then delivered it up to the Episcopal party. Learning, some time after, that two Presbyterian ministers from Virginia had preached to a congregation in New York without his license, he threw them both into prison, and afterwards brought them to trial for a misdemeanour ; but although the judge who presided at the trial exhorted the jury to return a special verdict. in order that the legal rule on this subject might be finally ascertained, the jury had too much sense and honesty to intrust the liberties of their country to other keeping than their own, and without hesitation acquitted the prisoners. In every quarter of the province, the governor offered his assistance to the Episcopalians in usurping possession of the ecclesiastical edifices that other sects had erected, and, to the disgrace of some of the zealots for Episcopacy, this offer was in various instances accepted, and produced the most scandalous scenes of riot, injustice, and confusion. But, happily for the unfortunate people who were exposed to the mischief of Lord Cornbury's administration, his conduct in other departments of government soon weakened his influence with all parties, and gradually deprived him of the power of instigating any portion of the community to harass or oppress the rest. It was discovered, that, not content with the liberal grants of money which the assembly bestowed on him for his private use, he had embezzled large sums appropriated to the construction of public works and the defence of the province ; and that, unable to subsist on his legitimate emoluments, even with the addition of official pillage, he had contracted debts to every tradesman who would lend him credit, and silenced or defied these creditors by the terror of his power or the privilege of his station, which exempted him from arrest.   Even after this discovery was made, he contrived to have some more of the public money intrusted to his hands, by alarming the assembly with pretended intelligence of an approaching invasion ; and the supply thus extorted was employed with as little fidelity as he had observed on prior occasions.

In vain the assembly proposed to establish a board of auditors to control the public expenditure and account for it to themselves ; and with as little success did they transmit a remonstrance against the general conduct of the governor to the queen.   Their application to her Majesty produced no other effect than some private instructions, which were said to have been communicated to Lord Cornbury ; their proposition to control the public disbursements was disallowed ; and when they insisted on a scrutiny of the governor's accounts, he warned them, in an angry speech, not to provoke him to exert " certain powers " which the queen had committed to him, and advised them to let him hear less about the rights of the house, as the house had no rights but what the grace and good pleasure of her Majesty permitted it to enjoy.   By such declarations, and a line of conduct closely conformed to them, he succeeded in alienating all his adherents, and finally in uniting all classes of the people in one common interest of opposition to himself. When he dissolved an assembly for its fidelity to the public interests, he found his influence no longer able to affect the composition of the assembly by which it was succeeded.   It was, perhaps, fortunate for the colonists that they were compelled to endure Lord Cornbury's misgovernment for a number of years [1702 – 1708], and till the lessons which it was well calculated to teach them were deeply impressed on their minds.   The governor had leisure to repeat the expedient of dissolving intractable assemblies, and the mortification of finding every succeeding one more stubborn than its predecessor ; till at last he convoked assemblies which absolutely refused to vote the smallest supply for the public service, except on condition that the governor should previously account for all his past receipts and disbursements of money, and (which was impossible) should refund all the sums he had embezzled, — preferring even an extremity so inconvenient to themselves, to the continuance of this corrupt and profligate administration.   The dissolute habits and ignoble tastes and manners of the man completed and embittered the disgust with which he was now universally regarded ; and when he affronted public decency by rambling abroad in the dress of a woman, the people beheld with indignation and shame the representative of their sovereign and the ruler of their country.

The inhabitants of New York were now invited, by a painful but salutary experience, to reflect on and deplore the folly and mischief of those dissensions that had once enabled such a wretch to enjoy influence among them, and successfully to incite them to harass and maltreat each other, that he might the more securely pillage and oppress them all.   His administration forcibly taught them the important lesson, that divisions among themselves were profitable only to the person who ought to be the object of their constitutional jealousy, — the royal governor ; and that union among themselves, founded on a sense of common interest, and maintained by the exercise of mutual good-will and forbearance, was essential alike to their tranquillity and independence.   This lesson was not addressed to them in vain ; and though the animosities formerly kindled were not entirely extinguished for many years, they never again reached the height which they had attained at the commencement of Lord Cornbury's administration.   This worthless personage continued for a number of years to remind the people by his presence of the salutary counsels they derived from his administration, even after they had obtained a deliverance from its burden.   In the year 1708, Queen Anne was at last compelled by the reiterated and unanimous complaints of New York and of New Jersey (where he was equally odious) to supersede his commission, and appoint Lord Lovelace his successor ; and no sooner was he deprived of command, than his creditors threw him into the same prison where he had formerly confined the victims of his tyranny.   Thus degraded from office by his public crimes, and deprived of liberty by his private vice and dishonesty, this kinsman of his queen remained a prisoner for debt in the province he had governed, till the death of his father, by elevating him to the peerage, and investing him with the dignity of an hereditary legislator of Great Britain, entitled him to his liberation.[1]   He then returned to Europe, where he died in the year 1723.[2]

Both before and after the British Revolution, the province of New York received large additions to the number of its inhabitants from all the various sources of emigration which were generated by oppression, poverty, and discontent, in the kingdoms of Europe.   The poor found here a country where their industry was highly valued, and all freemen enjoyed equal rights, — where, instead of being compelled to vie with each other for the boon of ill-rewarded employment,[3] their services were eagerly courted by the rich, and labor conducted them with certainty to ease and independence.   Among the later accessions of people were a number of Protestant refugees from France and of Presbyterians from Ireland.[4]   The metropolis of the province, which in the year 1678 contained about three thousand four hundred inhabitants, was found to contain nearly double that number in 1696 ; and the port, which at a former period owned no more than three ships and eight sloops, possessed in the last-mentioned year forty ships, sixty-two sloops, and an equal number of boats.[5]   The shipping of New York was promoted not merely by the increase of its inhabitants, but by the advantages of its situation, which enabled it to conduct nearly the whole foreign trade of Connecticut and New Jersey.[6]   The total population of the province amounted, in 1701, to about thirty thousand persons.[7]   Many of the first English colonists who repaired to this province, after the conquest of it from the Dutch, remained but a short time in it, and sought a refuge in New Jersey from the hostile inroads of the French and their Indian allies.   At the end of the seventeenth century, the people consisted of various races, — English, Scotch, Irish, French, and chiefly Dutch ; the great majority being Presbyterians and Independents.   The Dutch congregations continued at this time, and long after, to acknowledge subjection to the ecclesiastical authorities of Holland, from whom their ministers, in general, derived their ordination

---

[1] Smith. *History of the British Dominions in America.* This work, which I have frequently referred to, is an anonymous publication in quarto. It contains more ample and precise information than the composition of Wynne, and, like it, brings down the history and state of the colonies to the middle of the eighteenth century. It is more of a statistical than a historical work.

[2] *Biographia Britannica.*

[3] See Note XX., at the end of the volume.

[4] Smith. In 1710, three thousand palatines, flying from persecution in Germany, settled in New York. Ibid.

[5] Chalmers.   [6] Smith.   [7] Holmes.

to sacred functions. The Scotch Presbyterians, after repeatedly soliciting
a charter incorporating their congregation, and being continually disappointed by the interest and opposition of the Episcopal party, executed, in
the beginning of the eighteenth century, a grant of their meeting-house and
of the ground attached to it to the general assembly of the church of Scotland. The Episcopalians, though the least numerous class, enjoyed a charter of incorporation from the provincial assembly ; and the minister of their
church in New York had a salary of one hundred pounds a year, collected by
a tax on all the inhabitants of the city. For this privilege they were indebted
to the exertions of Governor Fletcher ; and they were elated by it to such a
degree of presumption, as to maintain that the province was subject to the
ecclesiastical dominion of the church of England, and that theirs was *the
religion of the state*, — a pretension that excited much jealousy among all
the Dissenters, and was passionately disputed by them. When the Episcopal
clergy became more numerous, they accounted themselves subject immediately to the Bishop of London, who maintained a commissary at New York.
They made an attempt at an after period to engross the privilege of solem-
nizing all marriages in the province, but found themselves unable to carry
this pretension into effect. Though all law proceedings in the provincial
courts were conducted in English, and an English free school was established in 1702, the Dutch language continued long to prevail among a considerable portion of the people. For many years public worship was celebrated in Dutch in some of the churches ; and in several counties the sheriffs
often found it difficult to collect as many persons acquainted with English
as were necessary to compose the juries in the courts of law. The English
that was generally spoken was much corrupted by intermixture of the two
languages.[1]

The subsistence of the Dutch language was less advantageous to the
province than the permanence of Dutch manners, attested by the sobriety of
deportment, and the peculiar attention to domestic cleanliness, order, and
economy, by which the descendants of the original colonists of New York
were long distinguished, and which their example communicated, in no slight
degree, to the other races of European settlers with whom they were latterly
associated. A printing-press was established at New York, in the year
1693, by a printer flying from the strange occurrence of Quaker tyranny
and persecution in Pennsylvania ; and a library was founded under the government of Lord Bellamont in the year 1700. But the schools in this
province were inconsiderable ; and although the wealthier families obtained

---

[1] Smith. The English, French, and Irish colonists seem to have acquired pretty early a
uniform character. The stronger nationality and more rigid manners of the Scotch, aided
by frequent accessions of their countrymen from Scotland, preserved their national peculiarities
longer unimpaired. " They preserve unaltered," says Dwight, " the character which they
brought with them. They are industrious, frugal, orderly, patient of hardship, persevering,
attached to government, reverential to religion, generally moral, and often pious. At the
same time they are frequently unwarrantably self-complacent, rigid in their dispositions, unbending in their opinions, sequestered, avaricious, ready to unchurch those who differ from
them, and to say, *Doubtless we are the people*." Dwight's *Travels*.

Even when intermarriages and the common influence of free institutions and national association shall have produced uniformity of character among all the race of American colonists,
the peculiar pedigrees of many particular districts will be preserved by their names In one
county of New York, almost every place bears the name of an Irish saint, city, county, or
mountain. A neighbouring district, originally planted by New Englanders, is divided into
parishes and settlements bearing the names of Unanimity, Frugality, Sobriety, Enterprise,
and the like. (Dwight.) It may be hoped that the recollection of such names as these last
will impress a corresponding bias on the sentiments and character of the inhabitants of the
region.

valuable instructors for their children among the numerous Protestant refugees from France, the great bulk of the people were strangers even to the first rudiments of science and cultivation, till the era of the American Revolution.[1]

If Britain had pursued a wiser policy towards this and her other American provinces, she might have obtained from their resources a considerable diminution, if not an entire removal, of the burden of her poor-laws.   But various circumstances contributed to disguise or diminish the attractions by which the colonial territories invited the resort of the industrious poor. The practice of transporting felons to America brought this country into disrepute with many whose information was not sufficiently exact to acquaint them with the insignificant amount of the evil, and the great preponderance of the advantages by which it was counterbalanced.   The historian of New York has ascribed to this cause the dearness of labor, and the increased importation of slaves which began to take place in the beginning of the eighteenth century.   Another obstruction to the colonization of this province by the free poor arose from the practices of many of the governors, who, in order to promote the royal interest in the assembly, were permitted to make large grants of land to their partisans and dependents, by whom it was again farmed out at exorbitant rates to the cultivators, or retained in a vacant and unproductive state in the hope of a future rise in its value from the general progress of culture and population.[2]

The provincial organs of government in New York were the governor, the council, and the assembly.   The governor, appointed by the king, was commander-in-chief by sea and land, and received from the provincial revenue a salary of about one thousand five hundred pounds, together with perquisites amounting to as much more.   The counsellors were appointed by the crown, but might be suspended by the governor.   They received no salaries, and acted as a privy council to the governor, besides performing the same legislative and judicial functions as the English House of Lords.   The members of assembly (elected by freeholders possessing lands or tenements improved to the value of forty pounds[3]) had a daily stipend for their attendance ; and to them, in conjunction with the council and the governor, was committed the privilege of enacting the provincial laws, which were required to be analogous to the jurisprudence of England.   The laws were communicated to the English privy council within three months after their enactment, and might, *at any time after*, be annulled by the king.   The governor was empowered to prorogue or dissolve assemblies at his pleasure ; to appoint judges ; to collate to all vacant ecclesiastical benefices ; and, with the advice of the council, to make grants of land, to be held of the crown by soccage tenure.   Besides subordinate courts of law, there was a supreme court at New York, of which the chief justice received a salary of three hundred pounds a year.   From its judgments an appeal was competent, in causes involving more than one hundred pounds, to the governor and council, and in causes where more than three hundred pounds was at stake, to the

[1] Oldmixon. Smith. Thomas's *History of Printing*. Winterbotham. Warden. Grant's *Memoirs of an American Lady*, &c. Mrs. Grant's descriptions of American manners are, in general, entirely fanciful and erroneous.
[2] Smith. " The governors were, many of them, land-jobbers, bent on making their fortunes ; and being invested with power to do this, they either engrossed for themselves, or patented away to their particular favorites, a very great proportion of the whole province." Winterbotham.
[3] *Laws of New York from* 1691 *to* 1718.

king and the privy council of England. Much uncertainty prevailed in the administration of civil justice, from ignorance and difference of opinion as to the extent to which English statutes and decisions should be admitted to operate as rules or precedents.[1]

By a law passed in 1700 for the purpose of checking the missions of the Jesuits among the Indians, it was decreed that every Jesuit, or other Catholic priest, coming voluntarily into the province, should be subjected to perpetual imprisonment, and, in case of escape and recapture, to the punishment of death. Slaves (by a law passed in 1702), except when assembled for labor, were forbidden to meet together in greater number than three, — a regulation which proved insufficient to prevent a formidable insurrection of these unfortunate persons in the year 1712. Masters were enjoined by law to baptize their slaves, and encouraged to do so by a provision that their baptism should not entitle them to freedom. Indeed, manumission of slaves was discouraged by a heavy fine. Slaves were disqualified from bearing testimony in criminal cases against any but slaves ; and no negro, Indian, or mulatto, even though free, could acquire the property of houses or lands. Any negro or Indian, conspiring the death of a white man, was capitally punished. Even though baptized, slaves were not considered to be properly comprehended in the denomination of Christians ; for by an act passed in 1702, and confirmed in 1708, there was offered a reward of twenty shillings to every *Christian*, and half that sum to every Indian or *slave*, killing a wolf in the provincial territory. In some of the colonial settlements of the Dutch (particularly at the Cape of Good Hope), the treatment of their slaves has been distinguished by the most barbarous cruelty. But milder manners and less inhuman laws prevailed at New York, where extreme severity was inflicted only at second hand, by selling unruly and troublesome negroes to the planters of Jamaica. Various laws were made from time to time against selling ardent spirits to the Indians. The extortions of usurers were repressed by an act passed in 1717, restricting the lawful interest of money to six *per cent*. This was repealed in the following year, when the exaction of eight *per cent*. was permitted.[2]

---

[1] Smith.   [2] *Laws of New York from* 1691 *to* 1718. Smith.

BOOK VI.

NEW JERSEY.

Sale of the Territory by the Duke of York to Berkeley and Carteret. — Liberal Frame of Government enacted by the Proprietaries. — Emigration from Long Island to New Jersey. — Arrival of the first Governor and Settlers from England. — Discontent and Disturbance in the Colony. — Renovation of the Titles to New Jersey. — Equivocal Conduct of the Duke of York. — Situation of the Quakers in England. — Sale of Berkeley's Share of the Province to Quakers. — Partition of the Province between them and Carteret. — Emigration of Quakers from England to West Jersey. — Encroachments of the Duke of York. — Remonstrance of the Quakers — causes the Independence of New Jersey to be recognized. — First Assembly of West Jersey. — The Quakers purchase East Jersey. — Robert Barclay — appointed Governor. — Emigration from Scotland to East Jersey. — Designs of James the Second against the Proprietary Governments — defeated by the Revolution. — Inefficient State of the Proprietary Government. — Surrender of the Provincial Patent to the Crown — and Reunion of East and West Jersey. — Constitution of the Provincial Government. — Administration of Lord Cornbury. — State of the Colony.

Of all the national societies in which mankind have ever been united, there is none (except the fallen commonwealth of Israel) [1] which can boast of an origin as illustrious as that which belongs to the provinces of North America. Almost all these provincial settlements have been founded by men whose prevailing motives were zeal for the advancement of religious truth, for the security of political freedom, or for the enlargement of the resources and renown of their country ; and all have been indebted for a considerable share of their early population to the shelter which they afforded from civil or ecclesiastical tyranny. The successful establishment of every one of them is a grand and interesting monument of human energy and fortitude ; for it was not accomplished without a generous and heroic conflict with the most stubborn habits of human nature, and the most formidable obstructions of difficulty, danger, and distress. The colonists of New Jersey, indeed, from their proximity and friendly relation to older colonial settlements, and from other advantageous peculiarities in their situation, were exempted from much of the hardship which elsewhere attended, in so many instances, the foundation of civilized society in North America. But the motives which conducted a great proportion of them to this territory were such as must be acknowledged to reflect the highest honor on their enterprise, and to ennoble the origin of New Jersey.

The territory to which this appellation belongs was first appropriated by the Dutch, of whose settlements an account has already been given in

---

[1] It is remarkable, that, among those of the colonists of North America who were most eager to trace a resemblance between their own situation and that of the Jewish emigrants from Egypt, the opinion should have first sprung up that the savage Indians were the offspring of one of the tribes of Israel. This opinion (which is supported by very strong probabilities) was not without its use, if it tended to abate that spiritual pride sometimes engendered by a belief of the possession of an especial degree of divine favor. It was early adopted by the New England divines, and was maintained, with much learning and ability, in a treatise by one Thorowgood, published at London in 1650, and entitled *Jews in America.* It was afterwards embraced by William Penn, the Quaker, and supported by him, and by many other distinguished writers. See, in relation to this curious subject, the Appendix to Stowe's translation of Jahn's *History of the Hebrew Commonwealth.*

the history of New York. It was included in the province to which this
people gave the name of New Netherlands, and had received a few Dutch
and Swedish settlers at the period of the conquest of the Dutch colony
by the English. Preparatory to this enterprise, as we have already seen,
Charles the Second granted a charter of American territory [20th March,
1664], including the whole of the Dutch occupation, to his brother James,
Duke of York; and as the king, in conformity with his pretension to an
antecedent right, which the intrusion of the Dutch could neither extinguish
nor suspend, thought himself entitled to bestow his grant before the territory
was actually reduced to his dominion, the duke, in like manner, regarded his
investiture as completed by the charter, and proceeded to exercise the powers
it conferred on him, without waiting till he had attained actual possession of
the soil. His charter, though much less ample in its endowments than the
charters which were previously granted to the proprietaries of Maryland and
Carolina, resembled these in conferring the province, and the powers of
government, on the proprietary and *" his assigns."* Various instances, both
in the history of the Carolinas and of New Jersey, demonstrate, that, in
conformity with this expression, the proprietaries regarded their functions less
as a trust than as an absolute property, subject to every act of ownership,
and in particular to mortgage and alienation; and, accordingly, the sovereignty of large provinces of the British empire in America was repeatedly
assigned by proprietaries to their creditors, or sold in the market to the
highest bidder. It was not till after the British Revolution that the legality
of these transactions was disputed; but, although the ministers of William
the Third maintained that they were inconsistent with the law of England,
which recognized an hereditary but not a commercial transmission of office
and power, the point was never authoritatively determined. The evil, in
process of time, produced its own remedy. The succession and multiplication of proprietaries occasioned so much inconvenience to themselves,
that, sooner or later, they were glad to bargain with the crown for a surrender of their political functions; and both in Carolina and in New Jersey,
the exercise of the power of assignation materially contributed to abridge the
duration of the proprietary government.

The first example of a sale of proprietary rights and functions was afforded by the Duke of York, in his conveyance to Lord Berkeley and Sir
George Carteret of a portion of the territory comprehended in the royal
charter which he had recently procured for himself. If he had deferred
the exercise of his ownership till he obtained possession of the country,
and a report of its condition from Colonel Nichols, whom he appointed its
governor, this partition would probably not have taken place. But, before
he had yet actually occupied any part of it, or possessed the information
requisite to enable him to conduct such a transaction with advantage to himself either as proprietor of the soil or as sovereign of the people, he consented to sell one of the finest districts which it embraced to two persons
who were, or supposed themselves, much better informed. Berkeley and
Carteret were already proprietaries of Carolina; and not contented with
this ample investiture, nor yet apprized by experience of the tardy returns
from colonial possessions, they were induced, by the representations of a
projector acquainted with the domain conferred on the Duke of York, to
believe that a particular portion of it would form a valuable acquisition.
How far the disjunction of this portion might be calculated to affect the in-

terest and value of the remainder was a point, which, for the honor of the purchasers, they must be supposed to have overlooked as completely as it was misunderstood by the vendor.　But, at a subsequent period, Colonel Nichols did not scruple to assert that the person by whose advice Berkeley and Carteret were induced to make the purchase had himself been an unsuccessful candidate for the patent which the Duke of York obtained, and that he revenged his disappointment by instigating those courtiers to an acquisition which he was aware would greatly depreciate the remainder of the duke's domain.　Be this as it may, the transaction that ensued, as it was very little creditable to either of the parties who engaged in it, proved in the sequel disadvantageous to them both.

It was only three months after the date of his own charter, that the Duke of York [23d and 24th June, 1664], by a formal deed of assignment, in consideration of " a competent sum of money," conveyed to Lord Berkeley and Sir George Carteret, and their heirs and assigns, that tract of land adjacent to New England, lying westward of Long Island, and bounded on the east, south, and west by the river Hudson, the sea, and the Delaware ; on the north by the forty-first degree and fortieth minute of latitude.　In compliment to Carteret, who had defended the island of Jersey against the Long Parliament in the civil war, the duke bestowed on this region the name of Nova-Cæsarea, or New Jersey ; and he transferred to the grantees every right and privilege, and all the powers of government, which he himself possessed under his charter from the crown.[1]

Having obtained, in this manner, the sovereignty of New Jersey, the first care of the proprietaries was to invite the resort of inhabitants to the province ; and their exertions for this purpose, though pursued with more eagerness than perseverance, disclosed some share of political sagacity.　In those colonial territories which present to adventurers no alluring prospect of sudden enrichment, and which must owe their cultivation to the steady enterprise and industry of permanent settlers, the strongest attractions are supplied by liberal provisions for the security of the civil and religious rights of mankind.　The recent history of New England had demonstrated that these attractions address themselves most prevailingly to that description of human character which is best fitted to contend with the difficulties of colonization, and that their operation is so forcible as to overpower the temptations even of superior climate and soil.　That the useful lesson thus afforded to the founders of colonies was not disregarded by the courtiers of Charles the Second has already appeared from some parts of the history of Carolina, and is still more plainly manifested by the first measures that were pursued by the proprietaries of New Jersey.　They hastened to compose and publish a system of institutions for the government of the province ; and, as their object was to exhibit a political fabric that should appear generally desirable and advantageous, they succeeded in framing a project which obtained a very favorable reception, and would have better deserved it, if the proprietaries had been legislating for an existing population.　It was, indeed, a singular competition which these proprietary governments engendered, — in which sovereigns and legislators found it their interest to vie with each other in

[1] Scot's *Model of the Province of East New Jersey.* Oldmixon. Samuel Smith's *History of New Jersey.* Chalmers. Colonel Nichols gratuitously acquits Berkeley and Carteret of any accession to the design of defrauding the duke. But Carteret did not always enjoy an unspotted reputation. In 1669, he was expelled the House of Commons for issuing, as treasurer of the navy, public money without legal warrant. Hallam.

the production of models of liberty, and in tendering to the acceptance of their subjects the most effectual securities against arbitrary power. Whatever doubts may be entertained of the dignity of their motives or the sincerity of their professions, and even supposing (as we reasonably may) that these professions were mere expedients to obtain a temporary popularity, and quite unconnected with enlarged or liberal views of policy and government, the measures which the various proprietaries actually adopted in pursuance of their purposes proved highly beneficial to the provinces of North America, and cherished in the minds of the colonists a warm attachment to political freedom, and an habitual conviction of their right to it.

The instrument which was now published by Berkeley and Carteret gave assurance to all persons who might settle in New Jersey, that the province should be ruled only by laws enacted by an assembly in which the people were represented, and to which the power of making peace or war, together with many other important privileges, was confided. In particular, it was promissorily stipulated by the proprietaries, " for the better security of the inhabitants in the said province, that they are not to impose, *nor suffer to be imposed*, any tax, custom, subsidy, tallage, assessment, or any other duty whatsoever, upon any color or pretence, upon the said province, and inhabitants thereof, other than what shall be imposed by the authority and consent of the general assembly." By another clause, of equal importance, it was provided, that " no person, at any time, shall be any ways molested, punished, disquieted, or called into question, for any difference in opinion or practice in matters of religious concernment, who does not actually disturb the civil peace of the province ; but all and every such person and persons may, from time to time, and at all times, freely and fully, have and enjoy his and their judgments and consciences in matters of religion, they behaving themselves peaceably and quietly, and not using this liberty to licentiousness, nor to the civil injury or outward disturbance of others ; any law, statute, or clause, contained, or to be contained, usage or custom, of the realm of England, to the contrary thereof in any wise notwithstanding." The import of these expressions could not be misunderstood ; and as they were promulgated without censure or disallowance from any quarter, it must be admitted that the colonization of this province was undertaken on an assurance, which the settlers were entitled to credit, of their being completely exempted from the jurisdiction of the English parliament, both in the imposition of taxes and the regulation of ecclesiastical affairs. The administration of the executive power, together with the prerogative of affirming or rejecting the statutes of the provincial assembly, was reserved to the proprietaries. To all persons resorting to New Jersey with the intention of settling in it there were tendered allotments of land, proportioned to the earliness of their arrival in the province, and to the numbers of their indented servants and *slaves ;* and for these allotments they were required to pay a quitrent of a halfpenny per acre after the year 1670, and to maintain one able-bodied male servant for every hundred acres in their possession. As the quitrents were deemed the private estate of the proprietaries, it was declared that all public expenses should be defrayed by general contribution. Such was the first political constitution of New Jersey. New provisions were added to it from time to time, by subsequent proclamations, and the whole code was denominated by the people *The Laws of the Concessions*, and regarded by them as their great charter, and as possessing a higher authority than even the acts of assembly, from not being subject to alteration or repeal.   An important addition was suggested by the pru- dence and equity of Philip Carteret, who was the first governor appointed by the proprietaries, and who, without any directions from his constituents to respect the rights of the aboriginal inhabitants of the province, judged it proper to obtain their acquiescence in the colonial plantation, by purchasing their titles to the several districts which were occupied.   The proprieta- ries had the wisdom to approve this policy, and some years after established the rule, that all lands should be purchased from the Indians by the governor and council, who were to be reimbursed by the planters, in proportion to their respective possessions.[1]

The conquest of New Netherlands had now been achieved by Colonel Nichols, who assumed, as lieutenant of the Duke of York, the administra- tion of the whole territory surrendered by the Dutch.   While yet unac- quainted with the duke's assignment to Berkeley and Carteret, he formed the design of colonizing the district they had acquired, and to this end granted licenses to various persons to make purchases of land from the ab- original inhabitants of New Jersey.   Three small townships were speedily formed in the eastern part of the territory, by emigrants chiefly from Long Island, who laid the foundation of Elizabethtown, Woodbridge, and Piscat- away ; and Nichols, who entertained a favorable opinion of this region, be- stowed on it the name of Albania, in commemoration of one of the titles enjoyed by his master.   But his hopes of rendering it a valuable appendage of the duke's possessions were soon interrupted by intelligence of the trans- action which passed it to its new proprietaries ; and the measures he had already pursued gave rise to disputes respecting the property of the soil, between the settlers whose establishment he had promoted and the proprie- taries who subsequently claimed their allegiance, which disturbed the peace of the province for more than half a century.   Nichols addressed an earnest remonstrance to the Duke of York, on the impolicy of thus multiplying statistical divisions, and of disjoining from his own domain a portion dis- tinguished above all the rest by the fertility of its soil, the commodiousness of its rivers, and the richness of its minerals ; and while he urged the duke to revoke a grant so prejudicial to his own interest, he predicted, what ac- tually ensued, that the undertaking of Berkeley and Carteret to colonize a vacant territory would disappoint their expectations of profit, and involve them in expenses from which only their remote posterity could hope to gather any beneficial fruit.   This remonstrance appears to have produced some impression on the mind of the duke ; but either it was insufficient to induce him to revoke the grant which he had executed, or he judged such revocation beyond his power ; and Nichols was reluctantly compelled to surrender the government of New Jersey to Philip Carteret [November, 1665], who arrived with a company of thirty emigrants from England, and established himself at Elizabethtown, which was regarded as the capital of the infant province.   Here for some years he ruled in peace over a desert which was gradually replenished with planters from the provinces of New York and New England, attracted by the inviting qualities of the country and the repute of the liberal institutions which its inhabitants were to enjoy.

It was a happy peculiarity of the lot of these colonists, that, establishing themselves in the vicinity of countries already cultivated, they escaped the

---

[1] Scot. S. Smith. Chalmers.

disasters and privations which afflicted so severely the first inhabitants of most of the other American provinces. Their proximity to the channels of commerce formed at New York, in particular, was considered a circumstance of no small advantage during the infancy of their settlement ; though, in process of time, it was less favorably regarded by them, as having contributed to prevent the rise of a domestic mart, which would have afforded still more effectual encouragement to their trade. Like the other colonists of North America, they enjoyed the advantage of transporting the arts and habits of industry from a crowded and civilized community, where they were carried to a high pitch of improvement, into the fresh bosom of a fertile and unoccupied region, which afforded them more liberal recompense and more unrestricted scope. Their exertions for the rearing of cattle and grain were speedily and amply rewarded by a grateful soil ; and their friendly relations with the Indians enabled them to prosecute their labors in undisturbed tranquillity, and to add to them a beneficial traffic in peltry with the roving tribes by whom the neighbouring forests were inhabited. Their connection with the sister colony of New York communicated to them the benefit of the alliance which subsisted between this colony and the powerful confederacy of the Five Nations ; and, as the influence of this confederacy extended to all the tribes in the vicinity of the new settlement, its inhabitants enjoyed the felicity of an entire exemption from Indian war. Recommended by the salubrity of its climate, in addition to so many other advantages, it will not appear surprising that New Jersey was soon considered a very desirable residence, and that its attractions were celebrated by early writers with higher commendation than any of the other American settlements obtained.

The proprietaries, still buoyed up with the hope of an ample revenue from their province, were not wanting in exertions to circulate the intelligence of its advantages both in Europe and America, and occasionally despatched from England vessels freighted with settlers and stores to reinforce the numbers and supply the wants of their people. [1665 – 1670.] But the period to which they looked for the fulfilment of their hopes was fated to demonstrate the fallacy of them ; and the scene of felicity which the province had hitherto presented was disagreeably overcast by the arrival of the day when the payment of quitrents was appointed to commence. [March, 1670.] The first demand of this tribute excited general disgust among the colonists, who expressed more unwillingness than inability to comply with it. A party among them, including the earliest settlers, who had occupied their lands under the authority of Colonel Nichols, refused to acknowledge the title of the proprietaries ; and, in opposition to it, set up titles which they had obtained for themselves from the Indians. It was easier for the governor to demonstrate the illegality of these pretensions, than to prevail with the people to abandon them. For two years he maintained an ineffectual struggle to enforce the claims of the proprietaries ; till at length the popular discontent broke forth in an insurrection which he found it impossible to withstand. He was compelled to return to England, stripped of his functions, which the colonists forthwith conferred on a natural son of Sir George Carteret [November, 1672], by whom their pretensions were abetted. Disappointing as this result must have been to the proprietaries, it was impossible for them to impute the blame of it to their governor, or to hesitate to replace him in the station from which he had been expelled. This measure, however, was retarded by the unexpected events of the following year [1673], when, New York again reverting to the dominion of Holland, New Jersey was once more reunited to the province of New Netherlands.[1]

The Dutch, as we have already seen,[2] did not long retain their acquisition, which was restored to Great Britain by the treaty of London. [1674.] But the reëstablishment of the proprietary governments into which the territory had been previously divided was thought to require some additional formality, and was not accomplished without a renovation of the titles by which those jurisdictions were originally created. Some doubts had already been suggested of the validity of the royal charter, which was granted to the Duke of York at a time when the Dutch government enjoyed a peaceable and unchallenged possession of the country ; and, however unwilling to acknowledge the force of this objection, and recede from a pretension that had been deliberately embraced by his brother and himself, the duke was prompted by his own interest to remove from men's minds a doubt so likely to obstruct the resort of emigrants to his domains. Another cause seems also to have contributed to turn his thoughts to the procurement of a new investiture. The remonstrances of Colonel Nichols led him to regard the grant he had made of New Jersey to Berkeley and Carteret with feelings of dissatisfaction, which were not diminished by the liberal institutions which these proprietors had conferred on their province, and the number of inhabitants whom this policy attracted to it from his own dominions. Whatever were the motives that withstood the gratification of his wishes, — whether he scrupled to commit the injustice and incur the dishonor of robbing two of the firmest adherents of his family, or doubted the support of the law or the king in such a proceeding, — it is manifest from his conduct that he entertained a desire to repossess himself of the New Jersey territory, without making any compensation to the parties who had acquired it. The Dutch conquest seemed to furnish him with an opportunity of removing the objections to which his own title was subject, without seeming to confess its original defectiveness ; and to afford him, at the same time, a decent pretext for divesting Berkeley and Carteret of their property, without disowning the grant by which he had bestowed it upon them, or incurring any obligation to indemnify them for its loss. It was pretended that the Dutch conquest extinguished the proprietary rights, and that the territory, unencumbered by them, now reverted to the crown. [June, 1674.] In conformity with this view, the duke applied for a new investiture, and found no difficulty in obtaining from the king a second charter, which recited the former grant, and confirmed to him all the domains which that grant embraced. He now appointed Andros his lieutenant over the whole reunited province ; and committing to this governor and a board of counsellors all the functions of legislative and executive power, established the same arbitrary sway in New Jersey that he had hitherto maintained in New York. But while he could thus meditate the meanness of despoiling his friends of a property which he had sold to them, he wanted either resolution or authority to effectuate his iniquitous views ; and, on the application of Sir George Carteret, scrupled not to promise a renewal of the grant of New Jersey. Yet, though ashamed to acknowledge his purposes, he was unwilling to abandon them [January, 1675] ; and while the execution of the grant was delayed, he commanded Andros to maintain his prerogative over the whole territory. Even when

---

[1] Douglass's *Summary*.   S. Smith.   Chalmers.   [2] Book V., Chap. I., *ante*.

he finally consented to restore New Jersey, he endeavoured to evade the complete performance of his engagement, and pretended to have reserved certain rights of sovereignty over it, which Andros seized every opportunity of asserting.

In the beginning of the year 1675, Philip Carteret, returning to New Jersey, resumed the government of the settlements formed in the eastern part of the province, from which he was expelled about two years before. The inhabitants, who had experienced, in his absence, the yoke of conquest and the severe rule of Andros, now received their old governor with demonstrations of good-will; and, as he postponed the payment of their quitrents, and published a new code of *concessions* by Sir George Carteret that confirmed all their privileges, a peaceable and contented subordination was once more established in the colony. The only subject of disquiet that occurred for several years arose from the arbitrary measures by which Andros from time to time obtruded the unjust pretensions of the Duke of York. Governor Carteret, in the hope of procuring to his people a share of the gains which the neighbouring colony derived from her commercial pursuits and relations, endeavoured to establish a direct trade between England and New Jersey. [1676.] But Andros openly resisted this attempt, as an injury to the traffic and the customs of New York; and, by confiscating the vessels that traded in opposition to his mandates, extinguished the New Jersey commerce in its infancy. In addition to this outrage, he endeavoured by various exactions to render the colonists of New Jersey tributary to his own government; and even launched into such extremity of insolence as to arrest Governor Carteret and carry him prisoner to New York. When complaints of these proceedings of his deputy were carried to the duke, he betrayed the same indecision and duplicity that characterized all his recent demeanour. He could not consent, he said, to depart from a prerogative which had always belonged to him; yet he directed that the exercise of it should be relaxed, as a mark of *favor and indulgence* to his friend, Sir George Carteret.[1] But the province was now divided into two proprietary jurisdictions; and it was in the western part, in which Carteret had ceased to have any interest, that the duke attempted to exercise in its greatest latitude his pretended prerogative. The circumstances attending this partition of the territory compose the most interesting portion of the early history of New Jersey.

Among the various dissenters from the church of England who had reason to complain of the ecclesiastical policy pursued by the ministers of Charles the Second, the Quakers incurred a large share of disappointment and persecution. During the last years of the protectorate of Cromwell, a number of Quakers, charged with offending against public order and decency, were committed to prison in sundry parts of England; and because the Protector refused or delayed to command their release, one of the leaders of the sect reviled him publicly in a rhapsody of malediction, which he concluded by tearing his own cap in pieces, as a symbolical prognostic that the government of the state would be rent from Cromwell and his family.[2] The accomplishment of this *prophecy* was the only gratification

---

[1] Douglass. S. Smith. Chalmers. Smith's *New York.*
[2] Cromwell, though in general he treated the Quakers with lenity (of which the impunity of this prophet may be adduced as an instance), could not entirely discard his suspicions of a sect in which some of his own most determined adversaries had enrolled themselves. That restless agitator, John Lilburn, in the midst of his opposition to Cromwell,

which the Quakers were permitted to derive from the abolition of the protectoral rule.   In the interval between this event and the Restoration, they experienced so much additional rigor, as again elicited from one of their number the prediction of another political revolution.   This severe treatment, partly occasioned by the aversion which the Presbyterian ministers and magistrates entertained for the doctrines of the Quakers, was also in part provoked by the frenzy and indecency with which many of the professors of these doctrines thought proper to signalize their contempt for the creed of their adversaries.[1]   To the committee of safety, in whose hands the supreme power was lodged, the Quakers were rendered additionally obnoxious by the progress which their tenets had made among the veteran soldiers of the Commonwealth, and the success with which George Fox interposed to prevent a body of these converts from joining the parliamentary forces who were marching to suppress an insurrection of the royalists in Cheshire.   They refused to give orders for the liberation of Quakers who were imprisoned by the magistrates as vagabonds and disturbers of the peace, or even to restrain the outrages of the populace, who in many places began to insult and molest the Quaker assemblies.

The advancement of General Monk to the supreme direction of affairs not only gratified these sectaries with the accomplishment of another prediction, but encouraged them to expect a lasting and favorable change in their own situation.   Monk issued a proclamation prohibiting farther disturbance to the peaceable meetings of Quakers, and he listened to their complaints with a demonstration of respect and attention which they had not been able to procure from his predecessors in authority.   The hopes inspired by this altered treatment were confirmed at the Restoration.   To the favorable regards of the king the Quakers were recommended by the complaints they preferred against every description of authority that had subsisted in England during the suspension of monarchy, and by the peculiar enmity they expressed against those who were also the prominent objects of his own dislike.   Their accusations of the government of Massachusetts, in particular, met with a gracious acceptance, and produced an order for the suspension of all farther severities against them in that quarter.   Upwards of seven hundred Quakers were released from various prisons in England, and assurance was given that a complete toleration of Quaker worship would be embraced and proclaimed by the legislature with all convenient speed.   The fulfilment of this assurance, however, was obstructed by certain of the king's ministers, who, though willing by delusive pretences to tranquillize all the Dissenters till the newly restored monarchy should be more firmly established, were secretly determined to enforce a strict uniformity of religious worship in Britain ; and before many months of the new reign elapsed, their purpose was effectually promoted by an event which suddenly extinguished whatever of court favor the Quakers had really or seemingly enjoyed.   Meanwhile, the sect, like all others, was indulged with an actual toleration, which was diligently improved by its founder and his wiser asso-

---

made a profession of Quakerism, and yet not only continued to write against the Protector's government, but long refused to promise that he would not employ his sword in aid of his pen.   Gough and Sewell.   Cromwell personally witnessed a great deal of Quaker extravagance.   He was interrupted, when presiding in parliament, by a Quaker, who exclaimed that he had a message from the Lord to the Protector.   Ibid.   And he beheld a female Quaker enter stark naked into a church where he was sitting with his officers at divine worship.   Hume.

[1] See Note XXI., at the end of the volume.

ciates in multiplying their converts, and introducing into their society a system of order and discipline that tended to curb the wild spirit which had transported so many votaries of Quakerism beyond the bounds of decency and sobriety, and exposed their profession in so many places to reproach and persecution. But this state of unmolested tranquillity, together with the hope of seeing it perpetuated by law, was quickly destroyed by a violent explosion of fury and fanaticism from a different body of sectarians. In some points, both of doctrine and practice, the *Fifth Monarchy men*, or *Millenarians*, bore a strong resemblance to the Quakers ; a temporal hierarchy was equally odious to both ; and both rejected, on all occasions, the ceremonial of an oath. The Millenarians, however, went a step farther than the Quakers, and held themselves entitled to employ force for the overthrow of every temporal supremacy that usurped the place and obstructed the advent of that spiritual and divine dominion which they eagerly desired and expected to ascertain.

George Fox, on the contrary, had taught, from the beginning of his ministry, that it was unlawful to employ aught else than spiritual weapons for the promotion of spiritual objects. But he was well aware that he had collected around him many of the wildest and most combustible spirits in the kingdom ; and the exaggeration and distortion of his own principles, exhibited in the demeanour of many of his own followers, together with numberless examples among the other sects and factions of which the times were prolific, forcibly taught him by what insensible gradations the minds of men, when thoroughly heated by religious or political zeal, are transported beyond a mere censorious estimate of institutions hostile to their views into the conviction of an especial call, or plain moral obligation, to attempt their subversion. It was therefore with no small alarm that Fox learned the projects which the Millenarians entertained, some time prior to the Restoration, of promoting by force of arms the establishment, or at least the recognition, of the Messiah's personal reign upon earth ; and he published, at the time, an earnest remonstrance to all his followers on the unlawfulness of designs, which, however remote from their distinctive principles, would prove, he feared, but too congenial to the spirit with which, in many instances, these principles were associated. But his exertions, whatever effect they may have produced on his own followers, failed to convince the public that there was any radical or solid distinction between the Quakers and the Millenarians ; and what probably contributed to increase his alarm, as well as to fortify the public prepossession, was, that the Quakers were encumbered by the accession of a restless band of partial and temporary adherents, the limits of whose faith they were unable to ascertain by reference to a creed, and who, flitting from sect to sect, according to the ebbs and flows of their own humor and caprice, remained only long enough with any one to infect it with their own levity and dishonor it with a share of their own reputation.

The insurrection that broke forth among the Millenarians, in the first year of the restored monarchy, proved exceedingly prejudicial to the interests of the Quakers, not only from the current opinion that the tenets of the two sectarian bodies were substantially the same, but from the plausible pretexts that were afforded to the adversaries of toleration, and the pledges which the government, no less alarmed than affronted, determined to exact from all classes of its subjects. The Quakers now became the objects of peculiar jealousy, from their refusal to give assurance of fidelity to the king by taking the oath of allegiance, and were assailed with a rigor and reality of persecution which they had never before experienced in England. They were at first included along with the Millenarians in a royal proclamation which forbade either of these classes of Dissenters from assembling under pretence of worship elsewhere than in parochial churches ; but they were soon after distinguished by the provisions of an act of parliament that applied exclusively to themselves. By this statute it was enacted, that all Quakers, refusing to take the oath of allegiance, and assembling, to the number of five persons above sixteen years of age, for the purpose of divine worship, should, for the first and second instances of such offence, incur the penalty of fine and imprisonment, and for the third should either abjure the realm or be transported beyond it. Nay, so violent and vindictive was the jealousy which the court now harboured against the Quakers, that, instead of employing the complaints of these sectaries as the handle for a quarrel with the obnoxious province of Massachusetts, it was determined to stir up the slumbering enmity of the colonists against them, and to invite the provincial government to a repetition of those very severities which had been so recently prohibited. For this purpose, it was signified to the governor and assembly of Massachusetts, by a letter under the hand of the king,[1] that his Majesty, though desirous that liberty of conscience should be granted to all other religious professors in the province, would be glad to hear that a severe law were passed against the Quakers, whose tenets and practices he deemed incompatible with the existence of civil government. These unfavorable sentiments were not long after exchanged by the king for a juster estimate of Quaker principles. In a conference which he granted to some of the leading members of the sect, he received assurances which satisfied him not only that this people had been unjustly confounded with the Millenarians, but that their tenets with respect to municipal government, including an absolute renunciation of the right of resistance, were such as he had reason to wish more generally diffused through his dominions. But this alteration in his sentiments produced no relaxation of the legal severities to which the Quakers were liable, and was attended with no other consequence than a familiar and apparently confidential intercourse between him and some of the leaders of the sectarian body, together with many expressions of regard and good-will on his part, which he was unwilling or unable to substantiate.

In the persecution that was now commenced against all classes of Dissenters, the Quakers were exposed to a more than justly proportioned share of severity, from the unbending zeal with which they refused to conform even in appearance to any one of the obnoxious requisitions of the law, and the eagerness with which they seized every opportunity of openly performing their forbidden practices, and signalizing their peculiar gifts of patient suffering and unconquerable perseverance. In every part of England the Quakers were harassed with fines and imprisonments ; and great numbers were transported to Barbadoes and to the American settlements,[2] where they formed a valuable addition to the English population, and speedily found that their persecutors, in expelling them from their native land, had unconsciously contributed to the amelioration of their lot. Instead of the

---

[1] *Ante*, Book II., Chap. III.

[2] In one vessel alone, which was despatched from England in March, 1664, sixty Quaker convicts were shipped for America. Williamson's *North Carolina.*

wild enthusiasts who formerly rushed with frantic zeal to New England in quest of persecution, there was now introduced into America a numerous body of wiser and milder professors of Quakerism, whose views were confined to the enjoyment of that liberty of worship for the sake of which they incurred the penalty of exile. In several of the American provinces, as well as in the island of Barbadoes, they experienced an ample toleration and a friendly reception from the magistrates and the inhabitants ; and even in those provinces where they were still the objects of suspicion and rigor, they contributed to render their principles less unpopular, by demonstrating with what useful industry and peaceful virtue the profession of them might be combined. Contented with the toleration of their worship, and diligently improving the advantages of their new lot, many of these exiles attained, in a few years, to a plentiful and prosperous estate ; and so far did they carry their willingness to reconcile their peculiar principles with the existing institutions and usages of the countries in which their lot was cast, that, in many instances, they united a profession of Quakerism with the purchase and employment of negro slaves. Perhaps the deceitfulness of the human heart was never more strikingly exhibited than in this monstrous association of the character of exiles for conscience's sake and the profession of universal meekness and philanthropy, with the condition of slave-owners and the exercise of tyrannical power. Yet in process of time much good was educed from this evil ; and the inconsistency of one generation of Quakers enabled their successors to exhibit to the world an example of disinterested regard for the rights of human nature, and an honest sacrifice to the requirements of piety and justice.

The principles of Quakerism continued meanwhile to propagate themselves in Britain to an extent that more than supplied the losses occasioned by the banishment of so many of their professors. Almost all the other Christian sects had sustained a decay of piety and reputation, from the share they had taken in the passionate disputes, the furious struggles, the dark intrigues, and vindictive severities that attended the civil wars ; and while the Quakers were distinguished by exemption from this reproach, they were not less advantageously distinguished by a rigorous persecution, of which they were the objects, and which enabled them to display, in a remarkable degree, the primitive graces of Christian character. It was now that their cause was espoused and their tenets were defended by writers who yielded to none of their contemporaries in learning, eloquence, or ingenuity, and who have never been equalled, or even approached, by any succeeding scholars of the Quaker persuasion. The doctrines that had hitherto floated loosely through the sectarian society were collected and reduced to an orderly system ; the discipline necessary to preserve from anarchy, and restrain the fantastic sallies which the genuine principle of Quakerism is peculiarly apt to suggest,[1] was explained and inculcated ; and in the midst of a persecution which drove many of the Presbyterians of Scotland to despair and rebellion, the Quakers began to add to their zeal and resolution

---

[1] Robert Barclay, author of the *Apology for the Quakers* and of a treatise on *The Anarchy of the Ranters*, has done, perhaps, more than any other writer of his persuasion to render Quakerism a methodical and rational system. Yet this eminent person, though remarkably distinguished for the strength and soundness of his understanding and the sedateness of his temper, soon after his conversion to Quakerism, betrayed in his conduct a strong taint of enthusiastic extravagance. He has himself recorded, that, on one occasion, having experienced a vivid impression of the duty of walking through the streets of Aberdeen in sackcloth and ashes, he could not be easy till he had obeyed the divine call, as he conceived it to have been.

that mild gravity of address and tranquil propriety of thought and conduct by which they are now almost universally characterized.

Yet was it long before the wild and enthusiastic spirit which had distinguished the rise of the society was banished entirely from its bosom ; and while it continued to exert its influence, a considerable diversity of sentiment and language prevailed among the Quakers.[1] This diversity was manifest, among other instances, in the sentiments that were entertained with regard to the duty of confronting persecution. While all the Quakers reckoned it unlawful to forsake their sectarian observances on account of the prohibition of their oppressors, there were many who esteemed it no less a dereliction of duty to abandon their country for the sake of a peaceful enjoyment of those observances in another land. Considering Quakerism as a revival of primitive Christianity, and themselves appointed to repeat the fortunes of the first Christians, and to gain the victory over a carnal world by evincing the fortitude of martyrs, they associated the success of their cause with the infliction and endurance of persecution ; and deemed the retreating from a scene where this evil impended over them to one where they might be exempted from it equivalent to the desertion of the contest in which the prevalence of truth or of error was to be decided. The toleration of their principles seemed to be less the object of their desire than the victorious spread of them ; and the success of Quakerism in England they reckoned incomplete without the downfall of the established hierarchy.[2] But there were others of more moderate temper and more enlightened piety, who, willing fully to sustain the character of the primitive Christians, justly deemed this character no way inconsistent with that conduct which was expressly prescribed to the objects of their imitation, in the divine direction, that, when persecuted in one city, they should flee to another. Disturbed in their religious assemblies, harassed and impoverished by fines and imprisonments, and withal continually exposed to a violent removal from their native land, as the consequence of a line of conduct which they held it their duty to pursue, — they were led to meditate the advantage of a voluntary expatriation with their families and their substance, and naturally cast their eyes on that transatlantic realm, which, notwithstanding the severities once inflicted on their brethren in some of its provinces, had always presented an asylum to the victims of persecution. Their regards were farther directed to this quarter by the number of their fellow-sectaries who were now established in several of the North American States, and the freedom, comfort, and tranquillity which they were reported there to enjoy.[3]

Such was the situation of the Quakers at the time when Lord Berkeley, alarmed by the insubordination of the planters of New Jersey, and dissatisfied with a possession which seemed likely to realize the forebodings of Colonel Nichols, offered his share of the province for sale. He soon received the proposal of a price that was satisfactory from two English Quakers, named Fenwick and Byllinge ; and in the year 1674, in accord-

---

[1] See Note XXII., at the end of the volume.

[2] In Neal's *History of the Puritans* there is preserved an account of a debate which took place in one of the churches of London between an English bishop and a party of these wilder professors of Quakerism, who willingly accepted the bishop's rash challenge to a public disputation. The debate was short, and soon degenerated into a reciprocation of scurrilous abuse, in which the bishop, finding himself by no means a match for his opponents, took to flight, and was pursued to his house by a mob of Quakers, vociferating at his heels, " The hireling flieth ! the hireling flieth ! "

[3] Gough and Sewell's *History of the Quakers.* Neal's *History of the Puritans.*

ance with their desire, conveyed the subject of the purchase to the first-mentioned of these persons in trust for himself and the other. Fenwick appears to have been unworthy of the confidence implied in this arrangement. A dispute soon arose between Byllinge and him with regard to their respective proportions of interest in the territory ; and, to avoid the scandal of a lawsuit, the two parties agreed to submit their pretensions to the judgment of William Penn, who now began to occupy a conspicuous place among the leaders and champions of the Quaker society. Penn found it easier to appreciate the merits of the case than to terminate the controversy ; for, after he had pronounced an award in favor of Byllinge, it required the utmost exertion of his address and authority to induce Fenwick to comply with it. Yielding at length to the solemn and earnest remonstrances of Penn, Fenwick consented to abandon his unjust plea ; and in the year 1675, with his wife and family and a small troop of Quaker associates, he set sail from England, and established himself in the western part of New Jersey. But Byllinge was now no longer in a condition to profit by the adjustment of the dispute. He had sustained such losses in trade, that it became necessary for him to divest himself of the whole of his remaining property for the indemnification of his creditors ; and as the most valuable part of this property consisted of his New Jersey purchase, he was naturally led to desire that its administration should be confided to the same eminent person whose good offices had recently contributed to ascertain and preserve it. William Penn, after some deliberation, agreed to undertake this duty, and, in conjunction with Gawen Laurie and Nicholas Lucas, two of the creditors of Byllinge, assumed the direction of their constituent's share of New Jersey.

The first care of Penn and his associates was to obtain a partition of the provincial territory between themselves and Sir George Carteret ; and as all parties were sensible of the disadvantage of a joint property, the division was accomplished without difficulty. The eastern part of the province was assigned to Carteret, under the name of East New Jersey ; the western, to Byllinge's assignees, who named their moiety West New Jersey. The administrators of the western territory then proceeded to divide it into a hundred lots, or *proprieties ;* ten of which they assigned to Fenwick, and the remaining ninety they proposed to sell for the benefit of the creditors of Byllinge. Their next and more important concern was to frame a political constitution for the future inhabitants of the province, which was promulgated under the title of *concessions,* or terms of grant and agreement, to be mutually embraced by the vendors and purchasers of the territory. This instrument adopted the provisions formerly enacted by Berkeley and Carteret for the exemption of the colonists from all taxes but such as their own provincial assemblies should impose on them, and for the security of religious freedom ; the clause by which this latter provision was introduced being prefaced by a general declaration, " that no men, nor number of men, upon earth, have power to rule over men's consciences in religious matters." It was appointed that the people should meet annually to choose one honest man, for each *propriety,* to sit in the provincial assembly ; that " these elections be not determined by the common and confused way of cries and voices, but by putting balls into balloting boxes to be provided for that purpose, for the prevention of all partiality, and whereby every man may freely choose according to his own judgment and honest intention"; and that every member of assembly should be allowed a shilling a day during the session, "*that thereby he may be known to be the servant of the people.*" That the representatives of the people should receive wages or salary from their constituents was a principle adopted from the beginning in almost every one of the North American States ; and, assuredly, never in the world were constituencies more adequately represented or more faithfully served. Every male colonist, it was announced, should enjoy the capacity of electing and being elected to sit in these assemblies, which were vested with the power to make, alter, and repeal laws, and to nominate, from time to time, a committee of assistants to carry the existing laws into execution. It was declared, that no man, except by the verdict of a jury, should be arrested, confined, or deprived of life, liberty, or estate. Imprisonment for debt was disallowed ; and a bankrupt, after surrendering his estate to his creditors, was to be free from their claims, and entitled again to exert his industry for behoof of himself and his family. Such is an outline of the composition that forms the first essay of Quaker legislation, and entitles its authors to no mean share in the honor of planting civil and religious liberty in America. "There," said Penn and his colleagues, in allusion to this fruit of their labors, "we lay a foundation for after ages to understand their liberty as men and Christians, that they may not be brought in bondage but by their own consent ; *for we put the power in the people.*"[1]

The publication of this instrument, which its authors accompanied with a special recommendation of the relative territory to the members of their own religious fraternity, produced an immediate display of that diversity of sentiment which had recently been manifested in the Quaker society. Of these sectaries, many prepared with alacrity to embrace the proposals of the trustees, and expressed the most exaggerated expectations of the freedom, prosperity, and happy repose that awaited them in the new settlement ; while others regarded with jealousy, and even stoutly opposed, a secession which they considered pusillanimous and discreditable. To moderate the expectations of the one, and to appease the jealousy of the other of these parties, Penn and his colleagues addressed a circular letter to the members of their society, in which they solemnly cautioned them against leaving their country from a timid reluctance to bear testimony to their principles, from an impatient, unsettled temper, or from any other motive inferior to a deliberate conviction that the Lord of all the earth providentially opened their way to New Jersey, and sanctioned their removal thither. They were admonished to remember, that, although Quaker principles were cherished and cultivated in the province, only Quaker safeguards could be interposed or relied on for their preservation ; and, in particular, that the religious toleration which was to be established must exclusively depend for its continuance on the aid of that Being to whose will they believed it agreeable, and must never be defended by force or violence against the arm of an oppressor. To this admonitory letter there was annexed *A Description of West New Jersey*, for the information of intending colonists, in which some trivial exaggerations that had been reported of the good qualities of the soil and climate were corrected, — but, in the main, a most inviting representation of the region was conveyed. This publication was certainly not intended to repress the ardor of Quaker emigration ; neither

---

[1] S. Smith. Chalmers. Clarkson's *Memoirs of Penn.*

had it any such effect. Numerous purchases of colonial estates were
made by Quakers in various parts of England ; and in the course of the
year 1677, upwards of four hundred emigrants of this persuasion transported
themselves to West New Jersey. Many of these were persons of affluent
estate, who carried with them their children and servants ; and along with
them were sent a board of commissioners, appointed by Penn and his colleagues to make partition of the lands, and engage the acquiescence and
friendship of the Indians. While the ship that carried out the first detachment of these emigrants lay in the Thames, on the point of sailing, it
happened that Charles the Second was passing by in his pleasure-barge.
Observing a number of Quakers on board, the king came alongside the
vessel, and inquired whither they were bound. Informed of their destination, he asked if they were all Quakers ; and, being answered in the affirma-
tive, invoked a blessing upon them and departed.[1]

On their arrival in America, the emigrants very soon discovered that the
danger of an arbitrary encroachment on their rights and liberties had not
been suggested to them in vain. Andros summoned them to acknowledge
the sovereignty of his master, the Duke of York ; affirming that his own
life would be endangered, if he should venture to recognize their independence without an express order from that prince. When they remonstrated against this usurpation, Andros cut short the controversy by pointing to his sword ; and as this was an argument which the Quakers were incapacitated from retorting, they submitted for the present to his violence,
and acknowledged themselves and their territory subject to the Duke of
York, till the issue of an application for redress, which they transmitted
to England. They were compelled for some time to endure the hardships
inseparable from the occupation of a desert land. But these hardships were
surmounted by industry and patience ; and their first settlement, to which
they gave the name of Burlington, soon exhibited a thriving appearance,
and was replenished with inhabitants by successive arrivals of additional
Quaker emigrants from the parent state. [1678.] It was observed in this,
as in most of the other infant settlements in America, that the success of
individual colonists was in general proportioned to the original humility of
their condition, and the degree of reliance which they placed on the resource of their own unassisted industry. Many who emigrated as servants
were more prosperous than others who imported a considerable substance
along with them. Inured to personal toil, they derived such ample gains
from it, as speedily enabled them to rise above a state of servitude, and
cultivate land on their own account ; while the others, subsisting too long
on their imported stock, and relying too far upon the hired labor of the
poor, were not unfrequently themselves reduced to penury. The first exertions of the colonists to procure themselves a livelihood were facilitated
by the friendly assistance of the Indians ; but a hostile attack was soon
threatened by these savages, who, in consequence of a dangerous epidemic
that broke out among them, accused their neighbours of having treacherously
sold them the small-pox. The danger, however, was averted by the influence of an Indian chief, who assured his countrymen that their forefathers
were afflicted with similar diseases, while as yet they had no intercourse

---

[1] S. Smith. Proud's *History of Pennsylvania*. This is a very scarce work. It evinces
great research, and abounds with valuable matter, unfolded with extreme dulness and prolixity.

with strangers, and that such calamities were not of earthly origin, but descended from heaven.[1]

Sir George Carteret, the proprietary of East Jersey, died in 1679 ; having derived so little benefit from his American territory, that he found it necessary to convey it by testamentary bequest to trustees, who were instructed to dispose of it for the advantage of his creditors.   The exemption which this district was permitted to enjoy from the dominion of the Duke of York increased the discontent with which the inhabitants of the neighbouring region of West Jersey endured an authority from which their right to be exempted was equally clear.   They had never ceased to importune the duke for a redress of this grievance ; and were at length provoked to additional warmth of complaint and urgency of solicitation by a tax, which Andros, in the exercise of his master's pretended sovereignty, attached to the importation of European merchandise into West Jersey.   Wearied with the continual importunity of these suitors, rather than moved with a sense of honor or equity, the unjust prince consented to refer the matter of their complaint to certain commissioners, by whom it was finally remitted to the juridical opinion of Sir William Jones. [1680.]   The remonstrance presented in behalf of the colonists of West Jersey, on this occasion, was prepared by William Penn, George Hutchinson, and several other coadjutors, chiefly of the Quaker persuasion, and breathes a firm, undaunted spirit of liberty, worthy of the founders of a North American commonwealth.   "Thus, then," they insisted, after a narrative of the titles by which the territory had been transmitted to them, "we come to buy that moiety which belonged to Lord Berkeley, for a valuable consideration ; and in the conveyance he made us powers of government are expressly granted ; for that only could have induced us to buy it ; and the reason is plain, because to all prudent men the government of any place is more inviting than the soil.   For what is good land without good laws ? the better, the worse.   And if we could not assure people of an easy and free and safe government, both with respect to their spiritual and worldly property, — that is, an uninterrupted liberty of conscience, and an inviolable possession of their civil rights and freedoms, by a just and wise government, — a mere wilderness would be no encouragement ; for it were a madness to leave a free, good, and improved country, to plant in a wilderness, and there adventure many thousands of pounds to give an absolute title to another person to tax us at will and pleasure."   Having adverted to the argument in support of the duke's usurped authority, they continued : — "Natural right and human prudence oppose such doctrine all the world over ; for what is it but to say, that people, free by law under their prince at home, are at his mercy in the plantations abroad ? And why ? because he is a conqueror there ; but still at the hazard of the lives of his own people, and at the cost and charge of the public.   We could say more, but choose to let it drop.   But our case is better yet ; for the king's grant to the Duke of York is plainly restrictive to the laws and government of England.   Now the constitution and government of England, as we humbly conceive, are so far from countenancing any such authority, that it is made a fundamental in our constitution, that the king of England cannot justly take his subjects' goods without their consent.   This needs no more to be proved than a principle ; it is an homeborn right, declared to be law by divers stat-

---

[1] S Smith. Proud.

utes." "To give up this," they added, "the power of making laws, is to
change the government; to sell, or rather resign, ourselves to the will of
another; and that for nothing. For, under favor, we buy nothing of the
duke, if not the right of an undisturbed colonizing; and that, as Englishmen, with no diminution, but rather expectation of some increase, of those
freedoms and privileges enjoyed in our own country: for the soil is none of
his; 't is the natives', by the *jus gentium*, the law of nations; and it
would be an ill argument to convert them to Christianity, to expel instead
of purchasing them out of those countries. If, then, the country be theirs,
it is not the duke's; he cannot sell it; then what have we bought?"
"To conclude this point, we humbly say that we have not lost any part
of our liberty by leaving our country; for we leave not our king nor our
government by quitting our soil; but we transplant to a place given by the
same king, with express limitation to erect no polity contrary to the same
established government, but as near as may be to it; and this variation is
allowed but for the sake of emergencies; and that latitude bounded by these
words, *for the good of the adventurer and planter.*"

In a subsequent part of their pleading,[1] they remark that "there is no
end of this power; for since we are by this precedent assessed without
any law, and thereby excluded our English right of common assent to taxes,
what security have we of any thing we possess? We can call nothing our
own, but are tenants at will, not only for the soil, but for all our personal
estates. This is to transplant, not from good to better, but from good
to bad. This sort of conduct has destroyed governments, but never raised
one to any true greatness." "Lastly, the duke's circumstances and the
people's jealousies considered, we humbly submit it, if there can be, in their
opinion, a greater evidence of a design to introduce an unlimited government, than both to exact an unterminated tax from English planters, and
to continue it after so many repeated complaints; and on the contrary, if
there can be any thing so happy to the duke's present affairs, as the opportunity he hath to free that country with his own hand, and to make us all
owers of our liberty to his favor and justice. So will Englishmen here
know what to hope for, by the justice and kindness he shows to Englishmen
there; and all men see the just model of his government in New York to
be the scheme and draught in little of his administration in Old England at
large, if the crown should ever devolve upon his head." Unpalatable as this
argument must doubtless have been to the British court, and to the counsellors of the Duke of York, it was attended with the most triumphant success.

The commissioners to whom the case was referred were constrained to
pronounce their judgment in conformity with the opinion of Jones, "that,
as the grant to Berkeley and Carteret had reserved no profit or jurisdiction,
the legality of the taxes could not be defended." In compliance with this
adjudication, the duke without farther objection resigned all his claims on
West Jersey [August, 1680], and in the amplest terms confirmed the assignment of this province to its new proprietaries. And as the reasons

[1] This curious document, which is extremely prolix (like most Quaker productions), and
enriched with some display of legal knowledge, is preserved at full length in S. Smith's *History*. It is remarkable that Chalmers has taken no notice of it. Winterbotham has given
an abridged and very inadequate version of it. That Penn concurred in the presentation of
the pleading is undeniable; and hence it may be fairly presumed that he assisted in its composition. But that he was the sole author of it, as some of his modern biographers have insinuated, is rendered extremely improbable by its style, in which not the slightest resemblance is discoverable to any of his acknowledged productions.

of this concession extended with equal and manifest application to East Jersey, he granted soon after a similar release in favor of the representatives of his friend, Sir George Carteret.[1] [September, 1680.] Thus the whole of New Jersey was promoted at once from the condition of a conquered country to the rank of a free and independent province, and rendered in political theory the adjunct, instead of the mere dependency, of the British empire. The powerful and spirited pleading, by which this benefit was gained, derives additional interest from recollection of the conflict then subsisting in England between the advocates of liberty and the abettors of arbitrary power. It would not be easy to point out, in any of the political writings or harangues of which that period was abundantly prolific, a more manly and intrepid exertion for the preservation of liberty than we behold in this first successful defence of the rights of New Jersey. One of the most remarkable features of the plea which the colonists maintained was the unqualified and deliberate assertion, that no tax could be justly imposed on them without their own consent and the authority of their own provincial assembly. The report of the commissioners in their favor, and the relief that followed, were virtual concessions in favor of this principle, which in an after age was destined to obtain a more signal triumph in the national independence of North America.

West Jersey now filled apace with inhabitants by the accession of numerous settlers, of whom a great proportion still continued to be Quakers. Byllinge, who received from his fellow-proprietaries the appointment of governor, not finding it convenient to leave England, granted a deputation of his functions to Samuel Jennings, by whom the first representative assembly of West Jersey was convoked. [Nov., 1681.] In this assembly there was enacted a code of *Fundamental Constitutions,* together with various laws for the protection of property and the punishment of crimes. By the Fundamental Constitutions, the assembly was empowered to appoint and displace all persons holding offices of trust in the province ; and the governor was restrained from proclaiming war, or contracting any engagement obligatory on the State, without the assembly's concurrence, and from withholding his assent to any of its ordinances. Assemblies were to be annually convoked ; and no assembly was to have power to impose a tax which should endure longer than a year. Of the laws that were enacted on this occasion, the most remarkable feature is a provision, that in all criminal cases, except treason, murder, and theft, the person aggrieved should have power to pardon the offender, whether before or after condemnation, — a provision of very questionable expediency, but probably intended to prevent the Christian requirement of forgiveness of injuries from being evacuated, as in most countries is practically done, by the supposed municipal duty which engages a man to avenge, in his capacity of a citizen, the wrong which as a Christian he is commanded to forgive. It was ordained (with departure equally wise and just from the practice in the parent state) that the landed property of every inhabitant should be responsible for his debts ; marriages were appointed to be solemnized by justices of the peace ; for the prevention of disputes with the Indians, the sale of spirituous liquors to them was strictly prohibited ; and for the encouragement of poor but industrious laborers, who obtained the means of emigrating from Europe by indenting themselves as servants to more

---

[1] S. Smith. Proud. Chalmers, *State Papers, apud eundem.*

wealthy planters, every such servant was authorized to claim from his master, at the expiry of his indenture, a set of implements of husbandry, certain articles of apparel, and ten bushels of corn.   To obstruct the resort of worthless and vicious persons to the province, a law was framed, requiring every new settler, under pain of a pecuniary fine, to give satisfactory evidence to a justice of the peace, that his change of residence was not the consequence of crime, nor an act of fraud, but that he was reputed a person of blameless character and sober life.   From this period till the dissolution of the proprietary government, the provincial assembly continued to be annually convoked.   It did not always confine itself to the exercise of the ample powers with which it was constitutionally endowed ; for when Byllinge soon after proposed to deprive Jennings, the deputy-governor, of his office, the assembly interposed to prevent this measure ; declaring that Jennings gave satisfaction to the people, and desiring him to retain his situation.[1]   The rule and ordinary practice of the constitution, however, was that the council of assistants to the governor were nominated by the assembly ; while the proprietaries appointed the governor ; and he, with the consent of the proprietaries, named his own deputy.

The success of their experiment in the western portion of New Jersey encouraged the Quakers of Britain to avail themselves of the opportunity now afforded of enlarging the sphere of their enterprise by the acquisition of the eastern quarter of that territory.   The close of Philip Carteret's administration in East Jersey was embittered by a renewal of the disputes that had once rendered him a fugitive from this province.   Even the release obtained from the Duke of York served but to furnish additional materials of discord between the proprietary government and the people ; for, instead of mutually enjoying the important benefit which it conferred, the two parties set themselves to debate, with extreme virulence and pertinacity, whether this instrument or the proprietary concessions in 1664 should be regarded as the basis of the provincial institutions.   Disgusted with these disputes, and perceiving that they were not likely to derive either emolument or satisfaction from a prolonged administration of the proprietary government, the trustees and executors of Sir George Carteret offered the province for sale to the highest bidder ; and, closing with the proposals of William Penn[2] [Feb. 1682], conveyed their rights over East Jersey to him and to eleven other persons of the Quaker persuasion.   The territory comprehended in this conveyance contained already a variety of settlements, inhabited by seven hundred families, or about three thousand five hundred individuals, exclusive of the inhabitants of certain remote and scattered plantations, who were computed to amount to at least half as many more. A great majority of the settlers were not Quakers ; and whether with the view of allaying the jealousy with which these colonists might regard a government administered exclusively by men whose principles differed so widely from their own, or for the purpose of fortifying their interest at the British court by the association of persons of influence in their undertaking, the twelve purchasers made haste to assume twelve other partners in the proprietary rights, and among others the Earl of Perth, chancellor of Scot-

[1] S. Smith. Proud.

[2] Though Penn thus became a proprietary of East Jersey, his connection both with its concerns and with those of West Jersey was henceforward almost merely nominal. He had now acquired for himself the province of Pennsylvania, which occupied all his interest, and diverted his attention from New Jersey.

land, and Lord Drummond of Gilston, the secretary of state for that kingdom.[1] In favor of these twenty-four proprietaries the Duke of York executed his third and last grant of East Jersey ; on receiving which, they appointed a council or committee of their own number to whom all the functions of the proprietary power were intrusted. [March, 1682.] To facilitate the exercise of their dominion, they obtained from Charles the Second a royal letter, addressed to the existing governor, council, and inhabitants of the province, unfolding the title of the proprietaries to the provincial soil and jurisdiction, and requiring all persons to yield obedience to their authority and laws.[2]

At the time when East Jersey thus became subject to Quaker administration (for the Quakers still formed a majority of the associated proprietaries), the inhabitants, by a diligent improvement of their local advantages, had generally attained a flourishing and prosperous estate. The greater number of them were emigrants from New England, or the descendants of New England men ; and their laws and manners, in some particulars, disclosed traces of this origin. The punishment of death was denounced by law against children striking or cursing their parents. Adulterers were subjected to flogging or banishment. Fornication was *punished*, at the discretion of the magistrate, by *marriage*, fine, or flogging. Nightwalking, or revelling abroad after nine o'clock of the evening, exposed the offenders to a discretionary punishment. A thief, for his first offence, was adjudged to restore three-fold the value of what he had stolen ; in case of frequent repetition of guilt, he might be capitally punished, or reduced to slavery. There was no law for the public support of religion ; but every township maintained a church and minister. " The people," said the first governor deputed to them by their Quaker sovereigns, " are generally a sober, professing people, wise in their generation, courteous in their behaviour, and respectful to us in office." So happily exempt were they from the most ordinary and forcible temptation to violence and dishonesty, that, according to the same testimony, there was not an industrious man among them whose own hands could not assure him a state of decent competence, and even of ease and plenty.[3] If we might rely implicitly on the opinion of this observer, we should impute the dissensions that had previously occurred in the province to the folly and mismanagement of Carteret and his associates in the government. But there is reason to believe that the blame of those dissensions was more equally divided between the people and their rulers. A headstrong and turbulent disposition appears to have prevailed among some classes, at least, of the inhabitants ; various riots and disturbances broke forth even under the new government ; and the utmost exertions of Quaker prudence and patience were required to compose them.

[1] From the dedication of Scot's *Model*, &c., *of East Jersey*, it appears that two other powerful Scottish nobles, Viscount Tarbet, afterwards Earl of Cromarty, and Lord M'Leod, became shortly after proprietaries of this province. In one of Oldmixon's lists of the proprietaries we find the names of Sir George Mackenzie, Lord Advocate of Scotland, whom his contemporaries justly denominated *The bloody Mackenzie*, and of West, the lawyer, who obtained an infamous distinction as a witness for the crown on the trial of Lord Russell.

[2] Scot. S. Smith. Chalmers.

[3] This testimony is confirmed by Gawen Laurie, who was the second deputy-governor under the Quaker administration. " There is not," he says, " in all the province a poor body, or that wants." " The servants work not so much by a third as they do in England ; and, I think, feed much better ; for they have beef, pork, bacon, pudding, milk, butter, and good beer and cider to drink. When they are out of their time, they have land for themselves, and generally turn farmers for themselves. Servants' wages are not under two shillings a day, besides victuals." S. Smith.

A law, enacted about four years after this period, reprobates the frequent occurrence of quarrels and challenges, and interdicts the inhabitants from wearing swords, pistols, or daggers.[1]

Among the new proprietaries of East Jersey was Robert Barclay of Urie, a Scottish gentleman, who had been converted to Quakerism, and, in defence of his adopted principles, had published a series of works that gained the applause and admiration of all Europe. Esteemed by scholars and philosophers for the extent of his learning and the commanding force and penetrating subtlety of his judgment, he was endeared to the members of his religious fraternity by the liveliness of his zeal, the purity of his character, and the services rendered by his pen to their cause. These services consisted rather of the literary celebration which he gave to the Quaker doctrines, than of any deeper impression of their influence upon mankind. For his writings in general are much more calculated pleasingly to entertain and dazzle the understanding, than to produce solid conviction, or sink into the heart. To the king and the Duke of York he was recommended not less by his distinguished fame and his happy genius and address, than by the principles of passive obedience professed by that sect of which he was considered a leader ; and with both the royal brothers, as well as with several of the most distinguished of their favorites and ministers, he maintained the most friendly and familiar intercourse. Inexplicable as such a coalition of uncongenial characters may appear, it seems at least as strange a moral phenomenon to behold Barclay and Penn, the votaries of universal toleration and philanthropy, voluntarily associating in their labors for the education and happiness of an infant community such instruments as Lord Perth and other abettors of royal tyranny and ecclesiastical persecution in Scotland.[2]

By the unanimous choice of his colleagues, Robert Barclay was appointed the first governor of East Jersey under the new proprietary administration. [July, 1683.] So high was the repute which he enjoyed, and so much advantage was anticipated from his superintendence of the colony, that his commission bestowed the office on him for life; and while it dispensed with his personal residence,[3] authorized him to nominate his own deputy. But the expectations which produced or attended his elevation were disappointed by the result ; his government (like that of Sir Henry Vane in Massachusetts) was brief and ill-fated, and calculated rather to lower than to advance his illustrious reputation. The most signal and beneficial event of his presidency was the emigration of a considerable number of his countrymen, the Scotch, to East Jersey, — a measure, which, however congenial it may appear to the circumstances of that oppressed and persecuted people, they were not persuaded to adopt but by dint of much exhortation and importunity. For, although a vast majority of the people of Scotland were dissatisfied with the Episcopal establishment which their king had forced upon them, and great numbers were enduring the utmost rigors of tyranny for their resistance to it, it was found no easy matter to persuade them to seek relief from their sufferings in a distant and perpetual exile from their native land.[4] In addition to the motives to emigration which the

[1] S. Smith.   [2] See Note XXIII., at the end of the volume.
[3] Oldmixon is mistaken in asserting that Barclay himself repaired and carried his family with him to the province. Barclay never was in New Jersey. Soon after his appointment, he sent thither his brother David, some of whose letters from the province are printed in S. Smith's *History.*
[4] Howbeit, we have seen (*ante,* Book IV., Chap. II.) a troop of Scottish emigrants con-

severities exercised by Lord Perth and the other royal ministers contributed to supply, the influence of Barclay and other Scottish Quakers was successfully employed in prevailing with their countrymen to accept an asylum
in East Jersey ; and thither, accordingly, a band of emigrants, chiefly from
Barclay's native county of Aberdeen, soon after resorted. [1684.] For
the purpose of rendering the Scotch more generally acquainted with the
state of the colonial territory and the nature of its institutions, and of inciting them to remove thither, it was proposed by the proprietaries to publish a historical and statistical account of it, with a preliminary treatise in
which the prevailing objections to emigration should be combated, and this
resource exhibited in a more favorable light than that in which the Scotch
were generally disposed to regard it.   From undertaking the entire or
avowed authorship of this performance Barclay was probably deterred by
knowing, that, as a Quaker, his estimate of the popular objections, some
of which were founded on religious considerations, would find little favor
with the bulk of his countrymen, as well as by unwillingness to entangle
himself with allusions to the existing persecution, which he could hardly
have characterized in a manner satisfactory at once to his own conscience
and to Lord Perth and others of his proprietary associates, who were actually at the time administering in Scotland the rigor of a law inflicting
banishment to the plantations on every person who declined to give evidence, when required, against the frequenters of conventicles.

To the work which was now composed and published, in furtherance of
Barclay's and his colleagues' design, it is probable that he contributed some
assistance ; and, indeed, the inequality of the performance attests that it was
not wholly the composition of a single author.   It was published as the
production of a Scottish gentleman, George Scot of Pitlochie, and bore
the title of *The Model of the Government of the Province of East New
Jersey in America.*   From various passages in this work, it appears that
many of the Scotch were prepossessed with the notion, that to emigrate
from their native land, without some extraordinary interposition of heavenly
direction, was an impious revolt from the lot which the Almighty had assigned to them.   In opposition to this view, a large and ingenious com-
mentary was made on the divine command to replenish and subdue the
earth ; and it was argued, that, as this was an eternal law, the duty to fulfil it
was of continual obligation, and required no additional manifestation of celestial sanction.   Among other incitements to emigration, it is remarked,
that " We see by nature trees flourish fair, prosper well, and wax fruitful
in a large orchard, which would otherwise decay if they were straitened in
a little nursery.   Do we not see it thus fall out in our civil state, where a
few men flourish best, furnished with abilities or best fitted with opportunities, and the rest wax weak, and languish, as wanting room and means
to nourish them ?   Now, that the spirits and hearts of men are kept in
better temper by spreading wide will be evident to any man who considers
that the husbanding of unmanured ground and shifting into empty lands
enforceth men to frugality and quickeneth invention ; and the settling of
new estates requireth justice and affection to the common good ; and the
taking in of large countries presents a natural remedy against covetousness,
fraud, and violence, when every man may enjoy enough without wrong or

ducted by Lord Cardross to Carolina in 1683. Probably the Scottish adventurers whom Cardross collected were persons of different character from those whom Quakers desired to attract to New Jersey.

injury to his neighbour." The heads of ancient families were exhorted to embrace this opportunity of cheaply endowing their younger sons with a more liberal provision in America than the laws and usages of Scotland enabled them to bestow at home.[1] In reply to an objection which had been urged, that a province governed by Quakers must be left unprovided of the means of military defence, it was stated that several of the proprietaries and many of the inhabitants did not belong to the Quaker persuasion, and that East Jersey already possessed a militia of 600 men. The argument derived from the severities inflicted by the British government on the Presbyterians is handled in a very courtly style. "You see it is now judged the interest of the government altogether to suppress the Presbyterian principles ; and that, in order thereto, the whole force and bensil of the law of this kingdom are levelled at the effectual bearing them down ; that the rigorous putting these laws in execution hath in a great part ruined many of these, who notwithstanding thereof find themselves in conscience obliged to retain these principles ; while, on the other hand, Episcopacy is by the same laws supported and protected. I would gladly know what other rational medium can be proposed, in these circumstances, than either to comply with the government, by going what length is required by law, in conforming ; or to retreat, where by law a toleration is by his Majesty allowed. *Such a retreat doth at present offer itself in America, and is nowhere else to be found in his Majesty's dominions.*" What an encomium on America, at the expense of every other portion of the British empire ! The work contains a minute account of the climate, soil, institutions, and existing settlements of East Jersey, and an elaborate panegyric on its advantages in all these particulars. As a farther recommendation of the province to the favor of the Scotch, Barclay [1685], displacing a deputy whom he had appointed, of his own religious persuasion, conferred this office on Lord Neil Campbell, uncle of the Marquis of Argyle, who repaired to East Jersey, and remained there for some time as its lieutenant-governor.

The efforts of Barclay and his colleagues were crowned with success. A great many inhabitants of Scotland emigrated to East Jersey, and enriched American society with a valuable accession of virtue refined by adversity, and of piety invigorated by persecution. The more wealthy of the Scottish emigrants were noted for the accompaniment of a numerous retinue of servants and dependents ; and, in some instances, they incurred the expense of transporting whole families of poor laborers, whom they established on their lands for a term of years, and endowed with a competent stock ; receiving in return one half of the agricultural produce.[2]

But James the Second now ascended the British throne ; and practically inverting the magnanimous sentiment that has been ascribed to a French monarch, he deemed it unnecessary for a king of England to respect the engagements of the Duke of York ; nor could all his seeming friendship

---

[1] Whether this advice was regarded or not, it is certain, that, both before and after the present period, many cadets of titled families, both in England and Scotland, resorted to America, where some distinguished republican heroes and patriots have sprung from the transplanted scions of feudal nobility in Europe.

[2] Scot. Oldmixon. S. Smith. The convulsions that preceded the assassination of De Witt and the triumph of the Prince of Orange in Holland drove many respectable Dutch families from their native land. Most of these exiles retired to North America. Sonmans, a member of the States General, had proceeded to England with this view, when he was overtaken by the sanguinary fury of the Orange faction, and murdered by their emissaries, as he was riding with Robert Barclay the Quaker, in the neighbourhood of London. His family, however, finally reached New Jersey. S. Smith.

for Barclay, together with all the influence of Lord Perth and the other courtier proprietaries, deter him from including New Jersey in the design which he had formed of annulling the charters and constitutions of the American colonies [1686]. A real or fictitious charge of smuggling was preferred to the English court against the inhabitants of the Jerseys ; and the ministers of James, readily seizing this handle, without farther ceremony caused writs of *quo warranto* to be issued against both East and West New Jersey, and directed the attorney-general to prosecute them with the utmost stretch of legal expedition ; assigning, as the explanation or apology of their conduct, the necessity of checking the pretended abuses " in a country which ought to be more dependent on his Majesty." Alarmed at this demonstration, the proprietaries of East Jersey presented a remonstrance to the king, in which they reminded him that they had not received the grant of the province as a benevolence, but had acquired it by purchase, and were encouraged to do so by the assurances of protection which they received from himself ; they declared that they had already sent thither several hundreds of people from Scotland ; and that they were willing to correct whatever might be found amiss in the conduct of affairs within the province, and particularly, if it would be satisfactory to his Majesty, would now require their provincial assembly to adopt the same regulations against smuggling that were established at New York. They entreated, that, if any change should be made in the condition of their province, it might be confined to a union of East and West Jersey in one jurisdiction, to be ruled by a governor whom the king might select from the body of proprietaries. [1687.] But James was inexorable ; and to their remonstrance returned no other answer than that he had determined to unite the Jerseys with New York and the New England States in one general government dependent on the crown and administered by Andros. Finding it impossible to divert him from his arbitrary purpose, the proprietaries of East Jersey were so far deserted of spirit and dignity, as not only to abandon a hopeless contest for the privileges of their people, but even to facilitate the execution of the king's designs against them, as the price of his consenting to respect their own private property in the colonial soil. [April, 1688.] They made a formal surrender of their patent on this condition ; and as James agreed to accept it, the prosecution of the *quo warranto* process was no longer needed for East Jersey, and was even suspended with regard to the western territory. Seeing no resistance opposed to his will, the king was the less intent on consummating his acquisition ; and while the grant of the soil to the proprietaries, which was necessary for this purpose, still remained unexecuted, the completion of the whole design was arrested by the British Revolution.[1]

Although the proprietary governments in New Jersey were preserved for a time from dissolution by this event, they never afterwards possessed vigor or efficiency. Robert Barclay, who seems to have retained during his life the government of East Jersey, died in 1690 ; but no traces of his administration are to be found after the year 1688 ; and from thence till 1692, it is asserted by Chalmers that no frame of government at all existed in New Jersey. The peace of the country was preserved, and the prosperity of its inhabitants promoted, by their own honesty, sobriety, and industry. Almost all the original proprietaries of both provinces had in the mean time disposed of their interests to recent purchasers ; and the proprietary associa-

---

[1] S. Smith. Chalmers.

tions became so numerous [1] and so fluctuating, that their policy was deprived
of proper concert and steadiness, and their authority obtained neither the
respect nor the affection of the people.   The appointment of new proprietary governors in 1692 proved the commencement of a series of disputes,
intrigues, and vicissitudes of office, which in a commonwealth more populous or less virtuous would probably have issued in civil war and bloodshed.   The government of New York, which, on account of its dependence
on the crown, was encouraged by King William to arrogate a preëminence
over the neighbouring chartered colonies, reckoned this a favorable opportunity of reviving, and even extending, its ancient pretensions in New Jersey,
whose inhabitants learned with equal surprise and indignation that the assembly of New York had included them in a taxation which it imposed on its
own constituents.   This last attempt, however, was not more successful
than the previous instances in which New York made similar efforts to
usurp an undue authority.   A complaint to the English government on the
subject was referred to the crown lawyers, who delivered an opinion that
produced an abandonment of the pretensions of New York.[2] [June, 1697.]
At length the disagreements between the various proprietaries and their respective adherents attained such a height, and were productive of so much
schism and confusion, that it was sometimes difficult, if not impossible, for
the people to ascertain in which of two or more rival pretenders to authority the legal administration was truly vested.[3]   Numerous complaints of
the inconvenience occasioned by this state of matters [1700] were addressed by the inhabitants of the Jerseys to the British court ; and the proprietaries themselves, finding that their seigniorial functions tended only to
disturb the harmony of the provincial community, and to obstruct their own
emoluments as owners of the soil, hearkened willingly to an overture from
the English ministers for a surrender of their powers of government to the
crown. [April, 1702.] This surrender was finally arranged and accomplished in the commencement of the reign of Queen Anne, who straightway
reunited East and West Jersey into one province, and committed the government of it, as well as of New York, to her kinsman, Edward Hyde,
Lord Cornbury.[4]

The commission and instructions which this nobleman received, on his
departure from England, present an abstract of the political state of New
Jersey from the resumption of its charter till the termination of its connection with the British empire.   The provincial government was appointed
to consist of a governor and twelve counsellors nominated by the crown,

[1] "The shares and parts of shares had been so divided and subdivided, that some of the
proprietors owned but *one fortieth part of a forty-eighth part of a twenty-fourth share.*" Pitkin.
[2] Sir John Hawles and Sir Cresswell Levinz were the lawyers consulted on this occasion.
The opinion they delivered was," that no customs could be imposed on the people of the
Jerseys, otherwise than *by act of parliament* or their own assemblies."
[3] Obedience was refused by a considerable party to one governor, because it was doubted if
a majority of the proprietaries had concurred in his nomination ; to another, because it was denied that his appointment had been ratified by the king ; and to a third (notwithstanding the
precedent of Barclay's and of Lord Neil Campbell's administrations), because, being a Scotchman, it was questioned if he were legally capable of holding office in an English colony.
[4] Oldmixon. S. Smith. Chalmers, *State Papers, apud eundem.* Although the proprietaries
persisted in terming this surrender a voluntary act, and asserting their right to have retained
the government if they had pleased so to do, they appear to have been swayed in some measure by the threat of an expensive suit with the crown, which had determined to bring the
validity of their pretensions to trial. In the instrument of surrender, the queen, while she
declares her gracious acceptance of the powers resigned to her by the proprietaries, expressly
refuses to acknowledge that these powers ever legally belonged to them.

and of a house of assembly, consisting of twenty-four members elected by the people. The sessions of this assembly were held alternately in East and in West Jersey. No persons were capable of voting for representatives in the assembly, but colonists possessing a hundred acres of land, or personal property to the value of fifty pounds ; and none were eligible, but colonists possessing a thousand acres of land, or personal property worth five hundred pounds. The laws enacted by the council and assembly were subject to the negative of the governor ; but if approved by him, they were to be immediately transmitted to England, there to be finally affirmed or disallowed by the crown. The governor was empowered to suspend any of the members of council from their functions, and to supply vacancies in their number ; and, with consent of this body, to constitute courts of law, to appoint all civil and military officers, and to employ the forces of the province in hostilities against public enemies. To the assembly there was communicated the royal desire, that it should impose taxes sufficient to afford *a competent salary* to the governor, to defray the salaries of its own members and of the members of council, and to support all the other provincial establishments and expenditure ; the prescribed style of all money bills being, that the sums contained in them were granted to the crown, with the humble desire of the assembly that they might be applied for the benefit of the province ; and all moneys so raised were to be paid into the hands of the receiver of the province, till the royal pleasure should be signified with regard to their actual distribution. The former proprietaries of New Jersey were confirmed in their rights to the estates and quitrents which they had previously enjoyed ; and none but they and their agents and surveyors were permitted to purchase lands from the Indians. Liberty of conscience was assured to all men, *except Papists.* Quakers were declared to be eligible to every municipal office ; and their affirmation was accepted in lieu of the customary oaths. The governor was invested with the right of presentation to all ecclesiastical benefices. He was required to extend particular favor and patronage to all ministers of religion in connection with the church of England, and to "take especial care that God Almighty be devoutly and duly served." It will excite more regret than surprise, to see combined with, and almost in immediate sequence to, this display of royal zeal for the interests of religion[1] and the honor of God, a requisition to the governor, that, in promoting trade, he should especially countenance and encourage the Royal African Company of England, — a mercantile association that had been formed for the piratical purpose of kidnapping or purchasing negroes in Africa, and selling them as slaves in the American and West Indian plantations. It was declared to be the intention of her Majesty " to recommend unto the said company that the said province may have a constant and sufficient supply of merchantable negroes at moderate rates " ; and the governor was required to compel the planters duly to fulfil whatever engagements they might contract with the company. He was farther directed to cause a law to be framed for restraining inhuman severity to slaves, and attaching a capital punishment to the wilful murder of them ; and to take every means in his power to promote the conversion of these unfortunate persons to the Christian faith. *All printing was prohibited* in the province without a license from the governor. In all lawsuits where the sum in dependence exceeded a hundred pounds, an appeal was admitted

[1] See Note XXIV., at the end of the volume.

from the provincial courts to the governor and council ; and when it exceeded two hundred pounds, a farther appeal was competent to the privy
council of England.[1]

The instructions to Lord Cornbury contain reiterated protestations of
the queen's sincere desire to promote peace, good-will, and contentment
among her American subjects ; but this desire accorded as ill with the disposition and qualifications of the individual to whom she remitted its accomplishment, as her professed anxiety to mitigate the evils of slavery did with
her actual endeavour to diffuse this mischievous institution more widely
in her dominions. Of the character and policy of Lord Cornbury we have
already seen a specimen in the history of New York. If the people of
New Jersey had less reason to complain of him, it was only because his
avocations at New York compelled him generally to delegate his functions
in the other province to a deputy ; and because the votaries of his favorite
institution, the church of England, were too few in New Jersey, and perhaps too honest and unambitious, to afford him the materials of a faction
whose instrumentality he might have employed in oppressing and plundering
the rest of the community. His distinguished name and rank, his near
relationship to the queen, and the advantage he derived from appearing as
the substitute of a government which had become universally unpopular,
gave him at first an influence with the people of New Jersey, which a
man of greater virtue might have rendered conducive to their felicity, and a
man of greater ability might have improved to the subjugation of their spirit
and the diminution of their liberty. But all the illusions that attended his
outset among them were speedily dispelled by acquaintance with his character and experience of his administration. From the period of his appointment till the recall of his commission, the history of New Jersey exhibits
little else than a detail of the controversies, now long forgotten, in which
he involved himself with the provincial assemblies ; and a display of the
spirit and resolution with which these assemblies resisted his arbitrary violence, condemned his partial distribution of justice, and exposed his fraudulent misapplication of the public money. To none of the inhabitants was his
administration more oppressive than to the Quakers, who were harassed
with numerous prosecutions for refusing, in conformity with their religious
tenets, to assemble at the musters of the provincial militia. Though he
was unable to place himself at the head of a party in this province, he prevailed, partly by bribery and partly by intimidation, on some of the provincial counsellors to subscribe an address to himself, commencing in these
terms : — " Your Lordship has not one virtue or more, but a complete
accomplishment of all perfections," — and expressing the most loyal abhorrence of the factious stubbornness of their fellow-colonists. This ridiculous
production, which he termed The Humble Address of the Lieutenant-
Governor and Council of New Jersey, proved satisfactory to the British
government, and enabled him for some years to defy the hatred of the colony. But at length, after repeated complaints, the queen was compelled to
sacrifice him to the universal indignation he had provoked ; but not till he
had very effectually, though most unintentionally, contributed, by a wholesome discipline, to awaken and fortify a vigorous and vigilant spirit of liberty
in two of the colonies which were most immediately subjected to the influence of the crown. He was superseded, in 1708, by Lord Lovelace, who

---

[1] S. Smith.

was at the same time appointed his successor in the government of New York.[1]

The attractions which the neighbouring province of Pennsylvania presented to the English Quakers, and the cessation which the British Revolution produced of the severities that had expelled so many Protestant Dissenters from both England and Scotland, prevented the population of New Jersey from advancing with the rapidity which its increase at one period seemed to betoken.   Yet, at the close of the seventeenth century, the province is said to have contained twenty thousand inhabitants, of whom twelve thousand belonged to East, and eight thousand to West Jersey.[2]   It is more probable that the total population amounted to about fifteen thousand persons.   Of these, a great majority were Quakers, Presbyterians, and Anabaptists.   The militia of East Jersey amounted, at this period, to 1,400 men.   There were two ministers of the church of England in the province ; but their followers were not sufficiently numerous and wealthy to provide ecclesiastical edifices.[3]   New Jersey is said to have witnessed an unusually long subsistence of varieties of national character among its inhabitants.   Patriotic attachment and mutual convenience had generally induced the emigrants from different countries to settle in distinct societies ; a circumstance which promoted among them the preservation of their peculiar national manners and customs.   Kalm, the traveller, has preserved a very agreeable picture of the rural life and domestic habits of his countrymen, the early Swedish colonists of New Jersey and Delaware.   They are said to have been less tenacious of their national peculiarities than the Dutch, and to have copied very early the manners of the English.   Notwithstanding some symptoms of a turbulent and refractory disposition which were evinced by a portion of the East Jersey population during the subsistence of the proprietary government, a much more reasonable and moderate temper seems to have generally characterized the people of both parts of the united province ; whereof a strong testimony is afforded in the harmony which attended their union by the act of the crown in 1702, and which even the mischievous agency of such a promoter of discord as Lord Cornbury was unable to disturb.   Though separated from each other by differences of religious denomination, the inhabitants of the eastern and western territories were assimilated by the habits of industry and frugality peculiar alike to the national character of the Scotch and to the sectarian usages of the Quakers ; and the prevalence of these habits, doubtless, contributed to maintain concord and tranquillity among the several races of people.   Yet they were always distinguished by the steadiness and ardor of their attachment to liberty, and a promptitude to assert those generous principles which had been interwoven with the earliest elements of political society in New Jersey.   It is disagreeable to remember that this manly appreciation of their own rights was not always accompanied with a proportionate consideration of the rights of others.   Negro slavery was established in New Jersey ; though at what precise period or by what class of the planters it was first introduced, we have not now the means of

---

[1] S. Smith.   " I confess," says Oldmixon, in the second edition of his work, " it gives me a great deal of pain, in writing this history, to see what sort of governors I meet with in the plantations."

[2] Warden's estimate of the population is much lower.   He says, that, until the peace of Utrecht, in 1713, New Jersey never possessed more than 16,000 inhabitants.   But his account of this province displays great negligence and inaccuracy.   Holmes reports the population to have amounted to 15,000 in the year 1701.

[3] Oldmixon.

ascertaining. In spite of the royal patronage which we have beheld this baneful system receive, it never attained more than a very insignificant prevalence throughout the territory. Even the Quakers in this province, as well as in Pennsylvania, became proprietors of slaves ; but their treatment of them was generally distinguished by a relenting tenderness and humanity ; and so early as the year 1696, the leading members of the Quaker society of New Jersey united with their brethren in Pennsylvania in recommending (though ineffectually) to their fellow-sectaries to desist from the employment or at least from the farther importation of slaves.[1] This interesting subject will demand more particular consideration in the history of Pennsylvania.

New Jersey, at the close of the seventeenth century, had been for some time in possession of an increasing trade ; but of the extent of its commerce at this period no accurate estimate can be formed. The exports from the province consisted of agricultural produce (including rice), with which it supplied the West India islands, furs, skins, and a little tobacco for the English market, and oil, fish, and other provisions, which were sent to Spain, Portugal, and the Canary Isles.[2] Blome, whose account of the American provinces was published in 1686, remarks, that the town of Burlington even then gave promise of becoming a place of considerable trade. The stateliness of the public edifices, and the comfort and elegance of the private dwellings that composed this town, are highly commended by a writer whose account of the province was published about ten years later than the work of Blome. It possessed already a thriving manufacture of linen and woollen cloth.[3] This manufacture, which was also introduced at an early period into Pennsylvania, so soon aroused the jealousy of the parent state, that in the year 1699 an act of parliament was passed prohibiting the exportation of wool and woollen manufactures from the American colonies, under a penalty of five hundred pounds for each violation of the law, in addition to the forfeiture of the offending ship and cargo.[4]

It is alleged by some writers, that, till a very late period, the inhabitants of New Jersey betrayed a general neglect of education, together with a coarse indifference to all improvement in the arts of life, and particularly in their system of agricultural labor. This reproach has been applied more especially to the descendants of the Dutch settlers. Yet the college of Princeton was founded so early as the year 1738 ; the people have always enjoyed a high reputation for piety, industry, economy, and good morals ; and no colonial community, even in North America, has witnessed a wider diffusion, among all classes of its inhabitants, of the comforts and conveniences of life.[5] It has been noted as a singular peculiarity in their manners, that women in this province engrossed for a long time a considerable share in the practice of the medical art, and, except in cases of great difficulty and importance, were the only physicians whom the inhabitants had recourse to.[6]

[1] Kalm's *Travels.* Winterbotham. Clarkson's *History of the Abolition of the Slave-trade.*
[2] Gabriel Thomas's *History of West New Jersey.* Oldmixon. Blome celebrates the excellence of the New Jersey tobacco.
[3] Blome. G. Thomas. Thomas, who was familiar with the grandeur of London, mentions, among other considerable edifices, " the great and stately palace " built and inhabited by a planter in the neighbourhood of Burlington. See Note XXV., at the end of the volume.
[4] Anderson's *Historical and Chronological Deduction of the Origin of Commerce.*
[5] Winterbotham. Warden.
[6] Warden. Whether this usage was the effect or the cause of the remarkable healthiness of the people of New Jersey may admit of a doubt. But it certainly betokens a remarkable degree of respect for the female sex. Of this sentiment another very singular testimony was afforded, even so late as the commencement of the nineteenth century, by a law which ex-

This usage reminds us of that romantic system of manners, during the prevalence of which the softness of female service was so often blended with the ministrations of medical science by the high-born damsels who graced the age of chivalry.

It was a fortunate circumstance for the inhabitants of New Jersey, that the conterminous Indian tribes were inconsiderable in number, and almost always willing to cultivate friendly relations with the Europeans. The gravity, simplicity, and courtesy of Quaker manners were particularly agreeable to those savages. Samuel Smith, the historian of this province, has preserved an account of a visit paid by an aged Indian king to the inhabitants of Burlington, in the year 1682. Being attacked during the visit with a mortal distemper, the old man sent for the heir of his authority, and delivered to him a charge replete with prudent and reasonable maxims. Thomas Budd, a Quaker, and one of the proprietaries of the province, was present on this solemn occasion, and " took the opportunity to remark that *there was a great God who created all things ; that he gave man an understanding of what was good and bad ; and after this life rewarded the good with blessings, and the bad according to their doings.* The king answered, *It is very true ; it is so ; there are two ways, a broad and a strait way ; there are two paths, a broad and a strait path ; the worst and the greatest number go in the broad ; the best and fewest in the strait path.* This king, dying soon afterwards, was attended to his grave, in the Quakers' burial-place in Burlington, with their national solemnities, by the Indians, and with tokens of respect by many of the English settlers." [1]

In the year 1695, the governor's salary in East Jersey was one hundred and fifty pounds ; in West Jersey, two hundred pounds. From the year 1702, when the two provinces were united and surrendered to the crown, till the year 1738, the government of New Jersey was always committed to the same individual who enjoyed the corresponding authority at New York ; and during that period the salary attached to the office of governor in New Jersey was six hundred pounds.[2]

tended the elective franchise in New Jersey to women. The New Jersey women, however, showed themselves worthy of the respect of their countrymen, by generally declining to avail themselves of this preposterous proof of it. Yet, according to the statement of Harriet Martineau, in her work entitled *Society in America*, a number of New Jersey women actually attended elections and gave their votes. The law that invited such absurdity was repealed a few years after its enactment. " I do not believe," says Dr. Dwight, " that a single woman, bond or free, ever appeared at an election in New England since the colonization of the country. It would be as much as her character was worth."

[1] Oldmixon. S. Smith.   [2] S. Smith.

BOOK VII.

PENNSYLVANIA AND DELAWARE.

CHAPTER I.

Birth and Character of William Penn. — He solicits a Grant of American Territory from Charles the Second. — Charter of Pennsylvania. — Object and Meaning of the Clauses peculiar to this Charter. — English and American Opinions thereon. — Penn's Policy to people his Territories. — Emigration of Quakers to the Province. — Letter from Penn to the Indians. — Penn's first Frame of Government for the Province. — Grant of Delaware by the Duke of York to Penn — who sails for America — his joyful Reception there. — Numerous Emigrations to the Province. — First Legislative Assembly. — Pennsylvania and Delaware united. — Controversy with Lord Baltimore. — Treaty with the Indians. — Second Assembly — new Frame of Government adopted. — Philadelphia founded. — Penn's Return to England — and Farewell to his People.

WILLIAM PENN, so renowned as a patriarch and champion of the Quakers, and a founder of civilized society in North America, was the son of that naval commander, who, under the protectorate of Cromwell, enlarged the British dominions by the conquest of Jamaica. [October 14, 1644.] This was the first colony that England acquired by her arms. New York was the next : for Acadia, though conquered in the interim by Cromwell's forces, did not then become an English settlement, and was surrendered by Charles the Second, soon after his restoration. It is another example of the strange concatenation of human affairs, that the second instance of the acquisition of a colony by the British arms should have been the means of introducing the son of the first conqueror as a Quaker colonist and a preacher of peace in America.

His father, who attained the dignity of knighthood and the rank of an admiral, was the descendant of a respectable English family. Devoting himself to the naval service of his country in the commencement of the civil wars, he espoused the cause of the parliament, and subsequently adhered to the fortunes of Cromwell. From a humble station in the service of these authorities, he was promoted to a dignified and important command ; and in the war with Holland, he coöperated in the achievements and partook the renown of the illustrious Admiral Blake. He gained the esteem of the Protector, and retained it till the failure of the expedition which he conducted against St. Domingo. It is asserted very confidently by some historians, and particularly by all the Quaker writers, that this disaster was occasioned by the fault of Venables, who commanded the land forces, and could not fairly be attributed to Admiral Penn : but Cromwell, who understood military affairs better than these writers can be supposed to have done, was so far from acquitting the admiral of blame, that he imprisoned him in the Tower, and never afterwards intrusted him with any public employ.[1] This circumstance, perhaps, contributed to the favor which he enjoyed at court after the Restoration ; when he scrupled not to accept title and employment from a government that stigmatized the service in which he was previously en-

---
[1] *Lord Clarendon's Life.* Holmes.

gaged, by the insults it heaped on the memory of Blake.[1] It is alleged of
him by Bishop Burnet, that he earned the friendship of the Duke of York,
with whom he commanded at sea in the Dutch war of 1665, by dexterously
enabling this prince to avoid a renewed action with the enemy's fleet, without having seemed to decline it. Other writers, and especially those who
profess the tenets or patronize the fame of his son, have affirmed that the
admiral owed his favor with the king and the duke to no other recommendations than those of his eminent valor and abilities. He was impeached, in
1668, by the House of Commons, for embezzling prize money ; but, from
some unexplained circumstance, the impeachment was permitted to drop.[2]

The favor which he enjoyed at court, whatever might be the source of it,
was so considerable, as to authorize the most ambitious hopes of the advancement of his son, and proportionally to embitter his disappointment at
beholding the young man embrace a profession of faith which not only excluded its votaries from official dignity, but exposed them to the severity of
penal law, the displeasure of churchmen, and the derision of courtiers. The
younger Penn's predilection for the Quakers, first excited by the discourses
of one of their itinerant preachers, was manifested at the early age of sixteen, with so much warmth and impetuosity, as to occasion his expulsion
from the University of Oxford. His father endeavoured to prevail with him
to abandon principles and manners so ill calculated to promote his worldly
grandeur ; and, finding arguments ineffectual, resorted to blows, and even
banished him from his house, with no better success. Along with the peculiarities of Quakerism, the young convert had received the first profound
impression which he ever experienced of the truth and importance of Christianity ; and both were for ever inseparably blended together in his mind.
The treatment he underwent from his father tended to confirm his belief
that Quakerism was a revival of that pure and primitive Christianity which
was fated to occasion the division of households and the dissolution of the
strongest ties of natural affection. At last, the admiral devised a method
of sapping the principles which he could not overthrow ; and, for this purpose, sent his son to travel, with some young men of quality, in France,
then the gayest and most licentious country of Europe. This device, which
reflects little credit on the parental concern by which it was prompted, was
attended with apparent success. Quakerism and Christianity were checked
alike, for a time, in the mind of Penn, who returned to his gratified father
with the manners of an elegant gentleman and the sentiments of a man of
pleasure.[3] But, having repaired, in the year 1666, to Ireland, in order to

---

[1] In alluding to the history and character of his father, William Penn is divided between a
natural elation at his republican honors, and an unwillingness to have him considered an associate of republicans and antagonist of royalty. " From a lieutenant," says the son, " he
passed through all the eminent offices of sea employment, and arrived to that of general about
the thirtieth year of his age ; in a time full of the biggest sea actions that any history mentions ; and when neither bribes nor alliance, favor nor affection, but ability only, could promote."
He adds, however, — " He was engaged both under the parliament and king ; but not as an
actor in the domestic troubles ; his compass always steering him to eye a national concern,
and not intestine wars. His service, therefore, being wholly foreign, he may be truly said to
serve his country, rather than either of these interests, so far as they were distinct from each
other." Proud's *History of Pennsylvania.* Oldmixon (2d edition) thus characterizes the admiral : — " He was a strong Independent, and so continued till the Restoration ; when, finding
religion and liberty at the mercy of their enemies, he very quickly made his peace with King
Charles and the Duke of York."

[2] Howell's *State Trials.*

[3] To reconcile this well authenticated conduct of the admiral with the interest which Quaker writers have displayed in defence of his reputation, it is necessary to remember that he

inspect an estate that belonged to his family in this country, it was here again his fate to meet with the same itinerant preacher who had exercised so much influence on him six years before, at Oxford.   His former designation of mind was now reproduced with deeper conviction and increased zeal and energy ; and speedily elicited from him a public, solemn, and resolute profession of his espousal of the principles and practices of the Quakers.   In vain were his father's instances once more repeated, and the temporal dignities which seemed only to wait his acceptance pressed with fond and pathetic earnestness on his regard. It was even in vain that the admiral, despairing of farther concession, restricted his solicitation to such a slender compliance with the usages of the world, as that his son should uncover his head in the presence of the king, the Duke of York, and his parents. Penn's eye was now elevated to the contemplation of objects so glorious and exalted as to eclipse the lustre of earthly grandeur and dissipate the illusions of temporal distinction ; and his resolution (hardened by an early experience of imprisonment, and other legal severities) was wound up to such a pitch of firmness and intensity, that he refused to lay even a single grain of incense on what he deemed an unhallowed altar of human arrogance and vanity.   He now devoted all the large resources of his capacity to the defence and propagation of the Quaker tenets, and sacrificed his temporal ease and enjoyment to the illustration of the Quaker virtues, — with a success that has gained for him a renown more brilliant and extended than the ambition of his father ever ventured to hope, or the utmost favor of his sovereign could have conferred.

It would not be easy to figure a more interesting career than that which is exhibited in the greater portion of his subsequent life.   He travelled over many parts of Europe, and even extended his personal labors to America ; and everywhere, from the courts of German princes to the encampments of Indian savages, we find him overcoming evil by good, and disarming human violence and ferocity by gentleness, patience, and piety.   In his exterior appearance and address, were combined, in an unusual degree, a venerable dignity and gravity of aspect, with a frank, cheerful simplicity of manner, and a style of language fraught with plainness, vigor, and good-humor. His face was a very uncommon one, and its lineaments, though by no means fine, were far from unpleasing, and were rendered by their peculiarity more deeply and lastingly impressive.   With the general corpulence which his frame attained as he advanced in years, his face underwent a proportional enlargement of its dimensions ; and while his eye expressed considerate thought and strength of understanding, the amplitude and regularity

is said to have died a convert to Quaker principles, and to have prophesied to his son that these principles, calmly and patiently supported, would finally triumph over all opposition. Proud. Clarkson.

It must be considered, also, that the demeanour of the young convert was not at first entirely unexceptionable.   From Oldmixon's account of Penn's expulsion from Oxford, it appears that his first espousal of Quakerism was signalized by a display of primitive Quaker turbulence. " He was a student at Christ Church, Oxon., when an order came down thither, after the king was restored, that the surplice should be worn according to the laudable custom of ancient times.   Young Mr. Penn having engaged the young Lord Spencer, his fellow-collegian, afterwards that great politician, Robert Earl of Sunderland, and some other young gentlemen, to join with them, they fell upon the students who appeared in surplices, and pulled them over their heads." Oldmixon (2d edition).

There is no account of William Penn having ever complied so far with the wishes of his father as to enter into the army.   Yet I have seen an original portrait of him in the house of his descendant at Stoke, in Buckinghamshire, representing him, at the age of twenty-two, attired in complete armor.

of the rest of his features seemed to indicate an habitual tranquillity of spirit. A mind so contemplative, and a life so active, — such a mixture of mildness and resolution, of patience and energy, of industry and genius, of lofty piety and profound sagacity, — have rarely been exemplified in the records of human character. The most pious and the most voluminous, he was also, next to Robert Barclay, the most learned and ingenious writer in defence of Quakerism ; and, at the same time, next to George Fox, the most indefatigable minister that the Quakers of Britain have ever possessed. He contrived to exhibit at once the active and passive virtues suitable to a champion and a confessor of Quakerism ; and the same prisons that witnessed his patient suffering for the rights of his brethren were also the scenes of his most elaborate literary efforts for their instruction. Among other Quaker peculiarities, his writings are distinguished by a tedious prolixity ; yet not much more so than the productions of the most celebrated contemporary authors of different religious persuasion. They abound with numerous passages replete alike with the finest eloquence and the most forcible reasoning, engaging benevolence and fervent piety. He was deeply infected with the doctrinal errors of the Quakers ; yet more deeply imbued with the spirit of divine truth than many who profess to hold it devoid of such appendages ; and, notwithstanding the tendency of these doctrinal errors to lead men who have thoroughly embraced them into frantic and indecent excesses, there were none of the Quaker leaders who contributed more signally than Penn to the establishment of a system of orderly discipline throughout the sectarian society. This was a work of such difficulty, and so repugnant to the sentiments of many who regarded discipline as an encroachment upon the sovereignty and freedom of spiritual communication, that all the influence of Penn's character and address, and all the weight he derived from his labors and sufferings, were requisite, and indeed barely sufficed, to its successful accomplishment. Except George Fox, no other individual has ever enjoyed so much authority in this society, or so fully sustained the character of a patriarch of the Quakers. Though his principles excluded him from the official dignities which his father had coveted for him, they did not prevent him from attaining a high degree of favor and consideration both with Charles the Second and his successor ; which he improved, to the utmost of his power, for the relief of persecuted members of the Quaker society. Whatever were the services of the admiral, the claim which they inferred was extended to his son ; nor was its efficacy impaired by his visible influence over a numerous body of men, whose avowed renunciation of the rights of resistance and self-defence could not fail to conciliate the regards of arbitrary princes.[1]

There exists, in all mankind, a propensity to unbounded admiration, arising from an indistinct glimpse and faint remaining trace of that image of infinite majesty and purity with which their existence connects them, and to which their nature once enjoyed a closer conformity than it has been able to retain. We may consider either as the expression of this propensity, or the apology for indulging it, that eagerness to claim the praise of faultless perfection for the objects of our esteem, which perhaps truly indicates a secret consciousness that it is only to excellence above the reach of humanity that our admiration can ever be justly due. This error has been exemplified in a very remarkable degree by the biographers of

---

[1] Proud. Clarkson's *Life of Penn*.

Penn, and the historians of his transactions and institutions in America. The unmixed and unmerited encomium, which his character and labors have received, originated, no doubt, with the writers of his own religious persuasion ; but, so far from being confined to them, it has been even exaggerated by writers of a totally different class, and whose seeming impartiality has contributed, in a remarkable degree, to fortify and propagate the illusion.   The Quakers have always enjoyed, with some infidel philosophers,[1] a reputation which no other professors of Christianity have been permitted to share ; partly because they were accounted the friends of unlimited toleration, and partly from an erroneous idea that their Christian name was but a thin mystical covering, which veiled the pure and simple light of reason and philosophy from eyes yet too gross to receive it.   Refusing to define their doctrinal tenets by a creed, and having already evacuated by allegorical interpretation some of the plainest precepts of the gospel, the Quakers were expected by their philosophical panegyrists to pave the way for a total dissolution of Christianity, by gradually allegorizing the whole of the Scriptures.   By the united efforts of these several tributaries to his fame, William Penn has been presented to the world as a character nearly, if not entirely, faultless ; as the author of institutions not less admirable for their wisdom than their originality, and not less amply than instantaneously productive of the gratitude and happiness of mankind.[2]   How exaggerated is this picture of the merit and the effects of his institutions will appear but too clearly from the following pages.   That the dazzling light with which his character has been invested was sullied with the specks of mortal imperfection is also a truth which it is more easy than agreeable to demonstrate.   But excellence, the more credibly it is represented, is the more effectually recommended to imitation and esteem ; and those who may be conscious of such infirmities as William Penn betrayed receive an important lesson, when they are taught that these imperfections neither inevitably obstruct, nor satisfactorily apologize for, deficiency of even the most exemplary virtue.

In the commencement of his very controversial career, Penn treated his opponents with an arrogance of disdain, and a coarseness and scurrility of vituperation, strangely inconsistent with the mildness of manners enjoined by the canons of Quakerism, and even with common decency and propriety.[3] It redounds to his credit that he corrected this fault, and graced his wisdom with an address replete with courtesy and kindness.   But another change that occurred in his disposition presents him in an aspect which it is less pleasing to contemplate.   Recommended to Charles the Second and this monarch's successor by a hereditary claim of regard, by the principles of

[1] Among others, Voltaire, Diderot, Raynal, Mirabeau, and Brissot. Hume, in his *History*, has treated the Quakers with little respect; but in his *Essay on Superstition and Enthusiasm* he has represented those sectaries as enjoying a perfect freedom from priestly bondage, and approaching the only regular association of deists in the world, — a representation which has doubtless contributed to the favor which the Quakers have enjoyed with the philosophers of France.

[2] See Note XXVI., at the end of the volume.

[3] Some instances of this failing have been preserved by his biographers. But by far the most remarkable occurs in the address which he himself prefixed to his report of his celebrated trial at the Old Bailey for preaching at a conventicle, and which is reprinted in Howell's *State Trials*. The ribaldry, which Penn on this occasion condescended to employ, was borrowed from a coarse jest of Oliver Cromwell. Penn retained through life a taste for pleasantry. An adversary of the Quakers having published a controversial work against them, entitled *The Quaker's last Shift found out*, Penn answered it by a treatise bearing the ludicrous title of *Naked Truth needs no Shift*.

passive obedience, — which, as a Quaker, he professed, and as a writer contributed widely to disseminate, — and by the willingness with which he and his fellow-sectaries alone, of all the British Protestants, recognized the despotic prerogative affected by the crown, of suspending the ordinances of the legislature, — he was admitted to a degree of favor and intimacy with those perfidious and tyrannical princes, which laid a dangerous snare for the integrity of his character and the rectitude of his conduct. It was natural that he and his friends, oppressed by the severe intolerance of parliamentary legislation, should regard with more favor the arbitrary power which was sometimes interposed for their relief, than the constitutional authority which was uniformly directed to their molestation. But the other Protestant Dissenters in general beheld with disgust and suspicion the boon of a temporary mitigation of legal rigor, which implied a power in the crown subversive of every bulwark of British liberty. As the political agent of his society, cultivating the friendship of a tyrant, and seeking a shelter under his prerogative from the existing laws, Penn occupied a situation regulated by no established maxims of duty, or ascertained principles ;[1] and becoming gradually familiarized with arbitrary power, he scrupled not to beseech its interposition in behalf of his own private concernments, and to employ, for the enlargement of his American territory, at the expense of the prior right of Lord Baltimore, the same authority which he had accustomed himself to respect as an engine of public good and religious toleration. Dazzled, rather than corrupted, by royal favor and confidence, he beheld nothing in the character of the British princes that reproved his friendship with them, or prevented it from becoming even more intimate and confidential, at a period when their tyrannical designs were already fully developed, their perfidy unmasked to every other eye, and the hands from which he solicited favors were imbrued with the blood of men whom he had loved as friends, and reverenced as the most estimable and illustrious characters in England.

While as yet the struggle between the popular leaders and the abettors of arbitrary power had not issued in the triumph of royal prerogative, Penn seemed to participate in the sentiments that were cherished by the friends of liberty. He addressed his supplications, for repeal of the penal laws against Dissenters, to the House of Commons ; he attached himself to Algernon Sydney, and endeavoured to promote his election in a competition with a court candidate for the borough of Guildford ;[2] and we have seen how he coöperated in the magnanimous vindication of the rights of West Jersey against the encroachments of the Duke of York. But when the cause of liberty seemed for ever to have sunk beneath the victorious ascendency of royal prerogative, he applied to the crown for that relief from the rigor of ecclesiastical law, which he had already practically avowed to be legally derivable from the parliament alone ; he beheld his friend Sydney perish on a scaffold, the victim of patriotic virtue, without any interruption of cordiality between himself and the court ; and when James the Second committed a far greater outrage on the rights of Magdalen College of Oxford than the encroachment he had attempted on the liberties of New Jersey, Penn's advice to the academic authorities was to

---

[1] That Penn did not acknowledge the same duties, as a politician, which he prescribed to himself as a Quaker, appears from his withdrawing from a state warrant that was issued for his imprisonment on a political charge by King William, (Proud) — an evasion which he never stooped to, when he was persecuted for his religious practices.

[2] Clarkson.

appease the king by apologies for their past conduct, which, at the same time, he acknowledged to have been not only blameless, but upright and commendable.[1] Nay, as if to render the change of his disposition still more signally conspicuous, he concurred with the other proprietaries of East Jersey in tamely surrendering the liberties of this province to the same prince, against whom, when supported by the spirit of better times, he had so strenuously defended the freedom of its sister colony.   Penn was voluntarily present at the execution of Mrs. Gaunt, an aged lady, renowned for her piety and charity, who was burnt alive for having given shelter to a person in distress, whom she knew not at the time to have been a fugitive from the rebel army of the Duke of Monmouth ; and at the execution of Alderman Cornish, who was hanged before the door of his own house, for a pretended treason, of which nobody believed him to be guilty.[2]   The only sentiment that he is reported to have expressed in relation to these atrocities was, that " *the king was greatly to be pitied* for the evil counsels that hurried him into so much effusion of blood."[3]   When it is considered, that, after all this, Penn's eyes were not opened[4] to the real character of James, and that, on the contrary, his friendship with the barbarous tyrant continued to subsist, and even to increase, till the very last, — it seems by no means surprising that his contemporaries should have generally regarded him as a secret abettor of all the monarch's designs for the reëstablishment of the church of Rome in Britain and the destruction of British liberty. It was, perhaps, fortunate for his fame that the public displeasure vented itself in this injustice ; the detection of which has contributed to shelter him even from the milder but more merited censure of an infatuated self-complacence and credulity, inspired by the flattering idea that he would ultimately render the royal authority entirely subservient to the accomplishment of his own religious and philanthropic views.

The character of William Penn has not escaped the charge of ambition,[5] — a charge which admits of such variety of signification, that perhaps no human being was ever entirely exempt from it.   If restriction to ends merely selfish constitute the depravity of ambition, a nobler and more generous range may be allowed to *make ambition virtue.*   Assuredly, Penn was neither conscious nor susceptible of that vile and vulgar aspiration that courts a personal distinction and superiority obtained by the depression and spoliation of mankind.   Of the wish to derive a reflected lustre from the happiness and improvement which others might owe to him, it is neither so easy nor so desirable to absolve him.   Nor, perhaps, was he wholly insensible to the influence of a temptation which this refined ambition is very apt to beget, — the desire of enlarging and perpetuating the authority by which

---

[1] Clarkson.   [2] Ibid.   [3] See Note XXVII., at the end of the volume.

[4] He published a book in favor of the king's attempts to establish toleration, even after James had so far disclosed his real views as to have intruded Roman Catholics into the government of the University of Oxford. He had recently before undertaken a secret embassy from the king to the Prince of Orange, in the hope of prevailing with this prince to give his sanction to the measures in behalf of toleration.   Clarkson.   Though unable to discern the designs of the king, he had not always been equally insensible to the dangers of Popery ; and, in the days of his patriotic fervor, wrote a pamphlet to animate the national rage against the pretended *Popish Plot.*   Ibid.

[5] An acute, but very partial writer, who boldly essays to beat down all Penn's pretensions to generous virtue, has characterized him as " a man of great depth of understanding, attended by equal dissimulation ; of extreme interestedness, accompanied with insatiable ambition ; and of an address in proportion to all these."   Chalmers.   Scarcely, if at all, more favorable are the sentiments expressed by Dr. Franklin and Jedediah Morse, with regard to the character of Penn.

such benefits might continue to be conferred by himself and his posterity. It has been alleged of more than one benefactor of the human race, that, confident of their good intentions, and habituated to power, they have coveted the possession of it somewhat too eagerly, as a peculiarly efficient instrument of human welfare.   But it is time to proceed from these prefatory observations on the character of this distinguished person, to a consideration of that portion of his life which is identified with the history of Delaware and the rise of Pennsylvania.

The circumstances by which the attention of Penn was first directed to the colonization of North America have already been unfolded in the early annals of New Jersey.   While he was engaged with his Quaker associates in administering the New Jersey government, he received such information of the fertility and resources of the country situated to the westward of the Delaware, as inspired him with the desire of acquiring a separate estate in this quarter. [June, 1680.]   For this purpose, he presented a petition to Charles the Second, stating his relationship to the deceased admiral, and his claim for a debt incurred by the crown to his father, at the time when Shaftesbury's memorable device was adopted, of shutting the exchequer ; soliciting, on these accounts, a grant of land to the northward of Maryland, and westward of the Delaware ; and representing, that, by his interest with the Quakers, he should be able to colonize the province, which might, in time, not only yield a revenue sufficient to extinguish his claims on the crown, but enlarge the British empire, augment its trade, and promote the glory of God by the civilization and conversion of the Indian tribes.[1]   This petition was referred to the Duke of York and Lord Baltimore, that they might report how far its object was compatible with their prior investitures. Both signified their acquiescence in Penn's demand, provided his patent should be so worded as to preclude any encroachment on their territories ; and the Duke of York added his recommendation of the petition to the favor of the crown.   Successful thus far, Penn transcribed from the charter of Maryland the sketch of a patent in his own favor [November, 1680] ; but the attorney-general, Jones, to whose opinion it was remitted, pronounced that certain of the clauses were "not agreeable to the laws here, though they are in Lord Baltimore's patent," and signified, in particular, that the exemption from British taxation, which Penn desired for his colony, was utterly illegal.   Compton, Bishop of London, at the same time, understanding that Penn, in soliciting his patent, described himself as the head of the English Quakers, interposed in the relative proceedings, for the protection (as he declared) of the interests of the church of England. [January, 1681.]   After some discussion of the points that had thus arisen, the Committee of Plantations desired Chief-Justice North, a person of considerable eminence, both as a statesman and a lawyer, to undertake the revision of the patent, and to secure, by proper clauses, the reservation of royal prerogative and parliamentary jurisdiction.   With his assistance, there was prepared an instrument which received the royal confirmation, and afterwards acquired much celebrity as the charter of Pennsylvania.[2] [March, 1681.]

---

[1] In a letter to a friend, about the same time, he declares his purpose in the acquisition of American territory to have been "so to serve the truth and people of the Lord, *that an example may be set to the nations*"; adding, "there may be room there, though not here, for such an *holy experiment.*"   Proud.
[2] Oldmixon.   Proud.   Chalmers.   Dillwyn (see Note XXVI.) *apud* Winterbotham.   Both

By this charter, which professed to be granted in consideration of " the merits of the father and the good purposes of the son," there was conferred on William Penn, and his heirs and assigns, that vast region bounded on the east by the river Delaware ; extending westward five degrees of longitude ; stretching to the north from twelve miles northward of Newcastle (in the Delaware territory) to the forty-third degree of latitude ; limited on the south by a circle of twelve miles drawn round Newcastle to the beginning of the fortieth degree of latitude. Penn was constituted the absolute proprietary of the whole of this territory, which was erected into a province by the name of Pennsylvania,[1] and was to be held in free and common soccage by fealty only, with the obligation of paying two bear-skins annually, and one fifth of all the gold and silver that might be discovered, to the king. He was empowered to make laws, with the advice and assent of the freemen of the territory assembled, for the imposition of taxes and other public purposes, — but always in conformity with the general strain of the jurisprudence of England ; to appoint judges and other officers to carry the laws into execution ; and to pardon and reprieve offenders, except in the cases of wilful murder and high-treason. In these cases, reprieve might be granted only till the signification of the pleasure of the king, — to whom there was also reserved the privilege of receiving appeals from the provincial tribunals in civil cases. The distribution of property, and the punishment of felonies, were to be regulated by the laws of England, unless and until different ordinances should be expressly enacted by the proprietary and freemen. Duplicates of all the provincial laws were to be transmitted to the privy council, within five years after they were passed ; and if not declared void by the council within six months after transmission, they were to be considered as finally ratified, and to become valid ordinances.

That the colony might increase by the resort of people, liberty was given to English subjects (those only excepted who should be specially forbidden) to remove to and settle in Pennsylvania ; and thence to import the productions of the province into England, "but into no other country whatsoever," and to reëxport them, within one year, — paying the same duties as other subjects, and conforming to the Acts of Navigation. The proprietary was authorized to divide the province into towns, hundreds, and counties ; to erect and incorporate towns into boroughs, and boroughs into cities ; and to constitute ports for the convenience of commerce, to which the officers of the customs were to have free admission. The freemen in assembly were empowered to assess reasonable duties on the commodities

---

Oldmixon (who was a personal friend of Penn) and Clarkson have asserted that Penn's efforts to obtain his charter were greatly obstructed by his profession of Quakerism. Of this I can find no evidence at all. Penn himself, writing to the Lords of Trade in 1683, says, " I return my most humble thanks for your former *favors in the passing of my patent,* and pray God reward you." Chalmers.

[1] Penn's account of this denomination is creditable to his modesty. Finding that the king designed that the name of Penn should form a part of the appellation of the province, he requested leave to decline an honor that might be imputed to his own vanity, and proposed the name of New Wales, which was objected to (most absurdly) by the under secretary of state, who was a Welshman. Penn then suggested Sylvania, on account of the woody surface of the region ; but the king declared that the nomination belonged to him, and that, in honor of Admiral Penn, the last suggested name should be enlarged into Pennsylvania. Clarkson.

"Hæc habet, et regio memorabile nomen habebit,
      Auctior auctoris in omne tempus sui ;
Qui fuit illustri proavorum stemmate natus,
      Sed virtute magis nobilis ipse sua."
                                        Makin's *Descriptio Pennsylvaniæ.*

laden or unladen in the harbours of the colony ; and these duties were granted to Penn, with reservation, however, to the crown of such customs as then were, or in future might be, imposed by act of parliament.   Penn was required to appoint an agent to reside in or near London, to answer for any breach of the trade laws which he or his people might commit ; and in case of such misdemeanour, he was to make satisfaction within a year ; in default of which, the king was to appropriate the government of the province, and retain it till due satisfaction were made.   The proprietary was required not to maintain correspondence with any prince or state at war, nor to make war against any prince or state in amity, with England.   By an article of the charter, which, perhaps, a strict adherence to his principles should have induced him to disclaim, he was empowered " to levy, muster, and train all sorts of men ; to pursue and vanquish enemies ; to take and put them to death by the laws of war ; and to do every thing which belongeth to the office of captain-general in an army."   He was farther empowered to alienate the soil to the colonists, who were authorized to hold their lands under his grants, notwithstanding the English statute prohibiting such sub-infeudations.   Assurance was given by the king, for himself and his successors, " that no custom or other contribution shall be levied on the inhabitants or their estates, unless by the consent of the proprietary, or governor and assembly, *or by act of parliament in England.*"   It was stipulated (in compliance with the suggestion of Bishop Compton), that, if any of the inhabitants, to the number of twenty, should signify their desire to the Bishop of London to have an Episcopal minister established among them, the pastor appointed for them by this dignitary should be allowed to reside and perform his functions without hindrance or molestation.   In case of the emergence of doubt with regard to the construction properly applicable to any part of the charter, it was declared that an interpretation the most favorable to the proprietary should always be admitted ; with the exclusion, however, of any supposition that might derogate from the allegiance due to the crown.[1]

Such is the substance of a charter on which was established the fabric of the Pennsylvanian government and laws, so renowned for their wisdom, mildness, equity, and liberality.   The cautious stipulations for guarding and ascertaining the British ascendency, by which this charter was distinguished from all preceding patents, were manifestly the offspring of the disputes in which the royal court had been for some time engaged with the colony of Massachusetts.   The provincial government of Massachusetts had deemed the Acts of Navigation inoperative within its jurisdiction, till they were legalized by its own ordinance.   But direct and steady obedience to them in Pennsylvania was enforced by the stipulated penalty of the forfeiture of the charter.   Laws had been passed in Massachusetts for a domestic coinage of money, and other objects, which were deemed inconsistent with the prerogative of the sovereign state.   For the prevention of similar abuse, or at least the correction of it, before inveterate prevalence should create habits of independence, it was required that all the laws of the new

---

[1] Proud. Chalmers. " It is remarkable," says Dr. Franklin, in his *Historical Review of the Constitution of Pennsylvania,* " that such an instrument, penned with all the appearance of candor and simplicity imaginable, and equally agreeable to law and reason, to the claims of the crown and the rights of the subject, should be the growth of an arbitrary court."   The trait would have been more remarkable, if this arbitrary court had been as much renowned for integrity in fulfilling, as for facility in contracting, engagements in favor of law, reason, and popular rights.

province should be regularly transmitted to England for the royal approbation or dissent. To obviate the difficulty that was experienced by the English government in conducting its disputes with the people of Massachusetts, who could never be induced to accredit an agent at the court without
much reluctance and long delay, it was required that a standing agent for
Pennsylvania should reside in London, and be held responsible for the proceedings of his colonial constituents. But the most remarkable provision,
by which this charter was distinguished from all the other American patents,
was that which expressly reserved a power of taxation to the British parliament.

Of the import of this much agitated clause very different opinions were
entertained, from the first, by the lawyers and statesmen of England, and
the politicians of Pennsylvania. In England, while it was denied that the
novel introduction of the clause into the charter of this province afforded to
any of the other colonies an argument against their liability to parliamentary
taxation, — it was, with more appearance of reason, maintained that its actual insertion in the present charter precluded even the possibility of an
honest pretension to such immunity on the part of the Pennsylvanians. Of
the very opposite ideas that were entertained on this subject by the colonists an account was rendered about a century afterwards by Dr. Franklin,
in his celebrated examination, as an agent of his countrymen, at the bar of the
British House of Commons. Being asked how the Pennsylvanians could
reconcile a pretence to be exempted from taxation with the express words
of a clause reserving to parliament the privilege of imposing this burden upon
them, he answered, — "They understand it thus : — By the same charter,[1]
and otherwise, they are entitled to all the privileges and liberties of Englishmen. They find in the great charters and in the petition and declaration
of rights, that one of the privileges of English subjects is, that they are
not taxed but by their common consent ; they have, therefore, relied upon
it, *from the first settlement of the province*, that the parliament never
would nor could, by color of that clause in the charter, tax them till it
had qualified itself to exercise such right by admitting representatives from
the people to be taxed."[2] That this reasoning was not (as some have
suggested) the mere production of Franklin's own ingenuity, nor even the
immediate growth of the era of American independence, but that it expressed the opinion of the earliest race of the Pennsylvanian settlers, is a point
susceptible of the clearest demonstration.

From the official correspondence between the royal functionaries in
America and the court of London, it appears, that, before the Pennsylvanians had existed as a people for seventeen years, the English ministry
were apprized of the general prevalence of these sentiments among them ;
and in the work of a contemporary historian of this province, who derived
his acquaintance with it from the communications of Penn himself, the right
of the colonists to elect representatives to the British parliament is distinctly
asserted.[3] It was only in the year preceding the date of the Pennsylvanian
charter, that Penn, in reclaiming for the colonists of New Jersey the privi-

---

[1] This is a mistake. The Pennsylvanian charter differs from all the others in not communicating an express assurance to the colonists of the rights and character of Englishmen. The
reason for this omission is said by Chalmers to have been, that the eminent lawyers, who
prepared the charter, deemed such declarations superfluous, and their import sufficiently inferred by general law.

[2] *Memoirs, &c., of Franklin.*

[3] See Note XXVIII., at the end of the volume.

lege of imposing taxes on themselves, had protested that no reasonable men would emigrate from England to a country where this advantage was not to be enjoyed ; and as the argument which he maintained on that occasion was founded entirely on general principles, and on what he regarded as the constitutional rights inseparable from the character of British subjects, without reference to any peculiarities in the charter of New Jersey, it is highly improbable that he believed the clauses peculiar to his own charter to admit of an interpretation that would have placed his favorite province beyond the pale of the British constitution, and deterred reasonable men from resorting to it.   We must either believe him to have entertained the same opinion that prevailed on this point among the colonists of his territory, or adopt the illiberal supposition of a historian[1] who charges him with making concessions, in treating with the crown, which he never intended to substantiate in practice.

Possessed of this charter, to which the king gave additional authority by a royal letter commanding all intending planters in the new province to render due submission to the proprietary, Penn directed his attention to the interesting concern of attracting inhabitants to his vacant territory.   To this end, he published a description of the soil and resources of the province, together with admonitions to those who were inclined to undertake its cultivation, and a statement of the conditions on which he was willing to deal with them.   The admonitions are almost precisely the same with those which he previously addressed to the intending emigrants to West Jersey ; and enjoin all persons, deliberating with regard to their removal, to have especial respect to the will of God, — to balance present inconvenience with future ease and plenty, — and to obtain the consent of their near relations, in order that natural affections might be preserved, and a friendly and profitable correspondence between the two countries maintained.   It was intimated to all who were disposed to become planters, that a hundred acres of land would be sold at the price of forty shillings, together with a perpetual quitrent of a shilling.   It was required, that, in disencumbering the ground of wood, there should be reserved one acre of trees for every five acres cleared ; and an especial recommendation was given to preserve oak and mulberry trees for the construction of ships and the manufacture of silk.   It was declared that no planter would be permitted to overreach or otherwise injure the Indians, or even to avenge, at his own hands, any wrong he might receive from them ; but that, in case of disputes between the two races, the adjustment of them should, in every instance, be referred to twelve arbitrators, selected equally from the Europeans and the Indians. The requisition of quitrents, in addition to the payment of a price, which proved ultimately so fertile a source of discord between the proprietary family and the colonists, was the only feature in this scheme that appeared objectionable to the religious fraternity of which Penn was a member ; but his influence with these sectaries was so great, and his description of the province so inviting, as more than to outweigh this disagreeable and unexpected condition.

Numerous applications for land were speedily made by persons, chiefly of the Quaker persuasion, in London, Liverpool, and especially in Bristol, where one trading association alone became the purchasers of twenty thou-

---

[1] Chalmers, who, in support of his opinion, remarks that not one of the laws and constitutions, enacted by Penn, or under his auspices, was ever submitted, according to the requisition of the charter, to the English court.

sand acres of the territory, and prepared for embarking in various branches of commerce which had relation to their acquisition. The prospect thus afforded, of an early replenishment of his province, invited the immediate attention of Penn to the form and fabric of its political constitution ; in the composition of which there could be room for little other labor than the exercise of a judicious selection from the numerous theoretical models which had employed the pens and exhausted the invention of contemporary writers, and from the various practical institutions by which the several proprietaries of American provinces had vied with each other for the approbation of mankind and the attraction of inhabitants to their vacant domains. In undertaking an employment so congenial to his disposition as the work of legislation, Penn seems to have been impressed with equal confidence in the resources of his capacity and the rectitude of his intentions, and touched at the same time with a generous sense of the value of those interests that were involved in his performance, and the expanse of liberty and happiness that might result from it. " As my understanding and inclinations," he declared, " have been much directed to observe and reprove mischiefs in government, so *it is now put into my power to settle one.* For the matters of liberty and privilege, *I purpose that which is extraordinary,* and leave myself and successors no power of doing mischief, that the will of one man may not hinder the good of a whole country." The liberal institutions that arose shortly after in Pennsylvania, and the happiness of which they were so largely productive, attested the sincerity and rewarded the virtue of this magnanimous design ; while the partial disappointment which it sustained, and particularly the mischief and dissension that arose from the degree of power that was actually reserved to the proprietary and his successors, forcibly exemplified the infirmity of human purpose, and the fallacy incident to all human expectations.

As several of the purchasers of land, in their eagerness to commence the new settlement, were prepared to embark before Penn had yet completed his legislatorial composition, it was necessary that they should be previously acquainted with the general scope, at least, of a work so deeply affecting their interests. A rough sketch of its principal features was accordingly prepared and mutually signed by the proprietary and these adventurers, who, being now assured of unlimited toleration,[1] and satisfied with the model of the political constitutions, no longer hesitated to bid adieu to a scene of tyranny, contention, and persecution, and set sail, in quest of freedom and repose, for Pennsylvania. [May, 1681.] Three vessels from London and Bristol carried out these first Pennsylvanian settlers, and along with them Colonel William Markham, the kinsman and secretary of Penn, who appointed him deputy-governor ; and certain commissioners who were appointed to confer with the Indians respecting the purchase of their lands, and to endeavour to form with them a league of perpetual peace. These commissioners were solemnly enjoined to treat the Indians with candor, justice, and humanity, and were intrusted with a letter from Penn to them, accompanied by suitable presents. The proprietary's letter signified to the

---

[1] It detracts not from the wisdom of Penn, but merely from the judgment and accuracy of those writers who have deemed the honor of practical virtue incomplete without the attribute of original invention, that this equitable principle of toleration had been already realized in America by Lord Baltimore and the Catholics of Maryland, and employed as a politic device by Lord Clarendon and his associates in Carolina, and by Lord Berkeley and Sir George Carteret in New Jersey. Clarkson is the only historian of Penn who has conceded to Lord Baltimore the honor of originating toleration in America.

Indians, that the great God and Power, who created all men and command-ed them to love and do good to one another, had been pleased to make a connection between Penn and America ; that the king of England had be-stowed on him a province there, but that he desired to enjoy it with the good-will and consent of the Indians ; that many wicked Europeans, he was aware, had treated the Indians very ill, but that he was a person of a differ-ent disposition, and bore great love and regard to them ; and that the peo-ple he now sent among them were similarly disposed, and wished to live with them as neighbours and friends.

Markham, at the head of one of these detachments of adventurers, proceeded, on his arrival in America [August, 1681], to take possession of an extensive forest, situated twelve miles northward of Newcastle, on the western side of the Delaware, whose waters contributed, with other streams of lesser note, to the salubrity of the air and the fertility of the soil. As this situation enjoyed the advantages of a civilized neighbourhood on the south and east, the colonists were not embarrassed with the difficulties which encumbered and disturbed so many of their predecessors in similar pur-suits ; and, animated by vigorous hope and steady resolve, they set them-selves diligently to prepare for the reception of the numerous emigrants who were expected to join them in the following year. Greater hardships were endured by another detachment of the first adventurers, who, arriving later in the season, disembarked at the place where Chester was afterwards built [Oct., 1681] ; and, the river having suddenly frozen before they could resume their voyage, were constrained to pass the remainder of the winter there. Markham now discovered a circumstance which had material in-fluence on the future conduct and policy of his patron. Penn had hitherto supposed that the whole of the Delaware territory, except the settlement of Newcastle and its appendages (occupied by the Duke of York as a de-pendency of his own province of New York), was really included in the Pennsylvanian charter, — a supposition which he entertained with a great deal of satisfaction ; for he was aware that this territory already contained a number of Swedish and English settlers ; and though doubtless he proposed to people his domains chiefly with Quakers, he was by no means insensible to the advantage of obtaining for himself an immediate accession of tribu-taries, and for his people a social connection with a race of hardy agricul-turists inured to colonial life and habits. He knew that the government of Maryland laid claim to the allegiance of a number of settlers whose planta-tions he believed to be included within his own chartered district of Penn-sylvania ; and he had instructed Markham to demand from Lord Baltimore a relinquishment of that pretension. Markham accordingly applied to the proprietary of Maryland, and readily accepted this nobleman's proposal to compare the titles of the two provinces and adjust their boundaries ; but discovering very speedily that Penn had in reality no other claim than what might be derived from the confused designation in his charter of the limits of his province, and that a literal construction of Lord Baltimore's prior charter, where the limits were indicated with greater precision, would evac-uate at once the pretensions both of Penn and the Duke of York, he de-clined all farther conference, and acquainted Penn with a discovery that threatened so much obstruction to his views.[1]

In the spring of the ensuing year [April, 1682], Penn completed and

---

[1] Proud. Chalmers. Clarkson.

delivered to the world a composition, the fruit of great research and profound reflection, entitled " *The Frame of the Government of the Province
of Pennsylvania.*" It was introduced by an ingenious preface, unfolding his
own views of the origin, nature, and objects of government ; wherein he de-
duces from various texts of Scripture the origination and descent of all
human power from God, the utter unlawfulness of resisting constituted authority, and, in short, "*the divine right of government,* and that for two
ends : first, to terrify evil doers ; secondly, to cherish those that do well ;
which," he continues, "*gives government a life beyond corruption,* and
makes it as durable in the world as good men shall be ; so that *government
seems to me a part of religion itself,* a thing sacred in its institution and
end." " They weakly err," he afterwards observes, " who think there is
no other use of government than correction, which is the coarsest part of
it." Declining to pronounce any opinion on the comparative merit of the
various political systems which had been exhibited to mankind in the practice of commonwealths or the speculations of philosophers, and remarking
that not one of these models was ever realized without incurring some alteration from the lapse of time or the emergency of circumstances, he advances this position, that " any government is free to the people under it,
whatever be the frame, where the laws rule and the people are a party
to these laws ; and more than this is tyranny, oligarchy, or confusion."
With close, though perhaps unconscious, transcription of the maxims ascribed by Plutarch to Lycurgus, he maintains that " governments rather
depend upon men, than men upon governments. *Let men be good, and the
government cannot be bad.* If it be ill, they will cure it. But if men be
bad, let the government be never so good, they will endeavour to warp and
spoil it to their turn. I know some say, ' Let us have good laws, and no
matter for the men that execute them. But let them consider, that, though
good laws do well, good men do better ; for good laws may want good
men, and be invaded or abolished by ill men ; but good men will never
want good laws nor suffer ill ones.[1] *That, therefore, which makes a good
constitution, must keep it ; namely, men of wisdom and virtue ; qualities,
that, because they descend not with worldly inheritances, must be carefully
propagated by a virtuous education of youth.*" In conclusion, he pro-
claims that " We [2] have, with reverence to God and good conscience to
men, to the best of our skill, contrived and composed the frame of this government to the great end of all government, *to support power in reverence
with the people, and to secure the people from the abuse of power, that they
may be free by their just obedience, and the magistrates honorable for their
just administration ; for liberty without obedience is confusion, and obedience without liberty is slavery.*" This production, which will always command respect for its intrinsic merits, excited the greater interest, at the
time of its emission, from being regarded as the political manifesto of the
party that had now become the most numerous and powerful among the
Quakers, and whose ascendency continued gradually to increase, till at
length the whole sectarian society, by dint of conversion or expulsion, was

---

[1] How they could refuse to suffer bad laws, under a frame of government excluding them
from a share in legislation, is a difficulty which he has not undertaken to solve, and which
indeed, his general anathema against all resistance to established authority renders perfectly
insoluble. It is true that he reproaches a government so framed with the character of tyranny ; but this reproach merely gives additional sanction to discontent, without giving any to
resistance.

[2] Some of the planters had coöperated with Penn in the composition of the frame.

moulded to a conformity with its opinions. Another party still existed, but was daily diminishing, which regarded with equal aversion the establishment of ecclesiastical discipline and the recognition of municipal government. The adherents of this party were willing to forbear from all forcible resistance to human violence ; but were no less resolutely bent against any voluntary coöperation with municipal authority ; and reproached the rest of their brethren with degenerating from original Quaker principles, and substituting a servile obedience to *the dead law without*, in place of a holy conformity to *the living law within*.

By the *constitutional frame* which followed this preface, it was announced that the government of the province should be administered by the proprietary, or his deputy, as president, and by the freemen formed into two separate bodies of a provincial council and a general assembly. The council was to be elected by the freemen, and to consist of seventy-two members, of whom twenty-four were annually to retire, and be replaced by a new election. In the council, the governor was to preside, invested with no other control than a treble vote. Thus composed, the council was to exercise not only the whole executive power, but the peculiar privilege which was annexed to the functions of the same state organ in the Carolinian constitutions, of prejudging and composing all the bills or legislative projects that should be presented to the assembly. The presence of two thirds of the members of the council was requisite to the composition of a quorum of this body ; and the consent of two thirds of such quorum was indispensable in all matters of importance. The assembly was to consist, the first year, of all the freemen; the next, of two hundred representatives elected by the rest : and this number was afterwards to be augmented in proportion to the increase of population. The legislative functions of the assembly did not extend to originating laws, but were restricted to a simple assent or negation in passing or rejecting the bills that might be proposed to them by the governor and council. They were to present sheriffs and justices of the peace to the governor, — naming double the requisite number of persons, for his selection of half. They were to be elected annually ; and all elections, whether for the council or the assembly, were to be conducted *by ballot*. Such was the substance of the constitution, or frame of government, which was farther declared to be incapable of alteration, change, or diminution, in any part or clause, without the consent of the proprietary or his heirs, and six parts in seven of the members both of the council and the assembly.

The mode of election *by ballot*, which has since become so general in North America, was first introduced there by the Puritans, and subsequently adopted into the constitutions of Quaker legislation, — by which we have seen it established in New Jersey, and now extended to Pennsylvania. This latter repetition of the experiment proved very unsatisfactory. The planters soon declared that they felt it repugnant to the spirit of Englishmen to go *muzzled* (as they were pleased to express themselves) to elections ; that they scorned to give their opinions in the dark, or to do what they seemed ashamed to avow ; and that they wished the mode of election to be so framed as to show that their hearts and their tongues agreed together. In consequence of these objections, Penn, perceiving (says Oldmixon) that the perfection of his institutions was not in accordance with the narrow capacities of human nature, consented to assimilate the Pennsylvanian to the English mode of election.

To the Constitutional Frame there was appended a code of forty conditional laws, which had been concerted between the proprietary and divers
of the planters before their departure from England,[1] and were to be submitted for approval or modification to the first provincial assembly.   This
code is a production far superior to the Constitutional Frame, and highly
creditable to the sense, the spirit, and the benevolence of its authors.
Among other regulations, it proclaimed that the rank and rights of freemen
of the province should accrue to all purchasers or renters of a hundred
acres of land ; to all servants or bondsmen who at the expiry of their engagements should cultivate the quota of land (fifty acres) allotted to them
by law ; and to all artificers and other inhabitants or residents paying scot
and lot to the government ; that no public tax should be levied from the
people, "but by a law for that purpose made" ; and that whoever should
collect or pay taxes not thus sanctioned should be held a public enemy of
the province and a betrayer of its liberties ; *that all prisons shall be
workhouses* ; that a thief should restore twice the value of his depredation,
and, in default of other means adequate to such restitution, should work as a
bondsman in prison for the benefit of the person whom he had plundered ;
that the lands as well as the personal property of a debtor should be responsible for his obligations, except in the case of his having lawful children, for
whose use two thirds of the landed estate were appointed to be reserved ;
that all factors and correspondents in the province, defrauding their foreign
employers, should, in addition to complete restitution, pay a surplus amounting to a third of the sum they had unjustly detained ; that no person should
quit the province, without publication of his intention, in the market-place,
three weeks prior to his departure ; that all dramatic entertainments, games
of hazard, sports of cruelty, and whatever else might contribute to promote ferocity of temper, or habits of dissipation and irreligion, should be
discouraged and punished ; and "that all children within this province, of
the age of twelve years, shall be taught some useful trade or skill, to the
end none may be idle, but the poor may work to live, and the rich, if they
become poor, may not want."   This last regulation, so congenial to primitive Quaker sentiment and to republican spirit and simplicity, was calculated not less to promote fellow-feeling than to repress pauperism and dependence.   It contributed to preserve a sense of the natural equality of
mankind, by recalling to every man's remembrance his original destination
to labor ; and while it tended thus to abate the pride and insolence of
wealth, it operated no less beneficially to remedy the decay of fortune peculiarly incident to wealthy settlers in a country where the dearness of all
kinds of labor rendered idleness a much more expensive condition than
in Europe.   It was farther declared that no persons should be permitted
to hold any public office, or to exercise the functions of freemen, but "such
as profess faith in Jesus Christ, and are not convicted of ill fame, or unso-
ber and dishonest conversation"; and that every man acknowledging the
one almighty and eternal God to be the creator, preserver, and ruler of the

[1] Markham, the kinsman and secretary of Penn, and afterwards governor of the province,
has ascribed the greater part of the constitutions of the Frame itself to the suggestions and
importunity of these persons, in opposition to the original intentions of the proprietary. In a
letter to Fletcher, the governor of New York (in May, 1696), Markham says, "I very well
know that it [the frame of government] was forced from him by *friends*, when, unless pleased,
and granted whatever they demanded, they would not have settled his country." *State Papers*,
apud Chalmers. It is plain from the preface, that Penn considered a future alteration of the
constitutions as far from unlikely.

universe, and professing to be conscientiously engaged to live peaceably and uprightly in the world, should be exempted from molestation on account of his more particular opinions and practices, as well as from obligation to frequent or support any religious assembly, ministry, or worship whatever.[1]

This composition having been published, the next care of Penn, suggested doubtless by his experience of the Duke of York's behaviour to the proprietaries of New Jersey, was to obtain from this prince an express release of every claim or pretence of jurisdiction over Pennsylvania ; nor did the duke refuse a concession so manifestly just, to the son of a man for whose memory he professed the highest regard. [August, 1682.] It was a stronger proof of this regard, and the fruit of much more importunate solicitation, which Penn obtained at the same time, in a grant of the Delaware territory,[2] whose thriving plantations he anxiously desired to annex to his extensive but uncultivated domains of Pennsylvania. Yielding to the urgency of Penn, and probably swayed, in some degree, both by sentiments of friendship, and by indifference for an estate which he held by a defective and uncertain title, and had never been able to render productive of revenue, — the duke now conveyed to him, by two separate deeds of gift, the town of Newcastle, with a territory of twelve miles around it, together with the tract of land extending southward from it along the Bay of Delaware to Cape Henlopen. This conveyance included not only the settlements originally formed by the Swedes and afterwards conquered by the Dutch, whereof the early history is blended with the annals of New York,[3] and to which Lord Baltimore possessed a claim which he had never been able to render effectual, but a large district which this nobleman's title equally embraced, and which his activity and remonstrance had actually reclaimed from Dutch and Swedish occupation.[4] Without adopting the harsh censure of a writer [5] who maintains that this transaction reflected dishonor both on the Duke of York and on Penn, we can hardly fail to regard it as a faulty and equivocal proceeding, or to regret the proportions in which its attendant blame must be divided between a prince distinguished even among the Stuarts for perfidy and injustice, and a patriarch renowned even among the Quakers for humanity and benevolence. The duke's patents assuredly did not include within his boundaries the region which he now pretended to convey ; and it was only to a part of it that he could transfer even the dubious title arising from casual occupation, in opposition to the formal grant and legal claim of Lord Baltimore.[6]

All things being now prepared for his own personal presence and agency in America, Penn himself set sail from England to visit his transatlantic ter-

---

[1] Proud. Oldmixon.

[2] Only a month before this favor was granted, Sir John Werden, the duke's secretary, signified to Penn a repetition of former refusals of it, and at the same time wrote to Dongan, the governor of New York, cautioning him to beware of the encroachments of Penn, whom he describes as " very intent on his own interest in these parts, as you observe." *State Papers, apud* Chalmers. The effect of the scenes of intrigue and controversy, which his views on the Delaware territory had produced and seemed likely still farther to prolong, is sufficiently visible on the mind of Penn. One of his letters to a friend, at this period, expresses an evident abatement of the fervor of his first impressions of the degree in which his colonial designs might be rendered conducive to spiritual ends. "Surely," he says, " God will come in for a share in this planting work, and that leaven shall leaven the lump in time. I do not believe the Lord's providence had run this way towards me, but that he has a heavenly end and service in it." Clarkson. " Less of the man of God now began to appear," says Dr. Franklin, " and more of the man of the world."

[3] *Ante*, Book V., Chap. I.　　　　　[4] *Ante*, Book III., and Book V., Chap. I.
[5] Chalmers.　　　　　　　　　　　[6] Oldmixon. Proud. Chalmers.

QQ *

ritory [September, 1682], in company with a hundred English Quakers, who resolved to unite themselves to their friends already removed to that quarter of the world.   Arriving on the banks of the Delaware, he beheld with great satisfaction the thriving settlements comprehended in his latest acquisition, and the hardy, sober, and industrious race of men by whom they were inhabited.   The population of that part of the Delaware territory which he succeeded in finally retaining against Lord Baltimore amounted already to three thousand persons, chiefly Swedes and Dutch;[1] and by them, as well as by the English settlers who were intermixed with them, and by the Quakers whom Markham had conducted thither in the preceding year, the proprietary was received on his arrival with a satisfaction equal to his own, and greeted with the most cordial expressions of respect and good-will.   The English rejoiced in their deliverance from the sway of the Duke of York; and the Dutch and Swedes were glad to renounce a connection that had originated in the conquest, first of the one, and afterwards of both their races.[2]   It was flattering to their importance to be united to a State that seemed then much less likely to overshadow them by superior greatness than either New York or Maryland; and whatever they might think of the justice of Lord Baltimore's pretensions, or of the equity of his administration, it was manifest that his power was unequal to divest the Duke of York of the dominion which this prince had now peaceably surrendered to the solicitations of William Penn.   Advancing to Newcastle, where the Dutch possessed a court-house, the proprietary convoked there a meeting of his new subjects; and, after a formal proclamation of his title to the soil and the political governance of the country, he explained to the people the objects of his visit to them, exhorted them to live in sobriety and mutual amity, and renewed the commissions of the existing magistrates.

The number of his colonists meanwhile was fast increasing around him. In the course of the present year, no fewer than two thousand emigrants, chiefly Quakers, arrived from England on the banks of the Delaware. Many of them were persons considerable by their rank and substance in the parent state; and all were men of some education and great respectability, and to whom the main inducement to forsake their native land was supplied by views of religious truth and duty, more or less enlightened, but unquestionably sincere and conscientious.   They needed all the influence of this noble principle to animate them to a brave endurance of the hardships they were compelled to undergo during the rigorous winter that followed their arrival.   Their sufferings were mitigated as far as possible by the hospitality of the Swedes; but many families were compelled to pass the winter in temporary huts or sheds; and the greater number of the new settlers had no better lodging than caves, which they dug for themselves on the banks of the river.   These hardships neither abated their zeal, nor were depicted by them in such a formidable light as to repress the ardor of their friends in Europe, who, in the course of the following year, continued, by successive arrivals, to enlarge the population of Delaware and Pennsylvania.   A valuable addition, in particular, was derived soon after from a nu-

[1] In one of Penn's letters the Dutch and Swedish inhabitants of Delaware are thus described : — " They are a plain, strong, industrious people; who have made no great progress in culture; desiring rather to have enough, than plenty or traffic. As they are people proper and strong of body, so they have fine children, and almost every house full." Proud. The Dutch had one and the Swedes three meeting-houses for divine worship in the Delaware territory. Ibid.

[2] *Ante*, Book V., Chap. I.

merous emigration of German Quakers, who had been converted to this form of faith by the preaching of Penn and his associates, and whose well-timed removal from their native land enabled them to escape from the desolation of the Palatinate. The exemplary piety and virtue by which these German colonists were distinguished in America formed an agreeable sequel to the happy intervention of Providence by which they were thus seasonably snatched from the rage of a tyrant and the impending ruin of their native country. There arrived likewise at the same time, or shortly after, a number of emigrants from Holland, a country in which Penn had already preached and propagated his doctrines.[1]

Seeing his people thus gathering in numerous and increasing confluence around him, Penn hastened to bind them together by a practical application of the social compact which he had devised. Having distributed his territory into six counties, he summoned, at a place which received the name of Chester, the first provincial parliament, consisting of seventy-two delegates. [December, 1682.] Here, according to the *frame* that had been concerted in England, the freemen should have attended in their own persons. But both the sheriffs in their returns, and the inhabitants in petitions which they presented to the proprietary, affirmed that the fewness of the people, their inexperience in legislation, and the engrossing urgency of their domestic concerns, rendered it inexpedient for them to exercise their political privileges ; and expressed their desire that the deputies they had chosen might serve both for the council and the assembly, in the proportions of three from every county for the council, and nine from every county for the assembly. From the circumstances of the people, the session of this first provincial parliament was necessarily short ; but it was distinguished by measures of considerable importance. The proprietary having expressed his approbation of the suggestions that were conveyed to him, an *act of settlement* was framed, introducing a corresponding and permanent change into the provincial constitution. With this and a few other modifications, the municipal scheme that had previously been announced was solemnly recognized and accepted. An *act of union* was passed, annexing the Delaware territory to the province of Pennsylvania ; and the rank of naturalized British subjects was conferred on the Dutch, the Swedes, and all other foreigners within the boundaries of the province and territory. This arrangement, which, at the time, was both the effect and the cause of mutual harmony, unfortunately contained within itself the seeds of future dissension and discontent : for Penn held the Delaware territory, not by a grant from the crown, but by an assignation from the Duke of York ; and when the efficacy of such a title to convey municipal authority came to be questioned, the people reprobated with resentful blame the wanton rashness, as they deemed it, of erecting the system of their civil rights and liberties on a foundation so precarious. All the laws that had been concerted in England, together with nineteen others, were adopted and enacted by the assembly, which, in three days, closed a session no less remarkable for the extent and importance of its labors, than for the mutual confidence, good-will, and general harmony that prevailed among men so diversified by variety of race, habit, and religious opinion. All united in expressing gratitude and attachment to the proprietary ; the Swedes, in particular, deputing one of their number

---

[1] " In this [1682] and the two next succeeding years, arrived ships, with passengers or settlers, from London, Bristol, Ireland, Wales, Cheshire, Lancashire, Holland, Germany, &c., to the number of about fifty sail." Proud.

to assure him *that they would love, serve, and obey him with all they had, and that this was the best day they had ever seen.*[1]

Among the many praiseworthy features of the code of laws that was thus enacted for Pennsylvania and Delaware, we have already remarked the particular wisdom of the provision for educating every native-born colonist to some useful trade or employment. But the points on which this code most justly claims the praise of original excellence and enlightened humanity are its provisions for the administration of penal law. Nor was there any point on which its regulations have been more efficacious, or more productive of lasting and extensive benefit to mankind. It was reserved for Quaker wisdom to discover, and for Quaker patience and benevolence to demonstrate, that, in the treatment of criminals, justice and mercy were not inconsistent virtues, nor policy and humanity incompatible objects of pursuit. Only two capital crimes, treason and murder, were recognized by the Pennsylvanian code ; and, in all other cases, the reformation of the criminal was esteemed a duty not less imperative than the punishment of his offence. To this end, it was ordained that *all prisons should be workhouses*, where offenders might be reclaimed, by discipline and instruction, to habits of industry and morality, and political benefit educed from the performance of Christian duty. The institutions that resulted from this benevolent enterprise in legislation have reflected honor on Pennsylvania, and diffused their advantages extensively in America and Europe.[2] Notwithstanding the strict injunctions in the royal charter, neither the code of laws which was now established, nor the alteration and enlargement which it subsequently underwent, was ever submitted to royal revision.

No sooner was the assembly adjourned, than Penn hastened to Maryland to vindicate that part of its proceedings which was necessarily offensive to Lord Baltimore, and, if possible, negotiate with this nobleman an amicable adjustment of their respective territorial pretensions. But he seems, from the beginning, to have been aware that such a termination of the dispute was not to be expected ; and, notwithstanding the grateful and approving sentiments with which he must necessarily have contemplated Lord Baltimore's tolerant policy, and the protection which the Quakers had experienced from it in Maryland, he plainly regarded him with a prejudice and suspicion not very creditable to his own candor and moderation ; finding matter of evil surmise even in the demonstrations of honor and respect which he received from his brother proprietary.[3] Lord Baltimore relied on the priority and distinctness of his own title ; while Penn defended a later

---

[1] Oldmixon. Proud. Chalmers.

[2] The Americans have subsequently carried, in practical application, the system of prison discipline perhaps as near perfection as the necessary evil of this corrective instrument will admit. But a nobler principle, aiming directly at the prevention of those vices that taint and destroy communities, has been cultivated with admirable genius, benevolence, and success, in New England. This happy instrumentality has been greatly improved and developed by the generous labors, as well as illustrated and recommended by the excellent writings, of Doctors Tuckerman and Channing of Massachusetts. The compositions of Tuckerman — especially (though it is difficult to particularize, where all are admirable) his sermon, in 1834, at the ordination of Barnard and Gray, and his introduction to the American translation of Degerando's *Visitor of the Poor* — are literary works which every wise and good statesman must earnestly desire to see widely spread and rightly appreciated in his country. We are taught thus how the coexistence of riches and poverty in the same commonwealth, instead of proving a divisive principle, the nurse of vice, misery, and social anarchy or arbitrary government, may be rendered a principle of union, the nurse of virtue, happiness, and social order.

[3] In an account of their conference, which Penn transmitted to England, he says, "I met the proprietary of Maryland, attended suitably to his character, who took the occasion, by his civilities, to show me the greatness of his power." Proud.

and more indistinct grant, on a plea which was suggested to him by the Committee of Plantations in England, — that it had never been intended to confer on Lord Baltimore any other territory but such as was inhabited by savages only, at the date of his charter ; and that the language of his charter was therefore inconsistent with its intendment, in so far as it seemed to authorize his claim to any part of the region previously colonized by the Swedes or the Dutch. Each of the competitors tenaciously adhered to his interest in property, which, with more or less reason, he considered his own ; and neither could suggest any mode of adjustment, save a total relinquishment of the other's pretensions. To avoid the necessity of recurring again to this disagreeable controversy, we may here so far anticipate the pace of events as to remark, that it was protracted for some years without the slightest approach to mutual accommodation ; that King Charles, to whom both parties complained, vainly endeavoured to prevail with the one or the other to yield ; and that James the Second, soon after his accession to the throne, caused an act of council to be issued for terminating the dispute by dividing the subject-matter of it equally between them. By this arrangement, which had more of equitable show than of substantial justice, Penn obtained the whole of the Swedish and Dutch settlements, and, in effect, preserved all that he or the Duke of York had ever been in possession of. These districts, annexed to his original acquisition, received the name of *the Three Lower Counties*, or *the Territories of Delaware*, in contradistinction to the remainder of the united domain, which was termed the Three Upper Counties, or Province of Pennsylvania.[1]

This busy year was not yet to close without an important and memorable scene, in which the character of Penn appears in a very different light from that which his controversy with Lord Baltimore reflects on it. The commissioners who accompanied the first detachment of emigrants had, in compliance with the proprietary's instructions, negotiated a treaty with the neighbouring Indian tribes, for the purchase of the lands which the colonists were to occupy, and for the assurance of perpetual friendship and peace between the two races of people. The time appointed for the ratification of this treaty now arrived ; and, at a spot where subsequently arose Kensington, one of the suburbs of Philadelphia, the Indian sachems, at the head of their assembled warriors, awaited in arms the approach of a Quaker deputation. To this scene William Penn repaired, at the head of an unarmed train of his sectarian associates, carrying various articles of merchandise, which, on their approach to the sachems, were spread on the ground. Distinguished from his followers by no other external badge than a sash of blue silk, and holding in his hand a roll of parchment that contained the confirmation of the treaty, Penn exchanged salutations with the Indians, and, taking his station under an elm-tree,[2] addressed them with the assistance of an interpreter. He assured them that the Great Spirit, who cre-

---

[1] Proud. Chalmers.

[2] This tree was long regarded with universal respect. During the war of independence, Lieutenant-Colonel Simcoe, who commanded a British force stationed at Kensington, when his soldiers were cutting down all the trees around them for firewood, placed a sentinel under Penn's elm to guard it from injury, — a singular tribute from a man who was engaged in violating the very principles of equity and peace of which the object of his consideration was respected as a memorial, and probably intended as a grateful compliment to the American Quakers, for supporting British tyranny against the liberties of their country. In 1810, the tree was blown down ; and a large portion of it was then conveyed to the seat of the representative of the Penn family at Stoke, near Windsor, in England, where, in 1828, I saw it in a state of complete preservation.

ated all men, and beheld the thoughts of every heart, knew that he and
his people sincerely desired to live in friendship and a perpetual commerce
of good offices with the Indians.   It was not the custom of his friends,
he said, to use hostile weapons against their fellow-creatures, and for this
reason they came to the conference unarmed.   Their intention was not to
do injury, and so provoke the Great Spirit, but to do good ; and in this
and every transaction with their Indian neighbours, to consider the advantage of both races of people as inseparable, and to proceed with all open-
ness, brotherhood, and love.   Having read, from the parchment record, the
conditions of the purchase, and the articles of compact, by which it was
agreed that all disputes between the colonists and the Indians should be adjusted by arbitrators mutually chosen, he delivered to the sachems the stipulated price,[1] and farther desired their acceptance, as a friendly gift, of the
additional articles of merchandise that were spread before them.   He then
invited them to consider the land which he had purchased as still common
to the two races, and freely to use its resources whenever they might have
occasion for them.[2]   He added, " that he would not do *as the Marylanders
did*, that is, call them children or brothers only ; for often parents were apt
to whip their children too severely, and brothers sometimes would differ ;
neither would he compare the friendship between him and them to a chain,
for the rain might sometimes rust it, or a tree might fall and break it ; but
he should consider them as the same flesh and blood with *the Christians*,
and the same as if one man's body were to be divided into two parts."
He concluded by presenting the parchment to the sachems, and requesting,
that, for the information of their posterity, they would cause it to be carefully preserved for three generations.   The Indians cordially acceded to these
propositions, and solemnly pledged themselves to live in love with William
Penn and his children as long as the sun and moon should endure.[3]

Thus was conducted a treaty of which Voltaire has remarked, with more
sarcasm than truth or propriety, that it was the only one between the Christians and the Indians that was not ratified by an oath, and that never was
broken.   Assuredly, no ceremonial altogether resembling the legal formula
of a Christian oath was employed by either of the contracting parties ; but
it is not easy to distinguish the solemn appeal that was made to the omnis-
cience and vindictive justice of a Supreme Being from the substantial interposition of a sacramental pledge ; nor would it be easy to cite another
treaty between the Europeans and the Indians in which such a pledge was
expressed with more or even with equal distinctness and formality.   In one
respect, indeed, the forbearance of Penn on this occasion to advert to
Christianity otherwise than as a mere nominative distinction may have contributed to the cordiality with which his propositions were received.   He
sedulously forbore every allusion to distinctive peculiarities or offensive
truths ; and in addressing men whom he considered as benighted heathens,[4]

---

[1] What this price amounted to has nowhere been recorded.   Penn, writing in the following year to some friends in England, represents it as *dear ;* and adds, " He will deserve the
name of wise that outwits them (the Indians) in any treaty about a thing they understand."
Proud.
[2] The same liberality was shown by the colonists of New England, where, as we learn from
Dr. Dwight, " the Indians were always considered as having a right to dwell and to hunt
within the lands which they had sold."   *Travels in New England*, &c.
[3] Oldmixon.   Proud.   Clarkson.
[4] In one of his letters to friends in England, he says of the Indians: " These poor people are
under a dark night in things relating to religion."   Proud.   The following adventure was
communicated by Penn himself to Oldmixon.   He was visiting an Indian sachem, and had

he descended to adopt their religious nomenclature, and more than insinuated that the Great Spirit of the Indians and the True God of the Christians were not different, but the same. But a much more respectable peculiarity of Quakerism than abstinence from oaths formed the most remarkable feature in this treaty with the Indians, and mainly contributed to insure its durability. Few instances have been recorded of greater magnanimity than was evinced in the explicit declaration of a race of civilized men, surrounded by a nation of warlike barbarians, that they renounced all the advantage of superior military skill, and even disclaimed the employment of every weapon of violence for the defence of their lives or the redress of their wrongs ; trusting the safety of their persons and possessions against human ferocity and cupidity to the dominion of God over the hearts of his rational creatures, and relying on his willingness to signalize this dominion in the protection of all who would exclusively rely on it.

The singular exemplification of Christian character in this respect, by the Pennsylvanian Quakers, was attended with an exemption no less singular from those contentions and calamities which Indian neighbourhood entailed on every other description of European colonists. The intentional injury of a Quaker by an Indian is an event almost, if not altogether, unknown in Pennsylvanian, and very rare in all American history. The probity of dealing, and courtesy of deportment, by which the Quakers generally endeavoured to maintain this good understanding, were aided by the distinctions of dress and manners by which the members of their society were visibly segregated from other men, and thus exempted, as a peculiar or separate tribe, from responsibility for the actions, or concern in the quarrels, of their countrymen. The inhabitants of many of the other colonies were no less distinguished than the Quakers for the justice and good faith that characterized their transactions with the Indians ; and the Catholic inhabitants of Maryland are said, in addition, to have graced these estimable qualities with the most conciliating demeanour. Yet none were able to obtain an entire exemption from Indian hostility, or to refrain from retaliatory warfare. The people of Maryland were sometimes involved in the indiscriminate rage with which certain of the Indian tribes pursued the hostilities they had commenced against the colonists of Virginia. But whatever animosity the Indians might conceive against the European neighbours of the Pennsylvanians, or even against Pennsylvanian colonists who did not belong to the Quaker society, they never failed to discriminate the followers of Penn, or *children of Onas*[1] (which was the denomination they gave to the Quakers), as persons whom it was impossible for them to include within the pale of legitimate warfare.

The friendship that was created by Penn's treaty between the province and the Indians, refreshed by successive acts of courtesy and humanity, endured for about sixty years, and was never seriously interrupted till near the close of the political supremacy of the Quakers in Pennsylvania. No feature in the manners of the Quakers contributed more efficiently to guard

---

retired for the night, when a young woman, the sachem's daughter, approaching his bed, lay down beside him. Penn was much shocked; but, unwilling to offend by rejecting an intended compliment, he lay still without taking any notice of her, till she thought proper to return to her own couch. A New England patriarch, in such circumstances, would probably have excited the enmity of the whole Indian tribe by his expressions of displeasure and reprobation.

[1] *Onas*, in the Indian tongue, signifies a pen. It came to be the Indian appellation of the governors of Pennsylvania, as *Corlear* was of the governors of New York. Proud.

them against Indian ferocity, than their rigid abstinence not merely from the use, but even from the possession, of offensive weapons,[1] enforced by their conviction of the sufficiency of divine aid, and their respect to the Scriptural threat, that all who take the sword shall perish by it. It was a different feature of Christian character that was exhibited by the Puritan colonists of New England in *their* intercourse with the Indians. They felt less indulgence for the frailty of the savages, than concern for their spiritual blindness, and abhorrence of their idolatrous superstition; they displayed less meekness of wisdom than the Quakers, but more of active zeal and missionary ardor. The Puritans were most concerned to promote the religious interests of the Indians; the Quakers, to gain their good-will. The Puritans converted a number of their heathen neighbours; the Quakers conciliated them all. It was unfortunate for the colonists of New England, that, asserting the lawfulness of defensive war, they were surrounded by numerous bold and warlike tribes, stimulated to acts of aggression, at first by their own ferocity and jealousy, and latterly by the intrigues of the French. It was a happy contingency for the planters of Pennsylvania, that the Indian tribes around them were inconsiderable in number, and either belonged to the confederacy or were subject to the influence of *the Five Nations*,[2] who were themselves in alliance with the sister colony of New York.

Nothing can be more exaggerated or inapplicable than the encomiums which numerous writers have bestowed on this celebrated transaction between Penn and the Indians. They have, with unhappy partiality, selected as the chief, and frequently the sole, object of commendation, the supposed originality of the design of buying the land from the savages, instead of appropriating it by fraud or force, — which last they represent as the only methods of acquisition that had been employed by the predecessors of Penn in the colonization of North America.[3] This is at once to reproach all the other founders of civilized society in North America with injustice and usurpation; to compliment the Indians with the gratuitous supposition that only bare justice on the part of the colonists was requisite to the preservation of peace between the two races; and to ascribe to Penn a merit which assuredly did not belong to him, and which he himself (though by no means deficient in self-complacency) has expressly disclaimed. The example of that equitable consideration of the rights of the native owners of the soil, which has been supposed to have originated with him, was first exhibited by the planters of New England, whose deeds of conveyance

[1] Herodotus (Book IV.) relates of a Scythian tribe, called the Argippæans, that "No man offers violence to this people; for they are accounted sacred, and *have no warlike weapon among them.*" These Scythian Quakers appear also to have studied an observable peculiarity of exterior, by eradicating all the hair from their bodies. Herodotus, indeed, represents them as born without hair; but we know that the same opinion was long, though erroneously, entertained with regard to the aborigines of America.

[2] Oldmixon. Chalmers.

[3] The Abbé Raynal declares, that Penn, by purchasing a conveyance from the Indians, in addition to his charter from the king of England, "is entitled to the glory of having given an example of moderation and justice in America, never so much as thought of before by the Europeans." Noble, in his *Continuation of Granger*, says, "He occupied his domains by actual bargain and sale with the Indians. This fact does him infinite honor. Penn has thus taught us to respect the lives and properties of the most unenlightened nations." It would be easy to multiply similar quotations. Even Mr. Clarkson, who acknowledges that Lord Baltimore, at least, preceded Penn in this act of justice, cannot refrain from complimenting Penn for soaring, in this instance, "above the prejudices and customs of his time." The most modest and moderate account of Penn's treaty which I have seen is that which claims Mr. Dillwyn (See Note XXVI., at the end of the volume) for its author.

from the Indians were earlier by half a century than his ; and was successively repeated by the planters of Maryland, Carolina, New York, and New Jersey, before the province of Pennsylvania had a name.   Penn was introduced to an acquaintance with American colonization by succeeding to the management of New Jersey, in which Berkeley and Carteret had already established this equitable practice ; and his own conformity to it in Pennsylvania was expressly recommended to him by Bishop Compton (whose interference we have remarked in the composition of the charter), and was publicly ascribed by himself to the counsels of that prelate.[1]

The continual arrival of vessels, transporting settlers to the colony from all parts of the British dominions, afforded frequent occasion to Penn for the exercise of the agreeable labor of surveying his territories, and appropriating to the purchasers their respective allotments of land. [1683.]   One of these allotments, consisting of a thousand acres, was a gift from the proprietary to his friend, George Fox, and formed the only landed estate which this venerable founder of Quakerism ever possessed.[2]   The greater number of the emigrants still continued to be Quakers, with the addition of some other Dissenters, withdrawing from the severities of persecution and the contagion of European vices ; and their behaviour in the colony corresponding with the noble motives that conducted them to it,[3] the domains of Penn exhibited a happy and animated scene of active industry, devotional exercise, and thankful enjoyment of civil and religious liberty. It appeared, however, that some worthless persons had already intruded themselves among the more respectable settlers ; and three men, who were now brought to trial and convicted of coining adulterated money, gave occasion to the first practical display of the mildness of Pennsylvanian justice.

Shortly before this judicial proceeding, the second convocation of the legislative assembly of Pennsylvania and Delaware had taken place. [March, 1683.]   In this assembly some new laws were passed, and certain anomalies in legislation were broached. It was proposed that all young men should be compelled by law to marry before a certain age ; and that no inhabitant of the province should be permitted to have more than two suits of clothes, one for summer and the other for winter ; but these propositions were, very properly, rejected. More wisdom was displayed in an ordinance which abrogated the common law with regard to the descent of lands, and enacted, that, in the succession of children to a father dying intestate, the eldest son should have no farther preference than a double share. However consonant it might be to feudal principles to bestow the fief undiminished upon the son who was first able to defend it, this policy was manifestly unsuitable to colonists, who, having a vast wilderness to cultivate, were in prudence obliged to multiply the incentives to exertion by an extensive diffusion of interest and property in the soil. An impost upon goods imported and exported was voted to the proprietary,[4] who acknowl-

---

[1] In a letter from Penn to the Lords of the Committee of Trade and Plantations in England (in 1683), he declares, that " I have followed the Bishop of London's counsel, by buying, and not taking away, the natives' land." Proud. This letter is also printed by Chalmers. Mr. Clarkson refers to it as containing Penn's statement of his controversy with Lord Baltimore, but has not thought that the credit of Penn would be advanced by its republication. It consists chiefly of an elaborate attempt to vindicate his own pretensions to the Delaware territory, and to interest the Lords of Trade to support them against Lord Baltimore's claims. Hence, perhaps, the readiness he evinces to compliment the Bishop of London.
[2] Fox disposed of this estate by his will. But he never was in Pennsylvania.
[3] See Note XXIX., at the end of the volume.
[4] This seems to refute the allegation of Dr. Franklin, in his *Historical Review of the Con-*

edged the kindness of the assembly, but wisely and liberally remitted the proposed burden on the province and the traders who resorted to it.   But the most important business transacted in this session was an alteration in the constitution of the State, which, unquestionably, from whatever cause, underwent in its infancy a fluctuation almost, if not altogether, unexampled in the history of the other colonial establishments.   William Penn having demanded of the members of council and assembly, "whether they desired to preserve his first charter, or to obtain a new one," they unanimously adopted the latter part of the alternative ; and with the assistance of a committee of these bodies, a new frame or charter was forthwith prepared. The chief purpose of this transaction seems to have been to legalize (according to Penn's ideas) the alteration introduced by the *act of settlement* passed by the prior assembly.   It was accordingly now provided, by a charter emanating from the proprietary, that the provincial council should consist of eighteen persons, three from each county, and the assembly of thirty-six, by whom, in conjunction with the governor, all laws were to be made and public affairs conducted.   But still no laws could be proposed in the assembly, except such as had been considered and prepared by the governor and council.   The only change in the distribution of power that was produced by this new charter was, that the governor, with his treble vote, necessarily possessed more control in a council of eighteen, than by the original frame he could have enjoyed in a council of seventy-two members.   The interests of freedom were, however, promoted by a grant, to all the inhabitants of the province, of unlimited liberty to hunt in uninclosed lands and to fish in all waters, " that they may be accommodated with such food and sustenance as God in his providence hath freely afforded " ;[1] and aliens were encouraged by a provision, that, in case of their dying without having been previously naturalized, their lands should, nevertheless, descend to their heirs.   The new charter was thankfully accepted by the representatives of the people, who closed their second assembly with expressions of undiminished attachment to the proprietary.

This assembly was held at the infant city of Philadelphia.   Soon after his arrival in the province, Penn had selected a commodious situation, between the rivers Schuylkill and Delaware, for the erection of the metropolis of Pennsylvania ; and, having regulated the model of the future city by a map,[2] he bestowed on it a name expressive of that brotherly love which he hoped would ever characterize its inhabitants.   Many of the streets he distinguished by appellations descriptive of the peculiar forest-trees that were cut down to make room for them, and which still continue to commemorate the sylvan original of the place.   The progress of the buildings of Philadelphia was a favorite object of his care, and advanced with such rapidity, that, in less than a year from its commencement, the in-

---

stitution of Pennsylvania, that "Penn prevailed with his first colonists to submit to his quit-rents, by holding out the delusive hope that they would supersede all public impositions for the support of government."

[1] This specification of the legitimate objects of hunting and fishing was probably intended to obviate the appearance of Quaker sanction of the pastime of the chase.   Sanguinary sports have always been deemed utterly repugnant to Quakerism.   Yet, at a later period, a Pennsylvanian Quaker was celebrated for possessing the only pack of hounds existing at the time in North America.   Cobbett's *Year's Residence in the United States.*

[2] In the *Connection of the History of the Old and New Testament,* by Dean Prideaux, there is a plan or model of the city of ancient Babylon.   "Much according to this model," says the dean, "hath William Penn, the Quaker, laid out the ground for his city of Philadelphia, in Pennsylvania ; and were it all built according to that design, it would be the fairest and best city in all America, and not much behind any other in the whole world."

habitants of a hundred substantial houses beheld [1684] from these structures of civilized life the caves whose rude shelter they had so recently
occupied ; and in the course of the following year the population of the
city amounted to two thousand five hundred persons.[1]

The remainder of the time spent by the proprietary, in his first visit to
his colony, was employed in conducting his controversy with Lord Baltimore ; in extending his treaties with the Indian tribes, to whom his presents
from time to time amounted in value to several thousand pounds ; in acting
as a minister among the Quaker colonists, and arranging the frame of their
sectarian practice and discipline ; and in impelling and directing the progress
of his favorite city of Philadelphia. He saw his religious society and
principles established in a land where they were likely to take a firm and
vigorous root and expand with unbounded freedom ; and institutions rising
around him that promised to illustrate his name with a lasting and honorable renown. In fine, he beheld the people who acknowledged his supremacy happy and prosperous, and seemed himself to enjoy his transatlantic retirement.[2] The only subjects of trouble or disappointment, which his
colonial project had yet produced, were, his dispute with Lord Baltimore,
and the failure of his efforts to guard the Indians from that destructive
vice which the vicinity of Europeans has always contributed to diffuse among
them. A law was passed against supplying those savages with spirituous
liquors ; but the practice had been introduced by the colonists of Delaware
long before Penn's arrival, and his attempts to suppress it proved ineffectual. The Europeans acknowledged the cruelty and injustice of this
traffic, and the Indians confessed their experience of its baneful effects ;
but neither could be persuaded to desist from it. It was attended with
the additional evil of confirming the Indians in their roving habits of life and
distaste for the discipline of civilization ; as the peltry they acquired in
hunting was the only commodity they were able to exchange with the colonists for rum and brandy.[3] The more valuable possessions and advantages
by which the colonists were distinguished were either lightly esteemed by
the Indians, or reckoned unworthy of the constant toil that was required to
procure them. In answer to the advice of the Europeans, that they should
betake themselves to a life of regular industry, one of the Indians begged to
hear some satisfactory reason *why he should labor hard all his days to make
his children idle all theirs.*[4]

In the midst of a scene of felicity as unmixed, perhaps, as any society
of human beings ever exhibited, Penn resolved upon returning to England,
in order to fortify, by personal solicitation, the interest which he possessed
at the English court, and which he was desirous to employ in furtherance
of his suit with Lord Baltimore, as well as for the relief of a number of his
Quaker brethren who were suffering in the parent state from an increased

---

[1] Oldmixon. Proud. Chalmers. Clarkson.

[2] In a letter to a friend in Engalnd, he says, "O, how sweet is the quiet of these parts,
free from the anxious and troublesome *solicitations*, hurries, and perplexities of *woful Europe ;*
and God will thin her ; the day hastens upon her." Proud.

[3] "An Indian," says Charlevoix, "who has once tasted brandy, never after applies himself
to fishing or agriculture. He thinks only of amassing furs in order to purchase the means of
intoxication."

[4] Oldmixon. Proud. S. Smith. "The Indians have a sovereign contempt for whatever is
not necessary, — that is, for the very things which we hold in the greatest estimation." Charlevoix. This is too broad an assertion. Proud, the Quaker, in one page compliments the Indians
for their stoical indifference to all finery whatever ; and in the very next condemns their
childish partiality for finery of apparel.

strictness in the execution of the penal laws against Nonconformists.[1]   In
preparation for this measure, he intrusted the administration of his proprietary functions to the provincial council, of which he appointed Thomas
Lloyd, a Quaker, to be president, and his own kinsman, Markham, to be
secretary ; and committed the distribution of justice, in conformity with
the existing laws, to Nicholas Moore and four other planters, whom he
constituted the provincial judges. [June, 1684.]   On the eve of his departure, and having already embarked, he addressed to Lloyd, and others
of his more intimate associates, a valedictory letter, which he desired them
to communicate to all his friends in Pennsylvania and Delaware.   " Dear
friends," he declared, " my love and my life is to you and with you ; and
no water can quench it, nor distance wear it out or bring it to an end.   I
have been with you, cared over you, and served you with unfeigned love ;
and you are beloved of me and dear to me beyond utterance.   I bless you
in the name and power of the Lord ; and may God bless you with his
righteousness, peace, and plenty, all the land over.   O, that you would eye
him in all, through all, and above all the works of your hands ! "   After ad-
monishing those to whom he committed the office of magistracy to consider
it as a sacred function and heavenly trust, he apostrophized his favorite city
with this votive benediction : — " And thou, Philadelphia, the virgin settlement of this province, named before thou wert born, what love, what care,
what service, and what travail has there been to bring thee forth, and preserve thee from such as would abuse and defile thee ! O, that thou mayest
be kept from the evil that would overwhelm thee ! that, faithful to the God
of thy mercies in the life of righteousness, thou mayest be preserved to the
end !   My soul prays to God for thee, that thou mayest stand in the day
of trial, that thy children may be blest of the Lord, and thy people saved
by his power.   My love to thee has been great, and the remembrance
of thee affects mine heart and mine eyes.   The God of eternal strength
keep and preserve thee to his glory and thy peace ! "   " So, dear friends,"
he thus concluded, " my love again salutes you all, wishing that grace,
mercy, and peace, with all temporal blessings, may abound richly among
you : — So says, so prays, your friend and lover in the truth, William
Penn."

At the period of the proprietary's departure from the province, Philadelphia already contained three hundred houses, and the population of Pennsylvania amounted altogether to six thousand souls.[2] Of the increase which
the population of the Delaware territory had undergone no memorial has
been preserved.

---

[1] The unfortunate consequences that attended Penn's withdrawment at this period from the
quiet of America, to plunge again into the *solicitations of woful Europe,* have rendered the
cause of this step a subject of some importance.   Oldmixon, who derived his information from
Penn himself, says, that he was determined, much against his will, to return, by tidings of the
persecution of the Quakers and other Dissenters in England ; and that " he knew he had
an interest in the court of England, and was willing to emp_oy it for the safety, ease, and welfare of his friends."   But Proud, who is by far the best authority on points of early Pennsylvanian history, declares that " the dispute between him and the Lord Baltimore before-
mentioned was what mainly occasioned Penn's return to England."   In a letter written
shortly after his arrival in England, Penn says that " he had seen the king and the Duke
of York.   They and their nobles had been very kind to him, and he hoped the Lord would
make way for him in their hearts to serve his suffering people, as also his own interest as it
related to his American concerns."   Clarkson.
[2] Oldmixon. Proud.

CHAPTER II.

Penn's Favor at the Court of James the Second. — Dissensions among the Colonists — their Disagreement with Penn about his Quitrents. — He appoints five Commissioners of State. — Rumor of an Indian Conspiracy. — Penn dissatisfied with his Commissioners — appoints Blackwell Deputy-Governor. — Arbitrary Conduct of Blackwell. — Displeasure of the Assembly. — Dissension between the People of Delaware and Pennsylvania. — Delaware obtains a separate Executive Government. — George Keith's Schism in Pennsylvania. — Penn deprived of his Authority by King William. — Fletcher appointed Governor. — Penn's Authority restored. — Third Frame of Government. — Quaker Accession to War. — Penn's second Visit to his Colony. — Sentiments and Conduct of the Quakers relative to Negro Slavery. — Renewal of the Disputes between Delaware and Pennsylvania. — Fourth and last Frame of Government. — Penn returns to England. — Union of Pennsylvania and Delaware dissolved. — Complaints of the Assembly against Penn. — Misconduct of Governor Evans. — He is superseded by Gookin. — Penn's Remonstrance to his People. — State of Pennsylvania and Delaware at the Close of the Seventeenth Century.

BIDDING adieu to the peaceful scene of his infant commonwealth, Penn transferred his presence and activity to the very dissimilar theatre of the court of England. [1685.] Here the interest which he possessed was soon increased to such a degree, by the advancement of his patron and his father's friend, the Duke of York, to the throne, that, in the hope of employing it to his own advantage and to the general promotion of religious liberty,[1] he abandoned all thoughts of returning to America, and continued to reside in the neighbourhood, and even to employ himself in the service of the court, as long as James the Second was permitted to wear the crown ; — a policy, which, in the sequel, proved extremely prejudicial to his reputation in England and to his interest in America. The first fruit of his enhanced influence at court was the adjudication that terminated his controversy with Lord Baltimore and secured to him the most valuable portion of the Delaware territory.[2] Fruits of a more liberal description illustrated his successful efforts to procure a suspension of the legal severities to which the members of his own religious society were exposed, and for the discontinuance of which he had the satisfaction of presenting an address of thanks to the king from all the Quakers in England.[3]

---

[1] The address of the Quakers of England to James the Second, on his accession to the throne, was conceived in these brief and simple terms : " We are come to testify our sorrow for the death of our good friend Charles, and our joy for thy being made our governor. We are told thou art not of the persuasion of the church of England, no more than we ; wherefore we hope thou wilt grant us the same liberty which thou allowest to thyself, which doing, we wish thee all manner of happiness." And yet these Quakers perfectly well knew that the prince whom they thus addressed was, at the time, and had for several years before been, waging a savage persecution against the people of Scotland for their dissent from a church from which he himself still more widely dissented.

[2] This adjudication was not so distinct as to prevent much subsequent dispute respecting the precise boundaries between Delaware and Maryland, which continued to distract the inhabitants on the borders of these provinces, till it was adjusted in 1750, by a decree pronounced in Chancery by Lord Hardwicke. Chalmers. Vesey's *Reports*. This decree was not finally executed till the year 1762, when " the inhabitants on the Pennsylvanian side, near the boundary, agreed to employ two ingenious English mathematicians, after their return from the Cape of Good Hope (where they had been to observe the transit of Venus in 1761), finally to settle or make out the same ; which was accordingly performed by them ; and stone pillars erected, to render the same more durably conspicuous." Proud.

Nothing was more common, for a long time, in the American provinces, than disputes arising from uncertain boundaries. A dispute of this nature between the townships of Lyme and New London, in New England, during the seventeenth century, was decided by a solemn pugilistic combat between four champions chosen by the inhabitants of the two places. Dwight's *Travels*.

[3] Proud. The civic company of *cooks* in London followed the example of the Quakers in thanking the king for his declaration of indulgence, by an address (published in the *London*

This year was signalized by an attempt, that originated with the annual meeting of the Quaker society at Burlington, in New Jersey, to communicate the knowledge (such knowledge as the teachers themselves possessed) of Christian truth to the Indians. These savages readily acceded to the conferences that were proposed to them, and listened with their usual gravity and decorum to the first body of missionaries who, in professing to obey the divine command to *teach and baptize* all nations, ever ventured to teach that baptism was not an ordinance of Christian appointment. Of the particular communications between the Quaker teachers and the Indians no account has been preserved ; but the result, as reported by a Quaker historian, was, that the Indians in general acknowledged at the time that what they heard was very wise, weighty, and true, — and never afterwards thought farther about it.[1] The first successful attempts to evangelize the Indian inhabitants of New Jersey, Delaware, and Pennsylvania were not made till towards the middle of the following century, when this work was undertaken by the celebrated David Brainerd, of New England, and by certain Moravians who had emigrated from Germany. Indian converts to Christianity have been gained in America by Catholics, Puritans, and Moravians ; but no instance has been recorded of the religious conversion of an Indian by Quakers.

Meanwhile, the emigration from England to Pennsylvania continued to flow with undiminished current ; the stimulus, that had been previously afforded by the rigors of ecclesiastical law, being amply supplied by the dislike and suspicion with which the king's civil policy was regarded, — by the accounts which were circulated of the prosperity enjoyed by the colonists of this province, — and by the common belief that Penn's interest with the king would protect its liberties from the general wreck in which royal tyranny had involved the constitutions of the other American colonies.[2] But this increase in the numbers of his colonists was now the sole satisfaction that they were to afford to the proprietary ; and his connection with them henceforward was clouded by disappointment, and embittered by mutual dispute. It was but a few months after his departure from the province, that a spirit of discord began to manifest itself among the planters. Moore, the chief justice, and Robinson, the clerk of the provincial court, neither of whom belonged to the Quaker society, had rendered themselves disagreeable to the leading persons of this persuasion in the colony. The first was impeached by the assembly of high crimes and misdemeanours, — and for refusing to answer the charge was suspended from his functions by the council ; while a very disproportioned censure was passed on the other, who, for what was deemed contemptuous behaviour in answering the questions of the assembly, was not only deprived of his liberty, but voted " a public enemy to the province and territories." Of the charges against Moore not a trace has been preserved ; but it is manifest that Penn considered them frivolous or unfounded. In vain he wrote to the authors of these measures,[3] entreating them to moderate their tempers, and forbear

---

Gazette) in which they protested that this act of power " resembles the Almighty's manna, which suited every man's palate ; and that men's different gustos may as well be forced, as their different apprehensions about religion."

[1] Proud.

[2] In 1685, the number of inhabitants of Pennsylvania was seven thousand. Warden.

[3] " For the love of God, me, and the poor country," he says in one of these letters, " be not so *governmentish*, so noisy and open in your dissatisfactions. Some folks love *hunting* in government itself." Proud.

from the indulgence of animosities so discreditable to the colony ; to value *themselves* a little less, and to honor other men a little more. The assembly answered by professions of the highest reverence for himself, accompanied by entreaties (unfortunately ineffectual) that he would return to live among his people ; but declared withal that they thought fit " to humble that corrupt and aspiring minister of state, Nicholas Moore."

The correspondence between the proprietary and this body, as well as the council, assumed in its progress an increasingly unfriendly complexion. To other causes of displeasure were added reports of the increased consumption of spirituous liquors among the colonists, — the intemperance which they propagated among the Indians thus recoiling upon themselves ; and complaints of various abuses and extortions committed by the officers whom Penn had appointed to conduct the sales of his land. But nothing else mortified him so keenly as the difficulty he experienced in obtaining payment of his quitrents, and the reluctance that was shown to comply with, or even bestow any attention on, his applications for the arrears of this revenue. The people in general had rather submitted to than approved the imposition of quitrents ; and, though prospering in their circumstances, and conscious of the expenses that the proprietary had incurred for their advantage, they were as yet only beginning to reap the first fruits of the far greater expenses incurred by themselves in purchasing their possessions from him, and in transporting themselves and their families, servants, and substance to the province. Much labor and expense was yet wanting to render more than a small portion of their lands productive of advantage to them ; and the summons now addressed to them to pay quitrents for the whole, and for this purpose to surrender the first earnings of their own hazard, hardship, and toil, to be expended by their proprietary in a distant country, was a measure ill qualified to obtain their favorable regard, and which the very munificence of the proprietary, that rendered it the more urgently necessary on his part, had by no means prepared them to expect. Penn had hoped that the council to whom he delegated his proprietary functions would have spared him the humiliating necessity of descending to a personal solicitation of quitrents from his people. But, so far were the council from demonstrating such regard for his delicacy or his interest, that they would give him no assistance whatever in the prosecution of his unpopular demand, and even forbore to take any notice of the remonstrances which he addressed to them on the neglect of their duty. [1685.] Astonished and indignant to find himself treated in a manner which he deemed so unjust and unmerited, Penn was provoked to reproach his people in a letter which forms a melancholy contrast to the beautiful valediction with which he had taken his leave of them, scarcely two years before. [1686.] He complained that the provincial council neglected and slighted his communications ; that the labor which he religiously consecrated to his people's good was neither valued nor understood by them ; and that their conduct in other respects was so unwarrantable, as to have put it in his power more than once to annul the charter he had bestowed on them, if he had been disposed to take advantage of their ungrateful folly. He declared that he was suffering much embarrassment by the failure of the remittances he had expected from America, and that this was one of the causes of his detention in England. His quitrents, he insisted, ought then to amount, at the very least, to five hundred pounds a year ; but he could not obtain a penny of this income. " God is my witness," he protested, " I lie not. I am above six thousand pounds out of pocket more than ever I saw by the province ; and you may throw in my pains, cares, and hazard of life, and leaving of my family and friends to serve them." If this statement be perfectly accurate, we are to believe that he had already sold a million acres of land in the province, and devoted twenty thousand pounds (the stipulated price corresponding to sales of that extent) to the public service, besides the additional expenditure which he mentions of six thousand pounds.

The proprietary's remonstrance, which was more especially addressed to the provincial council, having proved as unavailing as his preceding applications, Penn determined to withdraw from that body the management of his interests and the administration of the executive power, which he had committed to it on his departure from the province. Expecting more acivity from fewer ministers, and more affection to his service from other men, he resolved to confine the executive power to five persons ; and, in order to mark his sense of the injurious treatment of an individual who possessed his friendship and esteem, he hesitated not to appoint Nicholas Moore one of the officers by whom this important function was to be exercised. To Lloyd, the former president of the council, and three other Quakers, in conjunction with Moore, he granted, accordingly, a warrant or deputation investing them with the administration of the proprietary authority under the title of *commissioners of state.* [December, 1686.] He commanded them, in the very first assembly that should be holden after their instalment in office, to abrogate, in the proprietary's name, every law that had been enacted during his absence. He required them heedfully to note and check any tendency to disorder, dispute, or collision of powers between the several organs of government, and, for this purpose, to permit no parleying or open conference between the council and the assembly, but to confine the one to the exercise of its privilege of proposing laws, and the other to a simple expression of assent or negation. He charged them to act with vigor in repressing vices, without respect of persons or persuasions, — adding, " Let not foolish pity rob justice of its due, and the people of proper examples. I know what malice and prejudice say ; but they move me not. I know how to allow for new colonies, though others do not." He advised them, before ever *letting their spirits into any affair,* to lift up their thoughts to the Almighty Being who is never far from any of his creatures, and to beseech from this only source of intelligence and virtue the communication of a good understanding and a temperate spirit. He recommended to them a diligent care of the proprietary's interest, and a watchful attention to the preservation of their own dignity. " I beseech you," he said, " draw not several ways ; have no cabals apart, nor reserves from one another ; treat with a mutual simplicity, an entire confidence in one another ; and if at any time you mistake, or misapprehend, or dissent from one another, let not that appear to the people : show your virtues, but conceal your infirmities ; this will make you awful and reverent with the people." " Love, forgive, help, and serve one another," he continued ; " and let the people learn by your example, as well as by your power, the happy life of concord." [1]

---

[1] Proud. In a letter to these commissioners, some time after, he tells them : — " They that live near to God will live far from themselves ; and, from the sense they have of his nearness and majesty, have a low opinion of themselves ; and out of that low and humble frame of spirit it is that true charity grows. O, that the people of my province felt this gracious qual-

The new arrangement proved more conducive than might reasonably be supposed to the peace of the province, which appears for some time to have sustained no other interruption than what arose from the rumor of a conspiracy of the Indians for a general massacre of the colonists. [1687.] In the midst of the consternation which this report excited, Caleb Pusey, a Quaker, volunteered to repair to the spot where the conspirators were said to have assembled in preparation for their bloody enterprise, — provided five other persons deputed by the council would consent to accompany him, and to appear, as he purposed to do, unarmed before the Indians. [1688.] Never was the dignity and utility of moral courage more signally displayed ; nor ever was this virtue more happily contrasted with that moral cowardice, which, united (as it frequently is) with animal spirit and personal bravery, would, on such an emergency, have inspired counsels equally dangerous and cruel. On the arrival of Pusey and his magnanimous associates at the spot to which they were directed, they found only an Indian prince with a small retinue engaged in their ordinary occupations. The prince, to whom they related the cause of their visit, informed the deputies that the Indians were indeed disappointed to find that the price of a recent occupation of land was not yet fully paid to them ; but that, having perfect confidence in the integrity of the English, they were by no means impatient : he protested that the story of the projected massacre was a wicked fabrication, and that some Indian women who had contributed to give it currency deserved to be burned alive. One of the deputies having reminded the prince that the Indians and the English were the creatures of the same God, and equally the objects of his impartial benevolence, which he manifested by sending dew from heaven alike on their lands, and urged that the two races ought therefore to love one another, — the prince replied, " What you have said is true ; and as God has given you corn, I would advise you to get it in, for we intend you no harm." This amicable assurance, repeated by the deputies to their friends, delivered the province from an apprehension that had spread general dismay.

But Penn was far from deriving the satisfaction which he had expected from his commissioners of state ; and his letters continued to repeat, though in a milder tone than before, his complaints of the detention of his quitrents, the neglect of his communications, and the disregard of his services. " *I believe I may say,*" was his expression at this period, " *I am one of the unhappiest proprietaries with one of the best people.*" [1] From the numerous apologies contained in these letters for his continued residence in England, and his protestations that he found attendance at court as burdensome and disagreeable as the state of a slave in Turkey, it would seem that the people of Pennsylvania regarded his absence from them with much dissatisfaction. At length, Lloyd and some of the other Quaker commissioners desiring that he would release them from their functions, Penn conceived that some farther change was necessary in the form of the provincial government ; and, having determined to commit his authority and his interests to the more active management of a single individual invested with the

---

ity abounding in them ! My work would then be done, and their praise and my joy unspeakably abound. Wherefore, in the name and fear of God, let all old sores be forgotten as well as forgiven." Ibid.

[1] " It is none of the endearingest considerations," he adds in the same letter, " that I have not had the present of a skin, or a pound of tobacco, since I came over." Proud. Yet Penn condemned the use of tobacco, and vainly endeavoured to persuade the Quakers to renounce it. Clarkson.

rank of deputy-governor, he selected for this purpose Captain John Blackwell, one of Cromwell's officers, who had married the daughter of General Lambert, and was residing at this time in New England. The consequences of this appointment were, effectually, the reverse in all respects of those which had resulted from the preceding one ; but, unfortunately, they were much more disagreeable and pernicious. Blackwell was highly esteemed by Penn, and he probably exerted himself more diligently than his predecessors in the executive authority had done to vindicate the patrimonial interest of the proprietary ; but he provoked the indignation and disgust of the people by arbitrary and illiberal conduct. " Rule the meek meekly," was the instruction of Penn to him ; " and those that will not be ruled, rule with authority." But meekness was no part of the disposition of Blackwell ; and violence and intrigue were the chief engines of his policy.[1] He commenced his administration by endeavouring, not without effect, to sow discord among the planters, and to overawe the timid by a display of power. But he had mistaken the real character of the people over whom he presided ; and was taught, by the issue of an obstinate struggle, that the profession of Quaker meekness and submission is by no means inconsistent with the exertion of inflexible firmness and determination. Finding that White, the individual who had given most displeasure to Penn, by urging the impeachment of Moore, was chosen a delegate to the assembly, he resolved to debar him from attendance there ; and for this purpose caused him to be thrown into prison on the most frivolous pretences. A writ of *habeas corpus* was procured in behalf of White ; but the execution of it was long impeded by the devices of Blackwell.

Other practices, no less iniquitous and tyrannical, were employed by him for disabling men whom he disliked or suspected from performing the functions of members of the provincial council. To give the assembly time to cool, after the commission of these outrages, he deferred the convocation of it as long as possible, and at last opened its session with a speech conceived in the most haughty and imperious strain. [March, 1689.] His predecessors in authority had not considered it expedient to comply with the proprietary's desire of abrogating all the laws enacted in his absence ; but this measure was now announced by the deputy-governor with an insolence that would have discredited a more acceptable communication. The first act of the assembly was a remonstrance against his arbitrary conduct ; and the utmost that his influence could accomplish with some of the members of this body was to prevail with them to absent themselves from its sittings. This miserable device had no other effect than to provoke the assembly to declare that the secession of those members was a treacherous desertion of the public service. They voted, at the same time, a series of resolutions, importing " that the proprietary's absence, as it may be to his disappointment, so it is extremely to the people's prejudice ; that, as to the project of abrogating all the laws, he has no right so to do, because every law is in force that has not been declared void by the king ; that, even with the consent of the freemen, the proprietary can make no laws to

---

[1] Penn appears to have been deceived on this occasion by a repute of which Blackwell proved to be totally undeserving. He apologized to the people of Pennsylvania for the unhappy consequences that resulted from his misplaced confidence, by stating that he had acted for the best, and had not selected Blackwell till he found it impossible to prevail with any Quaker to accept the office of deputy-governor ; yet, he added withal, " I must say, I fear this peevishness to some friends (Quakers) has not arisen out of the dust without occasion." Proud.

bind the province, except in the way prescribed by the charter ; and that, as it is desirable, so it is also to be hoped, that no laws of any other make will be imposed upon the people." After a vain struggle with an opposition thus resolutely conducted, Blackwell was compelled to abandon his office, and depart from the province, leaving the executive authority once more in the hands of the provincial council, of which the presidency was resumed by Thomas Lloyd.[1] [Dec., 1689.]

The ferment that was excited during Blackwell's administration, whatever evil influence it may have exercised on the tempers of the colonists, had not the effect of retarding even in the slightest degree the rapid pace with which their prosperity was advancing. On the contrary, a more vigorous spring seemed to have been imparted to the industry and general progress and improvement of the community, — as if the energy that was aroused by the strong provocation of public spirit had diffused its influence through every occupation and department of life. It was in the present year that the first institution for the education of youth was established in Pennsylvania. This was called *The Friends' Public School of Philadelphia* ; at the head of it was placed George Keith, a celebrated Quaker writer ; and it was subsequently incorporated and enlarged by charters from the proprietary.[2]

It had been happy for Penn, if he had sooner discovered how detrimental to all his interests his long absence from the colony and residence at the English court must inevitably prove. The revolution of the British government that occurred in the close of the preceding year abruptly destroyed that precarious favor of a tyrant, for the sake of which he had risked his popularity in England and his influence in Pennsylvania, and which infatuated his understanding to such a degree that he even continued to correspond with the fugitive monarch after his expulsion from the throne. No satisfactory evidence has ever been adduced to prove that he was personally engaged in the plots that were formed at this period for the restoration of James ; but as he voluntarily lingered in England for some time after the revolution was accomplished, and never transmitted any instruction for proclaiming William and Mary in Pennsylvania, it is not improbable that he looked with some expectation to the success of those attempts.[3] To return to America was soon after put out of his power, by the consequences of the general suspicion which his conduct excited in England. [1690.] He was compelled to give bail for his appearance before the privy council ; and though he more than once succeeded in justifying himself from the charges adduced against him, yet, finding that farther accusations continued to be preferred, and that a warrant at length was issued for committing him to prison, he thought proper to sequester himself from public view, and to

---

[1] Proud. *Modern Universal History.* Franklin's *Historical Review of the Constitution of Pennsylvania.* Chalmers.

[2] Proud. Chalmers.

[3] In a letter, written by him to his friends in Pennsylvania in January, 1689, he says, " Great revolutions have been of late in this land of your nativity, and *where they may period* the Lord knows." He adds, that " to improve my interest with King James for tender consciences " had been the main cause of his detention so long in England. Proud. From a letter of Leisler, who at this period acquired much celebrity at New York (*ante,* Book V., Chap. II.), to Bishop Burnet, it appears that he accounted Pennsylvania one of the strongholds of the Jacobites in America, and that a considerable number of this party were then retiring from the other provinces to Pennsylvania and New Jersey. Chalmers. Smollett asserts that Penn was an accomplice in Lord Preston's plot for the restoration of King James. Similar charges against Penn have been preferred by the historians Burnet and Ralph.

live in a state of concealment. His name was occasionally inserted in the proclamations for the apprehension of suspected persons, issued from time to time by the English ministers ; who were, however, too deeply engaged in more pressing and important affairs, to have leisure as yet to attend to the concerns of his Pennsylvanian sovereignty. During this retirement, his repose was invaded very disagreeably by tidings of factious disputes and dissensions among his people, and particularly by the rupture that took place between Pennsylvania and Delaware, and separated from each other two communities, for the conjunction of which he had labored with a zeal that outstripped his usual equity and moderation.

The increasing strength and importance of Pennsylvania had gradually excited the jealousy of the people of Delaware, who beheld with impatience their own more ancient settlement verging into comparative insignificance, as the mere fraction of a younger but more thriving community. The members deputed to the provincial council at Philadelphia from Delaware complained that they were deprived of a just share in the direction of public affairs, and attempted by intrigue to counterbalance the preponderance of their Pennsylvanian associates. Privately assembling, without the usual formality of an official summons, in the council-room, they assumed plenary possession of the executive functions vested in the whole body, and issued warrants for displacing a number of public officers, and appointing others to fill their places. [September, 1690.] This transaction was almost instantly declared illegal and void by a council more regularly convoked ; but the waters of strife had now broke forth, and could no longer be stayed. Penn, alarmed at these dissensions, sought to mediate between the parties, and desired them to make choice of any one of the three forms of executive administration which they had already successively tried. He was willing, he said, to invest the executive power either in the council, or in five commissioners, or in a deputy-governor ; and their choice would be determined by the recollection of which of these they had found the most impartial in the distribution of municipal functions and emoluments. [January, 1691.] The Pennsylvanians at once declared themselves in favor of a deputy-governor ; and, anticipating the proprietary's approbation of their wishes, desired Lloyd to undertake the duties of this office. The Delaware counsellors, on the contrary, protested against this choice, and declared their own preference of a board of commissioners. They refused to submit to the government of Lloyd, and, withdrawing from the council, returned to Delaware, where their countrymen were easily induced to approve and support their secession. In vain Lloyd endeavoured, by the most liberal and generous offers to the Delaware colonists, to prevail with them to submit to an administration which he had reluctantly assumed, in compliance with the urgent and unanimous desire of the Pennsylvanians ; they rejected all his overtures, and, countenanced by Colonel Markham, declared that they were determined to have an executive government for themselves distinct from the institutions of Pennsylvania. Stung with vexation and disappointment at this result, Penn was at first inclined to impute the blame of it to Lloyd ; but soon ascertaining how perfectly disinterested and well-meaning the conduct of this worthy man had been, he transferred his censure to the Delaware counsellors, and bitterly reproached them with selfish ambition and ingratitude. Hoping, however, by gratifying them in their present desire, to prevent the rupture from extending any farther, he granted separate commissions for the executive government of Pennsylvania and Delaware to Lloyd and Markham ; the functions of legislation still remaining united in a council and assembly common to the two settlements. [April, 1691.] By the friendly coöperation of Lloyd and Markham, this anomalous machinery of government was conducted with much greater harmony and success than the peculiarities of its structure, and the causes from which they arose, seemed at first to portend.[1]

The following year [1692] was signalized in a manner still more discreditable to the province and offensive to the proprietary, by a violent dissension among the Quakers of Pennsylvania. This affair has been represented, by the party that proved weakest in the struggle, as a purely ecclesiastical quarrel, wherein their adversaries, worsted in spiritual, had recourse to carnal weapons ; and by the stronger, as a political effervescence, which the power of the magistrate was properly employed to compose. The disturbance originated with George Keith, a native of Aberdeen, in Scotland, a man remarkably distinguished by the vigor and subtlety of his apprehension, by an insatiable appetite for controversy, a copious eloquence, a vehement temper, extreme sincerity, and entire deficiency of candor. To his religious associates he was recommended by his numerous writings in defence of their tenets, and more particularly endeared as the champion of their quarrel with the churches, ministers, and magistrates of New England, — a country, which, by a numerous body of the Quakers, was long regarded with a feeling to which it is difficult to give any other name than that of vindictive dislike. He had travelled in that country as a Quaker preacher ; and, having sharpened by personal controversy with the people a previous resentment of their well remembered persecution of his spiritual kinsmen, he accumulated against them a hoard of animosity, which all the prolixity of his publications was incapable of exhausting. With an animated strain of invective and vituperation, which was reckoned very *savory* by the Quakers as long as it was directed against their adversaries,[2] he condemned the government of New England for the severities inflicted by it heretofore upon enthusiasts, with whose extravagance, as well as whose sufferings, it appeared that he himself was too much inclined to sympathize. Even those Quakers, who were imbued with the moderate spirit which of late had been gaining on their society, and allaying the frenzy that produced such deplorable results in New England,[3] were flattered by publications which artfully turned the shame of Quakerism into its glory, and added the honors of martyrdom to the other evidences of its claim to the character of a revival of primitive Christianity.

The favor and esteem of his fellow-sectaries had recommended Keith first to the appointment of surveyor-general of East Jersey, and more recently to the presidency over the Quaker seminary of education established at Philadelphia. From real conviction, from an inveterate habit of

---

[1] Proud. Clarkson. Penn expressed no disapprobation whatever of the conduct of Markham, of whom Proud, indeed, reports, that " he had the proprietary's confidence and esteem till his death " ; — whence, perhaps, it may be inferred, that the real purpose of Markham, in placing himself at the head of the factious counsellors of Delaware, was to retain over them an influence propitious to the authority of the proprietary.

[2] On a retrospect of his character, however, after they themselves became his adversaries, the Quakers discovered, that, even before his schism with them, and even in his treatment of the people of New England, he had " had too much life in argument," had " exhibited an unbecoming vanity on victory thereby obtained by him over his opponents," and altogether conducted himself " in a very extravagant manner." Proud.

[3] *Ante*, Book II., Chap. III.

controversy, or from ambitious desire to gain a still higher eminence among the Quakers than he had already attained, he began at length to utter censures of various abuses and corruptions which appeared to him to have depraved the system of Quakerism in Pennsylvania. He complained that there was a great deal too much slackness in the execution of Quaker discipline, and that very loose and erroneous doctrine was taught by many of the Quaker preachers. He insisted, that, as the infliction and even the violent resistance of evil was incompatible with Christian meekness and brotherly love, no Quaker ought to be concerned in " the compelling part of government," and much less to retain negroes in a state of slavery. His censures had in some respects a substantial reality, and in others at least a reasonable show, of just application, that rendered them only the more irritating to the minds of those whom he disturbed without being able to convert. Supported by a respectable company of adherents, and particularly in some of his views by the German emigrants, who from the first had protested against negro slavery as a monstrous practical departure from pure Christianity, Keith encountered the opposition which his new doctrines received from the majority of the Quakers, with as much unbridled vehemence as he had displayed in his previous contests with their common enemies. Impetuous, uncharitable, and immoderate, his address savored more of attack than of instruction ; he seemed never to distinguish between dissent and hostility, nor between men and their failings.

A regular trial of strength ensued between the two parties in the Quaker society [April, 1692] ; and the adversaries of Keith, finding themselves supported by a numerical majority, published a *declaration or testimony of denial* against him. In this curious production they expressed their deep regret of " the tedious exercise and vexatious perplexity " which their late friend, George Keith, had brought upon them. " With mourning and lamentation do we say, — How is this mighty man fallen ! — How is his shield cast away ! — How shall it be told in Gath ! — Will not the daughters of the uncircumcised triumph ? " They proceeded to accuse him of uttering against them " such unsavory words and abusive language, as a person of common civility would loathe " ; and in particular of having audaciously declared to them on various occasions, " and upon small provocations, if any," that they were *fools, ignorant heathens, silly souls, rotten ranters,* and *Muggletonians,* " with other names of that infamous strain ; thereby, to our grief, foaming out his own shame." They charged him with slandering Quakerism, by affirming that it was too often a cloak of heresy and hypocrisy, and that more diabolical doctrine passed current among the Quakers than among any other description of Protestant professors. As the climax of his contumacy, they alleged, that, when they had *tenderly dealt* with him for his irreverent language and disorderly behaviour, he insultingly answered, *that he trampled their judgment under his feet as dirt* ;[1] and that he had since established a separate congregation, whose proceedings ren-

---

[1] These very words, long before addressed by William Penn to an English magistrate, who was in the act of committing him to Newgate for refusing to take an oath, had been hitherto current and respected among the Quakers, as importing no more than a magnanimous contempt or decent disdain. However deficient in meekness and courtesy, they were certainly much less so than a great deal of the contemporary language that was exchanged between many of the Quaker writers and their adversaries. One Bugg, who had been a Quaker, having about this time quarrelled with and deserted the sectarian society, maintained with it a literary warfare that tended more effectually to provoke the mirth than to promote the edification of mankind. I have seen an address to Bugg, from his original associates, in which they greeted him with numerous abusive allusions to the unsavoriness of his name.

dered the religious repute of the Quakers " a scorn to the profane and the song of the drunkard."

Keith, who had now collected around him a numerous concourse of partisans, whom he styled *Christian Quakers*, while he bestowed on all the rest of the Quaker society the opprobrious title of *apostates*, promptly replied to this declaration by an address which contained a defence of himself and his principles, and an illustration of the various acts of apostasy wherewith he reproached his adversaries. This publication presented so ludicrous a contrast between the sectarian professions and the magisterial conduct of the rulers of Pennsylvania, that these Quaker politicians were transported by the perusal of it beyond the restraint of their favorite virtue, and fully convinced that what had been hitherto regarded as a mere ecclesiastical dispute ought forthwith to be resented as a political quarrel. They declared, that, though a tender meekness should undoubtedly characterize their notice of offences committed against them in their capacity of Quakers, yet a magisterial sternness was no less incumbent upon them, in the visitation of offences that tended to " lessen the lawful authority of the magistracy in the view of *the baser sort of the people.*" Keith, the author of the address, and Bradford, the printer of it, were both (after an examination which the other magistrates refused to share with their Quaker brethren) committed to prison ; Bradford's printing-press was seized ; and both Keith and he were denounced, by proclamation, as seditious persons, and enemies of the royal authority in Pennsylvania. Bradford, who relied on the protection of English constitutional law, compelled his prosecutors to bring him to trial for the offences they laid to his charge ; but though he was acquitted by the verdict of a jury, he incurred great pecuniary loss, and found himself so much oppressed by the dislike of a powerful party, that he was compelled to remove his printing establishment from Pennsylvania.

Keith was arraigned shortly after, along with Francis Budd, another Quaker, for having, in a little work which was their joint production, defamed a Quaker magistrate, by describing him as *too high and imperious in worldly courts.* They were found guilty, and sentenced to pay a fine of five pounds.[1] Retiring soon after to England, Keith published an account of the whole proceedings against him, in a pamphlet which he entitled "*New England Spirit of Persecution transmitted to Pennsylvania, and the pretended Quaker found persecuting the true Quaker.*" So extensive was his influence, both in England and America, that for some time it was doubted whether he and his friends, or the party opposed to them, would succeed in eclipsing the others, and securing to themselves the exclusive possession of the Quaker name. But the career of Keith, as a Quaker, was suddenly abridged, and his influence in the society completely overthrown, by a consequence which neither he nor his opponents had anticipated at the commencement of their disputes. In the course of his labors in that wide field of controversy which the attacks of his various adversaries in Pennsylvania and New England spread before him, Keith succeeded (to his own satisfaction at least) in refuting all the peculiar tenets that had ever been common to himself and the Quakers ; and, scorning to conceal the desertion of his original opinions, he hesitated not to declare himself a convert from the Quaker society to the church of England. This secession was a death-

---

[1] Penn, writing to a friend in America, declares that the report of this trial had excited much disgust in England, and induced many persons to exclaim against the fitness of Quakers to administer municipal authority. Proud.

blow to the influence of that party which had hitherto espoused his sentiments ; and which, henceforward, either gradually coalescing with a more
powerful majority, or peaceably submitting to a sentence of expulsion, contributed alike to the ascendency of principles which originally it proposed
to subvert.   When Keith finally declared himself the antagonist of Quakerism, he encountered the controversial hostility of William Penn ; but till
then the treatment which he experienced in Pennsylvania was a source of
the utmost regret and disapprobation to the proprietary.[1]

The government that arose from the revolution in England, having now
completed the arrangements that were necessary for its secure establishment
at home, had leisure to extend its cares to the colonial communities at the
extremity of the empire. [1693.]   In the annals of the other American
settlements we have seen instances of the avidity with which King William
and his ministers endeavoured to appropriate to the crown the nomination of
the provincial governors.   The situation of the proprietary of Pennsylvania,
together with various circumstances in the recent history of this province,
presented a favorable opportunity of repeating the same policy ; and, indeed,
furnished a much more decent pretext for it than had been deemed sufficient
to warrant an invasion of the rights of the proprietary of Maryland.   Penn
was generally suspected by the English people of adherence to the interests
of his ancient patron, James the Second ; and, in consequence of a charge
that was preferred against him of accession to a treasonable conspiracy in
favor of the exiled tyrant, he had absconded from judicial inquiry, and was
living in concealment.[2]   In Pennsylvania, the laws had been administered in
the name of the banished king, long after the government of William and
Mary was recognized in the other colonies ; and the dissensions which
Keith's schism had excited were magnified into the semblance of disorders
inconsistent with the honor of the British crown.   Fortified with such pretexts for the royal interposition, King William issued a warrant, depriving
Penn of all authority in America, and investing the government of his territories in Colonel Fletcher, who was likewise appointed governor of New
York.   Penn, regarding this proceeding as a tyrannical usurpation of his
rights, adopted the strange defensive precaution of writing to Fletcher, beseeching him, on the score of private friendship, to refuse compliance with
the king's commands ; but no regard was paid to this foolish solicitation,
and the government was quietly surrendered to Fletcher, who appointed,
first Lloyd, and afterwards Markham, to act as his deputy. [April, 1693.]

In the commission to Fletcher no notice was taken of the charter of
Pennsylvania ; and the main object of his policy was to obtain a recognition
of the unqualified dependence of the province on the crown.   This involved

[1] G. Thomas's *History of Pennsylvania.* Proud. Clarkson's *History of the Abolition of the
Slave-trade.* Thomas's *History of Printing in America.* Proud's account of these proceedings
bears evident marks of partiality. It is amusing to observe his grudge against Keith and Bradford, for having described a writing which they published, as the employment of their hours
of bondage *in the prison* to which professed Quakers had committed them.

George Keith, after his recantation of Quakerism and espousal of the doctrines of the
church of England, was sent back again as a missionary to America, by the English Society
for the Propagation of the Gospel ; and, in his labors to convert the Indians, is said to have
been much more successful than any of the votaries of his former tenets. Oldmixon.

[2] The author of the charge from which Penn withdrew himself was the notorious Fuller,
who was afterwards condemned to the pillory, for the detected (or at least pretended) falsehood of the charges which he had preferred against other distinguished persons. The suspicions entertained of Penn were strengthened by the conduct of his wife, who appears to have
paid frequent visits to St. Germains, and to have conveyed presents of money from the English
Jacobites to the exiled queen. Belknap's *American Biography.*

him in a series of disputes with the assembly, who unanimously voted a resolution, "that the laws of this province, which were in force and practice before the arrival of this present governor, are still in force "; but afterwards judged it expedient to acquiesce in the arrogation, that the liberty of conscience, which they owed to the wisdom and virtue of William Penn and themselves, was a boon derived from the grace and favor of the king. Farther than this the governor found it impossible to bend them to his wishes. One measure to which he strenuously labored to obtain their assent was a contribution of money in aid of the defence of the frontiers of New York against the arms of the French. Finding it necessary to reinforce by argument the authority of a royal letter which he produced, and in which the contribution was suggested [March, 1694], he reminded them that the military operations at this frontier contributed to the defence of the other colonies as well as New York, and that it was unjust to burden that province with the sole charge of measures which were indispensable to the general safety. He was aware, he said, that the Quaker principles which prevailed among the Pennsylvanians forbade not only the use of offensive arms, but the employment of money even for the support of defensive war; but he hoped they would not refuse to feed the hungry and clothe the naked, which were undeniably Christian virtues, and which the hunger and nakedness of the Indian allies of New York now presented them with a favorable opportunity of exerting. This ingenious casuistry, which the Quakers might justly have regarded rather as an affront to their understandings than a concession to their principles, proved, on the present occasion, quite unavailing, — to the no small displeasure of William Penn, who, on being reinstated in his government, reproached the assembly with their refusal to contribute towards the common defence, and desired that a sum of money for this purpose should forthwith be levied and remitted to New York.[1]

In addition to the other disappointments and misfortunes that befell the proprietary of Pennsylvania, he had now to lament a sensible decay of the credit which he had hitherto enjoyed with the members of his religious society in England. They reproached him with having *meddled more with politics, and the concerns of the English government, than became a member of their Christian body*; and would not admit the benevolent motives of his conduct, or the especial benefit which their own society had reaped from it, as a sufficient apology for the scandal it created and the evil example it afforded.[2] In the midst of so many adverse circumstances, — involving the estrangement of ancient friends, and the miscarriage of almost every scheme of temporal satisfaction which he had proposed to himself, — his retirement was penetrated by the grateful kindness of that illustrious man, whom once, in circumstances resembling his own present situation, he had endeavoured to befriend. John Locke, who was now in the enjoyment of considerable favor at the English court, persuaded of Penn's innocence, and mindful of the friendly intercession which Penn had made in his behalf with

---

[1] Proud. Dillwyn, *apud* Winterbotham.

[2] Lower, a Quaker, the friend of Penn, and in good repute with the rest of the society, undertook to mediate a reconciliation between them, and for this purpose composed the following apology, which was to be subscribed and distributed by Penn: — " If in any things, during these late revolutions, I have concerned myself, either by words or writings (in love, pity, or good-will to any in distress), *further than consisted with truth's honor or the church's peace,* I am sorry for it; and the government having passed it by, I desire it may be by you also." Clarkson. Whether this apology was presented or not is unknown; but a reconciliation took place shortly after between Penn and the Quakers.

King James, when Locke was an exile in Holland,[1] offered to employ his interest to procure him a pardon from King William.   But the dignity of Penn's virtue was rather elevated than depressed by adversity ; and emulating the magnanimity with which his own similar kindness had been formerly rejected by Locke, he protested, that, as he had done nothing blameworthy, he would not consent to stain his reputation by accepting a *pardon*.[2] The retirement thus virtuously preserved contributed no less to the refinement of his character than to the extension of his fame, and was signalized by the publication of a series of literary performances replete with learning, genius, and mild benevolence.   In a short time the clouds that had gathered around his fortunes began to disperse ; the Quakers became completely reconciled, and as much attached as ever to him ; and the good offices of Lord Somers, Locke, and other friends, coöperating with the justice of his cause, and the detection of (real or supposed) impostures committed by one of his accusers, succeeded in undeceiving the English court, and obviated every pretence for continuing to exclude him from the enjoyment of the privileges to which he was entitled by the charter of Pennsylvania.   A royal warrant was issued accordingly, for reinstating him in his proprietary functions [August, 1694] ; in the exercise of which, he forthwith invested his kinsman Markham with the office of deputy-governor of his whole territories, — thus again reuniting the executive administration of Pennsylvania and Delaware.[3]

Pennsylvania had continued to increase its population with such rapidity, that now the number of inhabitants (exclusive of negro slaves) was estimated at twenty thousand. [1695.]   A considerable change was observed, soon after the British Revolution, in the character of the emigrants resorting to this province, — who, though generally respectable persons, yet showed very plainly, in many particulars of their conduct, and especially in their reluctance to embrace the measures that were proposed for mitigating the evils of negro slavery, that views of temporal enrichment had operated more powerfully than religious zeal to conduct them to America.   The formality of apparel and simplicity of manners enjoined by the constitutions of the Quakers tended to purify their sectarian society, by confining its attractions to sober-minded men ; and peculiarly recommended the virtue of industry, by increasing its efficacy in conducting to a plentiful estate. But the temporal advantages thus closely associated with Quaker manners had latterly contributed to produce a practical relaxation of the strictness of Quaker principles, and to adulterate the motives by which the profession of these principles was inculcated.   The attractions of Pennsylvania as a sanctuary of liberty of conscience were comparatively diminished to the English Dissenters by the Revolution ; but its allurements in other respects continued unabated, and, by the widely diffused influence and correspondence of Penn, were promulgated in all parts of the British empire.   Already many emigrants, who in England found it difficult to gain a scanty livelihood, had in Pennsylvania amassed estates of considerable value. The accounts that were published in England of the liberal wages of labor in the province attracted thither a great many persons in the humblest walks

---

[1] *Ante*, Book IV., Chap. I.

[2] This was not the only point of similarity in the histories of these distinguished persons. Both had been the dupes of very bad men (Shaftesbury and James the Second), and both suffered unjustly for their connection with them. Both were expelled from the University of Oxford.

[3] Proud. Clarkson.

of life, who had the expenses of their transportation defrayed by wealthier individuals, to whom they engaged themselves as servants for a series of years. But the improvement in the condition of these people was so rapid, and they were so eager to enjoy the dignity of independence, that a scarcity of servants, and the exorbitancy of the wages that were necessary to retain free men in this condition, were continual subjects of complaint.[1] These circumstances, coöperating with the example of the neighbouring colonies, had originally introduced negro slavery into the province, and now continued to prolong the subsistence of this execrable institution, which, degrading servitude, and rendering it a condition still more uninviting to free men, promoted the causes whence itself had arisen. It required more virtue than even the Quakers were yet prepared to exert, in order to defend them from the contagion of this evil, and to induce them to divide the produce of their lands with their servants in such proportions as might have enabled them to employ only free labor in their cultivation.

During the interval that elapsed between the restoration of Penn to his proprietary authority [1696] and his second visit to his people, some change was introduced into the form of the provincial constitution. Markham had repeatedly pressed the assembly to authorize the levy of a sum of money, to be remitted to the governor of New York, for the support of the war, — or, as it was decently pretended, for the relief of the distressed Indians ; and Penn, in his letters from England, reinforced this application, by protesting that the preservation of the proprietary government would again be endangered by a refusal to comply with it. This appeared to the assembly a favorable opportunity of obtaining a change which they had long desired, in the distribution of the legislative functions between themselves and the governor and council ; and hinting plainly, that, without such equivalent, they were determined not to waive their scruples to a contribution for martial purposes, they compelled Markham to assent to a new act of settlement, which formed the third *frame* or system of the Pennsylvanian constitution. [November, 1696.] By this new compact, it was provided that from each county there should be chosen only two persons to represent the people in council, and four as their representatives in assembly ; the council being thus reduced in number from eighteen to twelve, and the assembly from thirty-six to twenty-four. It was farther stipulated that the assembly should be empowered to regulate its own adjournments ; and that it should be no longer confined to a simple assent or negation to legislative propositions originating with the governor and council, but should partake with them the privilege of introducing and discussing laws. On receiving this boon, the assembly passed an order for raising the sum of three hundred pounds, to be remitted to the governor of New York, *for the relief of the distressed Indians* on the frontiers of his province.[2] Governor Fletcher wrote to Markham in the following year, affirming that the money had been faithfully applied to the feeding and clothing of the Indians, and requesting a fresh supply for the same benevolent purpose. The assembly, in reply to this proposition, desired that their thanks might be conveyed to Fletcher for " his regard and candor to them " in applying their former subsidy to the use they had contemplated ; adding, that, although for the present they must decline imposing additional burdens on

[1] G. Thomas. Oldmixon.
[2] It was almost at the very same time, that Archdale, the Quaker governor of Carolina, introduced into this province a law for the formation of a militia. *Ante,* Book IV., Chap. II.

the province, they would always be ready to observe the king's farther commands, " according to their religious persuasions and abilities." Thus early did the Quakers experience the difficulty of reconciling their religious principles with the administration of political power. It was but a few years after, that, in answer to a requisition from Penn, in the king's name, for a subsidy avowedly destined to the erection of forts and batteries at New York, the Pennsylvanian assembly pleaded its poverty, and remonstrated against the partiality which imposed upon this people so many exactions from which other and older colonies were exempted, as the only reasons for deferring to comply with the king's commands, " so far as their abilities and religious persuasions shall permit." [1]   This reservation, which was always inserted on such occasions, for the honor of Quaker consistency, never prevented the Quakers of Pennsylvania from contributing, as the subjects of a martial monarchy, their full contingent to the sinews of war.   In voting grants of money which were expressly demanded as military subsidies, and which they well knew would be employed to impel the rage of war, and nourish the ferocity of savages whom they professed their anxious desire to pacify and civilize, it was always attempted, by the substitution of some other alleged purpose, to shift the sin and scandal of the transaction from themselves to their military superiors, or at least to draw a decent veil over concessions which they could neither withhold nor avow.[2]   The veil was not without its use, if it contributed to maintain among the Pennsylvanian Quakers that respect for their pacific tenets of which they made a more practical and honorable display in the succeeding century, when the attempts of the English government to extort from them a still more active and unequivocal coöperation with military measures induced them to sacrifice to their principles the possession of political power.

Accession to war, though the most important, was not the only instance in which the Pennsylvanian Quakers were compelled by the singularity of their situation to content themselves with a theoretical profession instead of a practical exemplification of their principles.   By the constitutions of Quakerism, they were restricted to the employment of a plainness of speech remote from the ordinary style of colloquial intercourse in the world, and totally inconsistent with the strain of elaborate homage, which, in regal governments, pervades the addresses of inferior magistrates and corporations to the throne.   This sectarian principle was always admitted to regulate their intercourse with the provincial governors, who were invariably addressed in the *plain language* of Quakerism by the Pennsylvanian assemblies.   But the same assemblies, in their addresses to the crown, and even in those of which the object was to solicit advantages and immunities to the Quakers, employed the usual style of official obeisance ; — the Quaker majority of the assembly taking care to adject to each address a declaration that they approved its substance, " but excepted against some part of its style." [3]

The affairs of the colony continued to glide on for some time in a

---

[1] Proud.

[2] Dr. Franklin mentions an instance, some years after, of a requisition addressed to the assembly of Pennsylvania, of the sum of two thousand pounds for the purchase of gunpowder ; to which the assembly replied, that, consistently with Quaker principles, they could not grant a farthing for such a purpose, but had voted two thousand pounds *for the purchase of grain.* Various instances of accession to war, still more unambiguous, on the part of the American Quakers, are related in Kalm's *Travels in North America.*

[3] Proud.   Similar instances of Quaker assent to the substance and dissent from the style of addresses occur in the transactions of the assembly of New Jersey.   S. Smith.

course of tranquillity, interrupted at length by an event which had been now too long deferred to be capable of producing the beneficial consequences which at one time were fondly expected to ensue from it, — the return of the proprietary to his American dominions. [1698, 1699.] On this second occasion, accompanied by his family, and professing his intention to spend the remainder of his life in Pennsylvania, his arrival was hailed with general, if not universal satisfaction, — of which the only visible abatement was created by the first visitation of that dreadful epidemic, the *yellow fever* (since so fatally prevalent), at Philadelphia.[1] Some young men, having ventured, in opposition to the commands of the magistrates, to salute the proprietary on his arrival with a discharge of artillery, performed this operation so awkwardly, as to occasion severe injury to themselves ; which was regarded by the Quakers as a providential rebuke of a tribute so unsuitable to a member of their fraternity. The very first transactions that took place between Penn and his provincial assembly were but ill calculated to promote their mutual satisfaction. In the history of some of the other settlements (and particularly of Carolina and New York), we have remarked that the American seas were at this time infested by pirates, whose prodigal expenditure of money in every place where they found shelter and entertainment, and whose readiness to assist in evading the obnoxious Acts of Navigation, recommended them too successfully to the countenance of many of the North American colonists. Pennsylvania did not escape this reproach, which Penn had already communicated in letters to the assembly, — who readily enacted laws against the practices imputed to their fellow-citizens, but at the same time issued proclamations declaring in the strongest terms that the imputations were unfounded. This disagreeable subject was resumed immediately after the arrival of Penn ; and though the assembly still complained of the injustice of the reproach, it was found necessary to expel from it one of its own members, the son-in-law of Colonel Markham, who was suspected of participating, or at least countenancing, piracy. Still more productive of discord were the frequent demands of pecuniary contributions for the support of a military establishment at New York, which Penn was compelled by the British government to address to his assembly ; and which were answered only by complaints of the hardship of these exactions, and protestations of the inability of the province to comply with them.[2] But the most remarkable disagreement that occurred between Penn and the assembly arose from the measures which he now suggested for improving the treatment of negro slaves, and correcting abuses that prevailed in the intercourse between the colonists and the Indians.

It was impossible that the flagrant evils of slavery, and the especial repugnance of such an inhuman institution to Christian morality, which Baxter, Tryon, and other writers had already pressed upon the attention of the Protestant inhabitants of Christendom, could escape the moral sense of

[1] Thomas Story, an eminent preacher among the Quakers, and afterwards recorder of Philadelphia, thus describes the impression produced by the prevalence of this epidemic : — " Great was the majesty and hand of the Lord ; great was the fear that fell upon all flesh : I saw no lofty or airy countenance, nor heard any vain jesting to move men to laughter ; nor extravagant feasting to excite above measure the lusts of the flesh ; but every face gathered paleness, and many hearts were humbled, and countenances fallen and sunk, as such that waited every moment to be summoned to the bar." Proud. How different this from Thucydides' description of the increased gayety and profligacy produced by the plague at Athens ! [2] Proud. Clarkson.

those benevolent sectaries who professed to study and exhibit a peculiar and almost literal conformity to the precepts of charity, humility, and self-denial, interwoven with the doctrines of the gospel. When George Fox, the founder of Quakerism, visited Barbadoes, in 1671, he found the members of his sectarian society within the island, as well as the other white inhabitants, in possession of slaves. "Respecting their negroes," he relates among his other admonitions to the Quaker planters, "I desired them to endeavour to train them up in the fear of God; as well those that were bought with their money, as those that were born in their families. I desired also that they would cause their overseers to deal mildly and gently with their negroes, and not use cruelty towards them, as the manner of some hath been and is ; and that, after *certain* years of servitude, they should make them free."[1] How conscientiously the Quakers complied with this admonition is attested by a law promulgated by the legislature of Barbadoes five years after, commanding those sectaries to desist from giving instruction to negroes, and, in particular, from admitting them to their religious assemblages ;[2] and how magnanimously they persisted to do their duty, in the face of this unchristian command, may be inferred from an ordinance very soon after enacted by the same legislature, imposing a penalty on any shipmaster who should bring a Quaker to the island.[3] The prosecution of such measures, and the adoption of a similar policy in others of the West India plantations, succeeded in banishing from these colonial settlements an example which might have been attended with the most beneficial consequences to the interests of the white inhabitants and the happiness of the negroes ; and compelled many Quaker planters to emigrate from the West Indies to America, whither they brought with them their modified opinions on the subject of slavery. Some of these Quakers perhaps entertained the purpose of an entire compliance with the admonition of Fox, by setting their negroes at liberty after *certain* years of servitude ; but this purpose was easily overpowered by the sophistry and temptation of self-interest, the contagion of general example, and the influence of evil habit in blunting the feelings of humanity.

By his acquisition of the Delaware territory, it is probable that Penn, on coming into possession of his American domains, found the system of negro slavery already established within them. During his first visit, it appears that a few negroes were imported into Pennsylvania, and were purchased by the Quakers, as well as the other settlers. While the scarcity of servants enhanced the temptation to this practice, the kindness of Quaker manners contributed to soften its evil and veil its iniquity ; and it was not till the year 1688, that the repugnance of slavery itself, however disguised, to the tenets of Christianity was first suggested to the Pennsylvanians by the emigrants

[1] Fox's *Journal.* An earlier and more uncompromising resistance to slavery was made by some of the clergy of the church of Rome, at St. Luis, in the year 1653. Southey's *History of Brazil.*
[2] Oldmixon. The preamble of this law sets forth, that, "Whereas many negroes have been suffered to remain at the meeting of Quakers as hearers of their doctrine, and taught in their principles, whereby the safety of this island may be much hazarded," &c. We find the legislature of Barbadoes, one hundred and fifty years after, enacting similar laws against the Methodist teachers and preachers, and declaring that their doctrines were fitted to turn the world upside down.
[3] Clarkson's *Abolition of the Slave-trade.* About sixty years later, Thomas Chalkeley, a renowned Quaker minister, in one of his visits to Barbadoes, having exhorted a meeting of the free inhabitants to treat their negro slaves with greater mildness (without presuming to breathe a syllable of objection against the institution of slavery), was fired at and wounded in open day by one of the planters of the island. Chalkeley's *Journal.*

who repaired to them from Germany. If it was natural for the Quakers to relish the connection which they habitually experienced between certain of their sectarian usages and temporal enrichment, it was not easy for them to avoid proportionally contracting at least a practical estrangement from whatever in their principles savored only of unproductive self-denial and depauperating virtue. But whatever taint their practice, as American planters, might have derived from human infirmity, they were still anxious, as an ecclesiastical society, to maintain the theoretical purity of their principles ; and accordingly, in compliance with the suggestion of the Germans, a resolution declaratory of the unlawfulness of slavery was adopted and published in the same year by the annual meeting of the Quakers of Pennsylvania. The effect of this deliberate homage to eternal truth and the immutable principles of justice and humanity was not carried beyond a practical exemption of the slaves of Quakers from evils not inevitably inherent in the condition of bondage. George Keith, as we have seen, made an attempt, in 1692, to bring the practice of his fellow-sectaries into closer accommodation to their theory ; but the arrogance of his demeanour and the intemperance of his language were ill calculated to recommend ungracious truth, or to promote the spirit of heroic sacrifice ; and the increasing number of the slaves, together with the diversities of character among the colonists (to which we have already adverted), rendered the emancipation of the negroes increasingly improbable. In the year 1696, the annual meeting of the Pennsylvanian Quakers repeated their former declaration, adding to it an earnest admonition to the members of their society to refrain from all farther importations of negro slaves ; but no other immediate effect resulted from this measure than an increased concern for the welfare of the negroes, who in some instances were admitted to attend divine worship in the same meeting-houses with their Quaker masters.

On his second arrival in America [June, 1700], Penn very soon perceived, that, from the varieties of character among his provincial vassals, and the inevitable tendency of absolute power to corruption and abuse, the negro slavery of Pennsylvania exhibited, in too many instances, the same odious features that characterized this barbarous institution in other places.[1] He was additionally mortified with the discovery of numerous frauds and abuses committed by the colonists in their traffic with the Indians. With the view of providing a remedy for both these evils, he presented to the assembly three bills which he had himself prepared : the first, for regulating the morals and marriages of the negroes ; the second, for regulating the trials and punishments of the negroes ; and the third, for preventing abuses and frauds in the intercourse between the colonists and the Indians. The assembly instantly negatived the first and last of these bills ; acceding only to that which related to the trial and punishment of their slaves. No account is transmitted of any discussion or debate on the bills which were rejected ; and, indeed, it is probable that the assembly, in this instance, were glad to confine themselves to the ancient formula of simply approving or rejecting the legislative overtures presented to them. But it is asserted (conjecturally, I suppose) by one of the biographers of Penn, that the feelings of the proprietary received *a convulsive shock* on the occasion. In proposing the bills, he had indeed been unanimously supported by his council, which consisted entirely of Quakers ; but he had seen them de-

---

[1] " Though Pennsylvania boasts her peaceful plain,
     Yet there in blood her petty tyrants reign." — Gregory.

cisively rejected by an assembly, of which a great majority consisted of persons of the same religious persuasion. Though disappointed of the more extensive influence which as a political legislator he had hoped to exercise, he was yet able, in his ecclesiastical ministry among the Quakers, to introduce into their discipline regulations and practices relative to the purposes of the rejected bills, the spirit of which, at least, was, by the example of this powerful sect, forcibly recommended to general imitation. Monthly meetings were appointed among the Quakers, for the religious and moral education of their negro slaves [1703]; and regular conferences were established with the Indians, for the purpose of communicating to them whatever instruction they would consent to accept. Penn finally obtained leave, or at least assumed the power, to make a treaty with the Indians, by which they acknowledged themselves subjects of the British crown and amenable to the provincial laws; and by which certain regulations were framed for preventing the frauds to which they were exposed in their commercial dealings with the white population.

Thus was preserved in the Quaker society a principle, which, about seventy years after, obtained the signal triumph of procuring emancipation to all the negroes in America belonging to Quakers; and thus, meanwhile, was cherished in the general body of the inhabitants of Pennsylvania such a sense of the unalienable rights and indissoluble obligations of humanity, as obtained for enslaved negroes in this province a treatment far kinder and more equitable than they enjoyed in any other part of North America, except the States of New England. Notwithstanding the encouragement afforded by the British government to the importation of negroes into all the American settlements, the slaves in Pennsylvania never formed more than a very insignificant fraction of the whole population of the province. Slavery subsisted longer in Delaware; and the slaves in this settlement, though not numerous, were rather more so than in the larger province of Pennsylvania.[1]

In addition to the other disagreeable impressions of which his second visit to America was productive, Penn had now the mortification of witnessing a revival of the jealousies between Delaware and Pennsylvania, and of experiencing the inefficacy of all his efforts to promote a cordial union between the inhabitants of these countries. As a remedy for their mutual dissatisfaction, he proposed a change in the frame of government; but the adjustment of this compact tended rather to inflame than to allay the existing

---

[1] Proud. Clarkson's *Abolition of the Slave-trade*. Clarkson's *Life of Penn*. Winterbotham. Warden. In the course of his ministerial labors at this time, Penn visited his Quaker brethren in Maryland, and was received in a friendly manner by his ancient adversary, Lord Baltimore, who with his lady accompanied him to a Quaker meeting. Penn regretted, for the sake of his noble companions, that the fervor of the meeting had subsided before their entrance; and Lady Baltimore declared herself disappointed of the *diversion* she had expected. He had also various interviews with the Indians, who listened to him willingly as long as he confined himself to general allusions to religion. But when he desired, on one occasion, to direct their minds to the search of an internal manifestation of the Redeemer of the human race, his interpreter declared that no words in the Indian tongue were capable of conveying such a notion. No words, indeed, of any human language are *of themselves* capable of adequately expressing the doctrines of the Holy Scriptures The understanding of an adult heathen recoils from the doctrine of *creation*, in which he perceives the difficulties that elude the consideration of many members of Christianized communities on whom the doctrine has been inculcated from their infancy.

To Penn himself the Indians very readily paid a degree of respect which they refused to extend to his religious tenets. Many of them believed him a being of higher order than the rest of mankind; "nor could they for a long time credit the news of his death, not believing him subject to the accidents of nature." Farmer's *View of the Policy of Great Britain*, &c.

animosities. He endeavoured to defer the extremity to which their disputes manifestly tended, by various acts of conciliation towards the weaker and more irritable party, and particularly by convoking at Newcastle, the metropolis of Delaware, another assembly, which was held in the close of the present year [1700]. But although he succeeded, after much adroit exertion, in obtaining from this assembly a subsidy for the support of his government, and made some progress in arranging with them the terms of a new charter or frame of government, — the mutual jealousies between the two settlements were displayed with such unreserve, that, in almost every debate, the Delaware representatives suggested and supported precisely the reverse of whatever was proposed or approved by the Pennsylvanians. The subsidy amounted to £ 2,000, of which £ 1,573 was the proportion imposed upon Pennsylvania, and the remainder upon Delaware. It was unwise, perhaps, of Penn to invite his people to the acceptance of a new social compact, at a time when they were so much heated by mutual irritation, and when the union between the two settlements was evidently so precarious. It afforded a pretext not long after for taxing him with converting the public distractions to his own advantage, and practising devices for the enlargement of his power, while the minds of his people were too much occupied with their mutual dissensions to perceive the drift of his proceedings.

But Penn had now determined again to leave America [1701], and return to England ; and while he naturally desired to have the frame of the provincial government finally established before his departure, his recent experience had doubtless impressed on him the conviction, that an extension of his own magisterial prerogative would render the constitution more instrumental to the welfare of the people, and afford a freer scope to the promotion of views and the exertion of influence impartially directed to the general advantage.

In the last assembly which he convoked before his departure [September, 1701], he had occasion to exert all his authority and address, in order to prevent the representatives of Delaware and Pennsylvania from coming to an open rupture, and also to guard his own interests in the sale and lease of vacant lands from an attempt of the legislative body to assume a control over them. Various laws were passed ; of which the most remarkable were those for the establishment of a post-office, for the punishment of the vices of *scolding* and drunkenness, for restraining the practice of drinking healths, and for the destruction of wolves. [October, 1701.] But the most important transaction on this occasion was the establishment of the new charter or frame of government, which Penn finally tendered to the assembly, and prevailed with a great majority of the members to accept, and even thankfully acknowledge. By this instrument, it was provided (in conformity with the municipal compact of 1696) that a legislative assembly should be annually elected by the freemen, and should consist of four persons from each county, or of a greater number, if the governor and assembly should so determine ; that the assembly should nominate its own officers, and decide with exclusive jurisdiction all questions relating to the qualifications and elections of its members ; that it should prepare legislatorial bills, impeach criminals, and redress grievances ; and possess all the other powers and privileges of a representative assembly, accordant with the rights of the freeborn subjects of England, and the customs observed in the

TT

British plantations in America. The governor was empowered to convoke, prorogue, and dissolve the provincial legislature ; to nominate his
council ; to discharge singly the whole executive functions of government;
and to share the legislative functions, by affirming or rejecting the bills of the
assembly.   The Pennsylvanian council differed from all the other provincial
councils in this respect, that it did not form a distinct branch of the legislature, but was considered as a court of assistants to the acting governor,
and a check on his authority,— rather a privy council than a senatorial
body.   It was declared that liberty of conscience was the inviolable right
of the colonists ; that Christians of every denomination should be qualified
to occupy the offices of government ; and that no act or ordinance should
ever be made to alter or diminish the form or effect of the charter, without the consent of the governor, and six parts in seven of the assembly.
But as it was now plainly foreseen that the representatives of the *province*
and those of the *territories* would not long continue to unite in legislation,
it was provided that they should be allowed to separate within three years
from the date of the charter, and should enjoy the same privileges when
separated as when united.   In exercise of the new authority thus vested
in himself, Penn nominated a *council of state*, to consult with and assist
the governor or his deputy, and to administer his functions in case of his
death or absence.   The office of deputy-governor [1] he bestowed on Colonel
Andrew Hamilton, who had formerly been governor of New Jersey.

One of the latest acts which Penn performed before his final departure
from America, the incorporation, by charter, of the city of Philadelphia,
has been justly charged with great illiberality ; though, according to the
apology which his friends have suggested for it, the blame must be divided
between himself and others.   By this charter he nominated the first mayor,
recorder, aldermen, and common councilmen of the city ; and, among other
privileges and franchises, empowered them to elect their successors in
office, and even to increase their own number according to their own discretion.   The city lands were granted to them, under the title of the Mayor
and Commonalty of the City of Philadelphia ; but the commonalty had no
share in the government or estate of the city ; the civic functionaries being self-elective, and not accountable to their fellow-citizens in any respect.
It has been asserted, that this municipal constitution, which was copied
from the charter of the town of Bristol, in England, was conceded by
Penn to the desires of certain of his colonists who were natives of that
place ; and it is admitted that the functionaries whom he himself appointed
were men of talent and integrity.   But the possession of power, divested
of control and responsibility, produced its usual effect on this corporate
society ; and the abuses engendered by its administration were, from a
very early period, a theme of continual discontent and complaint to the
inhabitants of the city and the provincial assembly.   Having concluded
these transactions, and once more renewed the engagements of peace and
good-will with the Indians, Penn addressed to his people a farewell couched
in friendly and benevolent terms, but far less tender and affectionate than
his former valediction ; and, embarking with his family, returned to England.[2] [October 31, 1701.]

[1] No mention is made of the royal confirmation of this appointment, which is expressly referred to in the appointment of Evans, the successor of Hamilton. By an act of parliament,
already noticed in the history of Maryland, it was requisite now that all the acting governors
in the proprietary jurisdiction should be approved by the king.
[2] Proud. Winterbotham. Dillwyn, *apud eundem.* Clarkson.

The only reason that Penn assigned to the colonists for this second departure was the intelligence he had received of a project of the English court to abolish all the proprietary jurisdictions in North America, and the expediency of his own appearance in England to oppose a scheme so derogatory to his interest ; but as he found, on his arrival in this country, that the measure had been abandoned, and yet never again returned to America, it seems very unlikely that this was the sole or even the main reason for his conduct.   The disagreements between himself and his colonists had rendered their intercourse far less satisfactory than he could have desired, and had induced him to supply the inadequacy of his own personal influence by a large addition to his political power ; and from the numerous demands of the British government for contributions in aid of military purposes, it was manifest that this power must be frequently exerted for the attainment of objects, which, as a professor of Quakerism, he could pursue with more decency and more firmness by the intervention of a deputy than by his own personal agency.   The disagreeable tidings that pursued him from America must have increased his aversion to return thither ; and the favor he enjoyed with Queen Anne, on her accession to the throne [January, 1702], perhaps reawakened the views and hopes that had led him once before to prefer the courtly shades of Kensington to the wild woods of Pennsylvania.   His attendance at court, however, was soon interrupted by the perplexity and embarrassment of his private affairs (arising from the fraud of his steward), which compelled him to mortgage his American territory ; and the same cause, uniting with increased dissensions between him and the colonists, induced him subsequently to treat with the British government for a sale of his proprietary functions.[1]   The completion of the bargain, however, was suspended by his sickness, and intercepted by his death, which transmitted the proprietary government to his descendants, by whom it was enjoyed till the period of the American Revolution.

Penn had scarcely quitted America when the disputes between the *province* and the *territories* broke forth with greater bitterness than before. The Delaware representatives protested against the charter ; and, refusing to sit in the same assembly with the Pennsylvanians, chose a separate place of meeting for themselves in Philadelphia.   After continuing for some time to indulge their jealous humor, and to enjoy whatever satisfaction they could derive from separate legislation, they were persuaded by the successor of Hamilton, Governor Evans (who was much more agreeable to them than to the people of Pennsylvania), to demonstrate a more reasonable temper [1703[2]], and to propose a reunion with the Pennsylvania assembly.

---

[1] He demanded as the price of this surrender twenty thousand pounds, but agreed to accept twelve thousand pounds.

[2] This year (if we may believe the representation of Colonel Quarry) was remarkably productive of crime in Pennsylvania.   In Quarry's *Memorial to the Lords of Trade*, it is stated that the jail of Philadelphia was then crowded with felons, and that justice was greatly obstructed by the refusal of Quaker judges, jurymen, and witnesses to take an oath ; insomuch, that at a recent sessions, where many guilty persons were indicted, only one murderer was convicted, and " all *Quakers and others* for rapes and less crimes were discharged."   Quarry's *Memorial*, in the British Museum.

From the *Journal* of Thomas Chalkeley, the Quaker, it appears that some of his fellow-sectaries in Pennsylvania were not exempt from occasional lapses into very immoral and disorderly conduct.   " It is worthy of commendation," he reports, " that our governor, Thomas Lloyd, sometimes, in the evening, before he went to rest, used to go in person to public houses, and order the people he found there to their own houses, till at length he was instrumental to promote better order, and did in a great measure suppress vice and immorality in the city."

But this body, provoked and disgusted at the refractory spirit which the Delaware representatives had already displayed, now refused to entertain their overtures of reconciliation. The breach thus became irreparable; and in the following year [1704] the separate legislature of Delaware was permanently established at Newcastle. In addition to the tidings of these prolonged disagreements and final rupture between the two settlements, Penn was harassed by complaints against the government of Evans, whose exertions to promote a militia, though they rendered him popular in Delaware, made him odious in Pennsylvania. Deriding the pacific scruples of the Quakers, Evans falsely proclaimed the approach of a hostile invasion, and invited all who were willing to defend their liberty and property to take arms against the enemy. A few individuals, and, among these, four Quakers, duped by this stratagem, flew to arms, and prepared to repel the threatened attack. But the chief effect of the proclamation was to cause many persons to bury their plate and money, and to fly from their homes; and the detection of the falsehood was followed by an impeachment of the governor, and of Logan, the secretary of the province, who, though innocent of accession to the fraud, made himself suspected by endeavouring to palliate the guilt of it. Penn, however, supported these accused officers, and thereby increased the displeasure that was gathering among his people against himself. He was now little disposed to consider with indulgence the conduct of the inhabitants of Pennsylvania; who, no longer engrossed with the interest of the discussions they had maintained with the people of Delaware, but perhaps animated by the temper which such discussions commonly imply or produce, began with very dissatisfied spirit narrowly to inquire into the whole course of their proprietary's policy with respect to themselves.

The assembly of Pennsylvania not only assailed him with repeated demands, that the quitrents, which he deemed his own private estate, should be appropriated to the support of the provincial government,[1] but transmitted to him a remonstrance, entitled *Heads of Complaint*, in which they alleged that it was by *his artifices* that the constitution of the province had been subjected to so many successive alterations; that he had violated his original compact by the recent enlargement of his authority so far beyond the limits within which he at first engaged to confine it; and that he had received large sums of money, during his last visit to the province, in return for benefits which he promised to procure, but had never yet obtained, for the people from the English government. They censured the original annexation of Delaware to Pennsylvania; reminding him that his title to the government of Delaware, not having been founded on a royal grant, was from the first extremely precarious; and *lamenting with great grief* that the privileges granted to the Pennsylvanians by his first charters were exposed to perish with the baseless fabric of the Delaware institutions wherewith he had associated them. Numerous extortions of his officers were at the

---

[1] " Penn's first purchases of land from the Indians," says Belknap, " were made at his own expense; and the goods delivered on these occasions went by the name of *presents*. In course of time, when a treaty and a purchase went on together, the governor and his successors made the speeches, and the assembly were at the expense of the presents. When one paid the cost, and the other enjoyed the profit, a subject of altercation arose between the proprietary and the popular interests, which other causes contributed to increase and inflame." *American Biography.* From the work of Proud it appears, that, long before Penn's death, the payments which the Indians were continually receiving were derived from assessments imposed by the provincial assembly on their constituents.

same time complained of; and these were attributed to his refusal, in the year 1701, to affirm a bill that had been framed by the assembly for the regulation of official fees. Probably some of the foregoing complaints were founded in misapprehension, or suggested by factious malignity; and, doubtless, the discontent, which both on this and other occasions was expressed towards the proprietary, owed in some degree its origin to the peculiar relation which he held to the members of his own religious society in the province. These persons had always regarded the civil and political institutions of Pennsylvania as subordinate to the establishment and patronage of Quakerism; and expected a degree of equality to result from the legislation of a Quaker minister, which they would never have looked for from a lawgiver of any other persuasion. His own assurances, at the beginning, that, in acquiring the province, his main purpose was to serve the cause and the people of God (which they understood to signify Quakerism and the Quakers), contributed to exaggerate their expectations in this respect.

Indignant at the charges levelled against himself, and prejudiced by this feeling against the accusers of Evans, Penn continued to support that worthless functionary, till his conduct had gone far to excite the people of Delaware to actual hostilities against their Pennsylvanian neighbours, in prosecution of an unjust demand of a toll on the navigation of the Delaware, which Evans suggested to them. Receiving complaints of this, as well as of other instances of official malversation, on the part of his deputy-governor, and having ascertained, by deliberate examination, that they were too well founded, Penn hesitated no longer to supersede Evans, and appointed in his place Charles Gookin [1708], a gentleman of an ancient Irish family, retired from the army, in which he had served with repute, and who seemed qualified, by his age, his experience, and the mildness of his manners, to give satisfaction to the people over whom he was sent to preside. Gookin carried with him an affectionate letter from Penn to the assembly, in which their recent disagreements were passed over without any other notice or allusion than was couched in an invocation for his people, as well as himself, of that humility with which men ought to remember their own imperfections, and that charity which they ought to extend to the infirmities of others. But the assembly proved far less placable and indulgent than he expected. [1709.] While they congratulated Gookin on his arrival, they reproduced in their address every murmur and complaint that they had ever before expressed. Their ill-humor was augmented by the number of applications which Gookin was from time to time constrained to make, in the queen's name, for contributions in aid of the various military operations that related more immediately to the American colonies. To all these applications the assembly invariably answered that their religious principles would not suffer them to contribute to the support of war; but, with mechanical regularity, they voted the sums that were demanded, as *presents* to the queen.

Finding his people more estranged from him and more obdurate to his overtures of conciliation than he had been willing to believe, Penn, now in his sixty-sixth year, for the last time addressed the Pennsylvanian assembly, in a letter whereof the reproachful tenor was moderated by a tone of calm solemnity and dignified concern. [April 29, 1710.] It was a mournful consideration to him, he said, that he was forced, by the ill usage and disappointment which had fallen to his share in this life, to speak to the people of *that province* in a language he once hoped never to have occasion to employ. In a strain of serious remonstrance, he appealed to them, if, at the expense of his own fortune and personal exertions, he had not conducted them into a land where prosperity and liberty, far beyond the common lot of mankind, had been made their portion ; and if this work of his hands had yielded him aught else than the sorrow, disquiet, and poverty, that now pressed heavily on his old age.[1] " I must desire you all," he proceeded, " in a serious and true weightiness of mind, to *consider what you are or have been doing ;* why matters must be carried on with these divisions and contentions ; and what real causes have been given on my side for that opposition to me and my interest which I have met with, *as if I were an enemy*, and not a friend, after all I have done. I am sure I know not of any cause whatsoever. Were I sensible you really wanted any thing of me, in the relation between us, that would make you happier, I should readily grant it, if any reasonable man would say it were fit for you to demand." He recapitulated, with minute deduction, the various alterations that the constitution of the province had undergone, and endeavoured to show that every one arose out of inconveniences of which all were sensible at the time, and which all had willingly united in thus correcting. It was right, he contended, that the proprietary, who was personally responsible to the crown for an administration conformable to the *royal charter*, should be vested exclusively with the executive power. He could no longer, he protested, impute the treatment he met with to honest misconception ; seeing that he had such injuries to complain of as repeated attacks on his reputation, — numerous indignities offered to him in writings sent to England by the hands of men who could not be expected to make the most discreet or charitable use of them, — insinuations against his integrity, — attempts upon his estate, — and disfavor shown to individuals (particularly Logan, the secretary of the province) on account of their reputed attachment to him. " I cannot but mourn," he added, " the unhappiness of my portion dealt to me from those of whom I had reason to expect much better and different things ; nor can I but lament the unhappiness that too many are bringing on themselves, who, instead of pursuing the amicable ways of peace, love, and unity, *which I at first hoped to find in that retirement*, are cherishing a spirit of contention and opposition, and, blind to their own interest, are oversetting that foundation on which your happiness might be built. Friends ! the eyes of many are upon you ; the people of many nations of Europe look on that country as a land of ease and quiet, wishing to themselves in vain the same blessings they conceive you may enjoy ; but to see the use you make of them is no less the cause of surprise." He concluded by declaring that the opposition he had encountered from the people of Pennsylvania now compelled him to consider more closely his own private and declining circumstances in relation to this province. He was willing to continue his kindness to them, if they should think him deserving of reciprocal regard. If it should be otherwise deemed by a majority of them, let them say so at once ; and he would know what he had to rely on.

---

[1] Notwithstanding this desponding strain, it is manifest, from Penn's competition with Locke for the praise of superior legislation (see a note to Book III., *ante*), that he was by no means insensible to the imperishable fame assured to him as the founder of Pennsylvania. The services of Penn were not only more liberally remunerated, but more gratefully remembered by his people, than were those of Lord Baltimore by the colonists of Maryland.

And yet he would hope that God might so direct them, by the impartment of heavenly wisdom and holy fear, that " we may once more meet good friends, and live so to the end."

This touching and forcible appeal was not fruitlessly addressed to the people of Pennsylvania. On all the more generous and considerate spirits in the assembly it prevailed with an efficacy at once instantaneous, profound, and enduring. Awaking to impressions of which faction had suspended the enjoyment without effacing the relish, they were touched with a tender remembrance of Penn's long labors and venerable age ; they began to cherish a filial devotion to the father of his country ; to excuse his frailties with a kind indulgence ; and to appreciate, with noble elation, their own interest in his distinguished fame. This revolution of sentiment was rapidly propagated throughout the province ; and its effect was apparent at the next annual election, when not one of the persons who had signalized themselves by their enmity to Penn, and encouraged the rest of their countrymen to think unfavorably of him, was elected a member of the provincial assembly. [Oct., 1710.] But it is more than doubtful if this gratifying proof of restored confidence and regard was ever known to its illustrious object, who was attacked shortly after by a succession of apoplectic fits, which, suspending almost entirely the exercise of his memory and understanding, prevented him alike from completing an arrangement he had made with the crown for the sale of his proprietary rights, and from receiving the intelligence that might have induced him to consider such an arrangement unnecessary.[1]

Little remains to be added to the view that has already been exhibited of the condition and institutions of Pennsylvania and Delaware, at the close of the seventeenth century. Pennsylvania retained the constitution defined by Penn's last charter, in 1701, till the era of American independence ; and Delaware continued to enjoy its own assembly, and to be subject to the executive administration of the governor of Pennsylvania, till the year 1755, when it was formally erected into a separate State, and endowed with a separate government. No fixed salary was allotted to the governor of Pennsylvania ; but sums of money were voted to him, from time to time, to defray the expenses of his government ; and the amount of these sums was proportioned to the favor he enjoyed with the representatives of the people. In the assembly which was held by Penn at Newcastle, in the close of the year 1700, the remuneration allotted to the members consisted of six shillings a day for attendance, and threepence per mile for travelling charges. The speaker's daily allowance was ten shillings. The meeting of the assembly was indicated by the ringing of a bell ; and any member entering half an hour after the appointed time was fined tenpence. The humane code of criminal law, which we have remarked among the first fruits of Pennsylvania legislation, continued in force till the year 1705, when it was abolished by Queen Anne, as too little consonant with the spirit of English jurisprudence ; but it was soon after reestablished by the same princess, at the intercession of William Penn. For the prevention of lawsuits, three functionaries were appointed by each county court of Pennsylvania, who were invested with the honorable title of *Peacemakers*, and the blessed office of mediating between contending parties, and accommodating their differences by friendly arbitration. Twice a year an *orphan's court*

---

[1] Proud. Chalmers. Dillwyn, *apud* Winterbotham. Oldmixon (2d edition). Clarkson. See Note XXX., at the end of the volume.

was held in every county for the inspection and regulation of the affairs of widows and orphans.[1]

Although Quakerism continued long to be the most prevalent religious persuasion in Pennsylvania, yet from a very early period the province had invited and gained the resort of Christian professors of various other denominations ; and an ecclesiastical edifice was already built in Philadelphia for the reception of a congregation of seven hundred persons attached to the tenets and ritual of the church of England.   Some displeasure was manifested by the Quakers at the first proposal of this Episcopal party to erect an organ in their church.   In the years 1698, 1706, 1709, and 1711, the population of Pennsylvania was augmented by successive emigrations supplied by the sect of Mennonists in Germany and Flanders.   These religionists, derived from the parent society of Anabaptists, resembled the Quakers in renouncing oaths and arms, and suffered, as the Quakers had once done, for the reproach which the frenzy of their sectarian parents had brought upon their tenets.   Apprized of the circumstances of these people, Penn conveyed to them information of the liberal institutions that were established in his proprietary domains ; and considerable numbers of them, partly for the sake of religious liberty, and partly with the hope of temporal advantage, transported themselves from Europe to Pennsylvania.   The Episcopalians, and most of the other colonists who were not professors of Quakerism, made frequent propositions for the establishment of a militia ; but the Quakers steadily refused to sanction such a proceeding by an act of the provincial government ; though all who deemed the use of arms lawful were permitted to train themselves, and to adopt every military precaution for their defence that was not inconsistent with peace and good order in the province.[2]   Most of the offices of government were filled by Quakers ; and neither the conduct of forensic controversy, nor the administration of judicial power, was deemed incompatible with their religious profession.[3]   Though they disapproved of oaths, the Quaker judges seem never to have hesitated to administer them to those witnesses who did not partake their scruples.   So early as the year 1686, a printing-press was established at Philadelphia ; and an almanac, for the following year, was printed at this press by Bradford.[4]

When the Swedish colonists first occupied Delaware, they found the country infested with wolves, whose ferocity was soon after inflamed to an extraordinary pitch by the mortality which the small-pox occasioned among the Indians, and the increased quantity of prey derived from the unburied corpses of the victims of this pestilence.   Both in Pennsylvania and Delaware, bounties continued to be paid for the destruction of wolves so late as the middle of the eighteenth century.[5]

[1] Warden. Clarkson. Oldmixon. Similar to the institution of the Pennsylvanian *Peacemakers* was the *Tribunal of Conciliation* established in Denmark, and described by Catteau in his *Tableau des Etats Danois.*
[2] Oldmixon. Proud.
[3] In the case of Kinsey, a Quaker lawyer (afterwards attorney-general and finally chief-justice of Pennsylvania), it was determined, after solemn debate, by the provincial government, that Quaker lawyers should not be obliged to uncover their heads in addressing the judges. Proud. Lord Fountainhall, a Scottish judge, in his published report of a legal decision pronounced by himself and his brethren, observes, that one of the parties in the case was the celebrated Robert Barclay of Urie, who pleaded in person for himself, and proved the victorious litigant. On this occasion (says Lord F.), Mr. Barclay stood within the bar *with his hat off*, " and gave to the president the compellation of *My Lord.*" Yet this was the same man who had perambulated Aberdeen in sackcloth and ashes.
[4] Thomas's *History of Printing in America.*
[5] Kalm's *Travels in North America.*

The *province* and the *territories*, but especially the former, enjoyed from an early period a thriving trade with the parent state, with the southern English colonies in America, and with the British West India settlements. Their exports consisted of corn, beef, pork, fish, pipe-staves, hides, tallow, and wool, to the West Indies ; horses and other live cattle to the southern plantations ; and peltry to England. Their direct trade with England was afterwards increased by the cultivation of tobacco, which was commenced under Blackwell's administration, and so rapidly extended, that, in the beginning of the eighteenth century, fourteen ships sailed annually with cargoes of that commodity from Pennsylvania. Their exports, however, were abridged in the year 1699 by an act of parliament (already noticed in the history of New Jersey) which prohibited the exportation of wool, whether raw or manufactured, from the American colonies. The province, at the same time, imported the produce of various English manufactures to the value of about eighteen thousand pounds a year, and yielded a revenue of three thousand pounds to the customs of the crown. The consumption of English manufactures would probably have been larger, but that the German colonists imported with them into Pennsylvania the manufactures of paper, linen, and woollen cloth.[1]

According to Oldmixon, whose history was first published in 1708, the total number of inhabitants within the domains of William Penn then amounted to thirty five thousand ; a computation which the author himself terms a modest one, and which, as it included Indians and negroes, was probably short of the truth. The town of Philadelphia, in 1696, contained more than a thousand houses, most of which are described as substantial structures of brick; and Newcastle, the metropolis of Delaware, in the beginning of the eighteenth century, possessed two thousand five hundred inhabitants.[2] For many years after its first occupation by the English, Pennsylvania continued to witness a rapid growth of its people, not only from a constant resort of emigrants, whom its attractions invited from all parts of Europe, but from a native increase more vigorous than any other society, since the infancy of the world, has ever exhibited. Gabriel Thomas, who published his account of this province in 1696, affirms that barrenness among women was unknown in Pennsylvania, and their celibacy, after twenty years of age, a very rare occurrence ; and that it was impossible to meet a young married woman there who had not a child in her body or one in her arms. The children born in the province he describes as in general " better-natured, milder, and more tender-hearted than those born in England." [3] The fertility of the soil, the general healthiness of the climate (notwithstanding the severe epidemics occasionally prevalent at Philadelphia), the liberal reward of labor, and the moral, frugal, and industrious habits, promoted by the powerful example of the Quakers, contributed to the production of this large increase, and rendered Pennsylvania distinguished, even among the North American communities, as a scene of happiness and virtue. The manners of a numerous portion of the first race of Quaker settlers, and of their immediate descendants, have been cited as

---

[1] G. Thomas. Oldmixon. Penn, *apud eundem.* In the *Descriptio Pennsylvaniæ* of Thomas Makin, the Pennsylvania farmer is represented as deriving both his food and raiment from the produce of his own possessions : —

" Esuriens, dulces epulas depromit inemptas,
Et proprio vestis vellere texta placet."

[2] Oldmixon. G. Thomas.   [3] G. Thomas.

a remarkable exemplification of courteous benevolence, corresponding to the purpose with which their migration to America was undertaken, — of facilitating the enjoyment of that affectionate intercourse which their sectarian tenets peculiarly enjoined. Some of the leading persons among the earliest Quaker settlers were men who traced their lineage to the stock of the most ancient nobility of England, and in whom a sense of ancestral distinction was so tempered with the meekness of genuine Quakerism, as to impart only a patriarchal dignity to their deportment. Their hospitality, in particular, was conducted with a grace and simplicity entirely patriarchal.[1] The people of Delaware appear to have been, in general, a less refined and enterprising, but not a less virtuous race. Penn himself has celebrated the good morals and sobriety of demeanour of the Swedish and Dutch agriculturists. The Swedish church at Wilmington is reputed one of the oldest churches in North America.[2]

Among the first race of Pennsylvanian settlers were various persons whose attainments in science and literature would have entitled them to an honorable distinction in the most refined and enlightened societies. James Logan, a Quaker, and secretary of the province, was the correspondent of the most illustrious scholars and philosophers in Europe ; and several of his works, written in the Latin tongue (particularly a treatise on the generation of plants, and another on the properties of light), were published with much applause at Leyden. He enriched Philadelphia with a valuable library ; and, in his old age, composed an admirable translation of Cicero's treatise *De Senectute*, which was afterwards printed with an encomiastic preface by Dr. Franklin. Thomas Makin, another Quaker, and one of the earliest settlers in Pennsylvania, produced, in the beginning of the eighteenth century, a descriptive and historical account of the province, in a Latin poem, entitled *Descriptio Pennsylvaniæ*,[3] exhibiting, with great force of thought and beauty of language, one of the most delightful pictures of national virtue and happiness that have ever invited the admiration of mankind.

---

[1] Warden. Galt's *Life of West*. "In the houses of the principal families, the patricians of the country," says Mr. Galt, " unlimited hospitality formed a part of their regular economy. It was the custom among those who resided near the highways, after supper and the last religious exercises of the evening, to make a large fire in the hall, and to set out a table with refreshments for such travellers as might have occasion to pass during the night ; and when the families assembled in the morning, they seldom found that their tables had been unvisited."

[2] Winterbotham.

[3] Proud. The original portrait of Makin bears some resemblance to the later and fanciful representation of the bard of Wyoming, who reports of his favorite Pennsylvanian settlement, that it long was ignorant of both war and crime, except from the testimony of European story, —

     " For here the exile met from every clime,
     And spoke in friendship every distant tongue." — Campbell.

APPENDIX I.

State and Prospects of the North American Provinces at the Close of the Seventeenth Century. — Sentiments and Opinions of the Colonists respecting the Sovereignty and the Policy of Great Britain, &c.

AT the close of the seventeenth century, the British settlements in North America contained a population of more than three hundred thousand persons, distributed among the various colonial establishments whose origin and early progress have engaged our attention.[1] The formation of these colonies is by far the most interesting event of that memorable age.[2]

" Speculative reasoners during that age," says a great historian, " raised many objections to the planting of those remote colonies, and foretold, that, after draining their mother country of inhabitants, they would soon shake off her yoke, and erect an independent government in America ; but time has shown that the views entertained by those who encouraged such *generous undertakings* were more just and solid. A mild government, and great naval force, have preserved, and *may still preserve, during some time*, the dominion of England over her colonies. And such advantages have commerce and navigation reaped from these establishments, that more than a fourth of the English shipping is at present computed to be employed in carrying on the traffic with the American settlements."[3] The apprehensions of depopulation to which this author has adverted are considered at greater length in the prior work of Oldmixon, who asserts that " on this argument are founded all the reasons to excuse the ill-usage the plantations have met with " ; and after combating the absurd and groundless alarm, appeals to the large increase already derived to the trade and the revenue of England from the colonies, as affording a juster and stronger reason for repairing that ill-usage, and introducing more liberal provisions into the English commercial code.[4] The apprehensions of American independence were no less the object of ridicule to the best informed writers, in the beginning of that century which was destined to witness the American Revolution. " It will be impossible," says Neal, " for New England to subsist of itself *for*

---

[1] From a comparison of the calculations of various writers, each of whom almost invariably contradicts all the others, and not unfrequently contradicts himself, I am inclined to think the following estimate of the population of the colonies at this period nearly, if not entirely, correct. Virginia, 60,000 ; Massachusetts (to which Maine was then attached), between 70,000 and 80,000 ; Connecticut, 30,000 ; Rhode Island, 10,000 ; New Hampshire, 10,000 ; Maryland, 30,000 ; North and South Carolina, 10,000 ; New York, 30,000 ; New Jersey, 15,000 ; and Pennsylvania, 35,000. Even writers so accurate and sagacious as Dwight and Holmes have been led to underrate the early population of North America, by relying too far on the estimates which the provincial governments furnished to the British ministry for the ascertainment of the numbers of men whom they were to be required to supply for the purposes of naval and military expeditions.

[2] See Note XXXI., at the end of the volume.

[3] Hume's *England*.

[4] Oldmixon, Introduct. Some part of this author's reasoning seems to have been derived from a work of William Penn, entitled *The Benefit of Plantations or Colonies*. Oldmixon refers to another work, in which the same topics had been enforced, entitled *Groans of the Plantations*, by Judge Littleton of Barbadoes. A still more distinguished writer on the same side of the question was Sir Dalby Thomas, an eminent merchant, and author of *An Historical Account of the Rise and Growth of the West India Colonies.*

some centuries of years ; for, though they might maintain themselves against their neighbours on the continent, they must starve without a free trade with Europe, the manufactures of the country being very inconsiderable ; so that, *if we could suppose them to rebel against England*, they must throw themselves into the arms of some other potentate, who would protect them no longer than he could sell them with advantage."[1]   So slightly were the colonies connected with each other, and so much of mutual repugnance was created by religious and political distinctions between them, that the probability of their uniting together for common defence against the parent state never occurred to this author.   Nor will this be deemed an impeachment of his sagacity, when we consider, that, seventy years afterwards, the prospect, which had then begun to dawn, of an effectual confederacy of those colonies against England, was declared by an eminent philosophical historian to be perfectly delusive and chimerical.[2]

If Hume had accurately examined the history and condition of the British colonies, or if Neal and Oldmixon had added to this acquirement the sagacity and penetration of Hume, it is probable that *he* would not have cited the *mildness* of the English government[3] as one of the circumstances that were likely to retard the independence of America, which he perceived must ere long ensue ; and that *they* would have discerned in the policy of the English government an influence strongly tending to counteract the principles that separated the American communities from each other, and to unite them by a growing sense of common interest and common injury in a confederacy fatal to the prerogative of the parent state.   Every added year tended no less to weaken the divisive influence of the distinctions imported by the original colonists into their settlements, than to enhance the sense of united interest, and to augment the *power* by which this interest might be sustained and defended.   The character of *generous undertakings*, which Hume justly applies to those colonial establishments, expresses a praise which the English government had no pretension to share with the private individuals by whom they were founded ;[4] and the mild policy, whether spontaneous or accidental, which permitted the liberal institutions erected by these men for themselves to continue in existence, tended rather to abridge than to prolong the British dominion, by nourishing in the colonies a spirit and habit of liberty repugnant to the unjust and oppressive strain of the British commercial restrictions.[5]   The colonial empire of Spain would not have boasted a longer duration than that of England, if her settlements in South America had enjoyed as liberal constitutions as the North American colonies. "The policy of Europe," says a writer who perhaps equalled Hume in political sagacity, and certainly excelled him in acquaintance with colonial history, "has very little to boast of, either in the original establishment, or, so far as concerns their internal government, in the subsequent prosperity, of the colonies of America."   Folly and injustice he pronounces to have been

---

[1] *History of New England.*   [2] Raynal's *America.*
[3] "Britain," says another historian, "behaved like an unnatural parent to her own colonies, and treated them like aliens and rivals."   Smollett's *England.*
[4] The colonization of Georgia, which did not occur till 1732, was the only instance in which the English government contributed to the foundation of any of the North American States.
[5] See an account of the commercial restrictions that were imposed prior to the British Revolution, and an examination of their policy, *ante*, Book I., Chap. III. To the restrictions there described, there was added, before the close of the seventeenth century, a prohibition (noticed in the histories of New Jersey and Pennsylvania) of the exportation of wool from the colonies.

the principles that presided over the formation of all the colonial settlements ; avarice of gold impelling the adventurers to the southern, and
tyranny and persecution promoting the emigrations to the northern parts
of America. The governments of the several parent states, he remarks with
truth, contributed little or nothing towards the plantation of their colonies,
and yet invariably attempted to enrich their own exchequers, and secure
to themselves a monopoly of the colonial commerce,[1] by regulations injurious to the freedom and prosperity of the colonists, — a policy in which the
particular procedure of England was distinguished only as somewhat less illiberal and oppressive than that of the other European states. "In what
way, therefore," demands this great writer, "has the policy of Europe contributed either to the first establishment or to the present grandeur of the
colonies of America ? In one way, and in one way only, it has contributed
a great deal. *Magna mater virum !* It bred and formed the men who
were capable of achieving such great actions, and of laying the foundations
of so great an empire ; and there is no other quarter of the world of which
the policy is capable of forming, or has ever actually and in fact formed,
such men. The colonies owe to the policy of Europe the education and
great views of their active and enterprising founders ; and some of the greatest and most important of them, so far as concerns their internal government, owe to it scarce any thing else."[2]

In the colonial establishments of the French, the Spaniards, and the
Portuguese, the royal government was stronger and more despotic, and
subordination was more strictly enforced, than in the relative parent states.
Illiberal institutions, remote from the power and splendor of the thrones
to which they were allied, required to be guarded with peculiar care from
the approach of opinions and practices that savored of freedom. It was
otherwise in the British colonies, where the grafts of constitutional liberty
that were transplanted from the parent state expanded with a vigor proportioned to their distance from the rival shoots of royalty and aristocracy
with which they were theoretically connected. Though a great diversity
of views and motives contributed to the foundation of these colonial communities, yet a considerable similarity of character and disposition was produced among their inhabitants by the similarity of the fortune which they
encountered, and of the social positions which they attained in America.
Not only did the British colonies enjoy domestic constitutions favorable to
liberty, but there existed in the minds of the great bulk of the people a
democratic spirit[3] and determination that practically reduced the power
of the parent state even below the standard of its political theory. Many
causes contributed to the production of this spirit, and to the nurture and
development of its vigor and efficacy. All the colonial charters were extorted, by interest or importunity, from princes noted for arbitrary designs
or perfidious characters ; and no sooner had the charters produced the
effect of collecting numerous and thriving communities in America, than
some of them were annulled, and all of them would have shared the same

---

[1] See Note XXXII., at the end of the volume.

[2] Smith's *Wealth of Nations.* See also Postlethwayt's *Universal Dictionary of Trade.*

[3] Colonel Quarry, in his *Memorial to the Lords of Trade,* in 1703, after reprobating the republican spirit that prevailed in Virginia, protested, that "Now or never is the time to maintain the queen's prerogative, and put a stop to those wrong, pernicious notions which are
improving daily, not only in Virginia, but in all her Majesty's other governments." "A frown
now from her Majesty," he adds, "could do more than an army hereafter." See also the
statements cited in Note XXVIII.

fate, if the dynasty of the Stuarts had endured a little longer.   The designs
of these princes were not sincerely or substantially repudiated by their successors.   For many years after the British Revolution, the American colonists were provoked to continual contests in defence of their charters, which
the English court made successive attempts to qualify or abolish.   These
defensive efforts, and the success with which they were generally crowned,
tended strongly to keep alive an active ,and vigilant spirit of liberty in
America.   The ecclesiastical constitutions and the religious sentiments that
prevailed in the majority of the provinces were no less favorable to the
growth of liberal and independent sentiments.   In Virginia, Maryland, and
Carolina, alone of all the   States, — in the first from its earliest settlement,
and in the others by unjust usurpation, — the church of England was possessed of a legal preëminence, and supported at the expense, not only of
its own adherents, but of all the other inhabitants, of whatever Christian
denomination.   In every one of the other States there existed, about the
close of the seventeenth century, either an entire political equality of religious sects, or at least a very near approach to it ; and in these States,
not only were the inhabitants, by their general character of Protestants,
the votaries of a system founded on the acknowledged supremacy of popular and individual judgment, — but the majority of them, belonging to that
class which in England received the title of Protestant Dissenters, professed tenets which have been termed *the Protestantism of the Protestant
faith*, and which naturally predispose the minds that harbour them to a jealous regard for civil liberty, and a promptitude to repel every arbitrary exertion of municipal authority.   Even the Episcopal churcn, where it existed,
whether as the preëminent establishment, or as one of many coequal associations, was stripped of the aristocratical appendages which it enjoyed in
the parent state, and exhibited neither a titled hierarchy nor a gradation of
ranks among the ministers of religion.   In civil life a similar equality of condition generally prevailed.   No attempt was ever made to introduce the
haughty privilege of titular *nobility* into any of the provinces except Carolina, where the institution soon withered and died.[1]   Unaccustomed to that
distinction of ranks which the policy of Europe has established, the people were generally impressed with a conviction of the natural equality of
all freemen ; and even in those provinces where negro slavery obtained
the greatest prevalence, the possession of this tyrannical privilege seems
rather to have inflamed and adulterated the spirit of freedom with a considerable tinge of arrogance, than to have contributed at all to mitigate its
ardor.   Slave-owners regarded every approach to the condition of slavery
with stern aversion and disdain.   Except that inhuman institution, every
circumstance in the domestic or relative condition of these provinces had
a tendency to promote industry, good morals, and impressions of equality.
The liberal reward of labor and the cheapness of land placed the enjoyment of comfort and the generous dignity of independence within the reach
of all the inhabitants ; the luxuries and official dignities of England attracted the wealthy voluptuary and the votary of ambition to that fitter
sphere of enjoyment and intrigue ;[2] and the vast *wastes* or uncultivated

---

[1] Yet the mysterious nonsense of *freemasonry* was introduced pretty early, and has continued to maintain a footing among the Americans.

[2] William Penn, in his treatise on *The Benefit of Plantations or Colonies*, declares, that
many persons, who had been constrained by poverty to emigrate, had returned with large fortunes, accumulated in the colonies, to reside in England.

districts attached to every province presented salutary outlets by which the population was drained of those restless, disorderly adventurers who were averse to legal restraint and patient labor, and who, in the roving occupation of hunters and *backwoodsmen* (as they have been termed), found a resource that diverted them from more lawless and dangerous pursuits, and even rendered them useful as a body of pioneers who paved the way for an extension and multiplication of the colonial settlements. Feudal tenures were little known in America, where almost every farmer was a freeholder and absolute proprietor of the ground which he cultivated. No trading corporations or monopolies restrained the freedom with which every man might employ his industry, capital, and skill; and no forest laws nor game laws confined the sports of the field to a privileged class of the community. No entails were admitted, to give adventitious aid to natural inequalities, and perpetuate in the hands of idleness and incapacity the substance that had been amassed by industry and talent.[1] Happily for the stability of American freedom, it was impossible for the first generation of colonists to succeed in rearing their settlements, and attaining a secure and prosperous establishment, without the exercise of virtues and the formation of a character that guarantied the preservation of the blessings to which they had conducted.[2] Even the calamities of French and Indian war, which long harassed some of the provinces, contributed to preserve a spirit and habits without which their people would probably have been unable, in the eighteenth century, to achieve their independence.[3] In Virginia we have already seen the preparations elicited by an Indian war rendered instrumental to a rebellion against the parent state; and the annals of New England and New York have shown us nearly half of the American provinces induced to unite their counsels and forces in common efforts against the French and their Indian allies. If the later settlements of New Jersey and Pennsylvania were exempted in some degree from the discipline of those hardships and difficulties with which the commencement of all the other settlements was attended, they were peopled chiefly by a class of religious professors whose habits and manners are peculiarly favorable to industry and good morals, and congenial to the spirit of republican institutions. The Quakers, indeed, have been much more successful in leavening American society with manners favorable to liberty than with principles allied to their own political doctrines.

To England the acquisition of these colonial settlements was highly advantageous. They enlarged her trade and revenues; they afforded a boundless field in which her needy and superfluous children might improve their condition and dissipate their discontent; and, finally, they created for her a new nation of friends interested in her happiness and renown, and of customers whose growing wants and wealth stimulated and rewarded the manufacturing industry of her domestic population. Every British emigrant to North America, by his secession from his native country, contributed to extend the imitation of her manners, the popularity of her literature, and the prevalence of her language,[4] character, and institutions; and the British

---

[1] At a subsequent period, the system of entails became prevalent in Virginia. Wirt's *Life of Henry.* It was productive of great dislike and jealousy between the aristocracy and the yeomanry of the province. Ibid. It was abolished three months after the declaration of American Independence.

[2] See Note XXXIII., at the end of the volume.   [3] See *Judges*, iii., 1, 2.

[4] "Our solid and increasing establishments in America, where we need little dread the inundation of barbarians, promise a superior stability and duration to the English language." Hume to Gibbon, 1767.

shoot, that with so much elaborate virtue was grafted on America, will reflect glory on the parent stem, when Britain herself may *sleep under the
shade of a mighty name.*   It was the calculation of Sir Josiah Child, that
every colonist, by the produce of his labor in the plantations, furnished
employment and maintenance to four persons in the mother country.   All
the nations of Europe derived advantage from the formation of the American settlements, which disburdened their territories of great numbers of
men, whom the pressure of poverty aggravated by defective civil institutions, and an aversion to the systems of their national churches inflamed
by ecclesiastical intolerance, must have rendered either martyrs or rebels in
their native land.   The emigration from the continent of Europe, and especially from Germany, to America, during the greater part of the eighteenth century, was much more copious than the emigration from England.
To the colonists the subsistence of their peculiar connection with England
was likewise attended with considerable advantage.   The acknowledged
sovereignty and implied protection of England deterred all other European
powers who were not at war with her from molesting them ; while their
chartered or traditionary constitution opposed (after the British Revolution) a barrier to gross and open encroachments of the parent state herself
on the provincial rights and liberties.   As their own strength and resources
increased, the benefit of England's protection was proportionally diminished,
while the inconvenience of her commercial restrictions, and of participation in her military policy, was more sensibly experienced.

A remarkable variety and indistinctness of opinion prevailed, both in Britain and America, respecting the precise nature and import of the political
relation that united the two countries.   It was at first the maxim of the
court, that the crown was the only member of the British constitution which
possessed jurisdiction over the colonies.[1]   All the charters were framed
in conformity with this view, except the charter of Pennsylvania.   The
colonists were by no means uniform in the sentiments they expressed on
this subject.   They all condemned the unjust power usurped over them by
the British parliament, when the Navigation Laws were passed ; and openly
asserted, on various occasions, that an act of the British parliament was
not obligatory, by its own mere intrinsic efficacy, on America.   Yet, in many
instances, they scrupled not to complain of their incidental grievances to
the houses of parliament, and to invoke the interposition of parliamentary
authority in their behalf.   The New England States alone perceived from
the first the advantage they might one day derive from adhering to the
maxim, that they were politically connected only with the king, and not at
all with the parliament ; and with singular prudence forbore to solicit favors
even from a parliament by which they were regarded with especial good-
will, lest they should seem to sanction parliamentary interference in their
concerns.   When the parliament enjoyed only an accidental existence, and
was frequently, indeed generally, opposed to the court, the English monarchs resolutely maintained their exclusive jurisdiction over the colonies.
When the parliament acquired greater power and stability, it compelled
both the court and the colonies to acknowledge its supreme legislatorial
jurisdiction.   The colonists murmured against the trade laws ; they fre-

---

[1] A bill having been introduced into the House of Commons, in the reign of James the
First, for regulating the American fisheries, Sir George Calvert, secretary of state, conveyed to
the House the following intimation from the king : — " America is not annexed to the realm,
nor within the jurisdiction of parliament ; you have, therefore, no right to interfere." *Colonial Tracts in Harvard Library, apud* Holmes.

quently evaded those obnoxious regulations ; and many persons still maintained that the parliament had no right to impose them. This opinion continued to prevail,[1] and would have been more generally and openly asserted,
if the colonists had been less overawed by the power of England, or had
received encouragement from the crown. But the English ministers were
now always (by a necessity of the constitution) possessed of a commanding majority in parliament, and found it easier and safer to act through
the instrumentality of this organ, than through a prerogative employed on a
variety of distant provincial assemblies. The Revolution of 1688 established firmly the supreme authority of the parliament, and consequently the
submission of America to its legislative control. No taxation of the colonies was *practically attempted* by the parliament, except what arose from
the regulation of commerce ; but an abstract right of indefinite taxation
was repeatedly proclaimed, and a power was assumed to alter the American charters, or at least to modify the constitutions which these charters had
created. There was one point, indeed, in which the relation of the colonies to the royal prerogative appeared still to be acknowledged. It was
not to the House of Lords, or to any of the ordinary tribunals of England, that appeals were preferred from the judgments of American courts,
but to the king in council ; and it was the same organ that enjoyed the
privilege of modifying and rescinding the provincial laws which were deemed
repugnant to English jurisprudence.[2]

Yielding not to conviction, but to necessity, — overawed by the strength
of Britain, — and embarrassed by the dangerous vicinity of the French in
Canada, — the colonists submitted to the power of parliament, and rendered
to it even that degree of voluntary acknowledgment which may be inferred
from numerous petitions for the redress of grievances.[3] Yet the submission
actually obtained was yielded with undisguised reluctance ; and the pretensions, in conformity with which that submission might be still farther
extended, were regarded with the most jealous apprehension. So early as
the year 1696, a pamphlet was published in England, recommending the
parliamentary imposition of a domestic tax on one of the colonies. This
suggestion was instantly and vigorously impugned by two responsory
pamphlets, in which the right of taxing the colonies was expressly denied to
a parliament in which they were not represented.[4]

There were various particulars in the supremacy exercised and the policy pursued by the parent state, that were offensive to the colonists, and
regarded by them as humiliating badges of dependence. The royal prerogative exerted in the nomination of certain of the provincial governors not

---

[1] See the statement of Colonel Nicholson, cited in Note XXVIII., at the end of the volume.

[2] Lord Mansfield repeatedly pronounced that it was within the competency of the English
Court of King's Bench to send a writ of *habeas corpus* into America; but he remarked that
this was a power which could rarely, if ever, be exercised with propriety. Stokes on the
Constitution of the British Colonies.

[3] When they became more wealthy and powerful, and found that the parliament was projecting to usurp their domestic taxation, they refrained from sending petitions to it, and presented them only to the king ; — see Franklin's *Works ;* — and at length boldly revived the
ancient maxim, "that the king, and not the king, lords, and commons collectively, is their
sovereign ; and that the king, with their respective assemblies, is their only legislator." Ibid.
Thus the Americans, in contending for their independence, finally took their stand on a principle originally introduced by despotic princes, and intended to secure the subjection of the
colonies to arbitrary government and royal prerogative.

[4] Gordon's *History of the United States.* "The pamphlets against taxation (said Lord Camden, in his speech in the House of Lords, April, 1766) were much read, and no answer was
given to them, no censure passed upon them ; nor were men startled at the doctrine." Ibid.

only created discontent in the provinces which were thus debarred from a privilege enjoyed by the inhabitants of the other States, but excited in those others a continual apprehension of being levelled in this respect with the condition of their neighbours. The manner, too, in which this royal prerogative was frequently administered, tended to render it additionally disagreeable. It was no less the interest than the duty of the parent state, that the provincial viceroys whom she appointed should be men whose talents and characters were fitted to communicate impressions of the dignity of her supreme dominion and the benevolence of her superintending care. Yet the general practice of the English ministers was to commit the royal governments to needy dependents, whose chief aim was to repair a shattered fortune, and to recommend themselves to their patrons by a headlong zeal for the assertion of every real or pretended prerogative of the crown.[1] In thus partially straining and illiberally exerting her power, the parent state pursued towards the colonies a policy at once unjust, offensive, and inefficient. It would perhaps have been more politic to have usurped the appointment of all the provincial governors, and to have bestowed these offices on men of splendid rank and fortune, salaried by the crown, and capable of maintaining in the provinces the appearance of a court.

The transportation of felons to America was also a practice of the British government, which the lapse of time and the multiplication of negro slaves rendered increasingly offensive to the colonists. We have seen the assembly of Maryland, as early as the year 1676, endeavour to obstruct the stream of vicious and perilous example which was thus directed by the parent state among the laboring classes of her colonial subjects. The assembly of Pennsylvania made an attempt to discourage the importation of convicts into its territory by imposing a duty of five pounds on every convict that should be imported. But it was not till a later period that the practice excited general disapprobation in America. So pressing in most places was the demand for laborers, that their moral character, and the terms on which they were obtained, were considerations to which the planters had not leisure to attend. Nay, in some instances, felons were not the only involuntary emigrants from England whose labor they appropriated. It became at one time a common practice for captains of vessels to entice ignorant persons, by flattering promises of wealth and preferment, to accompany them to America, where they had no sooner arrived, than they were sold as bondsmen to defray the cost of their passage and entertainment. So early as the year 1686, an order of council[2] was issued for the prevention of this practice. In process of time, all the provincial governments, and all the wealthy inhabitants of the provinces (especially of those in which negro slaves were most numerous), united in petitioning the British gov-

[1] Sir William Keith's *History of Virginia.* Williamson's *North Carolina.* We have already seen abundant confirmation of the testimony of these writers in the histories of Virginia, New York, and New Jersey. See the observations on the general effect of the English Revolution on the American colonies, at the close of the history of Virginia, Book I., Chap. III., *ante.*

[2] This document is preserved in the British Museum. The system of inveigling and kidnapping was not confined to England. It was carried on to a great extent in Suabia and other German cantons by Dutch factors, whom Raynal asserts to have been hired by the British government. But that this charge was unjust in some instances, and probably in all, may be collected from a curious and interesting article in the *Annual Register* for 1764.

Young persons of blighted reputation or feeble understanding were sometimes conveyed by their friends to the American plantations, in order to bury memorials of family disgrace. Benjamin, the eldest son of the poet Waller, appearing deficient in capacity, was disinherited by his father and sent to New Jersey. Johnson's *Life of Waller.*

ernment to discontinue the practice of sending felons to America;[1] but their complaints of this evil, as well as of the continued importation of additional negro slaves, were entirely disregarded. "Very early," says an American writer, "it had been the fashion to suppose, that the colonists, by emigrating, had lost a portion of their dignity, and that at best they should be regarded only as an inferior order of Englishmen, whose duty it was to labor for the glory and advancement of the nation."[2] One consequence that resulted from this arbitrary and degrading treatment was the existence of gross ignorance or illiberal prejudice with regard to the social condition of North America, in the minds of all classes of people in England.[3] Though persons connected with the colonies, by commerce or otherwise, might entertain juster notions of their condition, it is certain that till a very late period these territories were commonly regarded in England as wild, inhospitable deserts, infested by savages and beasts of prey, and cultivated only by criminals or by enslaved negroes and kidnapped Europeans. Though Bishop Berkeley prophesied a destiny of unequalled glory to this region, in his *Verses on the Prospect of planting Arts and Literature in America*, and though Thomson celebrated the happiness of the colonies, and their instrumentalness to the grandeur of the British empire,[4] the encomiastic strains of these writers were more than counterbalanced by the sarcastic and opprobrious imputations which were circulated by other and more popular authors.[5] The conquest of Louisburg from the French, in 1745, —

---

[1] An American patriot humorously proposed that a reciprocal transportation of American rattlesnakes to England should in equity be indulged to the colonists. Franklin's *Memoirs*.

[2] Burk's *History of Virginia*.

[3] Preface to Smith's *New York*. See Note XXXIV., at the end of the volume.

[4] " Lo ! swarming o'er the new-discovered world
    Gay colonies extend ; the calm retreat
    Of undeserved distress. . . . . .
    . . . Bound by social freedom, firm they rise ;
    Of Britain's empire the support and strength." — Thomson.

[5] Smollett alludes to the colonies of North America in the following strain : — " *The galleys of France abound with abbés ; and many templars may be found in our American plantations.*" *Count Fathom.* Among the bad company assembled at Bath, the same writer enumerates " planters, negro drivers, and hucksters from our American plantations." *Humphrey Clinker.* " Our people," he adds, " have a strange itch to colonize America, when the uncultivated parts of our own island might be settled to greater advantage." Ibid. Fielding sends his hero, *Jonathan Wild*, to fortify his vice and villany in Virginia ; and in various other allusions to the colonies, always represents them as the suitable refuge of *deserved distress*. In Reed's farce, *The Register Office*, a miserable Irishman is exhibited as on the point of being trepanned to America, to be there sold as a slave. A similar scene is depicted in Goldsmith's *Vicar of Wakefield*, where an unfortunate man of letters is nearly kidnapped by an insidious offer of being appointed " Secretary to an embassy from the Synod of Pennsylvania to the Chickasaw Indians." Even in this author's poem, *The Traveller,* where the expulsion of an English peasant and his family from their home is represented as an ordinary consequence of the pride and luxury of English landlords, the exiles are supposed to find a tenfold addition to their woes in North America. Nay, this strain seems not yet to have ceased ; and the grief of " heart-sick exiles " in America has been deplored by Sir Walter Scott in the nineteenth century. Alluding to the wild, melancholy song of Scottish Highlanders, this great bard observes, —
     " I thought how sad would be that sound
     On Susquehannah's swampy ground,
     Kentucky's wood-encumbered brake,
     And wild Ontario's boundless lake,
     Where heart-sick exiles in the strain
     Recalled fair Scotland's hills again." — *Marmion*.
Since the time when Waller and Marvell eulogized the tranquil retreat of Bermudas, I am not aware that any other British poets but Thomson, Mrs. Barbauld, Campbell, and Lord Byron, have celebrated the happy scenes and circumstances of American life. There is more of pathos than of animation in the strain in which my revered and amiable kinsman, the late author of *The Sabbath*, has, in that delightful poem, depicted the feelings of Scottish settlers in America. Emigrants may entertain, not properly a regretful, but a fond, and even melancholy, remembrance of their native land, amid circumstances far happier than that land could afford them.

an enterprise originally projected by the genius, and mainly accomplished by the vigor, of the government of Massachusetts, — was the circumstance that first prepared the people of England to receive more just impressions of the dignity and importance of the American provinces.

But no particular of the treatment which the colonists experienced from England, during the early part of their connection with her, was so generally offensive to them as the restrictions she imposed upon their trade and industry. This system not only disgusted them by its injustice, but seems in some instances to have perverted their sentiments and infected their counsels with a corresponding strain of selfish illiberality. In some of the commercial ordinances that were framed by the colonists, we may discern the reflection of that narrow and grasping spirit that pervaded the policy of the parent state, — a defensive or vindictive reaction of the illiberal principles to whose operation they were themselves exposed. An act of the assembly of Virginia, in 1680, imposed a duty on all tobacco exported from, and on all emigrants imported into, the colony in vessels not belonging to Virginian owners. By an ordinance of Massachusetts, a tonnage duty was imposed on all ships casting anchor in any port within its jurisdiction, excepting vessels owned by inhabitants of the State. A similar duty was imposed by the assembly of Rhode Island, in the year 1704, on all vessels not wholly owned by inhabitants of this colony. In 1709, the legislature of New York imposed a tonnage duty on every vessel of which one half did not belong to citizens of this State. By a law of Maryland, in 1715, the duties imposed on the importation of negroes, servants, and liquors were declared not to extend to cargoes imported in vessels whose owners were all residents in the colony. The legislature of the same province had eleven years before prohibited the collection of debts due to English bankrupts, till security were given that the claims of provincial creditors on the bankrupt's estate should first be wholly discharged.[1] Even the Pennsylvanians, who in this respect professed a more liberal consideration of the claims of foreign creditors than any of the other provincial communities, enacted a law for securing priority of payment from the estates of bankrupts to the inhabitants of their own province. Among other apologies for this policy with regard to the recovery of debts (which obtained a general prevalence throughout the colonies), it has been urged, with unquestioned and perhaps unquestionable accuracy, that the planters were commonly treated with great illiberality by the merchants to whom they consigned their produce in England, — who took advantage of their necessities, while the sales of provincial produce were in suspense, to lend them money at exorbitant interest, and on the security of their mortgaged plantations.[2] Almost all the American planters and merchants were continually in debt to their English correspondents ; and so partial was the parent state to their interests, that in the year 1758 she prohibited the province of Massachusetts from adopting the bankrupt law of England, lest its operation should be perverted to the injury of English creditors of American debtors. In 1701, the assembly of South Carolina imposed a duty of three farthings a skin on hides exported by the colonists in their own ships, but double this amount if the exports were loaded in English vessels,[3] — a distinction

[1] In the history of Maryland we have already seen the first instance of a law disabling all settlers from enjoying provincial offices till by residence for a term of years they might be supposed to have contracted provincial habits, views, and notions.
[2] See Note XXXV., at the end of the volume.
[3] In the year 1718, an act of the assembly of South Carolina imposed a heavy duty on

against which the English Commissioners of Plantations remonstrated, as an unjust discouragement of the commerce of England.[1] The Virginian act of 1680 had provoked similar remonstrances from the same quarter, and made the British nation feel that to practise injustice is to teach a lesson that often returns to plague the inventor.

In the year 1696, King William erected a new and standing council at London, of which the members were entitled the Lords Commissioners for Trade and Plantations. The governors of all the American provinces were required to maintain correspondence with this board, and to transmit to it the journals of their councils and assemblies, the accounts of the collectors of customs, and similar documents and articles of official intelligence. This requisition was obeyed by the governors who derived their functions from royal appointment, but met with very little attention in those colonies of which the governors were appointed by the people. In the year 1714, the attorney-general of England (Northey) acquainted the English ministers that it was not in their power to punish such neglect, and advised them to apply to parliament for an act commanding all the colonies to submit their laws to royal revision. His recommendation, however, was not adopted ; and a report of the Lords Commissioners, in the year 1733, announces that " Rhode Island and Connecticut, being charter governments, hold little or no correspondence with our office, and we are very little informed of what is doing in these governments ; they not being under any obligation to return authentic copies of their laws to the crown for its sanction or disallowance, or to give any account of their proceedings." [2]

There was a considerable variety in the civil and political constitutions of the several provinces at the commencement of the eighteenth century. In Maryland and Pennsylvania, the property of the soil and the administration of the executive power belonged to one or more proprietaries. This was also the situation of the Carolinas and New Jersey, till the surrender of their proprietary jurisdictions ; when the soil belonged to the proprietaries, and the executive power to the crown. In Massachusetts, the property of the soil was vested in the people and their representatives, and the executive power was exercised by the crown. In Virginia and New York, both the soil and the executive authority belonged to the crown. In Connecticut and Rhode Island, both the soil and every function of government were vested in the corporation of the freemen of the colony. These distinctions promoted frequent disputes respecting boundaries, in which the crown was supposed, and not without reason, to favor the claims of those States wherein its prerogative was greatest and the quitrents enlarged the royal revenue. But they exercised a more beneficial influence upon the colonists, in prompting them to canvass and discuss the merits of those systems of municipal authority, of which so great a variety was presented to their view, — and thus promoting among them a constant and

---

all British manufactures imported into this province. Similar acts were passed at the same time by the legislatures of Massachusetts and New York. They were all repealed by command of George the First. Hewit. Hutchinson. Smith's *New York.*

[1] *Abridgment of the Laws of Virginia. New England Ordinances Abridged. Laws of Rhode Island. Laws of New York. Laws of Maryland.* Oldmixon. Chalmers

[2] Anderson's *Historical and Chronological Deduction of the Origin of Commerce.* Chalmers. As a remedy for the defective correspondence which was anticipated between the colonies and the Board of Trade, an act of parliament was passed in 1696, declaring (in conformity with the colonial charters), " that all by-laws, usages, and customs, which shall be in practice in any of the plantations, repugnant to any law made in the kingdom relative to the said plantations, shall be void and of no effect."

animating circulation of political sentiment and opinion. All the provinces were nearly on the same footing in respect of the structure of that important organ of liberty, their representative assemblies.

No encouragement was ever afforded by the British government to the cultivation of science or literature in the American provinces, except in the solitary instance of a donation by William and Mary, in aid of the college which took its name from them in Virginia.[1] The policy of the parent state in this respect was thus delineated by one of the royal governors, in the beginning of the eighteenth century : — " As to the college erected in Virginia, and other designs of the like nature which have been proposed for the encouragement of learning, it is only to be observed in general, that, although great advantages may accrue to the mother state both from the labor and luxury of its plantations, yet they will probably be mistaken, who imagine that the advancement of literature and the improvement of arts and sciences in our American colonies can be of any service to the British state." [2] We have already beheld the instructions that were communicated to the royal governors by the British court, both prior and subsequent to the Revolution of 1688, to restrain the exercise of printing within their jurisdictions. Many laws were framed in New England, after that event, for enlarging the literary privileges and honors of Harvard College ; but they were all abolished by the British government.[3]

The first printing-press employed in North America was established in Massachusetts, in the year 1638. It was not till half a century later that printing commenced in any other part of British America. In 1686, a printing-press was established in Pennsylvania ; in 1693, at New York ; in 1709, in Connecticut ; in 1726, in Maryland ; in 1729, in Virginia ; and in 1730, in South Carolina. Previous to the year 1740, more printing was performed in Massachusetts than in all the other colonies together. From 1760 till the commencement of the Revolutionary War, the quantities of printing executed in Boston and Philadelphia were nearly the same. The first North American newspaper was published at Boston, by Campbell, a Scotchman, the provincial postmaster, in 1704. The second made its appearance in the same city in 1719 ; and in the same year, the third was published in Philadelphia. In 1725, New York, for the first time, published a newspaper ; in 1732, Rhode Island obtained the same advantage ; and after this period similar journals were gradually introduced into the other colonies.[4]

The press, in America, was nowhere entirely free from legal restraint till about the year 1755. In 1723, James Franklin (brother of Dr. Benjamin Franklin) was prohibited by the governor and council of Massachusetts from publishing *The New England Courant*, without previously submitting its contents to the revision of the secretary of the province ; and in 1754, one Fowle was imprisoned by the House of Assembly of the

[1] Dartmouth College, in New Hampshire, which was founded in the year 1769, received, indeed, some patronage from the British monarch, George the Third. But the object of royal patronage, on this occasion, was not the improvement of the colonists, but the instruction of the Indians.
[2] Sir William Keith's *History of Virginia*. I have termed Keith a royal governor. He was, it is true, the governor of a proprietary settlement, Pennsylvania. But the appointment of all these governors was now controlled by the necessity of royal approbation ; and Keith's nomination, in consequence of William Penn's mental incapacity at the time, proceeded altogether from the crown.
[3] Holmes.
[4] John Dunton, in the prospectus of the journal which he began to publish at London in 1696, states that there were then but eight newspapers published in England. None were published in Scotland till after the accession of William and Mary.

same province, *on suspicion* of having printed a pamphlet containing censorious reflections on some members of the government.   After the year 1730, there was no officer appointed in Massachusetts to exercise a particular control over the press ; but prior to that period, the *imprimatur* of a licenser was inscribed on many of the New England publications. The first postoffice created by British authority in North America was established by act of parliament in the year 1710.[1]

A country where labor was so dear, and proprietors of land were so numerous, as in North America, might, not unreasonably, be supposed peculiarly favorable to the growth of a skilful and economical system of husbandry.   While the dearness of labor restrained expensive cultivation, the general diffusion of the ownership of land enhanced and multiplied incitements to industry and improvement.   But the influence of these causes was counteracted by the cheapness and abundance of land, and the vast forests with which the whole country was overgrown.   Every man possessed land enough to afford him a sufficient subsistence by the simplest and coarsest agricultural process ; and a great deal of industry was absorbed in the operation of disencumbering the ground of wood.   Rotation of crops and the art of manuring obtained little regard from farmers whom the woodman's axe supplied with continual accessions of fresh and fertile soil to replace the portions that had been fatigued by culture.   Although every one of the settlements already possessed numerous substantial edifices of brick and stone, yet, from the dearness of labor and the abundance of wood, the greater number of dwelling-houses were everywhere constructed of this material, — a practice which was prolonged till a very late period by the erroneous notion that wooden houses contributed a better defence than stone buildings against the humidity of the atmosphere.[2]

In every state of society we may discern the operation of a levelling principle which restricts or counteracts the beneficial influence of favorable circumstances, and mitigates or countervails the pressure of circumstances unfavorable to human happiness and prosperity.   Density of population and the convergence of wealth and authority in a few hands promote the division, the neatness, and the mechanical perfection of labor.   Where wealth and population, on the contrary, are dispersed, and equality of rights prevails, the dearness of labor and the scarcity and independence of laborers obstruct the division of employments ; every man is constrained to dispense as far as possible with hired service, and, doing almost every thing for himself, to do much in a coarse and inferior style.   The mechanical workmanship is less perfect ; but a superior development of intelligence characterizes the workman.   In old and crowded societies, where aristocratical institutions prevail, hired labor produces the most elegant commodities, the finest and amplest provision of conveniences to the employers of the laboring classes ; in thinly peopled and improving communities, devoid of aristocratical institutions, it produces most advantage to the laborers themselves ; and of course in the latter, the general destination of mankind to labor is a circumstance more propitious to human happiness than in the former.   But in crowded and aristocratical states, the elegance which the wealthy and privileged classes are enabled to enjoy, from their own leisure and the cheapness and perfection of hired labor, de-

[1] Isaiah Thomas's *History of Printing in America.*   Holmes.   *Collections of the Massachusetts Historical Society.*

[2] Jefferson was the first who attempted to combat this error of his countrymen, in his *Notes on Virginia.*   In 1692, the legislature of Massachusetts enacted, that no building, exceeding certain dimensions, should be erected in Boston, but of stone or brick, and covered with slate or tile.   Holmes.

scends by imitation to the laborers themselves, and tends to refine the accommodations of their comparatively meagre estate ; while in communities thinly peopled and unacquainted with aristocratical distinctions, the rich have less leisure for the cultivation of refinement, and the poor are strangers to that dependence which begets imitation. Where labor is cheap, and laborers consequently much dependent on their employers, only neatness and economy can enable them to enjoy comfort ; social progression is slow ; the laborer is more likely to succeed in embellishing his actual condition than in rising beyond it ; and refinement of habits and manners, aided by the strong influence of imitation, is generally proportioned to advancement of condition. Where labor is dear, and dependence and aristocratical distinctions are unknown, a great deal of coarse comfort may consist with neglect of neatness and economy ; the very richness of the rewards of labor supplies a strong temptation to indolence and sensuality, which frequently overpowers the attractive hope of advancement ; and from the absence at once of models consecrated by public homage, and of a disciplined spirit of imitation, enlargement of estate is often greatly disproportioned to the polish and improvement of manners, tastes, and accommodations. Inelegant ease and slovenly plenty are said to have characterized the manners and circumstances of a considerable portion of the colonists of North America, and especially of the Middle and Southern States. This reproach has doubtless been exaggerated ; and even those who must be esteemed its unexceptionable supporters nave acknowledged the restriction which it derived from the influence of Puritan, Quaker, and latterly of Methodist and Moravian manners. The cultivation of the spirit and principles of Christianity is the most certain and the purest process that can be employed for the refinement of human tastes, manners, and habits. It is religion alone, which, teaching mankind duly to appreciate the dignity and felicity of their lot, preserves them from that worst of all evils, the abuse of blessings, causes the sentiment of liberty to impart elevation without arrogance, and the possession of wealth to refine without relaxing the springs of exertion.

America has owed to Europe not only a race of civilized men, but a breed of domestic animals. Oxen, horses, and sheep were introduced by the English, French, Dutch, and Swedes into their respective settlements. Bees were imported by the English. The Indians, who had never seen these insects before, gave them the name of *English flies* ; and used to say to each other, when a swarm of bees appeared in the woods, " Brothers, it is time for us to decamp, for the white people are coming." [1]

Every one of the provinces beheld the Indian tribes, by which it was surrounded, melt away more or less rapidly under the influence of a civilized neighbourhood.[2] In none of the provinces (with the exception, perhaps, of South Carolina) were wars undertaken against that unfortunate race

---

[1] Kalm. Morse, Art. *Kentucky.* Oldmixon asserts (2d edit.) that America had neither rats nor mice till the arrival of the European vessels. In the year 1701, a few camels were imported into Virginia in certain vessels from Guinea ; but the attempt to rear a breed of these animals in the colony proved unsuccessful. Oldmixon. Wynne.

[2] " So the red Indian, by Ontario's side,
Nursed hardy on the brindled panther's hide,
As fades his swarthy race, with anguish sees
The white man's cottage rise beneath the trees.
He leaves the shelter of his native wood,
He leaves the murmur of Ohio's flood,
And forward rushing, in indignant grief,
Where never foot has trod the fallen leaf,
He bends his course where twilight reigns sublime
O'er forests silent since the birth of time." — Leyden.

for the sake of conquest ; yet none of the colonies whose history we have hitherto traced, except New Jersey and Pennsylvania, were able to avoid altogether a contest, of which the issue was always unfavorable to the Indians.   Virginia was the only province of which the soil had been occupied without a previous purchase from the Indians ; and in South Carolina alone had the treatment which these savages experienced from an English provincial government been justly chargeable with defect of forbearance and humanity.   The hostile aggressions of the Indians were provoked not only by their own jealousy of the rapid progress of the colonial settlements, but by injuries which they sustained from particular individuals among the colonists, and which their political maxims and habits taught them to avenge by reprisals against the whole community to which those individuals were reputed to belong.   The back settlements of all the provinces, on account of their remoteness from the seats of justice, were naturally resorted to by the most worthless and disorderly classes of the emigrant population, — by fugitive felons and idle vagabonds, whose behaviour to their savage neighbours did not always coincide with the precepts of natural equity.   Scorning to complain of such wrongs, and unaccustomed to a limited or discriminative revenge, the Indians were too frequently incited by those private quarrels to general hostilities, which invariably terminated in their own discomfiture and destruction.   But the friendship of the colonists commonly proved no less fatal than their hostilities to the Indians.   The taste for spirituous liquors, which they communicated, was indulged by the savages with an avidity that amounted to frenzy ; and the European diseases which they imported, both from peculiarities in the physical constitution of the Indians, and from the unskilful treatment occasioned by their inexperience of such maladies, were productive of a havoc among the tribes that far outstripped all the power of human hostility.   A vitiated and debilitated habit of body spread through the people of every tribe in proportion to the closeness and duration of their intercourse with Europeans.   The peculiar mortality which the small-pox occasioned among the Indians has been ascribed by some writers to their practice of anointing themselves with bear's grease, in order to repel the attacks of noxious insects in summer, and to exclude the extreme cold of winter, — which is supposed to have repressed the cutaneous eruption requisite to a favorable issue of the distemper.   Guided, in this instance, by their own sensations, the Indians anticipated the Europeans in the use of the cold regimen in small-pox ; and the mortality that the disorder produced among them was at first erroneously ascribed to this practice.[1]   Even the acquired relish for superior comforts and finer luxuries, which might have been expected to lead the Indians to more civilized modes of life, was productive of an opposite effect, and tended to confirm them in savage pursuits ; as those luxuries were now generally tendered to them in exchange for the peltry which they procured by hunting.   Almost all the Indian tribes were engaged in wars with each other ; and all were eager to obtain the new instruments of destruction which the superior science of the Europeans had created.   Wielding this improved machinery of death with the same rage and fury that characterized their previous warfare with less efficacious weapons, their mutual hostilities were rendered additionally destructive by the communication of an invention, which, among civilized nations, has shortened the duration and diminished

---

[1] Kalm.

the carnage of war.   But as the intercourse of mankind with each other must always be mutually beneficial or mutually injurious, the Europeans themselves incurred the most serious disadvantage from their association with the Indians.   Besides the misery and desolation produced by the sanguinary hostilities of the savage tribes, the fraud, the vice, injustice, and hazard incident to the Indian trade depraved the manners and debased the disposition and character of almost all the colonists who engaged in it.   Europe received the vilest of human diseases from America, and in return communicated the small-pox.   How a civilized people may commingle with, or even inhabit the vicinity of, savage tribes, without mutual corruption and the declension and final extinction of the weaker race, is a problem which has hitherto eluded human solution.

At the close of the seventeenth century, the Indian tribes of New England could still muster ten thousand fighting men ;[1] those of New York, one thousand ; and those of Virginia, five hundred.   There were six thousand Indians altogether in Pennsylvania ; four thousand in North Carolina ; probably as many in South Carolina ; three thousand in Maryland ; and only two hundred in New Jersey.[2]

The danger which the European colonists must have incurred, during the infancy of their settlements, from a coalition between their negro slaves and the Indians, was obviated by the violent dislike and antipathy which long prevailed between these two degenerate races.   The gentle and effeminate Indians of South America were regarded from the first with scorn and disdain by the negro slaves of the Spaniards ; and the freer and hardier Indians of North America demonstrated the fiercest aversion and contempt for the negroes imported into the settlements of the English.[3]

---

[1] When Connecticut was first settled, there were computed to be twenty thousand Indians within its boundaries alone. Trumbull. In Gookin's *Historical Collections of the Indians in New England* some illustration is afforded of the rapid decline which these tribes sustained during the short interval between the settlement of the New England States and the year 1674. The Pequods were reduced from four thousand to three hundred warriors ; the Narragansets, from three thousand to one thousand ; the Pawtuckets, from three thousand to two hundred and fifty ; the Massachusetts (who have given their name to the principal State in New England), from three thousand to three hundred ; and the Pawkunnakuts, a tribe which had formerly numbered three thousand warriors, was almost entirely extinct. *Collections of the Massachusetts Historical Society.*

[2] Oldmixon. Warden. The most accurate, I believe, and certainly the most interesting, picture of Indian manners that exists in the English language is contained in that admirable production of learning and genius, Southey's *History of Brazil.* Much curious information respecting the history and language of the Indians has recently been given to the world in Albert Gallatin's *Synopsis of the Indian Tribes,*" &c., published in the second volume of the *Transactions of the American Antiquarian Society.*

[3] Soon after the middle of the eighteenth century, intermarriages began to take place between the negroes and the declining remnant of the Indian communities in Massachusetts ; and "the mixed race increased in numbers, and improved in temperance and industry." *Collections of the Massachusetts Historical Society.* About thirty years after, the historian of the Moravian missions relates that "the negroes and Indians intermarry without any scruple." Loskiel. "As for the usurpation of territory from the natives by the American States," says one of the most distinguished organs of literary, moral, and political criticism in England, "he must be a feeble moralist who regards that as an evil ; the same principle upon which that usurpation is condemned would lead to the nonsensical opinions of the Brahmins, that agriculture is an unrighteous employment, because worms must sometimes be cut by the ploughshare and the spade. It is the order of nature that beasts should give place to man, and among men the savage to the civilized ; and nowhere has this order been carried into effect with so little violence as in North America. Sir Thomas More admits it to be a justifiable cause of war, even in Utopia, if a people, who have territory to spare, will not cede it to those who are in want of room." *Quarterly Review.* See *Wisdom of Solomon,* xii., 3, 7.

NOTES

THE FIRST VOLUME.

NOTE I. Page 36.

THE important instruction, both moral and political, which may be derived from a consideration of the origin of the slave-trade, is forcibly depicted by that distinguished philanthropist (Thomas Clarkson) whose virtue promoted, and whose genius has recorded, the abolition of this detestable traffic. It is a remarkable fact, that the pious and benevolent Las Casas, actuated by an earnest desire to emancipate the feeble natives of South America from the bondage of the Spanish colonists, was the first person who proposed to the government of Spain the importation of negroes from Africa to America. His proposition was rejected by Cardinal Ximenes, who considered it unlawful to consign innocent people to slavery at all, and was, moreover, struck with the moral inconsistency of delivering the inhabitants of one country from a state of misery, by transferring it to the inhabitants of another. " After the death of Cardinal Ximenes, the Emperor Charles the Fifth encouraged the slave-trade. In 1517, he granted a patent to one of his Flemish favorites, containing an exclusive right of importing four thousand Africans into America. But he lived long enough to repent of what he had thus inconsiderately done. For in the year 1542, he made a code of laws for the better protection of the unfortunate Indians in his foreign dominions ; and he stopped the progress of African slavery by an order that all slaves in his American islands should be made free." This order was subsequently defeated by his own retirement into a monastery ; but " it shows he had been ignorant of what he was doing, when he gave his sanction to this cruel trade. It shows, when legislators give one set of men an undue power over another, how quickly they abuse it ; or he never would have found himself obliged, in the short space of twenty-five years, to undo that which he had countenanced as a great state measure. And while it confirms the former lesson to statesmen, of watching the beginnings or principles of things, in their political movements, it should teach them never to persist in the support of evils, through the false shame of being obliged to confess that they had once given them their sanction ; nor to delay the cure of them, because, politically speaking, neither this nor that is the proper season ; but to do them away instantly, as there can be only one fit or proper time in the eye of religion, namely, on the conviction of their existence." — Clarkson's *History of the Abolition of the Slave-trade.*

Louis the Thirteenth of France was at first staggered by the same scruples of conscience that prevailed with the Emperor Charles, and could not be persuaded to authorize the slave-trade till he was induced to believe that he would promote the religious conversion of the negroes by suffering them to be transported to the colonies. — Ibid.

NOTE II. Page 59.

CAPTAIN SMITH was so obnoxious to the leading patentees, that, even if he had remained in the colony, it is highly improbable that they would ever again have intrusted him with official authority. They neither rewarded nor reëmployed him after his return to England. They were bent on deriving immediate supplies of gold or rich merchandise from Virginia; and ascribed their disappointment in a great measure to his having restricted his views to the establishment of a solid and respectable frame of provincial society. This is apparent from many passages of his writings, and particularly from his letter to the patentees while he held the presidency. An honester but absurder reason, that prompted some of them to oppose his pretensions to office, was, that certain fortune-tellers had predicted that he would be unlucky; a prediction that sometimes contributes to its own fulfilment.

In various parts of his history, Smith applies himself to refute their unreasonable charges, and account for the disappointment of their expectations. For this purpose he has drawn a parallel between the circumstances of the Spanish and the English colonists of America. " It was the Spaniards' good hap," he observes, " to happen in those parts where were infinite numbers of people, who had manured the ground with that providence it afforded victuals at all times. And time had brought them to that perfection, that they had the use of gold and silver, and the most of such commodities as those countries afforded: so that what the Spaniards got was chiefly the spoil and pillage of those country people, and not the labors of their own hands. But had these fruitful countries been as savage, as barbarous, as ill peopled, as little planted, labored, and manured, as Virginia, their proper labors, it is likely, would have produced as small profit as ours. And had Virginia been peopled, planted, manured, and adorned with such store of precious jewels and rich commodities as were the Indies; then, had we not gotten and done as much as, by their examples, might be expected from us, the world might then have traduced us and our merits, and have made shame and infamy our recompense and reward."

Were we to confine our attention to the superficial import of this isolated passage, it would be difficult not to suppose that this excellent person was deterred less by want of inclination than by lack of opportunity from imitating the robberies and cruelties of the Spanish adventurers. But the general strain of his book, as well as the more credible evidence supplied by the whole scope and tenor of his life, would fully refute the unjust supposition. That he was unacquainted with the enormities committed by the Spaniards in Mexico and Peru may be collected from the praises he bestows on their exploits, and from his appealing to the glory of these exploits as an incentive that should stimulate the ardor of the English in the exercise of laborious virtue, and the prosecution of humble but honest emolument in North America. Thus nobly we find him expressing the sentiments of a mind which the condition of humanity did not exempt from being deceived, but which piety preserved from gross depravation or perversion : — " Who can desire more content, that hath small means, or but only his merit, to advance his fortunes, than to tread and plant that ground he hath purchased by the hazard of his life ? If he have but the taste of virtue and magnanimity, what to such a mind can be more pleasant than planting and building a foundation for his posterity, got from the rude earth by God's blessing and his own industry, without prejudice to any ? If he have any grain of faith or zeal in religion, what can he do less hurtful to any, or more agreeable to God, than to seek to convert those poor savages to know Christ and humanity, whose labors with discretion will triple thy charge and pains ? What so truly suits with honor and honesty as the discovering things unknown, erecting towns, peopling countries, informing the ignorant, reforming things unjust, teaching virtue, and gaining to our mother country a kingdom to attend her;

finding employment for those that are idle because they know not what to do; so far from wronging any, as to cause posterity to remember thee, and, remembering thee, ever to honor that remembrance with praise?" It is probably such expressions as these that have led certain writers to charge Smith with *enthusiasm*,— a term by which some persons denote every elevation of view and tone that religion imparts,— and by which many others designate every quality and sentiment above the pitch of their own nature.

Smith proceeds as follows:—"Then who would live at home idly, or think in himself any worth to live, only to eat, drink, and sleep, and so die; or consuming that carelessly his friends got worthily, or using that miserably that maintained virtue honestly; or, being descended nobly, pine, with the vain vaunt of great kindred, in penury; or, to maintain a silly show of bravery, toil out thy heart, soul, and time basely, by shifts, tricks, cards, and dice; or, by relating news of other men's actions, shark here and there for a dinner or supper," &c., "though thou seest what honors and rewards the world yet hath for them that will seek them and worthily deserve them?" He adds, shortly after, "It would be a history of a large volume, to recite the adventures of the Spaniards and Portugals, their affronts and defeats, their dangers and miseries, which, with such incomparable honor and constant resolution, so far beyond belief, they have attempted and endured, in their discoveries and plantations, as may well condemn us of too much imbecility, sloth, and negligence. Yet the authors of these new inventions were held as ridiculous for a long time, as now are others that but seek to imitate their unparalleled virtues."

I should contend neither wisely nor honestly for the fame of Captain Smith, were I to represent him as a faultless character, perfectly divested of the imperfections of humanity. The sufferings of others were able to provoke him to an intemperance, at least of language, which none of his own trials and provocations ever elicited, and with which none of his actions ever corresponded. Indignant at the cruel massacre of the Virginian colonists in 1622, long after he had left them, he pronounced in haste and anger that the colony could not be preserved without subduing or expelling the Indians, and punishing their perfidious cruelty, as the Spaniards had punished "the treacherous and rebellious infidels" in South America. These expressions afford a farther proof of the very imperfect acquaintance he had with the real circumstances that attended the subjugation of South America by the Spaniards. "Notwithstanding such a stern and invincible resolution as Captain Smith displayed," says an intelligent historian of Virginia, "there was seldom seen a milder and more tender heart than his was." Stith.

Smith expatiates at great length, and with much spirit and ability, on the advantages of colonial establishments in America; and propounds a variety of inducements to embark in them, appropriate to the various classes of society in England. Colonies he characterizes as schools for perpetuating the hardy virtues on which the safety of every state depends. He ascribes the fall of Rome and the subjugation of Constantinople to the indolence and covetousness of the rich, who not only passed their own lives in slothful indulgence, but retained the poor in factious idleness, by neglecting to engage them in safe and useful employment; and strongly urges the wealthy capitalists of England to provide for their own security, by facilitating every foreign vent to the energies of active and indigent men. He enlarges on the pleasures incident to a planter's life, and illustrates his description by the testimony of his own experience. "I have not been so illbred," he declares, "but I have tasted of plenty and pleasure, as well as want and misery. And lest any should think the toil might be insupportable, I assure myself there are who delight extremely in vain pleasure, that take much more pains in England to enjoy it than I should do there to gain wealth sufficient; and yet I think they should not have half such sweet content." To *gentlemen* he proposes, among other inducements, the pleasures of fishing, fowling, and hunting, to an unbounded extent ; and to *laborers*, the blessings of a vacant soil, of unequalled cheapness and unsurpassed fertility.   He promises no mines to tempt sordid avarice, nor conquests to allure profligate ambition ; but the advantages of a temperate clime and of a secure and exhaustless subsistence, — the wealth that agriculture may extract from the land, and fisheries from the sea.   " Therefore," he concludes, " honorable and worthy countrymen, let not the meanness of the word *fish* distaste you ; for it will afford as good gold as the mines of Guiana or Potosi, with less hazard and charge, and more certainty and facility."

I have given but a mere outline of Smith's exposition of this subject.   The details with which he has filled it up are highly interesting and well deserving of perusal.   I think there can be no doubt that he has treated the subject of colonization with more both of the practical skill of a politician and the profound sagacity of a philosopher, than Lord Bacon has shown in either or both of his productions, the *Essay on Plantations*, and the *Considerations touching the Plantation in Ireland*.

The name of Smith has not yet gathered all its fame.   The lustre it once possessed is somewhat obscured by time, and by the circumstances that left America so long to depend on England for the sentiments and opinions that literature preserves or produces, and consequently led her to rate her eminent men rather by the importance of their achievements in the scale of British than of American history.   But Smith's renown will break forth again, and once more be commensurate with his desert.   It will grow with the growth of men and letters in America ; and whole nations of its admirers have yet to be born.   As the stream becomes more illustrious, the springs will be reckoned more interesting.

Smith was born in the year 1579, and died on the 21st of June 1631.

NOTE III.   Page 62.

ROBERTSON's credit as a historian is not a little impeached by the strange inaccuracy of his account of Sir Thomas Dale's administration.   He not only imputes to the Company the composition and introduction of the arbitrary code transmitted by Sir Thomas Smith, but unfolds at length the (imaginary) reasons that prevailed with them to adopt a measure so harsh and sanguinary ; though of this measure itself they are expressly acquitted by Stith, the only authority on the subject that exists, and the very authority to whom Robertson himself refers.   Among the other reasons which he assigns is the advice of Lord Bacon, which he unhesitatingly charges this eminent person with having communicated, and the Company with having approved.   In support of an accusation so distinct and so remarkable, he refers merely to a passage in Lord Bacon's *Essay on Plantations*.   It would be well for the fame of Bacon, if all the charges with which his character is loaded were supported only by such evidence.   For *supposing* (which is doubtful) that this essay was published before the collection of Sir Thomas Smith's system of martial law, and *supposing* it to have been read by the compiler of that system, it is surely more than doubtful if the passage alluded to would yet support Dr. Robertson's imputation.   It merely recommends that a provincial government should " have commission to exercise martial laws, with some limitation " ; a power inseparable from such, and indeed from every system of government.   The twenty-fourth section of King James's second charter to the Company had already invested the provincial governors with " full power and authority to use and exercise martial law, in cases of mutiny or rebellion " ; and the preceding section of the same charter authorizes them, " in case of necessity," to rule, correct, and punish, according to their own " good discretions."   No blame can attach to the bare authorization of an extraordinary power, reserved in every society, for extraordinary occasions. What alone seems deserving of blame is Sir Thomas Smith's violent and illegal substitution of the most sanguinary code of martial law that was ever framed, in the room of the original constitution, and for the ordinary government of the colony ; and Dr. Robertson's very hasty and unfounded imputation of this measure to the act of the council and the advice of Lord Bacon. It had been well, if the council had paid more attention to the maxim of this great man, that " Those who plant colonies must be endued with great patience."

NOTE IV. Page 118.

An illustration of this remark may perhaps be derived from the apologetic theory philosophical slave-owners have introduced into the world, — that the negroes are a separate and inferior race of men ; a notion by which the degradation that human beings inflict on their fellows, in reducing them to the level of the brute creation, is charged upon God, whose word assures us that he created man after his own image, and that he fashioned all souls alike. Interest and pride harden the heart; a deceived heart perverts the understanding, and men are easily persuaded to consider those as brutes whom they deem it convenient to treat as such. The best refutation of this theory that I have ever seen is the production of an American writer. It occurs in Dr. S. Smith's interesting *Essay on the Causes of the Variety of Figure and Complexion in the Human Species.* See, also, on the same subject, Clarkson's *Researches, Antediluvian, Patriarchal,* &c.

In his *Notes on Virginia,* Mr. Jefferson has contended for the natural inferiority of negroes to white men. But I was assured by the Abbé Grégoire (formerly Bishop of Blois), that Jefferson, in a private letter to him, confessed that he had seen cause to alter this opinion. Anthony Benezet, the Quaker, himself a very ingenious and accomplished man, who had conversed extensively with negroes in America, and undertaken the education of a great number of them, pronounced, as the result of his experience, that this race is perfectly equal to the whites in all the endowments of nature ; the prevalence of an opposite opinion he ascribed partly to the debasing effect of slavery on the minds of the negroes, and partly to the influence of ignorance, pride, and cruelty on those white men, who, pluming themselves on a wide separation from the negroes, are incompetent to form a sound judgment on the capacities of this race. Vaux's *Life of Benezet.* Man (alas!) seems to be the only creature capable of provoking from his fellow-man such cruelty as the blacks have experienced from the whites.

Most of the advocates or apologists of slavery maintain that enslaved negroes are generally contented with their lot, — a statement, which, if correct, might well be cited in proof of the corrupting effect of slavery on ordinary minds. Who regards otherwise than with pity and contempt the depraved longings of the emancipated Israelites for a return to the ignominy of Egyptian bondage ? The contentment of a slave in his degraded estate proves that *the iron has entered into his soul.* " If thou mayest be free," says an inspired Apostle, " use it rather." A distinguished American writer, whom I respect so highly as to be unwilling to name him, on the present occasion, has so far misused his admirable ingenuity as to maintain that slavery may prove a blessing to the country in which it exists, and elevate human character by affording opportunity to the masters of generous self-control, and to the slaves of grateful recognition of the indulgent forbearance of their masters. To be consistent (an impossibility to a North American advocate of slavery), this accomplished writer should demand an alteration of the Lord's prayer, and, instead of the petition, " Lead us not into temptation, but deliver us from evil," propose as our orison, " Let us fall into temptation, that we may deliver ourselves from evil."

Many Americans, while they cling to the vile institution of negro slavery (asserting, with horrible sophistry, the *sacredness* of a man's pretension to an artificial right of property in the violent privation of another man's natural right of property in his own liberty), are eager to impute its existence, or at least its extent, among them, to the policy and conduct of the British government, in encouraging the slave-trade, and disregarding the remonstrances against it that were addressed to them by certain of the American provinces. But they urge this apologetic plea a great deal too far. Britain could not *force* her colonial offspring to become slave-holders, though she might (and did) facilitate their acquisition of slaves. "Every man," says the word of God, "is tempted, when he is drawn away of his own lust, and enticed." By far the greater part of the remonstrances unsuccessfully addressed to the British government were the suggestions of men who themselves possessed abundance of slaves, and who were desirous of preventing others from rivalling them in wealth, and from endangering the stability of slavery, by additional importations of negroes unaccustomed to the yoke. I have heard many slave-owners vehemently profess a sincere desire to discover some *practicable* plan of abolishing slavery; but almost invariably found that they required the *impracticability* of repairing long and enormous injustice without any atoning sacrifice or reparatory expense.

NOTE V. Page 148.

CHALMERS and Robertson have ascribed the slow increase of the colonists of New Plymouth to "the unsocial character of their religious confederacy." As the charge of entertaining antisocial principles was preferred against the first Christians by men who plumed themselves on exercising *hospitality to the gods of all nations*, it is necessary to ascertain the precise meaning of this imputation against the American colonists, if we would know whether it be praise or blame that it involves. Whether, in a truly blameworthy acceptation, the charge of unsocial principles most properly belongs to these people or to their adversaries may be collected from the statements they have respectively made of the terms on which they were willing to hold a companionable intercourse with their fellow-men. Winslow, who was for some time governor of New Plymouth, in his account of the colony, declares that the faith of the people was in all respects the same with that of the reformed churches of Europe, from which they differed only in their opinion of church government, wherein they pursued a more thorough reformation. They disclaimed, however, any uncharitable separation from those with whom they differed on this point, and freely admitted the members of every reformed church to communion with them. "We ever placed," he continues, "a large difference between those that grounded their practice on the word of God, though differing from us in the exposition and understanding of it, and those that hated such reformers and reformation, and went on in antichristian opposition to it and persecution of it. It is true, we profess and desire to practise a separation from the world and the works of the world; and as the churches of Christ are all saints by calling, so we desire to see the grace of God shining forth (at least seemingly, leaving secret things to God) in all whom we admit into church-fellowship with us, and to keep off such as openly wallow in the mire of their sins, that neither the holy things of God nor the communion of saints may be leavened or polluted thereby." He adds, that none of the settlers who were admitted into the church of New Plymouth were encouraged, or even permitted, to insert in the declaration of their faith a renunciation of the church of England, or of any other reformed establishment. Mather. It does not appear to me that these sentiments warrant the charge of unsocial principles in any sense which a Christian will feel himself at all concerned to disclaim. Whether the adversaries of these men were distinguished for principles more honorably social or more eminently charitable may be gathered from a passage in Howel's *Familiar Letters*, where this defender of royalty and episcopacy thus expresses the sentiments of his party respecting religious differences between mankind : — " I rather pity than hate a Turk or infidel ; for they are of the same metal and bear the same stamp as I do, though the inscriptions differ. If I hate any, it is those schismatics that puzzle the sweet peace of our church ; so that I could be content to see an Anabaptist go to hell on a Brownist's back." The ecclesiastical policy of the monarchs and prelates of England tendered a premium to the production of such sentiments. Howel's fervor for the church party did not survive the power of this party to reward him. After the fall of the English church and monarchy, he became the defender and panegyrist of the administration of Cromwell ; though, like Waller and Dryden, he returned in the train of fortune, when she returned to his original friends.

NOTE VI. Page 171.

The introduction of this feature into the portrait of Sir Henry Vane rests entirely on the authority of Burnet and Kennet (followed by Hume), who speak from hearsay. Ludlow, who knew Vane personally, bestows the highest praise on his imperturbable serenity and presence of mind ; and, with the sympathy of a kindred spirit, describes the resolute magnanimity with which at his trial he scaled his own fate by scorning to plead, like Lambert, for his life, and gallantly pleading for the dying liberties of his country. At his execution, when some of his friends expressed resentment of the injuries that were heaped upon him, — " Alas ! " said he, " what ado they keep to make a poor creature like his Saviour ! I bless the Lord I am so far from being affrighted at death, that I find it rather shrink from me than I from it. Ten thousand deaths for me, before I will defile the chastity and purity of my conscience ; nor would I for ten thousand worlds part with the peace and satisfaction I have now in my heart." Perhaps the deep piety and constant negation of all merit in himself, by which the heroism of Vane was softened and ennobled, may have suggested to minds unacquainted with these principles the imputation of constitutional timidity. At all events, this cloud, whether naturally attendant on his character or artificially raised by the envious breath of his detractors, has, from the admirable vigor of his mind and the unquestioned courage of his demeanour, served rather to embellish than to obscure the lustre of his fame.

Hugh Peters, like Sir Henry Vane, has been charged with defect of courage. Bishop Burnet, in particular, reproaches him with cowardice at his execution. Yet, in reality, his death was dignified by a courage such as Burnet never knew, and which distinguished him even among the regicides. After his fellow-sufferer, Cook, had been quartered before his face, the executioner approached him, and, rubbing his bloody hands, said, " Come, Mr. Peters, how do you like this work ? " Peters answered, " I thank God I am not terrified at it ; you may do your worst." Shortly before he died, addressing a friend who attended him, he said, " Return straightway to New England, and trust God there." Prefixed to a posthumous work of Peters, entitled *A dying Father's last Legacy to his Daughter*, is a poetical tribute to the author, thus concluding : —

> " Yet his last breathings shall, like incense hurled
> On sacred altars, so perfume the world,
> That the next will admire, and, out of doubt,
> Revere that torchlight which this age put out."

NOTE VII. Page 199.

THE accounts of the first conversations which the missionaries held with various tribes of these heathens abound with curious questions and observations that proceeded from the Indians in relation to the tidings that were brought to their ears. One man asked, Whether Englishmen were ever so ignorant of Jesus Christ as the Indians. A second, Whether Jesus Christ could understand prayers in the Indian language. A third proposed this question, How there could be an image of God, since it was forbidden in the second commandment. On another occasion, after Mr. Eliot had done speaking, an aged Indian started up, and with tears in his eyes asked, Whether it was not too late for such an old man as he, who was near death, to repent and seek after God. A second asked, How the English came to differ so much from the Indians in their knowledge of God and Jesus Christ, since they had all at first but one father. A third desired to be informed, How it came to pass that sea-water was salt and river-water fresh. Several inquired, How Judas could deserve blame for promoting the accomplishment of the purpose of God. One woman asked, Whether she was entitled to consider herself as having prayed, when she merely joined in her mind with her husband who prayed by her side. Another, If her husband's prayer signified any thing while he continued to beat his wife. Many of the converts continued to believe that the gods whom they formerly served had in reality considerable power, but were spirits subordinate to the true and only God; and when threatened with witchcraft by the Powwows for their apostasy, they said, "We do not deny your power, but we serve a greater God, who is so much above your deities that he can defend us from them, and even enable us to trample upon them all." One sachem sent for an Indian convert, and desired to know how many gods the English had. When he heard they had but one, he replied scornfully, "Is that all? I have thirty-seven. Do they suppose I would exchange so many for one?" Other sachems rejected the instructions of the missionaries with angry disdain, saying, that "the English had taken away their lands and were attempting now to make them slaves."

The efforts of missionaries among the Indians have always been obstructed by the erroneous ideas of *liberty* fondly cherished by these savages; who, professing the most exalted estimate of this blessing, and having its name continually in their mouths, have always ignorantly restricted it to a debased and impoverished sense "The Indians are convinced," says Charlevoix, "that man is born free, that no power on earth has a right to infringe his liberty, and that nothing can compensate the loss of it; and it has been found a very difficult matter to undeceive even the Christians among them, and to make them understand how, by a natural consequence of the corruption of our nature, which is the effect of sin, an unbridled liberty of doing wrong differs very little from an obligation to commit it, because of the strength of the bias which draws us to it; and that the law which restrains us causes us to approach nearer to our original state of liberty, whilst it appears to take it from us." Charlevoix's *Travels.*

NOTE VIII. Page 211.

" GEORGE FOX," says William Penn, doubtless with especial reference to the advanced age and matured character of the subject of his description, "was a man whom God endowed with a clear and wonderful depth, — a discoverer of other men's spirits, and very much a master of his own. The reverence and solemnity of his address and behaviour, and the fewness and fulness of his words, often struck strangers with admiration. He was civil beyond all forms of breeding in his behaviour, very temperate, eating little and sleeping less, although a bulky person."

The character of George Fox is certainly neither justly nor generally understood in the present day. His writings are so voluminous, and there is such a mixture of good and evil in them, that every reader finds it easy to justify his preconceived opinion, and to fortify it by appropriate quotations. His works are read by few, and wholly read by still fewer. Many derive their conception of his character from the passages which are cited from his writings by his adversaries; and of the Quakers not a few are content to judge him from the passages of a different complexion which are cited in the works of the modern writers of their own sect. I shall here subjoin a few extracts from his *Journal*, which will verify some of the remarks I have made in the text; premising this observation, that the book itself was first put into my hands by a zealous and intelligent Quaker, for the purpose of *proving* to me that it contained no such passages as some of those which I am now to transcribe from it.

Fox relates, that in the year 1648 he found his nature so completely new modelled, that "I knew nothing but pureness, innocency, and righteousness, being renewed up into the image of God by Christ Jesus; so that I was come up to the state of Adam which he was in before he fell. The creation was opened to me; and it was showed me how all things had their names given them according to their nature and virtue. I was at a stand in my mind whether I should practise physic for the good of mankind, seeing the nature and virtues of the creatures were so opened to me by the Lord. But I was immediately taken up in spirit to see another or more steadfast state than Adam's in innocency, even into a state in Christ Jesus that should never fall. The Lord showed me that such as were faithful to him in the power and light of Christ should come up into that state in which Adam was before he fell; in which the admirable works of the creation and the virtues thereof may be known through the openings of that divine word of wisdom and power by which they were made." In many of the disputes which he afterwards held with ministers and doctors, he maintained that he was, and that every human being, by cultivation of the spiritual principle within his breast, might become, like him, perfectly pure and free from all dregs of sin. He relates with complacency and approbation, that, having one day addressed a congregation of people at Beverley, in Yorkshire, the audience declared afterwards that it was an angel or spirit that had suddenly appeared among them and spoken to them. He conceived himself warranted by his endowments to trample on all order and decency. One Sunday, as he approached the town of Nottingham, he tells, "I espied the great *steeple-house;* and the Lord said unto me, Thou must go cry against yonder great idol, and against the worshippers therein." He accordingly entered the church, and, hearing the minister announce the text, *We have also a more sure word of prophecy*, and tell the people that by this was meant the Scriptures, whereby they were to try all doctrines, religions, and opinions, Fox adds, " I could not hold, but was made to cry out, ' O, no! it is not the Scriptures: it is the Holy Spirit.' " On another occasion, having entered a church, and hearing the preacher read for his text, *Ho! every one that thirsteth, come ye to the waters*, &c., Fox called out to him, " Come down, thou deceiver! dost thou bid people come freely and take of the water of life freely, and yet thou takest three hundred pounds a year of them for preaching the Scriptures to them?" Approaching the town of Lichfield, he declares he found himself spiritually directed to cast off his shoes, and in that condition walk through the streets, exclaiming, " Woe to the bloody city of Lichfield!" which he accordingly did. These examples are selected almost at random from numberless instances of similar proceedings recorded in his voluminous journal. Yet he strongly condemns the frantic extravagance of the *Ranters*, and relates various attempts he had made to convince them of their delusion. *Journal.*

William Penn, in the beautiful Preface which he wrote for this *Journal*, informs us that these Ranters were persons, who, " for want of staying their minds in a humble dependence upon Him that opened their understandings to see great things in his law, ran out in their own imaginations, and, mixing them with these divine openings, brought forth a monstrous birth, to the scandal of those that feared God." " Divers," he adds, " fell into gross and enormous practices, pretending in excuse thereof that they could without evil commit the same act which was sin in another to do." " I say," he continues, " this ensnared divers, and brought them to an utter and lamentable loss as to their eternal state ; and they grew very troublesome to the better sort of people, and furnished the looser with an occasion to blaspheme."

Fox himself relates some horrid immoralities of the Ranters, and that he had found it necessary to publish addresses conveying assurance to the world that these deluded persons were Quakers only in name. *Journal.* He applies the epithet of Ranters to many of those who called themselves Quakers in America. Some of Fox's chief associates and coadjutors appear to have become in the end Ranters, or something worse. Of these was James Naylor, long the fellow-laborer and fellow-sufferer of Fox, and whom Fox still terms a Quaker, at the time when he was in prison for blasphemy and obscenity. Fox alludes vaguely and sorrowfully to Naylor's errors and disobedience to him. When he found that Naylor would not give heed to his rebukes, Fox told him that " the Lord moved me to slight him, and to set the power of God over him." He adds, that it soon after happened to Naylor that " his resisting the power of God in me, and the truth of God that was declared to him by me, became one of his greatest burdens." *Journal.* Naylor had ridden naked into Bristol with a crew of insane followers, uttering blasphemous proclamations before him, and had gloried in the commission of abominable impurities. On his trial, he produced a woman, one Dorcas Earberry, who declared on oath that she had been dead two days, and was recalled to life by Naylor.

It is not easy to discover what part of the extravagance of Naylor was condemned by Fox and the proper body of the Quakers. We find Fox relating with great approbation many wild and absurd exhibitions by which Quakers were moved, as they said, to show themselves as signs of the times. " Some," he informs us, " have been moved to go naked in the streets, and have declared amongst them that God would strip them of their hypocritical professions, and make them as bare and naked as they were. But instead of considering it, they have frequently whipped, or otherwise abused them." *Journal.* Many such instances he relates in the *Journal*, with cordial commendation of the insane indecency of the Quakers, and the strongest reprobation of the persecutors who punished them for walking abroad in a state of corporeal nudity.

Fox taught that God did not create the devil. Yet, though the reasoning by which he defends this gross heresy would plainly seem to imply that the devil was a self-created being, there is another passage in his writings from which we may perhaps conclude that Fox's deliberate opinion was, that the devil was created by God a good spirit, but transformed himself by his own will into a wicked one. He records every misfortune that happened to any of his adversaries or persecutors as a judgment of Heaven upon them. He relates various cures of sick and wounded persons that ensued on his prayers, and on more ordinary means that he employed for their relief. It may be doubted if he himself regarded these as the exertions of miraculous power; but from many passages it is plain that they were (to his knowledge) so regarded by his followers, and the Quaker editor of his *Journal* refers to them in the Index under the head of " Miracles."

I think it not unreasonable to consider Quakerism, the growth of a Protestant country, and Quietism, which arose among Catholics, as branches of a system essentially the same; and Madame Guyon and Molinos as the counterparts of Fox and Barclay. The moral resemblance is plainer than the historical connection; but the propagation of sentiment and opinion may be effectually accomplished when it is not visibly indicated. Quietism was first engendered in Spain among a sect called the *Illuminati*, or *Alumbrados*, who sprang up about the year 1575. They rejected sacraments and other ordinances; and some of them became notorious for indecent and immoral extravagances. This sect was revived in France in the year 1634, but quickly disappeared under a hot persecution. It reappeared again, with a system of doctrine considerably purified (yet still inculcating the distinctive principle of exclusive teaching by an inward light and sensible impression), towards the close of the seventeenth century, both at Rome in the writings of Molinos, and in France under the auspices of Madame Guyon and Fénélon.

NOTE IX. Page 216.

BESSE, in his voluminous *Collection of the Sufferings of the People called Quakers*, relates, that Lydia Wardel, of Newbury, in New England, a convert to Quakerism, found herself inwardly prompted to appear in a public assembly " in a very unusual manner, and such as was exceeding hard and self-denying to her natural disposition, she being a woman of exemplary modesty in all her behaviour. The duty and concern she lay under was that of going into their church at Newbury naked, as a token of that miserable condition which she esteemed them in." " But they, instead of religiously reflecting on their own condition, which she came in that manner to represent to them, fell into a rage and presently laid hands on her," &c. He also notices the case of " Deborah Wilson, a young woman of very modest and retired life, and of a sober conversation, having passed naked through the streets, as a sign against the cruelty and oppression of the rulers. "

George Bishop, another Quaker writer, thus relates the case of Deborah Wilson. " She was a modest woman, of a retired life and sober conversation ; and bearing a great burden for the hardness and cruelty of the people, she went through the town of Salem naked, as a sign ; which she having in part performed, was laid hold on, and bound over to appear at the next court of Salem, where the wicked rulers sentenced her to be whipt." — *New England Judged*. The writings of Besse, Bishop, and some others, who were foolish enough to defend the extravagance that they had too much sense to commit, were the expiring sighs of Quaker nonsense and frenzy. They are still mentioned with respect by some modern Quakers, who praise, instead of reading them ; as the sincere but frantic zeal of Loyola and Xavier is still commended by their sly successors, who have inherited the name and the manners, without the spirit that distinguished the original Jesuits. With a great proportion of its modern professors Quakerism is far less influential as a doctrinal system than as a system of manners.

Since the infancy of Quakerism, various eruptions of the primitive frenzy have occurred. But they have all been partial and shortlived. The most remarkable occurred in Connecticut in the beginning of the eighteenth century. Even in the close of that century, as I was assured by a respectable person, who was a witness of the fact, a Quaker walked naked for several days successively at Richmond, in Virginia, *as a sign of the times*. Nathaniel Prior, a worthy Quaker of London, informed me, that, at a meeting of his fellow-sectaries at which he was present, in the beginning of the nineteenth century, one member, suddenly starting up, announced that he was directed by the Spirit to walk in Lombard Street without his breeches. He was instantly disowned and expelled by the Quaker Society. The progressive diminution of Quaker extravagance has been attended with a progressive increase of acknowledged insanity among the Quakers, — in whose society the numbers of the insane bear a greater proportion to the whole mass than in any other Christian sect or association.

It had been well if the government of Massachusetts had inflicted punishment on the disgusting violations of decency avowed by Besse and Bishop, without extending its severity to the bare profession of Quakerism. This injustice was occasioned by the conviction that these outrages were the legitimate fruits of Quaker principles; a conviction, which, it appears, the language even of those Quakers who were themselves guiltless of outrage, tended strongly to confirm. It is only such language on the part of the Quakers that can acquit their adversaries of the ingenious inhumanity that pervades the reasoning of persecutors, and holds men responsible for all the consequences that may be logically deduced from their principles, though rejected and denied by themselves. The apology of the magistrates of New England is thus expressed by Cotton Mather : — " I appeal to all the reasonable part of mankind, whether the infant colonies of New England had not cause to guard themselves against these dangerous villains. It was also thought that the very Quakers themselves would say, that, if they had got into a corner of the world, and with immense toil and charge made a wilderness habitable, on purpose there to be undisturbed in the exercises of their worship, they would never bear to have New Englanders come among them and interrupt their public worship, and endeavour to seduce their children from it; yea, and repeat such endeavours after mild entreaties first, and then just banishments to oblige their departure." Yet Mather deplores and condemns the extreme severities which were ultimately inflicted by his countrymen upon the Quakers. It was one of the privileges of Israel that *the people shall dwell alone ;* and the expected fruition of a similar privilege was one of the motives that led the Puritans to exchange the charms of their native land for the gloom of a desolate wilderness.

A story is told by Whitelocke strongly illustrative of the singularity with which the Quakers of those times combined all that was frantic in action with all that was dignified and affecting in suffering. Some Quakers at Hasington, in Northumberland, having interrupted a minister employed in divine service, were severely beaten by the people. Instead of resisting, they went out of the church, and, falling on their knees, besought God to pardon their persecutors, who knew not what they did, — and afterwards addressing the people, so convinced them of the cruelty of their violence, that their auditors fell a quarrelling among themselves, and beat one another more than they had formerly beaten the Quakers.

The Quakers have always delighted to exaggerate the persecutions encountered by their sectarian society. An illustrious French traveller has been so far deceived by their vague declamations on this topic, as to assert that Quakers were at one time *put to the torture* in New England. Rochefoucauld's *Travels.*

NOTE X.   Page 224.

Upon this occasion Cotton Mather observes : — " Such has been the jealous disposition of our New Englanders about their dearly bought privileges, and such also has been the various understanding of the people about the extent of these privileges, that, of all the agents which they have sent over unto the court of England for now forty years together, I know not any one who did not at his return meet with some very froward entertainment among his countrymen; and there may be the wisdom of the Holy and Righteous God, as well as the malice of the evil one, acknowledged in the ordering of such temptations."

Norton, before his departure for England, expressed a strong apprehension that the business he was required to undertake would issue disastrously to himself. Mather adds, " In the spring before his going for England, he preached an excellent sermon unto the representatives of the whole colony assembled at the court of election, wherein I take particular notice of this passage : — *Moses was the meekest man on earth; yet it went ill with Moses, 't is said, for their sakes. How long did Moses live at Meribah? Sure I am, it killed him in a short time! a man of as good a temper as could be expected from a mere man.*"

It might have been expected, that Norton, whose death was thus in a manner the fruit of his exertions to extend religious liberty in the colony, would have escaped the reproach of persecution. But he had given mortal offence to the Quakers by promoting the prosecutions against the Quaker enthusiasts in New England. And after his death, certain of those sectaries published at London *A Representation to King and Parliament*, wherein, pretending to report some *Remarkable Judgments upon their Persecutors*, they inserted the following passage : — " John Norton, chief priest at Boston, by the immediate power of the Lord, was smitten ; and as he was sinking down by the fireside, being under just judgment, he confessed the hand of the Lord was upon him, and so he died." Mather. The Romish fables, respecting the deaths of Luther, Calvin, Bucer, and Beza, are hardly more replete with folly, untruth, and presumption, than some of these Quaker interpretations of Providence. Their authors, like many other persons involved in religious contentions, or exposed to persecution for religion's sake, mistook an ardent zeal in behalf of what they esteemed divine truth for a complete subjection of mind to the divine will, and an entire identification of their views and purposes with it; practically regardless of their own remaining infirmity, and forgetting, that, while we continue to be clothed with humanity, we know only in part, and can see but darkly. Enlargement of view is always attended with increase of charity ; and the cultivation of our charity at once refines and enlarges our view.

NOTE XI. Page 226.

WINTHROP the younger was in the bloom of manhood, accomplished by learning and travel, and the heir of a large estate, when he readily joined with his father in promoting and accompanying an expedition of emigrants to New England. They were indeed, as Dryden said of Ormond and Ossory, "a father and a son only worthy of each other." Cotton Mather has preserved a letter written by Winthrop the elder to his son, while the one was governor of Massachusetts, and the other of Connecticut. I shall be excused for transcribing some part of an epistle so beautiful in itself, and so strikingly characteristic of the fathers of New England. " You are the chief of two families. I had by your mother three sons and three daughters ; and I had with her a large portion of outward estate. These are now all gone ; mother gone ; brethren and sisters gone : you only are left to see the vanity of these temporal things, and learn wisdom thereby which may be of more use to you, through the Lord's blessing, than all that inheritance which might have befallen you : And for which, this may stay and quiet your heart, that God is able to give you more than this ; and that it being spent in the furtherance of his work, which has here prospered so well through his power hitherto, you and yours may certainly expect a liberal portion in the prosperity and blessing thereof hereafter ; and the rather, because it was not forced from you by a father's power, but freely resigned by yourself, out of a loving and filial respect unto me, and your own readiness unto the work itself. From whence, as I do often take occasion to bless the Lord for you, so do I also commend you and yours to his fatherly blessing, for a plentiful reward to be rendered unto you.

And doubt not, my dear son, but let your faith be built upon his promise and faithfulness, that, as he hath carried you hitherto through many perils, and provided liberally for you, so he will do for the time to come, and will never fail you nor forsake you. My son, the Lord knows how dear thou art to me, and that my care has been more for thee than for myself. But I know thy prosperity depends not on my care, nor on thine own, but on the blessing of our Heavenly Father : neither doth it on the things of this world, but on the light of God's countenance through the merit and mediation of our Lord Jesus Christ. It is that only which can give us peace of conscience with contentation ; which can as well make our lives happy and comfortable in a mean estate as in a great abundance. But if you weigh things aright, and sum up all the turnings of divine providence together, you shall find great advantage. The Lord hath brought us to a good land, a land where we enjoy outward peace and liberty, and above all the blessings of the gospel, without the burden of impositions in matters of religion. Many thousands there are who would give great estates to enjoy our condition. Labor, therefore, my good son, to increase our thankfulness to God for all his mercies to thee, especially for that he hath revealed his everlasting good-will to thee in Jesus Christ, and joined thee to the visible body of his church in the fellowship of his people, and hath saved thee in all thy travels abroad from being infected with the vices of those countries where thou hast been (a mercy vouchsafed but unto few young gentlemen travellers). Let him have the honor of it who kept thee. He it was who gave thee favor in the eyes of all with whom thou hadst to do, both by sea and land ; he it is who hath given thee a gift in understanding and art ; and he it is who hath provided thee a blessing in marriage, a comfortable help, and many sweet children. And therefore I would have you to love him again and serve him, and trust him for the time to come.".

Winthrop the elder not only performed actions worthy to be written, but produced writings worthy to be read. Yet his *Journal*, or *History*, as it has been termed in the late edition by Mr. Savage, is very inferior in spirit and interest to his *Letters*. Winthrop the younger was one of the greatest philosophers of his age, the associate of Robert Boyle and Bishop Wilkins in projecting and founding the Royal Society of London, and the correspondent of Tycho Brahe, Galileo, Kepler, Milton, Lord Napier, Sir Isaac Newton, Sir Henry Wotton, and various others of the most distinguished characters in Europe.

NOTE XII. Page 242.

AMONG many interesting and romantic adventures related by Mather, Neal, Hutchinson, Dwight, and other New England writers, as having occurred during Philip's War, there is one incident which excited much wonder and speculation at the time, and has since derived an increase of interest from the explanation which it received after the death of the individual principally concerned in it. In 1675, the town of Hadley was alarmed by the sudden approach of a body of Indians during the time of public worship, and the people were thrown into a confusion that betokened an unresisted massacre. Suddenly a grave, elderly person appeared in the midst of them. Whence he came, or who he was, nobody could tell. In his mien and dress he differed from the rest of the people. He not only encouraged them to defend themselves, but, putting himself at their head, rallied, instructed, and led them on to encounter the enemy, who were defeated and put to flight. As suddenly, the deliverer of Hadley disappeared ; and the people were left in a state of perplexity and amazement, and utterly unable to account for this singular phenomenon. After his death, it was known to have been Goffe, the regicide, who dwelt somewhere in the neighbourhood, but in such deep sequestration that none except those who were intrusted with the secret were ever able to make the remotest approach to a discovery of his retreat. Whalley resided with him; and they had some years before been joined by another of the regicides, Colonel Dixwell. They frequently changed their place of abode, and gave the name of *Ebenezer* to every spot that afforded them shelter. They had many friends both in England and in the New England States, with some of whom they maintained a close correspondence. They obtained constant and exact intelligence of every thing that passed in England, and were unwilling to resign all hopes of deliverance. Their expectations were suspended on the fulfilment of the prophecies of Scripture, which they earnestly studied. They had no doubt that the execution of the late king's judges was *the slaying of the witnesses*, in the Apocalypse, and were greatly disappointed when the year 1666 elapsed without any remarkable event; but still flattered themselves with the notion of some error in the commonly received chronology. The strict inquisition that was made for them by the royal commissioners and others renders their concealment in a country so thinly peopled, and where every stranger was the object of immediate and curious notice, truly surprising. It appears that they were befriended and much esteemed for their piety by persons who regarded the great action in which they had participated with unqualified disapprobation. Hutchinson.

NOTE XIII. Page 243.

That the jealousy and suspicion with which the New England States were regarded by the English court had not slumbered in the interim may be inferred from the following passages extracted from the *Journal* of John Evelyn, the author of *Sylva*, who, in the reign of Charles the Second, was one of the Commissioners of Trade and Plantations. "26 May, 1671. What we the commissioners most insisted on was, to know the condition of New England, which appearing to be very independent as to their regard to Old England or his Majesty, rich and strong as they now were, there were great debates in what style to write to them; for the condition of that colony was such that they were able to contest with all other plantations about them, and there was fear of their breaking from all dependence on this nation; his Majesty therefore commended this affair more expressly." "Some of our council were for sending them a menacing letter, which those who better understood the peevish and touchy humor of that colony were utterly against." "6th June. We understood they were a people almost on the brink of renouncing any dependence on the crown." "3d August. The matter in debate was, whether we should send a deputy to New England, requiring them of Massachusetts to restore such to their limits and respective possessions as had petitioned the council; this to be the open commission only, but in truth with secret instructions to inform us of the condition of those colonies, and whether they were of such power as to be able to resist his Majesty, and declare for themselves as independent of the crown, which we were told, and which of late years made them refractory." "12th February, 1672. We also deliberated on some fit person to go as commissioner to inspect their actions in New England, and from time to time report how that people stood affected."

NOTE XIV. Page 290.

A good history of Harvard University, by its librarian, Benjamin Peirce, has been recently given to the world. In the collegiate establishment, says this author,

" the substantial properties of the English universities were retained, while their pompous and imposing ceremonies were in a great measure excluded." — " The first Commencement took place on the second Tuesday of August, 1642. Upon this novel and auspicious occasion, the venerable fathers of the land, the governor, magistrates, and ministers from all parts, with others in great numbers, repaired to Cambridge, and attended, with delight, to refined displays of European learning on a spot which but just before was the abode of savages." — " In looking over the list of early benefactions to the College, we are amused when we read of a number of sheep bequeathed by one man, a quantity of cotton cloth worth nine shillings presented by another, a pewter flagon worth ten shillings by a third, a fruit-dish, a sugar-spoon, a silver-tipped jug, one great salt, one small trencher-salt, by others ; and of presents or legacies amounting severally to five shillings, nine shillings, one pound, two pounds, &c., all faithfully recorded, with the names of their respective donors. How soon does a little reflection change any disposition we may have to smile into a feeling of respect and even of admiration ! What, in fact, were these humble benefactions ? They were contributions from the ' res angusta domi'; from pious, virtuous, enlightened penury, to the noblest of all causes, the advancement of education. The donations were small, for the people were poor ; they leave no doubt as to the motives which actuated the donors ; they remind us of the offering from ' every one whose heart stirred him up, and every one whom his spirit made willing, to the work of the tabernacle of the congregation '; and, like the widow's mite, indicate a respect and zeal for the object, which would have done greater things, had the means been more abundant." How much nobler these humble tributes than the munificent donations of bigot or robber princes to the colleges of Europe ! — " It was, perhaps, fortunate, that, for so long a period after the foundation of the College, and before many other institutions had sprung up to divide the attention of the public, this ' school of the prophets' should have experienced no individual patronage of sufficient magnitude to supersede the care and support of the community at large. Its long dependence on the whole people, by whom it was cherished with parental fondness, tended to secure and perpetuate their affection for the College, and even for learning itself; and to this circumstance may probably be traced, in some degree, that general interest in the cause of education for which New England has always been distinguished." Peirce.

In the course of the eighteenth century, the College was enriched by many liberal donations from individuals in Britain, as well as in America. The most notable of its British benefactors were Samuel Holden, governor of the Bank of England, a member of parliament, and a leading person among the English Dissenters, and a family named Hollis (Dissenters likewise), distinguished through successive generations for mercantile industry and opulence, and for the most generous, untiring, and judicious philanthropy. Peirce has preserved an interesting account of these and other friends and patrons of this venerable institution ; remarking of the Hollises in particular, with unexaggerated encomium, that they formed " one of the most extraordinary families that Providence ever raised up for the benefit of the human race." Such were the great merchants of Britain, before they were debauched by a rage for fashionable and aristocratical distinction.

Since the foregoing note was written, I have had the pleasure of reading a far ampler and superior history of Harvard University, by its excellent and accomplished president, Josiah Quincy. If every thing else that has been written about America should perish, that work would secure to New England a glorious and imperishable name. No other country ever produced a seat of learning so honorable to its founders as Harvard University, — and never did a noble institution obtain a worthier historian. President Quincy's account of the transition of the social system of Massachusetts, from an entire and punctilious intertexture of church and state to the restriction of municipal government to civil affairs and occupations, is very curious and interesting, and admirably fills up an important void in New England's history. Son of one of the ablest and most generous champions of his country's independence, President Quincy has given additional lustre to a name renowned at Runnymede and dear to the liberty and literature of North America.

NOTE XV. Page 331.

The following may serve as a specimen of these articles of complaint, and of the answers they received. — "IV. As no laws can be repealed but by the assembly, it is desired to know if the proprietary intended to annul a clause in the act for bringing tobacco to towns?" *Answer.* "The proprietary does not intend to annul the clause mentioned, without an act of repeal." "V. The attorney-general oppresses the people." *Answer.* "If such proceedings have been practised, the law is open against the offender, who is not countenanced by government." "VI. Certain persons, under a pretended authority from some militia officers, have pressed provisions in time of peace." *Answer.* "We know of no such offenders ; but, when informed of them, we shall proceed against them according to law and matter of fact." "VII. The late adjournment of the provincial court to the last Tuesday in January is a time most incommodious to the people." *Answer.* "At the request of the lower house, they will adjourn the provincial court by proclamation." Chalmers. Why Chalmers, who is generally displeased even with the most reasonable and moderate friends of American liberty, should term this ebullition of ill-temper and nonsense " a spirited representation of grievances," I am at a loss to discover. But perhaps no other writer has ever combined such elaborate research of facts with such temerity of opinion and such glaring inconsistency of sentiment, as the *Political Annals* of this writer display. The inhabitants of America, though little beholden to his respect for their rights or their character, owe the most important elucidation of their history to his industrious researches. Some of the particulars of his own early history may perhaps account for the peculiarities of his American politics. A Scotsman by birth, he had emigrated to Maryland, and was settled at Baltimore as a lawyer, when the Revolutionary contest (in which he adhered to the royal cause) blasted all his prospects, and compelled him to take refuge in England, where his unfortunate loyalty and distinguished attainments procured him a respectable appointment from the Board of Trade. The first (and only) volume of his *Annals*, a work intended to be the apology of his party, was composed while he hoped that the royal cause would yet prevail in America. Though too honorable wilfully to misrepresent facts, his mind was too much warped by prejudice to regard and appreciate them fairly. His labors were discontinued when the cause and party to which they were devoted had evidently perished. Though a strong vein of Toryism pervades all his pages, he is at times unable to restrain an expression of indignant contempt at particular instances of the conduct of the kings and ministers whose general policy he labors to vindicate.

NOTE XVI. Page 351.

That a gift will blind the discernment even of the wise, and pervert the words even of the just, is an assurance conveyed to us by unerring wisdom, and confirmed by examples among which even the name of Locke must be enrolled. If no gift could be more seducing than the deference and admiration with which Shaftesbury graced his other bounties to Locke, no blindness could well be greater than that which veiled the eyes and perverted the sentiments of the philosopher with respect to the conduct and character of his patron. In his memoirs of this profligate politician, not less fickle in his friendships than furious in his enmities, and who alternately inflamed and betrayed every faction in the state, Locke holds him up as a mirror of worth and patriotism; declaring, that, in a mild yet resolute constancy, he was equalled by few and exceeded by none; and that, while liberty endures, his glory will mock the assaults of envy and the ravages of time. While Locke reprobates the selfish ambition and elaborate fraud and duplicity with which Monk endeavoured to the last to obtain for himself the vacant dignity of Cromwell, he is totally insensible to any other feature than the *ability* of the more successful manœuvres by which Shaftesbury outwitted the less dexterous knave, and at length forced him to concur in promoting the Restoration. Locke has vaunted the profound sagacity with which Shaftesbury could penetrate the character and acquire a mastery over the talents and understanding of every person he conversed with. For his own vindication, it is necessary to regard himself in this performance as exemplifying the influence which he has ascribed to the object of his panegyric. When occasion required it, Shaftesbury could assume a virtue to which his talent lent a degree of efficacy that commanded universal admiration. When he was appointed to preside in the Court of Chancery, he was unacquainted with law, and had grown gray in the practice of fraud and intrigue. Yet, in the discharge of the functions of this office, he is acknowledged to have combined the genius of Bacon with the integrity of More; and the satisfaction that was derived from the legal soundness of his decrees was surpassed only by the respect that was entertained for the lofty impartiality of his judicial conduct. It seems, indeed, surprising that the two most ambitious politicians that have ever appeared in Great Britain, Wolsey and Shaftesbury, should have distinguished themselves so highly by the probity and wisdom with which they administered the functions of judges in a court of equity.

Among other marks of confidence bestowed by Shaftesbury on Locke, he employed him to choose a wife for his son, whose early marriage he anxiously desired; as the feebleness of the young man's constitution gave him cause to apprehend the extinction of his family. Locke, undismayed by the nice and numerous requisites which Shaftesbury directed him to combine in the object of his choice, fulfilled this delicate duty to his patron's satisfaction; and afterwards accepted the office of tutor to the eldest male offspring of the marriage, who signalized himself as the author of the *Characteristics*. (*Life of Locke*, prefixed to the folio edition of his *Works.*)

Shaftesbury was able to infect Locke with all his own real or pretended suspicions of the Catholics; and, even when the philosopher could not refrain from censuring the severity and intolerance of the Protestants, he expressed his regret that they should be found capable of "such popish practices." Not less unjust and absurd was Lord Russell's declaration, that massacring men in cool blood was so like a practice of the Papists, that he could not but abhor it; and Sir Edward Coke's remark, that poisoning was *a popish trick*. When Locke undertook to legislate for Carolina, he produced ecclesiastical constitutions not more, and political regulations far less, favorable to human liberty and happiness, than those which had been previously established by a Catholic legislator in Maryland.

Mr. Fox is much puzzled to account for Locke's friendship with Shaftesbury, and has attempted it very unsuccessfully.

It is strange that we should be obliged to prefer the testimony of an unprincipled satirist to that of an upright philosopher. Yet Dryden's character of *Achitophel* is undoubtedly the justest and most masterly representation of Shaftesbury that has ever been produced by friend or foe. So much more powerful is affection than enmity in deluding the fancy and seducing the judgment!

NOTE XVII. Page 401.

FOUNDERS of ancient colonies have sometimes been deified by their successors. New York is perhaps the only commonwealth whose founders have been assailed with ridicule from the same quarter. It is impossible to read the ingenious and diverting romance entitled *Knickerbocker's History of New York*, without wishing that the author had put either a little more or a little less truth into it ; and that his talent for humor and sarcasm had found another subject than the dangers, hardships, and virtues of the ancestors of his national family. It must be unfavorable to patriotism to connect historical recollections with ludicrous associations : but the genius of Mr. Irving has done this so effectually, that it is difficult for his readers to behold the names of Wouter Van Twiller, of Corlear, and of Peter Stuyvesant, without a smile ; or to see the free and happy colonists of New York enslaved by the forces of a despot, without a sense of ridicule that abates the resentment which injustice should excite, and the sympathy which is due to misfortune. Yet Stuyvesant was a gallant and generous man ; and Corlear softened the miseries of war and mitigated human enmity and suffering by his benevolence. Stuyvesant appears (see Miller's *Retrospect of the Eighteenth Century*) to have possessed an additional claim on the courtesy of a man of letters, derived from the respectability of his own attainments in literature. If Mr. Irving had confined his ridicule to the wars, or rather bloodless buffetings and squabbles, of the Dutch and the Swedes, his readers would have derived more unreproved enjoyment from his performance. Probably my discernment of the unsuitableness of this writer's mirth is quickened by a sense of personal wrong ; as I cannot help feeling that he has by anticipation ridiculed my topic and parodied my narrative. If Sancho Panza had been a real governor, misrepresented by the prior wit of Cervantes, his posterior historian would have found it no easy matter to bespeak a grave attention to the annals of his administration.

NOTE XVIII. Page 423.

THE charitable attempt of Chalmers to vindicate the character of this man, impeached and detested, not by one, but by every province over which he exercised the functions of government previous to the British Revolution, is totally unsuccessful. The main topic of apology is, that Andros merely executed the orders of his master, and sometimes ineffectually recommended more humane and liberal measures ; an apology which might be (as in fact it was) equally pleaded to justify the atrocities of Kirke and Jeffries in England, and of Graham of Claverhouse and Sir James Turner in Scotland. It is an apology that may sometimes exempt from punishment, but can never redeem honor, or avert reproach. When Turner was taken prisoner by the persecuted Scottish peasantry in Dumfrieshire, they were proceeding to put him to death for his cruelty ; but observing, from the written instructions found on his person, that he had actually fallen short of the severity which he was desired to inflict, these generous men arrested their uplifted hands, and dismissed him with impunity, but not without abhorrence. That Andros seems (from some counsel which he privately tendered to his royal patron) to have been willing at times to alleviate the burdens of the people only renders him the more culpable for his active subservience to a contrary policy, the mischief and odium of which he plainly discerned. It has been urged, with some color of probability, that the unanimous dislike which he provoked in New England inferred less of reproach to his personal character, than of repugnance between the previous habits of the people and the structure of that arbitrary system which he was appointed to administer among them. But the detestation he excited in New York, where the people were habituated to arbitrary government, admits not of this apologetical suggestion; which, even with regard to New England, is very slightly applicable, if admissible at all. James the Second displayed a sagacity that approached to instinct, in the employment of fit instruments to execute injustice and cruelty; and his steady patronage of Andros, and constant preference of his to any other instrumentality in the subjugation of colonial liberty, is the strongest certificate that could be given of the aptness of this officer's disposition for the employment for which he was selected. His friend and colleague, Randolph, boasted, that, in New England, Andros was as arbitrary as the Great Turk.

After the British Revolution, Andros conducted himself irreproachably as governor of Virginia. But William and Mary had not intrusted him with tyrannical power in this province; and the Virginians would not have permitted him to exercise it. His appointment to this situation, however, was an insult to the American colonies, and an illiberal measure of King William, who assuredly was not a friend (as, indeed, what monarch ever was?) to liberty, either in America or anywhere else.

Andros died at London in 1715, at a very advanced age.

NOTE XIX. Page 450.

THIS Jesuit accompanied the French commissioners who repaired to the head-quarters of the Five Nations to treat for peace. When the commissioners approached the Indian station, they were met by a sachem who presented them with three separate gifts (strings of wampum); the first, to wipe away their tears for the French that had been slain; the second, to open their mouths that they might speak freely; and the third, to clean the mat on which they were to sit, while treating of peace, from the blood that had been spilt on both sides. The Jesuit, who acted as the orator of the embassy, endeavoured to pay court to the Indians by imitation of their style of speech. "The war-kettle," said he, "boiled so long, that it would have scalded all the Five Nations, had it continued; but now it is overset and turned upside down, and a firm peace made." He recommended to them the preservation of amity with *Corlear* (the Indian title of the governor of New York); and having thus attempted to disarm their suspicions, uttered many injurious insinuations against this ally. "I offer myself to you," he continued, "to live with you at Onondaga, to instruct you in the Christian religion, and to drive away all sickness, plagues, and diseases out of your country." Though this proposition, which the French pressed with great urgency and address, was absolutely rejected, the peace brought them a deliverance from so much misery and fear, that, when a deputation of the sachems of the Five Nations arrived at Montreal to ratify the treaty, they were received with general acclamations of joy, and a salute from the artillery on the ramparts. The Indian allies of the French were highly offended with this demonstration of respect. "We perceive," they angrily observed, "that fear makes the French show more respect to their enemies, than love can make them do to their friends." Colden.

NOTE XX. Page 457.

DENTON, whose description of New York was published in 1702, gives a very agreeable picture of the state of the province and its inhabitants at this period. — "I must needs say, that, if there be a terrestrial Canaan, 't is surely here. The inhabitants are blessed with peace and plenty ; blessed in their country ; blessed in the fruit of their bodies and the fruit of their grounds ; blessed in their basket and in their store ; in a word, blessed in whatsoever they take in hand or go about; the earth yielding plentiful increase to all their painful labor." — "Were it not to avoid prolixity, I could say a great deal more, and yet say too little, to show how free are these parts of the world from that pride and oppression, with their miserable effects, which many, nay, almost all, parts of the world are troubled with. There a wagon or cart gives as good content as a coach, and a piece of their home-made cloth pleases better than the finest lawns or richest silks ; and though their low-roofed houses may seem to shut their doors against pride and luxury, yet how do they stand wide open to let charity in and out, either to assist each other or to relieve a stranger ! and the distance of place from other nations doth secure them from the envious frowns of ill-affected neighbours, and the troubles which usually arise thence."

What a contrast there is between this happy picture and the state of European society about the same period, as depicted by De Foe in the most celebrated of his romances ! — "I saw the world busy around me ; one part laboring for bread, and the other squandering it in vile excesses or empty pleasures " : — "the men of labor spent their strength in daily strugglings for bread to maintain the vital power they labored with ; so living in a daily circulation of sorrow ; living but to work, and working but to live, as if daily bread were the only end of a wearisome life, and a wearisome life the only occasion of daily bread."

NOTE XXI. Page 469.

FROM the writings of the modern historians and apologists of Quakerism, we might be led to suppose that none of the Quakers who were imprisoned by the magistrates of England at this period were accused of aught else but the profession of their peculiar doctrinal tenets, or attendance at their peculiar places of worship. But very different accounts of the causes of their imprisonment have been transmitted by some of the sufferers themselves ; and from the tenor of these, it is manifest that the only wrong which their authors sustained from the magistrates was, that they were committed to prison, instead of being confined in lunatic hospitals. One of the most remarkable of these compositions is the *Narrative of the Persecution of Solomon Eccles*, in the year 1659, written by himself, and dated from Newgate, where he describes himself as " a prisoner for the testimony of the Lord." This man, who was a Quaker, and a tailor in London, relates, that " It was clearly showed to me that I should go to the steeple-house in Aldermanbury the first day of the week then following, and take with me something to work, and do it in the pulpit at their singing-time." So, after much musing, " I purposed to carry with me a pocket to sew." He repaired to Edmund Calamy's chapel, and, watching his opportunity, with the proverbial dexterity of a Quaker, made his way into the pulpit. " I sat myself down upon the cushion, and my feet upon the seat where the priest, when he hath told out his lies, doth sit down, and, having my work ready, I pulled one or two stitches." When the people began to persecute him (i. e. to pull him down), he cared not if they had killed him, " for I was full of joy, and they were full of wrath and madness." He was carried before the mayor. " Then said he to me, 'Wherefore did you work there?' I said, 'In obedience to the Lord's commandment.' He said it was a false spirit: and said he, 'Where are your sureties?' I said, the Lord was my security." Accordingly, his *persecution* was consummated by a commitment to Newgate. "Now, *let all sober people judge* whether I did this thing out of envy against either priest or people. Yea, farther I say, the Lord lay it not to their charge who have said that I did it in malice, devilishness, and envy," &c. &c. This singular narrative is republished in Howell's *State Trials.*

NOTE XXII. Page 473.

Of this diversity the following instance may serve as a specimen. When the statute against the Quakers began to be generally enforced, George Bishop, a man of some eminence among them, remonstrated against it in these terms: "To the king and both houses of parliament, *Thus saith the Lord*, Meddle not with my people because of their conscience to me, and banish them not out of the nation because of their conscience; for, if you do, I will send my plagues among you, and you shall know that I am the Lord. Written in obedience to the Lord, by his servant, G. Bishop." Gough and Sewell. Very different was the remonstrance which William Penn addressed on the same subject to the king of Poland, in whose dominions a severe persecution was instituted against the Quakers. "Give us poor Christians," said he, "leave to expostulate with thee. Suppose we are tares, as the true wheat hath always been called; yet pluck us not up for Christ's sake, who saith, Let the tares and the wheat grow up until the harvest, that is, until the end of the world. Let God have his due as well as Cæsar. The judgment of conscience belongeth unto him, and mistakes about religion are known to him alone." Clarkson's *Life of Penn.*

NOTE XXIII. Page 482.

It is not difficult to understand how a friendly intercourse originated between the leading persons among the Quakers and Charles the Second and his brother. The Quakers desired to avail themselves of the authority of the king for the establishment of a general toleration, and for their own especial defence against the enmity and dislike of their numerous adversaries. The king and his brother regarded with satisfaction the principles of non-resistance professed by these sectaries, and found in them the only class of Protestants who could be rendered instrumental to the design of reëstablishing the faith and sway of the church of Rome by the preparatory measure of a general toleration. But how the friendly relation thus created between the royal brothers and such men as Penn and Barclay should have continued to subsist uninterrupted by all the tyranny and treachery which the reigns of these princes disclosed is a difficulty which their contemporaries were unable to solve in any other manner than by reckoning the Quakers conscious votaries, instead of deluded instruments, of bigotry and arbitrary power. The more modern and juster, as well as more charitable, censure is, that they were the dupes of kingly courtesy, craft, and dissimulation. They hoped to make an instrument of the king; while he permitted them to flatter themselves with this hope, that he might avail himself of their instrumentality for the accomplishment of his own designs.

Perhaps, since the days when the prophets of Israel were divinely commissioned to rebuke their offending monarchs, no king was ever addressed in terms of more

dignified admonition than Robert Barclay has employed in concluding the dedication of that erudite and ingenious work, his *Apology for the Quakers*, to Charles
the Second. " There is no king in the world," he bids the monarch remember,
" who can so experimentally testify of God's providence and goodness; neither
is there any who rules so many free people, so many true Christians : which thing
renders thy government more honorable, and thyself more considerable, than the
accession of many nations filled with slavish and superstitious souls. Thou hast
tasted of prosperity and adversity ; thou knowest what it is to be banished thy
native country and to be overruled, as well as to rule and sit upon the throne ; and,
being oppressed, thou hast reason to know how hateful the oppressor is both to
God and man. If, after all these warnings and advertisements, thou dost not turn
unto the Lord with all thy heart, but forget him who remembered thee in thy distress, and give thyself up to follow lust and vanity, surely, great will be thy condemnation." Yet, Charles gave himself up to lust and vanity without apprehending or experiencing any diminution of the regards of his Quaker friends ; and the
falsehood and cruelty that stained the conduct of both Charles and James rendered
them hateful to all men except the Catholics and the Quakers. The tortures inflicted, by the orders and in the presence of James himself, on the Scottish Covenanters must have been perfectly well known to Barclay. But perhaps his
sympathy with the sufferers was obstructed by the lamentable intolerance which
many of these unfortunate victims of bigotry themselves displayed. There were
few of them, who, even in the midst of their own afflictions, did not bequeath a
dying testimony to their countrymen against *the sin of tolerating the blasphemous
heresy of the Quakers.* See *The Cloud of Witnesses,* Woodrow's *History,* and
other works illustrative of that period.

Of the cajolery that was practised by King James upon the Quakers I think
a remarkable instance is afforded (very unintentionally) by Mr. Clarkson, in his
Memoirs of William Penn. In the year 1688, Gilbert Latey, an eminent Quaker
minister, having been presented by Penn to this prince, thanked him for his *Declaration of Indulgence* in favor of Quakers and other Dissenters ; adding an expression of his hope, that, as the king had remembered the Quakers in their
distress, so God might remember him in his distress. Some time after, when
James, expelled from England, was endeavouring to make head against his adversaries in Ireland, he sent a message to Latey, confessing that the Revolution
had approved him so far a prophet, inasmuch as the king had actually fallen into
distress. But Latey was not satisfied with this partial testimony, and reminded
James, that, as his life had been saved at the battle of the Boyne, the *prophecy*
that had been addressed to him was entirely fulfilled.

The Quakers, notwithstanding Pope's imputation of *slyness* to them, have
displayed amazing credulity in their intercourse with every tyrant who has thought
it worth his while to caress them. Since the death of James the Second of
England, no prince has gained a greater share of their good graces than the late
Emperor Alexander of Russia, who, during his visit to England, accompanied a
distinguished philanthropist of this persuasion to a Quaker meeting, and actually
convinced some of the leading members of the society that he himself was *in
heart a Quaker.*

NOTE XXIV. Page 487.

" THE truth is," said the accomplished grandfather of Queen Anne, " there
is naturally that absence of the chief elements of Christian religion, charity,
humility, justice, and brotherly compassion, in the very policy and institution
of princes and sovereign states, that, as we have long found the civil obligations

of alliance and marriage to be but trivial circumstances of formality towards concord and friendship, so those of religion and justice, if urged for conscience' sake, are equally ridiculous ; as if only the individuals, not any state itself, were perfectly Christian.   And I assure you, I have not been without many melancholy thoughts, that this justice of God, which of late years hath seemed to be directed against empire itself, hath proceeded from the divine indignation against those principles of empire which have looked upon conscience and religion itself as mere private, subordinate, and subservient faculties to conveniency and the interest of kingdoms, rather than duties requisite to the purchase of the kingdom of heaven.   And therefore God hath stirred up and applied the people, in whom only princes thought it necessary to plant religion, to the destruction of principalities, in the institution whereof religion hath been thought unnecessary."   Lord Clarendon's *Letters*.

NOTE XXV. Page 490.

GABRIEL THOMAS, the author of this pleasing little work (which is dedicated to Sir John Moore and Sir Thomas Lane, aldermen of London, and two of the principal proprietaries of West Jersey), was a Quaker, and the friend of Penn, to whom, at the same time, he dedicated a corresponding history of the province of Pennsylvania.   His chief aim in writing he declares to have been to inform the laboring poor of Britain of the opportunity afforded to them, by those colonial settlements, of exchanging a state of ill-rewarded toil, or of beggarly and burdensome dependence, for a condition at once more useful, honorable, prosperous, and happy.   " Now, reader," he thus concludes, " having no more to add of any moment or importance, I salute thee in Christ ; and whether thou stayest in England, Scotland, Ireland, or Wales, or goest to Pennsylvania, West, or East Jersey, I wish thee all health and happiness in this, and everlasting comfort (in God) in the world to come.   Fare thee well ! "

NOTE XXVI. Page 496.

THE following instance of the sensitiveness of the Quakers to the reputation of William Penn and his institutions I believe has never before been published, and I think deserves to be made known.   When Winterbotham undertook the compilation of his *Historical, Geographical, Commercial, ana Philosophical View of the American United States,* he was encouraged to pursue his labors by the assurance of numerous subscriptions, most of which were obtained from English Quakers.   The authorities which he consulted on the subject of Pennsylvania gave him an insight into the lamentable dissensions that had occurred between the founder of this province and his Quaker colonists, and induced him to form an opinion unfavorable to the equity of Penn and to the moderation of both parties. The historical part of his account of Pennsylvania was accordingly written in a strain calculated to convey this impression.   Unfortunately for him, this came to be known just when his work was ready for publication and delivery to the subscribers.   The Quakers instantly withdrew their subscriptions ; a step that involved Winterbotham in the most serious embarrassment.   The unfortunate author (then a prisoner in Newgate for seditious expressions of which he is now generally acknowledged to have been innocent) applied to the late William Dillwyn, of Walthamstow, and, throwing himself on the humanity of this venerable man, implored his powerful intercession with the members of his religious fraternity. By his advice, Winterbotham consented to cancel the objectionable portion of the work; and, in the place of it, there was substituted a composition on the same subject from the pen of Mr. Dillwyn. A few copies of the work in its original state having got into circulation, there was added to the preface in the remaining copies an apology for the error into which the author declared that he had been betrayed with regard to the character of Penn and his colonists. The Quakers, on being apprized of this, complied at once with the solicitation of their respected friend, and fulfilled their engagements with Winterbotham. This anecdote was related to me by Mr. Dillwyn himself. The composition which this excellent person thus contributed to Winterbotham's publication is characterized by his usual mildness and indulgence. Without denying the existence of unhappy dissensions in Pennsylvania, he suggests reasons for supposing that they originated in mutual misapprehension, and were neither violent nor lasting. An apologetical vein pervades the whole piece, of which the only fault is, that (unlike the generality of Quaker productions) it is a great deal too short. Mr. Dillwyn was a native of New Jersey, and had devoted much attention to the history of America. He has been celebrated (along with his friend and coadjutor in exertions to promote human liberty and happiness, Robert Grahame of Whitehill, father of the author of this *History*) in Clarkson's *History of the Abolition of the Slave-trade*.

NOTE XXVII. Page 498.

BISHOP BURNET relates, that Penn, in alluding to the executions of Mrs. Gaunt and Alderman Cornish, which he had attended as a spectator, said that " the king was greatly to be pitied ! " and endeavoured to palliate his guilt, by ascribing his participation in these and other atrocities to the influence that Jeffries had acquired over his mind. Unfortunately for the credit of this miserable apology, the king was not under the influence of Jeffries when he ordered and witnessed the infliction of torture on the Covenanters in Scotland ; and the disgrace into which Jeffries fell shortly before the Revolution, for refusing to gratify the king by professing the Catholic faith, and pretending to keep a corner of his conscience sacred from the royal dominion, shows how voluntary and how limited the king's pretended subjection to him truly was. It is related in the diary of Henry, Lord Clarendon, that Jeffries expressed his uneasiness to this nobleman at the king's impetuosity and want of moderation. When Jeffries was imprisoned in the Tower at the Revolution, he assured Tutchin (one of his victims, who came to visit and exult over him), that, on returning from his bloody circuit in the West of England, he had been " snubbed at court for being too merciful." Kirke, in like manner, when reproached with his cruelties, declared that they had greatly fallen short of the letter of his instructions.

For the credit of Penn's humanity, it may be proper to observe, that it was common, in that age, for persons of the highest respectability (and, among others, for noblemen and ladies of rank, in their coaches) to attend executions, especially of remarkable sufferers. See various passages in that learned and interesting work, Howell's *State Trials.*

NOTE XXVIII. Page 502.

COLONEL NICHOLSON, an active agent of the crown both before and after the English Revolution, who held office successively in many of the colonies, and was acquainted with the condition of them all, in a letter to the Board of Trade, in 1698, observes, that " A great many people of *all the colonies,* especially in those under proprietaries, think that no law of England ought to be binding on them, without their own consent; for they foolishly say, that they have no representatives sent from themselves to the parliament of England; and they look upon all laws made in England, that put any restraint upon them, to be great hardships." *State Papers, apud* Chalmers. It was probably in reference to the reports of Colonel Nicholson, that the Lords of Trade, writing to Lord Bellamont in the year 1701, caution him to watch and curb " the humor that prevails so much in proprietary and charter governments," — adding, that *" the independency they now thirst after is so notorious,* that it has been thought fit those considerations, together with other objections against these colonies, should be laid before the parliament." Belknap.

In the introduction to the historical work of Oldmixon (who boasts of the assistance and information he received from William Penn) we find this remarkable passage: — " The Portuguese have so true a notion of the advantage of such colonies, that, to encourage them, they admit the citizens of Goa to send deputies to sit in the assembly of the Cortes. And if it were asked, why our colonies have not their representatives, who could presently give a satisfactory answer ? " In the year 1809, during the struggle which the Spaniards were maintaining against the usurpation of the Emperor Napoleon, a proposal was broached in the Spanish councils that " the colonies be represented as an integral part of the empire " in the organs of authority within the parent state. This idea was subsequently realized to a certain extent, when the Spanish Cortes was convoked. Napier's *History of the War in the Peninsula.*

An extension of the right of electing members of parliament to a part of the realm which had not been previously represented there occurred in the thirty-fifth year of the reign of Henry the Eighth. The inhabitants of the county palatine and city of Chester complained, in a petition to the king, " that, for want of knights and burgesses in the court of parliament, they sustained manifold damages, not only in their lands, goods, and bodies, but in the civil and politic governance and maintenance of the commonwealth of their said county ; and that, while they had been always bound by the acts and statutes of the said court of parliament, the same as other counties, cities, and boroughs, that had knights and burgesses in the said court, they had often been touched and grieved with acts and statutes, made within the said court, as well derogatory unto the most ancient jurisdictions, liberties, and privileges of the said county palatine, as prejudicial unto the commonwealth, quietness, and peace of his Majesty's subjects." They proposed, as a remedy, " that it would please his Highness, that it be enacted, with the assent of the lords spiritual and temporal, and the commons in parliament assembled, that, from the end of the session, the county palatine shall have two knights for the said county, and likewise two citizens to be burgesses for the city of Chester." The complaint was thought just and reasonable, and the petitioners were admitted to send representatives to parliament.

Various instances of similar proceedings occurred in the reigns of this monarch's successors, — Edward the Sixth, Mary, and Elizabeth; the latter of whom created twenty-four new boroughs in England. In the reign of Edward the Sixth, a writ was directed to the inhabitants of Calais, requiring the return of a member of parliament for that town.

NOTE XXIX.   Page 517.

In the year 1684, there was published, by one of these emigrants, *The Planter's Speech to his Neighbours and Countrymen of Pennsylvania ;* a composition which reminds us of some of the productions of the early colonists of New England. "The motives of your retreating to these new habitations," says this writer, "I apprehend (measuring your sentiments by my own) to have been, —

"1st. The desire of a peaceable life, where we might worship God and obey his law with freedom, according to the dictates of the divine principle, unencumbered with the mouldy errors occasioned by the fierce invasions of tradition, politic craft, and covetous or ambitious cruelty.

"2d. That we might here, as on a virgin Elysian shore, commence or improve such an innocent course of life, as might unload us of those outward cares, vexations, and turmoils, which before we were always subject unto from the hands of self-designing and unreasonable men.

"3d. That, as *Lot*, by flying to little *Zoar*, from the ungodly company of a more populous and magnificent dwelling, we might avoid being grieved with the sight of infectious as well as odious examples, of horrid swearings, cursings, drunkenness, gluttony, uncleanness, and all kinds of debauchery, continually committed with greediness; and also escape the judgments threatened to every land polluted with such abominations.

"4th. That, as trees are transplanted from one soil to another to render them more thriving and better bearers, so we here, in peace and secure retirement, under the bountiful protection of God, and in the lap of the least adulterated nature, might every one the better improve his talent, and bring forth more plenteous fruits, to the glory of God, and public welfare of the whole creation.

"5th. And lastly, that, in order hereunto, by our holy doctrine, and the *practical teachings* of our exemplary abstemious lives, transacted in all humility, sobriety, plainness, self-denial, virtue, and honesty, we might gain upon those thousands of poor dark souls scattered round about us (and commonly, in way of contempt and reproach, called *heathens*), and bring them not only to a state of civility, but real piety; which, effected, would turn to a more satisfactory account, than if, with the proud Spaniards, we had gained the mines of Potosi."

"These thoughts, these designs, my friends, were those that brought you hither; and so far only as you pursue and accomplish them, you obtain the end of your journey." "Our business, therefore, here in this new land, is not so much to build houses and establish factories, and promote trade and manufactures that may enrich ourselves (though all these things in their due place are not to be neglected), as to erect temples of holiness and righteousness, which God may delight in." Among other advices which this writer proceeds to communicate, he recommends not only the refraining from all wanton waste of inferior animal life, but a total abstinence from animal food. Proud.

Such, says Proud, the historian of this province, were the views and motives of those who undertook the settlement of Pennsylvania. "But all things have their time; and both kingdoms and empires, as well as smaller states and particular persons, must die : *finis ab origine pendet.* Yet folly often shortens their duration, as wisdom and virtue prolong their more happy existence." Ibid. This last observation reminds us of the celebrated maxim of the Jewish Rabbi, Jochonan Hassandalar, who lived under the reign of the Emperor Adrian, — that every commonwealth formed in the fear of God flourisheth; for virtue is the life and bond of society, while vice ruins and dissolves it.

NOTE XXX. Page 547.

Of the condition in which Penn continued to linger for a number of years before his death an interesting picture is given by Thomas Story, the Quaker (whose account of the yellow fever at Philadelphia, in 1699, I have already noticed), who, arriving from America in 1713, paid a visit to all that remained of his venerable friend. "He was then," says Story, "under the lamentable effects of an apoplectic fit which he had had some time before; for his memory was almost quite lost, and the use of his understanding suspended, so that he was not so conversable as formerly, and yet as near the truth, in the love of it, as before; wherein appeared the great mercy and favor of God, who looks not as man looks. For though to some this accident might look like judgment, and no doubt his enemies so accounted it, yet it will bear quite another interpretation, if it be considered how little time of rest he ever had from the importunities of the affairs of others, to the great hurt of his own, and suspension of all his enjoyments, till this happened to him, by which he was rendered incapable of all business, and yet sensible of the enjoyment of truth as at any time in all his life. When I went to the house, I thought myself strong enough to see him in that condition; but when I entered the room, and perceived the great defect of his expressions from want of memory, it greatly bowed my spirit under a consideration of the uncertainty of all human qualifications, and what the finest of men are soon reduced to by a disorder of the organs of that body with which the soul is connected and acts during this present mode of being. When these are but a little obstructed in their various functions, a man of the clearest parts and finest expression becomes scarcely intelligible. Nevertheless, no insanity or lunacy at all appeared in his actions; and his mind was in an innocent state, as appeared by his very loving deportment to all that came near him. And that he had still a good sense of truth is plain by some very clear sentences he spoke in the life and power of truth in an evening meeting we had together there, wherein we were greatly comforted; so that I was ready to think this was a sort of sequestration of him from all the concerns of this life, which so much oppressed him, not in judgment, but in mercy, that he might have rest, and not be oppressed thereby to the end." Clarkson. Yet some writers have asserted, that, at this very time, Penn was engaged with the Jacobites in concerting plots in behalf of the Pretender. This allegation appeared the more plausible, as proceeding from the State Papers (published by Macpherson) of Nairne, an under secretary at the Pretender's court; although the statements in these papers are founded entirely on the reports sent to France by two obscure Jacobite spies in England.

William Penn lingered in this condition till the 30th of July, 1718, when he closed his long and laborious life. This event, though for many years expected, was deeply bewailed in Pennsylvania; and the worth of Penn honorably commemorated by the tardy gratitude of his people. Proud.

NOTE XXXI.   Page 551.

"The British nation, renowned through every age, never gained by all her conquests, even when her arms subdued France and thundered at the gates of Paris, such a valuable acquisition as her settlements in North America. To lawless power, to faction, and to party rage, these spreading colonies owed their firmest establishment. When the mother country was in the most deplorable situation, when the axe was laid to the root of the constitution, and all the fair blossoms of civil liberty were destroyed, — even then, from the bare trunk, despoiled of all its honors, shot forth these branches, as from a stock where native vigor was still kept alive." Wynne, *Introduction.*

A few such animated sentences as these, together with a compilation of statistical details from the numerous publications respecting America that issued from the English press shortly prior to the War of Independence, constitute the whole merit of the first part of Wynne's *History.* This writer is distinguished above every other historian with whose works I am acquainted, for the depth of his ignorance and the height of his presumption, for the monstrous inaccuracy of his statements and the folly and absurdity of his speculations. Among a numerous host of similar blunders, he describes the delusion of the New England witchcraft as one of the causes that led to the concession of the charter of Connecticut; he imputes the replenishment of North America to the enforcement of the penal laws against Dissenters by James the Second; and he congratulates England on the conquest of Canada, as an event that excluded the interposition of France in the approaching struggle with the North American colonies. But the charter of Connecticut was granted more than thirty years before the occurrence which he represents as having produced it; James the Second excited the displeasure and fears of his subjects, not by enforcing, but by unconstitutionally suspending, the penal laws against Dissenters; and the conquest of Canada not only accelerated the Revolutionary War, but insured the participation of France in it against England. He represents Colonel Dongan as having been governor of Massachusetts; and relates (with superfluous regret) that William Penn died in prison. Yet, in strains of most ridiculous superiority and condescension, he declares the purpose of his work to have been the reconciliation of England and her colonies, by dissipating that mutual ignorance in which he supposes their disputes to have originated. Dark indeed must have been the ignorance that exceeded his own.

The same remarks do not apply (or if so, far less forcibly) to the second part of Wynne's *History*, — which, whether from greater attention or from access to better materials, displays so much of accuracy and good sense, that it is not easy to believe the whole work to have been the composition of the same author.

NOTE XXXII. Page 553.

"It is remarkable," says a distinguished modern statesman and philosopher, " how exactly the history of the Carthaginian monopoly resembles that of the European nations who have colonized America. At first, the distant settlement could admit of no immediate restraints, but demanded all the encouragement and protection of the parent state; and the gains of its commerce were neither sufficiently alluring to the Carthaginian merchant from their own magnitude, nor necessary to him from the difficulty of finding employment for his capital in other directions. At this period, the colony was left to itself, and was allowed to manage its own affairs in its own way, under the superintendence and care of Carthage, which protected it from foreign invasion, but neglected its commerce. In this favorable predicament, it soon grew into importance; some of the Carthaginian merchants most probably found their way thither, or promoted the colonial speculations by loans; at any rate, by furnishing a ready demand for the rude produce.

" In this stage of its progress, then, we find the colony trade left free; for the first of the two treaties, prohibiting all the Roman ships of war to approach within a certain distance of the coast, allows the trading-vessels free access to all the harbours both of the continent and the colonies. This intercourse is even encouraged with the port of Carthage, by a clause freeing the vessels entering from almost all import duties. The treaty includes the Roman and Carthaginian allies; by which were probably meant their colonies, as well as the friendly powers; and the clause, which expressly includes the colony of Sicily, gives the Romans all the privileges in that island which the Carthaginians themselves enjoyed. At this period, it is probable that the commerce of Rome excited no jealousy, and the wealth of the colonies little avarice; although a dread of the military prowess of the former seems to have given rise to the negotiation.

" Some time afterwards, another treaty, conceived in a different spirit, and formed exactly upon the principles of the mercantile system, was concluded between those celebrated rival powers. The restrictions upon the navigation of the Roman ships of war are here extended and enforced ; the freedom of entry into the port of Carthage is continued, and into the ports of Sicily also ; the Romans granting to the Carthaginians like privileges at Rome. But the Romans are debarred from plundering, trading, or settling (a singular conjunction) upon the coast of Africa Propria, which was peopled by Carthaginian colonies, and furnished large supplies of provisions and money to the city. The same restriction is extended to Sardinia ; and trading-vessels are only permitted to enter the harbours of that colony for the space of five days, to refit, if driven thither by stress of weather. A singular clause is inserted, to which close analogies may be traced in the modern questions of neutral rights and contraband of war ; — if any Roman troops shall receive stores from a Carthaginian port, or a port in the provincial territories of the state, they are bound not to turn them against either the republic or her allies.

" The substance of this very singular document will suggest various reflections to my readers. I shall only observe, that we find in it the principles of the modern colonial system clearly unfolding themselves ; and that we have every reason to regret the scantiness of our knowledge of the Carthaginian story, which, in so far as relates to the commerce of that people, breaks off here, and leaves us no trace of the farther restrictions most probably imposed by succeeding statesmen upon the growing trade of the colonies." Brougham's *Inquiry into the Colonial Policy of the European Powers.*

NOTE XXXIII. Page 555.

THE most admirable and interesting of the British settlements in North America, and in an especial degree the provinces of New England, owed their social formation and earliest domestic guardianship to men devoted to the cultivation of piety, virtue, and all ennobling and humanizing knowledge. Such national parentage inevitably tended to the nurture and propagation of democratical spirit and authority ; a circumstance which must be propitious or unhappy to America (and consequently to all the world) in proportion to the preservation and spread, or the neglect and restricted operation, of the principles from which it originated. As democracy, in alliance with religion, morality, and liberal education, may be the greatest political blessing that human societies can receive ; so, united with impiety, profligacy, and ignorance, it must exert an instrumentality at once injurious to the true interests and disgusting to the sound judgment and good taste of mankind. From the example of various national societies, both ancient and modern, in which the principles of aristocracy have prevailed, it has been too rashly deduced, that the mass of mankind, in all numerous and civilized communities, *must* necessarily be corrupt, gross, ignorant, and depraved. It remains for America (and God grant it be her happy destiny) to teach a different and nobler lesson to the world. The recent institutions of infant schools, which have so wonderfully contributed to render the imitative disposition of children subservient to their moral and intellectual advancement, and the improvements in charitable practice illustrated in the writings of Tuckerman and Channing of Massachusetts, if diligently and generally prosecuted, appear sufficient to intercept the growth, or extinguish the prevalence, in social life, of the worst evils of poverty and of all the debasing principles of artificial aristocracy. The condition of the poorer classes of society, demanding that their education should commence at an age, which, among the wealthier classes, is generally reckoned unsusceptible of culture, and should be administered to large numbers of them together, was long accounted unpropitious to the diffusion of knowledge among them. But the genius of benevolence has recently discovered, in these very circumstances, a principle peculiarly promotive of the efficacy and the best effects of education. It may be hoped that this genius in alliance with the true interests of democracy will discern and exemplify (as no government is more fitted than a democratical one to do) the advantage of rendering the acquisition of the elements of education legally compulsory on every citizen of the commonwealth. " Knowledge," said the illustrious Washington, in his first address to congress as president of the United States, " is in every country the surest basis of public happiness. In one in which the measures of government receive their impressions so immediately from the sense of the community as in ours, it is proportionably essential."

NOTE XXXIV. Page 559.

A GOOD deal of irritation was excited in America, in the beginning of the eighteenth century, by a discussion that took place in parliament with regard to a project for the employment of felons in the royal dock-yards of England. A bill for this purpose was passed by the House of Commons, but rejected by the House of Lords, as tending to discredit his Majesty's service in the dock-yards. This was commented on with just displeasure by an American journalist, of whose lucubrations some specimens have been preserved in Smith's *History of New York*. By making felony a passport to the advantages of an establishment in America, says this writer, the number of criminals is multiplied in England ; and the misery of the industrious poor is aggravated by the discredit attached to the only certain means of improving their condition. He maintains that this policy is at once mischievous and insulting to the colonial settlements ; and that it would be much less injurious, and not more unjust, to burden them with the support of all the decrepit or lunatic paupers in England. " There are thousands of honest men," he continues, " laboring in Europe at fourpence a day, starving in spite of all their efforts, a dead weight to the respective parishes to which they belong ; who, without any other qualifications than common sense, health, and strength, might accumulate estates among us, as many have done already. These, and not the felons, are the men that should be sent over for the better peopling the plantations."

NOTE XXXV. Page 560.

FROM the time when one of the earliest assemblies of North Carolina prohibited the inhabitants of that province from accepting commissions to sue for debts due to foreigners, down to the present day, the North Americans have been charged with deficiency of strict and honorable justice in their commercial policy, especially with regard to the interests of creditors and payment of debts. To a certain extent, the reproach is doubtless well founded. But those who have endeavoured to account for it, by supposing that the commercial morality of the Americans was tainted by the frauds incident to the Indian trade, have assigned neither the most honorable nor the most ample and satisfactory explanation, — which may be derived, I think, partly from the circumstances mentioned in the text, and partly from the popular sources and consequent bias of American legislation. The majority of every people are debtors, or at least more akin to the condition of debtors than of creditors ; and hence, when the majority rules, the interests of creditors are rather reluctantly protected than cordially aided by the laws. In an aristocracy, where legislation is in the hands of a few, and these few are more akin to the class of creditors than of debtors, the pervading policy of commercial law is precisely the reverse. Men are always much more prone to prescribe than to practise wisdom and virtue. When the many rule, they legislate mainly for themselves, and are governed chiefly by considerations of self-interest, which are often illiberal and short-sighted. When the few rule, then men are legislating for others; and however self-interested the legislators may be, they are willing enough to acquire a cheap credit by imposing on their fellow-citizens the most strictly upright and honorable regulations. It is then that the sentiments of creditors give the tone to commercial legislation, and that the duties of debtors are most strictly unfolded and enforced by law. In human society, evil is often overruled to the production of good, and good perverted to the production of evil. The condition of the inhabitants of North America is eminently fraught with good; and only the controlling and purifying influence of strong Christian principle can exempt them from a proportional share of those abuses that constitute the guilt and the penalty of benefits irreligiously enjoyed.

END OF VOLUME I.